長白山上一高僧

妙覺山邊度眾生

指引迷津遵彼岸

極樂西方要共登

劉果濟（濟生）敬攝於一九七八年並題詩
Liu Guoji (Jisheng) respectfully took this photo in 1978 and wrote the following poem:

A high Sanghan from Eternally White Mountain
Crosses living beings over at Wonderful Enlightenment Mountain.
He guides the confused multitudes to reach the other shore,
So that they may together ascend to the Western Land of Ultimate Bliss.

1

以德感人心誠服
望之儼然即溫和

When virtue is used to influence people,
they accept with sincere hearts.
He seems stern, but is actually gentle.

威猛慈悲大丈夫
調伏眾生出迷途

Awe-inspiring yet compassionate is
　this great hero.
He tames and subdues living beings
　so they can find their way out of confusion.

無邊誓願利眾生
不可思議常在定

With limitless vows,
    he benefits living beings.
Inconceivably,
    he is constantly in samadhi.

常行無我波羅蜜
離諸法執行摩訶

Always practice the Paramita of
　No Self.
Having no attachment to dharmas
　is the Mahayana.

有緣無緣咸攝化

Those with and without affinities are all gathered in and transformed.

Great Parinirvana

大般涅槃

安詳示寂
Peaceful manifestation of stillness

於殯儀館念佛
Recitation of the Buddha's name at the mortuary

迎請法體回長堤聖寺
Reverently inviting the Venerable Master back to Long Beach Sagely Monastery

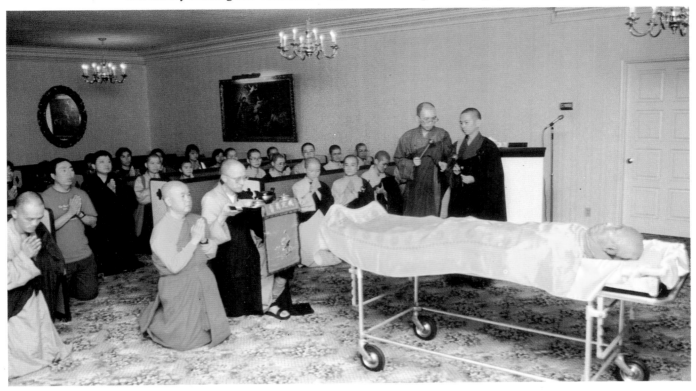

座下弟子恭候上人
Disciples respectfully wait for the Venerable Master

旭朗老法師主持入殮大典
Elder Dharma Master Xulang hosts the Ceremony for Placing the Body in the Casket

入殮後瞻仰上人
Reverently gazing upon the Venerable Master after the ceremony

緬懷師恩
Remembering the Venerable Master's kindness

恭送上人回萬佛聖城
Respectfully sending the Venerable Master off to the Sagely City of Ten Thousand Buddhas

Transporting the Casket to the Sagely City of Ten Thousand Buddhas

從長堤聖寺出發
Departing from
Long Beach Sagely Monastery

恭迎上人回山
Respectfully welcoming
the Venerable Master

敲大法鐘
Striking the great Dharma bell

擊大法鼓
Beating the great Dharma drum

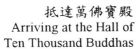

抵達萬佛寶殿
Arriving at the Hall of
Ten Thousand Buddhas

至誠頂禮上人九叩首
Bowing nine times in utmost sincerity
to the Venerable Master

比丘扶柩將入無言堂（在方丈室）
Bhikshus carry the casket towards the Hall of
No Words (at the Abbot's quarters)

安置於大般涅槃堂內（在無言堂）
Placing the casket in the Great Nirvana Hall
(in the Hall of No Words)

東北親屬
Relatives from Manchuria

一〇七歲的達摩瓦拉長老蒞臨
The Venerable Bhante Dharmawara, aged 107

明暘老法師恭敬瞻仰
Elder Dharma Master Mingyang reverently
gazing upon the Venerable Master

英國蘇美度法師（左二）與座下弟子前來禮敬
Venerable Ajahn Sumedho (2nd from the left) and disciple
from England paying respects

Final Ceremonies at the End of Forty-nine Days

圓
滿
七
七

於萬佛聖城
At the Sagely City of
Ten Thousand Buddhas

佛前傳供
Ceremony of Passing Offerings
before the Buddhas

四眾弟子虔誠傳供
The fourfold assembly of disciples
sincerely passes offerings

明暘老法師主持法事
Elder Dharma Master Mingyang
hosts the ceremony.

於長堤聖寺
At Long Beach Sagely Monastery

各寺住持參加讚頌大典
The Abbots of various monasteries attend the
Ceremony in Praise and Recognition

獻上最後的供養
Making the Final Offering

全體法師合影留念
A group picture of
all the Dharma Masters

The Memorial Ceremony

追思大會

拜華嚴懺
Bowing the Flower Adornment
Repentance

讚頌感恩
Ceremony in Praise and Recognition of
the Venerable Master's Kindness

憶念上人 (幻燈片放映)
Remembering the Venerable Master (slide show)

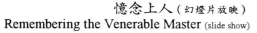

移靈祖師殿
Transporting the casket to the Hall of Patriarchs

貴賓致詞
Speeches by honored guests

參加大典的海內外信眾
The international assembly taking part in the ceremony

茶毗大典

諸山長老及四眾弟子傳供，
供養上人
The elder monks and fourfold assembly
of disciples passing offerings
to the Venerable Master

明暘老法師念封棺文
Elder Dharma Master Mingyang reads
the verse for sealing the casket

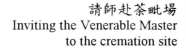

請師赴茶毗場
Inviting the Venerable Master
to the cremation site

門下出家弟子開始扶柩
The Venerable Master's left-home disciples begin to carry the casket

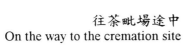

往荼毗場途中
On the way to the cremation site

入荼毗爐
Placing the casket into the crematory

得大自在

Attaining Great Ease

等待熱氣球攜帶骨灰升空
Waiting for the hot-air balloon
to carry the ashes into the air

覓師蹤跡，了不可得
The Venerable Master's tracks are
nowhere to be found

銘記師訓護正教，如來家業自承當
Firmly remember the Master's instructions and
protect the Proper Teaching.
Let us take the Thus Come One's mission
upon ourselves.

我從虛空來，回到虛空去

I came from empty space, and I will return to empty space.

23

Memorial Ceremonies Abroad

海外追思

加拿大華嚴聖寺信徒於涅槃堂
Devotees in the Nirvana Hall of Avatamsaka Sagely Monastery, Canada

馬來西亞紫雲洞觀音寺放大蒙山
The Great Meng Mountain Ceremony at Tze Yun Tung Temple, Malaysia

中國山東省汶上縣寶相寺舉行七期念佛法會
Baoxiang Monastery holds a Recitation Session, Wenshang County, Shandong Province, China

舍
利
光
燦

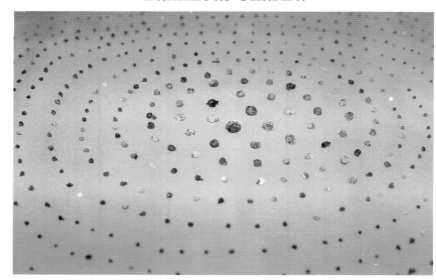

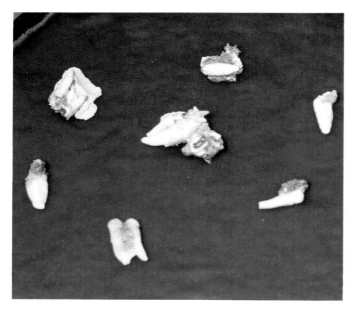

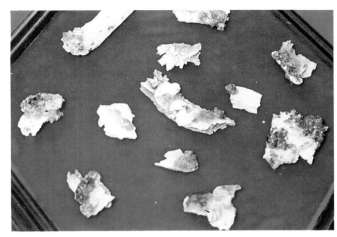

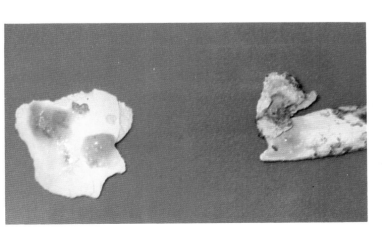

Remembering him upon seeing his things

阿彌陀佛像
（上人從東北時期就隨身攜帶供養）
Amitabha Buddha Image
(Beginning when he was in Manchuria, the Venerable Master always carried this image with him and made offerings to it.)

祖衣（圖一）
Samghati robe (photo 1)

祖衣（圖二）
Samghati robe (photo 2)

鉢（上人從虛雲老和尚增益受戒時所得）
Almsbowl given after ordination (given to the Venerable Master after he received the precepts a second time, for additional benefit, from the Elder Master Hsu Yun)

如意、拂塵、寶鐸、木杖等法物
A scepter, a whisk, a precious bell, and a wooden staff

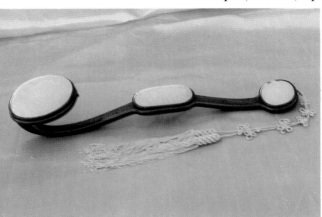

上人十六歲時的修省日記
The Venerable Master's Diary of Cultivation, written at age 16

Translation of diary contents:
I resolve to emulate the sages and worthies.
I resolve to accomplish great deeds.
The father is weak, so the son must be strong
To make a living to support our lives.

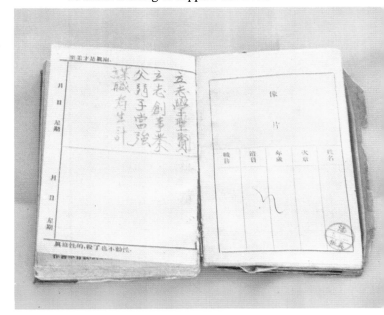

在香港時所用的南傳缽及茶杯
The Theravadan-style almsbowl and teacup that the
Venerable Master used in Hong Kong

年輕時曾用過的羅盤
A compass that the Venerable Master used in his youth

日常衣物
Clothing and articles for daily use

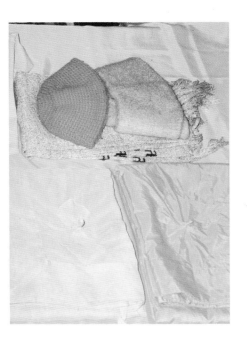

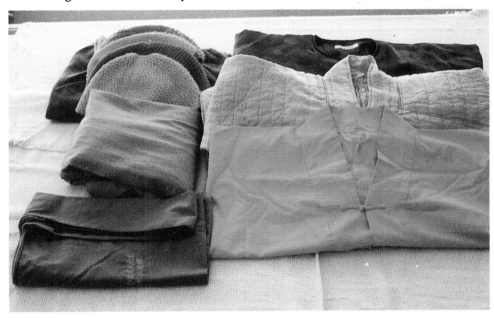

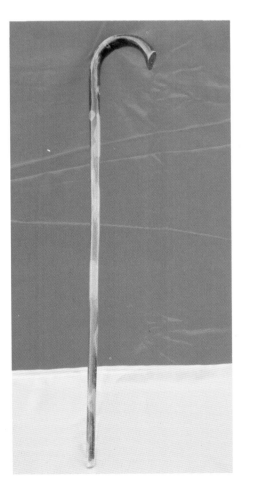

Precious Teachings in Calligraphy

World Peace
Written by To Lun

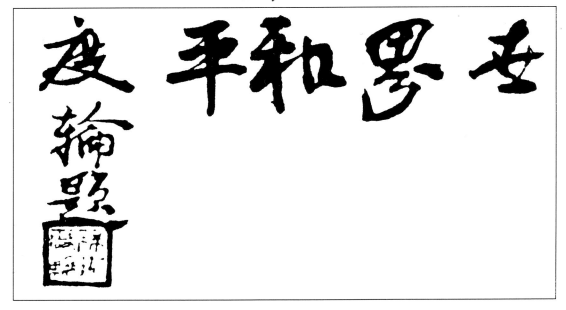

From the Preface to *Water Mirror Reflecting Heaven*

This is the reason I am writing *Water Mirror Reflecting Heaven*. But although it is easy to talk about this, it is not easy to do it. Why? If you want living beings to be good, you have to constantly remind them in their ear and bring it up to their face. You can tell them three times and instruct them five times, but still they do not obey instructions. If they encounter something evil...

One should dwell thus and bring forth the mind.
One should try one's best to become established
in order to accomplish one's work.

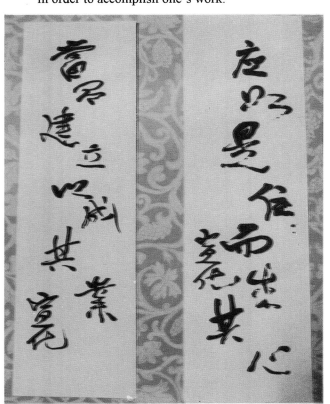

Flower

Buddha
Written by
the Mendicant

Adornment

Thus
Vajra Eye

Assembly

No calculating
A person of the Way
without a mind

33

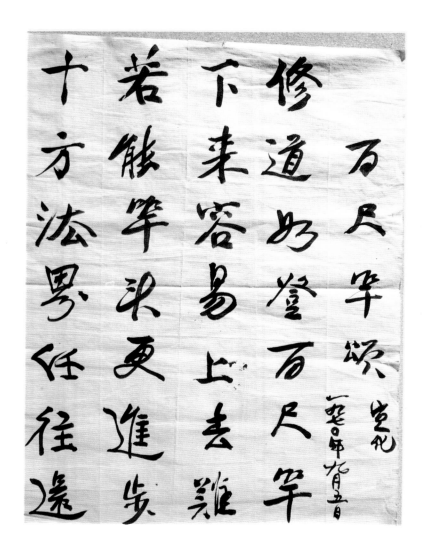

Verse of the Hundred-foot Pole
by Hsuan Hua   September 5, 1970

Cultivating the Way is like
    climbing a hundred-foot pole:
Sliding down is easy, going up is hard.
If at the top of the pole you take just one more step,
You'll be free to come and go
    in the ten directions of the Dharma Realm.

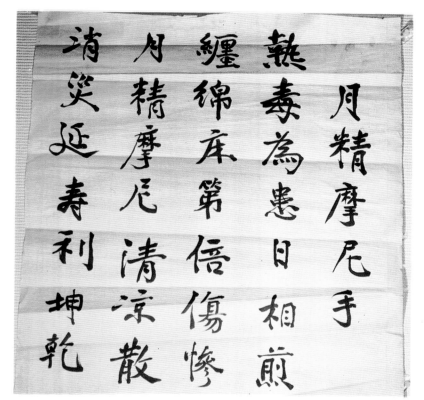

Verse for the Moon Essence Mani Hand and Eye

Afflicting one with fever poisons,
    they harass one every day.
To be confined to bed is even more tragic.
The Moon Essence Mani Jewel's refreshing medicine
Averts disaster, lengthens life,
    and benefits women and men.

34

Verse on the Wise, Foolish, True, and False
by Hsuan Hua

The wise seek the true and
  yet are not apart from the false.
The foolish cling to the false and
  are confused about the true.
Wise and foolish are two concepts with
  ten thousand different functions.
True and false are one suchness,
  unobstructed in substance.

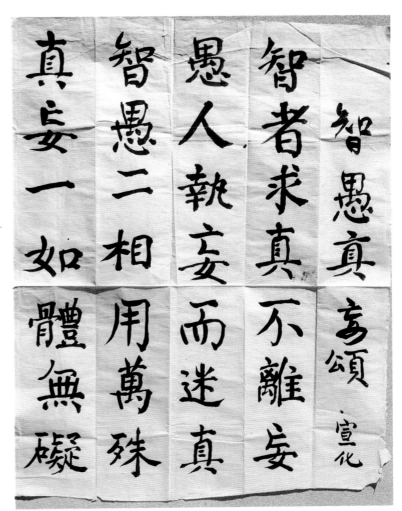

Guest-dust Verse

When the eighty-one
  delusions come to an end,
  the wild mind is put to rest.
Still the thoughts and reflect:
  Who is so busy?
Let the 84,000 afflictions come
  and go as they please.
Comfortable and without
  moving is the King of the
  Enlightened Nature.

August 29, 1970

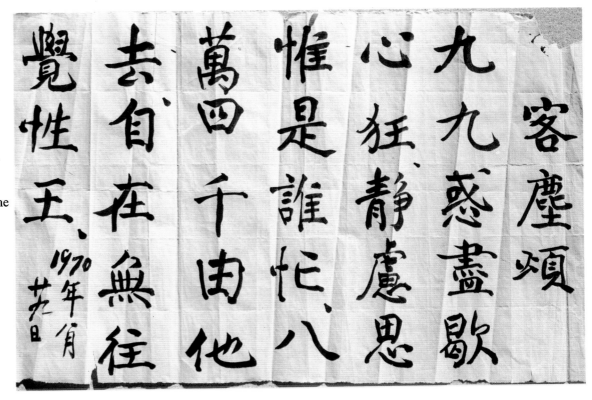

In commemoration of the relocation of the Buddhist Lecture Hall

The light shines everywhere.

May 16 in the year of *ren yan* (1962)

Written by To Lun

Diligence leads to achievement. Playing brings no benefit. Take care to avoid idleness And urge yourself on to succeed.

Hsuan Hua

In Memory of Upasaka
Zhang Daqian

You are foremost in
  Chinese painting, and you
  used to be my fellow cultivator.
In the past and present,
  in China and abroad, your name
  prevails throughout the cosmos.
Your popularity is universal,
  and everyone strives to be
  the first to see your work.
Like lightning travelling through
  space, high up to the heavens.
Guanyin manifests the appearance
  of a great hero.
Amitabha would personally praise
  this elder's countenance.
Although playfully roaming in
  samadhi is delightful,
Do not forget the purple-golden
  lotus in the West.

November 9, the year of
the Buddha 2999 (1972)

Written by mountain monk
Hsuan Hua

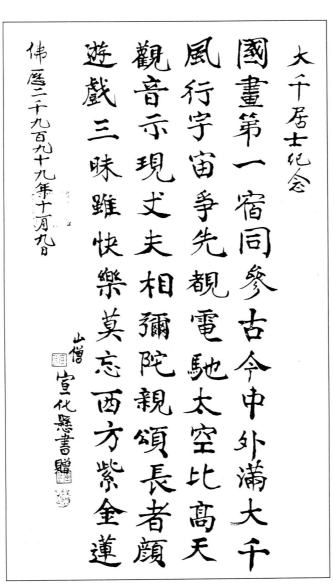

To endure suffering is
  to end suffering.
To enjoy blessings is
  to use up blessings.

Human Immortal

The Insane One

Verse in Praise of the Elder One's Image

The revival of the Buddha's teaching came from the Noble Yun,
The schools and Dharma doors are glorified again.
The Sangha all relied upon and drew near to him.
Thus, the Triple Jewel dwells in the world, reaching all sentient beings.
Though I'm a dull mountain-dwelling Sangha member,
I've received in transmission the seal of the Weiyang line.
"Thus it is, thus it is, and once more, it is thus."
We only pray that with kind eyes you will look on living beings.

Reverently composed by Disciple-in-Dharma-Transmission, To Lun

Verse in Praise of [Elder Master Hsu Yun's] Sharira

Five-colored in profusion are the solid seeds;
Perfectly forged, the myriad virtues, like the full moon.
Lustrous is the precept pearl, its clear light luminous.
Like mother-of-pearl, the samadhi gem, rare in hue.
Crystal like, the wisdom lamp, shining on the Dharma Realm;
The fruit of Prajna wisdom transforms the universe.
These lotus seeds, great and small, are as pure as jade—
Adornments of the collected virtues of the Vinaya.

Reverently composed by Disciple-in-Dharma-Transmission, Hsuan Hua

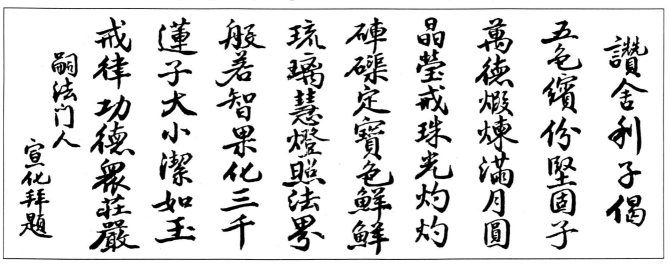

Your body and your mind are both manifested within the wonderfully bright, true, pure, and subtle mind. How is it that all of you have lost this fundamental wonder?

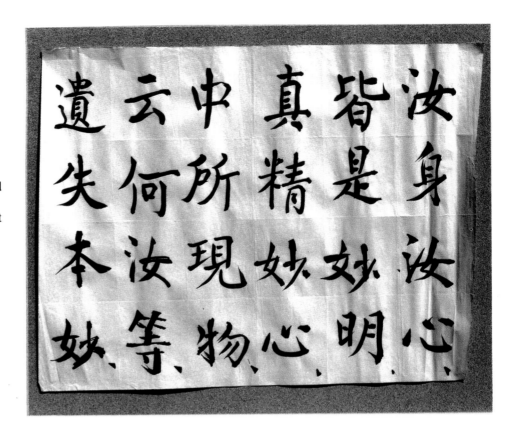

When form is mingled with false thinking, it takes the shape of a body. As conditions come together, there are internal disturbances which tend to gallop outside. Such inner disturbances are often mistaken for the nature of mind.

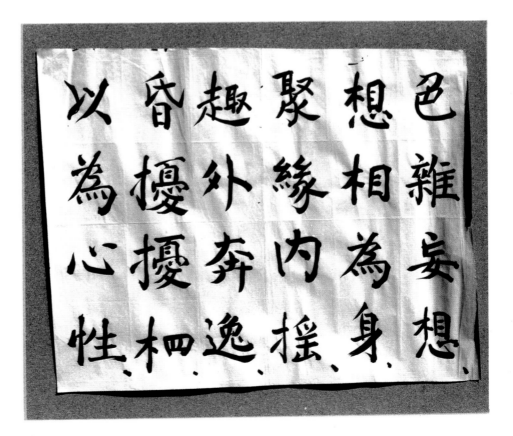

無聲的讚頌

On the completion of stillness by the
Elder Master Venerable Hsuan Noble Hua

Attaining great self-mastery

Mingyang, Abbot of the Yuanming Lecture Hall in Shanghai, China,
bows in mourning

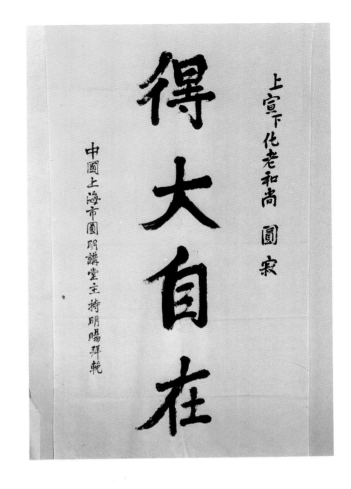

On the birth of the Elder Master Venerable Hsuan Noble Hua
in the Western Land of Eternal Stillness and Light

Nirvana without Residue

Zhenchan, Honorary Chairman, and
Mingyang, Chairman of the Buddhist Association of Shanghai, China,
bow in mourning

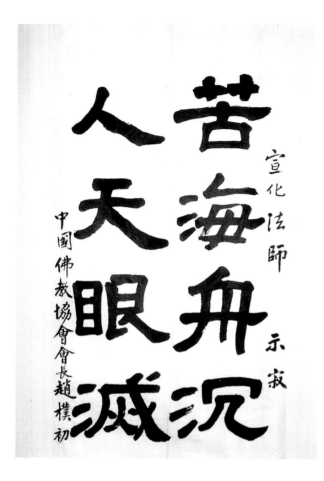

On the manifestation of stillness by Dharma Master Hsuan Hua

The ship has sunk in the sea of suffering;
The eyes of humans and gods have been put out.

Zhao Puchu, Chairman of the Buddhist Association of China

A prayer on the completion of stillness of the
Elder Master Hsuan Hua, To Lun

For seventy-eight years, his virtues were high and lofty.
All people put their hopes in him.
He proclaimed the teachings and propagated the Chan school.
His merit and virtue accomplished,
He went to Nirvana.

In an instant, he was relieved of his work in the mundane world.
His spirit roams in Buddha lands.
His compassionate resolve is vast and great.
Out of vast kindness, may he turn the boat around and
*   come back riding on his vows.*

Mingyang, Vice-chairman of the Buddhist Association of China,
Abbot of Longhua Monastery and Tiantong Monastery,
and the fourfold assembly of disciples
bow together

On the entering of stillness by the Elder Dharma Master Hsuan Hua

May he come back riding on his vows and
universally save living beings.

In respectful mourning,
Zhenchan, Vice-chairman of the Buddhist Association of China,
Chairman of the Buddhist Association of Shanghai

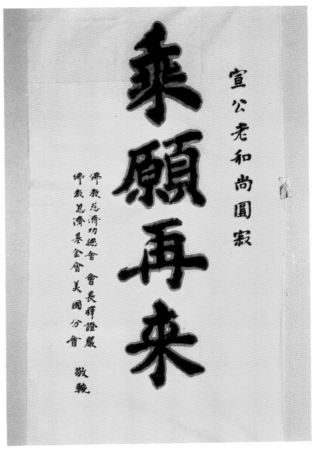

On the completion of stillness by the Elder Master Hsuan Hua

May he come back riding on his vows.

In respectful mourning by Shi Cheng Yen,
Director of the Buddhist Tz'u Chi Organization,
and the American branch of the Buddhist Tz'u Chi Foundation

For the spirit of Elder Dharma Master Hsuan Hua,
founder of the Sagely City of Ten Thousand Buddhas to view:

Ascending to the Buddha land

Written respectfully by Shi Manjue,
Director of the Vietnamese Buddhist Association of the United States,
in mid-summer of the year of *yihai* (1995)

On the rebirth of Elder Master To Lun
in the Inner Court (of Tushita Heaven)

He has understood his own affairs,
  so he renounced his life and departed;
Yet his affinities with living beings have not ended,
  and he must come back riding on his vows.

Zhiding leads the assembly of Hsu Yun Monastery
in respectful mourning

On the Nirvana of the Venerable Master To

The Bodhisattva is a clear and cool moon
Traveling in ultimate space,
Shining its light upon the Three Realms;
There is no place where the Mind-dharma fails to appear.

The eternal state is without appearance;
The eternal wisdom is without conditions;
He dedicates merit to the Way-place of those without affinities.

Joining his palms,
Bhikshu Shi Zhijue of Siming,
in the Brahma-sound Bodhimanda, Hualin Garden,
the Dharma Realm without affinities

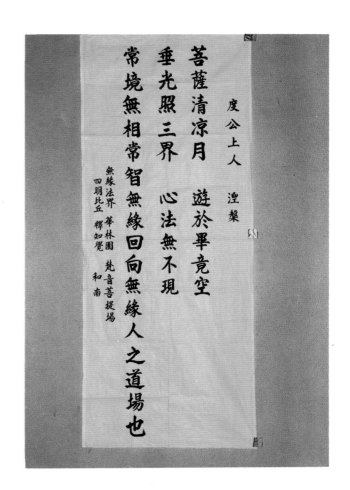

In Memory of the Venerable Master Hua's
Manifestation of Stillness

He practiced and cultivated the conduct of
*   Universal Worthy Bodhisattva.*
The broad door of the Dharma Realm harbors his vast,
*   sea-like wisdom.*

He vowed to continue the deeds of the ten thousand Buddhas.
The bright moon in the Sagely City shines
*   upon his Dhyana intent.*

In respectful mourning by the Shramana Shi Renjun

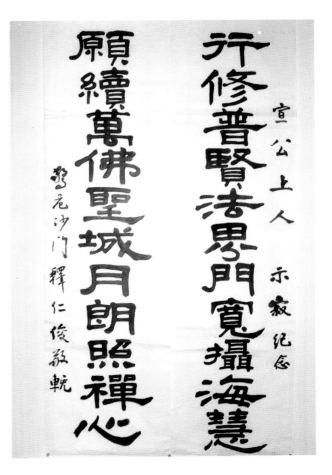

Written tearfully on the completion of stillness of
a lofty Sanghan of this age, the Venerable Master Hsuan Hua

Proclaiming the Dharma's principles,
Spreading the Dharma rain,
Bleeding and exhausting himself,
  he cultivates the sagely ground,
Planting Bodhi seeds at the foot of the mountain of
  Ten Thousand Buddhas.

Teaching multitudes of ignorant ones,
Saving multitudes of lives,
His monumental merit and vast deeds
  cause the grass and trees to thrive;
And he attains eternal life in the Land of Ultimate Bliss.

Buddhist disciples Xiaoling and Wujue of China
bow in mourning in the Flower City,
Mid-summer of 1995,
the 2539th year of the Buddha

Painfully mourning for the Venerable Master Hsuan Hua,
the Chairman of the Dharma Realm Buddhist Association
in the United States

The Venerable Master was a model for the world;
After his work was accomplished, he left like a cloud.

Committee for the Reconstruction of Baoxiang Monastery in
Shandong Province, China
July 10, 1995

On the completion of stillness by the Venerable Master Hsuan Hua

May he come back riding on his vows.

Changuang leads the assembly in respectful mourning
at the Dharma Light Monastery, Los Angeles

On the manifestation of stillness by the
Elder Master Venerable Hsuan Noble Hua

May he appear again to transform those with affinities.

The assembly of lotus friends at Great Enlightenment Lotus Society
bow in mourning

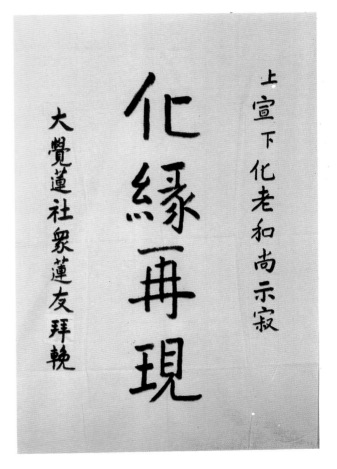

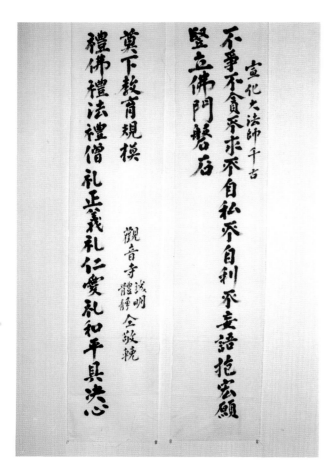

In eternal memory of the Great Dharma Master Hsuan Hua

Not fighting, not being greedy,
Not seeking, not being selfish,
Not pursuing personal advantage, and not lying:
Harboring vast vows, he laid a foundation for Buddhism.

Worshipping the Buddha, worshipping the Dharma,
Worshipping the Sangha, worshipping righteousness,
Worshipping benevolence, and worshipping peace:
With a resolute mind, he set down a model for education.

In respectful mourning by Chengming and Tijing of
Guanyin Monastery

On the completion of stillness of the Venerable Master Hua

Attaining great self-mastery

In respectful mourning by Shengliu
Wanyuan Monastery

On the manifestation of stillness by Dharma Master Hsuan Hua

Propagating the Proper Dharma,
He crossed the vast ocean to the West.
The Shakyan teaching has been established in North America,
And dragons and elephants pervade the four seas.

Transforming and saving multitudes of beings,
He benefitted the entire universe.
His work accomplished, he returned to the West,
But we hope he will come again riding on his vows.

Daguang leads his disciple Guanglin in respectful mourning
Thousand Flowers Lotus Society in Hong Kong,
Lingdu Hermitage in the U.S.A.

In eternal memory of the Great Dharma Master Hsuan Hua

At the old Gold Mountain, he propagated the Dharma
To universally save living beings.
At the City of Ten Thousand Buddhas, he laid the foundation
And then alone accomplished Bodhi.

In respectful mourning by Yanci of Hongfu Monastery and
Zhizang Monastery

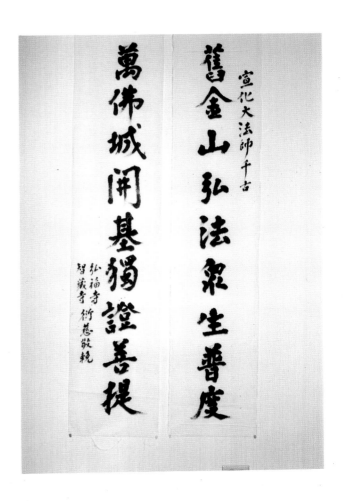

On the manifestion of stillness by the
Elder Master Venerable Hsuan Noble Hua

May he come again riding on his vows.

Weijing of Cien Monastery bows in mourning

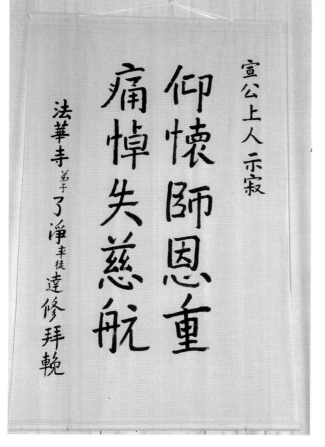

On the manifestation of stillness by the
Venerable Master Hsuan Hua

I respectfully remember the Master's deep kindness
And bitterly mourn the loss of the compassionate ship.

Disciple Liaojing of Dharma Flower Monastery
leads her disciple Daxiu to bow in mourning

On the Nirvana of the Venerable Master Hua

Permanence, Bliss, True Self, and Peace

Yinhai leads the fourfold assembly of Fayin Monastery
in respectful mourning

Respectfully mourning the
Elder Master Venerable Hsuan Noble Hua

His vows pervade the Dharma Realm;
Eternally he turns the wonderful Dharma wheel.

The fourfold assembly of disciples at Nanlin Monastery
bow in mourning

Respectfully looking to the spirit of
Elder Master Venerable Hsuan Noble Hua,
founder of the Sagely City of
Ten Thousand Buddhas and
the Dharma Realm Buddhist Association

Presented by Bhikshu Fuben,
Abbot of the Vietnamese Buddhist Pure Karma
Lotus Friends Blessings and Wisdom Temple
in America, and the lotus friends assembly
of that temple

The myriad dharmas are extinguished.

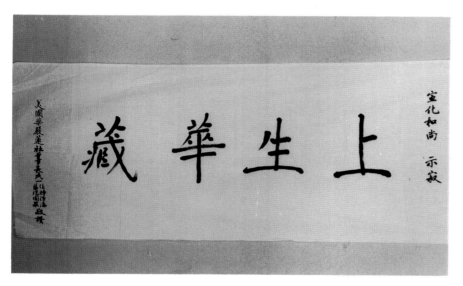

On the manifestation of stillness by
the Venerable Master Hsuan Hua

Ascending to birth in the Flower Treasury

Respectfully written by
Chengyi, Chairman of the Board;
Jinghai, Abbot; and
Yuanguo, Supervisor
of the Huayan Lotus Society of America

On the manifestation of stillness by
the Elder Master Hsuan Hua

Free to come and go

Daneng of Shengneng Monastery
of Los Angeles bows in mourning

Presented to the spirit of
Elder Master Venerable Hsuan Noble Hua,
founder of the Sagely City of
Ten Thousand Buddhas and
the Dharma Realm Buddhist Association

In respectful mourning by
Venerable Great Master Fuhui, the Abbot of
the Vietnamese Buddhist Blessings and Wisdom
Temple in Austria, and the fourfold assembly
of that temple

The substance and nature are perfect and bright.

On the Nirvana of our Teacher
Venerable Hsuan Noble Hua,
the founder of Instilling Goodness Elementary
School and Developing Virtue Secondary School
at the Sagely City of Ten Thousand Buddhas

A teacher and model for humans and gods

All faculty, staff, and students bow in respect

On the manifestation of stillness by
the Elder Master To

May he come back riding on his vows.

Shi Xuanyang of Miaojue Pure Hermitage
bows in respect

On the manifestation of stillness by
the Elder Master Venerable Hsuan Noble Hua

May he come again riding on his vows.

In respectful mourning by
Liaoyi (Daohai, Guoqing) of
Zhengjue Hermitage in Puli, Taiwan

On the manifestation of entering Nirvana by
the Venerable Master Hsuan Hua

Dwelling in great Nirvana

In respectful mourning by Shi Weijue,
Abbot of Lingquan Monastery in Wanli and
Zhonghe Chan Monastery
in Puli, Taiwan

On the completion of stillness by
the Venerable Master Hsuan Hua

Ascending to birth in the Buddhaland

Sanbao Monastery of Foguangshan and
the Foguan Association
in San Francisco

On the completion of stillness by
the Venerable Master Hsuan Hua

Unimpeded in mind

In respectful mourning by Kaizheng

On the completion of stillness by
the Venerable Master Hsuan Hua

The flower opens and the Buddha is seen.

In respectful mourning by Weijun, Abbotess of
Nanlin Monastery

On the Venerable Master Hsuan Hua's rebirth in
the West

He is guided to the Western Land.

In respectful mourning from
Hsi Lai Monastery of Foguangshan

On the completion of stillness of
the Venerable Master Hsuan Hua

With deeds of wisdom he rescued the world.

In respectful mourning by Chen Lifu

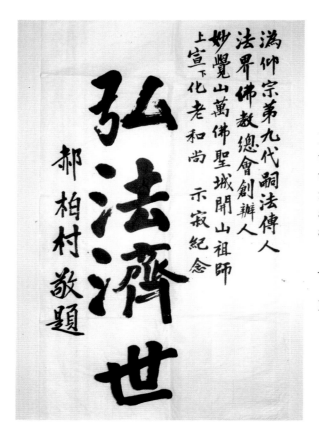

In memory of the manifestation of stillness by
the Elder Master Venerable Hsuan Noble Hua,
the ninth patriarch of the Weiyang Sect,
founder of Dharma Realm Buddhist Association,
and founder of the Sagely City of Ten Thousand Buddhas
at Wonderful Enlightenment Mountain

He propagated the Dharma to save the world.

Respectfully written by Hao Bocun

On the completion of stillness by
the Venerable Master Hsuan Hua

His teaching aided those in all directions.

In respectful mourning by Lin Yanggang

On the Venerable Master Hsuan Hua's
birth in the West

With enlightenment perfected,
he returns to truth.

In respectful mourning by Huang Zunqiu

On the completion of stillness by the Venerable Master Hsuan Hua

He propagated the way of the Sages
And was looked up to by the multitudes.
He transformed the common people,
And was equally respected by all the world.

Wu Junsheng joins his palms in respectful mourning

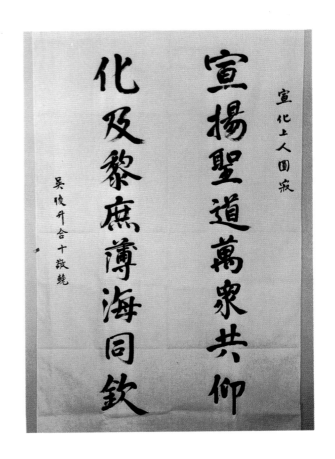

On the manifestation of stillness by
the Venerable Master Hsuan Hua

With enlightenment perfected,
he returns to truth.

In respectful mourning by Liang Surong

On the completion of stillness by the Venerable Master Hsuan Hua

He is reborn in the Pure Land.

In respectful mourning by Wang Jinping

On the manifestation of stillness by the Venerable Master Hua

The transformation of a Bodhisattva,
He propagated the Dharma and saved people
without being limited by national boundaries.

With the Six Principles and Three Guidelines,
He started schools and established teachings
to rescue the people of the world.

Chiang Chi-fu, Honorary Principal of
Developing Virtue Secondary School and
Instilling Goodness Elementary School,
bows in mourning

On the Venerable Master Hsuan Hua's birth in the West

He is reborn in the Pure Land.

In respectful mourning by Liu Songfan

On the completion of stillness of
the eminent Sanghan Hsuan Hua

Vast deeds and wonderful truth

In respectful mourning by Chen Lü-an

On the completion of stillness by the Venerable Master Hua

I have lost the proper path for asking about the Way;
I have lost a person who knew my heart.

In respectful mourning by Lichi, Yang Fusen

On the completion of stillness
by my Teacher,
the Venerable Master Hsuan Hua

May he come back riding on his vows.

In tearful mourning by disciple Zhou Guoli

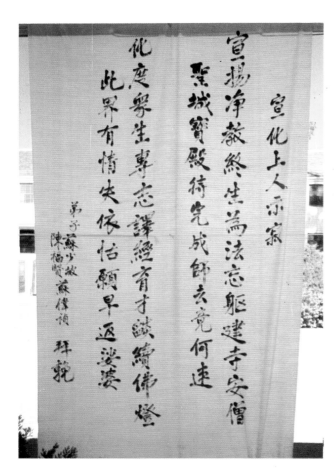

On the manifestation of stillness by the Venerable Master Hua

Propagating the pure teachings,
All his life he forgot himself for the sake of the Dharma,
Building monasteries and settling the Sangha.
The Jewelled Palace at the Sagely City awaits completion.
How soon my teacher has left!

Teaching living beings,
He dedicated himself to the translation of
*   the scriptures and education,*
Passing on the lamp of Buddhism.
The sentient beings of this realm have lost their refuge.
We hope he will quickly return to the Saha world.

Disciples Su Shaopo, Chen Fuxian, and Su Weizhen

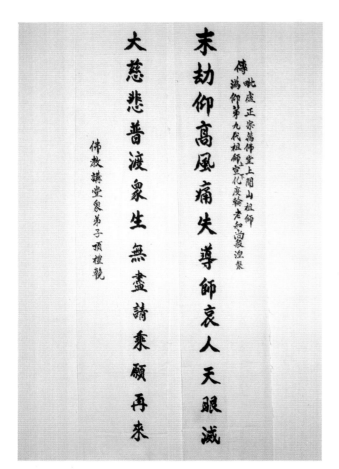

On the Nirvana of the Elder Master To Lun,
Venerable Hsuan Noble Hua,
the ninth patriarch of the Weiyang Sect,
the founder of the City of Ten Thousand Buddhas,
and the transmitter of the Vairochana Sect

In the final age, we look up to your exemplary style.
We have bitterly lost our guiding teacher,
And we mourn that the eye of humans and gods has perished.

With great compassion you save
The limitless living beings.
Please come back riding on your vows.

The assembled disciples of the Buddhist Lecture Hal[l]
bow in mourning

For the Venerable Master Hua

His kindness and compassion cross over all;
Believers are liberated and perfect the Right Enlightenment.
Transforming beings wherever he goes,
    his spirit remains intact;
Those who venerate him obtain blessings and
    awaken to the Unproduced.

Respectfully presented by Pan Xiuming
Written by Liu Yaoli in March 1994

On the pure, still quiescence of the Venerable Master

Without going, without coming, and without attaching,
    he propagated and transformed in the void,
    according with conditions.
With compassion, with vows, and with virtue,
    he acted as a vessel for crossing living beings over,
    responding to potentials.

Disciple Wong Guojun bows

KÍNH VÃNG

GIÁC LINH HÒA THƯỢNG

TUYÊN DƯƠNG CHÁNH PHÁP LẪY LỪNG TRONG BỐN BỂ

HÓA ĐỘ MUÔN LOÀI QUA KHỎI SÁU DƯỜNG MÊ

PHẬT LỊCH 2539

MÙA HẠ NĂM ẤT HỢI 1995

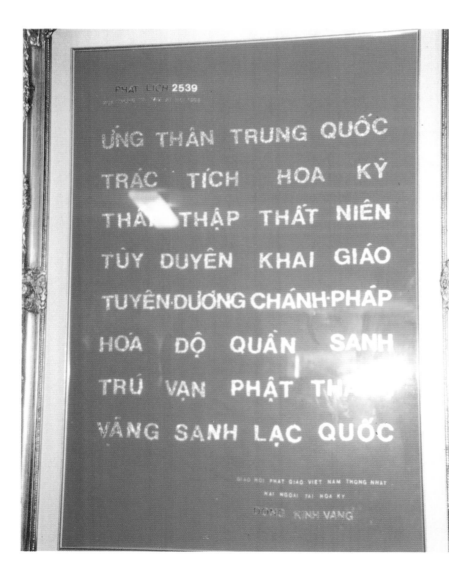

PHẬT LỊCH 2539

ỨNG THÂN TRUNG QUỐC

TRÁC TÍCH HOA KỲ

THẤT THẬP THẤT NIÊN

TÙY DUYÊN KHAI GIÁO

TUYÊN DƯƠNG CHÁNH PHÁP

HÓA ĐỘ QUẦN SANH

TRÚ VẠN PHẬT THÀNH

VÃNG SANH LẠC QUỐC

GIÁO HỘI PHẬT GIÁO VIỆT NAM THỐNG NHẤT
HẢI NGOẠI TẠI HOA KỲ

DƯƠNG KINH VANG

佛曆二五三九年
一九九五年仲夏

應身中國　卓錫美國
七十七年　隨緣開教
宣揚正法　化度群生
住萬佛城　往生樂國
美國越南海外佛教會敬輓

Mid-summer, the year of the Buddha 2539 (1995)

His response body appeared in China,
And he settled in America
Until his seventy-seventh year.
According with the conditions,
* he introduced the teaching.*
He proclaimed and propagated the Proper
* Dharma,*
Transforming and rescuing multitudes of
* beings.*
He dwelt at the City of Ten Thousand
* Buddhas*
And was reborn in the Land of Bliss.

In respectful mourning,
the Overseas Vietnamese Buddhist Association
in the United States of America

佛教國際諮詢中心
敬輓
覺靈和尚
宣揚正法磊落四海中　化度萬類出離六迷途

佛曆二五三九年
一九九五年仲夏

The International Buddhist Information Bureau
Respectfully mourns for the spirit of the Venerable Master

He proclaimed and propagated the Proper Dharma clearly throughout the four seas.
He taught and rescued the myriad species so that they could escape the six paths of delusion.

Mid-summer, the year of the Buddha 2539 (1995)

(1)　　　　　　　　　　　　(2)

(1)
Transcending all existence and
perfecting unsurpassed compassion

(2)
On the completion of stillness
of our kind teacher,
the Venerable Master Hsuan Hua

We have sadly lost our
great teacher.

A disciple of the Triple Jewel
bows in mourning

63

Myriads of Auspicious Signs

瑞相重重

放大光明照世間　胎卵濕化離倒懸
九界眾生成正覺　常樂我淨品自高

As great light is emitted to illuminate the world,
Those born from wombs, eggs, moisture, and transformation
　leave the destiny of hanging upside-down.
Living beings of the nine Dharma realms attain Right Enlightenment;
With permanence, bliss, true self, and purity,
　one is naturally noble in character.

六月十六日無言堂前
In front of No Words Hall on June 16

註：七月二十八荼毗日清晨迎請上人到祖師殿途中（65、66頁之圖① ② ③ ④）
Note: Photos ① ② ③ ④ on pages 65-66 were taken in the early morning of July 28, the day of the cremation, as the Venerable Master was being invited to the front of the Patriarchs' Hall.

①

②

③

④

七月二十八日傳供大典時
During the Ceremony for the Passing of Offerings on July 28

七月二十九日撒骨灰畢大眾合影時
As group pictures were being taken after the scattering of ashes on July 29

宣化老和尚
追思紀念專集

IN MEMORY OF THE
VENERABLE MASTER HSUAN HUA

第二册
Volume Two

宣化老和尚
追思紀念專集

第二冊

翻 譯
佛經翻譯委員會
出 版
法界佛教總會
佛經翻譯委員會
法界佛教大學

IN MEMORY OF THE
VENERABLE MASTER HSUAN HUA

Volume Two

Translation by the
Buddhist Text Translation Society

Buddhist Text Translation Society
Dharma Realm Buddhist University
Dharma Realm Buddhist Association
Burlingame, California U.S.A.

Published by:

Buddhist Text Translation Society
Dharma Realm Buddhist University
Dharma Realm Buddhist Association
1777 Murchison Drive,
Burlingame, CA 94010-4504

Second edition 1996

03 02 01 00 99 98 97 96   10 9 8 7 6 5 4 3 2

ISBN 0-88139-553-6

Translation by:
Buddhist Text Translation Society

Note: Pinyin is used for the romanization of Chinese words, except for
proper names which retain familiar romanizations.

Addresses of the Dharma Realm Buddhist Association's branch offices are listed
at the back of this book.

法界佛教總會・萬佛聖城
Dharma Realm Buddhist Association
The City of Ten Thousand Buddhas
2001 Talmage Road, Talmage, CA 95481-0217 U.S.A.
Tel: (707) 462-0939   Fax: (707) 462-0949

法界聖城
The City of the Dharma Realm
1029 West Capitol Ave., West Sacramento, CA 95691 U.S.A.
Tel: (916) 374-8268

國際譯經學院
The International Translation Institute
1777 Murchison Drive, Burlingame, CA 94010 U.S.A.
Tel: (415) 692-5912

法界宗教學術研究院
Institute of World Religions (Berkeley Buddhist Monastery)
2304 McKinley Avenue, Berkeley, CA 94703 U.S.A.
Tel: (510) 848-3440

金山聖寺
Gold Mountain Monastery
800 Sacramento Street, San Francisco, CA 94108 U.S.A.
Tel: (415) 421-6117

金輪聖寺
Gold Wheel Monastery
235 N. Avenue 58, Los Angeles, CA 90042 U.S.A.
Tel: (213) 258-6668

長堤聖寺
Long Beach Monastery
3361 East Ocean Boulevard, Long Beach, CA 90803 U.S.A.
Tel: (310) 438-8902

華嚴精舍
Avatamasaka Hermitage
11721 Beall Mountain Road, Potomac, MD 20854 U.S.A.
Tel: (301) 299-3693

金聖寺
Gold Sage Monastery
11455 Clayton Road
San Jose, CA 95127
Tel: (408) 923-7243

金峰聖寺
Gold Summit Monastery
233-1st Ave. West, Seattle, WA 98119 U.S.A.
Tel: (206) 217-9320

金佛聖寺
Gold Buddha Monastery
301 East Hastings Street, Vancouver, BC, V6A 1P3 Canada
Tel: (604) 684-3754

華嚴聖寺
Avatamsaka Monastery
1152 10th Street SE, Calgary, AB, T2G 3E4 Canada
Tel: (403) 269-2960

法界佛教印經會
Dharma Realm Buddhist Books Distribution Association
臺北市忠孝東路六段85號11樓
11th Floor, 85 Chung-hsiao E. Road, Sec. 6, Taipei, R.O.C.
Tel: (02) 786-3022

紫雲洞觀音寺
Tze Yun Tung Temple
Batu 5½, Jalan Sungai Besi, Salak Selatan, 57100 Kuala Lumpur, Malaysia
Tel: (03) 782-6560

前言

一本散爲萬殊

萬殊仍歸一本

　　當七七期滿，熱氣球載著上人骨灰遍撒虛空的剎那，一切似乎也都空了。上人曾說：「我是什麼，你們一點都不知道。」聖人的境界本非吾等凡夫眾生所能揣測，但是「千江有水千江月，萬里無雲萬里天」，對於每一位見過上人面，乃至只是聞過其名的人來說，上人隨類應化，平等攝受的悲心，都在這些眾生的心水中，現出一片皎潔的月光。因此儘管我們無法說盡上人的功德，吾等不肖弟子仍然勉力爲之，以述上人德行於萬一。

　　自《宣化老和尚追思紀念專集》第一冊，於上人圓寂七七紀念日出版以來，幸蒙諸山長老、大德耆宿，及眾弟子們踴躍來稿、惠賜佳作、鴻文墨寶、照片、資料等，佛經翻譯委員會才得以順利進行第二冊紀念專集之製作，實不勝感謝之至。此次專集包括追思大會、茶毗大典、輓聯、各界慰問函、上人墨寶、舍利、開示等文稿、照片，並初步整理收集了上人早期弘法教化之事蹟、圖片，及眾多弟子們感人的追思文稿。從這些事蹟與行儀，從映在每一位眾生心水中的月光，我們得以略窺萬里無雲萬里天的境界。

　　上人所給我們的，太多太多了，唯願藉此專集之出版，與一切有緣無緣的眾生，共同分享。我們深信上人的願力：「願一切眾生，見我面，乃至聞我名，悉發菩提心，速得成佛道。」必能使所有見聞者，都受到上人無私的月光，遍照眾生心水，「眾生心水淨，菩提影現中。」上人教化弟子，爲一切的眾生奉獻生命，是不求任何回報的，上人只希望我們也能：「利益一切的眾生，對所有的人好。」

一九九五年十月五日

Introduction

One root divides into ten thousand branches;
Ten thousand branches return to the one root.

When the Venerable Master's ashes were scattered into empty space from the hot-air balloon at the end of forty-nine days of holding memorial services, it seemed that everything was empty. The Master once said, "You don't have the slightest idea of what I'm all about." The state of a Sage cannot be fathomed by ordinary people. Nevertheless, "The waters of a thousand rivers reflect the moon; the sky is free of clouds for ten thousand miles." To people who have seen the Master or simply heard his name, the Master's individualized teachings and compassionate and equal acceptance of all are like the bright moonlight reflected in the waters of their minds. Knowing that we could never completely express the Master's meritorious virtue, we unfilial disciples have still tried to describe a small fraction of the Master's virtuous conduct.

Ever since the book *In Memory of the Venerable Master Hsuan Hua*, Volume One, was published during the memorial services, many elder Sangha members, greatly virtuous ones, and disciples have contributed essays, letters, calligraphy, photographs, and other material, enabling the Buddhist Text Translation Society to compile the second volume without difficulty. We deeply appreciate all these contributions. This second volume includes coverage of the Memorial and Cremation Ceremonies; elegies; letters; the Venerable Master's calligraphy and instructional talks; photographs of the Master's sharira; an initial compilation of stories and photos concerning the Master's work of propagating the Dharma and teaching disciples in America; and many touching memorial essays by disciples. From the moonlight which is reflected in the waters of living beings' minds by these records of the Master's life, we can get a small peek at the state in which "the sky is free of clouds for ten thousand miles."

The Venerable Master has given us so very much. We hope that with the publication of this volume, we can share what we have received with all living beings, whether or not they have affinities with us. We deeply believe the Master's vow: "I vow that all living beings who see my face or even hear my name will bring forth the Bodhi mind and quickly realize the Buddha Way." Those who see or hear of this volume will certainly benefit from the Master's unselfish moonlight, which shines universally in the waters of living beings' minds. "When the waters of living beings' minds are pure, the reflection of Bodhi appears." In teaching disciples and devoting his life to all living beings, the Master did not seek any reward. He hoped only that we would also benefit all living beings and be good to all people.

October 5, 1995

目 錄

前言
照片選輯

荊棘路

3　憶念雲公 — 前塵後際因緣如是
10　佛祖心燈
12　宣公上人行儀
25　華嚴境界
28　絕食祈禱
30　菩薩幻化 頭陀行跡
88　早期法總的點點滴滴
92　育良小學與培德中學校史
94　香港慈興禪寺
96　上人的阿彌陀佛像
98　臺灣法界佛教印經會

法界音

106　傳供疏文
108　封棺法語
108　舉火荼毗法語
109　長堤聖寺七七涅槃追思法會
110　讚頌追思暨荼毗大典
112　撒骨灰儀式
113　瞻仰舍利
114　追思大會後記
119　追思函

甘露雨

141　五大宗教互容互融
145　道
151　○：自性的大光明藏
155　本立而道生
158　做人的根本先要盡孝道
160　天下有德者居之

CONTENTS

Introduction

Photographs

A Road of Hardship

A Recollection of My Causes and Conditions with the Venerable Yun   3

The Mind Lamp of the Buddhas and Patriarchs   10

The Life and Deeds of Venerable Master Hua   12

The Flower Adornment State   25

Fasting and Praying   28

Transformation of a Bodhisattva, Footsteps of an Ascetic Monk   30

Details of the Early History of Dharma Realm Buddhist Association   88

History of Instilling Goodness and Developing Virtue Schools   92

Cixing Chan Monastery in Hong Kong   94

The Venerable Master's Amitabha Buddha Image   96

The Dharma Realm Buddhist Books Distribution Association in Taiwan   98

News from the Dharma Realm

The Eulogy of the Ceremony for Passing Offerings   106

The Ceremony of Sealing the Casket and Speaking the Dharma   108

The Ceremony of Lighting the Fire for Cremation and Speaking the Dharma   108

Conclusion of the Forty-nine-day Memorial Nirvana Ceremony at
Long Beach Sagely Monastery   109

The Memorial and Cremation Ceremonies   110

The Ritual of Scattering the Ashes   112

Viewing the Sharira   113

Evaluations of the Memorial Ceremony   114

Letters in Memoriam   119

Rain of Sweet Dew

The Five Great Religions Penetrate and Fuse with One Another   141

The Way   145

Zero: The Great Bright Store of Your Own Nature   151

When the Foundation Is Established, the Way Comes Forth   155

The Basis for Being a Human Being Is Filiality   158

One with Virtue Can Rule the World   160

163　眞正的科學就是佛教

166　佛法是很平實的

168　人心不可一日無喜神

172　千百年來碗裡羹　怨深似海恨難平

175　何謂正知正見？

177　出家未忘忠貞志

千江月

185　祝禱宣化長老早日乘願再來

188　時時刻刻不離老和尚的教導

190　精勤持淨戒　慈悲度眾生

192　光明照世爲所歸

193　巨星的殞落

194　宣化上人涅槃禮讚

195　願中美佛教友誼萬古長青

197　摩訶薩不管他

198　悼念度輪長老

201　與宣化上人的一段因緣

203　永恆的懷念

204　恭請乘願再來

205　師父像太陽一樣

206　上人究竟教了我們什麼？

209　漫談上人的教育觀

211　悼念叔公宣公上人

213　緬懷上人

214　我所認識的宣化上人

216　老法師與一個尋常人的友誼

219　結緣三年獲知音

233　感懷師父上人

234　六年切磋

236　一則公案的啓示

237　文以載道的上人

239　感師恩

244　最寶貴的教誨

245　幻化的生命

247　有求必應的師父

248　祈願上人乘願再來

True Science Is Just Buddhism 163

The Buddhadharma Is Ordinary and Honest 166

Our Heart Cannot Be Unhappy for a Single Day 168

For Hundreds of Thousands of Years, the Stew in
the Pot Has Boiled up a Resentment Very Hard to Level 172

What Are Proper Knowledge and Proper Views? 175

Though I've Left the Home-Life, I Haven't Forgotten My Heart's Allegiance 177

The Moon Reflected in a Thousand Rivers

Praying that the Venerable Elder Hsuan Hua Will Soon
Come Back Riding on His Vows 185

Never Apart from the Venerable Master's Teaching 188

Diligently Uphold the Pure Precepts; Compassionately Take Living Beings Across 190

His Light Shines upon the World and He Is a Place of Refuge 192

A Big Star Has Fallen 193

A Praise for the Venerable Master Hua's Nirvana 194

May the Friendship between Chinese and American Buddhism Last Forever 195

A Mahasattva Takes Care of Himself 197

In Memory of Elder Master To Lun 198

My Conditions with the Venerable Master Hua 201

In Eternal Remembrance 203

Respectfully Requesting the Venerable Master to Come Back Riding on His Vows 204

The Master Is Just Like the Sun 205

What Did the Venerable Master Teach Us? 206

The Venerable Master's Views on Education 209

Mourning My Grand-Uncle, the Venerable Master 211

In Memory of the Venerable Master Hua 213

The Venerable Master Hua As I Knew Him 214

The Elder Dharma Master's Friendship with an Ordinary Person 216

A Bosom Friend for Three Years 219

In Memory of Our Teacher, the Venerable Master 233

Six Years of Studying 234

Insights from a Chan Story 236

The Master's Literary Works Convey the Truth 237

In Gratitude to Our Teacher's Kindness 239

The Most Treasured Teaching 244

This Illusory Life 245

A Master Who Answers All Prayers 247

Praying that the Venerable Master Will Return on His Vows 248

249　生命的轉折

254　承教與蒙恩

258　夢的啓示

259　無題

260　面見菩薩　交臂錯過

262　上人的慈悲救拔

263　護持法寶

264　遊戲人間

266　老吾老以及人之老

267　我發願

268　弟子的追思

269　化悲痛爲力量

272　遙想當年佛教講堂

281　風範長存

283　懺悔的感應

284　醒悟的機會

286　仰之彌高

288　人天導師

294　片片的回憶

299　一個夢

300　巧把塵勞作佛事

302　佛法的啓示

304　明燈詠

305　福澤人天

306　我連一粒微塵的欲念都沒有

308　師父上人——大醫王

309　捨命爲佛事

314　普令眾生得法喜

316　上人知道每一個人的心

317　師父在不在身邊，都一樣

318　精進行　報師恩

320　正法住世當第一

321　我與上人的一段生活

323　我都是撿人家不要的

324　化化生生各自然

327　我遇到上人的因緣和感應

329　無私無畏護持正法

How My Entire Life Was Changed 249

Grateful for the Venerable Master's Teaching 254

Dream Revelation 258

Untitled 259

Face to Face with a Great Bodhisattva and Not Recognizing Him 260

The Venerable Master Compassionately Saved Me 262

Protecting the Dharma Jewel 263

Roaming Playfully in the World 264

Caring for My Parents and the Parents of Others 266

I Make These Vows 267

A Disciple Remembers 268

Transforming Grief into Strength 269

Distant Memories from the Buddhist Lecture Hall 272

His Exemplary Style Will Remain Forever 281

A Response from Repentance 283

The Opportunity for Awakening 284

The More You Gaze up at Him, the Higher He Becomes 286

A Guiding Master of Humans and Gods 288

Small Remembrances 294

A Dream 299

Doing the Buddha's Work in the World 300

Revelations of the Buddhadharma 302

Verse in Praise of the Illumining Lamp 304

His Blessings Nurtured Humans and Gods 305

I Don't Have the Slightest Speck of Desire 306

The Venerable Master—A Great Physician King 308

Renouncing His Life to Do the Buddha's Work 309

Bestowing Dharma Joy Upon Living Beings 314

The Venerable Master Knows the Mind of Every Single Person 316

Whether or Not the Venerable Master Is Here, It's All the Same 317

Practice Vigorously to Repay the Master's Kindness 318

Our First Priority: Preserving the Proper Dharma in the World 320

Life with the Master 321

I Always Pick Up What Others Don't Want 323

Every Phenomenon Comes into Being and Changes in its Own Natural Way 324

How I Met the Venerable Master and Some of the Responses I've Experienced 327

Selflessly and Fearlessly Protecting and Upholding the Proper Dharma 329

330　師父上人還活著
331　只盼來生新緣結
333　恩同父母
339　我的學佛心路歷程
341　「果能，你已來晚了！」
342　無能盡説佛功德
344　詠上人歌三首
347　盼了二十年，就差二十天
348　入道之門－－忍辱行
350　迷時師度
355　我與上人的一段緣
361　悄悄地我走了
362　行慈悲心　滿眾生願
366　他助不如自助
368　飛來天鵝綻蓮華
373　師父沒有離開我們
376　忘己濟群生
378　跟著上人走
380　盡你最大的努力！
383　哀痛與思念
384　宣公上人救了我
386　一眞一切眞
388　思念與感恩
390　感念吾師教誨恩
393　我的朋友－－師父
394　一切是考驗
396　我與慈悲聖者的巧遇
399　菩薩清涼月　常遊畢竟空
402　悲心切切望回心
406　寫在上人圓寂之後
407　你爲什麼要上天堂？
408　不留痕跡萬世宗
411　初發菩提心
413　幸運的選擇
414　往菩提大道邁進
415　上人的禮物
420　妙手回春憶上人
421　永恆的感恩

I Only Hope to Create New Affinities in the Next Life 331

As Kind as a Parent 333

My Experience in Studying the Buddhadharma 339

"Guoneng, You've Come Late!" 341

No One Could Ever Finish Praising the Virtues of the Buddha 342

Three Songs about the Venerable Master 344

Yearning for Twenty Years, Missing by Twenty Days 347

The Gate Leading to the Way—The Practice of Patience 348

When Confused, We Need a Teacher to Rescue Us 350

My Experiences with the Venerable Master 355

I Have Gone in Silence 361

Practicing with a Compassionate Mind; Fulfilling Living Beings' Vows 362

Being Helped by Others Is Not as Good As Helping Oneself 366

How the Swan Came and the Lotuses Bloomed 368

The Venerable Master Has Not Left Us 373

Forgetting Himself to Save the Multitudes 376

Following the Venerable Master 378

Try Your Best! 380

In Grief and Remembrance 383

The Venerable Master Saved My Life! 384

He Was True in Every Way 386

Remembrance and Gratitude 388

In Gratitude and Reminiscence of My Master 390

The Master—A Personal Friend 393

Everything Is a Test 394

My Close Encounter with a Benevolent Sage 396

The Bodhisattva Is a Clear and Cool Moon Constantly Travelling in Ultimate Space 399

Compassionately Hoping for a Turnaround of the Mind 402

Written after the Venerable Master Completed the Stillness 406

Why Do You Want to Go to Heaven? 407

He Left No Traces, But a Teaching that Will Last for Ten Thousand Generations 408

Bringing forth the Bodhi Resolve 411

A Fortunate Choice 413

Advancing towards the Great Bodhi Way 414

The Master's Gift to Us 415

The Venerable Master's Magnificent Transmission of a Cure 420

Eternal Gratitude 421

424　恩師宣化上人涅槃感言

426　菩薩的悲憫

427　易知難行的六大宗旨

428　鍥而不捨地追求

432　憶念恩師

433　追思短文

439　我將記住您的微笑

440　聞聲救苦的上人

441　宣公上人二三事

444　千百億化生

445　依稀夢中情

447　萬法唯心

448　我只能幫助真正需要的人

451　宣公上人的第十四大願

452　震撼我心的師父上人

454　真實的故事

455　發無上道心

457　參禪見佛

460　無盡的哀思

462　上人——我慈悲的導師

467　觀世音菩薩讓我重獲光明

469　恩師是照耀我的明燈

470　如電　如山　如海

472　夢中示教感慈恩

473　我不做生意

475　人與路

481　諸布施中　法布施最

482　流血汗　不休息

484　感恩與願望

486　虛空萬有

488　師父上人創校與教學之法

490　吾愛吾師

491　一切是考驗　看爾怎麼辦

494　夢中示教

495　煩勞迷者度慈航

497　法雨拾零

499　斷欲

501　善知識對我的教誨

On the Nirvana of Our Kind Teacher, the Venerable Master Hua 424

The Bodhisattva's Compassion 426

The Six Guiding Principles: Easy to Believe but Difficult to Practice 427

Never Give Up 428

In Remembrance of Our Kind Master 432

Commemorative Essay 433

I Will Remember You Smiling 439

The Venerable Master Hears and Responds 440

A Few Recollections of the Venerable Master Hua 441

A Hundred Million Transformation Bodies 444

Scenes from Dreams 445

The Myriad Dharmas Are Made from the Mind Alone 447

I Am Only Able to Help Those People in Real Need 448

The Venerable Master's Fourteenth Vow 451

The Venerable Master Hua, Who Stirred My Heart 452

A True Story 454

Bringing forth the Resolve for the Unsurpassed Way 455

Investigating Chan and Seeing the Buddha 457

My Boundless Sorrow 460

My Compassionate Teacher, the Venerable Master 462

Guanshiyin Bodhisattva Helped Me to See the Light Again 467

Our Benevolent Teacher Is the Bright Lamp that Shines on Me 469

Like a Thunderstorm, a Mountain, or an Ocean 470

Grateful for the Master's Guidance in My Dream 472

I Don't Do Business! 473

People and Roads 475

The Gift of Dharma Is the Highest of All 481

Not Sparing Blood or Sweat and Never Pausing to Rest 482

My Gratitude and Wishes 484

Emptiness and Existence 486

How the Venerable Master Established Schools and the Way He Taught Students 488

I Like My Teacher 490

Everything Is a Test to See What You Will Do 491

A Teaching in a Dream 494

Those Who Are Afflicted, Wearied, and Confused Ride His Ship of Kindness 495

Drops of Dharma Rain 497

"Cut Off Desire!" 499

The Good and Wise Advisor's Teachings for Me 501

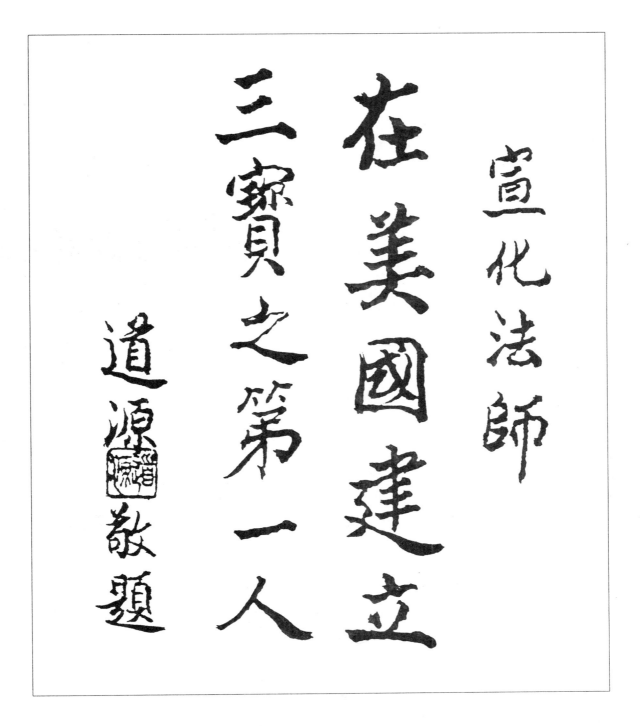

宣化法師

在美國建立三寶之第一人

道源敬題

Dharma Master Hsuan Hua, who is

the first person to establish the Triple Jewel in America

Respectfully written by Dao Yuan

憶念雲公
前塵後際因緣如是

A RECOLLECTION OF MY CAUSES AND CONDITIONS WITH THE VENERABLE YUN

釋度輪　Shi To Lun

長白山僧，黑水禪和，幼具道心，聞雙城王孝子常仁大師之孝德，影響而發願效法。晨夕禮佛畢，即向父母三叩首。初，人以為異，久則習慣成自然。後皈依三寶，深信佛教，親近常仁和尚（即雙城王孝子），每有啟發，頗感對機。繼之母逝，遂廬墓，即披剃出家。得悉曹溪南華寺祖庭，有禪宗大善知識上虛下雲老和尚主化，心嚮往之，而因關山阻隔，未克如願。

民國三十四年，日人投降，交通告便。至三十五年秋，八月中旬，束裝就道，偕果能、果舜二徒（果能參方不知消息，果舜自己焚身供佛），前赴曹溪親近雲公，途中備經艱苦，曉行夜宿，戴月披星，至長春（滿洲國時稱新京）般若寺，二徒留該寺，以待來年受具。余乃單人不帶衣物等件（所攜穿衣物不過五斤重而已），自往內地。

抵天津，住大悲院，聽倓虛老法師講《楞嚴經》。遇體敬法師，一同搭船至湖北正覺寺，同行共濟者有聖照、聖妙、照定、阮祥、潤慧、本知、覺知、融靈、靈觀、精戒等諸師，因而說偈曰：

> 同舟共渡十四僧，
> 眾皆尊貴我獨貧；
> 衲衣一食無他物，
> 任人毀謗與訶瞋。

在該寺充當淨頭、水頭、園頭、門頭

I am a monk from the Changbai (Eternally White) Mountains, a Chan cultivator from the Black Waters. I brought forth a resolve for the Way in my youth. Hearing of the filial piety of Filial Son Wang (Great Master Changren) of Shuangcheng (Twin Cities) County, I vowed to emulate him. Every morning and evening, after bowing to the Buddhas, I bowed three times to my father and mother. At first, they thought it strange, but after a while they became used to it. Later on, I took refuge with the Triple Jewel and had deep faith in Buddhism. I went to study under Great Master Chang Ren (Filial Son Wang of Shuangcheng County). The Great Master's instructions to me were always right on the mark. After my mother died, I built a simple hut by her grave and had my head shaved, leaving the home-life.

Hearing that the Elder Venerable Hsu Noble Yun, a great wise advisor of the Chan school, was teaching in Nanhua Monastery at Caoxi, I wished to go there. However, that would have involved a difficult trek through mountainous terrain. After the Japanese surrendered in 1945, transportation became more convenient. In the fall of 1946, in the middle of the eighth lunar month, I packed my bags and set out with two disciples, Guo Neng and Guo Shun. (I have no news of Guo Neng. Guo Shun cremated himself as an offering to the Buddhas.) We headed for Caoxi, wishing to draw near the Venerable Master Yun. The journey was very arduous. We walked during the day and rested at night, sometimes travelling even at night, until we reached Prajna Monastery in Changchun (which was called Xinjing, "New Capital," during the Manchu Empire regime). My two disciples remained at that monastery, waiting to receive full ordination the following year. Without carrying any extra clothes or luggage (the clothes I wore didn't exceed five pounds), I travelled alone towards the interior.

When I reached Tianjin, I stayed at Great Compassion Temple and heard Elder Dharma Master Tanxu lecture on the *Shurangama Sutra*. I met Dharma Master Tijing and rode in the same boat with him to Proper Enlightenment Monastery in Hubei. Also travelling with us were Dharma Masters Shengzhao, Shengmiao, Zhaoding, Yuanxiang, Renhui, Benzhi, Jiaozhi, Yongling, Lingguan, Jingjie, and others. I composed a verse which goes,

Fourteen monks rode in the same boat.
Honored and noble were they; only I was poor.
Donned in ragged robes, I ate one meal and had no extra possessions.
People could scold and slander me as they pleased.

At that monastery, I performed austerities and chores such as cleaning, boil-

、殿主、香燈等苦行任務，惟獨禪定功夫頗有相應。翌年，赴普陀山受具後，至蘇州靈巖山寺研究班學教。秋，至空青山參加禪七過冬，禮明觀和尚、了乘和尚。正月，起單抵滬，搭船復至湖北寶通寺，當搭船時，身上一文莫名。遇一癱瘓者，不能行，以〈大悲咒〉加持之，立癒，健步如初。故同舟旅客，皆生敬信，臨別贈金，得法幣七十餘萬元，於是赴曲江火車票不憂矣。至車站，邂逅周易大師，湖北人。詢之，亦云赴廣東南華寺親近虛老。問其有錢買車票否？曰：無。乃為其購票，同乘火車至馬壩。落車，周易云：肚餓。是時除用旅費外，尚存十餘萬元，全給周食早餐，而余身邊又一文莫名。

至南華寺，禮雲公，如嬰兒見母，如遊子歸家，數年仰慕之心，於此夙願克遂矣。初至，任祖師殿香燈。有智參法師時相過訪，道義相投，並向雲公推薦，謂為人才法器。公即延至方丈，令進戒律學院任監學法師，余不允。再三勉強。余曰：學人萬里參方，為了生死，親近善知識。老人如果能保證我了生死，雖赴湯蹈火，粉身碎骨，亦在所不辭。

公曰：自己生死自己了，自己吃飯自己飽，吾如云保證汝了生死，乃係騙汝，吾決不如此。雖然如是，修行當重內功外果，福慧雙修，方克有成，不可甘為自了漢，獨善其身，當兼善天下，行菩薩道，護持常住，為大眾服務，即可福慧雙圓，則生死自了。余仍不允。公曰：汝自東三省不遠萬里來親近吾，若不聽指揮，云何親近？至是，余乃允諾為職事。

平時祕察公之言行動作，與人無異，惟以身作則、刻苦自待，非常人所可企及。

春期傳戒，早板響時，則聞虎嘯之聲，自近而遠，此乃余親耳所聽者。諸法侶云：即皈依公之虎弟子也。逢戒期則回寺衛護道場，宿於後山洞中。戒期畢

ing water, tending the garden, watching the door, taking care of the Buddha-hall, and serving as verger. My skill in Chan samadhi increased greatly. In 1947, after going to Mount Potola to receive full ordination, I went to study the doctrines at the Buddhist Academy at Lingyanshan Monastery in Suzhou. In the fall, I went to Kongqing Mountain to take part in a Chan session and pass the winter. I paid respects to Venerable Mingguan and Venerable Liaocheng. In the first month of 1948, I left for Shanghai and then took a boat to Baotong (Precious Penetration) Monastery in Hubei. When I boarded the boat, I was penniless. On the boat I met a cripple who couldn't walk. When I recited the Great Compassion Mantra to aid him, he was immediately healed and could walk again. This evoked respect and faith from the rest of the boat's passengers. Before parting, they donated over 700,000 *fa bi* (monetary units). Thus I was able to buy a train ticket to go to Qujiang. At the train station I met Great Master Jouyi, a native of Hubei. When I asked him, he told me he was also going to Nanhua Monastery in Guangdong to draw near the Venerable Master Yun. I asked him, "Have you got money to buy a train ticket?" He said, "No." I bought him a ticket, and the two of us took the train to Maba. When we got off the train, Master Jouyi said, "I'm hungry." After paying for the train fare, I still had over 100,000 *fa bi*, which I gave to him to buy breakfast. Again, I was left penniless.

Upon reaching Nanhua Monastery, I bowed to Venerable Master Yun, feeling like an infant seeing his mother again, like a wandering son who returns home. After so many years of yearning admiration, I was finally able to fulfill my wish. When I first arrived, I was assigned to serve as verger in the Patriarch Hall. When Dharma Master Zhican came to visit, he and I found that we shared the same views on cultivation, and he recommended me to the Venerable Master Yun as a capable person and worthy vessel of Dharma. The Venerable Master Yun then summoned me to the Abbot's quarters and asked me to be Superintendent of the Vinaya Academy. I refused. He urged me three times. I said, "Your student has come ten thousand miles to meet the Good Knowing Advisor and in order to end birth and death. If the Venerable Master can guarantee that I will be able to end birth and death, then I wouldn't refuse your orders even if you told me to jump into a cauldron of boiling water, walk on fire, or give up my body and bones."

The Venerable Master Yun replied, "One ends one's own birth and death, just as one eats one's own food to fill oneself. If I were to say that I guaranteed that you will end birth and death, I'd be cheating you. I don't do that sort of thing. In cultivation, one should concentrate on inner skill and outer accomplishment. By cultivating both blessings and wisdom one will succeed. One should not be an independent Arhat, looking after only his own good. One should practice the Bodhisattva way for the good of all, support the monastery, and be of service to everyone. In that way, one may perfect blessings and wisdom and quite naturally end birth and death." I again refused. The Venerable Master Yun said, "You came all the way from northeast China to meet me. If you are not going to obey my instructions, why did you bother to come at all?" I then accepted the position.

I carefully observed the words and actions of the Venerable Master Yun and found them to be quite ordinary. What set him apart from ordinary people was his ability to set an example for others with his own practice and his willingness to take suffering and hard work upon himself.

During the spring precept-transmission, when the morning boards were struck, I heard with my own ears the roar of a tiger at first nearby and then off in the distance. My Dharma friends told me, "That is the tiger who took refuge with the Venerable Master Yun and became his disciple. It lives in a cave be-

，公獨自悄然返雲門監督建築工程。

是年暑假，余應江西南城黃鑄哉老居士之請講《彌陀經》，八月中旬回南華寺，九月中旬，土匪聚夥搶劫南華，破門而入南華戒律學院，余以身迎，彼等以槍指余心曰：打！打！余曰：為何欲打吾？匪曰：因你不開門。余曰：吾不開門，正因你們是來搶劫而非送禮，假使你是我之立場，你亦不肖開門耳。匪曰：拿支票來！余指所穿衲袍曰：你看！穿這樣破衣服的人，能有支票否？匪曰：誰有？余曰：我乃法師，彼等皆為學僧，吾既無錢，彼等更無矣。此房為吾所居，請到裡面看，何物合意，儘量取之，不吝也。

此際有懷一法師者，聽吾與匪侃侃而談，若無其事者然，即從房中出來，參加談話。匪即捨我而之他，亦如對我之狀。懷師見此，當下悲泣，低頭不敢仰視。匪亦曰：拿支票來！懷師云：到我房裡取去。於是前導入室，搜搶一空。

次日上課，懷師對眾學僧曰：南華百餘僧伽，皆存恐懼心，惟度輪法師毫無畏怖驚恐之意態耳。迨余上課時，對眾曰：懷師所說本寺惟吾無怖者，誤耳。據我所知，本寺有四人無怖。第一，六祖惠能大師，如如不動，了了常明，不瞅不睬，毫無其事。第二，憨山祖師，端然正坐，閉目養神，內外境空，人我雙忘。第三，丹田祖師，則探頭張望，一言不發，視其動靜，察其所安。第四，方是山僧度輪，既看且言，互相談話，慷慨激昂，惟亦無畏。說完，哄堂大笑。

不久，老人聞訊，由雲門趕來，召集全體學僧開會，出席者：為懷一法師、度輪法師，老人自為主席。學僧有祖印、雲妙、悟雲、宣揚、恆定、提揮、提廣、法亮、海龍、法慧、萬心、止空、法明、法開等三十餘人。當經土匪打劫之後，全寺震動，皆欲起單。公即席挽留懷師，懷師拒之；挽留同學，同學不聽。公見此情形，放聲痛哭，曰：吾盡

hind the mountain and always comes out to protect the monastery during the precept ceremonies.

After the transmission of the precepts, the Venerable Master Yun returned quietly and alone to Yunmen, where he was supervising the construction of buildings. That summer, I went to the district of Nancheng in Jiangxi to lecture on the *Amitabha Sutra* at the invitation of Elder Layman Huang Juzai. I returned to Nanhua Monastery in the middle of the eighth month. In the middle of the ninth month, a group of bandits who were intent on ransacking the monastery broke down the door and entered the Nanhua Vinaya Academy. When I went out to meet them, they pointed their guns at my chest and said, "We're going to shoot you." I said, "Why do you want to shoot me?" The bandits said, "Because you didn't open the door." I said, "I didn't open the door because you have come to rob me, not to give me gifts. If you had been in my place, you wouldn't have dared to open the door either." The bandits said, "Hand over your money!" I pointed at my ragged robe and said, "Look! Would someone wearing such tattered clothes have money?" The bandits asked, "Well, who does?" I said, "I'm the Dharma Master here, and all the rest are student monks. If I am penniless, surely they will be poorer yet. This room is where I live. You are welcome to look around and take whatever you like." Hearing me conversing with the bandits as if nothing were going on, Dharma Master Huaiyi came out from the inner rooms to join the conversation. The bandits promptly let go of me and seized him, giving him the same treatment they had given me. Master Huai burst into tears and hung his head, afraid to look up. The thieves then said, "Give us your money!" Master Huai said, "Go to my room and get it." They entered his room and took everything in it, leaving it empty.

The following day at class, Master Huai announced to the students, "Of the hundred or more monks at Nanhua Monastery, only one man showed no sign of fear—Dharma Master To Lun." When it came time for me to teach, I said, "Master Huai said I was the only one in this monastery who was not afraid. He was wrong. As far as I know, there were four people: First of all, the Sixth Patriarch, Great Master Huineng, sat unmoving in bright samadhi, without worrying or paying any attention, as if nothing were going on. Second, Patriarch Hanshan sat erect, nourishing his spirit with eyes closed, in a state of internal and external emptiness in which concepts of self and others were both gone. Third, Patriarch Dantian stuck out his head to take a look around and see what was going on, yet did not say a single word. The fourth one was me, the mountain monk To Lun, who not only looked but also spoke. I conversed with the thieves and got all excited, but I was not afraid either." After I said this, the class broke into laughter.

The news soon reached the Venerable Master Yun, who hurried back from Yunmen and called a general meeting. Present at the meeting were Dharma Masters Huaiyi and To Lun, and the Venerable Master Yun himself chaired the meeting. There were over thirty students, including Zuyin, Yunmiao, Wuyun, Xuanyang, Hengding, Tihui, Tiguang, Faliang, Hailong, Fahui, Wanxin, Zhikong, Faming, and Fakai. After the incident of the bandits, everyone in the monastery was unsettled and wished to leave. The Venerable Master Yun urged Master Huai to stay on, but he refused. He tried to detain the students, but they wouldn't listen. Under these circumstances, he broke down and wept bitterly. He said, "To the end of time, I will never again run a Buddhist Academy." Then he got up and returned to the Abbot's quarters. I was deeply moved and vowed to assume the duties of managing and continuing to run the Buddhist Academy. Later Master Huai went to Guangxi, and I became solely responsible for all the classes at the Nanhua Vinaya Academy.

未來際，永不辦佛學院矣！言畢，拂袖而起，逕返方丈。余大受感動，故誓將佛學院任務，荷擔起來，維持下去。後懷師赴廣西，南華戒律學院惟余一人負責課程。

至次年元旦，上書雲公辭去學院教務主任職，居於藏經樓閱藏，戒期勉任尊證阿闍黎，傳戒畢，隨公至韶關大鑒寺。公回雲門，命余可往雲門，余曰：諾！須先回寺便來。於五月初旬赴大覺寺，行山路，蚰蜒崎嶇，猶如蜀道。距雲門尚有二十餘里，天即黑矣。余獨行無侶，路徑生疏，實難前進。而前面忽有燈光，即向行去，始終距離百餘步遠近，及至無燈，視之，已至大覺禪寺山門口矣。恰在開大靜時間，余拍門而入，見公。公曰：何故如此晚遲？余告以故，及見燈光在前引導情形。公曰：奇哉！怪哉！山路日行無人引導，亦難認識，況夜晚行路不錯，太奇怪矣。即為安單，並云：在南華為班首，雲門亦仍為班首，上殿、過堂、坐禪，領眾薰修。

余往雲門不久，遂生濕氣，難於忍受，因向老人告假，欲赴廣州療治。公不許，曰：勿去！去則難返矣！余曰：不然，學人意志已決，一定要去。老人聞之，悽然淚下，握余手曰：去則不能再相會矣！余曰：病癒即返，請老人放心勿念！公曰：此去當為釋迦老子爭口氣，為歷代祖師建道場，前途光明無量，努力！努力！好自為之，勿負吾之期待，珍重而拜別矣。

余至穗赴港，掛單東普陀。七月，復返穗，掛單六榕，明觀和尚請余為堂主兼副寺。姑應之，準備中秋節後，重回雲門，孰料八月初旬，韶關易手，交通斷絕，不得已。八月十八晚，由謝寬輝、陳寬滿兩居士資助船費，復回香港，赴泰國考察南傳佛教，三十九年返港，遁跡隱於觀音洞中，如聾如啞，若癡若呆，每憶及老人臨行贈法語，悔當時弗聽知識訓誨，今欲復親近雲公，竟不可得，痛哉！痛哉！夫復何言。辛卯冬，

On New Year's Day of the following year (1949), I wrote a letter to the Venerable Master Yun resigning from my post as Dean of Academic Affairs at the Academy. I then stayed in the Tripitaka Hall and read the Tripitaka (Buddhist Canon). During the precept-transmission I was asked to be one of the certifying *acharyas*. Afterwards, I went with Venerable Master Yun to Dajian Monastery in Shaoguan. When Venerable Master Yun then suggested that I continue with him to Yunmen, I agreed to join him there but insisted on first returning to Nanhua. In the beginning of the fifth month, I set out for Dajiao Monastery (in Yunmen). The mountainous path was winding and narrow, similar to the roads in Sichuan province. Night fell when I was about twenty *li* from Yunmen. Since I was travelling alone, it was difficult to make progress on the unfamiliar path. Suddenly a lamp-light appeared before me, and I followed it. The light remained at a constant distance of about a hundred paces before me, and when I finally reached it, it disappeared. Looking around, I discovered that I had arrived at the very gate of Dajiao Monastery. Everyone had already retired. I knocked on the door, entered, and saw the Venerable Yun, who asked, "Why did you arrive so late?" I told him the reason and described how I had been guided by a lamp-light. The Venerable Yun said, "How remarkable! It is difficult enough to travel on these mountain roads during the day without a guide. How remarkable that you have been able to find your way in the pitch black of night! Very strange!" After arranging a place for me to stay, the Venerable Yun said, "You were the *panshou* (head of the assembly) at Nanhua, and you should continue to be the *panshou* at Yunmen. You should lead the assembly to cultivate during ceremonies, at mealtime, and sitting in meditation."

I had not been at Yunmen very long when I became ill because of the dampness of the weather. It was very hard to bear, and so I requested leave from the Elder Master to return to Guangzhou to recuperate. The Venerable Yun refused and said, "Don't go. If you do, it will be difficult to return." I said, "No. Your disciple has already made up his mind. He is definitely going." Hearing my words, the Elder Master was grieved to the point of tears. He took my hand and said, "If you go, we will not be able to meet again." I said, "I'll return as soon as my illness is healed. Please don't worry about me!" The Elder Master said, "After you have left, you should make every effort on behalf of Shakyamuni Buddha and establish Way-places to carry on the work of the Patriarchs of the past. The future is very bright. Push on, work hard. Conduct yourself well, and don't disappoint me. Take care. Goodbye."

I travelled to Guangzhou and then to Hong Kong, where I stayed at East Potola Monastery. In the seventh month, I returned to Guangzhou and stayed at Liurong Monastery. The Abbot Mingguan asked me to serve as the hall manager and assistant manager of the monastery. Since I planned to return to Yunmen after the mid-autumn festival (the fifteenth of the eighth month) I agreed to serve for the time being. But in the beginning of the eighth month, Shaoguan fell and the road was cut off, making it impossible to go back. On the night of the eighteenth of the eighth month, Xie Kuanhui and Chen Kuanman paid for my boat fare and I went to Hong Kong again. I travelled to Thailand to examine the southern transmission of Buddhism. In 1950 I returned to Hong Kong and went into seclusion in Guanyin Cave. I was as if deaf and dumb. Each time I thought of the Elder Master Yun's parting words, I regretted not having listened to the Good Knowing Advisor's advice. I wanted to go back to see the Elder Master, but it was impossible. Alas! What could be said? In the winter of 1951, I worked on the construction of Western Bliss Gardens (Xileyuan) Monastery. At the request of Luo Guoming, Chen Guofa, Tang Guoshan, Mai Guolian, Yuan Guolin, and other laypeople, I lectured on the *Earth Store Sutra*

修建西樂園寺，羅果明、陳果發、唐果善、麥果蓮、袁果林等居士為發起人，於通善壇講《地藏經》。次年秋，復於該壇講《金剛經》；越歲秋，於寶覺講《彌陀經》；後於西樂園寺講《楞嚴經》十四個月；復於某淨苑講《地藏經》。修建慈興禪寺，為雲公造生像，以示崇敬之至意，上書雲公，蒙付以正法眼藏，佛祖源流，以心印心，教外別傳，涅槃妙心，實相無相，真空不空之法。上承祖意，下化眾生，如此法乳深恩，時刻在念。

老人來函：令作功德，遂發願認捐雲居山真如禪寺大雄寶殿佛像等數萬元，並赴緬購買金箔為佛像裝金，計金箔三百餘盒（乃大盒）。公甚喜，屢函謝之。足見公對後輩之深意遠大，謙德不遑，薄己厚人，捨己從人，偉大精神，無上慈悲，崇高道德，至真平等，使人中心悅而誠服也。又函召余赴雲居，禪觀之中，知其欲委以真如之重任，以種種因緣，不克應命，至今遺憾不已。及成立佛教講堂，終日為弘揚大法而奔忙，更感分身無術，本擬將事務處理完善，付託有人，復親近老人，侍奉左右。

於己亥年七月間，聞公病劇，日夜不安，知有不祥之兆。先是戊戌歲，公攝法照，二目平視，雙眉數寸，可搭於耳際，余見而拜之。有感曰：公從來攝影皆閉目，今竟慈眼視眾生，如此改常，必有大變，不出一年，當可明白矣。於是請十方大德師僧，頂禮《消災延壽藥師寶懺》，延生普佛數日，並於報章發表消息，通知老人門下弟子，以期群策群力，眾志成城，有感斯通，無求不應。當即對眾開示云：此次為老人延生普佛，拜《藥師懺》等佛事，恐為最後一次，再無機會矣。聲音異常沉重而悲痛，所聽到之人，亦皆泣不成聲。旋雲居來信云：公病稍瘥，甚慰！

即專志命人設計繪畫老人畫傳集，精美國畫二百餘幅，洋洋數萬言，發揮老人一生超人道德，行願刻苦勤勞獨到之

at Tongshan Temple. In the fall of the following year, I lectured on the *Vajra Sutra* at that Temple. The fall after that, I lectured on the *Amitabha Sutra* at Baojue (Precious Enlightenment) Monastery. Later on I delivered a fourteen-month lecture series on the *Shurangama Sutra* at Western Bliss Gardens Monastery. Later I lectured on the *Earth Store Sutra* at another temple. I worked on the construction of Cixing Chan Monastery and had an image of the Venerable Master Yun carved as a token of my utmost reverence. I wrote to the Venerable Yun and received from him a document entitled "The Treasury of the Orthodox Dharma Eye: The Source of the Buddhas and Patriarchs"—the Dharma of the mind-to-mind seal which is transmitted outside the teaching, the wonderful mind of Nirvana, the real mark which is without marks, the true emptiness which is not empty. Following the intent of the Patriarchs above and teaching living beings below, I was constantly mindful of the deep kindness of this Dharma-milk. The Elder Master wrote to me, urging me to do meritorious works. I vowed to contribute several tens of thousands of dollars to pay for the Buddha images in the Jewelled Hall of Great Heroes of Zhenru Chan Monastery at Yunju Mountain. I also travelled to Burma and purchased more than three hundred large cartons of gold foil for gilding the Buddha images. The Venerable Yun was very happy and wrote repeatedly in thanks. This shows the vast extent of the Venerable One's deep concern for the younger generation. He is humble and never careless. He denies himself everything to be generous to others and renounces his own will to comply with that of others. His awe-inspiring spirit, his matchless compassion, his lofty virtue, and his absolutely genuine impartiality cause people to serve him happily and willingly.

I received another letter from the Venerable Yun instructing me to return to Yunju Mountain. While in Chan contemplation I came to know that the Elder Master wished to transfer the responsibilities of Zhenru Monastery to me, but for various reasons I could not heed the command. Even now my regret knows no bounds. The Buddhist Lecture Hall had just been established, and every day I was busy with the work of propagating the great Dharma. Since there was no way I could be in two places at the same time, I planned to go back to be with the Elder Master and attend upon him after I had taken care of matters satisfactorily and found someone to assume my responsibilities in Hong Kong.

In July of 1959, I received news of the Venerable Yun's grave illness, and day and night I was worried. I knew it was an inauspicious sign. I had noticed in the Venerable One's Dharma portrait of 1958 that his eyes gazed horizontally, and his eyebrows were several inches long, so they could have been tucked behind his ears. When I saw the portrait I bowed before it and was moved to say, "Every time the Venerable One closes his eyes for photographs, but this time the compassionate eyes are gazing on living beings. This is very unusual. It must be an indication of a major change. In less than a year it will be clear." Then I requested the greatly virtuous Sangha of the ten directions to bow, on behalf of the Elder Master Yun, the Jewelled Repentance of Medicine Master Buddha Who Dispels Calamities and Lengthens Life. I also arranged for several days of Universal Bowing to the Buddhas, and put a notice in the newspaper to let all the Elder One's disciples know, so that by the combined strength of the assembly's determination and sincerity a response would come to pass. At the time, I said to the assembly, "I fear that this is the last opportunity for us to practice Universal Bowing before the Buddhas, to bow the Medicine Master Repentance, and to perform other ceremonies for the Elder Master Yun." My voice was so laden with sorrow as I spoke these words that those who heard me also wept silently.

精神，以垂永範，啟迪後賢，萬古未來，有所楷式。不幸噩耗，竟爾於十月十六日（即農曆九月十五日）接獲專電通知云：老人慟於本月十二日下午一時四十五分鐘，安詳圓寂於雲居山真如禪寺，囑令後人勤修戒定慧，息滅貪瞋癡。為法忘軀，互相敬愛云云。

遽聞之下，不啻山頹地震，人世毀滅，劫火洞燃，不辨是夢是醒，為實為虛，如呆癡之木偶，似無識之泥像，久之乃知覺恢復，不勝悲悼！次日十七上午，召集本堂檀越，商議追思事宜。即席決定舉行佛七二十一天後，復舉行大般若七一百二十日，以昭追思而報法乳之恩。當即通電海外各法侶同參等，分別致電如三藩市佛教講堂、檀香山佛教會、星加坡佛教會、李俊承、畢俊輝居士等，加拿大詹勵吾居士，南洋各國，臺灣、緬甸、泰國、印度、錫蘭等地，以及世界佛教友誼會主席于振東居士等，計百餘封電報拍出，故各地風起雲湧，響應追思老人。遂以電話通知本港各佛教人士，十八日（即農曆九月十七日）在本港各報章公開發表消息，普告大眾。詎料因此招人妒忌，肖小誹謗，魔鬼猖獗，混亂視聽，一般自命為善知識者，亦甘附驥尾從而和之，良可嘆也！信乎善事多魔。

總之，知我者其為雲公乎？罪我者亦惟雲公乎？孔子作春秋而亂臣賊子懼，司馬修史記而作奸犯科者亡，余為雲公而致力，雖萬矛刺身，亦無所畏耳。請儘量發揮汝等之伎倆，至表歡迎接納，永嘉大師云：觀惡言，是功德，此即成吾善知識，不因訕謗起冤親，何表無生慈忍力。又云：從他謗，任他非，把火燒天徒自疲，我聞恰似飲甘露，銷融頓入不思議。然而當知因果不可思議，報應亦不可思議也。慎之！慎之！倘墮拔舌泥犁之苦，悔之晚矣！

農曆十月初四日，遣薛果鳳、馬果仙兩居士赴雲居迎舍利及靈骨供養。初七日，抵真如禪寺，獲舍利十餘顆，異彩

Then a letter came from Yunju saying: "The Venerable One is a little better. We are deeply relieved!" I immediately concentrated all my attention on finding an artist who could be commissioned for the painting of the Elder One's Pictorial Biography. The biography includes over two hundred exquisite Chinese brush drawings. In several tens of thousands of words, it sets forth the Elder One's life of superior virtue, his conduct and vows, the hardships he suffered, his toil, and his singular energy and spirit. The Elder Master is shown as an eternal model and guide for the sages to come. There has not been a model such as he in thousands of years. Unfortunately, death is inevitable. On October 16 (the fifteenth of the ninth lunar month), I received a telegram saying that on October 12 at 1:45 p.m., the Venerable One had completed the stillness at Zhenru Chan Monastery on Yunju Mountain. His instructions for those who would come after him were to diligently cultivate precepts, samadhi, and wisdom, and put to rest greed, anger, and stupidity; to forget themselves for the sake of the Dharma; to respect one another; and so forth.

When I heard this news, suddenly not only did the mountains collapse and the earth quake, but the whole world and everyone in it disappeared as the disaster of fire blazed through everything. I could not tell if I was dreaming or awake, if things were real or illusory. I was as dull as a puppet, as senseless as a clay image. After a while, when I came to my senses, I experienced an overwhelming grief. The next day, on the morning of October 17, I called together all the temple's donors to discuss arrangements for the memorial services. We decided to hold a 21-day Buddha Recitation Session followed by a 120-day Great Prajna Recitation Session. We hoped in this way to commemorate the Elder Master and to repay him for the kindness of the Dharma-milk he had given us. Then we sent telegrams overseas to inform Dharma companions in various parts of the world. Among those contacted were the Buddhist Lecture Hall in San Francisco; the Buddhist Association of Honolulu; Layman Li Juncheng and Laywoman Bi Junhui and others in Hawaii; Layman Zhan Liwu in Canada, and other disciples in Taiwan, Burma, Thailand, India, Ceylon, and other countries; and Layman Yu Jendong, Chairman of the World Buddhist Friendship Association. More than one hundred telegrams were sent out, and thus disciples throughout the world gathered in response to commemorate the Nirvana of the Elder One. Hong Kong Buddhists were contacted by phone, and on October 18, the newspapers in Hong Kong published the news.

Who would have thought that this would arouse people's jealousy! Evildoers began to slander and demonic ghosts went mad. They became so totally confused that they did not distinguish clearly what they saw and heard. Those self-proclaimed "Good Advisors" cleverly convinced not only themselves but impartial bystanders to follow along and join in their campaign. How pitiful! It is easy to believe the saying, "When deeds are good, the demons abound."

When all is said and done, I leave it for the Venerable Yun to decide: Have I done right? When Confucius wrote the *Spring and Autumn Annals*, the corrupt officials and thieves recoiled in dread. When Sima wrote the *Historical Records*, his exposes put an end to villains and criminals. I will devote all my strength to the Venerable Yun. Although ten thousand spears may pierce my body, I am absolutely not afraid. Proceed to aim your machinations at me. I will gladly withstand them.

Great Master Yongjia said, "Contemplate vicious words / As merit and virtue. / Then vicious words become one's Good and Wise Advisors. / Do not let abuse and slander arouse enmity or liking. / How else can the power of compassion and patience with nonproduction be manifest?" He also said, "Let others slander me; / I bear their condemnation. / Those who try to burn the sky only exhaust themselves. / When I hear it, it's just like drinking sweet dew. /

光明，五色繽紛；十六日由寺返，十八日下午至本堂。余率兩序大眾，香花迎接，頂禮叩拜皆大歡喜，余亦如釋重負，輕鬆愉快。

次日偕四居士：毛文達、李仲猷、薛、馬，奉舍利往訪岑老居士，商討專刊事。彼主張遲日出刊，以待海外文件。故此本刊現在始問世（編按：宣公上人在香港時期所製作的《虛雲老和尚涅槃專刊》）。今後尚希世界各國佛教徒眾，精神團結，互相敬愛。

老人遺偈曾云：

蝦恤蟻命不投水，
吾慰水族身擲江，
祈諸受我身願供，
同證菩提度眾生。

請各法侶，不必憂慮，
生死循業，如蠶縛繭，
貪迷不休，囚間憂喜，
欲除此患，努力修煉，
妙契無生，明通性地。
斷愛憎情，脫輪迴險，
參淨三學，堅持四念，
誓願圓成，質幻露電，
證悟真空，萬法一體，
離合悲歡，隨緣泡水。

吾死後化身畢。請各位將吾骨灰，碾成細末，以油糖麵共骨灰和好，做成丸果，請送放河中，以供水族，滿吾所願，感謝無盡！還債人虛雲頂禮。

以此作為吾等之準繩，向前邁進佛城，永不退轉於阿耨多羅三藐三菩提。

Thus smelted and refined, suddenly one enters the inconceivable." Therefore, everyone should be aware of the inconceivable functioning of the law of cause and effect and of the inconceivability of the resulting retribution. Take heed! When you fall into the Hell of Pulling Tongues, it will be too late to regret what you have done.

On the fourth day of the tenth lunar month, I sent two lay disciples, Xie Guofeng and Ma Guoxian, to Yunju to receive a portion of the Elder Master Yun's sharira (relics) and bones and bring them back so we could make offerings to them. On the seventh, the two disciples arrived at Zhenru Chan Monastery and obtained more than ten sharira of rare brilliance, which emitted a light of five colors. They set out on the return trip on the sixteenth and arrived at the Lecture Hall on the afternoon of the eighteenth. I led the great assembly in offering incense and flowers and making prostrations to the sharira. Everyone was extremely happy, and I felt as if a great burden had been lifted off my shoulders.

The next day four laymen—Mao Wenda, Li Jungyou, Xie Guofeng, and Ma Guoxian—accompanied me to take the sharira and call on the Elder Layman Chen to discuss the publication of a memorial book. Layman Chen suggested that the publication be delayed to allow time for the receipt of articles from overseas. Thus it is only now that this book has been published and circulated. I hope that Buddhists in all countries of the world will unite in spirit and respect one another.

The Elder Yun's verse of bequest reads:

Out of kind regard for the life of ants, the shrimp don't hop back in the water.
That I might pacify aquatic creatures, please toss my body in the river.
I pray that all who partake of my offering of body and vows,
Will in turn attain Bodhi and rescue living beings.

I hope that my Dharma companions will not be sad or worried about me.
Birth and death follow our karma, just as the cocoon binds the silkworm that has spun it.
If you do not put an end to greed and confusion,
*   you will remain entrapped by joy and sorrow.*
If you wish to be rid of this trouble, you should cultivate diligently and refine yourself
Until a wonderful tallying with the unproduced occurs
*   and you gain a thorough understanding of the mind ground.*
Through cutting off the emotions of love and hate,
*   you can be released from the dangerous turning wheel.*
As you work to purify the three studies, firmly hold to the four dwellings in mindfulness.
When your vows are perfected, your body is as illusory as a dew drop or a lightning flash.
When you certify and awaken to true emptiness, the myriad dharmas become one substance.
Separation and union, sadness and joy, are as unsubstantial as bubbles.

After I die and my body is cremated,
Please take the ashes of my bones
And grind them into a fine powder.
Mix the powder with oil, sugar, and flour,
Roll it into pellets and then place these in the river
As an offering to the aquatic creatures.
I will be forever thankful if you grant my wish.
Hsu Yun, one who repays his debts, bows in reverence.

Let us take this as our standard of conduct and continue advancing towards the Buddha-city, never retreating from our resolve to realize anuttara-samyak-sambodhi.

佛祖心燈

THE MIND LAMP OF THE BUDDHAS AND PATRIARCHS

本師釋迦牟尼佛

初祖摩訶迦葉尊者（天竺初祖）

二祖阿難陀尊者

三祖商那和修尊者

四祖優婆毱多尊者

五祖提多迦尊者

六祖彌遮迦尊者

七祖婆須密尊者

八祖佛陀難提尊者

九祖伏馱密多尊者

十祖脅尊者

十一祖富那夜奢尊者

十二祖馬鳴大士

十三祖迦毘摩羅尊者

十四祖龍樹尊者

十五祖迦那提婆尊者

十六祖羅睺羅多尊者

十七祖僧伽難提尊者

十八祖伽耶舍多尊者

十九祖鳩摩羅多尊者

二十祖闍夜多尊者

二十一祖婆修盤頭尊者

二十二祖摩拏羅尊者

二十三祖鶴勒那尊者

二十四祖師子尊者

二十五祖婆舍斯多尊者

二十六祖不如密多尊者

二十七祖般若多羅尊者

二十八祖菩提達摩大師（東土禪宗初祖）

二十九祖大祖慧可大師（東土禪宗二祖）

三十祖鑑智僧璨大師（東土禪宗三祖）

三十一祖大醫道信大師（東土禪宗四祖）

三十二祖大滿弘忍大師（東土禪宗五祖）

三十三祖大鑑惠能大師（東土禪宗六祖）

三十四世南嶽懷讓禪師

Original Teacher Shakyamuni Buddha

First Patriarch Ārya Mahākāśyapa (First Patriarch in India)

Second Patriarch Ārya Ānanda

Third Patriarch Śāṇakavāsa

Fourth Patriarch Ārya Upagupta

Fifth Patriarch Ārya Dhṛtaka

Sixth Patriarch Ārya Micchaka

Seventh Patriarch Ārya Vasumitra

Eighth Patriarch Ārya Buddhanandi

Ninth Patriarch Ārya Buddhamitra

Tenth Patriarch Ārya Pārśva

Eleventh Patriarch Ārya Puṇyayaśas

Twelfth Patriarch Mahāsattva Aśvagoṣa

Thirteenth Patriarch Ārya Kapimala

Fourteenth Patriarch Mahāsattva Nāgārjuna

Fifteenth Patriarch Ārya Kāṇadeva

Sixteenth Patriarch Ārya Rāhulata

Seventeeth Patriarch Ārya Saṅghanandi

Eighteenth Patriarch Ārya Gayāsata

Nineteenth Patriarch Ārya Kumārata

Twentieth Patriarch Ārya Jayata

Twenty-first Patriarch Ārya Vasubandhu

Twenty-second Patriarch Ārya Manorhita

Twenty-third Patriarch Ārya Haklena

Twenty-fourth Patriarch Ārya Āryasiṃha

Twenty-fifth Patriarch Ārya Basiasita

Twenty-sixth Patriarch Ārya Puṇyamitra

Twenty-seventh Patriarch Ārya Prajñātāra

Twenty-eighth Patriarch Ārya Bodhidharma
(First Patriarch of the Chan School in China)

Twenty-ninth Patriarch Great Master Dazu Huike
(Second Patriarch of the Chan School in China)

Thirtieth Patriarch Great Master Jianzhi Sengcan
(Third Patriarch of the Chan School in China)

Thirty-first Patriarch Great Master Dayi Taoxin
(Fourth Patriarch of the Chan School in China)

Thirty-second Patriarch Great Master Daman Hungren
(Fifth Patriarch of the Chan School in China)

Thirty-third Patriarch Great Master Dajian Huineng
(Sixth Patriarch of the Chan School in China)

Thirty-fourth Patriarch Chan Master Nanyao Huairang

Thirty-fifth Patriarch Chan Master Mazu Daoyi of Jiangxi

Thirty-sixth Patriarch Chan Master Huaihai of Baizhang

Thirty-seventh Patriarch Chan Master Linyou of Weishan
(First Patriarch of the Weiyang Sect)

宣化老和尚追思紀念專集

三十五世江西馬祖道一禪師
三十六世百丈懷海禪師
三十七世潙山靈祐禪師（潙仰宗第一世）
三十八世仰山慧寂禪師（潙仰宗第二世）
三十九世西塔光穆禪師（潙仰宗第三世）
四十世資福如寶禪師（潙仰宗第四世）
四十一世報慈德韶禪師（潙仰宗第五世）
四十二世三角志謙禪師（潙仰宗第六世）
四十三世興陽詞鐸禪師（潙仰宗第七世）
四十四世德清虛雲禪師（潙仰宗第八世）
四十五世宣化度輪禪師（潙仰宗第九世）

Thirty-eighth Patriarch Chan Master Huiji of Yangshan
(Second Patriarch of the Weiyang Sect)
Thirty-ninth Patriarch Chan Master Guangmu of Xita
(Third Patriarch of the Weiyang Sect)
Fortieth Patriarch Chan Master Rubao of Zifu
(Fourth Patriarch of the Weiyang Sect)
Forty-first Patriarch Chan Master Dezhao of Baoci
(Fifth Patriarch of the Weiyang Sect)
Forty-second Patriarch Chan Master Zhiqian of Sanjiao
(Sixth Patriarch of the Weiyang Sect)
Forty-third Patriarch Chan Master Ciduo of Xingyang
(Seventh Patriarch of the Weiyang Sect)
Forty-fourth Patriarch Chan Master T'e-ch'ing Hsu-yun
(Eighth Patriarch of the Weiyang Sect)
Forty-fifth Patriarch Chan Master Hsuan-hua To-lun
(Ninth Patriarch of the Weiyang Sect)

潙仰宗第八代祖虛雲德清演派五十六字：

Eighth Patriarch Hsu-yun T'e-ch'ing's 56-character Verse
for the Transmission of the Weiyang Sect:

詞德宣衍道大興，戒鼎馨遍五分新；
慧燄彌布周沙界，香雲普蔭燦古今。
慈悲濟世願無盡，光超日月朗太清；
振啓拈花宏潙上，圓相心燈永昌明。

The virtue of words proclaims in profusion and the Way greatly prospers.
The morality tripod's fragrance permeates with five shares renewed.
The wisdom flames fully pervade, enveloping worlds as many as sands.
The incense cloud everywhere masks the splendor of old and new.
Kindness and pity deliver the world with vows which have no end.
The light excels the sun and moon, bright and totally clear.
He revived the sect and held the flower to propagate the Wei.
The perfect mark of the mind-lamp is eternally glorious and bright.

禪宗金頂毗盧派源流訣

Verses on the Source and Lineage of the Golden-crowned Vairochana Sect of the Chan School

寶誌禪師演派二十八字：

Chan Master Baozhi's 28-character Verse for the Transmission of the Sect:

寶樹成行德蓮香，
志願極樂懷安養；
紫金憲古永遠在，
毗盧性海萬世昌。

The precious tree is erected; the lotus of virtue is fragrant.
The mind is resolved on Ultimate Bliss and longs for comfort and ease.
The example set by the purple-golden one in ancient times will always remain.
Vairochana's nature sea will flourish for ten thousand generations.

昌海禪師續派四十字：

Chan Master Changhai's 40-character Verse for the Continuation of the Sect:

聞定靜宗道，慈福眞法德；
正善印義祖，普弘信玄妙。
崇現本來少，性空圓明照；
思修常安果，親傳無爲教。

Samadhi and stillness of hearing are the sect's tradition.
Kindness and blessings are the true virtue of the Dharma.
Proper goodness seals the meaning of the patriarchs.
Universally propagate and believe in its profound wonder.
It's exalted manifestation has always been rare.
The nature is empty, perfect, and brightly illuminating.
Reflect upon and cultivate the fruition of eternal peace.
Personally transmit the unconditioned teaching.

宣公上人行儀

THE LIFE AND DEEDS OF VENERABLE MASTER HUA

釋恆通　Shi Hengtung

壹、出生

民初戊午年農曆三月十六日，宣公降生在中國東北吉林省雙城縣一個小村落裡姓白的農家。一出母胎，連哭三天，悲憫娑婆世界的眾苦充滿。十一歲，在荒野見一死嬰，開始省悟，欲出家修道，解決生死大事。

十二歲，向父母悔過，一心孝養。天天行叩頭，覺不夠，漸至增加向天地君親師叩頭，還覺不夠，更增加向一切眾生叩頭。早晚各一次，每次叩八百三十多個頭，共須五個小時。颶風也叩，下雨也叩，大雪來也叩，希望把壞人叩成好人，把亂世叩到太平。

十五歲，皈依哈爾濱三緣寺上常下智老和尚，正式為三寶弟子；親近三緣寺方丈上常下仁老和尚。直到十七歲，這期間雖只讀了兩年半的書，但因專一其心，過目成誦，所以貫通四書、五經、諸子百家、醫卜星相一切世法。又參禪習定，研究經典，故也透徹出世法。

十六歲時，開始為人講《六祖法寶壇經》、《金剛經》、《彌陀經》等，為不識字的人講說佛法。

十八歲時，因母親生病，輟學在家侍母。深體失學的苦處，所以創辦義務學校，一人全天候不休息地教育三十多個貧寒的孩子。

在求學期間，還參加很多慈善團體——佛教會、道德會、慈善會、理善勸戒菸酒會……。諸惡不作，眾善奉行，廣修救人濟世的菩薩道業。

貳、出家

十九歲，母親胡太夫人逝世。四月初八佛誕日，拜上常下智老和尚，在三緣寺披剃，

I. Birth

On the sixteenth day of the third lunar month in the year of Wuwu (1918), the Venerable Master Hua was born to a family called Bai in a small village in Shuangcheng County of Jilin Province, Manchuria, China. As soon as he was born, he cried continuously for three days out of pity for the beings who suffer in the Saha world. When he was eleven, he had an awakening upon seeing a dead infant left in the wilderness. He wanted to leave the home-life and cultivate the Way in order to resolve the great matter of birth and death.

When he was twelve, he began repenting of his faults to his parents and attended to them with filial devotion. He bowed to his parents every day. Later he felt it was not enough to bow to them, so he began to bow to the heavens, to the earth, to the Emperor, and to his teachers. He still felt it was not enough, so he gradually increased his bows until he was bowing to all living beings. He bowed every morning and evening, each time making more than 830 bows, which took five hours a day. He bowed even in the wind, rain, and snow, hoping to influence evil people to become good, hoping to bring peace to the chaotic world.

When he was fifteen, the Master took refuge with Venerable High Master Changzhi of Sanyuan Monastery in Harbin and became a disciple of the Triple Jewel. He drew near the Abbot of Sanyuan Monastery, the Venerable High Master Changren. He attended school for only two and a half years, until he was seventeen, but because he studied with single-minded concentration, he was able to recite a text from memory after reading it once. Thus he mastered the Four Books, the Five Classics, the texts of various Chinese schools of thought, and all worldly fields of knowledge, such as medicine, divination, astrology, and physiognomy.

At sixteen, the Master began to lecture on Sutras such as the *Sixth Patriarch's Dharma Jewel Platform Sutra*, the *Vajra Sutra*, and the *Amitabha Sutra*, explaining the Buddhadharma to those who were illiterate.

When the Master was eighteen, his mother became ill, so he quit school and stayed home to take care of her. Because he knew well the hardships that came from not receiving a complete education, he founded a free school and taught over thirty poor children from morning to night without rest.

During his years in school, the Master also took part in many charity organizations—the Buddhist Association, the Moral Society, the Charity Society, a society which exhorted people to quit smoking and drinking, and others. Refraining from all evil and practicing all good, he vastly cultivated the Bodhisattva work of rescuing people and saving the world.

II. Leaving the Home-life

When he was nineteen, his mother, Ms. Hu, passed away. On the eighth

受沙彌戒，名「安慈」，字「度輪」。
依止三緣寺方丈上常下仁老和尚。接虛
老法脈後，號「宣化」。出家三年，在
母墓旁守孝，人稱「白孝子」。

　　同年六月十九觀音誕，在佛前發下十
八大願。宣公一生實踐力行，圓滿這十
八大願：

稽首十方佛，及與三藏法，過去現在賢
聖僧。惟願垂作證，弟子度輪，釋安慈
，我今發心，不為自求人天福報、聲聞
緣覺，乃至權乘諸位菩薩。唯依最上乘
，發菩提心；願與法界眾生，一時同得
阿耨多羅三藐三菩提：

（一）願盡虛空、遍法界、十方三世一
切菩薩等，若有一未成佛時，我誓不取
正覺。
（二）願盡虛空、遍法界、十方三世一
切緣覺等，若有一未成佛時，我誓不取
正覺。
（三）願盡虛空、遍法界、十方三世一
切聲聞等，若有一未成佛時，我誓不取
正覺。
（四）願三界諸天人等，若有一未成佛
時，我誓不取正覺。
（五）願十方世界一切人等，若有一未
成佛時，我誓不取正覺。
（六）願天、人、一切阿修羅等，若有
一未成佛時，我誓不取正覺。
（七）願一切畜生界等，若有一未成佛
時，我誓不取正覺。
（八）願一切餓鬼界等，若有一未成佛
時，我誓不取正覺。
（九）願一切地獄界等，若有一未成佛
，或地獄不空時，我誓不取正覺。
（十）願凡是三界諸天、仙、人、阿修
羅、飛潛動植、靈界龍畜、鬼神等眾，
曾經皈依我者，若有一未成佛時，我誓
不取正覺。
（十一）願將我所應享受一切福樂，悉
皆迴向，普施法界眾生。

day of the fourth month, the Buddha's birthday, he left the home-life at Sanyuan Monastery under Venerable High Master Changzhi, received the Shramanera (novice) precepts, and was given the names An Tse and To Lun. He studied under Venerable High Master Changren, the Abbot of Sanyuan Monastery. When he received the Dharma-transmission from the Elder Master Hsu Yun, he was given the name Hsuan Hua. For three years after he left the home-life, he lived in a simple hut by his mother's grave in observance of filial piety. People called him Filial Son Bai.

On the nineteenth day of the sixth month (the anniversary of Guanyin Bodhisattva) of that year, he made eighteen great vows before the Buddhas. The Venerable Master Hua's life was a practical realization of these eighteen great vows.

I bow before the Buddhas of the ten directions, the Dharma of the Tripitaka, and the Holy Sangha of the past and present, praying that they will hear and bear witness. I, disciple To Lun, Shi An Tse, resolve never to seek for myself the blessings of gods or humans, or the attainments of Shravakas, Pratyekabuddhas, or high Bodhisattvas. Instead I rely on the Supreme Vehicle, the One Buddha Vehicle, and bring forth the Resolve for Bodhi, vowing that all living beings of the Dharma Realm will attain Utmost, Right, and Equal, Proper Enlightenment at the same time as I do.

1. I vow that as long as there is a single Bodhisattva in the three periods of time throughout the ten directions of the Dharma Realm, to the very end of empty space, who has not accomplished Buddhahood, I too will not attain Proper Enlightenment.

2. I vow that as long as there is a single Pratyekabuddha in the three periods of time throughout the ten directions of the Dharma Realm, to the very end of empty space, who has not accomplished Buddhahood, I too will not attain Proper Enlightenment.

3. I vow that as long as there is a single Shravaka in the three periods of time throughout the ten directions of the Dharma Realm, to the very end of empty space, who has not accomplished Buddhahood, I too will not attain Proper Enlightenment.

4. I vow that as long as there is a single god in the Triple Realm who has not accomplished Buddhahood, I too will not attain Proper Enlightenment.

5. I vow that as long as there is a single human being in the worlds of the ten directions who has not accomplished Buddhahood, I too will not attain Proper Enlightenment.

6. I vow that as long as there is a single asura who has not accomplished Buddhahood, I too will not attain Proper Enlightenment.

7. I vow that as long as there is a single animal who has not accomplished Buddhahood, I too will not attain Proper Enlightenment.

8. I vow that as long as there is a single hungry ghost who has not accomplished Buddhahood, I too will not attain Proper Enlightenment.

9. I vow that as long as there is a single hell-dweller who has not accomplished Buddhahood, I too will not attain Proper Enlightenment.

10. I vow that as long as there is a single god, immortal, human, asura, airbound or water-bound creature, animate or inanimate object, or a single dragon, beast, ghost, spirit, or the like of the spiritual realm that has taken refuge with me and has not accomplished Buddhahood, I too will not attain Proper Enlightenment.

11. I vow to fully dedicate all blessings and bliss which I myself ought to receive and enjoy to all living beings of the Dharma Realm.

（十二）願將法界眾生所有一切苦難，悉皆與我一人代受。

（十三）願分靈無數，普入一切不信佛法眾生心，令其改惡向善，悔過自新，皈依三寶，究竟作佛。

（十四）願一切眾生，見我面，乃至聞我名，悉發菩提心，速得成佛道。

（十五）願恪遵佛制，實行日中一食。

（十六）願覺諸有情，普攝群機。

（十七）願此生即得五眼六通，飛行自在。

（十八）願一切求願，必獲滿足。

結云：

眾生無邊誓願度
煩惱無盡誓願斷
法門無量誓願學
佛道無上誓願成

參、治疾病

宣公自幼就有俠義心腸，最不忍見人受苦，所以發願代一切眾生受苦。治好無數人的疑難怪病、致命絕症、瘟疫痢疾、鬼上身、業障病……等等，度化狐狸、龍、蛇、鬼神，甚至有千年樟樹來求皈、受戒。宣公說：不是我有什麼能力，或者神通妙用，這都是佛菩薩的加被。人有誠心，佛菩薩就有感應。

宣公在為人加持中，要人明白加持的意義：不要只知求人加被自己，人要自己先能加被自己，再去加被一切眾生，這才是真正的加持。

人為什麼誦經、念咒沒有感應？就因為打妄語，說假話。咒是真言，人能不打妄語，所說的話都是靈文，叫天天應，叫地地靈。宣公說：我是個最不會說話的人，只會講真話，講人不愛聽的話。專門破除迷信，也不怕得罪人，該說的話，到哪裡都要說；不該說的話，到哪裡都不說。就因為不打妄語，所以字字句句都有無邊的力量，能治有情眾生的病，也能治無情眾

12. I vow to fully take upon myself all the sufferings and hardships of all living beings in the Dharma Realm.

13. I vow to manifest innumerable bodies as a means to gain access into the minds of living beings throughout the universe who do not believe in the Buddhadharma, causing them to correct their faults and tend toward wholesomeness, repent of their errors and start anew, take refuge in the Triple Jewel, and ultimately accomplish Buddhahood.

14. I vow that all living beings who see my face or even hear my name will fix their thoughts on Bodhi and quickly accomplish the Buddha Way.

15. I vow to respectfully observe the Buddha's instructions and cultivate the practice of eating only one meal per day.

16. I vow to enlighten all sentient beings, universally responding to the multitude of differing potentials.

17. I vow to obtain the five eyes, six spiritual powers, and the freedom of being able to fly in this very life.

18. I vow that all of my vows will certainly be fulfilled.

Also:

I vow to save innumerable living beings.
I vow to eradicate inexhaustible afflictions.
I vow to study limitless Dharma-doors.
I vow to accomplish the unsurpassed Buddha Way.

III. Healing Illnesses

The Venerable Master Hua had the spirit of a knight-errant even as a child. He couldn't bear to see people suffering, so he vowed to take the suffering of all living beings upon himself. He healed countless people who were stricken with strange diseases, terminal illnesses, ghost-possession, sickness caused by karmic obstacles, and so forth. He influenced and saved foxes, dragons, snakes, ghosts, and spirits. Even a thousand-year-old camphor tree sought to take refuge and receive the precepts from the Master. The Venerable Master said, "This is not because I have some special ability or the wonderful function of spiritual powers. This is the aid of the Buddhas and Bodhisattvas. When people's minds are sincere, the Buddhas and Bodhisattvas will respond."

Whenever the Venerable Master bestowed aid, he wanted people to understand the meaning of bestowing aid: "You shouldn't only know how to seek aid from others. You should first be able to aid yourselves, and then you can bestow aid on all living beings. That's the true meaning of giving aid."

Why do people fail to obtain a response when they recite Sutras or mantras? Because they tell lies. Mantras are true words. If people can refrain from false speech, then whatever they say will be efficacious. If they call on heaven, heaven will respond. If they call on earth, the earth will be efficacious. The Venerable Master Hua said, "I am the worst speaker, because I only know how to speak the truth and say things that people don't like to hear. I specialize in destroying superstition, and I'm not afraid of offending people. If something ought to be said, I will say it wherever I go. If something should not be said, I will not say it no matter where I go. Simply because one does not speak falsely, every word and sentence one

生的病；本來要打颶風的，能令它不打颶風；本來有大地震的，結果也不震了；沒水的地方可以有水；沒雨的地方，可以下雨；有戰爭、災難的地方，能令它沒有戰爭、災難；有能變無，無能變有，這是因為真誠到極點，自然有感斯通，無求不應。

真理所在，一切天龍善神都來護持。
真理所在，一切諸佛菩薩都來護持。

肆、弘正法

　　一九四八年，赴香港弘法。一九六二年應邀來美，致力弘法、譯經、教育大業（全屬義務性質）。並建道場，收徒眾、立宗旨，奠定正法在西方的基石。

　　「可以一日不吃飯，不可一日不說法」，「只要有一口氣在，就要說法。」「人多也講，人少也講，一個人來還是講，沒人來，就講給鬼神聽。」宣公一生言行，時時刻刻，在在處處，都是最真實的說法。

一、身說法

　　（一）三年守墳，對父母盡孝。一生敬老懷幼，對眾生盡孝。見中國多難，不忍拋棄中國人的身分，來美三十多年，一方面全心利益美國國民，一方面堅持保留中國國籍，對兩國都盡忠。

　　（二）衣食住行儉樸到極點，節省各項物資能源，一雙鞋穿三十多年，一張面紙至少用三天以上，一生從沒為自己做過一件衣服，連過橋費都刻意儉省。米屑落地，拾起再吃，喝水要一滴不剩，吃的是無油無鹽最簡單的食物，甚至多次打長期餓七，把自身福德迴施所有眾生。沒有任何個人財產，一切供養轉做公用，連一根頭髮般的私心都沒有。

　　（三）從不擺架子，總把自己放在最低、最後。從十二歲就行叩頭法門，禮拜一切眾生，沒有一天停止。來到美國，還向弟子行叩頭法門，叩得弟子也敢講法了，叩得弟子也發願三步一拜了，叩得弟子也學習向毀謗宣

says has limitless power and can cure the diseases of sentient as well as insentient beings. If a hurricane is due to occur, it can be averted. If a great earthquake is supposed to happen, it can be prevented. In places without water, water will appear. In places where the rain doesn't fall, it will rain. Wars and calamities can be quelled. What exists can be made to disappear, and what doesn't exist can be made to appear. Because one is sincere to the utmost point, there is naturally a response to everything one seeks."

Wherever the truth is found, all the gods, dragons, and good spirits will come to protect it.
Wherever the truth is found, all the Buddhas and Bodhisattvas will come to protect it.

IV. Propagating the Proper Dharma

In 1948, the Venerable Master went to Hong Kong to propagate the Dharma. In 1962, he responded to an invitation to come to America where he devoted himself to the great tasks of propagating the Dharma, translating the Sutras, and administering education, all on a voluntary basis. He also built Way-places, accepted disciples, set forth principles, and lay the foundation for the proper Dharma in the West.

"I may go without eating for one day, but I cannot go for a day without speaking the Dharma." "As long as I have even one breath left, I will speak the Dharma." "I will speak whether there are many people or few. Even if only one person comes, I will still lecture. Even if no one comes, I will still lecture for the ghosts and spirits to hear." The Venerable Master's every word and every move, at all times and places, was the truest expression of Dharma.

A. Speaking the Dharma by Example

1. He stayed by his mother's grave for three years, thus fulfilling his filial duty to his parents. Throughout his life, he respected the elderly and cherished young people, thus fufilling his filial duty to all living beings. Seeing China going through difficult times, he couldn't bear to renounce his Chinese citizenship. During his thirty-some years in America, he devoted himself to benefitting Americans, while firmly insisting on maintaining his Chinese citizenship, thus being entirely loyal to both countries.

2. He was extremely sparing in his clothing, food, and dwelling, hoping to save the world's resources and energy. One pair of shoes could last him more than thirty years, and he would use the same napkin for at least three days. In his whole life he never had any clothes made for himself. He would even try to save on paying the bridge toll. If a grain of rice fell to the ground, he would pick it up and eat it. When he drank a glass of water, he would drink every last drop. He ate the plainest of food, cooked without oil or salt. He undertook long fasts many times, dedicating his own blessings to all living beings. He had no personal wealth or property, for he turned all offerings over to the general fund. He had not even a hairsbreadth of selfishness in his heart.

3. Not only did he put on no airs, he always put himself last and lowest. He began cultivating the Dharma door of bowing when he was twelve, bowing to all living beings every day without fail. After coming to

公的人叩頭了。到任何地方，走路，都要弟子先走，自己走在最後頭；講法，讓弟子先說，自己最後說；成佛，也是讓眾生先成，自己最後成。

（四）威儀具足，嚴中有慈，雙目低垂，兩手當胸，口常含笑，望之儼然，即之也溫！

（五）凡事不願麻煩別人，衣服自己洗，行李自己提，甚至病到要拐著拐杖才能行走時，仍不要人扶持。幾年來，抱病坐輪椅、搭機往返各道場說法期間，仍堅持自己揹行李，或放在膝上。宣公說：我就是要自立自強，不依賴任何人。

（六）宣公二六時常在定中，事來則應，事去則靜。在日理萬機之中，仍然從容不迫，氣定神閒。宣公說：我也不念經，也沒誦咒，我只是不打妄想。宣公做任何事，都是專一其心，弟子英譯有誤，宣公馬上糾正。對所有物件的放置，沒有忘失。對四眾弟子的姓名、背景、性情、習氣悉知悉見，從不錯亂。甚至自己一天內走了幾步路，都一清二楚。

（七）在美弘法多年，人稱「上人」、「全球第一高僧」，山東濟寧大學請求改成「宣化大學」，又有教授提倡成立「法界妙覺山研究會」來研究宣公事蹟……。但宣公表示：不要研究我，我不值得研究。你們應該去研究其他人，男的、女的、出家的、在家的、老的、少的、好的、壞的……，都記錄下來，將來可以教化人。我道不足感人，德不足化人，人家要的名字我不要。我不是「高僧」，不是「上人」，只是「下人」，歡喜在人人之下。人家不要的名字，就是我的名字，我叫自己是「活死人」、「墓中僧」、「小螞蟻」、「小蚊蟲」，甘願走在一切眾生的腳下。其實，一切名字都是假的，沒有什麼是真名字，不過是因時、因地、因人而有，這沒什麼了不得的，但人都著到名上，為它奔波勞碌。我生時死後，都不願人提我的名字，也不要人給我造靈塔、紀念堂，什麼痕跡也不留，我從虛空來，還要回到虛空去。

America, he also bowed to his disciples, bowing until they were no longer afraid to speak the Dharma, bowing until some of them vowed to make a pilgrimage of bowing once every three steps, bowing until his disciples were also willing to bow to the slanderers of the Venerable Master. No matter where he went, he always wanted his disciples to walk in front of him. He would walk behind everyone else. When he spoke the Dharma, he let his disciples speak first and was himself the last to speak. He also wanted all his disciples to attain Buddhahood before he did. He wanted to be the last one to attain Buddhahood.

4. He had perfect comportment. He was stern, yet kind. His eyes were ever lowered, his two hands remained folded at his breast, and a smile always touched on his lips. He appeared stern, yet when one came to have contact with him, he was gentle and kindly.

5. He never wished to trouble others. He washed his own clothes, carried his own luggage, and didn't want people to support him even when he was so ill that he had to lean on his cane to walk. Even in the last several years, when he had to use a wheelchair, he still insisted on carrying his own bag over his shoulder or on his lap as he travelled by plane to the various Way-places to speak the Dharma in his sick condition. The Venerable Master said, "I want to stand on my own feet and use my own strength. I don't want to be dependent on anyone else."

6. The Venerable Master was in samadhi twenty-four hours a day. He responded to situations as they arose and was calm when they were over. He handled the myriad affairs of the day naturally and easily. The Master said, "I don't recite any Sutra or mantra. I simply don't have any idle thoughts." The Venerable Master did everything with single-minded concentration. He would immediately catch any mistake his disciples made in translating what he said into English. He never forgot where he placed things. He remembered the names, backgrounds, dispositions, and habits of all his disciples and never got them mixed up. He even knew exactly how many steps he had taken on any given day.

7. During the many years that he propagated the Dharma in America, people called him 'Superior One' and 'The World's Foremost High Sanghan (Buddhist monk).' Jining College in Shandong province, China, wanted to change its name to "Hsuan Hua College." A professor founded the Wonderful Enlightenment Mountain Research Committee to study the life of the Venerable Master Hua.... Yet the Venerable Master said, "Don't study me. I'm not worth studying. You should study the lives of other people, be they male or female, monastic or lay, old or young, good or bad,...You should record their lives, for in the future these accounts can instruct people. I do not have sufficient virtue in the Way to influence people. I do not want the names that other people want. I am neither a 'High Sanghan' nor a 'Superior One.' I am just an 'inferior one' who likes to be below everyone else. The names that other people don't want, I take for my own. I call myself 'Living Dead Person,' 'Monk in a Grave,' 'Little Ant,' and 'Little Mosquito.' I wish to walk beneath the feet of all living beings. All names are, in fact, false. There are no true names. Names exist in response to the time, place, and person. They are no big deal. Yet everyone is attached to names and works tirelessly for their sake. While I am alive and after I die, I don't want people to mention my name, or build me any stupas or memorials. I don't want to leave any traces. I came from empty space, and I will return to empty space."

二、口説法

（一）在「法總」各道場：說法是為了認識真理，所以各道場每天都有講經或聽經的課程。「恆河的水，天天在流；萬佛聖城的法，天天在說。」宣公早期採用「主觀智能推動力」的方法，平等栽培四眾弟子，輪流練習請法、演說和講評。又時常主持「對聯課」，開啟弟子自性的智慧！

（二）隨緣遇事：觀機說法，對平民百姓，就說安分守本的法門；對學生，就說孝悌忠信、禮義廉恥，愛身、愛家、愛國的法門；對教授、校長，就說為教育而教育的法門；對政界人士，就說兩袖清風、愛民如子的法門。

（三）應邀演講：宣公不要個人名利，所以從不單獨赴請。但為訓練弘法人才，組成四眾訪問團，到海內外各國去參學。每日行程緊密，除例行早、晚課、上供外，拜懺、誦經、講開示、傳三皈五戒，做大悲、楞嚴法會，或會見信眾……，不空過一分一秒。宣公說：我們不是「旅遊團」，也稱不上「弘法團」，只是「訪問團」。我什麼也不懂，不夠資格來弘揚佛法；但歡喜跟在眾人後面，向各地長老大德來學習。

伍、建道場

宣公從中國到香港，又從香港來美國。發願「造人不造廟」，要造活祖師、活羅漢、活菩薩、活佛。所以在艱難困苦中，整修現成的建築物，用做度生的菩提道場。在無形的道場下功夫，不在有形的道場耗財力。可以說，「法總」各道場的外觀雖不是中國典型的寺廟，但內裡卻是真心修行人安居的淨土。

宣公又歡喜「拆小廟、蓋大廟」，成立「公共大道場」，每創建一個道場，就獻一個道場。宣公獻出萬佛聖城、法界聖城兩大道場，和「法總」所屬一切寺院，給全世界的眾生使用。來者不拒，不分國籍、種族、親疏、遠近、姓別、年齡、南宗、北宗……，

B. Orally Speaking the Dharma

1. At the affiliated Way-places of the Dharma Realm Buddhist Association: The Dharma is spoken to enable beings to recognize the truth. Therefore, each Way-place includes in its daily schedule a time for giving or listening to lectures on the Sutras. "The waters of the Ganges River flow day after day; the Dharma of the Sagely City of Ten Thousand Buddhas is spoken day after day." In the early period the Venerable Master used a method called "Developing Inherent Wisdom" to train the fourfold assembly of disciples on an equal basis. They would take turns to request the Dharma, give lectures, and evaluate lectures. The Venerable Master also regularly held classes on "Matching Couplets" to help his disciples activate the wisdom in their own natures.

2. According to conditions: The Venerable Master would always choose the appropriate Dharma to speak to the people he was facing. To ordinary people, he spoke of being content with their work and fulfilling their basic duties. To students, he spoke of filial piety, fraternal respect, loyalty, trustworthiness, propriety, righteousness, incorruptibility, and a sense of shame; of cherishing oneself, loving one's family, and serving the country. To professors and university presidents, he spoke of educating for the sake of education. To political leaders, he spoke of moral probity and of loving the people as if they were one's own children.

3. In accepting invitations to lecture: The Venerable Master didn't want personal fame. Because he wished to train other people, he never went to give a lecture alone. Rather, he would always bring a delegation of disciples on trips to study and learn in various countries. The daily schedule on these trips would always be very full. Aside from the usual morning and evening ceremonies and noon meal offering, there might be repentance ceremonies, Sutra recitation, lectures, transmission of the three refuges and five precepts, Great Compassion or Shurangama Dharma Sessions, or meetings with faithful followers. Not a single moment would be wasted. The Venerable Master said, "We are not a tourist delegation, nor can we be called a Dharma-propagation delegation. We are simply a visiting delegation. I don't understand much of anything, and I'm not qualified to propagate the Buddhadharma. I'm happy to follow behind everyone else and to learn from the Elders and Greatly Virtuous Ones of various places."

V. Establishing Way-places

The Venerable Master went from China to Hong Kong, and from Hong Kong to the United States. He vowed "to build people, not temples." He wanted to create living patriarchs, living Arhats, living Bodhisattvas, and living Buddhas. And so, under the most difficult of conditions, he renovated already-existing buildings to serve as bases for teaching living beings. He applied effort on the intangible and invisible Way-places instead of spending extravagant amounts of money on the physical and visible Way-places. Although the various Way-places of the Dharma Realm Buddhist Association do not look like traditional Chinese monasteries on the outside, within them one finds a Pure Land where true cultivators reside.

The Venerable Master also wished to "tear down small temples and build great temples" and to establish "large public Way-places." Every time he established a Way-place, he would offer it to others. The Venerable Master offered two great Way-places—the Sagely City of Ten Thou-

願護持各地真心的修行人都來共同辦道。宣公說：我們不是子孫廟，十方來，十方去，道場等待任何有德的人來主持，我只是個暫時看門的，我一個道場也沒有。

又說：佛教是人教、心教、眾生教、法界教，沒有個別的門戶。所以我也不屬於任何教派。耶、回、猶，一切宗教都在佛教裡面，我們隨時歡迎所有宗教來萬佛聖城舉行自己的儀式。每個教徒應該學習各教教主救世的悲願，互相幫助，共同建設世界宗教大團結的發源地，令一切眾生有所依歸，那麼世界的戰爭都會沒有了。

陸、收徒眾

宣公說：萬佛聖城龍蛇混雜、份子不齊，有修行的人，有不修行的人。我們要本著慈悲喜捨四無量心，對不好的人要更加照顧，把壞人感化成好人。

一、度出家弟子，不捨任何眾生

法賴僧傳，人能弘道，為了在西方奠定正法的堅固基礎，必須有正人來行持正法。所以，早期的收徒條件特別嚴格，必須是大學生，必須會背〈楞嚴咒〉；出家之後，必須會背《楞嚴經》，必須訓練講經說法、禪坐，必須吃苦耐勞……。

中期後，宣公為平等攝受一切眾生，就算善根只有一根頭髮那麼細的人，都會滿對方出家的願心。九十多歲的老人也收，令他們有所歸投；六、七歲的小孩也收，令他們善根增長；六根不具的人也收，成就他們出世淨緣。

二、度在家弟子，不爭任何一弟子

現代教界流行「參師」，一人皈依很多師父。宣公說：皈依一次就夠了，不要拜一個師父，又違背一個師父，拜這麼多師父，一個師父的話也不聽，這是沒有用的。不但影響法師間不和合，爭徒弟。更令教內只是同一班老教徒在打混，沒有新血輪，佛法就會衰亡了。

sand Buddhas and the Sagely City of the Dharma Realm, as well as all the monasteries affiliated with Dharma Realm Buddhist Association—to all the living beings in the world. He welcomed all people who came, not discriminating what nationality, race, sex, or age they were, whether or not they were related to him, how close or distant they were, whether they belonged to the northern or southern school, and so on. He was willing to support any sincere cultivator who wished to come and cultivate in the Way-place. The Venerable Master said, "We are not a family temple. People come and go from the ten directions. The temple is waiting for a virtuous person to serve as Abbot. I am merely a temporary doorkeeper. Not a single Way-place belongs to me."

He also said, "Buddhism is the teaching of people, the teaching of the mind, the teaching of living beings, and the teaching of the Dharma Realm. It has no sects or factions. I don't belong to any particular sect either. Christianity, Islam, Judaism, and all other religions are within Buddhism. We always welcome other religions to come to the Sagely City of Ten Thousand Buddhas to hold their services. Every religious person should study the compassionate vows that the founders of all religions made to save the world. Everyone should help one another and work together to establish a starting ground for the unity of the world's religions. Then all living beings will have a place of refuge, and wars will vanish from the world."

VI. Taking Disciples

The Venerable Master said, "The Sagely City of Ten Thousand Buddhas is a place where dragons and snakes mingle together. People are not all the same. There are cultivators, and there are people who don't cultivate. We should base ourselves on the four limitless thoughts of kindness, compassion, joy, and giving. We should especially take care of those who are not good, and influence bad people to become good."

A. In taking left-home disciples, he didn't renounce any living being
The Dharma depends on the Sangha for its transmission. The Way must be propagated by people. For the orthodox Dharma to have a strong foundation in the West, there have to be upright people who practice the proper Dharma. For that reason, the Venerable Master set extremely strict requirements for people who wished to leave the home-life under him: a college education and memorization of the Shurangama Mantra. After they left home, they had to memorize the Shurangama Sutra, practice lecturing on the Sutras and speaking the Dharma, practice sitting in meditation, and be able to endure suffering and toil....

After the middle period, the Venerable Master began accepting all living beings on an equal basis. As long as a person had even the tiniest bit of good roots, the Venerable Master would grant his or her wish to leave the home-life. He accepted people who were in their nineties, providing them with a haven of refuge. He also accepted six-and seven-year-olds, allowing their good roots to grow. He also accepted those who were crippled or impaired, allowing them to perfect the pure conditions for transcending the world.

B. In taking lay disciples, he didn't compete for a single disciple
In the modern Buddhist world, the trend is for people to take refuge with many teachers. The Venerable Master said, "Taking refuge with one teacher is enough. Don't take refuge with one teacher and turn your back on another. You take refuge with so many teachers, but you don't listen to any of them. This is useless. Not only does this cause disharmony

只要有真誠，宣公即使在病中，多人來，也辦皈依；一人來，也辦皈依，不怕煩，不怕累。

三、古來大德有立志不收徒眾的，以免因教化責任而誤了自身修持。而宣公是從不考慮自己，包容末世一切剛強頑鈍、難調難伏的根器。寧施頭目腦髓，也不捨棄任何一個眾生。

柒、立宗旨

來到萬佛聖城的人，都要守規矩，是龍也要盤起來，不可隨便降雨；是虎也要臥起來，不能隨便颳風。「法總」所有道場，共同學習行持宣公立下的三大宗旨、六大條款等，為修行的準則，而以萬佛聖城做總部的代表。

一、三大宗旨、六大條款

各道場四眾弟子在早晚課誦開始時，先要迴光返照，共念：

凍死不攀緣，餓死不化緣，窮死不求緣，隨緣不變，不變隨緣，抱定我們三大宗旨，捨命為佛事，造命為本事，正命為僧事，即事明理，明理即事，推行祖師一脈心傳。問自己是不是不爭？問自己是不是不貪？問自己是不是不求？問自己是不是不自私？問自己是不是不自利？問自己是不是不打妄語？問自己是不是吃一餐？是不是衣不離體？這是萬佛聖城的家風，任何人都不能改。

二、衣不離體

為遵守佛制，為護持僧相，宣公領導出家弟子時刻搭衣、持具、袈裟不離身，也破除自、他對好衣的貪著。

三、日中一食

飲食既費時又滋長貪心，妨礙修行，宣公依佛制，行日中一食，用缽吃飯。以清淡的大鍋菜、羅漢湯，做治饑渴病的良藥，七、八分飽就夠，不求多、不貪好，從食欲中得自在。

---

among Dharma Masters as they compete for disciples, it results in a situation where there are only the same old disciples stirring up confusion. There is no new blood in Buddhism. This will cause the Buddhadharma to perish."

As long as people were sincere, the Master would transmit the refuges to them even when he was ill. Undaunted by trouble or fatigue, he would hold the ceremony whether or not many people came.

C. Some of the greatly virtuous cultivators of the past vowed not to take disciples, fearing that their teaching duties would interfere with their own cultivation. The Venerable Master accepted all the headstrong, ignorant, and incorrigible beings of the Dharma-ending Age, never giving a thought to himself. He would rather give up his own brains, eyes, and marrow than renounce any living being.

VII. Establishing Principles

"Those who come to the Sagely City of Ten Thousand Buddhas have to follow the rules. Dragons have to coil up; they cannot make it rain whenever they please. Tigers have to crouch down; they cannot make the wind blow according to their whim." At the Way-places of Dharma Realm Buddhist Association, everyone strives to practice the Three Guidelines and Six Principles set forth by the Venerable Master, taking these as the standard in cultivation. The Sagely City of Ten Thousand Buddhas is the headquarters of the Association.

A. The Three Guidelines and Six Principles

At the beginning of the morning and evening ceremonies each day, the fourfold assembly of disciples must reflect upon themselves as they recite: "Freezing to death, we do not scheme. Starving to death, we do not beg. Dying of poverty, we ask for nothing. According with conditions, we do not change. Not changing, we accord with conditions. We adhere firmly to our three great principles. We renounce our lives to do the Buddha's work. We take the responsibility to mold our own destinies. We rectify our lives as the Sangha's work. Encountering specific matters, we understand the principles. Understanding the principles, we apply them in specific matters. We carry on the single pulse of the patriarchs' mind-transmission. Ask yourself: Is it the case that I don't fight? Ask yourself: Is it the case that I am not greedy? Ask yourself: Is it the case that I do not seek? Ask yourself: Is it the case that I am not selfish? Ask yourself: Is it the case that I do not pursue personal advantage? Ask yourself: Is it the case that I do not lie? Ask yourself: Do I eat just one meal a day? Do I always wear my precept sash? These form the tradition of the Sagely City of Ten Thousand Buddhas, and no one can change them."

B. Always Wearing the Precept Sash

In order to uphold the Buddha's regulation and preserve the appearance of the Sangha, the Venerable Master taught his left-home disciples to wear their precept sash (*kashaya*) at all times and to carry their sitting/bowing cloth. He also taught them to eliminate their craving for fine clothing.

C. Eating One Meal a Day at Noon

Food takes a lot of time to prepare and increases our greed, thus hindering our cultivation. Following the Buddha's regulation, the Venerable Master set down the rules of taking one meal a day and eating from an almsbowl (*patra*). The unseasoned pot of boiled vegetables and Arhat soup are excellent medicine for hunger and thirst. One should eat until

四、夜不倒單

睡眠昏沉，易增愚癡，宣公早年就長坐不臥，亦教弟子坐著睡眠，易於清醒，精進用功，從睡魔中得解脫。

五、持銀錢戒

錢是罪孽根，有錢就生一切妄想。宣公為護修行人的法，教弟子遵守佛制不摸錢，不蓄私財。僧眾沒有單金（公家每月發給僧人的費用），也不受私人供養。一切工作純是義務，有病、有公務，可申請公費支付。宣公說，能持銀錢戒的，就是真正的清淨福田僧。

六、無執事名份

各道場裡，四眾分工合作，一起學習，各盡職責，在法喜中同修共事，不在名利權力上明爭暗奪。沒有當家住持，都是守門人，平等平等。

七、男女界限嚴明

凡因公事面談或通電話，或傳遞文件，男女雙方須各有兩人以上為原則，令四眾弟子互相護持，斷除染緣，離欲清淨。辦事不離修道，修道不離辦事。

八、隨眾共修

早課、拜願、誦《華嚴經》、上供、〈大悲懺〉、晚課、聽經、咒心……是固定常課。另舉辦佛菩薩聖誕紀念法會、一年一度的敬老節、懷少節、護國息災大法會，或不定期的傳三壇大戒、水陸空大法會、宗教研討會……等特別活動之外，個人隨分隨力出坡做工、校內教學、翻譯經典、處理寺務、會談公議……，決不浪費光陰。

捌、辦教育

一、有一個道場，就要有一個學校

教育是一切世出世法的根本，法門無量誓願學，大家互為老師、互為學生，彼此學習。萬佛聖城設有育良小學、培德中學、法界大學、僧伽居士訓練班等教育機構。其他各

---

seventy or eighty percent full, no more. By not being greedy for large amounts of food or good flavors, one will be liberated from gluttony.

D. Not Lying Down at Night
The muddled state of sleep increases one's stupidity. The Venerable Master began the practice of never lying down when he was young. He also taught his disciples to sleep sitting up, so that they can easily stay alert and apply effort with vigor. In this way, they can free themselves from the demon of sleep.

E. Observing the Precept of Not Keeping Money
Money is the root of offenses. Once a person has money, he will have all sorts of fanciful thoughts. In order to protect cultivators, the Venerable Master taught his disciples to observe the Buddha's rule by not handling money or keeping personal wealth. The members of the Sangha receive no allowance and accept no personal offerings. Their work is purely voluntary. In case of sickness or temple business, they may apply for money from the general fund. The Venerable Master said, "Those who can observe the precept of not keeping money are truly pure Sanghans who can serve as fields of blessings."

F. No Concept of Rank or Hierarchy
In all the Way-places, the fourfold assembly of disciples work in cooperation and study together. Each fulfills his or her own duties. Filled with the joy of Dharma, everyone cultivates together. There are no positions of authority and no salaries. There are no struggles over name and gain. There is no Manager or Abbot. Everyone is a doorkeeper; everyone is equal.

G. A Clear Separation between Men and Women
Whenever the two sides have to meet face-to-face, talk over the phone, or exchange written matter, there must be at least two members present on each side. This rule allows the fourfold assembly to sever defiled conditions, protect one another, and remain pure and far from desire. Daily business is not apart from cultivation, and cultivation is inseparable from daily business.

H. Cultivating with the Assembly
The daily ceremonies include: the morning ceremony, bowing to the Buddha, reciting the *Flower Adornment Sutra*, the Noon Meal Offering, the Great Compassion Repentance, the evening ceremony, the Sutra lecture, and the recitation of the mantra heart. In addition to these, there are celebrations on the anniversaries of the Buddhas and Bodhisattvas, the annual Respecting Elders Day and Cherishing Youth Day, Dharma Sessions for Protecting the Nation and Quelling Disasters, Transmissions of the Three Platforms of Precepts, Water-Land-Air Dharma Sessions, conferences on religion, and many other special events. At other times, people work according to their strength and abilities maintaining the grounds, teaching in the schools, translating the Buddhist scriptures, handling temple affairs, holding meetings, and so on, certainly not letting the time go by in vain.

VIII. Working in Education

A. Every Way-place Is a School
Education is the foundation of all worldly and transcendental dharmas. Dharma-doors are limitless; we vow to study them all. We are all mutu-

分道場也多設有周末班或周日學校。

二、一律採行義務教學

老師不領薪、不罷工，學生為明理而讀書，不為名利。以儒教做基礎，以佛教為依歸，教育出真正的人才，來利益全世界。宣公說：不要錢的，才是真的。

三、實行男女分校

男女有別，無感情糾紛，能專心學習，能防止男女濫交、墮胎、離婚、問題兒童，乃至同性戀等社會病態的產生。「教育是最根本的國防」，能救人，救社會，可以徹底解決世界問題！

四、僧教育為首

出家人有責任做一切眾生的模範，必須把自己教化好了，才能負擔起教化他人的工作。所以宣公對出家弟子的要求和訓練特別嚴謹。

（一）順其所長，給予職責，學習做大眾的事。給每個弟子同等的機會，時時耳提面命，從旁扶助。

（二）隨時考試：邀請各國各界人士，到萬佛聖城及各分支道場，或講經、或上課，看看大家認識不認識。宣公說：要有擇法眼，是道則進，非道則退，擇善而從，不善而改。「一切是考驗，看爾怎麼辦？覿面若不識，須再重頭煉。」

（三）法無定法：法是死的，人是活的，不要抱著一條路跑到黑。宣公說：你們有自己的智慧，要相信自己，不要相信我。宣公作風自由民主，尊重每個弟子，不刻意立戒條。每當弟子隨有所犯，才順時應緣定規矩，保護行者的修持。

（四）為弟子鋪路：道場運作由自修式漸改為開放式，藉著敬老、懷少、慶生等活動，結合四眾，互相護持，堅固道場基礎，令弟子得以積累經驗，忍煩耐勞，動中生定，安住辦道。

ally teachers and students as we learn from one another. The educational institutions at the Sagely City of Ten Thousand Buddhas include Instilling Goodness Elementary School, Developing Virtue Secondary School, Dharma Realm Buddhist University, and the Sangha and Laity Training Programs. Many of the branch Way-places have weekend classes or Sunday schools.

B. Volunteer Teaching Is the Rule
Teachers receive no salary and do not go on strike. Their goal in studying is to understand principles, not to pursue fame and profit. With the Confucian teachings as the foundation and Buddhism as the final refuge, the schools aim to produce truly capable individuals who can benefit the entire world. The Venerable Master said, "Those who don't want money are the genuine ones."

C. Boys and Girls Study Separately
When boys and girls are separated, they can concentrate on their studies without emotional distractions. Thus the social ailments of promiscuity, abortion, divorce, juvenile delinquents, and homosexuality are completely avoided. "Education is the most fundamental national defense." If children are taught to save people, not kill people, this can resolve the world's problems at a fundamental level.

D. Sangha Education Is Foremost
It is the duty of left-home people to act as models for all living beings. They must do a good job of teaching themselves before they can take on the work of teaching others. The Venerable Master thus trained his disciples rigorously and demanded highly of them.

1. According to their own rate of progress, disciples were assigned duties and expected to learn to do the community chores. Equal opportunities were given to all. The Master constantly gave them both direct and indirect teachings and offered his support.

2. The Master gave them unexpected tests: He invited people from all walks of life and various countries to lecture on the Sutras and hold classes at the Sagely City of Ten Thousand Buddhas or the branch Way-places, to see if the assembly would recognize them for who they were. The Venerable Master said, "You must have the Dharma-Selecting Eye. If it's the Way, then advance. If it's not the Way, then retreat. Choose what is good and follow it. Take what is bad and change it in yourself. 'Everything is a test to see what you will do. If you don't recognize what's before your face, you'll have to start anew.'"

3. The Dharma is not fixed: "The Dharma is dead. People are alive. You shouldn't stick inflexibly to one road until you run into darkness." The Venerable Master also said, "You have to have your own wisdom and believe in yourself. Don't believe in me." The Venerable Master's style was democratic. He respected each disciple and didn't deliberately set down precepts ahead of time. When a disciple did something wrong, then he would make a rule according to the time and situation in order to protect the disciple's cultivation.

4. In order to pave the road for his disciples, the Venerable Master gradually made the cloistered monasteries more open to the public. By means of celebrations for respecting the elderly, cherishing youth, and birthday gatherings, he brought the laypeople and monastics together and encour-

（五）無盡的包容：不論弟子犯了多大的錯誤，只要一念懺悔，宣公沒有不原諒的。「真認自己錯，莫論他人非；他非即我非，同體名大悲。」宣公一向責己不責人，把弟子一切的過錯，一切的無明、業障、脾氣，都歸到自己身上，承擔所有人的罪業。

五、沙彌教育是僧教育的根本

宣公在其生命的最後一、兩年內，特別重視培養僧團中一批新出家的幼齡沙彌和幼齡沙彌尼，親自安排師資、課程，甚至抱病傳授「四十二手眼」法門，可說耗盡心血。希望在四眾弟子合作、護持下，這群年紀在六到十七歲之間的新生代，早做未來佛陀正法的大光明日，弘揚宣公慈悲喜捨的大願，引導眾生修菩薩道，了脫生死大苦。

玖、辦譯經

為了普及佛法到全世界，宣公早年就立願將三藏經典翻譯成各國的語言文字，這是一項千秋大業。宣公說：翻譯經典比往生淨土還重要。

一、宣公先用中文解經

宣公上人每次講經時，都是先背出一段經文，再逐句解說，不看經本，也沒有筆記，純是自性的流露。以大眾化為主，用通俗白話，深入淺出，令人人都聽得懂。宣公說：我講經只能講淺淺的，所以出版的書都叫「淺釋」。就像白水煮白菜，淡而無味，可是有益健康。

二、譯為其他語言

以英文最多，已經譯有百餘部，陸續有法文、西班牙文、越南文的譯本。目前以中英對照的新版書為目標，預計將來仍採中文配合其他語言，以雙語對照方式，進行中法、中越……等翻譯出版工作。

aged them to be mutually supportive. In this way he strengthened the monastery's foundation. Disciples gained experiences, learned to be patient and work hard, to stay calm in the midst of activity, and to reside securely in the practice of the Way.

5. The Venerable Master had infinite patience and tolerance. No matter how great a mistake a disciple might make, as long as he gave rise to one thought of repentance, the Venerable Master would forgive him. "Truly recognize your own faults. Don't discuss the faults of others. Others' faults are just my own. To be of the same substance with all is called great compassion." The Venerable Master always blamed himself instead of reproaching others. He took upon himself all the mistakes, ignorance, karmic hindrances, and bad tempers of his disciples. He shouldered everyone's karmic offenses.

E. The Education of Shramaneras (Novices) Is the Foundation of Sangha Education

During the last couple of years, the Venerable Master paid great attention to a group of young Shramaneras (novice monks) and young Shramanerikas (novice nuns) who had newly left the home-life. He personally arranged teachers and classes for them and even transmitted to them the Dharma-door of the Forty-two Hands and Eyes during his sickness. He exhausted his efforts on their behalf. It is hoped that, under the cooperation of the fourfold assembly, this group of young Sanghans, aged six to seventeen, will soon become the bright sun of the Buddha's proper Dharma, propagating the Venerable Master's great vows of kindness, compassion, joy, and giving; guiding living beings to cultivate the Bodhisattva path and end the great suffering of birth and death.

IX. Overseeing the Translation of the Buddhist Canon

Wishing to cause the Buddhadharma to spread throughout the world, the Venerable Master made a vow in his youth to see to the translation of the Tripitaka (Buddhist Canon) into all languages. This is an historic mission. The Venerable Master said, "Translating the Canon is even more important than being reborn in the Pure Land."

A. The Venerable Master's Explanations of the Sutras in Chinese

The Venerable Master would first recite a passage of Sutra from memory, then explain it sentence by sentence without looking at the text. He didn't have any notes, either. He just spoke directly from his own nature. His explanations were aimed at the general public. Using ordinary colloquial Chinese, he would explain profound principles in a way that everyone could understand. The Venerable Master said, "I only know how to give very simple explanations of the Sutras. That's why my published explanations are called 'Simple Explanations' (in Chinese). Like cabbage boiled in plain water, they are bland and tasteless, but good for one's health."

B. Translations into a Second Language

Over a hundred volumes of translations have been published, primarily in English, and also some in French, Spanish, and Vietnamese. The current goal is to publish bilingual books with Chinese and English side by side, and later to publish bilingual books with Chinese and another language, such as French or Vietnamese, side by side.

除書籍出版外，同時推展錄音帶、錄影帶的有聲出版，也朝著雙語對照的方向發展，目前已流通的以中、英為主。

四、成立譯經院

一九七三年成立國際譯經學院，一九九二年成立「法總」總辦事處。共同從事譯經、出版的四眾弟子，都是受宣公德行感召，由十方雲集而來，義務奉獻，不取任何回報！

拾、現病相

凡夫的病由業力而來，自作自受，有貪瞋癡，就有一切病。聖人的病是由願力而來。他作我受，眾生有病，所以菩薩有病。聖人三毒已去，沒有自己的病，但他願意代眾生受苦，把眾生的病承擔到自己身上，現種種果報相，希望眾生見病相、知病因，趕快修行。

宣公為護持四眾弟子的修行，不辭勞苦奔波於各道場之間，坐長程車，忍冷忍熱，處理一切繁雜瑣事。又時時為人加持，日夜損耗心神。十多年前早已積勞成疾，六年前病得連一級台階也上不了。當醫生診斷只剩七天的壽命時，宣公還是不休息，不看病，拄著拐杖、坐著輪椅，仍舊各處說法。兩年來病倒床上，起不了身，還在電話上教導弟子，在夢境中點化弟子。

宣公治好無數人的病，為什麼治不好自己的病？不是治不好，而是不願治。因為宣公一生從來不為自己做任何事，從沒有一念為自己的心。在色身痛到極點時，宣公仍然不幫助自己一點點。直到今年六月七日在醫院圓寂前，病痛沒有減輕，也沒有現瑞相，更沒有顯奇蹟，就這麼不留痕跡地為眾生轉成住壞空、生老病死的大法。

這實在是宣公對弟子們在行菩薩道時的一個最大的考試。無量劫來，菩薩為眾生捨身捨命，只有他人，沒有自己。能在這萬苦交煎、難忍能忍的示現當中，更堅定信念，不畏行菩薩道的辛苦，繼續勇猛向前的人，就是宣公洪爐烈火裡煉出來的唯一真金了。

C. The Development of Audio Publications

In addition to books, audio and video tapes are also being published bilingually. Currently, bilingual audio tapes are available in Chinese-English format.

D. The Founding of the International Translation Institute

At the International Institute for the Translation of Buddhist Texts, founded in 1973, and the Administrative Headquarters of the Dharma Realm Buddhist Association, established in 1992, monastic and lay disciples have gathered from all directions to work as volunteers in the translation and publication of Buddhist texts, without any form of compensation.

X. Manifesting the Symptoms of Illness

The illnesses of ordinary people are caused by karma. They receive the retribution for whatever karma they create. All their illnesses are due to greed, anger, and stupidity. The illnesses of a Sage arise from his vows. He undergoes retribution for karma created by other people. Because living beings are ill, the Bodhisattva is also ill. A Sage has already eradicated the three poisons. He himself has no illness, yet he wishes to stand in for living beings and take their suffering. He transfers their illnesses to his own body and manifests various symptoms of sickness, hoping that living beings will see sickness, realize the cause of sickness, and quickly cultivate.

In order to protect and support the cultivation of his left-home and lay disciples, the Venerable Master personally travelled from one Way-place to another, making long trips by car, enduring the cold and heat, taking care of a myriad miscellaneous affairs, and constantly bestowing aid upon people, thus exhausting his mind and spirit by day and by night. Over ten years ago, the Venerable Master had already become sick from overwork. Six years ago, he was so sick he couldn't even climb a single step. Even when the doctors diagnosed that he had only seven days left to live, the Venerable Master still refused to rest or seek treatment. Leaning on his cane and riding in a wheelchair, he continued speaking the Dharma in various places. Two years ago he was so ill that he couldn't get up from the bed, yet he still instructed his disciples over the phone or appeared in their dreams to teach them.

The Venerable Master had healed countless others. Why couldn't he heal himself? It wasn't that he couldn't, but that he wouldn't. The Venerable Master had never in his entire life done anything for himself. He had never had a single thought of concern for himself. Even when his body was sick to the extreme, he didn't help himself the slightest bit. Right up to the time he completed the stillness on June 7 this year, his illness and pain didn't subside; he didn't manifest any auspicious signs or miracles. Instead, without leaving any traces, he spoke for living beings the great Dharma of formation, dwelling, decay, and emptiness; of birth, old age, sickness, and death.

This was truly the greatest test that the Venerable Master gave his disciples on the Bodhisattva path. For limitless eons, Bodhisattvas have given up their bodies and lives for the sake of living beings. They think only of others and have no sense of self. Faced with this manifestation of bearing all kinds of unbearable suffering, one who is able to continue advancing bravely with increased faith, undaunted by the

宣公的一生，就是一部法界的華嚴大經王。在《華嚴經》〈佛不思議法品〉中說，諸佛世尊有十種廣大佛事：

「佛子。一切諸佛入涅槃時。無量眾生悲號涕泣。生大憂惱。遞相瞻顧而作是言。如來世尊。有大慈悲。哀愍饒益一切世間。與諸眾生爲救爲歸。如來出現。難可値遇。無上福田。於今永滅。即以如是。令諸眾生。悲號戀慕而作佛事。……諸佛世尊雖般涅槃。仍與眾生作不思議清淨福田。無盡功德最上福田。令諸眾生。善根具足。福德圓滿。是爲第十廣大佛事。」

rigors of the Bodhisattva path, is a unique gold nugget smelted in the Venerable Master's blazing furnace.

The Venerable Master's entire life was an enactment of the great king of Sutras, the *Flower Adornment Sutra* of the Dharma Realm. The "Chapter of the Inconceivable Dharma of the Buddhas" in the *Flower Adornment Sutra* says that the Buddhas, World Honored Ones, have ten vast and great deeds:

Disciple of the Buddha, when a Buddha enters Nirvana, limitless living beings wail and weep in grief and give rise to great distress and vexation. They look at each other and say, "The Thus Come One, the World Honored One, is greatly kind and compassionate. He pities and benefits all those in the world and is a source of refuge for all living beings. It is difficult to encounter the appearance of the Thus Come One. This supreme field of blessings is now gone forever. Since this is the case, all living beings mournfully cry out in yearning and do the work of the Buddha... Even when a Buddha, a World Honored One, enters Nirvana, he continues to be living beings' inconceivable and pure field of blessings, a supreme field of blessings of infinite merit and virtue, enabling all living beings to be replete in roots of goodness and perfect in blessings and virtue. This is the tenth vast and great deed of the Buddha.

華嚴境界

THE FLOWER ADORNMENT STATE

陳果傑　　Cecilia (Guojie) Chen

◆ 上人只知道有其他人，不知道有自己。

◆ 上人剛來美國舊金山中國城做墓中僧時，有時去垃圾桶撿菜吃，也從不覺得它有什麼不好。上人曾說：修道人不要吃得太好，吃得太好就不會修道了。

◆ 上人慈悲為懷，遠離八萬四千里外眾生們的悲聲、哀聲、苦聲、怨聲、嘆聲……，甚至於一掉眼淚，上人皆無所不知，無所不曉，聞聲救苦。

◆ 上人曾言：「我在舊金山一天，就不准舊金山地震！」而一九八九年舊金山大地震時，上人正在臺灣為護國息災舉行法會，馬不停蹄（其時上人禁食）。上人關懷災區眾生心切，地震發生後，立即返美，第三天又飛回臺灣，繼續為護國護民流血汗。

◆ 十幾年來，風雨無阻，不論天氣再炎熱，上人每月一次，從舊金山南下洛杉磯金輪寺弘法。那時師父乘坐的車子，又破又舊，又沒有冷氣。一路辛苦，路上連水也不喝，衲袍都汗濕透了，但是上人從無怨言。中途經過 Coalinga（屠宰牛的地方）時，上人還專門下車，遠遠面對著這一群群將被宰殺的數千隻牛的方向，唸唸有詞，慈悲地度牠們離苦得樂。

直到加拿大金佛寺成立後半年左右，上人才改為每隔一個月去洛杉磯一次。金佛寺成立之後，為了節省機票開支，上人也是坐車十八小時先至西雅圖，次日再坐三小時車到加拿大溫哥華，弘法數日後，又坐車回萬佛城。一路上來回，上人除了吃午餐之外，連水都不喝，非常辛苦，上人就是這樣地奔波於萬佛聖城與各個道場之間。

◆ The Venerable Master knew only that there were others; he didn't know that he had a self.

◆ When the Venerable Master was being a "monk in the grave" in San Francisco's Chinatown after he had just come to America, he would sometimes go to the garbage dump and take out vegetables to eat. He didn't feel there was anything bad about it. The Venerable Master said, "Cultivators shouldn't eat too well. If they eat too well, they won't cultivate."

◆ The Venerable Master has a compassionate heart. He completely knows and perceives the sounds of sadness, sounds of grief, sounds of suffering, sounds of resentment, sounds of sighing...even the shedding of a single tear of living beings, and even when they are more than 84,000 miles away. The Venerable Master hears their sounds and rescues them from suffering.

◆ The Venerable Master said, "As long as I am in San Francisco, I will not allow San Francisco to have an earthquake!" When a major earthquake occurred in San Francisco in 1989, the Venerable Master was in Taiwan, toiling nonstop to hold a Dharma Session for Protecting the Nation and Quelling Disasters (he was also undertaking a complete fast at the time). The Venerable Master was very concerned about the living beings in the earthquake zone, so he immediately returned to America. Three days later, he flew back to Taiwan to continue giving his blood and sweat to protect the nation and its people.

◆ For more than ten years, regardless of the wind, rain, or hot weather, the Venerable Master would travel once a month from San Francisco to Gold Wheel Monastery in Los Angeles to propagate the Dharma. The car that the Venerable Master rode in was battered, old, and had no air conditioning. Although his robes would be soaked with sweat after the uncomfortable journey, he never once complained. When they passed through Coalinga (where cows were slaughtered), the Venerable Master would get out of the car, face the several thousand cows who were doomed to be slaughtered, and recite for them, compassionately saving them and enabling them to leave suffering and attain bliss.

About half a year after Gold Buddha Monastery was founded in Canada, the Venerable Master started going to Los Angeles only every other month. After Gold Buddha Monastery opened, in order to save the money it would have cost to buy a plane ticket, the Venerable Master would travel by car for eighteen hours to Seattle, and then ride for three more hours the following day to reach Vancouver. After propagating the Dharma there for several days, he would then travel by car back to the City of Ten Thousand Buddhas. During those trips, except during his one meal at midday, the Master didn't even drink water. It was very difficult. That was how he travelled between the Sagely City of Ten Thousand Buddhas and the various Way-places, undergoing great suffering and hardship.

◆ 上人分分秒秒不辭辛勞，各處奔波，為法忘軀。我多年來常見到上人旅途十幾個小時，連水都不喝。每到一處，一進道場，通常會有法師頂禮後，即刻向上人呈報各項事務，有時連續一、二小時，或數小時之久，還有處理不完的公事、私事要馬上解決。上人連吃飯都沒有時間，更談不上休息，但也從未見過上人叫苦，他老人家一向任勞任怨，以身作則，不把自己的身體當一回事，每天就這樣流血流汗。

◆ 上人常常對我們說，不要把光陰空過了。在旅途上無論多辛苦、多遙遠，第二天上人總是一大早，有時早上兩、三點已開始在做事了。

◆ 上人不論去哪裡，無論是萬佛城裡或到遠地，從來未向居士開過口，要城外的人替他開車。

◆ 今年四月間（一九九五年）我有機會去朝上人在香港大嶼山的道場——慈興寺。從香港坐船一小時，下船後還要坐巴士一小時，然後再爬山一小時，才到了隱藏在深山裡，渺無人煙的慈興禪寺。想起當年上人為了建寺，為了工人的口糧，要坐船到香港去買米，然後背著沉重重的米袋，沿著陡斜的山坡回到寺裡。今天在寺廟，當年上人是如何艱辛的蹤跡，仍可四處看到。不免心酸，感慨萬千！

◆ 上人不單為世界和平絕食，也常因為弟子們剛強難調，發脾氣，起爭論而不吃飯。自己責怪自己沒有德行，沒有把弟子們教好。

◆ 法總每個道場的家風是法輪常轉，不論人多人寡，甚至沒有人聽經，也每天講經：一天不講經，就一天不吃飯。上人講法深入淺出，一針見血，因人說法，善巧方便，智慧如海，弟子們在師父開示後都說：「今天師父講的是我！」師父講法生動幽默，故弟子們聞法都不會打瞌睡。

◆ 上人苦口婆心，經常耳提面命，教弟子們，「不要自暴自棄，人人皆可成堯舜！」

◆ The Venerable Master toiled every minute and second, travelling from place to place, forgetting himself for the sake of the Dharma. Over the years, I have seen the Venerable Master travel for over ten hours without even taking a drink of water. Wherever he went, as soon as he arrived at the Way-place, the Dharma Masters there would bow to him and then immediately report to him on various matters. Sometimes this would go on for several hours, and there would still be endless temple matters and personal problems that required his immediate attention. The Venerable Master didn't even have time to eat, much less to take a rest. Yet I never saw the Master complain once. He always bore the toil and the complaints, setting an example with his own conduct. He didn't pay any heed to his body. Every day he exhausted himself like this.

◆ The Venerable Master often reminded us not to let our time go to waste. No matter how exhausting or long the journey was, the Venerable Master would always rise early the next morning. Sometimes he would start working at two or three o'clock in the morning.

◆ No matter where the Venerable Master was, whether he was in the City of Ten Thousand Buddhas or somewhere far away, he would never ask a layperson who lived outside the City to drive him somewhere.

◆ In April of this year (1995), I had an opportunity to visit Cixing Monastery—the Venerable Master's Way-place at Lanto Island in Hong Kong. From Hong Kong, I rode on the ferry for one hour, then took a one-hour bus ride, and finally climbed the mountain for an hour, before reaching Cixing Chan Monastery hidden deep in the mountains, where no trace of human dwellings could be seen. I think back to the time when the Venerable Master was constructing the monastery. For the sake of feeding the workers, he would take the ferry to Hong Kong to buy rice and then carry the heavy bags of rice over his shoulder and walk back up the steep slopes to the monastery. The Venerable Master's laborious pains can still be seen all about the monastery today. I cannot help feeling grieved and deeply moved!

◆ The Venerable Master not only fasted for world peace, he frequently also refused to eat when his disciples were stubborn and disobedient, lost their tempers, or got into arguments. He would blame himself for lacking virtue and failing to teach his disciples well.

◆ Each of the Way-places of the Dharma Realm Buddhist Association is characterized by the constant turning of the Dharma wheel. Whether there are many people or few—even if there aren't any—lectures on the Sutras are held every day. If there is one day the Sutras are not lectured, that day people should go without eating. When the Venerable Master spoke the Dharma, he penetrated it deeply yet expressed it in very simple words. His words were straight to the point. He employed skillful expedients and had ocean-like wisdom. After listening to the Venerable Master's talks, each disciple would say, "Today the Venerable Master was talking about me!" The Venerable Master spoke the Dharma in such a lively and humorous way that his disciples were never able to doze off during his talks.

◆ The Venerable Master remonstrated earnestly with his disciples, giving instructions in their ear or telling them to their face, teaching them, "Don't give up on yourself! Everyone can become like (the sage-emperors) Yao and Shun!"

◆ 在道場，上人規矩嚴格，教導弟子們時時刻刻要專一其心，努力辦道，眼睛不東張西望，口：不寒暄、閒聊，不說雜話、廢話，以免空過光陰，意：不向任何人攀緣，溜虛拍馬，以免障道。

◆ 上人講解《祖師傳》時，常常勉勵我們要逆潮流而行，做疾風中的勁燭，做一個頂天立地、出乎其類、拔乎其萃的人。從哪裡下手？就在行住坐臥，吃飯、穿衣、睡覺上用功。

◆ 上人是嚴師慈父，外表雖然很嚴肅，內心卻慈祥溫暖，對弟子們有無限的關懷，默默地照顧每一個人。

◆ 令上人最不快樂的事，是弟子們發脾氣。

◆ 有一天晚上，在聖城妙語堂講經時，沒有一個出家人願意上臺先講。講經結束後，從妙語堂回佛殿時，上人是跪著看大眾出門的，他嚴厲責罰自己，行無言之教。我不知當時有多少人知道師父的用心良苦。

◆ 上人有大智慧，處理一切事務不須思索，問題皆迎刃而解。

◆ 上人有驚人的記憶，根據周果立居士回想一九七〇年代，上人講解《華嚴經》長達九年，可以不用看經書，朗朗咨誦經文，一字不漏。

◆ 上人是我見過最自在的人，真正做到掃一切法，離一切相，沒有一切執著。不像我們凡夫念念不忘我做了什麼，我某年某月供養了什麼，我⋯⋯，我⋯⋯，我⋯⋯。

◆ 上人的境界不可心思，不可言議，寫再多也無法講完，無法真正表達上人的大慈、大悲、大喜、大捨、大勇、大智、大願、大行、大力⋯⋯。上人的境界是《華嚴經》的境界，唯有常靜心讀誦《華嚴經》，才能認識我們偉大的師父。在末法時代，能遇到上人，常常親近上人，是我此生最最幸福的一件事。

◆ In the Way-place, the Venerable Master set up strict rules and taught his disciples to concentrate single-mindedly at all times and diligently cultivate. One's eyes should not look around at random. One's mouth should not indulge in meaningless conversation, idle chatter, or irrelevant talk, as these are a waste of time. In order to avoid obstructing the Way, one's mind should not try to exploit conditions or curry favor from anyone.

◆ When the Venerable Master explained the *Lives of the Patriarchs*, he frequently exhorted us to go against the mainstream, to be brave candles in a strong gale, heroes, and outstanding people. Where should we begin? By applying effort while we are walking, standing, sitting, and lying down; while we are eating, wearing clothes, and sleeping.

◆ The Venerable Master was both a strict teacher and a kindly father. Although he appeared stern, his heart was gentle and warm. He cared infinitely for his disciples and silently took care of every person.

◆ What upset the Venerable Master most was to see his disciples lose their tempers.

◆ One night, during a Sutra lecture in Wonderful Words Hall, not a single left-home person was willing to go up to the podium and lecture. After the lecture was over and people were leaving Wonderful Words Hall to return to the Buddhahall, the Venerable Master knelt down by the doorway and watched the assembly walk out, reproaching himself sternly, bestowing a wordless teaching. I don't know how many people realized what great lengths the Venerable Master had gone to.

◆ The Venerable Master had great wisdom and handled all matters without conscious deliberation, resolving all problems at once.

◆ The Venerable Master's memory power was astounding. As Layman Zhou Guoli recalls, during the nine years that the Venerable Master explained the *Flower Adornment Sutra* in the 1970's, he was able to recite the text in a clear voice, without missing a single word and without looking at the book.

◆ The Venerable Master was the most carefree person I have ever met. He was truly able to "sweep away all dharmas and separate from all marks." He didn't have any attachment at all, unlike us ordinary people, whose every thought is about: "What I have done, what offering I made in a certain month of a certain year, what I..., I..., I..."

◆ The Venerable Master's state was inconceivable and ineffable. No matter how much I write, I will never be able to finish. It's impossible to truly express the Venerable Master's great kindness, great compassion, great joy, great renunciation, great courage, great wisdom, great conduct, great strength... The Venerable Master's state was the Flower Adornment State. Only through constant reading of the *Flower Adornment Sutra* with a calm mind will we be able to recognize our extraordinary teacher. The most fortunate thing in my life is that I have been able to encounter the Venerable Master and frequently draw near to the Venerable Master in this Dharma-ending Age.

絕食祈禱

FASTING AND PRAYING

譚果正　Stella Tam

大家都知道，上人願力之一是，無論他在哪裡住，那個地方一定平安無事。要是他離開了，那就不管了。所以上人抵美後，第一件事，就是要為給他機會做弘法利生事業的國家及人民祈福。

一九六二年，正值古巴核子危機。美國政府探悉蘇聯在古巴秘密建設飛彈基地。由於古巴是位於美國後門加勒比海中的一個島嶼，所以蘇聯此舉將會極端危害美國的安全。當時的美國總統甘乃迪立即採取行動，首先派出海、空軍阻止所有攻擊性武器運往古巴；另一方面卻考慮攻打古巴，先發制人。當時全美國人心惶惶，唯恐大戰爆發，核子戰爭，將會殺人無數。這一年九月，上人抵美還不到半年，突然間對大眾宣佈絕食五星期，祈求世界和平，為人民消災解難。

出人意料地，美國正要出兵之際，蘇聯突然同意和談。十月二十八日甘乃迪總統與蘇聯克魯雪夫總理雙方談判成功。十一月二日甘乃迪總統宣佈，蘇聯在古巴的飛彈基地已經開始拆除。

上人絕食期間，有兩位大約十三、四歲的男孩子，常追隨在上人左右，他們就是黃果仁和李錦山。黃果仁說：「上人每天只喝一杯水，最後兩星期，上人滴水不沾，還不斷地說法開示，沒有休息。普通人怎樣受得了？」

同年年底，上人又絕食五星期。以後上人又絕食三次，其中兩次為期兩週，一次為期一週。一九六三年上人到檀香山，在檀華寺又絕食兩星期。上人一連串打了十七個餓七，都是為祈禱世界和平，使美國人民免除戰爭之禍害。

一九六三年七月二十五日，英、美、蘇三國簽訂禁止核子試爆條約。大家都讚賞甘乃迪總統英明果斷，嚇怕老蘇，解脫危機。其中因果感應，只有明眼人纔能洞悉。上人從來都是默默地忍飢受苦，為解除眾生的厄難啊！

Everyone knows that one of Venerable Master's vows is that wherever he goes, that place will be peaceful and without trouble. Once he leaves the place, it is another matter. When the Venerable Master arrived in America, his first task was to pray for blessings on behalf of the country and people who had given him an opportunity to propagate the Dharma for the benefit of living beings.

The Cuban Missile Crisis occurred in 1962. The American government discovered that the Soviets were secretly building missile bases in Cuba. Since the island of Cuba was located in the Caribbean Sea, right at the "back door" of the United States, the Soviet move was a serious threat to U.S. security. President Kennedy took immediate action by deploying the U.S. Navy and Air Force to stop delivery of all offensive military weapons to Cuba. He was also considering an attack on Cuba. People all over America were very worried and feared that a major war would break out. A nuclear war would result in countless casualties. In September of that year, less than six months after the Venerable Master had arrived in America, he suddenly announced to the assembly that he would embark on a five-week fast in order to pray for world peace and to eradicate the disasters and hardships of the people.

Unexpectedly, just as the U.S. was preparing to deploy the troops, the Soviet Union suddenly agreed to negotiate. On October 28, President Kennedy and Soviet Premier Khrushchev successfully reached an agreement in their negotiations. On November 2, President Kennedy announced that the Soviet missile bases in Cuba were being dismantled.

During the Venerable Master's fast, he was often accompanied by two boys aged thirteen to fourteen. Their names were Jimmy Wong and Kim Lee. Jimmy recalls, "At first the Venerable Master drank a glass of water every day. In the last two weeks, the Master didn't drink a single drop, yet he continued speaking the Dharma without taking a rest. How could an ordinary person have taken that?"

At the end of that year, the Venerable Master fasted for another five weeks. Later on he fasted three more times. Two of the fasts were two-weeks long each, and the other fast was for one week. In 1963 the Master went to Honolulu and fasted for two weeks at Tanhua Monastery. Altogether he undertook seventeen weeks of fasting to pray for world peace and to help Americans avert war.

On July 25, 1963, Britain, the United States, and the Soviet Union signed a limited nuclear test-ban treaty. Everyone praised President Kennedy for his heroic and decisive action, which had intimidated the Soviets and resolved the crisis. Only those with wise discernment could see the hidden response of cause and effect. As always, the Venerable Master had quietly endured hunger and suffering in order to resolve the crises of living beings!

十方無量無邊界，所有一切諸眾生，
我皆救護而不捨，此無畏者行斯道。
　　　——《華嚴經》〈十行品〉

In limitless and boundless worlds throughout the ten directions,
I shall rescue and protect all living beings, without renouncing them.
This is the path practiced by the fearless one.

—Ten Conducts Chapter, the *Flower Adornment Sutra*

上人的一位美國籍弟子 Leland Eagleson 曾寫過一篇文章說：「有一件事是最難了解的，那就是上人為世界和平而絕食與解除古巴危機之間的關連性，可是對我來說，這關連性是非常清楚的，那就是『誠可格天』」。

Leland Eagleson 居士還將此事寫了一首詩，現在翻譯給大家看：

　　地球一線懸，聖者深憂感。
　　發大慈悲願，感動地與天。
　　消除戰火勢，鎮定人怖畏。
　　為眾救世界，已生或將生，
　　自由完其生。弟子應明識，
　　偉大慈悲者，恩德何其深！
　　此生本了結，得回獻此身。
　　機會再來臨，何不從善行？

Leland Eagleson, an American disciple of the Venerable Master, wrote an essay in which he said, "There is one thing that is difficult to understand: the conjunction of the Venerable Master's fast for world peace and the defusing of the Cuban Missile Crisis. In my mind the connection is clear: Heaven responded to sincerity."

Layman Leland Eagleson also wrote a poem to convey his understanding of the mystery:

The world hung by a slender thread,
Evoking a Sage's deep concern.

Heaven and Earth moved in response
To great and compassionate vows,

Quelling war's forces, stilling man's fears;
Saving the world for all living beings:

Living and not yet born,
Left free to choose their lives.

We disciples must understand
The depth of the debt we owe to
The greatly compassionate one.

How can we not offer up our lives
That once were nearly forfeited?

How can we not offer up good conduct
In homage to the chance freely given?

TRANSFORMATION OF A BODHISATTVA, FOOTSTEPS OF AN ASCETIC MONK

菩薩幻化　頭陀行跡

Compiled by Shi Hengchi　*釋恆持整理*

● **1950　Guanyin Cave, Furong Mountain, Hong Kong**
一九五〇年　香港　芙蓉山　觀音洞

When the Master returned to Hong Kong after a visit to Thailand, he was penniless. A layman helped him find Guanyin Cave—a small, dark hole in the face of the mountainside. Bending low to enter the mouth of the cave, the Master found a flat rock inside. He sat down on it and pulled his legs up into lotus posture. He had no furniture or utensils, no bedding or food; he had only his tattered, patched robe to wear.

The Master sat unmoving on the rock in the barren cave for several days and nights, only deciding to get up after about 100 hours of uninterrupted sitting. But when he tried to stand, he found that his legs wouldn't move. The Master paid no attention to his paralysis, but simply continued to sit on the rock in the dank cave. He remained in the full lotus meditation posture day and night for two full weeks, and then gradually began to recover the use of his legs.

訪問泰國回到香港時，上人已身無分文。一位居士替上人找到了觀音洞——在山邊一個又小又暗的洞，彎下身進入洞內後，上人在洞裡的一塊石頭平臺上，結雙跏趺坐。除了身上穿的那件滿是補丁的衲袍，上人一無所有。

上人在陰暗的山洞裡，不眠不食地連續坐了幾天幾夜，約一百個小時。當上人打算起身時，才發現雙腿已不能動了。上人並不在意他的麻痺，在陰濕的山洞裡，又繼續雙跏趺坐了兩個星期，雙腿才慢慢地恢復了活動。

Dong Putuo Monastery, Hong Kong
香港　東普陀寺

The Master with Upasaka Chen Xuelü, who wrote a year-by-year record of Venerable Master Hsu Yun's life and his biography, and Upasika Tan Guoshi, who with her sister Tan Guozheng, helped the Master establish the Sino-American Buddhist Association in the United States in 1959.

上人與岑學呂居士、譚果式居士。岑居士收集虛老的事蹟，撰寫了《虛雲老和尚年譜》。譚果式居士與她的姐姐譚果正居士，一九五九年在美幫助上人成立中美佛敎總會。

Western Bliss Gardens Monastery
The Master in a Group Portrait
西樂園寺
上人與信眾的團體照

The Master arranged for, planned, and supervised the construction of Western Bliss Gardens. He printed no announcements or advertisements; he asked for no donations; he dropped no hints to wealthy lay people; and he did not go begging from door to door. Standing firm in his guiding principles, he refused to take advantage of Hong Kong's affluence. His pure and lofty courage and determination inspired his disciples.

西樂園寺的建築工程，從最初的籌劃、安排，到監督施工，都由上人親自操勞。上人始終堅守他的宗旨，拒絕向富裕的香港社會攀緣，從不印通知、打廣告，更沒有一家一家去化緣。上人清淨、崇高的節操與志向，使弟子們深受感動。

● Western Bliss Gardens, Hong Kong
香港　西樂園寺

Since there was no water in the vicinity of Western Bliss Gardens, everyone in the area had trouble getting water to use. After the Master moved into Western Bliss Gardens, he found a crack in a stone at the base of the cliff behind the temple. He knelt before the Buddhas and Bodhisattvas and prayed for a sweet spring on the site. Every day he recited the Great Compassion Mantra before the cleft. Soon a little moisture appeared at the cleft.

由於西樂園寺附近沒有水源，民眾用水很困難。上人搬入西樂園寺後，在寺廟後邊崖壁底下的一塊石頭上找到了裂縫。於是，上人跪在佛菩薩面前，祈求湧出甘露泉。上人每天在裂縫前持誦〈大悲咒〉。不久，裂口處便開始濕潤起來。

● Western Bliss Gardens, Hong Kong
香港　西樂園寺

Gradually, drop by drop, the water began to flow. Sweet dew began pouring forth and flowing down to form an abundant pool. The serious problem of Western Bliss Gardens' water supply had been resolved by the Buddhas and Bodhisattvas.

慢慢地，水從一滴一滴，變成涓涓細流，向下流瀉，形成一個有豐足水源的水池。從此，西樂園嚴重的缺水問題，在佛菩薩的保佑下得到解決。

● **Western Bliss Gardens, Hong Kong**
香港　西樂園寺

When news of the miraculous spring spread, everyone in the neighborhood was astonished. How could water flow from a dry rock on that barren mountain?

　　當這件地湧清泉的神奇消息傳開以後，鄰里都感到非常驚異，一座光禿禿的山，水怎麼會從乾燥的石縫中湧出呢？

● Western Bliss Gardens, Hong Kong
The Master at Western Bliss Gardens sitting near the papaya trees

香港　西樂園寺
上人坐在木瓜樹旁

In the year that the Master landscaped Western Bliss Gardens with pine, papaya, and bamboo trees, a severe typhoon hit Hong Kong and the winds ripped out the newly-planted trees. At that time the Master laid down an ultimatum: "As long as I am in Hong Kong, there will not be any more typhoons. What happens when I leave Hong Kong is another matter, but as long as I am here, no more destructive storms will hit here."

After that, for more than ten years while the Master remained in Hong Kong, not a single typhoon struck the city. Time and again typhoon warnings were displayed, but each time the storm either died out or changed course. The immunity of the city was dramatically evidenced when on several occasions storms beat a straight course for Hong Kong, only to veer off suddenly from as close as fifteen miles offshore.

當年，上人建西樂園時，為美化環境，種植了松樹、木瓜、竹等各種植物。一場劇烈的颶風侵襲香港後，新種的樹都被吹倒了。上人因此發願說：「只要我在香港一天，就不准再有颶風發生。」

以後，上人在香港居住的十年之間，不曾有颶風侵襲香港。雖然一次又一次的，發出颶風警報，但每一次颶風都戲劇性地突然消失或轉移方向。

● Western Bliss Gardens, Hong Kong
The Master in a Group Portrait

香港　西樂園寺
上人與信眾的團體照

The photo reveals a vajra-shaped light supporting the Master.

這張照片中顯示有一道「金剛」形的光體撐托著上人。

宣化老和尚追思紀念專集

● **1953　Hong Kong**
　一九五三年　香港

Group portrait at Zhilian Jingyuan (Temple of Resolve to be Born in the Pure Lotus Land) commemorating the completion of the Master's lecturing of the *Sutra of the Past Vows of Earth Store Bodhisattva* in 1953.

　　志蓮淨苑團體照。紀念上人講解《地藏菩薩本願經》功德圓滿。

● **Hong Kong　香港**

The Master presiding at the Opening of Cixing (Flourishing Compassion) Monastery on Lanto Island

　上人主持大嶼山慈興禪寺開幕典禮。

● **Hong Kong**
香港

The Master seated at the door of the Buddhahall at Cixing Monastery on Lanto Island.

上人坐在大嶼山慈興禪寺佛堂門前。

● **l953　Hong Kong**
一九五三年　香港

The Master with the dragon he personally carved at Cixing Monastery, Lanto Island, Hong Kong.

大嶼山慈興寺。上人與親手雕塑的龍。

● 1953 Hong Kong
一九五三年　香港

During the renovating of the Monastery, an incident occurred involving jealousy. The new Bodhimanda had provoked the demon kings, and in 1953 a red-headed, green-bodied poisonous snake kept appearing at the Way-place. When Sangha members first saw it, they caught it in a barrel and took it several miles beyond the grounds, but before the party had returned, the snake was already back at the monastery. It was removed again, and reappeared again. Time and again the same thing happened. Once the snake was taken particularly far away, but when the lid of the barrel was lifted to release it, it was nowhere to be seen. Thinking this strange, the man who had taken the barrel away replaced the cover with a light tap, and suddenly the severed body of half a snake fell out. By the time the man had returned, however, the body had become whole once again and the poisonous snake was seen crawling in front of the Buddhahall where it coiled itself, lifted its head, and darted out its tongue.

Snakes belong to the class of dragons, and so the Venerable Master molded a golden dragon to perch on top of the dragon-subduing rock to the left of the monastery. Simultaneously the Master personally recited the Shurangama Mantra nonstop twenty-four hours a day for a week. After the golden dragon was complete, the poisonous snake was taken away and it never reappeared.

慈興禪寺剛改建時，發生了一件事情：新的道場使當地的魔王生了嫉妒。一九五三年時，便有一條紅頭青身的毒蛇，經常在道場出現。僧眾第一次看到牠時，將牠捉入一個大桶內，然後把牠帶到數里外釋放。在他們回道場之前，此蛇卻已先回到廟上。他們又把牠弄走，牠又回來，這樣反覆了數次。有一次，又將此蛇帶去更遠的地方。但將蓋子打開，準備放生時，卻找不著牠了。送蛇的人感到奇怪，把蓋子輕輕地拍一下，將桶蓋上。忽然，切斷的半截蛇身掉了出來。當送蛇的人回到廟上時，這條毒蛇的身體又復原了，有人看見牠爬到佛殿前，盤著身，昂頭吐舌。

蛇屬於龍的族類。所以，上人塑了一條金龍，棲守在寺廟左邊的降龍石上。同時師父用了一星期的時間，每天二十四小時持誦〈楞嚴咒〉。當金龍造好之後，又將這條毒蛇弄走，這次就沒再回來了。

● **Happy Valley, Hong Kong, 香港 快活谷**

The Master (at left of photo) with disciples on the roof of the Buddhist Lecture Hall.

上人與眾弟子在佛教講堂屋頂。

● **Buddhist Lecture Hall, Hong Kong, 香港 佛教講堂**

The Master shown on the porch of the Hong Kong Buddhist Lecture Hall, established in 1956.

上人攝於香港佛教講堂的門廊。講堂創立於一九五六年。

- **1961 Kingsgrove, Australia**
  一九六一年 澳大利亞 王樹城

Prior to coming to America, the Master spent a year in Australia.

　來美之前，上人曾在澳大利亞居留一年。

- **Burma**
  緬甸

The Master is standing in the second row beside the short monk in Theravada robes.

　上人站在一位個子較小的南傳僧人旁邊。

● Early l960's: Early Years in America
六十年代初：來美初期

The Master is showing San Francisco disciples the document titled "Treasury of the Orthodox Dharma Eye: The Source of Buddhas and Patriarchs," a transmission certificate of the Wei-yang lineage. The Venerable Master Hsu Yun sent this certificate to the Master (who was residing in Hong Kong) in May of l956. Elder Master Yun's letter, which accompanied the document says, "You, Venerable One, have concern for the preservation of the Dharma and for the continuation of the wisdom-life of the Buddhas and Patriarchs. I am sending you the Source, the inheritance of the Patriarchs' pulse, the Patriarchs' Way. Entrusted to you, it will prosper. This is my hope." The document bears this certification:

Transmitter of the Wei-yang Orthodox Lineage, the Elder Te-ch'ing Hsu-yun now bequeaths the Treasury of the Orthodox Dharma Eye upon the ninth generation, Dhyana cultivator Hsuan-hua To-lun, to be personally protected and maintained by him.

This photo also shows the incense-burn offering on the Master's chest in the shape of the character 卍 meaning "myriad," which is used in Buddhism to represent the Buddhas' myriad virtues.

　　上人讓弟子們看一份證書，上面寫著「正法眼藏　佛祖源流」，這是溈仰宗傳承的表信。一九五六年五月，上虛下雲老和尚將表信寄給當時住在香港的上人，同時附上的一封信裡寫著：「座下為法心切，續佛祖慧命，當滿座下之願，附寄源流俾承祖脈，祖道賴以重興，是所至望，專覆不盡　即頌。」證書上寫著：「傳溈仰正宗第八代，德清虛雲老人，今將正法眼藏，囑咐：第九代宣化度輪禪人善自護持。」

　　從這張照片上，可以看到上人在胸前燃的卍字。（卍字表佛之萬德莊嚴）

1960's
San Francisco
六十年代
三藩市

The Master teaching young men to meditate.
In front of the Master second from left is Kim Lee. At far right is Jimmy Wong. These two young men were devoted disciples who translated for the Master and served Buddhism in many ways during the early years in San Francisco.

上人教弟子們打坐。左邊第二位是李錦山，最右邊是黃果仁。上人早期在三藩市時，這二位虔誠的年輕弟子，爲上人做英語翻譯，並爲佛教做了很多事。

● **Early 1960's   San Francisco** — The Master leading a meditation period.
六十年代早期   三藩市 — 上人指導弟子們如何坐禪

Advocating full lotus posture and investigation of a meditation topic, the Master used many expedient teachings to help young students enter the Dharma door of Chan (Dhyana).

上人主張雙跏趺坐和參話頭，他會用很多善巧方便來啟發、幫助年輕學子，把他們引入修禪的法門。

An early lecture on the Dharma.

The Master spoke the Dharma and lectured on Mahayana Sutras all during his first six years in the United States, even though he was in semi-seclusion during that time.

早期講法。

在來美最初的六年中，上人雖然半閉關，但仍然一直開示、說法及宣講各種大乘經典。

● **1960's**
Buddhist Lecture Hall, San Francisco
六十年代　三藩市　佛教講堂

The hall was small and the young Americans, eager for the Dharma, packed it. This one room served as the lecture hall, dining hall, meeting room, meditation hall, class room, guest hall, and study area.

講堂雖小，卻擠滿了渴求佛法的美國青年。當時，這間房間不但用做講堂，同時還充做齋堂、禪堂、教室、閱覽室、會議室和會客室。

宣化老和尚追思紀念專集

1968　San Francisco
一九六八年　三藩市

Several times during that first summer, the Master received disciples. In July he transmitted the Three Refuges. Behind the Master is the white plaster Buddha image that he molded himself.

　那一年的夏天，上人收了好幾批弟子。七月，傳授三皈。上人後面的一尊白色石膏佛像，是上人親自塑造的。

1968　San Francisco
一九六八年　三藩市

End of the Shurangama Lecturing and Cultivation Summer Session. The Venerable Master's patient teaching and compassionate expedients awakened and inspired these young Americans according to their various potentials. The majority of these students began the summer with little or no understanding of Buddhism. At the end, most participants received the Five Precepts, and many received the Bodhisattva Precepts. They are shown here in robes and precept sashes with their bowing cloths.

　《楞嚴經》暑期講習班結業。暑期班開始時，這些美國年輕人多半對佛法沒有概念。經過上人耐心的教導和慈悲的善巧方便，這些人都得到了不同程度的啟發和覺悟。現在這些學生大多受了五戒，其中很多位還受了菩薩戒。從照片中可以看到，他們穿著海青和縵衣，及使用臥具。

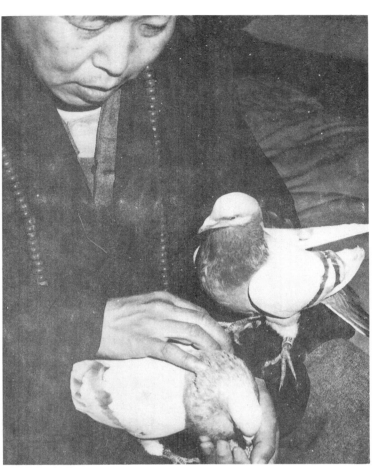

1968　San Francisco
Liberating Life

一九六八年　三藩市
放生法會

During the first such ceremony that these young Americans had ever witnessed, held on the roof of the Buddhist Lecture Hall, thirty-eight pigeons were released. All but two flew away. Those two pigeons stayed around and became regular participants in the activities at the Lecture Hall. The Master shed tears as he explained that these birds had been his left-home disciples during the Tang Dynasty (around 750 A.D.) in China.

　　這些年輕的美國人，是第一次見到這種法會，放生地點在佛教講堂的屋頂，一共有三十八隻鴿子。除了兩隻之外，其餘的都飛走了。留下來的兩隻鴿子，經常參與講堂的活動。上人在解釋這二隻鴿子是他唐朝時代（公元七百五十年）的出家弟子時，落淚了。

1968　San Francisco
一九六八年　三藩市

The Master gave them the names 'Twelve Causes and Conditions' and 'Seven Bodhi Shares,' and their dispositions were quite distinct. Seven Bodhi Shares was gentle, but Twelve Causes and Conditions was impatient and would often beat her wings against the Master, who taught her with wise and gentle kindness.

　　上人為兩隻鴿子分別取名為「十二因緣」和「七菩提分」。牠們的性情顯著地不同，「七菩提分」很溫和，「十二因緣」則很急躁，常常用牠的翅膀拍打以悲智來教化牠的上人。

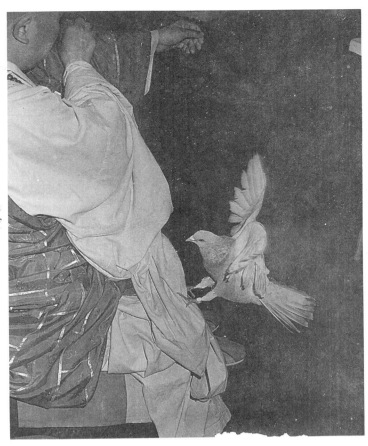

1968   San Francisco
一九六八年　三藩市

Or she would fly about in a rage if she didn't get what she wanted. The Master's wisdom and clever expedients in teaching the birds weren't lost on his human disciples, who suffered from many of the same afflictions.

當「十二因緣」不滿意時，會氣得飛來飛去。上人訓導這兩隻鳥的智慧及善巧方便，也令生爲人類具諸類似煩惱的弟子們，受益良多。

1968   San Francisco
一九六八年　三藩市

One of these afflictions was food, because many of the young American disciples, inspired by the Master's practice of taking only one meal a day, were trying to master that practice themselves.

吃是煩惱之一。很多年輕的美國弟子，受到上人日中一食的啓發，希望自己也能如是行持。

● 1968 San Francisco
一九六八年 三藩市

The Master wisely directed to the birds his teaching about greed for food. He fed them from a tall glass jar filled with the best of grains. At first the jar was filled to the brim and the two birds would happily perch on the rim and peck at the grain.

對於食物的貪求，上人給這兩隻鳥智慧的教導。他用一個高的玻璃瓶裝著最好的穀子，起初瓶子裝得滿滿的，兩隻鴿子可以站在瓶子的邊緣快樂地啄食。

● 1968 San Francisco
一九六八年 三藩市

Gradually the amount of grain in the tall glass jar decreased until the birds had to reach far into the jar, often unceremoniously losing their balance in the process, in order to get the food. The Master, shown here feeding the birds from a nearly empty jar, gave a 24-character calligraphy lesson every evening during the year 1969. He wrote out the *Shurangama Sutra* and combined many learning potentials into that single lesson, including stroke orders for Chinese characters, techniques of writing brush calligraphy, simple explanations of each passage of text, and development of disciples' memorization skills.

瓶內所放的穀子逐漸減少，直到鴿子得深入瓶中取食。很多次，為了吃到食物，他們失去平衡，很是狼狽。從相片中，可以看到上人用幾乎快空的瓶子在餵鴿子，同時也在教美國人書法。在一九六九年，上人每晚在書法班上，寫出《楞嚴經》的經文，每次教二十四個中文字。同時在一堂課中融合了許多學習的內容，包括中文筆順、寫毛筆字的技巧及《楞嚴經》的經文淺釋，同時也訓練了學生的背誦能力。

1969　San Francisco
一九六九年　三藩市

In that year, Saturday afternoon lectures were held at the Laywomen's Forest, located in the Richmond district of San Francisco. The Master placed an exquisite image of Earth Store Bodhisattva at that residence for Buddhist women and agreed to lecture the entire *Sutra of the Past Vows of Earth Store Bodhisattva.*

那一年，每星期六下午，上人都去「女居士林」講經說法。居士林座落於三藩市的列治文區。上人請了一尊莊嚴精緻的地藏菩薩聖像供奉在居士林。同時答應開講整部《地藏菩薩本願經》。

May 1970　San Francisco
The First Wesak (Buddha's Birthday Celebration) held by the Sino-American Buddhist Association (later called Dharma Realm Buddhist Association)

一九七〇年五月　三藩市
中美佛教總會（後稱爲法界佛教總會）第一次舉辦釋迦牟尼佛聖誕慶祝法會

More than 600 people gathered to bathe the Buddha in Union Square Park. Then the Sangha led a procession to the great hall (in the First Congregational Church) for the main celebrations of the day. The Master is shown here sitting inconspicuously in the primarily Western assembly as he watches his young monk and nun disciples lead participants in performing the traditional ritual of bathing the infant Buddha, which symbolizes the cleansing of our own natures.

六百多位信眾在聯合廣場的花園裡浴佛。隨後，僧眾領著隊伍進入大殿（在第一公理教會），開始這一天主要的慶典。上人很不顯眼地坐在信眾當中，看著他年輕的出家弟子，帶領信眾進行傳統的儀式：沐浴一尊佛像。藉此代表清淨我們的自性。

● Buddhist Lecture Hall, San Francisco
三藩市　佛教講堂

A typical and beloved gesture of the Master—bending close to his characters, cocking his head, and looking hard at them with a scrutinizing eye. He once told those attending his daily calligraphy class: "You can be developing your skill in everything you do. For instance, you may not perceive it, but for me, the process of writing calligraphy involves my breath. You can learn many things right in the course of living your daily lives."

　上人聚精會神在寫字。有一次，上人告訴每天來學書法的學生說，你可以在你所做的每一件事中，去發展你的技巧。譬如，或許你沒有察覺到，當我寫書法時，我甚至控制住自己的呼吸。其實，在日常生活中，你就可以學到很多東西。

● Roof of Buddhist Lecture Hall, San Francisco
三藩市　佛教講堂的屋頂

Circumambulating while reciting is one of the fundamental rituals that the Master taught his Western disciples. "Once we form the circle, then the positions of first and last lose their meaning. Last becomes first; first becomes last. Everyone can be first; everyone can be last. In the circle, there is no first or last." He used the circle as an analogy in teaching us about fighting, competition, ambition, and greed for name and position.

　繞行念誦，是上人教西方弟子們的佛教基本儀式之一。當我們圍成一個圓圈時，第一及最後的地位就失去其意義了。最後變成第一，第一變成最後。每個人都可以成為第一，每個人都可以成為最後。在一個圓圈裡，沒有第一與最後。上人用此做為譬喻，教導我們應該怎樣去看待鬥爭、競賽、野心及對名利地位的貪求。

● Thousand-Handed, Thousand-Eyed Guanyin Bodhisattva
千手千眼觀世音菩薩

The Guanyin Bodhisattva image that now presides at the City of Ten Thousand Buddhas first graced Gold Mountain Dhyana Monastery. At that time, the Guanyin Bodhisattva image was not yet gilded.

這尊觀世音菩薩聖像，目前安放在萬佛聖城的萬佛寶殿。在這之前，是供奉在金山禪寺。當時，這尊觀世音聖像尚未貼金。

● **Dining Hall, Gold Mountain Dhyana Monastery**
金山禪寺　齋堂

The lumber used to renovate Gold Mountain came as a response from Guanyin Bodhisattva. Guo Tung and Guo Tung Laughton, disciples of the Master, learned that an office building in downtown San Francisco was about to be renovated and that the wooden shelving needed to be removed. Anyone willing to remove the wood could have it free of charge. The Laughtons quickly informed Gold Mountain and crews of young disciples were sent to tear out the shelving.

The wood was the major material used in the initial renovation of Gold Mountain. The small pieces left over from major work were saved and used to make the tables and small wooden stools used in the dining hall at Gold Mountain. The Master's lesson to extravagant Westerners about the principle of reusing and not wasting was repeated again and again during the renovations of the Association's Way-places.

　　金山寺整修時使用的木頭，來自觀世音菩薩的感應。一天，上人的弟子，果同‧勞頓夫婦，得知三藩市鬧區有一所辦公棲要維修，需要拆走一些木架子，誰來拆除，木料就歸誰。果同夫婦立即通知金山寺，寺裡便派了弟子們去把木架子拆下並送回金山寺。

　　在開始整修金山寺時，這些木頭是主要的材料。其餘的小塊木頭則用來做齋堂的飯桌和小凳子。在整修很多法總道場時，上人一再地教導奢侈的西方人　不浪費、重複使用可用的材料。

- **Early 1970's San Francisco**
Passing the Offerings, Gold Mountain Dhyana Monastery

七十年代早期 三藩市
金山禪寺
傳供儀式

The Master directs the first Passing of Offerings Ceremony, while one of his Bhikshu disciples hosts the meal offering. From the very beginning, the Master trained his disciples by putting them in the leading roles and keeping a low profile himself, giving advice when needed.

上人指導第一次傳供法會，當時的一位比丘弟子爲法主。從一開始，上人就訓練他的弟子們站在領導的地位。自己則保持低姿態，在必要時給予輔導。

- **1973　San Francisco**
Grand Opening of the International Institute for the Translation of Buddhist Texts

一九七三年　三藩市
國際譯經學院開光大典

It was here that many of the first editions of the Buddhist Text Translation Society's English translations were completed. Instilling Virtue School (later known as Instilling Goodness Elementary School) was also founded here in 1976.

許多首版英譯佛教經典都是在這裡完成的。育良小學也於一九七六年在此成立。

● **1973   International Institute for the Translation of Buddhist Texts, San Francisco**
一九七三年　三藩市　國際譯經院

The Venerable Master is shown "opening the light" on the forty-two hands and eyes Guanyin Bodhisattva image that adorned and protected the Institute during the Grand Opening Ceremonies. The mantra he taught us to recite was *shi fo la shi fo la / to la tuo la / pin tuo la pin tuo la / chen tuo chen tuo / hu xin hu xin*" which is a section at the beginning of the Fourth Assembly of the Shurangama Mantra.

The Venerable Master's verse for *shi fo la shi fo la* says:

The Buddha Jewel universally illumines, emitting immeasurable light
That shines throughout the Dharma Realm and the treasury of empty space.
Having opened, revealed, awakened to, and entered proper knowledge and views,
They are the greatly enlightened kings who have attained unsurpassed Bodhi.

　　上人正爲一尊護佑、莊嚴譯經院的四十二手眼觀世音菩薩聖像開光。上人教我們念的咒語是：「什佛囉什佛囉。陀囉陀囉。頻陀囉頻陀囉。瞋陀瞋陀。虎信虎信。」此是〈楞嚴咒〉第四會開始的一段咒語。

　　上人爲「什佛囉什佛囉」所作的偈頌曰：「佛寶普放無量光，照遍法界虛空藏，開示悟入正知見，無上菩提大覺王。」

● San Francisco
Dharma Assembly at Gold Mountain Dhyana Monastery
三藩市
金山禪寺法會

Shown at far right is the Master, in the low profile that he early assumed as he allowed his disciples to act as Dharma Hosts and to learn by doing. Although the Master assumed a low-key role, he was ever-attentive to all aspects of monastic life and training and never failed to point out places that needed improving.

Without a doubt, the greatest strength he provided was his personal presence day in and day out, year in and year out, as he nurtured the seeds and tended the sprouts of Buddhism in the West.

圖中上人在右邊一個不起眼的角落。一開始，上人就讓弟子們在各種佛事及法會中充當法主，使他們得到訓練並取得實際的經驗。雖然上人只是扮演一個不起眼的角色，但他很注意寺院生活及訓練的種種細節，他總是能指出需要改進之處。

在西方培養、滋潤這些佛教的種子幼苗時，只要有上人在，就可以給人極大的鼓舞及力量。

● **San Francisco**

Gold Mountain Dhyana Monastery: Group Portrait including the California Dreamers

三藩市

上人與「加州夢幻者」（上人後排的成人及前排的小孩們）的團體照

The California Dreamers (adults shown standing in the row behind the Master and children sitting cross-legged in front) followed Sam Lewis (Sufi Sam), who sometimes paid his respects to the Master at the Buddhist Lecture Hall.

After Sam's untimely and premature death, many members of this group of California Dreamers had identical dreams of Sam, which occurred three times, all in the same night. Sam told them, "I now understand that I wasn't really qualified to be teaching you. I don't have any real accomplishment. I now regret that although I met Master Hua, I never studied with him. You should all go take refuge with him and become his disciples. He is qualified to teach; he has great accomplishment."

The next day, after comparing their dreams, the Dreamers called Gold Mountain Monastery and asked when the next Take Refuge ceremony would occur. After becoming disciples, they studied and worshipped together with disciples at Gold Mountain and sent their children to Instilling Virtue School when it opened in 1976.

山姆・路易斯是「加州夢幻者」的創立人。他曾到佛教講堂拜訪上人。

山姆不幸早逝之後，許多「加州夢幻者」的成員在同一晚上，一連三次夢到山姆告訴他們：「我現在才明白，我確實沒有資格教你們，因為我並沒有得到實證。我現在很後悔，雖然遇到了上人，卻沒有向他學習。你們都去皈依他。上人有資格教你們，他已得大成就。」

第二天，「夢幻者」們討論了這件事後，就給金山寺去電話，並問何時有皈依法會。皈依上人後，他們與其他的弟子們共同在金山寺研習佛法。而且一九七六年育良小學成立後，他們還將孩子送到學校來念書。

- **1973   San Francisco**
  Entering into Monastic Life Ceremony in November, Gold Mountain Dhyana Monastery

一九七三年 三藩市
十一月，金山禪寺剃度儀式

Shown standing behind the Master are six new Sangha members:

1. Heng Fu ('Blessings'), Guo Man, the donor of the Hong Kong Buddhist Lecture Hall [standing directly behind the Master];
2. Heng Fu ('Ax'), who as a layman went to an interview with the Master carrying an ax in a paper bag—a fact that went unnoticed by the Master's attending disciples until the Master himself asked that the bag be opened and its contents revealed [middle of three standing monks];
3. Heng Chen ('Precious'), who translated the Master's biography and the *Amitabha Sutra* into Spanish [beside Heng Fu/Guo Man];
4. Heng Kung ('Empty'), who fasted for seventy-two days, recited the Shurangama Mantra eight hours a day for a period of time, and could meditate for more than twelve hours at a stretch without breaking his full lotus posture [the tallest one in the photo];
5. Heng Lu ('Prosperity'), the only son of a businessman in San Francisco; and
6. Heng Chen ('Heavy'), a young woman from South Africa.

上人的背後，是六位新的出家眾。

（一）恆福（果滿），站在上人的正後方。她是香港佛教講堂的捐贈人。

（二）恆斧，三位站著的出家男眾當中，他是中間的那一位。他出家以前，有一次去訪問上人時，在紙袋裡裝了一把斧頭。上人的隨從弟子並不知道，直到上人親自叫他把紙袋打開，斧頭才露出來。

（三）恆珍，在恆福的左邊。她將《宣化上人事蹟》及《阿彌陀經》翻譯成西班牙文。

（四）恆空，他是照片中個子最高的一位。他打了七十二天的餓七。曾經有一段時期，他每天持誦八小時的〈楞嚴咒〉。他可以雙跏趺坐十二小時以上。

（五）恆祿，他是三藩市一位商人的獨生子。

（六）恆沈，來自南非的一位年輕女士。

● Gold Mountain Dhyana Monastery, San Francisco
Group Portrait with Professor and Mrs. Edward Conze and Professor and Mrs. Lewis Lancaster

三藩市　金山禪寺
上人與愛德華‧康薩教授及夫人、藍卡斯教授及夫人等的
團體照

Professor Edward Conze, the noted Buddhist scholar, was teaching at the University of Washington, Seattle, when Dr. Ronald Epstein wrote his Master's thesis based on his translation of the Venerable Master's Verses Without a Stand and Prose Commentary on the *Heart of Prajna Paramita Sutra.* At that time Bhikshu Heng Ching had also been studying with Professor Conze, but after the Shurangama Sutra Summer Session, he made his decision to enter into monastic life under the Master.

Professor Lewis Lancaster, the Director of the Buddhist Studies Department of the University of California at Berkeley, was also on Dr. Epstein's committee when he wrote his Doctoral dissertation based on his translation of the text and the Venerable Master's commentary on the "Seeking for the Mind in Seven Places" section of the *Shurangama Sutra.* Current with this photo, Bhikshuni Heng Yin was doing research under the direction of Professor Lewis Lancaster regarding the translation of the *Sixth Patriarch's Sutra* with the Venerable Master's commentary. This occasion was auspicious, as evidenced in the unusual triple appearance of an octagonal light canopy over the group.

　　愛德華‧康薩教授是西雅圖華盛頓大學著名的佛教學者。那時易象乾教授（法界佛教大學美洲區的校長）翻譯上人的《般若波羅蜜多心經非臺頌解》做爲其碩士論文的內容。恆靜也曾隨康薩教授上課，但在參加上人舉辦的「暑期《楞嚴經》講習班」後，決定追隨上人剃度出家。

　　藍卡斯教授，是柏克萊大學佛學系的主任。他是易象乾教授博士論文的主考委員之一。論文的內容取材於易教授翻譯《楞嚴經》中〈七處徵心〉的經文及上人的淺釋。恆隱當時是藍卡斯教授的研究生。正在翻譯《六祖壇經》的經文及上人的淺釋。照片中，大眾頭頂上的三個相互重疊的八角形影光，象徵著吉祥。

Redwood City, California

The Master invited by Professor Lewis Lancaster to speak to UC Berkeley students at a Redwood City Retreat

加州 紅木城

應藍卡斯教授的邀請，上人爲在紅木城進修的柏克萊加州大學學生講演。

The Master taught these young Western students the history of the word "Buddha," which in Chinese began as a transliteration *fo tuo ye* but was soon shortened to *fo*. Then, much to Professor Lancaster's amusement and scholarly appreciation, the Master suggested that had he been around at the time, he would have suggested that "Buddha" be rendered in Chinese as *bu da,* which means "Not Big." Because, the Master went on to say, Buddhas are not big and not small, and they neither come nor go.

上人爲這些青年學生講解「佛」字的來源。中文最初將「Buddha」音譯成「佛陀耶」，後來簡稱爲「佛」。上人說如果當時他在場的話，就會建議將「Buddha」翻成「不大」，因爲「佛」是不大、不小、不來，也不去的。藍卡斯教授很欣賞上人的說法，也覺得很有趣。

1974 Berkeley
一九七四年　柏克萊

The Master hosted a Dharma Gathering to Liberate the Living at the Berkeley Marina in 1974 on the Anniversary of the Enlightenment of Guanyin Bodhisattva.

The message of liberating the living: Oppression, wars, and killing can be rooted out without violence if we respect the right of beings to live and be free, and if we liberate them. By transforming our own hostile, aggressive, and jealous thoughts into hearts of compassion and peace; by liberating creatures whose lives are doomed, we can liberate ourselves and the world from the effects that killing karma brings about.

上人於觀世音菩薩成道日，在柏克萊水濱主持放生法會。

放生的意義在於：如果我們尊重其他眾生生存的權利及自由，並且將牠們放生，那麼世界上的壓榨、戰爭、殺戮，就可以不用武力予以根除。如果我們能將自己仇恨、妒忌、侵略的念頭，轉爲慈悲、祥和之心，並且將那些在死亡邊緣掙扎的眾生放生，那麼我們就能將自己及整個世界，從殺業所帶來的可怕後果中解脫出來。

● **Berkeley** — Liberating Life, Berkeley Marina
柏克萊 — 柏克萊水濱放生法會

In the early years of the Master's teaching, the assembly was primarily composed of Westerners who, regardless of their race and cultural backgrounds, knew virtually nothing about the traditional principles and practices of orthodox Buddhism. Thus, it was necessary for the Master to guide and direct, to teach and explain each procedure, ritual, ceremony and so forth over and over until the growing group of disciples who always followed him assimilated the knowledge and understanding. Here the Master is shown helping disciples and friends of the Dharma to arrange the crates, which contain birds about to be set free, into the form of the Chinese character for "Buddha" prior to the Liberating Life Ceremony.

　　上人來美後，早期的信眾，大多數是西方人。這些人來自不同的民族，有著不同的文化背景。他們對傳統的佛教原理、儀軌，一無所知。所以上人必須要加以引導，並再三解釋每一種佛事活動及法會的程序、儀式等等，直至他的常隨弟子們瞭解和吸收了這方面的知識。這是上人在放生法會上，指導他的弟子及信眾，把裝有鳥的箱子排成一個「佛」字。

As the number of disciples who wished to leave the home-life grew, the Master needed to find larger facilities. A portion of his time and energy and much of his blood, sweat, and toil were spent in searching for appropriate places and facilities to house Buddhist monasteries, translation institutes, schools and training centers, homes for the elderly, lay housing, temples, and lecture halls.

In those early days, the Master was always the first one up a mountain and the last one to tire as he out-paced and out-lasted all the young disciples during these hunting expeditions.

由於出家人數的增加，上人需要物色更大的道場。上人一生中，花了很多時間、精力、血汗，辛苦尋找適當的場所及設備，以便改建爲寺院、佛殿、講堂、譯經院、學校、訓練中心、老人院、居士林等。在早期覓地的日子裡，上人每次都是第一位爬上山頂和最後一位感到疲倦的人。而且比他所有的年輕弟子都走得快，堅持得最久。

- **1974 Seattle**
  The Master Hosting the
  World Peace Gathering
  一九七四年 西雅圖
  上人主持「世界和平
  聚會」

More than five hundred people joined the day's activities, sincerely uniting their minds in a single thought of peace.

五百多人參加了這次的活動。大家誠懇地心連心，一心一意祈求和平。

- **1974　Seattle**
一九七四年　西雅圖

The Gathering coincided with the arrival in the Seattle area of Bhikshus Heng Ju and Heng Yo, the two monks who executed the first Three-Steps-One-Bow pilgrimage. Two other monks, Bhikshus Heng Kuan and Heng Kung, joined the Gathering in the midst of their seventy-two-day fasts.

　值此「世界和平聚會」，兩位比丘，恆具及恆由，剛好完成第一次的三步一拜，抵達西雅圖。另兩位參與此會的比丘，恆觀及恆空，正在實行七十二天的絕食。

- ### 1974　Seattle
  ### 一九七四年　西雅圖

Bhikshus Heng Ju and Heng Yo, seeking for world peace, made a pilgrimage from San Francisco to Marblemount, Washington, that began in October 1973 and ended in August 1974. This was a great feat within the history of Buddhism.

　　比丘恆具和恆由——爲祈求世界和平，自一九七三年十月至一九七四年八月，從三藩市開始三步一拜，一直叩至華盛頓的大理石山。這是世界佛教史上的一大壯舉。

- ### 1974　Seattle
  ### 一九七四年　西雅圖

Bhikshus Heng Kuan and Heng Kung both fasted for seventy-two days consecutively (during which time they abstained from all food and drink with the exception of one cup of water a day).

　　Here the Master is shown with those two monks and Guo Hui Weber, who fasted for thirty-five days.

　　比丘恆觀及恆空——連續打了七十二天的餓七。（絕食的條件是：七十二天內，斷絕一切食物及飲料。每天只能喝一小杯水。）

　　照片中是上人與恆觀、恆空及魏果回。魏果回也打了三十五天的餓七。

● **Gold Mountain Dhyana Monastery, San Francisco**
三藩市　金山禪寺

The Master handing Bhikshu Heng Ju a piece of pie, celebrating the successful completion of his bowing pilgrimage from San Francisco to Marblemount, Washington. There's a story that goes with this.

As a layman, Heng Ju was learning to eat one meal a day, but it was hard. One evening as he returned from work, he stopped and bought a packaged pie and stuck it in the pocket of his coat. During evening lecture, he could think of nothing else but that piece of pie and could hardly wait for the lecture to be over so he could eat it.

After lecture, without telling a soul, he quietly slipped unnoticed up the fire ladder to the flat roof, and began strolling around. Opening his packaged pie at last, he took a huge bite. As he rounded the roof, he suddenly caught sight of the Master climbing over the edge of the roof from the fire ladder. The Master began to stroll the opposite way in the same circle and was headed right for him. Heng Ju's mouth was stuffed so full of pie that he couldn't speak. He could only nod his head in acknowledgment and keep on walking. Thus they passed each other three times as they strolled in opposite directions around the roof. Upon the third passing, the Master smiled and asked, "How do you feel?" With that he left the roof.

上人送一塊「派」給比丘恆具，慶祝他成功地完成了從三藩市至華盛頓大理石山三步一拜的壯舉。在此有個故事：

恆具尚未出家時，已學習日中一食，但覺得很困難。一天下午，當他下班回家時，停下來買了一塊包裝好的「派」，把它塞進大衣的口袋裡。當晚聽經時，他什麼也不想，只顧著想那塊「派」。他等不及講完經，就想吃它。

聽完經後，他沒有告訴任何人，自己靜悄悄地從防火梯溜到屋頂平台上，開始經行，最後終於打開「派」的紙包，咬了一大口。當他在屋頂上繞行時，忽然看到上人也從防火梯爬上屋頂。上人開始向相反的方向經行，正好面對恆具。當時，恆具口中塞滿了「派」，不能說話，他只能點頭向上人作禮，繼續經行。兩人迎面從相反方向在平台上繞了三圈。第三次時，上人笑著問他：「你覺得怎麼樣？」然後上人便下了屋頂。

1974　Saigon, Vietnam
一九七四年　越南　西貢

November. Phuong Guo Wu (shown at left in photo) was an international traveler who had visited almost every country in the world. She and her husband were based in Saigon, where their land holdings and businesses were extensive. A little while prior to the change of government in Saigon, the Venerable Master placed an unexpected call to Guo Wu, who was at home with her husband at the time. She was surprised at the long distance call and immediately asked if anything was wrong. "Nothing," replied the Abbot. It was a simple conversation in which the Master, speaking to both husband and wife, gently suggested that the couple might tie up their affairs and come to America a little sooner if there was nothing particular holding them there. Guo Wu and her husband did not follow the Master's suggestion but lingered on in Saigon. As a result of that delay, when the change of government came, more than half of the family holdings were lost.

十一月，上人的弟子方果悟（相片的左側），是個國際旅遊專家。幾乎走遍了世界上所有的國家。她與丈夫定居西貢。在西貢擁有生意及大片的土地。在西貢政變之前，有一次，上人突然打電話找果悟，當時她與丈夫都在家。她很驚異，馬上問上人發生了什麼事。上人回答說：「沒事。」在電話上，上人與他們進行了簡單的交談。上人溫和地向他們建議，提早將事業結束，遷移到美國去。但他們並沒有聽從上人的勸告馬上到美國去，而繼續留在西貢。結果，當越南易幟時，她家損失了一大半財產。

● 1975　Oregon
一九七五年　奧立岡

The Master led the four assemblies of young disciples in a Buddha Recitation Session under an open tent in the woods of Oregon. Himself an expression of Western Bliss, the Master explains the Dharma door of reciting Amitabha Buddha's name. The glow of a kerosene lamp sheds a canopy of light above the Master's head as he brings to life the method that leads to rebirth in the Pure Land.

　上人帶領四眾弟子，在奧立岡州的森林中，一個露天的帳棚裡，舉行爲期一週的念佛法會。帶著來自西方極樂世界的表情，上人講解念「阿彌陀佛」聖號的淨土法門。當上人正生動地講述求生淨土的方法時，一盞油燈發射出光芒，罩著上人的頭頂。

● Oregon　奧立岡

The Master is shown hosting the Great Transference of Merit performed on the Oregon Coast at the culmination of the Buddha Recitation Session held at Buddha Root Farm.

　The Master's expedients in introducing young Westerners to the Dharma were many. On this occasion, he moved the entire Buddha Recitation Session from the Oregon woods to the Oregon coast. Everyone is facing West as the sun sets at the end of the Amitabha Buddha session, vowing to attain rebirth in the Western Pure Land, and to transfer the merit to all living beings.

　上人在奧立岡海岸主持佛七後的大迴向。這是在「佛根地」這次佛七的高潮。

　上人用很多的善巧方便來接引西方青年進入佛門。在佛七結束時，上人將法會會場從奧立岡的森林移向海岸。與會的佛子們面向西下的夕陽，每個人都發願往生西方淨土，並將此功德迴向一切眾生。

The Master, Dharma Master Hui Seng, and the Master's left-home disciples speaking Dharma for university students.

Over the years, the Master spoke at many educational institutes including the University of California at Berkeley and at Davis; the University of Southern California, Los Angeles; Stanford University; the University of Wisconsin; the University of Minnesota; Humbolt State University; the University of Oregon; the University of Washington; the University of Hawaii; and the University of British Columbia.

上人、慧僧法師及出家弟子們爲大學的學生們講法。多年來，上人曾在許多教育機構講演佛法。包括柏克萊加大、戴維斯加大、洛杉磯南加大、史丹福大學、威斯康辛大學、明尼蘇達大學、漢堡大學、奧立岡大學、華盛頓大學、夏威夷大學、加拿大卑詩大學等等。

1976 Santa Clara

Central Park: The Master (seated at far left) speaks to young Americans about "Energies for Peace."

一九七六年　聖他克拉拉

中央公園：上人爲年輕的美國人講「和平的精神」

The Master's affinities with young Americans are evident in this photo. Wherever he went, young Americans were immediately attracted to his straight talk, his compassionate warmth, and his uncanny ability to communicate that transcended language and cultural barriers.

從照片中可以很明顯地看出，上人與美國年輕人的緣份。不管上人走到哪裡，他率直的談吐、慈悲的溫馨，還有跨越了語言及文化障礙的神奇溝通能力，會立刻吸引了這些年輕人。

1976 Santa Clara
一九七六年 聖他克拉拉

The Master's virtue moved young Americans, gently subduing their strong sense of independence and concept of "freedom," so that they willingly learned simple Buddhist rituals such as reciting Buddha's and Bodhisattva's names. Shown here, they follow the monks and nuns in circumambulation.

　　上人的德行感動了美國青年，並逐漸地降伏了他們強烈的獨立感及「自由」的觀念，使他們樂意學習佛教的儀軌，如持念佛菩薩聖號。照片中，他們隨著出家眾繞佛。

● 1976 San Francisco — The Master Presiding over Entry into the Monastic Life, Gold Mountain Dhyana Monastery
一九七六年 三藩市 — 金山禪寺上人主持剃度典禮

In 1976, four more young men and women made the resolve to enter into monastic life. They were the monks Heng Sure and Heng Shun, the nun Heng Chu, and another monk who was the first Asian to leave home with the Master since his arrival in the West.

　　在一九七六年，又有四位青年男女發心加入僧團。他們是恆實、恆順、恆居，另一位是上人來美後收的第一位亞洲出家弟子。

- ## 1970's   Gold Mountain Dhyana Monastery
Disciples listening to the Master's lectures on the *Avatamsaka (Flower Adornment) Preface, Prologue*, and *Sutra* at Gold Mountain Dhyana Monastery

七十年代　金山禪寺

弟子們正在聽上人講解《華嚴經疏序》、《華嚴經疏》及《華嚴經》

During this lecture series the Master encouraged disciples to do preparation. It was never known when the Master would call on a disciple to lecture that evening's passage first.

Earphones were used so disciples could listen to the Chinese while the English translation was being given. Simultaneously, other disciples were in a sound-proof booth typing the lecture into English as it was spoken in Chinese.

講經期間，上人鼓勵弟子們事先做好準備，因爲誰也不知道，何時上人會叫弟子出來講演。

使用耳機的目的，是爲了方便弟子們在翻譯英語時，同時可以聽中文。在隔音室，其他的弟子們，則一邊聽中文，一邊翻譯並打字成英文講稿。

● **1970's   San Francisco**
七〇年代　三藩市

The Master accorded with conditions in order to teach beings. That means that whatever the Master did was an expedient aimed at helping an individual or a group. It also means that often the things the Master allowed others to do for him were not necessarily things that he liked having done for him.

One example is how his disciples liked to serve the Master a cup of liquid during his Sutra lecture. For a while, one of the monks was very involved in serving the Master that cup of liquid. But in order to prepare this drink for the Master, he would miss evening recitation. The Master didn't like that, but at first he kept quiet. Later, he began to complain that the cup the monk served him was dirty.

Finally when that didn't work, the Master decided to use an expedient. One evening he drank most of the cup of liquid and then began to peer intently into the almost-empty cup. His intense interest in his cup was soon noticed by everyone. Then, while still examining the contents of the cup, he called Bhikshu Heng Ching up to the high seat, announcing that his cup had a bug in it and instructing him to look in the cup and then tell everyone what he saw. Heng Ching stared into the cup and then reported, "All I see is a bit of soggy dust fuzz in the cup."

"That's not dust! That's an insect!" argued the Master. "Pass the cup around for everyone to take a look!"

Heng Ching did as he was told. Those disciples who peered into the cup also saw what looked like a bit of soggy gray fuzz in the bottom of the cup. After the cup went around the room, it was placed back on the Master's table at the high seat.

The Master continued his lecture on the *Avatamsaka Sutra*, but whenever the translation was going on, he would pick up the cup and stare into it intently. Finally, he called Heng Ching back up again and said, "Look in the cup now and tell me what you see."

Heng Ching did as he was asked and reacted with amazement. "Why, there's a perfectly-formed insect in the cup!"

"Pass it around," the Master commanded, and Heng Ching did. What the disciples saw this time was indeed an exquisite insect perched on eight legs shimmering with multicolored iridescence, looking unlike any creature belonging to this world. That night everyone saw what they had never seen before while the tea-serving monk was taught a lesson: "I don't want to be the cause of your missing evening recitation!" explained the Master. "I don't have such blessings, and I don't want to have to bear the cause and effect

68   宣化老和尚追思紀念專集

上人隨緣度化眾生，上人所做的每一件事，都是爲了方便教化眾生。有時，上人讓別人爲他做事，但實際上這些事未必是爲他自己的需要而做的。

例如，上人講經時，弟子們喜歡爲上人準備飲料。有一段時間，一位出家弟子很殷勤地爲上人準備飲料，因此而不能做晚課。上人不喜歡這一點。起初上人不講話，後來他開始抱怨裝飲料的杯子是髒的。

當上人的抱怨沒有結果時，上人就採用另一種方便法。一天晚上，上人喝水後，留了一點水在杯子裡，然後就盯著這隻杯子看。所有聽課的人馬上就都注意到了。上人不停地看著杯子，然後叫恆靜走上講台。上人告訴他杯子裡有隻蟲，讓恆靜看了一下杯子裡面，然後向大家說看到了什麼。恆靜看了以後，說：「我看到的是一些濕濕的塵毛。」

「那不是灰塵！是蟲！」上人說：「傳下去讓每個人看看。」

恆靜依命而行。所有的弟子看到的，都只是一些濕透的灰色塵毛，在杯子底下。大家看完之後，杯子又送回上人的桌上。

上人繼續講《華嚴經》，每當英語翻譯時，上人就又拿起杯子來看。然後又叫恆靜上講台，問：「看看這杯子，告訴我你看見什麼。」

恆靜看了一下杯子，驚訝地說：「怎麼搞的，杯子裡居然有一隻蟲！」

「傳下去！」上人命令。弟子們這次所看到的，的確是一隻有著八隻腳、多彩漂亮的昆蟲。看起來不像是這個世間所有的生物。那天晚上大家都大開眼界，而那位很殷勤地爲上人準備飲料的弟子，也得到了一個教訓。上人事後解釋說：「我不願意成爲你缺席晚課的因，我沒有這份福報，我也不願意負這因果的責任。」

● 1976　City of Ten Thousand Buddhas
　　一九七六年　萬佛聖城

August. The Three Masters (with the Master as Precept-Transmitting Acharya) and Seven Certifiers signing precept certificates at the Second Threefold Ordination Ceremony (the first to be held at the City of Ten Thousand Buddhas).

八月，首次在聖城舉辦第二屆三壇大戒。上人爲得戒和尚，三師七證在戒牒上簽名。

● City of Ten Thousand Buddhas   萬佛聖城

The Sangha grows under the Master's guidance as more men and women enter into monastic life.

This photo was taken at the site of the present Long Life Hall, prior to its building, and commemorates the day when several more heads were shaved.

為上人的德行所感召，更多的善男信女，發心剃度出家，僧團人數逐漸增加。

這是為新落髮的弟子們舉行的慶祝會。拍照的地點是現在的延生堂。

● Blessing the Turtles
祝福烏龜

Already free, the turtles were loath to leave their benefactor. They surfaced and tread water, craning their necks to peer at the source of their mysterious liberation. Their obvious expression of gratitude brought a smile to the Master's face as he quietly extended his hands to bless them.

被放生的烏龜捨不得離開恩人，牠們浮上水面，伸長脖頸凝望著上人——釋放牠們的不可思議的本源。牠們明顯地表示感恩，令上人臉上露出微笑，默默地伸出手祝福牠們。

宣化老和尚追思紀念專集

1977 City of Ten Thousand Buddhas

The Master with Paul Cardinal Yubin

一九七七年 萬佛聖城

上人與天主教的
于斌樞機

When the Cardinal led a religious delegation to the City of Ten Thousand Buddhas in 1977, the Master advised him, "You be a Buddhist among the Catholics, and I will be a Catholic among the Buddhists." The Cardinal agreed.

當于樞機帶著他的宗教訪問團來到聖城時，上人對他說：「你做天主教裡的佛教徒，我做佛教裡的天主教徒。」于樞機同意了。

1977 Golden Gate Park — February. Dharma Gathering for Rain in Marx Meadow
一九七七年 金門公園 — 二月，馬克斯草地，求雨法會。

Procession into Golden Gate Park where services were held to try to end a two-year drought that had left California barren and desperate for rain.

參加法會的信眾，列隊走向在金門公園舉行的求雨法會，希望解除已持續兩年的旱災。嚴重的缺雨使加州成為不毛之地。

● 1977　Golden Gate Park
一九七七年　金門公園

Recitation of Guanyin Bodhisattva's name (the Bodhisattva who hears the sounds of the world) and of the special mantra for seeking rain were done alternately. Dharma talks explained simple principles of cause and effect. "Why hasn't it rained? Because we have been too selfish and greedy and we have wasted water. If we admit our mistakes and change, the sincerity of our repentance and reform can evoke a response." The crowd of participants grew and joined in the chanting, kneeling, and prostrations. Even while the mantra for seeking rain was being recited the clouds gathered and the wind picked up.

　　祈雨的人們輪流念誦觀世音菩薩聖號及求雨的咒語。講法開示因果的基本道理：「爲什麼不下雨？因爲我們太自私、貪心及浪費水。如果我們承認自己的過錯，並誠心地懺悔，就會有感應。」參與的大眾人數逐漸增加，大家在一起唱誦、禮拜。當大家念求雨的咒語時，天空開始滿佈烏雲，風也刮起來了。

● 1977　Golden Gate Park　一九七七年　金門公園

Did it rain? Yes it did. Early the following morning, rain was reported in Mendocino County (in the area around the City of Ten Thousand Buddhas), northern California. By 11:30 a.m. rain pelted San Francisco and the news reporters who had covered the Dharma Gathering for Rain returned to Marx Meadow for an on-the-spot report. "Right there was the altar where the Buddhists prayed for rain," she reported. "Now it was raining, just as they had sought, and where the altar had stood was a huge puddle of water." The Master did not go to Golden Gate Park. He stayed back, behind the scenes, directing the entire Dharma Assembly.

下雨了？是的。報導說，次日凌晨在北加州的曼都仙諾縣一帶（萬佛聖城所在地），已開始下雨。上午十一時半，大雨驟降三藩市。曾在當時採訪求雨法會的記者們，回到馬克斯草地，做現場報導：「這裡是佛教徒們設壇求雨的地方，現在已開始下雨。正如他們所祈求的一樣。放置佛桌的地方已經有一汪水。」上人雖沒有去金門公園，但他留在金山寺加持整個求雨過程。

- **Spring 1978   City of Ten Thousand Buddhas**
  Seminar on Death and Dying
  一九七八年春　萬佛聖城
  舉辦名爲「死亡與臨終」的座談會

- **Spring 1978   City of Ten Thousand Buddhas**
  一九七八年春　萬佛聖城

"Entwined Lovers," a portion of two naturally-formed tree roots, was one of the highlights of the Seminar on Death and Dying. Found on the grounds of the City of Ten Thousand Buddhas during that seminar, this tree trunk was shown to the Master, who explained that it was actually two lovers who, during their previous lives, had been so inseparable from each other that they made mutual vows to always be together in every life. Due to their karma, they ended up in this life as two tree roots that grew together in a perpetual embrace. The Master went on to explain the true principle of how sexual desire and emotional love are the root of death and dying and lead to endless transmigration in the paths of rebirth.

連理枝（愛結），這是自然結合在一起的兩節樹幹，同時也是「死亡與臨終」座談會的討論話題。這是座談會期間，在聖城裡找到的。有人將此木拿去給上人看，上人解釋說，過去有一對情人因爲太相愛了，他們發誓生生世世永不分離。因爲他們的共業，使他們形成兩棵永遠環抱在一起的連理枝。上人說，情愛是生死輪迴的根本。

- **l978　Malaysia**
The Master compassionately gathering in the faithful.

一九七八年　馬來西亞
上人慈悲接引虔誠的信眾。

- **Bay Area, California**
加州灣區

Much of the Master's time and energy was spent searching for land and facilities to serve as Way-places in the West. The Master's tireless zeal in establishing Buddhist communities, educational facilities, monasteries, and translation institutes was based on his vows that the Proper Dharma should prevail.

　　上人花了很多時間及精力，尋找建立道場的地方及設備。基於弘揚正法的願力，上人不知疲勞，歷盡艱辛逐步建立了佛教叢林、教育中心、寺院及譯經院等。

- **Great Compassion House, City of Ten Thousand Buddhas**
  Early Group Portrait of the Master with the Great Assembly in the courtyard of Great Compassion House.

萬佛聖城　大悲院
早期上人與四眾弟子攝於大悲院庭院。

- **City of Ten Thousand Buddhas** — The Master giving instruction in Chan Meditation during a Winter Chan Session

萬佛聖城 — 上人在冬季禪七開示

Every year at the City a Chan Session was held. Sessions were several weeks long, running from 3:00 a.m. until 12:00 midnight with hour-long sits broken by twenty-minute walks. A one hour rest period was allowed in the late afternoon. Under the Master's patient guidance, his disciples gradually learned the beginning techniques of meditation. Everyone dropped his/her duties to participate fully in these rare sessions. Things came to a standstill in mid-winter as everyone investigated Chan together.

　　每年冬天，萬佛聖城都要「打禪七」。這些長達數週的禪七，每次坐香一小時，接著行香二十分鐘，從凌晨三時到午夜十二時，只在傍晚休息一個鐘頭。在上人耐心地指導下，弟子們慢慢學會了打坐的入門技巧。一到冬天，所有的事情都停了，大家放下工作，全心參加這難得的禪七。

● **West Coast, America**
美國西岸

The Master with Bhikshus Heng Sure and Heng Chau during their Three-Steps-One-Bow Pilgrimage.

It was during this period that the Venerable Master established five of the Six Guiding Principles: no fighting, no greed, no seeking, no selfishness, and no pursuit of personal advantage. Later, in Vancouver, the Master added the sixth: no lying. Together these became the Six Guiding Principles of the Dharma Realm Buddhist Association.

上人探望三步一拜中的比丘恆實及恆朝。也就在這個時期，上人立下了「不爭、不貪、不求、不自私、不自利」的五大宗旨。以後在加拿大溫哥華，上人又加上一條「不打妄語」，成爲現在法界佛教總會的六大宗旨。

● **1978   Malaysia**
一九七八年   馬來西亞

When the Master went to Southeast Asia to propagate the Dharma, his delegation included Bhikshu Heng Chau (far left) and Shramanera Guo Tung (far right). During that visit to Malaysia, Bhikshu Heng Chau fell ill. Guo Tung also fell ill and joined him in the sick room. Heng Chau's illness became critical and the Master appointed Bhikshu Heng Sure to attend and keep 24-hour watch over him. One evening things were grave and Guo Tung, who had dozed off during his recitation of the Great Compassion Mantra, suddenly saw the Ghost of Impermanence come in, riding on a cold wind that all three monks perceived as it blew through the room. Wearing a tall hat and looking thin and foreboding, the Ghost of Impermanence announced to Guo Tung that it was his time to go. Guo Tung shivered with fear and picked up his recitation of the Great Compassion Mantra with life-and-death vigor. The Ghost disappeared.

Meanwhile Heng Chau had fallen into a semi-coma. Only the Master could arouse him when he came to visit in the late evenings despite his weariness at the end of long days of lecture tours with the delegation. The Master would compassionately take Heng Chau's hand, and at that gesture, Heng Chau would slowly open his eyes and become aware of his surroundings.

King Yama wanted him, and finally the Master had to use a mudra to write a mandate to King Yama. He said that this disciple was sincere and dedicated and that under no circumstances should King Yama take him yet. It took some persuasion, but in the end King Yama yielded and Heng Chau recovered. From these experiences, both monks learned about the dangers of false thinking and increased their cultivation of the mind-ground to try to prevent defiled thoughts

...rom entering.

After Heng Chau's recovery, the Master kindly advised him, "I had to use every effort to persuade King Yama to let you live on, and so all the merit and virtue you had amassed so far in your years as a monk has been used up. But don't worry, you can generate more. You should apply yourself diligently and work hard for the Dharma!"

上人在東南亞弘法時，比丘恆朝（左邊）及沙彌果童（右邊）也同行。在馬來西亞時，兩人都因病而住在病房裡。因恆朝的病變得很嚴重，上人就叫比丘恆實二十四小時守護著他。一天下午，果童在念〈大悲咒〉時，打起瞌睡來，他突然看見無常鬼乘著一股冷風而來，三位僧人都感覺到這股冷風。戴著高冒、瘦長的無常鬼對果童說，時辰已到，要果童跟他走。果童怕得發抖，在這生死關頭，立即精進地持念〈大悲咒〉，無常鬼便消失了。

當時，恆朝已陷入半昏迷狀態，只有上人能喚醒他。每次上人在一整天的巡迴弘法之後，還不顧勞倦也去探望他。上人會很慈悲地握著他的手，在這時，恆朝就慢慢地睜開眼睛，意識到周圍發生的事。

閻羅王要帶他走，最後上人用手印寫了個命令，說他的弟子虔誠地為佛教奉獻，無論如何也不能將他帶走。閻羅王最後被說服了，恆朝才逐漸復原。

從這次的經歷中，這兩位出家人知道了打妄想的危險，並更加地在心地上用功，防止污濁念頭侵入。

復原之後，上人很慈悲地告訴恆朝：「我盡了最大的努力來說服閻羅王，讓你繼續活著。因此你出家幾年所累積的功德已經用完了。但別擔心，你可以繼續積功累德，為佛法努力精進。」

● **Malaysia**
The Master seated at the door of a temple

馬來西亞

上人坐在某寺門前

The Master once wrote:

Walking, standing, sitting, and lying down,
Don't be apart from this.
To depart from this
Would be a mistake!

上人偈曰：「行住坐臥，不離這個，離了這個，便是錯過。」

● **No Words Hall,
City of Ten Thousand Buddhas**
The Master teaching a class on the Buddhist Patriarchs

萬佛聖城　無言堂
上人在爲弟子講解《佛祖道影》

The Master wrote eight-line verses for each of the Patriarchs.

His classes were conducted as part of the "Developing Inherent Wisdom" series, wherein disciples were required to explain the texts written on the board first in Chinese and English. Only after many disciples had practiced explaining the lesson would the Master finally give his explanation. Such classes often lasted four or five hours and were the arena for many kinds of learning, the Master's dedication to educating being one of the primary lessons.

The Master would teach very early in the morning (6:00 or 6:30 a.m.) for several reasons: (1) so the cooks could attend before they had to go to the kitchen; (2) so that teachers and students could attend before they had to go to school; and (3) so that he could finish his lesson and make the drive back to San Francisco in time to cross the Golden Gate Bridge toll-free. Sometimes the Master would teach in the evenings as soon as he arrived on the grounds after the long drive from San Francisco, without allowing himself time to rest and refresh himself.

上人爲每一位祖師寫了一首八句的偈頌。

上課時，上人以他特有的「主觀智能推動力」的方式來教導弟子們。多位弟子先用中、英文解釋事先在黑板寫好的課文，之後上人才開始講解。這種教課方式，有時延續四、五小時之久。我們在這些課裡學到很多重要的東西，同時也學到上人這種對教育的奉獻精神。

上人早晨很早就開始教課（六點或六點半），原因是：（一）煮飯的人可以先上課再去廚房。（二）老師及學生可以先來上課再去學校。（三）上人教完課回三藩市，可以趕得上過金門橋的免費時刻。

有時上人晚上從三藩市回到萬佛聖城，沒有給自己時間休息，就立即爲弟子上課。

● 1979   City of Ten Thousand Buddhas
一九七九年   萬佛聖城

The Master presiding as Precept-Transmitting Acharya during the Third Threefold Ordination Ceremony at the City of Ten Thousand Buddhas. Preceptees make full prostrations as the Master passes down the corridor of Great Compassion House.

上人爲第三屆三壇大戒的得戒和尚。這是上人經過「大悲院」的走廊時，戒子們向上人頂禮。

● 1979   City of Ten Thousand Buddhas — The Third Threefold Ordination Ceremony
一九七九年   萬佛聖城 — 第三屆三壇大戒

Shown here are the Three Masters and Seven Certifiers who transmitted the precepts (seated in middle row) and the newly precepted monks and nuns (seated on the floor). This Full Ordination Ceremony was unique in that the Transmitting Masters included Bhikshus from China, Vietnam, America, and Sri Lanka, representing both the Mahayana and the Theravada traditions.

這是授戒的三師七證（坐在中排）和新戒比丘、比丘尼（坐在前排）。此次的三壇大戒的戒師們有來自中國、越南、美國、錫蘭的比丘。這象徵著南傳、北傳佛教的統一與團結。

● 1979   City of Ten Thousand Buddhas
一九七九年　萬佛聖城

November. The Master opening the light on the Thousand-Handed, Thousand-Eyed Guanyin Bodhisattva in the Hall of Ten Thousand Buddhas.

The Master is surrounded by young American and Asian disciple-monks: (from left to right) Bhikshus Heng Tso, Heng Chau, Heng Wu, Heng Gung, and Heng Sure, and Shramanera Guo Erh.

十一月，上人於萬佛寶殿爲千手千眼觀世音菩薩聖像開光。

圍繞著上人的是年輕的美國及亞洲僧眾弟子：比丘恆佐、恆朝、恆無、恆貢、恆實及沙彌果爾。（從左到右）

● **City of Ten Thousand Buddhas** — The Master with Karmapa at the City of Ten Thousand Buddhas
萬佛聖城—上人與卡馬巴（西藏喇嘛）

The Karmapa's disciples tried to reach the Master several times by phone at Gold Mountain Dhyana Monastery, but the Master would not take the calls. Finally disciples were sent to see the Master in person. The Master also declined to see them. Eventually the disciples of the Karmapa left messages making it clear that the Karmapa's life was in grave danger due to his illness (cancer). The Master was informed of the situation and after that the Karmapa's illness went into recession.

Later, the Karmapa himself went to visit the Master, who was at the City of Ten Thousand Buddhas.

Wherever the Karmapa went, his disciples arranged an elaborate fanfare. This occasion was no exception. And so one carload of his disciples started out about one hour early so that they could reach the City first and arrange for flags, Tibetan trumpets, and so forth. Who would have guessed that their car would break down! It took them more than one hour to get back on the road, and they were terribly nervous because they knew they could never reach the City before the Karmapa did.

Thus, the Karmapa's entry into the City of Ten Thousand Buddhas was quiet and unheralded. Everyone was at lunch, including the Master. The Karmapa and his personal attendants had to come to the dining hall to find the Master, who calmly invited them to take a seat on the side until he finished his lunch.

Later, the Master walked with the Karmapa to the Master's quarters. Upon arrival in the Master's guest room, the Karmapa's disciples began to pull out beautiful cloths to cover his seat and to arrange other adornments. the Karmapa stopped them saying, "No! Not here! Put it away." Then the Karmapa took a simple seat at the side of the Master. A quiet discussion followed in which the Master urged the Karmapa to immediately cancel his commitments and shave his head to become a Bhikshu: to properly enter monastic life. The Master's unspoken meaning was that if the Karmapa could put down his prestige and reputation, he could get well and enjoy long life. But if he continued to do the "Anointing of Crowns" ceremony, he would expend too much of his own precious energy, and there could be no guarantee on his own life. The Karmapa was unable to heed the Master's advice and died not long after that interview.

卡馬巴的弟子們曾多次打電話到金山禪寺與上人聯絡，但上人都不接。最後他的弟子親自上門找上人，上人也拒絕接見。卡馬巴的弟子最後留言說，卡馬巴已經生命垂危（他患了癌症）。上人知道了這件事後，不久卡馬巴的病就開始好轉。

後來卡馬巴親自上萬佛聖城拜訪上人。他雖未明述來意，但不用說，來訪的目的是要對上人表示他的感恩之意。

卡馬巴每到一處，他的弟子們必事先安排一個隆重的場面，這次也不例外。所以，有一整車的弟子提前一小時出發，以便能在萬佛城做好各種旗幟、喇叭等的歡迎準備。沒想到他們的車子卻拋錨了。花了一個多小時，才又重新上路。他們非常緊張，因為他們知道他們無法比卡馬巴早到萬佛城。

所以，當卡馬巴到達時，萬佛城一片寧靜。當時，所有的人，包括上人在內，都在用午齋。卡馬巴與隨從必須親自上齋堂找上人。上人從容地請他們坐在一旁，直到上人用完午齋。

結齋後，上人與卡馬巴一齊走到方丈室。在上人的貴賓室裡，卡馬巴的弟子拿出漂亮的座布為他鋪座，並安排其他的裝飾。卡馬巴阻止他們：「不，這裡不用這個，拿走！」然後，卡馬巴就坐在上人旁邊的座位上。兩人平靜地交談著，上人勸卡馬巴放下一切，剃髮為僧，正式出家。上人的言外之意是，如果卡馬巴肯放下他的威望與聲譽，他的病就能好轉，壽命也可以延長。但如果繼續為人「灌頂」，他將消耗太多的寶貴精力，甚至無法保住自己的生命。卡馬巴並未接受上人的忠告，在這次訪問後不久就去世了。

● **City of Ten Thousand Buddhas**
The Master presiding in the Small Dining Hall
萬佛聖城
聖城的小齋堂

At the beginning, everything was simple and unadorned. Here, Bhikshu and Bhikshuni disciples join with the Master for the one meal of the day. The dining hall's wood-burning stove provided the only source of heat on the grounds of the City. Everyone warmed up during lunch.

　　初期的萬佛聖城，一切都很簡陋。上人在這裡與出家弟子們共用午齋。小齋堂裡有個燒木材的暖爐，是整個聖城唯一的熱源。每個人用齋時都感到很暖和。

● **No Words Hall,**
　City of Ten Thousand Buddhas
　萬佛聖城　無言堂

The Master displays his "playful samadhi" during his Shurangama Mantra class at No Words Hall, City of Ten Thousand Buddhas.

　　Each verse for each line of Mantra was full of principles to put into practice:

If you cherish others,
　　and they don't draw near to you,
　　take a look at your kindness;
If you respect others, but they don't reciprocate,
　　your reverence is not yet true.
Turn the light to illumine within,
　　and seek the answer inside.
The response and the Way intertwine;
　　don't be confused by God!

　　上人在無言堂講解〈楞嚴咒〉時，示現他的「遊戲三昧」。上人為每一句咒語都作了一首偈頌。這些偈頌富含很深的佛理。

　　　　愛人不親顧其仁，
　　　　禮彼弗答敬未眞；
　　　　迴光反照求諸己，
　　　　感應道交莫迷神。

• City of Ten Thousand Buddha
萬佛聖城

The Master seated outside the Abbot's
Quarters (K Building) at the City of Ten
Thousand Buddhas.

上人坐在方丈室外邊。

• December, 1985   City of Ten Thousand Buddhas
The Master with Dharma Master Haideng, an expert in "One Finger Skill."

一九八五年十二月　萬佛聖城
上人與海燈法師（海燈法師系以「一指禪」功聞名海內）

Dharma Master Haideng came to pay respects to the Venerable Master. Accompanied by Chinese officials who were promoting a
film about him, Dharma Master Haideng also took the time and energy to teach basic "Pure Youth Skill" (tongzigong) to the
Master's disciples, on the condition that they would not retransmit the skills or explain them for others.

The Master also arranged for Dharma
Master Haideng to lecture the "Four
Unalterable Aspects of Purity" from the
Shurangama Sutra, and praised his lectures,
saying that only those who are pure and proper
dare to explain that portion of the Sutra. In
order to show due respect to Dharma Master
Haideng, the Master himself and all his
disciples knelt to listen to the lectures.

海燈法師來美參訪上人時，中國政
府官員陪伴著他，來推銷有關海燈法
師的影片。海燈法師向上人的弟子們
傳授了基本的「童子功」。條件是：
不能外傳此功夫。

上人請海燈法師為四眾弟子講解《
楞嚴經》〈四種清淨明誨〉的經文。
上人很讚賞海燈法師的講演，並說唯
有清淨及正直者，才有勇氣講解這一
段經文。為了表示對海燈法師的恭敬
，上人親自帶領弟子們跪著聽經。

● **Late l980's**
The Master in Canada at Branch Way-places

八十年代末期
上人於加拿大分支道場

The Master was venerated by beings from nine Dharma Realms wherever he went. Those who could see would sometimes be given a glance into the realms beyond ordinary sight. Those who could not see but whose faith was deep also sensed the profundity of the Master's virtue in inspiring beings both visible and invisible. During this visit by the Master to the Associations' Way-places in Calgary and Golden, a dragon who had waited 2000 years for an opportunity to take refuge with the Master came seeking to become a disciple.

　上人無論到何處，都受到九法界眾生的尊敬，開了眼的人有時就可以看到這些肉眼所不能見的眾生。而那些看不到，但有深信心的人，也可以深深地感受到，上人感化那些有形、無形眾生的崇高德行。此次上人前往法總在加拿大之分支道場時，有一條龍在此地等了二千年，終於遇到皈依上人的機會，而成為上人的弟子。

宣化老和尚追思紀念專集

● 1987 City of Ten Thousand Buddhas
一九八七年 萬佛聖城

The Master greeting the seventy Bhikshus from China who came to perform the Water, Land, and Air Ceremony at the City of Ten Thousand Buddhas in 1987.

Dharma Masters Mingyang, Zhenchan and Miaoshan led the unprecedented delegation of monks from China, who performed the week-long intensive and elaborate ceremony which requires an Inner Platform and six Outer Platforms all staffed with monks and nuns who simultaneously perform rituals, ceremonies, and repentances and recite Sutra texts and the Buddha's name daily. At night the compassionate ceremony called "Flaming Mouths" was performed to liberate beings from suffering. All merit is transferred to rescue beings who died untimely deaths in the water, on land, or in the air.

應上人邀請，由明暘法師、眞禪法師、妙善法師率領了七十位僧眾，組成前所未有的中國佛教法務團，來到萬佛聖城舉辦水陸空大法會。

整個法會期間，全體僧眾每天在內壇、外壇（分爲六壇），同時進行誦經、念佛、拜懺。晚間是「焰口慈悲法會」，來超渡一切苦難眾生。法會的所有功德皆迴向給一切在水、陸、空冤死之眾生。

- **l987 City of Ten Thousand Buddhas**
The Master during the 1987 Water, Land, and Air Ceremony.

一九八七年　萬佛聖城

上人主持水陸空法會。

● 1989   Taiwan
一九八九年   臺灣

The Master led a delegation to Taiwan. The Master was fasting at this time to transfer merit to the living beings of Taiwan during the delegation's Great Compassion Dharma Assembly for Protecting the Nation and Eradicating Disasters. He fasted for over thirty days during which he made four trips across the Pacific by air (he returned to San Francisco after the earthquake and then flew back to Taiwan) and headed Dharma Assemblies in north, central, and south Taiwan. (The earthquake proved the Master's words, "For every day that I am in San Francisco, I will not allow an earthquake to occur in San Francisco.")

上人率弘法團赴臺灣舉行「護國息災大悲法會」期間，爲臺灣的眾生，他連續絕食三十多天。法會期間，因三藩市發生強烈地震，上人立即返美救災。然後又飛回臺灣，主持在臺灣北部、中部、南部地區的弘法演講大會。（這次地震應驗了上人以前所說的話：我在三藩市一天，就一天不准三藩市地震。）

● 1990   England
 The Master with Ajahn Sumedho, Abbot of Amaravati Buddhist Centre in England
一九九〇年   英國
上人與英國阿瑪拉瓦諦
佛教中心住持蘇美度法師

Ajahn Sumedho displayed deep reverence for and faith in the Master and often visited the City of Ten Thousand Buddhas and the Association's branches in order to draw near the Master and receive his guidance.

蘇美度法師很崇敬、信仰上人。時常訪問聖城及法總的各分支道場，以親近上人並接受上人的教導。

早期法總的點點滴滴

DETAILS OF THE EARLY HISTORY OF DHARMA REALM BUDDHIST ASSOCIATION

譚果式

Magdalena Tam

我生長在香港，是受英國式的教育。在我小學五年級時，因家父皈依度輪上人，而認識了佛教，繼而我也皈依了上人。中學畢業後，我本申請去澳洲念書，澳洲方面也批准了，但家父卻希望我到美國。我請示師父之後，師父說：「妳還是去美國好了。去美國，將來就會很美嘛！如果去澳洲，妳就會懊悔！」因此我便改向美方提出申請，沒想到只等了兩個月左右，就批准下來。

我姊姊（譚果正）比我早幾年來美留學。那時，她常寫信給師父，曾提到美國這裡沒有佛堂，只有道堂。所以師父就在一九五八年一月，我飛美之前，囑咐說：「妳和妳姊姊要好好地把佛法帶到美國。」

到了美國，我們就在呂宋巷找到一個地下室做為建佛堂的地方。請示了師父以後，在一九五八年成立了「佛教講堂」（師父在香港有佛教講堂）。最初登記註冊就叫「佛教講堂」（Buddhist Lecture Hall），中英文完全都照香港的。

每逢週末、週日，在這裡舉行各種佛事：講經、開示，還有念佛法會。起初，大都由我來講經。同時也邀請一些教授、老華僑來講法。來參加法會的，大部分都是從廣東四邑僑鄉移民過來的老華僑。

那時我們也沒有特別向大眾介紹師父的事。當時這些老華僑，看我們所做的佛事，聽我們所講的佛法，就知道我們在香港是曾受過訓練的。加上老一輩的華僑，都認識家父，就想，既然家父都會皈依這麼年輕的法師，可見這位法師必定有與人不同之處。另外，當時來美國留學並不是很容易的，尤其是女眾，所以這些人對我們姊妹都很尊重。

I was born and grew up in Hong Kong and received a British-style education. When I was in fifth grade, because my father took refuge with Venerable Master To Lun, I came to know Buddhism and later took refuge with the Master as well. When I graduated from high school, I applied to go to Australia to attend college, and my application was approved. My father, however, wished for me to come to America. When I sought the Venerable Master's advice, he said, "It's better if you go to America. It will be very beautiful! [In Chinese, 'America' is literally 'beautiful country.'] If you go to Australia, you will regret it! [In Chinese, one of the characters for 'Australia' sounds like the word 'regret.']" Hence I applied to study in America, and unexpectedly received approval within two months' time.

My elder sister (Stella Tam) came to the United States to study a few years earlier than I did. She often wrote letters to the Master and mentioned that there were only Taoist temples, no Buddhist temples, in America. And so before I flew to America in January of 1958, the Master instructed me, "You and your sister should do a good job of bringing the Buddhadharma to America."

When I arrived in America, I found a basement on Pacific Street [in San Francisco's Chinatown] where a Buddhist temple could be set up. After we asked the Venerable Master, we established the Buddhist Lecture Hall in 1958 (the Master had a Buddhist Lecture Hall in Hong Kong). The name we registered under was "Buddhist Lecture Hall"; both the Chinese and English names were identical with those used in Hong Kong.

Every weekend, there would be various Buddhist events: Sutra lectures, instructional talks, and sessions for reciting the Buddha's name. In the beginning, I gave most of the lectures on the Sutras. Some professors and overseas Chinese were also invited to give Dharma talks. Most of those who attended these events were immigrants from four counties of Guangdong Province.

We didn't make a special point of introducing the Venerable Master to the assembly. Yet when these overseas Chinese observed us leading Buddhist ceremonies and heard our explanations of the Buddhadharma, they knew we had had training back in Hong Kong. The older generation of overseas Chinese also knew my father, and they thought that if my father had taken refuge with such a young Dharma Master, that Dharma Master must be quite special. Furthermore, since it was not easy for students, especially girls, to come to America to study in those days, they regarded my sister and me with great respect.

我們姊妹因為在大學念書，只能週末去佛教講堂。所以講堂的鑰匙，就由比較發心的信眾去保管。當時所有的會員每個月都要繳會費，以便支付房租、水電費等。若有人不願意繳費，也不勉強。

來佛教講堂的信眾越來越多，他們都知道我們姊妹是皈依師父的，所以就有人想要皈依師父，經稟告師父後，師父就來函指定，哪一天，什麼時間打皈依，某某人的法名是什麼。我們就在美國這邊舉行皈依儀式，當時是由我來主持的。

我之所以熟悉這些佛事，是因為在香港時，師父曾請旭朗法師來教我們唱梵唄。師父說：「這位法師在東北是很有名的讚王，是數一數二的。」那個時候，誰想學唱誦都可以的，只是我比較年輕，學得也快，所以在香港時一些佛事大都由我做維那。甚至師父來美初期，一有皈依及法會等佛事，仍然由我做維那。後來師父在美有了出家的弟子，就叫我教他們唱念、打法器、作佛事、誦經等。之後，就由他們自行來主持。

一九六〇年初，基於絕大多數皈依師父的弟子，從未見過師父本人（只能從佛桌上看到師父的德相），因此便提出了，「請師父來美國弘揚佛法」的建議。徵得許多人的贊同及支援後，於是我姊姊便辦理申請師父來美的部份手續，並開始籌備資金。按照美國移民局規定，我們必須保證提供師父的來回機票（當時的機票是很貴的），及師父在美期間的一切生活費用，這樣才可以得到移民局的批准。

因為美國移民局的手續繁雜，師父來美國的事情，進展緩慢。信心不足的弟子，就開始懷疑我們是不是在騙錢什麼的……，於是要求退款。姊姊告訴我這件事後，我就說：「如果這個樣子下去，這事一定辦不成的。」於是我就一個個地對他們解釋，最後達成協議，擔保說：「如果師父不能來的話，所有的錢，一定原封不動退回。」並要他們在捐款的收據上簽字，並言明是給師父來美的費用。不久，師父來美的手續也被批准了，但師父來美以前，先去了澳洲一年（一九六一年）。

師父來美之前，我們先後搬了兩個地方。原本佛教講堂是在Pacific St. 租的店面，預備給師父來的時候用，因為這店面原做過長生店（棺材店），沒人敢租。我們因為用來做佛堂，不怕，因

Because my sister and I were attending college, we could only come to the Buddhist Lecture Hall on the weekends, so the key to the Lecture Hall was given to the more devoted laypeople to keep. All the members had to pay a monthly fee to help pay the rent and the gas, electricity, and water bills. However, no one was forced to pay against their will.

More and more laypeople began coming to the Buddhist Lecture Hall. They all knew that my sister and I had taken refuge with the Venerable Master, and some of them also wished to take refuge with the Master. We told the Master, who wrote back telling us on which day and at what time we should hold the refuge ceremony, and what each person's Dharma name would be. So we held the ceremony for taking refuge here in America, under my direction.

I was familiar with all these Buddhist ceremonies because in Hong Kong, the Master had asked Dharma Master Xulang to teach us to sing the Buddhist praises. The Master said, "This Dharma Master is a very famous cantor in Manchuria. He is one of the best." Everyone was welcome to learn to sing the praises, but because I was younger, I learned fast, and so I served as cantor for most of the ceremonies in Hong Kong. When the Master first came to America, I also served as cantor for all the refuge-taking and other Buddhist ceremonies. After the Master had left-home disciples in America, he asked me to teach them how to sing the praises, play the Dharma instruments, perform the ceremonies, and recite Sutras. After that, they were able to lead the ceremonies themselves.

In the beginning of 1960, almost all the disciples who had taken refuge with the Venerable Master had never seen the Master in person (they could only look at the Venerable Master's image on the altar). They proposed that we request the Master to come to America to propagate the Buddhadharma. After we gained the approval and support of many people, my sister and I initiated the process of applying for the Master to come to America. We also began raising funds. In order to gain approval from the U.S. Immigration Service, we had to prove that we could provide a roundtrip air ticket for the Master (in those days airfare was quite expensive) and all the Master's living expenses during his stay in America.

Due to the complicated procedures of the immigration service, the Master's trip to America was delayed. Disciples with insufficient faith began to suspect that we were cheating them and demanded their donations back. When my sister informed me of this, I said, "If this continues, we will never accomplish our goal." I went to each of them and explained the situation. In the end we reached an agreement and guaranteed them, "If the Master cannot come, we will return all the money untouched." We also had them sign their receipts and write down that the money was to pay for the Venerable Master's trip to America. Soon afterwards, the Master's visit to America was approved. However, before coming to America, the Master went to Australia for one year (1961).

Before the Master came to America, we moved twice. The Buddhist Lecture Hall had originally rented a storefront on Pacific Street where the Master could stay. It had been a coffin store before, and no one dared to rent it. Since we were going to use it as a Buddhist temple, we had no qualms about renting it. But when our lease was up, the landlord demanded that we move out. We looked at

此租下了。但合約期滿後，業主卻逼我們搬家。以後又找了許多地方，都不合適。而師父又快要來美國了，所以只好搬到 Clay St.，並將已租給人家做會社的地下室收回來（家父在美時所遺留下來的房子的地下室），好讓佛友們能夠有地方暫時集會。

就在此時，由於講堂內部不和，少數佛友們爭權奪利，甚至有一位居士煽動要成立董事會，目的是想讓在家人為中心的董事會，來執掌佛堂的一切行政事務。佛堂的主持法師要由董事會來聘請，法師們的職責，只是進行法事的安排，不能干預董事會。這樣的顛倒行事，把僧寶置諸度外，所以造成佛教講堂分裂成派。部份對佛教一知半解的佛教徒就另起爐灶，信心堅定的弟子們，則忍耐著，盼上人早日來美主持法務。

一九六二年三月，師父終於由香港，途經日本，在檀香山稍事停留後，飛抵美國舊金山（三藩市）。師父剛抵美國時，姊姊因回香港探親，而被美國領事館拒簽返美，而我臨時有急事須往美國東部，於是請余果興居士組成一團人到機場迎接師父。四月份，師父即開講《金剛般若波羅蜜多經》，並成立禪坐實習班，指導年輕人打坐。

由於地下室太潮濕，實在不適合住人。所以在附近另租一個住處，給師父居住。師父來美後，信眾日多，因此經一些老華僑的資助，在 Sacramento St. 租了一處地方，也就是「開平同鄉會」的樓上，就這樣佛教講堂便由原來的地下室搬遷該處了。

新的佛堂建立後，很多人來聽師父講經說法，也引來許多當地的華僑來聽經，也有很多人皈依了師父。在農曆七月，師父在那裡舉行虛雲老和尚圓寂週年的紀念法會，有很多原來皈依虛老的弟子，也紛紛來參加法會。那時已有幾個美國人常來親近師父。

之後，搬到 Sutter St.，這地方是一九六三年由弟子們籌款買的（講堂目前還保留著）。因為那地方靠近黑人區，所以比較便宜。但並沒有住很久，因為治安不好，交通也不方便，很少人去。所以才又搬到 Waverly St.，地點在中國城天后廟的樓上。

一九七〇年，師父買下了位於十五街的一幢床墊工廠，改裝後成立了金山禪寺。

many places, none of which were suitable. Since the Master was coming to America soon, we decided to move to Clay Street, reclaiming the basement that we had rented out to a tenant (the basement of a house that my father had bought when he was in America), so our fellow cultivators could have a place to meet.

At that time, there was some disharmony in the Lecture Hall. A few of the members wanted to seize power, and one layman even instigated a move to form a Board of Trustees of laypeople to handle the administration of the temple. His plan was to have the Board of Trustees engage Dharma Masters for the Lecture Hall, and for the Dharma Masters to only carry out the scheduled Dharma events and not serve on the Board of Trustees. This inverted plan would place the Sangha Jewel far from the center of control. Consequently, the Buddhist Lecture Hall divided into factions. Those who had only a partial understanding of Buddhism went off to start their own group, while disciples with firm faith patiently bore out the matter and hoped the Venerable Master would soon come to America to direct the temple's activities.

In March 1962, the Master flew from Hong Kong via Japan, stopped briefly in Honolulu, and landed in San Francisco. When the Master arrived in America, my sister had returned to Hong Kong to visit our family, and the American consulate had refused to issue her a visa to return to the United States. I was also temporarily called away to the East Coast on urgent business, and so I asked Layperson Yu Guoxing to form a group of people to welcome the Master at the airport. In April, the Master began lecturing on the *Vajra Prajna Paramita Sutra* and held a Chan meditation class to guide young people in meditation.

Because the basement was too damp and unfit for residence, another place was rented nearby for the Master to live in. After the Master arrived in America, his followers increased day by day. With the support of some overseas Chinese, the upper floor of the Kaiping Villagers Association was rented and the Buddhist Lecture Hall moved from the basement to the new location.

Many people came to listen to the Master's lectures on Sutras at the new temple, including many local overseas Chinese. Many people also took refuge with the Master. In the seventh lunar month, the Master held a Dharma Session Commemorating the Anniversary of Elder Master Hsu Yun's Completion of Stillness. Many people who had taken refuge with Elder Master Yun came to attend. By that time, there were several Americans who frequently came to draw near the Master.

Later, the Master moved to Sutter Street. The place was bought in 1963 with funds raised by disciples (the Lecture Hall is still there today). Because it was near a black neighborhood, it was cheaper. However, he did not stay there long, because it was not a very safe place, it was not easy to get there, and few people went. Later the Master moved to Waverly Street, to the upper floor of Tianhou Temple in Chinatown.

In 1970, the Master bought an old mattress factory on Fifteenth Street and renovated it. It became Gold Mountain Dhyana Monastery.

＊　　　＊　　　＊

Heng Tso

◆ When the Master was living on Sutter Street, he was very selective about whom he let into his rooming house. Word about his accomodations had gotten to the Haight Ashbury district, and sometimes hippies would come to try to rent a room, but the Master would refuse them. (Nick and Susan Mechling told me this many years ago.)

◆ In 1970 the Master bought Gold Mountain Monastery on Fifteenth Street. This three story brick building was probably built in the thirties or forties and had been a mattress factory before. Since repairs had not been made on it for many years, many windows were broken, the roof leaked, and most of the lights didn't work. Everything was covered with a thick layer of dust. However, the building was quite large when compared to the Buddhist Lecture Hall and provided lots of room for expansion. Because there was barely enough money to make the payments, all the Bhikshus, Bhikshunis, and laypeople worked on turning the place into a proper place for cultivation. Unfortunately, some people's minds were not very big, and they criticized the Master for getting such a large building. They said that the Buddhist Lecture Hall was already big enough. If this attitude had prevailed, there would be no Sagely City of Ten Thousand Buddhas today.

The next few years was a time of hardship. Money was very tight and the Sangha was growing; so an arrangement was made with a local market to provide all the nonsalable produce to the monastery for $1. Once a day someone would go to the market and pick up one or more boxes of yellowing vegetable leaves, bruised fruit, or other produce in various states of decay and take it back to Gold Mountain Monastery, where the cook would sort through this treasure for all that was edible. The Master says that was when they ate from the garbage.

Gold Mountain Monastery was also called the "ice box" because there was no heat. This three story building with solid brick walls held the cold very well. Oftentimes the building would be colder inside than it was outside.

恆佐

◆ 師父在 Sutter St. 住時，對前來租房子的房客，挑選得很嚴格。消息傳到嬉皮區之後，有很多嬉皮假意來租房子，都被師父給回絕了。（這是尼克和蘇珊在很多年前告訴我的。）

◆ 一九七○年，師父買下了位於十五街的金山寺。這幢三層樓房建造於一九三○至四○年之間，前身是一家彈簧床墊工廠，因年久失修，很多窗戶都破了，屋頂也漏水，電燈多半不亮，到處佈滿一層厚厚的灰塵。但與佛教講堂比較起來，可是大得太多了，有很多地方可以利用。當時的經濟來源不足，所以四眾弟子都得辛苦地自己動手修整一切。可是有些人的心量不大，他們埋怨師父買這麼大的地方，他們說佛教講堂已經過大了。但是如果當時順著他們的話，也就不會有今天的萬佛聖城了。

接下來的幾年，是很困難的。而僧團又在擴大，使得物質生活非常艱苦。當時中國城有些菜販同意用每天一塊錢的代價，將賣不出去、發黃的菜和水果賣給金山寺，而金山寺每天會有一個人，去市場拿那些發黃的菜葉、爛水果或其他壞掉的食物，帶回金山寺。負責煮飯的人就從這些寶貝中挑出可食用的部分，煮給大家吃。

當時金山寺是很有名的「冰箱」，因為沒有暖氣，這三層的磚房正好把冷空氣貯藏得很好，所以室內的溫度常常比室外還低。

HISTORY OF INSTILLING GOODNESS AND DEVELOPING VIRTUE SCHOOLS

育良小學與培德中學校史

Terri Nicholson 易果參

In the fall of 1975 Gold Mountain Monastery held a series of Candidates Nights for local candidates running in the November election. Among them was Carol Ruth Silver, who was then running for District Attorney. (She later served on the San Francisco Board of Supervisors for many years.) On the evening she came to speak, her adopted son, Ah-hwei, accompanied her. Ah-hwei was then five years old, and since he was originally from Taiwan, Ms. Silver was very concerned that he learn his original language and study about Chinese culture. After a long discussion of educational ideals she agreed to help us get a school started.

On March 1, 1976, Instilling Virtue Elementary School opened at the International Translation Institute, then located at 3636 Washington Street in San Franscisco. The school was to be bilingual (Mandarin Chinese and English), and to emphasize filiality (the importance of repaying the kindness of one's parents and teachers) and respect for one's elders. That first spring we began with eight students, both boys and girls, ranging in age from four to eleven. Besides Chinese, the students studied the required state curriculum, meditation, Sanskrit, and Chinese calligraphy, and participated in some of the daily Buddhist ceremonies.

By the next fall the number of students had doubled. The summer of 1977, the first summer program was held at the newly purchased City of Ten Thousand Buddhas in Talmage. For six weeks students lived at the City and combined academics with study of the Dharma, T'ai Chi Ch'uan, and other outdoor activities. The school then completed one more full year at the San Francisco location before moving to its present location at the City of Ten Thousand Buddhas. During that year students were also fortunate to meet Cardinal Yubin (they sang for him at the airport). At this time another very important principle of the school was established: all religions working together and respecting one another. (The Venerable Master said he would be a Buddhist Catholic and the Cardinal agreed to be a Catholic Buddhist.) To this day the student body of the school includes students of many different religions and nationalities. We teach students to be a good member of whatever religion they believe in and to be a loyal and worthwhile citizen of their own country. During these first few years the students also put on several plays and the first Buddhist musical, entitled "Sundarananda Finds the

一九七五年秋天，金山寺為參加十一月競選的人，舉行了一連串的候選人之夜，來參加的人包括競選地方檢察官的西佛女士（以後數年她曾擔任三藩市參事）。在西佛女士來演說那一晚，她把收養的兒子阿輝也帶來了。阿輝當時五歲，原籍臺灣，西佛女士十分關心她這位養子，能否學到他自己原有的語言及文化，我們當時談了很久關於教育上的看法，後來她答應幫我們成立一所學校。

一九七六年三月一日，育良小學成立，校址即在座落於三藩市華盛頓街三六三六號的國際譯經學院，以中英雙語教學，注重孝道、報父母師長恩、敬老。第一學期（春季班），共有男女八個學生，年齡由四歲至十一歲不等。除了中文課之外，學生學習範圍，包括加州政府規定的學校課程，打坐、梵文、中國書法，及部份佛教儀式。

秋季班開學時，學生人數增加了一倍。一九七七年暑假，第一次舉辦暑期班，班址即在剛於瑜伽市成立的萬佛城。學生在萬佛城住了六個星期，學習範圍融合了學科、佛法、太極拳及戶外活動。育良小學此後又在三藩市校址上了一年的課，之後即搬入萬佛城。在那一年中，學生有幸與于斌樞機主教見面（學生在機場曾為于樞機唱歌）。就在那個時候，學校樹立了一個重要的原則，就是一切宗教互相合作、互相尊重。（上人就在那時說，他要做佛教裡的天主教徒；于樞機也同意要做天主教裡的佛教徒。）學校學生來自許多不同宗教、國籍、背景，不論學生信仰什麼宗教，我們教導他們做自己教中的好教徒，做他們自己國家的好公民。在創校頭幾年中，學生演了幾齣話劇，及第一齣佛教音樂劇：「孫陀羅難陀找到了道」，這齣劇講佛陀的弟弟孫陀羅難陀怎樣出家。

一九七八年秋，學校遷至萬佛城。剛開始時，校中學生大部分都是原在三藩市時的舊生，週一至週五，在萬佛城住校；週六及週日，回三藩市家中。慢慢地

Way," the story of how the Buddha's half brother, Sundaranada, came to leave the home life.

In the fall of 1978 the school relocated to the City of Ten Thousand Buddhas. At first, most of our students were former students from San Francisco who boarded during the week and went home on the weekends. Gradually, however, the school became better known in the Ukiah local community and the number of local students increased. In the fall of 1981 Developing Virtue Secondary School opened its doors. This school also was dedicated to educating students in both academic excellence and moral integrity. Added to the teaching of filiality was the concept of good citizenship and encouraging students to seek careers that will benefit society as well as themselves.

In the fall of 1982 the school decided to adopt a policy of educating girls and boys separately in order to preserve their natural innocence and purity and to make it easier for them to concentrate on their studies. Since that time there have been separate boys' and girls' schools. Students are strongly encouraged to treasure the precious time of their youth, to study well and postpone emotional ties with the opposite sex until they are of a proper age to marry and form permanent relationships. (At least twenty years old for girls and thirty for boys.) At that time the children of families in the Buddhist Council for Refugee Rescue and Resettlement also attended our schools, adding a distinctly international flavor to the student body. These students, mostly from Vietnam, Laos, and Cambodia, studied with our students for three to six months before being resettled somewhere in the United States where jobs could be found for their parents. During the time they were here, they studied English, our ethics curriculum, and Western customs and lifestyle. Since many of them were Buddhist they felt very comfortable in our school and blessed the other students with contributions from their own countries and experiences. This program was discontinued by the U.S. government in 1986.

Instilling Goodness and Developing Virtue Schools have continued to grow and now have several branch schools, which have afterschool and weekend programs in Los Angeles, Vancouver, and also San Francisco. Another weekend program will begin this fall at the Sagely City of the Dharma Realm in West Sacramento, California. At the present time the schools at the City of Ten Thousand Buddhas have over 130 students (including over 30 boarding students from the U.S. and the international community) and there have been nearly forty high school graduates. The schools continue to emphasize the same principles of filiality, humaneness, righteousness, and good citizenship as well as upholding the six principles of not fighting, not being greedy, incorruptibility, not being selfish, not seeking, and not lying. In November 1992 the school also began to seek for teachers who are willing to volunteer their time and work without pay, devoting their lives to educating students with the highest integrity who hopefully will grow up to lead our country and the world.

，瑜伽市居民也開始知道了育良小學，所以來自當地的學生人數也逐漸增加。

一九八一年秋天，成立培德中學，校旨注重學術及道德之並進，在傳授孝道之外，又教導學生做好公民，鼓勵學生選擇，不但能利己也對社會有所利益的職業。

一九八二年秋天，學校開始男女分校上課，以保護學生的天真及清淨無邪，也為幫助學生能專心課業。強調學生應該珍惜年少的時間，好好用功，與異性間之情感可以緩一步發展，待到年歲適當時，再論婚嫁（女子二十歲，男子三十歲）。那時城中設有難民救濟中心，來自這些佛教家庭的孩子也就讀本校，為本校更增加了國際性的特色。這些學生大部份是從越南、寮國，和柬埔寨來的，他們在本校念了三至六個月之後，再搬移至父母就業之處定居。這些學生在本校就讀時，學習範圍包括英語、本校倫理課程、西方生活方式習俗。因為這些學生大都來自佛教家庭，所以很能適應我們學校。又因為他們來自國外，所以他們也將自己國家的特色及經驗，與本校其他學生分享。本城救濟中心於一九八六年結束。

育良小學及培德中學學生人數不斷增加，並在洛杉磯、溫哥華及三藩市設立了幾處分校，辦理課後教學及週末教學；在加州西沙緬度法界聖城，今年秋天也會辦理週末教學。萬佛城的育良小學及培德中學，有學生一百三十名，其中包括住校生三十名，都是由美國各地及海外來的，畢業生約有四十名。本校注重忠孝仁義，並遵守六大宗旨 —— 不爭、不貪、不求、不自私、不自利、不打妄語。一九九二年十一月，本校招請義務老師，自願奉獻時間工作、不受薪，致力以最高道德教育學生，希望他們長大後成為國家及世界的領袖。

香港慈興禪寺

CIXING CHAN MONASTERY IN HONG KONG

證慧　Zheng Hui

一九五一年春天，宣公上人於香港筲箕灣馬山頂，興建西樂園佛堂後，就發願要創建一座能夠容納更多僧眾用功辦道的道場。

慈興禪寺，座落在香港新界大嶼山，與周圍群峰相連，青蔥幽邃，人跡罕到。它是以前的國清禪院與一幢兩層別墅所併建的叢林。

當太平洋戰爭的砲火波及大嶼山，國清禪院被日軍焚燬。僧眾因此四散，只剩下半埋在瓦礫堆中的房架 —— 沒有門，沒有窗，也沒有屋頂；四壁頹圮不堪，千瘡百孔，生滿了野草。一九五三年秋，徵得國清禪院有關人士的同意，將該院的廟基施給了上人。兩層別墅，乃是董果耆居士皈依上人之後，慨然捐施的。別墅雖然較完整，但也因棄置太久，門窗俱失。這棟別墅與國清禪院比起來，只差樓蓋還沒有通天呢！殘破的程度，如同廢墟。然而上人是怎麼樣把它復興的呢？以下就是慈興禪寺興建的經過：

為了興建慈興禪寺，上人廢寢忘食，帶病四處奔走，餐風露雨，披星戴月。是凡雇工購材，造像備糧，無一不親手籌劃。上人有偈：

夜落靈會山，步出慈興寺，
孤月照貧僧，眾星拱北極。
世事如夢幻，知者嘆幾希，
勿為浮塵轉，許汝六根一。

別墅及客堂，早於一九五四年春，修繕竣工，是為慈興禪寺的左院。除大殿、左院、客堂外，復增修齋堂、關房、茅棚各一間。左有降龍石，右有伏虎溪，星羅棋布，格局勝佳，紅柱白牆，襯托於萬山叢綠

In the spring of 1951, after the Venerable Master Hua had constructed Western Bliss Gardens Temple on Horse Mountain in Xiaoqiwan, Hong Kong, he made a vow to construct a Way-place that would have space for more Sangha members to apply effort in cultivating the Way.

Cixing Chan Monastery is situated on Lanto Island in the New Territories of Hong Kong. It is surrounded by mountain ranges and hidden in a grove of trees, and people rarely venture into the area. The monastery is a combination of the former Guoqing Chan Cottage and a two-story villa.

When the fiery waves of the Pacific War reached Lanto Island, Guoqing Chan Cottage was burned down by the Japanese troops. As a result, the Sangha dispersed in all directions, leaving only the framework of the cottage half-buried under the rubble of tiles and gravel. There was no door, no windows, and no roof—the four walls were crumbling, full of holes, and covered with weeds. In the autumn of 1953, with the permission of the guardians of Guoqing Chan Cottage, the remains of the cottage were given to the Venerable Master. The two-story villa was the generous offer of Layman Dong Guoqi, who had taken refuge with the Master. Although the villa was in slightly better condition, it had been abandoned for so long that it too was missing its windows and doors, and the only thing that made it better than the Cottage was that its roof was still intact. How did the Venerable Master go about rebuilding these dwellings that were ruined to the extent of being like a wasteland? The following is an account of the renovation of Cixing Chan Monastery:

In order to rebuild Cixing Chan Monastery, the Venerable Master dispensed with sleep and forgot to eat. Despite his weakened condition, he travelled extensively during the day and night, even when buffeted by winds and drenched by rains. The selection of workmen, the preparation of materials, the commissioning of images, the laying-in of provisions—not one bit of the work did not spring from his efforts. The Venerable Master wrote a verse:

As night falls on Magic Mountain,
I step out from Cixing Monastery.
The lone moon shines upon the poor monk;
The stars encircle Polaris.
Mundane affairs are like dreams;
How few are those who know!
Don't be turned by the dusts;
Then your six sense organs may become one.

Repairs were completed on the villa and the guest hall early in the spring of 1954. These formed the Left Wing of Cixing Chan Monastery. Aside from repairing the Great Hall, the Left Wing, and the guest hall, the Master also constructed a dining hall, a room for practicing in seclusion, and a cabin. To the left is the dragon-subduing rock and to the right is the tiger-taming stream. The architecture is superb, with white walls and red pillars framed by the surrounding mountains. It truly can be said to borrow the efficacious atmosphere of heaven and earth, surpassing all other natural

中。真可以說是「奪天地之靈氣，超造化之天機」，實不亞於中國四大名山和八大小山的幽勝，就是和南華的六祖道場相比，也毫不遜色！

在修建慈興禪寺的過程中，有一則插曲：一九五三年時，有一種紅頭綠身的毒蛇，常出沒於道場。寺內僧眾，見則捕之，放入鐵桶，然後送至數里外放生。可是，每次送蛇的人還沒回來，這條蛇卻已先回來了，並且在顯眼的地方爬行；如此反覆多次。最奇怪的一次就是，送到目的地後，打開桶蓋一看，噫！蛇呢？覆桶輕敲，不多久，忽然看見有半截蛇身掉出。送蛇的人回到寺時，竟然看到那半截蛇身又變成一條完整的毒蛇，昂首吐舌，在佛堂前蜿蜒爬行了。

蛇是屬於龍類的。度公在東北時，曾有十位龍神皈依度公座下。因此，度公乃在慈興禪寺左院後左方嵯峨矗立的降龍石上，親自塑造金龍一條，呈張牙舞爪欲飛騰之狀。金龍塑成後，毒蛇遂不再出現。德可伏魔，誠然不虛！

伏虎溪，為一長約數里的澗水，在寺前右方；每逢雨季，山洪爆發，行人經此，倍感困難。因此，在此溪穿過「靈山道場」牌坊裡邊的道上，修一弓形石橋，橋下闢一方塘，做為放生池。從此，山水循路而下，不但無礙於行人，反而有利於愚癡的眾生。

從種種因緣上看，慈興禪寺的復興，實非偶然。千秋萬世，法門龍象定可輩出。舉凡用功修道之人，必心嚮往之，雲集而歸。慈興禪寺的將來，也必定在佛教史上寫下輝煌的一頁。

settings. It is certainly not inferior in grandeur to the famous four great mountains and eight small mountains of China. It is in all respects comparable to the appearance of Nanhua, the Way-place of the Sixth Patriarch.

The following incident occurred during the rebuilding of Cixing Chan Monastery:

During 1953, a red-headed, green-bodied poisonous snake kept appearing at the Way-place. When the Sangha members first saw it, they caught it in a barrel and took it several miles beyond the grounds, but before the party had returned, the creature had already appeared on the monastery grounds, crawling along in plain sight. This happened time and again. The strangest thing was that once, after the snake had been taken to its destination, the man lifted the lid of the barrel to release it, but it was nowhere to be seen. The man replaced the cover with a light tap, and soon the severed body of half a snake fell out. By the time the man had returned, however, the body had become whole once again, and the poisonous snake was seen crawling in front of the Buddhahall, where it lifted its head and darted out its tongue.

Snakes belong to the class of dragons, and when the Venerable Master was in Manchuria, ten dragons took refuge with him. Therefore the Venerable Master proceeded to shape a golden dragon on top of the dragon-subduing rock, to the left and behind the left wing of the monastery. He fashioned it with teeth bared and claws brandished in such a way that it appeared to be on the verge of flight.

After the golden dragon was complete, the poisonous snake never reappeared. It is certainly true that virtue can subdue demons!

The tiger-taming stream is a mountain torrent several miles long. It flows to the right of the monastery, and every rainy season the flash floods on the mountain presented countless problems for travellers. Because of the difficulty, at the place where the stream passed under the road which lies within the Lingshan Way-place Memorial Arch [halfway down the mountain from Cixing Monastery], the Master constructed a bow-shaped stone bridge and beneath the bridge hollowed out a pond, making a pool for liberating life. After that, the mountain waters had easy passage down, and not only did the stream no longer obstruct travellers, but it actually benefitted stupid living beings.

From these various incidents one can see that the rebuilding of Cixing Chan Monastery is no casual occurrence. For thousands of years and myriads of generations, generations of great Buddhist cultivators will certainly arise from here. All those who work hard cultivating the Way will be drawn to gather at this place. The future accomplishments of Cixing Chan Monastery will definitely make a brilliant page in the history of Buddhism.

上人的阿彌陀佛像

THE VENERABLE MASTER'S AMITABHA BUDDHA IMAGE

編輯部　　Editorial Department

Western Bliss Gardens was to be the resting place of the extremely efficacious and miraculous image of Amitabha Buddha that the Master had brought with him from Manchuria. It was the image he made obeisance to during his early years of cultivation, and as a result of the extreme purity of the Master's heart, the graceful porcelain figure had gradually undergone a miraculous transformation. As the Master continued to bow with ever-deepening sincerity before the image, a distinct rosy hue began to suffuse the once snow-white porcelain until it eventually took on the glow of living flesh. The connection between the Master and the miraculous image of Amitabha Buddha is one of utmost purity that far transcends the kind of attachment found in the realm of dualism.

In a most profound sense, the image could be said to be indispensable to the Master. Nevertheless, after the Master arrived in Hong Kong and began to meditate in Guanyin Cave, he had no appropriate place to respectfully make offerings to the Buddha-image, and he had to ask two Dharma Masters, who had a temple, to keep it for him so that it could be properly cared for, respected, and worshipped. The Dharma Masters accepted the image with the full understanding that they would return it to the Master when he had an appropiate place for it. During the period of more than a year that the Master spent meditating in Guanyin Cave, however, the two monks developed a fondness for the exquisite image and no longer wished to remember that it had only been loaned to them. They considered it their own.

When the Master decided to establish Western Bliss Gardens, it was Amitabha Buddha whom he called on to aid him in carrying out the work. Once he moved to the grounds and the construction of the temple began, he asked the two monks to return the image of Amitabha Buddha. Not wishing to comply, but lacking any justification for refusing his request, the two monks came to pay special New Year's greetings to the Master. Kneeling before the Master, they said ingratiatingly, "We just cannot bear to part with the Amitabha Buddha image, and so we have decided to kneel here until the Dharma Master consents to let us keep it." They knelt for five hours before the Master, who used many expedient means to bring them to their senses. He scolded. He shouted. He was pointedly rude to them. He picked up his tea pot and slammed it down on the floor in front of them. He hurled his tea cup against the wall, smashing it to smithereens. But even his most extreme attempts to teach and transform them were to no avail. The two remained rooted to the floor, sustained by their greed for the Buddha-image. Since he couldn't frighten them into waking up, the Master decided that at least he could physically remove them from the Buddhahall and perhaps jar them to their senses. Although each monk weighed over 200 pounds, he grabbed them under the armpits one at a time and dragged them outside. But by the time he had evicted one monk and had a good grip on the second, the first had

上人從滿州（東北）帶出來的阿彌陀佛像，神奇靈驗無比，原準備安置供奉在西樂園寺。上人在早年的修行中，虔心禮拜的就是這尊佛像。由於上人的心極其清淨，加上不斷至誠地恭敬禮拜，這尊磁製古雅的佛像，漸漸發生了奇蹟般的變化，佛像由原來的雪白色，漸漸地呈現出淡淡的玫瑰紅，乃至變成猶如真人般那樣栩栩如生。上人與這尊神奇佛像之間的關係，是神聖而不可思議的。

當上人剛到香港時，在觀音洞閉關。洞裡沒有合適的地方安置佛像，所以上人請附近寺廟的兩位法師代為保管佛像，以便好好保護、恭敬、禮拜、供養。兩位法師知道一旦上人有了合適的地方安置佛像，那尊佛像是要奉還上人的。上人於觀音洞閉關這一年多的時間裡，兩位法師對這尊珍貴的佛像生了大歡喜心，因而忘記了佛像只是暫時安置在他們那裡，反而認為這尊佛像原是屬於他們的。

在上人決定建立西樂園寺時，曾求阿彌陀佛來幫助他成就建寺的工程。在建寺工程開始以前，上人先搬到西樂園的工地去住。建廟的工程開始後，上人想請回這尊阿彌陀佛像。那兩位法師既不願順從，又沒有正當的理由拒絕，他們就在大年初一拜訪上人。他們跪在上人前，討好地說：我們離不開這尊阿彌陀佛像，所以我們要跪在這裡，直到上人答應讓我們保留這尊佛像。他們在上人面前跪了五個鐘頭。上人用盡了各種權宜之計，想讓他們神識清明。上人大聲訶責，甚至拿起茶壺摔在他們面前，又把茶杯擲到牆上摔個粉碎。即使用這樣極端的方法，也是徒勞。對那尊佛像的貪念使他們像生了根一樣地跪在那兒。既然威嚇也無法令他們覺醒，上人想，至少可以把他們拉出佛堂，這也許能使他們恢復神智吧！這兩位法師體重都超過二百磅重，上人把他們挾在腋下，一個一個地拉出去。可是才把一個拖了出去，要

returned and was kneeling once more. After the Master deposited the second monk on the doorstep and walked back to evict the first, the second was already following close at his heels.

Realizing that the two failed to understand the seriousness of the matter, the Master turned from the expedient to the actual and attempted to explain to the monks the nature of the ineffable, mysterious, and wonderful affinity which existed between himself and that spiritually efficacious Amitabha Buddha image.

"With that image I can realize Buddhahood. Without it, I cannot," he told them. "However" he added quietly, "if you want the image so badly, then take it." Heedless of the Master's first statement, the two monks only heard that at last the Master had relinquished the image. Satisfied, they got up and left. "Don't ever set foot in my door again," warned the Master as they departed.

But the Master had spoken the truth, and by the next day, in the absence of the Amitabha Buddha image, he had fallen seriously ill. Day by day his fever rose. Since he lived alone and few people even knew where to find him, there was no one to fix gruel or fetch water for him. As a result, he rapidly grew weaker and weaker, and his condition became grave.

Eventually Bhiksu Heng-yueh, who lived in the same temple as the two offending monks, learned of their outrageous display on New Year's Day and of the Master's subsequent illness. Heng-yueh carried the Amitabha Buddha image back to the Master, and with its return, the Master's illness subsided and the construction of the Bodhimanda progressed rapidly.

來對付第二個，第一個又跑了進來跪在那兒。等第二個被安置在門外台階上，回來要趕第一個，第二個又跟在他腳後了。

上人明白他們兩人不了解事情的嚴重性，上人放棄了方便法，以真實法試著向他們解釋，自己和這尊阿彌陀佛像之間不可思議的神奇緣份。有了這尊像，我才能成佛；失去了它，我不能。上人靜靜地補充：雖然如此，如果你們真是這樣想要，就拿去吧！這兩位出家人忽略了上人第一句話，只聽到上人願意放棄佛像。他們心滿意足，站起來走了。他們離開時，上人說：「別再進我的門！」

上人對他們講的是實話，由於失去了那尊阿彌陀佛像，上人第二天就病倒了，而且病得很重，日復一日他高燒不退。因為他獨居，很少人知道要去哪裡找他，更沒有人煮稀飯及倒水照顧上人。因此，上人很快地變得愈來愈虛弱，到了很嚴重的地步。

最後，和那兩位法師同住的恆越法師，得知兩位法師在大年初一無理取鬧，及上人因而病倒的事情之後，就把阿彌陀佛像請回來還給上人。佛像回來後，上人的病才漸漸好起來，建廟的工程也得以迅速進展。

臺灣法界佛教印經會

THE DHARMA REALM BUDDHIST BOOKS DISTRIBUTION ASSOCIATION IN TAIWAN

臺灣法界佛教印經會提供
Compiled by the Dharma Realm Buddhist Books Distribution Association in Taiwan

在臺北市忠孝東路六段八十五號萬商工業大樓的電梯旁，你每天都會看到這樣的情景：工作人員熟練地將經書放在小車上，推進上下忙碌的電梯裡。一批批的佛書送往十一樓，然後又從十一樓流通到臺灣、美國及世界各地。而在十一樓的佛堂內，法師們正領著大眾禮佛、拜懺。這裡就是美國法界佛教總會在臺灣的門戶——法界佛教印經會（以下簡稱「法界」）。它可以說是流通宣公上人中文法音的總站，不同版本的佛教經典、上人的開示錄及錄音帶，都是由這裡源源流出的。

「法界」地方雖小，但因敬仰宣公上人高德懿行，而弟子們盡心竭力護法的赤誠之心，卻是量周法界的。

大約十年前，發起人之一的陳老師第一次讀到上人的《放眼看世界》一書（當時上人的書在臺灣流傳很少），覺得書中的法，完全是由上人的自性中流露出來的。在深深受益，感動之餘，遂有印製、流通上人法音的念頭，並將此想法告訴了護持臺北行天宮的二十多位同參道友（下文稱老同修）。大部份的老同修都來自中下層人士，教育程度不高，家境清寒，有的人甚至是清潔工、小工。簡樸單純的他們，非常忠實地護持行天宮，因此當他們轉而為上人護法時，都事先擲杯請示關帝君，問問是否可行？經關帝君指示認同之後，他們才放下心來護持佛教正法，由此可見上人的懿德，何止通於人間！

在陳老師的領導下，大家節衣縮食攢集下來血汗錢，老同修們開始了「法界」最初的事業。陳老師白天忙碌於印經之事，為了節省印經費用，親自校稿，奔波於印刷廠、裝訂廠之間。晚上又要到夜校上班，業餘時間又教大眾讀

Beside the elevator of the Multi-Commercial Industrial Tower located at 85 Chung-hsiao E. Road, Sec. 6, Taipei, R.O.C., you will see the following scene every day: workers expertly loading Sutra books onto a small cart, which they then push into the busy elevator. Load after load of Buddhist books are transported up to the eleventh floor, and from there they are circulated to Taiwan, the United States, and other parts of the world. In the Buddhahall on the eleventh floor, Dharma Masters are leading the assembly in bowing to the Buddhas and bowing in repentance. This is the Dharma Realm Buddhist Books Distribution Association (DRBBDA)—the Taiwan gateway of the Dharma Realm Buddhist Association, headquartered in the United States. This is the main center for the circulation of the Venerable Master's Dharma in Chinese. An endless flow of various Buddhist Sutras and the Venerable Master's instructional talks and tapes comes forth from here.

Although DRBBDA occupies a small area, the sincerity of the devoted Dharma-protecting disciples who admire the Venerable Master's lofty virtue and conduct pervades the Dharma Realm.

About ten years ago, Ms. Chen, one of the initiators of DRBBDA, read the Venerable Master's *Open Your Eyes and Take a Look at the World* (at that time the Venerable Master's books were not widely circulated in Taiwan) and felt that the Dharma in that book had flowed forth from the Venerable Master's self-nature. She was deeply moved and had the idea of printing and circulating the Venerable Master's Dharma. She told her plan to over twenty friends who had been supporters of Xingtian Taoist Temple in Taipei. Most of these friends were lower-middle class, not well-educated, and had poor households. Some of them did janitorial and other menial work. These simple and honest folks had been loyal to the Xingtian Temple, and before they became the Venerable Master's supporters, they used an oracle to ask Lord Guan if it was okay. After Lord Guan had indicated approval, they supported the orthodox Buddhadharma without worries. This shows that the Venerable Master's virtue is certainly known beyond the human realm!

Under Ms. Chen's leadership, everyone pooled their hard-earned savings from scrimping on clothing and food and began the first business of DRBBDA. During the day, Ms. Chen busied herself getting the Sutras printed. In order to cut costs, she proofread the manuscripts herself and travelled back and forth between the printing company and the binding company. In the evenings she worked at the night school. In her spare time she taught the assembly to read the Sutras and understand their meaning. Sometimes she would be so busy that

經，瞭解經義。她有時忙得連續幾天均以饅頭充飢。為求印經順利，使正法流通於臺灣，每次印經前，陳老師又在凌晨一、二點，帶領著大眾去朝山。朝山時，陳老師一拜下去，大家要等很久很久才聽到引磬聲，才拜起來，大家都知道陳老師很辛苦，誰也不忍心叫醒她。

就這樣，老同修們風雨無阻，連續幾年在泥濘的山路上叩拜，完全憑著他們對佛法的那份信心、誠心，及堅忍不拔的毅力。

機緣成熟，陳老師並其他有心人士赴美國萬佛聖城，向上人請法的同時，懇請上人恩准，在臺灣成立專門流通上人法音的印經會。蒙上人慈悲同意，並賜名為「法界佛教贈經會」。

一九八三年十月二十六日，法界佛教贈經會正式成立。最早的會址位於臺北松山（另一位發起人家中的二樓），不久遷至臺北農安街（另一位老同修家的六樓）。

篳路藍縷，創業維艱，老同修們到市場去撿繩子、撿盒子、撿紙等，凡是一切對印經、包裝經典、運送經典有用的東西，他們能撿就撿，乃至於到批發市場，撿菜充飢。這一切無非是要節省經費，多印一些經。

因為位於六樓的會址，沒有電梯，搬運經書成了大問題。當時只要有一批經書出版，老同修們就全部聚集在一起，分工合作，用接力的方式將經書搬運至六樓。若是印刷廠沒按時送書來，大家不在時，那就相當困難了。只好靠少數在場的人，千辛萬苦地從一樓搬到六樓。經書在六樓被包裝後，為了節省郵資，許多年過半百的老同修們揹著經，或徒步、或騎腳踏車，親自將經書送到附近的會員家中。這種赤誠，曾經使路人非常感動，發心每月代送。如果聽說某地方有法會，他們就到會場去送經書，但是往往都被阻擋了，老同修們常常難過得淚水往肚子裡吞。

從一樓將經書搬到六樓，包裝後再搬到一樓寄送，很不方便。後來老同修們想出一個方法，那就是：經書一旦由印刷廠送來時，馬上在一樓的樓梯口包裝，隨即寄送。但這要動作迅速俐落，才不會妨礙交通。有幾次，眼看烏雲密佈，大雨即將來臨了，但是往往等到經書被包裝好送走的最後一分鐘，雨才嘩啦而下。老同修們深深覺得此事「不簡單」，天龍八部如

for several days in a row she would only eat mantos (steamed buns) to stave off hunger. In order to pray for successful printing so that the proper Dharma could circulate in Taiwan, each time before a Sutra was printed, she would lead everyone on a bowing pilgrimage at one or two o'clock in the morning. During the bowing, Ms. Chen would bow down, and everyone would have to wait a long, long time before they heard the handbell, signalling people to rise. Everyone knew Ms. Chen was exhausted and no one had the heart to wake her up.

Undaunted by wind and rain, these people went out on the muddy mountain paths to bow for several years like this, relying completely on their faith, sincerity, and perseverance towards the Buddhadharma.

When the conditions ripened, Ms. Chen and others travelled to the Sagely City of Ten Thousand Buddhas in America. When they sought instruction from the Venerable Master, they also sincerely requested the Venerable Master to permit them to establish an association in Taiwan exclusively to circulate the Venerable Master's Dharma. The Venerable Master kindly assented and bestowed the name "Dharma Realm Buddhist Books Distribution Association."

On October 26, 1983, Dharma Realm Buddhist Books Distribution Association was officially established. The first address was in Song Mountain, Taipei (on the second floor of the home of another one of the initiators). Soon it was moved to Nong-an Road (on the sixth floor of the home of one of the supporters).

"Blazing a trail and founding a business is difficult." They would go to the market to pick up discarded rope, boxes, paper, or anything else that could be used for printing, packaging, or delivering the Sutras. They picked up whatever they could, and they would even pick up vegetables to stave off their hunger. Their only wish was to cut costs and print a few more Sutras.

Because the sixth floor address had no elevator, it became a big problem to move the Sutras. Whenever a shipment of books was printed, they would all gather together and work cooperatively and pass the books from one person to the next to transport them to the sixth floor. If the printing company didn't deliver the books at the scheduled time and not everyone was around, it became very difficult. The few people who were on hand would laboriously carry the books from the ground floor to the sixth floor. After the books were packaged on the sixth floor, in order to save postage, many volunteers who were over fifty would carry the books and either walk or ride bikes to personally deliver them to members who lived nearby. Their sincerity moved some passersby, who volunteered to help them make deliveries every month. If they heard of a Dharma Assembly somewhere, they would deliver books to the place. Sometimes, when they were refused, the volunteers would sadly swallow their disappointment.

It was a lot of trouble to move the Sutras from the first floor to the sixth floor, package them, and then move them back down. Later they came up with a new method: As soon as the printer sent the books, they would package them by the stairwell of the first floor and immediately deliver them. However, they had to work quickly, or else they would block the people who were passing by. Several times, dark clouds filled the sky and it looked like a heavy rain was coming. But it would not be until the last minute, after the Sutras had been delivered, that it would suddenly begin to rain continuously. The volunteers thought this was not a casual matter. The gods, dragons, and the rest of the eightfold

此護法，老同修們常被感動得淚溼沾襟，護持正法的心，也就更堅固了。

這批「法界」拓荒者有二十幾位，大部份都是家庭主婦，有的甚至沒讀過書，不識字，但「下下人有上上智」，他們知道一定要緊跟著當代大善知識——宣公上人的腳步走。當時皈依上人，必須會背誦〈楞嚴咒〉。為此，她們就去夜校上識字班，走路時，坐公車時，都在念〈楞嚴咒〉，甚至打瞌睡時，也提醒自己趕快背誦〈楞嚴咒〉，就這樣，硬是把〈楞嚴咒〉背會了。

那時每個月，每人發一張誦持經咒、聖號或禮拜數量的日計表，以督促個人用功（此表沿用至今）。每個月底則於道場共修，並迴向功德。或舉行七天七夜輪班不停的〈大悲咒〉或〈楞嚴咒〉默念會。不論朝山、誦咒，或自修，大家都採用陳老師立的迴向文：

（一）迴向法界眾生，離苦得樂，了生脫死。

（二）迴向至尊師父上人法體安康，延年益壽，常住於世轉大法輪，教導更多的眾生歸覺路。

（三）懇祈諸佛菩薩息滅（某某）的貪、瞋、癡，並開智慧。

（四）法界佛教贈經會人材濟濟，師父上人的正法在臺流通順利。

他們純樸踏實、艱苦卓絕的護法、學法精神，不但使他們成為傳播佛法的使者，也點燃了自己的智慧之燈。現在他們不僅會背〈楞嚴咒〉，會讀誦經典，且佛號不離於心，更有幾位老同修後來成了上人的出家弟子，有些老同修的子女也跟著上人出了家。

一位六十六歲曾受過中文教育的老同修，將《楞嚴經》卷一到卷五背得滾瓜爛熟，速度比一般人照著經本讀誦還快。也有的人悟得「二分鐘送走煩惱」的妙訣，快樂地活在佛法中。還有一位老同修說：「不要說拜佛、念佛沒有感應，其實能到道場禮佛、拜懺、誦經，這就是最大的感應了，要好好珍惜這份善根。」

division were so protective of the Dharma. The volunteers were often moved to tears and became even more sincere in supporting the proper Dharma.

There were over twenty of these pioneers of DRBBDA. Most of them were housewives. Some had never been to school and were illiterate. However, "the lowliest of people have the highest of wisdom." They knew they had to follow closely in the footsteps of a great wise advisor of the age—the Venerable Master Hua. At that time, people who wanted to take refuge with the Venerable Master had to memorize the Shurangama Mantra. For this reason, they went to night school to learn to read, and while walking or taking the bus, they would recite the Shurangama Mantra. Even when they felt drowsy, they would remind themselves to quickly recite the Shurangama Mantra. In that way, they forced themselves to memorize the mantra.

Every month, to encourage progress in cultivation, each person would be given a sheet for recording his or her daily amount of recitations of Sutras, mantras, and holy names, and bows to the Buddha (this sheet is still being used today). At the end of every month they would gather in the Way-place to cultivate together and then dedicate the merit. They would also hold sessions for silent recitation of the Great Compassion Mantra or Shurangama Mantra in shifts for seven days and nights without break. Whether they were making a bowing pilgrimage, reciting a mantra, or cultivating alone, they would all use Ms. Chen's dedication:

1. I dedicate the merit to all living beings of the Dharma Realm, hoping they will leave suffering, attain bliss, and end birth and death.

2. I dedicate the merit to the most honored Venerable Master, hoping he will be healthy, live long, and always remain in the world to turn the great Dharma wheel, teaching more living beings to return to the path of enlightenment.

3. I sincerely pray that the Buddhas and Bodhisattvas will eradicate my greed, anger, and stupidity so that my wisdom will come forth.

4. May there be many talents in DRBBDA and may the Venerable Master's proper Dharma circulate in Taiwan without difficulty.

With their spirit of protecting and studying the Dharma with simple honesty and willingness to suffer inordinate hardship, they became the disseminators of the Buddhadharma. They also lit their own lamps of wisdom. Not only can they recite the Shurangama Mantra from memory, they can also recite Sutras and are ever mindful of the Buddha's name. Some of the volunteers later left the home-life under the Venerable Master, and some of the volunteers have children who left home with the Master.

One of the volunteers, a sixty-six-year old who graduated from high school, thoroughly memorized the first five rolls of the *Shurangama Sutra*. She can recite it from memory faster than most people can recite it looking at the text. Some people also discovered the secret two-minute formula for getting rid of afflictions and happily dwell within the Buddhadharma. One of the volunteers said, "Don't say that you don't have any response from bowing to the Buddhas or reciting the Buddhas' name. In fact, your coming to the Way-place to bow to the Buddhas, bow in repentance, and recite Sutras is already the greatest response. You

記得有一次他們去臺北木柵朝山，返家途中發生車禍，所搭的公車整部翻滾到山下。其中一位老同修在朝山時，腦子裡出現「翻車」的字眼，當時她並沒有在意，口裡仍念著觀世音菩薩聖號，繼續朝山。雖然車禍發生之後，她昏迷不醒，但是一點外傷也沒有，因為她上車時抱著睡袋。還有一位老同修本來也要搭這部公車，臨時被同伴拉下來：「你身體不好，要運動，跟我們一起走路。」結果逃過一劫。其他同車的老同修也化險為夷，可謂默默耕耘，默默感應。

嗟末法，惡時世，眾生福薄難調制，
去聖遠兮邪見深，魔強法弱多怨害，
聞說如來頓教門，恨不滅除令瓦碎。
　　　　——永嘉大師證道歌

在創辦「法界」的初期階段，臺灣佛教界中流傳許多中傷宣公上人的流言，也有不少人對上人有誤解。因此老同修莫不懷著如臨深淵、如履薄冰的心情，力排眾議，兢兢業業地流通佛典，弘揚正法。上人雖遠在美國，但許多老同修仍然能感應到上人的關注與悲心，他們對上人充滿無限的信心。

和上人初次見面的因緣，是在一九八一年，宣公上人返臺出席第三屆世界佛教僧伽大會，弘法會場設在濟南路民眾服務活動中心。在數千人擁擠的會場中，老同修們無法接近上人，只好遙望著上人，並在心裡表示願意皈依他老人家（關帝君也示杯，指示可以皈依老和尚）。

一九八八年，上人再次返臺弘法，儘管行程匆忙，時間緊湊，上人仍專程去「法界」探望大家。當時帶路的弟子不識路，在農安街附近走了很多冤枉路，都找不到「法界」，上人仍指示繼續尋找。最後終於找到了，上人一步一步親自登上六樓時，老同修正忙著搬運經書。對於上人突然地光臨，老實的他們歡喜得說不出話來：原來，上人和他們這麼近！雖然上人沒多說什麼，他們已深深地體會到上人無限的關懷與鼓勵。

法界佛教贈經會，抱著流通正法音的宗旨，遵循宣公上人的六大條款：不爭、不貪、

should cherish these good roots.

One time they went to Muzha, Taipei, to make a bowing pilgrimage. On the way home, the bus they were riding in overturned and rolled down the mountain. When one of the volunteers had been bowing, the words "overturned car" appeared in her mind. She didn't pay heed to it and continued reciting the name of Guanshiyin Bodhisattva and bowing. Although she was unconscious after the accident, she suffered no external injury because she had been holding her sleeping bag in the bus. Another volunteer had been about to take the bus, but at the last minute her colleague had pulled her off, saying, "Your health is poor. You can walk with us and get some exercise." Thus she escaped the danger. The other volunteers who were on the bus also came away without any serious injuries. It could be said that quiet, hard work results in quiet responses.

Alas! In the evil time
Of the Dharma-ending Age,
Living beings' blessings are slight; it is difficult to train them.
Far indeed from the Sages of the past!
Their deviant views are deep.
Demons are strong, the Dharma is weak;
Many are the wrongs and injuries.
Hearing of the door of the Thus Come One's Sudden Teaching,
They hate not destroying it as they would smash a tile.
　　　　—*The Song of Enlightenment* by Great Master Yongjia

When DRBBDA was newly established, there were many detracting rumors about the Venerable Master Hua in the Taiwan Buddhist world, and many people misunderstood the Venerable Master. Many of the volunteers were very cautious and nervous as they cleared up people's misunderstandings, distributed the Buddhist texts, and propagated the proper Dharma. Although the Venerable Master was faraway in America, many of the volunteers could sense the Master's mindful concern and compassion and had boundless faith in the Master.

The first time they saw the Venerable Master was in 1981. The Venerable Master came to Taiwan to attend the Third International Buddhist Sangha Conference, which was held at the People's Service Activities Center on Ji-nan Road. Several thousand people filled the auditorium, making it impossible for the volunteers to draw near the Venerable Master. They gazed at the Master from afar and wished in their hearts to take refuge with him. (Lord Guan had indicated through an oracle that they could take refuge with the Master.)

In 1988, the Venerable Master came to Taiwan again to propagate the Dharma. Despite his tight and hectic schedule, the Venerable Master paid a special visit to DRBBDA to see everyone. The disciple who was leading the way wasn't familiar with the road, and they circled about Nong-an Road without finding DRBBDA. The Venerable Master instructed them to continue searching. When they finally found the place, the Master personally walked up the steps to the sixth floor, where the volunteers were busily moving Sutra books. The Venerable Master's surprise visit made them speechless with delight: They didn't realize the Master was so close to them! Although the Venerable Master didn't say very much, they could feel the Master's boundless concern and encouragement.

The goal of DRBBDA is to circulate the Proper Dharma, and its members honor the Venerable Master's six great guidelines: no fighting, no

不求、不自私、不自利、不打妄語,以淨化社會風氣。「法界」在千辛萬苦中成長。過去社會一般贈閱的佛書,均不注重設計、印刷、裝訂,而「法界」所印的經書,均盡可能的求印刷設計的精美,也因此帶動了佛教界印行佛經時,提高品質的風氣。

一九八八年,上人終於在臺灣花蓮建立了第一座道場,帶給「法界」的老同修們,及陸續進來的工作人員一劑興奮劑。從此大家不顧路途遙遠,數次前往花蓮親近僧團,也希望僧團能到「法界」來主事,但是因機緣尚未成熟,而暫時作罷。

一九九〇年七月,「法界」遷移到北市林森北路一處較大的地方,更名為「法界佛教印經會」。其時應十方護法大德需要,由單純的印經轉變成多元化的弘法服務,諸如出版美國法界佛教總會的錄音帶、錄影帶,並舉辦兒童繪畫、英語班。同時邀請上人的出家弟子,定期拜懺、講法,及贊助法界佛教總會各項弘法活動。由於從事的弘法事務越來越多,越來越顯出法界的重要性。一向由居士主辦的「法界」,迫切地需要僧眾的領導。於是「法界」正式被納入美國法界佛教總會,成為法總在臺灣的另一個分支道場,「法界」終於歸隊了!

爾後林森北路的屋主急需房屋,老同修等又再度發揮他們的力量,廢寢忘食地為「法界」找一個永久的會址,以免不時遷移之苦。皇天不負有心人,一九九二年三月,終於在臺北市忠孝東路六段八十五號十一樓有了自己的新家。在擁擠嘈雜的臺北市,它算是一個良好的環境,光線充足,遠眺群山,視野遼闊。面積雖仍不敷使用,但卻免除了經常遷移的麻煩。有了一個穩定的所在,大家也可以在這裡安心辦道、印經、禮佛、拜懺、講經說法⋯⋯等,使法輪常轉。

一九九三年一月,上人回臺弘法時,有三十八人在「法界」從上人剃度出家,一時「法界」成為上人返臺弘法的焦點之一。

現在「法界」的日常活動,除每天由僧眾領導早晚功課、拜〈大悲懺〉、誦《華嚴經》、聽經及週末的兒童班外,每月亦定期舉行〈水懺〉(每月第一、三個星期日)、〈楞嚴咒〉

greed, no seeking, no selfishness, no pursuing of personal advantage, and no lying, which were established in order to purify and transform social trends. The development of DRBBDA took place amidst multiple hardships. In the past, the design, printing, and binding of free Buddhist books were not of very high quality. DRBBDA, on the other hand, sought to produce books of high quality design and printing, thus raising the standard of printing quality in the Buddhist world in general.

In 1988, the Venerable Master finally established a Way-place in Hualian, Taiwan, giving the original group of volunteers and incoming workers a dose of happiness. Despite the long distance, they would often go to Hualian to draw near the Sangha. They also hoped the Sangha members would take over the administration of DRBBDA one day. Because conditions were not yet ripe, they themselves were doing it for the time being.

In July of 1990, DRBBDA moved to a slightly larger place on Linshen N. Road in Taipei. Due to the needs of the Dharma-protecting laity, the Association's function evolved from simple printing of Buddhist texts to providing various services for the propagation of Dharma. For example, it began to publish audio and video tapes for Dharma Realm Buddhist Association in America, and to offer drawing and English classes for children. It also invited the Venerable Master's left-home disciples to regularly lead repentance ceremonies, give Dharma talks, and support various Dharma-propagation activities of the Dharma Realm Buddhist Association. As it began to sponsor more and more Dharma-propagation activities, its importance became increasingly obvious. DRBBDA, which had been managed by laypeople up to now, desperately needed the leadership of the Sangha. Hence DRBBDA officially became a branch of Dharma Realm Buddhist Association of the United States. It had finally joined ranks!

The landlord at Linshen N. Road urgently needed his building back, and so the volunteers again put forth their efforts, forgetting about sleeping and eating as they searched for a permanent location for the Association so that the trouble of having to move all the time could be avoided. Heaven will not disappoint those who are resolved. In March of 1992, they finally had their own home on the eleventh floor at 85 Chung-hsiao E. Road, Sec. 6, Taipei, R.O.C. In the crowded and noisy city of Taipei, it is in a very good setting—with ample light, a panoramic view, and mountains in the distance. Although the space was still too small, it resolved the problem of constant moving. Finally there was a fixed location where everyone could settle down and do their work—printing Sutras, worshipping the Buddhas, bowing in repentance, lecturing on the Sutras and speaking the Dharma, and so on, constantly turning the Dharma wheel.

In January of 1993 when the Venerable Master returned to Taiwan to propagate the Dharma, thirty-eight people at DRBBDA shaved their heads on the same day. DRBBDA became a focus of the Venerable Master's propagation of Dharma in Taiwan.

Every day at DRBBDA, Sangha members lead the morning and evening ceremonies, the Great Compassion Repentance, the recitation of the *Flower Adornment Sutra*, and the Sutra lectures. There are classes for children during the weekend. Every month there are regular events such as the Water Repentance on the first and third Sunday, the recitation of the Shurangama Mantra during the second week, and

（每月第二個星期）、佛一（每月第四個星期日）等法會。還有不定期於佛菩薩聖誕舉行的佛七、觀音七、地藏七，並《梁皇寶懺》等法會。隨著聞風而來的信眾日增，「法界」逐漸成為臺北地區上人的弟子們一個精神的寶所，並且越來越壯大了！

一群出身微寒，沒有受過多少教育，被人們視為沒有智慧的人，靠著他們堅忍的力量，建立起正法的流通站，將菩提種子撒向臺灣，撒向世界，使宣公上人的正法音，流進士、農、工、商各個階層。在時下物欲橫流的社會，上人的正法無異是一股清流，洗去了人心的濁垢，帶給社會一種明淨。這股清流也流向了監獄，使多少囚徒，改過自新，得到新生。「法界」的拓荒者，就是這樣默默地為社會，分擔起教化人心的工作。

「前人種樹，後人乘涼」，今天當我們讀著各種印製精美的上人開示、淺釋時；當我們聽著上人講法的法音時，怎能不飲水思源，怎能不珍惜前人的苦心，而生稀有想，效法想呢！

one day of Buddha's name recitation on the fourth Sunday. There are also special events such as week-long sessions for reciting the names of Amitabha Buddha, Guanyin Bodhisattva, or Earth Store Bodhisattva, and the Jewelled Repentance of the Emperor of Liang. With more and more people hearing about and coming to DRBBDA, it has gradually became a spiritual haven for the Venerable Master's disciples in Taipei. It has also become more and more flourishing!

Due to the persevering efforts of a group of humble folk who had received little schooling and were commonly regarded as ignorant, a center for the circulation of the proper Dharma was established. This center would disseminate the seeds of Bodhi in Taiwan and the rest of the world, enabling the Venerable Master's proper Dharma sound to be heard among scholars, farmers, workers, and businessmen. In this society of rampant materialistic desires, the Venerable Master's proper Dharma is a clear stream that washes the turbid filth from people's minds and brings a bright purity to society. This clear stream also flows into the prisons, inspiring many prisoners to reform and renew themselves. It was in this way that the pioneers of DRBBDA quietly worked for society, assuming the responsibility for teaching and transforming people's minds.

"The ancestors planted trees so their descendants could enjoy the shade." Today, when we read the beautifully printed books of the Venerable Master's instructional talks and explanations or hear the Venerable Master's lectures, how can we not appreciate the pains taken by those who came before us? Should we not cherish what they have done and strive to emulate them?

我自己的事情，不願意得到什麼利益，
只要對眾生有利益，我雖死不辭。
我看死和活，這都是一樣的，沒有什麼分別。
我能為法忘軀，這是佛弟子的本份。

I don't wish to benefit myself. If there is something that I can do to
benefit living beings, I want to do it, even if I have to die.
I see life and death as being the same, without difference.
I can forget myself for the sake of the Dharma.
This is the basic duty of a disciple of the Buddha.

傳供疏文

THE EULOGY OF THE CEREMONY FOR PASSING OFFERINGS

恭維

佛曆三千零二十二年七月初二，法界佛教總會萬佛聖城住持恆律領四眾弟子等，謹以香花素齋之儀，奠祭三緣堂及眞如堂上萬佛聖城圓寂開山祖師宣公老和尚之蓮座前，誄詞以讚之曰：

Eulogy

In the year 3022 of the Buddha, on the second day of the seventh lunar month, I, Heng Lyu, Abbot of the Sagely City of Ten Thousand Buddhas under the auspices of Dharma Realm Buddhist Association, represent the disciples of the fourfold assembly to make offerings of incense, flowers, and a vegetarian meal. In front of the Lotus Seat of the Venerable Master Hsuan Hua, the High Master of Three Conditions Monastery and True Suchness Monastery, and the Founder of the Sagely City of Ten Thousand Buddhas, who has completed the stillness, I present this eulogy:

大權示現　無來無去　末法無端　度生七紀

He manifested provisionally,
Neither going nor coming.
In the chaotic Dharma-ending Age,
He saved living beings for nearly eighty years.

虛老心傳　潙仰九祖　跡遍亞洲　德庇歐美

With the mind transmission from Elder Master Hsu,
He became the ninth patriarch of the Weiyang Sect.
His footprints covered Asia,
And his virtue protected America and Europe.

攜法西來　首次剃度　美國僧尼

He brought the Dharma to the West
And was the first to shave the heads
Of American monks and nuns.

雙語教育　東西普攝　弘宗說教　無分南北

Westerners and Easterners were both gathered in
With bilingual education.
He propagated the Chan school and expounded the teachings,
Making no distinction between north and south.

華嚴境界　楞嚴壇場　破邪顯正　夙夜匪懈

With the Flower Adornment state
And the Shurangama platform,
He smashed the deviant to reveal the proper,
Never resting even at night.

恭塑萬佛　普傳心法　翻譯經典　媲美羅什　功同玄奘　廣施法喜

Reverently molding ten thousand Buddhas,
He universally transmitted the Mind Dharma.
In translating the Sutras
He rivalled Kumarajiva,
And his merit equalled that of Hsuan Tsang.
The joy of the Dharma was vastly bestowed.

衣不離體　日中一食　夜不倒單　弘範毗尼

Always wearing the precept sash,
He took one meal a day at noon
And did not lie down at night,
Thus propagating and serving as an exemplar of the Vinaya.

育良培德　提倡忠孝　法界大學　改革風紀　和平使者

With Instilling Goodness and Developing Virtue Schools,
He promoted filial piety and fraternal respect.
He founded the Dharma Realm University,
Seeking to reform the social trend
As a messenger of peace.

敬老懷少　移風易俗　不改國籍　追本溯源

Respecting the elderly and cherishing the young,
He wanted to improve the customs.
Not changing his nationality,
He traced his roots back to their source.

三大條款　百千磨練　六大宗旨　信守不渝

Following the Three Great Guidelines,
He underwent myriads of ordeals.
Upholding the Six Great Principles,
His heart never wavered.

十八大願　大悲手眼　驚天動地

The Eighteen Great Vows
And the Greatly Compassionate Hands and Eyes
Startle heaven and move the earth.

今示圓寂　頓失宗師　人天長夜　草木同泣

Now he has manifested the completing of stillness,
And suddenly we have lost our great teacher.
The long night falls upon humans and gods,
And plants and trees weep together.

祈我宣公　乘願再來　一瓣心香　伏維尚饗

We pray that our Venerable Master Hsuan Hua,
Riding on his vows, will come again.
We offer this stick of incense and hope he will accept it.

封棺法語
The Ceremony of Sealing the Casket and Speaking the Dharma
明暘老法師主法　Hosted by Elder Dharma Master Mingyang

主法說法語：

葉落歸根見本源，浮生大夢了無痕；
從茲一夢渾無事，幻滅之時眞自存。

恭維
旅美近代高僧宣化度輪尊宿，誕生東北
，應跡哈市，菩提之樹早花，般若之燈
續燄，多年宏宗演教，一世弘法利生，
莊嚴國土，利樂有情，人天師表，四眾
楷模，愛國愛教，豐功至偉。建法幢於
處處，破疑網于重重，化弘美歐，度眾
生於億兆；宗說兼通，導群倫於萬千。
茲者，娑婆印壞，淨土文成，機薪既盡
，應火潛輝；果滿因圓，撒手便行。

主法者舉封條，說封棺法語：

一靈不滅等虛空，即是當人舊主翁；
無去無來常不動，青山原在白雲中。

舉條云：「封！」

The Dharma Host speaks Dharma as he grasps the staff;

Leaves fall and return to the root: one sees the original source.
This fleeting life is but a great dream—completely without traces.
In this one dream, there is nothing at all.
When the illusion ends, the truth continues to exist.

Respectful Announcement:

A noble Sangha member of contemporary times, the Elder Master Hsuan Hua To Lun, who traveled to America, was born in Harbin, Manchuria, China. The Bodhi tree bloomed early, and the Prajna lamp continued to shine. For many years he spread the religion and expounded the teachings. Throughout his life, he propagated the Dharma to benefit living beings, adorned countries and lands, and brought happiness and benefit to sentient beings. He was a teacher and model for humans and gods and a role model for the fourfold assembly. He loved the country and loved his religion, and his meritorious works were monumental. He raised the Dharma banner in place after place and destroyed the nets of doubt, layer by layer. He taught and preached in America and Europe, converting millions of beings. Having mastered both the Chan meditation sect and the teachings, he guided tens of thousands of people. Now, his imprint in the Saha world has perished, and his accomplishment in the Pure Land is complete. Since the wood of his conditions for teaching have burned up, the fire of his responses shines latently. The fruition is complete and the cause is perfected. He let go of everything and departed.

The Dharma Host raises the seal and speaks the verse for sealing the casket:

His spirit is unextinguished, equal to empty space—
The original owner of this person.
Neither going nor coming, perpetually unmoving,
The green mountains have always been in the white clouds.

With the seal raised, he says: "Seal it."

舉火荼毗法語
The Ceremony of Lighting the Fire for Cremation and Speaking the Dharma
明暘老法師主法　Hosted by Elder Dharma Master Mingyang

主法說荼毗舉火法語：

舉起三昧火，燒卻幻化身；
一塵都不染，清淨自安然。

高聲云：「燒！」

光明寂照遍河沙，十方世界共一家；
一念不生全體現，六根才動被雲遮。

The Dharma Host lifts the torch and recites a verse:

Lighting the fire of samadhi,
To burn the illusory body,
Not defiled by a single speck of dust,
One is pure and naturally at ease.

In a loud voice: "Light the fire!"

The light illuminates in stillness, pervading lands as numerous as the
　　Ganges' sands.
The worlds of the ten directions are all one family.
When not one thought arises, the entire substance manifests.
When the six faculties stir, one is covered by clouds.

法 界 音
News from
the Dharma Realm

長堤聖寺七七涅槃追思法會

CONCLUSION OF THE FORTY-NINE-DAY MEMORIAL NIRVANA CEREMONY AT LONG BEACH SAGELY MONASTERY

鄰虛塵
Lin Xuchen

為紀念「法界佛教總會」（以下簡稱法總）創辦人暨妙覺山萬佛聖城開山祖師上宣下化老和尚七七涅槃圓滿日，南加州四眾弟子特於一九九五年七月二十五日，在「法總」分道場洛杉磯的長堤聖寺，隆重舉辦國際齋僧大法會，藉茲盡孝報恩。

應供而來的大德，遍佈世界各國，計有中、美、英、法、越、泰、緬、柬埔寨、錫蘭、西藏等等，總數近一百七十位，其中百分之八十為比丘，可說是前所未有的盛會。其中戒臘最高者（五十五年）為錫蘭籍七十五歲的Hawanpola Ratanasara Mahathero 法師，又有來自英國的 Ajahn Sumedho（蘇美度）法師，隨團四人赴筵。 Dhammarajranutwat, Kongsophan, Umsum 等三位法師，特別撥冗與會，其戒臘都在五十以上，甚為稀有難得。另有臺灣司法院長林洋港的代表人余正昭先生，山東濟寧市人民政府僑務辦公室副主任暨寶相寺籌委會會長郭秋亞先生，中國歷史文化名城研究會常務理事楊春炳先生越洋而至。

當日上午開始讚頌儀典，以華語、英語、越南語、巴利文次第進行，梵唄清遠，莊嚴異常。護法居士恭辦素筵，謹遵佛制如法供養。齋畢，正午十二時，在「本師釋迦牟尼佛」聖號唱誦中，由十八位身著海青之居士代表法總四眾弟子一一虔誠獻禮。

供儀圓滿，「法界佛教大學」祖炳民教授致辭，歡迎諸山長老的蒞臨及加州各參議員、國會議員、市長等諸代表的赴會。祖教授並特別對宣公上人的生平事蹟作精要的簡介

In order to commemorate the completion of the forty-nine-day memorial service in honor of the Nirvana of the Venerable Master Hua, who was the founder of Dharma Realm Buddhist Association and of the Sagely City of Ten Thousand Buddhas at Wonderful Enlightenment Mountain, the fourfold assembly of disciples in southern California held an International Meal Offering Ceremony for the Sangha on July 25, 1995. This was also a way to express their filial piety and to repay the Venerable Master's kindness.

The virtuous Sangha members who came to receive offerings came from all over the world, including such countries as China, America, England, France, Vietnam, Thailand, Burma, Cambodia, Sri Lanka, and Tibet. There were nearly one hundred and seventy Sangha members, eighty percent of whom were Bhikshus (monks), making this an unprecedented event. The most senior Sangha member was Hawanpola Ratanasara Mahathero of Sri Lanka, who is seventy-five years old and has been ordained for fifty-five years. Venerable Ajahn Sumedho and three other Sangha members from England also attended the event. The Venerable Dharma Masters Dhammarajanutwat, Kongsophan, and Umsum, who have over fifty years in precepts, also travelled by plane and graced the event with their rare presence. Lin Yanggang, the Director of the Judicial Yuan of the Republic of China, was represented by Mr. Yu Zhengzhao. Coming overseas from Shandong Province, China, were Mr. Guo Qiuya (the Deputy Director of the Overseas Affairs Office of the People's Government of Jining City and the Director of the Baoxiang Monastery Committee) and Mr. Yang Chunbing (Standing Committee Member of the Research Institute of Historical and Cultural Cities of China).

Ceremonies in praise and recognition were conducted in Chinese, English, Vietnamese, and Pali in the morning. The pure sounds of religious chanting carried afar during these especially splendid ceremonies. The Dharma-protecting laity prepared a vegetarian banquet and made the meal offering in accord with the Buddha's instructions and the Dharma. After the meal, promptly at twelve o'clock noon as everyone recited the holy name "Fundamental Teacher Shakyamuni Buddha," eighteen laypeople wearing black robes, representing the fourfold assembly of Dharma Realm Buddhist Association, sincerely presented gifts to each Dharma Master.

At the completion of the offering ceremony, Professor John Tsu of Dharma Realm Buddhist University welcomed the guest Sangha members and elder masters and the representatives of various senators, con-

。續後，有多位各國法師上台開示。他們表示：世界必須有高度智慧的宗教領袖來領導，上人即是活生生的明證，他由修行而得圓滿究竟的智慧。正統佛教能以傳承於美國，這是上人最偉大的成就，故足以感召世界眾生的至心歸仰。但是上人自身則無任何執取，如鳥飛池塘，不留影跡，最是自在。福德具足者乃得遇上人，故弟子眾等，應善繼遺志，以上人悲心為己心，以上人悲願為己願。致力為一切眾生謀福。

恆實法師則舉了兩個例子，說明上人大小無礙的不思議境界，作為此次齋僧大會的結束。下午兩點二十分，齋筵圓滿，南北傳僧眾合影留念於長堤聖寺園苑，這是宣公上人宗教大團結的又一次實踐。下午三點啟建慈悲三昧水懺壇場，迴向功德於法界，俾一切眾生普沾上人深恩厚澤，如法修行，離苦得樂。

gressmen, and the mayor of Long Beach. Dr. Tsu also gave a brief sketch of the Venerable Master Hua's life. Then Dharma Masters from various countries also spoke. They pointed out that the world needs a religious leader of great wisdom to guide it, and the Venerable Master was a living example of this—he had cultivated and attained to the perfect, ultimate wisdom. The orthodox Buddhist tradition has been transmitted to America. This is the Venerable Master's greatest achievement. Therefore he was able to evoke the sincere trust of the living beings of the world. Even so, the Venerable Master never had any attachments. He was like a bird flying over a pool of water, not leaving any traces, free to the utmost. Only those replete with blessings and virtue were able to meet the Venerable Master. Therefore, as disciples we should continue to carry on the Venerable Master's will. Taking the Venerable Master's compassionate mind as our own mind and his compassionate vows as our own vows, we should dedicate ourselves to benefiting living beings.

To conclude this Meal Offering Ceremony to the Sangha, Dharma Master Heng Sure gave two examples to illustrate the Venerable Master's inconceivable state of the non-obstruction of great and small. When the ceremony drew to a close at 2:20 in the afternoon, the Sangha members from the Theravada and Mahayana traditions stood for group photographs in the garden of Long Beach Monastery. This was one more instance of the Venerable Master's advocacy of religious unity. At three o'clock in the afternoon, the ceremony for Compassionate Samadhi Water Repentance was begun, and the merit from it will be dedicated to all in the Dharma Realm in the hope that all living beings will benefit from the Venerable Master's deep, great kindness; cultivate according to the Dharma; leave suffering; and attain bliss.

讚頌追思暨荼毗大典
THE MEMORIAL AND CREMATION CEREMONIES

晁山　Zhao Shan

當代佛教高僧宣化上人於七月二十八日，在北加州萬佛聖城荼毗。兩千餘位自世界各地前來的信眾，在懷念追思的心情中，望著青煙裊裊上升。上人的肉身雖已火化，但「不為自己求利益，但願眾生得安樂」的精神，將永遠留在所有佛弟子的心頭。

二十八日上午七時起，佛教南北傳諸山長老已開始主持法會，將宣公上人的法體，自靈堂迎請至萬佛殿前的祖師堂。宣公上人是禪門溈仰宗第九代的祖師。來自美、加、歐、亞各國的兩千餘位信眾，包括宣公上人的多位美籍弟子，都放下工作、事業，專程前往萬佛聖城，參加上人的追思暨荼毗大典。

上午八時半，追思大會正式展開。首先由

The body of the Venerable Master Hua was cremated on July 28, 1995, at the Sagely City of Ten Thousand Buddhas in northern California. More than two thousand devotees from around the world watched mournfully as the blue flames rose higher inside the crematory. Although the Venerable Master's flesh body was cremated, his spirit of not seeking any benefit for himself and wishing only to bring peace and happiness to living beings will remain forever in the hearts of all Buddhist disciples.

At seven o'clock in the morning on July 28, Elder Masters from both Theravada and Mahayana traditions hosted a ceremony for inviting the Venerable Master from the Nirvana Hall to the Patriarchs' Hall in front of the Hall of Ten Thousand Buddhas. The Venerable Master Hua was the Ninth Patriarch of the Weiyang Sect of Chan Buddhism. The two thousand and some followers from the United States, Canada, and various Asian and European countries, including many of the Venerable Master's American disciples, put down their work and business in order to come to the Sagely City of Ten Thousand Buddhas to take part in the Memorial and Cremation Ceremonies for the Venerable Master.

The Memorial Ceremony itself began at eight-thirty in the morning.

來自中國大陸的「中國佛教協會」副會長明暘法師宣讀中國佛協會長趙樸初的唁電。

美國妙法院住持旭朗法師接著致詞指出，宣公上人在美國弘揚正法，不遺餘力。中國人到美國來開創道場，很不容易；上人開創了二十餘處道場，更是不容易。

一百零七歲的人瑞法師達瑪瓦若，則表示：「宣公上人的圓寂，彷彿一顆巨星的殞落，但另一顆新生的巨星將會繼起。」

西方出家人當中，戒臘最長（二十九年）的蘇美度法師，目前在英國有四處道場。他年輕時，曾前往泰國修苦行多年。宣公上人生前數次提及要弟子們學習蘇美度法師苦修的精神。蘇美度法師指出，宣公上人將正法帶到遙遠的西方，清淨的法永遠是真的不生不滅。蘇美度法師代表西方人，包括美國人與歐洲人，向宣公上人表達最崇高的敬意。

甘迺迪大學教授祖炳民宣讀前美國總統喬治・布希，以及加州現任州長威爾遜的弔唁信函之後，駐舊金山臺北經濟文化辦事處副處長傅迪宣讀了中華民國總統府資政林洋港與總統府秘書長吳伯雄的唁電。辦事處廖港民組長也陪同傅副處長前來。

萬佛聖城所在的曼都仙諾郡郡長富蘭克・馬可麥克曾經多次參加萬佛聖城舉辦的法會。這次也特地前來參加上人茶毗大典，以表達他對上人的敬意。加州選出的國會眾議員富蘭克・瑞格斯派代表德瑞爾・夏爾致詞表示，曼都仙諾郡及此地社區的日漸進步，是因為宣公上人在此住持。瑞格斯眾議員也是宣公上人治喪委員會的成員之一。

上午九時四十分，舉行「傳供儀式」。一百零八份供品，由兩千多位信眾接力傳送。這是宣公上人座下弟子，在上人火化前，最後一次獻上心意。

茶毗大典，於下午一時開始。上人的弟子與各界人士排隊魚貫進入祖師堂，一一瞻仰上人德相。三時正，上人的靈柩移往火化地點。兩千多人也隨同前往茶毗現場。在大眾虔誠的念佛聲中，明暘法師於四時二十分舉起火把，口誦偈語，大喝一聲：「燒！」這時宣公上人的四眾弟子紛紛跪拜，向這位精神導師的肉身告別。

Dharma Master Mingyang, the Vice-Chairman of the Chinese Buddhist Association in mainland China, started off by reading a telegram of condolence from the Chairman of the Association, Zhao Puchu.

Dharma Master Xulang, Abbot of Miaofa Temple in the United States, followed with a speech in which he pointed out that the Venerable Master Hua had not spared any effort in propagating the proper Dharma in America. He also said that it was not easy for a Chinese to come to the United States and found a monastery, much less over twenty monasteries.

The Cambodian Dharma Master Dharmawara, who is 107 years old, compared the Venerable Master's completion of stillness to the falling of a great star, but pointed out that the falling of this great star will make room for a new one.

Venerable Ajahn Sumedho, who is the most senior Western monk (ordained for twenty-nine years), currently oversees four monasteries in England. He practiced asceticism for many years in Thailand as a young man. When the Venerable Master Hua was alive, he often encouraged his disciples to learn Ajahn Sumedho's spirit in ascetic cultivation. Ajahn Sumedho pointed out that the Venerable Master Hua had brought the proper Dharma to the West from far away, and that this pure Dharma was eternally real, unborn and undying. Ajahn Sumedho offered his deepest respects to the Venerable Master on behalf of Westerners, including people of America and Europe.

Professor John Tsu of John F. Kennedy University read letters of condolence from George Bush, former President of the United States, and Pete Wilson, Governor of California. Following that, Fu Di, the Deputy Director of the San Francisco branch of the Taipei Economic and Cultural Office read telegrams of condolence sent by Lin Yanggang, Advisor to the President of the Republic of China, and by Wu Boxiong, Executive Secretary to the President. Deputy Director Fu Di was accompanied by the Supervisor of the Office, Liao Gangming.

Frank McMichael, the Chairman of the Board of Supervisors of Mendocino County, where the Sagely City of Ten Thousand Buddhas is located, has attended many of the Dharma assemblies held at the Sagely City. This time he especially visited the Sagely City to offer his respects to the Venerable Master by attending the cremation ceremony. Congressman Frank Riggs, who represents California in the U.S. Congress, sent Darrell Shull to speak on his behalf, saying that Mendocino County and neighboring areas owe their progress in part to the Venerable Master Hua's presence here. Congressman Riggs is also on the Memorial Committee in Honor of the Venerable Master Hua.

At 9:40 in the morning, the Ceremony for Passing Offerings was held. One hundred and eight offerings were passed from hand to hand among the two thousand and some devotees. This was the final offering to the Venerable Master by his disciples before the cremation.

The Cremation Ceremony began at one o'clock in the afternoon. The Venerable Master's disciples and people from all walks of life, over two thousand in all, lined up and walked into the Patriarchs' Hall one by one to gaze upon the Venerable Master's visage for the final time. At three o'clock, the Venerable Master's casket was carried to the cremation site by a procession of over two thousand people. At 4:20, as the assembly sincerely recited the name of the Buddha, Dharma Master Mingyang lifted the torch, recited a verse, and then shouted, "Light the fire!" The Venerable Master's disciples knelt and bowed, bidding farewell to their spiritual teacher.

宣公上人的骨灰，於七月二十九日上午，以熱氣球盛載升空，遍撒在萬佛聖城的上空。誠如上人在遺言中所交待的：「我來的時候什麼也沒有；走的時候，還是什麼也不要，在世上我不要留什麼痕跡。」

雖然宣公上人不要在世上留痕跡，但他老人家在西方弘揚佛法，翻譯佛經，開辦教育，感動了無數西方人，播下了菩提覺悟的種子，這已是無法磨滅的痕跡。宣公上人的美籍資深弟子之一，舊金山州大哲學系教授易象乾博士說得好：「雖然上人大部分的弟子都是中國人，但後人所記得他的，恐怕還是他將佛教帶到西方的事業。」

The Venerable Master Hua's ashes were scattered in the air over the Sagely City of Ten Thousand Buddhas from a hot air balloon on the morning of July 29. This was in accord with the Venerable Master's final instructions: "When I came, I did not have anything at all. When I leave, I still will not have anything. I do not want to leave any traces in the world."

Although the Venerable Master did not want to leave any traces in the world, by propagating the Buddhadharma in the West, translating the Buddhist canon, and founding schools, he has influenced countless Westerners and sowed the seeds of Bodhi (enlightenment). These are already traces that will never perish. Dr. Ron Epstein, a professor in the Philosophy Department of San Francisco State University and one of the Venerable Master's senior American disciples, aptly said, "Even though the majority of the Venerable Master's disciples are Chinese, the people of the future will probably remember him for his work to bring Buddhism to the West."

撒骨灰儀式
THE RITUAL OF SCATTERING THE ASHES
童欣慈　Tong Xinci

當代佛教高僧宣公上人於日前荼毗後，骨灰在七月二十九日由弟子們撒在萬佛聖城上空，圓滿宣公上人的心願：「我從虛空來，回到虛空去。」

七月二十九日上午八時正，千餘位宣公上人的弟子們，在萬佛聖城五觀齋堂前的大片草地上，等著熱氣球充氣，準備升空。

宣公上人座下的美籍出家弟子恆實法師、恆來法師與哥斯大黎加寶元寺住持真一法師，捧著宣公上人的骨灰，一同搭上熱氣球。

熱氣球於八時三十分冉冉升起，升至半空中時，只見搭乘熱氣球的法師們，將宣公上人的骨灰緩緩撒出。骨灰在空中迅速散開，彷彿縷縷輕煙，很快的與虛空融合為一。

這時，少數在場信眾痛哭失聲，高喊著：「師父，不要走；師父，不要走……」絕大部分的弟子繼續在莊嚴肅穆的念佛聲中，完成這項「圓滿大典」。

老和尚走了，走的方式正如他老人家生前曾說過的：「掃一切法，離一切相」。留給弟子們的，則是繼續弘揚佛法，翻譯經典與辦好教育等等重責大任。

On July 29, one day after the body of the eminent Buddhist monk Venerable Master Hsuan Hua was cremated, his ashes were scattered in the air above the Sagely City of Ten Thousand Buddhas by his disciples, fulfilling the Venerable Master's wish, "I came from empty space, and to empty space I will return."

At eight o'clock in the morning on July 29, over a thousand of the Venerable Master's disciples stood in the meadow in front of the Five Contemplations Dining Hall at the Sagely City, waiting for the hot air balloon to fill up and rise into the air.

Dharma Masters Heng Sure and Heng Lai (American disciples of the Venerable Master) as well as Dharma Master Zhenyi (the Abbot of Baoyuan Monastery in Costa Rica) boarded the hot air balloon, carrying the Venerable Master's ashes.

At eight-thirty, the balloon began to rise slowly into the air. The Dharma Masters riding in the balloon began slowly scattering the Venerable Master's ashes. The ashes quickly dispersed in the air, like undulating tendrils of smoke that soon merged into the void.

A few of the faithful who were present were choked with tears as they cried out, "Teacher, don't go! Teacher, don't go..." The vast majority of the disciples continued solemnly reciting the name of the Buddha, completing this Final Ceremony.

The Venerable Elder Master has gone, and the way he left accorded with his words when alive: "Sweep away all dharmas. Separate from all appearances." What he left behind for his disciples were great responsibilities—to continue propagating the Buddhadharma, translating the Buddhist Canon, carrying out the ideals of education well, and so on.

瞻仰舍利
VIEWING THE SHARIRA

龔同祚　Gong Tongzuo

北加州萬佛聖城於八月六日（農曆七月十五日），舉行一年一度的「盂蘭盆法會」。當天請出萬佛聖城開山祖師上宣下化老和尚的舍利，以供大眾瞻仰。

根據文獻記載，古印度人稱呼「米粒」為「舍利」。釋迦牟尼佛入滅火化後，有骨子，好像五色珠，光瑩堅固，大小如同米粒，所以稱之為舍利。佛經上也記載著，舍利是戒定慧所薰修，稀有難得，是最上福田。《金光明經》說：「是舍利者，即是修六波羅蜜功德所重。」因此，荼毘後得到舍利，是證明修行人在戒定慧方面有相當的成就。

宣公上人留有牙齒舍利，已數出來的舍利子有四千多顆，舍利花有數百朵。舍利顏色有素白、槐黃、翠綠、藏藍、玄黑等多種，其中有許多凝結在骨頭上的舍利，晶瑩光澤，一如翡翠玉石，十分稀有難得。尤其是牙齒舍利，宣公上人的一位弟子感動地說：「上人一生講經說法數萬會，難怪牙齒也燒出舍利！」另一位弟子也提到：「上人是真語者！實語者！所以牙齒都燒出舍利來。」

On August 6 (the fifteenth of the seventh lunar month), the annual Ullambana Festival was held at the Sagely City of Ten Thousand Buddhas in northern California. On that day the sharira (relics) of the late Elder Master Venerable Hsuan Noble Hua, founder of the Sagely City, were placed on public display.

According to historical records, the people of ancient India used the term "sharira" to refer to rice grains. After Shakyamuni entered Nirvana and his body was cremated, there were bone relics resembling five-colored pearls, luminous and hard, about the size of grains of rice, and they were called sharira. It is recorded in the Sutras that sharira are gained through being permeated by the cultivation of precepts, samadhi, and wisdom. They are very rare and serve as supreme fields of blessings. The *Sutra of Golden Light* says, "Sharira are what is important in the merit and virtue of cultivating the Six Paramitas." Therefore, the appearance of sharira after cremation proves that the cultivator has considerable attainment in precepts, samadhi, and wisdom.

The Venerable Master Hua's sharira (relics after cremation) include teeth sharira. More than four thousand sharira seeds and several hundred sharira clusters have been counted. The sharira are white, light yellow, green, blue, black, and other colors. Some of the sharira which are formed on the bones gleam like green jade; they are particularly rare. One of the Venerable Master's disciples, moved by the sight of the Master's teeth sharira, said, "In his life, the Venerable Master lectured on the Sutras and spoke Dharma in several tens of thousands of assemblies. No wonder his cremation yielded teeth relics!" Another disciple commented, "The Venerable Master only spoke true and actual words. That's why his teeth have become relics after cremation."

In Memory of Venerable Master Hua

追思大會後記

EVALUATIONS OF THE MEMORIAL CEREMONY

陳運璞 Yvonne Chen

宣公上人荼毗法會圓滿之際，法總佛教總會特別發出問卷，以蒐集各方善信的意見。計有一百位填寫，並交回、寄回問卷。答覆內容經統計如下：

人口資料

年齡：十九歲以下：　　　七人
　　　二十歲至二十九歲：　七人
　　　三十歲至三十九歲：　二十八人
　　　四十歲至四十九歲：　三十三人
　　　五十歲至五十九歲：　十二人
　　　六十歲至六十九歲：　九人
　　　七十歲以上：　　　　四人

答覆問卷者，年齡分布自七歲至八十七歲，而以三十歲至四十九歲年齡層的人數最多，合計為六十一人，將近三分之二。

性別：男眾：二十五人　　女眾：七十五人
　　　答覆問卷者，女眾為男眾的三倍。

身份：答覆問卷者，有十六位出家人（包括來自英國的南傳比丘數位），餘八十四人為在家眾。

宗教：佛教徒（八十二人）佔填寫本問卷者之絕大多數。道教與民間信仰有五人。基督教徒二人。另有十一人未答覆。

職業：答覆問卷的八十四位在家人當中，有七十六位填寫職業欄，其分類為：

商：（包括電腦、行政管理、金融、會計、
　　服裝、餐飲）：二十九人，佔了將近四成
家庭管理：十三人　　　學生：八人
醫護人員：七人　　　　教育工作：五人
科學／研究：五人　　　建築、工程：五人
退休：三人　　　　　　宗教工作人員：一人

Upon the completion of the Cremation Ceremony for the Venerable Master Hua, the Dharma Realm Buddhist Association distributed questionnaires to Buddhists from all places to collect their opinions. One hundred people filled out the questionnaire. The statistics of their personal data and a summary of their answers are as follows:

Distribution

Age: Under 19: 7　　20 – 29: 7
　　　30 – 39: 28　　40 – 49: 33
　　　50 – 59: 12　　60 – 69: 9
　　　Over 70: 4

The age distribution of those who filled out the questionnaire is from 7 to 87. Two-thirds of the people were between the ages of 30 and 49.

Gender: Male: 25　　Female: 75
There were three times as many women as men.

Status: There were 16 left-home people (including several Theravada Bhikshus from England) and 84 laypeople.

Religion: The overwhelming majority of those who filled out the questionnaire were Buddhists (82 people). Five were Taoists and followers of folk religions; two were Christians; and the religion of the remaining eleven is unknown.

Occupation: Seventy-six of the eighty-four laypeople answered this question. Their data is as follows:

Business*:	29　(nearly 40% of the pool)
Student:	8
Housekeeper:	13
Medical & Nursing:	7
Education:	5
Science/Research:	5
Construction & Engineering:	5
Retired:	3
Religious Worker:	1

*Including computer, administration, finance, accounting, clothing, and food and drink.

一、從何處來

一百位填寫問卷者，有六十七位來自臺灣，占了三分之二。其餘三分之一是分別來自英國、美國本土、加拿大、馬來西亞、新加坡、印尼和香港等地。

二、皈依

填寫問卷者有八十六位是宣公上人的皈依弟子。十二位並未皈依上人。兩位未答覆。

皈依時間：一九六十年至一九七九年： 五人
　　　　　一九八〇年至一九八九年：三十三人
　　　　　一九九〇年至一九九五年：四十三人
（其中有十一位是這次茶毗法會時皈依）

三、來過萬佛聖城否？印象如何？

五十二位以前曾經到過萬佛聖城，其中有七位特別指出，萬佛聖城現在增加許多花草植物，花圃也經過整修，樹下設置涼椅，變得更加美觀。來自臺灣的一位男居士認為，萬佛聖城的居住陳設雖然很簡單，「但比住五星級旅館還舒服」。有三位信眾認為萬佛聖城的規劃，管理尚須加強。

　　第一次來萬佛聖城的有四十五位，每一位都感覺萬佛聖城環境清幽，是修行的好地方。有七位認為萬佛聖城是人間淨土，極樂淨土。十三歲的陳靜仁還看到城內的動物（編按：有孔雀、松鼠、雉雞等）與人相處融洽。不過，有兩位居士對萬佛聖城早晚溫差很大的氣候感到不習慣。

四、親近上人的因緣

答覆這個問題的人，計有六十九位，其中以「親友介紹」最多，所佔比例約為答覆者的四成。

- 親友介紹：二十七人
- 閱讀上人書籍，萬佛城月刊「金剛菩提海」雜誌：二十人
- 上人赴各地弘法時前往聽法：十人
- 從法界佛教總會各分支道場（如金山寺、金輪寺、金峰寺、華嚴寺等多處）得知上人：八人
- 尚未聽聞上人時，已在夢中見到上人：二人（一位美籍人士，一位為華裔女居士）
- 從電視上看到上人講法：一人
- 從錄音帶聽到上人講法：一人

Questions

1. What country or state are you from?

Sixty-seven out of the hundred (two-thirds of the pool) were from Taiwan. The remaining one third came from England, various states of the United States, Canada, Malaysia, Singapore, Indonesia, Hong Kong, and other countries.

2. Did you take refuge with the Venerable Master? If so, when and where?

Eighty-six are the Venerable Master's disciples. Twelve people have not taken the refuge with the Master, and two did not respond to this question.

Date of taking refuge: 1960 – 1979:　5
　　　　　　　　　　　1980 – 1989:　33
　　　　　　　　　　　1990 – 1995:　43*

*Eleven took refuge during this Cremation Ceremony.

3. Have you been to the Sagely City of Ten Thousand Buddhas (CTTB) before? What is your impression of it this time?

Fifty-two had been to CTTB before. Seven of them noted that the City has been beautified by many well-pruned gardens, benches beneath trees, and so on. A laywoman from Taiwan said that although the living quarters in the City are simple, "It's more comfortable than a five-star hotel." Three people thought that the planning and administration in the City needed to be improved.

This was the first visit to the City for forty-five people. Every one of them felt that the environment was tranquil and that it was a good place for cultivation. Seven thought the CTTB was a pure land in the world, the pure land of ultimate bliss. Thirteen-year-old Chen Jinren saw animals (Editor's note: CTTB has peacocks, squirrels, pheasants, etc.) living in harmony with people. But two laypeople were unaccustomed to the great temperature difference between day and night in the City.

4. Would you like to describe your conditions with the Venerable Master?

Sixty-nine people answered this question. Forty percent said they came to know the Master through relatives or friends.

- Introduced through relatives and friends:　27
- Read the Master's books and the City's Buddhist magazine, *Vajra Bodhi Sea*:　20
- Attended a Dharma session held during a Dharma-propagation tour by the Master:　10
- Through various branch monasteries (Gold Mountain Monastery, Gold Wheel Monastery, Gold Summit Monastery, Avatamsaka Monastery and others):　8
- Saw the Master in dreams before hearing about him:　2 (Two laywomen, one American and one Chinese)
- Saw the Master speaking Dharma on television:　1
- Listened to the Master's taped talks:　1

五、得知上人圓寂後的感受

答覆這個問題的人士絕大多數（六十四位）都表示十分悲痛，震驚，頓失依怙，從此「問道失正路」。一位從事餐飲業的男居士慨歎：「人生已無希望。」有六位指出，從此更應精進，護持上人志願，跟著上人的六大宗旨做人。以戒為師，不負上人的教導。祈願上人早日乘願再來的有七位。來自臺灣的七歲小弟弟張兆誼的感受是：「上人圓寂後，就可以飛，可以成佛了。」

一位華裔出家人的答覆是八個字「使命完成，放下就走。」另一位義大利籍的南傳比丘的回答只有兩個英文字：「great peace（極大的和平）」，與一位居士的感受不謀而合：「弟子為師父高興，師父是真的自在了。」

有一位居士認為上人只是示現人生的生、老、病、死與無常，其精神是永遠不滅的，我們應當深思上人用心良苦的示現。

一位學科學的上人弟子說：「得知上人病痛五、六年，還不斷為我們說法，傳道，真是無限敬佩、仰望。」另一位化學家則認為上人示寂是：「很偉大，常替人治病，自己有病卻不管。」

一位基督徒的回答是「沒有感受，覺得上人並未離開」。

六、對下列各點之感想：

（一）對讚頌紀念法會講演辭的感想
填寫問卷者有五十一位表示對此項目感到滿意。其中有兩位指出講演辭「都是想說的話」。另有兩位指出「對師父認識更多」。

表示不滿意的有三位，他們認為講演辭是「客套話，不切實際，並建議：講內心話比讚頌更好。其中一位英國南傳比丘認為「少了一點什麼。演講者或許未能完全定下心來。

（二）對荼毗大典的感想
填寫問卷者有七十二位認為儀式安排得當，過程樸實不誇張，象徵上人的個性及力行實踐。一位客法師特別強調：「不可思議的事，我原本不會雙盤，在上人荼毗時，很容易的達成

5. What were your feelings upon hearing of the completion of stillness of the Venerable Master?

The majority (64) of those who answered this question said they were deeply grieved, shocked, or had lost their support, and that from now on "the proper path for asking about the Way is lost." One laywoman in the food and drink business sighed, "There is no hope left in life." Six people indicated that they should be more vigorous in upholding the Master's resolves, observing the Six Great Principles, and taking the precepts as their teacher, so that they will not fall short of the Master's teaching. Seven pray for the Master's early return in accordance with his vows. A seven-year-old boy, Chang Zhaoyi, said, "Now that the Master has entered the stillness, he can fly and become a Buddha."

One Chinese Sangha member answered with these few words, "The task being completed, he put it all down and departed." An Italian Theravada Bhikshu said, "Great peace." A British Dharma Master rejoiced that the Master could enter Nirvana, sharing the same feeling as a Taiwanese layperson who said, "This disciple feels happy for the Master, for he is now truly free and at ease."

Five people thought the Master was merely manifesting birth, old age, illness, death, and the impermanence of life. In their opinion, his spirit exists forever, and we should reflect on the Master's great pains to make this manifestation.

A disciple who studies science said, "When I learned that the Master had been ill for five or six years, and yet did not stop expounding the Dharma and propagating the Way, I felt unlimited reverence and admiration."

A chemist thought the Master's manifestation of stillness was "the Master's warning to us." She also felt the Master was "a great person who was constantly curing others' ailments and yet totally ignored himself when he too got sick."

A Christian said he "felt nothing because the Master has never left."

6. What are your impressions of:

A. Talks in Praise and Recognition of Our Teacher's Kindness
Fifty-one people indicated their satisfaction with this program. Two pointed out that all the talks were "words from the heart." Two others said that they "came to know more about the Master."

Three people expressed their dissatisfaction. They felt the talks were speeches of polite greetings and not practical. They further suggested that it is preferable to speak from the heart then speaking words of praise. A British Theravada Bhikshu felt the talks were "somewhat lacking: speakers perhaps not completely 'settled' in the situation."

B. Cremation Ceremony
Seventy-two thought that the ceremony was well arranged, and the process simple and not exaggerated, exemplifying the Master's character and practice. One visiting Dharma Master said emphatically that, "It's inconceivable. I could never sit in full lotus before, but at the Master's cremation I did it easily." The seven-year-old boy, Chang Zhaoyi, said that during the cremation, he "smelled a fragrance." One

。」七歲小弟弟張兆誼說，荼毗時，他「聞到一股香味。」另一位居士建議：「保留火葬設備。」

指出缺點的有四位，其中兩位認為，荼毗大典後期秩序稍亂。來自加拿大的黃果生感覺：「照相攝影的人太多。」

另有七位說，上人荼毗時，他們很難過甚至當場大哭。

（三）對撒骨灰的感想

荼毗大典次日，宣公上人的骨灰以熱氣球盛載升空，撒在萬佛聖城五觀齋堂前。答覆問卷者中，有七十三位認為儀式安排恰當，其中有四位認為，沒想到會用熱氣球升空的方法，很具創意。有兩位認為「這是空前的做法」，另有三位說他們「不敢看，因為很難過」。有一位信眾很遺憾上人的骨灰只撒在西方，沒有撒在亞洲。

有五位信眾認為「若能請回舍利供養，就更完美。」還有兩位信眾覺得這項儀式是上人對弟子示法，上人自己則是永遠不生不滅，得大自在。

（四）幻燈片介紹上人生平事蹟

五十八位信眾對幻燈片介紹表示滿意，其中有五位建議，若採用錄影帶介紹上人，效果當更理想。另有六位建議，將這套幻燈片製成記錄影片和書籍，以廣為流通。

（五）法會佛事

有六十九位信眾對上人荼毗大典各項法會佛事的安排表示滿意，其中一位甚至表示「非常莊嚴，好像在西方極樂世界。」

有兩位信眾特別喜歡《華嚴懺》，另一位信眾則對「三皈五戒」的印象最深。一位西方人士表示法會儀式很能治癒傷痛。

有四位人士表示有不圓滿之處，意見分列如下：
- 音響太大聲。
- 法會各項儀式安排太密集。但有一位人士則很滿意：「法會安排很密集，沒浪費時間。」
- 非專業攝影人員在佛殿前形成太多干擾。
- 佛殿不夠大。希望能蓋大一點的佛殿。

layperson suggested that the crematory be kept.

Four people pointed out areas for improvement. Two thought that the assembly order was a little disorganized after the cremation ceremony. Huang, Gwosheng from Canada felt that "there were too many photographers."

Seven people wrote that they felt very sad during the cremation and that they cried.

C. Scattering of ashes

The day after the cremation ceremony, the Master's ashes were lifted up into the air by a hot air balloon and scattered in the air in front of the Five Contemplations Dining Hall in the City. Seventy-two people thought the arrangement for the whole event was quite proper. Four people pointed out that they did not expect the use of a hot air balloon, which they thought was quite creative. Two indicated that "it was unprecedented." Another three people said they dared not watch because they were so sad. One Buddhist felt sorry that the Master's ashes were only scattered in the West and not in Asia.

There were five Buddhists who thought that if they could "bring some sharira back to worship, it would make it more perfect." Two people felt that this ceremony was a dharma manifested by the Master, while the Master himself is eternally neither existent nor nonexistent, and has attained great ease.

D. The Slide Show

Fifty-eight people expressed satisfaction with the show. Five suggested that if the introduction was done with video tape the effect would be more ideal. Six suggested that the slides be turned into documentary films and books for circulation.

E. Buddhist Ceremonies

Sixty-nine people felt the ceremonies were well arranged. One of them even indicated that they were "very adorned, as if we were in the Western Land of Ultimate Bliss."

Two people were especially fond of bowing the "Avatamsaka Repentance." Another person had a very deep impression of the transmission of three refuges and five precepts. A Westerner said, "I found the ceremonies very healing."

Four people indicated there were areas which needed improvement. Their opinions were as follows:
- The sound system was too loud, it was piercing to the ears.
- The schedule for the ceremonies was too tight causing people to run to and fro. (However, one person said she was happy that the schedule was tight so that not a bit of the time was wasted.)
- Too many interruptions from nonprofessional photographers in front of the Buddhahall.
- The Buddhahall was too small. "I hope we can build a larger hall someday."

七、這次經驗對您有何改變？

答覆這個問題的人士，計有五十九位。其中有三十三位指出「生死心更切，一切無常，更要加緊用功，依教奉行，遵行上人六大宗旨」。有十二位自認「對佛教有更深認識」，其中一位特別強調，這是她一生中，「第一次有機會誦《華嚴經》」（編按：上人示寂前，曾在遺言中交待弟子們要誦『華嚴經』，因此，上人示寂後，座下各道場均誦四十九天的《華嚴經》。一位女居士指出：「三天法會天氣酷熱如同說法：『三界火宅』，此生不修更待何時？」

另有五位指出，要好好護法，發菩提心，其中一位表示：「萬佛聖城必須加強建設成為美國最大佛教聖地，這任務是吾等弟子須全力以赴的。」

有八位善信認為「改變很大，以前執著的事也放得下。無論得到什麼，走的時候還是單獨一個」，「要學習這裡重視環保節儉，不浪費的做法。」

有兩位指出「要加強英文能力」。一位是來自臺灣的小兒科醫師，她參加了萬佛聖城的中英雙語早、晚課與法會佛事後，發現自己英語能力不夠，希望能買到英語錄製的佛經錄音帶，對英譯佛經也感興趣。（編按：宣公上人創辦的法界佛教總會出版了兩百餘本英譯佛經淺釋與上人開示，並有上人開示的中英雙語錄音帶。）另一位是出家人，她發願要學好英文，「才能在美國弘法，譯經、辦教育。」

八、一般感想

四十三位人士認為這次法會「非常圓滿，沒有任何不圓滿之處」，一位善信寫道：「第一次過了佛門禮佛、誦經的三天最好日子。」另一位六十五歲的老太太直捷了當地答覆：「我住得好，吃得好，希望有機會再來。」一位居士指出：「醫護中心很管用。天氣太熱，大會提供冷飲及濕紙巾，對在場的人幫助不少。」

7. Has this experience changed your life in any way?

Fifty-nine people answered this question. Thirty-nine of them pointed out that they regarded the matter of birth and death with increased urgency. Everything is impermanent; they feel they should work harder and practice in accordance with the teaching, following the Master's Six Principles. Twelve people gained a "better understanding of Buddhism." One of them said this was the "first opportunity she had to recite the *Avatamsaka Sutra* in her life." [Editor's note: Before the Master manifested stillness, he instructed disciples to recite the *Avatamsaka Sutra*. Thus after the Master entered stillness, all the branch monasteries recited the *Avatamsaka Sutra* for forty-nine days.] A laywoman indicated, "The scorching weather during the three-day Dharma session was speaking Dharma: 'The three realms are like burning house.' If one does not cultivate in this life when should one cultivate?"

Five people said that they wanted to do a good job in protecting the Dharma and bring forth the Bodhi mind. One of them said, "CTTB should be developed into the largest Buddhist holy ground in America. All of us disciples should dedicate ourselves to completing this task."

Eight people thought they had "changed their bad habits." For instance, "I had a bad temper before, but now I've improved." "I've made great changes. I'm able to put down prior attachments. No matter what one attains in life, one still leaves without anything when the time comes." "We must learn the thrifty lifestyle here, not be wasteful, and be more aware of environmental protection."

Two people said they wanted to "improve their English comprehension." After attending CTTB's morning and evening recitation as well as Buddhist ceremonies in two languages, a pediatrician from Taiwan found his English insufficient and hoped to bring back some English Sutra tapes. He was also interested in the translation of Buddhist Sutras into English. [Editor's note: Dharma Realm Buddhist Association founded by the Master has published over two hundred volumes of Buddhist Sutras with the Master's explanation in English. There are also tapes of the Master's instructional talks in Chinese and English translation.] One left-home person vowed to study English so that she could propagate the Dharma, translate the Sutras, and work on education in America.

8. General Impressions

Forty-three people thought the Dharma session was "perfect and there were no flaws whatsoever." One person wrote, "This is my first Buddhist experience of bowing and reciting, and these three days have been the best time of my life." A sixty-five-year-old woman said directly, "I slept well and ate well, and I hope to come back again." One layperson said, "The medical aid center functioned well. The wet towels and cold drinks provided by the responsible team helped many participants in the excessively hot weather."

中國佛教協會
THE BUDDHIST ASSOCIATION OF CHINA

Date:

宣化老和尚示寂赞颂委员会：

惊闻一代高僧宣化上人示寂，我会同人殊深哀悼。

宣化上人道尊德重，苦心创建万佛城，弘法利生，爱国爱教，毕生奉献，功垂千秋！

值此宣化上人追思大会及荼毗典礼之际，我会委托副会长明旸法师代表我会全体同人深表悼念，祝愿宣化上人暂归极乐安养，早日乘愿再来，广度一切有情。

中国佛教协会
公元一九九五年七月十九日

宣化老和尚示寂讚頌委員會：

驚聞一代高僧宣化上人示寂，我會同仁殊深哀悼。

宣化上人道尊德重，苦心創建萬佛城，弘法利生，愛國愛教，畢生奉獻，功垂千秋！

值此宣化上人追思大會及荼毗典禮之際，我會委託副會長明旸法師，代表我會全體同仁深表哀悼，祝願宣化上人暫歸極樂安養，早日乘願再來，廣度一切有情。

中國佛教協會
一九九五年七月十九日

To the Committee Honoring the Nirvana of the Venerable Master Hsuan Hua:

We were surprised and deeply grieved to learn of the manifestation of stillness by the contemporary high Sanghan, Venerable Master Hsuan Hua.

The Venerable Master Hua's virtue was lofty and exalted. He toiled to establish the Sagely City of Ten Thousand Buddhas. He propagated the Dharma to benefit living beings. He devoted his whole life to his nation and to Buddhism. His merit will be remembered for thousands of years.

Today is the Memorial and Cremation Ceremony for the Venerable Master Hua. We ask Dharma Master Mingyang to represent this Association in expressing our deep condolence. We wish that after a temporary rest in the Land of Ultimate Bliss, the Venerable Master will ride on his vows and come back soon to extensively rescue all sentient beings.

The Buddhist Association of China
July 19, 1995

萬佛城諸上善人：

　驚悉

宣化法師示寂，苦海舟沉，人天眼滅，曷勝痛悼！謹此致唁。伏祈諸上善人節哀順變，爲法珍重！

趙樸初

一九九五年六月十七日

To the superior ones at the Sagely City of Ten Thousand Buddhas

I was astonished to learn that Dharma Master Hsuan Hua manifested the stillness. It's as if the ship has sunk in the sea of suffering and the eyes of humans and gods have been put out. It is impossible to express my grief. I respectfully send my condolences. I hope you will restrain your grief and take care of yourselves for the sake of the Dharma.

Zhao Puchu
[Chairman of the Buddhist Association of China]
June 17, 1995

美國加州達摩鎮
萬佛城如來寺
恆律當家師等：

唁　電

　來電驚悉，老道兄上度下輪宣化長老於昨日下午三時圓寂，噩耗傳來，萬分悲痛。本堂今日正逢舉行法會之期，集合全體大眾念佛一天。下午二時，普佛一堂參加者一千餘人，祈願

法師花開見佛

，高登蓮位，佛國長春，倒駕慈航，乘願再來，廣度眾生。特此唁電，今撰輓聯壹副，因時間不及，先奉上輓聯稿（另紙電傳）

　宣化長老圓寂日期時間如有出入，請電傳以便更正

中國佛教協會副會長、上海市佛教協會名譽會長、上海龍華古寺、北京廣濟寺、寧波天童寺、福建西禪寺、莆田光孝寺、上海圓明講堂
方丈明暘率四眾弟子同頂敬輓

一九九五年六月九日

Telegram from the Yuanming Lecture Hall, Shanghai

To: Manager Dharma Master Heng Lyu and others
Tathagata Monastery
The City of Ten Thousand Buddhas
Talmage, California, USA

I was surprised to learn that my elder brother in the Way, the Elder Master To Lun Hsuan Hua, completed the stillness yesterday at three o'clock in the afternoon. When I learned this sad news, I was deeply grieved. Today we are holding a Dharma assembly and everyone is gathered to recite the Buddha's name for one day. At two o'clock in the afternoon we bowed to the Buddhas. Over one thousand people took part. We all wish that the Venerable Master will see the Buddha when the flower blooms and ascend to the lotus seat. But as he enjoys the eternal spring in the Buddhaland, we hope he will compassionately turn his boat around and come back again to vastly rescue living beings. I'm sending this telegram to express my condolence. I also wrote a mourning couplet today, but because there is not enough time, I am first sending a draft of it (on a separate telegram).

　If there is any error in the date or time of the Venerable Master's completion of stillness, please send us a telegram so that we can make the correction.

Ming Yang, leading the fourfold assembly of disciples, bows in respect
Vice-Chairman of the Buddhist Association of China
Honorary Director of the Buddhist Association of Shanghai
Abbot of: Longhua Ancient Monastery of Shanghai
　　　　　Guangji Monastery in Beijing
　　　　　Tiantong Monastery in Ningbo
　　　　　Xicang Monastery in Fujian Province
　　　　　Guangxiao Monastery in Putian, Fujian Province
　　　　　Yuanming Lecture Hall in the City of Shanghai

宣揚妙法　化度群生　人天眼目　濁世慧燈

Propagating the wonderful Dharma, he transformed and saved all lives.
He served as eyes for gods and people, as a light of wisdom in the turbid world.

慈航倒駕　苦海渡人　菩薩大願　世界和平

He compassionately turned back his boat to save people in the sea of suffering.
Peace in the world was the great vow of this Bodhisattva.

翻譯經典　廣集群英　法雨普潤　遺教長存

To translate the scriptures, he gathered all talents.
The Dharma rain moistened universally; his teachings will remain forever.

萬眾歸命　萬佛聖城　願垂救度　再轉法輪

The myriad beings seek refuge in the Sagely City of Ten Thousand Buddhas.
We hope he will bestow salvation and turn the Dharma-wheel again.

奉法界佛教總會佛經翻譯委員會來函痛悉
宣公上人圓寂謹綴俚辭藉誌哀思
後學妙首釋昌臻沐手敬書于中國四川樂至報國寺
一九九五年七月二十九日

Upon receiving the letter from the Buddhist Text Translation Society
of the Dharma Realm Buddhist Association, I learned with pain of the
Venerable Master Hsuan Hua's completion of stillness. With respect I
offer this poem to express my sadness and remembrance.

Written respectfully by Shi Changzhen of Baoguo Monastery, Lezhi
County, Sichuan Province, People's Republic of China. July 30, 1995.

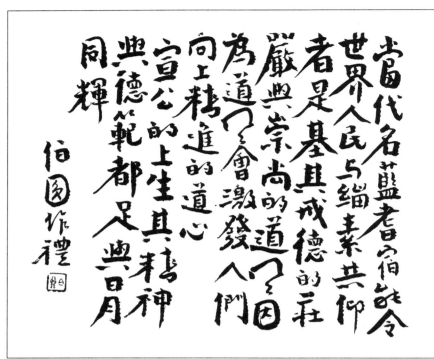

當代名藍耆宿，能令世界
人民與緇素共仰者，是基
其戒德的莊嚴與崇尚的道
行。因爲道行會激發人們
向上精進的道心。宣公的
上生其精神與德範，都足
與日月同輝。

伯圓作禮

This renowned elder of our time is looked up to by the people of the world, by monastics and the laity, because of his adornment in the virtue of precepts and his lofty conduct in the Way. His conduct in the Way inspires people to bring forth the resolve to advance with vigor towards the Way. Although the Venerable Hsuan has passed away, his spirit and his exemplary virtue make him equal to the sun and moon in brilliance.

Respectfully,
Bo Yuan

法界佛教總會國際譯經院同仁：

　　在法界佛教總會，宣公上人四十九天的喪期中，我深深地受到上人的弟子們的孝心所感動。

　　我也曾去過法總在加拿大溫哥華的分支道場，當時弟子們正在專心的誦《大方廣佛華嚴經》。在哪兒，我也觀察到上人的弟子們都很有紀律，及他們對上人的孝心。

馬來西亞檳城洪福寺主持釋文建
一九九五年九月二十六日

September 26, 1995

Dear Venerable Sirs,

During my stay in the Dharma Realm Buddhist Association, I really appreciated the filiality shown by the disciples towards the Venerable Master Hsuan Hua during the forty-nine days of mourning period.

I also visited Vancouver in Canada, Venerable Master Hsuan Hua's temple, where the disciples were seriously chanting the Flower Adornment Sutra. Over there, I also observed that the disciples were very disciplined and showed filiality to their Master.

Yours in Dharma,

Seck Boon Keng
Chief Abbot
Ang Hock See Buddhist Temple, Penang, Malaysia

宣公上人茶毗籌備會委員及諸四眾弟子們

本會已接到萬佛聖城主持宣公上人於農曆五月初十（佛曆二五三九年），公元一九九五年六月七日圓寂的消息。

在此謹代表駐美「越美佛教律學指導委員會」，及加州沙加美度「金光寺」四眾弟子，與諸仁者同爲已往生佛國的宣公上人祈禱。

南無大導師阿彌陀佛

Sacramento, June 21, 1995
Bhikshu Thich Thien Tri
Signed and Sealed

Vietnamese American Buddhist Congress
in the United States of America
The Vinaya Supervisory Commission
3119 Alta Arden Expressway,
Sacramento, CA 95825

The Chairman of the Vinaya Supervisory Commission
Director of the Directorate for Clerical Affairs
Vietnamese American Buddhist Congress in the U.S.A.
Abbot of the Kim Quang Temple
Sacramento, California

To

The Funeral Organization Committee,
Distinguished Disciples and Filial Family Members of
THE LATE VENERABLE HSUAN HUA
ABBOT OF THE SAGELY CITY OF TEN THOUSAND BUDDHAS

Distinguished Committee and Gentlemen:

We have been informed that the Great Elder Venerable Master Hsuan Hua, Abbot of the Sagely City of Ten Thousand Buddhas, has entered Nirvana on the Tenth Day of the Fifth Month of the lunar calendar, Buddhist calendar 2539, June 7, 1995.

On behalf of the Vinaya Supervisory Commission of the Vietnamese American Buddhist Congress in the U.S.A., and also representing the Sangha and the Laity of the Kim Quang Temple, Sacramento, California, we respectfully join with you, the Funeral Organization Committee, distinguished disciples and filial family members, in praying for the awesome entering into the Buddha Land of the Enlightened Spirit of the Most Venerable, Lord High Master Hsuan Hua.

Nam Mwo Great Guiding Master A Mi Two Fwo

Sacramento, June 21, 1995
Bhikshu Thich Thien Tri
Signed and Sealed

OFFICE OF THE GOVERNOR
State of California

July 11, 1995

TO: D.R. BUDDHIST ASSOCIATION IN AMERICA

I am sorry to know that the most venerable Dharma Master
Hsuan Hua has left this world, but given his profound spiritual
life, is now enjoying a greater and more permanent happiness.

He did many wonderful things in this world. He opened his
City of Ten Thousand Buddhas for refugees from Southeast Asia.
He gave flood relief and awarded scholarships to needy students.

He established an elementary and a secondary school as well
as a university. He established the International Translation
Institute, which translated more than 100 Buddhict texts and
sutras into English and other languages and has become the
translation center of Buddhist literature in the world.

People will forever remember his noble teaching on moral
principles and the world will show everlasting respect for his
spiritual life.

I am sure that the 27 Buddhist monasteries, temples and
spiritual centers established by him and the millions of
disciples and followers of this great holyman will continue his
spiritual work for the benefit of all mankind.

I extend my deepest sympathy and join you in prayers for
this great holyman.

Sincerely,

PETE WILSON

加州州長辦公室致佛教總會：

　　驚聞宣公上人圓寂，殊感哀悼之至。由於上人刻苦的修行，他現在正享受更廣大更恒久的快樂。
　　上人在世時，為善甚多：諸如開放萬佛聖城給東南亞難民居住、救助水患災民，及設立清貧學生獎學金等等。
　　上人還設立了小學、中學、大學。並創建了國譯經學院，將百餘部佛教經典譯成了英文和其他國家的語言，成為全球最大的佛教經典翻譯中心。
　　世人定會永遠記得上人的崇高教誨及道德典範。同時對他刻苦的修行表示永久的崇敬。
　　我更相信這位聖人所創建的二十七處道場的四眾弟子，和他的在世界各地的數百萬信眾，必定會繼續上人的事業，為人類做出更多的貢獻。
　　我謹獻上最誠摯的敬意，並與各位共同為這位偉大的聖人祈禱。

彼得・威爾孫　敬上
一九九五年七月十一日

　　　　　　　　　　　　　　　　　　　　　　宣化老和尚追思紀念專集

FRANK D. RIGGS
1st District, California

COMMITTEE ON
APPROPRIATIONS
SUBCOMMITTEES:
Agriculture, Rural Development and FDA
Energy and Water Development
Labor, HHS, and Education

COMMITTEE ON ECONOMIC AND
EDUCATIONAL OPPORTUNITIES
SUBCOMMITTEES:
Early Childhood, Youth and Families
Postsecondary Education, Training, and
Life-Long Learning

1714 Longworth Building
Washington, DC 20515
(202) 225-3311

DISTRICT OFFICES:

1700 2nd Street
Suite 378
Napa, CA 94559
(707) 254-7308

710 E Street
Suite 100
Eureka, CA 95501
(707) 441-8701

Congress of the United States
House of Representatives
Washington, DC 20515

June 20, 1995

Dr. John B. Tsu, President
Asian American Political Education Foundation

Dear Dr. Tsu:

Thank you for contacting my office to share news of the passing of Master Hsuan Hua.
I am honored by your request to serve on the Memorial Service Commitee, and I gladly lend
my name.

I understand the memorial service is scheduled for July 26th at the City of Ten Thousand
Buddhas in Talmage. I regret that my responsibilities in Washington will prevent me from
attending, but I have asked my field representative, Darrell Shull, to attend on my behalf and
present a short eulogy.

Again, I thank you for your thoughtfulness in contacting me. Please let me know if Cathy or
I may provide any additional assistance.

Sincerely Yours,

Frank Riggs
Member of Congress

祖教授：

感謝您告知我們關於宣化上人圓寂之消息。我感到很榮幸，能被邀為追思委員會的成員，而且我樂意被提名。

我知道追思大會將會在七月二十六日於萬佛聖城舉行。很遺憾的，因為我在華盛頓，有職責在身，使我無法參加此會。不過我會請 Darrell Shull 代表我去參加，並呈上一份簡短的頌詞。

再次的感激您的關切，通知我此事。假如您認為 Cathy 和我可以提供任何的支助，請您讓我知道。

美國眾議會議員法郎克·力各斯敬啟
一九九五年六月二十日

Congress of the United States
House of Representatives
Washington, D. C. 20515

Tom Lantos
California

July 3, 1995

The D.R. Buddhist Association
City of Ten Thousand Buddhas
Talmage, California, 95481-0217

Dear Members of the D.R. Buddhist Association:

My wife and I send you all our most sincere
condolences on the occasion of the loss of your
beloved leader, the Most Venerable Master Hsuan
Hua. His creative leadership, his deep wisdom,
and his caring for people has been a wonderful
influence on our community.

We are sure that the lives of many people and
communities have been better focused because
Master Hsuan Hua has lived among us.

Sincerely,

Tom Lantos

Tom Lantos
Member of Congress
TPL/abb

法界佛教總會會員法鑒：

在您們失去最敬愛之導師上宣下化老和尚的時刻，内人與我在此，向您們全體致至誠之哀悼。上人創造性的領導，深度的智慧，和對一切眾生的關切，賦予本社區不可思議的影響。

我們相信，許多人的生活和許多團體及社區，都已有更好的目標，因為上人曾經與我們生活在一起。

美國眾議會議員湯姆・藍多斯敬啓
一九九五年七月三日

The City of Burlingame

CITY HALL – 501 PRIMROSE ROAD
BURLINGAME, CALIFORNIA 94010

August 22, 1995

Committee Honoring the Nirvana of the
    Venerable Master Hsuan Hua
Dharma Realm Buddist Association
Sagely City of Ten Thousand Buddhas
2001 Talmage Road
Talmage, CA 95481-0217

Dear Reverent Disciples:

At its meeting of August 21, 1995, the Burlingame City Council observed a moment of silence and then adjourned its meeting in memory of the Venerable Master Hsuan Hua, founder of the Dharma Realm Buddhist Association.

Sincerely,

Judith A. Malfatti

Judith A. Malfatti
City Clerk

cc: Dharma Realm Buddhist Association
    1777 Murchison Drive
    Burlingame, CA 94011

法界佛教總會
上人四眾弟子道鑒：

在本年度八月二十一日的會議中，柏林根市議會在靜默片刻，並將會議暫延，以悼念法界佛教總會之創辦人上宣下化老和尚。

柏林根市議會書記
茉迪絲・瑪法蒂
一九九五年八月二十二日

**AMITA EDUCATION FOUNDATION
OF THE PHILS., INC.**

151 Kaliraya St., Quezon City (temporary office)
Tel. 731-3633; 732-2328; 732-0163; 712-2821; Fax 732-0171

June 27, 1995

The Abbot
The City of Ten Thousand Buddhas
2001 Talmage Road
Talmage, CA 95481-0217
U. S. A.

Dear Sir:

With sadness we learned of the "passing away" of Venerable Master Hsuan Hua.

In more ways than one, he was instrumental in the organization of AMITA EDUCATIONAL FOUNDATION OF THE PHILS., INC. He was our spiritual inspiration. We look up to him in our cultivation.

Venerable Master Hsuan Hua surely has gone to the other shore, but in our memories, he lives on.

Bows in respect,
AMITA EDUCATION FOUNDATION OF THE PHILS., INC.

CO YEK CHUAN
President

萬佛聖城執事：

我們深感哀傷地獲悉宣化上人圓寂的消息。他曾在各方面給予本組織以幫助。他是我們精神上的啟迪者，在修行上我們向上人看齊。

我們確信上人已經抵達彼岸，但他繼續活在我們的記憶中。

菲律賓阿彌陀教育基金會
會長 Co Yek Chuan
一九九五年六月二十七日

Ch'an
Meditation
Center

Institute of
Chung-Hwa
Buddhist Culture

90-56 Corona Avenue
Elmhurst, N.Y. 11373

(718) 592-6593
Fax: (718) 592-0717

July 21st 1995

The Committee Honoring The Nirvana of
    The Venerable Master Hsuan Hua
Sagely City of Ten Thousand Buddhas
2001 Talmage Road
Talmage, CA 95481-0217

Dear Committee Members,

We feel a great loss in the endeavor of spreading Buddhist Dharma in America with the Venerable
Master Hsuan Hua passed into the stillness on June 7, 1995.

We thank you for the notification you sent us in regards to the Dharma assembly to be held from July 26
through 28 in California in honor of the Venerable Master Hsuan Hua. Unfortunately we are unable to
participate in the assembly, and we are enclosing herewith our contribution of $200.00 in memory of the
Venerable Master Hsuan Hua. Please allocate our contribution in whatever category you see appropriate.

Once again, we would like to express the great loss we feel in the passing of the Venerable Master Hsuan
Hua. We hope all of the Venerable Master's disciples would now work even harder to spread his
teachings in the West, and the East, and Worldwide.

  In the Dharma,

Guo-gu Shi

Ven. Guo-gu Shi
Resident bhikshu
Program Coordinator

致宣公上人圓寂讚誦委員會
    我們感到上宣下化老和尚，於一九九五年六月七日
入滅，是在對美國致力弘揚佛法上的極大損失。
    感謝你們通知，將於七月二十六日至七月二十八日
在加州舉行對上人的追思大會。很遺憾的，我們無法
參加，在此附上兩百元以表對上人的追念。請隨所需
而使用此款。
    再次的，我們對上人的圓寂感到莫大的損失。我們
希望所有上人的弟子們，從現在起，更努力的在西方
、東方，乃至全世界弘揚上人的教誨。

中華佛教文化禪坐中心班主任
比丘釋果固（譯音）
一九九五年七月二十一日

INTERNATIONAL BUDDHIST INFORMATION BUREAU
OFFICIAL INFORMATION SERVICE
OF THE UNIFIED BUDDHIST CHURCH OF VIETNAM
25 rue Jaffeaux - 92230 Gennevilliers (France) •Tel.: Paris (1) 47 93 1081
Fax: Paris (1) 47 91 41 38

The Sagely City of Ten Thousand Buddhas
Dharma Realm Buddhist Association
Talmage, California. 95481-0217
United States of America.

Paris, July 22 1995

We are deeply grieved to learn that the Most Venerable Master TUYEN HOA entered Nirvana on June 7, 1995.

The Most Venerable Master made an inestimable contribution to the propagation of the Faith by making Lord Buddha's teaching accessible to the Western world. His merits are boundless, and his absence will be felt by Buddhists all over the world, regardless of their origins or nationality.

Yet, though the Most Venerable Master is departed, his teachings remain. They will continue to shine within each and every one of us as a guiding light.

On behalf of the International Buddhist Information Bureau in Paris, we present our most sincere condolences to you all, and pray that the spirit of the Most Venerable master TUYEN HOA will continue to guide us from the Pure Land, Sukhavati.

We have delegated Mr. Truong Phan, representative of the International Buddhist Information Bureau for California, to attend the funeral ceremonies on our behalf and pay our last respects.

法國越南聯合佛教會、國際佛教資訊局

　得悉宣公上人於一九九五年六月七日入涅槃，吾人深感痛惜。上人將佛陀的教誨帶給西方，在弘揚佛法上的供獻可以說功德無量。他在世上的消失對各國佛教界人士都是一個損失。

　雖然上人不在世上了，但他的教誨還留在世上。留在我們每一個人的心裡，像指路明燈一樣照亮亮著我們。

　我們代表巴黎國際佛教資訊局，在此表達我們至誠地哀悼，並希望上人在極樂世界的精神仍繼續指引我們。

　本局駐加州代表Phan先生將代表本會參加上人的讚頌示寂法會並表達我們的敬意。

Vo Van Ai
Director

國際資訊局主任　武文愛
一九九五年七月二十二日於巴黎

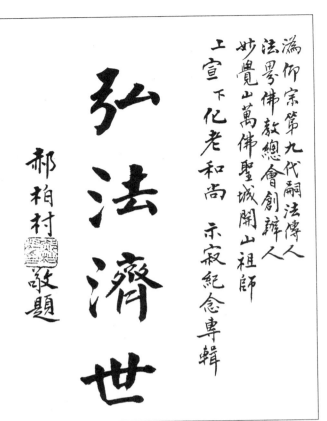

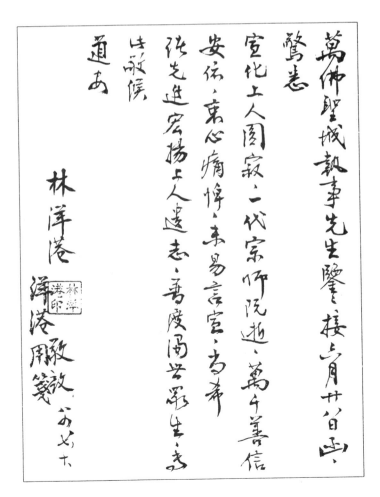

For the memorial book in memory of the manifestation of stillness by the Venerable Hsuan, Noble Hua, the Dharma-heir of the ninth generation of the Wei Yang Sect, the founder of Dharma Realm Buddhist Association, and the founder of the Sagely City of Ten Thousand Buddhas at Wonderful Enlightenment Mountain

He propagated the Dharma to save the world.

Respectfully written by Hao Bocun

To the Managers of the City of Ten Thousand Buddhas:

I received your letter dated June 28. I was shocked to hear that the Venerable Master Hua had entered Nirvana. The religious teacher of a generation has left the world.

Ten million faithful disciples have lost their place of reliance. My heart is deeply pained. It is difficult to express my feelings. I hope that you will carry on the Venerable Master's will and universally rescue all living beings in this turbid world.

With this note I convey my deepest respects. Peace in the Way.

Respectfully,
Lin Yanggang
July 10, 1995

Telegram of Condolence

To the Memorial Committee in Honor of the Venerable Master Hsuan Hua and the fourfold assembly of disciples of the Sagely City of Ten Thousand Buddhas and affiliated monasteries of the Dharma Realm Buddhist Association:

The Venerable Master Hua propagated the Way and transmitted the Dharma. His vows were profound. Now that he has manifested the stillness, we all recollect him in mourning. This telegram is to express our condolence.

Wu Boxiong
July 25, the eighty-fourth year of the Republic of China (1995)

總　統　府　用　牋

唁　電

宣化老和尚示寂讚頌委員會請轉法界佛教總會萬佛聖城暨各分支道場四眾弟子均鑒：宣公上人弘道傳法，願力精深，安詳示寂，毋任悼念，特電致弔。吳伯雄中華民國八十四年七月二十五日

（專供公務使用）

發電號 B 字84224 號
8分・7月25日10時20分
承辦者

萬佛聖城祕書處：

驚聞宣化上人大師圓寂，不勝悲痛，謹致沉痛哀悼。大師的不幸圓寂，是佛教界的重大損失。我們定努力弘揚佛法，勤奮工作，報答大師對汶上寶相寺恢復籌建盛舉的關懷與支持，盡早實現大師之遺願。將汶上寶相寺盡快修竣，使佛教聖物早入蓮座。宣化上人大師功德無量。至誠祈禱，惟願神遊蓮邦，面禮彌陀。

中國山東省汶上寶相寺籌建委員會
中國山東省汶上縣僑務辦公室
中國山東省汶上佛協籌委會
一九九三年六月十二日

The Office of the Sagely City of Ten Thousand Buddhas:

We are shocked and saddened to learn that Venerable Great Master Hua has completed the stillness. We are deeply grieved and in painful mourning. The Great Master's completion of stillness is a tremendous loss to Buddhism. We resolve to diligently propagate the Buddhadharma and work energetically to requite the Great Master's concern and support for the renovation of Baoxiang Monastery of Wenshang County and to realize the Great Master's wishes as early as possible. The renovation of Baoxiang Monastery of Wenshang county will be completed as soon as possible so that the holy relics of Buddhism can be placed on their altars. The Venerable Great Master Hua's meritorious virtues will be boundless. We sincerely pray and hope that his spirit is in the Lotus Land, paying homage to Amitabha Buddha.

Committee for the Renovation of Baoxiang Monastery
　in Wenshang County, Shandong Province, China
Overseas Affairs Office of Wenshang County, Shandong Province, China
Buddhist Fundraising Committee of Wenshang County,
　Shandong Province, China
June 12, 1995

驚聞噩音：

　　上宣下化上人圓寂，痛失依怙。
　　上人乃當代宗師，海內外共尊大德
，一生行頭陀行，戒定慧三學齊修。
今雖化緣已畢，回入常寂光土，弟子
受恩未報，涕泣悲哀！應轉悲痛為精
進，依教奉行，用報四恩。

　　　　中華人民共和國江蘇省鎮江市
　　　　弟子　果原　智參頂禮

To the Memorial Committee for the Venerable Master Hua

I was shocked to hear the sad news:
　　The Venerable Master Hua has completed the stillness, and we have painfully lost our place of reliance. The Venerable Master was a contemporary great master, and people in China and abroad respected him as one of great virtue. Throughout his life he practiced asceticism and cultivated the three studies of precepts, samadhi, and wisdom together. Although his affinities in teaching are finished and he has returned to the Land of Eternal Stillness and Light, as his disciples we have not repaid his kindness, so we are weeping in sadness. We should transform our sadness and pain into vigor and practice in accord with his teaching, using that to repay the four types of kindness.

Disciple Guo Yuan, Zhi Can bows in respect
Jenjiang, Jiangsu Province, The People's Republic of China

祖教授：您好

　　公務外出返濟後，驚悉上人圓寂，悲
痛萬分，遲致唁函，以表對上人無限哀
思。
　　九三、九四兩年，有緣在七月五日同
日兩度拜見上人，親耳聆聽上人開示，
受益終生。去年上人拖病體熱情接待我
們，並以巨資無償捐贈濟寧大學，使我
們無法以言語表達對上人的感激之情。
　　雖與上人接觸時間短暫，但我深深感
到上人是一位「保持國籍溯本源」的愛
國高僧。他注重教育，熱愛和平，濟世
救民，無私無畏的崇高境界和處世風範
，將永遠銘記在心，為我學習之楷模。
「慈悲喜捨度眾生，一塵不立淨自他；
隨緣履踐證菩提，求得證果亦弘法。」
　　寥寥數語，難表心情，拜託轉達對上
人的深深祈禱。

　　　　　　山東濟寧市政府及
　　　　　　濟寧大學代表
　　　　　　李衛國
　　　　　　一九九五年六月十五日

Professor Tsu:

How are you? After I returned to Jining from a business trip, I was shocked to learn of the Venerable Master's completion of stillness. I am deeply grieved, and I send this telegram to offer my condolences and to express my profound memories of the Venerable Master.
　　On July 5 of both 1993 and 1994, I had the opportunity to visit the Venerable Master and personally listen to his instructions, which will benefit me for the rest of my life. Even last year when he was sick, he still received us warmly and gave financial aid to this university. There are no words to express our gratitude to him. Although my contact with the Venerable Master was brief, I deeply feel that he was a patriotic Sangha member who "kept his nationality and traced his roots back to their source." He paid attention to education and was devoted to peace, rescuing the world and its people. We will always remember his state of egolessness and fearlessness and his model of handling affairs, and we will always learn from this model.

He crossed over living beings with kindness, compassion, joy,
　　and renunciation.
He cleared away the distinctions between self and others
　　until not a speck of dust was left.
Practicing in accord with conditions, he certified to Bodhi.
After attaining the proper fruition, he also propagated the Dharma.

These few words can hardly express my feelings. Please convey my deepest prayers for the Venerable Master.

Li Weiguo
Representative of Jining College and
Jining Municipal Government of Shandong Province
June 15, 1995

July 12, 1995

Dear Committee Members:

It was with great sorrow that my husband and I learned of the death of the Venerable Abbot. Our family grieves with you and shares your loss. The Venerable Abbot was, and will continue to be, a guide to so many people in their spiritual life and surely an inspiration to people around the world. On a more personal note, he was the mentor for our son, Dharma Master Heng Sure, and we are proud that we can call him our friend.

Since the early days of the group at Gold Mountain Monastery, the Venerable Abbot has been the leader of Heng Sure and the other young people who gathered around him for his wisdom and guidance. With his leadership, the organization has grown in influence and stature. We remember the excitement of finding the facilities that became the Sagely City of Ten Thousand Buddhas and other widely scattered temples that now are part of the Dharma Realm. With each new monastery came a new group of these followers to uphold the standards the Abbot has set.

We remember the Venerable Abbot as a kind, gentle man who never let sentiment stand in the way of teaching a lesson. My husband and I were very concerned when Heng Sure and Heng Ch'au set out on the Three Steps One Bow pilgrimage. Later, when we met the Abbot, we felt his deep compassion and knew that he and the Dharma had protected the monks on their journey.

Even though our meetings were few, we will miss the Venerable Abbot. His presence was always felt, and we are sure it will continue to be. You have been fortunate to have had such a remarkable person in your lives.

Sincerely,

Theodore O. & Deborah C. Metcalf

Theodore O. & Deborah C. Metcalf

委員會同仁們：

得悉上人圓寂之事，我和我先生皆感悲愴。我們一家也與你們同感失落。上人曾經是，也將是許多人精神生活上的領導者。以及必然是世上人類的啟迪者。就我個人而言，上人是我的兒子恆實師的一位輔導者。而且我們深感榮幸，可以稱呼他為一個朋友。

在早期的金山寺，上人一直是恆實師及其他年輕人的領導者。他們因上人的智慧和指導而跟隨在上人身邊。在上人的領導下，這個機構的影響力及發展，慢慢成長茁壯。我們還記得在物色現今的萬佛聖城及其他分佈各處的法總分支道場時，令人興奮的事。每一個新的道場，都有一群新的佛教徒渴望去聆聽上人的法音。現在也正是這些追隨者的責任，去護持上人所立下的準則。

我們記得上人是一位慈藹溫和的君子。他教導人時從不感情用事。在恆實師和恆朝師開始三步一拜時，我先生和我都非常地擔心。後來見到上人時，我們感受到他至深的慈悲。並且認知到上人與上人的法保護著旅途中的兩位比丘。

雖然我們與上人的接觸不多，我們也會懷念上人。過去我們覺得他在身邊，我們也確信這種感覺將會延續下去。你們一直是如此的幸運，在你們的生命中有著這樣一位不尋常的人物。

迪爾多‧麥克夫
黛柏拉‧麥克夫　敬上
一九九五年七月十二日

The International Translation Institute/
Buddhist Text Translation Society

To whom it may concern,

In response to your request, I am writing to relate our experiences with
the late departed Venerable Master Hsuan Hua. In 1973 I was enrolled
in Dr. Ronald Epstein's class in Buddhism at San Francisco State University. That September, at a seminar he hosted, my wife and I viewed
the Master for the first time. When the meeting ended, we got up from
our seats and stood in the aisle. At that moment we saw the Master
rushing up towards us, an enormous smile on his face. We were overwhelmed and turned and ran from the room.

We felt terrified, amazed; never had someone looked through us like
that. I had felt absolutely naked with my every fault exposed. And from
that moment on everything changed. We both agreed that this man displayed awesome powers and must certainly represent the true dharma.
We started investigating Chan and Pure Land Buddhism. Several
months afterwards we experienced insights that were sudden and profound.

During the winter session in 1981-82 at Wan Fwo Chan, we took
refuge with the Master before the Dharma Assembly in the 10,000 Buddhas Hall. As an artist, I was moved to begin painting a portrait of the
Master in seated meditation, against the backdrop of a view of the bay
area from on high, looking at the sun rise over the Berkeley Hills. It
was to represent the true dharma arising in the west.

For some reason it was never completed. The years went by, and even
though we constantly cultivated mindfulness and followed the dharma,
I couldn't bring myself to finish it. Several weeks ago while in my art
studio, I was suddenly compelled to bow three times before the picture
and heard myself take a vow to complete the picture once and for all.
This seemed a strange occurrence, and I mentioned it to my wife. One
week later we received your newsletter and learned for the first time
that the Master had died. This, combined with the incident I just mentioned, caused me immense sorrow as well as astonishment. We immediately made plans and went up to Wan Fwo Chan to bow and pay our
respects the following Saturday. Afterwards we felt as though a great
wave of energy had passed over and through us.

Yours in the Dharma,

Thomas Preble
Roberta Heidt
209 Lincoln Way #7
San Francisco, CA 94122
Phone: 415-665-3859

國際譯經學院

在你的要求下我作此回覆。講述我與近
日往生之宣化上人的經歷。在一九七三年
我選修了易果容博士在舊金山州立大學所
開的佛學課程。同年九月,在他所舉辦的
一個講習會上,我與內人初次遇見宣化上
人。於講習會結束時,我們起身離座,站
在走道上。在那時,我們看到上人面帶笑
容,急步的走向我們。我們因受寵若驚而
轉身跑出房間。

我們感到驚嚇且訝異,從未有人如此看
透我們。我覺得我的缺點完全赤裸裸的暴
露著。從那時起,一切都改變了。我們都
同意此人有股令人敬畏的力量,並且一定
是代表著正法。我們開始參禪與研究淨土
法門。幾個月之後,我們有了頓悟與深刻
的見識經驗。

在一九八二至一九八三年萬佛城的冬季
禪七,我們在萬佛殿的法會中皈依了上人
。身為一位藝術家,我因為受感動而開始
畫上人的禪坐畫像。其背景是三藩市海灣
的鳥瞰及旭日東昇的柏克萊山坡。這正代
表著佛法在西方升起。

基於某種原因,這畫並沒有完成。幾年
消逝過去了,雖然我們繼續不斷地修行正
念和遵循著佛法,我仍然無法完成這一幅
畫。幾個星期前,在我的畫室,我突然強
迫在畫前拜了三拜,並且聽到我自己發了
一個願,要一次完成這幅畫像。我告訴了
內人,這樁聽起來很奇怪的事件。一周後
我們收到一份通訊乍聞上人已圓寂。這消
息和前面所提到的事件使我極之哀傷與驚
訝。我們立刻計劃在下一個星期六去萬佛
城瞻仰上人。過後,我們覺得彷彿有一股
精力傳送到我們身上。

湯馬士・柏內伯
蘿柏塔・海特

萬佛聖城法界佛教總會

　　驚聞戒和尚宣公上人圓寂，
弟子莫不深感哀慟。
　　當此人心惶惶，動盪失序之
際，明燈闇然，痛失良師，弟
子之哀痛難以言喻。
　　謹電致上最深切至痛之慰問
，敬頌素安。

　　馬來西亞戒弟子
　　　　傳融　傳本　叩上
　　一九九五年六月十六日

Keow Hiang Lim Temple
No. 503 Hill Railway Road
11500 Penang, Malaysia
June 16, 1995

To Dharma Realm Buddhist Association, the Sagely City of Ten Thousand Buddhas:

　We were shocked to hear that our Upadhyaya (Precept Master), Venerable Master Hua, has completed the stillness, and we are deeply saddened.
　During this time when people are lost and unsettled, a bright light has gone out and we have lost our good teacher. There are no words to express our pain and sorrow.
　We respectfully send our deepest condolences and hope that everything is well.

Bowing in respect,
Disciples in precepts
Chwan Rong and Chwan Ben

宣化上人治喪委員會

驚聞靈訊：
　　宣化老法師圓寂，我們非常悲哀，痛
失大德，老法師道德戒行，馳名中外，
弘法美洲，功德威威。
　　願各位老法師，化悲痛爲力量，凝結
一心，建立完整寺廟，繼承遺願、弘揚
佛法、護持道場。

　　　鎮江市機械設備進出口公司
　　　　　　總經理　李鎮環

Committee in Memory of the Venerable Master Hua

I was shocked to hear the sad news:
　The Elder Dharma Master Hua's completion of stillness has left us in extreme grief. We are pained to lose such a Greatly Virtuous One. The Elder Dharma Master was renowned in China and abroad for his virtue and observance of precepts. The merit and virtue of his propagation of Dharma in America is truly monumental.
　I hope all of you Dharma Masters will transform your pain and sorrow into strength and unite singlemindedly to establish monasteries, carry on the Elder Dharma Master's resolves, propagate the Buddhadharma, and protect the Way-place.

Li Suohuan
General Manager, Jenjiang Export Company

祕書處法師慈鑒：
　　吾師宣公上人，昔年由港赴美，弘傳
佛教。在加州締造萬佛聖城，轉大法輪
，高樹法幢，開美國佛教之先河，功德
殊偉。
　　弟子等也遠蒙誨。突聞吾師已圓寂，
靈耗傳來，不勝哀痛！因未能奔喪，謹
在此長跪奉送，以表寸心。

　　　弟子侯果旭（明）
　　　　吳果園（世香）
　　　　林果河（錦河）　同頂禮
　　　一九九五年六月十三日

Correspondence Secretary/Dharma Master:

Our teacher, the Venerable Master Hua, left Hong Kong and went to America to propagate Buddhism many years ago. He established the Sagely City of Ten Thousand Buddhas in California, turned the great Dharma wheel, raised the Dharma banner on high, and opened the frontiers of American Buddhism, thus earning monumental merit.

We disciples also received his teaching from afar. When we heard the bad news that our teacher had already completed the stillness, we felt the utmost grief! Because we are unable to attend the funeral, we hereby kneel and respectfully send this letter as a token of our feelings.

Disciples Hou Guoxu (Ming), Wu Guoyuan (Shixiang), Lin Guohe (Jinhe)
bow together in respect
June 13, 1995

萬佛聖城禮鑒：

幹過去當周宣德居士及朱世龍在世時，曾由兩居士之介晉謁宣公大師數次，多承獎勵。其後當瑜伽市萬佛聖城完工後，亦曾偕內子及小女及女婿同到聖城禮佛。今年宣公生日曾經楊富森教授通知，云宣公可能來到此間長提接受慶壽。正準備前往，後因宣公健康不佳，未能受十方頂禮至用敬然。今由楊教授轉到訃聞，不勝悲感。謹具輓聯一紙，送陳左右，以誌敬仰。專此敬頌

法界前途無量

信士

勞幹謹致

一九九五年七月十五日

又上人遺囑將骨灰灑到虛空，此係上人謙遜節儉之意，是否可體諒十方信男信女之情，照一般人例將骨灰下葬，不建寺塔。比灑在空中，需要飛機者更為節省，未審可供考慮否？

宣公大師圓寂
On the completion of stillness of the Great Master Hua

令名溯遼海之濱　當茲弘法維艱　何處更聞獅子吼
濟世以修持為本　舉目橫流失序　追思遙寄鷲峰雲

We can trace his name back to the shores of the Sea of Liao.
In this time when it is so difficult to propagate the Dharma,
Where can we hear the Lion's Roar again?
To save the world, one must have cultivation as a basis.
Gazing at the chaos and disorder all around,
I send my recollections far away to Vulture Peak in the clouds.

To the Sagely City of Ten Thousand Buddhas:

When Upasakas Zhou Xuande and Zhu Shilung were alive, through their introduction I met the Great Master Hua several times and received much praise and encouragement from him. After the Sagely City of Ten Thousand Buddhas was completed in Ukiah, I went with my wife, daughter, and son-in-law to worship the Buddhas there. This year Professor Yang Fusen notified me of the Venerable Master's birthday celebration and said the Master might come to Long Beach to attend the celebration. I was planning to go. But the Venerable Master, for reasons of poor health, was unable to receive the worship of the guests from all directions. When I received the obituary from Professor Yang, my grief knew no bounds. I have sent a couplet in mourning to express my respect.

May the Dharma Realm have a limitless future.

Respectfully,
Lao Gan
July 15, 1995

Further, the Venerable Master instructed that his ashes be scattered in empty space out of a wish to be modest and frugal. However, I wonder if you could take the feelings of the faithful laity in the ten directions into consideration, and bury the Master's ashes according to ordinary custom, without building a temple or pagoda. That would be more economical than scattering the ashes in space, which would require a plane. Please consider this suggestion.

勞幹敬輓
In respectful mourning,
Lao Gan

仁心仁術，慈悲普度，攝導有緣歸覺海
善教善化，法雨均霑，接引無情入聖流

With humane hearts and humane practices,
Universally save all with kindness and compassion,
Guiding those with affinities to return to the sea of enlightenment.
With skillful teaching and skillful transformation,
Equally moisten all with the Dharma rain,
Leading those without sentience to enter the flow of sagehood.

五大宗教互容互融

THE FIVE GREAT RELIGIONS PENETRATE AND FUSE WITH ONE ANOTHER

宣公上人一九九二年二月二十二日對漢堡大學學生開示於萬佛聖城
The Venerable Master's talk to students of Humboldt State University
The Sagely City of Ten Thousand Buddhas, February 22, 1992

首先我要對大家說 happy new year，身體健康，精神愉快。從今天開始做一個新人，以前那個舊的習氣毛病，都把它留到去年，不要帶到新年來，不要帶到今年來。所以我們今年要做一個新人，有新的生命，有新的朋友，有新的生活，一切一切都要維新改良，所以說新年快樂！

各位善知識，各位不同宗教的善知識，各位不同國籍的善知識，各位不同年齡的善知識，這裡邊就包括各位兄弟姊妹，一切的青年、有為的朋友們，我們大家雖然國籍不同，種族不同，所信的宗教不同；可是我們都是人，那麼各有各的思想，各有各的信仰，也是都各有所長，各有所短。天主教有天主教的長處，也有它的短處；耶穌教也有它的長處，有它的短處；回教也有它的長處，有它的短處；孔教也有它的長處，有它的短處；佛教也有它的長處，有它的短處。長處是什麼？短處是什麼？這你去研究研究，都有的。

那麼孔、老、佛、耶、回這五大宗教，總起來說，就像五味似的。這五味有酸甜苦辣鹹，苦的雖然是很苦的，也有人願意吃。譬如佛教就很苦的，它講修苦行，講佛雪山打坐，六年只吃一麻一麥，那麼苦！可是也有人想要效法的。那麼有甜的，甜的這個宗教，就是對你有什麼利益，有什麼好處，所以也有人願意吃。不單願意吃，還很普遍的，很多人願意吃甜的，不願意吃苦的。酸的本來是不容易吃的，也有人歡喜吃酸的。辣的，那麼很辣的，可是也有人願意吃的，好像回教，我並不是毀謗回教，這回教講穆罕默德，穆罕默德一個手拿著香，一個手拿著槍，遇到善的他就燒香，遇到惡的他就放槍，那麼這個就比方是辣的。酸、甜、苦、辣、鹹，鹹的這個味道也不能吃多，你若吃多就會生病了，但是少少的，它是調味的，也有人願意吃的。

First I would like to wish all of you "Happy New Year," and I hope you are all healthy and in good spirits. I hope you all resolve to become new people starting from today and that you will leave all of your old bad habits behind with last year, and keep them from following you into the new year. This year we want to become new people. We want to renew our lives, find new friends, and renovate our lifestyle. In every way, we want to improve ourselves, and that's why I say, "Happy New Year to you all!"

I want to greet all Good and Wise Advisors of different religions, of different nationalities, of different ages. And this greeting includes all brothers and sisters, big and small, and all you talented young friends with bright futures. Although we all come from different nationalities, races, and religious faiths, yet we are people, all the same. We all have our differing thoughts, beliefs, strong points, and shortcomings. Catholicism has its strengths and weaknesses; Protestantism, Islam, Confucianism, and Buddhism all have their strengths and weaknesses. What are their strengths? What are their weaknesses? If you look into them, you will find each religion has both strengths and weaknesses.

The world's five great religions—Confucianism, Taoism, Buddhism, Christianity, and Islam—are just like the five flavors of food: sour, sweet, bitter, hot, and salty. Although bitter is bitter, some people still prefer its flavor. For example, Buddhism is very bitter, that is to say, it promotes ascetic practices. When the Buddha was meditating in the Himalayas, he ate only one sesame seed and one grain of wheat each day for six years. That's how tough his practices were, and yet there are people who are willing to try it out. There are other religions that advocate sweetness; they tell you what benefits will come to you, and what advantages you'll get by believing in it. Some people like to taste this flavor. In fact, it is very popular. Many people like sweet stuff and don't like bitterness. Although food of sour taste is basically not easy to eat, some people like sour food. Still others like to eat spicy food, no matter how hot it is. Take Islamic people, for instance. Now, don't get me wrong, I'm not slandering the Muslims. Islam talks about how Mohammed holds incense in one hand and a gun in the other. If he meets a good person, he burns incense for him. If he meets a bad person, he fires his gun. This is an analogy for hot, spicy food. You should

所以，這五大宗教我把它比成這個五味。這五味它的這個味，有好的，有不好的；不好的味道，就那麼辣的，也有人願意吃，那麼苦的也有人願意吃。我們人都是人，所以這五味有的人願意吃酸、甜、苦、辣、鹹，各有所好，所以說有長有短。在我的立場，認為這個味道是很好的，在另外的人立場呢，就說不好。宗教也是這個樣子，你再好的宗教，也有人毀謗；再不好的宗教，它也有人信仰，也有人讚歎。我這個很愚癡的見解是這樣子，所以我們誰信什麼宗教，是各有所好。

我記得臺灣這個樞機主教——于斌樞機，有一次他到金山寺來，也正趕上大約是六月十九觀音誕的時候，有一百五十多人參加一個宴會，來給他送行。我藉著這個宴會，對一百五十個佛教徒講，我說佛教是個古老的宗教，那麼有幾千年的歷史了，你們這些人信仰佛教，信仰這古老宗教，覺得不時髦了，不合乎潮代了，你們願意改變信其他宗教，現在是好機會，于樞機在這兒，你們隨時可以報名申請入教，改變你的信仰，這是我特別歡迎你們。說完了，我問大家有願意改變宗教的沒有？大家都說願意信這古老宗教。我問于樞機，我說：「于樞機，你敢不敢對你的信徒這樣講話？啊！他晃頭，他說：「我不敢講。」我說：「你還是有自私心哪！」他點點頭。這個不是他有自私，也不是我沒有自私，他有限制的，他上邊又有這個教皇，如果他這樣一說話，這個樞機就被免職了。所以講來講去，還是他歡喜他樞機這個王位，所以他不敢那麼樣講，所以佛教裡頭沒有教皇，無拘無束，沒有人來管，所以我隨便可以講講風涼話，所以我這言論自由。

佛教和耶穌教、天主教，孔老佛耶回這五大宗教，這也就像世界有這五行似的，金木水火土，各有所屬，互不相礙的，它是光光相攝，互容互融的。沒有你碰我，我就發了脾氣了；我碰你，你就不高興了，好像金木水火土，它是互相幫助的，也是互相障礙的。這互相幫助，就是各有所長；互相障礙，這就是各有所短了。宗教裡頭都有一些個黑暗，都有一些個不光明的事情，這是它的短處；也都有一些個長處，是它做事光明磊落。

我喜歡佛教就因為它是平等的，和人人都平等，上至佛菩薩、神，下至鬼，它是十法界都平等

eat salty foods in moderation, because too much sodium can make you sick. It can be used in small amounts to season food. Some people also like this flavor.

I use the five flavors as an analogy for the five religions. Although some of these flavors seem less palatable than others, such as hot and bitter, there are people who like these flavors best. So every religion has its strong points and its shortcomings, and people have their own likes and dislikes among the flavors of sour, sweet, bitter, hot, and salty. From my point of view, I feel this flavor is best. From your point of view, that flavor is unacceptable. Religions are just the same. The best of religions will still have people who criticize it, and the worst of religions will still have people who praise it and believe in it. This is my stupid opinion: People should follow the religion they prefer.

I recall the Catholic Cardinal from Taiwan, Paul Cardinal Yubin, who visited Gold Mountain Monastery on June 19, 1976, which was Guanyin Bodhisattva's birthday. There were over 150 people gathered to give him a farewell party. I said to the 150 people there, "Buddhism is an old-fashioned religion, with a history that is several thousands of years old. If you people who believe in Buddhism feel that it is too old-fashioned and not sufficiently up to date, and if you want to profess a different faith, you have an excellent opportunity before you. We have Cardinal Yubin among us today, and you can apply to transfer your belief and become a Catholic any time you like. I encourage any one of you to do so." Having said that, I asked whether there was anyone who wanted to change his religious belief. It seems they all wanted to stick with their old-fashioned faith. I turned to Cardinal Yubin and asked him whether or not he dared make the same statement to his followers. He shook his head and said, "No, I don't dare to say that." I said, "Well, then you still have a bit of selfishness left." And he nodded. My point was not to say that he was a selfish person, and I wasn't, but to point out that his hands were tied. He had the Pope's supervision above him, and if he made such a statement, he could have been fired from his job. When you get right down to it, he was still fond of his "royal" position as Cardinal. And that is why he didn't dare to make such an offer. There is no Pope in Buddhism, and no one controls anyone else or supervises anyone, so I enjoy freedom of speech; I can say what I please.

I could also compare the five great religions—Confucianism, Taoism, Buddhism, Christianity, and Islam—to the Five Elements that we find in the world: metal, wood, water, fire, and earth. Everything belongs to one or the other of them, and each element gets along in harmony, without obstructing the others. They cooperate smoothly, and penetrate and fuse with each other. The Five Elements work so that none of them ever says, "You bumped into me, and made me angry!" Metal, wood, water, fire, and earth help each other out and also hinder each other. When they help each other out, they all have their strong points. When they hinder each other, they each have their shortcomings. All religions have their shadowy aspects, which are their weaknesses. They also have their strengths, which are bright and out in the open.

Personally, I like Buddhism because it regards everyone as being equal. From the Buddhas, Bodhisattvas, and gods above down to

。十法界有佛法界、菩薩法界、聲聞法界、緣覺法界，這四聖法界，又有天法界，有人法界，有阿修羅法界，有餓鬼法界，有地獄法界，有畜生法界，各有它的界限。那麼彼此若明白了，這人都在十法界裡頭，都在這個大圓鏡智裡頭，你有多少智慧，你就是那一法界，屬於那一法界的。你有佛的智慧，就是佛；有菩薩的智慧，就是菩薩；有聲聞法界的智慧，就是聲聞；有緣覺法界的智慧，就是緣覺。看你這個智慧如何，你有智慧大的，那就是一個真正的覺悟者。真正覺悟者，那就和佛平等；你若沒有智慧，愚癡，那就和眾生平等，和眾生去劃成一個界限。

所以在佛教裡頭說：「是男子皆是我父，是女子皆是我母。」你若不明白道理的，說：「這是怎麼搞的？怎麼男子都變成你父親，女子變成你母親了？究竟哪個是你父親，哪個是你母親？」這是說，是男子前生或者都做過我父親，是女子或者前生都做過我母親，或者生生世世都做我的父母；不過這一投胎了，一改頭換面了，就大家互不認識了。它這個教義是廣的，不是那個狹義有限度的，它沒有限度，是無量無邊，平等自在的。這種的教義是小也可以說最小，大也可以說最大，它是無古無今無上下，極廣大盡精微。你可以說佛教是個小螞蟻、小蚊蟲那麼小，也可以說它是最大的，無量無邊那麼大。

那麼各宗教的聖人最初立教的宗旨，都是願意人好，他不會願意人互相毀謗的，你說我不好，我說你不好，這麼互相毀謗，他沒有這個思想。那麼後人就不懂的這個教義，不懂得聖人這個心、立教的宗旨，所以就演成爾為爾，我為我，互相攻擊，你攻擊我，我就攻擊你。若按著佛教的教義，我攻擊你，就等於我攻擊我爸爸一樣；你若攻擊我，就等於你攻擊媽媽一樣，這互相不應該的。所以我方才說，各有所長，各有所短，若都把這個短去了，保留這個長，這就是各宗教真正明白教義的教徒了，也真是創教教主的一個真正信徒了。耶穌教為什麼這麼普遍？就因為它的教徒講的道理也講得好，所以我認為馬太、路可這些個教徒，對耶穌教來講，是功勞很大的。

我又想起來這個于樞機，當時到我這兒來，就有一個居士請他吃齋，那麼我和他商量，他也答應了。到時候就到這個居士的家裡去吃齋，在正要吃的時候，就有一個人給送了一盤雞腿來。這

the ghosts below, those in the Ten Dharma Realms are equal. Within the Ten Dharma Realms there are the Buddhas, the Bodhisattvas, those Enlightened to Conditions, and Hearers—these are the Four Dharma Realms of Sages. There are also the Dharma Realms of gods, of humans, of asuras, of hungry ghosts, of hell-beings, and of animals. Each of them has its boundaries. When we understand one another, we will see that humans are all in the Ten Dharma Realms, in the Great Perfect Mirror Wisdom. The amount of your wisdom determines the Dharma Realm you belong to. If you have the Buddhas' wisdom, then you are a Buddha. If you have the wisdom of Bodhisattvas, then you are a Bodhisattva. Those with the wisdom of the Dharma Realm of Hearers are Hearers. Those with the wisdom of the Dharma Realm of Pratyekabuddhas are Pratyekabuddhas. It's all a question of your wisdom. Those who possess great wisdom are truly enlightened, and are the equal of the Buddhas. Those who lack wisdom and are stupid are the equal of living beings and belong in the realm of living beings.

There is a saying in Buddhism that goes, "All men are my fathers, and all women are my mothers." People who miss the principle will surely say, "Hey, how can all men turn into my father? How can all women turn into my mother? Exactly which mother and which father is mine?" The meaning here is that all men might have been my fathers in lives past, and all women might have been my mothers in lives past. Throughout countless lives in the past, they may have been my parents. We have experienced rebirth, and our names and faces have changed in the process, and so we no longer recognize each other. The teachings of Buddhism are vast and great, not narrow and small, not limited in any way, measureless and unbounded, equal, free, and comfortable. Such a teaching you might say is the smallest, yet it is also the greatest. It has no past and no present, no high and no low. It is both extremely vast and yet also ultimately fine. You could say that Buddhism is as small as an ant or mosquito, and you could also say it is the greatest—measureless and unbounded.

When the sages and saints founded each religion, their goal was for people to be good. They wouldn't have wanted people to slander one another. But people of later generations misunderstood the meaning of the teaching, the intent of the sages, and the principles upon which the religion was founded, and they pursued nothing but self-interest. They began to attack one another. For instance, I strike out at you and you retaliate. In the Buddhist teaching, for me to attack you is the same as attacking my own father. If you attack me, it's the same as attacking your mother. We should not do this to each other. That is why I said earlier that every religion has its strong points and its shortcomings. We must get rid of our shortcomings and maintain our good points. In this way, we are disciples who truly understand our religion. We are true followers of the founder of our religion. Why has Jesus' teaching spread so far and wide? It's because his disciples were eloquent preachers of his Gospel. For example, Matthew and Luke made a great contribution to Christianity.

I am reminded of one time when Cardinal Yubin came to my place and a layman invited him to a vegetarian lunch. We discussed the matter, and Cardinal Yubin agreed to go. We arrived at the

于樞機一看，就覺得不好意思，對這個送雞腿的人說：「我今天他們請我吃齋，你怎麼送雞腿來呢？」我說：「你們大家今天藉這個于樞機的光，你們都是佛教徒，平時都吃齋、不吃齋，我不知道。那麼今天這有人給送雞腿來呀！這是個好機會，你們誰願意吃雞腿的，今天都可以，我許可你們吃雞腿，你們若有什麼罪，都算我的。」于樞機當時就說：「那你要先吃啊！你若不吃，他們怎麼敢吃啊？」這于斌以這樣的難題來難我，我說：「好！我請你替我代表來吃這雞腿。」這于樞機說：「那好。」那麼誰願意吃雞腿的，就吃雞腿；不願意吃雞腿，就吃雞毛。

我們兩個，我和于樞機最初見到的時候，我說：「你應該做一個天主教的佛教徒。」他睜大了眼睛來看著我，認為很奇怪的，這麼樣講。我說：「沒有什麼奇怪的，我要做一個佛教裡邊的天主教徒，我們一交換這種思想啊！世界就沒有戰爭了，你信不信？」他想了有五分鐘吧！然後一拍大腿說：「好！我們就這樣幹！」從這個之後呢，他也拜佛了，所以我這是度了一個于樞機，他能把天主和佛教並行而不相悖，這是我很高興的一個事情。

所以我們兩個人一見如故，他和我的思想，我和他的思想，都彼此很接近的，可惜他正要把宗教互相聯合起來，就被天主叫回去了。他死了之後，我有一首詩紀念他，我也哭了一大場，今天不妨告訴告訴你們各位，我說：「天主啊！天主啊！你為什麼這樣不近人情啊？我剛剛有一個好朋友，志同道合的朋友，為什麼你這麼早把他叫回去了？」但是天主也不理我，唉！哭就哭啦！

好了，我今天就說這麼多。我父親、母親死了，我都沒有哭，于樞機死了，我哭了一場。我父親、母親死了，我都沒哭過，我是這麼一個不孝的人。好了，我今天班門弄斧，所說的都不知道對各位有沒有什麼利益？那麼就不多說了。

layperson's home, and when it came time to eat, a platter of chicken drumsticks appeared on the table. Cardinal Yubin was embarrassed, and said to the host who offered the meat, "They invited me to a vegetarian meal today. Why are you serving chicken drumsticks?" I said, "You folks can all take advantage of the Cardinal's presence here today. You are all Buddhists, and I don't know if you ordinarily eat only vegetarian food or not, but this is a good opportunity for anybody who wants to eat chicken legs to help yourselves. I will permit it today, and any bad karma that results will come to me instead of you." Cardinal Yubin said, "You will have to take the first bite, or else none of them will dare to eat the chicken." He put me on the spot like that. So I answered, "Please represent me, and eat my share of the chicken drumsticks for me." Cardinal Yubin said, "Fine." And so those who wanted to eat chicken drumsticks ate drumsticks, and those who didn't want to eat chicken drumsticks ate feathers.

The very first time I met Cardinal Yubin, I said, "You should be a Buddhist among the Catholics." He opened his eyes wide and stared at me, thinking that my statement was very strange. I said, "There's nothing strange about that. I will be a Catholic among the Buddhists. When we can share and exchange our ideas in this way, then there will be no more wars in the world. Do you believe it?" He thought it over for about five minutes and then slapped his thigh and said, "That's fine with me. Let's do it!" After that, he bowed to the Buddhas. That's how I took Paul Cardinal Yubin across. He made it possible for Catholicism and Buddhism to cooperate and get along together. This made me very happy indeed.

He and I felt an instant affinity with each other, since our thinking was so much alike. What a shame! Just as we were on the point of uniting our two religions, he was called back by God. After he died, I cried for a long time. I wrote a poem in his memory, too. I might as well tell you all today what I said at that time. I said, "God in Heaven! O God! Why don't you understand our feelings? I just made such a good friendship with a comrade in arms who truly understood my heart. Why have you called him back so soon?" But God paid no attention to me, so all I could do was cry.

Okay, I've said a lot today. When my own father and mother died, I didn't cry. But when Cardinal Yubin passed away, I really cried. I didn't even cry when my parents died. That is just how unfilial a person I am. Well, I've been blowing my own horn today, and I don't know if it's been of any value to you or not, so I'm going to stop here.

道

THE WAY

宣公上人一九八九年七月二十五日開示於夏威夷大學

A lecture by the Venerable Master Hua at the University of Hawaii on July 25, 1989

這次到夏威夷這個大島是臨時才決定的，得到這個大會的主席和各部的幹事人員看得起，所以今天也到這兒來說幾句話。至於講這道德倫理，世間所有一切都是在這個「道」裡邊。由道生，由德才能長，所以說：「道能生我，德能長我。」道德就是天地的一個正氣，道德就是人一個最優良的基礎，最優良品行的基礎，道德是我們每一個人本來具有的一種性德。所以老子一開始就說：「道可道非常道。名可名非常名。無名天地之始。有名萬物之母。故常無欲以觀其妙。常有欲以觀其儌。此兩者同出而異名。同謂之玄。玄之又玄。眾妙之門。」啊！有人聽到我念這一段文就說：「哦！這是《道德經》五千言的頭一篇，原來你是個老道，哦！怎麼你又做了和尚了？真是莫名奇妙！」這也就是「道可道非常道」，也就是「名可名非常名」。我們能說出來的，能做出來的，這不是個常道；那個常道是無名的，所以老子才說：「大道無名，大道無形，大道無情。」所以說：「大道無形，生育天地；大道無情，運行日月；大道無名，長養萬物。」它因為是萬物之母，所以你沒有法子給它起出個名子，這勉強給它起個名子就叫「道」，實際上，它根本連個「道」的名字也不可以有的。它就是我們每一個人的這種人性，也是我們要修行成佛的一個佛性，也就是一切眾生的眾生性，所以佛才說：「一切眾生皆有佛性，皆堪作佛，但以妄想執著不能證得。」

拿這個「道」字來講，這個上邊是「ヽ ノ」；本來「道」字上面這個「ヽ ノ」，可以說就是個「人」字。那麼人字，把它變了，於是乎就點成「ヽ ノ」，這是倉頡先師造字的時候，他來造的這個字。把這個「人」字一變化，就變成「ヽ ノ」，這「ヽ ノ」呢，就是一陰一陽；一個向上調，一個向下調，這叫一陰一陽，也就是無極生太極那個太極圖，那個陰陽魚，不過把它變

This time my coming to the large island of Hawaii was unplanned. Since the chairman and the various secretaries of this assembly have honored me, I have come here to say a few words today. On the topic of the Way, virtue, and human relationships, everything in the world is within the Way (dao). Everything is born from the Way, and then nurtured with virtue. There is a saying, "The Way can give birth to me. Virtue can foster me." The Way and virtue are the proper energy of heaven and earth. The Way and virtue are the most excellent foundation of people, a foundation of superlative character. The Way and virtue are the inherent virtue with which we are all endowed. Therefore, Laozi began by saying, "The Way that can be spoken of is not the eternal Way. The name that can be named is not the eternal name. The nameless is the beginning of heaven and earth. The named is the mother of all things. So, constantly without desire, one may perceive its wonders. Constantly with desire, one may observe its manifestations. These two came from the same source, but each bears a different name. Both are called mysteries, mystery upon mystery—the gateway to the manifold wonders." Ah! Some people, hearing me recite this passage, are saying, "Ha! This is the first section of the five-thousand-character *Classic of the Way and Virtue (Daodejing)*. So you're just an old Taoist! How did you become a Buddhist monk? Truly a mystery!" This is also "The Way that can be described is not the eternal Way," and "The names that can be named are not the eternal names." That which we can speak of or do is not the eternal Way. The eternal Way is nameless. Thus Laozi said, "The Great Way is nameless; the Great Way is formless; the Great Way is without sentience." And so it is also said, "The Great Way is formless; it produces heaven and earth. The Great Way is without sentience; it causes the sun and moon to orbit. The Great Way is nameless; it nurtures the myriad creatures." Since it is the mother of all things, you cannot give it a name. If it must have a name, you can call it the *dao* "Way." But in reality, it cannot even have the name "Way." It is every person's human nature. It is also the Buddha nature that makes it possible for us to cultivate and become Buddhas. It's also the living beings' nature of all living beings. Thus the Buddha said, "All living beings have the Buddha nature and can become Buddhas. It is only because of false thinking and attachments that they do not realize Buddhahood."

Let's talk about the character 道 *dao*. There are two short strokes ヽ ノ on the top. Originally, these two strokes are a transformation of the character 人 *ren* "person." When the ancient teacher Chang Jie was creating characters, he made this character. He transformed the character 人 *ren* into the two short strokes. These two short strokes represent yin and yang. When one is moved above and the other is moved below, it becomes the *taiji* diagram with the yin and yang fishes (when the Limitless 無極 *wuji* gives rise to the Absolute 太極

化不同了。那麼在人呢，這「ヽ╱」就等於人的二目；在天呢，就是日月，也就是陰陽。所謂「一陰一陽之謂道，偏陰偏陽之謂疾。」這個「道」，說起來，是無窮無盡的。因為這個陰陽變化、五行八卦，都是由「道」變出來的。

那麼在陰陽這「ヽ╱」下邊加一個「一」，這「一」是包羅萬有。這「一」，本來就是那個○字。說：「那個○字怎麼變成一了呢？」因為這個○字，它是個沒有數目，它是一個數目的本體，它是無大無小無內外，它是循環無端的，它是週而復始的。所以這個○字，你若加一個一，就變成十；你若加兩個○呢，就變成百；加三個○，就變成千；加四個○，就變萬。那麼你再加下去，百千萬億，無窮無盡的，你加多少○，那個數目就大一點；你加一點，就多一點，這叫一本散為萬殊，可是萬殊仍歸一本。這個○字加起來，越加越多，沒有完的時候；那你若不加呢，根本一個數目也不存在。你若一個數目不存在，那麼這就是無極，無極生太極。那麼不存在，可是這個○又斷了，這個○字一斷，把它不彎彎了，伸直了，就變成一個「一」字。

這個「一」字是「天得一以清，地得一以寧，人得一以聖。」人若得到這個「一」了，可以說就成聖人了。這個「一」是什麼呢？「一」就是「格物知至」格物那個「物」，把那個物欲革除了，這就能得到一了。所以佛經上也說：「得一萬事畢。」得到這個一了，萬事畢。可是得到這個一，你又把這個一要修成這個○字。這個○字，佛所放的光明，就是由這個○字放出來的。這也叫「大光明藏」，大光明藏就是由這個○字來變化的。那麼怎麼樣會變化呢？就是要得到一。怎麼樣得到一呢？你就要先格物，這一點呢，各位要注意。

格物，革除什麼物？就革除一切的物欲。譬如我們人有財欲，你把財欲這個思想革除去了，這沒有財欲了。色欲，你把色欲的思想革除去，就沒有色欲了。名有名欲，你把這個名的思想革除去了，就沒有名欲了。人人都想吃好東西，所以會不會修行，有沒有修行，你不要看旁的，你就看他吃東西，他是不是每一用刀的時候，他用刀叉是不是盡向好吃的那個東西叉？是不是那不好吃的東西，他就不叉了？用

taiji). It is just a different transformation. In terms of a person, the two short strokes represent a person's two eyes. In terms of heaven, they are the sun and moon, which are yin and yang. There is a saying: "A balance of yin and yang constitutes what is called the Way. An excess of yin or yang constitutes what is called sickness." The Way, if we were to describe it, is infinite and inexhaustible. The transformations of yin and yang, the five elements, and the eight trigrams are all produced by transformation from the Way.

Below the two strokes of yin and yang, there is the character 一 *yi* '1'. This 1 includes the myriad things within it. The 1 was originally a 0. "How did the 0 turn into a 1?" you ask. The zero is numberless; it is the fundamental substance of a number. It is neither great nor small, neither inside nor outside. It is a circle without a beginning. It goes around and comes back to the beginning. If you add a 1 to the 0, it becomes 10. If you add two 0s it becomes 100. Add three 0s and you get 1000. Add four 0s and it becomes 10,000. If you keep adding 0s, it becomes hundreds of thousands of tens of thousands of millions...endless and infinite. When you add a 0, the number increases. Each time you add a little, the number gets a little bigger. This is known as "one source dividing into ten thousand ramifications," but "the ten thousand ramifications all return to the one source." As you keep adding 0s, the more you add, the greater the number becomes, and there is no end to it. If you don't add any, then there isn't a single number to begin with. If not one number exists, then that is the Limitless 無極 *wuji*. The Limitless gives rise to the Absolute 太極 *taiji*. Nothing existed, but then the 0 was broken, straightened out, and became a 1 (一).

It is said of the One: "When heaven attains the One, it becomes clear. When earth attains the One, it is peaceful. When people attain the One, they become sages." What is the One? This refers to "eradicating desires and extending knowledge to the utmost." When you have gotten rid of material desires, you will attain the One. Therefore the Buddhist Sutras say, "When the One is attained, all things are finished." But once you attain the One, you have to cultivate to turn it into a zero. The light that the Buddhas emit comes from the zero. The Great Light Treasury is a transformation of the zero. How do you bring this transformation about? You have to attain the One. How do you attain the One? You must first get rid of material desires. Everyone should pay attention to this.

What material desires have to be eradicated? All material desires. For example, people have the desire for wealth. If you get rid of thoughts of desiring wealth, then you won't have any desire for wealth. If you get rid of thoughts of desiring beautiful forms, then you won't have any desire for beautiful forms. If you eradicate thoughts of desire for fame, then you won't have any desire for fame. Everyone likes to eat good food. To determine whether a person can cultivate or whether he has any cultivation, you don't have to look at anything else: just look at the way he eats. Is it the case that whenever he eats, he always forks up the good-tasting food while ignoring the food that doesn't taste so good? Or if he uses chopsticks, does he always use his chopsticks to pick up delicious food but refuse to eat food that isn't so delicious? Does he move the appetizing dishes closer to himself and push the unappealing dishes farther away? By observing just this, you can determine whether or not the person is a cultivator. If he is a

筷子，是不是他每一筷子都夾那個好吃的東西，那不好吃的東西，他就不想吃；好吃的東西，他把它挪到他的旁邊去，那不好吃的東西，他把它推得遠遠的？由這一點，你就能看出這個人是不是一個修道的人。若修道的人，他一定不會在這個飲食之間用功夫。所以他是好的也可以吃，不好的也可以吃；那麼有味的、沒有味的，都可以吃，他不選擇，不擇食。這就看出，不論你是修道的人也好，是讀書的人也好，是幹什麼，研究學問的人也好，他若專門那麼很饞的，那一定沒有什麼真功夫的。有真功夫，對這些個東西都不動心了；這是食欲。睡欲，貪睡眠，不夠睡了，就不行了，受不了了。他革除這五欲了，這才能談到一個格物。

格物然後才能知至，才能有智慧，觸類旁通，「事來則映，事去則淨。」這一種智慧，就像那個鏡子似的，什麼東西來了，它就現出來了，就照出來；去了，就沒有了。所以這是一個智慧的觀察力，你才能知至。

知至，然後要誠意；誠意，就是做任何的事情，都是畢恭畢敬，主敬存誠，絲毫不苟且，絲毫不馬虎，能以誠心誠意的這樣子。

誠意，過去就要正心；你心裡不要有邪念，不要今天想這一個五顏六色的東西，明天又想那個，總是在那兒想入非非。這個正心，心裡要有正知正見，要正念，《六祖壇經》上說：「正念之時，佛在室；邪念之時，魔在堂。」真正一個修道的人，不苟言笑，不能隨隨便便地這麼輕舉妄動，一定是三千威儀、八萬細行，都要具足了。所以不能同乎流俗，合乎污世，不能做這個鄉愿，德中之賊，不能這樣子，所以要誠意正心。

你能正心了，然後才能齊家；你若不能正心，你做事情都是那麼偏私，不能大公無私，你家庭裡都不佩服，那焉能治國呢？所以就不能治國；不能治國，就不能令天下太平。

所以這個三綱領就是要明德，明德就是把我們本有的德行瞭解了；瞭解了，然後才新民；新民，然後再止於至善。這三綱領、八條目，這是要在上面下功夫，來用功。所以格物、知至、誠意正心、修身、齊家、治國、平天下，這個是《大學》上所說的，清清楚楚的，不用東找西找的，喔！又這麼研究，那麼研究，研

cultivator, he certainly wouldn't waste his effort on food. He is able to eat good food as well as bad. Whether it is flavorful or flavorless, he can eat it just the same. He isn't picky about food. Whether a person is a cultivator, a student, or a scholar, regardless of what he does, if he is a glutton, then it's for sure that he doesn't have much skill in cultivation. If he had true skill, he wouldn't be tempted by these things. That's the desire for food. Then there's the desire for sleep. You may be greedy for sleep and not be able to take it if you don't get enough sleep. One must get rid of these five kinds of desire before one can be considered to have eradicated material desires.

After eradicating material desires, one can extend one's knowledge to the utmost, have wisdom, and be able to understand many things by inference. "When things come, one reflects them. When they are gone, one is pure." This kind of wisdom is like a mirror. When something comes along, its image appears in the mirror. When it passes, the image is gone. Thus, you must have wisdom to contemplate before you can extend your knowledge.

After one's knowledge is complete, one has to make one's thoughts sincere. To be sincere in thought means that whatever one does, one does it with an attitude of utmost reverence and earnestness. One is not casual or sloppy in the slightest. One is able to be sincere in mind and heart.

After one's thoughts are sincere, one must rectify one's mind. You should not have any deviant thoughts in your mind. You shouldn't be daydreaming all the time, thinking about the colorful attractions of the world day after day. To rectify the mind, you must have proper knowledge, proper views, and proper mindfulness. The *Sixth Patriarch Sutra* says, "When there is proper mindfulness, the Buddha is in the house. When there is deviant mindfulness, the demon is in the hall." A genuine cultivator does not talk or laugh casually. You should not move or act casually. You must observe the three thousand modes of awesome comportment and the eighty thousand subtle aspects of conduct. Don't go along with the crowd and follow the defiled ways of the world. Don't be an impostor, a thief among the virtuous. You have to be sincere in thought and rectify the mind.

Once you have rectified the mind, you can then regulate the family. If you cannot rectify your mind, if you do everything with a selfish motive and cannot be public-spirited, then your family will not respect you. If that's the case, then how can you expect to govern the country well? You cannot govern the country well, and so you cannot cause the world to be at peace.

The first of the Three Guidelines is to illustrate virtue. This means to understand our inherent virtue. Once we understand it, we can renovate the people. Once the people are renovated, we can rest in the highest excellence. The Three Guidelines and Eight Principles are where we should apply effort. Eradicating desires, extending knowledge, being sincere in thought, rectifying the mind, cultivating oneself, regulating the family, setting the country in order, and bringing peace to the world—this is explained very clearly in the *Great Learning*. There's no need to go looking east and west, investigating this way and that! You may investigate all you want, but if you don't actually practice it, it's no use at all. Once you understand the Three Guidelines and Eight Principles, you have to apply them, put them into practice, and actually carry them out yourselves. You can't just

究來研究去，你不實行，一點也沒有用的。所以你若明白這三綱領、八條目，就照著去做去，要躬行實踐，身體力行，要以身作則，不能說食數寶，不能口裡說說就算了，所以這個要真下功夫；真下功夫，就是躬行實踐。躬行實踐，要先從我身上做起，所謂「要想天下好，先從我身上做起。」我是世間人類的一份子，我還沒好呢！那麼怎麼能叫人家好？所以常常能律己，常常摩訶薩不管他，不要盡做這個洗衣機、照相鏡子。洗衣機盡給旁人往乾淨了洗，那個衣服洗乾淨，結果自己那個洗衣機外邊，塵土落得有多厚，它也洗不掉。那照相機只能照人家的相，而不能照自己的相。那個照相機，本身它不會照它那個照相機的相，這只是一個機器，一個物質。所以我們人為萬物之靈，人要以身作則，人要做人的一個好榜樣。

那麼這個天得一以清，天之所以為天呢，它因為有這個一；地之所以為地啊！因為它得到這個一了；人若得到這個一，就是聖人。這個「一」是什麼呢？就是革除物欲。聖人就是以禮制欲，所以顏淵問仁，子曰：「克己復禮。」克己復禮就是律己，就是自己要常常把自己內裡頭的心性，不要有邪念；外面的身體，不要有邪行；口裡說的，也不要說邪話，不要盡說一些個騙人的話，又似是而非啊，令人模棱兩可呀，或者這一種迷信的彩色，這都是一種沒能以身作則，才有這種行為。那麼一定要律己，你能律己，才能服人；你不能律己，所謂「其身正，不令而行；其身不正，雖令不從。」所以「正己而後教人，正己而後化人，正己而後助人。」你自己不正是不行的，所以說：「正念之時，佛在室；邪念之時，魔在堂。邪正具不立，常與白牛車。」

我們要克己復禮，才為「仁」。何謂克己復禮？孔子就說：「非禮勿視，非禮勿聽，非禮勿言，非禮勿動。」視聽言動都要合禮，不合禮的都不要去做去，這就是個「仁」。所以我們想修德行仁，就先要正己，然後才能有「仁」的表現。所謂「仁義禮智根於心」，那個仁義禮智它是在人的心裡頭生出來的，惻隱之心、羞惡之心、辭讓之心、是非之心。這是「惻隱之心，仁之端也；羞惡之心，義之端也；辭讓之心，禮之端也；是非之心，智之端也。」

talk about it and then forget it; that's like merely talking about food or counting others' treasures. You have to actually work at it. That means you have to honestly practice. To honestly practice means to start from yourself. As it is said, "If I want the world to be good, I have to start with myself." I am a member of the human race. If I'm not good, how can I tell others to be good? We should constantly discipline ourselves and be "Mahasattvas who pay no heed to others." You shouldn't be a washing machine or a camera. A washing maching can only wash others' laundry. It can wash their clothes clean, but it can't clean the thick coat of dust on its own exterior. A camera can only take pictures of other people; it can't take a picture of itself. The camera is only a machine, an object. Human beings are the most efficacious of all creatures. Therefore, we should set a good example. We should be a good model for other people.

When heaven attains the One, it is clear. Heaven is heaven because it possesses the One. Earth is earth because it has attained the One. If people attain the One, they become Sages. What is the One? It is the eradication of material desires. Sages use propriety to control desire. When Yan Yuan inquired about the meaning of humaneness, Confucius said, "Restrain yourself and return to propriety." This means to discipline yourself. It means to constantly keep your inner mind free of deviant thoughts, to keep your body from acting in deviant ways, and to avoid uttering deviant speech with the mouth. Don't tell lies, don't speak with duplicity, and don't say superstitious things. These kinds of behavior come about when you are not practicing honestly. You have to discipline yourself. Only then can you make people listen to you. If you don't discipline yourself, it is said, "When you are upright, people will do things without your having to order them. If you are not upright, then even if you order them, they won't listen." Therefore, "First rectify yourself and then teach others. First rectify yourself and then convert others. First rectify yourself and then help others." If you yourself are not upright, then nothing will work. Hence, "When there is proper mindfulness, the Buddha is in the house. When there is deviant mindfulness, the demon is in the hall. When neither deviant nor proper are established, one is constantly on the White Ox Cart."

We must restrain ourselves and return to propriety before we can have humaneness. What does it mean to restrain ourselves and return to propriety? Confucius said, "If it's not in accord with propriety, don't look at it. If it's not in accord with propriety, don't listen to it. If it's not in accord with propriety, don't talk about it. If it's not in accord with propriety, don't do it." Whatever we look at, listen to, talk about, and do just be in accord with propriety. If it does not accord with propriety, then we shouldn't act upon it. That's known as humaneness. If we want to cultivate virtue and practice humaneness, we must first rectify ourselves. Only then will humaneness manifest. As it is said, "Humaneness, righteousness, propriety, and wisdom are rooted in the mind." They are produced from within the mind, from the thoughts of sympathy, shame, yielding, and discrimination. "The thought of sympathy is the beginning of humaneness. The thought of shame and dislike of evil is the beginning of righteousness. The thought of yielding is the beginning of propriety. The thought of discriminating between right and wrong is the beginning of wisdom." It is said, "Humaneness, righteousness, propriety, and wisdom are rooted in the mind." Their basis is in the mind. "They produce a luminous quality which mani-

所謂「仁義禮智根於心」，它的根在心裡頭。「其生色也」，他有這種光澤的顏色，「睟然現於面」，睟然，「富潤屋，德潤身」，你真有德行了，你那是德光滿面，德潤身了。就是仁義禮智你充足了，你就有一種德光，對人人都有一種緣，所以其生色也，睟然現於面。「盎於背」，不但面上可以現出來，你那個形態，四肢百骸，都能現出來，盎於背。「施於四體」，那麼四體都能表露出來。表露出來，所以那德光照人，你有一種德光。所謂「有德人人欽，有道便為尊。」所謂「道高龍虎伏，德重鬼神欽。」你真若有道了，那個龍，是龍要盤起來，是虎要臥起來。這不是講迷信的話，你那個德行、道德的感應，那是「與天地合德，與日月合明，與四時合序，與鬼神合其吉凶。」這都是道德的充沛表現，所以說「根於心，睟然現於面，盎於背，施於四體，四體不言而喻。」不用說，人人都知道了。

所謂「充實之謂美」，仁義禮智信根於心，你若充實了，「之謂美」，這是個美人，因為人人都覺得和你有緣，有德人人欽嘛！有道便為尊嘛！這個人人都親近你，都歡喜接近你，所以這個德行是這樣的，這叫一個美人。這個美並不是擦擦胭粉，擦擦口紅，扮得那麼很美麗的，不是那樣；這天然的，有一種德光普照。那麼「充實而有光輝之謂大」，這是個大人，就超過這個美人了。「大而化之之謂聖」，你大，又能變化；變化，這就是個聖人。「聖而不可知之謂神」，這就是個神人。所以美、大、聖、神，這就是仁義禮智充滿了，才有這種的表現。我們為什麼有敵人？就因為我們仁義禮智沒有充滿。在佛教裡沒有敵人，佛教裡頭，都是有緣的人，和誰，你罵我，我不罵你；你打我，我不打你；你殺我，我不殺你；總而言之，不和人爭。「不爭不貪，福祿無邊；爭貪攪擾，罪孽不少。」所以，也不向外馳求，也不自私，也不自利，也不打妄語，什麼時候都是言而有信，這個是修行、做人必須具備的條件。

所以這個「一」字，就是那個○字的變化。○字的變化，你要修行呢，還要把它修成一個○字。這個○字就是無欠無餘，也沒有缺少的了，也沒有多的了，無欠無餘。這個境界要返

fests radiantly in the countenance." "Wealth enriches one's home. Virtue enriches one's body." When you have genuine virtue, the glow of virtue appears on your face and suffuses your body. When you are replete with humaneness, righteousness, propriety, and wisdom, you will have an aura of virtue and everyone will be drawn to you. Thus, the glow "manifests radiantly in the countenance, suffuses the back..." Not only does it appear in your face, it is also revealed in your figure and bone structure. It suffuses the back and "spreads to the four limbs." They are expressed even in the four limbs. Therefore, a virtuous light emanates from you. It is said, "When one has virtue, everyone respects one. When one has the Way, one is honored." There is a saying, "When the Way is lofty, dragons and tigers are subdued. When virtue is complete, ghosts and spirits are respectful." If you truly have the Way, then dragons have to coil up and tigers have to lie down. This is not superstitious talk. The response that comes from your virtuous conduct and morality is such that "your virtue unites with that of heaven and earth, your brightness unites with that of the sun and moon, your timing unites with the order of the four seasons, and your fortunes and misfortunes unite with those of the ghosts and spirits." These are the manifestation of the fullness of virtue. Thus, virtue is "rooted in the mind, manifests radiantly in the countenance, suffuses the back, and spreads to the four limbs. The four limbs express it without words." There's no need to speak about it. People can all tell.

As it is said, "Being replete with virtue is known as beauty." If humaneness, righteousness, propriety, wisdom, and trustworthiness are abundantly rooted in your mind, that is known as excellence. You are a beautiful person, because all people feel they have affinities with you. When one has virtue, all people respect one. When one has the Way, one is honored. Everyone draws near you and likes to be around you. This is what virtue is like. This is a beautiful person. This beauty is not a matter of applying blush and lipstick and dressing up prettily. This is a natural kind of virtuous light that shines forth. Then it is said, "Being replete to the point of radiance is known as greatness." A great person surpasses a beautiful person. "When one is great and can bring about tranformations, that is known as sageliness." If you are great and can transform yourself, then you are a sage. "When one is sagely to a point that cannot be known, that is known as divineness." One is a divine person. The manifestations of beauty, greatness, sageliness, and divineness are the result of being filled with humaneness, righteousness, propriety, and wisdom. Why do we have enemies? Because we are not filled with humaneness, righteousness, propriety, and wisdom. But in Buddhism, there are no enemies. Everyone is a person with whom we have affinities. If someone scolds me, I don't scold back. If someone hits me, I don't hit back. If someone kills me, I don't kill him. In general, we don't fight with others. "No fighting and no greed: boundless blessings and wealth. Fighting, greedy, and making mischief: one's offenses are not a few." Not seeking outside, not being selfish, not pursuing personal advantage, not lying, always telling the truth—these are the requirements for cultivating and being a human being.

The 1 is just a transformation of the 0. You have cultivate to turn it back into a 0. The 0 is neither deficient nor in excess. It does not lack anything, and it does not have too much of anything. To reach this state, one must return to the source, return to the inherent nature. If

本還原，就要返回到這個自性上來。能以返本還原，這是真正明白修道了，這就是那個「道」。

那麼「道」這個「一」字下邊，又有自己的「自」，那麼這個「道」在什麼地方呢？這個道在自己這兒呢！不要到外邊去找去。你花錢，也買不來這個道，無論你用什麼方法，用什麼手段，用什麼計策，都沒有用的，這個要「鐵匠對石匠，實打實著的。」要真正修行去，真正用功的，你差之絲毫，就謬之千里。所以要修這個道，這個道是在自己這兒。那麼合起來，這是個「首」字，這個「首者，頭也」，說是修行，這是人生頭一件重要的事情。那麼頭一件重要的事情，可是人人都把它忘了，所謂「清淨是福人不享，煩惱是罪個個貪。」天天都在求名、求利；求名的，就死到名上；求利的，就死到利上。死後了，也不後悔，還是覺得：「啊！我這一生啊，還沒有做好，等到來生我再努力，再接再勵。」那麼他就把修道都忘了，這個頭一件事忘了。

這頭一件事，你要修道，要怎麼樣呢？這所以用個「走」字，這要自己去修行去，自己去走去。這個「道」要自己去走出來的，所以說：「道是行的，不行何用道？德是作的，不作那有德？」你一天到晚叫：「欵！你要修行啊！你要修道。」叫旁人修道，自己把自己都忘了。叫旁人，說：「你作點功德啦！」盡叫旁人作功德，自己不做。這真是捨己為人，這個真是菩薩發心。所以你若不去做去，不行何用道？德是作的，不作那有德？什麼叫「德」？德就是利人；什麼是「道」？道就是不害人。你利人就是德，不害人就是道；你不要損人利己，這就是道德。你盡做一些個事情，損人利己，對人家有傷害，對自己有利益，這就沒有道德了，就缺道缺德了。所以這個道，要自己去行去，道是行的，不行何用道？德是作的，不作那有德啊？這個要躬行實踐，要實實在在去做去。我不懂得旁的，我只知道講一些個老老實實的話，這是「道德」兩個字，是要這樣的。「富潤屋，德潤身」，你有德行了，美大聖神那種光輝發外，那才是真正修道的一個人了。

所以我所說這個「道德」兩個字，不知道有什麼出入沒有？我想先請問請問大家有什麼意見？我若說得不對的地方，請大家多多指教指教。

you can return to the source, then you have truly understood how to cultivate the Way.

In the word 道 *dao*, below the "一" there is a 自 *zi* "self." Where is the Way? It is right within yourself! Don't look for it outside. You cannot buy it with money. No matter what method, what maneuver, what plan you use, it won't work. You have to be like "the blacksmith and the mason, whose every blow is right on the spot." You have to really cultivate and truly apply effort. If you're off by a hair, you'll miss by a thousand miles. So you have to cultivate the Way, and the Way is right where you are. Combining these elements, we get the word 首 *shou*, which means "head." This refers to cultivation. The most important thing in life is cultivation. Unfortunately, people have forgotten this most important matter. They have renounced the root to pursue the branchtips. As it is said, "Fame and profit are small matters, but all people like them. Birth and death are a great matter, but no one guards against them. Purity is a blessing, but no one enjoys it. Afflictions are offenses, but everyone craves them." Day in and day out, they chase after fame and profit. Those who seek fame will die in pursuit of fame. Those who seek profit will die in quest of profit. Even after they die, they feel no regret. They still think, "Oh! I didn't finish my business in this life. In my next life, I'll keep working hard and striving ahead." And so they forget about cultivating the Way. They forget this foremost matter.

How should you go about cultivating the Way? The character 道 *dao* has a "walking" element, indicating that one must cultivate and walk by oneself. You have to walk the Way yourself. So it is said, "The Way is to be walked. If one doesn't walk, how is it the Way. Virtue is to be practiced. If it is not practiced, how can there be virtue?" All day long you tell others, "Hey! You have to cultivate! You should cultivate the Way." In telling others to cultivate, you forget to do so yourself. You say to others, "Why don't you do some meritorious deeds?" All you do is tell others to do meritorious deeds, but you don't do any yourself. This is truly a case of renouncing oneself for others, a true Bodhisattva resolve. But if you don't practice, then what use is the Way? Virtue must be done. If you don't do it, how can there be virtue? What is virtue? Virtue consists of benefiting others. What is the Way? The Way is not to harm others. Your benefiting of others is virtue; your not harming others is the Way. If you don't harm others to benefit yourself, then that is morality. If you keep doing things that harm others and benefit yourself, then you have no morality. You lack the Way and virtue. So you yourself have to practice the Way. The Way must be walked. If one doesn't walk it, what use is the Way? Virtue must be done. If you don't do it, how can you have virtue? You must actually put it into practice and truly do it yourself. I don't understand anything else. I can only say these simple and honest words. This is what morality—the Way and virtue—are all about. "Wealth enriches one's house; virtue enriches one's body." Once you have virtue, that excellent, great, sagely, and spiritual light will emanate from you. Then you will be a genuine cultivator of the Way.

I don't know if my explanation of the Way and virtue is incorrect in any way. Does someone have an opinion? If I have spoken wrongly, I hope everyone will correct me.

◯：自性的大光明藏

ZERO: THE GREAT BRIGHT STORE OF YOUR OWN NATURE

宣公上人開示

A lecture by the Venerable Master Hua

眾生生於無始，死於無終，無始無終，就是在這個輪迴裡頭流轉生死。眾生在這個無始無終的輪迴裡頭，轉來轉去，轉去又轉來，就好像一粒微塵，忽然而天，忽然而地，忽然而人道，忽然而餓鬼，忽然而畜生，忽然而地獄，忽然而修羅。啊！這叫沒有一個開始的時候，也沒有一個終了的時候。什麼時候你若能證果成佛了，這是把這個生死的輪迴停止了。沒有成佛之前，都在這個輪迴裡轉。「菩薩有隔陰之迷，羅漢有住胎之昏」，就是你法身大士，示現人間，也有的時候被這個生死的流，流得頭昏腦脹的，不知道怎麼樣才能截斷這個生死的流。

我們這個生死，生了又死，死了又生，這是一個大生死。我們還有小生死，由生那一天，雖然有所生，但是也就有所死了。生出來那一天，就是把死的那一天，已經都準備好了，所以我們這一生，這是一個大生死。我們每一年過去了，這就一年就死了。所以生這一天，也就是死那一天，因為有生，所以就有死；若沒有生，也就沒有死了。

說這個「無始」，一般人所講的這個「無始」，就是沒有一個開始，沒有一個終了，是從無始劫以來，沒有開始那個劫以來；沒有開始那個劫，所以也就沒有終了那個劫。說來說去，這個「無始」是個什麼呢？「無終」是個什麼呢？就是我們人人都認識那個字，在英文就叫◯，在中文就叫◯（零）。那個◯字，是也沒有始，也沒有終；沒有一個開始，沒有一個最終了，它是一元化的，那個就是無始無終。這個無始，就是所謂的這個◯字。這個◯字，你把它割斷了，在一邊割斷了它，就變成一個「一」字，這是一個開始了，這有始了－－有了「一」就會有二，再加一個一就是個二，再加一個一就是三，再加一個一就是四，五，六，七，八，九，十，有十就會生百，有百就會生千，由千就變化成萬，由萬又變化出來十萬，百萬，千萬，萬萬，乃至於數不盡那麼多，這是一個數目的開始。

現在這個科學時代，由我們地球造的這個火箭，能

Living beings are born without a beginning, and die without an end. Without beginning and without end, they transmigrate, revolving in birth and death. Living beings revolve and turn in this beginningless and endless transmigration like dust motes: suddenly up in the heavens, suddenly down on the earth. Just as suddenly they are born as hungry ghosts, or humans, or animals, or hell-dwellers, or asuras. Ah! There is no time at which it all begins, and no time when it ends. It is only when you realize the fruition and become a Buddha that you stop transmigrating in birth and death. Before you become a Buddha, you keep revolving in transmigration. It is said, "Even Bodhisattvas get confused after having gone through rebirth; even Arhats become muddled after having dwelt in the womb." Even if you are a great knight of the Dharma body manifesting in this world, sometimes you may be confused by the current of birth and death and not know how to stop it.

Our birth and death, being born and dying, dying and being born again, is birth and death on a great scale. We also have birth and death on a small scale. There is the day we are born. Although we are born, we will have to die. The day of our death is already set the day we are born. Therefore, our life is birth and death on a great scale. Each passing year brings the death of that year. Thus if we are born one day, we will have to die one day, because once there is birth, there is death. If there is no birth, then there is no death.

As to the "beginningless," most people explain it as there being no beginning and no end. It refers to time without beginning; it started at a kalpa in the beginningless past, and goes to a kalpa in the endless future. What is without a beginning anyway? And what is without an end? This refers to something we all recognize; in English it is called zero, and in Chinese it is called O (ling). This O has no beginning and no end. It is the Absolute, without beginning or end. The beginningless is just the O. If you cut this O open, it becomes a "一" (the Chinese character for 'one'). This is the beginning. Once there is a one, there is also a two: when you add one to one, that is two. Adding another one makes three, and adding more ones makes four, five, six, seven, eight, nine, ten. From ten, a hundred is produced, and a hundred brings forth a thousand, a thousand transforms into ten thousand, ten thousand further transforms into one hundred thousand, one million, ten million, and a thousand million, up to infinity. That is the beginning of numbers.

In our modern scientific era, we can use rockets to launch satellites into space. The satellite revolves in its orbit in

打到太空去，入了太空軌道，在太空運行不息，在那兒流轉，這是一個有始。那麼由這個數目來推算，能把這個火箭送到太空去，這都是「有始」的作用，一個數學的變化。那麼有終沒有呢？現在還不知道什麼時候是個終。終的時候，就是這個成住壞空它「空」的時候，它是終；那麼這個成劫，是一個開始，成二十個小劫，住二十個小劫，壞二十個小劫，空二十個小劫，這也可以說是一個開始，一個終了。

那麼這一切眾生無始劫來，所有的眾生，你說從什麼地方來的？你來研究研究。就拿人類來說，你說，是先有男人？是先有女人？你說「先有男人」，沒有女人，男人怎麼會有？你若說「先有女人」，那麼沒有男人，怎麼又會有女人？這個是一個「無始」，不知道從哪個地方開始。就拿這個雞子來講，你說先有雞？是先有蛋？無始劫以來，沒有小雞子，啊，那麼怎麼會有了？說：「由蛋有的。」這個蛋，如果沒有雞，又怎麼會有蛋？這也研究不明白這個道理，這也就是由無始來的，人也就是由無始來的，由那個○字那兒來的。那麼由○字那兒來的，所以這是無始無終、無內無外、無大無小。這個○，你小，就是一粒微塵，你若把它擴大起來，就是一個法界，盡虛空、遍法界，沒有超出這個○字去，盡虛空遍法界，碎為微塵，那一粒微塵也沒有離開這個○字。所以這個○字，是生生化化之源，是無始無終的一個真空妙有的道理。這個○字擴大起來，變成虛空，變成法界，這是一個真空，你把它縮小了，變成一粒微塵；雖然微塵是小，這可是妙有。所以這個無始劫以來，就是沒有開始的時候。那麼這個○字，就是真空，就是妙有。你們各位想一想，你若明白這個道理，你就是明白真法；你若不明白這個道理，你還是糊塗人，沒有真正智慧。

這個○字，你若是開悟了，它就是大智慧光明；你要是沒有開悟，它就是一個無明。無明，也是這個○字；智慧光明，也是這個○字。所以這個無始無終、無內無外、無大無小。這個○字，大而無外，沒有再比它更大的，你若把它往大的寫，你看寫多大都可以；你若把它縮小的寫，寫多小都可以，所以大而無外，小而無內。那麼大而化之，就是清淨本源，妙真如性。小而藏之，你把它藏起來，也就是你最初那一念的無明，所以我講這個「無始」是這樣的講法。

space without stop. That is a beginning. With the help of numerical calculations, we are able to send rockets into space. That is the function of a beginning; it's a kind of mathematical transformation. Then is there an end? We don't know yet when the end will come. The end corresponds to the stage of emptiness in the four stages of formation, dwelling, decay, and emptiness. The kalpa (eon) of formation is a beginning. Formation lasts for twenty small kalpas. Then there is dwelling for twenty small kalpas, decay for twenty small kalpas, and emptiness for twenty small kalpas. One could say that this is a beginning and an end.

Where would you say all these living beings that have appeared since beginningless kalpas come from? Let's investigate. Take human beings, for example. Did man exist before woman, or woman before man? If you say man appeared before woman, then without a woman how could there be any men? If you say woman appeared before man, then without a man how could there be any women? This is the "beginningless"—we don't know where it started. Chickens are another example. Would you say the chicken came before the egg, or the egg before the chicken? For beginningless kalpas there were no chickens. Then how did one come into existence? We may say it was born from an egg. Well, if there were no chickens, how could there be eggs? Our investigation cannot provide a clear understanding of this principle; it comes from the beginningless. People also came from the beginningless, from the O.

This O is beginningless and endless; it has neither inside nor outside; it is neither big nor small. In its minutest aspect, the O equals a dust mote. If we expand it, it is equal to the Dharma Realm. To the ends of the empty space, throughout the Dharma Realm, nothing is beyond this O. If the empty space throughout the Dharma Realm is smashed into dust motes, not a single dust mote is apart from this O. Therefore, the O is the source of the myriad births and transformations. It is the principle of true emptiness and wonderful existence without beginning or end. When this O is expanded, it becomes empty space, the Dharma Realm. That is true emptiness. When it is shrunk, it becomes a dust mote. Though a dust mote is tiny, it is wonderful existence. Therefore, beginningless kalpas have no beginning. This O is true emptiness, and it is wonderful existence. All of you, think about this! If you can understand this principle, you understand the true Dharma. If you can't understand this principle, you're still a confused person, having no real wisdom.

If you have attained enlightenment, this O is great bright wisdom. If you haven't attained enlightenment, then it's ignorance. Ignorance is just the O, and great bright wisdom is also the O. Thus the O is beginningless and endless; it has neither inside nor outside; it is neither big nor small. It's so big there's nothing outside of it, nothing is bigger. When you draw this O, you can make it as big as possible, or as small as possible. Therefore, it is so big there's nothing outside it, and so small there's nothing inside it. Its bigness transforms into the pure and clean fundamental source, the wonderful true nature. Its smallness and hiddenness is the single initial thought of your ignorance. This is how I explain "beginningless."

Transmigrating in birth and death is the O. The so-called transmigration in the six paths is just revolving within the O.

在生死的輪迴裡邊，這個輪迴，也就是這個○字。所謂六道輪迴，都是在這個○字裡面轉來轉去，啊！沒有把這個○字打破了，生了又死，死了又生，不知多少個大劫在這個六道輪迴裡來轉，這叫生死久流轉。這個「久」字，你看看這是不是很可怕的，就是啊！它在輪迴裡轉來轉去。怎麼會久流轉？就是你那念念生、念念滅造成的，你一念染污心生出來了，就做畜生，做惡鬼，或者墮地獄；你再稍微清淨一點，或者做人，或者做阿修羅，或者升天，啊！這都是從你那個心念所造成的這個輪迴。那麼去受輪迴的果報，也因為我們的心已經造這種的業，才去受報。不是受報那個時候，才開始你這個受報這種業，是在你啊！往昔盡打妄想，你打天堂的妄想，就生天；打阿修羅的妄想，就做阿修羅；你打人道這個妄想，就去做人；打畜生道的妄想，就去做畜生；你打餓鬼道的妄想，就去做餓鬼；打地獄道的妄想，就去墮地獄。你要是盡造罪孽過，就墮落三惡道；你要是盡做善功德，就升三善道。這是大大概概地說一說這種意思，要是詳細說，盡未來際也說不能盡。所以這個世界，都是從眾生妄想所造成的，要是人人都沒有妄想了，這個世界就空了。

這一切眾生都不瞭解這個真空實相的法、真如實相的法、真空妙有的法，這都叫真實法。真空妙有的法，也就是方才我說那個○字。這個○字，這麼大個天地，是由○字而生；這麼大個世界，是由○字而生；這麼多的眾生，是由○字而生，這一切一切都是從這個○字生出來的。那個○字，因為它「不墮諸數」，它不在數內，超出數外，無始無終、無內無外、無大無小，「放之則彌六合，卷之退藏於密。」這個真實法，也就是這個真空妙有法；真空不空，為什麼它不空呢？它有妙有。妙有非有，它又不是有，為什麼它不是有呢？因為它還有真空，「真空不礙妙有，妙有不礙真空」，這個道理就是解決「先有男？先有女？」的問題，也就是解決「先有雞？先有蛋？」這個問題。這一切的問題都在用這個○字，就可以把它解決了，為什麼呢？這個○字是一個真空，真空裡邊能現出妙有，能現出一切物，妙有可是還沒有離開這個真空，這種境界你若沒有得到諸佛心印法的人，你不會明白的；你若明白諸佛以心印心這個法門，你就明白這種法了，所以說「不了真實法」。

眾生啊，都是頭上安頭，騎驢覓驢，啊！盡是向

Before this circle is broken, living beings are born and die, die and are born again, revolving in the O for countless great kalpas. This is called eternally revolving in birth and death. Don't you think this word "eternally" is horrifying? It is! You keep turning 'round and 'round in transmigration. Why do you revolve eternally? Because your thoughts are produced and extinguished one after another. When you give rise to one defiled thought, you become an animal, or a hungry ghost, or fall into the hells. If you incline toward purity, you may be born a human or an asura, or ascend to the heavens. All this transmigration is caused by your mind. Because our mind has created the corresponding karma, we receive the retribution of transmigration. Such karma does not start when we receive the retribution. In reality, you had lots of false thoughts in the past. With false thoughts about the heavens, you are born in the heavens; with false thoughts about asuras, you are born an asura; with false thoughts of being human, you are born a human; with false thoughts of animals, you are born an animal; with false thoughts of hungry ghosts, you are born a hungry ghost; with false thoughts of hells, you fall into the hells. If you always create offenses, you fall into the three evil paths; if you always establish wholesome merit and virtue, you ascend to the three good paths. This is just a general explanation. If I were to explain this in detail, I wouldn't be able to finish to the end of time. In short, this world is created from living beings' false thoughts. If no one had any false thoughts, then this world would be empty.

Living beings don't understand this Dharma of the real appearance of true emptiness, the Dharma of the real appearance of true suchness, the Dharma of true emptiness and wonderful existence. All of these are called actual Dharma. The Dharma of true emptiness and wonderful existence is just the O mentioned above. The great heaven and earth are produced from the O; so is this vast world, the numerous living beings, and all other things. Because the O does not fall into the category of numbers, it is not within numbers. It is beyond numbers or reckoning. It has no beginning or end, no inside or outside, no big or small. "When released, it fills the six directions. When rolled up, it retreats and hides away in a secret place." The actual Dharma is just this Dharma of true emptiness and wonderful existence. True emptiness is not empty. Why? Because it contains wonderful existence. Wonderful existence does not exist. Why? Because it encompasses true emptiness. It is said, "True emptiness does not obstruct wonderful existence; wonderful existence does not hinder true emptiness." This principle resolves the question of whether the man came first or the woman came first. It also resolves the question of whether the chicken came first or the egg. The O can solve all problems. Why? Because the O is true emptiness. From it, wonderful existence and the myriad things manifest. Yet this wonderful existence is not separate from true emptiness. Without having attained the Dharma of the mind-seal of the Buddhas you cannot understand this state. If you understand the mind-to-mind-seal Dharma-door of the Buddhas, you will understand this Dharma. Therefore, it is said, "The actual Dharma is not understood."

Living beings are forever adding a head on top of a head, or looking for the mule while riding on one. They all run around

外馳求，到外邊去找去，不知道迴光返照。這個真實法，是自性本具的，是自性恆具的，是自性本有的，不需要到外邊去找去；你到外邊找，找了八萬大劫，你也找不到。你要是迴光返照，當下就是！所謂「苦海無邊，回頭是岸」，也就是你向外去找，就是苦海無邊；你若向內來找，在你自性上用功夫，這就是回頭是岸。

我們人啊！這麼顛顛倒倒的，一天到晚，追逐妄緣，隨著六根、六塵去跑，不明白真實法。諸佛在常寂光裡邊，結雙跏趺坐入定，在定中啊！就要跑到這個世界上來，為什麼呢？看見你我他這個愚癡的眾生，太可憐了，啊！一天到晚都把真的忘了，只執著這個假的，不知道反迷歸覺，不知道反妄歸真，不知道借假修真，不知道反求諸己，非常的可憐。所以諸佛在那個定中，啊！生一種大悲心，來到這個世界上，指我們的迷途，可是我們這個人追逐妄緣，不認識這個真法，佛越給他說法，他越向後轉不停，把佛都著急得晃頭了。所以沒有法子啊！佛沒有法子怎麼辦呢？你回頭轉嘛？佛就迎頭趕上，再到你面前去，來教化你，所以「諸佛故興世」。

這種真實法，沒有任何的外道可以破壞的。你若明白真實法，這個真實法，是盡虛空遍法界，都在這個真實法裡邊包括著，無論你佛啊，魔啊，天魔外道啊，都是在這個真法裡邊包著，他跑不出這個法界的。所以，天魔外道也就要隨順正法，為什麼呢？他不能破壞這個正法。所以正法沒有人能可以破壞的；你能破壞，那它還不是真實法，真實法無可破壞。

自在大光明也就是那個○字，你修得圓滿了，大光明藏現出來了，自在大威神力、大光明藏都現出來了，這個大光明藏盡虛空遍法界。所以說普遍來指示世間一切眾生，了生脫死的法門、迴光返照的法門、還本返原的法門。就是你這個大智慧光明，把這個無明破了，顯出你本有的法性。你要是不相信的話，你只管試試看，到時候你就沒有法子不相信，你不相信，也要相信，因為它就是這樣子嘛，你有什麼方法可以不相信？啊！所以這個大光明藏是你自己本有的，不是旁人給你的，也不是諸佛給你的，是你自己本具的。

seeking outside, and don't know that they should reflect upon themselves. This true Dharma is inherent in the self-nature, it abides constantly and originally in the self-nature. One doesn't need to seek outside for it. If you go outside to try to find it, you can spend eighty thousand great kalpas and you still won't be able to find it. However, if you can return the light and look within, it's there instantly. It is said, "The sea of suffering is boundless, but a turn of the head is the other shore." That is to say, when you seek outside, just that is the boundless sea of suffering; when you reflect within and work on your self-nature, just that is the other shore you find upon turning your head.

We people are all upside down. From morning to night we pursue false conditions, follow the six sense organs and the six defiling objects, and do not understand the actual Dharma. In the eternal still light, the Buddhas enter samadhi in full lotus posture. They come to this world in their samadhi. Why? Because they see how truly pathetic we foolish living beings are, forgetting the real and clinging to the false. We don't know how to turn from delusion and return to enlightenment, how to turn from the false and return to the real, how to use the false to facilitate the cultivation of the real, and how to reflect upon ourselves. We are truly pathetic. Therefore, in their samadhi, all the Buddhas give rise to a greatly compassionate mind and come to this world to point out our confusion. However, we seek false conditions and don't recognize this actual Dharma. The more the Buddha speaks Dharma to us, the more we keep retreating. The Buddha shakes his head in frustration; he is at a loss. What can we do if the Buddha is at a loss? Well, you can turn around. When you do so, the Buddha will come face to face with you, to teach and transform you. Therefore, it is said, "Thus all Buddhas appear in the world."

This actual Dharma cannot be destroyed by any externalist ways. If you understand the actual Dharma, you know it encompasses everything throughout empty space and the Dharma Realm. Buddhas, demons, heavenly demons, and externalist ways are all included in this true Dharma; nothing is outside the Dharma Realm. Therefore, even the heavenly demons and those of externalist ways should follow and accord with the proper Dharma. Why? Because they are unable to destroy it. The proper Dharma cannot be destroyed by anyone. If one were able to destroy it, it wouldn't be the actual Dharma. The actual Dharma is indestructible.

The great brightness of self-mastery is just this O. When you have perfected your cultivation, the great bright store will manifest, the great awesome spiritual power of self-mastery will appear. This great bright store pervades empty space and the Dharma Realm. Thus the Buddha comes to universally guide all living beings in this world through the Dharma-doors of leaving birth and death, of reflecting upon oneself, and of returning to the source. Your great bright wisdom can shatter ignorance and reveal the inherent Dharma nature. If you don't believe what I say, just go ahead and try it out. When the time is ripe, you won't be able to disbelieve it. You'll believe it even if you don't want to. Because that's the way it is. How can you not believe? This great bright store is originally your own, it's not given to you by other people, nor is it given to you by the Buddhas. It is inherently yours.

本立而道生

WHEN THE FOUNDATION IS ESTABLISHED, THE WAY COMES FORTH

宣公上人一九八九年四月十二日開示於美國奧立岡州立大學

A lecture by the Venerable Master Hua at the University of Oregon on April 12, 1989

孔子說過：「三人行必有我師焉，擇其善者而從之，其不善者而改之。」由這幾句話，我們知道孔老夫子是一位空前絕後好學的學者，也是空前絕後的大教育家，也是空前絕後的一個大政治家。就由這幾句話，我們知道孔老夫子他一生是謙德不逾，什麼時候都沒有自滿的時候，沒有貢高我慢的時候。為什麼這樣說呢？就因為他說，三人行，那麼我有兩個師父，一個師父就是我要效法的師父，一個師父就是我不要效法的師父。就是擇善而從，他若有長處，我就要跟他學習；他若有短處，我就要改過，不要照著他那樣學。就是善者可以做我們的法，我們要效法他；不善者做我們的戒，我們要以他為戒師。所以今天我們做人，若能用這個理論，做為我們的座右銘，我們無人而不自得焉。那麼古人是這樣謙讓的德行，所以後人尊他為聖人，是有他的道理。

那麼又有人說：「眾人是我師」，說大家都是我的師父。「我是眾人師」，我也是一般人的師父。就是大家都是我的教授，我也是大家的教授，這互相學習，互相切磋琢磨，所以說我是眾人師。「時常師自己」，時常自己又要以自己為師，要每一天把自己所行所作，做一個簡短的檢討，看看我今天所行所作是否有當？是不是都合道理？是不是有不合道理的地方？所以自己常常反省。因為這個，所以曾子才說：「吾日三省吾身，為人謀而不忠乎？與朋友交而不信乎？傳不習乎？」

曾子他自己都說他不是一個很聰明的人，所以在《孝經》上說過：「仲尼居，曾子侍。子曰：『先王有至德要道，民用和睦，上下無怨，汝知之乎？』」說你知不知道這個啊？「曾子避席曰」，曾子站起來了，避席就是站起來，恭恭敬敬對孔老夫子就說：「參不敏」，說參我呀！很不

Confucius once said, "When there are three people walking, my teacher is bound to be among them. I select their good points and follow them. I take their bad points and change them in myself." From these words, we know that Confucius was a devoted scholar who was one of a kind. He was also a great educator who was in a class by himself. He was also a great statesman without equal. From these words, we also know that Confucius was humble and not careless. He never became conceited and arrogant. Why do I say this? Because he said that if there were three people, then he would have two teachers: one would be a teacher for him to emulate, and the other would be a teacher he wouldn't want to emulate. This is to select the good and follow it: If someone has good points, I will learn from him. If he has bad points, I will change them in myself and not imitate him. Those who are good can be our models, and we can emulate them. Those who are not good can be an example of what we should avoid. So if we can take this principle as our motto in being people, we will be at ease wherever we are. The ancients had this kind of humble and courteous virtue. Thus, it is not without reason that later generations have honored them as sages.

Someone also said, "All people are my teachers." Everyone is my teacher. "I am a teacher for all people." I am also everyone's teacher. Everyone is my professor, and I am also everyone's professor. We learn from each other and rub off on each other. "I always teach myself." I constantly act as my own teacher. Every day, we should briefly reflect on what we have done that day. "Were the things that I did today appropriate? Were they reasonable? Did I do anything unreasonable?" We should frequently examine ourselves. Thus Zengzi said, "I daily examine myself on three points—whether, in transacting business for others, I may have been not faithful; whether, in intercourse with friends, I may have been not sincere; whether I may have not mastered and practiced the instructions of my teacher."

Zengzi said of himself that he was not a very intelligent person. So the *Classic of Filiality* (Xiaojing) says, "Zhongni (Confucius) was seated and Zengzi was attending upon him. The Master said, 'The ancient kings had the highest virtue and the essentials of the Way. If these are used among the people, they will dwell in harmony and no resentment will arise between the ruler and his subjects. Did you know this?' Zengzi rose from his seat and said, 'Seng is not smart. How could he know this?'" He stood up and respectfully said to his Teacher, Confucius, "I, Seng, am very dull-witted. I'm not able to know about the highest virtue and the essen-

聰明的，「何足以知之？」我是還不夠知道這個先王的至德要道。民用它就能和睦，上下都沒有怨，沒有仇怨了，這是治國、修身、齊家的一個大法，曾參說他不夠聰明，不知道。那麼孔子就說了，說：「身體髮膚，受之父母，不敢毀傷，孝之始也。」

《論語》上又說：「君子務本，本立而道生，孝悌也者，其為人之本歟？」「君子務本」，君子他所要學習的，就是根本的道理，他所專務的是根本的道裡。「本立而道生」，你根本若立住了，就是根深葉茂，本固枝榮。那麼道生就是根生，道生也就是本立了，本立而道生。「孝悌也者，其為人之本歟？」那麼做人的根本，我們必須要溯本窮源，知道我們做人應該注意的是什麼？我們人應該追求根本，根本是什麼呢？就是「孝悌」這兩個字。孝 —— 孝順父母；悌，就是悌敬長上，這是做人的頭一件要務。頭一件的要務並不是學成了，賺的錢賺得多，這是重要的；我們要把這個孝悌做到圓滿，這是我們第一件事。做人子女的不孝順父母，這叫忘本，忘本的人根本就沒有懂得怎麼叫人，所以我們做人第一個條件要孝順父母。

在西方，英文裡邊並沒有很顯著地說明孝順父母這個道是什麼。孝順父母就是報恩，報根本我們應該報的恩。我們這個身體是父母給的，我們必須要保護這個身體，令他思想健全，身體健康，思想健康，行為健康，一切一切都健康。不可毀傷，不可以用我們父母給的這個身體去做犯法的事，去做不守禮儀的事，要循規蹈矩，按步就班，做一個實實在在真實的人。

我們做人的基礎是什麼？我們做人的基礎，就是仁義道德忠孝。這個孝是我們每一個人出生以來，耳濡目染所應該注意的，就是這個孝道。你若能盡孝道，天主是歡喜你；你若能盡孝道，這菩薩是歡喜你；你若能盡孝道，佛是歡喜你；你若能盡孝道，父母一定不會對你發脾氣的；你若能盡孝道，和兄弟姊妹一定不會爭利益。孝道是天地的靈魂，是做人的一個基礎。

忠，我們要忠於國家。忠於國家要大公無私，至正不偏。我們愛護自己的國家，要保衛自己的國家，而不要心心念念想要去侵略旁人的國家。我們只保衛自己的國家，這也就是忠；我們要是想侵略旁人的國家，這也就是不忠。為什麼呢？

tials of the Way of the ancient kings." If the people can use this, then they will be in harmony and there will be no enmity between the government and the people. This is the great Dharma for governing a nation, cultivating oneself, and regulating the family. Zengseng said he was not intelligent enough to understand it. Then Confucius said, "We received our body, hair, and skin from our parents and dare not harm them. This is the beginning of filiality."

The *Analects* say, "A superior person attends to the foundation. Once the foundation is established, the Way comes forth. Are not filiality and fraternal respect the foundation of a person?" A superior person studies the fundamental principles. He devotes his attention to the fundamental principles. "Once the foundation is established, the Way comes forth." When the foundation is established, then the roots will be deep and strong, and the leaves and branches will flourish. The coming forth of the Way is also the coming forth of the root, the establishing of the foundation. "Are not filiality and fraternal respect the foundation of a person?" We must trace back to the source and know what we should pay attention to in our human life. What are the roots that people should seek? Filiality and fraternal respect. We should be filial to our parents and respectful to our elders. This is the most important human obligation. The most important matter is not finishing our studies and making a lot of money. We must fulfill our obligations of filiality and fraternal respect—this is our top priority. If we are not filial to our parents, then we are said to have forgotten our roots. People who forget their roots basically don't understand what it means to be human. Therefore, our foremost human obligation is to be filial to our parents.

In the West, in English there isn't a very obvious explanation of what it means to be filial to one's parents. Being filial to parents means repaying their kindness, the fundamental kindness which ought to be repaid. Our bodies were given to us by our parents. Therefore, we must protect our bodies, making sure that our thoughts are wholesome, our bodies are healthy, our ideas are healthy, our conduct is healthy, and we are healthy all-around. We cannot harm our bodies. That means we cannot use our bodies, given by our parents, to do things that break the law or go against the rules of etiquette. We have to follow the rules, do things in the proper way, and be true and honest people.

What is the human foundation? It is humaneness, righteousness, the Way, virtue, loyalty, and filiality. From the time of our birth, the concept of filial piety should be instilled in each of us and we should pay attention to it. If you can be filial, Lord God will be pleased. If you can be filial, the Bodhisattvas will be pleased. If you can be filial, the Buddhas will be pleased. If you can be filial, your parents won't get mad at you for sure. If you can be filial, you certainly won't compete for advantages against your brothers and sisters. Filial piety is the spirit of heaven and earth and the human foundation.

We should be loyal to our country. To be loyal to the country, we have to be public-spirited and unselfish, perfectly fair and just. We should cherish and protect our own country and not think about invading other countries in thought after thought. If we only protect our own country, then we are being loyal. If we invade other countries, then we are not being loyal. Why is this? If you invade another country, you have to use the lives and wealth of your own

你侵略旁人的國家，你要先用自己國家的人命、財產，去向人家搏鬥、作戰、殺人，所謂「爭地以戰，殺人盈野；爭城以戰，殺人盈城。」你爭這個土地，把滿地都鋪滿了人的死屍，殺人盈野；爭城以戰，你爭著去攻打人的城池，把人家城池裡邊的人，也給殺盡了，這殺人盈城。這叫「率土地而食人肉」，這是在那兒吃人呢！「罪不容於死」啊！這是犯死罪的。你犯死罪，這對自己的國家不忠，對其他人的國家也不智，沒有智慧。

我們做人時時刻刻都要用慈愛的心，來愛護一切人，用這個仁愛人的心來對待一切人。做事情要衡量衡量，對自己有利益的事情，不要做那麼多；對人家有害的事情，更不應該做。所以我們要把「仁義道德忠孝」這六個字，能推而廣之，擴而充之，這就是得到做人基本的條件，把做人的這個地基建立起來。你把人的基礎建立起來，你這個人一生都是健康的，既身體健康，精神也愉快，不會憂愁得、煩惱得把頭髮也白了，眼睛也花了，耳朵也聾了；完了，自己還不覺悟，莫名其妙，這一生是很糊塗就過去了。

country to fight, make war, and kill others. There is a saying, "If war is waged over a piece of land, the slaughtered will fill the wilds. If war is waged over a city, the slaughtered will fill the city." If you fight over land, the ground will be covered with corpses. If you attack a city and massacre the people inside it, the city will be filled with the dead. This is known as "using the country's resources to devour people's flesh." It's the same as eating people! "Death is insufficient punishment for this crime." Ah! This is a capital crime. If you commit this capital crime, you are not being loyal to your own country, and you are not being wise in your dealings with other countries.

We should always maintain a kind and compassionate attitude and cherish all people. We ought to be benevolent towards everyone. We should take stock of what we do. We should do fewer things to benefit ourselves and not do anything that harms others. We have to develop and expand the qualities of humaneness, righteousness, the Way, virtue, loyalty, and filiality—these are the basic requirements for being a person. We should establish this human foundation. Once we do that, we will be healthy all our lives. We'll be healthy in body and happy in spirit. It won't be the case that we're worried and afflicted to the point that our hair turns white, our eyes grow blurry, and our ears go deaf. It won't be that even when it's all over, we still don't wake up—we're still as puzzled as ever, having spent our entire lives in muddled confusion.

做人的根本先要盡孝道

THE BASIS FOR BEING A HUMAN BEING IS FILIALITY

宣公上人一九九三年元月四日開示於臺灣法界佛教印經會

A lecture by Venerable Master Hua
at the Dharma Realm Buddhist Books Distribution Association on January 4, 1993

我們做人，人要是沒有做好，都是不能成佛的，所以必須把基礎建立起來。什麼是做人的基礎？做人的基礎是孝悌忠信禮義廉恥，這八種是做人的根本，所以孔子說：「君子務本，本立而道生；孝悌也者，其為人之本歟。」那麼做人的根本先要盡孝道，先要敬老尊賢，看所有的老人都是等於我的父母一樣，中年人都像我的兄弟姊妹一樣，青年人則像我的子女一樣，能這樣看，這才是懂得怎麼樣做人。因為這個，古人才說：「老吾老以及人之老，幼吾幼以及人之幼。」敬老尊賢，尊重賢人，再能恭敬有道的人，這是做人的根本。

〈禮運大同篇〉上說：「故人不獨親其親，不獨子其子，使老有所終，壯有所用，幼有所長，鰥寡孤獨廢疾者，皆有所養。」在古來古聖先王，有道的明君，都是這樣治理天下。文王發政施仁，必先周濟鰥寡孤獨這四類人，所以周朝人民享受太平。文王能以天下像一家似的，世界像一體，所以沒有彼此親疏遠近的分別，這叫大同世界的開始。我們做人都要本著這種心理來學佛，你如果有這麼大的心量志願來學佛，佛一定會護持你；你要是不這樣去做，你就是念佛、拜佛，然後常常發脾氣，這也是無有是處的，於佛教得不到什麼利益。

我不會說什麼高談闊論，只希望每一個人都能把脾氣布施出來，這是你真正的布施。你要是不能布施你的脾氣，這與佛道一定不相應的。

今天我頭一次到這兒來和你們各位見面談話，因為在飛機上也沒有睡覺，昨天晚上也沒有睡覺，今天又有很多人來見我，所以覺得很累。我不多說了，說得太多，你們都忘了，也是沒有用的；說得少，你們記住一句，真能去躬

If we do not do a good job as human beings, we cannot become Buddhas. Therefore, we must lay the foundation. What is the foundation for being a human being? It is: filial piety, fraternal respect, loyalty, trustworthiness, propriety, justice, modesty, and a sense of shame. These eight principles are the basis of being a human being. Confucius said: "The superior person devotes himself to the foundation. Once the foundation is established, the Way comes forth. Filial piety and fraternal respect are the foundation for being a human being." To have the basis for being a human being, first of all you must be filial. Respect the elderly and the worthy. Regard all elderly people as your own parents, all middle-aged people as your own siblings, and all young people as your own children. If you have this attitude, then you understand how to be a person. Thus, the ancients said, "I take care of my own elders and children and extend the same care to others' elders and children as well." Respecting the elderly, honoring the worthy, and venerating those who have attained the Way—these are the basis for being a human being.

The Chapter on the "Great Commonwealth of Peace and Prosperity" in the *Book of Rites* says "People cherish not only their own parents and children, but cherish the parents and children of others as well. The elderly live their last years in happiness, able-bodied adults are usefully employed, and children are properly raised. Widowers, widows, orphans, the childless aged, the crippled, and the ailing are well cared for." In ancient times, all the sages, worthy kings, and virtuous and wise emperors governed the nations in this way. When King Wen implemented policies with kindness, he always first gave aid to widowers, widows, orphans, and the childless aged. Therefore, the people of the Zhou Dynasty enjoyed peaceful times. King Wen was able to regard the country as one family and the world as one body. Thus there were no distinctions between you and I, between near and distant relatives, or between those who were close and those who were far. That was the beginning of a commonwealth of peace and prosperity. We should study Buddhism with this kind of spirit. If you are studying Buddhism with such a magnanimous spirit and resolve, the Buddha will surely protect and support you. If you do not have this kind of spirit—if you recite the Buddha's name and bow to the Buddha, yet constantly lose your temper, then you will not be able to obtain any benefit from Buddhism.

I do not know how to speak about lofty theories. I simply hope each one of you can give away your temper. That is true giving. If you cannot give away your temper, you will not be able to practice the Buddha's path effectively.

Today is the first time I have come here to talk to you. Since I didn't sleep on the plane, didn't get any sleep last night, and had a lot of

行實踐，真能去認真行孝悌忠信禮義廉恥，再加上不爭、不貪、不求、不自私、不自利、不打妄語，這是把佛教的路邁出頭一步，第二步你們更應該努力勇猛精進，祝你們各位早成佛道。

visitors today, I feel very tired. I will say no more. If I said too much, you would all forget and it would be useless. If I say less and you can remember even just one sentence and truly put it into practice—sincerely practice the virtues of filial piety, fraternal respect, loyalty, trustworthiness, propriety, justice, modesty, and sense of shame, as well as not fighting, not being greedy, not seeking, not benefiting yourself, not being selfish, and not lying—this would be the first step in studying Buddhism. The second step is to work hard and advance vigorously. I hope you all attain Buddhahood soon!

天下有德者居之

ONE WITH VIRTUE CAN RULE THE WORLD

節錄自宣公上人開示

Excerpts from lectures by the Venerable Master Hua

◆ 諸惡莫作，眾善奉行。對有利於民，無不行之。要為老百姓謀幸福，不是為個人謀幸福。「大道之行也，天下為公。故人不獨親其親，不獨子其子。」如果能依照這〈禮運大同篇〉去做，國家就可以治好。

◆ 最好是甚麼都不要，那才是真正為民服務，競選也不要用錢去競選。我現在要找知音，就是找不要錢而治國的，這樣能做清官，兩袖清風，愛民如子。國家如此才能強盛，有一點自私都不夠資格治國。我說這話，誰願意信，我也這麼說，不信我也這麼說；有人聽過我也這麼說，沒人聽過我也這麼說，我也不管你高不高興。

◆ 天下有德者居之，無德者失之。你看古來中國的領導者，是帝王也好，是什麼也好，都是寬容大度，那個度量一般人比不了。唐朝為什麼有貞觀之治？唐太宗他就因為能任用敵人－－用魏徵，言聽計從，還一點也不狐疑他，所以他有貞觀之治。

◆ 「國家將興，必有禎祥；國家將亡，必有妖孽。現乎蓍龜，動乎四體；禍福必先知之，善必先知之，不善必先知之。」商湯王他自己告罪，向上帝來告罪，他說：「曰予小子履」，說我這個小子叫湯履，「敢用玄牡」，用一個黑牛，「敢昭告於皇皇后帝。朕躬有罪。無以萬方。萬方有罪。罪在朕躬。」他說我一個人有罪，你不要給加到我老百姓身上；如果老百姓有罪，都是因為我沒教化好他們，你把他們的罪業都加到我身上，我一個人承受的。古聖明王都是這樣的，來勇於改過，勇於認錯，納諫如流，這才是真正這個人民的一個榜樣、領導者。

◆ Don't do any evil. Do only meritorious acts. Do only the things that benefit people. You should work only for the people's welfare, not for your own. "When the Great Way prevailed, every person was a part of public society, and the public society belonged to everyone. People not only loved their own parents and children, but loved the parents and children of others as well." If you can follow this chapter on *The Explication of Great Unity through the Functioning of Propriety*, then you will be able to govern the nation well.

◆ To want nothing at all is the best—that's to truly serve the people. Don't use money to get elected. I am looking for a friend who understands me, one who can govern the country without taking money. Such a person can be a pure official. He does not hoard money and loves the people as if they were his children. That's the only way the country can become strong. If a person has even a vestige of selfishness, he is not qualified to govern the country. I say this whether or not you believe it. I say it whether or not you like to listen. I don't care if you are happy or not.

◆ One with virtue can rule the world. One without virtue will lose his power. If you study the leaders of ancient China, be they emperors or other rulers, you will see they all had great tolerance. Their capacity for benevolence was much greater than that of ordinary people. Why was the Zhenguan reign period of the Tang Dynasty so illustrious? It was because Emperor Taizong was able to use his enemy Wei Zhen, to follow his advice faithfully without the slightest trace of doubt. That's why the Zhenguan reign was so successful.

◆ There is a saying: "If the country is about to prosper, there will be auspicious omens. If the country is about to perish, there will be evil portents. The oracles will manifest signs, and the people's actions will be affected. Thus, calamities and blessings can be known in advance. Good and evil can also be known in advance." King Tang of the Shang Dynasty appealed to the Lord on High, saying "I, this little boy, Tang Lyu, offer up a black cow and address the Supreme Lord. If I have offenses, do not punish the people. If the people have offenses, it is because I have not taught them well, and you should punish me for their offenses. I alone should take the blame." The renowned sage-kings of ancient times courageously reformed themselves, confessed their mistakes, and accepted criticism with grace. They are truly good models and leaders.

◆ 在上者，要對下推心置腹，愛人如己，必須教老百姓安居樂業。老百姓你搶我奪，不是幸福。以前周恩來在的時候，夜不閉戶、路不拾遺。臺灣一個小地方，再治不好，人人都瘋狂，人都不擇手段想賺錢，這是不祥之兆。臺灣現在像南宋臨安時期，偏安小地方，大家爭名奪利；岳武穆那樣的人，反而被殺，「國有賢良，國運必昌」，忠臣義士反而被殺，是不對的。治國，必須從古以來回憶，什麼時候安寧，哪個朝代對老百姓愛民如己，一定昌盛。互相用心機，是來之不善。「做豆腐置河窪地，漿來水去。」像共產黨用手段得天下，來之不善，將來內部必亂。「夫人必自侮，而後人侮之」，自己不健全，人必侮之。「不爭、不貪、不求、不自私、不自利、不打妄語」是最好的方法，可是愚癡的人都不敢用。

◆ 要大公無私，不貪贓，不受賄，要聰明正直，為民服務。

◆ 想要世界好，和每一個國家好，政府一定要愛護人民，保護人民，一切的問題都用理智，而不用一種剛強，或者鎮壓的手段；要用很理智的，互相溝通，互相瞭解，不能互相格格不相入。好像做政府的，你若沒老百姓，根本就不需要政府。

◆ 愛國並不是說我愛我的國，我把我這個國家擴張我的版圖，而征服全世界，這是一個愛國的，這簡直是一個國賊。因為你每一個國家，如果想擴張你的版圖，你也想擴張你的版圖，而要吞併其他人的國家；他也想要擴張他的版圖，要吞併其他人的國家。好像日本人侵略中國，結果他自己受到原子彈這個災難，無條件投降，這就是一個大錯而特錯。我們每一人不知道這種錯誤，而還要用這個強權和武力來解決問題，這是一個大錯而特錯的。我們每一個人真正愛國，真正愛自己的家庭，愛自己國家的人民生命財產，就應該要注重教育。

這個教育，你把小孩子教育明白了，他知道怎麼樣做人，他知道怎樣愛身、愛國、愛家，那麼乃至於愛全世界的人類，這才是真正治理國的一個方法，不是要用陰謀手段去壓迫旁人

◆ Those who are above should place their trust in and love those below them as they love themselves. They should enable the people to dwell in peace and find satisfaction in their work. If the people compete with and rob one another, it is not a sign of prosperity. When Zhou Enlai was still around, doors didn't have to be locked at night and things lost on the road were not picked up by others. Now, even such a small place as Taiwan cannot be governed well. All the people are going wild and using every possible means to make money. This is not an auspicious sign. Taiwan's situation resembles that of the Southern Song dynasty when it was confined to the small area of Ling-an and everyone was fighting for fame and benefit. And a [loyal commander] like Yue Wumu was killed. "If the nation has worthy and good people, it will surely prosper." It is not right for loyal ministers and righteous heroes to be killed. In governing a nation, we must remember that from ancient times till now, whenever there was peace and order, whenever the dynasty's rulers loved the people as they loved themselves, that period was certain to be prosperous. If people scheme and plot against each other, they gain things by unwholesome means. "If you make tofu and set it by the marsh, it was made with water and will be washed away by water." For example, the Communist Party took over the country by force. Since they used crooked means, there is sure to be conflict in the Party later on. "A person must insult himself before other people will insult him. If you are not healthy, people will certainly insult you." The best method is not to fight, not to be greedy, not to seek, not to be selfish, not be pursue personal advantage, and not to lie. However, stupid people dare not use it.

◆ One must be public-spirited and unselfish. One should not be greedy for bribes, nor should one take bribes. One must be intelligent, upright, and straightforward in serving the people.

◆ For the world and every nation to be well off, the governments must love the people and protect the people. They must use reason to deal with problems, not forceful or oppressive measures. They must use reason to communicate with and understand one another. They shouldn't be completely separated and unable to conform to one another. If a government didn't have any people to govern, then there would be no need for it.

◆ To love one's country doesn't mean to say, "I love my country, so I want to expand the national boundaries and take over the whole world." With this attitude, you are nothing but a traitor. Consider what would happen if every country wanted to expand its territory and swallow up the other countries. For example, when the Japanese invaded China, they suffered the disaster of the atomic bomb and surrendered unconditionally. They had made a serious mistake. None of us recognize this kind of mistake, however, and so everyone still wants to resolve problems with brute force and military power. This is a great mistake. If we all truly love the country, truly love our own families, and truly cherish the lives and property of the people of our country, then we ought to put emphasis on education.

The genuine way to govern the country is to educate children so that they know how to be good people and how to love themselves,

，而令旁人結果就不服了。所以我們在這個時代，大家趕快要把睡覺這種思想覺悟了它，不要再以為用欺騙的手段，用愚民的政策，可以就愚弄人，來統治人，這是錯誤的，這是大錯而特錯的。

所謂「以力服人者，非心服也，力不贍也。」你以那強暴的手段去壓迫人，那個人不會真正服從你。你一定要用仁義待人，那麼「以德服人者」呢？「衷心悅而誠服也」，你真正對人好，那個人不會反你的。你要是口頭上說對人好，而事實和你說的不一樣，那老百姓在什麼時侯也不能佩服的。這個國家的人民，你在上邊的人，「君子之德風，小人之德草，草上之風必偃。」你要是真正對老百姓好，沒有一個人會反的。所以你若不對老百姓好，你若假的呢，那始終是壓不住的，始終是會有人反的。

their country, their families, and all the people in the world. It is not to use secret plots to oppress other people, because people will refuse to submit. Therefore, in the present time, everyone should quickly awaken from their sleep. Don't think that you can fool people and govern them with policies that cheat them and treat them as idiots. This is wrong. It's a serious mistake.

There is a saying, "If you cause people to submit by force, it is not a true submission from the heart, but only because they have not the strength to resist." If you oppress people with violent measures, they will not truly accord with you. You have to treat people with humaneness and righteousness. "If you cause people to submit by virtue, they will joyfully and sincerely submit." If you are truly good to people, they will not disobey you. If you say you are good to people, but the facts prove otherwise, then the people will never respect you. "The virtue of a superior person is like the wind. The virtue of petty people is like the grass. When the wind blows, the grass bends." If you truly treat the people well, none of them will oppose you. If you do not treat them well, if you are false, then you won't be able to keep them down. People are bound to oppose you.

眞正的科學就是佛教

TRUE SCIENCE IS JUST BUDDHISM

宣公上人一九九三年年一月十日開示於臺灣臺北工業技術學院

A lecture by the Venerable Master
Taiwan Institute of Industrial Technology on January 10, 1993

我也沒有讀過科學，也沒有讀過哲學，所以對於這個Science（科學）、philosophy（哲學），都是一個門外漢。今天你們各位要求講這個題目，這真是強人所難。雖然如此，我略說幾句，是不科、也不學、也不哲的話。什麼叫科學？什麼叫哲學？這兩個名詞都很抽象的，為什麼呢？科學，是屬於慧性，哲學是屬於理性。這慧性和理性沒有一個進步，也沒有一個退步，它都是宛然存在的，在聖不增，在凡不減。

什麼叫慧學？慧學就是「戒定慧」這個「慧」。你想要有真正的智慧，首先必須要有定力，才能分辨是法、非法，善法和不善法；你想要有定力，先要持戒。持什麼戒呢？這個戒，就是止惡防非的，我們「諸惡不作，眾善奉行；自淨其意，是諸佛教。」這屬於慧性。說「諸惡不作」，誰都知道，那有什麼慧性？「眾善奉行」，也誰都知道，怎麼又能講得上慧性呢？你若能「諸惡不作」，就是個戒力；你若「眾善奉行」，就是個慧力。你有戒力了，中間產生一種定力；定力可以支配這個慧力，這個慧性，智慧之性。

談起這個科學，我是門外漢，可是我說幾句行家話。科學，是無窮無盡的。五百年以前，人家就懂得科學。在中國來說，三千年以前已經有人懂得科學。軒轅黃帝發明指南車，這是在四、五千年以前就發明了；直至今日，東、西方還是根據指南針來判定方向，這都是一種科學的產品。中國的科學，在周朝以前，很早已經有火炮、火藥；可是那時候，不用它來打仗、作戰，用它來鳴炮舉聲，這表示事情的隆重。那時候中國就有科學的發展，乃至於墨子那時候，就發明飛機，但它的名詞不叫飛機，叫飛雁。可是中國人做事，好讀書不求甚解，發明了一種東西，他不向深了去研究，所以日久又都忘了，這在歷史上可考據的。漢朝諸葛亮造「木牛流馬」，也不吃草，

Since I never studied science or philosophy, I am an outsider to these subjects. You are really giving me a difficult task by asking me to speak on these subjects. Nevertheless, I will say a few unscientific and unphilosophical words. What is science? What is philosophy? These two terms are very abstract. Science deals with wisdom, and philosophy deals with reason. As for wisdom and reason, there is no progress and no retreat in them. They exist in completion, with neither more in sages, nor less in ordinary people.

What is the study of wisdom? It refers to the wisdom in the three-fold study of precepts, concentration, and wisdom. If you want to have real wisdom, you must first have concentration. With concentration you can distinguish true dharmas from false dharmas and good dharmas from bad dharmas. To obtain concentration, you must first observe the precepts. What are the precepts? The precepts guard against wrongdoing. We should follow the saying: "Do no evil, practice all good, and purify your own mind. That is the teaching of the Buddhas." This is considered wisdom. You say, "Everyone understands the principle of doing no evil. How can that be wisdom?" "Anyone can understand the principle of practicing only good. How is that wisdom?" If you can do no evil, then you have the power of the precepts. If you practice only good, then you have the power of wisdom. Once you have the power of precepts, the power of samadhi arises. The power of concentration can regulate the power of wisdom, the nature of the wisdom.

I am an outsider to science, but I will say a few "professional" words. Science is limitless and inexhaustible. Five hundred years ago, people already understood science. For example, in China over three thousand years ago, there were already people who understood science. Xian Yan, the Yellow Emperor, invented the compass four or five thousand years ago, and it is still being used today to tell direction in both the East and the West. Such things are the products of science. Very early on in Chinese science, before the Zhou Dynasty, they had cannons and gunpowder, but they didn't use them in warfare. They would just set off the cannons a few times to celebrate important occasions. Science was already developing in China then, and by the time of Mocius, the plane was already invented. Instead of calling it a plane ("flying machine" in Chinese), they called it a "flying goose."

Although the Chinese people like to study, they do not try to deepen their understanding. They invent something, but do not investigate it deeply, so after a long time, it is forgotten. There is historical evidence for this. In the Han Dynasty [206 B.C. to A.D. 24], Zhuge Liang [a brilliant military strategist] built wooden horses and oxen that could transport food and supplies for the army with-

也不吃料，也不睡覺，就能運輸糧草給軍人用。
（編按：木牛流馬宛然如活者一般；上山下嶺，各盡方便。後人有詩讚曰：「劍關險峻驅流馬，斜谷崎嶇駕木牛；後世若能行此法，輸將安得使人愁？」）到現在嘛，把這個方法也都失去了。這都是屬於科學。

這科學，五百年以前的科學研究，說科學是這個樣子；等到五百年以後，又變了樣子，以前所發明的又都沒有用了，所以這個道理是無窮無盡的。說科學有進步，它不是進步的時候，人才知道；就不進步的時候，它也存在的，就是因為我們人智慧、智力達不到這種境界，所以不知道這科學。

電腦，這也屬於一種科學的結晶，可是我們人現在迷到電腦上了，用電腦來賺錢。若懂得電腦了，就能賺不少錢；不懂得電腦，就要失業了。我在十多年以前就對人講過，我說這個電腦不如神腦。神腦不是用電來支配，是用自己的智慧來駕御它。你有智慧了，什麼問題都迎刃而解，能當機立斷；沒有智慧，愚癡的人，學的東西不會很圓滿。所以這個神腦，我們每一個人都有，不用錢去買，你把神腦若會用了，那又超過那個電腦了。可是現在一般人研究的科學，也不知道有個神腦。這個神腦是自性具足的，不需要到外邊找。

這個哲學也是一種理性，講這個道理，合乎邏輯、不合乎邏輯？這兩種的學問，有的研究來、研究去，愈研究愈迷糊，研究到老死，也沒研究出個所以然；等到再世為人，把所研究的又都忘了，又是要從頭練過。所以說科學、哲學它是宛然存在的，並沒有什麼進步和退步。退步、進步，這都是我們人心在那兒分別。我在各位科學家面前講的話，你們聽得出一定是個外行所講的。

真正科學是什麼呢？不爭是科學，不貪是科學，無所求是科學，不自私那是真科學，不自利那也是真正哲學，再不打妄語。若有這六種毛病，不管研究什麼，研究來、研究去，都是在皮毛上打轉轉，愈研究愈迷惑，沒有一個頭緒，所謂循環無端，無窮無盡的。那麼與其無窮無盡，我們何不返本還原，把我們這個神腦修理好了。這時候，不動而知天下，無所不知，無所不明，這所謂「而一旦豁然貫通焉，則眾物之表裡精粗無不到，而吾心之全體大用，無不明矣！」你真能修

out needing to eat hay or grain or to sleep. [Note: These wooden oxen and horses were just like live ones; they could travel up and down the mountains and valleys, providing a convenient source of transportation. Later, a verse was written in praise of them: "Wooden horses were driven through the dangerous peaks of Jianguan. Wooden oxen were driven up the narrow, twisted paths of the rugged, steep mountains. If future generations can use this method, how could anyone worry about transportation?"] Although that technology has now been lost, it was also a scientific development. In speaking of science, we must realize that the scientific research of five hundred years ago defined science a certain way, but that definition has changed after five hundred years. What was considered a scientific invention in the past is no longer used now. So the principles are endless and inexhaustible, and when we say there is progress, it does not mean that we invent something new. Even when there is no progress, the principle is always there. It is just that our wisdom and intelligence may not have reached that kind of state, and so we are unaware of that kind of science.

Computers are also a result of science, but nowadays everyone is infatuated with computers, and many are using them to make money. If you understand computers, you can make a lot of money, but if you don't, you might lose your job. Over ten years ago, I said that the computer ["electronic brain" in Chinese] cannot beat the "spiritual brain" which runs not on electricity, but on our own wisdom. If you have wisdom, then you can resolve any problem right away. Fools who lack wisdom cannot learn anything well. Each one of us has a spiritual brain. We don't need to go out and buy one. If we know how to use our spiritual brain, then it can surpass the electronic brain—the computer. However, those who study science today don't know about the spiritual brain, which is inherent in their own nature and need not be sought outside.

Philosophy deals with reason, with the study of what is logical and what is not. The more people study this kind of knowledge, the more muddled they become, until they grow old and die without having reached any conclusion in their studies. When they are reborn as people in their next life, they will have forgotten everything they studied previously and will have to start all over again.

Science and philosophy exist by themselves, and there is no such thing as their progress or decline. Progress and decline are just discriminations that we make. As all of you scientiests can tell, I am just speaking the words of an outsider.

What is true science? Not fighting is science; not being greedy is science; seeking nothing is science; being unselfish is true science; not pursuing personal profit is true philosophy, and so is not lying. If you have these six faults, then no matter how much research you do, you are just circling around on the surface. The more you study, the more muddled you get, and you will never get a handle on it. It never ends, but just goes on and on. Wouldn't it be better for us to return to the source and improve our spiritual brains? Then, without making a move, we would understand the universe. Nothing would be beyond our knowledge. As it is said, "one suddenly penetrates everything and understands all the inner and outer, coarse and fine aspects of the myriad phenomena, as well as the overall great functioning of one's mind." If you can

習定力、修習戒力、修習慧力，戒、定、慧，這是科學、哲學的一個根本。可是我們人在這個地方恐怕都忽略了，沒注意這個。沒有注意這個，所以就像在那個輪子裡轉轉似的，轉來轉去，找不著出頭的地方。

我們要研究科學、哲學，首先一定把這個本身的科學、哲學，研究徹底明白了。你自己本身的問題，還沒明白，就只是到外面去找。研究、研究，用多少錢來研究，研究來研究去，也是沒有什麼成就。因為你捨本逐末，沒能在心地法門上用功夫。你向外馳求，到外邊去找去，外邊找來的都不是的。

我說的話一定很多人不願意聽的，說：「你講來講去，真是荒唐透頂！我從來就沒有聽過人家講科學、哲學，說要由戒定慧上著手。戒定慧那是你們和尚的事情，與我們科學、哲學有什麼關係？」你因為沒找到根本，就認為這是和尚的事。和尚根本也是個人，他是由人而做和尚的，我們大家不要忘了，「人同此心，心同此理」，不要認為這有什麼了不起。

真正的科學就是佛教，佛教包羅萬有，再沒有什麼學問超過佛教了。所以你若想廣博多聞，要先來研究佛法；你把佛法了解了，研究科學也容易，研究哲學也容易，因為你開大智慧了，一切問題都迎刃而解。

我說的，如果有點道理嘛，你們各位就不妨試一試；若沒有道理呢，就算我浪費你們每一個人的時間，你把它忘了！

truly cultivate precepts, concentration and wisdom, they are the fundamentals of science and philosophy. I'm afraid we have neglected them and paid no attention to them. We are just spinning in circles, round and round, unable to find a way out. In studying science and philosophy, we should first thoroughly investigate the science and philosophy of our own selves. If you study what is outside, without first understanding your own problems, then no matter how much money and effort you expend in your research, it will come to nothing. This is because you are abandoning the root to pursue the branch tips. You are looking outside instead of applying effort internally, in the mind. If you search for and study the Dharma external to your mind, what you find will not be the real thing.

I am sure some people are objecting, "What you are saying is totally absurd. We've never heard anyone say that science and philosophy should be based on precepts, concentration, and wisdom. Precepts, concentration, and wisdom are the business of monks—what do they have to do with science and philosophy?" It is just because you haven't found the root that you think they are the business of monks. Actually, monks are just people, and it is people who become monks. It is said, "People's minds are all the same, and all minds follow the same principle." You shouldn't think what I said is a big deal.

The true science is just Buddhism. Buddhism encompasses the myriad things, and there is no field of study which goes beyond Buddhism. Therefore, if you want to study widely, you should first investigate the Buddhadharma. Once you understand the Buddhadharma, it will be easy to study science and philosophy, because you will have great wisdom, and all problems will be solved as soon as they arise.

If what I have said makes sense, you can try it out. If it doesn't make sense, then I have wasted everyone's time, and you should forget it.

佛法是很平實的

THE BUDDHADHARMA IS ORDINARY AND HONEST

宣公上人一九九三年八月七日開示於國際譯經學院

A lecture by the Venerable Master Hua
on August 7, 1993 at the International Translation Institute

各位善知識，我們學佛主要不要在佛教裡造罪業。如果造了罪業，這就是得不償失；你在佛教裡頭，應該立功、立德、立言，不要造罪業。在佛教裡頭，一天到晚就給旁人洗衣服，盡說其他人的不是、不對，這是學佛最大的毛病，也是造罪業造得最多的地方。我們本照直心是道場，不爭、不貪、不求、不自私、不自利、也不打妄語，你若能這樣，庶幾乎不會在佛教裡再造罪業。

這一點是我們每個人要特別注意的，你不注意這一點，那就是不懂佛法呢！佛法都是善良的，不是叫你在佛教裡頭造是造非的。你要能以「擇善而從，不善而改；是道則進，非道則退。」這個法，「是法平等，無有高下。」你若懂佛法的，一舉一動、一言一行，都是佛法；你若不懂佛法，天天念經、念佛，也是沒有用的。因為你心裡頭，妒忌、障礙在那兒滿肚子都是。你看看！嫉妒、障礙、貢高我慢在心裡頭裝滿了，那你還能懂佛法嗎？不懂佛法了！佛法就是很平實的，直心是道場，不用轉彎抹角。那麼你直心是道場啊！這個收功效，看著是沒有什麼收穫，實際上這就是你在真正修行的路上走呢！

所以古人說：「道在邇，而求諸遠；事在易，而求諸難。」本來這個「道」離著你很近，你不認識，要到遠的地方去找道，甚至於去找密宗，又去找什麼 secret school，這都是白搭功夫，枉勞神哪！你盡往外找，那都不是的；你迴光返照，反求諸己，那當下就是，就是道。所以道在邇，而求諸遠，向遠的地方去求道。事在易，這個什麼事情本來很容易的，很容易就解決它；而求諸難，認為這是很不容易的，自己把這個界限就劃出來了，所以永遠也不能解決這事情的問題，你認為它很難，很高深

All Good and Wise Advisors:

In studying Buddhism, the most important thing is to avoid creating offenses in Buddhism. If you create offenses, then what you gain does not make up for what you lose. You should establish merit, virtue, and teachings in Buddhism, not create offenses. The greatest flaw that students of Buddhism have, the place where they commit the most offenses, is in washing others' clothes all the time—always pointing out the faults of others. We should follow the motto that "the straight mind is the Way-place" and not contend, not be greedy, not seek, not be selfish, not pursue personal benefit and not tell lies. If you can do this, then you won't create any offense karma in Buddhism.

We should pay special attention to this point. If you don't pay heed to it, then you simply don't understand the Buddhadharma. The Buddhadharma is wholesome and good; you shouldn't be stirring up rumors in Buddhism. You should be able to: "Select what is good and follow it; / Take what is bad and change it. / If it is the Way, then advance upon it; / If it is not the Way, then retreat from it." "All dharmas are equal and level, without high or low." If you understand the Buddhadharma, then each action or movement, every word and deed, is the Buddhadharma. If you don't understand it, then even if you recite the Sutras or the Buddha's name every day, it's all useless. That's because your mind is full of jealousy and obstructiveness. Take a look! With your mind full of jealousy, obstructiveness, and arrogance, how can you understand the Buddhadharma? You simply can't! The Buddhadharma is something very ordinary and honest. The straight mind is the Way-place. Don't act in a crooked way. The straight mind is the Way-place! It may seem that you gain nothing, but in reality, you are already walking on the path of true cultivation!

The ancients said, "The Way is near, but people search afar; the task is easy, but people make it difficult." Originally, the Way is very close to you, but you fail to recognize it and want to look for it in distant places. Your search may even take you to the Secret School. This is all a waste of effort and energy. If you keep looking outside, you won't find it. Return the light and shine within. Seek within yourself: you'll find the Way right here. The Way is near, but people search afar. They seek the Way in distant places. It's basically an easy task, a simple matter to resolve, but people make it difficult. They decide that it is very difficult, so they limit themselves and never resolve the problem. They think it's very hard, very deep. Actually, the Way is very ordinary. The ordinary mind is the Way. We should realize that all dharmas are the Buddhadharma, and none can be obtained. If you think that something can be attained, you are an

的。這個「道」都是很平常的，平常心是道。我們要知道一切法皆是佛法，皆不可得，你若有一個所得，那就是外道了；心外求法，名為外道。

你行、住、坐、臥，舉動行為管自己，行住坐臥不離家，就是要用克己復禮的功夫。什麼叫克己復禮的功夫？就是非禮勿視，非禮勿聽，非禮勿言，非禮勿動。不合乎禮的事情，我不看它，勿視；非禮勿聽，不合乎道理的話，我不要聽它；非禮勿言，不合乎道理的言論，我也不說；非禮勿動，不合乎道理的事情，我絕對不做的。你能這樣子，就是求仁得仁，求智慧得智慧，不用繞圈子向遠的地方去找，回頭就是；苦海無邊，回頭就是彼岸；你不能回頭，那你怎麼能到彼岸呢？

所以我們做人的道理先把它做好了，我們不爭、不貪、不求、不自私、不自利、不打妄語，能以謹守這六個條款，這就是我們佛教徒的本份，我們都應該這樣子去做去。我們佛教徒，掛個招牌是佛教徒，但是一天到晚經經營營的，經之營之這麼不休息地去求，到頭來啊，「金銀堆成山，閉眼全都撂；空手見閻君，悔心把淚掉。」你這個時候知道，這一生悠悠蕩蕩地把光陰都空過了。你看！這多可惜呀！你要好好修行修行，自性的光明現前、自性的智慧現前，這才是真正佛教徒的本份；你沒有開智慧，這什麼時候都是在門外站著的。

outsider—one who seeks the Dharma outside the mind.

In every move you make, mind your own conduct. Whether moving or still, sleeping or awake, do not leave the true mind. This is the skill needed to "restrain oneself and comply with propriety." What kind of skill is this? It consists of not looking at what is improper, not listening to what is indecent, and neither speaking nor acting without observing propriety. I won't look at anything which does not accord with propriety. I won't listen to words that do not accord with principle. I won't make any comments that go against principle. I shall never perform deeds that do not accord with principle. If you can be this way, you will attain humaneness when you seek it, and you will obtain wisdom when you seek it. There's no need to go around in circles or to seek afar. It's just a turn of the head. The sea of suffering is boundless; a turn of the head is the other shore. If you can't turn around, how can you get to the other shore?

So we should first follow the principles of being a good person, and strictly uphold the Six Principles—not contending, not being greedy, not seeking, not being selfish, not pursuing personal advantage, and not lying. These six guidelines are the basic duty of every Buddhist. This is what we should do. Don't advertise yourself as a Buddhist and then scheme to attain things all day long. When the time comes, "You pile up mountains of gold and silver, but when you close your eyes in death, you have to cast them aside. Empty-handed, you go to see King Yama. Filled with remorse, you can only weep." Only now do you realize that you have frittered away your life. Isn't it pitiful! Cultivate well, and the light and wisdom of your inherent nature will appear. This is the responsibility of a real Buddhist. Before you attain wisdom, you are still standing outside the door.

人心不可一日無喜神

OUR HEARTS CANNOT BE UNHAPPY FOR A SINGLE DAY

宣公上人一九九四年二月六日開示於國際譯經院

A lecture by the Venerable Master Hua
at the International Translation Institute on February 6, 1994

各位善知識，我也學祖教授，給你們各位早祝一個新年快樂，Happy New Year! 我們新年快樂了，要是舊年快樂不快樂呢？我們要年年都快樂，月月都要快樂，日日都要快樂，時時刻刻都要快樂。為什麼要快樂呢？這快樂並不是吃點好東西，這就快樂了；也並不是穿一件好衣服，我們就快樂了；也不是買一輛最漂亮的車，我們快樂了；也不是住一棟好房子，就快樂了。

什麼我們應該快樂？我們應該自性常常地知足，所謂知足常樂，能忍自安，知足常足，我們要時時刻刻都要知足。我們做人了，比那一切的畜生都有智慧，有靈知靈覺，一切的一切都超過畜生，這我們就應該知足了。我們知足，就快樂了，就沒有煩惱。所以這不是過年要快樂，是時時刻刻都要 happy（快樂），不要煩惱，那麼這樣子才能「栽培心上地，涵養性中天。」你能心地光明了，性天也光明了，這個光明就是佛的光明。我們為什麼沒有現出這光明？就因為我們沒能真正栽培心上地，涵養性中天。所以在佛教裡頭，你若能常常快樂，這就是修行。

那個《菜根譚》上說：「光風霽月，草木欣欣」，光風霽月的時候，這個風也有和風；霽月，沒有什麼雲。草木欣欣，這個草木都覺得欣欣向榮，很快樂的。「怒雨疾風」呢？你要是天發了脾氣，下大雨；下大雨這等於天哭一樣，天在那兒也發愁了，怒雨。疾風，刮那個颶風，刮那個颱風。刮這個風啊，不要說人哪，就那個禽鳥，禽是禽獸，鳥是飛鳥，戚戚，牠們也都在那兒不快樂了。所以說：「光風霽月，草木欣欣；怒雨疾風，禽鳥戚戚，故天地不可一日無和氣，人心不可一刻無喜神。」天地要是下大雨啊、刮大風啊，這都是不和了。天地不可一日無和氣，都要有這個和暖的風，這種祥瑞的氣。

人心不可一刻無喜神，時時刻刻都要歡歡喜喜

All Good and Wise Advisors, Happy New Year! Like Professor Tsu, I would like to wish all of you a Happy Chinese New Year in advance! We say, "Happy New Year!" Should we be happy in the old year? We ought to be happy year after year, month after month, day after day, and moment after moment. Why should we be happy? Happiness does not mean we eat some delicious food and feel happy. Nor does it mean we wear nice clothes, and that makes us happy. Nor is it that we buy a fancy car, or live in a fine house, and that makes us happy.

How should we be happy? In our own natures, we should always be content. As it is said, "Knowing contentment, one is always happy. Able to be patient, one is naturally at peace." We should always be content. In every moment and at all times, we ought to be content. We human beings have more wisdom and more spiritual awareness than animals. We surpass them in every respect. For that reason, we should be content. If we are content, we will be happy and without afflictions. So not only should we be happy when celebrating the new year, we should be happy and free of afflictions all the time. That way, we can "cultivate the ground of the mind and nurture the sky of the nature." If you can make the ground of your mind bright, and the sky of your nature bright, this brightness is the brightness of the Buddha. Why haven't we manifested this brightness? It's because we have not truly been able to "cultivate the ground of the mind and nurture the sky of the nature." Therefore, according to Buddhism, if you can be happy all the time, just this is cultivation.

In *Vegetable Root Discourses,* it says, "With the brilliant wind and unclouded moon, the grass and trees are delighted." At this time, there is a gentle breeze, a clear moon, and few clouds. The grass and trees all thrive and flourish, feeling very joyful. What about "the furious rain and strong wind"? If heaven gets angry, it rains heavily. The falling rain symbolizes heaven's tears; heaven is feeling sad. The strong wind refers to a hurricane. When a hurricane blows in, not to mention people, even the birds and beasts are distressed and unhappy. So it says, "With the brilliant wind and unclouded moon, the grass and trees are delighted. With the furious rain and strong wind, the birds and beasts are woeful." Therefore, heaven and earth cannot exist for a day without harmony. A person's heart cannot be for a moment without happiness. If there are rainstorms and gusty winds, then heaven and earth are not in harmony. "Heaven and earth cannot exist for a day without harmony." There should always be a gentle breeze and an auspicious energy.

"A person's heart cannot be for a moment without happiness." In

宣化老和尚追思紀念專集

的。那彌勒菩薩，你對他怎麼樣，他也不生煩惱。他說：「老拙穿衲襖」，我這個沒有知識的老人，老拙，很拙笨的一個人。穿衲襖，穿一件補補釘的衣服。「淡飯腹中飽」，我吃的粗茶淡飯，吃飽了這個肚子就好了。所以他那麼大肚子，用手常常拍拍肚子：「看我這肚子裡飽了！」「補破好遮寒」，我這衣服破了，我就把它補起來，補個補釘，好遮寒，我遮這個寒。「萬事隨緣了」，什麼事情來了，事來則應；什麼事情去了，事去則靜，萬事隨緣了。「有人罵老拙」，有人他若罵，說：「你這個老怪物！你這個老不死的！」「老拙只說好」，我這個笨的老人，就說好、好、好，你罵我是最好的！有人罵老拙，老拙只說好。「有人打老拙」，有人要是來打我，「老拙自睡倒」：你打我，我躺那地方給你打，像睡著了似的。「唾在我面上」：你吐在我臉上一口口水，「憑它自乾了」：叫它自己乾到臉上，我也不擦它。這樣怎麼樣？「我也省力氣」：我也省擦你這口水的力量，「你也無煩惱」，你吐到我臉上，我也不回吐，向你起對待，你也無煩惱。「這樣波羅蜜」：這樣的波羅蜜，「便是妙中寶」，因為一般人都不會用這種波羅蜜，這種到彼岸的方法，便是妙中寶，這是妙中之妙，寶中之寶。「若知這消息」，你若知道這個道理，這個消息，這個訊息啊！「何愁道不了」，你怎麼能不成道呢？你道業一定成就的。

祖教授講這個慈悲，和中國儒教的仁慈。其實儒教是講「忠恕」的，天主教和耶穌教他們是講「愛」，他們就「博愛」。這個「博」字也是個豎心旁，這個「愛」字也有個心，在那個愛的中間，在心裡頭。道教是講「感應」，它雖然說「清淨、無為」，要修自然之道，「人法地，地法天，天法道，道法自然。」這是《道德經》上說的。那麼實際上呢，它的教義就是「感應」兩個字。佛教呢，是「慈悲」。儒、釋、道這三教，都是沒離開這個「心」；若離開這個「心」，就沒有教了。

所以儒教是講「忠恕」，忠是忠以持己，恕是恕以待人。持己，是我做什麼事情，對人要有忠心，要盡我的忠心，這是培植自己品德的一個基本條件。恕以待人，恕是原諒其他的人，其他人有什麼錯處，要有原諒、寬恕其他人的這種思想。那麼你能忠以持己，你的人格就清高了；你能恕以待人，你對人就有利人的思想，對人都不苛求，對誰也不苛求。這是儒教的，它沒離開這個「心」，你看「

our hearts, we should be happy and joyous all the time. We should be like Maitreya Bodhisattva, who never becomes afflicted, no matter how people treat him. He said, "The Old Fool wears a patched cloak." I am a dumb old man who doesn't know anything. The clothes I wear are patched up rags. "He fills his belly with tasteless food." "It is all right if I can get full with simple meals," he says. So he often pats his big belly and says, "See how full I am!" "He mends his clothes to keep out the cold." When my clothes are torn, I mend them. "And lets the myriad things go by." When things come up, he responds; when things are gone, he is still. He handles the myriad things according to their conditions. "If someone scolds the Old Fool..." If someone scolds him, "You old freak!" "The Old Fool just says, 'Fine!'" This old fool will just say, "Good, good. It's great that you're scolding me." "If someone beats the Old Fool, he falls down and goes to sleep." If someone beats me, I lie there and take the beating, as if I were asleep. "If someone spits on his face, he lets it dry by itself." If you spit saliva on my face, I let it dry up by itself. I won't wipe it off. How is it? "That way, he saves his strength, and you don't get afflicted." I save the energy of having to wipe it off. When you see that I do not react or try to spit back at you, you don't be afflicted either. "This kind of Paramita is the jewel within the wonderful." Ordinary people do not know how to apply this Paramita, this way to get to the other shore. This is the wonderful of the wonderful, the treasure of the treasures. "If you know this news, why worry about not realizing the Way?" If you know this principle, how could you not accomplish the Way? You will surely accomplish the Way!

Professor Tsu was talking about compassion and about humaneness in China's Confucianism. Actually Confucianism advocates loyalty and forgiveness. Catholicism and Protestantism talk about universal love. The Chinese character 博 "universal" has a vertical heart (mind) radical 忄, and the character 愛 "love" also has a heart 心 in the middle. Love is in the heart. Taoism talks about influence and response. Although it advocates "purity and nondoing" and cultivating the way of Nature, wherein "People emulate the earth, the earth emulates heaven, heaven emulates the Way, and the Way emulates Nature," as quoted in the *Daodejing* (*Classic of the Way and Virtue*), the teaching of Taoism focuses on influence and response. Buddhism promotes kindness and compassion. These three religions—Confucianism, Buddhism, and Taoism—are not beyond the mind. Apart from the mind, there is no religion.

Confucianism advocates loyalty and forgiveness. Loyalty means to conduct ourselves honestly. Forgiveness means to be forgiving of others. To conduct ourselves honestly means that, in whatever we do, we should be faithful to others. We should do our best to be loyal. This is basic to cultivating our character and virtue. To be forgiving of others means to pardon others. If they make mistakes, forgive them, and be tolerant. If you can conduct yourself honestly, your character will be pure and noble. If you can forgive others, you will benefit others and not pick on them. This is the teaching of Confucianism, which is not beyond the mind. The Chinese characters for "loyalty" 忠 and

忠恕」兩個字，底下都是「心」字。

道教是「感應」，他做什麼事情是憑感應。怎麼叫感呢？是感而遂通；應呢？是無求不應，誰有求於他，他都答應了。「有感斯通，無求不應」，這是感應兩個字，感應道交。什麼叫感應呢？譬如這個電，你那個地方也裝上電了，欵！它就放光了，這就是「有感斯通，無求不應。」也就是你那個心裡想什麼，他這兒也知道了。這是互相心裡那個電能有所感應，如是感應，感應如是，這是「有感斯通，無求不應」，你求什麼能得什麼。你真誠心了，就有感，就能通，通達到神明了。

這個道教裡講感應，所以老君才寫《感應篇》，這《感應篇》一開始就這麼說：「老君曰：福禍無門，唯人自召」，這就是感應，它禍也沒有個門，福也沒有個門，你自己做善事就有福，做不善事就有禍，所以說福禍無門，唯人自召。「善惡之報，如影隨形」，善惡的果報，就像人的身體，有個影子常常跟著你跑，你走到什麼地方，你那影子就到什麼地方。善的報也像如影隨形，惡的報也像如影隨形，善惡之報，如影隨形。

是以天地有司過之神，天地都有年值、月值、日值、時值，有四值功曹。四值功曹就是年、月、日、時，都默默中有神在那兒管著的。所以「是以天地有司過之神，因人所犯輕重，以奪人算，算減則貧耗。」以奪人算，以奪人這個壽命；奪人算了，就是這個人本來應該活長命了，忽然間短命了，這個叫算。這個一紀是十二年，這叫紀算。算減則貧耗，你若算、壽命短了，你就也窮了，什麼禍患都來了，飛災橫禍啊、疾病啊、口舌啊，什麼都來了。這是感應篇，它是「有感斯通，無求不應」，所以這個道教講感應。

佛教就講「慈悲」，什麼叫慈？慈就是無緣大慈，無緣就是對你沒有緣的，你也對他慈悲，不管他對你好不好，你都對他慈悲，這叫無緣大慈。沒有緣嗎？沒有緣，才要用慈悲，這是無緣大慈。同體大悲，怎麼有大悲心呢？這個大悲心就是同情心，就是看人家的苦，就像自己受的，如同身受一樣，這所以叫悲天憫人。慈悲喜捨，因為慈能予樂，慈就能給眾生樂；悲能拔苦，因為你有同情的心了，就能把眾生的苦惱都給它拔除去，這也就是愛人如己。

耶教、天主教它講這個「博愛」。博是個豎心

"forgiveness" 恕 both have a mind radical at the bottom.

In Taoism, everything depends on influence and response. What is meant by influence? It means, "With influence, there is a connection." What is meant by response? It means, "There is a response to every prayer." Anyone who prays will get his prayers answered. This is describing the interchange in the Way between influence and response. What is meant by influence and response? Take the example of an electric current. When the electricity is hooked up somewhere, there can be light. This is what is meant by: "With influence, there is a connection. There is a response to every prayer." It also means that others can know what you are thinking. There is mutual influence and response between people, like an electric current running between their minds. Whatever you seek, you will get. If you are really sincere, you will have influence and be able to connect with the gods and spirits.

Taoism talks about influence and response, and thus Laozi wrote the "Essay on Influence and Response," which begins, "The Elder Superior One says: Blessings and calamities have no door, but people bring them upon themselves." That is influence and response. There is no door for blessings and calamities to enter through. If you do good deeds, you will have blessings. If you do evil, you will suffer calamities. "The retribution for good and evil follows one like a shadow." The rewards for good deeds and retributions for bad deeds are just like the shadow of your body, which follows you everywhere. Wherever you go, your shadow goes along with you.

Thus heaven and earth have gods in charge of offenses. Heaven and earth have four gods in charge of the year, month, day, and hour, respectively. There are always gods and spirits quietly and invisibly supervising everything. "Thus heaven and earth have gods in charge of offenses. They reduce people's allotted life spans according to the gravity of their offenses. When one's life span is reduced, one meets up with poverty and waste." To reduce people's life spans means to shorten their lives. One *ji* 紀 is a period of twelve years, and we speak of reducing life spans in terms of *ji*. With your life span shortened, you will also become poor, and you'll suffer all kinds of misfortunes, accidents, sicknesses, and bad reputation. The "Essay on Influence and Response" says, "With influence, there is a connection. There is a response to every prayer." Therefore, Taoism talks about influence and response.

Buddhism talks about kindness and compassion. What is kindness? It means being kind to those with whom one has no affinity. That is, you should be kind and compassionate to people who feel no affinity with you, no matter how they treat you. It is especially when there is no affinity that we must be kind to people. This is kindness for those without affinities. There's also the great compassion of being one with all. How can we have great compassion? Great compassion is a feeling of pity and sympathy. When we see others suffering, we also suffer. This is known as commiserating with the world's people. We should practice kindness, compassion, joy, and giving, because by being kind, we can make living beings happy, and by being compassionate, we can sympathize with living beings and alleviate their suffering and afflictions. We should love people as much as we love ourselves.

，它這個心放到旁邊了；這個愛，心放到中間了。所以它這個愛，就講得甚至於接近男女這種愛。男女的愛是一種不清淨的愛，是一種染污的愛；真正清淨的愛，沒有這個染污在裡頭夾雜著。那麼耶穌教一天到晚喊愛、愛、愛，對誰都講愛心！愛心！這個愛不需要口頭上來高高地盡唱這個愛的口調，愛的這種歌曲。真正的愛，是無形無相的，無所表的。不是像男女這個男貪女愛，這個叫愛，這都是世俗的一種「男女居室，人之大倫。君子之道，肇端乎夫婦。」這都是這種的世間法。若出世法的愛，就沒有這種染污的念頭在裡頭。所以你們各位要真正懂得這個愛的範圍是怎麼回事。男女愛，這是一個愚癡的愛；出世的愛，那是對眾生真正的愛。

In Protestantism and Catholicism, there is the concept of universal love. The character "universal" has a vertical "heart" radical on the side, and the character "love" has a heart in the middle. The way they explain "love," it is very close to the love between a man and a woman. The love between a man and a woman is an impure love, a defiled kind of love. Love that is truly pure does not have any defilement in it. In Christianity, they preach "love, love, love" all day long, saying that we should love everyone! There's no need to holler the slogan of "love" or sing the tune of "love." True love is invisible and formless. It has no external expression. It's not like the romantic love between a man and a woman, which is based on worldly notions: "A man and a woman dwelling together is the basic human relationship. The Way of a superior man begins with the relationship of husband and wife." This is all worldly dharma. Transcendental love has no room for defiled thoughts. Therefore, we should all understand what the true scope and definition of love is. The love between a man and a woman is a stupid kind of love, whereas love that transcends the world is a true love for living beings.

千百年來碗裡羹
怨深似海恨難平

FOR HUNDREDS OF THOUSANDS OF YEARS,
THE STEW IN THE POT HAS BOILED UP
A RESENTMENT VERY HARD TO LEVEL

宣公上人一九八九年七月二十一日開示於夏威夷大學

A lecture by Venerable Master Hua at the University of Hawaii on July 21, 1989

現在這個世界上，殺生的人也太多，救生的人是太少了，那麼人人都只知道殺生，人人就都忽略了放生。因為殺生，你殺他，他也要殺你，互相報仇，互相製造五濁惡世這個輪迴，所謂冤冤相報何時了。古人有這麼幾句話說：「千百年來碗裡羹，怨深似海恨難平，欲知世上刀兵劫，試聽屠門夜半聲。」我們人應該依照孔老夫子的話來做人，說：「見其生不忍見其死，聞其聲不忍食其肉，是以君子遠庖廚也。」這「千百年來碗裡羹」，從千百年到現在，這麼一碗的羹湯，你也喝這碗羹湯，我也喝這碗羹湯，這碗羹湯就是用肉來做的羹湯。「怨深似海恨難平」，這股怨氣啊，在這一碗羹湯裡頭，那個仇恨比海都深，所以恨難平，這個怨恨心不容易把它平息了。「欲知世上刀兵劫」，想要知道世界上為什麼有刀兵、水、火、瘟疫流行，這個戰爭的痛苦，殺人流血，互相這麼尋仇報怨，為什麼呢？就因為殺生殺太多了。所以你若不明白，「試聽屠門夜半聲」，你到那個屠宰場聽一聽，那屠宰場半夜的時候是個什麼聲音 —— 豬也叫，羊也哭，牛也在那兒嚎，都是在那兒要求，說：「饒命吧，老大爺呀！饒命吧，老祖宗啊！饒命吧，老佛爺啊！」都在那兒叫，但是我們人也視而不見，聽而不聞，也不管三七二十一，就照殺可也。這一殺呀，那個牛羊豬那一念的瞋恨心，將來也就要報仇雪恨，所以演成世界戰爭這種的災難，種種的意外死亡，這都是由殺生造成的。

可是這個還報不完，現在最厲害的就是人這個 cancer（癌）病，又是種種的的怪病，為什麼生

In the world today, there are too many who take life and too few people who save lives. Everyone knows only how to kil!. Everyone has neglected to liberate life. When you kill someone, he will want to kill you back. This mutual revenge leads to the cycle of rebirth in the world of the five turbidities. When will this cycle of mutual vengeance ever come to an end? The ancients have said, "For hundreds of thousands of years, the stew in the pot / Has boiled up a resentment very hard to level. / If you want to know why there are calamities and wars in the world, / Just listen to the sounds from a slaughterhouse at midnight." We should base our lives on the words of Confucius: "When I see those who are alive, I do not wish to see them die. When I hear their sounds, I cannot bear to eat their flesh. Therefore a gentleman does not go near the kitchen." For hundreds of thousands of years until now, there's been a pot of stew. You've eaten from the pot of stew and so have I. This stew is a meat broth. It contains a resentment which is deeper than the sea, which is very hard to level. It's not easy to subdue these feelings of enmity. Do you want to know why there are wars, floods, fires, and epidemics in the world? What is the reason for the suffering, killing, and bloodshed brought on by wars? Why do people seek each other out to take revenge? Because there has been too much killing. If you don't understand, just go near the slaughterhouse and listen to the sounds that come from there at midnight—the pigs calling out, the lambs crying, the cows wailing...They are all there pleading, "Please spare our lives, Mister! Please spare our lives, Elder! Please spare our lives, Buddha!" But we pretend we don't see or hear them crying out, and we go ahead and kill them without a second thought. As soon as we kill them, the one thought of hatred that those cows, sheep, and pigs give rise to will lead them to seek revenge in the future. This leads to disasters such as world wars and all kinds of accidental deaths. These all result from the taking of life.

However, even such retribution is not enough. Now the most devastating things are cancer and all kinds of strange diseases.

的呢？就是吃肉吃得太多了。吃肉吃得太多，那個肉裡頭，尤其現在這空氣也染污了，地球也染污了，那麼水的性質也都染污了，水質都染污了。在這個染污的空氣，染污的地球，染污的水裡邊，生出一切的東西來，都帶著一種毒的性質，那麼等到動物吃到這種的飲食了，它有一種毒氣在裡頭藏著，沒有發作出來，我們人要是把這個動物的肉給吃了，這種毒傳染到人的身上，所以就生種種怪病，種種不治之病。

那其中不是偶然它生這種難治之病，都是因為有怨魂在那兒想要討命債。所以我現在到處看見很多小鬼，到處都想要要人的命，都想叫人生種種的怪病。這些個小鬼就是還沒有做完全一個人，就被人墮胎給殺了，所以這些小鬼都是更厲害。它在那地方不是把人的心臟給弄破了，再不就肝臟給弄壞了，腎臟、膽臟，把你五臟先給你破壞了，所以你想不死，也是辦不到了。為什麼他這樣子毒辣呢？就因為它先先被你殺了，所以它現在要來報仇。報仇這一類的病，你怎麼樣用什麼醫生，中醫、西醫也治不好的，就是混吃等死，等到最後那一口氣斷了，然後再去報仇去。我現在給你們大家說的，這是真經真典哪！

那麼再要知道啊，我對人再說恐怕有人不願意聽了，可是我犯這個毛病，我不管人願意聽、不願意聽，我就願意說，我就願意說人家不願意聽的話，所以到這兒來的人應該先有心理的的準備，說：「我不願意聽的，也忍耐一點，聽一聽，看他倒是說什麼？」這個是什麼話呢？我用中文來解釋這個「肉」字，這個肉字裡邊就是一個四方的口，四方的口，底下那一橫不加上，就張著口呢！張著口幹什麼呢？吃人呢！所以「肉字裡邊兩個人」，說裡邊有個人字，外邊又有個人字，足見這個肉是離不開人的，可是人不要離不開肉。這是一個吃肉的人，一個被吃的人，所以一個就出頭，出去這口了；一個人就在那個口裡邊，可是這口也沒有閉上，這個人字還會流出去，流出去還可能再做人；再做人，所以就吃這個吃肉的人，這互相吃。所以說肉字裡邊兩個人，「裡邊罩著外邊人」，裡邊的這個人和外邊這個人是有連帶關係的，「眾生還吃眾生肉，仔細思量是人吃人」，那麼既然是人吃人了，這個人會不會是我的朋友呢？不知道；那會不會是親戚呢？不知道；會不會是我的父母祖先呢？不知道。那麼在這個不知道裡邊，這個問題就很多的，所以

Why have these appeared? Because people have eaten too much meat. Nowadays, the air is polluted, the earth is polluted, and the water is also polluted. This polluted air, polluted earth, and polluted water have produced a toxic substance, and when animals eat food which contains this kind of toxin, the poisonous energy passes into their system. Although it may just stay in their bodies and not take effect, if we eat the meat of these animals, the poison will pass into our bodies and cause us to develop all sorts of strange and incurable diseases.

These diseases which are hard to cure do not happen by chance. Behind them, there is a ghost with a grievance who wants the person's life in payment. So now I see a lot of little ghosts everywhere, trying to make people pay with their lives or causing them to suffer various strange diseases. These little ghosts were fetuses who were aborted before they had a chance to develop into complete human beings, so they are very ruthless. They may rupture people's hearts, or injure their livers, kidneys, or gall bladders. They destroy your five organs so that you have to die whether you want to or not. Why are they so malicious? Because you killed them first, and now they want to take revenge. Diseases caused by vengeful ghosts cannot be cured no matter what kind of doctor, Chinese or Western, you see. All you can do is take your meals and wait for death. After you take your last breath, it's your turn to seek revenge. What I'm telling you is the most genuine Sutra!

If I say more, people may not want to listen. However, I have a fault which is that I'm willing to say something regardless of whether or not people want to hear it. I'm especially willing to say the things that people don't want to hear. So those of you who have come here should prepare yourselves psychologically. You should tell yourself, "I don't want to listen, but I'll be patient for a little while and see what he has to say." What do I want to say? I want to explain the character 肉 for 'meat' in Chinese. This character 肉 has the element 口 'mouth,' but the bottom line is left out, meaning that the mouth is open! Why is the mouth open? To eat people! So, "In the character for 'meat,' there are two people." There is a character 人 'person' inside and another 人 'person' outside. This shows that meat is inseparable from people. However, people should not be inseparably attached to meat. This represents a person who is eating the meat and a person who is being eaten. One person's head is sticking out of the mouth, and the other person is inside the mouth. But since the mouth is not closed, that person may fall out. When he falls out, he may become a person again. When he becomes a person again, he will go and eat the person who was eating meat. They mutually devour each other. So, there are two people in the character for 'meat', and "The one inside is covering the one outside." The person inside and the person outside are bound up in this relationship. "Living beings eat the flesh of living beings. If you reflect on it carefully, it's just people eating people." Since it's people eating people, might that person be my friend? I don't know. Could it be my relative? Don't know. Could it be my father, mother, or ancestor? Don't know. This "not knowing" presents a lot of problems, so it would be best it

我們大家最好不吃肉。

除了不吃肉，還有一個最要緊的、不生病的要訣。不生病的要訣是什麼呢？就是要沒有脾氣。誰若能沒有脾氣，誰的病，就是那冤冤相報它也不容易找你來了。因為你那兒一發脾氣，啊！這露出來一個窟窿，那鬼就鑽進來了；鬼鑽進，你病就愈生愈厲害了。這是要訣，你們誰若想不生病，活得健康長壽，就是不吃肉，不要發脾氣，再不抽菸，不喝酒，這都是養生之道。不要把身體弄壞了，百病纏身，那時候找醫生，還要用錢，也不一定治得好，你說麻煩不麻煩？

everyone didn't eat meat.

Aside from not eating meat, there's another essential secret to preventing sickness. What is it? Not losing one's temper. If you don't have a temper, then your karmic creditors who want to take revenge by making you sick will have a hard time finding you. But as soon as you get mad, there's a hole for the ghost to get in. Once the ghost finds its way in, your illness becomes more and more severe. If you want to be healthy, long-lived, and free from illness, the secret is not to eat meat, not to lose your temper, and not to smoke or drink. These are all ways to stay healthy. You shouldn't ruin your body and bring all sorts of illness on yourself. If you do, then you'll have to find a doctor and pay him money, and still he might not be able to cure you. Isn't that a lot of trouble?

何 謂 正 知 正 見 ？

WHAT ARE PROPER KNOWLEDGE AND PROPER VIEWS?

宣公上人一九九四年三月五日對柏克萊加州大學中國佛教青年會學生開示於萬佛聖城
The Venerable Master Hua's talk to the Chinese Buddhist Association of the University of California at Berkeley
on March 5, 1994, at the Sagely City of Ten Thousand Buddhas

各位年齡長的善知識，各位正在壯年的善知識，各位正在青年有為的善知識：

所謂善知識就是知道正當的法，認識不正當的法。那麼知道正當和不正當，我們每一個人就應該擇善而從，不善而改，是道則進，非道則退，要具有擇法眼，要具有正知正見。所謂正知正見就是對人類有益處的事情，我們去做；對人類有害處的事情，我們不要做。不單對人類是如此，乃至於對一切的眾生都是如此，若能這樣子，我們這個人是沒有白做；不能這樣子，不能認識真理，我們這個人可以說是白做人一場。為什麼呢？也不知道做人的根本是什麼？也不知道這生活要怎麼樣？那麼我們人生活在世間上，是要幫助其他的人，而把自己忘了，這才對人類、眾生類，乃至於國、家、個人，推而廣之，到全世界，我們要利益其他的人，不要利益自己。為什麼呢？自己是一個小範圍，其他的人和眾生，這是全體的，是整個人類的利益。要為個人做打算，那大可以什麼事情也不要做了；我們個人是吃不了多少，穿也穿不了多少，住也只是「大廈千間，夜眠不過八尺；良田萬頃，日食只是三餐。」

那麼萬佛城的人，無論出家人、在家人，出家人都是一天吃一餐，在家人有的也是吃一餐，那麼有一些個居士，也學萬佛城的出家人一天吃一餐。為什麼要這樣子呢？因為這個世界的食糧不夠了，我們願減少我們自己所用的食糧，給這個世界人類多留一點食糧。說：「這個你不吃那麼多，旁人也不一定得到。」不管他得到、不得到，這是一種物質不滅，我們少吃一點，給世界多留一點糧，這一點心，這就是利益世界，這就是幫助這個世界。

說：「這個是我辦不到的。」不單你辦不到，他也辦不到，為什麼呢？人都是自私，每天要把自己吃飽了、穿暖了，自己受一點苦就覺得吃虧了。其

All elderly Good and Wise Advisors, all Good and Wise Advisors in the prime of life, and all young and promising Good and Wise Advisors:

A Good and Wise Advisor is one who knows what is proper Dharma and what is improper Dharma. Knowing what is proper and improper, we should follow what is good and change what is bad. If it's the Way, we should go upon it. If it's not the Way, we should retreat from it. We must have the vision to discriminate the Dharma, and we must have proper knowledge and views. Having proper knowledge and views means we should do what is beneficial to people and avoid doing what harms people. Not only should we be this way towards people, we should be this way towards all living beings. If we can do this, then we haven't been people in vain. If we can't be this way and can't recognize true principle, then we have been people in vain. Why? Because we don't know the basis of being a person or how we should live. We live in the world in order to help others and forget ourselves. We want to benefit all people, living beings, the country, the family, ourselves, and the entire world. We want to benefit others, not ourselves. Why? Because the self is a small scope. All people and living beings are the whole substance. If we only calculate for ourselves, then we can probably get by without doing much of anything. We ourselves cannot consume that much food or wear that many clothes. As for a place to live, we may have a mansion with a thousand rooms, but at night we only take up eight feet of space. We may have ten thousand acres of fields, but we can only eat three meals a day.

At the City of Ten Thousand Buddhas, the left-home people eat one meal a day, and so do some of the laypeople. Why do they do this? Because there's not enough food in the world. We wish to eat less food ourselves and leave some more for the other people in the world. You might say, "Even if you don't eat that food, others may not get to eat it." Whether they get it or not, the food doesn't disappear. If we eat less and save more for others, we are helping the world.

You say, "I can't do this." Not only you, but other people can't do this either. Why not? Because people are all selfish—every day they have to eat their fill and wear enough to be warm. If they suffer even a little bit, they feel they've taken a loss. But actually, living in this world, "Enduring suffering puts an end to suffering." It's because we have suffering that we suf-

實怎麼樣？人在這個世界上，受苦就是了苦，我們有苦才要受苦。說：「你怎麼知道你有苦？」你問問你自己有沒有脾氣？有沒有無明、煩惱？這無明、煩惱就是因為德行不夠，所以才動無明，發脾氣，生煩惱。所以佛才說，種種無明是苦根哪！無明、煩惱、發脾氣，這都是一種苦的根本；苦根除盡善根存，你若把這苦根都了了，善根就長出來了。所以才說「受苦是了苦，享福是消福。」我們有福報，自己不享受，把這福報分給一切的人類，一切的眾生。我們享福是消福，你有福報，你把它享盡了，就沒有了；你若不享受，把它分給旁人，也好像我們有飯吃，有很多沒有飯吃的人，有很多國家的人都飢餓而死，也不知每天有多少；有很多國家的人沒有衣服穿，我們減省一點穿的衣服，把它迴向給全世界這個困苦的人、困苦的眾生，這就是幫助這個全世界。

可是我們雖然這樣做，還不需要居功，不需要說：「啊！我這樣做，我有了功德了！」善欲人見，不是真善；惡恐人知，便是大惡。」善是孝順，惡－－萬惡淫為首，死路不可走。這個淫亂的行為，就是一種罪惡、邪惡，可是現在的人都往這條路上鑽，想辦法都要恣行淫欲，所以世風就日下了，人心就不古了，那麼一天就不如一天了。在古來，人心樸厚，沒有這麼多邪惡的行為，所以也沒有這種奇奇怪怪的，又什麼cancer（癌）病啦，又是愛死病啦，又是種種奇奇怪怪的不治之症。現在人還不覺悟，說這個病是怎麼樣怎麼樣生出來的。這都是人太邪惡了，邪惡不善才有這種的災難。我們可以看一看現在世界的天災人禍，不一而足，過了水災，就是火災；過了火災，又是風災；過了風災，又是地震，哦！這種種奇奇怪怪的飛災橫禍都來了，這就因為人心太邪惡了。我們趕快覺醒，喚醒全世界的人，要擇善而從，不善而改，是道則進，非道則退。我們要有正知正見，要有擇法眼，知道黑的是什麼，白的是什麼；不要迷迷糊糊的、糊糊塗塗的，把這一生就混過去了，這是太可惜的事情了。

fer. How do you know you have suffering? Ask yourself if you have a temper, ignorance, and afflictions. If you have these, it's because you don't have enough virtue. That's the reason you are ignorant, get angry, and become afflicted. So the Buddha said, "All kinds of ignorance are the roots of suffering." Ignorance, anger, and afflictions are the roots of suffering. "When the roots of suffering are eradicated, what are left will be roots of goodness." Once you put an end to the roots of suffering, good roots will grow. Thus it's said, "Enduring suffering puts an end to suffering. Enjoying blessings uses up blessings." If we have blessings, we should share them with all living beings, instead of enjoying them by ourselves. If you enjoy all your blessings, then you'll use them up and you won't have any more. If you don't enjoy your blessings, you can share them with others. For example, we have food to eat, but there are many people who have nothing to eat. In many countries, countless people starve to death every day. In many countries, people don't have clothes to wear. We can be more frugal in our own clothing, and transfer the benefit to all the suffering living beings in the world. Then we are benefiting the world.

Even so, we shouldn't get attached to our merit. We shouldn't say, "Since I did this, I have merit and virtue." "Good deeds which are done hoping others will see are not truly good. Evil done fearing others will find out is great evil." Good refers to filiality. As for evil, "Of the myriad evils, lust is foremost. Don't walk this road to death." Licentious behavior is deviant and evil, but nowadays everyone is taking this path. They all find ways to indulge in lust. So the morality of the world declines day by day, and people's hearts do not follow the example of the ancients. Each day is worse than the day before. In ancient times, people's hearts were good, and there wasn't so much deviant and evil behavior. All these strange and incurable diseases such as cancer and AIDS didn't exist. People still haven't realized why these diseases occur. These calamities happen because people are too deviant, evil, and immoral. Take a look at the manmade and natural disasters in the world; they occur one after the other. After a deluge, there comes a great fire. After a fire, there's a hurricane. After that there's an earthquake. Ah! All kinds of perverse disasters are occurring. This is because people's hearts are too malicious. We should wake up quickly ourselves, and then wake up all the people in the world. We must follow the good and change the bad. Follow the path, and retreat from what is not the path. We must have proper knowledge and views, and the vision to judge the Dharma, so that we can tell black from white. Don't be so muddled and confused that you let your life pass in vain. That would be a great pity.

出家未忘忠貞志

THOUGH I'VE LEFT THE HOME-LIFE, I HAVEN'T FORGOTTEN MY HEART'S ALLEGIANCE

宣公上人一九九三年一月十二日開示於臺北縣立體育館

A lecture by the Venerable Master at the Banqiao Stadium, Taipei County, Taiwan, on January 12, 1993

今天也是有所感觸，願意把我心裡頭的話，對你們各位講一講。你們願意聽，就聽一聽；不願意聽呢，可以退席的。什麼話呢？我到美國已經三十多年了，中間經過的年、月、日、時，也不算短了，不論是美國人、中國人，都希望我改變我的國籍，入美國的國籍，做為美國的公民。說是美國的護照，走遍天下都是最方便的；美國的公民，走遍全世界，都是受人恭敬的。中國護照那個性質就不同了，拿中華民國的護照，到共產黨的國家裡頭去，共產黨就不願意給簽證，共產黨就歧視；拿中國人民政府的護照，到各處更令人怕，不是怕他國大、人多，而是怕他這個法律有問題。所以趕快入美國籍，這是好的。

那麼三十多年來，官方、民方都有很多人，向我來提議這個問題。可是我因為是中國人，我不論共產黨，還是國民黨，他們把國家弄得怎麼樣低落，我還是中國人。報紙上說：「我若不是共產黨，不會流浪到海外。」我並不是怕共產黨，跑到海外來的。可是我在東北的時候，從哈爾濱到了吉林，我走出來的時候，還可以出來；想要回去嘛！就要路條。我不是在共產黨的範圍內居留，所以這個路條，我就沒有法子找去，所以回不去了。回不去，我從吉林又到錦州。我離開哈爾濱，哈爾濱就被共產黨佔領了；我到了吉林，吉林還有國民黨在那兒駐守；等我一到錦州，吉林和哈爾濱就不通了，交通斷絕了。我又到長春，到了長春，吉林又不能回去了。那麼到遼寧，本來想要回哈爾濱，可是人人都是很關心我，叫我不要回去了。那麼這樣子我就到了天津，住在大悲院，那時候還是一個沙彌。以後從天津就到上海，上海以後就到武昌，一路一路的，我前步走了，後步就被共產黨給佔領了。這麼樣子，等我到了廣州，舊曆八月十八那天，我從廣州又到了香港。那麼八月二十，大約我走了三天之後

Today I have some feelings and would like to tell you what has been on my mind. If you want to listen, fine. If you don't want to listen, you may leave. What is it I want to say? I have already been living in the United States for over thirty years, which is not a short time. Both Americans and Chinese people have been suggesting to me that I change my nationality and become an American citizen. They say that having an American passport makes it convenient to travel anywhere in the world. Americans are respected wherever they go, but it's different with a Chinese passport. If you have a passport from the Republic of China, the Communists will not grant you a visa to enter their country. The Communists will discriminate against you. If you have a passport from the People's Republic of China, people will be even more afraid of you wherever you go. They are afraid not because China is a big country with a large population, but because the government might give them trouble. So the best thing is to become an American citizen as soon as possible.

In these thirty-some years, both officials and civilians have suggested this to me. I am still a Chinese, regardless of how terrible and underdeveloped China might become under the Communists or the Nationalists. The newspapers said that if it were not for the Communists, I would not be wandering abroad. Well, it certainly wasn't out of fear of the Communist Party that I went abroad. In Manchuria, when I left Harbin and went to Jilin, I was free to go. When I wanted to return, they required a special pass. Since I did not have a residence in the Communist area, I had no way to obtain a pass, so I couldn't go back. From Jilin, I went to Jinzhou. After I left Harbin, it was taken by the Communists. When I arrived in Jilin, the Nationalist Party was still in control there, but communication was cut off between Jilin and Harbin. When I went to Changchun, it was impossible to return to Jilin. I went to Liaoning and thought about returning to Harbin. Everyone was very concerned and urged me not to go back. I then went to Tianjin and stayed in the Great Compassion Temple. At that time I was still a Shramanera (novice monk). Later I left Tianjin and went to Shanghai, and afterwards to Wuchang.

All along the way, as soon as I left a place, that place would be occupied by the Communists. In this way, I arrived in Guangzhou on the eighteenth of the eighth lunar month. From there I went to Hong Kong. About three days after I left, Guangzhou was also captured by the Communists, and after I arrived in Hong Kong there was no way to return to Guangzhou.

，廣州也被共產黨佔領了。就這樣子到了香港之後，再回廣州也回不去了。這是時節因緣所湊合的，我並不是怕共產黨。我生來是一個天不怕、地不怕、神不怕、鬼不怕的人，我也不怕美國人說中國話。那麼這樣子到了香港，在香港住了十多年。我大約是一九四八年到了香港，等到一九六二年就到了美國。在香港的期間，到過澳洲、緬甸、泰國、新加坡都到過。可是我到處都不受人歡迎，為什麼呢？我這個人沒有什麼人緣，誰見到我，就都遠遠地跑，出家人、在家人都是。

這麼樣子，我一九六二年到達美國，在美國最初住到一個地下室裡邊。這個地下室有門沒窗戶，白天是黑的，晚間當然更是黑的啦！就等於在墳墓裡頭住一樣的。所以我到了美國之後，我自己嘲笑自己，給自己起個名字，就叫「墓中僧」。在墳墓裡頭的一個和尚。為什麼叫這麼個名字呢？我因為自己不願和人爭名，不願意爭利，不願意和人爭勝負，我就等於在墳墓裡頭一樣。在東北的時候，我出家之後，曾經也有一個名字，叫什麼呢？叫「活死人」。為什麼叫活死人呢？因為我人雖然活著，我不和人爭名奪利，不和人爭，我也不貪。我這一生啊！無論做任何的事情，我不求代價的，不拿錢的，所以叫活死人。這個人雖然活著，也就等於死了一樣，到了美國又叫墓中僧。大學裡請我去講演，我也是用墓中僧的名義去講。

那麼這樣子經過一段時間，等到一九六八年 ——就是現在隨團來的這位易教授、易博士、易居士，我也不知叫他什麼名字好。那麼就遇著他了，不過他不是一九六八年遇著的，大約一九六六年哪？是六五年？這我記不清楚了。遇到他，以後他到臺灣來學習中文．我就叫他到臺灣訪尋善知識，來皈依三寶，因為他是一個猶太人。他到臺灣，我介紹他幾個法師，他各處都去了，都覺得沒有緣；不是人沒有緣，是錢沒有緣。他說臺灣這兒佛教都是要錢的，我皈依誰，就要紅包。他也沒有多少錢，就不皈依了，回去就要求皈依我，我說：「你可以慢慢等一等。」

以後他就從西雅圖，帶來大約三十多個人，有讀博士的，有讀學士的，有讀master（碩士）的。這大約有三十多個人吧！，還有一些個不讀書的人，也都一起來，因為他在美國人緣還不錯，介紹他們都來聽講《楞嚴經》。在講《楞嚴經》的期間是暑假班，講了九十六天。以後就有些人從西雅圖轉學

This was brought about by a combination of time and circumstance. It was certainly not the case that I was afraid of the Communists. In all my life, I have never feared heaven, earth, ghosts or spirits. Nor am I afraid of Americans who speak Chinese! I lived in Hong Kong for over ten years. I arrived in Hong Kong in 1948, and came to the United States in 1962. When I was residing in Hong Kong, I visited Australia, Burma, Thailand, and Singapore. However, I was not welcome anywhere I went. Why? I do not have much affinity with people. People see me and run far away. Left-home people and laypeople all react this way.

In 1962 I came to America, and in the beginning I lived in a basement. The basement had a door but no windows. It was dark in the daytime and even darker at night. It was like living in a grave. I made fun of myself after coming to America and called myself "The Monk in the Grave." Why did I take this name? I did not want to fight with others for fame and profit, nor triumph over them. It was just as if I were in a grave. In Manchuria, I had another name after I left home, which was "The Living Dead Person." This is because although I was alive, I did not fight with others for name and gain. I was not greedy. In all my life, no matter what work I do, I have never asked for wages or taken any money. That is why I was called "The Living Dead Person." Even though I was alive, I was as good as dead. In America, I called myself "The Monk in the Grave." When I was invited to lecture at the universities, I used the name "The Monk in the Grave." After a time, in 1968, I met a person who is in the delegation—Professor Epstein, Dr. Epstein, Upasaka Epstein—I don't know what I should call him. Actually it was 1965 or 1966 that I met him, but I do not remember exactly when. Then he came to Taiwan to study Chinese. I told him to look for a Good and Wise Advisor in Taiwan and to take refuge with the Triple Jewel, for he was Jewish. I introduced him to several Dharma Masters in Taiwan, and he visited them, but felt no affinities with them. It wasn't the people that he felt no affinities for, but the money. All the Buddhist activities in Taiwan require money. No matter what teacher he wanted to take refuge with, he was expected to give a donation (in a red envelope). Since he hardly had any money, he didn't take refuge. He returned and asked to take refuge with me. I told him to wait awhile.

Later on, in 1968, he brought more than thirty people from Seattle, some of whom were candidates for Ph.D., Bachelor's, and Master's degrees. Others who were not students also joined the group. He had pretty good affinities with Americans, and he invited them to hear my lectures on the *Shurangama Sutra*. I lectured on the *Shurangama Sutra* for ninety-six days during summer vacation (1968). Later, some of the students from Seattle transferred to San Francisco, including Dr. Epstein. They moved to San Francisco, and I was lecturing on the Sutras and speaking the Dharma every day. My vow is that as long as I have one breath left, I will lecture on the Sutras and speak the Dharma. When I have no breath left, I will stop speaking. So even though I am sick now, I still put forth my greatest effort to

轉到三藩市來，這個易博士他也是其中之一。

那麼轉到三藩市，由那時起，我天天都在講經說法。我的願力是有這一口氣存在，我就要講經說法；等這口氣沒有了，就不講了。所以我現在雖然有病，我還是盡我的最大努力，給大家來說法。我知道大家不一定願意聽我所說的法，可是我也不能因為多數人不願意聽，我就不講了。我還是就有一個人他願意聽我說法，我也講；甚至於沒有人聽，我還是自己對鬼來講，對神來講，對一切有靈性的來講，這是我一個大概、簡單的意思。

所以我看見報紙說：「這個宣化是一個流浪漢。」不錯，我現在是流浪漢。雖然中華民國也不一定要我這個國民，共產黨也不一定要我這個國民，因為國家多我一個不多，少我一個不少。可是我是中國人哪！我就要念舊，我這個人就是不忘舊，所以我寫了一首詩不是詩，偈不是偈，就叫它很簡單的幾句話。我現在從美國回到臺灣，我不是講經說法的，我不是弘法的，我是訪問來的，我是向所有的耆德高僧來學習的。我也不是高僧，也不是耆德，報紙上這麼稱呼，這是我愧不敢當的名詞。我以前在年輕的時候，想要創革命，可是沒有能成功，我以後就不問政治的興衰啦！治亂啦！不問了！我已經是活死人，又是一個墓中的和尚，和一般的和尚，我是比不了的。一般的和尚都有道有德，在那兒弘揚佛法，我是弘揚佛法不夠資格的人，所以我沒有資格來弘揚佛法，我是跟著大家來學習。那麼現在最後，我要把我這幾句淺白淡語，對大家說一說。我說：

中華混亂數十年，傷時感事淚成泉，
此生愧具回天手，往昔難彈落日弦，
世途崎嶇人鬼詐，官海浮沉彼此煎，
出家未忘忠貞志，不改國籍溯本源。

我這八句俚語、八句淺白淡語，是說明了我這個思想，說明了我這個行為，說明我這個志願。我可以略略解釋一下，說：

「中華混亂數十年」，這是說的我們中國人在這個水深火熱裡頭度生活，還不自覺，還不存報國的心。我怎麼說臺灣有這個累卵之勢，為什麼呢？都是各自為政，不團結。商人發財發得很多，應該盡忠報國，可是對國家都不相信。怎麼證明他不相信呢？因為他投資到外國去，把自己國內的力量都分

speak the Dharma for everyone. I know everyone doesn't necessarily want to listen to the Dharma I speak, but I can't keep silent even if the majority of the people don't want to listen. As long as one person wants to listen, I will speak the Dharma. Even if there is no one listening, I will still speak for the benefit of the ghosts, spirits, and all spiritual beings. That is my intention in general.

The newspapers say that Hsuan Hua is a vagabond. That's right, I am a vagabond, because the Republic of China (Taiwan) doesn't necessarily want me as a citizen, nor does the Communist Party (Mainland China). I am not a significant addition or a significant loss to either country. I am a Chinese person, and I care about my roots. I am a person who cannot forget the past, so I wrote a few simple words, which cannot be considered poetry. I have come to Taiwan from the United States, not to lecture the Sutras or propagate the Dharma. I have come to visit and to learn from all the Venerable Sanghans and Greatly Virtuous Ones. I myself am neither a Venerable Sanghan nor a Greatly Virtuous One. The newspapers have given me those names, but I do not deserve them. In my youth, I wanted to start a revolution. I never succeeded in doing it, and afterwards I paid no more attention to the political situation. I was already a "Living Dead Person" and a "Monk in the Grave" and could not be compared to ordinary monks. Ordinary monks have virtue in the Way and are able to propagate the Buddhadharma. I do not have the status to propagate the Buddhadharma, so I want to learn from everyone else. Now I want to speak about the simple lines that I wrote.

China has been in turmoil for decades.
Anguished by the affairs of the times,
*   my tears flow like a river.*
I regret that in this life, I haven't been able to turn the tide
*   of events.*
In the past, I failed to play the lute of the setting sun.
The roads of the world twist and turn, as people and
*   ghosts deceive each other.*
The sea of politicians surges and rolls, as they fight
*   each other.*
Though I've left the home-life, I haven't forgotten
*   my heart's allegiance.*
Not changing my nationality, I trace my roots back to
*   their source.*

These simple lines explain my ideals, my conduct, and my resolutions. I shall explain them briefly.

China has been in turmoil for decades. This says that the Chinese people, not realizing that they are living in deep waters and hot fires, still do not know to be loyal to the country. I say that Taiwan is like a pile of eggs; do you know why? Every person is out for himself. They are not united. The business people who have struck it rich and made a lot of money should loyally do all they can to repay the kindness of the land. None of them believe in the country. What proof is there? They invest all their money in other countries, thus scattering the wealth of their own country abroad.

撥到外國去，這商人不夠忠心。你就富稱敵國，你沒有報國的思想，這還是窮人啊！這是不懂道理的人，不愛護國家，只是自私自利，這是一點。

老百姓雖然說有的信佛了，但是不信的還是很多，這對於國家是一個損失。老百姓若真正都信佛、拜佛、懂得因果了，他就不會去殺人放火呀！偷盜啊！強搶啊！販毒啊！投機取巧啊！玩大家樂呀！賭股票啊！不會有這樣的行為，這是國家一個不祥的預兆。還有學生，根本把教育都忘了，只在皮毛上轉轉，把孔教置諸腦後，沒有人提倡孝悌忠信、禮義廉恥、忠心愛國這種的道理，都是在求名求利上用功夫，這一點也是國家的不祥之兆。

那麼人都不知道愛惜自己的生命財產，隨便揮霍撩亂，這對國家也是大不祥的一個地方。民為邦本，本固邦寧。這對國有種種的不祥、種種的不利，這是我所以說臺灣有這個累卵之勢，很危險。這不是大言聳聽，令人故意來害怕，不是這樣的，所以說中華混亂數十年。現在，發財的人有，哪一個能以把財產都捐獻給國家？這個財產小的不算；財產大的，我在臺灣，沒有聽說哪一個為國捐獻所有的財產，沒有，都是為自己自私自利，留著給兒孫後代。其實你這個兒子若比你強，

> 養子強如父，
> 你留財做什麼？

他比你有志氣、有本領，你能發財，他比你更發得大，你給他留那麼多幹什麼？所以說

> 兒孫自有兒孫福，
> 莫為兒孫做馬牛。

你錢再多，死了帶不進棺材去。我這個話誰都聽過，可是人人都不注意這一點，這個邏輯學人人都忘了。都是在那兒爭啊、貪啊、求啊、自私、自利、打妄語。我說的是說大多數，不是說少數。你不要以為有人也願意捐所有財產給國家，這都是少數的，不多。所以說中華混亂數十年。

「傷時感世淚成泉」，我傷嘆這個時候，又感慨這個世間的事，所以淚成泉。很多聰明人不做

So the business people are not loyal enough. Even if you're as wealthy as everyone else put together, if you have no sense of loyalty to your country, then you are still a poor person! You are a person who does not understand principle, who does not love his country, and who knows only to be selfish and self-benefitting. That's one point.

Although some of the citizens have come to believe in Buddhism, there are still many who do not, and that is a great loss to the country. If the ordinary citizens truly believed in the Buddha, bowed to the Buddha, and understood cause and effect, they wouldn't go out to commit murder, set fires, rob, or deal in drugs. They would not be opportunistic and play the lottery or stock market. They wouldn't engage in such activities. The fact that they do is an unlucky sign for the country. Moreover, students have totally forgotten about education, and they work only at a superficial level. They have pushed the teachings of Confucius to the back of their brain, and no one advocates filial piety, fraternal respect, loyalty, trustworthiness, propriety, righteousness, incorruptibility, a sense of shame, and the principles of being loyal to the country. Instead, everyone puts their efforts into seeking fame and profit. That is another unfavorable sign for the country.

If people do not cherish their own lives and wealth, and spend them recklessly, that is very bad for the country. It is said, "The people are the foundation of the country. If the foundation is solid, the country will be at peace." This behavior is unfavorable and unbeneficial to the country in many ways. That's why I say Taiwan is like a pile of eggs. It is in a dangerous situation. I'm not talking big in order to make people excited to listen, and I'm not saying this just to scare people. That's not my intent. I said, "China has been in turmoil for decades." Among those who have made big fortunes, who has been able to offer all his wealth to the country? Those who have small assets don't count. I'm talking about those who have great fortunes. In Taiwan, I haven't heard that anyone has contributed all his money to the country. People are all out for themselves—selfish and self-benefitting—leaving their wealth to their children and descendants. Actually,

> *If the son is as capable as the father,*
> *Why should the father leave wealth for the son?*

If your son has more ambition and skill than you, then he must be able to make even more money than you, so why should you leave so much wealth for him? It is also said,

> *Your children have their own blessings.*
> *There's no need to be a slave for them.*

No matter how much money you have, you can't take it to the grave when you die. Everyone knows this, but no one pays any attention to it. Everyone has forgotten it and just goes on fighting, being greedy, seeking, being selfish, pursuing personal gain, and lying. I'm talking about the vast majority, not just a few people. Don't say that there are those who are willing to give all their wealth to the country. Such people are rare. There are not many at all.

That's why I say: "China has been in turmoil for decades." An-

聰明事，做糊塗事；很多糊塗人想做聰明事，他不知道怎麼樣做，這是一種不圓滿的地方。

「此身愧具回天手」，說我這一身哪、盡這一個身體。愧具回天手，我沒有回天的手段。我若有回天的手段，我應該把中華民國、中華人民共和國都想法子，令他們都知道怎麼樣救國、治國，怎麼樣治理天下，怎麼樣才能做一個堂堂大國的風度？

「往昔難彈落日弦」，我以前為什麼要創革命呢？我因為看見日本人侵略中國，是太不公平，所以我想要創革命打日本人。可是我始終也沒有走上那條路，因為這個，我就不過問世事了。

「世途崎嶇人鬼詐」，那麼我又看見世途崎嶇，世間這個道路崎嶇難行、彎彎曲曲的、很危險的。人鬼詐，中國人對於「鬼佬」是互相欺詐，「鬼佬」也學會了，對中國人也用這種手段，以牙還牙，你欺騙我，我也欺騙你，全世界成一個互相欺騙的世界。

「宦海浮沉彼此煎」，這個做官的都是在那兒排除異己。你是我這個黨，是我這個派，我就用我這個自私自利的心，來提拔你。你若和我不是一黨一派，我就排斥你，令你抑鬱不得志。所以宦海浮沉彼此煎，彼此互相熬煎。

「出家未忘忠貞志」，我雖然出家了，我沒有忘掉忠心為國的這種思想，我不能改變我的志氣。我是中國人，永遠是中國人，我生生世世、在在處處都要是中國人。等中國人真正強大了，那時候我或者已經不在了，或者還在；不管在不在，我希望我這一生，最低限度不改變我的國籍，我不貪任何的便宜和方便。

所以說「不改國籍溯本源」，我不改變我自己的國籍，我還沒有忘本。這是我幾句淺白的話，你們各位大約對我稍微會瞭解一點。

guished by the affairs of the times, my tears flow like a river. Saddened by the times, I lamented the affairs of the world. Many intelligent people do not do intelligent things. Instead, they do muddled things. Many muddled people want to do intelligent things, but they don't know how. This is a sad situation.

I regret that in this life, I haven't been able to turn the tide of events. In this life, I have no way to turn back the tide of destiny. If I did, I should want to enable both the Republic of China and the People's Republic of China to know how to govern the country and deal with the world, and how to have the deportment of a great country.

In the past, I failed to play the lute of the setting sun. Why did I want to start a revolution? I saw China being invaded by Japan, and I felt that it was too unjust, so I wanted to lead a revolt against Japan. I was never able to carry out my plans, so later I put the world's affairs behind me.

I also saw that: The roads of the world twist and turn. In this world, the roads are crooked and hard to travel. They are very dangerous. As people and ghosts deceive each other. The Chinese people would cheat the foreigners any way they could. The foreigners learned the tricks from the Chinese and cheated the Chinese in turn, "taking a tooth for a tooth." People cheated each other and the world became a place of mutual deceit.

The sea of politicians surges and rolls, as they fight each other. The politicians formed cliques and excluded those who were different. They promoted those of their own group, out of selfishness and desire for personal gain. Those of other cliques were left out and frustrated in their attempts to realize their aims. So "the sea of politicians surges and rolls, as they fight each other." Political leaders harassed and tormented one another.

Though I've left the home-life, I haven't forgotten my heart's allegiance. Although I've left home, I haven't forgotten my loyalty to the country. I am Chinese, and I'll always be Chinese. In every life, in every place, I am Chinese. When China truly becomes great and strong, I may or may not be around. Whether I am still living or not, I hope that throughout my life, at the very least, I will not change my nationality. I am not greedy for convenience.

Not changing my nationality, I trace my roots back to their source. I will not change my citizenship, and I will not forget my roots. These are some simple lines that I wrote. Now all of you can probably understand a bit about me.

我是一隻小螞蟻，
甘願走在一切眾生的腳底下；
我是一條道路，
願所有的眾生走在我身上，
從凡夫地，直達佛地。

I am a small ant that wishes to crawl beneath the feet of
all living beings. I am a road that wishes all living beings will walk
upon me and travel from the stage of ordinary beings to the
stage of Buddhas.

祝禱宣化長老早日乘願再來

PRAYING THAT THE VENERABLE ELDER HSUAN HUA WILL SOON COME BACK RIDING ON HIS VOWS

釋明暘　Shi Mingyang

接到美國加州萬佛聖城寄來的訃告，獲悉法界佛教總會創辦人、妙覺山萬佛城開山祖師、佛教溈仰宗第九代傳人宣化長老，於西曆一九九五年六月七日（農曆乙亥年五月初十日）三時十五分，安詳示寂於美國洛杉磯，世壽七十有八。法界總會四眾弟子，恪遵長老遺教，於萬佛聖城及各分支道場－－舊金山金山聖寺、洛杉磯金輪聖寺、西雅圖金峰聖寺、加拿大金佛聖寺與華嚴聖寺等，舉行《大方廣佛華嚴經》及念佛法會四十九永日，迴向長老早日乘願再來，普度眾生。並於一九九五年七月二十六日至七月二十八日，每日上午七時起，在萬佛聖城舉行三天追思大會暨荼毗典禮。我被推為宣化長老示寂讚頌委員會委員，專程赴美參加追思大會及荼毗典禮，衷心祝禱宣化長老早日乘願再來，普度眾生。

宣化長老原籍中國吉林省雙城縣。一九四八年受虛雲老和尚傳法，為禪宗溈仰宗第九代傳人。駐錫香港十餘年後，一九六二年赴美弘法。三十多年來，宣講大乘經典三十餘部，並由他的弟子將佛教經典譯成英語、越語等多種文字，逾一百多部。在北美洲、東南亞、港、臺等地廣為傳播。共創辦道場二十七所，皈依弟子遍布世界各地。

長老一身戒律精嚴，更重身教，在萬佛城和各道場樹立不爭、不貪、不求、不自私、不自利、不打妄語的六大宗旨，為僧俗弟子所尊敬。他還提倡教育事業，在萬佛城設立了中、小學及法界佛教大學。

一九八七年五月，為安排由北京廣濟寺、上海龍華寺僧眾組成的七十人大型僧伽

Upon receiving the obituary notice sent by the Sagely City of Ten Thousand Buddhas in California, U.S.A., I came to know that the Venerable Elder Hua, founder of the Dharma Realm Buddhist Association and the Sagely City of Ten Thousand Buddhas at Wonderful Enlightenment Mountain, and the ninth patriarch of the Weiyang Sect of Buddhism, had peacefully manifested the stillness in Los Angeles, U.S.A., at 3:15 p.m. on June 7, 1995 (the tenth day of the fifth lunar month of the year *yi hai*) at the age of seventy-eight. The fourfold assembly of disciples at the various branches of Dharma Realm Buddhist Association (Gold Mountain Sagely Monastery in San Francisco, Gold Wheel Sagely Monastery in Los Angeles, Gold Summit Sagely Monastery in Seattle, Gold Buddha Sagely Monastery and Avatamsaka Sagely Monastery in Canada, and others), following the Elder One's last instructions, recited the *Flower Adornment Sutra* and the Buddha's name for forty-nine days, praying that the Elder One will soon return on the power of his vows and universally save living beings. From July 26 to 28, 1995, beginning at 7:00 a.m. each day, the Sagely City of Ten Thousand Buddhas held a three-day Memorial and Cremation Ceremony. I was asked to be on the Committee in Honor of the Nirvana of Venerable Master Hua, and I came to the United States especially to attend the Memorial and Cremation Ceremony. I sincerely pray that the Venerable Elder Hua will soon return on his vows and universally save living beings.

The Venerable Elder Hua was a native of Shuangcheng County, Jilin Province, China. In 1948 he received the Dharma-transmission from the Elder Master Hsu Yun and became the ninth patriarch of the Weiyang lineage of the Chan Sect. In 1962, after living in Hong Kong for over ten years, he went to America to propagate the Dharma. Over the next thirty-odd years, he expounded more than thirty Mahayana Sutras and his disciples published over one hundred volumes of translated Buddhist texts in English, Vietnamese, and other languages. These publications have been widely circulated in places such as northern California, Southeast Asia, Hong Kong, and Taiwan. He founded twenty-seven Way-places, and his disciples are found in all parts of the world.

The Elder One maintained the precepts strictly throughout his life and emphasized the importance of teaching by example. At the City of Ten Thousand Buddhas and other Way-places he established the six great principles of no fighting, no greed, no seeking, no selfishness, no pursuit of personal advantage, and no lying, which are held in respect by both monastic and lay disciples. He also promoted educational activities and founded elementary and secondary schools and the Dharma Realm Buddhist University at the City of Ten Thousand Buddhas.

In May of 1987, preparation began for the trip of a seventy-member delegation of monks from Guangji Monastery in Beijing and Dragon Flower Monastery in Shanghai to go to America to hold the Water, Land, and Air

法務團赴美，舉行水陸空大法會一事，我與中國佛教協會教務部主任王新居士，及國務院宗教事務局趙昌明先生等，先期赴美就壇場佈置、單資結緣等問題，與宣化長老等具體商討。為七月即將在萬佛城舉行的水陸空大法會做好準備。在宣化長老躬自率眾參加下，從七月十八日起至二十四日，連續舉行了整整七晝夜的水陸空大法會，功德圓滿。

這不僅是新中國成立以來，我國佛教界首次組織大型法務團，到國外舉行規模盛大的佛事活動。在中國佛教向外傳播的歷史上，也是前所未有的。體現了我國宗教信仰自由政策和對外開放政策，在國外產生了巨大影響，宣化上人真是功德無量。我在一九八九年十月八日上海「解放日報」上，發表了一篇「萬佛城的掌聲」，記述其事。宣化長老的名字從此為國內四眾弟子所熟悉，他的《法華經》、《楞嚴經》、《金剛經》等講義淺釋，在國內也被大量翻印，法雨普及，促使了正法久住。其後，我多次到美國參加萬佛聖城的傳戒等活動，與宣化長老攜手合作，弘揚聖教。

在宣化長老四十九天的涅槃法會圓滿後，九月十八日至二十三日還將舉行傳戒法會，由我任說戒和尚，恆實法師任羯磨阿闍黎，恆來法師為教授阿闍黎。宣化長老一生嚴持戒律，萬佛聖城僧眾以道風嚴謹著稱。例如中國僧伽法務團抵萬佛城時，上人率眾長跪相迎，這是佛教中最高的禮節。在生活上，萬佛城的僧眾日中一食，夜不倒單，提倡艱苦樸實的作風，贏得信眾的尊敬。《華嚴經》說：

戒是無上菩提本，應當具足持淨戒。
若能堅持於禁戒，是則如來所讚歎。

戒，是獲得無上正等正覺大菩提的根本。根本不固，一切難成。好比建築房屋，地基不鞏固，一遇風雨就易倒塌。三無漏學，戒是基礎，由戒生定，由定發慧。釋迦世尊在《遺教經》中說：「汝等比丘。於

Ceremony. I and Layman Wang Xin (the Director of Religious Affairs of the Buddhist Association of China) and Mr. Zhao Changming of the Religious Affairs Department of the National Affairs Assembly went to America in advance to set up the platform and discuss the questions of expense with the Venerable Elder Hua. We made the necessary preparations for the Water, Land, and Air Ceremony to be held at the City of Ten Thousand Buddhas in July. Under the personal guidance of the Venerable Elder Hua, the assembly participated in the Water, Land, and Air Ceremony, which lasted continuously for seven days and nights and concluded successfully.

Not only was this the first time since new China was established that Chinese Buddhism sent a large delegation abroad to hold such an elaborate Buddhist ceremony, this was also unprecedented in the history of the outward propagation of Chinese Buddhism. It was an actualization of China's policies of freedom of religion and of open exchange with other nations and was of great influence abroad. The Venerable Master Hua's merit is truly immeasurable. I described the event in the article "The Sound of Applause at the City of Ten Thousand Buddhas" in Shanghai's *Liberation Daily* on October 8, 1989. Since then the Venerable Elder Hua's name has become widely known among Buddhists in the mainland, and his explanations of the *Dharma Flower Sutra, Shurangama Sutra, Vajra Sutra,* and other Sutras have been reprinted in great volume within the country. His Dharma rain reaches everywhere, perpetuating the Proper Dharma. Later, I went to America several times to take part in the ordination ceremonies and other activities, working hand in hand with the Venerable Elder Hua to propagate the holy teachings.

After the forty-nine-day ceremony in honor of the Venerable Elder Hua's Nirvana, there will be an ordination ceremony from September 18 to 23, with myself as the Precept-speaking Master, Dharma Master Heng Sure as the Karma Acharya, and Dharma Master Heng Lai as the Teaching Acharya. The Venerable Elder Hua strictly maintained the precepts throughout his life, and the Sangha of the Sagely City of Ten Thousand Buddhas is well-known for their strict practice. For example, when the Chinese Sangha Delegation arrived at the City of Ten Thousand Buddhas, the Venerable Master led the assembly to kneel and welcome us. This is the most exalted form of courtesy in Buddhism. The monks and nuns at the City of Ten Thousand Buddhas take only one meal a day, never lie down to sleep, and promote a style of practice that is bitter and austere, thus evoking the respect of the laity. The *Flower Adornment Sutra* says:

Precepts are the unsurpassed foundation of Bodhi.
One should completely uphold the pure precepts.
If one is able to persevere in upholding the precepts and rules,
Then one will be praised by the Thus Come Ones.

The precepts are the foundation for obtaining great Bodhi—the unsurpassed proper, equal, and right enlightenment. If the foundation is not firm, it will be difficult to accomplish anything. It is like building a house: If the foundation is not solid, the house will collapse in a storm. Of the three nonoutflow studies, precepts are the foundation. From the precepts, samadhi arises; and from samadhi, wisdom can come forth. The World Honored One, Shakyamuni, said in the *Sutra of the Final Teaching,* "Bhikshus, after my Nirvana, you should cherish the Pratimoksha." Pratimoksha refers to precepts. It is also translated as 'separate liberation' and 'liberation in every place.' The precepts taken by the seven assemblies of

我滅後。當尊重珍敬波羅木提叉。」波羅提木叉就是戒律，又譯別解脫，或譯處處解脫。七眾佛弟子所受戒律，能免過非，各別解脫身口七支的惡業，所以各別解脫。世尊又說：「戒是正順解脫之本。故名波羅提木叉。因依此戒。得生諸禪定及滅苦智慧。」

為使佛陀「以戒為師」的聖訓得以延續，在宣化長老涅槃法會圓滿之際，舉行傳戒，意義非常深遠。

在讚頌宣化長老無量功德的同時，我們應當學習上人的高貴品質，實踐他所提倡的不爭、不貪、不求、不自私、不自利、不打妄語的六大宗旨，繼承他的遺志，把法界佛教總會萬佛聖城辦得更好。

祝禱長老早日乘願再來，使佛日增輝、法輪常轉。

上海市佛教協會名譽會長
上海市龍華寺方丈
上海市圓明講堂住持明暘

disciples can prevent them from making mistakes and separately liberate the Seven Limbs of the body and mind from evil karma. Thus, they are called the precepts of separate liberation. The World Honored One also said, "Precepts are the basis for proper and compliant liberation. Thus they are called Pratimoksha. By relying on precepts, one gives rise to Chan samadhi and the wisdom that extinguishes suffering."

In order to carry on the Buddha's instruction to "take the precepts as our teacher," the transmission of precepts is being held at the conclusion of the ceremonies in honor of the Venerable Elder Hua's Nirvana. The significance of this is extremely deep and far-reaching.

At the same time that we praise the Venerable Elder Hua's limitless merit and virtue, we should strive to imitate the Venerable Master's noble character, practice the Six Great Principles that he promoted—no fighting, no greed, no seeking, no selfishness, no pursuing personal advantage, and no lying—carry on his vows, and make Dharma Realm Buddhist Association and the Sagely City of Ten Thousand Buddhas even better.

I pray that the Venerable Elder will soon come back riding on his vows, causing the Buddha's sun to shine ever brighter and the Dharma wheel to constantly turn.

Mingyang,
Honorary Director of the Buddhist Association of Shanghai
Abbot of Dragon Flower Monastery of Shanghai
Abbot of Yuanming Lecture Hall of Shanghai

（一）

高僧赴美結良因，
舊友新知格外親；
遠涉重洋弘聖教，
鵬飛異域播梵音。
如來寺裡如法行，
萬佛城中萬事興；
功德圓滿光史冊，
千秋偉業耀當今。

(1)

A lofty Sanghan went to America to create good causes
Whether old friends or new acquaintances, everyone liked to draw near him.
He crossed the vast ocean to propagate the holy teaching.
He flew to a distant foreign land to spread the pure sound.
In Tathagata Monastery, people cultivate in accord with the Dharma;
At the City of Ten Thousand Buddhas, the myriad things flourish.
The perfection of his merit and virtue will shine in the pages of history.
His great deeds will endure for a thousand autumns and illuminate the present.

（二）

妙覺山前鐘鼓聲，
達摩鎮畔有高僧；
度輪長老悲心切，
宣化沙門慈願深。
廣施門開興水陸，
無遮會啓利有情；
廣大宏誓深似海，
乘願重來度眾生。

(2)

The bell and drum are struck at Wonderful Enlightenment Mountain.
In the town of Talmage, there was an eminent Sanghan.
The Venerable Elder To Lun's compassion was earnest.
The Shramana Hsuan Hua's kind vows were profound.
Opening the door of extensive giving, he hosted the Water Land Ceremony.
With an assembly open to all without restriction, he benefited sentient beings.
His vast, great vows are as deep as the sea.
We hope that, riding on his vows, he will return to save living beings.

時時刻刻不離老和尚的敎導

NEVER APART FROM THE VENERABLE MASTER'S TEACHING

明暘老法師　一九九五年七月二十六日開示於萬佛聖城宣公上人讚頌追思法會

A talk by Elder Dharma Master Mingyang on July 26, 1995
at the Sagely City of Ten Thousand Buddhas

律法師、各位法師、各位居士：

我今天奉了大和尚的指示，要我今天晚上和大家見見面，和大家介紹一點我與宣公老法師的認識過程；但是我因為年紀大，講話不清楚，希望各位多多原諒。

我剛剛接到恆律大和尚送給我一本宣公老法師追思紀念的專集，我把它打開一看，他功德是非常地偉大，他在世界上做了大量的貢獻，是不可思議的境界，即是大菩薩乘願再來的。

我自從一九九五年六月七日，得到宣公老和尚涅槃的消息，我們在中國上海的敎友，都感到非常地悲傷。這一天我們圓明講堂正在紀念圓瑛老法師，有兩三千人都知道這個悲痛的消息。我們這一天就在上海圓明講堂將紀念圓瑛老法師紀念會，改為悼念宣公大德長老法會。有兩三千人專門念一堂佛，紀念宣公老和尚。吃過飯，打了一場普佛，來紀念宣公老和尚。這一天有很多的敎友，原在圓明講堂參加法會，都參加了這個紀念宣公老法師的紀念大會，或參加普佛。這一天，中國佛敎協會趙樸初會長，唁電的兩句話：「苦海舟沉，人天眼滅。」非常地哀悼。

上人生前說：「我從虛空來，回到虛空去。」這也是《金剛經》的要義。我希望在座的各位法師、居士，把老法師最後「我從虛空來，回到虛空去」的話，請大家記在心中，隨時隨地都離不開老法師的遺敎，隨時隨地都像親近老法師一樣地分不開。

這什麼意思呢？就是說虛空廣大圓滿，周遍法界，我們每一個人都不能離開虛空，我們能生存在世界都靠著虛空；沒有虛空，我們就不能生存。我們做了老法師的弟子，經常得到老法師的敎導，把老法師所講的種種

Dharma Master Lyu, all Dharma Masters, and all laypeople:

Today, following the Abbot's instructions, I have come to meet with everyone tonight and talk about how I came to know the Venerable Master Hua. However, I hope you will forgive me for not speaking clearly because of my advanced age.

A little earlier Abbot Heng Lyu gave me a copy of the memorial book in honor of the Venerable Master Hsuan Hua. As soon as I opened the book and began to read, I realized that the Venerable Master's merit and virtue are extremely great. He made a great contribution to this world. His state was inconceivable. He certainly was a great Bodhisattva who came back riding on his vows.

Ever since the news of the Venerable Master Hua's Nirvana was received on June 7, 1995, many Buddhists in Shanghai, China, have felt extremely sad. On that day, at the Yuanming Lecture Hall we happened to be commemorating the Anniversary of the late Elder Dharma Master Yuan Ying. Two to three thousand people were present, and they all heard this sad news. So right in that Dharma Assembly, we began a memorial ceremony for the Greatly Virtuous Elder Master Hsuan Hua. Two to three thousand people recited the Buddha's name in the morning in memory of the Venerable Master Hua. After lunch, we also held a universal bowing session in memory of the Venerable Master. On that day, many Buddhists who had come to the Yuan Ming Lecture Hall to attend the Dharma Assembly all participated in the memorial ceremony for the Elder Dharma Master Hua and in the bowing ceremony.

That day was just as Chairman Zhao Puchu of the Buddhist Association of China described in his telegram of condolence: "It's as if the ship has sunk in the sea of suffering, and the eyes of humans and gods have been put out." We all felt extremely grieved.

The Venerable Master said when he was alive, "I came from empty space, and I will return to empty space." This is also the essential meaning of the *Vajra Sutra*. I hope all the Dharma Masters and laypeople who are present will remember in their hearts these last words of the Elder Dharma Master, "I came from empty space, and I will return to empty space." At all times and places, do not be apart from the Elder Dharma Master's last teaching. It should always be inseparable from you, just as when you used to draw near the Elder Dharma Master.

What does it mean? It means that empty space is vast, great, and perfect, pervading the entire Dharma Realm. None of us can be apart from empty space. We rely on empty space to exist in the world. Without empty space, we wouldn't be able to exist. As disciples of the Elder Dharma Master, we often received teachings from him, and we should remember in our hearts all the things he said. If we do that, then at all times and places we will be able to see the Elder Dharma Master as if he were right in front of us.

話，要記在心中，那我們就時時刻刻、在在處處，都能見到老法師如在目前。

老法師在這兩句話下面，還有幾句話，他不是說「諸佛的母親──《華嚴經》」、「正法的妙用──楞嚴經」、「如來的家法，就是正法眼藏」，老法師最後這三句話是什麼意思呢？就是說《華嚴經》希望大家多念、多看、多研究，這是諸佛母親，能夠出生無量的諸佛。諸佛的母親，《華嚴經》；正法流遠呢，就是《楞嚴經》。《楞嚴經》裡講什麼道理呢？講非常主要的道理。所以要使正法永遠常流下去，永遠不息，就可以多研究《楞嚴經》。老法師所講的多少「不」，希望大家一生中間把老法師所講的不爭、不貪、不求、不自私、不自利、不妄語中六個「不」字，都記在心中，多研究《華嚴經》，多看看《楞嚴經》。諸佛的母親、正法的妙用、佛教的家風，大家記在心中。這就是宣化老法師雖然過去了，他的遺教，他的法語，還有很多留在世間，還有很多的事業，都在世間。希望各位法師，都在恆律法師和恆實法師、各位老師兄領導下，團結起來，把老和尚的事業，更加發揚光大發達，更加一天比一天興隆起來；才不辜負老法師一番的心血，他做了許多的功績，交代各位。

因為我今天沒有很好的準備，剛剛翻開追思紀念文章看一看，老法師的幾句話非常非常重要，真是如來的正法眼藏，真是真理；希望大家把老法師這幾句話，永遠記在心中，就是我們時時刻刻不離老和尚的教導，時時刻刻紀念老和尚講的願望。所以他十八大願中間，最後的一個願，就是他所有的願，統統得到圓滿成功。所以各位如能照這樣做下去，就是老法師十八大願中所講的，他真正得到各位弟子們大力支持、大力擁護。

因為時間關係，我不多講，我跟老法師多年的交情，不是一句、二句話講得完，我想在座各位已經都看到、聽到我們多年的交情，我這次怎麼來的呢？我受到恆律法師一再地邀請。我在上海百忙中間，無論如何要到萬佛城來給老法師送行，祝他老人家發的願，獲得滿願，法會順利，佛事莊嚴，一切如意。謝謝各位。最後感謝恆律法師、恆實法師、在座各位法師，謝謝大家！Bye-bye. Sayonara!（再見！）

The Elder Dharma Master also said some other things after that sentence. He said, "The mother of all Buddhas is the *Flower Adornment Sutra*"; "The wonderful function of the proper Dharma is the *Shurangama Sutra*"; and "The Tathagata's Dharma is the Proper Dharma Eye Treasury." What is the meaning of these last three statements of the Elder Dharma Master? He hoped that everyone would spend more time reciting, reading, and studying the *Flower Adornment Sutra*, which is the mother of all Buddhas and can give birth to all the limitless Buddhas. So, the *Flower Adornment Sutra* is the mother of all Buddhas. To perpetuate the proper Dharma, use the *Shurangama Sutra*. What principles does the *Shurangama Sutra* discuss? It talks about very fundamental principles. If we want the proper Dharma to stay forever and never decline, we can spend more time studying the *Shurangama Sutra*. The Elder Dharma Master talked about many "no's." I hope everyone will remember for their whole life the six no's that the Elder Dharma Master spoke about—no fighting, no greed, no seeking, no selfishness, no self-benefitting, and no lying. I also hope everyone will spend more time studying the *Flower Adornment Sutra* and reading the *Shurangama Sutra*. The mother of all Buddhas, the wonderful function of the proper Dharma, and the tradition of Buddhism—everyone should remember these in their minds. Even though the Elder Dharma Master Hsuan Hua has already passed away, his teachings and his words of Dharma are still very much in the world. Much of the work that he has done is still in the world. I hope that all of you Dharma Masters will unite under the leadership of Dharma Master Heng Lyu, Dharma Master Heng Sure, and your elder Dharma-brothers, so that you can propagate the Venerable Master's endeavors, causing them to become more flourishing with each passing day. Only then will you not be ungrateful for the Elder Dharma Master's bitter toil. His numerous achievements have been passed on to you.

I was not very well prepared for today's talk. I just opened the memorial collection and skimmed through the essays. Those statements of the Elder Dharma Master are extremely important. They are truly the Tathagata's Proper Dharma Eye Treasury. They are the genuine truth. I hope everyone will cherish these words of the Elder Dharma Master in their hearts forever. Then we will never be away from the Venerable Master's teachings for a moment. At all times we will be remembering the Venerable Master's wishes. Among his Eighteen Great Vows, the last one is that all his vows will be fulfilled. If all of you can follow this, then the Venerable Master will truly obtain the full strength and complete support of his disciples in realizing his Eighteen Great Vows.

Due to the limited time, I will not say too much. My friendship with the Elder Dharma Master goes back many years, and it cannot be summed up in a couple of sentences. I think all of you have seen or heard about our friendship of many years. How did I come this time? I received repeated invitations from Dharma Master Heng Lyu, and so despite my busy schedule in Shanghai, I was determined to come to the Sagely City of Ten Thousand Buddhas to bid farewell to the Elder Dharma Master, to pray that the vows he made will be fulfilled, that the ceremonies will be orderly and splendid, and that everything will turn out well. Thank you all. Finally I'd like to thank Dharma Master Heng Lyu, Dharma Master Heng Sure, and all the Dharma Masters who are present. Thank you, everyone! Bye-bye. Sayonara!

DILIGENTLY UPHOLD THE PURE PRECEPTS;
COMPASSIONATELY TAKE LIVING BEINGS ACROSS
精勤持淨戒　　慈悲度眾生

英國永生佛教中心蘇美度法師　一九九五年七月二十七日開示於萬佛聖城宣公上人讚頌追思法會
A talk by Venerable Ajahn Sumedho of the Amaravati Buddhist Centre in England
on July 27, 1995 at the Sagely City of Ten Thousand Buddhas

Whenever I would come to the United States, I'd always make a point of coming to see Venerable Master Hsuan Hua wherever he was. I would go to the Gold Wheel Temple in Los Angeles, to the temple in San Francisco, or come here. In 1989, I invited the Venerable Master to England, and when he arrived at our monastery of Amaravati with a retinue of Bhikshus and Bhikshunis, we were very delighted and pleased. Strangely enough, though the Chinese community has existed in Britain for several hundred years, in 1989 there were no Chinese monks or Chinese temples in England. I remember searching in London, trying to find, in the Chinese community, any sign of a temple or Buddhist group. We could hardly find anything that you could call Buddhism among the Chinese community in Britain. It was greatly compassionate of the Master to come to England at that time, because now there is definitely a renewal of interest in the practice of the Dharma among the Chinese community.

It's very important to recognize the monastic form as something that is not understood very well by Western people. Both here in America and in Europe, the idea of a Buddhist monk or nun is considered very strange. Once people really understand the purpose and intent of our life, most people respect what we're doing. But there are very few Masters that inspire Westerners to live the holy life in the monastic form. The Venerable Master Hsuan Hua was one of these great teachers who by his own example and his own compassion could encourage and inspire Western people to take on the restraining life of the Buddhist monk and Buddhist nun and to live it for liberation and for compassion, for liberating all sentient beings. My teacher in Thailand was also one of these great beings who could inspire Western people to see the value and the beauty that lies in living the life of the Shramana [Buddhist monastic].

In 1992 Ajahn Chah died, and now the Venerable Master Hsuan Hua has died, and what we have is the memory of both these great teachers. This memory is something to respect and honor. A ceremony like this gives all of us who have known the Venerable Master or heard of him an opportunity to come together. All of us from various parts of this planet have assembled together at this time and place to honor the memory of this great being. The memory of a great teacher—instead of seeing it in terms of grief and sorrow and loss—is something to inspire us,

每次來美國，我一定要去見一見上人，不管上人在什麼地方。他在洛杉磯金輪寺，我就去金輪寺；在舊金山，我就去舊金山；在萬佛城，我就去萬佛城。

一九八九年，我邀請上人到英國訪問。當上人帶領多位出家眾，到永生佛教中心時，我們感到十分欣悅。雖然中國人在英國定居已有數百年的歷史，但奇怪的是，直到一九八九年，英國還沒有中國的僧侶或寺廟。我們曾到倫敦的中國人社區裡，尋找佛教團體或寺廟，卻不曾看到一點佛教的跡象。上人慈悲為懷，於一九八九年到英國弘法，此後當地的中國人，也開始對佛教發生了興趣。

我們應該認識到，西方人對佛教的制度並不太瞭解。不論在美國或歐洲，對佛教中比丘、比丘尼的概念，非常陌生。可是一旦人們真正瞭解了出家的目的和意願之後，多數人都能尊重出家僧眾的修行。但是，只有少數的大師能夠激發西方人，來過這種神聖的出家生活。宣公上人就是這樣的一位大師，以身作則，以慈悲心鼓勵西方人，為了自己的解脫，也為了慈悲救度一切有情眾生，去接受佛教比丘、比丘尼那種嚴謹的生活方式。

我在泰國的師父，也是這樣一位能感化西方人，使西方人認識佛教沙門生活價值的人。

我的師父於一九九二年往生，現在宣公上人也走了。留給我們的是對這兩位大師的回憶，這種回憶充滿了敬仰和尊崇。今天的追思紀念大會，讓所有認識上人的人，從世界各地來到這裡，有機會聚在一起，共同追思憶念這位偉人。在追憶這位大師時，我們不應徒然悲傷哀嘆，而應振奮起來，鼓勵自己，立志於自身的開悟、解脫。我發覺，雖然我的

to awaken us, to encourage us, towards our aspiration for liberation and enlightenment in our own lives. I find that even though Venerable Ajahn Chan has died and now the Venerable Master Hsuan Hua has died, this gives me even more encouragement and purpose in my monastic life, because I appreciate all that they've done for all of us over the many years and probably many lifetimes. This is not to be just dismissed and ignored, but to be contemplated and reflected upon to give us that extra energy and inspiration and the ability to fulfill our own intentions in our lives as Buddhists.

I want to express my joy at being able to come to the cremation of the Venerable Master. I have to rush back, because this is our *vassa* [summer retreat] time, in which we cannot stay away from the monastery for more than seven nights.

My association and my memories of the Venerable Master have always been precious to me, and even though he has passed away, this only increases the bonds and the respect we feel for each others' communities. Talking to the venerable monks here, I don't feel that this will be my last appearance at the Sagely City of Ten Thousand Buddhas. May you all be free to develop this life of moral restraint and of cultivation of the Way, so that you may be free from all forms of selfishness and self-delusion, all forms of desire, and all forms of suffering, and that you may all realize Nibbana. Thank you.

*　　　*　　　*

A Magnificent Living Example of the Dharma

July 28, 1995

I just want to express the gratitude from the Western side of Buddhism to the Great Master, who inspired us all and gave us so much during his lifetime. It's a great gift from the Asian continent to the Western world, these venerable sages that choose to live and share their wisdom with us in the Western world. I think this kind of gift and great compassion is something beyond compare. It is what you might call "foreign aid at its very best." I will always remember and treasure this.

Also, in reflecting on the body of the great Master this morning, I had a marvelous insight into the way he would say he was always living like a dead man anyway. The truth, the pure Dharma, that which is real and true, was never born and never dies. Even though the Great Master, in terms of conventions of our language and our perceptual range, is such that we see Venerable Master Hua as having died and passed away, what we really loved and respected is still present with us, and that is the True Dharma that he was always pointing to and of which he was a magnificent living example. I just want to say again what gratitude we all feel—here in America and Europe—for the great gifts that the Venerable Master gave to us.

師父和宣公上人都走了，但他們卻為我的出家生活留下了更多的鼓勵和努力的目標。我很感激他們在過去多年，甚至多生中為我們所做的努力。我們不應忘記，更不應該忽略，而應該觀照、反省，並從中汲取精力、靈感及能力，而成就我們的道業。

能來參加上人的荼毗大典，我深感榮幸。但是我得趕回去，因為現在正是我們結夏安居的時候，我們離開寺廟的時間，不得超過七個晚上。

我跟上人的交往及對上人的懷念，對我來說是十分珍貴的。上人雖已不在了，但是我們之間的聯繫，以及僧團間的相互尊重，卻不斷地增長。和這兒的出家人交談以後，我相信我還會回到萬佛城來。希望你們大家能自在地持戒修行，能從自私、妄想、一切欲望和所有的痛苦中解脫出來，早證涅槃。謝謝！

上人是真理最真實莊嚴的化身

一九九五年七月二十七日

我想從西方佛教的立場，向上人表示感恩。他老人家一生中給我們的啟發及奉獻，這正是亞洲給西方世界最大的禮物。這些聖人來到西方，讓我們分享他們的智慧，我想這樣慈悲的奉獻，是沒有人可以相比的，這也可以說是「最好的國際支援」，我會永遠懷念、珍惜這一切。

今天早上去瞻仰上人之後，我心中突然明白了為什麼上人常說：「我就是一個活死人。」因為法本來無生無滅，雖然從感官、從世間的立場來看，我們說上人圓寂了。但是我們所尊崇的真理－－這是上人時常教導我們的，而他自己也正是真理最真實莊嚴的化身，仍然活生生地在我們眼前。最後，我想再一次向上人表示感激，他老人家給我們歐美西方世界這份最大的禮物。

HIS LIGHT SHINES UPON THE WORLD AND HE IS A PLACE OF REFUGE

光明照世爲所歸

Ven. Dr. K. Sri Dhammananda JSM, D.Litt. Malaysia

達摩難陀法師

I was deeply saddened to learn of the untimely demise of the Venerable Master Hsuan Hua which occurred on 7th June 1995. I have had the good fortune to be associated with him and enjoyed his warm hospitality during my visit to him on the occasion when I attended the opening ceremony of the City of Ten Thousand Buddhas in 1979. I am happy to recollect that the Late Venerable Master Hsuan Hua reciprocated that visit by being my guest of the Buddhist Maha Vihara in Kuala Lumpur, Malaysia, soon after that. Throughout my association with him my respect and admiration for his humility, intelligence, dedication, energy and warmth knew no bounds.

I am proud to recognize the tremendous service that the Late Venerable Master Hsuan Hua had rendered during his lifetime in the cause of Buddhism. Although he was an orthodox follower of the Mahayana School of Buddhism, he nevertheless displayed a great openness of mind and recognized the transcendental essence of the Teachings of the Enlightened One. Although not English educated, he was able to bring the sublime teachings of the Buddha to the West and thereby inspired both Easterners and Westerners to follow his discipline and devotion to the study of the Dharma. His was a dynamic personality that inspired his followers, both monks and nuns as well as laypeople, to follow the path of discipline, virtue and wisdom that he himself had trod throughout the seventy-six years during which he manifested himself in this earthly form.

He devoted his tremendous energy not only towards the noble task of teaching, but also to that of developing the more tangible, physical aspects of Dharma Practice. His greatest contribution in this area was the building of the magnificent edifice called the City of Ten Thousand Buddhas, which will long endure to symbolize the presence of the sublime Dharma in the West. It is not only a place of worship and a meditation centre; it is also a University and a renowned Buddhist Research and Translation Centre. Many millions of sentient beings will benefit from the work done at this centre for a long time to come.

Following in the footsteps of the great Chinese Buddhist Missionaries of the past like Fa Hsien and I Ching, the Late Master Hsuan Hua travelled widely not only in the West but also in Asia as well, spreading the Dhamma in far-off places like Hong Kong, Singapore, Malaysia and Taiwan where he established Buddhist Centres for the study and propagation of the Dhamma. In Malaysia there are many members and devotees who respect him and try to emulate the footsteps of the great Master Hsuan Hua.

The demise of Master Hsuan Hua is indeed a great loss to all of us. But we can learn even from his passing away of what our Lord Buddha had

宣公上人於一九九五年六月七日離世，我對上人的早入涅槃，感到非常難過。本人很有幸認識上人，並於一九七九年萬佛聖城開光典禮時，承他盛情款待。不久之後，上人來訪馬來西亞吉隆坡十五碑佛教寺院，成為我的座上賓，以酬上次我去萬佛城拜訪上人。這件事我現在回想起來，都還覺得很高興。在與上人交往之後，我對於上人待人的謙虛、睿智，做事時孜孜不倦、充滿活力，對人的溫和親切，更加地敬仰了。

本人有幸能知道宣公上人一生中，對佛教所做出的極大貢獻。雖然上人信仰大乘佛教，但上人的胸襟廣大開闊，並深知大覺者出世教化的精義。上人雖沒有受過英語教育，卻能將佛法崇高的教義帶到西方，因而啟發了東、西方人士跟隨他嚴謹自律和專心致志的精神，來學習佛法。他對座下的人，不論出家、在家，都極有影響力，能把他們調教得都走上他本人在一生中，以身體力行的戒德與智慧之道。

上人不僅致力於神聖的教化工作，同時也建立了壯觀的萬佛聖城，並發展成西方佛法的象徵。聖城不只是禮拜、打坐的中心，也是一所佛教大學，也是一個聞名的佛教研究翻譯中心。其成績將使未來千千萬萬的有情眾生都蒙受利益。

步著過去法顯、義淨等佛教大師的後塵，宣公上人足跡遍及西方和亞洲，遠至香港、新加坡、馬來西亞和臺灣弘揚佛法，建立道場。在我們馬來西亞有很多信徒尊

reminded us—that all of us are subject to the triple suffering of ~~j~~ati (Birth), Jara (Decay) and Marana (Death). No one can stop ~~t~~hat. We must therefore endeavour to renew our efforts to follow ~~i~~n the footsteps of the Late Master and work diligently to free our~~s~~elves from the bonds of Samsara, the endless round of rebirths.

May he, like all of us, be freed from worldly suffering and may ~~h~~e attain final Nirvanic bliss.

敬上人，並想追隨上人。

宣公上人的離世真是大家的損失。但從他的離世，我們仍可學習到佛陀所提醒我們的人生三苦：生苦、壞苦（老病）和行苦（死）。這是無人得以倖免的，我們必須重新努力，精進追隨上人的腳步，以便脫出無休止的輪迴纏縛。

但願上人和我們一樣，都能免於世間之苦，證得涅槃之樂。

A Big Star Has Fallen
巨星的殞落

A talk by Venerable Bhante Dharmawara during the Memorial Ceremony for the Venerable Master Hua
on July 28, 1995 at the Sagely City of Ten Thousand Buddhas
達摩瓦拉法師　一九九五年七月二十八日
開示於萬佛聖城宣公上人讚頌追思法會

The most venerable Mahatheras and Maha Upsakas and Upasikas: A big star has fallen. On account of that, we are gathering here to express our gratitude for the good that the big star has left behind. Now the fall of the big star makes room for another star. I am quite sure we are thinking of the big star, and our love for the big star has not ended with his fall. But we have to understand that the fall of the big star has provided room for the second one, and I am sure the second one will not fail to perform his duty to replace the loss. I am sure we have much to gain by the new one. This is my understanding. Thank you so much for giving me time.

諸山長老、各位尊貴的法師、居士：

因為一顆巨星的殞落，所以今天大家同聚一堂，對巨星所遺留下來的恩澤，表達我們的感恩。我相信巨星雖然殞落，但我們對的它的懷念與敬愛是無盡的，我們應該明白一顆巨星的殞落將使另一顆巨星升起，而第二顆巨星將會繼續這份工作，彌補我們今天的損失，相信從新的巨星那兒我們將得到更多，這是我所瞭解的。謝謝各位給我機會說幾句話。

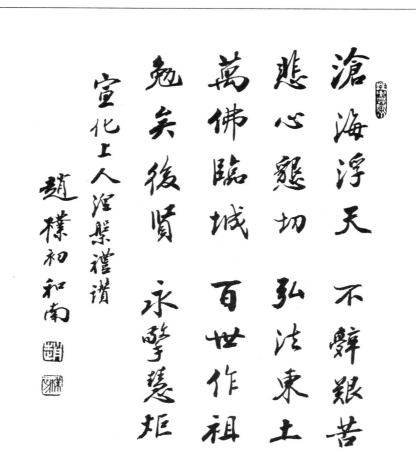

滄海浮天　不辭艱苦　悲心懇切　弘法東土
Between the vast sea and the lofty heavens,
Undaunted by toil and hardship,
With earnestness and compassion,
He propagated the Dharma in the land to the east.

萬佛臨城　百世作祖　勉矣後賢　永擎慧炬
Ten thousand Buddhas grace the City.
He was the patriarch for a hundred generations to come.
Carry on, worthy followers:
Forever raise aloft the torch of wisdom.

宣化上人涅槃禮讚
A Praise for the Venerable Master Hua's Nirvana

中國佛教協會趙樸初和南
Zhao Puchu joins his palms in respect
The Buddhist Association of China

願中美佛教友誼萬古長青

MAY THE FRIENDSHIP BETWEEN CHINESE AND AMERICAN BUDDHISM LAST FOREVER

沉痛悼念宣化上人

In Mournful Remembrance of the Venerable Master Hua

釋真禪　Shi Zhenchan

當聽到大洋彼岸的佛教高僧宣化上人圓寂的噩耗時，悲痛之情，油然而生。因遠隔重洋，不能親自前往吊唁，除命我所住持的各大寺僧眾舉行哀思法會，誦經迴向外，謹撰短文一篇，以示沉痛的哀悼。

十多年以前，即一九八四年，我和上海龍華寺方丈明暘法師、普陀山普濟寺方丈妙善法師等三人，應美東佛教總會應行久夫婦的邀請，前往美國紐約參加大乘寺玉佛寶塔落成和佛像開光典禮。宣化上人得知後，一連幾次打電話邀請我們前往萬佛城作客。盛情難卻之下，我們接受邀請前往參訪，受到隆重而又熱烈的接待。宣化上人親自率領眾弟子們，以紅地毯的規格迎接我們。

宣化上人對我們非常熱情，與我們晤談甚久。他對我說，他於一九七五年買下了一所本來是療養院的地方，然後改造成為弘揚佛法的基地，即現在的萬佛聖城。這是很不容易的，可說是歷盡了艱辛。他還說，他的最終目的，是要把萬佛聖城建設成為世界佛教的中心，以促進東西方文化的交流。聽了宣化上人的這些介紹，我們內心非常感動。

就在我們訪問他以後的第二年（一九八五年）春天，他就派遣了萬佛城數位美籍尼師到我們上海玉佛寺訪問。這些尼師在玉佛寺受到熱情、親切的接待。在參觀、訪問中，他們對玉佛寺殿堂建築的雄偉和佛菩薩像的莊嚴表示讚賞，對信徒、遊客的眾多和香火旺盛的情況感到驚訝。他們之中好多人在臨別時都說：「這次訪問給我們留下了深刻的印象。」

When I heard the sad news that the eminent Buddhist monk on the other side of the ocean, the Venerable Master Hua, had completed the stillness, grief welled up in my heart. Due to the great distance, I was not able to personally attend the memorial service. Aside from telling the Sangha members at the various monasteries of which I am the Abbot to hold mourning ceremonies and to recite Sutras and transfer merit, I am writing this short essay to express my heavy sorrow and grief.

More than ten years ago, in 1984, Dharma Master Mingyang (the Abbot of Dragon Flower Monastery in Shanghai), Dharma Master Miaoshan (the Abbot of Universal Salvation Monastery at Mount Putuo), and I attended the celebration of the completion of the Jade Buddha Pagoda and the inauguration of the Buddha image at Mahayana Monastery in New York at the invitation of Mr. and Mrs. Ying Xingjiu of the Eastern American Buddhist Association. When the Venerable Master Hua found out about this, he made several phone calls inviting us to go to the City of Ten Thousand Buddhas as guests, and since we could hardly refuse him, we accepted the invitation. We were given a solemn yet fervent reception. The Venerable Master Hua himself led his disciples in giving us a red-carpet welcome.

The Venerable Master treated us with great warmth. He conversed with us for a long time. He told me that he had bought what was originally the site of a hospital in 1975 and converted it into a base from which to propagate the Buddhadharma—presently the Sagely City of Ten Thousand Buddhas. This was a very difficult task. He endured great hardship and toil. He also said his final goal was to build the Sagely City of Ten Thousand Buddhas into a center for world Buddhism, where the cultural exchange between East and West could be furthered. We were very deeply moved by the Venerable Master's words.

In the spring of the following year (1985), the Venerable Master sent several American nuns from the Sagely City to visit Jade Buddha Monastery in Shanghai. We received them warmly at Jade Buddha Monastery. During their tour and visit, they praised the architectural magnificence of the Buddhahall and the adorned images of Buddhas and Bodhisattvas of Jade Buddha Monastery. They were surprised by the great numbers of devotees and tourists that came to the monastery and the prosperity of the temple. Upon leaving, many of them said, "This visit has left a deep impression."

The American nuns' successful visit to Jade Buddha Monastery in Shanghai and other places made the Venerable Master extremely pleased, and in the summer of that year, he personally paid a visit to his native country. When the Venerable Master arrived at Jade Buddha Monastery, I led all the monks—over a hundred in number—to welcome

數位美籍尼師到上海玉佛寺等地參訪成功，使宣化上人十分高興，於當年的夏天，親自回祖國大陸訪問。當宣化上人來到我們上海玉佛寺時，我親自率領全寺僧眾一百餘人，從山門夾道歡迎他至方丈室，使他深受感動。在玉佛寺的方丈室裡，時任上海市宗教事務局的王宏逵副局長拜見了他，向他宣傳了大陸宗教信仰自由政策和上海佛教的概況，他聽了非常高興。事後他對我們講，你們上海佛教呈現出生機勃勃的景象，這是與國家的護持分不開的。

一九八七年三月，宣化上人來信委託中國佛教協會，邀請高僧大德組團赴美國萬佛城主持水陸空大法會。中國佛教協會研究後，決定由北京廣濟寺和上海龍華寺組成七十人的大型中國僧伽赴美法務團，前往萬佛城參加水陸空大法會。一九八七年七月，由明暘法師任團長，我任顧問的中國廣濟寺、龍華寺僧伽赴美法務團到達美國舊金山萬佛聖城。當時，我們帶去了水陸空法會需用的「水陸軸子」等各種法器和僧服袈裟，還準備了《妙法蓮華經》、《大方廣佛華嚴經》等八十多部佛經，共裝九十七箱，重達二點五噸。當我們到達舊金山機場時，宣化上人親自率領約二百名四眾弟子，長跪合掌，五體投地，口稱佛號，恭敬地迎接我們。

萬佛城啟建的水陸空大法會，連續舉行了七晝夜。每天清晨起，法師們就在各個壇場（包括內壇、大壇、華嚴壇、楞嚴壇、法華壇、淨土壇和諸經壇等）誦經拜懺，響亮的法音縈繞屋樑，場面隆重而又莊嚴。

我國佛教界組織這樣的大型僧伽法務團飛渡重洋，到國外去舉行如此盛大規模、莊嚴隆重的佛事，不僅在新中國建立以來是第一次，而且在中國佛教向外傳播史上也是空前的。上人說：「我們相信，二十一世紀是佛教走向世界的時代。」在法會結束後的歡送會上，宣化上人還滿懷激情地賦詩抒懷：

中美文化互交流，兩國友誼傳萬秋；
明暘尊者續慧命，真禪長老展鴻猷。
各位龍象齊努力，十方檀越盡歸投；
水陸法會今圓滿，法音遍佈永無休。

the Venerable Master from the path at the front gate all the way to the Abbot's quarters. He was deeply touched by this. In the Abbot's room, he met with the Deputy Director Wang Hongkui of the Religious Affairs Bureau of the City of Shanghai, who explained to him the national policy of religious freedom and the conditions of Shanghai's Buddhism. The Venerable Master was extremely happy after hearing him. Later he said to me, "The flourishing of Shanghai's Buddhism is inseparably related to the protection of the entire nation."

In March 1987, the Venerable Master Hua wrote a letter requesting the Buddhist Association of China to invite a delegation of eminent and greatly virtuous Sangha members to go to the City of Ten Thousand Buddhas to host the Water, Land, and Air Ceremony. The Buddhist Association of China decided to ask Guangji Monastery in Beijing and Dragon Flower Monastery in Shanghai to form a seventy-member Chinese Sangha Delegation to travel to the City of Ten Thousand Buddhas to attend the Water, Land, and Air Ceremony. In July 1987, the Sangha Delegation from Guangji Monastery and Dragon Flower Monastery, led by Dharma Master Mingyang and myself as an advisor, travelled to the Sagely City of Ten Thousand Buddhas near San Francisco. We brought with us the "Water-Land axle-tree" and various Dharma instruments and equipment, sashes for the Sangha, and over eighty Buddhist Sutras including the Wonderful Dharma Lotus Flower Sutra and the Great Means Expansive Buddha Flower Adornment Sutra. These things filled ninety-seven cases and weighed 2.5 tons. When we arrived at the San Francisco airport, the Venerable Master Hua led two hundred disciples of the fourfold assembly in giving us a reverent welcome, kneeling with joined palms, making prostrations, and reciting the Buddha's name.

The Water, Land, and Air Ceremony at the City of Ten Thousand Buddhas lasted for seven days and nights. Early every morning, Dharma Masters would begin reciting Sutras and bowing in repentance at the various platforms (Inner Platform, Great Platform, Flower Adornment Platform, Shurangama Platform, Dharma Flower Platform, Pure Land Platform, and All Sutras Platform). The clear sound of the Dharma resounded through the buildings, and the whole scene was solemn and adorned.

Not only was this the first time since new China was established that Chinese Buddhism had sent such a large Sangha Delegation across the ocean to hold such a splendid and magnificent Buddhist ceremony in another country, it was an unprecedented event in the entire history of the propagation of Chinese Buddhism.

The Venerable Master said, "I believe that the twenty-first century will be an age during which Chinese Buddhism spreads to the world." During the farewell meeting after the Ceremony, the Venerable Master was very moved and presented us with a poem on his feelings:

With this Chinese and American cultural exchange,
The friendship between the two countries will endure for
*   ten thousand autumns.*
The Venerable Mingyang perpetuates the life of wisdom;
The Elder Zhenchan carries out vast plans.
All of you dragons and elephants (outstanding individuals)
*   should work hard together,*
And the faithful donors of the ten directions have come to take refuge.
The Water-Land Ceremony is now complete;
The sound of the Dharma spreads everywhere and
*   will never fade away.*

宣化上人已經離開我們圓寂了。從此佛教界減少了一位德高望重的高僧，我也失去了一位佛門好友。今天，我們緬懷宣化上人，應該學習他不辭勞苦，遠渡重洋，為法忘軀的勇猛精神，學習他那為增進中美佛教友誼的無私無畏精神。

宣化上人，永垂不朽！

盼他早日乘願再來，弘法利生，化度人間。

真禪撰於玉佛寺般若丈室
一九九五年七月

The Venerable Master has already completed the stillness and left us. The Buddhist world has lost an eminent Sanghan of lofty virtue, and I have lost a good Buddhist friend. Today, as we remember the Venerable Master Hua, we should strive to emulate his spirit of sacrificing himself for the sake of the Dharma and crossing over the ocean without fear of toil and suffering

The Venerable Master's example will live forever!

We hope he will come again, following his vows, to propagate the Dharma and benefit beings, to teach and save those in the world.

Written by Zhenchan, July 1995, Prajna Abbot's Hall, Jade Buddha Monastery

摩訶薩不管他

A MAHASATTVA TAKES CARE OF HIMSELF

高果宗　Gao Guozong

舊的金峰聖寺是個老舊的房子，很高，破破的外表看來根本不像個寺廟，可是裡面卻是住著真正修行的人，這種不重視外表，只重真心修行的道場真是難得，於是我就看上了這個道場。

這個道場是萬佛聖城上宣下化老和尚所創辦的道場之一，他是眾所尊敬的得道高僧，是我的皈依師父。老和尚一向主張越窮越好，越窮越好修行。因為物質的享受只能使人墮落，只有真正放下物質的享受，才能完成精神的超越。也就是死了才是真活，因此禪宗主張要大死一番，也就是斷盡一切欲念，不起心不動念，才能真正明心見性，才能智慧大開。

我曾到萬佛城去拜見上人，他老人家很慈悲地送我一樣寶貝，他說：「你自己沒有弄乾淨，不要去管別人。」這句話真是受用不盡。其實我們眾生就是因為自己沒有弄乾淨，才會去管別人；真地自己能弄乾淨了，也就不會去管別人了，也就是能成佛的時候了。因為這句話太好了，故特別提出來與大家共享。

Gold Summit Sagely Monastery is a very tall, old building. Its dilapidated exterior certainly does not seem like that of a Buddhist monastery. However, there are genuine cultivators inside. This kind of Way-place, which values honest cultivation and pays no attention to external appearance, is truly rare. That's why I had my eyes on this Way-place.

This Way-place is one of the Way-places founded by the Elder Master Venerable Hsuan Noble Hua of the Sagely City of Ten Thousand Buddhas. He is a high Sanghan who has attained the Way, and he is the Master with whom I have taken refuge. The Venerable Master has always maintained that the poorer one is, the better. The poorer one is, the easier it is to cultivate. Materialistic enjoyments can only cause people to fall. One can attain spiritual transcendence only when one has truly renounced materialistic enjoyments. Only by dying can one become truly alive. The Chan School maintains that one must undergo a great death—sever all thoughts of desire and not allow random thoughts to stir the mind—before one can truly understand the mind, see the nature, and bring forth great wisdom.

I once paid a visit to the Venerable Master at the City of Ten Thousand Buddhas. He very compassionately gave me a treasure. He said, "Before you have cleaned up yourself, don't mind others' business." This statement is truly of inexhaustible benefit. Actually, the reason we mind others' business is that we haven't cleaned up our own act. If we have truly made ourselves clean, we won't mind others' business anymore. We will also become Buddhas at that time. Because this statement is so wonderful, I wanted to share it with everyone.

悼念度輪長老

IN MEMORY OF ELDER MASTER TO LUN

釋知定　Shi Zhiding

度輪長老，法名安慈，度輪是其別名。五十年代中，虛雲老和尚授以溈仰宗第九代嗣法傳人，法名宣化；俗姓白，中國東北吉林省雙城縣人氏。長老幼年出家，勤修苦行；奉母至孝，慈母棄養，曾廬墓三年，人稱白孝子。惜因生逢末紀，處斯兵慌馬亂之秋，故披剃許久，尚未圓具。直至一九四七年才闖關萬里，受盡千辛萬苦，抵達普陀山，秉受了三壇大戒。之後，聽聞當代禪宗泰斗虛雲老和尚在曹溪重興祖庭，開堂說法。於是又不辭勞苦，跋山涉水，於一九四八年到達廣東南華寺。南華寺是年剛好春期傳戒，長老又再報名補戒，由此可見長老對戒律的重視。

我和宣化長老的認識，是在一九四八年南華寺戒堂中。彼時我當開堂，開堂的職責除教授出家人行住坐臥的一切規矩外，戒堂中的一切大小事務，亦在管轄範圍之內。而受戒弟子若有疑問或難題，向我請教，當然盡我所知為彼等解答。當時，我覺得度輪法師為人謙恭識禮，威儀整齊，動止安詳，知是法門龍象，真獅子兒，他日必有一番大振宗風之舉也。在南華寺我所辦的戒律學院，缺少一位好監學，此一職位，需要一位品學兼優之人，方堪勝任。戒期圓滿後，我即商請度輪法師出任斯職，一談即就。度老接任斯職，盡忠盡責，直到離開南華寺。

一九四九年最後一日，我到香港。在香港佛教聯合會，又與度輪法師相遇，真是有緣，處處能相逢。當時度老是以成元法師為領導，正在辦理赴泰國留學僧手續。

度老自從泰國返港定居後，即積極展開弘法利生工作。先是在港島西灣河創建「西樂園寺」，以三根普被之念佛法門，接引初機；後於跑馬地購買十二樓，建立「香港佛教

The Elder To Lun (his title), whose Dharma name was An Tse, in the 1950's was given the official transmission as the Ninth Generation Patriarch of the Weiyang Sect, by the late Venerable Elder Master Hsu Yun, and was given the certified name of Hsuan Hua (Proclaiming and Transforming). The Master was born in Manchuria, China, in Jilin (Auspicious Forest) Province in Shuangcheng (Twin Cities) County. His family surname was Bai (White). The Master left the home-life when he was young, and diligently cultivated ascetic practices. He was extremely filial toward his mother, and practiced filial piety by her graveside for three years after she passed away. People called him Filial Son Bai. He was born in the beginning of the century (1918), but because the country was facing a pending war, he did not receive the Complete Precepts until 1947, many years after leaving the home-life. He had to travel a long distance and underwent all kinds of hardships and difficulties before he reached Potola Mountain where he received the Complete Precepts.

After receiving the Precepts, the Master heard of the Venerable Elder Hsu Yun, a Patriarch of the Chan School who was at Cao Creek giving lectures and speaking the Dharma in order to revive the teachings of the sect. The Master, undaunted by the hardship and great distance, set out on his travels and headed towards the Province of Guangdong, and arrived at Nanhua Monastery in 1948. Coincidentally, during the spring of that year, the monastery was going to hold a Precept Transmission. The Master signed up to receive the Precepts, once again. From this, it is clear that the Master placed great emphasis on the precepts.

I met the Master in the Precept Hall at Nanhua Monastery in 1948. At that time, I was a teacher of the preceptees. My job included not only teaching the comportment and rules to the preceptees, but also all of the affairs that went on in the Precept Hall. If any of the preceptees had doubts or other problems, I did my best to try to help them resolve them. At that time, I noticed that Dharma Master To Lun was very humble and knew the rules of propriety. He had awesome comportment and his manner was calm. I knew that he was a vessel for the Dharma (literally: a dragon, an elephant, a real lion's son), and in the future could certainly do a good job to cause the School to flourish. At that time, I had established the Vinaya Academy at Nanhua Monastery and had not found anyone who was capable of filling the position as supervisor. To fill such a position, one needed to have character and learning. After the completion of the Precept Platform, I approached Dharma Master To Lun and requested that he fill this position. He agreed right away. After he took on this position, he was always attentive to his responsibilities until he left Nanhua Monastery.

At the end of 1949, I traveled to Hong Kong where I met the Master again at the Hong Kong United Buddhist Association. It is true that when you have affinities with people, you will always come together with them at any place. At that time, Dharma Master Chengyuan led a group of Sanghans from Hong Kong to Thailand, and the Master was among them.

講堂」，顧名思義，這是弘揚大經，普利上根利智，兼及普羅大眾。而且僧人又多一處掛單之所。度老在港除開單接眾、弘經演教外，還印送經典、流通法寶。

記得有一次，印送八十《華嚴經》，寫信請我助印。我接信後，覆信承認助印六十部。度老若有餘假，亦經常應邀前往東南亞及澳洲雪梨、墨爾本等地，宣揚法化，利導群生。

一九六二年，度老前來美國弘法，途經夏威夷，停留兩週。我略盡地主之誼，妥為照料，並舉行歡迎會，多次請度老對此地四眾弟子開示。

度老在夏威夷逗留兩星期後，就直飛三藩市。至一九九三年，於此悠悠三十幾個歲月之中，我們各為如來事業忙，彼此未曾見過面，不過，知道他老弘法的事業很成功，很光輝！心裡頭也覺得很高興！我們雖然久未見面，但度老卻常常有電話來，請我去萬佛聖城講經，但我每次均因事務繁忙而辭謝。

一九九三年六月，我因事赴丹佛「科州佛教會」，回程途經三藩市，特別赴萬佛聖城，拜訪多年未見的老友。誰知撲了一個空，原來度老已經去了洛杉磯金輪寺。出乎意料之外，只怪自己冒昧，未曾預先通知一聲，就貿貿然前往，至此唯有悵然而返。

我離開萬佛聖城之後，度老的弟子馬上電告長老。度老知道我到了三藩市，於是就打電話到三藩市各寺廟找我，結果第三日與我聯絡上電話，他請我去洛杉磯長堤；因我必須乘當日下午七點鐘的飛機返夏威夷，他的拳拳盛意，只有五衷銘感而已！後來，他邀請我去看看國際譯經學院的設備，我答允了。在當天下午二時到達譯經院後，由恆實法師等數位法師接待，參觀了原有之譯經院及新購入的兩座樓宇，非常宏偉壯觀，設備完善。將近五點，我們才參觀完畢；臨別又蒙恆實法師奉師命贈送紀念禮物，並邀請我下次有機會到譯經院講《心經》。

是年（一九九三年）八月二十日下午一時許，度公忽然在虛雲寺出現，我見到他，覺得很愕然；問他何時到的，為什麼不事先通知我去接機？他說：「昨日到，我又不是外人，何須須接。」我們許久未見面，要談的話自然很多

Once the Master returned from Thailand and settled down in Hong Kong, he actively began to propagate the Dharma. The first thing he did was to establish Xileyuan (Western Bliss Garden) near Xiwanho (West Bay River), where he used the Dharma door of reciting the Buddha's name (which can reach all those with sharp, dull, and in between faculties) to gather in those who were new to Buddhism. After that, he acquired the twelfth floor of a building in Paomadi (Horse Race Track), and established the Buddhist Lecture Hall. From this name you can see that this is the place where he wanted to propagate the Great Vehicle Sutras and gather in those with sharp faculties and also all living beings. Another benefit from establishing this Wayplace was that left-home people had a place to stay. Dharma Master To Lun not only lectured on the Sutras and spoke the Dharma, but also distributed Sutras so that they would widely circulate. I remember there was one occasion when the Elder To Lun wrote to me asking for help, because he wanted to print *The Avatamsaka Sutra.* I wrote back and said that I would help with sixty sets. Whenever the Elder To Lun had time, we would accept invitations to travel to Southeast Asia and to cities such as Sidney and Melbourne in Australia to propagate the Dharma and benefit living beings.

In 1962, the Elder To Lun went to the United States. He stopped over in Hawaii for two weeks, where I prepared a welcoming committee for him and asked him to speak Dharma for the four-fold assembly many times.

After spending two weeks in Hawaii, the Elder To Lun then flew directly to San Francisco. For the next thirty years we did not have occasion to see each other again, but I was pleased that he was very successful in propagating the Dharma. Although we didn't see each other during that time, he often phoned me and requested that I come to the City of Ten Thousand Buddhas to give lectures on the Sutras. Regretfully, I had to decline, because I was very busy. In June 1993, I went to Denver to the Buddhist Association of Colorado, and on the way back to Hawaii, I stopped off in San Francisco and made a special trip to the City of Ten Thousand Buddhas to see my old friend whom I hadn't seen for so many years. However, he wasn't there. He had already gone to Gold Wheel Monastery in Los Angeles. I hadn't expected this and could only blame myself for being so reckless and not giving advance notice. I had no choice but to leave in great disappointment.

After I left the City, the Elder To Lun's disciples notified him that I had been there. Once the Elder To Lun knew that I had come to San Francisco, he made phone calls to all the temples in San Francisco looking for me, on the third day, he found me. He then invited me to go to Long Beach, but I had to catch a seven o'clock plane back to Hawaii that evening. I could only decline his goodwill invitation in regret. Then he invited me to take a look at the International Translation Institute, and I accepted the invitation. I arrived at the Institute at two o'clock that afternoon. Dharma Master Heng Sure and several other Dharma Masters were there to receive me. They gave me a tour of the Institute, as well as two other newly purchased buildings which were very spacious, impressive, and well-equipped. We finished the tour at around 5:00 p.m. Upon leaving I was presented with a gift by Dharma Master Heng Sure, on behalf of the Elder To Lun. I was also invited to give lectures on *The Heart Sutra,* upon my next visit to the Institute.

On August 20 of the same year (1993), around one o'clock in the

，但始終離不了「邀請我去萬佛聖城講經」的話題。他老明白地對我說：「為著表示我的誠意，我這次親自來請您去萬佛城講經！」我的回答是：「一切事都要看因緣而定，因緣成熟，我一定會去的。」我們談了整個下午，才盡歡而散。真想不到我們這一次的聚會，竟是最後的見面；而此次的分別，竟成永訣！

近日來聞說長老四大失調，法體違和，現在於長堤調養中，吾人總以為長老為法為人，吉人天相，自然會早占勿藥。想不到九五年的六月十六日，竟有噩耗從萬佛城傳來，調度輪老和尚六月七日於長堤安然圓寂！這一消息，彷如晴天霹靂，聞者莫不震驚！往者已矣，夫復何言！度輪長老的般涅槃，不但是佛教的損失，亦是眾生一大損失，是以應該同聲悲悼！祈禱長老，乘願再來，饒益有情！

afternoon, the Elder To Lun suddenly appeared at Hsu Yun Monastery. I was surprised to see him. I asked him when he had arrived and why he hadn't let me meet him at the airport. He said that he arrived on the previous day, and that he wasn't an outsider so there was no need to go and meet him at the airport. We hadn't seen each other in a long time, and so naturally there were many things to say. However, during the conversation he kept inviting me to go to the City of Ten Thousand Buddhas to lecture on the Sutras. He told me clearly, "In order to show my sincerity, this time I have personally come to invite you to go to the City of Ten Thousand Buddhas to lecture on the Sutras." I said that everything depends upon causes and conditions, and when those causes and conditions are ripe, I certainly will go. We talked the whole afternoon, before we parted. I never expected that this would be the last time that we would see each other; that the departure would be eternal.

Recently, I had heard that the Elder To Lun was not in good health, and was staying in Long Beach in convalescence. I had thought that he would certainly recover quickly, because he was such an extraordinary person. I did not expect that news would arrive from The City of Ten Thousand Buddhas on June 16, 1995, that the Elder To Lun had completed the stillness on June 7, 1995. This news struck like a thunderbolt. Everyone who heard it was shocked. There were no more words left to say. The Elder To Lun's Nirvana is not only a loss to Buddhism, but is a great loss to all living beings. We should all mourn, but also pray that he will return riding on his vows to save all living beings.

一九九五年七月八日　　July 8, 1995

有刹仰住或傍覆　麤妙廣大無量種
菩薩一發最上心　悉能往詣皆無礙

菩薩勝行不可說　皆勤修習無所住
見一切佛常欣樂　普入於其深法海
——《大方廣佛華嚴經》〈初發心功德品〉

There are abiding kshetras facing upwards, or facing downwards;
Coarse, wondrous, or wide, of limitless kinds.
The Bodhisattva who first brings forth the most supreme mind
Is able to go to all of them without obstruction.

The Bodhisattva's superior conducts are ineffable.
He cultivates all of them without dwelling anywhere.
He sees all Buddhas and is continuously blissful,
And universally enters the most profound ocean of Dharma.

Chapter on The Merit and Virtue from First Bringing Forth the Mind, the *Flower Adornment Sutra*

與宣化上人的一段因緣

MY CONDITIONS WITH THE VENERABLE MASTER HUA

釋開證　Shi Kaizheng

十幾年前，宣化上人第一次由美國返臺弘法。那時候佛教界知道他的人不多，而他對臺灣佛教也不太了解。由於人面不廣，臺灣佛教界也少有人關懷協助他。有一天他帶了五、六個洋徒弟來到高雄宏法寺，我請他駐錫宏法寺並以禮相待。同時也安排他在高雄講經弘法，他老人家非常高興，此段因緣使他老人家對宏法寺留下深刻的印象。

本人對佛教有個理念：「應多關懷整個佛教，尤其應多關懷、敬重在國外弘法的法師。」當時本人對宣化上人並不了解，但認為他在美國弘法並非易事。所以應該盡可能地給予關懷和照顧。我非常地欽佩他能度化一些洋人出家，因為當時在中國佛教中，還沒有洋人出家的。他可說是第一位度化洋人的中國和尚。

宣化上人是第一個將中國佛教的種子，撒播在美國人心田裡的中國法師，也可說是在美國弘揚佛法的先鋒。由於度化洋人的忍耐力，令我深深佩服他，這即是我認識他的最初因緣。

為了實地考察中國佛教在美國發展狀況，及廣結法緣，本人於一九八八年第一次訪美。七月二日由西雅圖到舊金山的金山寺拜見老和尚。次日，老和尚派弟子帶領我們參觀萬佛城。萬佛城佔地很大，可惜當時並未全面開發。老和尚因為曾經來過宏法寺的因緣，對本人很熱誠地招待，他親自開他巡山用的三輪車，載我環山遊覽聖城全景。

宣化上人是位苦行僧，生活極淡薄：日中一食，夜不倒單，並粗衣素食。隨他出家的弟子都效仿他的苦行方式，因此孕育出萬佛城特殊的道風。

早年，他曾親近民初高僧倓虛老和尚研習《楞嚴經》，對《楞嚴經》有很深入的了解；並認真地修持〈楞嚴咒〉。因此出現了一些奇異的事蹟與靈感，有時也為眾生降魔、除病。他

Several decades ago, the Venerable Master travelled from America back to Taiwan to propagate the Dharma. Not many people in the Buddhist world knew of him then, and he didn't know very much about the Buddhism in Taiwan either. Because the Venerable Master was little known, there were few Taiwan Buddhists who were concerned about or supported him. One day he brought five or six Western disciples to Hongfa Monastery in Kaohsiung. I invited him to stay at Hongfa Monastery and Lixiang Monastery, and also arranged for him to lecture on Sutras and speak the Dharma in Kaohsiung. The Master was extremely happy about this, and he retained a deep impression of Hongfa Monastery for this reason.

I have an ideal for Buddhism: "We should be concerned with the entirety of Buddhism. We should especially be concerned with and respect Dharma Masters who propagate the Dharma abroad." I didn't know much about the Venerable Master Hua at that time, but I knew he was propagating the Dharma in America, and I knew it wasn't easy. Therefore, I thought I should show concern and be hospitable to the best of my ability. I very much admired him for having influenced some Westerners to leave the home-life, for no Westerners had ever left the home-life in Chinese Buddhism at that time. He could be considered the first Chinese monk to convert Westerners.

The Venerable Master was the first Chinese Dharma Master to sow the seeds of Chinese Buddhism in the minds of American people. He could also be called a pioneer in propagating the Buddhadharma in America. His patience to convert Westerners won my deep respect. Those were the initial conditions of my acquaintance with him.

In order to investigate the actual conditions of the development of Chinese Buddhism in America and to create extensive affinities in the Dharma, I visited the United States for the first time in 1988. On July 2, I travelled from Seattle to Gold Mountain Monastery in San Francisco to pay my respects to the Venerable Master. The following day, the Master asked a disciple to take me to visit the City of Ten Thousand Buddhas. The City of Ten Thousand Buddhas occupies a very large area, but unfortunately it was not completely developed then. Because the Venerable Master had been to Hongfa Monastery in the past, he treated me with the warmest hospitality and drove me around in his three-wheeled golfcart on a tour of the entire City.

The Venerable Master was an ascetic monk. His lifestyle was extremely frugal: he took one meal a day, did not lie down at night, wore coarse clothing, and ate simple, vegetarian food. His left-home disciples emulate his ascetic practices, and thus this special tradition of the City of Ten Thousand Buddhas was established.

In his early years, he drew near the eminent monk, Elder Master Tanxu, and studied the *Shurangama Sutra* under him. He had a deep understanding of the *Shurangama Sutra* and diligently cultivated the Shurangama Mantra. Consequently there were some rare events and responses. Sometimes he would subdue demons and heal diseases for

的弟子也認為他有神通，而寫出一些有關他
的事蹟。他老人家偶爾也會說些好像神通的
話。在萬佛城與他一席長談之後，我發現他
那些「好像神通」的話，是度眾的善巧方便
。我們要知道老和尚到美國弘法度眾，的確
經歷過一段困苦的時間。當時美國對中國佛
教瞭解甚少，所以不難想像他最初在美國度
化眾生的艱辛了，由此可見他堅忍不拔的毅
力了。

老和尚有他自己的修行觀念，尤其注重戒
行與威儀，特別痛惡教內不如法的事。對於
教界看不慣的事，都直心地批評，也因此引
起佛教界對他有不同的看法，甚至不受歡迎
。老和尚也常責備自己在家、出家的弟子，
說起來也是出於對弟子的關心，和求好心切
罷了。事實上，過份嚴格的要求，難免導致
誤會和引起不滿。

就本人對老和尚的瞭解而論，他能隻身到
美國，做為佛教在美國的拓荒者，澹泊苦行
、刻苦奮鬥、莊嚴道場、嚴格道風、翻譯經
典、教化眾生，這些都是功不可滅的事實。

老和尚性格耿直，常直言批評他人。我曾
經給予建議：「您老人家到臺灣弘法利生，
應該廣結善緣，且多說些好話，少作批評。
」老和尚笑一笑，謙虛地說：「依教奉行。
」這足以顯出他樸直可愛的地方，想來也是
他護教心切所致吧！別人的看法如何我不知
道，總之，我個人對他是特別地欣賞、敬佩
，並由衷地讚歎。

老和尚已圓寂了，我希望他的弟子們能維
持萬佛城嚴謹的家風。當然，若需要創新之
處也要創新。尤其是洋弟子們應把師父傳下
來的法，發揚光大，讓佛光普照到美國人的
社會及每個家庭，使萬佛城在美國佛教的歷
史上留下光輝的一頁。

開證　寫于宏法寺
一九九五年八月十五日

living beings. His disciples came to believe that he had spiritual powers
and recorded some of the events of his life. Occasionally he would also
say something that seemed to indicate he had spiritual powers. After
having a long conversation with him at the City of Ten Thousand Buddhas, I discovered that those comments that seemed to imply spiritual
powers were expedients that he used to teach living beings. We must
realize that when the Venerable Master went to America to propagate
the Dharma and teach people, he went through a very difficult period.
At that time Americans had very little understanding of Chinese Buddhism, so it's not difficult to imagine the hardships he went through
teaching living beings in the very beginning. We can also see his unwa-
vering determination and resolve from this.

The Venerable Master had his own views on cultivation. He especially emphasized the precepts and rules of deportment and was deeply
pained by Buddhists who did not practice according to the Dharma. He
would bluntly criticize the things he felt were wrong, and as a result he
came to be regarded as different and even unwelcome by those in the
Buddhist circle. Out of his concern for them, the Venerable Master often
scolded his left-home and lay disciples, wishing for them to improve.
However, overly strict demands may lead to misunderstanding and dis-
content.

Speaking from my own understanding of the Venerable Master, he
went to America alone and opened the frontier of Buddhism in America.
He practiced austerities and worked energetically in hard situations, establishing adorned Way-places and a strict style of cultivation, translating the Buddhist scriptures, and teaching living beings. The merit of
these deeds will never perish.

The Venerable Master was extremely straightforward, and he often
criticized others bluntly. I once suggested to him, "You have come to
Taiwan to propagate the Dharma and benefit beings. You ought to
widely create good affinities. You should say pleasant things more often
and not criticize so much." The Venerable Master smiled and humbly
said, "I'll obey your instructions." This reveals an endearing aspect of
his character. I think it must also be his sincerity in protecting the teaching. I don't know what other people's opinions are, but I feel particular
admiration and respect for him, and wholeheartedly praise him.

Now that the Venerable Master has completed the stillness, I hope his
disciples will preserve the strict traditions of the City of Ten Thousand
Buddhas. His American disciples in particular should widely propagate
the Dharma transmitted by the Venerable Master, enabling the Buddha-
light to shine throughout American society and in every American family, so that the City of Ten Thousand Buddhas will write a glorious page
in the history of American Buddhism.

Kaizheng
Written at Hongfa Monastery
August 15, 1995

永恆的懷念

IN ETERNAL REMEMBRANCE

遼寧省營口市佛教廣心庵住持釋嚴峻暨四眾弟子敬頌
佛曆二五三九（一九九五）年七月二十五日

Respectfully submitted by Abbotess Shi Yanjun and the fourfold assembly of disciples
of Guangxin (Vast Mind) Buddhist Convent, City of Yingkou, Liaoning Province
July 25, the year of the Buddha 2539 (1995)

一盞智慧的明燈在萬佛聖城熄滅了！當代佛它最真誠的一位弟子宣化老和尚突然離開了我們！這訃信令我們十分哀痛！我等做為老和尚故里東北遼寧的佛子，更充滿深深的哀思！

老和尚可稱得上一代聖僧，具備諸佛的慈悲。他以宏願降生到難聞佛法的冥闇邊地。這冥闇因老和尚的慧光而被驅除，使大眾見到了諸佛的靈光。這靈光依緣運行到哪裡，哪裡便除卻了愚闇。這靈光跨過萬頃波濤的太平洋，來到了彼岸，在那物質文明極度發達的國度，人們對六塵妄境中形形色色的物質相執著得最堅固的地方，靈光使彼岸的那種以偽為真、以妄為實、以非為是的顛倒慣性，再倒回來，使那裡的眾生皈依三寶，入於淳淨的法性，這是多麼巨大的法力啊！

佛教所謂正法、像法、末法，是相對的。老和尚在萬佛聖城中，秉承歷千劫而不古的佛陀遺教，實行傳統的日中一食，以夜不倒單來懾伏睡眠煩惱，使西方竟成了正法的道場，這真是舉世無雙，曠劫稀有的奇蹟！對老和尚之德行，我們一敬再敬，一拜再拜，永久禮敬不輟，以成就永恆的懷念！

我們未曾親覲老和尚的德相，但多次拜讀過老和尚的開示，受益非淺，銘刻於懷。

老和尚雖離開了我們，但這盞般若明燈永遠不會熄滅，他會長久照徹我們的身心，我們願依戒法的尺度而精進不懈，為菩提淨業自強不息！

我們願以清淨的身、語、意業，念念相續，無有疲厭地，對上宣下化老和尚加以虔誠地禮敬、讚歎、供養！

恭喜老和尚常樂我淨！

A bright lamp of wisdom has gone out at the Sagely City of Ten Thousand Buddhas! The Venerable Master Hua, one of the true disciples of the Buddha in this age, has suddenly left us! This obituary brings us great sorrow! As Buddhists from Liaoning, in the Venerable Master's native Manchuria, we are deeply filled with grief!

The Venerable Master could be called a holy monk of this age, for he had the compassion of the Buddhas. With his vast vows, he came to be born in this dark land where it is difficult to get to hear the Buddhadharma. The darkness was dispelled by the light of the Venerable Master's wisdom, allowing everyone to see the spiritual light of the Buddhas. Wherever this spiritual light spread, it would get rid of the darkness of delusion. This spiritual light crossed over the vast Pacific ocean and arrived at the other shore, in that country of highly developed material civilization. The people in that place are strongly attached to the various forms of material objects of the world of sense. The spiritual light enabled the beings in that land, who were accustomed to taking the counterfeit to be genuine, the wrong to be right, and the false to be true, to make a turnaround, take refuge in the Triple Jewel, and enter the pure Dharma nature. How enormous is the power of the Dharma!

The Buddhist terms Proper Dharma, Resemblance Dharma, and Ending Dharma are relative to each other. At the Sagely City of Ten Thousand Buddhas, the Venerable Master maintained the Buddha's timeless teachings, practicing the traditional rules of eating one meal a day and not lying down at night to subdue sleep and afflictions. Thus a Way-place of the Proper Dharma came to be established in the West. This is truly an unparalleled feat in the world, a rare miracle throughout the ages! We pay respect to him over and over, and bow again and again, paying homage forever without rest, in order to show our eternal remembrance of the Venerable Master's virtuous character.

We have never seen the Venerable Master in person, yet we have respectfully read the Venerable Master's *Instructional Talks* many times. We have gained profound benefit from them and engraved them in our hearts.

Although the Venerable Master has left us, this bright lamp of Prajna will never go out and will constantly shine upon our bodies and minds. We vow to vigorously practice according to the standards of the precepts, resolutely carrying out the pure work of Bodhi!

We vow to use our pure bodies, mouths, and minds to sincerely pay homage to, praise, and make offerings to the Venerable Hsuan, the Noble Hua, in thought after thought without weariness!

We congratulate the Venerable Master for realizing permanence, joy, true self, and purity!

恭請乘願再來

RESPECTFULLY REQUESTING THE VENERABLE MASTER TO COME BACK RIDING ON HIS VOWS

沈家楨　C. T. Shen

中國傳統的佛教，由中國法師正式傳入美國，是一九六〇年以後的事。經過了三十多年的弘揚，佛教在美加各地的華人社會中日益昌隆，信徒日益增加。而華人所創辦的佛教寺院和社團，也逐漸增加，到一九九五年中已發展到一百八十多個。但做得不夠的是，多數的寺院和社團，全是以華人為弘法對象，未能攝化美國人士。而宣化上人是少數能突破華人社會圈子，將佛法弘傳給美國人最有成就的法師之一。上人座下有許多美國籍的出家弟子，都能吃苦耐勞，一心向道，實在不可多得。

認識上人已三十多年了。宣化上人曾接受邀請，兩次帶領多位美籍弟子駐錫紐約菩提精舍，舉行「中文佛典英譯的討論會」。當三藩市的金山寺．從一所舊工廠中甫新成立時，蒙上人告知建立佛教大學的願望，培養僧才的堅決意志，並強調在美弘法應以美國人為主要對象。幾十年來，上人為弘揚佛法、續佛慧命，所做的努力及艱辛，實非常人可及，令我衷心欽佩，至今不忘。

據我所知，上人是出生於中國東北農村，生性穎悟，事親至孝，自幼有孝子之稱。十九歲喪母，感於人生無常而披剃出家，在故鄉弘化，感應極多。一九四五年東北中日戰爭結束後，他行腳參訪，朝禮普陀山，繼而南下廣東，親近禪門大德虛雲老和尚。老和尚一見許為法器，命他擔任南華戒律學院教務主任；並傳他溈仰宗法脈，為溈仰宗第九代傳人。上人早年出家時，法名度輪，這「宣化」二字，是虛雲老和尚賜他的。

一九四九年秋，上人到香港弘化，先後十餘年，其間曾到過東南亞和澳州。一九六二年飛錫美國，在舊金山創設金山寺。由於法

The formal transmission of Chinese orthodox Buddhism to America happened after 1960. After more than thirty years of propagation, the number of Buddhists in the increasingly thriving Chinese societies throughout the United States and Canada has grown day by day, and the number of Buddhist temples and societies founded by Chinese people has increased to over 180 in 1995. However, most of these temples and societies have been propagating the Dharma only to overseas Chinese people, and have not managed to attract and influence Americans. The Venerable Master Hua was one of the most successful of the few Dharma Masters who broke out of the overseas Chinese circle and transmitted the Buddhadharma to Americans. Many of the Venerable Master's left-home disciples are Americans, all of whom are able to toil and bear hardship and to single-mindedly apply themselves to their practice. This is truly a rare achievement.

I have known the Venerable Master for over thirty years. The Venerable Master twice accepted an invitation to stay at Bodhi Hermitage in New York to host a Conference on the English Translation of Chinese Buddhist Texts. During those times the Master told us about his resolves. Even though he was living at that time at Gold Mountain Monastery in San Francisco, which was in a refurbished old factory, he had vowed to establish a Buddhist University. He also stressed that the propagation of Dharma in the United States should be aimed primarily at Americans, and he was determined to create and nurture a Sangha here. This won my whole-hearted admiration, and even to this day I have not forgotten. His hard work and accomplishments and his unity of resolve and conduct over these several decades are not something that ordinary people would be capable of.

According to my understanding, the Venerable Master was born in a farming village in Manchuria, mainland China. He was intelligent by nature and very filial to his parents. People called him a "filial son" ever since he was young. His mother died when he was nineteen, and feeling that life was very fleeting, he shaved his head and left the home-life. He taught and influenced people in his native village and brought about many responses. After the Sino-Japanese War in Manchuria ended in 1945, he travelled to and visited other monasteries, paid homage at Potola Mountain, and then continued southward to Guangdong, where he drew near to the Elder Master Hsu Yun, an eminently virtuous master of the Chan School. At their first meeting, the Elder Master acknowledged him as a vessel for the Dharma and appointed him as the Dean of Academic Affairs at the Nanhua Vinaya Academy. Elder Master Yun also transmitted the Dharma-lineage of the Weiyang Sect to him, making him the ninth patriarch of Weiyang. When the Venerable Master left the home-life in his youth, his Dharma name was To Lun. The Dharma name Hsuan Hua was given to him by the Elder Master Yun.

In the fall of 1949, the Venerable Master went to Hong Kong to propa-

緣殊盛，許多美國青年皈依於上人座下，剃度出家，帶動了美國青年學佛的風氣，而上人也繼金山寺之後，先後創設了中美佛教會、國際譯經院等機構，並在美國其他地區建立道場。

一九七六年開始，在加州瑜伽市創立了佔地規模宏大的萬佛城（佔地四百八十八英畝），並得到加州政府的批准，創辦了法界佛教大學，並發行出版各種語言文字的佛教經典。

和上人最後一次會晤是在舊金山，那時他已示疾。他告訴我尚有許多計劃想做，可是這世已來不及了。我不加思索地回覆了一句：「當乘願再來。」彼此會心一笑。

gate the Dharma and teach people. He stayed there for over ten years, also visiting Southeast Asia and Australia during that time. In 1962, he came by plane to America and founded Gold Mountain Monastery in San Francisco. Because of the supreme Dharma affinities, many young Americans came to take refuge and to leave the home-life with the Master, starting a trend of studying Buddhism among young Americans. After establishing Gold Mountain Monastery in San Francisco, the Master also established such organizations as the Sino-American Buddhist Association and the International Institute for the Translation of Buddhist Texts, as well as other monasteries at other locales in the United States.

In 1976, he founded the City of Ten Thousand Buddhas on four hundred acres of land in Ukiah, California. The Dharma Realm Buddhist University was opened with approval from the California government, a monthly journal was produced, and English translations of Buddhist texts were published. The Venerable Master's vows were actively beginning to be realized.

The last time I saw the Venerable Master was in San Francisco, when he was already manifesting illness. He indicated that he still had many plans he wanted to carry out, but that he didn't have time in this life. Without thinking, I replied, "You should come back riding on your vows." We smiled at each other in understanding.

師父像太陽一樣

THE MASTER IS JUST LIKE THE SUN

小沙彌尼　釋果瑩
Young Shramanerika Shi Guoying

師父像太陽一樣，
太陽的光和熱，使萬物茁壯生長。
師父的慈悲，幫助眾生脫離苦海，脫離這痛苦的世界。
為了眾生，師父不知疲倦，甚至重病纏身。
但師父卻不幫他自己。
師父的偉大精神，令每個人讚歎不已！他值得大家學習。
師父的慈悲就好像蓮花一樣，出於污泥而不染！

The Master is just like the sun.
The light and warmth of the sun cause the myriad things to sprout and grow.
The Master's compassion helps living beings to escape the sea of suffering and leave this world of misery.
For the sake of living beings, the Master forgot his own weariness and even became gravely ill.
Yet the Master didn't help himself.
The Master's magnanimous spirit evokes endless praise from all!
Everyone should learn from him.
The Master's compassion is like a lotus flower, growing from the mud but remaining undefiled!

WHAT DID THE VENERABLE MASTER TEACH US?
上人究竟教了我們什麼？

Snjezana Akpinar, Chancellor of the Dharma Realm Buddhist University
法界佛教大學校長　阿匹納

In asking "What did the Venerable Master Hua teach?" one seems to step into shoes which are more than several sizes too large. It is not easy to answer that question, no matter which way we try to address it. That is probably why I decided to start from a beginning which is very personal. I see it as part of my attempt to understand Buddhism and explain it when the need arises. The most obvious part of the Master's teaching, in my view, is the attitude of East towards West and vice versa. The Venerable Master showed us how to cultivate an ability to spot well ingrained stereotypes which our own cultures and civilizations carry within them and impose on us from a very early age. When speaking within the sphere of education, particularly when children are involved, that should not be so hard to achieve. For Westerners one of the cures could be stories from distant lands, be they India, China, or Japan, as well as stories written by those who went to such distant places and wrote about them when they returned. For Easterners the cure, I presume, would lie in the opposite approach, stories about the West. One must never lose track, however, no matter how nice distant tales may be, that there are also those who see it all here and now, and are capable of illustrating the obvious by telling children and grown-ups stories about our immediate surroundings. But, it is still up to each one of us to continue in the same vein and find the inner courage to go beyond a particular point of view.

At first I thought that I should not write anything on such complicated subjects, that what the Venerable Master has taught is beyond words, so why keep on talking and telling others what to do? It is not my place. There are enough eloquent people around, and it is always the same. I do not wish and cannot be a judge in instances like these. The Venerable Master's influence changed a whole generation of Westerners and Easterners, both here in the New World and in the Old one. I always felt somewhat awkward when asked to speak, anyway. Whenever invited to sit next to the Venerable Master I was sure that hidden within the invitation there was a sincere wish to help me, and that the university and all other educational endeavors were only secondary. Actually I never seriously discussed all this, it was easier to go along to the best of my capacities, and it is impossible to resist such sincere wishes.

So after all of this I would like to explain that here I do not intend to analyze the Venerable Master's intentions, nor my own, since I am very incapable to do that, I never approached such sublime heights. Nevertheless, even without trying very hard it is not that impossible to spot the different points of view among all of his disciples. It is out of such ambiguities that I decided to write a few words and in this manner return to some of my own feelings and

在回答「上人究竟教了我們什麼？」這個問題時，人都會覺得好像穿了一雙大了幾號的鞋子那樣。這個問題無論由那一方面來談，都很難回答，所以我決定從我本人開始講起，這也是我試講一下我對佛教的瞭解。上人最明顯的教誨是上人對東西文化交流的態度。上人教我們怎樣有能力來分辨從小就深植於我們心中，我們文化中所固有的是非觀念。就教育兒童來講，這點不難做到。對西方人而言對治的方法之一，則是介紹遙遠的國度如印度、中國或日本的故事，或是由那些去過這些地方的人撰寫的故事。對東方人來說，其對治之道我想就是介紹西方的故事了。但不論遠方國度的故事如何引人入勝，我們也不要迷失了自己。因為也有的人，不但能在自己的地方眼前當下，就可以找到相類似那些故事中所欲闡述的道理。這些人並且還能夠利用我們身邊周遭的事情來闡述那些故事的要旨。但是這不得不靠我們每一個人同心協力，以堅毅不拔的精神來超越某些觀念。

起先我不想討論這麼複雜的主題，因為上人的教誨不是語言所能形容的。所以怎麼能夠盡在口頭上告訴別人該怎樣怎樣的，我不在其位不行其事。況且還有許多能言善道的人可以講，我判斷力也不夠，也不想判斷上人對這一代的人所產生的影響。

不論新世界的人，或舊世界的人，也不論是東方人、西方人都因他而有所改變。每次有人請我就這個題目談話，我都覺得很尷尬。每當上人說法時，讓我坐在他旁邊時，我都知道上人是誠心藉此幫助我。其他辦教育、辦大學等種種的事情都是因這個而起的。事實上，我從來沒有很認真地思考過這件事，因為別人怎麼安排我就盡力配合著做，這樣比較容易，而且我也不可能拒絕上人要幫助我的好意。

我正要解釋一下，我不打算分析上人的意向，

thoughts about the whole issue of education. I may be able to draw some conclusions not only about the Master's vision of a university, but also about the current activities in the fields of Buddhist studies in particular and religious studies in general, things I somehow stumble upon in spite of myself.

All of us who have been around Buddhism and the Venerable Master long enough learned to approach cliches and pre-packaged ideas with great caution. This goes for the whole spectrum, from the simplest to the most complex of thoughts. I believe that most of us have learned to steer away from prejudices, to spot them. This attitude in itself should be enough of a guide through anyone's life. It gives a general and freeing direction, an open door. But, as in anything that concerns our world, the next step is also very important. One could approach it in the following manner: Fine, we are now free, the door is open, but now what? What are we to do with our knowledge, and will we have enough strength to withstand? how far away from the open door do we dare to go? Some of us have natures that are more energetic and temperamental and are steadily pushed into battle for the sake of righteousness in an immediate manner full of indignation. Such people do not allow themselves to skirt political issues and "engagement" with the world and its struggles. Actually the word "engaged" is probably not well chosen here, but I cannot think of a better way to word this whole aspect of our nature. It is my private attempt to explain something complex in an easy way.

This country is full of such vigorous and "engaged" attitudes. I also am often attracted to such thoughts, mostly because of a sense of indignation felt by most of those who want the world to be a better place. But, if viewed from the point of view of the Venerable Master, at least as I perceive it, it is exactly these feelings which create the stumbling stones that we should avoid. Or, to word it in a better way, we should be aware of the existence of such stumbling stones and behave more cautiously exactly because they happen to be on our path. These obstacles should be viewed, if possible, from a healthy distance in order to grasp their totality through very broad perspective and at any given moment. That seems to be the only way a human being may be able to untangle himself from the "thicket of views" and the "jungle of views" as the Blessed Buddha had said, with a minimum of bruises and consequences to ourselves and our surroundings. Only then may we hope to reach a somewhat higher, clearer plateau. I am not a psychologist and I cannot explain all of this. Even this much is already too much, I fear. I can only quote, off the top of my head, as a further illustration of the same point, a letter which my father once long ago wrote to his brother and the rest of his family explaining why he decided to become a monk (my uncle at the time was horrified):

There are some very refined and subtle reasons, very hard to perceive and even harder to understand unless

也不打算在這裡分析我自己的意向，我沒有能力分析也不打算分析，我從來也沒有過這樣不平凡的能力。但是在上人徒弟之中，很容易就碰到持有不同見解的人，就是因為這些不一樣的見解，我所以決定講幾句話，同時也談談我自己對教育的看法。我或者可以就上人對教育上的觀點，和偶然之中注意到的目前一般宗教界的活動講幾句話，特別是現在目前的佛教研究情形。

凡是和佛教有所接觸的人及跟著上人的人都知道，不論就最簡單的事或最繁複的思想，我們在遇到沿以成習的觀念和想法時，都要謹慎小心。我相信現在我們大家在遇到偏歧的見解時，都能夠辨別得出而不受其左右。能有這樣的態度，在我們一生中都足以做我們的指引，使我們不再受局限，而能有所抉擇。接下來人可能會問：很好！現在我們可以自由抉擇了，門打開了，我們不再受局限了。但是我們應該怎麼抉擇呢？我們怎樣利用我們的所學所知呢？我們會有足夠的力量站起來嗎？我們該走多遠啊？有的人本性驍勇，能為正義而戰。這樣的人會過問政治上的事，也會積極參與這個世界上的事。我講得不很適當，但是我也想不出一個更好的說法來形容人性中的這一面，我這只是將一件複雜的事簡簡單單地解釋。

這個國家充滿了這樣驍勇和願意參與的態度。我自己也常常為這樣的態度吸引著，主要是因為我也想這個世界變好。就如同大部份凡是想這個世界變好的人都會持有一種義憤感。

但是假如由就我所知的上人觀點來看，本著這種態度的話，這種「態度」正是我們所應避免的，因為這種態度反而會成為「絆腳石」。或者應該換個方法講比較好一點，可以這麼說，我們應該留意這樣的「絆腳石」，而且應該特別小心，因為這些絆腳石就會在我們所走的路上出現。假如可能的話，對這些障礙，我們應該保持一個相當的距離，以便可以由一個比較寬廣的角度來看清其整體性。這大概就是唯一的方法，我們可以由佛陀所稱的「見刺」及「見林」中拔出腿來，而不會把自己，或把周遭的環境弄得滿是創傷。那時我們才有希望能達到一個更高更清楚的層次。我不是心理學家，也不能講出什麼道理來，講得雖然不多，恐怕也已經過多了。我只能隨口引述一封信，做為更進一步闡明我的論點。這封信是家父很久以前寫給他的兄弟和家人的，解釋他決定出家的原因（我的叔叔當時嚇壞了），信中說：

有一些很微細、很不容易覺察得到，也不容易瞭解的理由，除非你過那一種生活方式，或者懂得

you live a certain kind of life and have some sort of talent for the contemplative life. By this I mean a capacity to slow your thoughts down so that the sheer strength of the stream does not carry you away and throw you against some rock.

In these last years, since having lived at the City of Ten Thousand Buddhas, I began to glimpse the contours of that answer. What helped me most, was the steady onslaught of the "engaged" Buddhists, Islamists and others who very energetically mill around Berkeley and occasionally visit the City of Ten Thousand Buddhas. Many of the inhabitants of the City in the face of such attitudes patiently carried on with their cultivation. I tried to protect and criticize both, and somehow convinced myself that the Venerable Master put up with me in the hopes that I will derive some better degree of clarity from the whole issue.

The life of the Venerable Master remains a true example of how we can live in the truth, as Gandhi once had said. It is a way of life which helps us let go of our tight grips and our wishes to hold on to the our various "views" and points of view. It is Buddhism itself, and it can also be defined as a religious approach in the true sense of that word—an approach which stems from a certain foreknowledge, an awareness, based (for want of better words) on a co-feeling, an empathy, toward all living beings, a sort of filter built into, hopefully, the majority of living beings. I often imagine it as a primordial sieve, all of us should try and clean every once in a while. The action of cleansing is exactly that superhuman effort which demands that we be constantly aware, awake, and watchful. All religions are, in their essence, systems and methods which teach us how to do this more effectively. The effort and insight gained by such efforts should help us surpass all the "isms" and biases and multitudes of words. There are simply no words, they do not exist, which could describe all of these things.

As good Buddhists we also need to cultivate an awareness of the process of disintegration: from the withering of leaves falling around us to the greater and more striking phenomena. It is a process which at first strikes us as being frightening, but after a while we may also get the feeling that the death of a human being is one last educational tool, usually employed by parents to teach their children how to grow up. None of us, no matter how hard we may try to avoid such a lesson, is ever capable of escaping it.

過一種富於冥想的生活。我的意思是說，如果你有能力將你的思想緩慢下來，使得這股潮流的力量不會將你載走，把你沖激到岩石上。

最近在萬佛城住了幾年，我開始對上述的話略有些瞭解，但是對我幫助最大的，還是這些擠在柏克萊，有時也會到萬佛聖城來的佛教中的參與者及回教徒，還有其他的一些人。許多住在萬佛城的人在遇到這樣的態度時，都還是很有耐心地繼續自己的修行。我對這兩邊的人都保護，有時也指出他們不對的地方，但我也相信上人寬容我，是希望我能因這些事而變得更明白事理。

上人的一生是「怎樣生活在真理中」（甘地所說）的一個好榜樣。這種生活方式能幫我們怎樣放下我們總想要執著的不同的「見」和觀點，佛教本身講的就是這個，宗教的真義也在這裡。這種做法是基於一種與眾生同體的覺知，像是在我們身體裡邊裝了過濾器。我常常把這種生活方式想成一種過濾器，我們大家每過一段時期都應該來清掃一下。這種清掃的過程，是超人的一種努力，使得我們經常處於覺明了知的狀態之中，所有宗教的本質、制度、方法，都是教我們怎樣更有效地做這種清掃工作。經過這種努力之後所得的洞察力，可幫助我們超越所有的「主義」、「教條」、歧見和語言。世上沒有語言可以表達出來這種事情。

做為好的佛教徒，我們也必須要修習一種對「壞滅」的覺知；由我們身邊落地的枯葉到更明顯的現象，這種現象在開始時讓人覺得驚嚇，但是過了一會，我們就會覺得人的死亡是一個最終的教育工具。一般做父母的都會用到這個工具，來教導他們的孩子們如何成長，不管我們怎樣努力，都逃避不過這堂課的。

清淨大願恆相應　　樂供如來不退轉　　人天見者無厭足　　常為諸佛所護念
——《大方廣佛華嚴經》〈初發心功德品〉

With pure, great, and appropriate vows,
He delights in making offerings to the Thus Come Ones without retreating.
People and gods never grow weary of seeing him,
And he is always one of whom the Buddhas are protective and mindful.

Chapter on The Merit and Virtue from First Bringing Forth the Mind, the *Flower Adornment Sutra*

漫談上人的教育觀

THE VENERABLE MASTER'S VIEWS ON EDUCATION

法界佛教大學亞洲區校長　何伯超

一九九五年七月二十七日講於萬佛聖城宣公上人讚頌報恩法會

A talk given by Paicho Ho, Asian Chancellor of Dharma Realm Buddhist University, in the Ceremony in Praise and Recognition of the Venerable Master Hua's Kindness at the Sagely City of Ten Thousand Buddhas on July 27, 1995

各位法師、各位貴賓、各位善知識、各位同修：

今天我們為紀念宣公上人，舉行追思法會。我在這裡報告一下上人的恩德，也就是集結上人的嘉言懿行，做為弟子們的追思與效法。自從上人圓寂以後，我們都感到無限地悲痛與慚愧。因為上人的偉蹟，如河海的汪洋，並非每個人在短時間所能盡述。萬佛聖城出版的書刊，如：《金剛菩提海》、《智慧之源》、《上人開示錄》、《上人事蹟》，以及上人著作與各種英文佛經淺釋，都記載著上人的言論與思想。經由多位法師與善知識，詳加編輯與翻譯，都已盡了完善的責任。我現在僅能就我個人親近上人所體會與瞭解的意見，簡單地向各位提出報告，尚請多加指正。

首先我報告個人參加法界大學工作的因緣：遠在一九八五年，我在臺灣擔任專科學校校長時，因事來美訪問，特別到金山寺拜訪上人。因為我也是雙城人，在家鄉時久聞上人盛名。第一次會面，上人即邀我赴聖城參觀法界大學，並親切希望我在臺灣退休後，能夠前來參加教育工作。我當時感到非常意外與榮幸，因為我已皈依三寶多年，如能在退休以後，對佛教事業有所貢獻，我是很樂意的，所以我立即承諾，感謝上人期待之德意。自從一九八八年在臺灣退休以後，即來法界大學服務，迄今已滿七年。我個人非常慚愧未能盡到責任，其中原因很多。

就我平時瞭解，上人對於教育方面的訓示，約分以下各點，恭述如後：

一‧上人認為教育是做人的根本，也是世界的根本。

All Dharma Masters, all guests of honour, all good knowing advisers and and fellow cultivators:

Today, we gather here in this Assembly Commemorating the Venerable Master Hua. I'll give a report on the Venerable Master's virtuous kindness by collecting the Master's fine words and deeds, for the purpose of commemoration as well as to set forth a moral standard of conduct for everyone. All of us are extremely grieved, and remorseful over the passing into stillness of the Venerable Master. His remarkable deeds are as vast as the ocean; one would not be able to describe them exhaustively in a brief interval of time. Publications of the City of Ten Thousand Buddhas, such as *Vajra Bodhi Sea*, *Source of Wisdom*, *Instructional Talks* and *Records of the Life* of the Master, and other works written by the Master, as well as various explanations of Sutras by the Master, document the Master's speeches and lines of thought. These works have already been edited and translated. The following is a brief report that relates my personal opinion of, and experience with, the Venerable Master. Kindly correct me if I make any mistake.

Firstly, I shall talk about the conditions concerning my appointment by the Dharma Realm Buddhist University. In 1985, I was the principal of a technical college in Taiwan. When I came to visit America, I called on the Venerable Master at Gold Mountain Monastery. As I am also from Shuangcheng County, Manchuria, I had heard of the Venerable Master long ago. In our first meeting, the Venerable Master invited me for a tour of the University at the City of Ten Thousand Buddhas, and cordially invited me to join the educational service at the University after my retirement. I was surprised, yet honored; as I had taken refuge with the Triple Jewel for many years, if I could contribute to any Buddhist work in any possible way, I would be most willing. So I accepted the offer immediately and thanked the Venerable Master for his high expectation of me.

I have been working in the Dharma Realm Buddhist University for seven years since 1988, after my retirement in Taiwan. Due to several unforeseen circumstances, I regret that I have not been able to live up to the Venerable Master's expectation or to fulfill my responsibilities.

The following is a summary of my understanding of the Venerable Master's exhortations and instructions with regard to education:

1. The Venerable Master said that education is the foundation of humankind, as well as the foundation of the world at large.

二・佛教是教育的根本。

三・發展佛教要從教育著手。鼓勵青年立志做
　　大事，以發心救世為己任。

四・發展教育是上人一生的願力。

五・提倡道德教育，以孝道為首要。

六・教育青年，應啟發其內在的智慧。

七・實行六大宗旨：不爭、不貪、不求、
　　不自私、不自利，不打妄語。

八・提倡義務教育，擴大教育範圍。

　　我們歸納以上的訓示中，可以知道上人對於教育工作期待的殷切。現在上人示寂，離開我們西去，所謂人生無常，如露亦如電。我們都感到非常地悲痛。但是上人的形體雖化，他的精神與音容笑貌，永留人間。我們做為弟子們的責任，應當永遠秉持上人的大願，和合團結，續佛慧命，共同為弘揚佛法與發展教育事業而努力。我們虔誠祈禱上人慈航倒轉，乘願再來，能為我們建立人間樂土、華嚴世界。

2. Buddhism is the foundation of education.

3. In order to propagate the Buddhadharma, one has to begin with education. Encourage young people to bring forth their resolve and take on the responsibilities of saving the world.

4. Education was the Venerable Master's life long ambition.

5. Promoting moral education and establishing filial piety are some of the primary goals of moral education.

6. Educate young people, and inspire them to bring forth their inherent wisdom.

7. Practice the six guiding principles of: not fighting, not being greedy, not seeking, not being selfish, not pursuing personal advantage, and not lying.

8. Promote volunteer education, and expand the scope of education.

From the foregoing, we learned of the high expections of the Venerable Master with respect to education. Now, the Venerable Master has manifested entering into stillness and has left for the Western Land. Life is impermanent, like dew drops, like a lighting flash. We are extremely sad. Although his physical body has disappeared, his spirit and expression forever remain. As disciples of the Venerable Master, we ought to uphold his great vows, be harmonious and united, carry on the Buddhas' wisdom life, strive and work together to propagate the Buddhadharma, and promote education. We sincerely pray that the Venerable Master will ride on his vows and compassionately return to establish a pure and blissful human world as well as the world of Avatamsaka (Flower Adornment).

已住如來平等性　　善修微妙方便道
於佛境界起信心　　得佛灌頂心無著

兩足尊所念報恩　　心如金剛不可沮
於佛所行能照了　　自然修習菩提行

——《大方廣佛華嚴經》〈初發心功德品〉

He already abides in the level nature of the Thus Come Ones;
He well cultivates the path of the subtly wondrous skill-in-means.
Towards the state of the Buddhas, he gives rise to a heart of faith,
And he receives the Buddhas' anointing his crown, with a mind devoid of attachments.

At the place of the Doubly Perfected Honored Ones,
He is mindful of repaying their kindness.
His mind is like Vajra indestructible.
He can clearly comprehend the Buddhas' conduct
And spontaneously cultivate the conduct of Bodhi.

Chapter on The Merit and Virtue from First Bringing Forth the Mind, the *Flower Adornment Sutra*

悼念叔公宣公上人

MOURNING MY GRAND-UNCLE, THE VENERABLE MASTER HUA

白明志　一九九五年七月二十八日講於萬佛聖城宣公上人讚頌報恩法會

A talk given by Bai Mingzhi in the Ceremony in Praise and Recognition of the Venerable Master Hua's Kindness at the Sagely City of Ten Thousand Buddhas on July 27, 1995

海內外的各位法師、各位居士：

今天大家懷著萬分悲痛的心情，參加這次懷念師父上宣下化老和尚的追思大會。宣公上人十九歲出家，為了弘揚佛法，使佛教發揚光大，居留香港多年，到過許多國家。為了把佛法弘揚全世界，一九六二年來到美國，把佛法傳到西方，使很多的美國人懂得佛法，佛法的種子在每個人心中深深地紮根。

上人一生十分堅苦樸素、勤儉節約，一件衣服要穿很長的時間，連上人往生時穿的一雙鞋，也是幾年前穿過的。上人曾經說過：「我走的時候，就穿這雙鞋。」可以想像上人是多麼地節省。

至今上人到美國已經三十三年了，經過千辛萬苦，流血汗、不休息，共建立了二十七處道場，講經說法無數次。幾年前，上人身體健康就不太好，卻仍然抱病講經說法，很多人都不知道。上人出家時發了十八大願，要代眾生受苦，所以一生中受的苦很多。

上人離開家鄉將近六十年，只有在一九八六年時回國一次。到了家鄉，家鄉的親人才有機會第一次見到上人。我來了美國幾次，一九九四年七月五日和太太一起來。七月末，上人在洛杉磯住院，我們曾多次去探望，上人對我們十分親切，常常和我們談話。因為我平時和上人講話都稱上人為「老爺」。記得去年十月，有一次我們兩人與上人談話，上人說他的左胳膊有時非常痛。我告訴上人：「老爺，希望您身心早日恢復健康，我願為您受一切痛苦。」上人說：「你不要這樣講，有時說話是很靈的。你生病了，誰照顧你？」並要我們好好學習佛法。上人又說，一個人活一生並不容易，要做一個好人。

All Dharma Masters and laypeople:

Today, we gather here and participate in this Memorial Ceremony for the Venerable Master. All of us are extremely sad. The Venerable Master left home at the age of ninteen. In order to propagate the Buddhadharma and enable the Buddhadharma to flourish, he lived in Hong Kong for many years and visited many countries in the world. For the sake of spreading the Buddhadharma to all parts of the world, he came alone to the United States in 1962, spreading the Buddhadharma to the West, enabling many Americans to understand the Buddha's teaching. The seed of Buddhadharma has been deeply planted in everyone's mind ground.

The Venerable Master was very simple, hardworking, and thrifty, and endured much hardship all his life. For example, he could wear one robe for many years. And the pair of shoes he wore when he entered stillness had been worn for several years. From these incidents, we can infer that the Venerable Master was indeed very thrifty.

It has been thirty-three years since the Venerable Master came to America. After much hardship, toil, sweating, and bleeding, he established a total of twenty-seven Wayplaces, and gave many Dharma talks and Sutra lectures. Several years back, the Venerable Master fell ill, but he continued to give Dharma talks and Sutras lectures. Many people were not aware of this situation. When he left the home life, He made eighteen great vows, including one in which he vowed that he would stand in for and suffer on behalf of all living beings. As a consequence of this vow, he endured much sufferring during his life.

In 1986, the Venerable Master went back to China and visited his hometown, after having been away for nearly sixty years. His relatives in China had the opportunity to see him for the first time. I have been to America several times. On the fifth of July, 1994, I came to America again with my wife. At the end of July, the Venerable Master fell ill and was hospitalized in Los Angeles. We visited him many times at the hospital. The Venerable Master was very friendly and kept talking to us. I would address him as 'Grandpa' during our conversations. In October of last year, during one of our conversations, the Master told us that he sometimes felt great pain in his left shoulder. I said, "Grandpa, I hope you get well soon. I am willing to stand in for you and take all your suffering." The Master told me not to make such promises, for whatever we say might come true. "If you were to fall sick, who would take care of you?" He advised us to study the Buddhadharma well. He said that it is no easy matter to live one's life, and that one should aspire to be a good person.

On the twenty-fourth of March, we visited the Venerable Master

今年三月二十日，我們再去探望上人，上人的病情已經很嚴重了，躺在床上連坐都坐不起來，講話也很吃力。上人的手和我的手緊緊地握在一起，很久都捨不得放開。上人對我說：「我病重成這個樣子，也沒有叫人告訴你們，怕大家為我擔心著急。」四月七日，上人病情加重，再次住院，直到六月七日圓寂。在這兩個月當中，我們與法師一直都留在醫院護理照料。

現在上人的肉身雖然離開了我們，但上人嚴明的戒律和六大宗旨永遠存在。上人一生弘揚佛法，獻身佛教，為佛教事業做出偉大的貢獻，上人的精神將永遠地活在每個人的心中。

宣公上人老爺，您安息吧！

謝謝大家！阿彌陀佛

again. The Master was very ill then, lying on the bed and unable to even sit up. He also had difficulty talking to us. The Venerable Master held my hands tightly for a long time He did not let them go. He said that although he was so ill, he had not asked anyone to inform us about his illness, because he didn't want us to worry about him. On the seventh of April, the Venerable Master's condition worsened, and he was hospitalized again. For the two months from that day until he passed away on the seventh of June, we and the other Dharma Masters nursed and took care of him.

Although the Master's physical body has left us, his strict discipline, precepts, rules of deportment, and the Six Guiding Principles will remain forever. The Venerable Master propagated the Buddhadharma and committed himself to the Buddha's teaching for his entire life. He made important contribution to the Buddha's mission, and his spirit will remain forever in our memory.

The Venerable Master, Grandpa, may you rest in peace!

Thank you. Amitabha

知眾生心無生想　　了達諸法無法想
雖普分別無分別　　億那由剎皆往詣
無量諸佛妙法藏　　隨順觀察悉能入
眾生根行靡不知　　到如是處如世尊
　　　　——《大方廣佛華嚴經》〈初發心功德品〉

He knows the minds of living beings, without the thoughts of living beings;
He penetratingly understands Dharmas without having thoughts of Dharmas.
Although there are differences, everywhere he is without discriminations,
As he travels to all the millions of nayutas of kshetras.

With the treasury of the wondrous Dharmas of limitless Buddhas,
He accords, contemplates, and enters.
He knows all living beings' basic practices, and
Reaches a place like that of the World Honored One.

Chapter on The Merit and Virtue from First Bringing Forth the Mind, the *Flower Adornment Sutra*

宣化老和尚追思紀念專集

緬懷上人

IN MEMORY OF THE VENERABLE MASTER HUA

中華民國立法院副院長　王金平

Wang Jinping, Vice-director of the Legislative Yuan of the Republic of China

驚悉師父上宣下化老和尚，於一九九五年六月七日（夏曆乙亥年五月初十）安詳示寂於美國洛杉磯。凡我萬佛聖城四眾弟子，以及聽聞識知上人者，莫不感念嘆息，心祝登彼極樂。

宣公上人糸出禪宗一花五葉之溈仰，乃溈仰宗第九代嗣法傳人。當年為維繫祖庭禪法於不墜，離開大陸，經由香港遠赴美國，而創立萬佛聖城。至今分支道場遍佈北美，開中國人西方弘法之先河，觀其功業仿如當年達摩祖師之自印度東來中土，振宗風，廣流傳而裨益世道人心。

溈仰門風，苦行潛修，上人秉承傳統，日中一餐，食無味無油的飯菜，數十年如一日，不以為意，而專心致志修習智慧，實踐文殊精神，早已臻於智慧之大成就，是為「大智」者。同時發願弘法，實踐普賢精神，遍具眾德，願行廣大，更是一「大行」者。以此「大智」、「大行」擴為菩薩行。不論「布施度」、「持戒度」、「忍辱度」、「精進度」，「禪定度」均達於化境，亦即以智慧主導五度，以五度莊嚴智慧，能於當世自覺覺人，解除苦難，普度眾生。

緬懷上人，萬德具備，一代宗師，倏爾倒駕慈航，惟色身涅槃，精神永在。凡我後學末進，尤應紹承道業，發揚光大。偈曰：「法輪常轉，如來無窮」，而東土何來？美西何往？傳彼禪宗，萬古留芳。

I was startled to learn that the Venerable Hsuan, Noble Hua, peacefully manifested the stillness in Los Angeles on June 7, 1995 (the tenth day of the fifth lunar month in the year of *yihai*). All the disciples in the fourfold assembly at the Sagely City of Ten Thousand Buddhas and all those who have seen, heard, or known the Venerable Master, without exception, must sigh and wish that he has reached the other shore of ultimate bliss.

The Venerable Master Hua was the ninth generation patriarch of the Weiyang Sect, one of the five branches of the Chan School. In order to uphold the lineage of the Chan teaching and keep it from declining, he left mainland China, passed through Hong Kong, and travelled far away to America to found the Sagely City of Ten Thousand Buddhas, whose affiliated monasteries are now spread across North America. As the first Chinese to propagate the Dharma in the West, his merit was as great as that of Patriarch Bodhidharma, who left India and came to China, where he revived the Chan School and propagated it widely so that it could benefit the world and people's minds.

The Weiyang Sect is characterized by ascetic practices and quiet cultivation. The Venerable Master inherited both of these traditional attributes, taking only one meal a day of unseasoned food cooked without oil. It was this way every day for many decades, but he didn't mind. He concentrated on the cultivation of wisdom, realizing the spirit of Manjushri Bodhisattva, who attained wisdom long ago. Thus he was one of great wisdom. At the same time he made vows to propagate the Dharma, realizing the spirit of Universal Worthy Bodhisattva, who is endowed with the myriad virtues and whose vows and conduct are vast and great. Therefore he was one of great conduct. With this great wisdom and great conduct expanded to become the Bodhisattva conduct, he attained the ultimate state in the perfection of giving, the perfection of upholding precepts, the perfection of patience, the perfection of vigor, and the perfection of concentration. He also used wisdom to guide the practice of these five perfections, and used these five perfections to adorn wisdom. In this age, he was able to enlighten both himself and others, to rescue those who were in suffering and hardship, and to extensively save living beings.

I cherish memories of the Venerable Master as being one replete with the myriad virtues, a great Master of this age. He suddenly turned the boat of compassion around and went back. Although his physical body entered Nirvana, his spirit will be here forever. We students who come after him should inherit his work in the Way and make it flourish. A verse says, "The Dharma wheel turns constantly; the Thus Come One is inexhaustible." Where did he come from in the East? Where has he gone to in the West? He perpetuated the lineage of the Chan School so that it would continue for endless generations.

我所認識的宣化上人

THE VENERABLE MASTER HUA AS I KNEW HIM

山東濟寧大學董事會董事　李衛國　一九九五年八月八日

Li Weiguo, Member of the Board of Trustees, Jining College, Shandong Province

August 8, 1995

我有幸曾兩度在美國拜會宣化上人，巧合的是，一次在一九九三年七月五日，一次是九四年七月五日，宣化上人曾說：「這是機緣！」一九九三年五月得悉宣化上人有意在中國辦教育的信息，並首先選中了孔孟之鄉——濟寧。這是我有緣認識宣化上人的直接原因。

兩度拜會宣化上人，都是由美國甘乃迪大學校董祖炳民先生引見的。在與宣化上人的接觸中，我衷心感到宣化上人待人慈祥、和善，知識淵博，見解深刻，充滿智慧。他雖然是出家人，卻反對迷信，提倡內在的修行，而不是向外求。雖然他是佛教領袖，卻主張宗教之間應消除門戶之見，平等共處。他雖然可四大皆空閉門修心養性，卻慈悲為懷，憂國憂民，為了世界能「刀槍入庫，馬放南山」而祈禱，為人類和平幸福而奉獻；他雖然身居國外，卻保持國籍溯本源，關心祖國的教育事業，他曾表示：為了中國的教育事業，自己可以粉身碎骨。他把「不貪、不爭、不求、不自私、不自利、不妄語」做為教育的宗旨和立人之本：鼓勵我們以他那種：「沒有錢可以辦有錢的事」的精神去辦好教育。教育青年人要愛國、愛家、愛身，要為國家做些事情，要做青年的楷模。

更使我難忘的是，一九九三年我去洛杉磯拜會上人後，他得知我要在舊金山停留一天，特意飛回舊金山，在萬佛聖城安排午宴接待了我。九四年我再度去美國拜訪時，他不顧病體，親自安排我們的行程和生活，每天打電話詢問我們休息得怎樣，生活是否習慣，關懷備至，體貼入微。更使我感動的是，在我們訪美期間，宣化上人決定由萬佛城向濟寧大學、寶相寺捐贈美金二十萬元，這樣大數額的海外捐款，在濟寧是第一次。

做為一個普普通通的中國人，能得到宣化上

I had the fortune of visiting the Venerable Master Hua twice in the United States. Coincidentally, the first time was on July 5, 1993, and the second time was on July 5, 1994. The Venerable Master said, "These are opportune conditions!" In May of 1993, we learned that the Venerable Master Hua wished to carry out education in China and his first choice for a site was Jining, the hometown of Confucius and Mencius. This was the direct cause of my acquaintance with the Venerable Master Hua.

My two visits with the Venerable Master were arranged by Dr. John Tsu, a trustee of Kennedy University in the United States. During my contact with the Venerable Master Hua, I was left with a deep impression of the Master's kind and friendly manner towards others, his profound and vast erudition, his penetrating views, and his full wisdom. While he was a Buddhist monk, he opposed superstition and emphasized inner cultivation rather than external seeking. While being a Buddhist leader, he advocated the elimination of sectarian views and an equal status for all religions. He could have gone into seclusion to cultivate his mind and nature, regarding the four elements as empty, but instead he had a compassionate spirit—he cared for the country and people, prayed that the world would put its weapons away and set the war-horses out to pasture, and contributed to the peace and well-being of humankind. Even though he lived abroad, he preserved his citizenship, going back to his roots. He cared about the educational system of his fatherland. He once said that for the sake of China's education, he was willing to sacrifice his body and bones. He made "no fighting, no greed, no seeking, no selfishness, no pursuit of personal advantage, and no lying" the principles of education and the basis for people to establish themselves on. He encouraged us to adopt his attitude that "even without money, we can do the things that require money" in carrying out the work of education. We must teach young people to love their country, love their families, and cherish themselves. We must do some work for the country and set a good example for the young people.

I will never forget that after I paid a call to the Venerable Master in Los Angeles in 1993, when he found out I was going to stay one day in San Francisco, he flew back to San Francisco and arranged to have lunch with me at the Sagely City of Ten Thousand Buddhas. During our visit in 1994, he neglected his own sick condition and personally arranged our itinerary and accomodations. Every day he would call to inquire if we had rested well and if we were used to the living conditions. He showed the utmost concern for our well-being, down to the smallest details. I was even more moved when during our visit in America the Venerable Master decided to have the City of Ten Thousand Buddhas make a contribution of US$200,000 to Jining College and Baoxiang Monastery. It was the first time that Jining had ever

人這樣的高僧大德的厚愛和恩典，絕不是我個人的機緣，這是宣化上人對中國人民的深情厚誼。

宣化上人的圓寂給我們留下了無限的哀思，我們將永遠懷念他。他愛國重教，熱愛和平，齊世救民，無私無畏的崇高境界和處事風範，將成為世人的楷模。

> 慈悲喜捨度眾生，
> 一塵不立淨自他；
> 隨緣履踐為菩提，
> 圓得正果亦弘法。

received such a large contribution from overseas.

Although I am just a common Chinese person, I was treated with warm hospitality and kindness by the Venerable Master Hua, such a lofty and virtuous Sanghan. This is not due to my personal conditions. This is an expression of the Venerable Master's deep sentiment and generous friendship for all Chinese people.

I feel boundless grief for the Venerable Master's completion of stillness. We will remember him forever. He loved his country and valued Buddhism. He was devoted to peace and to saving the world and its people. His exalted state of selfless courage and his exemplary manner of doing things will be a model for the people of the world.

> *With kindness, compassion, joy, and giving, he was a hero who*
> *saved the multitudes.*
> *Without attaching to a single speck of dust, he purified himself*
> *and others.*
> *According with conditions, he truly practiced for the sake of*
> *Bodhi.*
> *He perfectly attained the Proper Fruition and propagated the*
> *Dharma as well.*

> 諸趣差別想無量　業果及心亦非一
> 乃至根性種種殊　一發大心悉明見
>
> 其心廣大等法界　無依無變如虛空
> 趣向佛智無所取　諦了實際離分別
>
> ——《大方廣佛華嚴經》〈初發心功德品〉

All the destinies are different, with thoughts measureless;
The karmic results and minds are also not of one kind.
Up to and including the various differentiations of the root natures:
Upon first bringing forth the great mind,
Once can clearly see them all.

The mind is vast and expansive, equal to the Dharma Realm,
Without reliance and unchanging like space.
One tends toward the Buddha's wisdom without any grasping,
And comprehends the limit of reality, without discriminations.

Chapter on The Merit and Virtue from First Bringing Forth the Mind, the *Flower Adornment Sutra*

老法師與一個尋常人的友誼

THE ELDER DHARMA MASTER'S FRIENDSHIP WITH AN ORDINARY PERSON

程曦教授

Professor Cheng Xi

在常人眼光中看來，特異出眾的人士，也許會是只從大處著眼的人。其實未必然，人在大的方面顧得到，小的方面也顧得到，才能成就事業。用平等的態度看人，對人的瞭解才深。

像我這樣一個並不太活躍的疏懶人，能結識宣化（度輪）老法師，這樣一位一天到晚多方弘法的忙碌人，並不足為奇。在香港召集的「大般若經重印討論會」上，我與宣化（度輪）老法師曾有一面之識。自從那次會面，至今已有幾十年了。

三十五、六年之前，我印了一本小書，叫做《程氏新禪語》。印了一千本與人結緣。後來老法師看到了，又用同樣的紙張、款式，印了五千本。那年秋天，我去了英國劍橋，就沒與老法師見過面了。老法師在美期間，又讓萬佛城刊物的編輯們把《程氏新禪語》選錄轉載了若干條，刊登在上面。那個期間，我又印出了《設問語錄》，老法師看到之後，又讓他的門人，將此書譯成英文刊登出來。老法師對這些小書的垂青，一直使我深記在心。

法界佛教大學草創，我的名字也出現在名單上。在以後的幾個暑期中，我也偶然去教了幾回書，並在道場中小住，頗感清靜。

我在第一次對萬佛城的聽眾談話時，就盡可能用平實的語氣，談了一些眼前的問題。事後老法師向我說：「老實人，出了名了。」

老法師不止一次勸我在將來搬到萬佛城法界佛教大學去定居教書，也曾讓旁人向我說過。我有一次是這樣用譬喻來回答的：「我不敢開將來的支票」，原因是開了就得全兌現，目前未必能保證他日張張支票都能兌現，所以先不開。

我在美國中西部住了二十多年。如果當時移動

Ordinary people may think that an outstanding person is one who only pays attention to great matters. Actually, this is not the case. A person must be able to take care of great matters as well as small matters if he wants to accomplish great deeds. By regarding all people with a fair attitude, one will be able to understand them better.

Thus, it is not so strange for someone like me who's rather idle and not very active to know the Elder Master Hsuan Hua (To Lun), a person who is busy propagating the Dharma from morning to night. I first met the Venerable Master Hua at the Conference on the Reprinting of the *Great Prajna Sutra* held in Hong Kong. Several decades have passed since that meeting.

Thirty-five or thirty-six years ago, I printed a small book called *New Chan Talks by Cheng*. I printed 1000 copies and gave them to people for free. When the Elder Dharma Master saw it, he printed 5000 copies using the same kind of paper and format. After I went to Cambridge University in England, I didn't meet the Elder Dharma Master again for a while. During the time he was in the United States, the Elder Dharma Master also had the editors of the monthly journal of the City of Ten Thousand Buddhas print selected passages of my book. Meanwhile I printed another book called *Questions and Answers*. When the Elder Dharma Master saw it, he again told his disciples to translate it into English and publish it in the journal. I will always deeply remember the Elder Dharma Master's liking for these small books.

When the Dharma Realm Buddhist University was in its initial stage, my name also appeared on the name list. I would occasionally go to teach there in the summers and stay at the monastery, which gave me a quiet and peaceful feeling.

The first time I spoke with the audience at the City of Ten Thousand Buddhas, I tried to speak in as ordinary a way as possible as I discussed some current issues. Afterwards the Elder Dharma Master said to me, "A modest person—you are now well-known."

More than once, the Elder Dharma Master exhorted me to move to the City of Ten Thousand Buddhas to live and teach at the Dharma Realm Buddhist University. He also asked other people to suggest this to me. I once replied with an analogy: "I dare not write a check for the future." The reason was that if I wrote it, I would have to be able to cash it. Since I couldn't guarantee that I would have the money to cash every check in the future, I didn't write it.

I have lived in the Midwestern United States for over twenty years. If I wanted to move, it would take me at least six months to

，不說旁的，就說二十多年來的紙張，一張一張
的看一遍，就得用半年以上的時間。無法說走就
走。有一次老法師說是可以派兩位在家弟子來幫
我搬東西。我就說搬東西容易，處理沒有秩序的
紙張難，沒敢說做就做。人既不開遠期支票，當
前也就暫求心安了。

老法師的道場，中外出家徒眾，都日中一食，
規矩很嚴。外客在裡面短期住時，晚間可以到齋
堂吃預先準備好的飯食。我在萬佛城小住時，有
時老法師也派人送餅乾來，可謂關心備至。

我曾對老法師說過幾次，有外客住在這道場裡
，可能感到自慚形穢，因為看到出家人們儘量往
清淨處做，而自己在外界很難避免世俗的污濁，
看了人家的精嚴戒行，而己身覺得望塵莫及，不
免有望洋興嘆的情形。

幾年前我有一次帶著病到加州看老法師，老法
師很快就派人把我送去一位中醫的診所，又用電
話一再關照醫師，加意診治。草藥拿到長堤聖寺
，他的徒弟們細心煎好了藥，放到溫而不涼的水
瓶，端了進來，我一口氣就喝光了。由這件事，
可以看到道場裡的人士們，除去慈悲為懷的表現
之外，熱心、細心，也是外界人士，所未必能想
像的。

我每次到老法師的住處，多是上天下地的閒談
，近幾年來，他對人說，我是他的老朋友。這個
「老」字，我可以勉強接受，但是他偶然稱我做
「平生知己」，則令我慚愧汗顏，萬萬不敢當了
。

我曾對人說過，如果我本來值三十分，後來到
值三十二分，那就有些進境了。如果人一下子先
看成值八十分的人，那我就算值得多過三十二分
，也自覺見不得人了，何況本來離三十分還遠呢
。

幾十年來，我從不曾送禮物給老法師。至於捐
給法界總會法界佛教大學的小貢獻，則是例外。
老法師對我這個自奉清簡的書生境況相當瞭解。
常常問起我有新作品要印行沒有，我知道他的門
下有幾位居士有印書的知識、技能，諸多方便。
可是我為避免打擾他人，書自己抄寫、複印、裝
訂，於心更安，所以近年印出的小冊子，都由自
己包辦，沒有麻煩各界的熱心人士，這些小冊子
。又多屬有關文藝之作，自問於道場無甚用處，
所以不如親力親為，自己去印。至於老法師對我

look at all the papers that have accumulated over the past twenty-
some years, not to mention anything else. I can't just pick up and
leave. The Elder Master once said he could send two lay disciples
to help me move my things. I said moving was easy enough; taking
care of the disorganized papers was the difficult part—I didn't dare
to promise I could do it. Since I can't write a check for the future,
at present I can only seek temporary peace of mind.

The Chinese and Western disciples at the Elder Dharma Master's Way-places eat one meal a day and follow very strict rules.
When guests come to stay, they can go to the dining hall in the
evening to have dinner which is prepared in advance. Sometimes
the Elder Dharma Master would also send people to deliver crack-
ers to me. He showed the utmost concern.

Several times I said to the Elder Dharma Master that when
guests come to the Way-place, they may be ashamed of their own
impurity. They see the monastics striving to be as pure as possible,
and yet they themselves find it hard to avoid the turbidity of the
mundane world. When they see others practicing such strict self-
discipline, they feel they cannot match up. Thus, they end up feeling discouraged.

Several years ago I went to visit the Elder Dharma Master in
California when I was sick. He immediately had someone send me
to a Chinese medical clinic, and then he kept calling the doctor,
paying special attention to my treatment. After the medicinal herbs
were taken back to Long Beach Sagely Monastery, his disciples
carefully boiled the herbs, poured the decoction into a thermos, and
brought it to me. I drank it down in one gulp. This shows that the
people in the monastery, aside from being kind and compassionate,
have a warmth and devotion which people outside the monastery
cannot imagine.

Whenever I went to the Elder Dharma Master's place, we would
talk about everything under the sun. In recent years he told others
that I was his old friend. I can barely accept the adjective "old," but
for him to occasionally call me his "bosom friend" makes me extremely remorseful, and I certainly dare not acknowledge such a
title.

I once said, "If I am worth thirty points and later I come to have
a value of thirty-two points, then I have made some progress. But
if someone suddenly judges my value to be eighty points, then even
if I were worth over thirty-two points, I would feel very ashamed,
how much the more since I'm still far from being even thirty
points."

In all these decades, I have never given the Elder Dharma Master a present, aside from making small contributions to Dharma
Realm Buddhist University. The Master seemed to understand my
situation as a "scholar living a simple life." He often asked me if I
had any new writings to print. I know that he had several lay disciples who were knowledgeable and skilled at printing books. However, I didn't want to trouble others and felt more comfortable writing out, copying, and binding the books myself. Thus I personally
printed the small booklets I've written in recent years, without
troubling others despite their eagerness to help. Morever, since
these booklets are mostly on artistic and literary themes and not of
much use in a monastery, I decided it would be better to print them

的關懷，對文化教育的熱心，我則是一樣的銘感於心。

　　我最後一次同老法師見面，是在去年（一九九四年）的夏天。我飛到洛杉磯時，有老法師的門人到機場去接，然後送我到長堤聖寺。我同老法師談得很好。臨走之前，有外客去拜訪，其中有一位擅長醫療筋骨的中醫師。老法師在百忙中讓客人替我看看左臂的扭傷。經過一番推拿，我臂部的筋好像有一個扣給解開了，幾個月來，從無此輕鬆的感覺。從此左臂上下恢復了靈活。我這次做客人，真是受益甚多。我住的州，並沒有住著這樣的中醫師，不到加州，很難得到這種方便。老法師那裡，偶然有這樣的外客，我才在偶然的機會中，得到這麼大的幫助。

　　像我這樣愚昧魯鈍的人，居然可以和老法師一談就是幾個鐘頭。在陌生的旁人看來，可能會以為我是個健談之客。其實這與健談、不健談無關。只是衝口而出，全無機心就是了。若在外界魚龍混雜的環境中，一不小心，說話太直率，惹了生事的人，就可能有遠離事實的傳言加在自己的頭上。倘去辯解，則白白浪費時間。我對於這種情形，初時也認為應該辯解，後來則主張不去理會那些無謂之言談，也不必去討論。這樣一來，就算本來健談的人士，也表現不出能說會道的長處來了。至於在老法師的面前，我則不用辯解任何問題，老法師早就知道我的真性格。我不必有什麼談話藝術，言辭無所保留。所以一談就暢暢快快，直言無隱，因而時間也就拉長了。

　　當我在病中看到報紙上關於宣化老法師圓寂的報導，真是料不到的。從未想過他走得竟然這樣快，這樣早。眾人的震驚也是必然的。我這裡疾病纏身，不能去給老法師送行。愧怍又有何用，只得在昏花的眼睛約略看得見的情形之下，模模糊糊的寫了這幾張稿子，遙致敬意。

with my own labor. The Elder Dharma Master's concern towards me and his enthusiasm for cultural education shall always remain in my memory.

The last time I saw the Elder Dharma Master was in the summer of last year (1994). I flew to Los Angeles and was picked up at the airport and taken to Long Beach Sagely Monastery by the Master's disciple. I had a very pleasant chat with the Master. Before I left, some other guests came to visit the Master, including a Chinese herbal doctor who specialized in treating bone and ligament problems. The Elder Master, despite being very busy, asked the guest to examine a sprain in my left arm. After a massage, it seemed that a knot had been released in my arm. I had not felt so comfortable for several months. After that my left arm regained its former agility. On that visit, I really benefitted greatly. In the state where I live, there are no Chinese herbal doctors. If I hadn't gone to California, it would hardly have been so convenient to receive such treatment. Because that guest happened to visit the Elder Dharma Master, I had an unexpected opportunity to be helped in such a great way.

Such a dull person as myself could actually engage in a conversation with the Elder Dharma Master for several hours. A stranger observing us might have thought I was a talkative visitor. Actually, it has nothing to do with whether I am talkative or not. I would just say whatever came to mind, without any deliberation. In the outside world where it's difficult to distinguish the good from the bad, as soon as one makes a slip of the tongue and speaks too frankly, offending the mischief-makers, one may become the subject of rumors that are far from the truth. At that point, to try to explain oneself would simply be a waste of time. I didn't think it necessary to explain myself to begin with, and later I decided to simply ignore such senseless talk. Under such circumstances, even a talkative person would find it hard to demonstrate his eloquence. However, with the Elder Dharma Master, I didn't have to explain or defend myself on anything. He understood my true nature long ago, and I didn't have to pay heed to the art of conversation. I had no reservations. And so I conversed very freely with him, speaking plainly and not hiding anything. Because of this, our conversations always lasted a long time.

When I read about the Elder Dharma Master Hsuan Hua's completion of stillness in the newspaper, I was truly taken by surprise. I never expected him to leave so soon, so early. Of course, everyone is certain to be shocked. I am seriously ill here and cannot go to say good-bye to the Elder Dharma Master. Feeling ashamed is of no use, so as much as my blurred vision has allowed me to, I have blurrily written these few pages as a brief expression of my respect.

結緣三年獲知音

A BOSOM FRIEND FOR THREE YEARS

蠡縣癡翁傲樵楊富森　一九九五年八月十四日

The dull old man from Li County, Jinquiao, Yang Fusen

August 14, 1995

一九九一年的春天，有一天，我應約去看望老友胡果相女士。她對我說，她已皈依佛教十幾年了，她的師父是宣化上人。她問我認識不認識，我說：「久聞大名，可是始終沒有會過！」她又問我：「有沒有興趣到法界佛教大學教書？」我回答說：「我已經退休八年了，我不想再教書了。」

她告訴我：「佛教大學是宣化上人創辦的，上人的弟子中有些是外國人，他們不懂中文，可是很想知道中文，佛教大學總也找不到一位可以教中文的老師；您現在已經退休了，而且身體健康，精力充沛，能不能看在老朋友的份上，去佛教大學義務幫忙幾個月？他們非常需要像您這樣一位老師。」

我這個人一向是「有求必應」的，何況是老朋友相邀，我不好意思說「不」字。可是，我是一個基督教徒，對佛教只有片面的認識；因此，我感到躊躇。

果相知道我在猶豫不決，於是改了口氣說道：「這麼辦吧：我請您和您的夫人去萬佛城看一下，如果可能的話，先和師父（宣化上人）碰個面；然後再決定，好不好？」

我答應了她的建議。我雖然是個基督徒，可是我並不是那種所謂「思想狹窄」、「死硬派」的宗教狂，我相信世界上真理只有一個，可是追求真理、到達真理的道路不僅一條；因此，在我的心目中有容忍和同情其他宗教的態度和「空間」。我所結交的朋友當中，有很多是猶太教徒、回教徒、天主教徒，和佛教徒。何況我很好奇，我很想多交朋友；我很想多知道一點佛教和這位大名鼎鼎的佛教高僧。我答應了，先去萬佛城看看，再做決定。果相高興極了，幾天之後，她說飛機票已經買好了，請我和老伴（劉金定女士）先去參觀萬佛城。

長話短說，我們去了萬佛城；很湊巧，在那裡我們遇到了祖炳民教授，和幾位老友（有唐德剛教授，謝覺民教授，陸鏗先生等）。我們在萬佛城住了

In the spring of 1991, I went to visit my old friend Mrs. Helen Woo, who told me that she had been a Buddhist for more than ten years and that her teacher was the Venerable Master Hua. She asked me if I knew him. I said, "I've long heard of his esteemed name, but I have never met him." She asked me, "Would you be interested in teaching at Dharma Realm Buddhist University?" I replied, "I retired eight years ago, and I don't want to teach again."

She told me, "Dharma Realm Buddhist Association was founded by the Venerable Master Hua, and the Master has some Western disciples who don't know Chinese and want to learn. The Buddhist University has never managed to find a Chinese teacher. You are retired, but still very healthy and full of energy. As a favor for a friend, would you be willing to volunteer your services at the University for a few months? They really need a teacher like you."

I've always been one who cannot refuse any request, especially one from an old friend. I would have felt embarrassed to say "no." However, because I was a Christian and had only a very superficial knowledge of Buddhism, I felt rather hesitant.

Helen knew I could not decide, so she made another suggestion: "How about this? I can take you and your wife to the City of Ten Thousand Buddhas to have a look, and if possible, meet the Master. Then you can decide. Okay?"

I consented. Even though I am a Protestant Christian, I'm not one of those narrow-minded, die-hard religious fanatics. I believe that while there is only one truth, there is more than one path leading to that truth. And so I have a tolerant and sympathetic attitude towards other religions. I have many Jewish, Muslim, Catholic, and Buddhist friends. What is more, I was very curious and eager to make more friends. I really wanted to know more about Buddhism and about this renowned lofty Buddhist master. So I agreed to first visit the City of Ten Thousand Buddhas and then make my decision. Helen was delighted. A few days later, she told me she had bought the plane tickets and invited myself and my wife (Ms. Liu Jinding) to tour the City of Ten Thousand Buddhas.

To make a long story short, we went to the City of Ten Thousand Buddhas. By coincidence, we met Professor John B. Tsu and several other old friends there (including Professor Tang Degang, Professor Xie Jueming, and Mr. Lu Jian). We stayed overnight at the City. Unfortunately we didn't get to see the Venerable Master. Helen said, "The Master is in the hospital

一夜，可惜，我沒有會到宣化上人，果相說：「師父正在一家醫院休養，不能見客。」我心裡稍感遺憾，真所謂「乘興而去，掃興而回。」回來的路上，我們參觀了國際譯經學院，在那裡，我也會到當時的佛教大學校長。

次年（一九九二）五月份，果相又打電話給我說：「師父已經出院，很想見你。」她問我願不願意和上人會面。我毫不猶豫地回答：「當然願意。」

果然，一星期之後，果相買好了飛機票，又約我和老伴去柏林根國際譯經學院去會晤宣化上人。

一九九二年五月二十日（星期三）上午九時半，我們三人（胡果相、老伴劉金定和我）到達柏林根，師父的弟子恆實法師和阿匹納博士（新任法大校務長），前任校務長 Chancellor 祖炳民教授等前來迎接，向我們表示歡迎之意。十分鐘後，我們到二樓的一間小會客室，拜見禪宗三藏高僧宣化上人。我見了上人鞠躬示敬，宣公坐在那裡，雙手合十，微笑相迎，低聲說道：「請坐，請坐。」我和老伴告坐之後，和宣化上人互道寒暄，他問我家鄉籍貫；當他問到我的歲數時，我說：「我屬馬，民國七年生人。」他聽了微微一笑，說道：「我也屬馬，咱們倆同歲。」然後，他又問我：「哪個月生的？」

我回答道：「陰曆三月。」

「三月哪一天？」師父又問。

「三月十三」我說出了我的生日。

師父聽了，又笑了笑，然後說道：「你比我大三天，我是三月十六生的。」（我們談到這兒的時候，忽然間在座的都靜了一靜，微笑，低著頭，彼此望了一下。我最初不明白，後來，胡果相居士告訴我，那是他們頭一次知道師父的生年月日。按照佛教的教規，出家人從來不告訴別人自己的年紀的。可是，師父竟破例的把他的生年月日告訴了我，大概是因為我把我的生年月日告訴了他。）

然後，師父又問我啟蒙的經過，我說我是在我們村子（河北省蠡縣南齊村）的私塾啟蒙的，念的是《論語》、《孟子》、《三字文》和《百家姓》。宣公聽了，又微笑了。他告訴我說，他只念了兩年半的書，也是從四書五經啟蒙的，《古文觀止》、《唐詩》等等，他全都念過，且還能背得滾瓜爛熟；他還讀過醫書，常給人家治病。

說到這裡，我將買來的一本書（即《元曲小令五十首》的英譯本）和近年我寫的一些打油詩和對聯

and cannot receive visitors right now." I felt a bit regretful. It was truly as the saying goes, "I went in high spirits and returned in disappointment." On the way back, we stopped to visit the International Translation Institute, where I met the president of the Buddhist University.

The following year (1992) in May, Helen called me again and said, "The Master has left the hospital and would like to meet you." She asked if I wanted to meet the Venerable Master. I replied without hesitation, "Of course!"

One week later, Helen bought the plane tickets and made an appointment for me and my wife to meet the Venerable Master Hua at the International Translation Institute in Burlingame.

On Wednesday, May 20, 1992, at nine o'clock in the morning, the three of us (Helen; my wife, Ms. Liu Jinding; and myself) arrived in Burlingame. Dharma Master Heng Sure (the Venerable Master's disciple), Dr. Akpinar (the newly appointed Chancellor of the University), former Chancellor Dr. John B. Tsu, and others welcomed us. Ten minutes later, we walked into a small meeting room on the second floor and met the eminent Chan Master and Tripitaka Master, Venerable Hsuan Hua. I bowed in respect to the Venerable Master, who placed his palms together and smiled in welcome. In a soft voice, he said, "Please take a seat." My wife and I seated ourselves and began telling the Master about ourselves. He asked me what village and province I was from. When he asked my age, I said, "I was born in the year of the horse, the seventh year of the Chinese Republic." He smiled and said, "I was born in the year of the horse, too. We are the same age." Then he asked, "What month were you born in?"

I replied, "The third month of the lunar calendar."

"What day of the third month?" asked the Master.

"The thirteenth day of the third month," I said, telling him my birthdate.

The Master smiled some more and said, "You are three days older than I am. I was born on the sixteenth day of the third month." (At that point in the conversation, the others who were present became quiet, smiled, lowered their heads, and glanced at each other. I didn't understand why then, but later, Helen told me that was the first time they knew the Master's date of birth. In Buddhism, left-home people are not supposed to reveal their age to others. The Master made an exception and told me his birthdate, probably because I had told him my birthdate.)

The Master then asked about my schooling. I told him I was educated in a private school in my village (the village of Nanji in the district of Li, Hebei Province). I had studied the *Analects*, *Mencius*, the *Three Character Classic*, and the *Hundred Surnames*. The Venerable Master smiled as he listened. He told me he had only had two and a half years of schooling, and that he had also studied the Four Books and Five Classics, the *Definitive Anthology of Ancient Essays*, the *Tang Odes*, and so on. He had studied all of these and moreover was able to recite them fluently from memory. He had also studied the treatises on Chinese medicine and had often healed people.

I then gave the Venerable Master a book entitled *Fifty Odes*

送給師父做為「見面禮」，師父立刻也送我他寫的詩和一套《華嚴經》。他聽說我喜歡寫詩和對聯，他也把他寫過的兩首詩背給我聽，一首是紀念周恩來的，一首是諷刺毛澤東的。（註：這兩首詩，大家都熟悉了，而且也都能背誦，我就不重複了。）

他告訴我，他常給弟子們上對聯課，他出上聯，讓弟子們對下聯；他以為這是一項極好的文字訓練，幫助增進弟子們的思考能力。

還沒等我答話，師父又說：「我給你（們）出一個上聯，看看你能不能對下聯。」我點頭同意。師父說：上聯是

白水泉中一大天

我立刻會意，這上聯的妙處是用「泉」「天」兩字，把它們分開來，再湊成一句。下聯也應該照樣做才行。

我從小的時候就喜歡像「對聯」這樣的文字遊戲，我讀過很多對聯、門聯，甚至輓聯，而且搜集了多種這類的書籍。我記得一副對聯，它的上聯和師父所出的上聯幾乎相同，那副對聯是：

白水泉邊女子好，少女更妙；
山石岩下古木枯，此木成柴。

上聯用的是「泉」，「好」，「妙」三字；下聯用的是「岩」，「枯」，「柴」三個字；分開來，再湊成一起，成一句話。因此，我立刻寫下「山石岩下」四個字；作為下聯的前一半；為了對上聯的「一」字，我想到了「二」這個數字；接著我忽然想到「夫」這個字，因為「夫」和「天」字幾乎一樣；「天」是「一」和大拼成的，「夫」應該是「二」和「人」拼成的；可是，怎樣才能對「一大天」呢？

我正在琢磨不定的時候，師父在旁邊看到了，他知道我在為難，於是忍不住地給我提示，說道：「二人夫不就成了嗎？」我恍然大悟，「二人夫」就是「二人的丈夫」正配「一大天」。因此，我是在座第一個交卷的人，對聯就成了：

白水泉中一大天，
山石岩下二人夫。

from the Yuan Dynasty (in English) and a collection of poems and couplets that I had written in recent years, as a token of our first meeting. The Master immediately gave me a book of verses written by himself and a set of the *Avatamsaka Sutra*. He had heard of my penchant for writing poems and couplets, and he recited two poems that he had written: one was in memory of Zhou Enlai, and the other was in ridicule of Mao Zedong. (Note: Everyone is familiar with these two poems and can recite them from memory, so I will not repeat them here.)

The Venerable Master told me that he regularly taught a class on matching couplets to his disciples. He would give them one line and have them come up with a second line to form a couplet. He considered it to be an excellent language drill that also improved their thinking power.

Without waiting for me to respond, the Master said, "I'm going to give you all a line of verse. Let's see if you can match it with a second line." I nodded my head in assent. The Master gave this line:

In the white-water spring, there is one great sky.

I immediately noticed that the wonder of this line lies in the fact that the words for 'spring' 泉 and 'sky' 天 are decomposed and then put back together. The second line would have to have the same characteristic to match it.

Ever since my youth, I loved to play word games such as that of matching couplets. I had read many matched couplets, couplets pasted on doors at the New Year, and even funeral couplets, and collected many books on the subject. I remember one couplet in which the first line was very close to the line given by the Venerable Master. It went:

Beside the white-water spring, a girl is nice;
a young girl is even more wonderful.
Beneath the mountain-rock boulder, an old tree is withered;
this wood can serve as firewood.

The words 'spring' 泉, 'nice' 好, and 'wonderful' 妙 in the first line and the words 'boulder' 岩, 'withered' 枯, and 'firewood' 柴 in the second line are decomposed into elements and the recombined to make sentences. So I immediately wrote down the words "Beneath the mountain-rock boulder" as the first half of the second line. To match the word 'one' in the first line, I thought of the number 'two.' Then I suddenly thought of the word 'man' 夫 because it is almost the same as 'sky' 天. 'Sky' 天 is formed by combining 'one' 一 and 'great' 大. 'Man' 夫 should be the combination of 'two' 二 and 'people' 人. But how could I match the phrase "one great sky"? Sitting next to me, the Master saw me puzzling over this and couldn't restrain himself from giving me the answer: "Wouldn't the phrase 'two (people) men' do?" It suddenly hit me: 'Two (people) men' was a precise match for 'one great sky.' Thus, I was the first one to turn in my paper. The resulting couplet was:

In the white-water spring, there is one great sky.
Beneath the mountain-rock boulder, there are two men.

師父看了，點頭，微笑不語。

我們談話的時候，果相兩三次提醒師父是午齋的時候了，宣公出家以來，六十年如一日，每日一餐（日中一食），夜不倒單；可是這一天，我們談話的時間早已超過了中午，因為談得投緣（彷彿兩人恨相見之晚），師父並不理睬果相的提醒，繼續興高采烈地談個不休。直到下午兩點多鐘，宣公上人才恍然覺到該是吃齋的時候了，我兩人的談話才告終止。（註：這是第二次師父破了自己的教例。）後來果相告訴我，師父和弟子們談話時，很少超過二十分鐘；初次見面的友人，尤其如此，可是，這一天，師父和我的談話竟超過四個鐘頭，打破了以往的慣例。這使我想起了晉朝時高僧慧遠和詩人陶淵明的故事：陶淵明和慧遠和尚是好朋友，他經常去山中廟裡拜望慧遠禪師，依照慣例，慧遠和尚送來訪的客人到山下，山下有一條小溪，名叫虎溪，慧遠和尚送客人到虎溪為止，從不越過虎溪；可是有一次，他送陶淵明下山，兩人邊走邊談，興緻極濃，走到山下，陶淵明越過虎溪，慧遠和尚也隨著他走過虎溪，等到陶淵明向他拱手告別的時候，慧遠和尚才覺悟到，他竟越過了虎溪，打破了自己的慣例。

The Master looked at it, nodded, and smiled without saying anything.

During our conversation, Helen reminded the Master two or three times that it was time for lunch. Ever since he left the home-life, the Venerable Master had, for sixty years, consistently observed the practices of eating one meal a day at noon and of sleeping sitting up. Yet on that day, our conversation lasted until way past noon. Because we were so engrossed in our dialogue, as if deploring the fact that we had not met earlier, the Master paid no attention to Helen's reminders and continued talking in a happy and animated manner. Only when it was past two o'clock did the Venerable Master vaguely realize that it was time to eat, and so our conversation came to an end. (Note: This was the second time the Master made an exception to his rules.) Later Helen told me the Master rarely talked for more than twenty minutes at a time with his disciples, how much the less a friend he had just met. Yet on that day, the Master talked with me for more than four hours, breaking his usual custom. This reminds me of the story of the great Buddhist monk Huiyuan of the Jin dynasty and the poet Tao Yuanming. They were close friends. Tao Yuanming often went up the mountain to visit the Venerable Huiyuan in the monastery, and following the custom, Venerable Huiyuan would accompany his guest down the mountain as far as a small creek named Tiger Creek. The Venerable Huiyuan would never go beyond Tiger Creek. One time, however, they were so engrossed in their conversation that when they reached the foot of the mountain, Tao Yuanming crossed Tiger Creek and the Venerable Huiyuan followed right after him. It was only when Tao Yuanming placed his palms together to salute him that the Venerable Huiyuan realized that he had crossed Tiger Creek and broken his own custom.

*   *   *

經過那次（首次）和宣公上人長談之後，我心中不但對宣公有極深刻的印象，而且起了讚佩景仰之情！雖然他只讀過兩年半的學校，可是他對我國的四書五經造詣極深，不要說別人，連我這個曾獲得博士學位而且在大學教授四十年的人，和宣公相比，我真覺得「自愧弗如！」正因為他的德行極好，修養極深，超過一般出家人之上，虛雲老法師才選拔他為禪宗溈仰派第九代傳人；正因為他的眼光遠大，他才隻身一人遠渡重洋，來到異邦（美國），弘揚佛法；在我國佛教記載中，除了唐朝的鑑真和尚遠渡重洋到日本弘揚佛法之外，宣公應是第二位不辭勞苦，遠涉重洋，把佛法傳播給異邦人士的高僧。

不但如此，宣公更想改善美國的教育，在萬佛城他創立了育良小學、培德中學，和法界佛

That long conversation with the Venerable Master on our first meeting left a deep impression on my mind and evoked my profound admiration and respect for him. Despite having received only two and a half years of schooling, his attainment in the Four Books and Five Classics of China was extremely profound. Even someone such as myself, a Ph.D. with forty years' teaching experience in universities, felt ashamed of my inadequacy compared to him. It was because his lofty virtue and deep cultivation surpassed those of ordinary monks that the Elder Dharma Master Hsu Yun chose him to be the ninth generation heir of the Weiyang lineage of the Chan Sect. Because of his far-reaching vision, the Venerable Master crossed the ocean alone and came to a foreign land (America) to propagate the Buddhadharma. In the history of Chinese Buddhism, the Venerable Jianzhen of the Tang dynasty was the first monk to cross the ocean and propagate the Dharma in Japan, and the Venerable Master Hua is the second eminent Buddhist monk who endured toil and hardship in order to cross the ocean and spread the Dharma to the people of another country.

The Venerable Master Hua also wished to improve American education, so he established Instilling Goodness Elementary School, Developing Virtue Secondary School, and Dharma Realm Buddhist Uni-

教大學，正因為我對上人起了敬仰之心，因此在和他長談之後，我立刻決定，應邀去萬佛城，重執教鞭，再奏弦歌。

一九九二年八月，我和老伴到達了萬佛城。在法大我開了三門課，一門是初級中文，一門是高級古文，而另一門是初級古文（每週星期三晚間上課，這樣城中的四眾都可以選修）。

上人聽說我已經來到萬佛城授課，非常高興，告訴校務長阿匹納說，要聘我為法界佛教大學校長；我聽了，婉言拒絕。上人對我說：「你既然不願意當校長，那麼，我另外給你一個稱號，我稱你為「校尊」好了。我佛如來被人稱為「世尊」，就是說，全「世」界的人都「尊」敬他；你稱為「校尊」，就是說全「校」的人都應該「尊」敬你的。」於是，從此以後，在法大我就被稱做「校尊」了。

我原計劃在法大教一學期，可是，一學期過後，全校的學生（僧伽四眾在內）一致挽留我再教一學期，我只好答應了；結果我在萬佛城住了整整一年。

在這一年中，我們的生活非常愉快；對來萬佛城教學這件事，我曾寫了一首打油詩，略抒我的感受：

有緣來到萬佛城，弦歌再繼喜盈盈。
宣公德行孚眾望，蠡叟心志羨群雄。
讀書學道應習練，拜佛誦經重修行。
甚喜庭院深且靜，落葉滿園秋意濃。

*　　　*　　　*

我和老伴兒並沒有住在萬佛城裡，主要的原因是我倆還沒有養成素食的習慣。學校為我們購置了一棟平房，就在萬佛城的旁邊，只隔一條小溪，因為幾年沒下雨，小溪都乾涸了，所以我們可以穿過小溪，就走到萬佛城的後園。

我們很喜歡那兒的環境，既清幽，又安靜，和我們在洛杉磯的住屋相比，真可說是城鄉之別；房子本身不算太大，可是後面的院子很大，原來的房主在後院種了二十三棵核桃樹，也種了四種不同的葡萄樹，我們住進的時候正是中秋，核桃和葡萄都結實累累，看了令人喜愛不已。我曾作了一首詩，描述院中的情景：

versity at the City of Ten Thousand Buddhas. Out of my great esteem for the Venerable Master, immediately after my first meeting and long conversation with him, I decided to accept his invitation to go to the City of Ten Thousand Buddhas and take up the duties of teaching again.

In August of 1992, my wife and I arrived at the City of Ten Thousand Buddhas. I taught three classes at Dharma Realm Buddhist University (DRBU): Elementary Chinese, Advanced Classical Chinese, and Beginning Classical Chinese (taught on Wednesday evenings so that the fourfold assembly in the City could attend).

When the Venerable Master heard that I was giving classes at the City of Ten Thousand Buddhas, he was very happy and told Dr. Akpinar, the Chancellor pro tem, to ask me to serve as Chancellor of Dharma Realm Buddhist University. I politely declined. The Venerable Master said, "Well, if you aren't willing to be Chancellor, I will give you another title: 'The Honorable One of the University.' That means everyone in the University should honor and respect you." From that point on, I was known to those at DRBU as 'Honorable One.'

I had originally planned to teach for one semester, but when the semester ended, the entire student body of the University (including the Sangha) requested me to stay on and teach one more semester. I had no choice but to agree, and so I ended up staying at the City of Ten Thousand Buddhas for an entire year.

That year was a very happy one. Here is a poem giving my impressions on teaching at the City of Ten Thousand Buddhas:

I've had the conditions to come to the City of Ten Thousand Buddhas
To play my music and sing in continued joy.
Venerable Hua's virtue wins the trust of the multitudes;
The resolve of the old man from Li County is to praise the heroes.
Pursuing studies and practicing the Way, we should refine ourselves.
Bowing to the Buddhas and reciting Sutras, we stress cultivation.
I delight in the yard's profound tranquility.
Fallen leaves cover the ground; it is deep in the autumn.

*　　　*　　　*

My wife and I didn't actually live in the City of Ten Thousand Buddhas, mainly because we had not yet become accustomed to a totally vegetarian diet. The University bought a one-story house right next to the City for us to stay in. We were separated from the City by a stream, which had dried up due to several years of drought, and so we simply had to cross the stream to reach the back of the City.

We were very pleased with the secluded and peaceful surroundings. It was a great contrast to our residence in Los Angeles. The house itself was not large, but it had a spacious backyard. The original owner had planted twenty-three walnut trees and four varieties of grapevines in the backyard. We moved in during mid-autumn, and the walnut trees and grape vines were laden with fruit. The sight of this delighted us to no end. I wrote a verse describing our yard:

秋雨初停藍滿天，
移居小鎮頗悠閑。
院內葡萄多甜脆，
門前花草漸枯乾。
胡桃遍地須人撿，
種籽盈籠待鳥啣。
陶公常道田園美，
我今方悟靖節言。

「註：陶公指的是晉代詩人陶潛，字淵明，諡靖節。」

During the height of autumn, we came for the first time, when the
  skies were blue.
How leisurely we are in this small town to which we have moved!
Grapes sweet and crisp fill the yard;
The plants by the door are gradually withering.
Walnuts cover the ground with no one to gather them;
Seeds fill the feeder, waiting for birds to eat them.
The Elder Tao often spoke of the beauty of fields and gardens;
I finally understand the words of that man of quiet integrity.

(Note: The Elder Tao refers to the Jin dynasty poet Tao Qian. His other name was Yuanming, and he was posthumously known as Jingjie 'quiet integrity.')

* * *

上人並不長住在萬佛城，因為分支道場有六、七處，所以宣公必須到各道場巡迴宣揚聖道，教導弟子。可是我剛到萬佛城講課的時候，師父正巧也到萬佛城小住數週。在萬佛城的時候，除了為弟子們開示之外，每週必上一堂對聯課；他知道我對作對聯很有興趣，於是約我參加，我欣然答應了。可是，他提醒我，對聯課一般是在清晨五時上課，「你能起得來嗎？」他笑著問我。「當然，沒問題，我可以起得來。」我硬著頭皮回答。

果然，一天朱建和小友打電話來，通知我，「明天早上五點鐘，師父上對聯課，請校尊來參加。」

第二天清早，我趕到城裡，參加師父的早課；我沒有料到，那天師父出的上聯正是：

楊校尊授洋文楊洋同音不同字。

我到達妙語堂的時候，堂中已擠滿了人，師父端坐在講台上，等他把上聯寫在黑板上之後，輕輕地問弟子們：「楊校授來了嗎？」我剛進了妙語堂，悄悄地坐在後面，聽到了師父的問話，我才站起來答道，「我來了。」師父聽了一笑。

我一看師父出的對聯，心中明白，我當然要對個下聯；我找了半天，想不出答案；忽然間，靈機一動，我想起了師父曾提到過，他和天主教樞機主教于斌不但是小同鄉而且是好朋友，我立刻寫出下聯：

于教主唱漁歌于漁異形且異義。

The Venerable Master didn't always stay at the City of Ten Thousand Buddhas, because there were six or seven major Way-places and he had to go around to each one to expound the holy teachings and instruct his disciples. However, when I first began teaching at the City of Ten Thousand Buddhas, the Master also happened to come to the City for a temporary stay of several weeks. Whenever he was at the City, in addition to giving instructional talks to his disciples, he would teach a class on matching couplets every week. He knew of my great interest in matching couplets and invited me to take part. I joyfully accepted. Then he reminded me that the class was held at five o'clock in the morning and asked with a smile, "Can you get up in time?" "Sure, I can get up, no problem," I insisted.

One day, my young friend John Chu called and said, "The Master will be teaching a class on matching couplets at five o'clock tomorrow morning and invites you to attend."

Early the next morning, I hurried into the City to join the Master's morning class. To my surprise, the Master gave the following line as the first line:

The Honorable Yang teaches foreign language (yang wen);
Yang and yang are two different words with the same sound.

When I arrived at Wonderful Words Hall, the hall was already filled with people. The Venerable Master was sitting upright on the speaker's platform. After he had written the first line on the blackboard, he softly asked his disciple, "Has Professor Yang arrived?"
I had just entered the hall and quietly taken a seat in the back. Hearing the Master's question, I stood up and answered, "I'm here." The Master smiled.

As soon as I saw the line given by the Master, I knew that I was supposed to come up with a matching line. I pondered for a long while but couldn't think of an answer. In a sudden flash of inspiration, I remembered the Master saying that he was not only from the same village as the Catholic Cardinal Yubin, but also a good friend of his. I immediately wrote the second line:

Cardinal Yu sings fishing (yu) songs;
Yu and yu are different in form as well as meaning.

宣化老和尚追思紀念專集

＊　　　＊　　　＊

到了第二個禮拜，師父又開了對聯課，我當然又去參加了。（雖然起了個大早，還有些不習慣。）這次，師父出的上聯是：

劉金童舉金刀揮利劍刀刀劈空不見血。

我一看，心中明白，原來師父又用我老伴兒的名字做為上聯，可是他大概不好意思用全名（我老伴兒的名字是劉金定）所以改用劉金童（而不是劉金定），讓弟子們對下聯。我明白師父的用意，可是我怕弟子們不瞭解聯中的微妙。我也對上了，我的下聯是：

信言之做言人亂講話人人譏罵未成名。

（註：我曾寫了一篇自傳，用毛筆寫的，呈給師父供參考；因此，師父知道我的身世和家庭情況。）

第三個星期，我又去上師父的對聯課，這回他出的上聯是：

楊雨辰震西將軍克敵制勝如探囊取物。

我一看，心中又明白了，原來這次師父用我兒子的名字編成上聯，讓弟子們對。（註：我兒子的名字是楊西震。我相信除了師父之外，弟子們不會知道我兒子的名字。胡果相居士知道因為我曾把我的小傳寄給她一份。）

我對了兩個下聯；一個是：

胡白水泉中妖怪興風作浪竟傷天害人。

另一個下聯是：

吳古月胡北醫師懸壺濟世以捨己爲人。

到了第四個星期，師父出的對聯不再是我家人的名字了，而是祖（炳民）教授的名字，上聯是：

祖教授孫國父祖孫兩人誰老誰少誰知道。

The following week, the Master gave another class on matching couplets, and of course I went to attend (even though I still wasn't used to getting up so early.) This time, the Master gave the following as the first line:

> *Golden Lad Liu (Liujintong) raised the golden knife and brandished the sharp sword;*
> *With every thrust of the knife, he slashed the air with no blood seen.*

As soon as I saw it, I understood. The Master was using my wife's name as the subject of the first line, but he probably felt it would be impolite to use her full name (her name is Liu Jinding) so he used 'Liu Jintong' instead. Although I understood the Master's intent, I'm afraid his disciples didn't grasp the wonderful meaning hidden in the line. I matched it with the line:

> *It was told in a letter, but the letter writer spoke recklessly;*
> *Every person scolded and ridiculed him,*
> *so he didn't become famous.*

(Note: I once wrote an autobiographical sketch using Chinese brush and presented it to the Venerable Master. Thus, the Master knows the details of my personal life and family.)

The third week, I again participated in the Master's matching couplets class. The Master gave the following line to be matched:

> *Yang Yuchen, the general who shocked the West, conquered enemies and won battles as easily as one digs into a pocket to take something out.*

When I saw it, I understood it at once. The Master had composed the line based on my son's name. (My son's name is Yang Xizhen [Editor's note: Xizhen 西 means "one who shocked the West," and the words *Yu* 雨 and *chen* 辰 when combined form the word 'shock' 震.] I don't think any of the Master's disciples knew my son's name. Helen Woo knew because I had given her a copy of my autobiographical sketch.)

I came up with two matching lines. The first one is:

> *Hu Baishui, the freak in the spring, stirs up the wind and makes waves, doing nothing but hurting heaven and harming the people.*
> [Note: *Bai* 白 and *shui* 水 combine to make the word 'spring' 泉.]

Another matching line says:

> *Wu Guyue, a doctor from Hubei, suspended the pot and saved the world, renouncing himself for the sake of others.*
> [Note: *Gu* 古 and *yue* 月 combine to make the word *Hu* 胡.]

In the fourth week, the Master's line was no longer based upon the names of my family members. Instead it mentioned the name of Professor John Tsu. It said:

> *Professor Tsu ('grandfather') and Founding Father Sun ('grandson'): Of the grandfather and the grandson, who is old and who is young—who knows?*

我對的下聯是：

男醫生女護士男女兩位孰好孰壞孰品評。

我在萬佛城的一年中，我參加了十幾堂師父的對聯課，獲益匪淺；我同意師父的想法，作對聯是訓練思考的最佳途徑。

諺云：「禮尚往來」又說：「來者不往，非禮也。」宣公既然出了上聯，讓大家（包括師父宣公在內）對下聯，那我也就出了我的上聯：

萬佛城萬佛成佛佛光普照。

四眾弟子們看了這個上聯，都低頭細想對個下聯，但是半天沒人能對得上；宣公確是一位名家，稍加思索，立刻在黑板上寫了下聯，即

千花山千仙獻花花香遠播。

我自己也百思不得要領，想了半天，也想不出合適的下聯來。因此，我越加讚佩宣公的技藝高人一等。

有一次，當四眾弟子們正在絞盡腦汁想下聯的時候，我正好站在師父的旁邊，他低聲地對我說道：「你可知道濟顛和尚的故事？」我說不知道。師父就說，在濟顛和尚出家以前，他住在丈人家，生活拮据，情緒不佳；有一天，他的丈人看到他這個樣子，就給他出了一個上聯：

寄寓客家牢守寒窗空寂寞。

濟顛僧看了，知道丈人在諷刺自己；於是稍加思索，就寫了一個下聯：

迷途遠避退還蓮逕返逍遙。

寫完之後，沒有多久，他就出家當了和尚。

我以為這個故事頗饒趣味，因此記在這裡，作為紀念。

正因為師父曾用我和我的家人寫成上聯，我也不甘示弱，就用師父的法號作了一副對聯：上聯是

宣揚佛法化育英才老禪師德高望重人景仰。

My matching line was:

A male doctor and a female nurse: of the man and the woman, who is good and who is bad—who can judge?

During the year I spent at the City of Ten Thousand Buddhas, I participated in more than ten matching couplets classes given by the Master and derived considerable benefit. I agree with the Venerable Master's view: matching couplets is an excellent way to train one's thinking.

It is said, "Propriety must be observed mutually." It is also said, "If one does not return the favor, then one has not observed propriety." Since the Venerable Master gave everyone (including himself) so many first lines to match, here's my first line:

At the City of Ten Thousand Buddhas, ten thousand Buddhas attain Buddhahood; the Buddhas' light shines on all.

The disciples lowered their heads and tried to think of matches, but no one came up with anything for a long time. The Venerable Master, however, was a genuine expert. After brief consideration, he wrote the following second line on the board:

At the Mountain of a Thousand Flowers, a thousand immortals offer up flowers; the flowers' fragrance wafts afar.

I racked my brains but couldn't come up with a suitable matching line myself. Thus, I stood in even greater awe of the Venerable Master's outstanding skill.

One time, as the disciples were racking their brains trying to come up with a match, I happened to be standing at the Master's side. He spoke to me in a low voice, "Do you know the story of Venerable Jidian?" I replied that I didn't. The Master then told me before the Venerable Jidian left the home-life, he was living in his fiancee's. He was poverty-sticken and moody. One day, his fiancee saw his condition and gave him a line of verse to match:

Living here as a guest, you are accompanied only by the loneliness of the chilly window.

Venerable Jidian knew that his fiancee was making fun of him, and with hardly a thought, he composed a matching line:

Going far away to escape the road of delusion, I shall return to the lotus path of leisure.

Not long afterwards, he left the home-life and became a monk.

I found this story very interesting and have recorded it here so that it will be remembered.

Since the Venerable Master had used my name and the names of those in my family in his couplets, I wasn't going to be outdone, so I used the Master's Dharma name in a matching couplet. The first line goes:

Proclaiming and propagating the Buddhadharma, teaching and nurturing superior talents, the Elder Chan Master has lofty virtue and high repute, and people all look up to him.

下聯是：

度脫罪愆輪轉紅塵大和尚心平氣和合郡歡欣。

遺憾的是，我做好了，沒敢呈給師父請他指正，我只告訴了胡公浩兩三個小友，希望他們還記得這副對聯。

＊

在萬佛城的時候，有一次宣公上人和我倆談話，他提到他辦學的心願，問我有沒有什麼主意；我就把我的想法通盤告訴上人。回到住所，我把我的建議寫成一篇「萬言書」呈給上人參考，沒過幾天，師父告訴我，「我非常同意你的辦學方案。」

我的建議是：在法界佛教大學名下，先成立兩個研究院，一個是佛學研究院，另一個是中國文化研究學院，這兩個學院合併成為一所「至聖研究學院」，作為法大的分校，建立在灣區附近。佛教總會已經在聖瑪提奧（San Mateo）買到一所房屋，即原來的基督教青年會舊址，師父說，可以把這所房子改建一下，做為至聖學院的校址。可惜，因為種種原因，改建一事並未成功。這是三年前的舊話了，至今想起來，我仍感遺憾。

＊

宣公上人不但在美國弘揚佛法，改革教育，而且倡導敬老尊賢的美德。一九九二年十二月二十日，法界佛教總會發起第一次敬老節，在洛杉磯的天恩素食餐廳舉行。宣公上人為這場盛宴命名為「尊老重賢敬德壽筵」，邀請了當地七十歲以上的老人參加。他並且做了一副壽聯，懸掛在餐廳中間，壽聯是：

尊老重賢　耆年壽考　福慧雙圓
學佛習聖　耄耋齡高　道德齊臻

橫批是：　松柏長青

此外，師父還寫了一首七律，詩云：

The second line says:

Rescuing and liberating those bound by offenses, turning the wheel amid worldly defilements, the Venerable Abbot is calm and peaceful and the multitudes are delighted.

I regret that I never presented this couplet to the Master to ask for his critique. I only told Howard Hu and two or three other young friends. I hope they remember this couplet.

＊　　＊　　＊

While I was living at the City of Ten Thousand Buddhas, the Venerable Master once mentioned to me his wish to set up and administer schools and asked me if I had any thoughts on this. I spilled my thoughts to the Master, telling him all my ideas. After I returned to my residence, I wrote out my suggestions in ten thousand words and submitted it to the Master. In a few days, the Master told me, "I quite agree with your proposal for setting up a school."
(Note: My proposal was to set up two graduate institutes under Dharma Realm Buddhist University; one would be a Buddhist Studies Institute and the other a Chinese Culture Institute. Together, they would be called the Zhisheng Graduate Institute and would be a branch of DRBU in the Bay Area. The Dharma Realm Buddhist Association had purchased a former YMCA building in San Mateo. The Master said it could be renovated and serve as the site of the Jhirrsheng Graduate Institute. Unfortunately, for various reasons the renovation was not successfully completed. Those were the plans of three years ago. Even today, I am filled with regret when I think of them.)

＊　　＊　　＊

The Venerable Master Hua not only propagated the Buddhadharma and began educational reform, he also promoted the virtues of respecting the elderly and honoring the worthy. On December 20, 1992, the Dharma Realm Buddhist Association held the first Celebration for Respecting the Elderly at Tian En Vegetarian Restaurant in Los Angeles. The Venerable Master Hua called the luncheon "A Birthday Banquet to Revere the Elderly, Esteem the Worthy, and Respect the Virtuous." Seniors over seventy were invited to attend. The Master also wrote a matched couplet, which was hung in the dining hall. The couplet said:

Respect elders and honor the worthy
for their seniority and longevity,
thus perfecting blessings and wisdom.
Learn from the Buddhas and study with the sages,
and at the advanced age of seventy or eighty,
one will attain the Tao and virtue.

The horizontal title read: "Evergreen like the pine and cedars."

尊老重賢孔孟訓，
學佛習聖釋子傳。
耆年壽考祖師教，
耄耋齡高天地寬。
福慧雙圓黎民慶，
道德齊臻草木歡。
竹梅冰雪愧予志，
松柏長青祝君安。

　我早已告訴上人，在洛杉磯我們十位退休的大學教授，組織了一個午餐會，定名為「十老還童」會，每月舉行一次聚餐，仿效當年的「竹林七賢」的故技，也效法王羲之（右軍）等人的「蘭亭」會聚；我們這十名成員有吳俊升先生、王師復先生、丁驌先生、楊治全先生、李邁光教授、丁時範教授、胡國材先生、鐵鴻業教授、楊訓苕教授，和我。其中吳俊升先生最年長，那年已有高壽九十一歲，楊訓苕教授是我們的小弟弟，剛剛七十歲（虛歲），其餘八位都在七十歲之間，可以說是七老八十的老人了。師父叫我傳話，約請眾學人參加盛會。那天除了丁驌教授因事不克出席外，其餘還童會的「老人」們都來了，真個是濟濟一堂，十分熱鬧。

　那天的敬老會中，最年長的壽星是一百零四歲柬埔寨籍的 Dharmawara 法師，其次應該是吳俊升教授了。為了表示敬重，宣公請這幾位老人坐在首席。那天正趕上白玉堂老先生（宣公的三哥）八十歲的誕辰，我當場做了一首白話詩，給「三哥」祝壽；我的詩是：

人生七十很平常，八十應是少年郎。
生活九十才開始，願君福壽永綿長。

　我高聲朗誦，大家聽了，同聲喝采。我還領導會眾唱「生日快樂歌」，為在座的老人慶祝生日。

　師父並在國際譯經院定期講座的法會上，宣佈在每年農曆十一月二十七日前後一天的假日，舉行一年一度的敬老節。

The Venerable Master also wrote another eight-line verse with seven characters to a line:

> To respect elders and honor the worthy is the instruction
> of Confucius and Mencius.
> To learn from the Buddhas and study with the sages is the teaching
> transmitted by the disciples of Shakyamuni.
> Seniority and longevity are reached through the
> Patriarchs' teachings.
> At the advanced age of seventy and eighty,
> one knows the vastness of heaven and earth.
> When one perfects blessings and wisdom, all people rejoice.
> When one attains the Tao and virtue, even the grass and trees are
> delighted.
> The bamboo and plum tree, which endure the ice and snow,
> put my resolve to shame.
> I wish all of you good health, resembling the pine and cedar,
> evergreen.

I had told the Venerable Master that ten retired professors, including myself, had formed a club called Ten Seniors Returning to Youth in Los Angeles that met for a monthly luncheon. This club is modeled after the Seven Immortals of the Bamboo Grove and the gathering of Wang Yizhi and his followers. The ten club members included Mr. Wu Junsheng, Mr. Wang Shifu, Mr. Ding Xian, Mr. Yang Zhiquan, Professor Li Maiguang, Professor Ding Shifan, Mr. Hu Guocai, Professor Tie Hongye, Professor Yang Xuntiao, and myself. Mr. Wu Junsheng is the eldest. The year of the birthday banquet, he was already ninety-one. Professor Yang Xuntiao is our "little brother"—he's only seventy. The other eight members are also in their seventies—already very elderly. The Master asked me to invite all of them to the banquet. The entire club came except for Mr. Ding Xian, who had another engagement. Thus, there was a full house at the banquet hall and everyone was bubbling with excitement.

The eldest guest at the birthday banquet was the 104-year-old Bhante Dharmawara from Cambodia. The second eldest was probably Mr. Wu Junsheng. The Venerable Master Hua invited these elders to sit at the table of honor. That day also happened to be the eightieth birthday of the Venerable Master's brother, Mr. Bai Yutang. I extemporaneously composed a verse for his birthday:

> It's very ordinary for people to live to seventy years.
> At eighty, one is still a young man.
> When one reaches ninety, life has just begun.
> I wish you blessings and eternal life!

I recited the verse aloud and everyone applauded. Then I led everyone ing singing "Happy Birthday" for all the seniors.

During his talk at the International Translation Institute, the Venerable Master later announced that a Celebration for Respecting the Elderly would be held every year around the twenty-seventh day of the eleventh lunar month.

*　　　　*　　　　*

最難忘懷的是一九九三年四月，那年正是我七十五歲的生日，自然也是師父上人的生日。弟子們，特別是胡果相居士，很想慶祝師父的七十五華誕，可是她深深地知道，依照佛門法規，一個出家人決不允許慶祝生日的，何況宣公是這樣一立德行崇高的禪宗潙仰宗的第九代傳人，當然不會答應弟子四眾為他過生日的。於是她私自和我商量（胡果相和我是三十年的老友），總要想個法子，為師父慶賀他的七十五誕辰。我立刻想出了一個妙計，我說，不如讓我的家人為我慶生日，我請師父參加我的生日會，我可以在會上宣佈，我們同時也是慶祝師父的華誕，這樣給他一個驚奇，（英文是 surprise）

「不知你覺得怎麼樣？」我問果相。

果相說：「這個主意不錯，不過，這樣不太好，因為我們要對師父說實話；不然，我們不是犯了『不打妄語』的戒律了麼？」

長話短提，果相果然對師父說出為我過生日的原意，也提到我要求師父和我一起過生日的心意。沒想到師父答應了，不過，他提出，要把我的名字放在前面，把他的名字放在後面。

四月四日那天，在洛杉磯的長堤聖寺舉行了第一次為師父慶生的法會。師父興緻勃勃，事前為慶生會作了一副對聯，上聯是：

光頭禿眉銀鬚飄灑南極仙翁降臨祝蝦賀禧。

下聯則是

輪耳寬額赤膽忠誠十方英俊赴宴源遠流長。

橫匾是：東西聚餐大同快樂長幼歡筵

師父把對聯作好之後，吩咐朱建和居士，讓我把對聯寫好；我當然欣然從命，雖然我的書法不怎麼樣，可是師父叫我寫，不請他人代筆，足見他對我的厚愛。

四月四日正好是我的農曆生日（三月十三日），也是我的兒子（楊西震）的農曆生日（他的陽曆生日是四月十日）；相當地湊巧。四月中，胡果相、胡果實伉儷也過生日，真是難得。（果相提醒我，不要提出她倆的生日。）

為了慶賀師父的誕辰，我送給師父一首詩，親筆寫好，裝上鏡框，當場送給宣公做為紀念；我的賀詩寫的是：

Another occasion that I will never forget was in April 1993. It was the time of my seventy-fifth birthday, which was also the Venerable Master's birthday. The Master's disciples, particularly Upasika Helen Woo, wished very much to celebrate the Master's seventy-fifth birthday. However, she was well aware that, in the Buddhist custom, a left-home person would never permit his birthday to be celebrated. How much the less would the Venerable Master, the eminently virtuous Ninth Patriarch of the Weiyang Sect, allow his disciples to celebrate his birthday. Therefore, she discussed the matter with me in private (for we have been friends for thirty years) and tried to think of a way to celebrate the Master's seventy-fifth birthday. I had a bright idea. "How about if my family holds a birthday party for me and I invite the Venerable Master to come? Then during the party, I will announce that we are also celebrating the Master's birthday. It will be a surprise! What do you think?" I asked Helen.

She said, "Not a bad idea. But we have to tell the Master the truth. Otherwise we'll be breaking the precept against lying."

To make a long story short, Helen told the Master of her original intention to celebrate my birthday and mentioned that I wished my birthday and the Master's birthday to be celebrated together. Unexpectedly, the Master agreed, on one condition: that my name be placed before his name.

The first Dharma assembly to celebrate the Venerable Master's birthday was held on April 4 at Long Beach Monastery in Los Angeles. The Master was in high spirits. Earlier on, he had composed a couplet for the occasion. The first line said:

Bald-headed and without eyebrows, his silvery beard flying freely,
The God of Longevity descends to offer congratulations on this birthday.

The second line said:

With noble ears and broad foreheads, in utter devotion and loyalty,
The eminent ones of the ten directions join the banquet to continue the lineage.

The horizontal title read:

East and West congregate, in the happiness of perfect unity, at a joyful banquet for old and young.

The Master told John Chu to ask me to write the couplet in Chinese calligraphy, and I happily complied. Although I'm not a great calligrapher, the Master asked me and not someone else to write the couplet; thus I felt he showed great affection for me.

It was a great coincidence that April 4 happened to be my lunar calendar birthday (the thirteenth of the third lunar month) and also the lunar calendar birthday of my son (Yang Xizhen) (his birthday on the Western calendar is April 10). Helen and Wesley Woo were also celebrating their birthdays in April. This was truly rare. (Helen asked me not to mention their birthdays.)

To honor the Master's birthday, I presented him with a poem that I had written by hand and framed. It says:

宣揚佛法渡重洋，
化育英才利萬邦；
上界菩薩發智慧，
人間導師啓愚盲。

（這是一首「藏頭詩」，每句的第一個字讀在一起，正是宣化上人四字。）

師父聽了，點頭微笑，席間不加思索，立刻回贈我兩首詩；第一首是：

博治淹貫一通儒，
聲音清朗展鴻圖。
富國植林樵吾材，
修身齊家壯志足。

第二首則是：

精神充沛豪氣壯，
蠡縣癡翁幽默奇。
山僧笨拙撰俚句，
祝君百歲更無疑。

（註：我為了那首詩，想了好幾天，最後才僥倖想出了四句。而師父上人在會上即席口占七言絕句兩首，讀起來鏗鏘有聲，語意深奧，真不愧是一位博學高士，我自嘆弗如了。）

*

據果相說，那天到會的不下千人，佛堂上和後園中都坐滿了賀客，真應了師父的聯句所說的「十方英俊赴宴，源遠流長」那句話了。

一九九三年七月，我在法大的教授任務完成之後（本來只答應教一學期，後來經學生們的要求，我又教了一學期，共一學年），我們回到洛杉磯，再度過退休生活。可是，正趕上師父也來到長堤聖寺小住，於是我別出心裁想和宣公聚會幾次，不是閒談，而是藉機會多認識師父的心路歷程，多聆聽他的教益，以便多增進我們之間的友誼。我深深地相信，自從宣公上人和我結交以來，他從來沒有把我當做外人，卻把我當做一個知音密友。每當他住在萬佛城的時候，除了經常上他的對聯課之外，我們常常談話，師父對我無話不談，我對師父自然

To propagate the Buddhadharma, you came across the ocean.
You nurture superior talents and benefit all nations.
A Bodhisattva of the higher realm, you inspire our wisdom.
A teacher in the world, you guide the foolish and blind.

(Take the first word of each line in Chinese, and you get "Venerable Master Hsuan Hua.") When the Venerable Master heard me read it, he nodded and smiled, and spontaneously composed two poems for me. The first poem goes:

Widely learned and erudite, he is such a penetrating scholar.
His clear, resonant voice opens up a bright future.
Enriching the country and planting the woods,
    he trains the talented.
He cultivates himself, regulates his family,
    and has great aspirations.

The second poem says:

With full energy and a magnificent spirit,
The sentimental old man from Li County has a unique sense
    of humor.
The dull-witted monk from the mountain composed
    these rustic lines
To wish you a hundred years for sure.

(It took me several days of hard thinking before I came up with the four lines of my poem. The Venerable Master, right during the celebration, was able to spontaneously compose seven-character verses that are both pleasant to read aloud and deeply meaningful. He fittingly deserves to be called an erudite scholar, and I sigh that I cannot match up to him.)

*   *   *

According to Helen, at least a thousand people attended the celebration. Both the Buddhahall and the garden were seated to capacity. It was truly as the Venerable Master's couplet said, "The eminent ones of the ten directions join the banquet to continue the lineage." In July 1993, after my professorial duties at the Dharma Realm Buddhist University were finished (originally I had agreed to teach for one semester, but at the request of the students, I taught an additional semester, completing one full academic year), I returned to my retirement life in Los Angeles. Just at that time, the Venerable Master happened to take up temporary residence at Long Beach, so I entertained the idea of getting together with the Master a few times, not just for idle conversation, but to get to know the Master better, to become familiar with his thinking and experiences, to listen to his teachings, and to further our friendship. I can say with absolute conviction that ever since the Venerable Master met me, he never regarded me as an outsider. Rather, he treated me as an intimate friend. Whenever the Master was at the City of Ten Thousand Buddhas, in addition to attending his matching couplets classes, I had numerous conversations with him. The Master discussed everything under the

也是無話不說，有時候還常常開個玩笑，以博他一笑。是的，弟子們，特別是胡果相居士，也從旁觀察到，每逢我們兩人閒談的時候，師父常常是笑口常開，臉上永遠帶著歡愉的笑容。他離開萬佛城的時候，不論在柏林根，或是在長堤聖寺，他總是打電話來，問我的生活近況。有一次我聽到他的聲音，我就隨便說一句：「一日不見，如三秋兮。」師父聽了，哈哈大笑，說道：「你可不能用這樣的字眼兒，因為那是男女談情的話。」我立刻說：「我們兩人也可以談情啊，友情啊，不對嗎？」師父笑而不答。

當然，我以認識宣公上人這位高僧為榮，七十五歲那年，我曾寫了一首「七五有感」的詩：

人生七十已平常，七五應是少年郎。
名利全拋心安順，是非不惹免彷徨。
讀書每感時光短，問道宜存志氣昂。
晚年欣逢知音友，共奏弦歌伴夕陽。

為了「問道」，為了更瞭解這位知音友，我提出了和宣公談話的這個要求，沒料到師父慨然應允；這樣，從七月開始到九月初旬，我們二人曾談過十幾次的話。最初只是我們兩個人在長堤聖寺的二樓會客室談天，後來，柏林根和萬佛城的弟子們聽到了這件事，也要求師父准許他們旁聽，於是，最後兩次是在長堤聖寺的佛堂舉行，當地的弟子們也可以前來旁聽，萬佛城和柏林根兩地的弟子們則用電話傳播；弟子們也可以隨時發問，師父也是有問必答，情況非常歡洽。

我最初的用意是打算從師父的口中得以認識師父這一生的修道經過，這樣，我可以根據他的口述，編寫一部「宣化上人的傳記」。遺憾的是，九月中師父必須去其他道場巡迴開示，我們之間的談話就只好暫停了。

*　　　*　　　*

此後，每逢師父來到長堤聖寺，我一定和他會面。有一次，他的一位老友程曦教授來長堤聖寺拜望上人，住在長堤聖寺，師父知道我和

sun with me, and so naturally I also talked about everything with the Master. In fact, I often joked with him, hoping to make him laugh. His disciples, particularly Laywoman Helen Woo, also noticed that whenever the two of us were together, the Master always had a smile on his face. When the Master was not at the City, whether he was in Burlingame or Long Beach, he would regularly call me and inquire about my life. Once when I heard his voice on the phone, I casually said, "One day without seeing you is like three autumns." Hearing my words, the Venerable Master laughed and said, "You can't use that expression. Those are words of affection used by lovers." I replied, "The two of us can also use words of affection to express the affection of friends, right?" The Master laughed and didn't answer.

Of course, I am honored to have known the Venerable Master Hua, such an eminent monk. In my seventy-fifth year, I wrote a poem entitled "Feelings at Seventy-five":

It's very ordinary for people to live to seventy years.
At seventy-five, I am still a young man.
Renouncing all fame and gain, I've set my mind at ease.
Avoiding gossip and mischief, I save myself from
    worry and agitation.
As I immerse myself in studying, I feel the time is short.
When inquiring about the Way, I should have a lofty resolve.
In the latter part of my life, I'm happy to have met
    a bosom friend.
As companions in the sunset of life, we make music
    and sing together.

With the aim of "inquiring about the Way" and understanding my bosom friend better, I asked the Venerable Master if I could interview him. What I didn't expect was that the Venerable Master would generously assent. Thus, from the beginning of July to early September, we met ten times. At first, it was just the two of us chatting casually in the meeting room on the second floor of Long Beach Sagely Monastery. Later, when disciples at Burlingame and the City of Ten Thousand Buddhas heard about it, they asked the Venerable Master if they could also listen in. Thus, the last two meetings were held in the Buddhahall at Long Beach Sagely Monastery. The local disciples were invited to participate, and disciples at the City of Ten Thousand Buddhas and Burlingame were hooked up with a long-distance telephone call. Disciples were allowed to ask questions at any time, and the Venerable Master would answer them. It was a very joyful occasion.

My original intent was to gain a better understanding of the Venerable Master's lifetime of cultivation through his own words. Based on his words, I could then write a *Biography of the Venerable Master Hua*. Unfortunately, because the Venerable Master had to travel to the other Way-places to give instructional talks, our interviews were temporarily interrupted in mid-September.

*　　　*　　　*

Every time the Venerable Master came to Long Beach Sagely Monastery after that, I would always meet with him. One time, his old friend Professor Cheng Xi paid a call on the Master and stayed at Long Beach Sagely Monastery. The Master knew that Professor Cheng Xi

程曦教授是老同學，所以打電話來，約我和程兄見一次面，我立刻趕去長堤，大家相見，歡慰異常。師父當年在香港弘法的時候，就和程曦交成道友，時常往還。程曦和我同是燕京大學畢業生。我在匹茲堡大學任教的時候，曾約程教授到匹大教暑期學校（程教授在愛荷華大學任教多年，直到退休為止），因此我們也相當熟悉。

還有一次，洛城有四、五十人皈依師父，當天晚上師父邀我為這些新皈依的弟子們講話，我也為此感到莫大的光榮。

又有一次，楊作相居士從天津來洛城拜謁師父，宣公也特別邀我參加在金輪寺舉行的晚間法會，並要我坐在首席，給會眾們講話。

在萬佛城的那一年，除了在他的對聯課上，師父總邀我站在講台上，幫助他改正弟子們所寫的下聯之外，每次他給弟子們在佛堂中開示，宣公總是約我參加，坐在他的左側，而且給弟子四眾們講話。

還有一次，萬佛城附近的漢堡大學的學生到萬佛城來參觀，師父特別叫我給學生們講話。我記得我曾用太平洋做比喻，我說：「過去我們所認識的太平洋，早已因為現代科技的發達，已經不是什麼「洋」，而應該稱做「太平河」了；而中國就在「河」的對岸，中國對美國來講，已經不是什麼「外國」，而是「近鄰」了：耶穌曾對門徒們說：「你應該愛鄰人」；所以，我們不應該對中國存有歧視的念頭……」，我說完了那段話後，我偷眼看看師父，只看到他點頭微笑示意，似乎對我的談話表示讚許。

這樣的例子，多得不可枚舉，我相信三年以來，自從我和宣公結緣以來，他對我的一言一行瞭若指掌，而我對他的德行學識，也佩服得五體投地。我曾經和師父相約，等我們兩人年逾八十之後，我們攜手隱退林下，那時候，我們有的是時間交往，我也有的是時間向他領教佛教的奧祕，他也有的是時間以詩詞自娛，你做我和，以文會友。沒想到他竟離我先去。噩耗傳來，使得我欲哭無淚，我只能用下面的輓聯，略表我的哀悼！

問道失正路，
知音少一人！

and I were old classmates, so he called me and arranged for me to see my classmate. I hastened over to Long Beach, and we had an extremely happy reunion. During the period when the Master was propagating the Dharma in Hong Kong, he and Cheng Xi had become good friends and had often visited each other. Cheng Xi and I are both graduates of Yenjing University. When I was teaching at the University of Pittsburgh, I arranged to have Professor Cheng Xi come to the University of Pittsburgh to teach summer school. (He taught at the University of Iowa for many years before he retired.) Thus, we know each other quite well.

Another time, forty or fifty people took refuge with the Venerable Master in Los Angeles. That evening, the Venerable Master gave me a great honor by inviting me to speak to those disciples who had newly taken refuge.

On another occasion, when Upasaka Yang Zuoxiang came from Tianjin (China) to pay his respects to the Venerable Master, the Master invited me to take part in the Dharma assembly in the evening. He asked me to sit at the front and speak to the assembly.

During my year at the City of Ten Thousand Buddhas, whenever the Venerable Master held a class on matching couplets, he would ask me to stand on the stage and help correct the matching lines written on the board by his disciples. Every time the Master gave an instructional talk to his disciples, he would also have me sit on his left and speak to the disciples.

Another time, the Venerable Master asked me to speak to students from the nearby Humboldt State University who had come to visit the City of Ten Thousand Buddhas. I remember using the analogy of the Pacific Ocean. I said, "Due to the advances of modern scientific technology, the Pacific Ocean as we knew it is no longer an "ocean." We should rather call it the "Pacific River," and China is on the other bank of this "river." From America's standpoint, China is no longer a distant foreign country, but a close neighbor. Jesus said to his disciples, 'Love thy neighbor.' Thus, we should not hold prejudices against China..." I finished speaking and stole a peek at the Venerable Master. He nodded his head and smiled, as if expressing approval for my words.

Examples like these are too numerous to relate. In the three years that I have known the Venerable Master, I believe that he has understood my every word and deed as clearly as the palm of his hand. I, in turn, have felt the utmost respect for his virtuous character and erudition. Once I made a plan with the Master to retreat into seclusion in the woods when we both turned eighty. At that time, we would have ample time for friendly conversations. I would have plenty of time then to seek instruction from him in the mysteries of Buddhism. He would also have plenty of time to compose verses for his own amusement. We would compose things together and be friends brought together by literature. I never expected that he would leave before I did. When I heard the sad news, I wanted to cry but no tears came. I can only use the following couplet to express my grief:

Seekers of the Way have lost the proper path;
I have lost a bosom friend!

感懷師父上人

IN MEMORY OF OUR TEACHER, THE VENERABLE MASTER

恩師已騎白象去，他日慈悲乘願來；逝者如斯動天地，德被群情濟眾生。

Our teacher has left, riding on a white elephant.
We hope that one day he will come back riding on his vows.
The one who passed away was such that he could shake heaven and earth.
His virtue protected and rescued all living beings.

普為世間常宣化，甘稱螞蟻作度輪；守靈成就白孝子，弘法西來墓中僧。

He proclaimed and transformed universally for those in the world.
He was willing to be an ant and a ferry.
Staying by the grave, he became known as Filial Son Bai.
Coming to the West to propagate the Dharma, he was the Monk in the Grave.

慈悲流盡血和汗，喜捨怎言休與息？震法雷兮擊法鼓，鬼哭神號幻化奇。

With compassion, he exhausted his blood and sweat.
With his joy and renunciation, how could he think to rest?
The Dharma thunder rumbles and the Dharma drum is struck.
Ghosts and spirits wail; the transformations are unusual.

生老病死視兒戲，語默動靜演真理；開權顯實決了義，財色名利巧作題。

Birth, old age, sickness, and death are but child's play.
In speech and silence, in movement and stillness, he proclaimed the truth,
Opening the provisional to reveal the actual and ultimate meaning.
Wealth, sex, fame, and profit were the topics of his skillful teaching.

常把恩師當明鏡，六大宗旨永銘記。法輪常轉歸故里，慧日破黯大雄力！

We should always take our kind teacher as a bright mirror
And remember the Six Great Principles.
As the Dharma-wheel constantly turns, he returns to his homeland.
His sun-like wisdom breaks through the darkness; his strength is heroic.

果卿、果霖弟子眾等至心頂禮於中國天津　一九九五年八月六日
Disciples Guo Qing, Guo Ling, and others bow sincerely in Tianjing, People's Republic of China on August 6, 1995

六年切磋

SIX YEARS OF STUDYING

釋化來　Shi Hualai

平凡瑣碎妙在常，聖行址跡眾心詳；孜孜兀兀七八載，空空蕩蕩東西洋。
眾眼望穿渾無跡，客心神往卻空房；天人失依渴乳哺，玉箸何期大王膳。

The wonder lies in ordinary, trifling affairs.
The deeds and footsteps of a Sage are known by all.
I wandered arduously for seven or eight years
In the vast expanse between the eastern and western shores.
People may exhaust the limit of their vision, yet can find no trace.
Although visitors come in yearning, they find an empty house.
Gods and humans have lost their refuge and are thirsty for his milk.
When can our jade chopsticks reach the royal feast?

緣起

五臺歸來，接到萬佛聖城的邀請書，幾經挫折，才拿到護照。忽又接到宗教事務處的通知，不准出國，要繳回護照。是菩薩加被，才安然來城。這一轉一折，正好促成我能常住聖城。頌曰：

五臺歸來喜氣隆，
上人邀我會群雄；
長風翩翩鐵鳥度，
源頭瀅瀅活水通。

初會

一天，一位老比丘進來，揹一只僧袋，在床上坐下，我便頂禮。

我獻上帶來的禮物。第一件茶葉。他說：「你來的不巧，我昨天已戒茶。」聽他的口氣，我知道是師父上人本人。這使我體會到師父謙光可掬。

第二件禮物，是虛雲老和尚與映徹和尚的題字照片。並且說：「虛老曾經給我回封信

Beginnings

When I returned from Mount Wutai, I received a letter inviting me to the Sagely City of Ten Thousand Buddhas. After several complications, I finally got my passport. Then I was suddenly notified by the Religious Affairs Office that I was not allowed to leave the country and had to surrender my passport. With the aid of the Bodhisattvas, I finally made it to the City. This turn of events caused me to decide to stay in the Sagely City permanently. A verse says:

Returning from Wutai, I am filled with joy.
The Venerable Master has invited me to join the heroes.
Flying through the wind, the iron bird brings me across.
The source is sparkling and the water bubbles forth.

The First Meeting

One day, a Bhikshu came in carrying a monk's bag over his shoulder. He sat down on the bed, and I made obeisance to him.

Then I offered up the presents I had brought. The first was a pack of tea leaves. He said, "You didn't come in time. I decided to quit tea yesterday." From his way of speaking, I knew it was the Venerable Master himself. This made me aware of the Master's humor.

The second present was a signed photograph of Elder Master Hsu Yun and Master Yingche. I said, "The Elder Hsu once wrote a letter back to me." The Venerable Master said, "It wasn't written by the Elder Hsu!" I was very shocked. In all these years, I've encountered all sorts of difficulties and temptations to sin, but because I took the Elder Master's letter as my standard, I wasn't moved and remained as pure and true as before. So I argued, "It's the Elder Hsu's way of speaking. No one else could simu-

。」師父說：「那不是虛老寫的！」我非常吃驚。歷年來，受盡顛沛流灕，各種誘惑，我之所以能夠不為境轉，純真如故，就是以虛老的信為楷模。於是辯道：「是虛老的口氣，別人代不了。」師父不假思索，隨口答道：「是虛老說的，別人寫的。」應變之速，我無法窺期端倪。這使我體會師父的直心直意。

第三件禮品，是毛筆。師父說：「是大阿辟嗎？」我沒有聽過這名稱，沒有回答。取出毛筆，遞上。師父說：「是大阿辟。」

第四次則呈上兩樣東西，一幅對聯，一幅立軸。立軸，是我在大陸的師父親手畫的阿彌陀佛像。師父說：「沒有落款不要！」一幅對聯則收下了，目前掛在師父的文物展覽館裡。對聯，是兩年前寫的，師父看了日期，不勝驚訝。我說：「對聯是兩年前寫的，落款是來美時才加上的。不過這對聯有一不尋常的經歷：在大陸時，我住處的樓上失火，火燒掉了對聯後面糊在竹笆上的紙，而對聯卻得幸留存下來。」這對聯的內文是：「九品度眾生，威德無窮極。」有人說：「對聯掛在譯經院二樓。」

禮物呈畢。談話中，師父說：「邀請的事，是法總搞的，我不知道。」（指法界佛教總會邀請我的事）我於是拿出邀請書，將他老人家的簽名指給他看，他沒再說什麼。

最後師父說：「師訪徒三年，徒訪師三年。」這使我體會師父到的事實求是，一絲不苟。頌曰：

初會切磋約六載，期滿歸去圓無在；
寒雁有信同形影，秋水無痕寂去來。

師訪徒

一次，在辦公大樓小課室內，師父對男界法師說法。師父問：「化來法師，你的背怎麼駝得這樣，被人壓迫的嗎？」隨即加持，我沒有重視。果浩居士說：「師父加持是不簡單的，你要重視。」恆律師說：「你以牆壁為準，將頭和背依牆壁成一直線，就這樣鍛煉。」幾年的努力，頭能抬起來。

當時上課時，有一位居士供養師父一瓶花旗蔘。師父隨手拿給我說：「化來法師，供養你。」

late it." The Master shot back, "It was dictated by the Elder Hsu and written by someone else." His quick response left me without a clue. This allowed me to perceive the Master's forthrightness.

The third present was a Chinese calligraphy brush. The Master asked, "Is it the large *api* type?" I had never heard of that name and didn't answer. I took out the brush and presented it. The Master said, "It's a large *api*."

Fourth, I presented two things: a couplet and a vertical scroll.

The vertical scroll was a painting of Amitabha Buddha done by my master in mainland China. The Master said, "It's not signed, so I won't take it." He accepted the couplet. It is now in the Master's exhibition room. I had written the couplet two years ago. The Master saw the date and was quite surprised. I said, "The couplet was written two years ago. I signed it after coming to America. This couplet has an unusual history. When the floor above me caught fire in the place where I was living in the mainland, the fire burned all the paper on the bamboo screen on which the couplet had been pasted, but the couplet was luckily left untouched." The couplet said, "Saving living beings with the nine grades, his awesome virtue is inexhaustible." Someone said that now the couplet is hanging on the second floor of the Translation Institute.

I had finished offering up all the presents. During our conversation, the Master said, "It was the Association that invited you. I didn't know about it." (He was referring to my being invited by Dharma Realm Buddhist Association.) I took out the letter of invitation and pointed out the Master's signature to him. He didn't say anything. Finally the Master said, "The Master visits the disciple for three years, and the disciple visits the Master for three years." This made me realize that the Master went by the facts and was completely serious. A verse says:

After the first meeting, I studied with him for about six years.
When it was over, he returned to perfection and was nowhere.
Like the winter geese bringing their message, the shadow never
    leaves its form.
Like the autumn water without any ripples, he comes and goes
    in stillness.

The Master Visits the Disciple

One time, the Venerable Master was lecturing to the Dharma Masters on the men's side in a small classroom in the Main Administration Building. The Master said, "Dharma Master Hualai, why are you so hunchbacked? Were you bullied by people?" The Master immediately bestowed aid, but I didn't take it seriously. Upasaka Guohao said, "The Master's aid is not that easy to come by. You should value it." Master Heng Lyu said, "Use the wall as your standard. You should practice trying to make your head and back line up straight against the wall." After several years of hard work, now I can lift my head.

During the class, a layperson gave a bottle of American ginseng to the Venerable Master. The Master immediately passed it to me,

這使我體會到師父的愛無偏袒。

我與大陸居士通信曾提過這事：當師父說法時，不點名的批評了。類似的批評，還有三次：其一，房間雜亂，其二，早餐後未結齋，其三，偷看報刊上的裸體照。這使我體會到師父的教育細緻耐心。

對聯課也是師父教化四眾的方式：

修行必先習太極拳，鍛煉身心。（師父）
學道務早識平常心，融會動靜。（化來）

觀音耳根圓通，無音不聞。 （師父）
持地心眼明達，有地皆淨。 （化來）

這使我體會到師父的融會萬法，妙用無窮。

saying, "Dharma Master Hualai, here's an offering for you." This made me see that the Master's kindness is without favoritism.

In my letter to a layperson in mainland China, I mentioned that the Master had criticized me without bringing up my name during his lectures. There were three points of criticism: First, having a messy room. Second, not doing the end-of-meal chant after the noon meal. Third, sneaking a look at nude pictures in a newspaper. This made me realize the Master's attention to details and patience in teaching.

The Venerable Master also used the class on matching couplets to teach the fourfold assembly:

In cultivation, one must first learn taijiquan and discipline the body and mind. (The Master)
In studying the Way, one must early on recognize the ordinary mind and interfuse movement and stillness. (Hualai)

Guanyin attained perfect penetration through the ear; there is no sound he doesn't hear. (The Master)
Earth-Upholding's mind and eyes are bright and penetrating; every piece of ground is pure. (Hualai)

This made me realize the Master's perfect understanding of the myriad dharmas and the inexhaustibility of his wonderful functioning.

一則公案的啓示

INSIGHTS FROM A CHAN STORY

潘志鴻　Pan Zhihong

有關師父上人的圓寂，眾說紜紜，因此想起一則公案。

昔日蘇東坡與佛印禪師一齊打坐，一炷香後，蘇東坡問佛印禪師曰：「我坐得如何？」
禪師曰：「如佛。」
接著禪師反問東坡曰：「吾又如何？」
東坡捉狹曰：「如牛糞。」
蘇東坡回到家中與蘇小妹眉飛色舞談及此事。
小妹答：「你輸矣！」
東坡曰：「為何？」
小妹曰：「禪師心中有佛，而你卻是牛糞。」

《華嚴經》云：「若人欲了知，三世一切佛，應觀法界性，一切為心造。」各位讀者，對於上人的圓寂，你的見解又是如何呢？

People have been saying many things about the Venerable Master's completion of stillness, and this reminded me of a Chan story:

One day Su Dongpo and Chan Master Foyin were meditating together. After an hour of sitting, Su Dongpo asked the Chan Master, "How am I sitting?" Chan Master Foyin replied, "Like a Buddha."

The Chan Master in turn asked Su Dongpo, "And how about me?" Su Dongpo answered jokingly, "Like cow manure."

When Su Dongpo returned home, he exultantly told Su Xiaomei (his sister) the story. Xiaomei replied, "You lost!"

Su Dongpo asked, "Why?" Xiaomei said, "The Chan Master has a Buddha in his mind. You have cow manure in yours!"

The *Avatamsaka Sutra* says, "If people want to know the Buddhas of the three periods of time, they should contemplate the nature of the Dharma Realm. Everything is made from the mind alone." Each of you can reflect upon the Venerable Master's Nirvana: What is your opinion?

文以載道的上人

THE MASTER'S LITERARY WORKS CONVEY THE TRUTH

恆實法師　一九九五年七月二十七日開示於萬佛聖城宣公上人讚頌追思法會

A talk by Dharma Master Heng Sure on July 27, 1995 at the Sagely City of Ten Thousand Buddhas

Many people have sat here in the last few days, and will continue to do so, talking about their memories of their teacher, talking about the Master's contributions to education, to translation and Sutra lecturing, propagating the Dharma, creating the Sangha, making Way-places, and so on. Everyone has said what was on their heart, and we have many more to hear later today. But I wanted to share something that I think is rare.

Probably not many people today, if they were asked what was the Venerable Master's outstanding feature, would say, "The Master was a poet without peer. He was a literati, a writer, an editor, a social commentator, and a historian without peer." And yet the Venerable Master wrote an eight-line verse for every line of the Great Compassion Mantra and every line of the Shurangama Mantra. He wrote the Verses without a Stand for the *Heart Sutra*. He wrote verses for the Patriarchs, adding to Elder Master Hsu Yun's *Lives of the Patriarchs*. He wrote not only verses but excellent rhymed essays. He was a master of prose and verse. The Master's scattered writings, occasional verses, and songs number in the hundreds. One of the things about the Master that has touched me the most is his contribution to literature, in the form of songs, essays, and poetry.

The Master would teach a matching couplets class, in which he would put the first line on the board regarding a state or a situation or a disciple's habits, and invite everyone else to come up and add the second line. It was amazing how just the few Chinese characters of your couplet line could reveal your character, your nature, your shortcomings, your literary skill, your education... He even had children who were not able to speak Chinese come up and put matching couplets on the board that were surprisingly sophisticated in form and refreshingly pure and straight in content. It was a wonderful experience to have the Master teach couplets. It's probably the first time in any American Way-place that a Buddhist teacher has done this (and maybe the first time in Chinese Buddhist history for a long time). So this is just to point to one aspect of our teacher that I think needs to be remembered.

What kind of a poet was he? I'd like to tell a very personal story, because it shows the way the Master taught. Perhaps many people who talked today never actually got a teaching from the Abbot, and they don't what it was really like to be on the receiving end of his teaching—how bittersweet that experience could be. So I'd like to talk about how the Abbot taught me and caught my mind in a place where I didn't even know I was vulnerable. This was on a bowing pilgrimage I did with another monk. We got to a place called Half Moon Bay on the coast. I was bowing along when something inspired me and I wrote down a poem. I thought, "That's a pretty good poem. Boy, I can

在過去幾天裡，人們在這裡談論他們記憶中的恩師上人，及上人對教育、翻譯、講經、弘法、建立僧團、道場等等所做的貢獻。我相信大家還會繼續討論下去。每一個人都說出了他們的心裡話。稍後我們還有機會聽到更多心聲。在此想與大家分享我認為不平凡的一些事。

如果我們問，什麼是上人的特色？也許不會有太多的人說：上人是一位不可望其項背的詩人、文學家、作家、編輯家、社會評論家、歷史學家……。為每一句〈大悲咒〉及〈楞嚴咒〉作一首八句的偈頌；並作《心經非臺頌解》；為祖師們作了偈頌，編入了虛雲老和尚編輯的《佛祖道影》。上人不但作偈頌，也作韻律優美的詩詞。上人的墨寶、詩詞、歌曲、對聯，數以千計。上人最讓我感動的事情之一，是他透過歌曲、詩詞，對文學所作的貢獻。

上人對「對聯」時，會把描述一種境界或弟子習氣的上聯，寫在黑板上，然後要大家對下聯。很不可思議的，寥寥的幾個中國字就能顯示出一個人的性格、優缺點、文學技巧、教育程度等等。上人甚至能使不會說中文的小孩子上前去，在黑板上寫出格調不俗、內容新鮮的對聯。上人教的這門課，是一個非常美好的經驗，美國的佛教史上恐怕是開天闢地的頭一遭，在中國佛教史上也恐怕是久遠以來的頭一回。這裡我只是指出我認為需要記得的恩師的其中一面。

上人是怎樣的一位詩人？我想跟大家講一個私人的故事。從這個故事可以看出上人的教導方式。今天發言的人，恐怕有很多都從來沒有真正地、直接地被上人教導過，所以不曾體會到上人的教導是什麼滋味——是如何地苦樂參半。這裡我想談談上人是如何地，在甚至我不自知是不堪一擊的心地上，逮到我而且教導了我。那是我與另一位出家眾三步一拜，拜到一

write Chinese poetry! This really has captured my state. I'm going to give it to the Master next time I see him." We hadn't seen the Master for about three weeks. When you're cultivating alone, it's really easy to get into a state and think you're hot stuff. My poem went like this: (This is the English translation.)

Words are false; books are many.
Energy is precious, and Buddhas are few.
Still dreaming? Stop talking.
Do no more false thinking.
After awakening, cross living beings over in everything you do.

Pretty good poem, huh? I was working on it—which is called false thinking—I should have been bowing, not thinking about what a great poet I was. I thought, "Well, someday I'll have a chance to read it to the Master." At lunchtime, a familiar station wagon pulled off the road; it was the Master and some other people. After the meal, I cleared my throat and said, "Master, I wrote a poem! Could I read it to you?" He said, "Hmpf! *You* wrote a poem? All right, let's hear it." So I said my poem. He said, "Not bad. But I want to change it." He said,

Your words are false, your excuses are many.
Value your energy, and you can become a Buddha.
You're still dreaming? Really stop talking,
  and do no more false thinking.
After awakening, you'll see all along that
  there hasn't been a single word in it anywhere.

Right on the spot! It took him less than a minute. He turned my own words around and pointed right at my false thinking. My wonderful poem was scattered to the wind. He made it not only a better poem, but exactly the right teaching for my mind. It was like looking in a mirror. Here I'd been, very proud of myself, and in the blink of an eye, the Master showed me—"See? False thinking. Go back to work." So this is the Master—the poet, the literati, and the teacher.

個叫半月灣的海岸時，我靈感突發作了一首詩。當時心裡想：「這首詩好棒。哇！我能用中文寫詩了！這首詩真正地表達了我的境界。詩的內容是這樣的：

言詞虛幻經書多，精神實貴稀有佛，
夢中止語離妄念，覺後盡氣爲眾説。

不錯嘛！是不是！我在思考－－那叫妄想－－我應該一心一意地拜，而不是想自己是了不起的詩人。我對自己說：「我會有機會念給上人聽的。」午齋時，一輛眼熟的旅行車靠路邊停了下來，是上人及其他一些人。結齋後，我清了清嗓子說：「上人，我寫了一首詩，我念給您聽好嗎？」他說：「哼！你作了一首詩？好罷，念來聽聽。」我就念了。「不錯，可是我要改一改。」上人說：

言詞虛幻狡辯多，寶貴精神可成佛，
夢中止語無差念，覺後原來一字沒。

一針見血！而只花了不到一分鐘的時間。上人用我自己的話，轉過來直指我的妄想，我那美妙的詩就在風裡化為烏有。上人不但將這首詩改得更好，而且對我來說是一個最恰當不過的教訓。如照鏡子一樣，我在此孤芳自賞，深以為傲，而在眨眼的瞬間，上人就給了我一個棒喝：「看了！打妄想！還不趕緊努力。」這就是上人：詩人、文人、教師。

念念莫忘生死苦　　心心想脱輪迴圈
虛空粉碎明佛性　　通體脱落見本源

宣公上人作

In every thought, never forget the suffering of birth and death.
In every aspiration, yearn to escape from the wheel of transmigration.
Obliterate empty space and understand the Buddha-nature.
Cast off the entire substance and see the original source.

by Venerable Master Hua

感 師 恩

IN GRATITUDE TO OUR TEACHER'S KINDNESS

章果慶　Sam Jing

觸目心驚跳，習氣毛病跑；
若不勤修行，累劫業示現，
則恐難入道，成佛難上難。
師父領進門，修行在個人；
成佛也由它，墮落也由它，
萬法唯心造。

When we set eyes upon him, our hearts palpitate in fear.
And all our bad habits and faults flee.
If we don't cultivate diligently,
Then the karma of many past eons will manifest
And it will be difficult to enter the Way.
Becoming a Buddha is the most difficult of difficult things.
The teacher leads us in the door,
But we ourselves must cultivate.
It's through our own mind that we become Buddhas
It's also because of our mind that we fall.
The myriad dharmas are made from the mind.

記得在一九八七年五月第一次到萬佛聖城的時候，這是第一次接觸佛教及初次見到師父的機緣。當我的雙眼接觸到師父目光的一剎那，我的心臟好像給人重重地打了一下，心裡是又驚慌是又恐怖，好像過去歲月中所犯的錯誤，所做的錯事都呈現在師父面前，一點也沒有機會隱藏。自己本身的習氣毛病都急急忙忙地從身體裡逃跑出來。回家之後，就主動對太太說以後不喝酒了，對於本來具有貪杯本性，而又有絕不放棄品酒習慣的我，也想不通為什麼會有這樣地改變。

後來有機會接近師父，蒙師父教化，才體會出師父的威德是盡虛空遍法界。而我們凡夫俗子面對師父目光時，就像面對照妖鏡一樣。我們沒有正知正見，不知正道的方向。我們的行住坐臥及為人處世，時時都具有習氣毛病。而師父把我們一一點破，耳提面命。記得師父常說：「為什麼有人怕我，因為他心裡有鬼，自己有愧，所以怕我。」

脾氣須彌山，我執又障道；
若能拋棄它，消失於虛空，
開門見西方，一步入佛國。

脾氣使人生煩惱。我在還沒有見到師父之前，脾氣就像須彌山那麼高、那麼大，一點小事就沒有耐心，就發脾氣。

I remember when I went to the Sagely City of Ten Thousand Buddhas for the first time in May of 1987 (that was my first contact with Buddhism and the first time I saw the Venerable Master), the instant my eyes met the gaze of the Venerable Master, I felt as if my heart had been dealt a heavy blow. I was both startled and frightened. It was as if all the mistakes and wrong deeds I had done in the past were presented before the Venerable Master. I didn't have any chance to hide. All of my personal habits and faults sprang forth from my body in a rush. When I got home, of my own initiative I told my wife that I would never drink alcoholic beverages again. Given my fondness for drinking and my habit of wine-tasting, which I would never have given up before, I couldn't imagine why such a change had taken place in me.

Later on, I had opportunities to draw near the Venerable Master and receive the Master's teachings. It was then that I began to perceive that the Venerable Master's awesome virtue exhausted the bounds of empty space and pervaded the Dharma Realm. When ordinary people face the Venerable Master's gaze, it is like facing a demon-spotting mirror. We lack proper views and proper knowledge and do not know the direction of the proper path. Whether we are moving or still, sleeping or awake, interacting with people or handling affairs, we are never apart from our bad habits and faults. The Venerable Master points out each of our problems, constantly telling and reminding us. I recall the Venerable Master often saying, "Why are some people afraid of me? Because they have ghosts in their hearts. Since they themselves are ashamed, they are afraid of me."

Temper is like Mount Sumeru.
Attachment to self is an impediment to the Way.
If these things are discarded
So that they vanish into thin air,
Then as easily as opening a door, one sees the Western land.
In one step, one enters the Buddha country.

A bad temper causes people to give rise to afflictions. Before I met the Venerable Master, my temper was as high and as great as Mount Sumeru. I would lose my temper over a trifling matter.

記得第一次到萬佛聖城參加法會，當午齋及皈依之後，師父都會坐在大殿內接受大眾頂禮及供養，接引大眾。當時我非常不懂事，自己問自己：「怎麼大家都給師父磕頭？」於是我勉為其難地跪在師父面前問師父：「我的脾氣很壞，不知道怎麼改？」師父的反應是搖一搖頭說：「沒有脾氣。」我很愚癡，不懂師父所說的意思，還笨笨地跪在師父面前幾分鐘才離去。回家就和太太討論，我太太說：「師父的意思是要你絕不發脾氣。」我當時說：「那怎麼可能？」

但是我現在要說：「我一定要盡最大的力量去做到。」為什麼？因為煩惱即是菩提，愚癡代表黑暗，智慧代表光明。師父是光明的象徵，他引領大家離開黑暗，走向光明。所以時時刻刻提醒大家不要發脾氣。

五欲不能除，六根塵六識，
妄想及執著，愚癡不見性，
若能去執著，則能得自在；
想去極樂國，何愁到不了。

我在沒有信佛前是音樂的愛好者，高中大學都喜好把玩樂器，而偏好的音樂是搖滾音樂（魔樂），尤其喜愛把玩吉他。皈依師父以後，還是捨不得放棄彈吉他，偶爾也會把玩一下。

記得有一次，是在赴萬佛聖城參加法會的前一天晚上，做完晚課之後，獨自一人想彈一下吉他，正陶醉在吉他的音樂中，太太來提醒我說：「我們已經皈依師父，應該專心修行，不應該彈吉他。」當時我的心情就像一個小孩，正在玩一個他最喜歡的玩具，突然被大人沒收一樣地憤怒。於是就順手把吉他向梳妝台摔去，並且很憤怒地說：「以後不彈了！打壞以後也沒得彈！」完全失去理性。

次日，參加萬佛城法會，在午齋之前，我照例到大齋堂察看音響系統。突然師父出現面前帶著慈祥的笑容對我說：「章先慶，你來幫我拿一樣東西。」於是我就很恭敬地跟隨師父到齋堂後面一間房子，師父把櫃子打開說：「就是這個東西！」當我看到櫃子裡

The first time I went to the Sagely City of Ten Thousand Buddhas to attend the Dharma session, I remember that after lunch and after the refuge ceremony, the Venerable Master would sit in the Buddhahall and allow people to bow and make offerings to him, gathering in people in this way. Because I didn't understand anything at the time, I thought to myself, "Why is everyone bowing to the Venerable Master?" I reluctantly knelt in front of the Master and said, "I have a very bad temper. How can I change?" The Venerable Master's reaction was to shake his head and say, "Have no temper." Not understanding the meaning of the Master's reply, I stupidly knelt in front of him for several more minutes before leaving. After I got home, I discussed it with my wife. My wife said that the Venerable Master's meaning was, "You should not lose your temper no matter what." At the time I said, "How could that be possible?"

However, now I want to say that I will try my very best to do this. Why? Because afflictions are just Bodhi. Stupidity represents darkness and wisdom represents light. The Venerable Master symbolizes light. He leads everyone to leave darkness behind and to walk towards the light. That's why he is always reminding everyone not to lose his or her temper.

If one cannot get rid of the five desires,
Then the six sense faculties, six sense objects,
*   and six consciousnesses appear.*
With false thoughts and attachments,
One is made stupid and cannot see the nature.
If one can cast off attachments,
Then one will be at ease.
If one wishes to go to the Land of Ultimate Bliss,
What need is there to worry that one cannot reach it?

Before I became a Buddhist, I was a music lover. During high school and college, I liked to play music, and my favorite kind of music was rock-n-roll (demonic music). I especially enjoyed playing the guitar. Even after I took refuge with the Venerable Master, I couldn't give up the guitar—I would still play it occasionally.

I remember once, the night before we were going to the Sagely City of Ten Thousand Buddhas to participate in a Dharma session, after I had finished evening recitation, I had an urge to play the guitar. Just as I was intoxicated by the guitar's music, my wife reminded me, "We've already taken refuge with the Venerable Master. You should concentrate on cultivation and not be playing the guitar." At the time I felt as indignant and angry as a little kid who is playing with his favorite toy when it is suddenly confiscated by an adult. So I flung the guitar at the dresser and retorted angrily, "I won't play it anymore in the future. If it gets broken, I won't be able to play it anyway." I had completely lost my sense of reason.

The next day we went to take part in the Dharma session at the Sagely City. Before the noon meal, I went into the dining hall to check the sound system as usual. Suddenly the Venerable Master appeared in front of me and said to me with a kind smile, "Sam Jing, please help me carry something." I very reverently followed the Master to a small room in the back of the dining hall. The Master opened up a cabinet and said, "This is it." I was shocked to see a guitar lying in the cabinet. I was scared out of my wits, to put it mildly. The Venerable Master said, "A certain Dharma Master used to be very attached to his guitar, so five years ago I

放了一把吉他，我嚇了一大跳，用「屁滾尿流」來形容絕不過份。師父說：「某某法師以前很執著吉他，五年前被我沒收了，現在他明白道理，我就把它還給他，可以拿去做一些有利學生的事。」

從這一件事可以告訴我們，師父的法身是隨時與我們同在，而我們每犯一次錯誤師父都會明察秋毫。在我們修行過程中，師父也對每個不同根器的弟子以不同的方式開示、教化，要我們看破放下五欲，不要被六根、六塵、六識所轉。如果能放下而不執著，就能自在而不罣礙，而依願往生淨土，也是指日可待。

> 貢高與我慢，修行之大忌。
> 斷自己善根，拒絕他善言，
> 不能入正見，亦不入正道。
> 如此修行者，必與魔為鄰。

師父在開示我們時，形容自大的人就像「臭」（由自大兩字組合）一樣的令人討厭。佛的慈悲是大家都想去親近。在修行過程中，自大、自滿是障礙修道之最。

記得在一九八七年，還沒有皈依之前，在家裡就對我岳母說：「我不認為有向他人下跪的必要，因為我都不對我父母親下跪，我為什麼要給師父磕頭？」就在那個星期天　師父在Mission College（米慎學院）開示，開示後，大家都在給師父磕頭，我前思後想要不要去磕頭，最後像有一種無形的力量驅使我向前頂禮師父。師父就對我說：「你這麼大個子，給我磕頭，不怕丟臉？」我嚇了一大跳，心想：「師父怎麼知道我在家說過的話？」事後檢討起來，當初不願下跪磕頭，就是貢高我慢的本性。師父即時加以開示教化，降服我、提拔我，讓我從無知愚癡的世界走向正道，我才有今天；要不然，不接受教化，繼續生活在錯誤的思想裡，永遠是沒有機會走上修行的正道。

記得在一九八八年間，在金山寺每逢星期六下午，師父都會坐在佛殿前的沙發。當時有機會親近師父，和師父對談少許。

took it away from him. Now he understands the principles, so I am going to return it to him. He can use it in activities that are beneficial to students.

This incident shows that the Venerable Master's Dharma body is constantly with us. Every time we make a mistake, the Venerable Master sees it clearly down to the last detail. In the course of cultivation, the Venerable Master also uses different methods to instruct and teach his disciples according to their individual dispositions. He wants us to see through and renounce the five desires and not let ourselves be turned by the six sense faculties, six sense objects, and six consciousnesses anymore. If we can successfully put them down and not cling to them, then we will be at ease and free of impediments. According to our vows, in no time we will certainly be born in the Pure Land.

> *Arrogance and self-conceit*
> *Are absolute taboos in cultivation.*
> *They cause you to cut off your own good roots*
> *And refuse to listen to good advice from others.*
> *You will not be able to develop proper views,*
> *Nor enter the proper path.*
> *Such cultivators will certainly end up*
> *Next door to the demons.*

Once when the Venerable Master was instructing us, he described people with big egos as being "stinky" [in Chinese, the character for "stinky" is composed of the characters for "self" and "big"] and therefore repulsive to others. On the other hand, the Buddha's kindness and compassion makes everyone want to draw near him. In the course of cultivation, an inflated ego and self-conceit are the greatest impediments to practicing the Way.

Before I took refuge in 1987, I remember saying to my mother-in-law at home, "I don't think there's any need for me to kneel in front of anyone else. I don't even kneel in front of my parents, so why should I bow to the Venerable Master?" That Sunday, the Venerable Master gave a Dharma talk at Mission College. After the talk was over, everyone was bowing to the Venerable Master, and I was deliberating over whether I should go bow or not. Finally, there seemed to be an invisible force pushing me forward, making me bow before the Master. The Venerable Master said, "You're such a tall guy. Aren't you afraid you'll lose face by bowing to me?" I was shocked, thinking, "How did the Master know what I had said at home?" Later I analyzed the matter and realized that my unwillingness to kneel and bow was due to my arrogant character. Because the Venerable Master immediately instructed, taught, and subdued me, pulling me out of my deluded, ignorant world and setting me on the proper path, I am where I am today. If I had been unable to accept his teaching, I would have continued living with my mistaken notions without ever getting an opportunity to walk on the proper path of cultivation.

I also remember that during the year of 1988, the Venerable Master would sit on the sofa in front of the Buddhahall every Saturday afternoon at Gold Mountain Monastery. On those occasions I had the opportunity to draw near to the Venerable Master and converse with him a little bit. I was rather naive, thinking that I had read the Venerable Master's books and gained some insight from them. I had gotten rid of some of my vices—drinking, meat-eating, and gambling—and smugly thought I was quite pure. So once I asked for instruction from the Venerable Master, saying, "I don't have enough samadhi power." The Master shook his head and

而我不知天高地厚，自以為看了一些師父的書，有一點心得，又改了一些壞毛病：酒、肉、賭，也滿以為自己很清淨了。於是有一次就問師父：我的定力不夠。師父搖一搖頭，給了我一個不軟不硬的釘子說：「你還談不上定力！」是的，我還談不上定力，因為我還沒有持戒嚴謹，當然還談不上定力。由師父指點，知道自己要學習的還多著呢！唯有虛心求教，才能獲益，自大自滿，猶如井底之蛙淺浮短視。

又記得在一九八九年，隨師赴臺灣花蓮弘法，在訪問慈濟醫院之前，師父一再提醒在家居士不可貢高我慢，要恭敬證嚴法師，可見師父時時都在提醒我們不可傲慢的重要。

又於一九八八年，隨師弘法於桃園妙法寺，因來訪人太多，屢次入師父房內報告，每天都要受到師父責罵，但我知道師父在考驗弟子，以及驅散弟子的貢高我慢心態。

這些寶貴的經驗，都足以告訴我：一個人不能夠謙虛及卑下，是不能成就道業的。因此，如果人自大，即使能精通詩書經典，修行到最後，還是做了魔的眷屬。

> 吾在憂患中，徬徨無著落，
> 師父暗助之，徒兒恩澤被，
> 事過已多時，方知師所為；
> 盃感師恩德，矢志遵師訓。

自從研究所畢業之後，進入了電子公司任職工程師。在沒有接受師父教化之前，我不懂得道理，不會做人，而結了許多惡緣，時常生活在人我是非的煩惱裡而不能自拔。皈依師父後，還是有一些煩惱，在公司任職的主管常常出難題，使我有想離開公司的想法。但是一連數個月寄出的求職信猶如石沉大海，公司又急於精減用人，雙重壓力之下，痛苦不堪。在一個星期六，到金山寺去求見師父，當我把實情秉報師父時，師父說：你再繼續去找工作。接著的這一星期，就有三個面談，而且三個工作都獲得。我馬上到金山寺拜謝師父，師父說：「不用謝！」我知道一個道理，凡是對師父有信心的弟子，在弟子有困難的時候，師父一個意念就會在暗

put me off neither gently nor harshly, saying, "You're not ready to talk about samadhi yet." It's true, I'm not ready to talk about samadhi, because I haven't been able to maintain the precepts strictly yet. So of course I'm not ready to talk about samadhi. From the Venerable Master's instruction, I realized that I still had a lot to learn! The only way to learn would be to seek instruction humbly. With self-conceit and arrogance, one is like the shallow and short-sighted frog at the bottom of a well.

I also remember when I accompanied the Venerable Master to Hualien, Taiwan, to propagate the Dharma in 1989. Before we went to visit the Mercy Salvation Hospital, the Venerable Master repeatedly reminded the laypeople that we should be respectful to Dharma Master Cheng Yen and not be proud or arrogant. The Venerable Master was always reminding us of the importance of not being arrogant. Also, in 1988 when I followed the Master to propagate the Dharma at Wonderful Dharma Monastery in Taoyuan, because there were many visitors I had to go into the Master's room to report to him many times. Every day I was scolded by the Master, but I knew the Master was only testing me and driving away my arrogance and conceit. These valuable experiences have told me that if a person cannot be humble and lower himself, he will not be able to accomplish his work in the Way. If a person is self-conceited, then even if he were to master the classics and Sutras, he would still end up in the retinue of demons after all his cultivation.

I was in worry and difficulty.
At a loss for what to do.
My teacher helped me without my knowing,
Bathing me with his kindness.
Only after a long time
Did I learn that this was my teacher's doing.
In gratitude to my teacher's grace,
I resolve to follow his teachings.

After graduating from graduate school, I got a job as an engineer in an electronics company. Before I encountered the Venerable Master's teaching, I didn't understand any principles and didn't know how to be a proper human being. I created many bad conditions with people and constantly lived amidst the afflictions of self and others, rights and wrongs, without being able to pull myself out. After I took refuge with the Venerable Master, I still had some afflictions. My supervisor in the company where I worked often gave me difficult problems to deal with, and that caused me to think of leaving the company. However, the job application letters that I mailed out over several months' time seemed to have sunk to the bottom of the sea like stones. At the same time, the company was trying to cut down its staff. Under this double-sided pressure, I felt extremely miserable. One Saturday I went to Gold Mountain Monastery and requested to see the Venerable Master. When I told the Venerable Master my situation, he said, "Keep trying." The following week, I had three interviews and three job offers. I immediately went to Gold Mountain Monastery to bow to and thank the Venerable Master. The Master said, "No need to thank me." I know one thing: As long as a disciple has faith in the Venerable Master, when he is in difficulty, in a single thought the Venerable Master will invisibly come to his aid, and after the matter he will not acknowledge that he did anything, either.

中幫助，而且事後還會不承認是他做的。

　　在六年之後，我自己出來創業，而這個創業的機緣又是師父的引領。當國際譯經學院遷至柏林根市之初，師父曾指示需要一些家具，希望看機緣購置做為將來用。於是我就常常注意拍賣的消息，在購買中，我發現有一些儀器是和我的工作有關，我可以進入這個行業。

　　在我是工程師時，常有個心願：「只要有一種工作可以夠家用，有多一點的時間為道場做事那就好了。」師父知道弟子有這樣的願望，指引我一條路讓我滿願。直到我自己創業後，才發現這一步一步都在師父安排下實現。弟子永遠記得師父對我的恩德。對師父的恭敬，是五體投地。

　　師父現在圓寂了，我們更應該拿出「以戒為師」的態度來躬行實踐六大宗旨，讓大家能在師父的精神感召下，更加團結，復興聖教。

Six years afterwards, I started my own business. Actually, it was under the Venerable Master's guidance that the conditions for starting a business ripened. When the International Translation Institute first moved to Burlingame, the Venerable Master said that some furniture would be needed and that if the opportunity arose, we should purchase some for future use. So I kept my eyes open for auctions. In purchasing furniture, I discovered some equipment related to my work, so I could enter that line of business.

When I was an engineer, I often wished I could have a job that would support my family so I'd have more time to work for the Way-place. The Venerable Master knew about my wish and guided me onto that path, allowing me to fulfill my wish.

It was only after I had my business that I realized all this was made possible by the Venerable Master's step-by-step guidance. I will forever remember the kindness the Venerable Master has bestowed upon me. I venerate the Venerable Master with all my heart.

Now that the Venerable Master has completed the stillness, we should more than ever, with the attitude of "taking the precepts as our teacher," respectfully practice the Six Great Principles. Let everyone unite under the Venerable Master's spiritual inspiration to make the holy teaching flourish again.

最寶貴的教誨

THE MOST TREASURED TEACHING

凡是男子皆是我父，凡是女子皆是我母

All men are my fathers, and all women are my mothers.

蘇美月
Su Meiyue

我自從學佛之後，改變了很多。尤其是師父上人解了我多年來的一個心結。怎麼說呢？

一九九三年，在由師父上人倡辦的首屆的敬老會上，我擔任招待。師父上人在開示中說，他對他的父母做得不夠圓滿，所以他對待年長者，是男的便視為是他的父親；是女的便視為他的母親。這段話使我生大慚愧。在我的觀念裡，生我、養我的，才是我真正的父母，我才應該孝順他們。至於對婆婆，我也並非不孝順，可是在心底始終認為，為什麼要孝順別人的父母？既沒生我，又沒養我。

我婆婆今年已經八十八歲了，她早年守寡。我雖然從未頂撞過婆婆，平常表面上我還是尊敬她的，人家也都說我是最孝順的媳婦。可是我總覺得她對子女和我要求太多，所以為她做事也從不是發自真心的。

自從聽師父上人開示以後，去年回臺灣探望婆婆，我就很溫柔、很孝順地，叫她一聲「媽媽！」我告訴她：「媽媽，我沒有孝順您，我對您太不好了……」她老人家八十多歲了，我很高興她那時仍很清醒，能聽到我的懺悔，並回答我說：「妳很好，妳很孝順……」，她的這句話使我很放心。我牽著她的手，切水果給她吃，看著她老人家吃得津津有味，心中十分安慰。

「凡是男子皆是我父，凡是女子皆是我母」，師父上人的這句話深深地打動我的心，這是上人留給我的最寶貴的教誨。過去我總是不明白，為什麼我付出這麼多，別人還對我有要求？還對我有不愉快的批評？現在，我不會像以前那樣總要求別人，反而儘量付出、儘量去做，總會得到一個很圓滿的結果。

I've changed a lot since I began studying Buddhism. This is especially because the Venerable Master untied a mental knot that I'd had for many years. How is this?

In 1993, I worked as an usher in the first Celebration for Respecting the Elderly held by the Venerable Master. During his talk, the Master said that since he had not been filial enough to his parents, he would treat all elderly men as his fathers and all elderly women as his mothers. This statement made me feel very ashamed of myself. In my view, only those who bore me and raised me are my real parents, and they are the only ones to whom I ought to be filial. As for my mother-in-law, though I have never been unfilial to her, deep down in my heart I have always thought: "Why should I be filial to someone else's parents? They didn't give birth to me, nor did they raise me."

My mother-in-law is eighty-eight years old this year. She was widowed at a young age. I have never talked back to my mother-in-law, and I always appear to be respectful to her. People all say that I'm the most filial daughter-in-law. But I've always felt that she demanded too much from her children and from me, so I am never genuinely sincere when I do things for her.

After hearing the Venerable Master's lecture, I was very gentle and filial to my mother-in-law when I went to visit her in Taiwan last year. I called her, "Mother!" I said, "Mother, I have not been filial to you. I have not treated you well..." I am glad that even though she is over eighty, she still has a very clear mind and could hear me repent. She said to me, "You are very nice, very filial..." Her words put me at ease. As I held her hand, sliced some fruit for her to eat, and watched her eating the fruit with relish, my heart was greatly comforted.

"All men are my fathers, and all women are my mothers." These words of the Master's have profoundly touched my heart. This is the most treasured teaching the Master has given me. In the past, I could never understand why people always asked for more and criticized me when I had already given so much. Now, I no longer ask from other people as I used to. On the contrary, I try my best to give, and I always have a very satisfactory outcome.

幻化的生命

THIS ILLUSORY LIFE

田季訓　Tian Jixun

一九八九年，上人返臺弘揚佛法。吳博英賢
伉儷亦隨眾同行。數日後，於臺北邀集其好友
宋榮松醫師、黃清源伉儷等相聚，乃有覲見上
人之議，黃清源兄以因緣難值，遂電召愚夫婦
同往。

有一天，上人率眾前往金山農場，途中，吳
先生談及上人此次返臺原因之一，係接受立法
委員王金平先生捐獻六龜鄉別墅一棟，作為道
場。該別墅經重新修整後，煥然一新，待法師
們進駐。其時，吳先生逐個檢視房間至浴廁時
，一推門，嚇然見地上躺了一條龜殼花大蛇，
便急忙關上門，怕它出來傷人。令人奇怪的是
，廁所是新裝修的，窗門未啟，地上鋪有瓷磚
，僅有的一個下水孔，又有密柵覆蓋，蛇是怎
麼進來的呢？

吳先生趕緊到廚房去拿火箝，打算將蛇挾出
。回到有蛇的房間，推門一看，竟然杳無蹤影
。正感到疑惑時，有位法師見吳先生神情有異
，便問他怎麼了，吳先生告訴法師房間有蛇的
事。法師卻寬慰他說：「上人無論至何地，都
有龍天護法相隨，你所見的蛇其實是條龍，牠
能顯能隱。你不要驚怪，我們早習以為常。你
也不必拿火鉗趕牠，不管牠就是了。」

吳先生聽了以後，頗不以為然，卻也無法反
駁，就對我們說：「等下見了上人當面問問，
看上人怎麼說。」大家深為驚訝，也不知其所
以然。

在金山農場，我們依序頂禮供養上人後，上
人跏趺坐，慈祥的問我們有什麼問題。上人對
宋醫師、黃夫人的問題作了詳細的開示。然後
，上人笑著回答了吳先生有關蛇的疑問：

你們聽說龍蛇混雜嗎？這條蛇就是現個相
給你們看看而已。我在香港的時候，有一
天，一個東北籍老鄉來看我，他也是我以
前的皈依弟子。我們異地相逢，非常高興

When the Venerable Master returned to Taiwan to propagate the Buddhadharma in 1989, Mr. and Mrs. Wu Boying also joined the group.
Several days later, they called together their good friends Doctor Song
Rongsong, Mr. and Mrs. Huang Qingyuan, and others in Taipei, and
had the idea of meeting with the Venerable Master. Because this was
such a rare opportunity, my colleague Huang Qingyuan then called my
wife and me and asked us to join them.

One day, the Venerable Master led a group to Jinshan Farm. During
the trip, Mr. Wu mentioned that one of the reasons the Venerable Master had come to Taiwan was to accept a house in Liugui offered by
Wang Jinping, a member of the Legislative Assembly. The house
would be used as a monastery. After a complete renovation, it looked
like new and was ready for the Dharma Masters to move in. Mr. Wu
went around the house looking at each room. When he opened the
door to the bathroom, he was scared stiff by the sight of a large poisonous snake with a tortoise-shell pattern on its skin lying on the floor.
He closed the door at once, fearing the snake would come out and
harm people. He thought it strange because the bathroom was newly
renovated, the windows hadn't been opened, and there was only a covered drain in the tiled floor. How could the snake have gotten in?

Mr. Wu hurried to the kitchen to get a pair of tongs with which to
pick up the snake. When he returned to the room where the snake had
been and opened the door, it was gone. As he was puzzling over this,
a Dharma Master noticed his bewildered expression and asked him
what was the matter. Mr. Wu told him about the snake in the room.
The Dharma Master consolingly said, "Wherever the Venerable Master goes, he is followed by dragons, gods, and Dharma-protecting spirits. The snake you saw was really a dragon. It can appear and disappear at will. Don't be startled. We've long been used to such things.
You don't have to chase it away with those tongs. Just ignore it."

Mr. Wu didn't quite believe what he heard, but he couldn't very
well argue. He said to us, "In a little while when we see the Venerable
Master, we can ask the Master and see what he says." Everyone was
very surprised and didn't quite know what to think.

At the Jinshan Farm, we bowed and made offerings to the Venerable Master. The Master, who was sitting in full lotus, asked us kindly
if we had any questions. He gave very detailed instructions in response
to the questions of Doctor Song and Mrs. Huang. Then the Master
answered Mr. Wu's question about the snake with a smile:

Have you heard the expression "dragons and snakes mingling
together"? This snake was just manifesting a form for you to see,
that's all. When I was living in Hong Kong, one day an old
friend from my village in Manchuria came to see me. He had
taken refuge with me before. We were extremely happy to see
each other again in another land. Before he left, I asked him to

。臨走時，我要他以後常來道場參加活動，他卻說：『我以後可不來了，你看廟門口的桃樹葉上好多大蛆，好嚇人哪！』我也就對他說：『龍蛇混雜嘛！你要是怕牠們，我叫牠們離開，保證你明天來一條也看不見。』結果他第二天來參加法會，真的一條也沒有了，就是這樣嘛，給你們現個相看看，沒有什麼嘛。

吳先生跟大家聽得似懂非懂，也不知該怎麼再問。因上人有其他客人來訪，我們便恭敬頂禮告退了。

是龍？是蛇？乃至是蛆蟲？皆是幻現的妄相。是彼幻？或是我們自心所幻？抑或是彼此因緣互結的幻中之幻？龍蛇混雜，龍與蛆蟲混雜，賢聖僧與凡夫亦混雜。上人的幻軀離眾生而去，是此滅而他生？抑或是他生即是此生？

come often to join the activities in the Way-place, but he said, "I won't be coming back anymore. The peach tree by the door of the monastery is covered with caterpillars. They scare me to death!" I said to him, "It's just dragons and snakes mingling! If they scare you, I'll tell them to leave. I promise that when you come tomorrow, you won't see a single one." The next day when he came to attend the Dharma session, they were indeed all gone. So you see, they are just taking form for you to see. It's no big deal.

Mr. Wu and everyone else listened without really understanding, but didn't know how to ask further. Because there were other guests waiting to see the Venerable Master, we bowed in respect and took our leave.

Was it a dragon? Or a snake? Or a caterpillar? These are all illusions. Is it an illusion on its part or on the part of our own minds? Or is it an illusion within illusions arising from the affinities between it and us? Dragons mingle with snakes, and dragons mingle with caterpillars. Worthies and sages also mingle with ordinary people. The Venerable Master's illusory body has left living beings. Has it died here and been born elsewhere? Or is it that when it is born elsewhere, it is also born here?

其心堅固難制沮　　趣佛菩薩無障礙
志求妙道除蒙惑　　周行法界不告勞

大悲廣度最無比　　慈心普遍等虛空
而於眾生不分別　　如是清淨遊於世
——《大方廣佛華嚴經》〈初發心功德品〉

His mind is solid and difficult to defeat,
He tends toward Buddha's Bodhi without obstruction.
He resolutely seeks the wondrous path which dispels delusions,
And he travels throughout the Dharma Realm without mentioning his toil.

Great compassion which widely takes beings across is most incomparable.
His kind heart pervades everywhere and is equal to space,
Yet he doesn't discriminate between living beings,
With purity like this, he travels in the world.

Chapter on The Merit and Virtue from First Bringing Forth the Mind, the *Flower Adornment Sutra*

有求必應的師父

A MASTER WHO ANSWERS ALL PRAYERS

釋恆樂
Shi Hengle

這些都是我出家以前的事。

一九八九年的一天，打算用我的一筆津貼來供養師父。可當時沒有人陪我去銀行領錢，內心又害怕被搶，就對著師父的照片合掌，祈求平安順利。當我領款後去金佛聖寺，一踏進門，就看見師父從樓上下來，問我說：「有事嗎？」我正不知錢要放在那兒較安全？這時馬上將錢取出供養師父。師父說：「ＯＫ！」我頂禮而退。

一九九二年，想去萬佛聖城拜萬佛寶懺，可是找不到同行的人。就對著師父的照片說：「師父啊，今年我恐怕不能到萬佛城去參加萬佛寶懺了，因為我不懂英文，又沒有人帶我去。」過了兩天，一位法師從西雅圖到金佛聖寺辦事，師父要她回萬佛聖城，我即隨同到聖城拜懺。

一九九一年七月十三日下午，我去萬佛聖城受菩薩戒，新受比丘尼戒的戒子們步出戒壇後，在家居士跪在祖師殿前等候戒師們出來合照。我不見師父出來，內心極難過，想師父身體一定很不舒服，也無心吃晚飯作晚課。回宿舍洗衣休息。七點半再回佛殿聽經時。遠遠見到師父披著淺黃色袈裟，從祖師殿慢慢走入佛殿。我趕到佛殿想向師父頂禮，師父卻不見了，而其他人仍都坐著。我拜過佛，即走到祖師殿，見兩位法師在那兒，即問說：「剛才師父來過啊？」她們說沒有。我告訴她們我看見師父了。她們說：「因為你想念師父，所以師父就化身讓你看到。」

The following events happened before I left the home-life:

One day in 1989, I planned to make an offering of money to the Venerable Master. I didn't have anyone to accompany me to the bank, and I was afraid of being robbed, so I placed my palms together before the Master's photo and prayed everything would go well. I withdrew the money and then went to Gold Buddha Sagely Monastery. As soon as I stepped in the door, I saw the Master coming down the stairs. He asked me, "Is something the matter?" I had just been wondering where to put the money so it would be safe. I immediately took the money out and offered it to the Master. The Master said, "OK!" I then bowed and withdrew.

In 1992, I wanted to go to the Sagely City of Ten Thousand Buddhas to participate in the Jewelled Repentance before Ten Thousand Buddhas, but I hadn't found anyone to accompany me. I faced the Venerable Master's photo and said, "Master, I probably can't go to the Sagely City to join the Jewelled Repentance before Ten Thousand Buddhas this year, because I don't know English and there's no one to take me." After two days passed, a Dharma Master came from Seattle to Gold Buddha Sagely Monastery to take care of some matters. The Venerable Master wanted her to go to the Sagely City of Ten Thousand Buddhas, and so I went with her to bow in the repentance ceremony.

In the afternoon of July 13, 1991, I went to the Sagely City of Ten Thousand Buddhas to receive the Bodhisattva precepts. After the newly-ordained Bhikshunis walked out of the Ordination Hall, the laypeople waited in front of the Patriarchs' Hall for the Precept Masters to come out and to be photographed with us. When I didn't see the Venerable Master come out, I felt very bad. I thought the Master must not be feeling well. I didn't feel like eating dinner or going to evening recitation, and so I went back to the dorm to wash my clothes and rest. When I was walking back to the Buddhahall at 7:30 p.m. to hear the Sutra lecture, I saw the Master in the distance, wearing a yellow sash and walking slowly from the Patriarchs' Hall into the Buddhahall. I rushed to the Buddhahall to bow to the Master, but the Master had vanished, and the other people were still sitting down. After bowing to the Buddhas, I walked into the Patriarchs' Hall. Seeing two Dharma Masters there, I asked them, "Did the Venerable Master just come by here?" They said no. I told them I had just seen the Master. They said, "It must be because you were thinking of the Master that the Master manifested himself for you to see."

祈願上人乘願再來

PRAYING THAT THE VENERABLE MASTER WILL RETURN ON HIS VOWS

賴秋貴　Lai Qiugui

六月十日，從美國杜興華居士的國際電話中，得知宣化上人往生的消息後，心中頓失依覺失落、徬徨而不能自己。

雖然一直都無緣親睹上人慈顏，但上人之德澤與風采卻早已深植我心，欽仰已久了！

上人旅居國外，但從他老人家屢次不辭辛苦，千里回國，或為宣揚佛法，或為消災祈福……，足見其心永繫著，關懷著生活在這塊土地的人，而在上人深入淺出的慧語，更是點化了無數人的迷思與困頓。他老人家懷著一顆出世之心，引入世之道，在其引導下，讓佛法進入我們日常生活中，讓我們清楚的感覺到「佛在心中」及佛法的奇妙與親近。

如今，他老人家已功德圓滿。在此，讓我們誠摯的向他誦持一聲「阿彌陀佛」，願上人快去快回，乘願再來，繼續帶領護持我們。

On June 10 I received a long distance call from Upasika Sherry Chen informing me of the Venerable Master Hua's passage into stillness. Instantly my mind was thrown into a turmoil and I was beside myself.

Although all along I have not had the affinities to enable me to draw near the Master's compassionate countenance, still the Master's beneficent virtue and supreme deportment reached deep into my heart long ago. I have admired him for so long!

The Master left his country and lived elsewhere, and yet he traveled thousands of miles to return many times despite the hardships and suffering that such travel brings. He would come to propagate the Buddhadharma, or to dispel disasters and pray for blessings. We can know from this that he was always concerned about the people who make their living on this island [Taiwan]. And with his wise words that seemed so simple but went so deep, he was further able to touch and change countless people's confusions and difficulties. The Master uses his transcendental mind to lead people to walk on the Path within the world. He brought the Buddhadharma into our daily lives. He helped us clearly realize that "The Buddha is in our minds" and brought us close to the wonder of the Buddhadharma.

Now the Master's merit and virtue are perfected. And so let us all sincerely recite "Amitabha Buddha" with the hope that the Master, who left so soon, will come back soon. Riding on his vows, may he come again and continue to guide and protect us.

菩薩具足妙智光　　善了因緣無有疑
一切迷惑皆除斷　　如是而遊於法界
——《大方廣佛華嚴經》〈初發心功德品〉

The Bodhisattva perfects the wondrous wisdom light,
And well comprehends causes and conditions without any doubts.
All confusion and delusion are completely cut off:
In this manner he travels throughout the Dharma Realm.

—Chapter on "The Merit and Virtue from First Bringing Forth the Mind," the *Flower Adornment Sutra*

生命的轉折

HOW MY ENTIRE LIFE WAS CHANGED

釋恆佐　Shi Heng Tso

I first met the Venerable Master in December of 1967 when I was eighteen years old. At that time he was living in a temple occupying the fourth floor at Waverly Place, in San Francisco's Chinatown. The background for my first meeting with the Venerable Master goes as follows:

Upon graduation from high school, Steve Mechling, my good friend at the time, and I traveled together first to Mexico and then Hawaii. While living in Hawaii, Steve corresponded with his eldest brother, Nick Mechling, who was living on Sutter Street in the same building as the Venerable Master. Steve told me that Nick would go listen to the Venerable Master lecture on the Sutras every week and would also mention various things about the Venerable Master in his letters. Because I was living the life of a carefree surfer, I didn't really have much interest in what Steve told me. However, after a very profound religious experience in the dormant volcano, Haleakala, on the island of Maui, I became very interested in spiritual pursuits and wished to find a teacher who could explain such things. I enjoyed living the surfing life, but the pressures of possibly being drafted to fight in Vietnam and the profound religious experience I had just gone through forced me to take my existence more seriously.

Around Christmastime, Steve and I left Hawaii to return to California where we planned to enroll in college and settle down. [Editor's note: During the Vietnam War, high school graduates in the United States could avoid the draft by enrolling in college.] Following Steve's suggestion we decided to first go to San Francisco to visit his brother before returning to our homes in Los Angeles. Little did I know how much this decision would change my entire life.

When we arrived in San Francisco, it was already dark and very cold. We didn't know anything about the city. With suitcases and sleeping bags in tow, we took two buses to get to Nick and his wife Susan's house. We were quite excited and talked late into the night. One plan we made was to go soon to the Buddhist Lecture Hall to meditate and hear the Master lecture.

At that time the Master was lecturing on Monday and Wednesday evenings and also on Sunday afternoons. The evening lectures, scheduled from eight to nine o'clock, were preceded by one hour of meditation. Those who attended were mostly young Americans. Because the Master lectured in Mandarin Chinese, a couple of boys in their late teens, Kim Lee and Jimmy Wong, were always present to translate.

The first lecture we attended was in the evening. I remember climbing the three long flights of very squeaky stairs to the Buddhist Lecture Hall and entering to find a few people seated on bowing cushions facing the walls. There was a strong smell of Chinese incense and the room was dimly lit. After meditating for most of an

我第一次見到師父，是在一九六七年十二月；那年我十八歲。當時師父住在三藩市中國城天后廟街內一幢小房子的四樓。拜見師父的因緣如下：

高中畢業後，會同好朋友史帝夫・麥克林，到墨西哥、夏威夷去玩。在夏威夷時，史帝夫和他住在三藩市的大哥尼克・麥克林通信。那時，尼克和師父一同住在沙特街。史帝夫告訴我，每星期尼克都去聽師父講經，並且在信中常提到師父的各種事蹟。當時我正沉醉於玩沖浪板，所以對師父的教誨沒什麼興趣。可是自從在毛依島哈里卡拉死火山，我有一次奇妙的宗教經驗之後，開始對宗教產生了好奇，並希望有一位師父能解釋這些事情。我雖然喜歡沖浪運動，但在可能被徵兵調往越南的壓力下，以及那次靈異經歷，逼使我更嚴肅地去正視自己的存在。

耶誕節前夕，我和史帝夫從夏威夷回到加州，打算找所大學安頓下來。（註：在越戰時期，美國實行徵兵制，高中畢業生如果上大學就可以不當兵。）史帝夫建議，我們先到三藩市去探望他大哥，然後再回洛杉磯的家。沒想到，此行改變了我的一生。

當我們到達三藩市時，天已經黑了。對三藩市，我們一無所知。揹著行囊，轉了兩趟車，才來到尼克和蘇珊的住所。大家興致很好地談到深夜，並決定盡快到佛教講堂去打坐、聽經。

當時，師父每星期一、三晚上和星期天下午講經，晚上八點至九點講經之前有一個小時打坐。參加的人多半是美國年輕人。因師父不會講英文，有兩個二十歲左右的中國青年金・李和吉米・王替師父翻譯。

記得那天晚上第一次聽經，踩著吱吱作響的長樓梯，我們來到位於三樓的佛教講堂，室內光線很暗，有一股很濃的燃香味。看到有幾個人面對牆壁坐在拜墊上。一小時之後，聽到有人敲引磬，燈光轉亮。大約有十五人在這一小時內陸續到達。這時師父坐在四張小方桌拼成的長條講桌的

hour, someone rang a small handbell and more lights were turned on. A few more people had come during the meditation period and now there were about fifteen people present. The Master sat at the head of a long table formed of four small tables pushed together and proceeded to give a very animated lecture. I don't remember a single word he said. In fact I didn't have much of a feeling for him or Buddhism at the time. I arrogantly thought to myself that enlightenment is a serious business, but the Master's lecture didn't seem to confirm my feelings.

After we returned to Nick and Susan's house, we talked about the evening's experience. I asked Nick if it was possible to go and talk with the Master. I wanted to discuss my volcano experience with him. Both Nick and Susan, to my surprise, encouraged me to call him. So, the next day I called and asked the Master if I could come for a visit. His response was very warm and encouraging, and he asked me to come the next evening.

The next evening, when Steve and I reached the temple, we timidly pushed the door open. It was dimly lit as before. The Master was sitting on a bowing cushion facing the door and motioned for us to come over to him. Then he directed us to each get a bowing cushion and sit down on either side of him. The first thing he asked was if we could sit in full lotus position. I said I could because I had started practicing about a month earlier. The Master looked at my legs and said I was sitting with the wrong leg on top and that I should reverse them. I did this with a little more difficulty, and then we proceeded to talk about all kinds of things.

Because we didn't know any Chinese and couldn't understand the Master's English very well, we had some difficulty communicating at first. However, the Master has many ways to communicate, and it didn't take long for us to become totally enthralled with what he was saying and doing.

At one point, the Master took my left hand and put it next to his left hand. Then he used his right hand to point out the similar lines on the palms of our hands. Right then something clicked inside, and I knew what he was saying. Because my entire life to that point had been so foreign to that of a monk's lifestyle, I didn't know how I could ever conduct myself in the proper manner, but still I found myself asking the Master if I could be a monk. The Master replied that becoming a monk was a lifetime commitment and not to be taken lightly. After some more discussion, the Master said I could leave home if I got my parents' permission.

Towards the end of our conversation, the Master said I could take a translation of the *Sixth Patriarch Sutra* from a shelf to my right and borrow it to read. Forgetting that I had been sitting in full lotus, I stood up abruptly and fell down just as fast. In the past I had been able to keep my legs up for just a few minutes at most. Because I was so concentrated this time, I had completely forgotten about the pain in my legs and didn't even realize that they had gone numb. Fortunately I didn't hurt myself.

After a week, Steve and I hitchhiked south to our homes. When we mentioned our plan to become monks to our parents, there was a lot of concern in both households. Steve's mother convinced him that he should wait a bit, and my parents wanted me to go see their local pastor and a psychologist. I complied with their wish and

前端，開始了生動的講演。那一次，我一點也記不起說法的內容，實際上，當時我對師父以及佛教並沒有什麼認識，而且還傲慢地認為，開悟應該是神聖的事，但師父的講演並沒有令我信服。

回到尼克和蘇珊的住處，交換了一些心得後，我便問能不能單獨和師父約個時間，談談我在夏威夷的靈異經歷。出乎意料的是，尼克和蘇珊鼓勵我打電話給師父。第二天，師父在電話中很慈祥地請我隔天晚上去。

第二天晚上，我和史帝夫來到講堂，輕輕推開佛教講堂的門，室內的燈光依然很暗，師父坐在拜墊上，面對著門，師父示意我們靠近他，要我們拿兩個拜墊坐在他的兩邊。師父首先問我們，會不會雙跏趺坐？我說會，因為在一個月前，我已開始學習打坐。於是我盤起腿來。師父對我說，我的腿盤錯了，應該把姿勢改過來。對我來說，改過來有點困難。師父和我們談了很多，因為我們完全不會聽中文，故剛開始時聽不慣師父的英文，但師父會用各種方法讓我們瞭解，不久，我就被師父的言行深深地吸引住了。

在談話中，師父將我的左手掌與他的相比，用右手指出兩隻手掌的掌紋很相似。突然我的心震動了，我明白師父的意思。雖然當時我的生活方式與出家人很不相同，我不知如何正確地去行持，但我還是問師父是否可以出家。師父說出家是很嚴肅的事，是終生的決定。討論後，師父說，只要父母允許，我就可以出家。

談話將結束時，師父說在我右邊的架子上有英譯的《六祖壇經》，我可以借去看。當時我忘了自己仍是雙跏趺坐，故一站起來就跌倒了。在這之前每次頂多盤幾分鐘，這次居然坐了半個小時。這次由於太專心，根本忘了痛，甚至連腳麻了都不知道，幸虧沒受傷。

一星期之後，史帝夫和我搭便車回到了家鄉。當我們提出出家的請求時，雙方家長都非常憂慮。史帝夫的媽媽說服他，要他緩一緩。我的父母則要我去見牧師和心理學家。我順從了他們，經過多次溝通以後，達成協議，等我大學畢業後再出家。大家這才鬆了一口氣。

耶誕節之後，我和史帝夫駕著我的小車，回三藩市同師父一塊住，並跟上人學習。師父知道我們不能馬上出家，就建議我們先去三藩市州立大註冊。但當時註冊期已過，於是有人叫我們到金

after numerous conversations, agreed to wait until I graduated from college before becoming a monk. I think all of us were relieved with this decision.

After the Christmas holidays, Steve and I drove my Volkswagen bug back to San Francisco to live and study with the Master. When we told him of our decision not to leave the home-life right away, he suggested that we enroll in college. We checked into City College of San Francisco but found that registration was already closed. At someone's suggestion, we enrolled at College of Marin, north of the Golden Gate Bridge, rented a small house nearby, and began our studies in a couple of weeks. This was the beginning of a long relationship that continues to this day. What follows are many experiences and teachings the Master has provided.

Many things happened during the winter and spring of 1968. Many people drew near the Master and were taught by him. Janice Vickers Storss (Gwo Jin) came from Texas, and Nancy Lovett, Steven Lovett's (Heng Gwan) wife, returned to the United States from Taiwan. Spring break also brought a few students from the University of Washington including Ron Epstein, Jon Babcock, Steve Klarer, Randy and Theresa Dinwiddie, and Loni Baur (Gwo Yi), who came to the Buddhist Lecture Hall to attend a meditation session. Because our spring break did not coincide with the others', Steve and I could only attend for the weekend. However, even just two days of meditation made us feel extremely happy.

Besides the Master's lectures on Monday and Wednesday evenings, Joe Miller also lectured on Tuesday evenings. Because we were full-time students living thirty miles away from San Francisco, Steve and I could not attend all the lectures. When we could, we would go into the city around four or five o'clock to visit with the Master and others for a while before the evening meditation and lecture. This was a very good chance to investigate many basic questions. One time the Master asked me about my girlfriends. He said sex should wait until marriage. During the late 1960s, the sexual revolution had changed everyone's thinking, and this was not something I expected to hear. That was my first glimpse of the real teachings of Buddhism.

One afternoon Janice Vickers Storss and Nancy Lovett told us they were going to take refuge. That afternoon the Master asked Steve if he was interested, and I requested to be included as well. The Master consented and set a date. On February 7, 1968, just three days before my nineteenth birthday, the four of us took refuge with the Master and formally became disciples of the Triple Jewel. The ceremony lasted for about an hour, and the Master did his own translation.

In the spring of 1968, my parents came to visit us and to see who this person was who had caused me to change so much. As was the case when anyone's parents come, the Master was happy to meet them. Unfortunately, on the afternoon of their visit, the only one there to translate was Alice Lum, one of the Master's disciples from Hong Kong whose English was not very good. During the conversation she got quite flustered. My mother, who can be very direct, asked the Master, "What are your credentials, and where are you from?" The Master replied that she should ask me, her son. My mother wanted to get to the bottom of things, and she thought

門大橋以北的馬林大學註冊，並在校外租了一間小房子，兩星期以後學校開學。從那時直到現在，我們就沒離開過師父。以下是我們與師父朝夕相處時的點滴回憶：

一九六七年冬天到一九六八年春天之間，發生了很多事情。有好些人來到師父的身邊，接受師父的教誨。如德州的珍‧費克爾斯（果進），史帝夫‧婁威特（恆觀）的俗家妻子南希‧婁威特從臺灣來到美國。春假期間，從西雅圖華聖頓大學來了一批學生，包括朗‧艾卜斯汀（易象乾）、約翰‧貝克、史帝夫‧柯爾、朗帝及德瑞莎‧丁威帝、朗尼‧鮑爾（果逸）在佛教講堂打禪七。我和史帝夫的春假時間與其他人不同，故我們只在週末去打坐兩天，但我們仍覺身心非常愉快。

除了每星期講經外，師父每星期一、三講經，星期二則由裘‧米勒負責演講。史帝夫和我因要上學，加上住的地方離佛教講堂有三十哩遠，所以不能每天去聽經。但我們盡力每個星期進城四到五次。而且每次都提前去佛教講堂，為了能在打坐講經之前，和師父及其他同修討論一些根本的問題。有一次，師父和我談及有關婚姻的事。師父說，結婚之前不應該有性行為。這與美國社會中普遍存在的性解放觀念，非常不一樣。這是我第一次真正瞭解佛教的戒律。

有一天下午，南希和珍告訴我們，師父希望她們皈依。那天下午師父問史帝夫是否願意皈依？我也請求要皈依師父，師父同意了，於是約好了時間。就在一九六八年二月七日，我十九歲生日的前幾天，和其他三人皈依了師父，成為一名正式的三寶弟子。皈依儀式舉行了約半小時，師父親自當翻譯。

一九六八春季，我的父母來會見宣公上人──這位改變我一生的人。師父像對其他人的父母一樣，高高興興地歡迎我的父母。不巧的是，那天下午在與師父的交談中，只有一位來自香港的愛麗絲‧何作翻譯，她的英文講得不太好，而我母親個性又很直，結果使愛麗絲非常為難。我母親問師父：「有沒有什麼證件可以證明你的來歷？」師父回答說：「妳應該問問妳的兒子！」愛麗絲無法應付，我媽媽又非要盤根問底不可。正僵持不下時，裘‧米勒和他的太太剛好進來。裘是個留著山羊鬍子，講話風趣的人。他用戲劇化，

the direct route was the correct way to deal with the situation. Unfortunately, Alice couldn't cope, but just when it looked like we had reached an impasse, Joe Miller and his wife walked in the door. Joe, a white-haired man with a goatee and a vaudeville past, proceeded to explain Buddhism in his own dramatic self-styled way. When the conversation ended, my mother was quite turned around and left with a satisfied feeling. However, my father was still somewhat suspicious.

Sometime during the spring, the Master announced that there would be a Shurangama Sutra summer study session held at the Buddhist Lecture Hall. It would last all summer and single men could stay in the temple and others could stay at another house or on Pine Street. Immediately after school was out, Steve and I went home for a short visit and then went back to the temple to attend the session.

During the session, the meals were taken care of by two people each week. Everyone also took turns washing dishes and cleaning up. Three meals were served each day, but as the Master encouraged us to eat a vegetarian diet and take one meal a day, more and more people began to skip dinner and breakfast. The Master also urged us to stop bad habits like smoking cigarettes and other substances. By the end of the summer, many of us had begun following his instructions, and when it came time to take the precepts, those with long hair and beards cut their hair and shaved off their beards. Many of the women also cut their hair shorter.

At the beginning, Kim Lee translated the evening lecture, but after a week or so, those attending the session full time began to translate for all the lectures. The translators were Ron Epstein, Paul Hansen, Jon Babcock, Steve Klarer, and Julie Plant. They all took turns and spent a lot of time preparing before each lecture. At that time, I wasn't aware of any internal conflicts. One day, however, none of the translators showed up and the Master had to translate for himself. The tapes for the afternoon lecture on the 4th of July are testimony to this.

After the summer session, Steve and I went back to school at College of Marin. An estate within walking distance of the school was looking for a caretaker, and I was tempted to move there, but when I discussed it with the Master, his reply stopped me cold in my tracks. He said, "If you move from here, you will not come back." Therefore, I decided to remain living at the Buddhist Lecture Hall and commute to school.

*　　　　*　　　　*

The Venerable Master devoted his time to many different things, and everything he did was to benefit living beings. I remember going with him to the park to feed hungry birds.

In the mid 1970s California suffered through a severe drought. During those years, I sometimes had the opportunity to drive the Venerable Master to different places in the San Francisco Bay Area. One particular day, my three year old daughter and I (I was still married at the time) came to pick him up early in the morning. After he climbed into the car, the Master asked me if I knew of any lakes in Golden Gate Park. I said I knew of a few, and he said, "Let's go take a look." After showing him three or four, he selected one smaller lake that was a bit more secluded than the others we had seen. As we got

別具風格的方式向我父母解說什麼是佛法。拜會結束時，我母親的態度完全改變，離去時相當滿意，但我父親仍然不太相信。

那年夏天，師父宣佈暑假將舉辦「楞嚴經講習班」，將持續整個暑假。單身男士可住在廟裡，其他的人則住另一幢房子或都板街。講習班在六月初開課，在我們的學期結束之後。史帝夫和我回家打個轉，就又回到廟裡參加那次講習班。

講習期間，每星期有兩個人負責煮飯、洗碗和清掃，其他的人也輪流。每天供應三餐。由於師父鼓勵大家吃素，日中一食，漸漸地大家都開始練習日中一食。師父又勸大家戒掉吸菸、吸毒的壞習慣。暑假結束時，多數的人都可以遵守這些規則了。到受五戒時，大家都剃了鬍子，剪短了頭髮，很多女生也都把頭髮剪短了。

講習剛開始是由李錦山擔任翻譯，以後就由全勤上課的人，如朗尼、約翰、保羅、史帝夫、裴帝等人輪流翻譯，翻譯之前每個人都花很多時間準備。當時我並不知道弟子之間有些小摩擦，直到有一天看到師父自己在翻譯，我才知道他們之間的不和。當年七月四日下午的講經錄音帶中，還保留有師父自己翻譯的記錄。

開學時，剛好有位同學的父母想找有宗教信仰的學生，替他們管理一些產業，同時提供免費的住屋。由於離學校很近，所以我很想搬去，但一和師父商量，心裡就涼了半截。師父說：「你如果搬出去，就不會再回來了。」所以我決定仍住在佛教講堂，每天開車去上學。

上人的時間都花在利益眾生上，他做的每一件事，都是為利益眾生而著眼。我想起有一回我跟上人到公園去餵餓鳥。

一九七〇年代中期，加州乾旱得嚴重。那段時期，我常有機會駕車載著師父到舊金山灣區各地方。那時我還是在家人，有一天一大清早，我帶著三歲的女兒去接師父。師父進入車中後問我在金門公園裡有沒有湖，我說有幾個湖。師父說他要去看看。看了四、五個之後，師

out of the car, from the canvas shopping bag he often took with him when he went out, he pulled a plastic bag full of left-over bread and said, "We are going to feed the birds."

Walking over to a bench and sitting down, he instructed us to recite the Great Compassion Mantra as we fed the birds. In no time we were surrounded by hundreds of birds including different kinds of gulls, loons, and ducks. they flew all around us grabbing the bread as we threw it in the air. Sometimes they landed on our shoulders as they fought to get closer to the food source. We must have looked like three flowers being swarmed by a hive of bees. A couple of gulls were the most aggressive, and the Master teased them by tossing bread in the opposite direction. Then all three of us would laugh at their foiled attempts to steal the bread from the other birds. This feeding went on for about twenty minutes until the bread ran out. After the last crumb was eaten, we got up to leave and the Venerable Master said, "They are very hungry." I reasoned it was probably a result of the drought. The very next day we did the same thing.

The Master didn't just lecture Dharma. He taught by doing, and his classroom was the Dharma Realm. Although he was lecturing the *Avatamsaka Sutra* eight times per week, establishing new monasteries, helping numerous people with their problems, and probably doing a lot of other things we weren't aware of, he still took time to feed birds that were suffering from the results of a drought. For him no matter was too small to tend to, and no matter was too big. His only wish was that we learn to be that way too.

One final observation: The way the birds acted with the Master was quite extraordinary. They were all over us seeking a handout. I didn't realize how unusual their behavior was until about two years later, when I returned to the same pond to again feed the birds. I expected them to swarm around me as they had done before, but this time only a few birds appeared, and they kept their distance.

父選了一個地點比較隱秘一點的小湖。我們下車之後，師父從他出門時不離身的一個帆布袋裡，拿出一個塑膠袋來，裡面裝滿了吃剩下的麵包，師父對我說：「我們餵鳥去！」

我們在一個座椅坐下後，師父叫我們一面餵鳥，一面念〈大悲咒〉。不一會兒，我們身邊就圍上了幾百隻鳥，有不同種類的海鷗、鸄鵋、鴨子，這些鳥在我們周圍飛著、搶著我們扔向空中的麵包。有的時候這些鳥會停在我們的肩膀上，搶著近前吃麵包。我們三個人看起來像似三朵被蜜蜂包圍著的花一樣。有幾隻海鷗比較兇猛一點，所以師父就把麵包往他們相反的方向丟去。牠們想從別的鳥那裡搶麵包，而又搶不到的樣子，惹得我都笑了。這樣子餵了二十分鐘，麵包也完了，我們準備走的時候，師父忽然說：「牠們很餓。」我猜可能是乾旱的關係。第二天，我們又去餵了一次。

師父不僅講經而已，師父以身作則，以法界為教室。雖然師父一星期講八次的《華嚴經》，又建寺廟，幫人解決困難，還做了許多我們不知道的事情，但是師父還找時間來餵那些因乾旱而受罪的鳥。再小的事，師父也不忽略，但他也不嫌事情大。

我還注意到一件事，這些鳥和師父在一起時，表現得很不平常，牠們圍著我們要東西吃。當時我沒有覺得這些鳥的行為有什麼不尋常。大概在二年後，我又回到那個湖邊去餵鳥。起先我還以為這些鳥也會像上次那樣包圍著我，結果只有少少幾隻鳥過來，而且還離得遠遠的。

西方佛法露曙光　東度眾生壽而康
悟得本來無生面　與爾同登萬佛邦

宣公上人作

In the West, the Buddhadharma radiates a bright light of dawn;
As in the East, it rescues beings and bestows long life and health;
If you can awaken to your basic identity, your unborn being,
On the spot you ascend together to Ten Thousand Buddhas' Land.

by the Venerable Master Hua

IN GRATITUDE FOR THE VENERABLE MASTER'S TEACHINGS
承教與蒙恩

釋恆音　Shi Hengyin

The first time I saw the Venerable Master was in December 1989, when he led a delegation to give a lecture and meditation retreat at the University of Texas, where I was a student. I remember being deeply impressed by the Master's account of how he started bowing to his parents, and to heaven and earth, the king, his teachers, and all living beings. I had never heard of anyone doing this in the modern world.

After the lecture, my father and I went up to the Master. Many people were bowing to him. My father introduced himself and frankly told the Master he had not understood much of the Dharma lecture. The Master gently replied, "Listen to the Dharma more, and you'll understand."

Many people took refuge with the Master. Later on, a Buddhist Association was formed at the University of Texas, with about thirty members, and meetings were held every Friday.

When I found out about the City of Ten Thousand Buddhas (CTTB), I was very excited, for it seemed full of hope and proper energy, in contrast to the greed, hatred, and ignorance of the ordinary world.

I ordered dozens of books from the Buddhist Text Translation Society of CTTB, mostly English translations of Sutras with the Master's commentary, and spent most of my days in the University library, reading them and meditating. These books were so different from other books I'd read; they were pure and inspiring, and contained true principles and proper Dharma in every line.

In June 1990, I went to the City of Ten Thousand Buddhas for a Chan Session. When I arrived, I was directed to Wonderful Words Hall, where the Venerable Master was giving a class on matching couplets. Later, the Master personally came to give instructions and start the Chan Session. During the seven days of the session, as I walked 'round and 'round the Chan Hall, I reflected deeply on my past mistakes and decided to make a new start in life, with the Dharma as my guide. I vowed to go back to the City as soon as possible.

Back in Texas, I renounced a $10,000 fellowship in graduate school and told my parents I wanted to transfer to Dharma Realm Buddhist University, to which they agreed.

In October 1990, I went with three Buddhist friends to attend a Guan Yin Session. All during the trip, I sincerely recited the Great Compassion Mantra. When the Venerable Master stood watching the assembly file into the Daoyuan Hall for the lecture,

第一次見到上人是在一九八九年十二月，上人到德州大學來講法，教靜坐。那時我是該校的學生。師父講了他向天地君親師和一切眾生磕頭的因緣，令我留下了很深的印象。在這個世界上，我從來沒有聽見過有人這樣做的。

上人講完法後，我和父親到上人跟前，有很多人在向上人頂禮。父親介紹了他自己，並且說大部分的開示他都沒聽懂。上人很溫和地回答：「聽多一點法，就會明白的。」當天很多人皈依上人；後來德州大學也成立了佛學社，約有三十多位社員，每週五定期集會。

當我發現萬佛聖城時，我真是興奮極了。萬佛城好像充滿了希望與正氣，與一般世界上的貪瞋癡完全不同。我請了萬佛聖城譯經委員會所出版的幾十本書，大多是上人解釋經典的英譯本。以後的一段時間，我都在學校圖書館看這些書，也在那裡靜坐。這些書的內容既純淨又富有啟發性，句句講的都是真理與正法，與我所讀過的書完全不同。

一九九○年六月我到萬佛聖城參加禪七。我到達後，有人教我去妙語堂，那時候上人在那裡上對聯課。在禪七開始時，上人親自開示，並起七。禪七行香時，我在禪堂裡一圈圈地走著，深自反省自己往昔的錯誤。之後，我決心依照佛法開始一個新的人生。我又發願要盡快再回聖城。回德州後，我放棄了研究所一年一萬元的獎學金，準備轉讀法界佛教大學，我父母他們也同意了。

一九九○年十月，我和三位佛友到萬佛城來打觀音七，在途中我一心虔誠誦念〈大悲咒〉。一天晚上，在大眾排班進入道源堂聽法時，上人在一邊站著看，當我經過上人身邊時，他抬了抬眼，好像在告訴我，他知道我的心願。觀音七後，我就決定留住聖城。

一九九○年底，上人率團到歐洲弘法，回來後即

he seemed to look up as I passed, as if in recognition of my prayers. After that session, I decided to stay on at the City.

At the end of 1990, the Venerable Master led a delegation to Europe, and became gravely ill when he returned. Day and night, the assembly took turns reciting mantras for the Master's health. This emphasis on sickness and impermanence led me to make the resolve to leave the home-life at the earliest opportunity. The opportunity came unexpectedly soon, and I left home a couple months later, on January 1, 1991.

For the next two years, since the Master was very ill, we hardly ever had a chance to see him or to hear him lecture. I often felt sad and envied the earlier disciples who had been lucky enough to receive the Master's personal guidance. I never expected that one day, the Master would recover from his illness and resume his busy schedule of teaching his disciples and propagating the Dharma, but that is what happened.

In the fall of 1992, the Venerable Master went to Gold Summit Monastery in Seattle. Although he was still not fully recovered, the Master lectured at the International Translation Institute in Burlingame in the morning, then flew to Seattle, where he gave a lecture, sat through the lectures of many disciples, and transmitted the Three Refuges in the evening. I remember looking at the Master during the Refuge ceremony, as he stood holding the flower and incense. He looked about ready to fall over in fatigue, and yet he would not quit. This was the spirit of "not sparing blood or sweat, never pausing to rest."

In December of 1992, the Venerable Master held the first Celebration for Respecting Elders in Los Angeles, and a busload of us went down from CTTB and the International Translation Institute (ITI) to attend it. On the overnight bus trip, I fell asleep, and when I woke up, probably due to the cold draft, my left arm was numb and stayed with the wrist bent inwards. Since there was no pain, I thought the numbness would go away by itself. But the next morning, it was still numb. Some Dharma brothers massaged it for me, to no avail. That day, the Master came to Gold Wheel Monastery, where we were staying, but I was too shy to approach him, for he was surrounded by many people. That evening, a Dharma brother reported my arm's numbness to the Master on the phone, and the Master reproached us for not letting him know earlier. The next day was the big celebration at the restaurant. The Master instructed that I go early to the restaurant and said he would arrange for an acupuncture doctor to treat me.

The next day, when we arrived at the restaurant, the doctor had not arrived yet. The Master was already sitting with several guests and called for me to go up. Smiling gently, he massaged my arm and told me I should exercise more and massage it myself to get the circulation going again. The Master's hands were very warm and strong, while mine was cold and stiff. Later, the doctor examined me, gave me acupuncture, and prescribed Chinese herbs to bolster my weak constitution. The Master instructed me to stay in Long Beach until January, when the Master would be leading a delegation to Taiwan. For those few weeks, with my hand paralyzed and useless, I tended to be rather moody. One evening I was feeling especially low. All of a sudden, the phone rang. It was the Master,

病重。在萬佛城,大眾日夜輪流持咒為上人的健康祈求。因為那次疾病與無常的示現,使我發心盡早出家。因緣成熟得也快,二個月後,在一九九一年的一月一日,我就圓頂了。

接著兩年上人示疾,大家很少聽到他老人家講法,也很少能見得到他老人家。那時我覺得很難過,我也很羨慕上人早期的弟子們,能蒙上人親自教誨。幸好後來上人病好了,又繼續忙碌地教化眾生,弘揚佛法。

一九九二年秋天,上人到西雅圖金峰寺講法。那時雖然上人身體還沒有完全復元,並且上午在柏林根譯經學院,就已經說了一上午的法,接著又飛到西雅圖說法。在眾多弟子講法的法會中,上人從頭到尾一直都坐在那裡聽著。晚上又打三皈依,在打皈依時,上人得站起來拿著香花請聖,我看到上人那時累得快要倒下去了,可是上人總也不歇息,這就是上人「流血汗,不休息」的精神。

一九九二年十二月,上人首度在洛杉磯慶祝敬老節。一輛大巴士載著萬佛城和譯經院的人南下參加。途中我們在巴士上過夜,可能因為受風寒,醒來後我的左手臂麻痺,而且手腕向內彎曲。因為不覺得痛,所以我以為過會兒就會好的。可是第二天早晨還是覺得麻痺,師兄弟為我按摩也不管用。那時我們住在金輪寺,上人來的時候,有許多弟子圍著他,我不好意思上前問上人。晚上有師兄在電話中,向上人報告我手麻痺,上人責怪為什麼不早說。第二天就是大型壽筵慶祝會,上人交待要我提早到會,他會安排針灸師為我醫治。

第二天我們到時,醫生還沒來,但是上人早已和幾位客人坐在一起。上人叫我上去,他很溫和地笑著,按摩我的手臂,並且告訴我要多運動、多按摩,讓氣血流通。上人的手非常溫暖有力,而我的手則又冷又僵。後來醫生來了,就為我針灸治療,開藥滋補我虛弱的體質。上人又讓我留住長堤,等一月份上人率團同去臺灣。以後幾個星期我因為手臂癱瘓無用,所以覺得很鬱悶不樂。有一天晚間我情緒特別低沉。忽然電話鈴響了,是上人打來的,他問我覺得怎麼樣,叫我別擔心,手很快就會好的。他還問我知不知道在譯經院有封父親的來信,我答不知道。上人說他們來時會帶下。最後上人說:「Good Night(晚安)

who asked how I was, told me not to worry, and reassured me that my arm would get better soon. The Master also asked me if I knew my father had sent me a letter to ITI. I said I didn't know, and the Master said they would bring it down to Long Beach when they came. Finally, the Master said "Good night" in English. That brief phone call came right when I needed it; it cheered me up completely.

Before the trip to Taiwan, the Master often called and asked about my condition. During the trip to Taiwan, the Master told me to get plenty of rest and not worry about attending all the ceremonies and also said I could eat breakfast if I wanted. Yet during that trip, the Master exhausted himself with a tight schedule of travel, meetings, and lectures, while letting his disciples take it easy.

After the Taiwan trip, I was taken to another doctor in Oakland, and my arm soon got better. Yet the Master continued to stress that not only I, but all his disciples, get enough exercise. Once he even gave a matching couplet on the benefits of tai-chi to cultivation and said we should all learn tai-chi from a certain tai-chi teacher, which I did for a while.

In mid-1993, I moved to Long Beach Monastery. When my parents, sister, and a friend, none of whom were Buddhist, came to visit me, the Master invited them to stay at the monastery and treated them like his own family. The Master asked what my sister liked to do, and when I said riding horses was her favorite activity, the Master said he used to ride the wild horses in Manchuria, too, standing on their backs! With my parents, the Master talked about China and explained Great Master Buxu's verse predicting the major events of a hundred years in China, which they found extremely interesting.

In November of 1993, the Master led a delegation to New York and Maryland. During the trip, the Master admonished me for always having my head down and asked me the reason. I said it was because I often felt guilty for all the bad things I'd done in the past. That opened the opportunity for me to repent to the Master of many impure deeds from my past, which had been weighing heavily on my mind. To each thing I repented of, the Master would listen seriously, and then exclaim, "That's nothing. People in the world all make that mistake. As long as you can change, everything's OK. I can be responsible for your offense." The Master immediately cleared away all the guilt, and made me see that my problem and the suffering it brought was actually the problem and suffering of all deluded living beings. Therefore, I ought to expand my mind and resolve to help all living beings put an end to suffering. I felt relieved and infinitely touched by the Master's vast compassion.

At first, I did not want to write anything, because I felt I could not accurately record the events, and perhaps others would find them fussy and trivial. Also, there are too many teachings and impressions received from the Master that there would be no way to express them fully. However, I finally decided to try to write something to express my gratitude to the Master as his disciple.

Although we are living in the so-called Dharma-ending Age and living beings' roots are dull and inferior, I feel that we are truly lucky to have met the Venerable Master. For the sake of establish-

！」簡短的一通電話，把我的勁全提起來了！上人這通電話，就在我最需要鼓勵的時候打來的。

去臺灣之前，上人也經常以電話詢問我的狀況。訪臺時，上人則要我儘量多休息，不用掛心參加法會，我如果要吃早餐的話也可以。上人常囑咐弟子們多休息，而自己的行程、會議與講法，則安排得緊湊之至。從臺灣歸來後，我去看屋崙的一位醫生，手臂很快就好了。上人強調要所有弟子們多做運動，一次，上人還以太極拳對修行有幫助為題，來出對聯，要大家跟城內的一位太極拳老師學習。所以我也練了一陣子太極拳。

一九九三年中，我搬入長堤聖寺。一日，父母、妹妹和一位朋友來訪，他們都不是佛教徒，上人邀他們在寺裡住下，如待家人。上人問我妹妹有何喜好，我答妹妹最好騎馬。上人說在東北時，他也騎野馬，而且還是站在馬背上！上人對我父母談了中國，又談了步虛大師的中國近百年預言詩，還解釋給他們聽，他們都聽得津津有味。

一九九三年十一月，上人率團往紐約州與馬利蘭州弘法時，上人責備我頭總是低垂，問我為什麼？我答自己因為羞愧往昔所做種種惡事。這給了我一個機會，向上人懺悔我過去不清淨的行為，減輕了我心頭的重擔。我所懺悔的每椿事，上人都聽得很仔細，每當我懺悔一椿事，上人就會說：「那沒什麼，世界上的人都犯那個錯，只要你能改過，一切都沒問題的，我可以為你擔當。」我的罪惡感頓時消除了，上人也讓我明白了我自己的問題和痛苦，也正是所有顛倒眾生的問題和痛苦。所以我應該擴大我的心量，立志幫助所有的眾生解除痛苦。從那以後我就覺得鬆快了許多，上人無量的慈悲使我非常感動。

本來我不打算寫紀念文，因為我以為自己沒有辦法能夠表達得清楚這些事情，而且別人也可能覺得沒什麼大意思。再說，上人給我的教化太多太多了，影響也是很深很深的，講也講不完。但是最後我還是覺得應該講一講，以表示我對上人的感激，也盡盡我做弟子的心。

雖然我們生在末法時代，眾生根器也很頑劣，但是我們有幸能遇到上人，實在是很難得的。上人為了把佛教的正法傳到西方來，寧願自己「流血汗，不休息」、捨生命。上人年事雖高，他修行精進的程度，與為佛教所做的貢獻，遠勝過他年輕的弟子們，這是我們都該深覺慚愧的。上人

ng the Proper Dharma in the West, the Master "spared no blood or weat, and never paused to rest." At his advanced age, he was infinitely much more vigorous and dedicated than his much younger disciples, for which we should be deeply ashamed. He didn't pass up any opportunity to teach living beings, and he spoke the Dharma in every word and deed. It is only that we are too stupid to understand and accept his teachings.

The Master fearlessly proclaimed the Proper Dharma and denounced corrupt practices wherever he saw them, out of a wish to train people to have discerning judgment so that they would not be led astray. He also bent over backwards to help those who wished to become better people. His virtue influenced people to change their faults and become good. Morever, unlike ordinary people, the Master had no self, no greed, and no desires. There was only great kindness and compassion for all living beings, for he considered living beings to be one with himself. The Master often said, "Truly recognize your own faults. Don't discuss the faults of others. Others' faults are just my own. Being one with all is called great compassion." Understanding this, how can we continue to discriminate between ourselves and others, bickering endlessly about who is right and who is wrong? Shouldn't we urge ourselves to recognize the darkness and filth in our own minds and then reform and renew ourselves?

不放棄任何一個教化眾生的機會，他老人家一言一行無不是在說法，只是眾生都太愚癡，無法理解，無法接受。

上人宣演正法，無畏無懼，指出各種腐敗的行為，也是為了培養世人的擇法眼，以免誤入歧途。對一心想學好的人，上人無不全力幫助，運用德行影響人們改過遷善。上人大公無私、無貪無欲無我，不同於一般人。他老人家所有的只是對眾生廣大平等的慈悲，因為上人視眾生和他都是一體的。上人常說：「真認自己錯，莫論他人非，他非即我非，同體名大悲。」明乎此，我們怎麼還可以在人我是非中爭執不休，拔不出腿來呢？怎麼還可以不鞭策自己，看清自己內心的黑暗面、骯髒面，而改過自新呢？

無罣礙名真放下　　再無恐怖業障除
遠離顛倒生相破　　夢想粗細沙惑如
三障消融圓三德　　六根互用證六通
會此妙想親受用　　知者易悟昧難途

宣公上人《般若波羅密多心經非台頌解》

Having no impediments is the true letting go;
When fear is no more, the activity-obstacles depart.
Distortion left far behind, the characteristic of production perishes;
The coarse, fine, and dust-and-sand delusions of
*   your dream-thoughts become Thus.*
The three obstacles are dissolved, the three virtues perfected.
The six faculties are used interchangeably,
*   certifying the attainment of the six psychic powers.*
When you are capable of this wonderful truth,
*   you personally experience its benefit;*
Those who know easily enlighten; those who are ignorant take a difficult path.

From the Venerable Master Hua's Verses without a Stand for the *Heart of Prajna Paramita Sutra*

夢 的 啓 示

DREAM REVELATION

莊春蓮　Zhuang Chunlian

我學佛學了好多年，但從沒到佛寺參加過什麼法會或是團體佛教活動之類的。只是平常抽點時間在家誦誦〈大悲咒〉、佛號而已。

一九八八年十一月十六日，一個偶然的機緣，得知有個法會在大溪的一座妙法寺舉行。那天我搭車、問路、換車，折騰了老半天，終於找到了妙法寺。正當走到「大雄寶殿」時，迎面有一位法師從佛殿走了出來。他後面跟著一大群的信徒，每人都是同樣的表情，那就是歡喜和崇拜。我後來才知道法會剛好結束。正在懊惱自己真是沒福氣，第一次到佛寺參加法會，卻只看到法會結束的場面。這時好多信眾都在填什麼表，我拿來看了看，好像每個人都在填，那我也填一份好了。

過了約十天，居然收到一本「皈依三寶證明書」，大概翻了一下，就塞到抽屜裡頭。第二年十月某一夜晚，夢見自己走呀走的，看到一間小屋子，裡面好像很多人。於是我好奇地擠呀擠的，擠到前面，想看個究竟？看到一位老人，留著白髮，白長鬍子，右手拿著一隻白拂塵，閉目盤腿而坐，面帶微笑。這時老人輕輕甩動一下拂塵，只見他後頭上冒出一陣白煙。哇！他哪是凡人？他是仙呀！……「阿蓮！」後面有人叫著，「你要皈依嗎？你一定要皈依這位法師哦！」我說：「哪位？」原來是二嫂，她拿著一本書，翻開指著一張手上拿著白拂塵的法師照片給我看。頓時我感到很面熟，正在想是否在哪裡見過，夢就醒了。這才想起去年寄來的，一年都沒再勤過的皈依證。找了老半天終於找到，那位拿著拂塵盤腿而坐的法師，不就是和夢中二嫂一再叮嚀的，要我皈依的師父完全一樣嗎？原來他就是宣公上人。

那一天很巧合的又得知，上人下星期要返臺舉行護國息災法會。這一次我一大早就到了妙法寺。終於完成了正式的皈依儀式，成為一個名符其實的皈依弟子。後來也遵師父的要求，

I have studied Buddhism for many years, but had never gone to Buddhist temple to take part in any Dharma session or Buddhist group activity. I would simply recite the Great Compassion Mantra or the Buddha's name at home when I had time.

On November 16, 1988, I happened to hear that there was going to be a Dharma session at a monastery in Daxi (Taiwan). That day I got on the bus, asked for directions, changed buses, and finally got to the monastery. Just as I was about to walk into the Buddhahall, a Dharma Master came walking out of the Buddhahall. He was followed by a crowd of devotees, all of whom wore the same expression of joy and worshipful respect on their faces. Then I found out that the Dharma session had just ended. I was frustrated with my poor blessings: The first time I came to a Buddhist monastery to attend a Dharma session, I only made it in time to see the end of the session. Many people were filling out some kind of application. I took an application as well, and since everyone seemed to be filling one out, I also filled one out.

After about ten days had passed, I received a Certificate of Taking Refuge with the Triple Jewel. I skimmed through it and then put it away in a drawer. In October of the following year, one night I dreamed that I was walking and walking, and I came to a small house in which there seemed to be a lot of people. Being curious, I crowded my way in to see what was there. I saw an old man with white hair and a white beard, carrying a white whisk in his right hand. He sat in full lotus posture with his eyes closed and a smile on his face. Just then, the old man lightly waved the whisk and a puff of smoke rose from his head. Ah! He was no common person! He must be an immortal! "Lian!" Someone behind me was calling my name. "Are you going to take refuge? You must take refuge with this Dharma Master!" "With whom?" I asked. It was my second sister-in-law, holding a booklet and showing me a photo of a Dharma Master holding a whisk. I thought he looked very familiar. As I was trying to think of where I had seen him before, I woke up. Then I remembered the refuge certificate that I had received in the mail a year ago and hadn't looked at since then. I looked for a long time before finding it. Wasn't that Dharma Master sitting in full lotus with a whisk the same one my second sister-in-law was urging me to take refuge with in my dream? It was the Venerable Master Hua.

That day, I happened to find out that the Venerable Master was coming to Taiwan next week to hold a Dharma Session for Protecting the Nation and Quelling Disasters. This time I arrived at the monastery early in the morning. I finally finished the formal ceremony for taking refuge and became a true disciple in refuge. I also followed the Master's requirement and bowed to the Buddha 10,000 times. Three years later, I took my two sons to take refuge with the

禮佛一萬拜。第三年，我把兩個兒子也帶去皈依宣公師父。

我想慈悲的師父一定是發覺他居然有個有名無實的笨弟子，故特來託夢與我，因而消除了我差點搬上的，欺騙三寶的罪名。現在師父圓寂了，我要化悲憤為力量，照上人的教誨時時記得那六大宗旨的真言。

Venerable Master as well.

I think the compassionate Venerable Master must have discovered that he had a foolish disciple who was a disciple in name only, so he appeared in my dream and prevented me from committing the offense of cheating the Triple Jewel. Now that the Master has completed the stillness, I shall transform my sadness into strength and follow the Master's teaching to always remember the truth of the Six Great Principles.

無 題

UNTITLED

果衡　Guo Heng

經云：「生死與涅槃。凡夫及諸佛。同為空華相。」空中本來無華，何來相？凡夫執著四大和合之體為身相，六塵緣影為自心相。四大分散稱之為死，四大不調稱之為病。四大調伏是健康之體。若四大分散，妄身何處？即知此身並無實體，和合為相，實同幻化。我等於無生中，妄見生滅，是故流轉生死，以假作真，認賊作父。

諸佛菩薩破此妄執而證涅槃，如《壇經》云：「不起凡聖見。不作涅槃想。二邊三際斷。常應諸根用。而不起用想。分別一切法。不起分別想。」這就是凡聖情亡，人我兩空，物來則現，物過不留，如如不動，了了分明，涅槃清淨，或稱真如實體。名異實同，亦稱如來知見，知則常知空寂，見則即見無生。無生故無滅，無滅故無處所。此真如佛性，在聖不加，在凡不減，本自具足，只因迷悟不同，故有分別。

度輪師父的真如法性，何曾離開過娑婆世界！何曾離開過我們！不必因師父走了，而過份悲哀，自暴自棄。應繼續師父平生志願，將佛法發揚光大，才不負師父對我等之期望。願共勉之！

The Sutras say, "Birth and death and Nirvana, ordinary people and Buddhas are all but images of flowers in space." Space originally had no flowers; where did the images come from? Ordinary people take the aggregate of the four elements to be their body and the shadows of the six sense objects to be their own mind. The dispersal of the four elements is called death, and the imbalance of the four elements is called sickness. When the four elements are regulated, one's body is healthy. When the four elements disperse, where is the false body to be found? Thus we know that this body has no real substance. It is merely a temporary coming together of elements. In reality, it is an illusion. In the state of the unproduced, we falsely see production and destruction, and thus we flow and turn in birth and death, taking the false to be true and taking a thief as our father.

The Buddhas and Bodhisattvas destroyed this false attachment and realized Nirvana. The *Platform Sutra* says, "Do not give rise to views of ordinary people or sages. Do not have the concept of Nirvana. Put an end to the two sides and three limits. You should constantly use the faculties, but not have the thought of their use. Discriminate all phenomena, but have no thought of discrimination." That is, the sentiments of ordinary people and sages are put to an end, self and others are both empty. When things arise, there is an appearance. When they are gone, they leave no trace. This is the purity of Nirvana, which is thus and unmoving, clear and understanding. It is also called the real substance of true suchness. The names are different but the reality is the same. It is also called the knowledge and vision of the Thus Come One. 'Knowledge' refers to constantly knowing the empty stillness. 'Vision' refers to the vision of the unproduced. Because it is unproduced, it is also undestroyed. Being undestroyed, it has no location. This Buddha-nature of True Suchness is neither more in sages nor less in ordinary people. It is inherently within us. Discriminations arise only because of the difference between confusion and enlightenment.

When has the Venerable Master To Lun's Dharma-nature of True Suchness ever left the Saha World? When has it ever left us? There's no need to indulge in excessive grief and give up hope just because the Master has gone. We should continue to follow the Master's lifelong vows to make Buddhism flourish. That way, we won't let the Master down. Let us urge each other on!

FACE TO FACE WITH A GREAT BODHISATTVA AND NOT RECOGNIZING HIM

面見菩薩 交臂錯過

Chen Guomei
陳果梅

The last thing I remembered in the operating room was the nurse putting an anesthetic mask over my face. The next thing I saw was the Venerable Master standing in the operating room. He was standing in a different plane. His appearance was certainly awesome and magnanimous. "Shr Fu, how did you know about this operation?" I asked him, because I don't remember telling him about it. I had the notion that the operating room in a maternity hospital was an "unclean place." "Shr Fu, isn't this place unclean for you to be around?" The Venerable Master just brushed this silly notion of mine aside with his arms. The operation commenced then. I realized how frantic the surgeon was as he seemed to cut deeper and deeper without finding a solution. This made me feel that life is in a delicate balance when you are there lying on the operating table looking at a surgeon who appears to be "lost in the woods." The Venerable Master was showing me that surgical operations are the result of one's karma and that karmic obstacles can obstruct a surgeon in performing even a seemingly simple and minor operation. It was only with the Venerable Master's intervention that the surgeon was able to proceed smoothly. The Venerable Master directed the whole operation. During the difficult part of the operation, the Venerable Master helped me recite the Great Compassion Mantra, the names of Guanyin Bodhisattva, Medicine Master Buddha, and the Venerable Master.

The Venerable Master's appearance was very awesome and magnanimous, and he appeared to be holding the whole world together with his unselfish and tireless efforts. Even though he appeared to be disappointed that people were not listening and following his Dharma instructions, he nevertheless continued to tirelessly and compassionately "take living beings across." The Venerable Master said, "Everything there is to know has been said and recorded in my books." The point is that people do not believe or only "half-believe," or simply chose to ignore his instructional talks. This scenario is similar to Shakyamuni Buddha trying to convince living beings to detach themselves from playing in the "burning house," as narrated in the *Wonderful Dharma Lotus Flower Sutra*. Our attachments to this "burning house" have made us ignore the advice of Shakyamuni Buddha. This is the very reason we are born as humans and we will continue to be reborn in the six realms of suffering until such time as we see through this attachment to the "burning house" and listen to and follow the instructions of the Buddha.

The Venerable Master said that everything is cause and effect. He

在手術室裡，當護士將麻醉面罩罩上我的臉之後，我便失去知覺了。之後我看見上人站在手術室中。他不像是我們這個世界上的人，他的樣子也很凝重肅穆。我記得並沒有告訴上人這次手術，所以我問上人：「師父，您怎麼知道我動手術？」我以為醫院裡產科手術室是個不乾淨的地方。所以我又問：「師父，這個地方是不是太髒了？上人能待嗎？」上人用手勢把我這個愚笨的問話揮開。這時手術開始了，我感覺到手術醫生很惶恐，他越割越深，但仍找不出解救的方法。我躺在手術檯上看著醫生，顯得不知所措，使我覺得生命是這樣的脆弱。上人讓我知道一個人動手術，是由他的業招感來的。一個人的業障，會使得最簡單的小手術，都不能順利進行。幸虧有上人的加護，這位外科醫生才能順利的做完了手術。其實，整個手術的過程都操縱在上人的手裡。在手術最困難的時候，上人加持著我誦〈大悲咒〉，念觀世音菩薩、藥師佛名號，及上人的名號。

上人的外表威嚴肅穆，看起來好像整個世界都掌握在他手裡。以他的無私不倦使整個世界不致散失。有時上人看起來好像對眾生失望，因為我們都不聽他的話，但他還是慈悲不捨地救度眾生。上人說：「所有該知道的都在我的書裡呢。」雖然眾生或者不相信，或者半信半疑，或者乾脆不理上人的開示。這就好像《妙法蓮華經》中的譬喻：釋迦牟尼佛要說服「火宅」中的眾生出離，勿在宅中嬉戲。我們對「火宅」的執愛，也使我們不顧釋迦牟尼佛的忠告。上人曾說任何事都有其「因果」，并為我們講解因果的道理。還叫我讓全世界的人都要明白因果的道理，並且照著他的書學習。上

has explained about causes and effects. The Venerable Master asked me to inform the whole world about the reality of cause and effect and to learn from his books. The Venerable Master says in his books that karma will not be off by a hair's breadth and karmic retribution is unbiased and cannot be brought out. The Venerable Master was teaching cause and effect and great compassion when he said,

Truly recognize one's faults,
Do not talk about others' faults.
Others' faults are my own.
To be one with all living beings is truly Great Compassion.

When the anesthetic began to fade my reaction was to tell the whole world that we are face to face with a Great Bodhisattva and yet do not recognize him. What occurred during this operation was conveyed to the Venerable Master in person. The Master just compassionately smiled.

The least we can do is to protect and uphold the Venerable Master's Six Great Principles and his instructional talks, especially on cause and effect, and to hold them dearly in our daily lives. Only then will we be able to deserve the Venerable Master's compassionate smile. As we read this article, we can be assured that his Dharma Body continues to compassionately save all living beings. Just as he helped me so during the operation, should we want to assist him?

人在他書裡說：「業報是絲毫不爽的，不會有偏差的，是不能逃避的。」從上人說的：

真認自己錯，莫論他人非，
他非即我非，同體名大悲。

之中，上人是在教導我們「因果」的道理及大慈大悲的精神。

當我從麻醉中甦醒過來之後，我很想向全世界宣佈：「菩薩就在我們面前，但是我們都不認識。」後來我親自將手術檯上的事向上人報告過，上人笑而不答。

我們至少應該時刻護持上人的六大宗旨和開示，特別是有關「因果」的道理。只有這樣我們才能看見上人慈悲的笑容。我們可以確定，上人的法身，還是在慈悲地救度眾生，一如上人在手術室幫助我一樣，難道我們不願幫助上人嗎？

十方眾生悉慰安　一切所作皆真實
恆以淨心不異語　常為諸佛共加護

過去所有皆憶念　未來一切悉分別
十方世界普入中　為度眾生令出離
　　——《大方廣佛華嚴經》〈初發心功德品〉

He pacifies all living beings of the ten directions,
All that he does is true and actual.
He always has a pure mind an does not use wrong speech,
And is constantly aided and protected by all Buddhas.

He is completely mindful of everything in the past,
He totally differentiates everything in the future;
Universally he enters the worlds of the ten directions,
In order to rescue living beings and effect their escape.

Chapter on The Merit and Virtue from First Bringing Forth the Mind, the *Flower Adornment Sutra*

上人的慈悲救拔

THE VENERABLE MASTER COMPASSIONATELY SAVED ME

李果記　Li Guoji

我的法名是李果記，是一九八八年七月六日，在加拿大卡加利的華嚴聖寺皈依師父－－宣公上人的。皈依後，我就開始茹素念經，差不多每天都到佛堂念經或做事。在一九九〇年，醫生告訴我，我患了子宮癌。我病了兩星期在家裡，沒有到佛堂去。當時華嚴聖寺的主持法師覺得奇怪，就向一位佛友詢問我的情況。當他知道我的病情後，就親自打電話給當時在萬佛城的另一位法師，並請他轉告師父上人。師父得悉後，很慈悲地讓法師轉告說：不要緊，此病無大礙。請華嚴寺的弟子們為他誦經，然後迴向就可以了。

就這樣，在我進醫院以前，華嚴寺的佛友們為我念了很多經。在這期間，我曾夢見師父三次。有一次，我夢見師父拿了一些藥草給我的朋友。還叫她煎給我喝。我在醫院住了二十幾天，頭三天做檢查和電療。休息兩星期之後，又做了三天的電療。做了這次治療後。我的病一直好轉。直到現在已經五年了，我的身體一直很好，沒什麼其它的病。所以我照常的上佛堂念經做事。

今年三月份，我去醫院做例行的檢查。早上八點多，在醫院的候診室，我一邊等候一邊念著觀世音菩薩的聖號。當時候診室內有很多病人在等著見醫生。突然間，我看到師父上人和一位住在華嚴寺的徐老師走了近來。我立即跪下向師父禮拜。師父一直往前穿走過了候診室，便消失了。這時，護士來叫我進去作檢查。當我出來時，差不多是十一點了，候診室的人全都走光了。我想這一定又是師父慈悲來救度這些病人了。

這幾年來，每逢萬佛聖城有大法會，我都去參加。有幾次，在頂禮師父的時候，我懇求師父醫治我的病。師父每次都在我的頭上打三下。當我回去再做檢查時，醫生總驚奇的問我，是否吃了別的藥。我說沒有，只是喝了大悲水

My name is Li Guoji, and I took refuge with the Venerable Master Hua on July 6, 1988 at the Avatamsaka Sagely Monastery in Calgary, Canada. After taking refuge, I became a vegetarian and started to recite Sutras. I also went to the monastery almost every day to recite Sutras or to work. In 1990, my doctor told me I had cancer of the uterus. I was sick for two weeks, during which I stayed home and didn't go to the monastery. The Dharma Master who managed Avatamsaka Sagely Monastery at the time thought it strange and asked a Buddhist friend how I was. When he found out about my sickness, he called Dharma Master Heng Chang at the City of Ten Thousand Buddhas and asked him to notify the Venerable Master. When the Venerable Master was informed, he kindly asked Dharma Master Heng Chang to pass this message: "Don't worry. The disease is not serious. Have the disciples at Avatamsaka Monastery recite Sutras for her, and she'll be okay."

Before I entered the hospital, the Buddhist friends at Avatamsaka Monastery recited Sutras for me for a long time. During that time, I dreamed of the Venerable Master three times. One time, I dreamed that the Master gave some medicinal herbs to my friend and told her to make a decoction for me to drink. I stayed in the hospital for over twenty days. The first three days, I had examinations and electrotherapy. After resting for two weeks, I was given three more days of electrotherapy. After that treatment, I recovered steadily. It has been five years, and I have been quite healthy, without getting any other diseases. Thus I have been going to the monastery as usual to recite Sutras and work.

In March of this year, I went to the hospital for a regular checkup. At a little after eight o'clock in the morning, I was in the waiting room reciting the name of Guanshiyin Bodhisattva and waiting to be called. There were many sick people waiting to see the doctor. All of a sudden, I saw the Venerable Master and Mr. Yu, who lives at the Avatamsaka Monastery, walk in. I immediately got on my knees and began bowing to the Master. The Master walked through the waiting room and disappeared. Right then, the nurse called me in for my checkup. When I came out again at around eleven o'clock, the waiting room was empty. I thought the Venerable Master must have compassionately come to save all those sick people.

In the past few years, I went to the Sagely City of Ten Thousand Buddhas to participate in several major Dharma sessions and celebrations. During those times, when I bowed to the Venerable Master, I would sincerely pray to the Master to cure my sickness. Each time the Master would hit my head three times. When I returned and went for a checkup, the doctor would always ask me in surprise whether I had taken some other medicine. I would say, "No, I just drink Great Compassion Water and recite Sutras and mantras." The doctor is puzzled because I have recovered so fast.

，念經，持咒。醫生覺得很奇怪，因為我的病好得這麼快。

我今天之所以能再在佛前念經，持咒，完全是師父上人的慈悲救拔，兩位法師的慈悲關懷，和華嚴寺佛友們的功德。

阿彌陀佛。

My being able to recite Sutras and mantras today is completely due to the Venerable Master's compassion, the concern of the two Dharma Masters, and the merit of my Buddhist friends at the Avatamsaka Monastery. Amitabha Buddha.

PROTECTING THE DHARMA JEWEL

護 持 法 寶

Barbara Dorney Waugh (Kuo Hsu) 果須

When I first met the Venerable Master Hsuan Hua, I barely noticed him. I was at a weekend conference on Buddhism sponsored by the University of California. The conference was held in La Honda, located in a forest setting near the ocean. On the second evening of the conference, the Master entered the hall accompanied by some of his American disciples. His appearance was very ordinary and unassuming and I didn't pay much attention to him. Instead I was fascinated by the sight of five American-born monks and nuns who had recently left home under the Master's guidance.

Everything changed when the Master began to speak. His words stood apart from anything I had ever heard for their clarity and wisdom. I was moved to tears by what he said. It was like a dam had burst. I cried for hours. I realized I had been waiting all my life to meet this person.

In the twenty-five years since, I have heard the Master speak many times and I have never heard him say anything that did not ring true. He spoke the Dharma tirelessly and at every opportunity. He did not ask for money when he spoke and he did not exclude anyone from the Buddha's Teachings. Whenever I asked him for help with a problem, he always did what he could to assist me. Not only did he help me, he helped all the members of my family in countless ways. I can't imagine what my life would be like now, without the benefit of his kindness and compassion.

Now that the Master has gone, I feel that it is more important than ever to support his efforts to bring the Buddha's Teachings to the West. The Master exhausted his life for this purpose and left behind as his legacy a great Dharma-treasury. It is up to his disciples to preserve this treasury and make it available to all who seek it, in the same spirit that the Venerable Master made it available to us.

July 10, 1995

當我第一次見到師父宣化上人時，我根本沒注意到他。當時我去參加加州大學主辦的，討論佛教的研究會。研究會的地點在近海的一座森林中。研究會第二天晚上，師父在他的美國弟子陪伴下走進會場。師父看起來非常非常普通，一點也不起眼，我倒是對跟隨師父出家的五位美籍比丘、比丘尼十分好奇。

當師父一開口講話時，我對他的印象立刻完全改觀。師父的話，既清晰又有智慧，和我以前聽過別人的講法完全不同。師父的話感動得我眼淚直流，就像水壩決堤般。我哭了好幾個鐘頭，也明白這輩子終於等到了我應該拜見的師父。

在過去的二十五年裡，我聽過師父講法很多次，每次講的都是真實不虛。師父利用每個機會，無倦地講法。師父講話時，既不開口跟人要錢，也不把任何人關在佛法門外。每次我有問題請師父幫忙，他總是盡力而為，師父不但幫我的忙，他還以各種方法來幫助我的家人。若不是受惠於師父的慈悲，我真不知道自己今天會是怎樣個局面。

現在師父圓寂了，我覺得當務之急是繼承師父的遺志，把佛法在西方廣泛傳播。為這個目的，師父竭盡一生的心力，為我們留下來那麼多的佛法寶藏。師父讓我們有機會認識佛法，現在做弟子的責任是繼續護持這些寶藏，並和其他尋寶的人分享。

一九九五年七月十日

遊戲人間

ROAMING PLAYFULLY IN THE WORLD

常懺　　Constant Repentance

因為一個因緣，使我有幸能參與道場的設計，從而能親近上人，體會上人無所不在的**觀機逗教**，和經典所謂的應機說法！

記得第一次拿設計圖請上人過目，並與上人討論時，上人倒拿著設計圖，一副似看非看，似懂非懂的樣子。我心裡想：「上人怎麼會這樣？」上人瞧也不瞧我，邊看邊冒了一句話：「法無定法！」

石破天驚的一句，將我所有的疑惑都震得**煙消霧散**！每思及此，不禁想起香嚴禪師頓悟時，遙拜溈山老人所云：「和尚大悲，恩逾父母！」誠哉斯言。

之後，又跟師父溝通過幾次，針對大雄寶殿要蓋多大，位置，形狀……等等，師父一一指示。有一天，建築師帶來了一份完全不同的設計，師父聽完解說，只幾分鐘便說：「O.K.！」我一聽，先是一愣，旋即又是一個**震撼** —— 沒有任何執著！

"Everything is O.K. No Problem!"（一切都沒有問題！）是這樣，無所罣礙！從此不論是開會，或上人開示都更能明了師父的一言一行。

有些人，總是捧師父的話：師父說……
有些人，師父說什麼就做什麼……
有些人，凡事都要等師父的指示……有些人，以為師父不知道自己的意圖……
也有一些人以為：師父年紀大了，眼、耳都不靈，會不會老糊塗了？
更有些人以為，他能幫師父治病……

的確是法無定法 —— 無有定法名阿耨多羅三藐三菩提，亦無有定法如來可說；佛以一音演說法，萬物隨類各得解；心生種種法生，真真假假，那個是真的？那個是假的？師

Because I was involved in the design of Way-places, I had the opportunity to draw near the Venerable Master. I came to see how the Venerable Master always contemplated the potentials and bestowed teachings, and to understand what the Sutras mean by "speaking the Dharma according to the situation."

The first time I brought some architectural drawings to show to and discuss with the Venerable Master, the Master held the drawings upside down. He seemed to be looking and yet not looking at them. He seemed to understand and yet not understand them. I thought to myself, "Why is the Master acting this way?" The Master ignored me, and as he looked at them he said, "There are no fixed dharmas!"

That startling statement chased all my doubts away! Whenever I think of this, it reminds me of how when Chan Master Xiangyan was suddenly enlightened, he bowed to the Elder One of Mount Wei and said, "O greatly compassionate Master, your kindness is greater than that of my parents!" How true his words are!

Afterwards, I had several discussions with the Venerable Master regarding the size, location, structure, and other aspects of the Jewelled Palace of Great Heroes. The Master gave instructions on each of these aspects. One day, the architect brought a radically different design. Only a few minutes after hearing his explanation, the Master said, "OK!" I was shocked, and then I realized that the Master has no attachments whatsoever!

"Everything is okay. No problem!" That's the way he was, without any worries or hangups! From then on, I could understood the Master's every word and move better, whether he was in a meeting or giving a lecture.

Some people always quote the Master: "The Master said..."
Some people do whatever the Master says...
Some people wait for the Master's instructions before they do anything...
Some people think the Master doesn't know their plans...
Some people think: The Master is getting old, and his sight and hearing aren't very good. Won't he just be an old fogey?
And some people think they can cure the Master's sickness...

Truly, there are no fixed dharmas—there is no fixed dharma called Anuttarasamyaksambodhi, and there is no fixed dharma spoken by the Thus Come One: The Buddha proclaimed with a single sound, and the myriad creatures understand according to their kind. When the mind arises, all kinds of dharmas arise, unreal and real. What is real? What is unreal? The Master used every expedient—speaking this way and that, saying what he means or saying the opposite of what he means, manifesting the angry appearance of a Vajra spirit, manifesting sickness, or giving spontaneous teachings.

No wonder the patriarchs of the past urged cultivators to cultivate

父真是用盡了一切的方便 —— 左說右說，正說反說，或現金剛怒目相，或現病相，或不經意的點撥……

毋怪乎歷來祖師都勸勉行者，須在大叢林共修。在萬佛聖城，形形色色，法無定法，隨大眾演戲、看戲，藉事鍊心。也許就因一句很平常的話、或是當師父對別人開示、對話時，一剎那的相應，都勝讀萬卷經書。不分國籍種族，不論老弱殘病，皆應機接引，隨緣度化。在萬佛聖城的幾年，耳聞目睹上人種種遊戲神通，出世、入世方便法打成一片，實在令人嘆為觀止！

只是，多少人慕名而來，多少人又離去不復再來。很多人不能深切體會到，萬佛聖城是如何地殊勝，是怎樣一個能讓行者無憂無慮修行的，不可多得的道場。甚至攜家帶眷的，都能跟著上人在濁世中走上自性清淨的解脫道。誠如上人所說的：在法水裡泡，泡久了就一點一點明白了！

要泡多久呢？法無定法，各有各的因緣。而我自知不天天泡，是回不了家的，乾脆搬進萬佛城了！惟願有緣人：但念無常，皆能及早回聖城，共沐法浴，共證菩提，阿彌陀佛！

together in large monastic communities. At the Sagely City of Ten Thousand Buddhas, there are all sorts of people and no fixed dharmas. Along with the assembly, one acts in the play, watches the play, and cultivates the mind in the situations that come up. It may be an ordinary statement, or a momentary insight gained when the Master was instructing and speaking with someone else, but it was worth more than reading ten thousand volumes of Sutras! The Master accepted all kinds of people according to their potentials and taught them according to conditions, regardless of their nationality or race, regardless of whether they were old, weak, sick, or handicapped. In the few years I've been at the Sagely City of Ten Thousand Buddhas, I have observed the Venerable Master's playful use of spiritual powers and his merging of worldly and transcendental expedient means. Truly, it is the height of perfection!

How many people have come upon hearing the good name? How many have left, never to return? Many people have failed to truly realize what a rare and supreme Way-place the Sagely City of Ten Thousand Buddhas is. It is a place where cultivators can cultivate without any worries. Even those with families to raise can follow the Venerable Master in this turbid world and walk the path of liberation to return to the pure inherent nature. As the Master said, "If you soak in the Dharma water, after soaking a long time you'll gradually come to understand!"

How long must we soak? There are no fixed dharmas. It depends on each person's conditions. As for myself, I knew that if I didn't soak every day, I wouldn't be able to return home. So I thought I might as well move into the City of Ten Thousand Buddhas! I hope those with affinities will be mindful of impermanence and return to the Sagely City as soon as possible to bathe in the Dharma and realize Bodhi together. Amitabha Buddha!

念念眞誠念念通，
默默感應默默中；
直至山窮水盡處，
逍遙法界任西東。

宣公上人作

When every thought is sincere, every thought penetrates;
In silence, responses are quietly received.
When you reach the end of the mountains and rivers,
You are free to roam throughout the Dharma Realm.

by Venerable Master Hua

老吾老以及人之老

CARING FOR MY PARENTS AND THE PARENTS OF OTHERS

釋恆謹　Shi Hengjin

有人是這樣描述美國的：「少年人的天堂，青年人的戰場，老年人的墳墓。」眾生為家庭、為社會、為國家忙碌了一生，最後的歸宿都是墓地，真讓人感到悲哀！在不重視老人的西方社會，老人的晚年尤其淒涼。可是在萬佛聖城，卻有一塊屬於老人的福地、天堂。

從下面的例子，可以看出師父對老人的慈悲大愛：

若干年以前，在臺灣聽了一位長老講經以後，蒙發了出家念頭，並表示願成為長老座下的弟子。長老問：「今年多少歲？」回稟：「六十五歲。」長老答：「在家念佛修行是一樣的，不必出家啦！」聽到這個回答，心中頗覺遺憾！直到第二年，得以在上人座下剃度出家後，才了卻了我這樁心願。

一位同修與年輕外孫同來聖城拜見上人後，祖孫同時向上人要求出家。當時老人請示上人，她年已八十，又不識字，上人能恩准出家嗎？上人嘆口氣說：「唉！百歲也要度哇！」老人如願得償，與外孫同蒙剃度。老人非常勤勞，外表雖略顯老態，但身體健康、步履輕快。出家後精進不懈，不說閒言浮語。每晨二時即起，背誦〈大悲神咒〉一百零八遍，學誦《彌陀經》，早晚各二萬彌陀聖號，並修習師父傳授的「四十二手眼」。老人每日爭做佛前供水、供花、供果等事，同修見她喜歡做香燈工作，即隨喜老人。老人如今已八十七高齡，身體雖然瘦小，仍很康寧。居士們見之，無不讚歎老人家，都祝福老人家能如願往生西方，親叩彌陀。

又有一位老人，已是九十二歲的高齡了，也是非常幸運地蒙師父恩准出家。老人身體雖健，但手腳已不靈便。上人派一位年輕的居士，照顧其飲食起居。

上人年輕時，因侍親至孝，鄉人譽為白孝

Some people described the United States in this way: "A heaven for children, a battleground for young people, and a grave for the old." People are busy all their lives for the sake of their families, the society, and the country, but their final refuge is always the graveyard. How depressing! In Western society, which does not value its elderly, the plight of old people is particularly sad. Yet at the Sagely City of Ten Thousand Buddhas, one can find a blessed land, a heaven, for old folks.

The following account will illustrate the Venerable Master's compassion towards the elderly.

Several years ago, after listening to a certain Elder Master lecture on the Sutras in Taiwan, I conceived the wish to leave the home-life and told the Elder Master I would like to become his disciple. The Elder Master asked, "How old are you this year?" I said, "Sixty-five." He said, "Reciting the Buddha's name and cultivating at home is the same. There's no need to leave home." Hearing his answer, I was filled with despair! It was only the following year that I shaved my head and left home under the Venerable Master, thus fulfilling my wish.

A fellow cultivator and her young grandson came to visit the Venerable Master at the Sagely City. Afterwards, grandmother and grandson simultaneously requested the Venerable Master's permission to leave the home-life. The elderly woman was already eighty and illiterate. Would the Venerable Master be so kind as to allow her to leave home? The Venerable Master sighed and said, "Even those who are a hundred years old need to be taken across!" The elderly woman's wish was granted, and she and her grandson left home together. She is extremely diligent. Although her age shows slightly, her body is healthy and she walks with quick, light steps. After leaving the home-life, she has been very vigorous and never indulges in idle talk. She rises at two o'clock every morning and recites the Great Compassion Spiritual Mantra 108 times. She is learning to recite the Amitabha Sutra. Every morning and evening she recites the holy name of *Amitabha Buddha* twenty thousand times. She also cultivates the Forty-two Hands and Eyes transmitted by the Venerable Master. Every day she rushes to make offerings of water, flowers, and fruit to the Buddhas. Her fellow cultivators see how much she likes to take care of the altar, and they follow her wishes. This year she is eighty-seven. Although she is small and slender, she is still healthy. All the laypeople who see her praise her and wish that she will be reborn in the West as she has vowed and personally bow to Amitabha Buddha.

Another elder, who was already ninety-two years old, was also extremely fortunate to receive the Venerable Master's kind permission to leave the home-life. Although she is healthy, her hands and feet are not agile. The Venerable Master assigned a young laywoman to prepare her food and attend to her needs.

When the Venerable Master was young, he was known as Filial Son Bai to the villagers because of filial piety towards his parents. The Venerable Master also showed the utmost concern and respect for elderly people. At the Sagely City of Ten Thousand Buddhas, the elderly reside in the newly renovated Tower of Blessings. They are allowed to take three meals, following the Buddha's instructions for the elderly. Thus the elderly have the opportunity to concentrate on reciting Sutras, bowing to the Buddhas, and reciting the Buddha's name.

We elderly are deeply grateful to the Venerable Master for his compassion and concern. We wouldn't have been cared for so well even at home. We vow to be reborn in the Western Land of Ultimate Bliss. Once we see Amitabha Buddha, what worry is there that we won't become enlightened? After enlightening to the nonproduction of dharmas, we will return by the power of our vows to help the Venerable Master propagate the Buddhadharma and lead all living beings to realize Bodhi together. Only then will we have repaid a tiny bit of the deep kindness of the Buddhas, the Bodhisattvas, and the Venerable Master.

子。上人也極為關切尊重老年人，在萬佛聖城，上人將老人們安頓在修葺一新的福居樓，並體諒老人們年老力衰，特為其開緣三餐。因此老人得以專心誦經、禮佛、念佛。

老人們都從心裡感激上人的慈悲與關愛之心。即便是在家裡，亦不可能得到如是的照顧。故我等發願，願生西方極樂世界。但得見彌陀，何愁不開悟。悟無生法，乘願再來。助師弘揚佛法，普度眾生，共證菩提，略報佛菩薩上人深恩於萬一也。

I MAKE THESE VOWS
我 發 願

小沙彌尼　釋果成
Young Shramanerika Shi Guocheng

The Venerable Master had Eighteen Vows. They are all very great, just like Earth Store Bodhisattva's vows: "If the hells are not empty I will not become a Buddha." Therefore we should cultivate diligently and not make the Venerable Master wait too long. I have never seen anyone who could replace such a wonderful high Sanghan. I'm really sad, because I left the home-life only a year ago, and now the Venerable Master has entered Nirvana. The Venerable Master was so compassionate that he came to this Saha world and took the sufferings of living beings upon himself.

What the Venerable Master liked best was to see us all cultivating diligently, holding the Six Principles, and changing all our bad habits, especially me. I resolve to fulfill the following vows:

1. I vow to respect all people.
2. I vow that I will not argue with anybody.
3. I vow that I will be filial to my parents.
4. I vow that I will not blame others.
5. I vow that I will change my big temper.
6. I vow that I will not look for others' bad points.
7. I vow that in every life I will follow the Venerable Master's teaching.

上人有十八大願，願願都很偉大。就如同地藏王菩薩的大願一樣，地獄不空誓不成佛；所以我們應該精進修行，不能讓上人等得太久。我從來就沒有見過任何一個人可以代替這樣一位高僧。我很幸運能跟上人出家，但是我很悲傷，因為我才出家一年，上人就入涅槃了。上人太慈悲了，所以他來此娑婆世界代眾生受苦。

上人所喜歡的是看到我們都能精進修行，遵守六大宗旨，改變所有的壞習氣，尤其是我。我發願要圓滿下列之願：

一、願尊敬一切人
二、願不和一切人爭吵
三、願孝順父母
四、願我不埋怨別人
五、願改我的脾氣
六、願不找別人缺點
七、願生生世世都跟隨上人

A DISCIPLE REMEMBERS
弟子的追思

Loni Baur 　果逸

When I came to meet the Master I knew only two things: (1) that I was hopelessly lost in a world full of suffering, and (2) the Master could teach me the way to escape suffering and how to help others escape.

Season upon season, year after year, the Master tirelessly expounded the scriptures of the wonderful Dharma, and his disciples studied them. But more than that, we learned from every word and every action of the Master, because he truly lived the words he taught. Kindness, compassion, joy, and giving are words. But we whose lives the Master has touched know, beyond the words, how he recognized, nourished and brought forth in each of us the very best and brightest part of our natures.

Some years back, I dreamed that I had floated off to the end of the universe. I looked back at the earth, a tiny, far-off speck. As I stood there in the blackness, with stars all around, I looked down and noticed what I was standing on: it was an eye. And the eye was sitting in the palm of a hand. And the hand, I realized, was our Teacher's hand. Then I heard his voice, kindly and amused, saying, "See? You can run... You just can't run away."

當我初遇上人時，只知兩件事：第一，在這多苦的世界，我已絕望地迷失；第二，上人能教我離苦，並教我助人離苦。

上人年年月月講經說法，永不疲厭，弟子們則隨著。上人更言行如一，以身作則；上人的一言一行，我們都學習。慈悲喜捨是文字，但受到上人影響的都知道，在文字之外，上人是怎樣地認識我們、培育我們、顯露我們自性中最好、最光明的一面。

幾年前，我夢見自己在宇宙的盡頭掉落下去，我回頭看地球，已經成了一粒小小的微塵。我站在一片黑暗之中，周遭圍繞著眾星，我向下一看，發現自己站在一隻眼睛上，這隻眼睛又生在一隻手上，而這隻手竟是師父上人的手，我又聽見上人的聲音：「你看！你可以跑，可是你跑不掉。」

梵語禪那波羅蜜，
此云靜慮細進參；
山高水深無所畏，
始知天外別有天。

宣公上人作

Dhyana Paramita is a Sanskrit term
Meaning still reflection and subtle investigation.
The mountains are lofty and the waters are deep, but there is nothing to fear;
One begins to know that beyond this world is another world.

by Venerable Master Hua

化悲痛爲力量

TRANSFORMING GRIEF INTO STRENGTH

莊果江　Zhuang Guojiang

上人圓寂的消息於六月上旬傳來之後，對四眾弟子而言可說是晴天霹靂。這也是眾生福報不夠，不能等到上人百歲燃身供佛。這位當代的大善知識就這麼離開了我們。

雖然上人已經走了，我們應該要化悲痛爲力量，仔細想想那些是師父一再叮嚀我們要奉行不移的？哪些是師父已做，但尚未完成的志業呢？諸如此類都是我們應該繼續努力的目標。筆者將自己盡可能想到的，提供給大家做參考：

（一）做好經典翻譯工作。上人到西方弘揚佛法，就是希望能把佛經翻譯成英文及世界上其他各種語言，以使全球的人類都有機會學習佛法。可是翻譯經典的工作並不只限於出家眾。出家眾應是翻譯的主力，但在家眾亦可衡量己力，每月或每季固定捐資給位於柏林根市的國際譯經學院。大家有力出力，有錢出錢，繼續這項神聖的任務。

（二）這幾年上人臥病期間，萬佛城發生了許多事情，這些事情相信都是上人對弟子們的考驗。雖然，那時候弟子們並不能過關，以後，大家更要記取教訓奉行不移。如搭衣、日中一食、六大宗旨等萬佛聖城的家風和「依法不依人」等。

（三）天天不忘持誦〈楞嚴咒〉。上人一再強調《楞嚴經》和〈楞嚴咒〉的重要性。上人曾說：「法滅時〈楞嚴咒〉先滅，也就是《楞嚴經》先沒有了。那時這些妖魔鬼怪出興於世，各得其所……。因此，我主張每一位佛教徒都要把〈楞嚴咒〉念熟，並且能背誦，天天誦持〈楞嚴咒〉。這就是保持正法不滅，就是正法住世。」蓮因寺的懺公也曾提及：在家人誦持〈楞

When the news of the Venerable Master's completion of stillness arrived in mid-June, it was like a peal of thunder in the blue skies to the fourfold assembly of disciples. Living beings did not have sufficient blessings to see the Venerable Master live to be a hundred and then burn his entire body as an offering to the Buddhas. This great Good Knowing Advisor of modern times has left us.

Although the Venerable Master has gone, we should transform our grief into strength. We should carefully think: Which things did the Master keep reminding us to practice without changing? Which resolves did the Master already start to carry out but did not completely realize? These are all goals towards which we should continue to strive. I offer the following points that I have thought of for everyone to consider:

1. We should carry out well the task of translating the Buddhist scriptures. The Venerable Master came to the West to propagate the Buddhadharma because he hoped to translate the Buddhist canon into English and all other languages of world, so that people around the globe would have the opportunity to study the Buddhadharma. The work of translating the Buddhist canon is not restricted to left-home people. While left-home people should be the main strength, laypeople can also contribute according to their ability, making a monthly or quarterly donation to the International Translation Institute in Burlingame. Those with manpower can contribute their strength, and those with money can make a financial contribution to enable this holy work to continue.

2. During the last few years when the Venerable Master was bedridden with illness, there have been many incidents at the City of Ten Thousand Buddhas. I believe these incidents were all tests that the Venerable Master gave his disciples. Even though his disciples didn't pass the test then, in the future everyone must take the teachings from these tests and practice without deviating from them. These teachings include: wearing the precept sash, eating one meal a day at noon, the six great principles and other special traditions of the Sagely City of Ten Thousand Buddhas, and the principle of "relying on the Dharma, not on an individual."

3. Recite the Shurangama Mantra without fail every day. The Venerable Master emphasized the importance of the *Shurangama Sutra* and the Shurangama Mantra over and over. The Venerable Master said, "When the Dharma perishes, the Shurangama Mantra will be the first to disappear; that is, the *Shurangama Sutra* will be the first Sutra to go. At that point the demons, ghosts, goblins, and weird creatures will thrive in the world and be able to do as they please... Therefore, I propose that every Buddhist should recite the Shurangama Mantra every day and become so familiar with it that they can recite it from memory. This is to protect the Proper Dharma from extinction, to keep the Proper Dharma in the world." Venerable Master Chan of Lianyin Monastery also said, "Laypeople who recite the Shurangama Mantra are simply left-home people with hair." When one is not familiar with the Shurangama Mantra, it may take twenty minutes to

嚴咒〉，就是頭頂戴髮的出家人。」誦〈楞嚴咒〉不熟時，可能需要二十分鐘左右。若是熟練後，不打法器，大概只要四五分鐘。在家人每天早課不打法器，熟練的話，誦持楞嚴、大悲、十小咒大概只要十分鐘。再加《心經》、發十大願王和念佛，這樣也和各叢林所做的早課相去不遠。

虛雲老和尚曾說：「天天誦持〈楞嚴咒〉，來生得七世的大富貴。」我們並不是為了求來生的福報而誦〈楞嚴咒〉，而是為了讓正法久住。希望大家都能發這樣的願：「願生生世世不管到那一個世界去投胎，只要那個世界有《楞嚴經》和〈楞嚴咒〉在，就要學習《楞嚴經》，天天誦持〈楞嚴咒〉。」另外上人也曾進一步的指出《楞嚴經》中的二十五圓通、四種清淨明誨和五十種陰魔等，都是值得大家仔細去研究的地方。

（四）上人圓寂前交待可誦《華嚴經》一七或七七。足見上人對《華嚴經》的重視。我們不只要在四十九天中誦，過了四十九天後，有空還是要好好地研究《華嚴經》。相信有「經中之王」和「金輪王」之稱的《華嚴經》，必有其值得聞、思、修之處。

（五）繼續支持由上人所倡導的，有關教育、道德等方面的活動。如「敬老懷少節」的推動、對育良小學、培德中學的支持。若是在家居士，要注重對小孩子的道德教育。要求自己的孩子不要一味地求名求利。有機會甚至可讓他們學習萬佛聖城的「弟子規」，或是到育良小學、培德中學接受教育。

另外有一點是，上人一九九三年回臺灣弘法後，有關個人的感想。在上人開示結束以後，有許多人談到他們的病苦或不如意的事，想請上人加持，祈求消災免難。上人差不多每次都答：「求觀世音菩薩」或「求觀世音菩薩加被」。後來上人又補充：「只要誠心的求，一定會有感應的。」其實學佛的人生活上有不如意的事，只要拿出真誠心來求，稱誦諸佛菩薩的聖號，或者是阿彌陀佛、或者是觀世音菩薩或是地藏王菩薩，只要誠心的求、稱念諸佛菩薩的聖號，必可消災免難。

recite. If one is very familiar with it and doesn't use any Dharma instruments, it only takes four or five minutes. If laypeople do not use Dharma instruments during the morning ceremony, then they probably need only ten minutes to recite the Shurangama Mantra, the Great Compassion Mantra, and the Ten Small Mantras. If they also recite the *Heart Sutra*, the Ten Great Kings of Vows, and the Buddha's name, they will not be too far from the standard morning ceremony of large monasteries.

The Venerable Master Hsu Yun said, "If one recites the Shurangama Mantra every day, one will have great wealth and honor in the next seven lives." We are reciting the Shurangama Mantra not for the sake of blessings in our next life, but for the sake of allowing the Proper Dharma to stay in the world. I hope everyone can make a vow like this: "I vow that in life after life, no matter what world I am born in, if the *Shurangama Sutra* and the Shurangama Mantra exist in that world, I will study the *Shurangama Sutra* and recite the Shurangama Mantra every day." The Venerable Master also pointed out that it is worth our while to carefully study certain sections of the *Shurangama Sutra,* such as the Twenty-five Sages Describing Their Perfect Penetrations, the Four Clear Instructions on Purity, and the Fifty Skandha Demon States.

4. Before the Venerable Master completed the stillness, he indicated that we could recite the *Flower Adornment Sutra* for seven days or for forty-nine days. This shows how highly the Venerable Master regards the *Flower Adornment Sutra.* Not only should we recite it for forty-nine days. After those forty-nine days, we should study the *Flower Adornment Sutra* well when we have the time. I am sure we will find it worthwhile to listen to, reflect on, and cultivate the *Flower Adornment Sutra*, which is known as the King of Sutras and the Gold Wheel King.

5. We should continue to support the educational and ethical activities that the Venerable Master promoted. This includes observing the Celebration for Respecting Elders and Cherishing the Young, and supporting Instilling Goodness Elementary School and Developing Virtue Secondary School. Laypeople should emphasize the ethical education of children and make sure their own children are not avidly pursuing fame and profit. If they have time, they can teach their children the "Rules for Being a Student" used at the Sagely City, or enroll their children in Instilling Goodness Elementary School and Developing Virtue Secondary School.

I also had a personal feeling when the Venerable Master went to Taiwan to propagate the Dharma. After the Venerable Master had finished his talk, a number of people spoke of their illnesses and troubles and requested the Master to bestow aid upon them and dispel the calamities. The Venerable Master almost always said, "Pray to Guanshiyin Bodhisattva (the Bodhisattva who contemplates of the world's sounds)," or "Pray for aid from Guanshiyin Bodhisattva." Later the Venerable Master added, "As long as you pray sincerely, you'll definitely receive a response." If people who study Buddhism encounter difficulties in their lives, all they have to do is sincerely pray by reciting the names of the Buddhas and Bodhisattvas. They may recite Amitabha Buddha's name, Guanshiyin Bodhisattva's name, or Earth Store Bodhisattva's name. As long as they pray and recite sincerely, the calamities and difficulties will disappear.

In the *Flower Adornment Sutra's Chapter on the Conduct and Vows of Universal Worthy*, there is a passage describing the tenth great vow:

《華嚴經普賢行願品》中，闡述第十大願時有一段經文這樣描述說：

復次善男子。言普皆迴向者，從初禮拜乃至隨順所有功德，皆悉迴向盡法界虛空界一切眾生。願令眾生常得安樂，無諸病苦，欲行惡法，皆悉不成，所修善業皆速成就，關閉一切諸惡趣門，開示人天涅槃正路。若諸眾生因其積集諸惡業故，所感一切極重苦果，我皆代受，令彼眾生悉得解脫，究竟成就無上菩提……。

上人十八大願的中第十二願：願將法界眾生所有一切苦難，悉皆與我一人代受。上人可說是，徹底實踐了普賢菩薩十大願王中的「普皆迴向」之願。

上人已經走了，我們在感傷之餘，對於他老人家的諄諄教誨要奉行實踐，對於他老人家未完成的使命要繼續完成，將佛法及上人的理念發揚光大，如此方不負他老人家辛勤的教導。正如一首偈頌：「菩薩清涼月，常遊畢竟空，為償多劫願，浩蕩赴前程。」這應可做為上人的寫照。濃縮民國初年揚州高旻寺來果禪師朝夕所發四十八願中之前三願：「希望正法能久住，不遭魔侵，也希望有更多的佛菩薩，不捨弘慈乘願再來，教化眾生。」

Moreover, Good Man, to universally transfer all merit and virtue is explained like this: All of the merit and virtue, from the first vow, to worship and respect, up to and including the vow to constantly accord, I universally transfer to all living beings throughout the Dharma Realm and to the limits of empty space. I vow that all living beings will be constantly peaceful and happy, without sickness or suffering. I vow that no one will succeed in doing any evil, but that all will quickly perfect their cultivation of good karma. I vow to close the doors to the evil destinies and open the right paths of humans, gods, and Nirvana. I will stand in for beings and receive all the extremely severe fruits of suffering which they bring on with their evil karma. I will liberate all these beings and ultimately bring them to accomplish unsurpassed Bodhi...

The twelfth of the Venerable Master's eighteen great vows says, "I vow to fully take upon myself all the sufferings and hardships of all the living beings in the Dharma Realm." The Venerable Master can be said to have fully put into practice the vow "to universally transfer all merit and virtue" among the Ten Great Kings of Vows of Universal Worthy Bodhisattva.

The Venerable Master has already left. Above our feelings of grief, we should follow the Master's earnest teachings, carry out the missions that the Master did not finish, and cause the Buddhadharma and the Venerable Master's ideals to flourish. Then we will not have been ungrateful for the Venerable Master's painstaking teaching. It is as the verse says, "The Bodhisattva is like a clear and cool moon constantly travelling in ultimate space. In order to fulfill vows made over many eons, he energetically advances on his way." This is the portrayal of the Venerable Master. Chan Master Laiguo of Gaomin Monastery in Yangzhou, Nongsuo, in the early years of the Republic of China, made forty-eight vows every morning and evening. The first three vows were: "I hope the Proper Dharma will remain for a long time and not be attacked by demons. I also hope more Buddhas and Bodhisattvas will not renounce their vast kindness and will follow their vows to come back and teach living beings."

說法偈
The Gatha of Speaking Dharma

佛法妙理本無説　　覺後一字更嫌多　　惟因眾生迷障重　　善巧方便來説説

The wondrous principles of the Buddhadharma are basically unspeakable.
After awakening a single word is too much.
It's only because living beings have deep confusion,
That they are spoken as skillful expedients.

宣公上人作
by Venerable Master Hua

DISTANT MEMORIES FROM THE BUDDHIST LECTURE HALL

遙想當年佛教講堂

Tim Testu (Kuo Yu)　　果逾

I was intrigued by the Abbot. The ordinary things he did made such a profound impact on me that I often found myself weeping with joy. And he was very, very funny.

我常被師父所吸引，師父的日常行為對我造成莫大的影響。師父常使我喜極而泣，師父實在是非常有趣的一個人。

*　　　　　*　　　　　*

One afternoon a very deliberate and hard-looking woman, with a bunch of tough-looking friends in tow, came in for the Master's Sutra lecture. Their vibes were bad. These people did not appear sincere; they looked angry. One wore a leather belt with chrome spikes sticking out. The Abbot, long-since accustomed to strange-looking Westerners, spoke the Dharma in his usual manner, and when finished, asked if anyone had questions. The woman stood up.

"I have two questions," she announced. "First of all, this world has millions of people who are starving to death. Every day thousands die of hunger. What does Buddhism think about this? And what is your position in this regard?

"Secondly, the world is filled with implements of nuclear destruction. The major powers have way more weapons than they'll ever need, enough to blow up the whole world many times over, yet there never seems to be enough. What do you think should be done about all this?"

The Abbot smiled patiently and waited for the translator to repeat the question. After a short silence he calmly replied with his delightful deadpan humour, "There's really a single solution to both of these problems. Take all the extra bombs and drop them on the overpopulated areas." The women gasped in shock. Everyone else roared with laughter.

But then the Master went on to answer what was undoubtedly the real issue. He said that basically there is no problem, and that is the official Buddhist position. Unfortunately, however, people are not satisfied with this state, so they go out and create problems for themselves where originally none existed. Basically everything is okay, but we make it not okay. The point of Buddhism is for each of us to try to reach this special state of "no problem." When we are able to dwell in the midst of all problems and at the same time realize there are no problems, then we've arrived. Buddhism, for the most part, remains apolitical.

某日午後，有位表情嚴肅的婦女，跟著一批不苟言笑的朋友，來聽師父說法。來者不善，看他們的表情，一點誠意也沒有，好像很生氣的樣子。其中一位腰部繫了條皮帶，上面絡黃的長釘突出來。師父老早對這些裝束怪異的西方人見怪不怪，照常說法。開示圓滿時，讓大家提問題，這位女士就站起來了，她說：「我有兩個問題。首先，全世界成千上萬的人因饑餓而死亡，每天有上千的人餓死。佛教對此現象如何解釋？你對這件事情所持的立場如何？第二，世界上充滿了核子武器的設備，幾個強國所擁有的核子武器和設備，足以毀滅世界好幾次不止，卻仍嫌不足。你覺得該如何處理這些情形？」

師父微笑著，耐心地聽完翻譯，停了一下，師父很幽默地回答說：「這兩個問題其實還真有一個解決的方法，把多餘的炸彈丟到人口過剩的地方去就好了。」這些女士聽後一驚，其他的人則笑得前仰後合。

師父接下來回答她的問題。師父說，其實並沒有什麼問題，這也正是佛教所持的立場。很遺憾的，一般人對此並不瞭解，在無事中去製造事端。本來一切都好好的，都沒有問題，問題是我們製造出來的。佛教就要每個人達到這種「沒有問題」的境界。當人們處在問題當中，卻明瞭實際上根本沒有什麼問題時，那就已到達了目的地。佛教本質上是不介入政治的。

When the lecture ended, everyone seemed satisfied with the answer.

The incident reminded me of the line in the Tennessee Williams movie, "Night of the Iguana." Richard Burton asks Ava Gardner why her Chinese cook always says *Meiyou wenti!* every time he is asked a question or told something to do.

Ava throws back her head and laughs. "*Meiyou wenti?*" she says. "That's 10,000 years of Chinese philosophy in two words!"

"Really? Well, what exactly do those two words mean?" asks Richard.

"No problem!" smiles Ava.

*   *   *

On another beautiful summer afternoon, after the noisy rhythm and clatter of ceremonies, when everyone was settled in elbow-to-elbow for the lecture, I overheard the Abbot quietly turn to layman Jones and tell him to keep a particularly close eye on people. He warned him to carefully watch the door because there was someone in the building who planned on stealing. Jones seemed to quickly forget what the Master had said, but I didn't. Maybe I felt the Abbot was also talking to me—he had a way of doing that. His mind was not singularly impeded like the rest of ours. He was aware of his connections and could read people from the inside. I was now sure of this powerful wisdom and looked for it in everything he said.

When the lecture ended, the ancient hall erupted into the usual hubbub of chitchat and socializing. Sure it was outflowing, a big release of energy, but folks just felt too darn high to contain themselves. While everyone indulged in their tête-à-tête, including Jones who'd forgotten what the Master had told him, I noticed a middle-aged Asian woman sneak into the vestibule off the main hall and try to rifle the donation box. It was like a living dream: first the prophecy, then the reality. The Master's mind flowed in and out of the future seamlessly, and he was taking us all along for the ride.

I alerted Jones, who quickly rushed in, grabbed the money from her hands, and shooed her out of the temple. The Master had already gone to his tiny room behind the altar, but his words echoed in my mind. He knew what this person was going to do before she did it! Amazing! It was as natural for the Master to read her mind, or my mind, or anyone's mind, as it was for me to speak English. How did he do it? And why was he revealing himself to me? Would I be able to do this kind of stuff if I cultivated? These incidents caused my heart of faith to grow astronomically. I really believed in Buddhism. I decided I was going to learn more about this amazing Abbot and his wondrous Buddhadharma.

*   *   *

開示結束後，看來大家對師父的回答都很受用。

這件事情，使我想起田納西・威廉斯的電影「大蜥蜴之夜」中的對白：李查・波頓問愛娃・嘉那，為什麼每次有人問她的中國廚子問題時，或是要他去做什麼時，總是說：「沒有問題！」愛娃・嘉那仰頭一笑說：「沒有問題？這句話濃縮了中國數千年哲理的精華。」「真的？那到底這話是什麼意思？」李查問道。愛娃笑著說：「沒有問題！」

*   *   *

另有一次，法會結束後，大家正要坐下來聽師父說法時，我聽到師父對一位瓊斯居士說，要他注意，因為大眾中有人要來行竊。瓊斯好像立刻就忘了師父的交待，但我卻沒忘，因為我覺得師父同時也在交待我。要知道－－師父總有辦法讓我有這種感覺。師父的心不像我們只能單向溝通，師父清楚地知道他與眾生的因緣，而且可以看透每一個人。我確認師父有如此的智慧，並去印證他說的每句話。

開示結束後，大家在講堂裡互相問好。這種現象當然也是一種「漏」，但是大家都很興奮，不能自已。當大家聊得正起勁時，瓊斯完全忘了師父的交待。我注意到一位亞洲中年婦人，偷偷跑到佛堂的走道去動功德箱。這真像在做夢，先是聽到預言，接著事實就呈現在眼前。師父易如反掌地遊走於現在和未來之間，並有意無意地讓我們多少瞭解其不可思議的境界。

我提醒瓊斯，他趕緊將錢從那婦人手中拿回，並要她離開。此時，師父早已回到佛堂後面小小的寮房去了。這件事卻一直縈繞在我腦海中。師父在這位婦女下手之前，就知道她想幹什麼，真是不可思議！你我心裡在想什麼，師父都明白。就好像我講英文般地容易。師父怎麼會有這種能力呢？他為什麼讓我知道他的能力呢？假如我修行的話，是否也會有這種能力呢？這類事情使我信心大增。我真正相信佛法。我決定要更深入地去認識師父和師父的妙法。

*   *   *

One day, just to start the ball rolling, I informed the head monk that I wanted to become a disciple of the Master and that I wanted to take the five precepts. He informed the Master of my intentions. A couple of days later the Abbot approached me and said there was going to be a "Take Refuge" ceremony in a few minutes. He asked me if I really wanted to do it. I told him I was sure. He smiled and returned to his room. The ceremony was about to begin when one of the American monks came rushing out and informed me that if I wanted to take refuge I'd have to shave my beard.

Now, I had grown quite attached to my beard in the short time I'd had it. It made me seem tough and masculine. Dark and curly, it was part of my chosen identity. Suddenly I was forced to make a choice. What was more important: some scruffy facial hair, or taking refuge with the Everlasting Triple Jewel? I quickly ran into the bathroom and shaved off my beard—I even gave my long hair a trim. When I came out, the ceremony was up and running.

A couple of other Americans also took refuge. The Abbot, using some method known only by himself, gave us names from a choice of about 50,000 Chinese characters. I'd noticed that it was uncanny the way the names somehow applied to the people who received them. For example, one disciple was named Kuo Li. He didn't know what it meant, but after the ceremony he gave the Master a present of lapis lazuli, a precious stone he had kept in his private collection for many years. No one knew he had the stone, or that he was going to give it to the Master. Later, when he looked up his name in the Chinese dictionary, he found that it meant lapis lazuli!

I took refuge with the Buddha, the Dharma, and the Sangha, choosing the Master as my teacher, and was given the name Kuo Yü (He who goes beyond the limit). I loved my new name and was very proud of it, for I had gone beyond the limit all my life and didn't plan on stopping now. After the ceremony, a bunch of Cantonese ladies were milling around the hall. The Master came out, and they drew near him like iron filings to a magnet. The Master looked at me and started laughing.

"Look at this stupid Westerner!" He said. "He just shaved off his nice beard so he could take refuge with me. Ha!"

My face stung with embarrassment, but there was nothing I could do to bring back the beard. I sulked over to a meditation pad to hide my feelings. I'm sure I felt a chunk of my ego fall off. My identity was going south, and there was little to take its place.

* * *

Over time I found the Abbot to be very gentle with most people, but there were a few he had to lay into. That's when I heard the expression, "First comes the honeymoon, then comes the Dharma!" He taught each one of us according to our individual natures, using "no fixed Dharma," employing a radically non-dogmatic approach within the framework of a highly traditional religion.

"Why is there wisdom?" He often asked. "Because the stupid make their mark!"

Using this principle, the Master challenged our ignorant ac-

首先，我告訴一位執事的比丘，我想皈依師父並受五戒。他把我的意思轉告了師父。幾天後，師父告訴我，一會兒就有皈依儀式。他問我是否真想皈依，我的回答是肯定的。他笑了笑轉身回到寮房去。皈依儀式開始前，一位美籍比丘對我說：「假如你真想皈依的話，得把鬍子刮掉。」

我對所留的鬍子是蠻得意的，黑而捲曲的鬍子是我自己選擇的形象，使我看起來有陽剛之氣。突然之間，我得做個決定，是保留臉上的鬍子？還是皈依三寶？我立刻跑進洗手間把鬍子刮掉，順便把長頭髮修了一下。當我走出來時，皈依儀式已經開始了。

同時還有幾位美國人皈依。師父用他自己才知道的方法，在五萬個中國字裡為我們選法名。我發現每個人跟他的法名中間有種奇妙的聯繫。比方說，有位弟子的法名叫果璃，他也不知道果璃的意思。皈依後，他把自己珍藏多年的一顆琉璃送給師父。事先沒人知道他有琉璃，也沒人知道他要送師父琉璃。後來，他查中文字典，想明白自己名字的意義時，才發現「璃」就是琉璃。

我皈依了三寶，選擇師父做我的老師，法名果逾（超越極限）。我對這個法名既滿意又得意。因為我正在超越自己的極限，也不打算停止。皈依儀式結束後，有幾位講廣東話的婦女還在講堂裡，師父走出來，她們立刻像鐵沙見到磁鐵般被吸引了過去。師父看著我就笑起來了。「看看那個愚癡的西方人，他剛把好好的鬍子刮掉，好跟我皈依三寶！哈！」

我滿臉窘相，但沒有辦法讓鬍子再長回來。於是我把脾氣轉移到拜墊上來掩蓋自己的情緒，我的自尊心受到了傷害。

日子久了以後，我發現師父對一般人都很溫和，但有些人卻需要師父的調教。我曾聽別人說：「蜜月過去後，就是講佛法了！」師父在傳統宗教體制下，以非教條式的方法對我們觀機逗教。

師父常問：「為什麼會有智慧？」「因為愚癡者著相。」

師父對我們的無明，觀機逗教，以智慧來教化我們。師父也不會對我們解釋他的教學方法。前一分

tions. We created the ignorance from nothing, and the Master responded from the depths of Wisdom Store. And he certainly didn't explain all his unusual techniques. One minute he'd scold someone at the top of his voice, the next instant he'd gently inquire of someone else. Most people's emotions ran like hot and cold water from a tap. The Master tried, it seemed, to lure us into the inconceivable ground of enlightenment beyond opposites. His occasional anger, if that's what one could call it, seemed real, yet he had no attachment to it. He could burst forth with tremendous blasts of power, shaking the windows and rattling the walls, and then relinquish it all the moment it left his lips. He went after our attachments, not our being; our self, not our Self-Esteem; our ghosts, not our Buddha-nature. We were volunteers—this was no place to take things personally. The Master performed Perfect Wisdom Mirror Service, helping us view our selves truly for the first time. He once conceded that his job was to get us oscillating between opposites: between good and bad, fear and love, happy and sad, inside and out, so on and so forth, until we got to where we no longer lurked in the illusions of opposites, the world of dualities, the idea of a separate self in an "outside world." We had to find the middle ground that was no ground in our true self-nature that was no self-nature.

*　　　*

The Master made free use of what he called his "radar" to teach from "the inside out." This put him universes beyond other so-called "masters" who tried to teach from the outside in. How could they possibly teach when they didn't have the ability to see what their disciples were doing behind their backs?

"Don't get the wrong impression," the Master said. "I'm really a nobody, a big nothing, a living dead man. You all want to be first, number one. I want to be last. You all are so smart, while I am cultivating my way to stupidity.

Just remember, you can cheat your teacher, you can cheat yourself, but you can't cheat the Buddhas and Bodhisattvas. If you want to try, however, go ahead and check it out."

He gave the Buddhas and Bodhisattvas credit for everything.

*　　　*

Small Novice was an American disciple who received a lot of verbal "beatings." This poor fellow had particular difficulty following the rules and stopping his outflows. One night, as the story goes, Small Novice became filled with the desire to go "outside" and do something. Now, many of us had wrestled with that one, but he actually decided to act upon it. Donning civilian clothes, including a wool cap to cover his bald head, Small Novice slid down a drain pipe from the fourth floor balcony, landed on a third floor balustrade, and fled down the fire escape into the night. He was gone several hours doing

鐘他還在大聲訶斥某人，下一分鐘他已經殷殷地問及另外一人的情況。一般人的情緒就像水龍頭的水有冷有熱。師父想帶領我們進入一個超越對立的，不可思議的開悟境界。

師父偶爾發脾氣——所謂的脾氣，看起來像是真的，師父卻一點也不執著它。師父「動怒」時，有強烈的震撼力。可是話一旦出口，他的脾氣也就消了。師父追究的，是我們的執著而不是本性；是我們的自我而不是自尊；是我們身上邋遢的東西而不是佛性。我們願意受他的調教，但你也不能認為師父是衝著你來的。師父用他的大圓鏡智來幫助我們真正地觀照自己。他曾說他的任務就是教我們在好壞、愛憎、憂喜、內外等兩者間來回，一直到我們不為「對立法」所迷惑。在「對立」的世界，我們必須尋得「中道」，但是在真正的自性中，卻無「中道」可言，亦無「自性」。

*

師父常用他所謂的「雷達」式的方法，「由內而外」教化。這種教化方法比其他「由外而內」教化的師父高明了許多。這些師父連徒弟在他們的背後做些什麼也不知道，怎麼能當師父呢？

師父說：「別搞錯了，我實在是個無名小卒，什麼都不是，是個活死人。你們都想爭先、做第一，我願意當墊底的。你們都很聰明、優秀，我是在愚癡上修。不過你們要記住，你們能騙得了師父、騙得了自己，可是騙不了佛菩薩。假如你們想試的話，請便。」

師父把所有的功德都歸於佛和菩薩。

*

一位美國小沙彌常受到師父「口頭鞭策」。這可憐的傢伙很不守規矩。放不下向外馳求的心。故事是這樣的：一天晚上，小沙彌決定到外面的世界去玩一玩。其實我們很多人也有這個念頭。但他是真地付諸於行動。穿上在家人的衣服，戴頂羊毛帽，然後沿著水管從四樓陽台爬到三樓的欄杆，再利用防火梯，在黑夜中

God knows what. Just before morning services he snuck back into the building the same way he went out.

No one saw him leave, no one saw him return, and he told no one about his big adventure.

The next day, however, the Master approached him and asked, "Where did you go last night?"

"Nowhere, Shrfu," replied the trembling monk.

"Then what were you doing on the bus?" inquired the Abbot. As always, whenever the Abbot spoke, everyone in the little room listened intently. This was definitely going to be another teaching experience.

"I, I, I, don't know," cried the Novice.

"Just who is it that doesn't know?" yelled the Abbot.

"I, I, I don't know."

"Who gave you the cigarette?"

"I, I can't remember," wailed the monk.

"Why were you talking to that girl on the bus?"

Small Novice's face turned deep purple. "How did you know?" he cried in astonishment.

"How do I know?" yelled the Abbot. "I'll tell you how I know…. Did you know?"

The young monk looked flabbergasted.

"Well, did you know?" the Abbot yelled again.

"Yes."

"Then that's how I know!" There was a prolonged silence.

"Just remember!" counselled the Abbot, "You may be able to cheat yourself, but you can't cheat the Great Assembly!"

*　　　*　　　*

The Master explained to us that in the golden age of Buddhism, during the T'ang dynasty, teachers had to beat their disciples into enlightenment. He said, however, that in America we were too soft, and Buddhism was too new. There was no way he could physically beat us, even though he was sure we needed it, and that undoubtedly it would do us some good. If he did, we'd all just run away, so his "beatings" would have to be mental, mind to mind. Just like the Patriarchs, but without the stick. If we wanted to get enlightened and obtain Samadhi, we'd have to toughen up and learn to take it. Most of us really wanted these "beatings." The Master's verse addressed this principle, and he repeated it to us over and over again.

Everything is a test
To see what you will do;
If you don't recognize what's before your face
Then you must start anew.

The Master informed us that in the future he might test us. We wouldn't know if it was real or a test, however, because he wasn't going to explain everything—we'd have to do our own figuring out. Some of these tests would be very hard to take, he warned, but we shouldn't fear a little suffering. Most of us would run away, he pre-

消失了蹤影。幾小時過去了，誰也不知道他做了些什麼事。早課開始前，他按著出去的路線又摸了回來。

沒有人看到他離開，也沒有人見到他回來。他也沒有跟任何人提到他的行蹤。

第二天，師父問他：「昨晚你上那兒去了？」「那裡也沒去，師父。」小沙彌發抖地回答。師父問：「那你在巴士上做什麼？」師父每次講話時，房間裡每個人都專心聽著。這絕對是師父要教化我們的好時機。「我…我…我不知道。」小沙彌說。「到底是誰不知道？」師父大聲說。「我…我…我不知道。」「誰給你香菸的？」「我記不得了。」小沙彌在哀泣。「你為什麼和巴士上的小姐聊天？」

小沙彌的臉都發紫了。他驚異地問道：「你怎麼知道？」師父大聲地說：「我怎麼知道？我告訴你我怎麼知道的……，你自己知不知道？」小沙彌大吃一驚。師父再大聲地問：「怎麼樣，你自己知不知道？」「知道。」「那就是我怎麼會知道了。」接下來是一片死寂……。

「記住！」師父勸道：「你可能欺騙得了自己，但是你無法欺騙大眾。」

*

師父說，在唐朝，也就是佛教的全盛時期，祖師為使弟子們開悟，不惜用棒打的方式。但在美國，佛教是新的宗教，弟子們也太軟弱。雖然他認為我們欠揍，而且打對我們也有益處，但師父不會真地打我們。假如師父真地打我們，大家一定全都跑光了。所以他所謂的「打」完全是精神上的，以心對心的，就像以前的祖師一樣，只是沒有用棒喝而已。假如我們真想開悟、得三昧，我們就得堅強起來，學著去接受善知識的棒喝。很多人都曾經想挨師父的「打」。師父有首偈頌一再對我們提示：

一切是考驗，看爾怎麼辦？
覿面若不識，須再重頭煉。

師父說以後他會考考我們。我們卻不知道那是真的考驗，還是什麼。他不會為我們解釋每件事情，我們必須自己去琢磨。他說，有些考

dicted, but that was no problem. We could run all we wanted—there was no way out of the universe. When we got tired, he'd be waiting for us; his door was open. He would neither beg us to come in, nor ask us to leave.

Some of the elder disciples asked if they could test the newer people to "help" them along the road to enlightenment. The Master blasted that false thinking, saying that he would be the only one making up the tests. Besides, most tests would arise of themselves, from within and without. If we didn't pass them, we'd get to start anew. Furthermore, our enlightenment, should we ever experience it in this lifetime, wouldn't be considered genuine unless certified by a true Master, a Master certified by the lineage of sages reaching back to the original teacher, Shakyamuni Buddha.

Thus, if we wanted it, we were going to get it. Those who stayed could count on being "beaten," cajoled, pushed, pulled, inspired, and empowered into enlightenment. No need for fear. Most of us recognized the beatings as manifestations of the highest form of compassion. Those who kept an open mind, who patiently practised, and who acted sincerely would get a response—a response exactly commensurate with the practice. Those who stuck around would experience incredible states, see things never before seen, and have some awfully rocky territory to navigate on the road to enlightenment .

*   *   *

Like many others who arrived at the Buddhist Lecture Hall in the late sixties and early seventies, I carried with me a lot of bad habit energy. Actually, I had them all beat in that department. But thanks to the Master, most of us were able to give up drinking, smoking, drugs, meat-eating and many other dark attachments. To help displace this ugly *Ch'i*, the Master filled our minds with ancient words of wisdom: the teachings of the Patriarchs, Ch'an talks, words of Dharma. The meditation periods worked hand in hand with the talks to bring about a centering effect, a vacuum of emptiness into which the teachings could flow. Just by sitting still, the six senses—the abilities to see, hear, smell, taste, touch, and think—became pure and enhanced. Perhaps we'd develop psychic powers, attain the ability to see into the past and future, or be able to read people's minds. Most of all, we had the opportunity to enter Samadhi, experience Satori, an aperçu—to become Buddhas.

To get there, however, we'd have to go far beyond the nonchalant, McDonald's-type meditations so popular in America, the kind where people dozed off in chairs with their legs dangling down. Sure, these methods could make a person feel better. They provided a nice little battery charge. But how could anyone have the gall to market short naps? Our Abbot was teaching the incredible process leading to the ending of the cycle of birth and death.

驗很難，但我們也不怕受苦。他預言很多人會跑掉，但這無關緊要。因為不管我們怎麼跑，也跑不出這個宇宙，等我們跑累了，他的門總是開著的。他會等我們的。他既不會求我們進去，也不會趕我們走。

一些資深的弟子問師父，是否可以讓他們來考驗新的弟子，幫助他們早日開悟。師父打破這種妄想，說只有他才能考驗我們。此外，這些考驗不是由內，就是由外產生的。假如我們通不過，就得重頭來過。假如我們這輩子真地開悟的話，還得由本師釋迦牟尼佛一脈相承的賢聖僧祖師印證，才算是真正開悟。

如果真想要得師父訓誨的話，我們會得到的。留下來的弟子知道，他們會受師父的鞭策，以各種不同的方式走向開悟之道。不需要害怕。大多數的人都認為這種鞭策是師父的大悲心的高度體現。以開放的心胸認真的修行，篤實的人會得到和修行相當的感應。那些留下來的弟子，也會經歷到一些不可思議的境界，見所未見。通向開悟的道路是非常崎嶇、漫長的。

我和其他在六十年代與七十年代之間，走進佛教講堂的人一樣，帶著很多惡習氣。感謝師父，我們大多數都能戒酒、戒菸，不再吸毒、吃肉，也戒掉很多其他的壞習慣。師父用很多充滿智慧的禪語和法語及祖師的教誨，來熏習我們的心靈，把壞習氣除掉。打坐和開示也相得益彰，在寂滅中可以真正領悟到師父的教誨。靜坐時，六根（眼、耳、鼻、舌、身、意）清淨了。此時，或許我們可以得到神通，明白過去和未來，或是能有他心通。但主要的是我們有機會能進入三昧，有悟道的經驗，乃至成佛。

要成佛，首先我們要比在美國很流行的那種漠不關心、打坐時入夢鄉，兩腿從椅子上垂下來的「麥當勞」式，更精進。「麥當勞」式的打坐方式的確可以讓人感覺舒服些。這是種充電。但是有誰人斗膽推銷這種小睡修行法？師父教我們的是了生脫死不可思議的方法。

After innumerable hours of sitting, the muscles and tendons in my legs gradually rearranged themselves. On occasion, I could sit for the full hour in half lotus, even though it was painful, and every once in a while I could twist into full lotus for a few minutes. Still, the waves of false thought arose from nowhere, and I continued to be lost in them. Helpless to stop this spurious flow, I indulged in trying to sort things out. I spent countless hours trying to make sense of my life, but the thoughts continued to flow like smoke from a fire. I'd follow one particle up until it disappeared, and then immediately grasp onto the next ash that came floating by. I tried regulating my breath, counting my breath, reciting special mantras, staring at the floor, rolling my eyeballs, and everything else I could think of, but my brains just kept smoking away.

Eventually, however, I discovered some techniques for clearing the mind. Shrfu taught us the sweeping dharma. When thoughts popped up, rather than get lost in them, we could brush them away. This was very subtle and difficult work. Sometimes the thoughts seemed quite profound, and indeed they were, but as far as meditation goes, they were just more dust, so we swept them away and they lost their power over us.

All these changes, of course, were happening in a very short period of time. I wasn't really aware of how these processes were working. We weren't just "studying" Buddhism, we were living it, and even though just beginners, were already reaping some of the rewards of practice.

*   *   *

The Abbot devoted his primary energy to the left-home people. We laypersons were free to learn from them and to benefit from their mistakes; they made plenty. The Abbot alternated between building them up, nourishing their egos and attachments, and then letting them fall back down, leaving only, one hoped, a shiny Buddha-nature. It was certainly fun to watch. Sometimes he'd pick a tiny little thing they'd done, and then seem to blow it all out of proportion. No one, for example, could ever forget the famous cottage cheese incident, when a tall, silver-tongued American monk manipulated a laywoman into offering some cottage cheese. For the next few weeks the Master would resurrect the incident again and again to drive his point home, showing us how the monk was acting like a "*P'an Yuan* (Climbing on Conditions) Ghost," and how we were all caught up in the three evils of greed, hatred, and stupidity. The way to get rid of those evils was by practising morality, concentration, and wisdom. In the midst of all this serious teaching we'd often be laughing through rivers of joyous tears.

The monks and nuns had put themselves in a position to be taught. They had no beards, no hair, no clothes, no money, no anything. They'd taken a giant leap of faith, leaving the world and its dust behind. I was a little jealous. I wanted special atten-

打坐了無數小時後，似乎覺得腿上的筋、肉慢慢地重新組合了。偶而也能單盤坐上一小時。雙盤腿會痛，偶爾也能坐上幾分鐘。但是心中的，不知從何而來的妄念，使我迷失。妄念既然難以止息。我就乾脆面對它們。我花了很多時間去了解我生命的意義，但是妄想仍像從火中冒出來的煙。我會抓住一個「粒子」一直到它消逝為止。立刻又再抓住下一「粒子」。我注意呼吸、練習數息、念咒、瞪地板、轉眼珠、用盡心思，但妄想仍念念不斷。

我終於發現一種技巧，可以清淨心念。師父曾教過我們一種掃除妄想的法門。妄念生起時，不要被妄念所轉，可以把它掃到一邊去。這是一種既微妙又困難的修行方式。不過，有時這些念頭很奧妙，事實上也真是如此。從打坐的觀點來看，這些念頭不過是些塵埃罷了，只要把它們掃到一邊，它們對我們也無可奈何。

前面我所提到的，都是很短的時間裡發生的。我也不是很清楚這整個過程的運作。我們不只是「學習」佛法，我們是活在佛法裡。雖然我們只是初學者，卻已經開始收穫了。

師父集中他的精力來教化他的出家弟子。在家弟子則可以從他們身上，甚至他們所犯的錯誤中學習－－錯誤還不少呢。我們看到師父一方面不停地在塑造他的出家弟子；一方面「滋養」他們的自我和執著，然後教訓他們。希望經過這種歷練後，顯現出耀眼的佛性。觀察這種琢磨過程是很有意思的。有時候，師父會挑一件小事，小題大作的教訓一番。比方說，令人難忘的有名的「白乳酪事件」。有位個子高高的、口才很好的美國比丘，唆使一位在家女居士供養一些白乳酪。以後好幾個星期，師父反覆提及這件事。為的是要我們真正明白這位比丘的行為無異於攀緣鬼。我們一直都困在貪瞋癡三毒裡。去除三毒的方法就是勤修戒定慧。在這些師父嚴肅的教誨中，常常伴著的是成行快樂的眼淚和笑聲。

比丘和比丘尼處於一種受教化的位置。他們不能蓄鬍子、留頭髮，不能穿華麗的衣服，積蓄錢財…

tion from the Master; I ached for it. For the time being, however, I contented myself with just sitting back and watching the show. My brief moment in the spotlight would come.

…。他們一無所有。在信力上，他們跨出了很大的一步，把世間的一切和煩惱通通拋棄。我有些嫉妒，我想得到師父的注意，非常想。然而到目前為止，對當個旁觀者的角色也很滿意，總會輪到我上台當主角的時刻。

* * *

The Abbot especially encouraged his monks and nuns to cultivate the "Awesome Manner."

"Don't walk around with your heads lowered, going 'Mee-mee, moo-moo'!" Don't act like a bunch of frogs!" he said. "Walk tall and proud, be fierce and fearless, and emit blazing light. Walk like the wind! Sit like a bell! Stand like a pine!"

The Abbot certainly demonstrated The Awesome Manner himself. Though his mind was still, many people trembled when in his presence. This was because of their demons within. Those with a pure mind, with nothing to hide or be ashamed of, had no trouble being around the Master.

The American monks and nuns could sit in full lotus without moving for the full hour meditations. I was still scared of the sitting meditation pain. I didn't feel I'd ever make a breakthrough. When it was 10:00 PM and lights out, I was ready to lie down and stretch those legs; I had my limits. These other people seemed to never stop cultivating. Even at night, when they were allowed to sleep, they'd stay up into the wee hours working on translations. And all this on only one meal a day!

師父特別告誡比丘、比丘尼們要注意威儀：「走路不要低著頭，迷迷糊糊的。不要像一群青蛙。走路時抬頭挺胸。要勇猛無畏。要有光采。行如風。坐如鐘。立如松。」

師父本身威儀具足。雖然他如如不動，很多人在師父面前會發抖，這都因為他們有魔障的關係。心清淨的人，沒什麼好隱瞞的人，一點也不怕師父。

美國比丘、比丘尼們可以雙盤打坐整整一小時。可是我還是怕腿痛，我覺得沒辦法突破。晚上十點熄燈後，我已經打算躺下來伸伸腿了。我的體力是有限的。其他的人好像永遠不停地在修行。甚至熬夜至清晨，來做翻譯工作。這些行者還都是日中一食呢！

* * *

Although Buddhism was now my religion of choice, it occurred to me that I didn't have to turn my back on Christianity. On the contrary, by following the precepts of Buddhism, I had become a better Christian than ever. For one thing, I was not "living in sin," but learning to "know, love, and serve God." My whole idea of God changed, however. I no longer thought of "Him" as some eighty-foot tall, long-haired guy in the sky, but as a cosmic force pervading me and the universe, a force beyond all opposites, including birth and death, with which I would have a chance to reunite if I practised the principles of Buddhism. Why wait to go to heaven; I could experience God and "heaven" right in this life. We didn't have to be lambs any longer; in Buddhism we could be lions. I liked the idea of faith, practice, and results in this life. But Christianity had its wonderful purpose in the world, and most religions had the power to help people grow spiritually. Even groups as radical as the Hare Krishnas were taking druggies off the streets and making them clean up their act, eat vegetables, and start thinking of someone else besides themselves. Shrfu taught us that all these religions were lights taking away the darkness of the world. So I gratefully took the love, compassion, knowledge and wisdom bestowed on me from all the virtuous nuns, brothers, priests, and my good Catholic family, and used it as a foundation for Buddhist studies.

雖然佛教是我所選擇的宗教，但是我也不需要摒斥基督教。相反地，因為守了佛教的戒律，我成為更好的基督徒。比方說，我不會「活在罪中」，但是學著去「瞭解、愛和侍奉主。」可是我對神的定義完全改變了。我不再認為神是一位住在天上，八呎高，有長髮的傢伙。祂是宇宙的一股力量，籠罩著我和整個宇宙，超過一切對立－－包括生死。假如我修習佛法也許有一天可以和祂重聚。何必等著上天堂？我在這一世也可以有同樣的經驗。我們也不必再是羔羊，佛教裡我們可以當獅子。我喜歡在這一生就看到信仰、修行的結果。但是基督教在這個世界上也有其積極的意義。大部份的宗教都能幫助眾生精神層面的成長，即使急進的宗教份子也幫助吸毒者，要他們重新振作、吃素，為別人著想。師父說這些宗教都是驅除世界黑暗的光明。因此我心存感激地接受所有善良的修女、神父、修士和我天主教家人所給予我的愛、悲憫、知識和智慧，做為我學習佛法的基礎。

At the Buddhist Lecture Hall we were free to create our own spiritual program from 84,000 mysterious Dharma Doors. The Master encouraged us to see through everything as false, illusory, and empty, and asked that we let go of it all, even to the point of letting go of Buddhism. "There are no fixed Dharmas!" he often said. "Your mind should be like empty space." So, with my heart resolved on Bodhi, I let go of my past and moved forward into territory unknown. Together, with brothers and sisters of like mind, I was on an extraordinary journey to the roots of consciousness. Each of us alone, yet together, shared a common bond of faith. It was, as the Abbot taught, our good roots and our vows from past lives bringing us back together. We were extremely fortunate to meet with this opportunity. We were all on a spiritual roll and the Abbot was blowing people's minds, tirelessly turning the awesome Dharma Wheel, sharing this magnificent treasure with everyone.

在佛教的八萬四千法門中,我們可以任意挑選適合自己的修行方法。師父要我們看一切事物都是假相、幻覺、都是空的。要我們一切放下,連佛法都要放下。師父常說:「法無定法!你們的心應該像虛空。」就這樣我發了菩提心,放下過去,邁向未知的領域。我和其他的同修,共同走在追求意識本源的特別旅途上。我們彼此間都有相同的體認,就如同師父說的,我們的善根和往世所發的願力,又把我們聚集在一起。我們很幸運的能遇到這個機會,行進在這精神隊伍中。師父不疲不厭地轉大法輪啟發著我們,和大家分享無上的法寶。

勉某禪人,發願三步一拜,祈求世界和平

宣公上人作於一九七三年十月十九日

美國金山寺,青年僧材,濟濟多士,維護正法,各擅專長。今汝能發人所未發之弘願,行人所未行之聖行。三步一禮,十方常住,佛法僧寶,以此虔誠懇切之真心,祈求世界和平,必有大感應。惟發心容易,滿願或難,然不要自餒。抱定堅誠恆,向前邁進。一千英里路,只是法界之一小步耳。決定不達到目的,不休止,具其勉諸即贈偈曰:

難行能行是聖行,難忍能忍乃真忍;十方諸佛從此出,八萬菩薩接踵來。

吹大法螺施號令,振寶錫杖化慳貪;功圓果滿凱旋日,衲為吾徒送餅餐。

An Exhortation to a Dhyana Cultivator Who Vowed to Bow Every Three Steps for World Peace

Composed by the Venerable Master Hua on October 19, 1973

At Gold Mountain Dhyana Monastery, in the United States of America, the Sangha is young and numerous. They concentrate on safeguarding the proper Dharma, and each one has his particular good points. Now you have made a vow never made before, and will practice Sagely conduct which has never before been practiced, bowing every three steps to the eternal Jewels of the Buddha, Dharma, and Sangha throughout the ten directions. Because your sincerity and earnestness in seeking for world peace is genuine, you will certainly evoke a magnificent response. Although your initial resolve came easily, it may be difficult to fulfill your vows. Don't give up; remain firm, sincere, and constant. The thousand miles over which you will pass is only one small step within the Dharma Realm. Be resolved not to cease until you have reached your goal. Raise up your spirits! I leave you this verse of parting:

Practicing what is difficult to practice is the conduct of the Sage;
Enduring what is hard to endure is the genuine patience.
All Buddhas throughout the ten directions have walked down this road,
And the eighty-thousand Bodhisattvas have followed right along.
Blow the magnificent Dharma conch, and raise up the cry;
Shake your precious tin staff, transform stingy greed.
Your work complete, the result full, return amidst songs of triumph—
Then I'll give my disciple a meal of berry pie.

風範長存

HIS EXEMPLARY STYLE WILL REMAIN FOREVER

陳果雄　Chen Guoxiong

一代高僧宣化上人於一九九五年年六月七日在美國洛杉磯圓寂，巨星遽殞，世人同悲！所幸在西天上，卻亮起了另一顆巨星，照耀大地，永遠指引眾生所應遵循的光明大道！這一顆巨星，壯麗、明亮，將成為弘揚佛法，拯救芸芸眾生的永久象徵！

我在許多年以前，就已景仰師父宣化上人長年苦行修持的聲名，但是苦無機會晉謁，暢聆教益。直到一九八九年間，師父返臺弘法，始得面謁師父，終償宿願。

一九九〇年夏季，兒女赴美國萬佛聖城參加夏令營活動，結訓後，留在萬佛聖城，分別就讀培德中學與育良小學。此後，我每年均趁著赴美探親的機會，晉見師父。蒙師父親切慈祥的昭示，心中均有所感應，受益良多，使我在工作上以及進德修業上均能得到許多啟迪並有許多進步！

師父曾經開導我說：

一、要做個好公務員，祇要對人民有利益的事情，在職責範圍內，就應該努力、放手去做，多為國家、社會，盡心盡力，無私無我！

二、心中不要生煩惱，以靜心養性！

三、不要發脾氣，以免自生煩惱，自亂步驟！

四、凡事只要是對的，就應該盡心盡力去做，不管他人的評論是非！

五、要多念佛，以消業障！

我始終牢牢記住師父對我的告誡，因此，使我在許多困難境況中，都能化險為夷，轉危為安，因此覺得師父給我的這些教訓彌足珍貴！

師父在弘揚佛法時，經常以「不爭、不貪、不求、不自私、不自利、不妄語」六大宗旨，諄諄告誡眾生，其悲天憫人的精神和一生無我無私，篤踐力行，弘揚佛理、佛法的風範，令

The eminent Sanghan Venerable Master Hua completed the stillness in Los Angeles on June 7, 1995. A great star has fallen, and the people of the world mourn together! Yet we rejoice that in the Western skies, another great star has lit up and shines upon the earth, forever guiding living beings towards the great, bright path which they should follow. This great star is magnificent and luminous, and will forever be a symbol of the propagation of the Buddhadharma and the salvation of living beings.

I began admiring the Venerable Master Hua's practice of good deeds and cultivation many years ago, but unfortunately did not have the opportunity to meet him and listen to his teachings in person. It was not until 1989, when the Venerable Master came to Taiwan to propagate the Dharma, that I was able to finally realize my wish to meet him.

In the summer of 1990, my son and daughter went to the Sagely City of Ten Thousand Buddhas in America to attend the summer camp. After it was over, they remained at the Sagely City and attended Developing Virtue Secondary School and Instilling Goodness Elementary School. On my yearly trips to America to visit them, I would also pay a visit to the Master. I responded deeply to and derived great benefit from the Master's kind advice. It was a source of inspiration to me and allowed me to make great progress both in my work and in my cultivation.

The Master counseled me as follows:

1. Be a good public servant. As long as something is beneficial to the people and is within your scope of duty, you should exert yourself and try your best to do it. Exhaust your mind and your efforts for the sake of the country and society, and be without a self.

2. Don't allow afflictions to arise in your mind. Calm your mind and nurture your nature.

3. Don't get mad, for if you do, you will become afflicted and cause yourself to stumble.

4. As long as something is right, you should try your best to do it and not care about what other people say.

5. Recite the Buddha's name more, in order to get rid of karmic hindrances.

Because I have firmly remembered the Master's admonitions to me, I've been able to resolve many crises and difficulties, transforming danger into peace. For this reason, I consider these teachings the Master has given me to be treasures!

When the Master propagated the Buddhadharma, he often exhorted living beings to follow the Six Great Guidelines—no fighting, no

人蕭然起敬！多年來，我切實恪遵師父的六大宗旨，使我在生活言行、工作態度和為人處世各方面，均有所依循，不至迷失了方向，實在感激不盡！

師父雖然長年在美國弘法，但是他老人家卻心懷祖國，尤其是極為關懷臺灣社會眾生的一切，終其一生，一直保留中華民國國籍，未入美國籍，並且始終珍藏著一面青天白日滿地紅的國旗，足見其熱愛國家，熱愛同胞，令人感動！

一九六二年，師父初抵美邦，適值古巴飛彈危機，他老人家為化解國際災厄，曾斷食五週。民國七十八年師父返臺弘法，見到此間社會眾生，流於奢侈虛榮，人民沈迷功利，耽於聲色，生活腐化，不禁發出誠摯的呼籲，不顧自己身體的孱弱，斷食三週，以消弭眾生貪、瞋、癡的念頭，以求眾生在茫茫人生苦海中，迷航知返，同登彼岸！凡此，益足以表現師父悲天憫人，犧牲奉獻的偉大情操和拯救眾生的堅定理念！今日在這社會秩序紊亂，暴戾成風、金錢掛帥，人心惶惶不安的時候，他老人家上述的六大宗旨，無異是給人們當頭棒喝，痛下針砭，其風範將長在人心！

關於宣化上人的弘法貢獻，佛教界及各方均已有詳細的論介，我不贅述。我所要說的，是他老人家苦口婆心弘揚佛法的風範，教我、助我許多，令我深為感激！今後自當更加切記他老人家的種種開示，不斷充實我的人生，盡心盡力，從事工作，以求毋負師父對我的殷殷叮嚀和深切的期望！

greed, no seeking, no selfishness, no pursuit of personal advantage, and no lying. His compassion for the world's people and his lifelong conduct of selflessness, honest practice, and propagation of the Buddhadharma has won people's respect! Over the years, I have earnestly followed the Master's Six Great Guidelines, and they have served as a guide for my daily speech and conduct, for my attitude at work, and in all aspects of social interaction, thus preventing me from going astray. For this, I am endlessly grateful.

Although the Master propagated the Dharma in America for many years, he was always mindful of his homeland. He was especially concerned about the living beings of Taiwan. To the end of his life, he kept his citizenship in the Republic of China and didn't become an American citizen. Moreover, he always treasured and kept a flag of the Republic of China (showing a white sun on a blue sky, with a red background). His ardent patriotism and love for his fellow countrymen moved people's hearts.

In 1962, soon after the Venerable Master arrived in America, the Cuban Missile Crisis broke out. In order to avert the potential disaster to the country, he fasted for five weeks. In 1989, when the Master returned to Taiwan to propagate the Dharma, he saw that people were pursuing luxury and vanity, deluded by utilitarianism, attached to fame, and living in corruption. Not only did he earnestly cry out from the depths of his heart, but he ignored his weak health and fasted for three weeks. He did that in order to dissolve living beings' thoughts of greed, anger, and stupidity and to rescue them from the vast sea of human suffering, so that they could turn away from delusion and ascend to the other shore! This was a manifestation of the Venerable Master's compassion for the world's people, his great spirit of self-sacrifice, and his firm resolve to save living beings. In today's chaotic society in which violence has become a trend, money reigns supreme, and people's minds are flustered and unsettled, the Master's Six Great Guidelines go straight to the heart of the problem. His exemplary style will remain in people's hearts forever!

Regarding the Venerable Master Hua's contributions in the propagation of Dharma, the Dharma Realm Buddhist Association and others have discussed this in detail, and I will not say more. What I want to say is, the good example that he set with his earnest propagation of the Buddhadharma has taught me and aided me greatly, and I am deeply grateful! From now onwards, I will remember the Master's counsel even more firmly, continue to enrich my life, and carry out my work to the best of my ability, so that I will not fail to follow the Master's earnest remonstrations and fulfill his sincere expectations of me.

肝中若無火　何病都能躲　即此妙伽陀　亦被置高閣　娑婆訶

宣公上人作於一九九三年五月十四日

Purge the fire in your liver, and avoid all disease;
Such a wonderful cure-all medicine: Set on the shelf and forgotten! Suo po he!

Composed by Venerable Master Hua on May 14, 1993

懺悔的感應

A RESPONSE FROM REPENTANCE

恆君　Shi Heng Jun

平時上人教導我們要不發脾氣，遵守六大宗旨，不爭、不貪、不求、不自私、不自利、不妄語。初學佛法總覺我沒脾氣，可是一遇著境界，考驗就來了！

總覺我是對的，別人不對，應該照我這樣的方法去做，而引起自己的爭心，與人爭我對你錯，爭來爭去，罵來罵去，引起無明，貪心，瞋心。旁邊的人看不順眼，也互相得罪了。於是造成了不可原諒的錯。他們都討厭我，遠離我，不肯原諒我時，我方覺錯了。我跪在上人的照片前，以誠懇心叩頭，懺悔我錯了，我不該無理得罪了長輩，起了瞋心，也起了無明，造成了大錯，損害了大眾和合。我很傷心，懊悔不該發脾氣，而又不知該怎麼辦才好時，突然腦波出現了一句話：「不用擔心，會慢慢好的，多念佛。」此時我的心始平靜下來，而念起佛號。感謝佛菩薩，我明白了，我應該去向被我得罪的人懺悔。

The Venerable Master always taught us not to lose our tempers and to follow the six guiding principles—no fighting, no greed, no seeking, no selfishness, no pursuing of personal advantage, and no lying. As a beginner in Buddhism, I tended to feel that I didn't have a temper. Yet when a state came up, it was always a test!

I always felt that I was right and others were wrong, and that people should do things my way. This brought on a fighting attitude and I started arguing with others. Bickering and scolding back and forth, ignorance, greed, and hatred came forth. When others disagreed with what I said, they also became offended. I ended up committing an unforgiveable mistake. It was only when they all detested me, stayed away from me, and refused to forgive me that I realized I was wrong. I knelt in front of the Venerable Master's photo and sincerely prostrated myself. I repented of my wrongs, admitting that I shouldn't insult my elders for no reason, give rise to hatred and ignorance, and commit such a great offense of disturbing the harmony of the assembly. I was very sorry and vexed. I shouldn't have lost my temper. Just when I didn't know what I should do, these words appeared in the mind, "Don't worry, everything will be all right soon. Recite the Buddha's name more." I calmed down and started to recite the Buddha's name. Thanks to the Buddhas and Bodhisattvas, I understand now. I should go and repent to the people I offended.

疾病呻吟苦
Groaning in the Agony of Sickness

苟延殘喘度餘生　老疾纏綿痛苦中　日進飲食如服毒　夜宿病榻賽僵蟲

夢中屢逢無常鬼　醒來難覓救護神　人命呼吸還知否　速返清淨自在城

I linger on, breathing with difficulty, spending the remainder of my life
Amidst the suffering of old age and disease.
During the day, when I eat my meals it is like taking poison;
At night, I lie on the sickbed like a dead worm that has gone stiff.
In my dreams, I often encounter the Ghost of Impermanence;
When I awaken, I cannot find a god that can save my life.
Don't you know that life is a matter of going from one breath to the next?
Quickly return to the City of Pure and Ultimate Bliss!

宣公上人作於萬佛寶殿　一九九二年十二月廿五日
Composed by Venerable Master Hua in the Hall of Ten Thousand Buddhas
December 25, 1992

醒悟的機會

THE OPPORTUNITY FOR AWAKENING

Tam Chu Bui

As a young person, it was through the family culture and tradition that I had contact with Buddhism--its temples and its environments.

Although I had tasted vegetarian food, I had never really questioned or understood the profound meanings connected with eating meat or the importance of being a vegetarian. Needless to say, I was a meat lover: beef steak, Mongolian beef, roast duck...you name it!

At that time, I did not know Master Hua personally. I had seen him once, and gotten only a quick glance at that, in 1994. It was through my sister, who has a profound respect for the Master, that I know about his books. In July 1995, during my stay in California, I visited the City of Ten Thousand Buddhas (CTTB) and, for the very first time, saw Master Hua closely. I respectfully bowed three times.

My second visit to CTTB was the most memorable visit of my life. I came to CTTB with doubts and some false thinking. I feared the discomfort, the food without meat, the hot weather, and the long hours of praying. I feel ashamed of my false and negative thinking. Yes, shame on me!

Although my first day at the temple was difficult, to my surprise, I quickly became a full vegetarian for the rest of my five-days' stay without any complaints and without thinking about meat. During those five days, I learned more about Buddhism and its culture and rules than ever before. I saw Bhikshus and Bhikshunis living in such harmony. I saw the people full of respect for the Master and Buddhism. The temple environment was in such harmony that one felt easily at peace. I even saw a peacock listening to the entire evening lecture on the biography of the Master. The next morning I witnessed the same peacock walking slowly but elegantly to the Vietnamese altar and bowing respectfully to the Buddha. I was moved at that scene. I felt so small compared to that peacock so elegant. I attended not all but most of the ceremonies and prayers. I tried to follow along even though I did not understand a single word of it. I have to emphasize this point: I do not speak, read, or write Chinese; however I enjoy singing along in the prayers, especially the four o'clock morning ceremony.

On July 26, I heard about the special ceremony for taking refuge under Master Hua. Even though I had heard so much good about the refuges, their meanings and their importance, and despite people telling me that it was the last opportunity, the very last chance, to have Master Hua as my Master, it seemed that nothing could convince me or motivate me to join the ceremony. I had the whole day to register, but I waited until the very last second and it was simply too late to register. In the Buddha hall, I prayed silently and with deep thinking. I talked silently

由於我出生的家庭背景和傳統，使我有機會和佛教、佛寺及佛教環境有所接觸。

我也嚐過素食，但是我從來沒有懷疑過，也不瞭解肉食的背後的真相和素食的重要性。不提也知我是愛肉食的人，不論是牛排或蒙古烤肉或鴨，只要你叫得出的肉食，我都喜歡吃。

那時我還不認得上人，在一九九四年我曾瞥見過他一次。經過姊姊的關係，才知道上人的一些書，我姐姐對上人有著深深的敬意。一九九五年七月我在加州時，我去了萬佛城，也是第一次有機會這麼近地看見上人，恭敬禮拜三下。第二次來聖城時，是我一生中最值得紀念的事。我是帶著懷疑和妄想來到聖城的。我怕那兒的種種不舒服，那兒沒肉的素食，酷熱的天氣，長時間的祈禱。我自己也對我的「虛幻負面的念頭」感到一份慚愧。

雖然我在廟上的第一天很困難，但是我自己也覺得奇怪，後來的四天我很快就習慣了素食，一點困難也沒有，吃肉的事連想都不想。在這五、六天之中，我對佛教及其他文化規矩知道得更多了，我看到比丘、比丘尼和諧地生活著，我碰見的人都對上人及佛教充滿敬意，廟裡的環境使人覺得祥和自在。我注意到一隻孔雀在晚間聽講解上人的事蹟。

第二天我又看見那隻孔雀好像佛一樣地優雅漫步，走向以越南文誦經的佛桌前禮拜，使我很感動。跟那隻孔雀那份優雅比起來，我覺得自己真是很渺小。我雖沒參加城裡所有的儀式，但大部份我都參加了。我聽不懂，但還是儘量隨喜參加。在這裡我要強調一下，我既不會說，也不會講，更不會寫中文，但是我還是很喜歡跟著唱誦，尤其是早上四點的早課儀式。

七月二十六日那天，我聽說有皈依上人的儀式，雖然我聽過許多關於皈依的意義及其重要性，也不管別人怎麼告訴我這是最後一次做上人弟子的機會，我有一整天的時間去登記，但是我還是無動於衷，一直到最後一秒鐘我才決定要皈依，但已經太遲

to Master Hua, asking him to bless me, and that if this ceremony was the opportunity and the right time for me to take refuge, then I would accept his decision. Among the crowd, a friend of my sister came forth to ask me if I had already registered for the ceremony. After my explanation, she told me if I wanted to, I could attend the ceremony. I did. It was only during the refuge ceremony that I discovered who Master Hsuan Hua was. His wisdom and his generosity touched my heart profoundly. I then understood the meaning of taking refuge and the responsibilities it involves. To my surprise, at the end of the ceremony, I got a certificate. A Dharma Master said, "After taking refuge, outside we will be the same, but inside we will have already changed."

Today, three weeks after that ceremony, I realize that what the Dharma Master said is true. Indeed, somehow I have changed inside since then. It is incredible and I do not know how to explain it. The result is: I am not afraid of ghosts any more for I now understand who they are. I can eat and enjoy vegetarian food, for I simply started to love it. I simply have no desire to eat meat. I am not a good follower, for I cannot simply obey and believe without questioning and understanding first. I feel I have so much to learn. There is so much to understand, to learn, and to do. But first I have my 10,000 bows to finish!

了，不接受登記了。我到佛殿裡深深思慮，默默祈禱。我輕聲對宣公上人請求著，假如今天的我是應該皈依的，我會皈依。在人群中我姐姐的朋友看到我了，她問我我登記皈依沒有，又說假如我正想皈依的話，我可以去參加皈依儀式，所以我就去了。一直到皈依時我才知道宣公上人是誰，上人的寬洪大量，他的智慧深深地打動了我的心，那時我才瞭解皈依的意義和責任。我沒想到皈依完後，我還拿到了一張皈依證。法師說：「皈依之後，外表我們沒有改變，但內裡我們已經不同了。」今天在我皈依三星期之後，我才瞭解到法師講的話是多麼真實，的確我內裡從那日以後是改變了，這實在是不可思議，我也不知該怎麼講才好。我只知道我現在不怕鬼了，因為我知道鬼是什麼。

我現在不但可以吃素，而且還深深地喜愛素食了，我根本就不再想吃肉了。我不太容易聽話，因為我不能對自己不懂的事無條件接受。我覺得我還有許多要學的，要知道的，要做的，但是我最先要完成的是拜完一萬拜！」

果功畫
Drawings by Sarah Kennedy Owen (Kuo Kung)

THE MORE YOU GAZE UP AT HIM, THE HIGHER HE BECOMES

仰 之 彌 高

釋恆賢　Shi Heng Hsien

The Venerable Master would occasionally tell us that none of us really understood what he was doing. An early teaching we received was when the Venerable Master lectured the Preface to the *Flower Adornment Sutra* by National Master Qing Liang. He showed us how National Master Qing Liang had taken a classical quotation from the Confucian *Analects* as the basis for a portrayal of the inconceivability of the *Flower Adornment Sutra*. In the *Analects*, someone asks Confucius' disciple Yan Hui what his Master's state is. Yan Hui replies, "The more you gaze up at him, the higher he becomes." To describe the *Flower Adornment Sutra*, National Master Qing Liang changed the quote to read: "Too high is it for gazing," meaning there is no way you can possibly see how high it is.

Another repeated teaching was that "everything's a test to see what you will do." During the forty-nine days after the Venerable Master entered Nirvana, each day I listened to tapes of instructional talks that the Master had given. Since I didn't have many tapes, I ended up listening to the published tapes of talks by the Venerable Master during Dharma propagation tours, and listening to the same tapes over and over. On those tapes, the Venerable Master tells the story of the philosopher Zhuang Zi returning home and encountering a woman along the road fanning a grave. When Zhuang Zi asked her why she was doing that, the woman replied that the grave was her husband's. They had been so devoted to each other that she would be embarrassed to remarry before her former husband's grave was dry, so she was fanning it so it would dry more quickly and she could remarry sooner.

When Zhuang Zi arrived home, he reported the incident to his own wife, who assured him she would never do such a thing. Shortly after, Zhuang Zi fell ill and died, and during the mourning period a handsome young man came to the house wishing to study with Zhuang Zi. Upon learning that the philosopher had died, the young man requested to stay for a while to study Zhuang Zi's books. Zhuang Zi's wife became enamored of the young man, but the young man said he could not become involved with her when Zhuang Zi's coffin was right there in the house. The wife assured him it was no problem, and broke open the coffin to prove it—only to find Zhuang Zi fully alive inside, confronting her with behaving even worse than the lady who had fanned the grave. It had all been a test.

師父有時會跟我們講，說我們都不瞭他葫蘆裡賣的是什麼藥。最早聽到這種說法，是師父在講解清涼國師所註解的《大方廣佛華嚴經疏》時。師父說清涼國師引用孔子《論語》裡的一句話，來形容《華嚴經》不可思議的境界。《論語》裡記載有人向孔子的門生顏回他老師的境界為何。顏回答曰：「仰之彌高，望之彌堅。」清涼國師稍稍改了這句話－－高不可望－－來形容《華嚴經》的境界，意思是說盡我們的全力也無法一窺究竟。

師父另一則耳提面命的教誨是「一切是考驗，看你怎麼辦？」師父入涅槃後四十九天的喪期裡，每天我都聽師父開示的錄音帶。我手中錄音帶有限，所以我反覆聽的是由萬佛城出版發行的開示。錄音帶裡師父講的是：莊子在回家的路上，碰到一位婦女拿著扇子對著一座墳搧。莊子問她在幹什麼？這位婦女回答說墳裡躺的是她丈夫。在他生前，他們夫婦十分恩愛，但是現在他的墳地還沒乾，她就想改嫁了，覺得有點不好意思，所以趕緊努力的搧以便可以早日改嫁。

莊子到家後，把這件事告訴他太太，太太則向他保證她永遠也不會做出這種事。不久之後莊子生病死了。在守喪期間，有位面貌俊美的年青男子慕名來向莊子拜師求學。聽到哲人已逝，這位年青男子則要求留下來研習莊子的著作。莊子太太愛上這位年輕男子，但是他卻說莊子的棺木還停在家裡，他實在沒辦法和她有進一步的發展。莊子太太再三向他保證沒有問題，甚至劈開棺木來證明所言不虛。一掀開棺木，看到莊子好好的活著，並怒責他的太太比那位墳上搧風的婦女行為還要過火。這一切都是考驗。

故事的重點在於：人類的感情都是暫時的。師父在弘法的時候曾多次講述這故事。我反覆的聽著同一卷錄音帶，幾星期裡聽了二、三十遍。師父的涅槃，至少對我自己而言，具有某種特殊的意義，雖然我並不

The point of the story is that emotional love is transitory, and the Venerable Master told the story many times on the tours. But I was listening to the same tapes over and over, and when I had heard the story twenty or thirty times in the space of a few weeks, I had to face the fact that there must be a pointed message for me, at least, connected with the Venerable Master's passing. We have been trained in the Venerable Master's Dharma like children just learning to read and write, and now the Venerable Master has gone away for a while—to see what we will do. Will we pass the tests, or will we give way to seeking for personal advantages and easy solutions? There are many things to carry on, the significance of which we only dimly perceive. We have had only a glimpse into the Venerable Master's vision for the propagation of the Buddha-dharma. To pass the tests we should be true to the Venerable Master's vision, grow up in his Dharma, and do our best to assure that the Venerable Master's teachings remain in the world.

知道他到底意味著什麼？

　這則故事還有更深一層的意義。在師父的法裡，我們就像小孩子學讀、寫一樣，師父現在走開一下，就是要看看我們如何應對？我們能過關嗎？還是我們會向個人的名聞利養或是任何其他好處讓步？很多責任我們要扛下來，其重要性我們也不是完全清楚。對師父宣揚佛法的弘觀，我們也只有一點概念。想通過這場考驗，我們得老實面對師父宣揚佛法的弘觀，在佛法中成長茁壯，並盡一已之力以肯定師父的教化常住於世。

了知一切空無我　　慈念眾生恆不捨
以一大悲微妙音　　普入事間而演說

放大光明種種色　　普照眾生除黑暗
光中菩薩坐蓮華　　為眾闡揚清淨法
　　——《大方廣佛華嚴經》〈初發心功德品〉

He understands that everything is empty and without a self,
He has kind thoughts for living beings
without ever forsaking them.
He enters the world everywhere and proclaims
A single, subtly wondrous sound of great compassion.

He emits great light of various colors,
Which universally shines upon living beings and eradicates their darkness,
Within the light are Bodhisattvas seated upon lotus flowers,
Who for the sake of the multitudes,
Proclaim Dharmas of purity.

Chapter on The Merit and Virtue from First Bringing Forth the Mind, the *Flower Adornment Sutra*

人天導師

A GUIDING MASTER OF HUMANS AND GODS

法明　Dharma Brilliance

臺灣曾有老修行（曾果佛），一生篤信佛教。八十九歲退休前，要筆者向師父陳情，希望能夠到萬佛聖城去住。又因為與筆者係三代世交，情誼深厚，希望在聖城時能由筆者負責照顧她的起居。於是一九九〇年，趁著上人回臺灣訪問時，筆者向師父呈報此事。師父一聽，就問她住在哪裡？要去看她！弘法期間，行程緊湊，師父卻因為她誠懇之心，毫不考慮自己。這也是師父時時胸懷「流血汗，不休息」的一個例證。在筆者勸阻之下，師父便說可以抽空約她來見。

果佛居士見到師父上人時，聲聲呼喊「師父大慈大悲！師父大慈大悲！」師父賜坐於身旁，一邊軟言慰問其生活起居，一邊以手摩她頭頂，達半小時之久。談話之中，師父一再表示歡迎她，並要她一切不用擔心。告辭出來，心中宿願以及種種憂慮都得消除，多日後，老人家歡喜之情未見消散！

果佛居士晚年孤苦，無處可依，來美後體弱力衰，只能投靠師父。次年，等她到萬佛聖城時，筆者已落髮並往溫哥華金佛聖寺幫忙。隨她前來照顧作伴的周居士，突然有私事，必須回臺處理。筆者當時正好由加拿大返聖城受菩薩戒。見此情形，以為出家人照顧在家人有所不便為由，向師父呈報了此事。受戒數日後，筆者準備搭灰狗巴士返金佛聖寺。此巴士一天只有一班，每天固定停在一便利商店前待客。可是，那天在車站，左等右等，總不見車的蹤影，問旁人也說未見到。等了兩個小時，才打聽到車已離去。原來那天它改停在超市後方。地方就那麼一點點大，居然錯過了龐大的巴士，真怪，只好返回聖城內。

入大殿禮佛時，便在殿前佈告欄看到徵人照顧她的啟事。我驀然明白，一定是此因緣，而不能前往金佛聖寺。後來知道照顧她並無不妥，遂自告奮勇，再報告上人。這就是師父上人

There was an elderly cultivator in Taiwan named Ceng Guofo ("Fruit of the Buddha") who was a devout Buddhist all her life. Before she retired at the age of eighty-nine, she asked me to tell the Venerable Master that she hoped to move to the Sagely City of Ten Thousand Buddhas to live. Because of her close relationship with my family for three generations, she hoped I would take care of her at the Sagely City. When the Venerable Master visited Taiwan in 1990, I reported this to him. As soon as the Master heard it, he asked where she lived and wanted to pay a visit to her! The Venerable Master had a very tight schedule of Dharma propagation, but he completely disregarded himself for the sake of her sincerity. This is one example of the Master's constant attitude of "not sparing blood or sweat and never pausing to rest." At my urging, the Master then agreed to have her come and meet him instead.

When Laywoman Guofo met the Venerable Master, she exclaimed over and over, "Greatly kind and compassionate Master! Greatly kind and compassionate Master!" The Venerable Master asked her to sit beside him. For about half an hour, as he gently inquired about her life, he rubbed the crown of her head with his hand. During the conversation, the Master welcomed her to the City many times and told her not to worry about anything. By the time she said goodbye, her worries had completely disappeared. Many days later, her happiness was still evident!

In her old age, Laywoman Guofo had been solitary and in hardship, without a place of refuge. Coming to America in poor health, she could only depend on the Venerable Master. When she came to the Sagely City of Ten Thousand Buddhas the following year, I had already left the home-life and gone to Gold Buddha Sagely Monastery in Vancouver to help out. Laywoman Zhou, who had come with her to the Sagely City to take care of her, suddenly had to return to Taiwan for personal reasons. At that time I returned to the City to receive the Bodhisattva Precepts. When I found out about the situation, I thought it might be inappropriate for a left-home person to take care of a layperson, and I told the Venerable Master about this. Several days after taking the precepts, I planned to take the Greyhound Bus back to Gold Buddha Sagely Monastery. The bus came only once a day and would stop in front of a convenience store to pick up passengers. That day, I waited and waited at the bus stop, but the bus didn't show up. When I asked someone else, he said he hadn't seen it either. After waiting for two hours, I asked and found out that the bus had already gone. As it turned out, the bus had stopped behind the supermarket that day. In such a small place, it would have been difficult to miss such a huge bus passing by. How strange! I could only go back to the City.

As I was going into the Buddhahall to bow, I saw a notice on the bulletin board outside seeking a volunteer to take care of Laywoman Guofo. I instantly knew this had to be why I hadn't been able to go to

以他的神通妙用，來成就果佛居士的願望，後來筆者與她朝夕相伴，一直照顧到為她送終。

師父上人不但慈悲攝受，並消除她面對老死的憂懼。在她往生前一個月還答應她出家，授以沙彌尼戒，賜號恆聖，使她在來生菩提道上增一勝因。師父來者不拒，大慈大悲，拔苦與樂，使她在人生最後數月，能在萬佛聖城更加精進日夜念佛。她的例子，全世界只能在萬佛城見到。師父上人度生真是沒有局限，沒有分別的！

師父上人常常告訴弟子們，凡是生活有困難的老年人，他都歡迎他們到萬佛城來。他說自己在東北時，雖被人稱為白孝子，但是以前侍奉父母未盡至孝，所以現在願意照顧他人的父母。這種老吾老以及人之老的無私心，其實正是師父一生奉持佛戒，「孝順父母師僧三寶，孝名為戒。」的又一例證。

筆者住在老人院的期間，知道師父經常來老人院探望，或時以他人供養給師父的食物，與老人家們分享。叫人為老人院加裝暖氣，並令專人負責老人院的飲食。有一次，上人還特別為老人的飲食，開示大眾如何調製合宜消化的菜餚。那份關懷倍至，體貼如微，一時一刻未曾捨離！

Gold Buddha Sagely Monastery! Later I found out that there was nothing inappropriate about my taking care of her. So I volunteered myself and informed the Venerable Master. The wonderful functioning of the Venerable Master's spiritual powers had fulfilled Laywoman Guofo's wish. Later I became her constant companion and took care of her until she passed away.

The Master not only gathered her in, but relieved her of the fears of old age and death. One month before she died, he allowed her to leave the home-life, transmitted the novice precepts to her, and gave her the Dharma-name Heng Sheng ('Sage'). She thus planted a supreme cause for her progress on the Bodhi Way in her next life. The Master, who never rejected anyone who came to him, used great kindness and compassion to alleviate suffering and bestow happiness. In the last few months of her life, she recited the Buddha's name with even greater vigor at the Sagely City of Ten Thousand Buddhas. One may search all over the world, but one will find an example like hers only at the Sagely City of Ten Thousand Buddhas. The Venerable Master's salvation of living beings is truly without limit or discrimination!

The Venerable Master often told his disciples that any elderly person who led a difficult life was welcome to live at the Sagely City of Ten Thousand Buddhas. He said that although people had called him "Filial Son Bai" in Manchuria, he had not fulfilled his filial duties to his parents, so he wished to take care of others' parents. This selfless attitude of treating all parents as one's own parents is yet another example of the Venerable Master's lifelong adherence to the Buddhist precepts: "One should be filial to one's parents, teachers in the Sangha, and the Triple Jewel. Filiality is known as precepts."

While living in the home for the elderly, I discovered that when the Venerable Master came to the City, he would often come to visit the elders himself, or share with them the food that others had offered to him. He had a heating system installed in the home and also appointed a person to prepare food for the elderly. One time, the Venerable Master even gave an instructional talk to the assembly on how to prepare food that could be easily digested by the elderly. The Venerable Master's concern for the elderly was such that his thoughts never left them even for a moment!

*   *   *

師父一生中所經歷過的每一件事情，無論是個人的或是道場的，大小鉅細，他無一不記得清清楚楚。下面舉一件一九八九年師父上人回臺灣訪問時發生的事情：

一位居士在花蓮向大眾訴說有關上人的故事：他說，一九八九年他到萬佛聖城參加法會。法會結束後，他到辦公室去辦事，當時師父也在那兒。上人慈祥和藹地對他說：「你要小心自己的皮夾啊！不要再弄丟了！」聽到此話，他大吃一驚，不禁脫口而出：「師父，您還記得我？」

The Venerable Master remembered every single thing, whether great or small, whether it involved an individual or a Way-place, that ever happened in his life. The following incident happened during the Venerable Master's visit to Taiwan in 1989:

A layman from Hualian related a story involving the Venerable Master: He said that he had gone to the Sagely City of Ten Thousand Buddhas in 1989 to attend a Dharma session, and after it was over, he went to the Administration Office. The Master was also in the office and very kindly said to the layman, "You should be careful with your wallet. Don't lose it again!" When the layman heard this, he was shocked and asked, "Master, you still remember me?"

Twenty years earlier, he had come to the Sagely City of Ten Thousand Buddhas to attend a Dharma session. He had been carrying his life savings in his wallet. One day, he suddenly discovered that he had lost the wallet. He had rushed to the office to ask the Master for help. Bodhi-

原來在二十年前，他也是到萬佛聖城參加法會，當時身上皮夾內裝著的，大約是他一生的積蓄。一天，他發現皮夾不見了！氣急敗壞地趕到辦公室去求師父。菩薩行無畏施！師父告訴他不要急，會找到的。後來果然找回了皮夾，裡面東西都沒丟。使他感到意外的是，師父上人弟子眾多，而他並不是個熱心的護法，也沒有經常親近師父。他說：「我這麼沒沒無聞，無關重要的弟子。二十年後，師父居然還記得我，並提醒我小心注意，實在不可思議！」師父實實在在地注意著、關心著，照顧著他的每一個弟子。他更明白的告訴我們一心修行，早成佛道，他自會在後邊為我們善後一切！

*　　　*　　　*

我們師兄弟，跟隨師父上人後，不論時間長短，或多或少都曾有過這樣的經歷：生活上各種困難、病痛、憂慮，師父都會為你著想，替你解決。若有誰犯了錯誤，心中不安樂，只要告訴師父，師父以大雄大力大慈悲，一一攝受而去。筆者仍記得，受沙彌戒前一夜的懺摩，每個人可以將以前做過的種種錯事，向法師懺悔清淨，以便能得一個清淨戒體重新做人。那天晚上，在三寶前恭敬頂禮，觀想師父，將自己的錯事一一說出，從此果然解脫了！

弟子們在師父面前，都是透明體，不只今生今世的言行心思，就是多生多劫以來的，也無法在師父眼前遁藏。正因為如此，眾生在急難時、病痛時，他都能悉知悉見而咸令果遂。

對弟子們不在心地上修淨梵行，犯過，縱任惡習增長，師父上人是絕不講情面的。師父的弟子中，也有因不能忍受師父的鐵面無私的教化，清苦嚴屬的家風，而離去的也不在少數。師父對弟子來去的原則是「參方不留，還俗不留」。

外人毀謗批評師父時，師父從不解釋，也不辯解，反而要弟子叩頭禮謝那些批評的人。師父不像世人重現實，求利益，他看重的是修行。

為了弘揚佛法，師父時時都在培養人才；提拔人才時，師父是平等一如，給每一個弟子都

sattvas practice the giving of fearlessness, and so the Master told him not to worry, that he would find it. On his return trip, he found his wallet, and none of the money had been touched. He was surprised, for the Master had so many disciples, and he himself was not a devoted Dharma protector who often drew near the Master. He said, "I'm such a nobody, not an important disciple, yet twenty years later, the Master remembered me and reminded me to be careful. Incredible!" The Venerable Master's vow is that, as long as any disciple of his has not become a Buddha, he will not become a Buddha. This is not an empty vow. He is constantly paying attention to, concerned about, and taking care of all his disciples. He clearly told us that we must single-mindedly concentrate on cultivation and quickly accomplish Buddhahood, and that he will follow behind us, taking care of our unfinished affairs!

*　　　*　　　*

All of us who are disciples of the Venerable Master, no matter how long or short a time we have followed the Master, have our own experiences: the Master took care of all the difficulties, illnesses, and worries that we encountered in our lives. If we were uneasy at heart because we had made mistakes, all we had to do was tell the Venerable Master, and with his great heroic power and great compassion, he took our worries and problems one by one and made them disappear. He was truly the best kind of insurance! I remember the evening before I received the Shramanera precepts, there was a repentance ceremony during which each preceptee was allowed to confess and repent of their offenses so that he or she could receive the pure precept substance and become a new person. That night I bowed respectfully before the Triple Jewel, contemplated the Venerable Master, and confessed all of the wrong things I had done. After that, I was truly liberated from them!

In front of the Venerable Master, all of his disciples were transparent. They could not conceal from him their words, deeds, and thoughts, not only of the present life, but of many lives and many eons. Because of this, he completely knew what every living being's needs were and fulfilled those needs.

Yet when his disciples committed offenses and indulged in bad habits, failing to cultivate pure conduct on the mind ground, the Venerable Master didn't show them any courtesy. Quite a few of his disciples left because they could not endure the Venerable Master's style of teaching, which demanded that they face reality and bravely change their faults. The Master's principle was not to detain those who wished to go elsewhere or return to laylife.

When people slandered or criticized the Venerable Master, he never tried to explain himself. He instructed his disciples to bow and thank those people and not defend him. The Venerable Master was not like worldly people, who only see the immediate reality and seek profit. What he valued was cultivation.

In propagating the Buddhadharma and in training and promoting capable people, the Venerable Master was fair and equal, giving every

有學習的機會。例如，有時他派差事給弟子時，有經驗、能幹的人他不叫，反而給予新手機會。讓弟子有機會自己去體驗，去認識，去學習。

數十年來，師父開示時，在他法座旁邊，都設弟子座位，並且讓弟子們先講。他為了培育講法人才，時時刻刻提攜後進，即使應邀到美國白宮內的場合，亦復如是。每次法會後，師父必殷殷垂問弟子們講法內容，使弟子們不由得生起於法應慎重之心。師父就是這樣來造就各種人才。筆者雖愚魯，不學無術，卻也承蒙師父多方面的訓練。

*　　　*　　　*

在宣揚正法的萬佛聖城各分支道場，修行有三大條款，就是「凍死不攀緣，餓死不化緣，窮死不求緣。」師父教弟子：「出家人不可見到居士發心，就打居士的主意，不可這麼沒骨頭的。我要價值幾百萬的東西都不跟人講的，都是他們需要什麼要跟我說。各處攀緣的人不配做我的徒弟……。出家人總要有清高的行為，要為世界立法，不是為名利。」

師父很年輕在東北修行時，就發願持日中一食。可當他參訪其他叢林時（當時的叢林是過午不食，可以吃早粥），他的方便法是：頭一天吃早粥，第二天就不吃了。就有人問：怎麼不吃粥啊？我說：「我一吃粥就肚痛，大概自己業障重吧？」旁人聽了也就說：「嗯！你真業障重，不能吃粥！」師父上人曾經有半年沒有飯吃的記錄，在艱難困苦中磨鍊自己的金剛志，任何境界都不能動搖他向道的志願：「凍死迎風站，餓死挺肚行」！

師父上人說「僧家不比世情濃」，「我世間法什麼都會，但都不教你們，我是一個很堅強的人。」可是，師父唯恐他的弟子像師父一樣窮，他總是一再叮嚀弟子們要恭敬三寶，供養三寶，要種福田。師父也教導他的弟子要惜福「當年我在道德會時，吃馬鈴薯都是連皮吃的，這是我十六、七歲在道德會學要節約物質」

師父所講的法，都是他躬行實踐得到的經驗，教導我們怎樣才能以不堅固的肉身換取金剛

disciple a chance to learn. For example, when there was a job assignment, he didn't call on those who were experienced and capable. Rather, he gave newcomers a chance. He gave his disciples the opportunity to experience, recognize, and learn on their own.

For several decades, whenever the Venerable Master gave a Dharma talk, he would always place seats for his disciples beside his own seat and would let his disciples speak first. In order to train people to speak the Dharma, he always gave his disciples a chance to practice. He did this even when he was invited to the White House. After each Dharma lecture, he would ask in detail about what his disciples had said in their talks, inspiring his disciples to naturally give rise to respect for the Dharma.

*　　　*　　　*

At the branch Way-places of the Sagely City of Ten Thousand Buddhas, which propagate the Proper Dharma, there are Three Great Guidelines: "Freezing, we do not scheme. Starving, we do not beg. Dying of poverty, we ask for nothing." The Venerable Master taught his disciples, "When left-home people see a layperson bringing forth the resolve, they cannot scheme to get something from him. They cannot be so lacking in self-respect. When I'm going to buy something that costs several million dollars, I don't mention it to anyone. Rather, they come to me when they need something. People who go around exploiting conditions are not fit to be my disciples... Left-home people should always conduct themselves in a lofty way, setting a good example for the world, but not being out for fame and profit."

When the Venerable Master was cultivating in Manchuria in his youth, he vowed to maintain the rule of taking only one meal a day at noon. When he stayed at other monasteries (the rule in most monasteries was not eating after noon, but monks could eat rice gruel in the morning). His expedient method was to eat the morning gruel on the first day, but not after that. People would ask him, "Why don't you eat gruel?" He said, "I get a stomachache as soon as I eat it. Probably my karmic obstacles are too heavy." Others hear his excuse and say, "Ah, your karmic obstacles must be really heavy! You can't even eat gruel!" The Venerable Master once went for half a year without eating. In the midst of difficulty and suffering, he forged his Vajra resolve. No state could move his resolve for the Way: "Freezing, I stand facing the wind. Starving, I stick out my stomach and walk."

The Venerable Master said, "The sentiments of the Sangha family are not as heavy as worldly emotions." "I have mastered all worldly skills, but I don't teach you. I'm a very strong person." Yet the Venerable Master feared his disciples would be as poor as he, so he always reminded his disciples to respect the Triple Jewel and make offerings to the Triple Jewel—they must plant fields of blessings. The Master also taught his disciples to cherish their blessings: "Back in the days when I was in the Moral Society, I ate potatoes with the peels on them. That was when I was sixteen or seventeen and I wanted to be thrifty at the Moral Society."

The Dharma that the Master spoke came from his own experience and true practice. He taught us how to exchange our perishable flesh

不壞的法身；以不恆常的凡夫心換取常住的真如佛性。

　　師父曾立下志願，一切應得的福報，願迴向一切眾生。他由亞洲到美洲，赤手空拳，三十年來興建大小二十七處道場，造福廣大眾生。為應未來弘法事業的需要，他更經常忙於選地點設道場。有一次看完某新道場回來，他說：「我這都是在為你們打天下。」

　　一九六二年，師父隻身遠渡重洋來到美國。在不聞佛法的西方，為度化哪怕是為數不多的美國弟子，師父真正的實踐了「難忍能忍，難行能行」。

　　一九六八年，在為期九十六天的楞嚴法會上，師父除了每天全天講經外，還要買菜做飯、侍候茶水。為了在預定時間中使法會圓滿，由每天講一次，增加到每天四次，師父曾說：「……我就天天煮飯、燒菜、烹茶，沒有人幫助我，每天服侍三十多人。家庭式的四口爐台，我一個人做，大家都愛吃得很，每天吃個精光。可是廚房裡，我也做得乾乾淨淨的。最後一天，才有人來幫忙拿碗，從裡面拿出來，把盤碗就打爛了。」由於東西方人因文化語言、個性習慣等背景的差異，使佛法在美國的弘傳倍感困難，尤其是培養美國的出家眾弟子。師父早期來美弘法度生的那份艱辛，寂寞，委屈，唯師父自己心中才知。師父曾描述：「登天難，也不難；叫公雞生蛋難，也不難。教美國人學佛法真是難。」

　　【註】從跟隨上人多年的居士處得知：上人在辦楞嚴班講習班時，之所以既講經又做種種炊事，實在是因為他見到有些弟子根基深厚，一心要栽培他們。要令大家心無旁鶩地用功，以成就法器。以致有美國人在一個月內就把艱深拗口的〈楞嚴咒〉背下來的佳話。

＊　　　＊　　　＊

　　師父上人度化弟子，有言傳、身教，還有許多是無言的。見到能做該做的事，師父從不會指使弟子去做，而是馬上動手自己去做。弟子一見當然知道要去做了。對這些弟子，他會加上這麼一句：「你們不要儘做表面功夫，不要見我做才做。」

bodies for the Dharma body of indestructible Vajra and how to exchange our impermanent, worldly minds for the eternal Buddha nature of true suchness.

The Master vowed to dedicate all his blessings to all living beings. From Asia, he came empty-handed to America and established twenty-seven Way-places of various sizes in thirty years in order to create great blessings for people. Considering the needs of the future propagation of the Dharma, he frequently went out to choose appropriate sites for the establishment of Way-places. Once, after going out to look out a new Way-place, he said, "I'm doing all of this to win the empire for you."

In 1962, the Master came across the ocean to America on his own. In the West, where people had not heard of the Buddhadharma, the Master genuinely "endured what was difficult to endure and practiced what was difficult to practice," in order to teach his American disciples, even though they were only a few.

During the 96-day Shurangama Dharma Session in 1968, the Master not only lectured on the Sutras every day, he also did the grocery shopping, cooked, and supplied tea and drinks. In order to complete the session on schedule, the Master increased the number of lectures from one per day to four per day. The Master said, "Every day I cooked, made tea, and boiled water. No one helped me. Every day I served over thirty people. I used a family-style stove with four burners. I did the cooking alone, and everyone had a good appetite. The food was always completely finished every day. I also kept the kitchen clean and tidy. It was not until the last day that someone helped me carry the dishes out of the kitchen, and he broke them in the process." Due to the differences in culture, language, character, and customs between Easterners and Westerners, propagating the Buddhadharma in America was an inordinately difficult task, especially when it came to teaching American left-home disciples. Only the Master himself knew the hardship, loneliness, and injustice that he suffered when he first came to America to spread the Dharma and save beings. The Master once described it thus: "Ascending to the heavens is hard, but not that hard. Getting a rooster to lay eggs is hard, but not that hard. Teaching Americans to study the Buddhadharma is truly hard."

Note: According to those who followed the Venerable Master for many years, the reason the Venerable Master lectured on the Sutra and did all the chores during the Shurangama Lecture and Practice Session was that he saw some of his disciples had a very good foundation and he wished to nurture them. He wanted everyone to apply effort without distraction so that they could become vessels of the Dharma. There were even some Americans who memorized the difficult Shurangama Mantra in one month.

＊　　　＊　　　＊

The Venerable Master taught his disciples both verbally and by example. Many of his teachings were wordless. When he saw something that should be done, the Master never told his disciples to do it. He would immediately do it himself. When his disciples saw this, they would of course know what they should do. The Master would then say to them, "You should not apply effort only on the surface. You shouldn't do it just because you see me doing it."

師父上人會治眾生各種各樣身病、業障病、煩惱病。他聽到某某人有病苦，經常最先的反應就是淡淡地問：「他現在在哪裡？」師父的治病救人，是隨時隨地、不收分文。而且替人治了病，還不願意教人知道。有一次，師父的一位弟子來向師父道謝，說：「師父，弟子又夢到您穿著紅袍戴著寶冠，給弟子加持，弟子病就好了。」師父就馬上接口：「嘿！你說的那一套，我都不相信。你如果給我說去，你的病就又要犯了。」使得弟子不知何以報答他。

師父心裡只有眾生，唯獨沒有想到他自己：吃沒有油鹽的食物；一張餐巾紙可以用幾天；穿破舊的衲衣；多年來所積的果儀都悉數做為獎學金，供在家、出家弟子讀書用；所有法界佛教總會所屬的道場財產，永遠都屬於佛教的。

師父所闡述的佛教經典，深入淺出，使人易於融會貫通。因為直心，師父說話不拖泥帶水，切中要點。為教化眾生，導以真實之法。細細推敲其中蘊涵的道理，會發覺淺顯中包藏著無盡的深義。正如師父的外表憨厚樸實，內在卻非常深沉，聰明睿智！

希望所有誤解、毀謗宣化上人的人，聽聽事實，不要混淆他人的視聽，又壞了自己的慧命！

師父的作風 - - 平實、直樸。
師父的天性 - - 無拘無束，任運自然，
　　　　　　　毫無造作。
師父的胸懷 - - 清清白白，坦坦蕩蕩，
　　　　　　　無私無畏！

The Venerable Master could cure living beings' physical illnesses, illnesses caused by karmic obstacles, and illnesses of afflictions. Whenever he heard that someone was sick, his first reaction was usually to ask, "Where is he now?" The Master healed and saved people whenever and wherever he saw the need, and he never accepted a penny in return. When he had cured someone, he didn't want the person to know. Once, a disciple went to thank the Master, saying, "Master, I dreamed again that you came, wearing a red sash and a jewelled crown, to aid me, and then I recovered from my illness." The Master immediately said, "Eh! I don't believe a word you say. If you keep saying such things about me, your sickness will recur." And so his disciple was left not knowing how to repay him.

The Master had only living beings on his mind. He never thought of himself. He took bland food that had no oil or salt. He could use the same napkin for many days. His robes were old and worn. He used the money offerings saved up over the years as scholarships for his lay and left-home disciples to study in college. All of the Way-places and properties of Dharma Realm Buddhist Association belong permanently to Buddhism.

The Master explained the profound principles of the Buddhist scriptures in such a way that people could easily understand them. His mind was straightforward, and so his words were sincere and to the point; he didn't beat around the bush. He taught and guided living beings with the true and actual Dharma. If one reflects carefully, one discovers that his simple words contain limitless and profound meanings. Likewise, while the Master's appearance was honest and simple, his mind was extremely profound, keen, and wise!

I hope the people who have misunderstood and slandered the Venerable Master Hua will listen to the facts and not confuse others and destroy their own wisdom!

The Master's style: honest, straightforward, and sincere.
The Master's disposition: unfettered, spontaneous, and effortless.
The Master's heart: pure, peaceful, unselfish, and without fear!

萬物因道生　　得者自通靈　　悟徹本來體　　一通一切通

宣公上人看六祖大師和神秀大師之偈頌而作

All the myriad creatures come forth from the Tao.
One who gains the Way personally touches the magic;
Awaken completely to your deepest, fundamental identity,
And when one penetrates, all alike connect.

Composed by Venerable Master Hua after reading the verses
of the Great Master the Sixth Patriarch and Great Master Shenxiu

片片的回憶

SMALL REMEMBRANCES

張果遷　一九九五年八月十六日
Theresa Tsai (Chang Guoqian)
August 16, 1995

一九八三年元月初十，是上人替弟子選定的皈依日期。上人給弟子取法名「遷」時，對弟子說：「出於幽谷，遷於喬木。希望你的心量要大。」又說：「你現在是四十一歲，佛教裡，你是一歲。」皈依的那天，上人又讓法師給了我好多書，都是上人的開示及佛經淺釋。我如獲至寶，心中充滿喜悅及感恩。皈依完畢，我帶著輕鬆、愉快的心情離開了金山寺。下樓時，聽見上人站在門口說：「你終於回來了。」

January 10, 1983, was the day the Venerable Master chose for me to take refuge. When the Venerable Master gave me the Dharma-name Qian "to move," he said, "Come out of the lonely valley and move to the tall tree. I hope your mind will be all-encompassing." He then said, "You are forty-one years old. In Buddhism, you are one year old." The day I took refuge, the Venerable Master directed a Dharma Master to give me many books, all of which were the Venerable Master's Dharma Talks and explanations of the Sutras. It was as if I had obtained a treasure. My heart was filled with joy and gratitude. After the refuge ceremony, I left Gold Mountain Monastery in a state of light-hearted bliss. As I was walking downstairs, I heard the Venerable Master, who was standing in the doorway, say, "You've finally come back."

*

*　　*

在去金山寺（舊址）的路上，我曾想，我有很多的困難及煩惱，準備等會兒向上人討教。來到金山寺跪拜上人後，上人示意我在他左邊的椅子坐下，很久很久……，上人似乎進入禪定。不知過了多久，我抬起頭來說：「師父，剛才我有很多的問題，怎麼看到您後，好像什麼問題都沒有了。」上人聽了，也笑起來。在上人房裡坐了兩個多鐘頭，感覺卻好像一瞬間，我真有點捨不得離去。

上人說：「你不想走囉！」

回家的路上，我感覺身心都非常清淨。好像我以往的罪業，上人都替我洗刷掉了。

On the way to Gold Mountain Monastery (the old location), I thought to myself: "I have a lot of difficulties and afflictions. In a little while I'm going to ask the Venerable Master for advice." After I arrived at Gold Mountain Monastery and bowed to the Venerable Master, the Master motioned for me to take a seat on his left. I sat there for a long, long time. The Master seemed to have entered samadhi. I don't know how much time passed, before I finally looked up and said, "Master, I had a lot of problems before, but after seeing you, it seems all my problems are gone." These words made the Venerable Master smile. I sat in the Venerable Master's room for two hours, but it felt like an instant. I felt a bit reluctant to leave.

The Venerable Master: "You don't feel like leaving!"

On the way home, I felt extremely pure in body and mind. It was as if the Venerable Master had washed away all my karmic offenses from the past.

*

*　　*

一時很難描述，我身邊的這位出家人。他，外表很不起眼。無語時，如入禪定，回答問題時，卻充滿智慧。我愈來愈覺得他不是一位平凡

It would be very difficult to describe the monk beside me. His external appearance is quite ordinary. When he is not speaking, he is constantly in Chan samadhi. Yet the answers he gives are full of wisdom. More and more, I feel that he is not an ordinary person. I feel as if I

294

的人。又覺得自己像在作夢：在這塵世間，真的會有這樣的聖者？他好像隨時會在我面前消失，我不由自主地說：「師父，您是佛。」上人頓了一下，小聲地說：「你不要到處去給我宣傳。」

*　　　*　　　*

又有兩次，在金山寺，看見上人又是接見信眾，又是給弟子們上課，未曾停止過。有一天，上人坐在最後一排，聆聽在家弟子翻譯，我終於忍不住說：「師父，您要休息啊！」上人站起身，甩了一下右手，很堅毅地說：「為法忘軀！」往講台上走去。

*　　　*　　　*

一次，去金山寺拜見上人，天氣非常寒冷。見到上人不時用手掌抹去流出來的鼻涕。不久我去萬佛城，在外面繞佛時，亦看到上人同樣用手掌擦抹流出來的鼻涕。上人刻苦，儉省到連一片手紙都捨不得用，弟子被深深地感動了。

*　　　*　　　*

第一次拜見上人

弟子：我最近讀了很多佛教的書。
上人搖頭：「也不能隨便看。」上人用右手指了一下右頭。「他們認為是這樣，咦！是這樣」上人又用右手指向下指，說：「就這樣寫下去了。」

*　　　*　　　*

弟子：他們說您很兇，會罵人。
上人：我不但會罵人，還會打人呢！

*　　　*　　　*

am dreaming: Could there really be such a sage in this mundane world? He seems about to vanish before my eyes at any moment. I cannot help but say, "Venerable Master, you are a Buddha." The Master remained silent for a while, and then whispered, "Don't you go around advertising me."

*　　　*　　　*

On two other occasions at Gold Mountain Monastery, I saw the Venerable Master meeting with faithful laypersons and holding class for disciples, never once taking a break. One day the Master was sitting in the last row listening to a lay disciple's translation. I couldn't restrain myself from saying, "Venerable Master, you must get some rest!" The Master stood up, extended his right hand, and said firmly, "Forget yourself for the sake of the Dharma!" Then he walked towards the lecture podium.

*　　　*　　　*

Once when I visited the Venerable Master at Gold Mountain Monastery, it was very cold. I noticed the Master constantly wiping the mucus from his nose with the palm of his hand. Later at the City of Ten Thousand Buddhas, when we were circumambulating outside, I also saw the Venerable Master using his hand to wipe away the mucus from his nose. The Master lived so austerely, not even wishing to waste a piece of tissue. I was deeply touched.

*　　　*　　　*

The First Time I Met the Venerable Master

Disciple: "I've read many Buddhist books."
The Venerable Master shook his head: "You can't read things at random." The Master pointed at the right side of his head with his right hand. "They think it is this way: 'Ah! So this is how it is.'" The Master then pointed downwards with his right hand and said, "So that's how they set it down in writing."

*　　　*　　　*

Disciple: "They say you're very fierce and that you scold people."
Venerable Master: "I not only scold people, I also beat people!"

*　　　*　　　*

拜見上人時，我不停的流淚。心想：上人為了眾生，什麼都捨了；上人為了眾生，什麼都受了；上人的崇高德行，使弟子感激涕零！

上人：好多人見到我都哭了。

＊　　　＊　　　＊

讀了虛雲老和尚的年譜。

弟子：「什麼是舍利子？」

上人：「是由戒、定、慧薰修而成，不要在這上面貪著。我死了以後，要把身體火化了，骨灰撒在虛空中。」上人抬起右手，在空中示意。

＊　　　＊　　　＊

師父替弟子做了一件事，滿了弟子的願。

弟子：謝謝師父。

上人：不用說謝。

＊　　　＊　　　＊

弟子問了一個不當的問題。

上人：哎！你 waste（浪費）掉你好多 gasoline（汽油）啊！（示意弟子不要在這無謂的事上執著。）

＊　　　＊　　　＊

弟子：什麼是佛？

上人：什麼都沒有。

＊　　　＊　　　＊

上人：佛教是真理，不是迷信。你要名，就死在名上。你要利，就死在利上。

＊　　　＊　　　＊

While visiting the Venerable Master, I can't stop weeping. I think to myself: "For the sake of living beings, the Venerable Master has renounced everything. For the sake of living beings, the Venerable Master has undergone everything. The Venerable Master's lofty virtue makes me cry in gratitude!"

Venerable Master: "Many people cry when they see me."

＊　　　＊　　　＊

I read the year-by-year account of the Elder Master Hsu Yun's life.

Disciple: "What are sharira?"

Venerable Master: "They are formed from the cultivation and permeation of precepts, samadhi, and wisdom. Don't be greedy for or attached to them. After I die, I want my body to be cremated and my ashes to be scattered in empty space." The Venerable Master gestured in the air with his right hand.

＊　　　＊　　　＊

The Venerable Master did something for me, granting my wish.

Disciple: "Master, thank you."

Venerable Master: "No need to say thanks."

＊　　　＊　　　＊

I asked an inappropriate question.

Venerable Master: "Ah! You've wasted a lot of your gasoline!" (He was telling me not to be attached to senseless things.)

＊　　　＊　　　＊

Disciple: "What is the Buddha?"

Venerable Master: "There's nothing at all."

＊　　　＊　　　＊

Venerable Master: "Buddhism is the truth, not superstition. If you want fame, you will die for fame. If you want profit, you will die for profit."

＊　　　＊　　　＊

看到上人的十八大願，我流淚了。

「度得完嗎？」弟子問。

「度不完。」上人回答。

眼淚又奪眶而出，為上人的願力感動而落淚。

「我盡我的心嘛！」上人在電話那頭說。

（一九八三年剛學佛，所以弟子問了這個問題。）

*　　　*　　　*

在電話裡，

上人問：「你最近怎麼樣？」

我微笑回答：「我在無事忙。」（當時我在航空公司服務）

上人說：「你在忙無事！」

我無語，慚愧，直到現在仍沒有放下。

*　　　*　　　*

上人：你要多幫助人，在暗處裡幫助，事後也不要讓他知道。

*　　　*　　　*

告訴了上人，弟子當時的工作職務。

上人：你不要拿權勢去壓迫人，要以身作則地去感化人。

*　　　*　　　*

弟子：師父，我希望我母親能信佛。

上人：那要看你了，看你怎麼感化她了。

*　　　*　　　*

弟子：我希望我母親的病能好起來。

上人：多念觀世音菩薩，要真心誠意地念才會有感應。

是的，上人待每一位弟子都是真心誠意的！

Seeing the Venerable Master's eighteen great vows, I cried.

"Can you finish saving them?" I asked.

"No," replied the Master.

I cried some more, moved by the Venerable Master's vows.

"I just try my best!" the Venerable Master said over the phone.

(This was in 1983, when I had just begun studying Buddhism. That's why I asked this question.)

*　　　*　　　*

On the phone:

Venerable Master: "How have you been lately?"

I smiled and replied, "I've been busy over nothing." (I was working for an airline.)

Venerable Master: "You've been busy doing nothing important!"

I was speechless and ashamed. Even today, I haven't put things down yet.

*　　　*　　　*

Venerable Master: "You should help people. Help them secretly and don't let them know afterwards that you've helped them."

*　　　*　　　*

I told the Venerable Master about my job responsibilities.

Venerable Master: "You shouldn't use power to pressure people. You have to use your personal example to influence others."

*　　　*　　　*

Disciple: "Venerable Master, I wish my mother would believe in Buddhism."

Venerable Master: "That depends on you. It all depends on how you influence her."

*　　　*　　　*

Disciple: "I hope my mother will recover from her illness."

Venerable Master: "Recite the name of the Bodhisattva Contemplator of the World's Sounds (Guanshiyin) more often. You have to recite with complete sincerity in order for there to be a response."

Indeed, the Venerable Master treated every disciple with wholehearted sincerity.

＊　　　＊　　　＊

去萬佛城回來，上人問我如何？我說還沒有準備好，上人在電話裡說：「瓜不甜，不好吃。」忽然提高聲音問：「這是什麼？」我回答：「還沒有看破、放下和自在。」

是的，弟子罪業深重，這個執著何時能破？

After I returned from the City of Ten Thousand Buddhas, the Venerable Master asked me how it was. I said I wasn't ready yet. The Master said over the phone, "If the melon is not sweet, it doesn't taste good." Then he raised his voice and asked, "What does this mean?" I answered, "I still haven't seen through things, put them down, and become free."

Yes, this disciple's offense karma is deep and heavy. When will I be able to break my attachments?

＊　　　＊　　　＊

一九九〇年八月三十一日，上人赴臺灣弘法，我去機場送行，上人見到我說：「你回來了？」我搖頭回答：「飛機上不去！」（按：筆者本來要返臺參加一位長輩的喪禮）上人接弟子說：「我替你去了。」（當時聽了很茫然，不明白上人的意思。）

On August 31, 1990, the Venerable Master was going to Taiwan to propagate the Dharma, and I went to the airport to see him off. The Master saw me and asked, "You came back?" I shook my head, "I couldn't get on the plane!" (Note: I had originally planned to go back to Taiwan to attend the funeral of an elder.) The Venerable Master said, "I went for you." (When I heard this I was very confused and didn't grasp the Master's meaning.)

＊　　　＊　　　＊

自上人涅槃後，弟子悲淚長流不能自己。幾天前，去金山寺拜〈地藏懺〉，帶回一本一九八六年三月份的萬佛城月刊《金剛菩提海》雜誌，第二十二頁，上人如是說：「……你若持戒律，就不會哭；不持戒律的人，就會常常哭……」啊！上人在跟弟子說法呢！弟子在此頂禮上人。

After the Venerable Master's Nirvana, I wept without being able to stop. A few days ago, I went to Gold Mountain Monastery to bow the Earth Store Repentance. I took home with me a copy of the March 1986 issue of *Vajra Bodhi Sea*, the monthly journal of the City of Ten Thousand Buddhas. On page 22, the Venerable Master said, "...If you held the precepts, you wouldn't cry. People who don't hold the precepts cry all the time..." Ah! The Venerable Master was speaking the Dharma to me! Here, I bow in respect to the Venerable Master.

＊　　　＊　　　＊

上人：有些人，想求得長生不老。人，那有不死的呢！

Venerable Master: "Some people seek to live forever and never grow old. How can there be a person who doesn't die?!"

＊　　　＊　　　＊

弟子：師父，我很愛乾淨，每次都用好多水洗東西。
上人：洗到什麼都沒有了。

Disciple: "Venerable Master, I'm very fussy about cleanliness. I always use a lot of water when I wash things."
Venerable Master: "Wash until there is nothing left."

＊　　　＊　　　＊

一個夢

A DREAM

釋恆繼　Shi Hengji

在今年年初，忽然接到妹妹的電話，說她做了一個夢：「夢中她看見太陽從天上一直往下墜，然後掉落下來。當時我在她旁邊，於是她問我，為何太陽會墜落下來？我回答：『因為西方的諸佛菩薩，要迎接我師父到西方極樂世界去。』所以我要通知妳，會不會妳師父發生什麼事了？」

當時不敢相信這夢境，希望不是真的。等到了美國，不時的注意師父的病況。直到接到師父圓寂的消息，事後才想起這個夢。師父上人當時要降臨這世界時，其母也做了阿彌陀佛顯現的夢境。現在師父度眾生之緣盡了，又回到他原來的地方，相信他的精神永在，還是隨緣應機度眾生。

At the beginning of this year, I suddenly received a telephone call from my sister who told me that she had had a dream. In the dream she saw the sun fall straight down out of the sky and set. At that time I was beside her and she asked me, "Why has the sun set?" I answered, "Because the Buddhas and Bodhisattvas of the West want to welcome my Teacher to the Western Land of Ultimate Bliss." And so she called me to see if something had happened to my Teacher.

At the time I didn't want to believe that dream—I hoped it couldn't come true. After I arrived in America, my attention was always directed towards the state of the Master's illness. It was only after receiving the news of the Master's Nirvana that I remembered this dream. At the time when the Master was about to be born in this world, his mother also had a dream in which Amitabha Buddha appeared. Now the conditions that brought the Master here to take living beings across have ended, and he has returned to the land where he came from. I believe his spirit will remain eternally and that he is still according with conditions and responding to opportunities to rescue living beings.

受想行識如空色　　再呼舍利汝諦聽
是諸法空相無性　　不生不滅寂然通
不垢不淨離污染　　不增不減悟玄中
湛然靜極超造化　　頓覺我法本圓融

宣公上人《般若波羅密多心經非台頌解》

Feeling, cognition, formation, and consciousness are like emptiness and form.
Again he calls, Shariputra, pay attention, listen!
All dharmas are empty of characteristics, lacking a nature of their own.
Not produced, not destroyed, the principle silently pervades.
Not defiled, not pure, the nature is separate from corrupting filth;
It neither increases nor diminishes enlighten to the mysterious Middle Way.
In the pure and deep ultimate silence, all creation is transcended:
A sudden awakening to the original perfect fusion of self and dharmas.

From the Venerable Master Hua's Verses without a Stand for the *Heart of Prajna Paramita Sutra*

巧把塵勞作佛事

DOING THE BUDDHA'S WORK IN THE WORLD

千笈　Qianji

無緣大慈　同體大悲

記得六年前美國中西部乾旱，加州也因久旱無雨而嚴重缺水。為了求雨，弟子們一起到萬佛城求觀世音菩薩保佑，早日降甘露水，並求師父為眾生祈雨。師父說：「只要大家誠心念〈大悲咒〉，可望早日降雨於乾旱之地。」於是大家滿心歡喜的回去，三餐照吃，〈大悲咒〉照念。約一星期，滴雨未下，弟子心中納悶，便到金山寺去請問師父，順便帶一箱剛上市的櫻桃，準備供養師父及法師。沒想到，師父為了祈雨已好幾天不吃飯了。師父說：「如今因人心壞，世界也壞，天龍八部，護法善神也不護了，絕食是為了迴向給眾生，以求降雨。」此時我才明白佛菩薩（師父）悲心切切，將眾生的業，眾生的苦，承擔到自肩上，化慈悲的力量為清涼的甘露水。雨，終於從天而降，使乾涸的大地得到雨水的灌溉，也令眾生無明的心田得到法雨的滋潤與智慧的灌溉。雨，越下越大，而師父，卻越來越瘦了……。

道高龍虎伏，德重鬼神欽

有一天隨師父上山，師父坐在弟子車上。弟子的車緊跟前面的一輛車子，快到目的地時，由於前面的車子走錯了，我也跟著走錯了。師父突然問：「怎麼啦？」弟子說：「師父，前面的車子走錯了。」師父又問：「怎麼知道他走錯了呢？」弟子回答：「因為他又再回到原來的那條路上。」師父於是說：「盲目跟隨總有錯的。」這件事使我悟出「盲修瞎煉是會走錯路的！」

上了山，我們的車穿過一片紅木林，來到山上的一片平地，四周青山環抱著綠水。前面有一座古老的房子。為了禮貌，師父令我前去和主人打個招呼，我走上前去，還未按門鈴，就

Great kindness for those without affinities;
Great compassion of being one with all

I recall that about six years ago, there was a drought in the Midwest. California was also suffering a serious water shortage due to drought. In order to seek rain, we hastened to the City of Ten Thousand Buddhas to pray to Guanshiyin Bodhisattva to protect us and quickly send down a rain of sweet dew. We also beseeched the Venerable Master to seek rain on behalf of living beings. The Master said, "If the assembly sincerely recites the Great Compassion Mantra, a rain of sweet dew will soon fall on the drought-stricken areas." So everyone happily went home and continued eating their three meals a day and reciting the Great Compassion Mantra. After about a week, not one drop of rain had fallen. I anxiously went to Gold Mountain Monastery to ask the Venerable Master about this, and I brought a box of cherries that were new on the market to offer to the Venerable Master and other Dharma Masters. I didn't know that the Venerable Master had already gone for several days without eating in order to pray for rain. The Master said, "Because people's minds are corrupt and the world is corrupt, the gods, dragons, and rest of the eightfold division of Dharma-protecting good spirits are not offering protection. I am fasting in order to dedicate merit to living beings and pray for rain." I then understood the compassion of the Buddhas and Bodhisattvas (the Venerable Master) in taking the karma and suffering of living beings upon themselves, transforming the power of compassion into refreshing sweet dew. The rain finally poured from the heavens, watering the parched earth. The mind-ground of living beings was also moistened by Dharma rain and irrigated with wisdom. The rain fell heavier and heavier. Meanwhile, the Venerable Master grew thinner and thinner...

When the Way is lofty, the dragons and tigers are subdued;
When virtue is great, ghosts and spirits are respectful

One day when I was driving the Master up a mountain, I was following the car in front of us very closely. When we were almost to our destination, the car in front took a wrong turn and I followed it. The Master suddenly asked, "What happened?" I said, "Master, the car in front took a wrong turn." "How do you know?" the Master asked. I replied, "Because it turned around and came back to the original road." Then the Master said, "If you blindly follow others, you will always go wrong." This incident made me realize that if we cultivate blindly, we will also go astray!

When we had ascended the mountain, I drove through a grove of redwoods and came to a meadow. The green mountains on all sides surrounded a spring. In front of us was an old house. For the sake of courtesy, the Master asked me to go say hello to the owner. Before I could ring the doorbell, a vicious dog chased me back and I nervously

波一隻惡狗狂追回來，我情急之下就躲到師父後面，臉色發青地說：「師父，房子裡一定沒有人，要不然，狗叫那麼大聲，怎麼不見有人出來？」師父說：「有人，有人。來，我們一起上去看看。」此時這隻惡狗看到師父向前走，竟然一步步往後退，真是不可思議。我當時心中納悶：師父到底跟牠說了什麼話呢？卻聽到師父對著狗說：「How are you?」（你好嗎？）狗不出聲的一直跪在原地不動，目送著師父走過。這時，主人也出來了，帶領我們四處參觀，往山上更高的地方走去。這裡也有幾隻大狗和一大群火雞。牠們看到師父，都靜悄悄的連叫也不叫了。這時我在想，到底師父跟牠們說了些什麼呢？突然聽到師父說：

修行人應該要修到所有的動物都不怕⋯⋯。

這時我才明白，一個修行人真正修到連一點點的鬥心和微細的殺念都沒有的時候，遇到再兇猛的動物，也能化暴戾為祥和。

這大概就是聖人（師父）與凡夫（弟子）之間的差別吧！想著想著，弟子又問：「應如何修呢？」師父說：「按六大宗旨修。」此時我突然改變話題請問師父：「這座山這麼高，怎麼還有水呢？」師父說：「此地的祥瑞之氣，乃是因為在此修行的一切眾生，皆不犯貪之故。所謂『凡心死，道心生』。修道功夫，修一天便有一天的功德。」弟子問：「如何積功德？」師父說：「為善不為人知，所謂『聰明乃是陰騭助，陰騭引入聰明路；不行陰騭使聰明，聰明反被聰明誤。』更要時時懺悔，如果以往所造之業沒有了，就能成就所有的功德。」弟子問：「如何修才能像師父一樣的有大智慧呢？」師父說：「先修無漏。」弟子：「由何修起？」師父說：「先由你的心，所謂『禪到無心便是道』。」此時才明白〈永嘉大師證道歌〉所云：「心是根，法是塵，兩者猶如鏡上痕，痕垢盡除光始現，心法雙忘性即真。」

筆者曾跟隨師父踏遍北加州的山山水水，親聆師父的若干珍貴的教誨。每回憶及此，弟子常悲淚長流。如今師父雖已長揖人間，可是師父留給弟子的，無盡的法益及深邃的智慧。

hid behind the Master. My face had turned greenish, and I said, "Master, the house must be empty. Otherwise, with the dog barking so loudly, why haven't we seen anyone come out?" The Master said, "There's someone there. Come, let's go take a look together." When the mean dog saw the Master approach, amazingly, it began backing up, step by step. "Just what did the Master say to it?" I wondered. Then I heard the Master say, "How are you?" to the dog. The dog crouched down and watched the Master walk by, not making a sound. By then, the owner had come out and showed us around the property, taking us to a place higher up on the mountain. At that place there were also several large dogs and a flock of turkeys. When they saw the Master, they became totally quiet and didn't call out. What had the Master said to them? As I was wondering, I suddenly heard the Master say,

Cultivators should cultivate to the point that they don't fear any animal at all...

Then I understood. When a cultivator has cultivated to the point that he doesn't have the slightest inclination to fight or kill, he can influence fierce animals to become peaceful.

That must be the difference between a sage (the Venerable Master) and an ordinary person (me)! I mused about this, and then asked, "How should one cultivate?" The Master said, "Cultivate according to the six great principles." I suddenly changed the topic and asked, "How can there be water on such a high mountain?" The Master said, "The auspicious energy of this land is due to the fact that the living beings cultivating here have no greed. As it is said, 'When the ordinary mind dies, the mind for the Way comes forth.' For every day one cultivates, one gains a day of merit." I asked, "How should one amass merit?" The Master said, "Do good deeds without letting anyone know. As it is said, 'Intelligence is aided by secret good deeds. Secret good deeds lead you on the path to intelligence. If you fail to perform good deeds in secret and merely rely on your intelligence, you will be outsmarted by your own intelligence.' You should repent at all times. When the karma you created in the past disappears, then all merit and virtue will be accomplished." I asked, "How can one cultivate to be as greatly wise as the Master?" The Master said, "First cultivate to be without outflows." I asked, "How should one start?" The Master said, "Start with your mind. As it is said, 'When one meditates to the point of having no mind, that is the Way.'" Then I understood the line in Great Master Yongjia's *Song of Enlightenment*: "The mind is the root; / Dharmas are dust. / The two are like streaks on a mirror. / When the streaks are entirely removed, light begins to appear. / When mind and dharmas are both forgotten, / Then the nature is true."

I went with the Venerable Master to visit many mountainous areas throughout northern California and obtained many precious teachings from the Master. Thinking of this always makes me cry. Although the Master has now left the world, he has left behind Dharma of endless benefit and profound wisdom.

佛法的啓示

REVELATIONS OF THE BUDDHADHARMA

白景學　Bai Jingxue

世人多數都為酒色財氣所迷惑，而修行的人就是要戒掉酒色財氣。酒是穿腸毒藥，色是括骨鋼刀，脾氣是下山猛虎，財是惹禍根苗。

我沒學佛法以前，酒色財氣總困擾著我，無論做什麼事都向「錢」看，吸煙、喝酒樣樣少不了。有了錢，歡天喜地，大魚大肉猛吃。沒錢，脾氣就來了，有錢三隻眼，沒錢一臉黑。

南無觀世音菩薩，大慈大悲，教化救度一切有緣人。一九八五年有人從萬佛城帶給我《修行者的消息》、《宣化上人開示錄》、《地藏經》等佛教書籍，閱讀之後，我開始拜佛、念經，懺悔我以往的過錯，從內心深處改掉壞習慣，眼不見嘴不饞，耳不聽心不煩，真念佛無間斷。

有一次，法界佛教總會給我的信提到，「宣化上人每日一餐，不吃油鹽的菜，白水煮豆腐、麵條，替天下人受苦，幾十年如一日……」那次的來信，對我的教育極其深刻，我對佛法有了認識，而且潛移默化地影響和改變我的內心世界，我決心皈依三寶，自利利他，自度度他。

往昔所造諸惡業，
皆由無始貪瞋癡，
從身語意之所生，
一切我今皆懺悔。

Most worldly people are deluded by wine, sex, money, and anger. Cultivators want to abstain from wine, sex, wealth, and anger. Wine is a poisonous drug that burns the intestines. Sex is a sharp knife that cuts to the bone. Anger is a ferocious tiger coming down the mountain. Money is the root of disasters.

Before I studied Buddhism, I was caught up in wine, sex, money, and anger. No matter what it was, I would be looking for money. I also smoked, drank, and had other bad habits. When money came, I was as happy as could be and would feast on fish and meat. When I had no money, I would lose my temper. With money, I had three eyes. Without money, I would be in a black mood.

The greatly kind and compassionate Guanshiyin Bodhisattva teaches and rescues all people with whom he has affinities. In 1985 someone brought back some Buddhist books from the City of Ten Thousand Buddhas for me, including *News of True Cultivators*, *Instructional Talks of the Venerable Master Hua*, and the *Earth Store Sutra*. After reading them, I began bowing to the Buddhas, reciting Sutras, and repenting of my past mistakes. I deeply reformed of my bad habits. Since I didn't look, my mouth didn't water. Since I didn't listen, my mind wasn't afflicted. I truly recited the Buddha's name without interruption.

One time, a letter came from the Dharma Realm Buddhist Association saying, "The Venerable Master Hua eats one meal per day. He doesn't eat foods seasoned with oil or salt, but takes only tofu and noodles boiled in plain water. He has been doing this every day for several decades, enduring suffering on behalf of the people of the world..." That letter afforded me a very profound teaching. I began to understand the Buddhadharma and was unconsciously influenced to change the inner world of my mind. I resolved to take refuge with the Triple Jewel, to benefit myself as well as others, to rescue myself as well as others.

For all the evil deeds I did in the past,
Based on beginningless greed, anger, and delusion,
And created by body, speech, and mind,
I now repent of them all.

*　　　*　　　*

我背誦〈大悲咒〉和《地藏經》，有時候，連有沒有吃飯都忘記了。一九八七年的某一天夜裡，我做了一個夢，夢見在整個地球上面，全部長著聳入雲天的松林，我的身體忽然像長了翅膀一樣飛向天空，向西方飛去，往著極樂世

When I am reciting the Great Compassion Mantra or the *Earth Store Sutra* from memory, sometimes I even forget about eating. One night in 1987, I had a dream: The surface of the entire planet was covered with pine trees that reached up into the clouds. I seemed to have grown wings and was also flying upwards in the western direction, towards the Land of Ultimate Bliss. Suddenly, a large hand grabbed my right foot and pulled me from the sky back to a piece of land that

界去。突然，有一隻大手拉住我的右腳，把我從高空拉回到只有一百多平方米的地面上，周圍仍舊是又高又大的松樹。我看見西北角的地面上，有一位長髯老者，手拿拂塵，正在打坐念佛。隨後，從西南方向的上空，南無觀世音菩薩手拿淨水瓶和柳枝，飄飄然落在西南角的地面上，觀音菩薩告訴我，那位念佛的老者，就是南無地藏王菩薩，此夢不可思議。

我與太太一起修行，每天念〈大悲咒〉和《地藏經》，念南無地藏王菩薩一千遍，拜南無觀世音菩薩一○八拜。拜佛時，觀想蓮池海會佛菩薩就在眼前。今後，更要精進學佛法，勤修戒定慧，息滅貪瞋癡，丟掉一切妄想，多做善事，利益一切有情眾生。

was only a hundred square meters in area. All around, there were regular pine trees both tall and short. In the northwestern corner, I saw a long-bearded old man holding a whisk and sitting in meditation reciting the Buddha's name. In the next moment, in the southeastern direction, I saw Guanshiyin Bodhisattva holding a vase of pure water and a willow branch and floating down from space to land on the southeastern corner. Guanshiyin Bodhisattva told me that the old man who was reciting the Buddha's name was Namo Earth Store King Bodhisattva. It was an inconceivable dream.

My wife and I cultivate together. Every day we recite the Great Compassion Mantra and the *Earth Store Sutra*, recite Namo Earth Store King Bodhisattva 1000 times, and bow to Namo Guanshiyin Bodhisattva 108 times. When we bow, we contemplate that the Lotus Pool Assembly of Buddhas and Bodhisattvas is right before us. From now on, we will study the Buddhadharma even more vigorously. We will diligently cultivate precepts, samadhi, and wisdom; put to rest greed, anger, and delusion; get rid of all false thoughts; and practice more good deeds to benefit all sentient beings.

為令眾生得出離　盡於後際普饒益
長時勤苦心無厭　乃至地獄亦安受

福智無量皆具足　眾生根欲悉了知
及諸業行無不見　如其所樂為說法

——《大方廣佛華嚴經》〈初發心功德品〉

In order to cause living beings to escape,
He universally benefits them, exhausting the boundaries of the future,
For a long time he toils, yet his mind is without repulsion,
To the extent that he also calmly endures the hells.

His blessings and wisdom are limitless and totally perfected.
The roots and desires of living beings are all known to him,
As well as all of their karma and actions,
He speaks the Dharma for them as they like it.

Chapter on The Merit and Virtue from First Bringing Forth the Mind, the *Flower Adornment Sutra*

明燈詠

VERSE IN PRAISE OF THE ILLUMINING LAMP

果覺　Guo Jue

師父！我將對您的感恩，化做法輪，轉向十方，以善巧的智慧，導航迷失的眾生。

師父！我將對您的緬懷，化成佛陀，慈光微笑，以方便的橋樑，指引夜路的行人。

師父！我將對您的尊敬，化爲春風，大地醒覺，以普施的法露，喚起沉睡的心靈。

師父！我將對您的諄誨，化現燈塔，高懸虛空，以慈悲的祥光，做駭浪中的光明。

詠不盡，恩師的德；報不盡，恩師的訓，點滴懷澤，常潤襟衫。

是長夜，天上明星；思不絕，慧命相繼。若無此緣，道必枯竭。

更如是，願應相契；行當依，法脈流芳。無以爲報，常倚師行。

慚愧弟子　果覺　拜述

Shr Fu, I wish to transform my gratitude with regard to your kindness, into a Dharma wheel, turning in the ten directions,
Using the wisdom of expediency, to guide and save living beings who have lost their way.

Shr Fu, I wish to transform my memory of you into the Buddha, smiling with the radiance of compassion,
Serving as bridges of convenience, to show the way to travellers in the night.

Shr Fu, I wish to transform my respect towards you, into the spring breezes, causing the earth to awaken,
Bestowing the Dharma dew universally, to wake up souls that are sound asleep.

Shr Fu, I wish to transform your exhortation and teaching, into a lighthouse, hanging high up in empty space,
Using the auspicious radiance of compassion, to serve as bright light amongst treacherous tidal waves.

Unable to exhaustively praise the virtue of my kind teacher,
Unable to exhaustively repay the admonition provided by my kind teacher
These are small incidents in remembrance of my teacher's kindness, which constantly moisten my clothes.

It is a long night, with bright stars in the sky;
My thoughts flow without cease, passing on the wisdom life in succession.
Without this affinity, the Way would wither and come to an end.

Moreover, I wish that our minds will mutually coincide.
Following you in all I do, I wish to perpetuate the lineage of the Dharma.
I have no way to repay your kindness, except to follow you in walking the Path.

Written respectfully by remorseful disciple Guo Jue

宣化老和尚追思紀念專集

福澤人天

HIS BLESSINGS NURTURED HUMANS AND GODS

林果本　Lin Guoben

一九八六年我以慕道者的心情，開車載著父親、大嫂，由舊金山出發，前往朝禮萬佛聖城。在聖城，面對莊嚴肅穆的萬佛寶殿，面對上人：「凍死不攀緣，餓死不化緣，窮死不求緣」的壯誓，一代高僧的嶙峋風骨，令我無限欽佩，無限嚮往。

一九九一年萬佛城三壇大戒的時候，我再次去到萬佛聖城，在那裡第一次見到上人，向他頂禮三拜。其後，尋尋覓覓了多年，直到一九九四年，才有因緣在加州長堤聖寺，皈依在上人的座下。由一個慕道者成為佛門弟子，我走了整整八年。

其後，又見過上人幾次。上人那如炬的目光，如強力的探照燈，往往使我不敢正視，因慚愧而低下頭來。上人那懾人的神采，無私的悲懷，洞悉世事的智慧法語，往往寥寥數語，卻已使我五內震動，沉思良久。

當頑冥的我，正想更深入地理解佛法，實踐上人的微妙法門時，上人卻捨報歸去。

六月中，隨上人的靈車回到萬佛聖城。在無言堂瞻仰上人的遺容時，一股莫名的酸楚，湧上心頭：今日一別，重逢不知何世！抬頭仰望上人的法相，那無言的說法，彷彿在告訴我這一切就像電光石火，無常幻化，紅塵、色身，終究如鏡花水月，轉眼成空呀！

「願將法界眾生，所有一切苦難，悉皆與我一人代受。」上人以他瘦弱的色身，承擔眾生無盡的苦難，這種無私無我，大悲大慈的菩薩行願，真可謂「光超日月，德越太虛。」上人傳給後人的法，將「留福澤於人間天上，宣化日於此界他方。」上人的大悲願力，莊嚴了佛國淨土，成就了無量無邊的眾生。「菩薩所緣，緣苦眾生」，祈願上人在佛國淨土，有朝一日，乘願再來，重入娑婆，廣度有情。

In the spirit of one who admires the Way, I drove my father and my sister-in-law from San Francisco to the Sagely City of Ten Thousand Buddhas in 1986. At the Sagely City, the dignity of the Hall of Ten Thousand Buddhas, the Venerable Master's great vows: "Freezing, we do not scheme. Starving, we do not beg. Dying of poverty, we ask for nothing," and the upright appearance of this eminent monk won my boundless admiration.

During the Threefold Ordination Ceremony in 1991, I again went to the Sagely City, where I met the Venerable Master for the first time and made three bows to him. Afterwards I searched for many years, but it was only in 1994 that I had the affinity to take refuge with the Venerable Master at Long Beach Sagely Monastery. It took me a full eight years to turn from an admirer of the Way to a Buddhist disciple.

After that, I saw the Venerable Master several more times. The Master's gaze was like a torch or a powerful searchlight. I usually lowered my head in shame and didn't dare to meet his gaze. The Master's arresting presence, his unselfish compassion, his wise words of Dharma which stem from a total understanding of all worldly affairs, and his awesome demeanor have shaken me up and caused me to ponder deeply.

Just when I, this dullard, wished to deepen my understanding of the Buddhadharma and to practice the Master's wonderful Dharma-door, the Master renounced his life and departed.

In the middle of June, I followed the vehicle carrying the Venerable Master's casket back to the Sagely City of Ten Thousand Buddhas. When I was gazing at the Venerable Master's face in No Words Hall, an indescribable feeling of bitterness welled up inside me: Now that he is gone, in which life will we be able to meet again? I looked up at the Venerable Master's portrait, and it seemed to speak the Dharma wordlessly, telling me that everything is like a lightning flash or a spark of fire, temporary and illusory; the world and this body are ultimately just like reflections of flowers in a mirror or the moon in water—they will vanish in an instant!

"I vow to take upon myself the sufferings and hardships of all living beings in the Dharma Realm." With his thin and feeble body, the Venerable Master took upon himself the inexhaustible miseries of living beings. Such unselfish, selfless, greatly compassionate, and greatly kind Bodhisattva conduct and vows have "light exceeding that of the sun and moon, and virtue surpassing the limits of outer space." The Dharma the Venerable Master has handed down to future generations will "leave blessings for those in the world and in the heavens; proclaiming and transforming like the sun shining everywhere." The Venerable Master's greatly compassionate vows have adorned the Buddhas' Pure Lands and brought limitless and boundless living beings to accomplishment. "The affinities of Bodhisattvas are affinities with living beings in suffering." We hope the Master will one day, from the Buddhas' Pure Land, ride upon his vows to return to the Saha World to cross over sentient beings on a vast scale.

I Don't Have
the Slightest Speck of Desire

我連一粒微塵的欲念都沒有

釋恆順

Shi Hengshun

The Venerable Master's state is something that cannot be fathomed by even Arhats of the fourth stage of Enlightenment who have already transcended the cycle of birth and death. So how can we common people understand him? (The Master said this on August 6, 1974 during a Chan session a few days after I had started to live at Gold Mountain Monastery.)

In 1986 when the Master made what I believe was his first visit to Indonesia—one morning the Master came out of his room and looked at a Dharma brother and myself and said, "You don't have the slightest idea about what I am about." I'm afraid that the situation today, as I write these words, is still quite the same.

In late 1976 or early 1977, after I had first become a Bhikshu, the Master once told me as I knelt before him in his guest room, "I don't have the slightest speck of desire." The Master said this in his very calm ocean-like voice as he held his thumb and forefinger together signalling a speck. I know that the Master was speaking about a reality that was his normal experience.

The Master influences people more than anything else with his everyday behavior. For approximately fifteen years I was in constant close contact with the Master. Whenever I had a problem, there is always a memory of the Master doing or saying something which resolved the problem.

During that time one thing which stood out for me about the Master was his vigor. No matter what we were doing or where we were going, the Master was always reciting. Whether he was reciting mantras or Sutras or both doesn't matter. The Master always cultivated with incredible vigor. He said never neglect your "homework," meaning cultivation, no matter what you are doing.

When he was lecturing the *Flower Adornment Sutra* he said that even in his sleep he would be reciting that Sutra.

The Master's teaching is so difficult to fathom. Once he continuously reprimanded a young American resident at the old Gold Mountain Monastery to stop looking around at this and that all the time. He reprimanded the thirteen or fourteen year old like this for a year or two. Then one day the Master told the boy, who by then was a little novice, that from then on it was his job to look at everyone who came through the door for the evening lecture on the *Flower Adornment Sutra*. As soon as he

即使是生死已了的四果阿羅漢也不能瞭解上人的境界，我們凡夫又如何能知道。一九七四年八月六日，在金山寺的一次禪七開示中，上人曾作如是言。那時我剛搬入金山寺才幾天。

一九八六年，記得上人第一次訪問印尼時。有一天早上，上人從他的房間出來，看著我和一位師兄說：「我是什麼，你們一點都不知道！」直到今天我動筆寫這篇文章時，我相信還沒有人真知道上人到底是誰。

在一九七六年底左右，我初為比丘時，有一次，在上人的客房裡，我跪在上人的面前，上人以他慣有的、平靜深遠如海洋似的聲音說：「我連一粒微塵的欲念都沒有。」並以大姆指及食指作一種手勢表示微塵。我知道上人是在講他自己日常經驗中的一種實情。

上人日常的行為，對周圍的人影響很深。大概有十五年的時間，我和上人十分接近。在我記憶中，每當有什麼問題時，總是由上人出面，講幾句話，或做些什麼就解決了。

那一段時間，我記憶中最深刻的是上人精進的程度。上人隨時隨地都在誦咒，或者誦經。上人修行精進的程度是驚人的。上人說，不管我們在做什麼都不要忽略了功課，就是指我們的修行而言。

當上人講解《華嚴經》時說，即使在睡眠時，他也還在誦《華嚴經》。

上人的教誨有時令人不易瞭解。比如有一次，上人多次責備一個當時住在金山寺的美國孩子，叫他不要總是東張西望。這個孩子當時大概十三、四歲，上人責備了他大概一兩年。後來這個小孩子出家做了小沙彌。有一天上人對他說，以後凡有人晚間來聽《華嚴經》的時候，他要「觀」這個人的來歷，這就是他的工作。這位小沙彌自然依教奉行，立

obeyed the Master's instructions, his spiritual eye opened and the Master would often have him describe what he saw during the lectures to the assembly.

Now would it work that way with us? Of course not. This just shows how dynamic and alive the Master's lectures were. The interaction of the Enlightened Master's mind with that of his faithful students is not something one can read in a book.

The only text I can think of which aptly describes this state is "Entering the Dharma Realm Chapter" in the twenty-first roll of the *Flower Adornment Sutra*. It relates the pilgrimage of the pure youth Good Wealth and his visits to fifty-three Good Spiritual Counselors. The visits represent the inconceivable interaction of Enlightened Bodhisattvas with great vows and accumulated good karma with the affinities and karma of the youth.

Each taught him differently and represented a certain level on the path to Enlightenment. Yet these levels were not levels that they were limited to, rather it was merely the way their karmic affinities played out with those of Good Wealth's. So it is with the Master's interaction with the literally measureless people and other beings who had the good fortune/karma to meet or be taught by him.

Simply one teaching, like the Master's "Return the Light" verse, can take a person all the way. It can enable one to transcend the cycle of birth and death, and then be able to turn the wheel of wondrous Dharma for others by one's very existence. That is, one's every move and thought will then embody the Buddhadharma so that one naturally influences others. What is true is not thought about or planned. The way to truly change the world outside is only by changing one's own mind!

刻他就開了眼。上人在講經的時候，就常叫他描述他看見了些什麼。

這當然不表示我們也都有這樣的際遇，不過這說明了上人的開示是多麼活潑生動。一位開悟了的大師和他虔誠的弟子心靈之間的交互感應，不是語言所能描述的。

我認為只有在《華嚴經》第二十一卷「入法界品」中，善財童子五十三參善知識品中，才恰當地描述了上人的這種境界。這種有宿昔善根、開了悟又發大願的菩薩與善財童子的緣及業，兩者間的交互感應是不可思議的。

每一位善知識教得都不同，每一位都代表開悟道上某一種的程度，並不是說他們就受限制於該種程度，而是因為善財童子的業緣之故，需用這種程度教導。

上人與無量有緣有幸能遇到上人，並受上人教化的眾生其感應道交，亦是如此。

又如上人那首迴光返照的偈頌，能使我們超越生死，然後又示現生死度諸眾生。也就是將佛法在自己的言行思想中表現出來，因而自然而然地就能影響他人。凡用心意想得到的皆不是真如，我們只有先改善自己的內心，才能改善外面的世界。

隨順思惟説法界　　經無量劫不可盡
智雖善入無處所　　無有疲厭無所著
——《大方廣佛華嚴經》〈初發心功德品〉

Complying with their thoughts he speaks of the Dharma Realm,
Passing through limitless kalpas which cannot be exhausted.
Although his wisdom well enters,
He is without a dwelling place,
Being without weariness, satiation, or attachments.

Chapter on The Merit and Virtue from First Bringing Forth the Mind, the *Flower Adornment Sutra*

師父上人 —— 大醫王

THE VENERABLE MASTER — A GREAT PHYSICIAN KING

李果櫻　Li Guoying

我的二哥李果煜大約在一歲的時候，得了一個怪病，常常無緣無故地扁桃腺發炎，發燒，抽筋，看了很多的醫生都沒有好轉，媽媽非常擔心。因為有兩位醫生的說法不一樣。一位醫生要哥哥服藥直到二十多歲才能停止，但服了一段時間藥，還是老樣子。母親因此又帶他找另一個醫生，那一位醫生則說立刻停止服藥，因為這種藥有副作用。當時媽媽很徬徨，不知如何是好？

一九七八年，師父上人率團到馬來西亞的吉隆坡弘法時，有一位善知識告訴我們，師父上人在鶴鳴寺講法及傳授三皈五戒。我們全家就去見師父和受三皈依。後來母親告訴師父上人，有關二哥的情形，師父很慈悲加持了他，然後說：「這孩子沒有問題，不要擔心了！」從這次加持之後，說也奇怪，哥哥的病竟然不藥而癒。當時我還很小，這件事是母親告訴我的。但是在我的心裡，師父的慈愛和悲心是多麼多麼廣大、可敬。我們要好好地學習師父，不要浪費寶貴時光。

My brother, when he was one year old, he suffered from an unusual disease. After seeing many doctors, his condition still did not improve. The symptoms included fevers, cramps, and infected tonsils. Because these symptoms occurred so irregularly, my mother was very worried. There were two doctors with different opinions. One doctor suggested that my brother stay on medication until he was twenty years old. However, my brother did not get any better after taking medication for a period. Then my mother took him to the other doctor, who suggested that he stop the medication, because it would have negative side effects on him. My mother was worried and confused. She did not know what to do.

In 1978, the Venerable Master Hua and his disciple came to Kuala Lumpur, Malaysia. At the time, a good advisor told my parents that the Venerable Master was giving a lecture and transmitting the Three Refuges and Five Precepts at Chaming Temple. My family went to see the Venerable Master and to receive the Three Refuges. Then my mother told the Master about my brother's situation. The Venerable Master compassionately said, "This kid is OK, don't worry!" After this, miraculously, my brother got better and better each day and finally recovered fully. I was very young then, and my mother told me this true story. I thought the Venerable Master's compassion was so vast and worthy of respect. We should study hard to be like him, and not let the precious time pass in vain.

宣揚正法一脈傳，
化解眾生永飢寒；
上天娑婆度不盡，
人仁慈悲苦裡安。

　　　　　——釋恆寰

He proclaimed and propagated the Proper Dharma, transmitting the single pulse;
He resolved living beings' eternal hunger and cold.
One can never finish saving beings in the heavens above and the Saha world;
With humaneness, kindness, and compassion, he bestowed peace among the suffering.

　　　　　——· Shi Henghuan

宣化老和尚追思紀念專集

捨命爲佛事

RENOUNCING HIS LIFE TO DO THE BUDDHA'S WORK

譚果正　Stella Tam

眼睛充滿了淚水，心裡填塞著悲傷！面對著太平洋澎湃的巨浪，思潮起伏，獨個兒想著：最疼愛我的高年老父，和共同學佛的母親及弟妹；慈祥而嚴峻的師父－－僅認識兩年，卻把我毫無目標的生存意識，穩住在有意義的人生上；還有一群年齡相仿、朝夕相處的師兄弟們。臨行時師父的叮嚀：「爲教爭光。」總在我耳邊縈繞著。

事隔多年，現在回想起來，他老人家費了多少心血，用盡心機、不求報酬地教導我們這一群十多歲最難管教的大孩子，成爲思想、品德良好的社會公民；師父對每個人用不同的方法，使我們在燈紅酒綠的香港社會裡，仍能不動搖，堅定自己是佛教徒的承諾，這實在是不容易的。

師父上人，爲了培養年輕一代的佛教徒，費盡心機。上人曾通宵達旦地與我們交談；曾爲我們留下最好吃的松子仁；也曾因爲給我們講公案，而冷落了他的上賓。爲使我們循規蹈矩，上人可以扳起臉孔整天不吃不喝；也曾嚴厲責罰我們的誤入歧途，到今天才真正明白了他老人家的苦心。回想自己修行的路程，覺得未報師恩，也辜負了自己。只好抱著來者仍可追的心情，盡此一生，爲佛教的發揚光大而努力。

上人無論走到哪裡，總有一群孩子追隨著。他老人家培養年輕的一輩，從不計較付出多少心血，十個人中，九個沒出息，他不在乎。他的希望是只要有一個能成法器，就可以代代相承，把佛教發揚光大。上人要求徒弟，不論在戒律或修持上，都要篤行實踐，不得馬虎，要直心是道場。所以受不了的人，出了家也自願捨戒還俗。上人曾說：「萬佛城是來不自由，去自由。」

爲了把佛法弘揚到世界上每個角落，上人盡心盡力訓練四眾弟子講經說法。記得年輕時在香港，上人要求師兄弟們，輪流用廣東

With tear-filled eyes and a heart filled with sadness, I faced the waves of the Pacific Ocean and thought of my elderly father who loved me so dearly, my mother and siblings who had studied Buddhism together with me, my compassionate yet stern Master—although I had only known him for two years, he had transformed my aimless existence into a life full of meaning—and the Dharma friends of the same age who had been my constant companions. The Master's last instructions before I left echoed in my ears: "Bring glory to Buddhism."

Now, many years later, I reflect back on how much time and energy he devoted to teaching and nurturing us—a group of unruly young adolescents—to become citizens of wholesome character and ideals. The Master used a different method to teach each individual, enabling us to firmly maintain our responsibilities as Buddhists in face of the decadent temptations of Hong Kong society. What he did was not easy at all.

Hoping to groom a young generation of Buddhists, the Venerable Master exhausted every means. He spoke with us all night. He saved the most delicious pine nuts for us to eat. Sometimes, he even neglected other important guests in order to tell us stories. In order to get us to follow the rules, the Venerable Master could appear very stern and not eat or drink anything for the whole day. He would scold us severely if we strayed down the wrong path. It is only now that I have come to truly understand his great pains. Reflecting on the course of my cultivation, I feel I have not repaid my teacher's kindness and have let myself down. I can only look to the future and work hard to bring glory to Buddhism.

No matter where the Venerable Master went, he was always followed by a group of children. He spared no effort to nurture the younger generation. Even if nine out of ten of his students failed, he wouldn't have minded. His hope was that if even one person could become a vessel for the Dharma, then the teaching would be passed down from generation to generation and Buddhism would flourish. Whether it was holding the precepts or cultivating, the Master encouraged his disciples to practice in earnest and not be casual. He taught that the straight mind is the place of the Way. Thus, those who could not take it would voluntarily renounce the precepts and return to lay-life. The Master once said, "It's not easy to come to the City of Ten Thousand Buddhas, but one is free to leave at any time."

For the sake of propagating the Buddhadharma to every corner of the world, the Venerable Master did his best to train his left-home and lay disciples to expound Sutras and speak the Dharma. I remember that during my youth in Hong Kong, the Venerable Master asked us to take turns translating his lectures into Cantonese. In the beginning I had stage fright, and I'd be so nervous that my hands would shake so that I couldn't even take notes properly. Yet I could hardly disobey the Master, so I forced myself to do it. This kind of training afforded me inexhaustible benefit and laid the foundation for my later career in education.

話翻譯他所講的經典。最初因為怯場，而怕
得手都發抖，連筆記都記不好，但師命難違
，只好硬著頭皮上。經過這種訓練後，卻得
益無窮，也奠定了自己後來順利從事教育事
業的根基。

要傳播佛教，一定要講經說法。當時每逢
週末，香港佛教講堂都有佛教講座。佛教講
堂的設立，不單單是為大法師，也為了培養
未來的小法師。上人要求他的弟子，無論男
女老幼都要講，連六十多歲的老太婆，每次
都是念同樣的一首偈也是講。不用筆記，直
心而發，隨口而出地講解佛法，是上人訓練
弟子們講經的獨特手法，這種方法一直持續
到現在。

上人在美國三藩市成立金山寺後，仍然天
天講經，所謂「一天不說法，一天不吃飯。
」在國際譯經學院，每週日由一位比丘，一
位比丘尼，一位優婆塞及一位優婆夷帶著腹
稿，對著百餘人講法。怕出醜嗎？這只是一
種法，法本無生，何醜之有？

記得萬佛城成立的初期，上人為弟子們講
課，同時叫弟子們出來說法。但誰也沒有那
個膽量，大家都怕講錯，也怕那種場面。你
能想像得到嗎？上人竟然跪在課室門前，向
弟子們頂禮，說自己教導無方，所以弟子不
聽他的話，不肯站出來說法。弟子們慚愧得
無地自容，誰還敢不依教奉行呢！上人就是
用這種方法，來培養未來的弘法人材，以使
佛教發揚光大！

後來，上人進一步創辦法界佛教大學，以
造就有志於佛教的知識份子；設立培德中學
，訓練忠孝愛國的佛教徒和良好公民；開辦
育良小學，灌輸孝悌仁愛的思想，在幼小的
心靈，播撒慈悲的種籽。上人將別人供養他
的果儀，提供給在名校攻讀博士或碩士學位
的弟子們。這種不自私、不自利的為教精神
，做弟子的，除了敬佩、效法之外，怎敢躲
懶偷安、不為發揚光大佛教而努力呢？

凡讀過《宣化上人開示錄》的人，都知道
上人是怎樣解行並重的。他老人家說到做到
，言行一致。所以，除了鼓勵四眾弟子研究
經典外，更注重的，就是嚴持戒律。出家眾
除了年齡老邁者，其餘都是日中一食，很多
弟子都夜不倒單。因為持戒才能生定生慧，
有了智慧才能善用方便，度化眾生。

If the Buddhadharma is to be propagated, the Sutras have to be expounded and the Dharma has to be spoken. There would be lectures every weekend at the Buddhist Lecture Hall in those days. The Buddhist Lecture Hall was established not only for the elder Dharma Masters, but also to groom the young Dharma Masters of the future. The Venerable Master required all his disciples to speak, whether they were male or female, young or old. Even an old woman in her sixties who always recited the same verse would speak. The Venerable Master trained his disciples to lecture on the Sutras in a unique way: He encouraged us to speak straight from the heart, to open our mouths and say what we thought, without using notes. This method is still being used today.

After the Venerable Master established Gold Mountain Monastery in San Francisco, he continued lecturing on the Sutras every day. As he said, "If I do not speak the Dharma for one day, I will go without food that day." At the International Translation Institute, he would have one Bhikshu, one Bhikshuni, one Upasaka, and one Upasika go up and speak the Dharma to an audience of over a hundred. What if they were bashful? This is only a Dharma. The Dharma is basically unproduced, so how can there be bashfulness?

I remember that when the City of Ten Thousand Buddhas was first established, the Venerable Master would hold classes for his disciples and would also ask his disciples to go up and speak the Dharma. Yet no one had the guts to do so. They were afraid of saying something wrong and afraid of being in front of so many people. Can you imagine what happened? The Venerable Master actually knelt at the door of the classroom and bowed to his disciples. He said it must be because he was an ineffectual teacher that his disciples didn't listen to him and were afraid to go up to speak the Dharma. His disciples were so ashamed and remorseful, yet had no place to hide; who would have dared to disobey then? The Venerable Master used this method to train people so that in the future they will be able to propagate the Dharma and cause Buddhism to flourish.

Later, the Master founded Dharma Realm Buddhist University to educate individuals who are committed to Buddhism. He also set up Developing Virtue Secondary School to teach students to become good citizens who are filial and loyal to the country. He opened Instilling Goodness Elementary School to instill the virtues of filial piety, fraternal respect, humaneness, and love and to sow the seeds of kindness and compassion in children's minds. The Master would pass the money offerings that people gave him to his disciples who were studying for their Master's or doctoral degrees at well-known universities. Seeing the Venerable Master's unselfish spirit of dedicating himself completely to the Teaching without seeking personal benefit, we as disciples should certainly admire and strive to emulate it. How could we be lazy and not work hard to make Buddhism flourish?

Those who have read the Venerable Master's *Instructional Talks* know that the Master was one who emphasized both understanding and practice. He practiced what he preached. While encouraging his left-home and lay disciples to investigate the Sutras, he stressed even more the strict observance of precepts. With the exception of those who are very old, the monastics eat only one meal a day and many of them do not lie down at night. Only by upholding the precepts can one develop concentration and wisdom, and only with wisdom can one skillfully apply expedients to teach living beings.

上人說法的目的，是要弟子明白佛教的宗旨，而依教修行，這樣才能成為一位名符其實的法師。如果只是在佛學名相上進行探討，那只是將佛教當做一門學問來研究，而沒有實際地信解行證，以致一生錯用了功夫。

例如有些唯識學者，在解釋「六根」時，僅從眼、耳、鼻、舌、身、意的生理構造和作用著眼，而上人對「六根、六塵、六識」的講解，卻是根據佛教經典的理論，而強調「一根既返源，六根成解脫」的道理。研究唯識的人，在名相上對「貪、瞋、慢、疑」解釋得很清楚，但上人卻非常具體的，教我們怎樣去除我們自身的貪心、瞋心和無明。上人告訴我們，每當貪瞋癡的念頭一起，當下就要覺察到，念念去除惡法，念念增長善法。最後瞭解「一切法無我」，而達到「法法本無法，無法法亦法」的境界。讀了上人講解的《百法明門論淺釋》後，我才體會到，應該怎樣去消除自己的無明，改正自己的缺點。所以，上人培養出來的法師，不但能講經說法，也能嚴持戒律。

宣公上人用深入淺出的方式，來闡述佛教經典的深奧義理。在美國佛教講堂，第一次暑期佛學班，上人開講的是《楞嚴經》。《楞嚴經》是佛教中的一部重要經典。經中有言：佛法將滅時，第一部將消失的經典就是《楞嚴經》。上人曾說：「《楞嚴經》是正法的代表，是一部照妖鏡。」有人說《楞嚴經》是偽經，上人據理駁斥。因為《楞嚴經》是修行路上的明燈，所以邪魔外道要把它撲滅。為了破除邪惡者的讖語，上人曾經發誓說：「如果《楞嚴經》是偽經，我願意永遠下地獄。」還有誰像上人這樣，捨命護持正法，護持佛所說的經典！所以上人的弟子都認真地背誦、研習《楞嚴經》和〈楞嚴咒〉。希望我們學佛人同心協力，護持《楞嚴經》，護持佛的正法。

上人年輕時，就已胸懷光大佛教之志。所以，當年在大陸東北時，結廬守孝，日夕參禪，艱苦卓絕，因此道業突飛猛進。

當上人去廣東南華寺，參拜禪宗耆宿虛雲老和尚時，老和尚對上人非常器重，並

The Venerable Master's aim in speaking the Dharma was to let his disciples understand the principles of Buddhism and to cultivate according to them. Only then would they live up to the title of Dharma Master. If they were to engage only in the study of Buddhist terminology, then they would be treating Buddhism as a branch of knowledge to be investigated, rather than as a process of faith, understanding, practice, and certification. They would then spend their lives applying effort in vain.

For example, when explaining the "six sense faculties," some scholars of Consciousness-Only only give an explanation of the biological structure and function of the eyes, ears, nose, tongue, body, and mind. The Venerable Master bases his explanation of the "six sense faculties, six sense objects, and six consciousnesses" on the doctrines found in the Buddhist Sutras and emphasizes that "when one faculty returns to the source, all six faculties are liberated." While Consciousness-Only scholars give very clear theoretical definitions of the terms greed, anger, stupidity, pride, and doubt, the Venerable Master very practically tells us how to get rid of the greed, anger, and ignorance in our own minds. The Venerable Master tells us that as soon as a thought of greed, anger, or stupidity arises, we must detect it right away. In thought after thought, we must get rid of evil dharmas and increase wholesome dharmas. Finally, we will understand that "all dharmas are without self" and reach the state of seeing that "all dharmas are originally devoid of dharmas, yet in the voidness of dharmas, the dharmas are still there." After reading the Venerable Master's explanation of the *Shastra on the Door to Understanding the Hundred Dharmas*, I finally understood how I should go about getting rid of my own ignorance and correcting my shortcomings. The Dharma Masters trained by the Venerable Master not only know how to lecture on the Sutras and speak the Dharma, they also strictly maintain the precepts.

The Venerable Master Hua gave simple, easy-to-understand explanations that reveal the profound meanings and principles of the Buddhist Sutras. During the first summer session at the Buddhist Lecture Hall (in America), the Venerable Master lectured on the *Shurangama Sutra*. The *Shurangama Sutra* is an important Sutra in Buddhism. The Sutras say that when the Buddhadharma is about to perish, this Sutra will be the first to disappear. The Venerable Master said, "The *Shurangama Sutra* represents the Proper Dharma. It is a demon-spotting Dharma." Some people claim that the *Shurangama Sutra* is inauthentic, but the Venerable Master rationally exposes the errors of such an argument. Because the *Shurangama Sutra* is a bright lamp illuminating the path of cultivation, the deviant demons and externalists all want to extinguish it. In order to refute the prophecies uttered by evil people, the Venerable Master vowed, "If the *Shurangama Sutra* is inauthentic, I'm willing to fall into the hells forever." Who else can be like the Venerable Master in renouncing his life to protect and maintain the Proper Dharma and the Sutras spoken by the Buddha? Thus, the Venerable Master's disciples diligently memorize and study the *Shurangama Sutra* and the Shurangama Mantra. I hope the students of Buddhism will unite their hearts and strength to protect and uphold the *Shurangama Sutra* and the Buddha's Proper Dharma.

When the Venerable Master was young, he had already set his mind on propagating Buddhism and causing it to prosper. Back in Manchuria, China, he built a simple hut by his mother's grave and stayed there in observance of filial piety. He sat in meditation day and night and underwent incredible hardships. As a result, he made swift and courageous progress in cultivation.

選擇上人為潙仰宗第九代傳人。（潙仰宗承傳曾經中斷，由虛老再續法脈，為第八祖，演派五十六字，並作傳法偈贈與上人。）師父改「度輪」為「宣化」，是尊重虛老的厚意，上人很少跟別人說他是潙仰宗的傳人。

上人參禪有很高的境界，一九四七年在中國大陸空青山打禪七時，曾與明觀老和尚對坐了七十天。但是，上人教化弟子卻儘量勸他們念佛，原因是念佛法門，「三根普被，利頓全收」，任何人都可以腳踏實地做去，到臨終時便往生西方。末法時期，眾生根性下劣，如果單憑日本禪和小乘止觀的靜坐方式來教導弟子，很容易導致他們誤以為這樣就可以即生開悟，了生脫死，糊里糊塗地虛度此生。所以古來禪宗大德如永明禪師就教人念佛，近代的虛雲老和尚參禪開悟，仍然教人修行淨土法門。

宣公上人平生大願之一，是要將佛教經典譯成各國文字，傳播世界各國。因此成立了國際譯經學院，結集了眾多的雙語人才，由於他們的辛勤努力，使師父的願望逐步實現。

回憶在香港時，上人常給我們講佛法。他老人家不但對我們解釋「三寶」是什麼，他也對我們講道教《七真傳》裡面，聰明誤事的邱長春和毀容學道的孫不二等人的故事，做為我們修行的借鑑。並以《射雕英雄傳》裡面憨直的郭靖和詭智的黃容為例，來告訴我們做人的選擇。

有時上人的開示直接了當，一針見血。譬如他解釋「無明緣行，行緣識……」中的「無明」時，就單刀直入地指出，那就是淫欲心。他說：「這個無明是什麼？」他以最簡單的字眼來代入，那就是淫欲心。《楞嚴經》上說：「淫心不除，塵不可出。」由此可以知道，如果不斷除愛欲的念頭，是不能了脫生死的。

一旦我們具有這種正知正見，也就可以辨別所謂男女雙修、不出家、有妻兒，一樣可以成活佛的話，皆是邪說。凡夫俗子最好還是出家修行、嚴持戒律，方才容易修成正果。

荷擔佛陀的家業，乃是佛門弟子的本分

When the Venerable Master went to Nanhua Monastery in Guangdong to pay homage to the eminent Venerable Elder Master Hsu Yun of the Chan School, the Elder Master regarded the Venerable Master very highly and chose him to become the Ninth Patriarch of the Weiyang Sect. (The transmission of the Weiyang Sect was once interrupted. Elder Master Hsu resumed the lineage as the Eight Patriarch, composing a fifty-six character verse for the continuation of the lineage. He also composed a Dharma-transmission verse for the Venerable Master.) The Master changed his name from "To Lun" to "Hsuan Hua" in order to honor the Elder Master Hsu's sincere wish. The Venerable Master seldom told others that he had received the transmission of the Weiyang Sect.)

The Venerable Master's state in Chan meditation was very high. During a Chan Session at Kongqing Mountain in mainland China in 1947, he sat for seventy days with Elder Master Mingguan. Yet the Venerable Master always exhorted his disciples to recite the Buddha's name, because the Dharma door of Buddha recitation "aids those of superior, average, and inferior faculties and gathers in both the sharp and the dull." Anyone who honestly practices can be reborn in the Western Land at the time of death. Living beings in the Dharma-ending Age have inferior faculties. If the Master had only taught his disciples the meditative practices of Japanese Zen or the contemplations of the Small Vehicle, they could easily have been misled to think that those practices can lead them to become enlightened and to end birth and death in this very life, and then they would spend their lives in confusion. Therefore, since ancient times, the Greatly Virtuous Ones of the Chan School, such as Chan Master Yongming, have exhorted people to recite the Buddha's name. The Elder Master Hsu Yun of contemporary times became enlightened through Chan meditation, yet he also taught people to cultivate the Pure Land Dharma door.

One of the Venerable Master's lifelong vows was to have the Buddhist scriptures translated into all languages and propagated to all nations of the world. To this end he established the International Institute for the Translation of Buddhist Texts and brought together many people with bilingual abilities. Due to their hard work, the Venerable Master's vow is gradually being realized.

I remember the Venerable Master explaining the Buddhadharma to us in Hong Kong. He not only explained what the Triple Jewel was, but also told us stories from the Taoist book *Lives of the Seven Immortals* of such people as Qiu Changchun, who was too intelligent for his own good, and Sun Buer ("non-dual"), who disfigured her face in order to cultivate the Tao. These stories served to teach us about cultivation. The Master also used the stories of the honest and frank Guo Qing and the crafty Huang Rong from the *Lives of Eagle-Shooting Heroes* to tell us about the choices of life.

The Venerable Master's talks would sometimes be very straightforward, hitting the nail right on the head. For example, in explaining the word "ignorance" in the cycle where "ignorance conditions activity, activity conditions consciousness,....," the Venerable Master pointed out directly that ignorance is simply lust. "What is ignorance?" he asked. He put it in the simplest words: It is just lust. The Shurangama Sutra says, "If one does not get rid of lust, one cannot leave the dust (worldly defilement)." Thus we know that if we do not eradicate thoughts of lust, we cannot be liberated from birth and death.

Once we possess such proper knowledge and views, we will be able to tell that "paired cultivation between men and women" and the idea that one can become a living Buddha by getting married and having children and not

。上人曾說：基督教是在耶穌死後，其門徒將基督教的教理宣傳到世界各地，才使基督教成為最大的宗教。宣公上人也盼望他的每一個弟子，能承擔起紹隆佛法的重任，彼此之間不要有宗派門戶之見。因此，萬佛聖城內的四眾弟子，是禪、教、律、密、淨五宗並修的，也從不歧視抨擊道、耶、儒、回等別的宗教。只有佛教相互團結一致，共同努力，才能實現佛陀的訓誨。

自從中國大陸實施共產主義後，佛教僧尼大量南來香港。宣公上人及很多大德法師們不遺餘力地弘揚佛法，使佛教在香港呈現出生機蓬勃的景象。再沒有人見了出家人就吐口水，說不吉利的話；年輕一輩也掀起了學習佛法的熱潮，佛教青年團，義學組織，慈善醫院等紛紛建立。由此可見，僧侶們只要團結一致，就能使佛法流入每個人的心中。希望美國的佛教徒也能屏除門派之見，為佛教在全世界發揚光大，為使末法變為正法，而盡到每個佛教徒應有的責任，也是弟子們報答宣公上人「代眾生受苦」的弘願深恩，以師志為己志的第一大步。

leaving the home-life are deviant theories. For ordinary people, it is still better to leave the home-life and strictly uphold the precepts. Then, it will be easier to cultivate and attain the proper fruition.

The duty of a Buddhist disciple is to carry on the Buddha's legacy. The Venerable Master said, "After Christ died, his disciples propagated Christ's teachings to all parts of the world, and thus Christianity became the largest religion." The Venerable Master hoped every Buddhist disciple would take upon his own shoulders the great responsibility of spreading the Buddha-dharma and not pay attention to sectarian differences. Thus, at the Sagely City of Ten Thousand Buddhas, the fourfold assembly of disciples cultivate the five sects of Chan, Doctrine, Vinaya, Esoteric, and Pure Land together, and they have never shown prejudice against Taoism, Christianity, Confucianism, Islam, or other religions. The Buddha's teaching can be actualized only through the united and cooperative efforts of all schools of Buddhism.

After mainland China became Communist, Buddhist monks and nuns went south to Hong Kong in great numbers. The Venerable Master Hua and many other greatly virtuous Dharma Masters devoted their complete energy to propagating the Buddhadharma. Thus the Buddhadharma in Hong Kong showed signs of great vitality. No longer did people spit upon seeing left-home people or say unlucky things about them. The young generation developed an enthusiastic interest in studying the Buddhadharma. Many Buddhist youth groups, free schools, charity hospitals, and so forth were established. From this we can see that as long as the Sangha is united, it can cause the Buddhadharma to flow into every person's heart. I hope American Buddhists will also set aside sectarian differences and do their best to cause Buddhism to flourish throughout the world and to turn the Dharma-ending Age into the Proper Dharma Age. This is also the first big step that disciples should take in taking the Master's resolve as our own resolve and repaying the Master's deep kindness for making the great vow to stand in for living beings and take their suffering.

三世諸佛家中生　　證得如來妙法身
普爲群生現眾色　　譬如幻師無不作
——《大方廣佛華嚴經》〈初發心功德品〉

He is born in the family of the Buddhas of the three periods of time,
And is certified to the Thus Come Ones' wondrous Dharma Body.
Universally for the sake of the flocks of beings,
He appears in many forms, just like a magician,
There is nothing he cannot do.

Chapter on The Merit and Virtue from First Bringing Forth the Mind, the *Flower Adornment Sutra*

普令眾生得法喜

BESTOWING DHARMA JOY UPON LIVING BEINGS

初果蓮　Chu Guolian

師父上宣下化老和尚圓寂的消息，使很多人震驚，而我心裡卻生出許多感慨，為什麼呢？因為師父是背負著眾生的業力而走的。眾生終日都在造孽，不僅沒有機會去懺悔，又隨時造新殃。若無善根遇到正法，是無法懺悔所做的種種惡業的。師父大慈大悲，替眾生擔待業力。作為師父的弟子，我們要常深思師父留給我們的教誨，並效法、實踐他老人家的宏願。

今年三月二十五日皈依佛門，也可說是師父的「末代」弟子，因為來道場（指臺灣法界佛教印經會）一年多，從未舉行過皈依儀式。早聽說師父要返臺弘法，可是後來聽說他病了。他老人家派了他兩位弟子來到臺灣。在一次法會上，兩位法師簡單介紹了他們出家的經過，之後就是請信眾問問題。

其中有位信眾問到關於夢境之事，法師答道：我們現在（現場）也是在作夢。頓時使我想起曾經夢見師父的事：記得去年十月中旬有緣來到道場後，愕然發現這就是我喜歡的，我所要尋找的道場，心中很高興，決定每星期日到道場（因平時上班），參加各種佛事活動。

初次見到師父法相時，有一種說不出的感覺，彷彿曾經認識；一聽法音，師父率直的口氣，令人倍感親切，所以想要皈依師父。但又聽說皈依師父的人，必須要拜一萬拜，他老人家才收。當時覺得很奇特，從未聽說過這樣的事情，真是奇怪，心想這位師父很了不起，拜就拜吧！於是在住的地方佈置成一個簡單的小佛堂，把觀世音菩薩和老和尚的法相安置好，加上一只小香爐，然後開始頂禮，規定一天一百拜。

拜了幾星期後，有一天夢見師父穿著深咖啡色衲袍（衣服陳舊），也在一張簡單佛桌前，桌面上放著一張黑白照片，旁邊有許多人，我站在前面，人們對我說：「來，給我的師父叩頭！」其他的人就跪下去了，我看大家都跪下去，我也就跟著跪下去了，當我起身之際就夢醒了。此時是

The news of the Elder Master Venerable Hsuan Noble Hua's completion of stillness has shocked many people. I am filled with melancholy. Why? Because the Master was bearing the karma of living beings when he left. Living beings commit sins to the end of their days. Not only do they have no opportunity to repent, but they constantly create new offenses. If they do not have the goot roots to meet the Proper Dharma, then they have no means to repent of all the evil deeds they have done. Our greatly kind and compassionate Master bore the karma of living beings upon his own shoulders. As his disciples, we ought to deeply reflect on the teachings the Master left us, and try to emulate and realize his vast vows.

I took refuge on March 15 of this year (1995). I could be considered a disciple of the "late period" of the Master, because during the one year or so that I've been at the Way-place (Dharma Realm Buddhist Books Distribution Association in Taiwan), there has not been a refuge-taking ceremony. We had long heard the Master was coming to Taiwan to propagate the Dharma, but later we heard he was ill. He sent two left-home disciples to Taiwan. During the Dharma session, the two Dharma Masters briefly related how they left the home-life and then let the audience ask questions.

Someone asked about dreams, and one Dharma Master replied, "We are dreaming right now." All of a sudden this reminded me of a dream of the Master that I'd had. When I came to this Way-place in mid-October of last year, I discovered with surprise that it was what I liked, the Way-place I'd been looking for. I felt delighted and resolved to come every Sunday (because I had to work during the week) to participate in the various Buddhist activities.

When I first saw the Master's image—I can't describe my feeling—it was as if I knew him before. When I first heard the Master speaking the Dharma in his straightforward way, I felt very close to him, and so I wanted to take refuge with the Master. But then I heard that to take refuge with the Master, one had to bow 10,000 bows. I had never heard of such a thing before and thought it very odd. However, the Master is so extraordinary, I thought, so I might as well bow! I set up a small altar in my home with images of Guanshiyin Bodhisattva and the Venerable Master, plus a small censer, and then began to bow a hundred bows a day.

After I'd bowed for several weeks, I had a dream one night in which I saw the Master wearing a dark brown, old robe. He was in front of a simple altar. The altar had a black-and-white photograph on it, and there were many people beside it. I was standing in the front, and some people said to me, "Come and bow to our Master." The other people knelt down, and I followed suit. Just as I was rising from the bow, I woke up from the dream. It was 4:20 in the morning. I suddenly thought this must be the Dharma body rescuing and teaching people; it corresponded to the couplet under the

清晨四點二十分，突然想到上人法身度化人群。可說是應驗了師父法相兩旁的題字：「慈悲普度信者得救成正覺，過化存神禮之獲福悟無生」的感召。真是奇妙！之後，逢見熟人就述說，讓別人也瞭解到一萬拜的感應。

師父的德行是在無形中度化、教化人們，我也相信他老人家遺言中說的話：「我現在好像兩個人，一個人現在仍然到處救度眾生；我這一個人，我是不會管他的，我不會幫助自己的。」這也是提醒我們要不斷學習精進，弘揚佛法，力行誓願，學習他老人家以身作則的德行。雖然無法做到像師父那樣完美，至少我們皈依師父的弟子，無論在家、出家都要遵守「以戒為師」，尤其是五戒，相信佛教定會住世，正法教義永垂不滅。

雖然師父的色身，我們是見不到了，但弟子們若認真地修行，他老人家會很高興、精神奕奕地在我們左右護持；祈求所有聽聞及未聽聞宣公上人者，都能受師父之名的庇佑，並把正教、正法發揚光大。

阿彌陀佛！

Master's image: "His kindness and compassion cross over all; / Believers are liberated and perfect the Right Enlightenment. / Transforming beings wherever he goes, his spirit remains intact; / Those who venerate him obtain blessings and awaken to the Unproduced." How rare and mysterious! Afterwards, I would relate my dream to those I knew, letting them know about the responses from the ten thousand bows.

The Master's virtue crosses over and teaches and transforms people invisibly. I believe what he said in his final instructions: "Right now I'm like two people. One person is still going around rescuing living beings. But this person who is me, I don't care about him. I won't help myself." This is a reminder to us that we never stop learning, being vigorous, propagating the Buddhadharma, realizing our vows, and learning the Master's virtue of genuine practice. Though we cannot be as perfect as the Master, as the Master's lay and left-home disciples, we should at least "take the precepts as our teacher," especially the five precepts. Then I believe the Buddhadharma will certainly remain in the world and the teaching of the Proper Dharma will never perish.

Though we can no longer see the Master's physical body, if we cultivate diligently, he will be very happy and will energetically protect us and stay beside us. I pray that those who have heard and who have not heard will all receive the Master's protection and cause the orthodox teaching—the Proper Dharma—to flourish.

Amitabha Buddha!

修菩提道
Cultivating the Bodhi Way

菩提大道直又直　　不可彎曲莫倖致　　真心求法必感應　　假意因循浪費時
勇猛精進忍弗退　　布施持戒修智宜　　有日完成波羅蜜　　十方諸佛會蓮池

The Great Bodhi Way is straight as can be.
Don't let yourself get sidetracked or try to find a shortcut.
If you seek the Dharma with a true heart, there's sure to be a response.
If you are insincere and negligent, you're just wasting time.
Advance vigorously, be patient, and don't retreat!
Practice giving, uphold the precepts, and cultivate wisdom.
One day you will complete the journey to the other shore
And join the Buddhas of the ten directions at the lotus pool.

宣公上人作
by Venerable Master Hua

THE VENERABLE MASTER KNOWS THE MIND OF EVERY SINGLE PERSON

上人知道每一個人的心

Shi Heng Gu　釋恆古

The scope of the Venerable Master's life work has been tremendous, and his disciples number in the hundreds of thousands, both East and West. I never had sufficient good roots to get to know the Master personally, but when our group of Shramaneras and Shramanerikas left the home life in October, 1994, at Long Beach Sagely Monastery, we were fortunate enough to have him preside over the ceremonies. His countenance was serious and solemn, as befitted the occasion. In my case, his presence elicited no special emotional response, but gave rise to a still, clear, and alert mind, as well as a solid awareness of being on the right path.

I was also aware that probably no one in the assembly could fathom his state—he seemed to be the "inscrutable Chinaman" par excellence. At the same time I felt that he knew the mind of every single person in that gathering. Thus there was no need for questions or answers, audiences or appeals. His vast mind already knew and acknowledged everything. This was just the way things were. He knew what we needed to advance on the Way, and in a brief Dharma talk told us unequivocally what to focus on: real, personal cultivation. "If you fail to cultivate, even having Shakyamuni Buddha as your teacher won't be of any use."

The Master's Dharma-body pervades everywhere and takes beings across universally—and this body does not come or go. I have not felt his absence. On the contrary, after the Master's return to the City of Ten Thousand Buddhas in June, I have felt a subtle presence about the City, and my deepest feeling is that of gratitude, even awe, that we have managed to meet such a Good and Wise Advisor in this day and age, and got to know the proper Dharma.

The Venerable Master has disciples who have studied under him for ten, twenty, even twenty-five years. He also has disciples who have never met him. In spite of that, many people have opened profound wisdom, even opened the five eyes, just by sincerely studying his books and talks. After I had left home, a Bhikshuni asked me how I dared to take this step without having ever met the Master before. I answered: "I've read the Master's book; I've seen his Way-places; I've met his disciples," and I felt these were quite sufficient grounds to base my decision on. To me, the life at the Way-place is where the Master's Dharma is embodied, put to practice, lived out in the midst of ordinary, daily circumstances. This is where we are tried and tested, this is where advance or retreat on the Way takes place.

上人的事業是很廣大的。上人在東、西方的弟子就有幾十萬，我自歎善根不足，沒有緣份親近上人。但在去年（一九九四年）十月，我們在長堤聖寺剃度出家的沙彌及沙彌尼們十分幸運，因為是上人主持剃度大典。那天上人非常肅穆莊重，威儀具足。雖然有上人在場，並沒有激起我情感上的特別反應，倒是因為覺得自己走對了路，而心裡感到很明白、很平靜。

法會中，可能沒有人真正知道上人的境界，上人可以說是「高深莫測」的。我也感覺到上人知道在場每一個人的心，所以我們一切的問題、一切的求訴、要求面談等等，都是沒有必要的。上人廣大的心量裡，已經什麼都知道了。他知道我們在道上應該怎樣前進，上人在簡短的開示中，很明白地告訴我們修行時，該注重些什麼，一點也不含糊。上人說：「假如你不修行，就是釋迦牟尼佛做你的師父，也沒有用！」

上人的法身遍一切處，普度眾生。這個法身是無來無去的，我一直到現在仍不覺得上人不在了。六月上人「回」聖城時，我反而有一種上人在聖城的感覺。在我心靈深處，常有一種感激、訝異之情，因為在今天這個時代，我們居然還能幸運的遇到這樣一位大善知識，得聞正法。

上人座下有的弟子已經追隨上人多年，有的超過二十五年；也有的弟子卻連上人的面都還沒見過。雖然沒見過面，但因為誠心研習上人的開示，許多人也開了智慧，甚至於開了五眼。我出家之後，有一位比丘尼師兄問我，為什麼連上人的面都沒見過，就敢跟隨上人剃度出家？我回答：「因為我看過上人的書，看過上人的道場，見過他的弟子們。」這就足夠使我做出決定了。對我來說，上人的道場就是上人法的所在，是修習上人法的地方，是將上人的法在日常生活中表現出來的地方，是考驗我們

Just as the Sixth Patriarch Hui Neng prophesied over sixty years ago, appearing by the Master's graveside hut in Manchuria, China, the Master's untiring efforts have made proper Dharma self-perpetuating in the West. The responsibility of carrying on this legacy lies now with us, all of his disciples. No matter whether we are old or fledgling disciples, whether we ever met the Master or not, we can and should resolve to meet him again. Life after life we can vow to meet him, recognize him, follow him, and dedicate our lives to upholding the proper Dharma.

的地方。我們是向前進呢？還是往後退？在上人的道場中就可以決定。

正如六祖惠能大師，於六十多年前在中國東北，對上人說的預言，因上人的辛勤努力，使正法在西方得以流傳下去。現在繼承上人大法的責任，落在我們所有做弟子們的肩上，我們不論是老弟子或新進的弟子，也不論是否見過上人的面，都應該發願立志，生生世世都要再找到上人、認識上人、追隨上人，並將自己的身心性命奉獻出來維護正法。

師父在不在身邊，都一樣

WHETHER OR NOT THE VENERABLE MASTER IS HERE, IT'S ALL THE SAME

釋恆布　　Shi Hengbu

師父在我身邊，我固然看得到他，聽得到他的教導；就是師父不在我身邊時，我也曾經看見過師父，聽得到他的教導。

一九九四年十二月，在花蓮彌陀聖寺，我見到圖書館新進的一批書中，有一本藥書附有圖案，我極喜歡，又不知去哪裡買？而這本書尚未編號，倘若可以不還回去，存在我身邊那是我最高興的。不料次日吃中飯時，卻聽到師父大聲地說：「圖書館的書，不能自己收起來。」幸虧師父即時的教導，否則我必犯盜戒，真是愚癡。

一九九五年六月九日晚上七點多，我隨大眾在殯儀館念佛，師父已經躺在那兒三天了，而我進去時，卻見到師父披著紅色袈裟從走道進入大廳。

When the Venerable Master was here, of course I could see him and hear his teachings. Even though the Venerable Master is not here, I have also seen him and heard his teachings.

In December of 1994, a new shipment of books was sent to the library of Amitabha Sagely Monastery in Hualian, and I noticed an illustrated book on medicinal herbs there. I was delighted, but didn't know where I could buy a copy. The book had not yet been catalogued. If I could keep it with me and not return it, how happy I'd be. Unexpectedly, at lunch the following day, I heard the Venerable Master say in a loud voice (on tape): "The books of the library cannot be kept personally." If it hadn't been for the Venerable Master's immediate instruction, I would have transgressed the precept against stealing. What a fool I was.

A little after seven o'clock on June 9, 1995, I was at the mortuary reciting the Buddha's name with the assembly. The Venerable Master had already been lying there for three days. When I went in, I saw the Master wearing a red *kashaya* sash and entering the main hall from the corridor.

精進行，報師恩

PRACTICE VIGOROUSLY TO REPAY THE MASTER'S KINDNESS

釋恆霞　Shi Heng Hsia

六月七日，一個讓人永遠難忘的悲痛日子。一代賢聖僧示寂。一個月來，弟子們心中所承受的那種壓力，那份感受，是難以用筆墨形容的。

剛剛聽到上人圓寂的消息時，心中雖然很震驚，但仍不願相信那是真的。愚癡的我，竟認為那是上人教化頑劣弟子的方法之一罷了。並不時的告訴自己，上人是入定了，會再回來的，老人家不會捨棄我們的。

然而當我趕到長堤參加入殮大典，瞻仰上人遺容後，方才夢醒了。希望落空了，心中百感交集，腦子一片空白，渾渾噩噩地，手足無措有如孩子遽失父母，船隻失去燈塔，世界失去光明。一切都無所依，變色的日子中只知落淚，卻理不出一點頭緒，情緒低落之極。

幼時，因祖母篤信佛法之故，偶而於假期中陪她到寺院禮佛，當時未識佛教義理之浩瀚淵深，亦不懂恭敬三寶。對僧人更視為是三百六十行中之一行，與世人無二無別的。每當見省吃簡用的祖母，將子女孝養的財物往廟上送，還認為她真傻，迷信過了頭。

直到恩師的出現，才使我這個業障深重，善根淺薄，不信佛法的人，改變觀念，改寫人生，捨俗出家。若非上人德行所感，若非上人慈悲攝受，此生不可能成為出家人。奈何自己福薄業重，雖於上人座下出家，卻非他老人家親自披剃。恩師僧臘雖長達六十年之久，而我卻只跟隨了三年多。

當上人於聖城親自教授四眾弟子時，我無緣恭逢其盛，聆聽教誨；當上人抱病臥床時，雖想探病請安，最終也只能對著上人的法相，遙遙祝願！這種種的際遇，使自己一再捫心自問：今生何以與善知識的因緣如此淺薄？又該如何方能培植跟隨善知識的善根呢？

June 7 will always be an unforgettable day of sadness. A holy and virtuous monk of this age manifested the stillness. It would be hard to describe in words the pressures and feelings in the hearts of his disciples in this last month.

Although I was quite shocked when the news of the Venerable Master's completion of stillness came, I refused to believe that it was true. How foolish I was! I thought it must be one of the ways the Venerable Master used to teach his dull-witted disciples. I kept telling myself, the Venerable Master has entered samadhi and will come out again. He wouldn't leave us.

When I went down to Long Beach to attend the ceremony for placing the Venerable Master's body into the casket, after gazing upon the Venerable Master, I finally woke up from my dream. My hopes vanished and a tumult of feelings arose. My mind was a blank. I was bewildered and at a loss for what to do, like a child who has lost his parents, like a ship that has lost sight of the light tower, like the world without light. I had nothing to rely on, and could only cry for days. I couldn't come to terms with what had happened. Emotionally, I had hit bottom.

When I was young, during vacations I would sometimes accompany my grandmother, a devout Buddhist, to a temple to worship. I didn't understand the vastness and profundity of the Buddhist doctrines then, nor did I understand enough to venerate the Triple Jewel. I thought of monkhood as only one of the many professions, and considered monks to be no different from worldly people. When I saw my frugal grandmother send the money her children have given her to the temple, I thought she was as stupid and superstitious as could be.

It was only when I met the Venerable Master that I, a person of deep karmic hindrances and scanty good roots who didn't believe in the Buddhadharma, changed my mind, redirected my life, and renounced the worldly home. If it hadn't been for the Venerable Master's virtuous influence and compassionate acceptance, I could not have become a left-home person in this life. However, due to my scarce blessings and heavy karma, although I left the home-life under the Venerable Master, the Master did not shave my head himself. And although the Master had been in the Sangha for sixty years, I followed him for only a little over three years.

When the Master personally taught the fourfold assembly of disciples at the Sagely City, I didn't have the affinities to be there and hear his teachings. When the Venerable Master was lying sick in bed, although I wanted to visit him, I could only face his image and wish him well from far away! These circumstances cause me to ask myself, "Why did I have such slight affinities with my Good Knowing Advisor in this life? How should I foster the good roots that will enable me to follow my Good Knowing Advisor in the future?"

Although one may say that the Venerable Master's Dharma body is everywhere and his disciples need not be attached to the Master's physical

雖說上人的法身是無所不在的，做弟子的不須執著師父的色身，然此超然的境界實非我所能及。所幸尚有上人的法相可禮拜、法音可聆聽，如今只能以此培植善根、薰習佛種性，學習上人精神於萬一。

上人的德行人無能及，修行境界之高無人能知，而濟世度人的事蹟，更是眾所周知、處處可聞的。雖然我未能親身經歷這些事，但目睹僧團中的人物，從目不識丁的文盲，到擁有碩士、博士學位的學者；從年輕力壯到老弱病殘者，或曾有劣跡惡行者，上人一律平等慈悲攝受，盡收為弟子。所謂菩薩心廣大如虛空。

萬佛聖城的三大宗旨，凍死不攀緣、餓死不化緣、窮死不求緣、不變隨緣、隨緣不變，推行祖師一脈心傳。六大條款，不爭、不貪、不求、不自私、不自利、不打妄語。這是上人教我們的修行方針，也是持戒的精神所在。

上人的圓寂，正是對四眾弟子的考驗。眼見師兄弟們有的絕食以請佛住世，有的欲追隨上人之後，有的則仍忙於道場的工作以報師恩……。這一切境界，是道非道，或進或退，全憑師父平日所教導的：「擇法眼」，亦如師兄的告誡：「你們要自己照顧自己了！」是的，離鄉背井，遠渡重洋來到聖城，就是為了親蒙師父耳提面命，當頭棒喝。若此時尚不知遵從師訓，嚴持律儀，苦行精進，以了脫生死，豈不愧對生身父母的養育之恩，愧對法身父母的賜予慧命！

body, that kind of elevated state is beyond me. Fortunately, we can still bow in homage to the Venerable Master's image and listen to his Dharma. These are the only things we can use as we foster our good roots, saturate our Buddha seed-nature, and learn to have a little bit of the Venerable Master's spirit.

While the Venerable Master's virtue is unparalleled and his state of cultivation is so lofty that no one can fathom it, his deeds to rescue the world and save people are known by all. Although I did not personally witness those deeds, I see that the members of the Sangha range from illiterate folks to Master's degree and Ph.D. holders; from the young and strong to the aged, feeble, sick, and crippled; and even those who committed vile and evil deeds in the past. Out of compassion, the Venerable Master accepted them all as his disciples. As it is said, the Bodhisattva's mind is as vast as empty space.

The Three Great Principles of the Sagely City of Ten Thousand Buddhas are: "Freezing, we do not scheme. Starving, we do not beg. Dying of poverty, we ask for nothing. According with conditions, we do not change. Not changing, we accord with conditions. We carry on the single pulse of the patriarchs' mind-transmission." The Six Great Guidelines are: no fighting, no greed, no seeking, no selfishness, no pursuing personal advantage, and no lying. These are the principles of cultivation that the Venerable Master taught us, and within them lies the spirit of the precepts.

The Venerable Master's completion of stillness is a test for the fourfold assembly of disciples. Some Dharma brothers have been fasting to request the Buddha to dwell in the world; some want to follow after the Venerable Master; others continue working busily in the Way-place to repay the Master's kindness... In all of these states, we must rely on the Dharma-selecting Eye that the Venerable Master taught us to have in order to discriminate between the Way and what is not the Way and to decide whether to advance or retreat. As one Dharma brother warned, "You have to take care of yourselves!" Indeed, we have left our hometowns and crossed the ocean to come to the Sagely City, hoping to personally receive the Venerable Master's teachings, direct and indirect, or even drastic measures to arouse us from stupidity. If we still fail to honor the Master's instructions, strictly uphold the precepts, and vigorously practice asceticism in order to end birth and death, won't we be disappointing the parents of our physical body for their kindness in raising us? Won't we be disappointing the parent of our Dharma body for his kindness in giving us our wisdom life?

普賢菩薩偈
Verse on Universal Worthy Bodhisattva

虛空有盡　我願無窮　充滿法界　遍入微塵　處處示現　剎剎化身　皆證菩提　圓大覺尊

Empty space may come to an end, but my vows will not be exhausted.
They fill up the Dharma Realm and pervade every mote of dust.
He appears in all places, manifesting transformation bodies in every land
To cause all living beings to realize Bodhi and accomplish great and perfect enlightenment.

宣公上人作
By the Venerable Master Hua

正法住世當第一

OUR FIRST PRIORITY:
PRESERVING THE PROPER DHARMA IN THE WORLD

李克勤　Christine Lee

師父上人雖然色身不在，但是他老人家的法、如來的家業仍住於世，我等在家居士仍忠心護持如來家業，愛護師父他老人家細心調教的出家四眾弟子，如護眼珠，一如師父上人他老人家在世一般。為什麼？因為法賴僧傳。千言萬語亦拂不去失去大慈悲父的悲慟，唯有團結四眾弟子延續如來家業、萬佛聖城家風，令正法住世為上首。

希望在多生多劫後，我們大家都有能力可以幫助師父上人他老人家，分擔眾生的業力。有道是：

我願好比香水海，我志好比彌山高；
海深不可沒我願，山高不可擋我志；
吾等心願佛亦知，正法住世當第一。

Even though the Venerable Master's physical body is gone, his Dharma and the mission of the Thus Come One (Buddha) are still in the world. We laypeople should loyally support the Thus Come One's mission and protect the Venerable Master's left-home disciples, whom he so carefully taught, as if protecting the pupils of our own eyes, as if the Venerable Master were still alive. Why? Because the Dharma depends on the Sangha to transmit it. No amount of words can console us in our grief at losing our greatly compassionate father. The only thing we can do is unite the fourfold assembly of disciples so that they can carry on the Thus Come One's mission and the tradition of the Sagely City of Ten Thousand Buddhas, thus maintaining the Proper Dharma in the world. That is our first priority.

I hope that many lifetimes and many eons later, we will all be able to share the Venerable Master's burden of taking on the karma of living beings. A poem says,

Our vows are like the Sea of Fragrant Waters;
Our resolve is as high as Mount Sumeru.
Though the sea is deep, it cannot drown our vows;
Though the mountain is high, it cannot block our resolve.
The Buddhas also know our wish:
Preserving the Proper Dharma in the world is our first priority.

已住究竟一乘道　　深入微妙最上法
善知眾生時非時　　為利益故現神通
——《大方廣佛華嚴經》〈初發心功德品〉

He already abides in the ultimate path of the one vehicle,
And deeply enters the subtly wondrous and most superior Dharma.
He knows well what is and is not appropriate for living beings,
In order to benefit them he manifests spiritual penetrations.

Chapter on The Merit and Virtue from First Bringing Forth the Mind, the *Flower Adornment Sutra*

LIFE WITH THE MASTER
我與上人的一段生活

Richard Josephson (Guo Hang)　　果航

When I arrived back in the U.S. from India, I went to the San Francisco Zen Center to practice Buddhism. But, after only a week I became discouraged because I was used to a much more vigorous practice. One of the people there told me of Gold Mountain. He said that few people go there because the practice is so difficult. I went to Gold Mountain the following day, and the first thing I saw on the wall was a picture of the Master Hsu Yun. I enquired about the picture and a monk there told me that Master Hua carried his lineage, but unfortunately the Master was on a South American tour and would not return for two months. I said that this was no obstacle, and I waited in the Buddha Hall for two months, sleeping under the stairs.

My practice during my earlier years at Gold Mountain was the recitation of mantras and cleaning the temple, and this is what it remained for the entire ten years I was with the Master.

It is difficult to relate a sudden awakening or a sudden non-awakening to another because the interaction between a ripe student and his teacher (or circumstance) is a very personal one. For example, Master Hsu Yun had a major awakening when hot tea was accidentally poured on his hand. The cultivation that ripened Master Hsu Yun's mind for his awakening took many months and his state of mind at that moment was unique to Master Hsu Yun. If this were not the case, anyone who had hot tea poured on his hand could obtain enlightenment. Having no sudden awakening to share, I would like to share a sudden non-awakening. As painful as non-awakenings were they too formed an important part of my cultivation.

I once handed the Master a gatha that read: "To see Amitabha in the Western Pure Land; how can this be done when facing East?" At that time, I was in charge of the meditation hall at Gold Mountain and always faced East during my many hours of daily meditation. The question put to the Master was from my heart and not merely a Zen game. In order to appreciate the Master's reply, one has to know something of the Master's third floor room at Gold Mountain. The walls and ceiling were supported by offerings from lay people, which included thousands of bars of soap and toothbrushes, piled everywhere with no order whatsoever. When one visited the Master's room he would often stick his hand in one of the piles and give you something. The Master couldn't read the English labeling, and never looked anyway, but nevertheless it often seemed as if the Master gave you just what you needed.

For the weeks that followed my giving the Master my gatha, I continued my meditations awaiting the Master's reply. Unfortunately I didn't recognize it when it came unexpectedly one day as

從印度回來之後，我到舊金山的「禪中心」去修學佛法。一星期後我就氣餒了，因為我已經習慣於更精進的禪的訓練。有人介紹我去金山寺，他說很少有人去那兒，因為金山寺的要求非常嚴格。第二天，我就去了金山寺，我一眼就看到牆上掛著虛雲老和尚的像。我問那是誰？一位出家人說，金山寺的住持宣公上人，就是承傳了虛老的法脈。不巧的是，上人去了南美，要兩個月才回來。我說沒問題，就在佛殿裡等了兩個月。晚上就睡在樓梯下。

早年我在金山寺的修行，包括持咒及打掃寺院。以後追隨上人整整的十年日子之中，也都是這樣。

對別人講頓悟、或者頓然不悟的情形，是很困難的。一個根熟的弟子與師父（或與環境）之間的溝通屬於個人的事情。如虛老因開水燙手，茶杯落地，豁然大悟。當下虛老的心境是他自己獨有的，是經過長期的用功修行，才達到的那種開悟的境界。否則，任何人只要被開水濺到手，豈不是都能開悟了！我個人沒有頓悟的經驗與諸位分享，但是可以談談我的頓然不悟。雖然頓然不悟是很痛苦的感受，但是這些經驗，卻形成我修行中重要的部分。

有一次，我給上人看一首偈頌：「面對東方而坐，怎能見西方淨土彌陀佛？」那時，我管理金山寺禪堂。每天我面對東方，坐禪數小時。這個問題，是從我心裡流露出來的，不是所謂的禪機。為了讓你們能理解上人稍後給我的回覆，我必須先介紹一下上人三樓寮房的情況：房間裡，從牆一直到天花板雜亂地堆滿了信徒的供品（肥皂、牙刷等等）。每當有人探望上人時，上人會隨手取出一樣東西送給來人。上人既不懂英文，也不看東西上的標籤，可是每次上人送的東西，都正是對方所需要的。

我呈給上人那首偈之後的幾個星期，我還是照

I sat meditating alone in the Buddhahall. The Master used to be able to break my meditation by looking at me. As I meditated in the hall he caused me to be aware of his presence on the far side of the hall near the office. He began walking towards me. He looked very different. He was expressionless, deep in trance, and not looking at me. But as he passed my bench he gave me a toothbrush. Then he continued on to circumambulate the Buddha, still deep in trance, in reverse direction, with the Buddha on his left. Only Shr Fu and myself were in the Buddhahall. I looked a moment at the toothbrush, saw nothing peculiar about it, and put it under my meditation bench. Shr Fu continued around the Buddha in reverse circumambulation.

A week passed before I thought to have another look at the toothbrush. I then realized, with my heart in my stomach, the brand name of the toothbrush: Dr. West.

One of the Master's most important teachings was that a disciple should not attach to "marks" or the form of a practice. Shr Fu helped us to realize a lofty purpose in our practice. When Heng Ju left to bow over a thousand miles to see his mother he failed after a single day. He didn't have the right motivation to sustain his pilgrimage. However, after he returned defeated to Gold Mountain, the Master gently directed Heng Ju's viewpoint from a purely selfish and egotistic one, to a lofty and altruistic one—World Peace. After that, Heng Ju completed his bows from San Francisco to Marblemount, Washington.

Now that Shr Fu is no longer with us, it is our duty as his disciples to make sure that Shr Fu does not become a mere memory. I personally feel a deeper sense of urgency to spread Buddhism now that Shr Fu is gone than I did when the Master was still with us. Shr Fu has carried his torch (his body) for as long as he could, doing the work of a Bodhisattva. Now he has passed the torch on to all of us. It is not only our duty as disciples to carry on the Master's work, but also the best way we can honor our Teacher.

Every day do something in honor of the Master and allow that seed to sprout. Shr Fu taught Dharma to all of us who have been touched by him. That very special feeling that each of us feels in his heart for the Master is his Dharma transmission. Without trying to intellectualize it, allow it to work through you.

If someone were to ask me what is the most important thing I gained from being with the Master for ten years, I would have to say that it is my deep conviction that I am Buddhist and my faith in the Buddhist teachings. When I first entered Gold Mountain, the idea of obtaining enlightenment seemed very remote and impossible. I was more concerned with ending this life's afflictions. But, after years with the Master my aim changed. I now understand that one must resolve to cultivate to end birth and death and realize the Bodhisattva ideal. Shr Fu pushed us all to "do what others cannot do," so that we might have an experiential awareness of the truth of Buddhism rather than a merely intellectual one. Woven within all my daily thoughts is a Buddhist thread, a thread that holds the fabric of my being together, and Shr Fu within my heart. The conviction that I am a Buddhist is unshakable.

常坐禪，等待上人的回覆。遺憾的是，當上人的回覆突然來到時，我正在坐禪，並沒有意識到。平時，上人只要注視著我，就可以打斷我坐禪。那天我正在坐禪，上人遠遠地站在辦公室那一邊，但我仍然注意到了。上人向我走來，看起來和平時不太一樣，面無表情，彷彿在定中，也不看我，當上人經過我的坐墊時，遞給我一支牙刷。然後繼續繞佛，還是在定中，但是是反方向繞佛（反時鐘方向）。當時，佛殿裡只有我們兩個人。我看了一下那支牙刷，看不出有什麼特別，就把它放在我的坐墊下，上人仍在反向繞佛。

一個星期後，我又拿出那支牙刷來看，這才大吃一驚，牙刷的牌子是「西方醫生」。

上人最重要的教誨之一：是要弟子們不要著相，或執著於某一種修行的形式。上人幫助弟子們確認修行中的崇高目標。當恆具到一千哩外去探望他母親時，只拜了一天，就失敗了。因為他的動機不純，無法繼續朝聖的旅程。回到金山寺後，上人溫和地幫助恆具從自私、自利的觀點，轉變成高尚、利他的觀點——世界和平。之後，恆具師才得以完成他從舊金山到華盛頓州大理石山的三步一拜。

現在上人走了，我們做弟子的要更加努力，不要讓上人成為記憶中的人物。比起上人在世時，我個人更急切的想將佛教發揚光大。上人用整個的一生，舉著大火炬（他的身體），行菩薩道。現在上人將火炬傳給我們，繼續上人的未完的事業，不僅是我們做弟子的責任，也是最好恭敬上人的方法。

我們每天應做點事，來表示對上人的尊敬，並且讓菩提種子發芽。師父對所有他遇見的人都施以教化，每個人心中對上人的那份特殊的感受，就是上人教給我們的法。用這個法來幫助我們，不要用心意識去瞭解它。

假使有人問我，跟隨上人十年，我學到的最重要的東西是什麼？我一定回答：我對佛教的信心，及我是佛教徒的堅定信念。

當我首次踏入金山寺時，覺得開悟是根本不可能的事。我所關心的，是要了卻今生的煩惱。跟隨上人數年後，我的目標改變了。我認真的發心修行，以了脫生死，證菩薩道。上人鼓勵我們「行人所不能行」，是讓我們去實踐佛法，而不只是從理念上去瞭解佛法。上人和他所教的佛法已經深深的植入我的心中，並將伴隨我一生。我對自己是佛教徒的信念，是絕對不會動搖的！

我都是撿人家不要的

I ALWAYS PICK UP WHAT OTHERS DON'T WANT

釋恆居　　Shi Hengju

曾經從上人的講話錄音聽到：「我都是撿人家不要的。」這句話令我感動不已。也就是人家不願意做的事情，不願意吃的苦，他都默默地去做，去承擔。別人不收的弟子，他也願意收。

由這句話裡，覺得自己很慚愧。什麼都想挑好的，吃的想挑好的，穿的要挑好的，用的要挑精緻的，做事想要挑輕鬆的，……凡此等等。凡是都要挑好的，這就是「自私」。因此希望能效法上人這種精神，從日常生活上吃的，用的，穿的上面一點一滴去做，學著「吃虧和忍讓」，希望這個被撿來的「垃圾」能變成「有用的資源」。如果人人都效法上人這種「我都是撿人家不要的」精神，相信我們的道場，乃至整個國家社會，都能充滿和諧安詳的氣氛。

In the tapes of the Venerable Master's Dharma talks, I heard him say, "I always pick up what others don't want." This statement touched me profoundly. He quietly does the things that other people aren't willing to do and takes the suffering that they aren't willing to take. He also accepts as disciples the people that others aren't willing to accept.

This statement makes me feel very ashamed. I always choose the best of everything: I choose good food to eat, nice clothes to wear, fine things to use, easy work to do, and so on. Always choosing what is good amounts to selfishness. Therefore, I hope to emulate the Venerable Master's spirit. Beginning with what I eat, use, and wear in daily life, bit by bit I want to learn to take losses and yield to others. I hope I can turn the garbage I pick up into useful resources. If every person can learn the Venerable Master's spirit of picking up what others don't want, I believe that not only our Wayplace, but the entire society and country, will be filled with harmony and peace.

小小蚊蟲性慳貪　　累生習氣仍纏綿
損人利己為能事　　欺善怕惡到處誇
靈殘墮落受果報　　癡執冥頑吮血逃
佛眼觀之可憐憫　　循業受生慎勿學

　　　　　　——宣公上人作

Teeny tiny mosquito, you're so stingy and greedy by nature.
You're still engulfed in habits accumulated in life after life.
You were good at nothing but harming others for your own sake.
Everywhere you went, you bullied the good and gave in to the evil.
Finally, your soul split and you fell to undergo your retribution.
Still adhering to your stupidity and stubbornness,
　　you suck people's blood and then flee.
In the Buddha's eyes, you are truly pitiful.
As is our karma, so is our birth. Take care not to follow this example!

By Venerable Master Hua

化化生生各自然

EVERY PHENOMENON COMES INTO BEING AND CHANGES IN ITS OWN NATURAL WAY

羅果英　Lo Guoying

師父上人的圓寂，帶給弟子們無盡的哀思與悲慟。因為每一個弟子，都衷心祈盼師父能久住娑婆，時時刻刻為弟子開示修行的妙理。師父生前弘法講經時，總是深入淺出地解釋經典中深妙智慧，並諄諄告誡我們依循佛陀的教誨去身體力行。在弟子們面前，他老人家永遠呈現出的是，慈悲和藹，至誠懇切。讓弟子們心中感到無比地清淨祥和，而拳拳服膺，五體投地，頂禮膜拜。

回憶十二年前，我帶女兒移民美國，住在洛杉磯。幾年後，覺得生活很無聊，想回到臺灣去，便把這念頭稟告師父。師父關切地說：「要是妳們沒有別的理由，只是感到無聊，我將在舊金山開一間素食館，你們母女兩個可以去那裡幫忙。」就這樣，我為師父的慈悲所感動，毅然和女兒遷到舊金山，並在萬佛君康素食館工作了三年多。寫到這裡，心中泛起了無盡的感激之情，是師父的慈悲喜捨，使我母女在茫茫的人海中找到了依止。現在，我們全家都在灣區安居樂業。此恩此德，弟子闔家永生難忘難報。

記得有一年，我和女兒參加萬佛聖城的山門開光盛典。各地來參加法會的信眾不下數千人，盛況空前。在聖城的十幾天，我們母女得到萬佛的加被，佛法的薰修，使業障得以消除。從師父上人的開示中方知，培養慈悲心必須由素食開始。

素食不但能幫助持不殺生之戒，還能除病延壽。師父提倡素食，贊助開設素食館，希望眾生不食眾生肉，是真正大慈大悲的菩薩行。從那年起，我和女兒便在佛前發願，吃長素，不沾葷腥。而我的良性腫瘤也漸漸消失。如果我未遵循師父的教誨，繼續食肉的話，也許就難逃刀劫或命劫了。所以，師父是我的再生父母

The Venerable Master's completion of stillness has brought endless sadness and grief to his disciples. Every disciple hoped that the Venerable Master would remain in the Saha world forever to instruct us on the wonderful principles of cultivation. When the Venerable Master propagated the Dharma and lectured on the Sutras, he always made the profound wisdom of the Sutras easily accessible to us and earnestly exhorted us to practice in accord with the Buddha's teaching. The elder one was ever kind, gentle and sincere, giving disciples an incomparable sense of purity and peace and causing us to pay homage with the utmost reverence.

Twelve years ago, my daughter and I immigrated to America and were living in Los Angeles. A few years later, I was feeling very bored and restless and wanted to return to Taiwan. When I told the Venerable Master, he said, "I'll be opening a vegetarian restaurant in San Francisco. If the only reason you want to go back is because of boredom, you and your daughter can go help out at the restaurant." Moved by the Venerable Master's compassion, the two of us moved to San Francisco and worked at the Ten Thousand Buddhas Chun Kang Vegetarian Restaurant for over three years. In writing this, I feel boundless gratitude to the Venerable Master for his kindness, compassion, joy, and giving, which allowed my daughter and I to find a refuge in this vast human sea. Now our whole family is happily living and working in the Bay Area. Our family will never be able to forget or to repay this kind favor.

One year, my daughter and I went to attend the Opening Light Ceremony for the Mountain Gate at the Sagely City of Ten Thousand Buddhas. Several thousand people from around the world came to attend this unprecedented event. For the dozen or so years that we have known the Sagely City, my daughter and I have received the Sagely City's aid and have been influenced by its cultivation of the Buddhadharma, enabling our karmic hindrances to disappear. From the Venerable Master's instructional talks, we have learned that compassion begins with a vegetarian diet.

Vegetarianism not only helps us to maintain the precept of not killing, but also cures illness and extends life. By promoting vegetarianism and opening a vegetarian restaurant in the hope that living beings will stop eating the flesh of other living beings, the Venerable Master is truly practicing the Bodhisattva's great kindness and compassion. That year, my daughter and I both made vows before the Buddhas that we would become vegetarian and no longer touch meat products. The tumor on my conscience thus gradually disappeared. If I had not followed the Venerable Master's advice and had continued eating meat, it would probably have been difficult to avoid having an

、使我的法身慧命得以延續。

有一天，聽完上人講經後，我們十多個弟子圍坐在師父身旁，向師父請示有關修行的問題時。一位弟子問師父，聽說在無言堂裡，供奉著一顆師公上虛下雲老和尚的五彩舍利，能讓弟子們瞻仰膜拜嗎？師父微笑著說：「如果不是特別的紀念日，我是不輕易讓大家瞻仰的，以後有機會再讓你們參拜吧！」按理，我們應該知趣，不再請求了。可是，為強烈的願望所驅使，我們這一群膽大的弟子，再次向慈父般的上人懇求，允許我們參拜師公的舍利。就這樣，師父竟破例答應了弟子們的懇求。大家選了幾個代表，跟隨師父進入無言堂樓上，去恭請師公的舍利。師父躬自奉持師公的舍利寶塔，慢慢步行到觀音殿內，將師公的舍利塔恭敬地放在供檯上。於是在場的弟子們列隊膜拜瞻仰師公的晶瑩舍利，如願以償。

此情此景，仍然清晰縈留於弟子的腦海。如今弟子瞻仰膜拜的，卻是師父的舍利，讓弟子怎不黯然神傷，悲從中來！

一天，有弟子問師父，妙覺山萬佛城的佔地數百畝，可惜我們沒有看到聖城的全景，頗有不識聖城真面目之憾。師父聽了之後，很高興地說：「明天就帶你們去看萬佛城的真面目。」翌日上午，師父叫人安排一部車，載我們到了後山。後山的樹林翠綠青鬱，山上還有一大片核桃果園。師父迎著微風，站在山丘上用手指著說：「那個地方，是要蓋一座大雄寶殿的。大雄寶殿是紅柱黃琉璃瓦，寺外環繞七重行樹，寺前有七寶池，內有八功德水，是個理想的極樂淨土，希望將來的出家和在家弟子，都可以在那兒暮鼓晨鐘精進修行，同證菩提佛果。而且該山形勢頗佳，將來會有出類拔萃的聖僧祖師出現。」回憶及此，師父的莊嚴法相又出現弟子面前，音容宛在。

如今，師父上人的肉體雖然離開我們了，師父的法語卻仍然縈繞於弟子的耳際：「捨己為人，不求名聞利養；為法忘軀，躬行實踐；發揮華嚴法髓，闡揚大乘要義；和藹處世，平易近人……真有智者，絕不自讚。真有德者，絕不誹謗人。」

師父是以不來亦不去的無言大法來教化眾生的。所以師父特別在遺言中告訴弟子們說：「

operation or losing my life. The Venerable Master is truly our parent, helping us to extend the wisdom life of our Dharma bodies.

One day after listening to the Venerable Master lecture on a Sutra, over ten of us disciples were sitting around the Master asking questions on cultivation. One disciple told the Master he'd heard there was a five-colored sharira of the Elder Venerable Master Hsu Noble Yun in No Words Hall. He asked if we could go to behold it and bow to it. The Venerable Master smiled and said, "If it's not a special celebration, I don't casually allow people to see it. You'll have an opportunity to bow to it later on." We should have heeded the Master's wish and not made the request again. Yet, driven by our fervent wish, this group of bold disciples again sincerely requested the Venerable Master, who was like our kind father, to allow us to go bow to the Elder Master's sharira. And so the Venerable Master made an exception and granted our request. We chose a few representatives who followed the Venerable Master upstairs in No Words Hall to pay reverence to the Elder Master's sharira. The Venerable Master personally carried the Elder Master's sharira and slowly walked into the Guanyin Hall, where he reverently placed it on the altar. Then the disciples lined up and bowed and gazed upon the Elder Master's dazzling sharira, just as they had wished.

That scene remains clearly etched in my mind. How can I not be grieved by the fact that I am now beholding and bowing to the Venerable Master's sharira?

One day, a disciple said to the Venerable Master: The City of Ten Thousand Buddhas at Wonderful Enlightenment Mountain covers several hundred acres. It's too bad we can't get an overall view of the Sagely City and recognize how the Sagely City really looks." Hearing this, the Venerable Master happily said, "Tomorrow I'll take you to see the City's true appearance." The following morning, the Venerable Master arranged for a car to take us to the mountains in the back. There were lush green woods and a large walnut grove in the back mountains. Standing at the top of a hill facing the breeze, the Venerable Master pointed with his hand and said, "Over there, we're going to build a Jewelled Palace of Great Heroes. It will have red pillars and glazed yellow roof tiles. The temple will be surrounded by seven rows of trees. There will be seven jewelled pools filled with water of the eight meritorious virtues in the front of the temple. It will be an ideal Pure Land of ultimate bliss. I hope the left-home and lay disciples of the future will cultivate vigorously there from morning to evening and together attain the Bodhi fruit (Buddhahood). This mountain has a fine shape. An extraordinary monk and patriarch will appear there in the future." As I recollect this, the Venerable Master's adorned image appears before me. I can still see the Master's face and hear his voice.

Although the Venerable Master's physical form has left us, his words of Dharma are still in my ears. "Renounce yourself for the sake of others. Don't seek fame and profit. Forget yourself for the sake of the Dharma. Practice truly. Express the marrow of the Flower Adornment Dharma; expound the essential meaning of the Great Vehicle. Get along with people and be amiable...Those who are truly wise would never praise themselves or slander others."

The Venerable Master is teaching living beings the wordless great Dharma of neither coming nor going. And so he gave these final instructions to his disciples: "After I have gone... Scatter my ashes in

我走後，……把我的骨灰撒到虛空去，旁的事情我也不要，記得不要給我造什麼塔、什麼紀念館。我來的時候什麼也沒有，走的時候還是什麼也不要。在世上，我不要留什麼痕跡！我從虛空而來，回到虛空去。」

緬懷追思之餘，做為師父的弟子，應該以佛心為己心，以師志為己志，盡己所能地去實踐師父的三大宏願：弘法、譯經、教育，使師父的大願義舉，後繼有人；也只有這樣才能真正報答師恩於萬一！

有一首禪偈，正可以讚歎師父的行誼、風範：

> 風帶泉聲流谷口，山和雲影落潭心；
> 一痕春水一縷煙，化化生生各自然。

empty space, and don't do anything else. Remember, don't build any stupas or memorials for me. I had nothing when I came, and I don't want anything after I'm gone. I don't want to leave any traces in the world! I came from empty space, and I'll return to empty space."

Beyond thinking of the Venerable Master longingly, as disciples we should take the Buddha-mind as our own mind and our Master's resolve as our own resolve. We should do our best to carry out the Venerable Master's three great vows: to propagate the Dharma, to translate the Buddhist Canon, and to work on education. We should cause the Venerable Master's great vows and deeds to be passed on to the future. Only then will we be able to repay a slight fraction of the Venerable Master's kindness.

There is a Chan verse that aptly praises the Venerable Master's conduct:

Carrying the sound of the spring, the wind blows through the valley.
The mountains and clouds are reflected in the deep lake.
An expanse of springtime water and a curl of rising smoke:
Every phenomenon comes into being and
　　changes in its own natural way.

彌勒菩薩
Maitreya Bodhisattva

你要問我笑甚麼　　我先問你哭什麼
哭笑原非中道義　　執著兩邊做甚麼
一口喝盡愁怨水　　雙眼看破名利人
菩薩面目無人識　　交臂失之自蹉跎

If you ask me why I'm laughing,
Let me first ask you why you're crying.
Crying and laughing are not the Middle Way.
Why should we be attached to the two sides?
In one gulp, he swallows the tears of sorrow and resentment.
His two eyes see through those who involved in fame and gain.
No one recognizes this Bodhisattva. They all miss him at arm's length.
They are still wandering about wasting time.

宣公上人作
by the Venerable Master Hua

How I Met the Venerable Master and Some of the Responses I've Experienced

我遇到上人的因緣和感應

吳家境　Goh Kahkeng

I met Venerable Master in Kuala Lumpur, Malaysia, in 1978 at the Chinese Assembly Hall where the Venerable Master was lecturing on the *Sutra of the Past Vows of Earth Store Bodhisattva*. It was just a five-minute encounter from a distance, but I felt attracted to the Master momentarily. At that time, I was new to Mahayana Buddhism and did not know much Chinese, either spoken or written, so I did not stay on to listen to the Master's lecture, but went home with my wife.

Later on, one of my friends gave me a copy of the *Sixth Patriarch's Platform Sutra* in English from the City of Ten Thousand Buddhas. After reading this Sutra, I became fascinated with the Master because there was a short history of the Master in the few pages at the front of the Sutra. I could understand the Master's profound commentary of the Sutra, and it immediately strengthened my faith in the Mahayana school, after having been a Theravada Buddhist for about ten years because of my English educational background. Consequently, I made a resolve to meet the Master again and seek his teaching of the Dharma.

This resolve was fulfilled in 1979 when I came to San Francisco for a convention given by my company. Armed with the address of the Gold Mountain Monastery, I paid a visit to the Monastery on the day I arrived in San Francisco. From there I got directions to go to the City of Ten Thousand Buddhas (CTTB) and took a Greyhound bus to CTTB that same afternoon. When I reached CTTB, it was late evening. I joined in the evening recitation, after which the Master allowed me to bow to him at close range. I cried when I stepped into CTTB, and I cried again several times during the evening recitation and when I was bowing to the Master. It was as if I had returned home and met a long-lost parent and teacher. The Master kindly gave me a meditation topic to think about, and that made me more keen to draw close to the Master.

At the conclusion of my company's convention, the Master invited my wife, my son, and me to have lunch at Gold Mountain Monastery. There, I listened to the Master's words of great wisdom and was also introduced to some of the Dharma Masters who were having lunch together with the Master. One of the Dharma Masters, an American, recited the Great Compassion Mantra, which made me want to learn the Mantra, too. That is how I was motivated to recite the Great Compassion Mantra within the few following months. I bought some books published by the Dharma Realm Buddhist Association and studied them when I returned home. Those books deepened my understanding of the True Dharma propagated by the Master, and I made

我是在一九七八年，吉隆坡的中華大會堂中，聽上人講《地藏菩薩本願經》時，第一次見到上人。由於不會中文，所以沒留下來聽，只遠遠的看了大約五分鐘，就同太太回家了。但當時就有一種似曾相識的親切感，那是我剛開始接觸佛教。

不久，我的一位朋友送我一本從萬佛城請的英文版《六祖壇經》。由於上人深入淺出的解釋，和其中對上人生平的簡述，深深地引起我對上人的欣悅之情，也加強了我對大乘佛教的信心。因為我所受的教育關係，我在過去十年一直是信仰小乘佛法的。但這本英文的《六祖壇經淺釋》加深了我對大乘佛法的信仰，我發願，願能再瞻仰並追隨上人，學習佛法。

一九七九年我的願望實現了。我服務的公司派我到舊金山開會。我先有了金山聖寺的地址，所以我到舊金山後，當天就去了寺裡。下午即搭巴士到達了萬佛聖城。我在晚課後終於有機會向上人叩頭。我一踏進萬佛城，眼淚就掉下來了。晚課當中，又忍不住地哭了好幾次，當我向上人叩頭時也在哭。我覺得好像浪子又重見到了久別的父母和師長一樣。上人很慈悲地給了我一個公案去思索，使我更渴望能接近上人。

在開會結束之後，上人讓我和太太、兒子到金山寺午餐。並介紹認識了一同進餐的法師，也聆聽了上人充滿大智慧的開示。席中有一位美國法師唸了一遍〈大悲咒〉，這使我下了要唸〈大悲咒〉的決心，也促使我在以後的幾個月中將〈大悲咒〉唸下來。在金山寺請了許多法界佛教總會出版的書，回家研讀之後，使我更一步的深入瞭解了上人所弘揚的正法，當時我又發了一個願要再回萬佛城向上人學習。

another resolve to return to CTTB to learn from the Master.

In 1981, my desire to learn from the Master became so intense that I came alone to the CTTB at my own expense. During this trip I had several miraculous or wonderful responses which I am pleased to share now.

I came to CTTB in 1981 with eight questions to ask the Master. I kept those questions in my pocket hoping that I could ask the Master in person. However, when I arrived at the CTTB, the Master was giving an afternoon lecture after the meal offering. I was led to listen to the lecture by one of the Dharma Masters. As I was listening to the lecture, I realized that all my questions were already being answered by the Master, even before I had the chance to ask him personally. I was filled with joy and reverence for the Master. So, I thought that my mission had been achieved, and I asked the Master's consent to let me move on to another place. However, the Master told me that I should stay on longer to learn more from him. Obediently I stayed on and learned a great deal about Chan meditation and the remarkable way of life of the Sangha in CTTB.

My stay in CTTB that time was extended to one whole month as I realized that more and more of my questions about life, birth, and death were answered in the most inconceivable ways, such as during the morning and evening recitations, during Dharma talks by the Master himself or his disciples, as well as in all the sayings posted on the walls in the dining hall, the Buddha hall and Tathagata Monastery, where I was given a room to stay.

One other very important thing happened during this time. That is, one day before I left my home in Kuala Lumpur to come to the CTTB, my thirteen-year-old son had had a fall from the bicycle he was riding. I had crudely treated his wounds and dressed them up in my own way. I did not know that his wounds had become infected while I was in the CTTB. In the third week of my stay in CTTB, my wife telegrammed me and I called home to speak to her. She told me that my son's wounds had developed into very bad sores and his body also had rashes like shingles. She had taken him to see many doctors (both Chinese and Western), but none of them could heal him. She asked me to return home immediately to help her handle the problem. She also asked me to ask the Master to help. I decided not to return home until the following week because I wanted to participate in the seven-day recitation of Guanyin Bodhisattva's name, which was beginning the next day. I told her to bow to the Buddhas, Bodhisattvas, and the Master at home and ask them for help. She did that, and within the next three days, she found a doctor who could heal my son's wounds. That experience increased her faith in Buddhism and the Master. At the end of the seven-day recitation, the Master announced to the assembly during lunch that when the participants went home, everything would be all right. When I returned to Kuala Lumpur two days later, I found my son back to normal.

我想向上人學習的願望越來越強烈，終於在一九八一年，我自費單獨前往萬佛城，這一次旅程，我有許多奇妙的感應，我願在此與大家分享。

當時我口袋裡裝了八個寫好要問師父的問題，當我到達聖城時，上人正在做午後開示演講。一位法師領我前去聽講。沒想到正在開示中，我的八個問題都得到了圓滿的答覆。我甚至沒有機會把問題從口袋裡拿出來呢！我當時心裡充滿了欣喜，及對上人的仰慕。此行的目的既已達到，就請求上人指示下一步該做什麼？上人說我應該再多住些時候，多學習學習。於是我就遵命在萬佛城住了下來，學了許多有關參禪打坐的事，也見習了城裡僧眾很不平凡的生活方式。

在這一段期間當中，我發覺不論是在做早晚課、打坐、繞佛、念佛，或是聆聽上人及其弟子的開示時，以及在閱讀齋堂、佛殿和我住的如來寺牆上所掛的標語時，我心中對有關生命、生死等的疑問，很不可思議地，就那麼一點一點地得到解答了。因此我將在聖城居留的時間延長至一個月。

在這段時間還有一件值得一提的事是：在我離開吉隆坡往萬佛城的前一天，我十三歲的兒子騎腳踏車摔傷了，當時我就自己給他消毒上了藥。到了萬佛城的第三個星期，我太太打電報要我立刻回去，因為兒子的傷口發炎得很厲害，看了許多中西名醫都不見好轉，她還要我去向上人救助。但我決定要多留一個星期打觀音七，便回電報給妻子，要她在家中禮拜佛菩薩，求上人加持，她答應照辦。三天之後，她果然找到了一位醫生，治好了我兒子的傷口。這使她對佛法及上人的信心大增。打完觀音七後，在午餐時，上人告訴大家：凡參加打七的，回去一定萬事吉祥。果然，兩天後我回吉隆坡見到兒子時，他健康如昔。

無私無畏護持正法

SELFLESSLY AND FEARLESSLY PROTECTING AND UPHOLDING THE PROPER DHARMA

釋恆豐 Shi Hengfeng

在一個偶然的機會裡，讀到上人的事蹟和開示錄，以及上人十八大願，受到深深的震動，因而發心修行。知道上人是真正的善知識，因此決心跟隨他走上菩提道。一九八六年，我終於滿足了一直嚮往的心願——跟上人出家了。

上人來美後，每天都講經說法，首先開講《楞嚴經》。古人說：「開悟的楞嚴，成佛的法華。」上人說此經能幫助我們開大智慧，並鼓勵四眾弟子要背誦《楞嚴經》、研究《楞嚴經》、講說《楞嚴經》，推廣《楞嚴經》到每一微塵處。因此當時有不少弟子會背誦《楞嚴經》。上人同時也要求弟子們背誦、研究、推廣〈楞嚴咒〉，並說：「世界上若無〈楞嚴咒〉，妖魔鬼怪則會肆無忌憚，橫行於世。但世界上若有〈楞嚴咒〉，則旁門左道，魑魅魍魎，山妖水怪都還有所恐懼，不敢公然出世作亂。」上人還詳細地解釋了每一句〈楞嚴咒〉，便於學習者能深入的了解〈楞嚴咒〉。虛雲老和尚也說：「修行人如果能背誦一部《楞嚴經》，修行就不會走錯路了。」一定要會背誦《楞嚴經》，這是我今生的一大願望。對誹謗《楞嚴經》是偽經的人，上人訶責甚嚴：「四種清淨明誨正是破群魔的照妖鏡。」又說：「保證《楞嚴經》是真經，如果《楞嚴經》是偽經，我願墮地獄。」上人這種大公無私的護教精神，為我指出了修行大道。

其次，上人又用了九年的時間，講完《華嚴經》。他曾說：「一日不講經，一日不食。」為我們弟子做出榜樣，為復興聖教而流血汗，不休息。

這是我跟隨上人出家後的點滴體會。現在上人圓寂了，我願有生之年一定學好佛法，廣利有情，以報師恩。

By chance, I read the Venerable Master's biography and instructional talks, as well as his eighteen great vows. I was deeply moved and resolved to cultivate. I knew the Venerable Master was a genuine wise teacher, and so I was determined to follow him on the path to Bodhi. In 1986, I finally fulfilled my long-held wish—leaving home with the Venerable Master.

After the Venerable Master arrived in America, he lectured on the Sutras and spoke the Dharma every day. He began by lecturing on the *Shurangama Sutra*. The ancients said, "The Shurangama is for opening wisdom. The Dharma Flower is for attaining Buddhahood." The Venerable Master said this Sutra can help us open great wisdom. He encouraged the fourfold assembly of disciples to memorize the *Shurangama Sutra*, investigate the *Shurangama Sutra*, expound upon the *Shurangama Sutra*, and propagate the *Shurangama Sutra* into every dust mote in space. Quite a few of his disciples were able to recite the *Shurangama Sutra* from memory. The Venerable Master also urged his disciples to memorize, study, and propagate the Shurangama Mantra. He said, "If the Shurangama Mantra did not exist in the world, then the demons, ghosts, goblins, and weird creatures would not be afraid and would wreak havoc in the world. If the Shurangama Mantra is in the world, the deviant cults, ghosts, goblins, and sprites will be afraid to come out and openly make trouble in the world." The Venerable Master explained each line of the Shurangama Mantra in detail, allowing students to gain a deep understanding of the mantra. The Elder Master Hsu Yun said, "If cultivators can memorize the *Shurangama Sutra,* they will not go astray in their cultivation." My one great vow in this life is to be able to recite the *Shurangama Sutra* from memory.

Towards those who slander the *Shurangama Sutra*, saying that it is inauthentic, the Venerable Master sternly reproaches, "The Four Clear Instructions on Purity are a demon-spotting mirror that destroys the deviant hordes." He also said, "I guarantee that the *Shurangama Sutra* is an authentic Sutra. I vow to fall into the hells if the *Shurangama Sutra* is false." The Master's public-spirited and unselfish attitude towards protecting the teachings points out the great path of cultivation for us.

In addition, the Venerable Master spent nine years lecturing on the *Flower Adornment Sutra*. He said, "If I don't lecture on the Sutras one day, I will not eat on that day." He set an example for his disciples, not sparing blood or sweat and never pausing to rest in his efforts to make the sagely teaching flourish.

These are some small feelings that I've had since leaving the home-life with the Venerable Master. Now the Venerable Master has completed the stillness. I vow that for the rest of my life, I will study the Buddhadharma well and widely benefit living beings in order to requite the Master's kindness.

THE MASTER IS STILL ALIVE
師父上人還活著

Sandra Miner (Kuo Yi) 果儀

Since I first heard of Venerable Master Hua's death, I keep waiting for what I expect will be an inevitable emotional sadness to descend on me—the kind of sadness that usually happens when an important person in one's life dies. But aside from a few tearful moments now and then when thinking about him, no heart-wrenching sadness, no sense of irreplaceable loss occurs. And slowly I realize that although his physical presence is gone, I don't really experience him as dead. The most important aspects of him are alive and will continue. Because of him, thousands of us in the U. S. and overseas have been introduced to Buddhism. Because of him, many temples exist. His teachings will continue through his monks, nuns, and lay disciples. The translated and published sutras will reach many others. His physical self is gone and will be missed, but all of us, his disciples and students, are evidence that he was here and significantly changed our lives with his teachings.

自聽到宣公上人圓寂的消息後，我就在等待一個無法避免的哀傷情緒的降臨－－那種通常在一個人失去了他生命中的重要人物時感到的哀傷。可是除了在想到師父時唏噓數回外，沒有痛不欲生的哀傷。也沒有感到無法彌補的損失。慢慢的，我了解雖然上人的肉身已經走了，可是我沒有真正的感覺到他死了。因為上人的精神是活著的，而且是永遠的活著。因為上人，才使千萬個美國人及海外的我們得以認識佛教。也因為上人，很多寺廟得以建立。上人的教導，將由四眾弟子們延續下去。將會有更多的人讀到已翻譯出版的經書。雖然師父已經走了，而且我們也很想念他。但是所有我們這些弟子，就是上人曾住世並且以他的教導，使我們的生命產生重大改變的明證。

觀察眾生如幻夢　以業力故常流轉　大悲哀愍咸救拔　爲說無爲淨法性
菩薩所住希有法　唯佛境界非二乘　身語意想皆已除　種種隨宜悉能現
——《大方廣佛華嚴經》〈初發心功德品〉

He knows living beings are like an illusory dream;
Because of the force of karma they always flow and turn.
With great compassion and pity he rescues and pulls them out.
For their sakes he explains the unconditioned pure Dharma nature.

The Bodhisattva abides in rare Dharmas;
They are solely the states of the Buddha,
Not those of the two vehicles.
His body, mouth, and mind have been completely renounced.
According to various kinds of opportunities,
He is able to manifest.

Chapter on The Merit and Virtue from First Bringing Forth the Mind, the *Flower Adornment Sutra*

只盼來生新緣結

I ONLY HOPE TO CREATE NEW AFFINITIES IN THE NEXT LIFE

釋恆剛　　　Shi Heng Gang

師父圓寂的訊息傳出後，我一直不相信那是真的。不，那不是真的！一定又是師父跟我們這些徒弟玩遊戲，要考驗考驗我們，看我們是不是又懈怠、偷懶了。

過幾天，師父就會出定了。我要趕快去念佛、拜佛，求師父不要走。有好幾天，我都恍恍惚惚、漫無目的的：走路不像走路，吃飯不像吃飯，念佛不像念佛。渴望能聽到有關師父的好消息，那怕是一點點。直到從洛杉磯長堤聖寺傳來的傳真中，得知要把師父的靈柩運回聖城時，我才相信：那是真的！我頓時悲傷地哭倒在佛殿裡。

以前，曾有好多機會可以見到師父，但都因為不想打擾他老人家而錯過了。尤其在師父重病期間，更不願意讓師父為弟子的事，消耗太多的精力。自己內心的業力障礙，也是未去謁見師父的原因之一，沒想到如此一來，竟然永遠不能再叩見師父，親臨教誨了。

從出家到現在，有好多年，一直有一種難以抗拒的心理，就是很怕見到師父，也不知道為什麼這樣。別人想見都見不到，可我卻很怕見師父。因為，每當師父出現時，弟子常常沒有充分的心理準備，淚水會不由自主地奪眶而出。結果往往使自己覺得很難堪。這也許是過去造下的罪業太深，以至於一見到師父，那種深深的悔恨、愧疚之心就由然而生？！我會因此而悲慟很久。

我有時真的不知如何去面對師父：弟子的快樂、悲傷、憂愁，師父都知道得清清楚楚，甚至當你一動念、一打妄想，師父馬上就知道了：「師父，您等我，再等我二十年，等我證果了您再走好不好？」過了幾天，師父真的回來說，他要活到一百歲。沒想到，師父就是如此慈悲的，滿足眾弟子的願望，那怕是一個妄想。

從師父平時教導弟子的言談，舉止中，可以看得出，師父是位很剛毅又真實的人。他說話很真，真到別人輕視他、罵他，他都無所謂。即使對徒弟也一樣，有時他可以當著大眾，毫不留情地

Ever since the news of the Venerable Master's completion of stillness came out, I haven't been willing to believe that it is true. No, it can't be real! The Venerable Master must be playing another game with his disciples, testing us to see if we are being lax or lazy.

In a few days, the Master will surely come out of samadhi. I must quickly recite the Buddha's name, bow to the Buddha, and beg the Master not to go away. For quite a few days, I was lost in a daze, without a goal. When I walked, it didn't seem like walking. Eating didn't seem like eating. Reciting the Buddha's name didn't seem like reciting the Buddha's name. I yearned to hear even a little bit of news of the Venerable Master. When the announcement came from Long Beach Sagely Monastery saying that the Venerable Master's casket would be sent back to the Sagely City, I finally believed the news was real! I was so overcome with grief that I broke down crying in the Buddha Hall.

There had been many opportunities when I could have seen the Venerable Master, but I missed them all, because I didn't want to disturb him. When the Master was sick, I especially didn't want him to spend a lot of energy worrying about the affairs of his disciples. It was also because of the karmic hindrances in my own mind that I didn't go to see the Master. I didn't realize then that I would never have another chance to bow to and see the Master and listen to his instructions in person.

For many years, from the time I left the home-life until now, I've always had an inconquerable fear of seeing the Venerable Master. I don't know why I felt this way. Other people wanted to meet the Master but seldom had the chance, while I was afraid of meeting him. This was because when the Venerable Master showed up, I was often caught psychologically unprepared. My tears would fall uncontrollably, making me feel very embarrassed. Perhaps this is because I created very deep karmic offenses in the past, and so when I saw the Venerable Master, those deep feelings of regret and guilt would well up all at once! I would remain depressed for a long time afterwards.

Sometimes I really didn't know how to face the Venerable Master, because he seemed to know the happiness, sadness, and worry in my mind very clearly. In fact, the Venerable Master knew immediately what I was thinking as soon as I thought it: "Master, wait for me for another twenty years. Wait till I certify to the fruition before you leave, okay?" A few days later the Venerable Master sure enough came back and said he would live to the age of one hundred. I hadn't realized that the Master was so compassionate, fulfilling my wish even though it was just an idle thought.

You could tell from the Venerable Master's speech and conduct that he was a very resolute and honest person. The words he spoke

訓斥弟子的一點點毛病，只為了教弟子往真的修行。另一方面，就算他的徒弟已經修得很好了，他也不會輕易誇獎他。因為師父滿意自己的徒弟，就如同滿意自己一樣。

師父為弘法利生，往來奔波於世界各地，所以弟子已習慣於不能經常見到師父了。可是這一次，師父是真地走了，永遠地離開了。

師父，當您乘願再歸來時，還願意教化您的弟子嗎？師父，我是一個如此不孝敬的弟子，沒能認真地去實踐您所弘傳的大法。

師父：「樂莫樂兮共相知，悲莫悲兮生離別；今生與師緣未了，只盼來生新緣結。」

*　　　*　　　*

在舉行追思法會及荼毗大典的那幾天，天氣熱得像在火爐裡一樣。儘管暑氣逼人，四眾弟子仍然很虔誠地從海內外各地趕來參加儀式，瞻仰上人最後的遺容。

望著師父慈悲的遺容，心裡想到：「躺在靈柩裡的那位老人家，直到最後他還念念不忘地教化我們：「修行要吃苦、要忍耐，不要發脾氣，吃苦才能了苦，享福是消福，苦盡才有甘來。」

當師父的靈柩緩緩地從祖師殿出來時，靈柩後面繫了好幾條黃色帶子，為著是讓弟子們握著，它象徵著扶著師父的靈柩一樣。當我握著彩帶跟著師父走的時候，突然感覺到，握著黃色帶子的意義，是非常深刻的！這似乎告訴我們，團結就是力量！看到師兄弟們手緊緊握在一起，心裡的感動，真地分不清楚是流汗，還是流淚。這種團結的心，相信是會自始至終永遠跟隨著師父的：會永遠去完成師父的遺願。

眼睜睜看著師父的法體被送進去焚化爐，永遠消失在虛空中。雖說是一具臭皮囊，弟子仍然很難去面對這個嚴酷的事實。

眾生的欲望與執著是永無止盡的，面對著師父的法體雖倍感傷心，但不管師父是否在我們身邊，都應該念念不忘師父的法，念念不忘師父的教誨。

were so true that he didn't care if other people looked down upon him or slandered him. He had the same attitude even towards his disciples. Sometimes he would pick on the minor faults of his disciples in front of the assembly, only wishing for us to become more true in our cultivation. Even if his disciples were very good in their cultivation, he wouldn't casually praise them, because being satisfied with one's disciples is the same as being satisfied with oneself.

In order to propagate the Dharma and benefit beings, the Venerable Master would travel around the world, so I was used to not seeing the Master on a regular basis. But this time, the Venerable Master is gone for good. He has left forever.

Master, when you come back riding on your vows, will you still be willing to teach your disciples? Master, I'm such an unfilial and disrespectful disciple. I haven't been able to truly practice the great Dharma that you propagated.

Master: "There's no greater happiness than having known you. / There's no greater sadness than being apart from you. / My affinities with my Master in this life have not ended yet. / I only hope to create new affinities in the life to come."

*　　　*　　　*

During the few days of the memorial and cremation ceremonies, it was as hot as a furnace. Despite the oppressive summer heat, the fourfold assembly of disciples still sincerely came from all parts of the world to join the ceremonies and behold the Venerable Master for the last time.

As I gazed at the Venerable Master's kind visage, I thought, "That elder one lying in the casket still remembers to teach us, even at the very end: 'In cultivation one must take suffering and be patient. One should not lose one's temper. Enduring suffering, one puts an end to suffering. Enjoying blessings, one uses up blessings. After the suffering ends, the sweetness comes...'"

As the Venerable Master's casket was slowly carried out of the Patriarchs' Hall, numerous yellow ribbons attached to the back end of the casket were unrolled and given to disciples to hold. Holding the ribbon symbolized carrying the casket. As I grasped the ribbon and walked along behing the Venerable Master, I suddenly realized the profound significance of holding the ribbons. It was telling each of us that there is strength in unity! Seeing my Dharma-brothers with their hands together holding the ribbon, I was deeply touched and couldn't tell if I was sweating or crying. This spirit of unity will always follow the Venerable Master and always serve to realize the Master's wishes.

With wide-open eyes I watched as the Venerable Master's body was placed in the crematory, and as it vanished forever into thin air. Although it was but a stinking skin bag, I found it very difficult to face this cruel fact.

There is no end to the wishes and attachments of living beings. Although we are saddened by the sight of the Venerable Master's body, regardless of whether or not the Master is physically beside us, we should never forget the Master's Dharma and his teachings for even a thought.

恩同父母

AS KIND AS A PARENT

黃林英姿寫於一九九五年八月二十日

Written by Huang Linyingzi (Erlina Hajardi) on August 20, 1995

一九九五年七月一日，我與定咸法師在雅加達會面。談話中，法師突然提及宣公上人圓寂的事。如晴天霹靂，我被震驚得呆住了。「什麼？上人已圓寂？不可能！我不信，定是謠言。」為了證實這一點，法師馬上電詢馬來西亞某佛寺。答案是確實的。上人怎麼會這麼快就離開了我們？老人家不是立願，若活到一百歲願焚身供佛嗎？老人家對我恩同父母，我還不曾有任何回報。本打算近一兩年之間邀請上人來棉蘭弘法，以了卻我十年前的這椿心願。如今，一切都成了泡影。雖是因緣不足，但也是我太大意，近年來因種種因素，太久沒和上人聯繫所致。悲哀、自責、後悔全襲上了心頭，熱淚盈眶，心痛如絞。幸好我的兒子是上人的皈依弟子，和金山寺的一位居士很熟，從電話中獲知上人要四十九天後才荼毗。在悲傷中，這消息帶給了我一絲的安慰，總算我還能見到上人的遺容。

參加荼毗大典後，在返印尼的途中，無論在飛機上、汽車上、旅館裡，或是在香港姊姊家中，每一思及上人的離開，便泫然欲淚。從《上人追思紀念專集》中看到「徵文」啟事，我願意將上人給予我的，如父母般慈愛的關照寫出來，讓讀者從中窺見上人深切的悲憫之心，以及譯經弘法的崇高的使命感。

一九八一年，我帶女兒去臺灣念書（兒子成家在臺灣），由媳婦的介紹，間接地認識了一位佛友。她對宣公上人推崇備至，並給了我一張金山寺和萬佛城的卡片。由於她的推崇，引起了我對上人及萬佛城的敬仰。故返棉後，每日早晚課必祈求，有朝一日能拜見上人及參觀萬佛聖城。心誠則靈，我的願望終於實現了。

一九八五年正月，我因事赴美，到金山寺拜見了上人。當時，佛殿裡靜悄悄的，沒一個人，當我點了香，跪在地上祈禱後，抬起頭來，

On July 1, 1995, I met with Bhante Aryamaitri in Jakarta (Indonesia). During our conversation, Bhante suddenly mentioned the Venerable Master Hua's completion of stillness. I felt as if I'd been struck by a sudden flash of lightning out of the blue; I was shocked senseless! "What? The Venerable Master has completed the stillness? It can't be! I don't believe it. It must be a rumor." In order to confirm it, Bhante immediately telephoned a Buddhist temple in Malaysia. They said it was true. How could the Venerable Master leave us all so soon? Didn't he vow that if he lived to be a hundred, he would burn his body as an offering to the Buddhas? He was as kind to me as a parent, and I have never done anything to repay his kindness. I had planned to invite the Venerable Master to come to Medan (Indonesia) to propagate the Dharma in the next two years, in order to fulfill a vow that I made ten years ago. But now, it's all turned into bubbles and shadows. Even though the conditions weren't sufficient, it's also because I was too negligent. For various reasons, I didn't keep in touch with the Venerable Master in recent years. I am filled with grief, self-reproach, and regret; tears fill my eyes and my heart aches so much. Fortunately, my son is the Venerable Master's disciple and knows a layperson who goes to Gold Mountain Monastery. Over the phone, he found out that the Venerable Master's body would be cremated only after forty-nine days. This news consoled me slightly. At least I would get to see the Venerable Master's visage.

On my way back to Indonesia after attending the cremation ceremony, whether it was in the plane, in the car, in the hotel, or in my sister's home in Hong Kong, I wanted to weep each time I thought of the Venerable Master's departure. When I saw the "Call for Papers" in the book *In Memory of the Venerable Master Hsuan Hua*, I wanted to write about how the Venerable Master had cared for me as tenderly as a parent. I hope the reader will perceive the profound sincerity of the Venerable Master's compassionate heart and the nobility of his mission to translate the Sutras and propagate the Dharma.

In 1981, I took my daughter to Taiwan to attend school. (My son's family was also in Taiwan.) Through my daughter-in-law, I came to know someone who is Buddhist. She praised the Venerable Master highly and gave me a card of Gold Mountain Monastery and the City of Ten Thousand Buddhas. Based on her recommendation, I came to hold the Venerable Master and the City of Ten Thousand Buddhas in high regard. After I returned to Medan, at the end of the morning and evening ceremonies each day, I always prayed that I would be able to pay respects to the Venerable Master and visit the City of Ten Thousand Buddhas one day. Sincerity brings a response—my wish finally came true.

In January of 1985, I went to America on business and stopped by

才發現左邊靠牆的長凳上坐著一位老和尚，一位美籍和尚跪著和他說著話。我想那必是宣公上人了。等那位法師離開後，我走向前去向老人家頂禮。他問我：「從什麼地方來啊？叫什麼名字？妳今年多大啊？」我都一一回答了。老人家右手的手指稍動了幾下，便說：「你啊，吃了很多的苦啊！受了很多的折磨啊！」好厲害！不愧為大修行者！一眼之下，便能道出我二十幾年來辛、酸、苦、辣的遭遇。如果不具慧眼，誰敢如此肯定地說？因從外表看來，我不像一個吃了很多的苦，受了很多折磨的人呀！心中不禁油然生起了對老人家的敬佩！接著老人家對我作了一些簡略的開示，如不貪、不自私、不自利……等等。當時我心中不明白上人為何對我說這些，因為我並非那類的人啊！後來才知道那是萬佛聖城的六大宗旨。

離開金山寺之前，我對上人說，想去參觀萬佛城。上人說：「我才從萬佛城回來呢！不過，你搭灰狗車就可抵達。」「但我第一次來美國，人地生疏，我不懂呀！」上人稍頓了一下，說：「那妳星期四來好了（兩天後）。要帶一些衣服，妳要在那兒過夜的。」我好高興！臨走前，我送給上人兩本我的著作的英文版。一本是我翻譯的英譯本，其中一本是我寫的《讓我們認識佛教》（這是為棉蘭婆羅浮圖佛寺住持出家十五週年寫的）。

星期四那天，如約抵金山寺。寺中已有十幾個人。用過了午餐不久，信眾一個一個向上人頂禮就回去了。最後，只剩下我一個人，當時心中很奇怪，上人不是叫我今天來嗎？是我聽錯了？或去不成了？心中充滿著失望。於是問一位美籍法師，法師說：「去啊！上人就帶妳一個人去啊！」帶我一個人去！我幾乎不敢相信自己的耳朵。上人竟然這麼地慈悲，真令我感激涕零！

去萬佛聖城途中，上人的聲音從後座傳來：「林居士，妳怕暗嗎？」「不怕啊！」「萬佛城路上沒電燈的啊，妳不怕？」「上人，我不怕。」「妳怕冷嗎？」「冷，我倒是很怕哦！」我的怕冷是天字第一號的。據電台報導，那年是美國三十年來最冷的冬天。

車抵萬佛城已是晚上。果然路上黑漆漆的，要用手電筒照路。抬頭一望，天好似很低，滿

Gold Mountain Monastery to pay a visit to the Venerable Master. The Buddhahall was quiet and empty of people. After I had lit incense and knelt to pray, I looked up and only then did I realize that an elderly monk was sitting on the long bench by the wall to my right, and an American monk was kneeling before him and talking with him. "That must be the Venerable Master Hua," I thought to myself. After the other Dharma Master had left, I walked up to bow to the elder monk. "Where are you from? What's your name? How old are you this year?" he asked. I answered each question. The elder monk moved the fingers of his right hand slightly, and then said, "You have suffered greatly! You've gone through many tribulations!" How sharp! He's certainly a great cultivator! In a single glance, he could tell me about the bitterness and grief I'd encountered for twenty-odd years. How could he have spoken so positively if he didn't have the Eye of Wisdom? My appearance certainly doesn't indicate that I have suffered a lot or gone through many tribulations! I couldn't help but respect this elder monk! The Venerable Master then gave me some simple instructions, telling me not to be greedy, not to be selfish, not to seek personal benefit, and so on. I didn't understand why the Master was telling me these things, because I wasn't that sort of person! Later I found out these were the Six Guiding Principles of the Sagely City of Ten Thousand Buddhas.

Before I left Gold Mountain Monastery, I mentioned to the Master that I wished to visit the City of Ten Thousand Buddhas. The Master said, "I just got back from the City! But you can take the Greyhound bus to get there." "This is my first time in America. I don't know the place, and I don't know how to get there!" The Master paused, and then said, "Then come back on Thursday (two days later). Bring some clothes along, because you'll be staying overnight." I was so happy! When I was about to leave, I gave the Master two English books that I'd written. One was an English translation that I'd done, and the other was called *Getting to Know Buddhism* (which I had written on the fifteenth anniversary of the leaving home of the Abbot of Vihara Borobodur in Medan).

That Thursday, I went to Gold Mountain Monastery as planned. There were over ten people at the Monastery. After lunch, one by one the laypeople bowed to the Venerable Master and departed. In the end I was the only one left. I thought it was kind of strange: Hadn't the Venerable Master told me to come on that day? Did I hear wrong? Or was the trip cancelled? I was filled with disappointment. I then asked an American Dharma Master, who said, "You're still going! You're the only one the Venerable Master is taking along!" "He's taking me alone?" I could hardly believe my ears. The Venerable Master's utter kindness made me want to cry!

On the road to the City of Ten Thousand Buddhas, the Venerable Master's voice came from the backseat: "Laywoman Lin, are you afraid of the dark?" "No." "The streets in the City of Ten Thousand Buddhas aren't lighted. You're not afraid?" "Venerable Master, I'm not afraid." "Are you afraid of the cold?" "Yes, I'm quite afraid of the cold." I was the world's number one for being afraid of the cold. According to the weather report, that year's winter was the coldest one America had had in thirty years.

It was already nighttime when the car reached the City of Ten Thousand Buddhas. It was indeed pitch black in the streets. One

天的星斗亮晶晶的，好美的天空！

在我被帶入一間單人房後，聽著法師介紹宿舍內情形時，突然在暗淡的燈光下看到上人走過來，手上拿著一包東西，後面跟著開車的居士。一到房門口，上人就指著手上那包東西說：「這是電毯子，要給妳用的，才不會冷。」我一看，那是一條原封不動全新的毯子，一定是某居士供養給上人用的。我怎麼敢用呢。於是我說：「不必啦，上人，床上已有三條毛毯子，而且我身上穿有衛生衣，棉衣好幾件，該不會冷的。」上人又說了：「不行，妳從熱帶地方來，一定會很怕冷。妳只要蓋這條就夠了。」我仍然再三地不敢接受。上人又問：「怎麼？我帶來了，妳不用？」口氣裡充滿著失望。這好比是一個慈父，怕孩子嚴冬受寒，但孩子卻非常固執，不能領會慈父的一片愛心，慈父怎能不失望呢？於是我趕緊說：「好的，我用！我用！謝謝上人的慈悲！」看上人的神情，好似在對我說：「嗯！這就對了！」

我住的房間，電插頭距我的床太遠。上人一邊在跟那位居士講如何移床的事，一邊吩咐法師帶我去用晚餐。在記憶當中，轉身出去之前，好像看到上人竟也親自動手幫忙呢！

那天晚上，我是唯一的用餐者。有一在家女居士在幫忙熱稀飯，法師則一面幫我拿麵包、乳酪、蘋果等等一大盤，一面頻頻地用華語招呼我：「坐下，不要客氣。」法師的慈悲親切讓我非常感動！

用完餐回寢室盥洗，不知道怎麼能得到熱水，只好用那寒徹骨的冰水，馬馬虎虎地洗一洗。回到房裡，全身瑟瑟發抖，牙齒打顫。但一將電毯子蓋上後，頃刻之間，一股暖流流暢周身，舒適非常。在這麼溫暖的被窩裡，本該很快進入夢鄉，但我卻睡不著，躺在那兒，盡是流淚。那是深切的、感恩的熱淚！淚珠兒就這樣不停地淌下來，也不知淌了好久才矇矇朧朧地睡著了。上人啊！上人！您老人家這份慈父般的恩情真叫我刻骨銘心，畢生難忘啊！

在萬佛城住了兩夜。我很歡喜萬佛城的清靜，是修行者的理想地方。遺憾的是沒參觀戒壇。離開萬佛城之前，上人問起，才知道是法師沒帶我參觀。上人似乎也感遺憾，但當時時間已不允許了。

歸途中，上人問我要不要住在美國？我知道老

needed a flashlight to shine the way. When I looked up, the sky seemed very low. The entire sky was filled with twinkling stars—a beautiful sight!

After I was taken to a single room, the Dharma Master explained the dorm situation to me. Suddenly, in the dim light I saw the Venerable Master approaching with a package in his hand. The laywoman who had driven us was following behind him. When the Master reached the door of my room, he pointed to the package and said, "This is an electric blanket for you to use, so you won't feel cold." I saw that it was a brand new blanket, still unopened and untouched. It must have been an offering to the Venerable Master from some layperson. How could I presume to use it? I said, "Venerable Master, I don't need it. There are three heavy blankets on the bed already, and I'm wearing thermal underwear and several layers of cotton. I shouldn't be cold." The Master said, "No. You're from a hot climate, so you'll certainly fear the cold. Just use this blanket, and it will be enough." I declined a second and a third time. The Venerable Master asked, "What? I've brought it, and you won't use it?" His voice was full of disappointment. He was like a concerned father, afraid lest his child freeze in the severe cold of winter; yet his child was very stubborn and failed to understand his father's concern. How could the father not be disappointed? I hastily said, "I'll use it! I'll use it! Venerable Master, thank you for your kindness!" The Venerable Master's expression seemed to be telling me, "Ah, now you've done the right thing!"

In my room, the electrical outlet was too far away from the bed. The Venerable Master was talking with the laywoman about moving the bed, while at the same time telling the Dharma Master to take me to dinner. Before I turned around to leave, I seem to remember the Venerable Master actually helping to move the bed!

That evening, I was the only person who took dinner. A laywoman had cooked the meal. While the Dharma Master helped me to get a plate full of food—bread, cheese, an apple, and so on, she said to me in Chinese, "Please sit down. Don't be polite." I was deeply touched by the Dharma Master's kindness and concern.

After I finished dinner, I went back to the dorm to wash up. I didn't know how to turn on the hot water, so I had to use the freezing water to wash myself more or less. When I returned to my room, my whole body was shivering and my teeth were chattering. But as soon as I got under the electric blanket, in an instant, a warmth spread throughout my body—extremely comfortable. Snuggled under such a warm blanket, I ought to have entered the dreamworld very quickly. However, I couldn't fall asleep. As I lay there, my tears kept falling—tears of deep gratitude. The tears kept flowing without stop. I don't know how long it was before I finally fell asleep. Oh Venerable Master! Your fatherly kindness will forever be engraved in my heart—I will never be able to forget it!

I stayed at the City of Ten Thousand Buddhas for two nights. I loved the purity of the City. It is an ideal place for cultivators. My only regret was that I didn't get to visit the Ordination Hall. Before I left the City, the Venerable Master asked and found out that the Dharma Master didn't take me to visit it. The Venerable Master also seemed to feel regret, but there was no time to go then.

On the return journey, the Venerable Master asked me if I

人家是要我參加譯經的行列。承蒙上人的看重，讓我感到無上的榮幸！譯經是一項神聖的、偉大的、艱鉅的工作，非常人所能勝任。但慚愧得很，我的中英文都是所謂的「半桶水」，而且我有八個兒女，先夫尚在，仍需我的照顧。再說，當時棉蘭的佛教還需要我，我於是婉謝了上人的盛意。但上人仍然是那麼慈悲，在我離開三藩市前，還贈送了好多的佛書給我，如《楞嚴經淺釋》、《修行者的日記》、《開示錄》……等。

在一次與上人的談話中，我曾邀請上人來印尼弘法（卻沒說明是印尼的棉蘭）。老人家很慈悲的微笑著說：「可以啊！不過我來時是十幾個人的。」我頓住了，因為家裡經濟能力有限。況且過去幾年當中，為了擴建棉蘭婆羅浮圖佛寺，我曾向各界人士募捐，到最後，人們怕見到我這「稅務官」，於是邀請之事就擱下來了。

大概是一九八六年，臺灣廣欽老和尚圓寂後的那段時間，上人率兩位弟子來雅加達。因沒申請到簽證，移民廳不准入境。幸蒙 Sunter Agung 小乘佛寺擔保，才被准許入境。我兩位住在雅加達的妹妹都去拜見了上人。上人對她們說，他來印尼是應一女居士（指我）的邀請。又說：「如果妳姊姊知道我來了，她一定會來的。」事情太不湊巧，偏偏我那時在新加坡，沒有人通知我，直到我回到雅加達後才知道這件事。哦，上人，他老人家大慈大悲，知道我心有餘而力不足，故自動地來印尼要滿我的心願。可是老人家的用心竟白費了。我心中的難過，不能言喻！一方面痛責自己太糊塗，竟忘了告訴上人我住在棉蘭，另一方面為棉蘭眾生婉惜，沒有因緣聆聽菩薩示現的大善知識的教誨。

一九八七年，我創立了「佛教慈愛會」，又打算建立佛教醫院。七個月後，先夫突然逝世。他的逝世，使我在籌款方面失去了一得力的支持者；再加上種種的壓力，以致我出現 Parkinson 綜合症的早期症狀。女婿是醫生，除了開藥之外，並勸我暫放下佛教醫院的事。大女兒陪我到美加旅遊，那是一九八八年四月份左右。路經臺灣時，板橋蓮社社長趙女居士告訴我，從上人的書中，她發現有幾個字有錯誤（校對或記錄上）。雖只幾個字，卻很重要。我也有同感。所以託我帶去美國給上人看。

根據行程，我們只能在萬佛聖城住一夜，若稿

wanted to live in America. I knew that he wished me to take part in the work of translating Sutras. I felt tremendously honored by the Venerable Master's consideration. The translation of Sutras is a sacred, noble, and very difficult task, not something that can be done by ordinary people. However, I'm ashamed to say that my Chinese and English are both mediocre. And my eight children and my husband still needed me to take care of them. What's more, the Buddhism of Medan still needed me. So I politely declined the Venerable Master's generous offer. The Venerable Master was still kind to me, and gave me many Buddhist books, such as the *Shurangama Sutra* with commentary, *News of True Cultivators*, and *Talks on Dharma*, before I left San Francisco.

During a conversation with the Venerable Master, I once invited him to come to Indonesia to propagate the Dharma (without specifying that the place was Medan, Indonesia). He very kindly said with a smile, "Okay! But when I come, it'll be with ten or more people." I was at a loss, because my family's financial resources were limited. This was especially true since I had been raising funds for the expansion of Vihara Borobodur in the past few years, and people had become afraid of me for being a "tax collector." So the matter of the invitation was set aside.

Probably it was in 1986, around the time that Elder Master Guangqin completed the stillness in Taiwan, that the Venerable Master and two disciples came to Jakarta. Because they had been unable to get visas, the immigration office refused to admit them. Fortunately, Sunter Agung, a Theravadan Buddhist temple, sponsored them and so they were able to come in. My two sisters who lived in Jakarta both went to pay respects to the Venerable Master. The Master told them he had come to Indonesia at the invitation of a certain laywoman (me). He said, "If you sisters know of my coming, she will surely come, too." Unfortunately, I happened to be in Singapore and no one notified me. I didn't find out until I returned to Jakarta. Ah, the Venerable Master's great compassion! He knew I really wished to invite him but didn't have the means, so he came to Indonesia on his own initiative to fulfill my wish. But his kind gesture was in vain. It's impossible to describe how bad I felt! I reproached myself for being so stupid and forgetting to tell the Master that I lived in Medan. I also grieved for the people of Medan, who didn't have the conditions to listen to the teachings of a greatly wise teacher who was the manifestation of a Bodhisattva.

In 1987, I founded the Buddhist Compassion Society (Yayasan Mettayana Buddhis) and made plans to build a Buddhist hospital. Seven months later, my husband suddenly passed away. With his death, I lost a powerful source of support in fundraising, and with the addition of various other pressures, I began showing symptoms of Parkinson's disease. My son-in-law's doctor not only gave me a medical prescription but also urged me to drop the Buddhist hospital project. My eldest daughter accompanied me to take a holiday in America and Canada. That was around April of 1988. When we passed through Taiwan, Laywoman Zhao, the director of the Banqiao Lotus Society, told me that she had discovered some typographical errors in the Venerable Master's books. Although it was only a few characters, they were very important characters. I agreed with her, and so she asked me to show them to the Venerable Mas-

件的事情耽誤了，那麻煩可就大了！所以到聖城的第二天午後，我去總辦公室請求謁見上人。法師說上人在休息，不可打擾。我說：「我有要事要和上人說！」法師說：「告訴我就可以，我會替妳轉達。」我說：「可是，法師啊！話要我親自對上人說才行的呀！而且今天下午我們得回三藩市，因為……。」再怎麼說，就是不行。女兒說：「算了吧，媽。」我說：「任務還沒達到，怎麼可以走？」情急之下，禁不住衝口而出地說：「法師，是否可以告訴上人我的名字？也許上人會歡喜接見我的。」當時，法師以一種很怪的眼神看著我。也難怪他的眼神怪。話說出了口，連我自己也覺得聽起來，好像我是何方神聖似的。但這也是事出無奈呀！終於法師說：「好吧，我試打電話問問看。」沒多久，法師回來，笑瞇瞇地說：「稍等一下，師父就要來了。」

果然一會兒，便看見老人家坐著一輛四方形兩輪無蓋的木車子（記憶中是這樣的）。車子的右手有一手柄，上人便擎著那手柄前後推動著車向我們駛來。待上人進入辦公室坐下後，我們向上人頂禮，上人慈悲地叫我們坐著談。我先將趙居士所託之事稟報了上人，然後談了一些其他的事。我又重新邀請上人到印尼棉蘭弘法。老人家說，最好由我組團來萬佛城參觀，就像馬來西亞曾組團來萬佛城一樣。我答應回去便組團。（但返棉後數月便罹患了一種怪病，國內外中西醫都束手無策，拖了兩三年才痊癒，因此沒有履行諾言。）

當我向上人告辭時，老人家問怎麼不多住幾天？我告訴了原委，老人家也不再多說。從辦公室出來後，本想請法師替我們租車回三藩市，正好碰見那位第一次載我到萬佛城的居士，載了幾位香港來的信徒，上人就交代那位居士載我們回三藩市。途中我向那位居士表示很過意不去，太勞累了她了。「不要緊」，她說：「妳是上人的貴賓嘛！」貴賓！多觸目的字眼！我何德？何能？何等身份？能被上人視為貴賓？不！不是貴賓！我告訴她說，這是上人的慈悲！上人像慈父般地愛護我，照顧我！

古人說：「滴水之恩，當以湧泉相報。」上人對我，恩深似海。可我卻沒有什麼回報，那怕一點點。雖佛門中講諸事皆有其因緣，但邀

ter when I went to the United States.

Our itinerary only allowed us to stay at the City of Ten Thousand Buddhas for one night. If we were delayed because of the text, it would be a great hassle. So in the afternoon of our second day at the City, I went to the Administration Office to ask to meet personally with the Venerable Master. The Dharma Master said the Venerable Master was resting and could not be disturbed. I said, "I have something very important to tell the Venerable Master." He said, "You can tell me, and I will tell the Venerable Master for you." I said, "But Dharma Master, I must speak personally to the Venerable Master! And we have to go to San Francisco this afternoon, because..." No matter how I pleaded, there was no way. My daughter said, "Why don't you forget it, Mom?" I said, "I haven't done what I have to do. How can I go?" In my agitated state, I couldn't stop myself from blurting out, "Dharma Master, could you just tell the Venerable Master my name? Maybe the Venerable Master would like to see me." The Dharma Master gave me a strange look, but I didn't blame him, for even to me, my words sounded like I was some kind of god or sage. But I had no choice! The Dharma Master finally said, "Okay. I'll call the Venerable Master and ask." In a short while he returned and said with a smile, "Please wait a moment. The Master is coming."

In a short while, I saw the Venerable Master seated in a rectangular, two-wheeled, uncovered wooden car (that's how I remember it looking). There was a lever on the right-hand side of the car, and the Master moved it back and forth to steer the car towards us. After the Venerable Master had come into the Administration Office and seated himself, I bowed to him, and the Master kindly told me to sit down and speak. I first reported the matter that Laywoman Zhao had entrusted to me, and then we talked about other matters. I again invited the Venerable Master to come to Medan, Indonesia, to propagate the Dharma. He suggested that I organize a group tour to the City of Ten Thousand Buddhas, as the people from Malaysia had done. I promised to do so when I went back. (But after I returned to Medan, I came down with a strange sickness for several months, which Chinese and Western doctors both domestic and abroad treated to no avail. It took two or three years for me to fully recover, and so I failed to carry out my promise.)

When I said goodbye to the Venerable Master, he asked why I didn't stay a few more days. I told him I had other obligations, and he didn't say more. When I walked out of the office, I planned to ask the Dharma Master to help me rent a car to return to San Francisco. I happened to see the laywoman who had driven us to the City the first time. She had just brought several Hong Kong disciples to the City, and the Venerable Master arranged for her to take me back to San Francisco. On the way I told the laywoman that I felt very embarrassed to give her so much trouble. "Don't worry," she said, "You're an honored guest of the Venerable Master." Honored guest! What striking words! What virtue and ability and status did I have that the Venerable Master considered me an honored guest? No! I wasn't an honored guest! I told her, "This is just the Venerable Master's compassion—his fatherly concern and protection towards me!"

The ancients said, "If one receives a drop of kindness, one should repay it with a bubbling spring." The Venerable Master's kindness to

請上人蒞臨印尼棉蘭一事，一拖再拖，的確是我的疏忽，以致使棉蘭眾生錯過瞻仰、親近上人的機會。每思及此，便悲悔交集，熱淚盈眶。

上人荼毘大典結束後，返印尼的途中，在香港最後的一個晚上，正傷感時，突然一個念頭閃過腦際：「對了，何不將上人的《追思紀念專集》翻印推廣？上人在世時，棉蘭的眾生雖然沒有福報，得以親近這位大菩薩示現的大善知識，如今卻可以從《追思紀念專集》裡，去多方面的感受上人偉大無我的精神，感人肺腑的十八大願，願代眾生受苦的大悲心，以及上人如何恩澤弟子們的扣人心弦的記述。……還有上人以他大智大勇、不畏艱辛而創立的，功德巍巍流芳萬世的譯經聖業。

從此專集，讀者定會產生親聆上人教誨，法喜充滿的感受。目前，翻印正進行中。願藉此能聊報上人的深恩於千萬之一！

願上人早日乘願再來！我堅信老人家必定再來，因老人家就是大願地藏王菩薩啊！

願上人的教化不僅能在西方的國家發揚光大，更願能普及全球！

me was as deep as the sea. Yet I haven't done anything to repay him. Although the Buddhist view is that all things have their conditions, the matter of inviting the Venerable Master to come to Medan was delayed time and again. It is because of my negligence that the people of Medan did not get the opportunity to behold and draw near to the Venerable Master. Every time I think of this, I feel regret, and tears of grief fill my eyes.

On my way back to Indonesia after the Venerable Master's cremation ceremony, during my last night in Hong Kong, in the midst of my grief, a thought suddenly flashed through my mind: "I know, why don't I reprint the book *In Memory of the Venerable Master Hsuan Hua* and circulate it widely? Even though the people of Medan didn't get to meet the Venerable Master—this greatly wise teacher, the manifestation of a Bodhisattva—when he was alive, they can read this book and be moved by the Venerable Master's magnanimous and selfless spirit, his eighteen great vows, his compassionate wish to take the sufferings of living beings upon himself, and the touching accounts of his kindnesses towards disciples...and his wise and courageous pioneering efforts to translate the Sutras—this is a sacred deed of monumental merit that will be remembered for endless generations."

Reading this book, one will surely feel that one is listening to the Venerable Master's teachings in person and be filled with the joy of the Dharma. The book is currently being reprinted. I hope that this will help me repay a small portion of the Venerable Master's kindness!

I wish the Venerable Master will ride upon his vows and quickly return! I have firm faith that the Venerable Master will return, for he is Earth Store King Bodhisattva of Great Vows!

I wish that the Venerable Master's teachings will not only flourish in the West, but will spread around the globe!

爲千手千眼觀世音菩薩開光説法
Opening the Light Verse for Thousand-handed, Thousand-eyed Guanyin Bodhisattva

千眼照見千手伸　接引眾生出迷津　普願含識俱離苦　摩訶般若彼岸登

A thousand eyes observe and a thousand hands reach out
To direct living beings who are confused at the crossroads.
He vows that all sentient beings will leave suffering.
And ascend to the other shore with Maha Prajna.

宣公上人作
by Venerable Master Hua

我的學佛心路歷程

MY EXPERIENCE IN STUDYING THE BUDDHADHARMA

王果益

Wang Guo Yi

當我幼小時，每到中國新年的除夕，媽媽一定到寺廟去酬神，為的是討個家宅平安，生意興隆。祖母在一年中的重要節日，會到寺廟中住上一日一夜。祖母多次選我陪她去。記憶中最深刻的一次，我陪祖母住廟，我在甜睡中被鐘鼓聲吵醒，只見燈光、燭光全亮，比丘尼在大殿誦經。因此自小我對寺廟的佛、菩薩、金剛、羅漢的塑像就都敬畏有加。甚至高中時，我到天主教書院就讀，也沒有改變我尊敬佛菩薩的態度。

以後到了美國，念書、畢業、工作、養育孩子，忙中又忙，無暇向精神領域及人生哲理深入探討。偶而忙中抽空，把孩子們帶到基督教堂作禮拜，也為的是參加中國人的社團活動。我們把孩子們送到基督教主辦的學前幼兒班，除了讓他們學習外，也希望他們中規中矩地學做人。當最小的孩子就讀幼稚園時，我才開始有一點閒情探索人生。

我是個念醫藥的人，對宗教鬼神這個問題，抱著可有可無的態度。但是我對於神通、特異功能、鬧鬼、起死回生的記載，抱著很大的好奇心。這時正是家姊積極學習佛法的時候。我不時向家姊借有關佛法的書籍閱讀，我因此相信有神通這一回事：跟著我又閱讀《向知識分子介紹佛教》一書，使我能將佛法與中國風俗傳統的迷信分析清楚。接著我開始閱讀上人的開示錄和經典淺釋，我才知道我已浪費了人生幾十年的珍貴時間，一無所聞，等到現在才聞得師父述說佛法的甘露。後來，我不能止步了，只知要往佛法這一條修道之路走。當我皈依上人的那天，家婆、丈夫也一起皈依：不到三年，女兒和兒子也自願皈依三寶，做師父的弟子了。

記得初皈依上人的第一個星期，我曾作一個夢，夢到自己飄到一個很殊勝的地方，氣氛很莊嚴，是一座寺廟，我是旁觀者，沒有人理我，我也不吵人。寺宇的建築物以金、黃、紅為主色，很

When I was little, on every New Year's Eve, my mom would take me to the temple to thank the spirits in order to ensure that our family would be peaceful and our business would prosper. On important holidays, my grandmother would stay overnight in the temple. She always chose me to accompany her. One of my deepest memories is of being awakened by the sound of bells and drums when I stayed in the temple with my grandmother once, and seeing the nuns reciting a Sutra in the Buddhahall, which was brightly lit with lamps and candles. I have always felt a deep awe for the images of Buddhas, Bodhisattvas, Vajra-spirits, and Arhats. Even when I was studying in a Catholic high school, I continued to feel reverence for the Buddhas and Bodhisattvas.

After I went to the United States where I attended college, graduated, and began working and raising my children, I was so busy that I had no time to look into spiritual subjects or the philosophy of life. Occasionally I would bring my kids to church, but we went mainly to take part in the activities of the Chinese community. We sent our children to a Christian preschool, hoping that they would learn to be good people. When my youngest child entered preschool, I finally had some time to delve into the meaning of life.

Since I had studied medicine in college, I paid no attention to religion and the question of whether God or ghosts exist. But I was extremely curious about spiritual powers, supernatural abilities, possession by ghosts, and the dead coming back to life. My elder sister was vigorously studying the Buddhadharma, and I often borrowed Buddhist books from her. Reading those books convinced me that spiritual penetrations were real. Later on, I read a book called *Introducing Buddhism to the Intelligentsia*, which helped me to distinguish between Buddhism and superstitious Chinese beliefs. When I started to study the Venerable Master's Dharma talks and his commentaries on the Sutras, I realized that several precious decades of life had gone by without my hearing the wonderful sweet dew of the Master's Dharma. I knew only that I wanted to walk the path of cultivation prescribed by the Buddhadharma. The day I took refuge with the Triple Jewel under the Venerable Master, my mother-in-law and my husband also took refuge; less than three years later, my daughter and son also took refuge and became disciples of the Venerable Master.

Less than a week after I took refuge, I dreamed that I flew up to a sublime place, a temple with an adorned atmosphere. I seemed to be an onlooker, for no one paid any attention to me and I didn't bother anyone else either. The buildings of the temple were mainly golden, yellow, and red in color. The place was very bright. When I went up to the second floor, I saw people working there in silence. Suddenly I was in the main hall on the first floor, standing at the back of the hall. I saw more than ten monks wearing yellow robes with red

光亮。我在二樓，看見每個人在工作，不說話。忽然間，我到了一樓的大殿，在殿後觀看，只見殿前有十多位比丘，穿著黃袍，披上金紅色的袈裟。我只感覺安宜舒靜。

再說吃素的經驗。上人一直教導我們吃素的好處，最大的慈悲是不吃眾生肉。我曾向住持法師借了《蓮池大師戒殺放生文圖說》回來看，讀了此書後，我便立願吃長素。吃素時的初三個月，我馬上覺得血液循環非常舒暢，精神比前飽滿，體力又很充沛。

上人很重視《楞嚴經》和〈楞嚴咒〉，住持法師常鼓勵同修們背誦〈楞嚴咒〉，所以我也將〈楞嚴咒〉背了。記得當我快背熟〈楞嚴咒〉的那一個星期，只覺得附在我身上的塵垢一層一層地飛走，離開我的軀體。我感覺身體很潔淨和輕便，這種感覺持續了有一個月之久。

以上是我學佛的因緣。我是個後知後覺的普通人，我初時不懂佛法，不明因果，年輕時為鞏固生活基礎而忙；到了中年生活基礎有點安定，才開始探索人生之謎。最初只是為了好其神通事蹟：在機緣成熟了，就遇上正信佛法，又覺得相見恨晚。試問人生有什麼比「生命從何而來？人死向何去？」這個問題更重要？上人的啟示教誨，句句是金玉良言。如何了生脫死、離苦得樂，應該是我們修行的目標。我願自己能遵照上人的教誨，用毅力克服自己不良的宿習和惡業，專一修行，朝向正道而行。

sashes on top. I felt peaceful and comfortable.

The Venerable Master has taught us the advantages of being a vegetarian, and that the greatest form of compassion is to refrain from eating the flesh of living beings. I once borrowed an illustrated book on liberating life and abstaining from killing written by Great Master Lian Chi. After reading it, I resolved to always be a vegetarian. During the first three months of being vegetarian, I felt an immediate improvement in my blood circulation and an unprecedented amount of energy.

The Venerable Master emphasizes both the *Shurangama Sutra* and the Shurangama Mantra. The Dharma Masters in the monastery also encouraged cultivators to memorize the Shurangama Mantra, and so I memorized the Shurangama Mantra as well. I still remember the week I was almost done memorizing the mantra, I felt the dust falling away from my body layer after layer. The feeling of purity and lightness lasted for over a month.

This is how I came to study the Buddhadharma. I am an ordinary person who began without any understanding of the Buddhadharma or the law of cause and effect. When I was young, I was busy consolidating my livelihood; in my middle age, when my livelihood became somewhat settled, I started to investigate the puzzle of life. It started with a curiousity about psychic powers, and when the conditions ripened, I encountered the proper Dharma. I regret only that I didn't encounter it earlier. What could be more important than the questions of "Where do I come from? Where am I going after death?"? Each word of the Venerable Master's teachings is full of wisdom. To know how to leave suffering and attain bliss and how to end birth and death should be the main goal in our cultivation. I vow to follow the Venerable Master's teaching, overcome my bad habits and evil karma with determination, cultivate single-mindedly, and walk upon the proper path.

富貴五更春夢，功名一片浮雲；眼前骨肉已非真，恩愛反成仇恨。
莫把金枷套頸，休將玉鎖纏身；清心寡欲脫紅塵，快樂風光本分。

Wealth and honor are but a springtime dream at dawn.
Fame and position are a wisp of floating cloud.
The blood relations of the present are temporary.
Love and affection soon turn to hate.
Don't drape your neck with golden chains,
Or bind the body with shackles of jade.
With a pure mind and few desires, you can transcend the world.
The scenes of happiness are originally yours.

「果能，你已來晚了！」

"GUONENG, YOU'VE COME LATE!"

釋恆耐一九九五年七月三十日寫於萬佛聖城
Written by Shi Hengnai on July 30, 1995 at the Sagely City of Ten Thousand Buddhas

師父上人的圓寂，留給我的，除了深深的哀慟，便是無盡的感恩！

一九七九年的一天，是我第一次來到萬佛聖城。當時天氣非常寒冷，又是清晨，所以我就到房間睡覺休息。睡夢中，聽到上人對我說：「果能，你已來晚了！」我回答說：「未晚。」醒來之後，我不知道這個夢意味著什麼。直至上人圓寂的消息傳來，我才真正體會到，我真地來得太晚了！正當我現在渴求這位明眼善知識的教誨時，他卻走了……。所謂「人身難得，中國難生，佛法難聞，善知識難遇。」

以前，我並沒有真正意識到師父上人是一位不可多得的明眼善知識，以至於並不珍惜在師父身邊的寶貴機會，內心覺得自己是那樣地目光短淺，那樣地可悲！

阿彌陀佛

The Venerable Master has completed the stillness. Aside from being deeply grieved, I am filled with boundless gratitude!

One day in 1979, I came to the Sagely City of Ten Thousand Buddhas for the first time. The weather was very cold and it was very early in the morning, so I went to my room to sleep. In a dream, I heard the Venerable Master say to me, "Guoneng, you've come late!" I answered, "I'm not late." After waking up, I didn't know what the dream meant. Only when I heard the news of the Venerable Master's completion of stillness did I understand that I really had come too late! Right when I was seeking the teaching of this Bright-eyed Wise Advisor, he left... As it is said, "It is difficult to obtain a human body, difficult to be born in a central country, difficult to get to hear the Buddhadharma, and difficult to encounter a wise advisor."

I never really recognized that the Venerable Master was a one-of-a-kind Bright-eyed Wise Advisor before, and so I didn't cherish the precious opportunity I had to be near the Master. I was truly short-sighted and pitiful!

Amitabha Buddha

或現始修殊勝行　或現初生及出家
或現樹下成菩提　或為眾生示涅槃

——《大方廣佛華嚴經》〈初發心功德品〉

Perhaps he manifests to be beginning his cultivation
of the most supreme conducts.
Or maybe he manifests birth, or leaving home.
Or he manifests realizing Bodhi under the tree,
Or for the sake of living beings, he manifests entry into Nirvana.

—Chapter on "The Merit and Virtue from First Bringing Forth the Mind," the *Flower Adornment Sutra*

無能盡説佛功德

NO ONE COULD EVER FINISH PRAISING THE VIRTUES OF THE BUDDHA

釋恆日　Shi Hengri

無論是《宣化上人事蹟》，或是眾多弟子們對師父上人的描述文稿，弟子們對這位恩師的認識也只能說是「滄海一粟」。因為凡有體相的，都有限量，師父上人所作皆辦，一切所行無有形相，非凡夫肉眼能見到。師父上人是「菩薩再來，遊戲人間，華嚴境界，普度一切。」從上人十八大願中，我們可感覺到上人那種無私、無我、大同悲心不可思議的境界。被上人攝受營救的眾生，真有無量無邊，不可數不可說那麼多。其功德之大一如《華嚴經》所說：

> 剎塵心念可數知，大海之水可飲盡，
> 虛空可量風可繫，無能盡説佛功德。

師父上人本身就是一部《無字真經》，凡接觸過上人的人，皆依其根性不同而有所領悟，各有所獲，一切眾生同蒙法益。若有不識者，惟其業深重，若是毀謗者，更顯其愚昧，因果還自受。師父上人雖然走了，但他的法仍存在，一種無形的力量，在默默中加持、示法、教化著弟子們，相信每一個人都親身體會到那種不可思議的感受，各沾法益。大善知識選擇去留之時，所現之法必有其涵義存在。意義何在，那就依各人與上人之緣去剖解了。

接到上人圓寂消息時，是驚！是悲！是疑！總之，不希望（不敢相信）那是事實，猶存一絲希望上人是在三昧定中，再過兩天他老人家就會出定。直至消息正式公佈，知道事實已無可挽回，那種失去慈父的失落感令弟子欲哭無淚。回憶師父上人，弟子感慨萬分，覺有愧於恩師，未曾盡孝於他老人家……。

Even with the *Biography of the Venerable Master Hsuan Hua* and the essays on the Venerable Master written by his disciples, our recognition of our kind Teacher can only be considered a drop in the great ocean. This is because anything with form and appearance is limited. The Venerable Master has accomplished whatever he had to do. All his deeds are without form and appearance, not something that the eyes of ordinary people can perceive. The Venerable Master is "a Bodhisattva come again, roaming through the world in the Flower Adornment state, saving all living beings." From the Venerable Master's Eighteen Great Vows, we can sense his inconceivable state of selflessness and great compassion of oneness with all. The Venerable Master's salvation of living beings is truly limitless and boundless, unreckonable and ineffable. The immensity of his merit and virtue is described by this verse in the *Flower Adornment Sutra*:

> *You might count every thought, numerous as atoms in all lands;*
> *You might drink entirely the mighty oceans deep;*
> *You might measure all of space, or harness fast the wind;*
> *But no one could ever finish praising the virtues of the Buddha.*

The Venerable Master himself is a "Wordless True Sutra." All the people who come in contact with him gain insights and benefits according to their individual dispositions. All living beings share in the benefit of Dharma. If there are those who do not recognize him, it is because of their heavy karma. Those who slander him reveal their own stupidity and will have to undergo the retribution. Although the Venerable Master has departed, his Dharma is still here. There is an invisible force silently aiding us, revealing the Dharma and teaching us. I think each person has experienced this kind of inconceivable feeling and received the benefit of Dharma. When a Great Wise Advisor selects his time of going, the teaching he manifests is certain to contain profound meaning. As to where the meaning lies, each person must analyze it for himself based on his own conditions with the Venerable Master.

When I first heard the news of the Venerable Master's completion of stillness, I was shocked, sad, and doubtful. In general, I hoped it wasn't true. I had a thread of hope that the Venerable Master was in samadhi and would come out in a few days. When the official announcement was made, I knew that it was an undeniable fact. Feeling that I'd lost a kind father, I wanted to cry but the tears wouldn't come. Thinking of the Venerable Master, I was filled with melancholy. I felt remorseful to my kind teacher, feeling that I hadn't been filial to him...

When I beheld the Venerable Master, it immediately made me think of the visage of the Sixth Patriarch. I also heard my Dharma brothers

第一眼瞻仰師父上人時，心中剎那想起「六祖大師」真身面容，又聽聞師兄弟們個人之感觀，有人認為上人現的是「金剛身」，令弟子聯想起《金剛經》中一句四字名言：「一切有為法，如夢幻泡影，如露亦如電，應作如是觀」。以前讀過這部經典，但因我腦筋遲鈍，始終沒法領會經中般若深意。上人示現的種種幻化，使弟子深深體會到，世上一切有形、有相、有感覺之萬物，實如夢幻泡影無常，一眨眼間便消逝無跡。雖然上人已超凡入聖，又會神通妙用，且能代眾生苦，消災延壽，可是菩薩的化身也是虛幻的，免不了要受色身之壞苦。一切假相都是由眾生的業幻化出來的。所以善知識常常勸導我們要藉假修真，不要執著這個臭皮囊。

在末法時期能遇到師父上人，並蒙攝受出家，弟子慶幸一生沒白活，就算生命將盡，心願亦滿矣！沒料到師父上人早示涅槃，他老人家色身雖滅，但真身始終未曾捨離弟子們。更感恩於上人的慈悲，無時無刻不在轉法輪演說微妙法，給與弟子們安慰與鼓勵。弟子們慶幸能親睹大善知識現身說法，當永銘心中，畢生不忘。這一切因緣都不是那麼簡單巧合的，所謂百千萬劫難遭遇今已遇，若再不珍惜此生好好修行，等到三災來臨時，恐怕已來不及了。

師父上人以凡夫僧相示入涅槃，為的是啟示弟子們，苦不堪言的生老病死。猶如上人所說，人生真的好像就是在演戲一樣，生命是如此地脆弱短促，大家應該要趕緊用功修行，念念莫忘生死苦，心心想脫輪迴圈，三界火宅不宜久留。

> 恩師雖去其法長存，
> 師恩未報菩提不退，
> 盡未來際誓續師緣，
> 與師同行歸命虛空。

talking about their own impressions. Some people thought the Venerable Master was manifesting the Vajra body. This reminded me of the verse in the *Vajra Sutra* which says: "All conditioned dharmas / Are like dreams, illusions, bubbles, and shadows / Like dewdrops and lightning flashes. / One should contemplate them thus." I had read this Sutra before, but because I'm very dull, I never grasped the meaning of Prajna in the Sutra. The various transformations manifested by the Venerable Master made me realize that all of the physical and visible phenomena in the world are as fleeting as illusions, bubbles, and shadows. They vanish in the twinkling of an eye. Although the Venerable Master has already transcended the worldly plane and entered the state of a Sage, although he possesses the wonderful functioning of spiritual powers and can take the sufferings of living beings upon themselves, dispelling disasters and lengthening their lives, the transformation body of a Bodhisattva is also false and cannot avoid the suffering of physical decline. All false appearances are produced from the karma of living beings. Thus the Wise Advisor always exhorts us to use the false to cultivate the true and not to cling to this stinking bag of skin.

I rejoice that I haven't lived in vain, for I have met the Venerable Master and been permitted to leave home and become a nun in this Dharma-ending Age. Even if my life were to end now, my wishes have already been fulfilled! I didn't expect the Venerable Master to manifest Nirvana so soon. Although his physical body is gone, his true body has never left his disciples. I am also grateful for the Venerable Master's compassion. He is constantly turning the Dharma wheel and proclaiming the subtle and wonderful Dharma, comforting and encouraging his disciples. We rejoice that we have been able to see the Greatly Wise Advisor speaking the Dharma in person. We will always remember his teachings. It has not been easy for all these causes and conditions to come together. They are difficult to encounter in a hundred million eons, but we have encountered them. If we fail to cultivate diligently in this life, when the three disasters arrive, it will be too late.

The Venerable Master manifested as an ordinary monk entering Nirvana in order to teach living beings about the unspeakable suffering of birth, old age, sickness, and death. As the Master said, life is truly like a play. Life is just this fragile and fleeting. Everyone should hurry to apply effort in cultivation and not forget the suffering of birth and death for an instant. In every thought we should wish to escape the cycle of transmigration and not linger in the burning house of the Triple Realm.

Although our kind teacher has gone,
his Dharma will always remain.
Before we have repaid our Teacher's kindness,
we must not retreat from Bodhi.
To the ends of time, I vow to continue my affinities
with my Teacher
And return to empty space together with my Teacher.

THREE SONGS ABOUT THE VENERABLE MASTER
詠上人歌三首

Janice Vickers Storss (Guo Jin)

果進

Our Teacher's Guiding Light
Fall, 1977

We never in this wide wide world
Would have ever found the way,
But for our teacher's guiding light
Turning nighttime into day,
Turning nighttime into day.

He has given us his life and light,
He has given soul and breath
So that we may cultivate the Way
And transcend birth and death,
And transcend birth and death.

He has made a vow for living beings
So we all can go before,
That he would not go to Buddhahood
Till we reach the other shore,
Till we reach the other shore.

Like a Vajra Mountain, pure and clear,
With wisdom like the sea,
His body is the Dharma Realm,
He is comfortable and free,
He is comfortable and free.

We never in this wide, wide world
Would have ever found the way,
But for our teacher's guiding light
Turning nighttime into day,
Turning nighttime into day.

指路明燈　　　一九七七年秋作

在這個廣大的世界裡，
我們永遠找不到出路，
幸有上人為指路明燈，
將黑夜轉成白日，
將黑夜轉成白日。

他給了我們，他的生命和光，
他的靈魂和呼吸，
所以我們可以修道，
可以了生脫死，
可以了生脫死。

他為眾生發了願，
所以我們可以先他而行。
他誓不取正覺，
如果我們不到彼岸，
如果我們不到彼岸。

清淨如金剛山，
智慧如大海，
他的化身即法界，
自由又自在，
自由又自在。

在這個廣大的世界裡，
我們永遠找不到出路，
幸有上人為指路明燈，
將黑夜轉成白日，
將黑夜轉成白日。

Man of the Way
Spring, 1978

He can fly, he can fly
Like the clouds in the sky,
He can fly…

He put everything down
Like a rock upon the ground,
Put it down…

He can let it all pass
Like the wind in the grass,
Let it pass…

Cuz everything's OK,
Said the man of the Way,
Everything's OK ….

修道人
一九七八年春作

他能飛行，他能飛行，
一如流雲行空，
他能飛行……

他放下一切，
如石墜地，
放下一切……

他能讓一切飄然逝去，
如風過草際，
飄然逝去……

因爲怎樣都好。
這修道人説：
怎樣都好……

Gone
June, 1995

Out of this world
And into the sun,
Away from the many,
And one with the one

For us he was human
In our time and place;
In splendid perfection
Is revealed his real face.

Neither coming nor going
In the Dharma so right
A ray of the Buddha's
Own infinite light

He who came not
Seems to us to have gone.
Amitabha, Amitabha,
Amitabha lives on.

Amitabha, Amitabha,
Amitabha lives on.

逝
一九九五年六月作

從地球上消失，
回歸太陽，
從萬殊中離去，
與一本合一……

在我們的時空裡，
他爲我們示現人身，
在大圓滿之中，
他示現本來面目。

不去亦不來，
法爾如是，
他是佛本然的一線無盡光。

他好像走了，
其實他根本沒有來，
阿彌陀佛，阿彌陀佛，
常在的阿彌陀佛。

阿彌陀佛，阿彌陀佛，
常在的阿彌陀佛。

We disciples are deeply grieved because he's no longer here. We may be feeling bereft, like Dharma orphans. But when we finish our sadness we can take heart, because this magnificent man whom we all (dare I say) adored has left each of us with a vast inheritance. I am speaking of the treasures of the Bodhisattva Way, repeating the Sacred Names, taking and keeping Precepts, holding Mantras, learning the Sutras, and all the other principles and Dharma Doors he taught.

Knowing him turned our life-paths from downward spirals to upward ones; put our minds right-side-up; gave us profound peace and secure in the face of mortality. Time and again we saw him heal broken hearts and give hope and courage. He urged us on into a bright, infinite future, to share the wisdom of the Buddha-nature's inherent bliss with other creatures of the Dharma Realm. It's our good fortune to carry out his will. And this and more are ours, if we believe and continue on the Way.

Janice Vickers Storss (Gwo Jin)
July 1995

弟子們深感悲傷，因為上人不再住世了。我們頓失依怙，如同佛法中的孤兒。在我們的悲痛稍為遏止之時，或可在這位敬愛的偉人，所留給我們每一個人的廣大遺產之中，找到慰藉：如行菩薩道這個法寶、念佛號、受戒持戒、持咒、習教，還有無量無量他教我們的其他法門。

他將我們的生命，由下沉的漩渦中迴轉向上。將我們顛倒的心撥正，在面對死亡時，他使我們深得和諧與安全。一次又一次，他撫慰我們破碎的心，給我們希望和勇氣，激發我們向光明的前途前進，與法界一切眾生共享本具佛性之智慧，我們有幸能克紹上人遺業，努力前進。

果進
一九九五年七月

諸苦逼迫各相攻　聚集招感自不同
惟滅可證究竟樂　是道應修悟法空
三轉四諦法輪運　七覺八正意念勤
一旦貫通成聖果　偏眞有餘乃化城

宣公上人《般若波羅密多心經非台頌解》

Each of the sufferings exerts pressure, and all attack together,
Accumulating is feelings which beckon, each unlike the other.
Only through extinction can the ultimate joy be attained.
Therefore, this is the way that should be practiced
*　　to awaken to the emptiness of dharmas.*
Through three turnings of the Four Truths the Dharma-wheel revolves,
Seven shares in enlightenment, the eightfold upright Path,
*　　intention, mindfulness, and diligence.*
One day connect right through and ripen the fruit of sagehood,
Partial truth with residue is just a conjured city.

From the Venerable Master Hua's Verses without a Stand for the *Heart of Prajna Paramita Sutra*

盼了二十年，就差二十天

YEARNING FOR TWENTY YEARS, MISSING BY TWENTY DAYS

徐岱 Xu Dai

我總算還見了上人一面！

我來自大陸廣州，是早年國立中央大學校友。七十年代初，就已讀到有關上人：獨闖美國，弘揚佛法，近似鑑真大師的偉大壯舉。我開始日日夜夜思念上人和萬佛城，並盼望有一天能見到上人，親聆教誨。直到一九九五年六月二十八日，才得到赴美機會（應美國醫學學術交流會之請）。到洛杉磯一下飛機，我就打聽，卻驚悉上人已於六月八日圓寂了，盼了二十年，只差二十天，唉……！（臺灣一位師姐，找了兩年就找到了，真有福氣！）

總算沒白來美國一趟：在荼毗前舉行的法體告別儀式上，最後終於見到了上人！今天我又要隨團返回洛杉磯。臨別前，向總會和各位法師，表表我這位學佛四十年小螞蟻的願望：

（一）當願眾生都學好《楞嚴經》裡，觀音教導的耳根圓通法門，成就楞嚴大定（即上人所說「菩薩清涼月，常遊畢竟空」）。

（二）當願眾生都早日到達阿彌陀佛極樂世界（也就是上人十八大願中，「眾生不成佛，他不取正覺」之遺願）。

（三）當願世界早日變成常寂光淨土（華嚴偈頌「一切唯心造」，只要人人都念佛，淨土即在人間，即在眼前）。

At least I got to see the Venerable Master!

I am an alumnus of the National China Central University in Guangzhou, mainland China. As early as the 1970's, I read of the Venerable Master's lone journey to America to propagate the Buddhadharma, a feat similar to that of Dharma Master Jianzhen. I began to think of the Venerable Master and of the City of Ten Thousand Buddhas day and night. I hoped that one day I might meet the Venerable Master and hear his teachings in person. It was not until June 28, 1995, that I had an opportunity to go to America (at the invitation of the American Medical Academic Exchange Society). As soon as I got off the plane in Los Angeles, I made inquiries and was shocked to hear the Venerable Master had completed the stillness on June 8. After yearning for twenty years, I had missed by only twenty days. Ah! (A Dharma sister from Taiwan found the Venerable Master after only two years of searching—how lucky she is!)

Still, I didn't come to America in vain. During the farewell ceremony preceding the cremation, I finally got to see the Venerable Master! Today I have to go back to Los Angeles with my group. Before I leave, I'd like to share with the Dharma Masters some vows of this little ant who has studied Buddhism for forty years:

1. I vow that all living beings will learn the Dharma-door of perfect penetration through the ear that Guanyin Bodhisattva teaches in the *Shurangama Sutra* and realize the Great Shurangama Samadhi. (As the Venerable Master said, "The Bodhisattva is like the clear and cool moon, constantly travelling in ultimate space.")

2. I vow that living beings will soon reach Amitabha Buddha's Land of Ultimate Bliss (Among the Venerable Master's Eighteen Great Vows, this is his vow that if living beings have not become Buddhas, he will not attain the Right Enlightenment.)

3. I vow that the world will soon turn into the Pure Land of Eternal Stillness and Light. (A verse in the *Flower Adornment Sutra* says, "Everything is made from the mind alone." If everyone recites the Buddha's name, then the Pure Land is in the world, right in front of us.)

容恕我罪慈氏忍　　原諒他非大悲心　　平等願力精進行　　智慧禪定戒珠明

宣公上人作於一九八四年三月十日萬佛城

Forgive my offenses with kindly patience.
Pardon his wrongs with a greatly compassionate mind.
With vows of equality, advance vigorously.
With wisdom and samadhi, the precepts pearl is bright.

Composed by the Venerable Master Hua on March 10, 1984, at the City of Ten Thousand Buddhas

入道之門 —— 忍辱行

THE GATE LEADING TO THE WAY—THE PRACTICE OF PATIENCE

枯道人　Ku Dao Ren

在萬佛城與各分支道場之間來來去去、忙忙碌碌，及至長住萬佛城，如此幾年下來，所見所聞，真是令人讚歎，卻也有點兒感慨。讚歎是無窮盡的⋯⋯，感慨的則是：幾十年來，從世界各地，慕名的也好，修行的也好，縱使在城內住下的也一樣，仍然有許多人不能體會其殊勝何在？多少人在遇到第一關時，就拂袖而去；多少人隨風而飄；多少人跟著老師父跑來跑去，逐相而求。就算是好幾年了，這其中看不透的，也大有人在。佛法難起，真真是如此呵！

而師父雖已年邁，仍是不厭其煩，很有耐性地隨機而教化之。《地藏經》云：「若有善男子、善女人，於佛法中一念恭敬，我亦百千方便度脫是人，於生死中速得解脫。」只是芸芸眾生，其性剛強，雖調難伏，各有所執，師父又能等多久呢？自己若不能迴光返照，即便在師父旁邊轉一輩子，又如何呢？

學人皆知千經萬論，只為破執著、除妄想而已；四聖諦也好，六度萬行也好，慈心下氣也好，不發脾氣也好⋯⋯，說來說去都是一樣的，「方便有多門，歸元無二路。」然「理則頓悟，事須漸修」，這漸修最重要的，就是一層一層的忍辱關；能忍才能入道，能忍才能得到佛法的受用；所以經云：天上人間不管多大的力量，也不能夠勝過忍辱，一切布施、持戒所不能比。忍辱之人，有大力，乃能荷擔如來家業！

回想當年師父在大殿誦《地藏經》，就有人來考驗他，之前的虛雲老和尚，那更不用說了。記得師父曾問：如果有人罵長堤聖寺，或者罵師父，你們怎麼辦？標準答案：跟他磕三個頭。只是啊！聽歸聽，當事情在平常的生活中顯現時，不管是夫妻之間，家庭之間，或道場之間，就都忘了迴光返照。「一諍便生四相心

While coming and going at the City of Ten Thousand Buddhas, helping at the branch temples, and living at the City, what I've seen and heard over the past few years truly inspires my praise, but I'm also a bit dismayed. My praise is endless....What dismays me is that for several decades, people from around the world have been coming to the City, perhaps attracted by the name, perhaps to cultivate, or even to live in the City, but many still cannot understand how rare and supreme it is. How many have left in anger upon encountering the first barrier? How many have been drifting with the wind? How many have been following the Elder Master around, chasing after superficial images and seeking along the line? Even after spending many years in the City, many still do not understand. Truly, it is difficult for the Buddhadharma to arise!

Even though the Master is advanced in years, he still tirelessly teaches and transforms living beings according to their potentials. Just as it says in the *Earth Treasury Sutra*, "If good men and good women in the future have a single thought of respect toward the Buddhadharma, I shall use hundreds of thousands of expedient devices to save them so that they may quickly attain liberation from birth and death." The problem is that living beings are obstinate and difficult to subdue; each has his own attachments. How much longer can the Master wait? If we cannot return the light and reflect within, then even if we spend our whole lives near the Master, what use is it?

Learners know that the myriad sutras and shastras are meant to break attachment and eradicate false thoughts. Be it the Four Noble Truths, the Six Paramitas, kindness and humility, or not losing one's temper...they are all the same. "There are many expedient doors, but only one road back to the source." "One can enlighten suddenly to principles, but the actual practice is gradual." In gradual cultivation, most important are the tests of patience which come one after another. Only with patience can one enter the Way and benefit from the Buddhadharma. Thus, a sutra says, "In the heavens and human realm, there is no strength greater than patience; giving and holding precepts cannot compare with it. Patient people have great strength, and can shoulder the work of the Tathagata."

I recall the Master reciting the *Earth Treasury Sutra* in the Buddha Hall, and people coming to test him. The Venerable Hsü Yun who preceded the Master endured even more. I also remember the Master asking, "What would you do if someone were to scold your teacher or slander Long Beach Monastery?" The correct answer was: kowtow to him three times. Although we've been listening to the sutra lectures, when things happen in our daily lives, whether between spouses, family members, or Way-places, we forget to return the light and reflect within. "As soon as we contend, the four marks arise." "Whether you are right or not, you must recognize your own faults." "If you want to

」、「有理無理，須認自己錯」、「要學好，冤孽找」……一樣也用不上，更別談磕三個頭了。我們打坐、拜佛、誦經等，修了半天，結果連試題來了都不知道，這不是很遺憾嗎？一如師父所言：一切是考驗，看你怎麼辦，對境若不識，須再重頭煉！學佛學了半天做個學者，又有何用？試想，修行若無考驗，那究竟我們要修個什麼？心淨佛土淨，一切的境界，就是來讓我們觀照自己還有沒有貪瞋痴的種子。佛言：「慎勿與色會，色會即禍生。」誠然，學人若不能看透是非的表象，就很難契入法界的實相。君不見觀世音菩薩也曾化身面燃大士－－大鬼王，來度化阿難尊者，我們又怎知眼前找我麻煩的、罵我的、給我臉色看的不是菩薩示現？天龍護法來考驗我們的呢？或者冤親債主大化小來解冤結的呢？如果我們還像俗人一般論是、論非、講道理，那就失之交臂，枉費學佛一場了！

萬佛城之所以為萬佛聖城，不僅僅是我們所想的「應該」都很親切、很慈悲，都能以布施、利行、愛語、同事來攝受眾生；更進一步的，有著種種的逆增上緣來考驗我們，增長我們的道業；所謂龍蛇混雜，天龍八部大演戲法，諸佛菩薩神通妙用，又豈是我們肉眼所見、凡夫所識的表象而已？

正法在西方要建立起大法幢，是必須真修行人來共同紮根的。「忍辱有大力」，忍辱不能過，焉能入真道？捫心自問：怎麼一句話，一個臉色，都受不了？不是「本來無一物」嗎？怎麼盡是被識想、風動、幡動所迷惑呢？《證道歌》不也云：「觀惡言是功德，此則成吾善知識；不因訕謗起冤親，何表無生慈忍力。」所以，智者見其勝，恰似飲甘露，愚者自不識，此是妙中寶！能轉物即如來，說歸說，末學也是生活在大考、小考中，戰戰兢兢，只是眼見仍有許多人，不明究理，為表象所惑，忘失菩提，乃至徒增口業，故略陳管見。但願來萬佛聖城的諸位學人，常存一切無求的忍辱心，不為境界所轉，保證「透得此門，出塵羅漢。」

be good, all your creditors show up..." We can't apply any of these, let alone kowtow three times. We meditate, bow to the Buddha, recite sutras, and cultivate for a long time, yet we don't recognize problems when they come. Isn't it pathetic? As the Master says, "Everything is a test to see what you will do. If you don't recognize what's before you, you'll have to start anew." If we just study Buddhism for a long time and become scholars, what use is that? Just think: if there were no tests in our cultivation, what would we be cultivating for? When the mind is pure, the Buddhaland is pure. All states are opportunities for us to reflect within to see if we still have the seeds of greed, anger, and stupidity. The Buddha said, "Be cautious not to associate with lust. When one associates with lust, calamities arise." Truly, if learners cannot see through the superficialities of right and wrong, it's hard to tally with the reality of the Dharma Realm. Don't you know that Guanyin Bodhisattva manifested as the Great Ghost King Burning Face to save the Venerable Ananda? How do we know that the people who trouble us, scold us, and give us nasty looks are not manifestations of Bodhisattvas or Dharma-protecting gods and dragons coming to test us, or our grieving relatives and creditors making big issues small and untying knots of past hatred? If we still act like ordinary people, arguing about rights and wrongs, then we're missing the point, and learning Buddhism in vain.

The City of Ten Thousand Buddhas is the way it is, not just how we think it "should be"—warm, compassionate, and gathering in living beings with charity, beneficial conduct, kind words, and working together. Going a step further, it has various adverse conditions to test us so that we will advance in our cultivation. The dragons and snakes mingle; the gods, dragons and the rest of the Eight Divisions put on a great show; and the Buddhas and Bodhisattvas use the wonderful functioning of spiritual penetrations. How could it only be the appearances which ordinary people see with their ordinary eyes?

To raise the great banner of proper Dharma in the West, true cultivators must lay the groundwork together. Patience is a great strength. Without patience, how can we enter the true Way? Let's ask ourselves: why can't we bear a few words or a nasty look? Isn't it true that, "Originally, there's not a single thing"? Then why are we deluded by our conscious thoughts, by the movement of the wind and flag? The *Song of Enlightenment* says, "Contemplate vicious words as merit and virtue, and they become one's good advisors. Do not let abuse and slander arouse enmity or liking. How else can the power of compassion and patience with non-production be manifest?" The wise see what is supreme as if drinking sweet dew, while the dull don't recognize the treasure within the wonderful! If one can turn things around, then one is just the Tathagata. However, words are still words. I, the last to learn, have also been gingerly going through big and small tests, but I see many who don't understand the principle and are deluded by appearances, thus losing their Bodhi resolve and increasing their mouth karma. Therefore, I've expressed my limited views, hoping that all learners who come to the City can be patient, seek nothing, and not be fooled by states. Then it is guaranteed that, "If one can get through this gate, one will become an Arhat who transcends the world."

迷時師度

WHEN CONFUSED, WE NEED A TEACHER TO RESCUE US

萬佛聖城育良小學、培德中學男校校長　顏亞日

Agis Gan, Principal of Developing Virtue Secondary and Instilling Goodness Elementary Boys Schools,
The Sagely City of Ten Thousand Buddhas

　　每一個人的人生旅途是不一樣的。但生命是寶貴的。這是因為「人身難得」。對我來說，更難得的是有緣遇到佛法，在茫茫的人海中遇到了宣公上人。上人常說，他是一隻「小螞蟻」。我想這句話的意義很深。有誰能知道世界上有多少螞蟻？而在螞蟻中，要找到你所尋找的那隻「小螞蟻」，真是難之又難。若不是往昔所種下的因緣，又怎能互相碰面？這就是所謂的命中註定吧？

　　遇到上人以後，我的一生起了很大的變化。心路歷程經受了一次又一次的考驗，掙扎及衝擊。生命是頑強的，心靈是冥頑的。過去做過什麼我不知道？來世將會怎樣更不清楚？今生應該怎樣做則茫然，這是多麼地危險！所以「迷時師度」此時顯得非常重要。就這樣，那種無形的力量，一步一步引導我來到了萬佛城。事情是怎樣開始的呢？這也算是感應吧！

　　我本名叫顏亞日。法名果日。一九五一年生於馬來西亞。我母親懷我時曾想墮胎。但我命不該絕，懷胎十個月，生下了「我」。小時多病，貪生怕死，有時聽到天災人禍之事，晚上必定做惡夢，半夜醒來找媽媽。家境貧困，我是家中唯一幸運讀上大學的人。一九七六年，我在馬來西亞大學物理學（教育）系畢業後，到離開家鄉四百里外的地方當中學教師。在那段時間，我不知什麼是佛法，卻對回教（伊斯蘭教）很敬佩，因為他們教理強調清淨。我的學生百分之九十八是回教徒，我羨慕他們有所皈依。

　　一九八二年，我開始接觸佛法，隨緣皈依會緣法師。當年我的大女兒出世不久，每到黃昏必大哭不止。岳母認為其中必有原因，要我夫婦把家中的「四面佛」送到佛教會開光。當天是佛誕日。會緣法師問我皈依沒有？我問什麼

Everyone is travelling the same path of life. Each person's life is precious because "the human body is hard to obtain." And I have been even luckier in that I have encountered the Buddhadharma, and moreover, among the multitudes of people, I have met the Venerable Master Hua. The Master often says that he is a tiny ant. To me, this statement carries deep meaning. Who could count all the ants in this world? And how extremely difficult it would be to find this one particular tiny ant among all those ants. If it were not for conditions developed in the past, how could I have met him? It must have been fate.

After meeting the Venerable Master, my life underwent a great change. My heart and soul underwent repeated tests and I was troubled by inner struggle and conflict. Life is full of perversity, and the mind is very stubborn. What a dangerous situation we are in, not knowing what we did in previous lives, not knowing what will happen in lives to come, and not knowing what we should be doing in this life. It is of utmost importance that we have a teacher to guide and rescue us when we are thus confused. And that is why an invisible force has guided me step by step to the City of Ten Thousand Buddhas. How did it all begin? Could this be a response?

My name is Agis Gan, and my Dharma name is Guo Ri. I was born in 1951 in Malaysia. When my mother conceived me, she considered getting an abortion. But it was not time for me to die, and so after a ten-month pregnancy, I was born. I was afflicted with many illnesses in childhood and was always scared of dying. Whenever I heard people talking about disasters or accidents, I would always wake up from nightmares in the middle of the night and seek my mother's protection. My family was poor, and I was the only one who was fortunate enough to be able to study at a university. I graduated from the Department of Physics Education at the University of Malaysia in 1976 and later became a teacher at a high school that was four hundred miles from my hometown. During that time, I didn't know anything about the Buddhadharma, but I respected and admired Islam, which emphasizes purity. Ninety-eight percent of my students were Muslims, and I envied them for having a belief to rely upon.

In 1982 I began to have contact with Buddhism, and I took refuge with Dharma Master Hui Yuan. At that time my first daughter had just been born, and she would usually cry nonstop at dusk every day. My mother-in-law thought there had to be a reason behind this and suggested that my wife and I send our four-faced Buddha image to the Buddhist association to have an initiation ceremony performed on it. The day we went happened to be the Buddha's birthday, and Dharma Master Hui Yuan asked me if I had taken refuge. I asked him what

是皈依？什麼是三寶？法師說：「若只拜佛像，不皈依三寶只能是佛教的同情者。」我為之震驚。於是，在內人向信徒們問明事理後，我偕同內人一起皈依。

同事黃礦光居士見我心誠，介紹我認識了楊果新居士。得知師父上人在美國成立了萬佛聖城，及師父的出家弟子完成三步一拜的壯舉。因此心生仰慕，借了《度輪禪師事蹟》閱讀。讀完之後，感嘆自己為窮教師，沒有能力到美國萬佛聖城一遊。

一九八三年，我搬遷到雪蘭莪州加影埠執教。當時想，見不到上人，先向他求皈依也無妨。於是寫信向師父求授皈依。出乎所料之外，師父竟然答應了，並指示我與妻子，早晚在佛前拜願兩個鐘頭，師父將在聖城為我二人授三皈依。當天正好是本師釋迦牟尼佛聖誕日。

一九八五年，妻子鼓勵我移居聖城，協助師父為佛教出力。我於是寫了一封信給師父，師父回答說：「機緣成熟時，水到渠成。」所以當時便暫時放棄這個打算。過後不久，達摩難陀上座尋找自願者到獄中傳教。我與內人都接受了這項工作。因為心中不安，所以去信向師父上人請示。師父開示說：「正人說邪法，邪法也正；邪人說正法，正法也邪。」因此，便安心的工作了兩年左右。

一九八六年，內人發心想到聖城參加萬佛寶懺法會。當時手上儲蓄不足，心中非常難過，不過還是讓她先報名。到要出發的時日，儲蓄竟然正好湊足，結果成行。在法會期間，內人體驗了聖城的清淨生活及高尚的道風。同時也有諸多感應，有留連忘返之意。臨走時向觀世音菩薩求願，讓我明年有機會到聖城一趟。回馬來西亞以後，內人念念不忘聖城，期望將來能到聖城來。我心中卻不以為然，認為她能有機緣出國到美國去，已算是幸運了。來年的機會如何先別夢想。豈料第二年，我真的也到聖城來了。

一九八七年，在師父的邀請下，我專程來聖城參加了水陸空大法會及世界宗教會議。在飛機上，半睡半醒中，彷彿看見了師父上機迎接我們，身邊還跟了一位年輕不知法號的比丘。到聖城後，發現聖城真有此比丘。遇到師父時心想，師父的弟子不計其數，不知師父記得我

taking refuge meant and what the Triple Jewel was. He answered, "If you bow to the Buddhas, but fail to take refuge with the Triple Jewel, you can only be considered a Buddhist sympathizer." I was astonished, and so, after my wife and I asked about the details of the matter, we both took refuge with Dharma Master Hui Yuan.

My colleague, Upasaka Huang Shiguang, seeing my sincerity, introduced me to another layman, Michael (Guoxin) Yang. From him I learned that the Venerable Master had founded the City of Ten Thousand Buddhas in the United States, and that his disciples had just completed a pilgrimage of prostrating themselves every three steps. Full of admiration, I borrowed a copy of the book *The Records of the Life of Dhyana Master To Lun*. After reading it, I lamented that I was only a poor teacher who did not have the resources to make a trip to the City of Ten Thousand Buddhas in America.

In 1983, I moved to Kang, Selangor, and took a teaching post in the school there. At that point, I reasoned that since I wasn't able to meet the Venerable Master, I could at least first request to take refuge with him. I wrote a letter to the Master requesting to take refuge, and to my complete surprise, the Master agreed and also instructed my wife and me to bow to the Buddhas for two hours each day, in the morning and evening. The Master also told us he would let us take refuge at the City of Ten Thousand Buddhas. The day we took refuge was Shakyamuni Buddha's birthday.

In 1985, my wife encouraged me to move to the City and help the Master by doing some work for Buddhism. So I wrote a letter to the Master and received the Master's reply: "When the conditions are ripe, the matter will take care of itself." Therefore I temporarily set this matter aside. Afterwards, Dr. K. Sri Dhammananda Mahathera was looking for volunteers to preach in jail. My wife and I agreed to take on this job, but we felt a bit uneasy, so we wrote a letter requesting advice from the Master. The Master instructed, "When an upright person speaks deviant dharma, the deviant dharma becomes proper; when a deviant person speaks the proper Dharma, the proper Dharma becomes deviant." Our minds were set at ease and we worked for about two years.

In 1986, my wife brought forth the resolve to attend the Ten Thousand Buddhas' Jewelled Repentance Ceremony. At that time I felt very bad because I didn't have enough savings, but I still told her to go ahead and register first. By the day she was to leave, I had saved up enough for her to make the trip. During the repentance session, she experienced the pure life and lofty practices of the City, as well as many responses, and consequently she didn't feel like returning to Malaysia. Right before she left the City, she prayed to Guanyin Bodhisattva to give me a chance to come to the City in the following year. After she returned to Malaysia, she could not forget the City and wished to come back. I didn't have the same hope, for I thought she was already lucky enough to go to the United States that year and there was no need to dream about getting another chance in years to come. I never expected that I would also come to the City the following year.

In 1987, upon the Master's invitation, I made a special trip to attend the Water, Land, and Air Dharma Assembly and the World Religions Conference. On the plane, when I was half-asleep, I saw the Master board the plane and welcome us. There was another monk,

否？更何況未曾與師父見面。當時向師父介紹說：「我是亞日，馬來西亞來的。」師父說：「你姓顏，是不是？」使我驚喜萬分。在聖城期間，我問師父：「我能為聖城做什麼？」師父回答說：「不要只為聖城，應該為佛教做事。」再問師父能做什麼，師父回答說：「拔草。」後來又問：「我的妻兒怎麼辦？」師父答道：「我也不知道。」

回到馬來西亞後，我的學生們看到水陸空法會的照片，都讚嘆不已。也有佛學會的學生，向聖城索請經書，喜愛閱讀。有一位同學畢業後竟然發心，到臺灣「正法佛學院」修學佛法。她現在已出家，在萬佛聖城跟師父上人做弘法利生的工作。

一九八八年十一月，師父又來馬來西亞弘揚正法。留下恆蘇師在馬來西亞辦理法務。有人建議應該在馬來西亞找尋一塊土地，若有固定道場的話，師父來弘法也方便。當時楊果新居士向內人談起時，內人忽然想起曾夢見師父說，在附近的「武來岸」有道場，而且將在此弘法。便和楊果新居士一起去視察，果然有人要出售一塊山地。楊果新之兄便發心把地買下來，後來上人改名為「如來岸」。不久，恆蘇師應邀，到舍下為大眾說法，來聽法者有七十多人。當晚法師離去，我法喜充滿的入眠。在夢中，竟然看見韋馱尊天菩薩現身：先是來到一所古廟，韋馱菩薩的身像已被塵封。菩薩的手先發紅光，接著全身塵脫而現出雄偉的將軍像。菩薩要我先喝一碗清水，然後從我雙脅下一撐，便把我帶到虛空中去。菩薩要我上下前後左右觀看，我看見四面八方都是無盡的虛空，頭頂腳下有各種世間看不到的朵朵彩雲。前方更有白雲顯現的清晰龍頭。我心中不解，便回頭看韋馱菩薩，此時菩薩竟然不知所去。我又回到了古廟。

此後，我對師父弘法的工作更加有信心。一九九二年四月，法界佛教訪問團又來馬來西亞，此次舉辦萬佛寶懺。我便發心請假協助工作，為期三個星期。後來吉隆坡的道場也搬遷到現在的紫雲洞。八月間，紫雲洞組織訪問團到聖城參加第二次水陸空大法會。內人又想參加。我說我們那間小屋子已賣了，如果你想去，不如四個孩子也一起帶去，讓他們有機會到萬

whose Dharma name I didn't know, standing beside the Master. After I arrived at the City, I discovered that the Bhikshu in my dream really existed. When I saw the Master, I thought to myself: "The Master has countless disciples; I wonder if he will remember who I am, especially since we have never met." Then I started introducing myself to the Master, saying, "My name is Agis, and I came from Malaysia." The Master said, "Your last name is Gan, right?" I was utterly astonished and delighted. During my stay in the City, I asked the Master, "What can I do for the City?" The Master replied, "Don't work only for the City; work for Buddhism." When I asked again what particular work I could do, the Master said, "Pull weeds." "How about my wife and children?" I asked. The Master replied, "I don't know, either!"

After I went back to Malaysia, I showed pictures of the Water, Land, and Air Dharma Assembly to my students, who praised it greatly. Some of the students in the Buddhist Association also ordered Sutras and books from the City. One of my students, after graduating from school, brought forth the resolve to study the Buddhadharma at the Proper Dharma Buddhist Academy in Taiwan. She has already left the home-life at the City and is now working to propagate the Dharma to benefit living beings.

In November, 1988, the Master again went to Malaysia to propagate the proper Dharma. Later he assigned Dharma Master Heng Su to stay in Malaysia to manage the Buddhist affairs. Some people suggested that we look for some land and establish a Way-place in Malaysia so that it would be convenient for the Master to go and propagate the Dharma. When Upasaka Yang Guoxin mentioned this project to my wife, she suddenly recalled a dream she had in which the Master had a Way-place in nearby Broaga and was propagating the Dharma there. She and Upasaka Yang went to look at the land there; unexpectedly, it was up for sale, so Upasaka Yang's brother bought it. Not long after that, we invited Dharma Master Heng Su to my place to give a lecture, which more than seventy people attended. After he left, I was filled with the joy of the Dharma and went to sleep. That night, Wei Tou Bodhisattva appeared in my dream: At first, I was in an old temple and Wei Tou Bodhisattva's image was covered with dust; then his hand began to emit red light and gradually, the dust fell away from his body and he appeared as a majestic general. The Bodhisattva first wanted me to drink a bowl of clean water; then he grasped me under both armpits and lifted me into the air. The Bodhisattva wanted me to look around. I saw endless space in all directions; under my feet and over my head were colorful clouds never seen before in the world; in front of me was a dragon's head appearing within the white cloud. As I was puzzling over all of this, I turned my head to look for the Bodhisattva, but he had already disappeared. Then I returned to the old temple again.

From then on, I brought forth deeper faith in the Master's work of propagating the Dharma. In April of 1992, another delegation from Dharma Realm Buddhist Association came to Malaysia and held a Ten Thousand Buddhas' Jewelled Repentance Ceremony. I requested a leave of absence from work and worked as a volunteer during the three weeks of the ceremony. After the ceremony, the temple in the Kuala Lumpur moved to Tze Yun Tung Temple. In August, a group from Tze Yun Tung Temple went to the City of Ten Thousand Buddhas to attend the second Water, Land, and Air Dharma Assembly.

城一遊，旅費也沒有問題。當時我們所憂愁
的是：一個大人帶著四個孩子，簽證那天，我
們帶著戰戰兢兢的心情到美國大使館去，大使
館人員竟然和顏悅色地批准了。

到了聖城，孩子竟然非常喜歡，而且申請留
下在中小學讀書。我在馬來西亞收到信後，緊
張起來，孩子的讀書費用怎辦？後來又想，如
果能在聖城讀上二、三年，費用沒有了再回來
也沒關係。因此，便在十一月假期間到聖城探
望他們。法師建議我辭去教職，到聖城當義務
老師。內人也說師父答應我到聖城教書。因此
，我便申請為法界佛教大學的學生，可以一面
學佛法，一面教書。

一九九三年二月，法大的入學通知函來了，
我心中開始掙扎。去還是不去？去的話，要先
辭去穩定的工作，奔向一個還不知會怎樣的前
程，而且是一家六口，非常難做出決定。不去
的話，我又不願意讓孩子及自己失去親近佛法
的機會。做出決定後，另一個矛盾又出現了，
辭職需要六個月，而學生簽證要在出發前兩個
月內才能申請。萬一辭職了，學生簽證又不批
准，兩頭都落空了怎麼辦？到時工作沒有了，
去聖城又不成行，那怎麼好呢？後來還是下定
決心，把辭職信交上。如此東奔西跑了六個月
，先收到批准辭職的信，然後學生簽證也批准
了。一時才放下心中的那塊石頭。那個時候內
人已從聖城回到馬來西亞，我們便急忙的把家
中可賣可送的東西都賣送出去，一起帶著最小
的女兒，來到了萬佛聖城。

聖城的一切，是那麼的熟悉。麒麟精舍的後
面，竟然是我以前在水陸空法會中夢見過的松
樹林。我夢見過一行行的比丘站滿松樹林，黃
又橙色袈裟，非常莊嚴，他們正在向前方走去
。而我現在正好就住在麒麟精舍。

現在，我的感受更多了。師父上人是多麼的
慈悲偉大，他為佛法肩負各種重擔而不言倦。
整個佛教事業，是靠他自己以硬骨頭支撐、建
立起來的。信徒給他的協助，並不足以把整個
事業建立起來。以前的高僧大德，依靠皇帝建
立道場、翻譯經典。美國的社會，哪來的皇帝
？哪來那麼多的供養？而現在眾多出家及在家
弟子，為了佛教事業，放棄了有收入的工作。
這麼多的道場，怎樣維持？師父上人除了弘法

My wife again wanted to go with them. I said that since we had sold our small house, the travelling expenses would not be a problem and she might as well take the four kids and give them a chance to visit the City. Our only worry was getting the visas for an adult with four children. We were a bit apprehensive going to the U.S. Embassy, but the officer was very agreeable and granted the visas.

When they arrived at the City, my children liked it very much and applied to stay and attend elementary and secondary school there. When I received their letter back in Malaysia, I worried about their tuition, but then thought: Perhaps they can study at the City for two or three years until the money runs out and then return to Malaysia. I went to visit them in November that year. Some Dharma Masters suggested that I resign from my job and become a volunteer teacher in the school at the City. My wife also told me that the Master had agreed that I could teach in the school. Therefore I applied to become a student at the Dharma Realm Buddhist University (DRBU), so that I could study the Buddhadharma at the same time that I taught in the school at the City.

In February of 1993, DRBU sent me a letter of acceptance and I started to debate whether or not to go. If I went, I would have to quit my job and go to place with an unknown future; besides, not only I, but my family—all six of us—faced the same problem. It was very hard for me to make a decision. If I didn't go, I didn't want them and myself to miss the chance to draw near to the Buddhadharma. After I made up my mind to quit my job, another problem came up: I had to send in my resignation six months in advance, but I could only apply for a student visa two months before I planned to leave the country. What if I quit my job and then my visa application was rejected? What would I do if I had no work and yet couldn't go to the City? In the end, I still decided to hand in my resignation. In this way, I was busy running here and there for six months. First I received a letter approving my resignation, and later my student visa was also approved. Only then was I able to heave a sigh of relief. My wife also returned from the City, so we hurriedly sold whatever could be sold, gave away the things that could be given, and came to the City with our youngest daughter.

Everything in the City seems so familiar to me. The view behind Unicorn House is exactly the same view of the pine forest that I'd seen in my dream when I attended the Water, Land, and Air Dharma Assembly. I also dreamed that many Bhikshus were walking in single file through the forest, wearing their yellow-orange sashes and looking very adorned. And now I was actually living in Unicorn House.

After all this, I found out more things. The Venerable Master is so compassionate and magnanimous. For the sake of the Buddhadharma, he undertakes all kinds of hardship and never once complains of weariness. It is because of his incorruptible character and moral fortitude that the entire range of Buddhist activities has been established. Even all the help provided by his disciples is not enough to set up all the activities of Buddhism. In ancient China, the emperors built Way-places for high monks to carry out the translation of Sutras, but nowadays in America, where can you find such an emperor? Where can you find a multitude of disciples to make offerings? How can we maintain so many Way-places, where so many left-home people and laypeople devote themselves to working for Buddhism without any income? Aside from making possible the propagation of Dharma and the translation of Sutras, the Venerable Master must also worry about and devote his efforts to

及翻譯經典的工作之外，也要為佛教事業的經費而操心，這不是一般人能做到的。

　　法界佛教總會需要更多的人發心出錢出力。已發心的人更應該團結一致，群策群力，使組織結構更加完善。並為這個機構打下一個穩定的經濟基礎。在師父上人的領導下，制定出一個長遠的目標與規劃。為確保將來佛教的發展，建立起穩定的基礎，為正法佛教開拓一個光明的前程。

paying for the expenses of Buddhist activities. This is not a job that an ordinary person would be able to do well.

Dharma Realm Buddhist Association needs more people to contribute their strength and money. Those people who have already come forth to help should unite and work together to establish a better system for our organization and give our organization a stable financial basis. Under the Venerable Master's leadership, we should make longterm plans and goals to establish a solid foundation for the future development of Buddhism and open the way to a bright future for the proper Dharma.

佛力無量此亦然　譬如虛空無有邊
爲令眾生得解脫　億劫勤修而不倦

隨順涅槃寂滅法　住於無諍無所依
心如實際無與等　專向菩提永不退

——《大方廣佛華嚴經》〈初發心功德品〉

The Buddha's power is limitless, and his is the same way;
Just like space, it has no boundaries.
In order to cause living beings to obtain liberation,
For a million kalpas he diligently cultivates,
Yet does not become weary.

He goes along with the still extinct Dharma of Nirvana,
Dwelling without striving and without any reliance.
His mind, like ultimate reality, is unequaled.
He only goes towards Bodhi without ever retreating.

Chapter on The Merit and Virtue from First Bringing Forth the Mind, the *Flower Adornment Sutra*

MY EXPERIENCES
WITH THE VENERABLE MASTER
我與上人的一段緣

Susan Mechling
麥蘇珊

My first experience with the Master was when I came to Sutter Street to rent a room. I had heard there was a Buddhist monk there who kept everything peaceful and quiet, and although I wasn't a Buddhist, that was just the sort of environment I wanted for my work—drawing and painting. After meeting him, I told him I wanted to rent a room and he showed me a very dilapidated room on the third floor that was too big, too dark, and kind of moldy. Because it was too high in price, being $20 over my limit, I reluctantly said I couldn't rent it. Then we went down to the second floor where he showed me a smaller room that had perfect natural lighting, was freshly painted, had an easel in the corner and newly varnished floors. I was immediately set on it and asked the price, which was $5 over my limit. Even so, I said, "I'll take it." Then he asked me, "Are you a student?" I said, "No." He said, "You are a student. I like students," and then quoted me a price $5 lower.

Later, after becoming his disciple or "student," I found out that "the Abbot," as we knew him, had planned to rent out rooms on that floor to "students of Buddhism." Another thing I found out much later (after marrying my husband, Nick, who was my next-door-neighbor on the floor) was that Nick had painted the room and cleaned it when he rented that room and the one next door, then had closed it off and given it back to the Abbot to rent out to a potential "student." Nick had also added the easel.

Before marrying Nick, one day as I was working concentratedly on a drawing of a very fancy doorknob in my room with the door open, all of a sudden I noticed that the Abbot was there watching me draw. A few seconds later, he said, "What are you doing?" I said, "I'm drawing this doorknob," and added, "It's not easy for me to do this." He then said, with emphasis, "Work hard!" and left the room abruptly. I've never forgotten that moment and try to keep it in mind. He wanted me to remember how I was concentrating and try to work hard.

Another time, I was putting something in the trash in the kitchen, and the Abbot came up, took a half-gallon milk carton out of the trash, stepped on it with his foot until it was flat, and then replaced it in the trash, indicating that's what should be done. Usually, he didn't interfere in anyone's business, but might walk through at any time of the day, catching one in a moment of living.

Nick and I were married by the Abbot at the Buddhist Lecture

和師父的第一次接觸，是我去薩特街租房子。雖然我並非佛教徒，卻喜歡安靜的地方以方便我作畫。聽說有位佛教和尚有平安寧靜的房子分租，就去見這位和尚。問明來意之後，師父帶我到三樓一間對我來說太大、太暗又很破舊，有點霉味的房間。由於價錢太高，比預算多了二十元，於是我只好很不情願的表示租不起。於是師父又帶我到二樓一間剛油漆過，又換了新塑膠地板，光線充足大小適中的房間。屋角居然還有個畫架，價錢雖然比預算多了五塊錢，我馬上就說：「我租了。」師父問我：「妳是個學生嗎？」我答：「不。」他說：「妳是個學生，我歡喜學生。」然後主動降價五塊錢。

等我皈依師父後，才知道這位方丈（那時我們這樣稱呼師父）是要把這些房間，租給學習佛法的學生。和尼克結婚後才知道，原來尼克把兩間住房（尼克住我隔壁）都租下來，油漆粉刷之後，還給師父一間，讓師父可多收個學生，畫架也是他加進去的。

在舉行婚禮之前，有一天我正開著門，聚精會神的畫著一個很別緻的門把。突然間，發覺師父正看著我畫畫，看了一會後，師父問：「妳在做什麼？」我說：「我在畫這個門把。」馬上又補充一句：「這門把很不好畫。」師父很慎重地說：「要努力！」就離開了。我永遠忘不了那一刻的感覺，師父是要我記得當時那種專心致志用功的境界。

又有一次是我到廚房倒垃圾，師父走過來，從垃圾桶裡拿出一個裝牛奶的空紙盒，用腳踩平後，再丟回垃圾箱。表示要這樣來處理垃圾。師父平常是不會過問任何人的事情的，但偶爾會在日用平常中觀察弟子。

我和尼克的婚禮是在佛教講堂內舉行的。尼克認識師父兩年了，師父是他在這個世界上最尊敬的人

Hall on Sutter Street. Nick decided that he wanted the Abbot to marry us because he had known him for about two years and respected him more than anyone else he knew. I was not sure what it would be like so we decided only to invite those who lived in the building. After asking the Abbot when the ceremony would be, we notified all our friends in the building of the appointed time (2 p.m. on September 15, 1966). We were told to be ready earlier, as the Abbot wanted to talk with us around noon. I was wearing a white dress and had a bouquet of flowers, but since it was just for an informal few minutes, I left my heels upstairs (since one never wore shoes in the Lecture Hall).

We were asked to bow, and I placed my bouquet in a vase on the altar as an offering. Next, the assembly, in Chinese black and brown robes, started reciting in Chinese and bowing. We bowed with them and then knelt. This kneeling continued for about half an hour, but it seemed longer, since I didn't understnd the words and wasn't used to kneeling. The sound of the knocker and bells and chanting was very compelling, though, and I maintained an erect posture until the end of the ceremony (which I later found out was the Eighty-Eight Buddha's Repentance Ceremony)

The Abbot then asked us to come up before the assembly, facing them on either side of him. He began to ask us some questions. He asked me, "Susan, do you love Nick?" I needed to really consider becuse somehow a shallow answer wouldn't do. It had to be the "whole truth" as in court. After a moment of consideration, I said, "Yes." Next, he asked me, "Will you love him tomorrow the same as you do today?" I answered "Yes" again after another moment of thought. He asked Nick the same two questions which he also answered affirmatively. Then we were married. The Abbot then gave us a few words of positive predictions for the future, and then some of the Chinese laypeople offered speeches of congratulations in Chinese, which were then translated into English.

I was glad that the wedding had already taken place because in the quiet of the temple with only the anonymous laypeople and the Abbot, I had been able to really concentrate well on answering the Abbot's two questions. The ceremony and our own words made a very strong impression on me and I never forgot them. They have influenced the entire course of my marriage to Nick (now at the 28-year point).

After continuing to live in the building for about a year, we moved around the time the Abbot sold it. After the Abbot moved away, it seemed as though his protection was no longer over the building, and it was no longer peaceful or wholesome. Later we went to listen to lectures at the building where the Abbot had moved to on Waverly Street.

In 1967, Ron Epstein, who had left for Taiwan for a year to study Chinese around the time we married and who later earned a Master's degree at the University of Washington, returned to San Francisco with some friends from U.W. to introduce them to the Abbot. Mostly American students of Chinese, many of them had taken courses in Buddhist philosophy as well, so this was their chance to meet a real Buddhist monk who, moreover, lectured on the Buddhist sutras. They all came to the temple and visited for a week or two, during which time, we had ceremonies, meditation and lectures.

In the summer of 1968, at the request of Ron and his friends, the Abbot began a lecture series on the *Shurangama Sutra*. The hours

，所以他請師父為我們證婚。這次的婚禮，我們只邀請了同屋居住的人。遵照師父的指示，婚禮時間是一九六六年九月十五日下午兩點，並通知了所有的來賓。師父要人通知我倆中午十二點去見他，他有話要告訴我們。我以為只是去和師父說幾句話，就穿了一件白色的洋裝，拿了一束花，赤著腳就去了（通常我們在講堂裡是赤腳）。

師父叫我們兩個先拜佛，我就把那束花插在供佛案上的花瓶裡供佛。然後一些穿海青的中國人，用中文唱誦及拜佛。我們隨他們一起拜，拜完後，大家就跪在那兒。我們在前面也跟著跪，由於我不瞭解佛教的結婚儀式，加上不懂中文，也不習慣跪著，雖然只有半個鐘頭左右，就好像跪了好久似的。雖然很不習慣聽法器的敲打聲及唱誦，但我仍然一動不動跪在那兒，直到儀式結束（後來才知道是〈八十八佛懺悔文〉）。

師父要我們站在大眾的前面。他問我：「蘇珊，你愛不愛尼克？」我有一種被審問的感覺，想了一會才謹慎地回答：「是的。」接著，他又問：「明天你是否也能像現在這麼愛他？」我又想了一會才肯定說：「是的。」師父也問了尼克同樣的問題，尼克也很堅定地說：「是的。」禮畢，我倆分坐在師父的兩邊，接受師父和其他中國居士的祝福，並有英文翻譯。

我很慶幸婚禮能夠在肅穆莊嚴的佛堂中舉行，由師父證婚，幾位居士在旁邊觀禮，讓我專心思考師父問的兩個問題。這個婚禮及我們自己的誓言，給我好深刻的印象，畢生難忘，也給了我們至今二十八年的婚姻很大的影響。

一年以後，師父售出我們婚後所住的那棟樓房。在師父搬出以後，似乎失去了師父的加持，整幢樓完全失去了原有的平靜、莊嚴。以後我們就去位於天后廟街的師父住處聽經。

一九六七年，有一位曾到臺灣學過中文，又具有華盛頓大學碩士學位的朗‧艾卜斯汀（易象乾），帶了許多華盛頓大學的中文系、佛教哲學班的朋友來三藩市，拜見這位佛教界的大德。他們來住了一兩個禮拜，那時我們就舉辦法會、打坐參禪及講經。

一九六八年暑假，在朗和他的朋友要求下，師父開講《楞嚴經》。時間是每天由早上六點

were from six in the morning to nine in the evening each day, and Nick and I attended as well. At that point, Nick was working full time for Western Electric and could only attend after work from five to nine o'clock. I was taking notes so I could explain to him what happened the rest of the time.

The Abbot helps people very effectively but with a minimum of moralizing. As an example, here's how he helped me stop smoking. I had smoked for about six years, and almost from the time I started, I tried to stop, but without success. Once, soon after moving to his building on Sutter Street, I had a lit cigarette in my hand when the Abbot passed through our hall. I quickly hid it behind my back like a guilty kid. Afterward, I wondered why I reacted so reflexively. He did have a strong presence, but at that time I didn't know his views on smoking. "Why was I so ashamed?" I thought.

Later, on one occcasion, the Abbot asked me with a strange tone to his voice, "You like smo—king?" I said, "No, not really." I wondered afterward—why was I doing something I didn't like? Finally, after marrying Nick, I was making serious efforts to stop smoking. Once, a few hours after I had smoked my first cigarette in three weeks, I was at the temple on Waverly Place, standing at the front end of a long side hallway. The Abbot was at the back end, about twenty feet away. He said with that same sly tone, "You been smo—king?" Of course, I said, "Yes," with a certain degree of consternation.

We were attending lectures regularly. One day during a lecture the Abbot began an uncharacteristic discussion of the practice of smoking, stating that when so many people in the world were going hungry, spending so much on packs of cigarettes which one simply smoked for the sensation of it, was a real shame. He actually seemed to be aiming his comments at someone else, but the argument really hit my conscience, and I decided to stop smoking. (I still have a mental image of him saying that.) I had made the resolve, but I felt it would help if I told the Abbot. I told him I had decided I could quit until I was thirty (I was twenty-four, so that meant six years). His eyebrows went up and there was palpable pause. Then he said, "Why not for your whole life?" He had timed his question perfectly. I said, "You're right! All right, I'll stop for my whole life." Before that when I saw or smelled cigarettes, I wanted to smoke. I would even have dreams about finding and smoking cigarettes. But from then on, even when I saw or smelled them I had no interest and I had no further tempting dreams.

We became Buddhists after about two years of attending lectures, meditation and ceremonies. We both had questions we needed to resolve and neither of us was inclined to be "easy to convert." What convinced us to follow the Abbot's teaching and, through him, the Buddha's teaching, was the example he had given us before our very eyes. Living in the same building for one and three years respectively, attending his lectures three or so times per week, and meditating in his hall, as well as spending all day every day for two months in his presence was enough to convince us that he was who he said he was.

Most of the time, he didn't define himself, but we noticed that there were all the things he did not do—he didn't smoke, he didn't drink, he ate only vegetarian food. He was not greedy, he was not out for personal gain. He did not seem to be attracted to others of the opposite or the same sex. He tried to help those in need, but he recognized those who were not doing the right thing and was able to say

到晚上九點,我和尼克也參加了。當時尼克在電力公司上班,所以只能在下午五點到九點去聽講,其他時間就由我記筆記再講給他聽。

師父不太用教條式的方法來教化他的弟子。以戒菸的例子來說吧,我抽了六年的菸,幾乎從一開始就想戒掉,但總不成功。在我搬進薩特街不久,有一次手上拿著一支點著的菸,師父突然的出現在走廊上,我就像犯錯的孩子似的,本能的把香菸藏到背後。事後回想起,雖然師父並沒有對我說過不能抽菸,可我為什麼一見到師父就把菸藏起來?為什麼覺得那麼慚愧?

又有一次,師父用一種奇怪,甚至有點幽默的語氣問我:「你歡喜抽——菸?」我說:「並不是真的喜歡。」事後,我也覺得不能理解,為什麼要做自己不喜歡的事?結婚之後,終於決定戒菸。戒了三個星期之後,實在忍不住抽了一根菸。幾小時後,在狹長的走廊盡頭碰到師父。雖然隔了二十呎遠,師父仍舊用那種幽默的語氣問我:「你抽菸了?」我狼狽的回答:「是。」

有一天講經時,師父好像並沒有針對誰,提到世界上還有很多人都沒飯吃,卻居然有人花這麼多錢抽菸!(師父當時說話的那種神態,仍然深印在我腦海裡。)由於良心受到譴責,我是真下定決心要戒菸。於是對師父說:「我決定三十歲以前不再抽菸。」(當時我二十四歲。)」師父眉毛抬得老高說:「為什麼不是永遠?」問得好!我說:「好!永遠不抽。」說也怪,從那之後,看到別人抽菸也不心動了(在這之前連作夢都在找菸)。

我們夫妻倆都是不容易教化的頑固份子,到底是什麼使我們接受師父,接受佛法的?

師父很少告訴我們有關他的事情,和師父住在一起的四年時間裡,我們每週至少聽經三次,更有兩個月,是整天的和師父在一起打坐。我們親眼目睹到師父言行一致,嚴格執行六大宗旨(不爭、不貪、不求、不自私、不自利、不打妄語),以及師父不抽菸、不喝酒、素食、不偏愛任何人,幫助每個需要他幫助的人。有人做錯事,他一眼就看出,只要幾句話就可讓那人良心發現。很多人看到師父,莫名其妙地覺得駭怕,這種人多半是做了虧心事,心裡

thing that (usually) reached their consciousnesses. Sometimes people would get really scared of him for no apparent reason. These were usually people who were not doing the right things, or at least in their own minds were not doing the right things. Later, upon taking the precepts from him, we learned that indeed, following the precepts can help a great deal in one's cultivation—without them, it can be like taking one step forward and then three steps back.

In the two years before the Shurangama Sutra Session, I attended lectures but I did not take notes, thinking that I wanted to listen and absorb the material, and taking notes would interfere with that. Once I noticed a visitor diligently taking notes, and I asked the reason after the lecture. He answered that although some of the material in the lecture was beyond his level of understanding at the moment, that in the future when he knew more it might be clearer. By that time, however, he would have forgotten this lecture. Therefore he wanted to take notes now so that in the future he might understand better. That seemed like a good idea, so I began trying to take notes.

Eventually during the spring before the Sutra session, I began taking notes more, but still it was a conflict for me. Nick suggested I ask the Abbot if it was a good idea to take notes. He said, "Yes, and also you should write as small as possible." Then I began taking notes in earnest as did Nick. Soon I discovered another benefit of notetaking. Listening to Chinese was difficult for me since I didn't understand the language. When I was only listening to Chinese, sometimes I got sleepy. It helped to try to write down words and phrases of Chinese as I heard them. During the translation into English, I began to write very small and then I leave spaces where I couldn't keep up. That enabled me to go back and try to fill in during the Chinese. In short, because of what the Abbot told me, I found myself not only awake most of the time, but also the owner of some readable and fairly complete notes since I had so much time to polish them.

That spring Nick suggested asking the Abbot to teach me Chinese. The Abbot asked me which kind I wanted to learn, regular spoken or written as in the Buddhist texts. I said, "Written as in Buddhist texts" because spoken could be taught by anyone, but who would be better qualified than a Buddhist monk to teach from the Buddhist texts? He held lessons outside the temple on the landing where he had a blackboard. He wrote the characters on the blackboard, and we copied them. I remember Jan Vickers, Lonnie Bauer, Steve Mechling, and Gary Linebarger came as well as Nancy Lovett.

He wrote the characters before we came and only emerged to explain them after we had finished copying them. First he would say the sound of each character as he pointed to it. Once I asked how to spell the sound of a character. He said to spell it any way we wanted, just so we could read how to say it." In a way, the Abbot's limited language was a help because the few words he did say really stuck. Also he had to use expression and motions to help him explain, and these were very impressive to the consciousness.

Once he told me that many people didn't know how to cook properly and that rather than throw a bunch of chopped-up vegetables into a wok seething with oil, the correct way to cook them was in a pan with very little oil on relatively high heat for just a few minutes stirring constantly with a wooden spoon or chopsticks and adding some salt. Then to add a small amount of water, cover and turn the flame low until done. That is the way I cook to this day. He told me not to use a metal spoon in a metal pan or aluminum cooking pots as either one could lead to cancer. He said once that

有鬼。

等受了戒以後，則更深刻地體會到戒律在修行中的重要性。假如沒有戒律，就好比進一步退三步。

在聽師父講《楞嚴經》以前，有兩年時間，我聽經時只想儘量吸收，不願分神去作筆記。一次，問一個很勤奮的作筆記的聽眾，他說：「很多內容雖然我現在聽不懂，但抄下來以後，可作為以後修行的參考。」有道理！我開始記筆記。關於作筆記，我曾經請教過師父，師父說：「應該要寫筆記，並且要儘量把字寫得小一點。」從此我和尼克很認真地作筆記。意外的，發現作筆記的另一個好處。由於不懂中文，所以在聽講中文部份時往往會打瞌睡。自從開始作筆記後，不但不打瞌睡，而且有了完整、清楚的筆記可讀。

那年的春天，尼克請師父教我們中文。師父問我們要學哪一種中文，普通話還是佛經？我說：「佛經的中文。」因為普通話誰都可以教，可是有誰比師父更有資格，以佛經作為中文教材呢？師父在佛堂外面階梯間的駐腳台給我們上課。在上課以前，師父先把黑板寫滿，等我們都抄完了，他才開始講解。師父教我們發中文字的音，每當師父覺得我們發音沒問題了，就給我們解釋字義。我問他怎樣用英文拼音，他說隨便怎麼拼，只要我們能唸正確就好。師父只會講一點英文，只好以手勢及表情來解釋經文。這樣的講解，確實是在八識田中種下很深的印象。師父所說的短短的幾句英語，都能牢記在心。

後來師父又教我們練習毛筆字，練了一陣以後，師父告訴我們應該先用鉛筆練習。他在折成小方塊的大張舊報紙上寫毛筆字，師父是站在講台前，面對著佛寫字的。通常都是寫一些經文。有一次師父把整段經文倒過來寫，寫完之後完全看不出來是倒著寫的。

除了教我們中文、書法以外，師父甚至教我們怎麼作飯。他告訴我正確的炒菜方法是，先在炒菜鍋裡放一點油，等油熱了

all food should be cooked, and I asked, "Even fruit?" He said, "Yes." I can also remember when he told me not to throw away celery leaves, that they were good for soup.

Once as I was serving some food during the session, I was feeling angry. As I set some food down near him, he noticed my anger and asked, "You angry?" I said, "Not really, just mad at myself." He said, "In Buddhism you are not even supposed to be angry at yourself."

Then, after finishing the pronunciation of the passage, he would go back through and explain the meaning. I had decided to use brush and ink, as did some others. After seeing the initial attempts at brush-painting the characters he said, "You should use a pencil until you really know the characters." Eventually the Abbot gave calligraphy lessons. He would take a large piece of newsprint folded in many squares, and standing at the foot of the lecture tables, facing the altar area, he would write characters on it from the Sutras with a brush and ink. One time, he wrote the whole quotation backward and did it perfectly so that it looked as it would normally.

While living at the house, I decided to do some clean-up work in the garden, and began sweeping up leaves, raking, and so on. One of the disciples, a young woman with very strong feelings, got upset at my doing this, and said I was injuring all the small insects and ants. She felt I should stop immediately and not engage in such things. I felt torn between my desire for order and cleanliness and her accusations. I asked the Abbot about this dilemma. He said, "I like a nice garden. It's okay to sweep and rake, just go slowly."

The admonition to "go slowly" is one I have heard from him many times, and it is a good one. It can be applied to many things. As I'd be coming up the four flights of stairs to the temple (on Waverly) there was a small caged in area at the top of the stairs. Quite often he'd be there sitting. And as I reached the top of the stairs, he'd say, "Slowly, slowly." I always wondered why he said it twice like that—only later did I discover that in Chinese, "Slow down" is man-man, the character for slow repeated.

Occasionally, he would ask someone (any of us at various times), "What are you doing?" This would almost invariably come at a time when we were a bit off in some way. I also noticed that he would very pointedly and slowly ask children, "What—are—you—do...ing?" but not in a very serious or mean way. It was a real conciousness-raiser.

Once when a large and important ceremony was to take place, there were many sitting clothes to make out of red, yellow and black material. I spent a lot of time including the last night before the ceremony making sitting cloths—copying one made from blue, red and black. On my sample, I noted that the black strip on one side was a bit wider than on the other side, so I decided that whoever had made it just hadn't done a good job. I made sure that all of my sitting cloths had equally wide stripes of black on either side. I was quite proud of the result.

The next day, before the ceremony, while the large room was crowded with people, literally standing-room-only, the Abbot asked loudly, "Who made all these sitting clothes?" Bursting with pride but not wishing to be boastful, I hesitated, then came closer and said I had made them. He then said, "These are all wrong! The black strip should be wider on this side—look, you can't fold them up properly!" This was very embarrassing and led me to always feel a bit uneasy about anything I do. It seems as if the minute one becomes too self-congratulatory, that's the time to

後再放菜。用木杓或筷子翻攪，再加鹽加水，蓋上鍋蓋，用小火燜熟。師父說不要用鐵鏟炒菜，也不要用鋁鍋煮東西，容易得癌症。師父也曾說過所有的食物都應該煮熟了吃，我問：「連水果都包括？」他說：「是的。」記得師父叫我不要把芹菜的葉子丟掉，芹菜的葉子可以做很好的湯。

有一次法會時，我不知為什麼生氣，當我端菜經過師父身旁時，他注意到了我的情緒，就問：「你在生氣？」我說：「沒什麼，只是在生自己的氣。」他說：「在佛法中，你甚至不可以生自己的氣。」

一次，在打掃院子裡的落葉、枯枝時，有一位年輕的女弟子很激動的要我馬上停止打掃，因為那樣會傷害許多昆蟲、螞蟻。我雖很同意她的顧慮，但又不能容忍院子的髒亂，於是就去問師父，師父說：「我歡喜看院子整整齊齊的，掃掃院子沒問題，掃慢一點，小心一點就好了。」師父常說，「慢一點」這句話，在生活中非常有用。每當我們上四樓的佛堂時，師父常會坐在樓梯邊的一個缺口處，看到我們上樓太快時，就會說：「Slowly!Slowly!」（慢一點！慢一點！）我常覺得很奇怪，為什麼要說兩遍，後來才知道是中文「慢慢」的意思。

師父常常突然會用英文問我們：「What are you doing?」（你在做什麼？）那通常都是我們心裡有鬼的時候。我也注意到，師父在對小孩子說「What are you doing?」這句話時，會把聲音提高、拖長。其中沒有含一點惡意或顯得很嚴肅。卻很有發人深省的作用。

一次大法會的前夕，我負責用紅、黃及黑布縫製「具」（臥具）。我發現作為樣品的黑色布條寬了一點。心想，做樣品的人也太粗心了。所以我在把每一條紅、黃、黑條子都裁成對稱的尺吋的同時，很得意自己能糾正這個錯誤。第二天，法會開始之前，佛殿站滿了人，師父忽然大聲地問：「這『具』是誰做的？」我興奮地以為這回一定會被表揚，故作謙虛的走上前去說是我做的。師父說：「都做錯了，這邊一條黑條應該比其他的要寬一點，才能折疊成形。」我當時真想

watch out. Also it made me aware of the value of double-checking rather than assuming someone else made a mistake.

After being married for more than ten years and having no children, I became discouraged. Then I thought maybe it was just as well not to have any. I decided to go and tell the Abbot about my realization. He assured me that it was a good idea to have children—and at least two of them. He told me that if I wanted to have children, I should recite "Namo Guanshiyin Pusa." I did this, and before long was pregnant with our first son, Nicholas. The pregnancy went well, but we had not yet told the Abbot we were having a baby. Nevertheless, one night around the fifth month Nick woke me up at around 4 a.m. and recounted a dream in which he saw the Abbot dressed in his red and gold sash standing bathed in golden light while behind him there was a golden background which radiated different colors of golden light. He told Nick that we would have a healthy, intelligent baby boy.

Nick didn't tell me until some time after Nicholas was born, but there was another part of the dream; that Nick should watch out for us since there would be some difficulty with the birth. Apparently one part of the baby's body would be unusually large—so much so that some people might feel there was an abnormality—but not to worry because it was just a sign of greater intelligence. Nick was afraid this part would frighten me, so he kept it to himself. Because of difficulties in labor, Nicholas was born by caesarian section at Merrit Hospital in Oakland. The doctors were amazed at his very large head. He weighed nine pounds and four ounces, but was long and slim. Because of hospital regulations involved with his birth, we were unable to hold and comfort him for many hours, although he remained alert.

I was glad we had been reassured in the dream about Nicholas, because although his head remained very large for his size, it was never a worry for us. At six weeks he saw the Master at Gold Mountain Monastery for the first time, and was calm and alert enough for him to hold him. He named him Guo Ma (Fruit of Carnelian) at the City of Ten Thousand Buddhas at two months of age because he was born in the year of the Horse (Ma).

About four years later, I became pregnant again with our second son, Christopher. Near the time of his birth, my doctor was concerned about the size of the baby. He warned me that there was the possibility of another caesarian section. Nick suggested asking the Abbot what to do to ensure a healthy and trouble-free birth. Master Hua told us to recite "Namo Guanshiyin Pusa." I asked, "When should we recite, before or during the birth?" He said, "Before and during—as much as possible."

We followed his advice. During labor, I could not recite well, so it helped me that Nick recited continuously. At a difficult time in my labor, I was reminded to recite, and I did. As I turned on my side, Christopher was suddenly being born without a problem. We bathed Christopher and were able to hold him and be with him from the start. He weighed ten pounds and was also a long slim baby with a large head. We were very happy that he didn't have to go through the trauma of a difficult birth as had Nicholas, and he was a peaceful baby with very high coloring. We brought him to visit the Abbot at two weeks of age, who named him Guo Dan (Cinnabar) because of his red coloring.

Those are some of my experiences with the Venerable Master.

找個地洞鑽進去。從那以後，我做事再也不那麼自以為是，並懂得當下要觀照，要再次的檢討自己，不要馬上斷定對方犯了過失。

和尼克結婚十年都沒有孩子。失望之餘，自我安慰地想：沒有孩子也許比較好。當我告訴師父時，師父說他保證有孩子並不是件壞事，他說我至少得有兩個小孩。師父又說，如果我想要小孩，應當常念「南無觀世音菩薩」。果然不久就有身孕了。當我懷孕五個月時，還未告訴師父。有一天清晨四點，尼克夢見師父身披紅色祖衣，在一片五彩金光中，告訴尼克將有一個健康、聰明的男孩子誕生，只是孩子身體的某一部分將會很大，因為特大，會令人覺得不正常。那特大的部份是代表智慧。當時尼克怕我擔心，並沒有告訴我這個夢。後來果然是剖腹生產，孩子（尼古拉）有一顆連醫生都稱奇的大頭，雖然重九磅四盎司，但很瘦很長。由於醫院的規矩，好幾小時後，才將他送來給我們看。幸好事先尼克在夢中得到師父的保證，否則真要為他那個超級大頭擔心死了。尼古拉六個星期大時，我們才第一次帶他去見師父，他很乖巧的讓師父抱著。兩個月大時，在萬佛城，師父給他取名叫果瑪，因為他是馬年生的。

四年之後，我又懷了第二個兒子克利斯多弗。臨到產期時，醫生曾警告我，由於孩子太大可能又要剖腹產。尼克建議去問師父，要怎樣才能平安生產。師父要我們念「南無觀世音菩薩」，我問：「是產前還是生的時候唸？」師父說：「都要念得越多越好。」我們遵行不誤，但在生產時，我痛得很厲害，不能好好地念聖號，尼克就大聲不停地念給我聽，當我側過身體便生了一個十磅重，同樣大頭瘦長的孩子，這一次沒有受生尼古拉時的各種驚恐。兩個星期大時，抱克利斯多弗去見師父，師父取名為果丹，因為他的皮膚是紅色的。

這就是我和上人的一段緣。

悄悄地我走了

I HAVE GONE IN SILENCE

吳耀鴻　Wu Yaohong

輕輕地我走了，正如我輕輕地來嗎？上人剛出生時，便痛哭娑婆世界的苦；離開世間時，也帶走了無數眾生的苦，示現重疾而去。

上人一生盡心辦道，代天宣化六大宗旨：不爭、不貪、不求、不自私、不自利，不打妄語；開創正法道場，讓無數有緣的迷夢眾生，前來親近善知識及聽聞佛法。就這樣使我慢慢地洗面革心，得到新生。雖然不能立即放下所有的壞習氣，但也知道有「止於至善」的一刻。

悄悄地我走了，正如我悄悄地來嗎？上人自懂得生死事大後，便發願出家，躬身力行，鑽研經典、辦義學、訪明師，尋真相。在這拜金主義的社會中，貪瞋癡氾濫的眾生界裡，到處樹法幢、擊法鼓、說實語、流血汗、不休息，目的就是要普度一切有緣眾生，同登極樂國。

念佛是誰？誰是我？不管誰！不管我！二六時中，行住坐臥，不離一句阿彌陀佛。

苦海無邊，欲海難填，幸虧上人為我們留下六把降魔劍，讓愚魯的弟子們做為保真衛命之用。至於會不會靈活地學以致用，全在當人。

I have left quietly, just as I came quietly, right? When the Master was first born, he wept for the suffering beings in this Saha world. When the Master left the world, he took with him the suffering of countless living beings, manifesting serious illness.

The Master devoted his entire life to cultivating the Way. He promoted the Six Great Principles of: no fighting, no greed, no seeking, no selfishness, no pursuing of personal benefit, and no lying. The Master also established many Way-places for the Proper Dharma, thus enabling the multitudes of deluded living beings who have affinity with him to draw near to good knowing advisers, as well as attend Dharma talks. In this way, I gradually learned to repent and reform, and I began a new life. Although I could not let go of all my bad habits yet, I did experience moments of "arriving at ultimate wholesomeness."

I have left in silence, just as I came in silence, right? After the Master realized the importance of the matter of ending birth and death, he resolved his mind on leaving the home-life. He investigated the Sutras diligently, and practiced the principles with all his might. He also promoted voluntary education, searched for wise teachers, and aspired to uncover the real mark. In this materialistic society, among living beings who are preoccupied with greed, hatred and stupidity, the Master erected Dharma banners and hit the Dharma drum wherever he went. He told the truth, toiled hard, and never rested, so that he could universally take across all living beings who have affinity with him, causing them to be reborn in the Land of Ultimate Bliss.

Who is reciting the Buddha's name? Who am I? Don't mind who! Don't mind me! Twenty-four hours a day, whether one is walking, standing, sitting, or reclining, one is never from the single phrase "Amitabha Buddha."

The sea of suffering is boundless. The sea of desire is hard to fill. Fortunately, the Master has left behind six swords for subduing demons, so that his dull disciples can protect their nature and life. As for whether one knows how to make use of what one has learned, it all depends on individual.

眞誠頌

修道必須具眞誠　虛僞自欺難欺神　時刻愼獨存正念　暗室屋漏莫虧心

宣公上人作於一九八二年二月十日

Verse on Sincerity

In cultivating the Way, one must have a sincere mind.
If you are false, you may cheat oneself, but it's hard to cheat the spirits.
Be cautious when you are alone and always maintain proper thoughts.
Don't do anything that goes against your conscience in a dark room.

Composed by the Venerable Master Hua on February 10, 1982

行慈悲心　滿眾生願

PRACTICING WITH A COMPASSIONATE MIND; FULFILLING LIVING BEINGS' VOWS

楊秋生　Chiou-Sheng Yang

六月七日中午，和朋友通電話，不知怎地突然提起師父，說起師父種種的好。下午誦完經，約兩點多時，我靜靜地地站在佛堂前，看著師父的相片，直站到去接小孩放學。

第二天早上，朋友打電話來，說師父已於六月七日下午三點十五分圓寂。

掛上電話，放聲大哭，哀痛逾恆！難道昨天，心靈深處已感應到師父要走了，捨不得，趕著去見他最後一面？

我只是哭，什麼事都無法做。心裡想，師父去了，我們不都成了孤兒？日後在修行的路上，誰還能像師父一樣，心心念念都是我們，不斷的關懷、指引我們？一位師姐了解我，抑制著悲慟告訴我，走的是師父的肉身，師父的法身還在。只要心靜意誠，自然可以感受到師父的。

木然地走到前院，蹲在地上拔野草。只有做這樣單純、機械式的粗工，才能抑制住不斷掉下的淚水。突然，我覺得四周異常的溫暖，強烈地感覺到是師父，師父的金身暖暖的包圍著我，讓我知道他還在，他就在我的身邊，不要再哀傷，不要再害怕！

十五日黃昏，朋友都走光了，或南下扶靈，或北上幫忙，以待次日在萬佛聖城迎接師父靈柩。我很哀傷，因為我沒法子出門。那天夜裡，我夢見我去扶柩！我又落淚了！師父，只有師父才知道我，他永遠滿我的願！

在生活周遭裡，是誰心心念念都是我們，一直滿我們的願呢？我想，只有父母了！

因此第一次，我在萬佛聖城見到師父，就有一種強烈的感覺——他是我爸爸！看見他只想衝上前去，趴在他的膝上，痛痛快快地哭一場，讓他的大手輕拍我的肩，說：乖，不哭！不哭！

On June 7, I was on the phone with a friend at noon, and I don't know why, but we started talking about our Teacher, Venerable Master Hua, and about all the ways in which he was wonderful. In the afternoon, after I finished reciting a Sutra a little after two o'clock, I stood quietly in front of the Buddha shrine and gazed at the Master's photograph until I had to go pick up my child after school.

The next morning, my friend called to tell me that the Venerable Master had already completed the stillness at 3:15 p.m. on June 7.

After hanging up the phone, I burst out crying in extreme sorrow and grief. Could it be that yesterday I had already felt instinctively, deep down in my heart, that the Master was going and couldn't bear to part with him, and so I hurried to see him for one last time?

There was nothing I could do but cry. I thought, now that the Master has gone, haven't we all become orphans? On our path of cultivation, who will be able to constantly think of us, care for us, and guide us the way the Venerable Master did? One of my Dharma-sisters knew that I was trying to restrain my grief and told me that it was only the Master's flesh body that was gone; his golden body is still here. If we are calm and sincere, we will naturally feel the Master's presence.

I walked woodenly into the front yard and squatted down to pull weeds. Only by doing such simple chores could I hold back the tears that fell without stop. Suddenly I became aware of an unusual warmth all around me. I had the strong feeling that it was the Master—the Master's golden body enveloping me in its warmth, letting me know that he was still around, that he was right beside me, and I shouldn't be sad or afraid anymore!

On the evening of the fifteenth, my friends were all gone. They had either gone south to escort the Venerable Master's casket, or they had gone north to help out, because people would be welcoming the Venerable Master's casket to the Sagely City of Ten Thousand Buddhas the following day. I was very sad because I couldn't go. That night, however, I dreamed that I also went to escort the casket!

My tears fell again! The Master knows me, and he always grants my wishes!

In our lives, who thinks of us in every thought and always fulfills our wishes? I think only our parents do. Thus, the first time I went to the Sagely City of Ten Thousand Buddhas and saw the Master, I had a very strong feeling that he was my father! When I saw him, I just wanted to run up to him and sit on his knee and have a good cry, and let him pat my shoulder with his big hand and say, "Now, be good. Don't cry, don't cry." That day, I had brought my child along, and I only wanted to let him draw near the Master. I didn't even know that we were supposed to bow. When my child walked up to the Master, the Master raised his big hand and very

那天，帶著孩子去，只想讓孩子親近他，我甚至不懂得要頂禮。孩子走上前去，他舉起大手來，極端嚴肅地就在孩子的頭上拍打。因為用力，袖子翩然，拍在頭上砰然作響。從沒有人見過師父對一個才五歲的孩子的頭，這樣用力地拍打。起初，大家都因為聲音大，忍不住笑起來，後來眼見師父一下接一下，神情異常嚴肅，一個個都斂起笑容，靜肅起來。師父拍了五下，專注地對著孩子說：「要乖、要乖乖哦！」師父的聲音似帶哽咽，我驚訝地看著他，他的眼裡彷彿有淚。我受到極大的震撼！我不過是一個徬徨的母親，我對佛法一無所知，而師父，卻有我所不能瞭解的至情和悲心！

那天，以為下午舉行皈依儀式時，可以向師父頂個禮。不料，下午是由別的法師代為舉行皈依儀式，沒能給師父磕頭，心裡一直覺得很遺憾。而那天夜裡，我夢見師父身著袈裟，端坐在一個廣場上，身旁、身後，或坐著、或站著許多出家人。天地一片亮光，亮到彷彿是正午陽光就在他身後，萬丈光芒，街邊幾棵樹的葉邊，泛著金邊，閃閃發光。廣場前許多的出家人和在家人都向他頂禮膜拜，兩邊路上只有幾個行人，看到他，也都跪下頂禮，我和孩子也跟著跪拜頂禮。是師父滿我的願啊！

從那時起，我開始研究經書、做功課，也開始學習如何真正做人！初學佛，總不得要領，老往外求。求心愈切，事情愈不能迴轉。有一回因求見師父心切，在大殿竟逾矩，師父臉一拉，微慍，說：「儀式開始了，去拜佛！」我一方面覺得向來規規矩矩的我竟逾矩，感覺極為羞慚，一方面因被拒，心裡很難過，頭一低，眼淚就湧出來，在眼眶裡打轉。師父見了，臉一鬆，和藹溫和地對我說：「去，去拜佛！多拜佛，多拜佛！」

我低著頭，反反復復回想著那一幕，突然，我想通了！原來，學佛是不能往外求的，而是要藉著拜佛多反觀自照！我想起第一次師父對我說的話：事情所以會這樣，都是因為因妳而來！多多迴光反照。

是啊！欲知前世因，今生受者是。看自己，不都明白了嗎？唯有從內心懺悔起，才有消業的可能。各人果報各人償，往昔所造諸惡業，無人可代受。想起從前，我和許許多多不明事

sternly hit my child on the head. Because the Master used such force, his sleeve flapped as he brought his hand down on my child's head with a loud whack. No one had ever seen the Master hit the head of a five-year-old so forcefully. At first, because the sound of the whack was so loud, people couldn't help but smile. However, when they saw the Master bring his hand down again and again with an unusually stern demeanor, they stopped smiling and became serious. The Master hit my child five times and said to him very intently, "You have to be good! Be good!" The Master's voice seemed to be choked with sobs. In surprise, I looked at the Master and saw that his eyes were filled with tears. I was shocked! I was only an agitated mother who knew absolutely nothing about the Buddhadharma, and the Master's deep tenderness and compassion was beyond my understanding.

I had planned to bow to the Venerable Master that day in the afternoon when the ceremony for taking refuge was held, but unexpectedly, the ceremony was held by another Dharma Master who stood in for the Venerable Master. I regretted very much that I didn't get to bow to the Venerable Master. That night, I had a dream in which I saw the Master wearing his *kashaya* sash and sitting very properly in an outdoor plaza surrounded by many left-home people who were sitting or standing. The atmosphere was very bright, as if the noon sun were right behind the Master giving off brilliant rays of light. The leaves of the trees along the road were also edged with gold and dazzling. There were many left-home people and laypeople in the plaza bowing to the Master. A few people who were walking by along the roads on both sides also knelt down when they saw the Master and bowed. My child and I joined them to kneel and bow. The Master had granted my wish!

That was when I began to study the Sutras and to cultivate—and I also began to learn how to really be a human being! As a beginner in Buddhism, I always failed to catch the main point and continually went seeking outside. The more sincerely I sought, the more of a mess things became. Once when I saw the Venerable Master, because I was seeking very sincerely, I actually disregarded the rules in the Buddhahall. The Venerable Master's countenace hardened and with a slight trace of displeasure, he said, "The ceremony has already begun. Go bow to the Buddhas." I felt very ashamed on the one hand, because I had presumed to break the rules when I was usually very good about following the rules. On the other hand, I felt very bad about being rejected by the Master, and tears brimmed in my eyes as I lowered my head. When the Master saw this, his countenance softened and he gently told me, "Go, go bow to the Buddhas. Bow to the Buddhas more."

When I put my head down and recollected that scene, all of a sudden, it dawned upon me! I realized then that in studying Buddhism, we cannot seek outwardly. We have to use the method of bowing to the Buddhas to reflect upon ourselves! I remember what the Master said to me the first time: "Things are the way they are all because of you! Try to reflect within yourself as much as you can!"

Yes! If one wants to know about the causes one planted in past lives, just take a look at the effects one is receiving in this life. When we look at ourselves, isn't it very clear to us? The only way to wipe out our karma is to repent within our own mind. Each person has to pay for his own causes and effects. No one can stand in for us to take the retribution for all the evil karma we created in the past. I remember joining the multitudes of ignorant people who knew only to seek for

理的人，只曉得求師父，不知道師父為了眾生，揹了多少業！難怪我曾夢見年事已高的師父還揹著我走！

師父四處弘揚佛法，平日要處理的事情又多。我們去萬佛聖城，單程就要三個多小時，要見師父一面並不容易，而每次心裡有事，或者想念師父，就會夢到師父。夢裡，他總會告訴我一些佛理，醒來後慢慢參，參透後，受用無窮。雖不常見他，卻感覺到和他親，他親如父，而我是孺慕之子。雖說他對弟子的用心，他話中的真義，我似乎頗能心領神會。然而修行道上，理能頓悟，事相上仍須漸修，對於自己的經常懈怠，常覺愧對師父，不可原諒！而他一遍一遍地包容我們，指引我們，對我們從不放棄希望。許多見過師父的人都說，看到師父都覺得師父像自己的爸爸，我想，那是因為師父的慈悲吧！他的大慈大悲，洗滌我們塵垢的身心，讓我們在徬徨中有了依靠。任何時間、任何地方，只要想到有師父在，我們就可安心了！

師父用各種方法誘導眾生，多年來心力交瘁，透支過甚。有時候，才聽說師父正積勞成疾，怎麼又見他奔波海內各道場，弘法利生，為法忘軀。他甚至經常絕食多日，將功德迴向給眾生。他從來沒有為過自己，已然病重不支了，仍說：「我甚至不會用一根手指頭的力量，來幫助這個躺在病床上的自己！」

六月七日下午三點十五分，無私無我、大慈大悲的師父 —— 宣化上人，將無盡福報迴向法界，入大涅槃。想到師父為眾生這樣不顧自己，心情豈是「哀慟」兩個字可以形容的！淚無法停止，心無法安定，飯吃不下，夜裡輾轉不能成眠⋯⋯。

翻開皈依證，仔細體會師父的十八大願，看到他的第十一願「願將我所應享受一切福樂，悉皆迴向，普施法界眾生。」以及第十二大願「願將法界眾生，所有一切苦難，皆悉與我，一人代受。」他的悲、他的願、他的行，一如菩薩，而今，他走了，眾生何所依？

心裡只是想著師父、師父⋯⋯。

help from the Master. We didn't have any idea of how much karma the Master had already shouldered on behalf of living beings. No wonder I dreamed that my Master, already advanced in years and experience, was still carrying me on his back as he walked!

The Venerable Master went everywhere propagating the Buddha-dharma and took care of a myriad affairs on a daily basis. Moreover, it was a three hour trip to the Sagely City of Ten Thousand Buddhas. Thus, it was not easy to get to see the Master face-to-face. Yet whenever something was troubling me, I would dream of the Master. In my dream, the Master would always tell me some Buddhist principles. After I woke up, I would gradually delve into them. And when I understood them, they afforded me endless benefit. Even though I didn't get to see the Master often, I felt very close to him. He was as close as a father, and I was like a little child.

Even though I can say I grasped the Venerable Master's intent and the truth of his words, on the path of cultivation, there can be sudden enlightenment to the principles, but we must cultivate gradually in actual practice. Due to my habitual laxness, I often feel remorse towards the Venerable Master and feel that I cannot be forgiven. And yet he always tolerantly accepts and guides us, never giving up on us. Many people who knew the Venerable Master have said that when they met the Master, they felt as if he were their very own father. This must be due to the Master's kindness and compassion! His great kindness and compassion cleansed our minds and bodies of filth and defilement, allowing us to feel that we have something to rely upon in our distress. No matter when and where, as soon as we think of the Master's presence, we can stop worrying.

The Venerable Master used all kinds of methods to teach and guide living beings. Over the years, his strength declined and he overexhausted himself. Sometimes we would hear that he was ill from overwork, and then we would see him travelling to various Way-places both domestic and abroad, propagating the Dharma to benefit beings, disregarding his own well-being for the sake of the Dharma. He regularly embarked on fasts lasting for many days, dedicating the merit to all living beings. He never did anything for himself. Even when he was no longer able to hold up, he said, "I wouldn't even use the strength of one finger to help this body of mine which is lying on the sickbed!"

On June 7 at 3:15 in the afternoon, our selfless and unselfish, greatly kind and compassionate teacher, the Venerable Master Hua, dedicating his inexhaustible blessings to the entire Dharma Realm, entered great Nirvana.

When I think of how he did everything for living beings without any regard for himself, my heart is sorely grieved. I can't stop crying, and my mind cannot find peace. I have no appetite, and I toss and turn all night long, unable to sleep...

Opening my certificate of taking refuge, I carefully study the Venerable Master's eighteen great vows. I see the eleventh vow: "I vow to fully dedicate all blessings and bliss which I myself ought to receive and enjoy to all living beings of the Dharma Realm" and the twelfth vow: "I vow to fully take upon myself all sufferings and hardships of all living beings in the Dharma Realm." His compassion, his vows, his conduct—are just like those of a Bodhisattva. Now that he is gone, upon whom can living beings rely?

宣化老和尚追思紀念專集

十七日上午，到萬佛聖城瞻仰師父。

念佛聲中，站在靈柩前，定定地看師父。師父完全變了一個樣子——我震驚得連淚都止了——師父和六祖一模一樣！所有的悲哀、傷慟、徬徨、恐懼，全在這一剎那間粉碎！我突然想起二祖慧可初見達摩祖師時中間的一段對話：

慧可：「我心未寧，乞師與安？」
達摩：「將心來，與汝安。」
慧可：「覓心了不可得。」
達摩：「我與汝安心竟。」

此時，我的心得到前所未有的安定，不由得衷心慨歎：大師就是大師！師父將我的身心都安頓好了！

走出方丈室，想起那天夢見師父，師父掙扎起身問：「師父走了，今後大家怎麼辦？」我回答說：「當以戒為師。釋迦牟尼佛將入涅槃時，阿難以四事問佛，其中一問是『我們以後將依什麼為師？』釋迦牟尼佛答道：『要以戒為師。』戒，就是戒律，大家要守戒律。」

師父無私地奉獻了一生，留給弟子的是哀慟、是追思、是感恩，以及完美的風骨和修行榜樣。

師父從虛空來，又回到虛空去，因此，我知道，今天師父才是真正地無所不在。

In my mind, I can only think of the Master, the Master...

On the morning of the seventeenth, I went to the Sagely City of Ten Thousand Buddhas to gaze upon the Venerable Master's visage.

As the sound of the Buddha's name filled the air, I stood calmly before the casket gazing at the Venerable Master.

The Master's appearance was totally changed—I was so shocked that even my tears stopped—the Master looked just like the Sixth Patriarch!

All of my grief, sorrow, distress, and fear vanished in an instant!

I suddenly thought of the dialogue that took place when the Second Patriarch Hui Ke met Patriarch Bodhidharma for the first time:

> Great Master Hui Ke: "My mind has not been calmed. I beg the Master to calm it for me."
> Patriarch Bodhidharma: "Bring me your mind and I'll calm it for you."
> Great Master Hui Ke: "I've searched for my mind and it cannot be obtained."
> Patriarch Bodhidharma: "I've already calmed your mind for you."

At that time I felt an unprecedented calmness of mind, and I couldn't help but sigh to myself: "A Great Master is just that! The Master has already put my body and mind at ease!"

Walking out of the Abbot's quarters [where the Venerable Master's Nirvana Hall was set up], I thought of the dream I had of the Master, in which the Master struggled to sit up and asked, "After I leave, what should everyone do?"

I answered, "We should take the precepts as our teacher. Right before Shakyamuni Buddha entered Nirvana, Ananda asked the Buddha about four questions. One of them was, 'Whom shall we take as our teacher in the future?' Shakyamuni Buddha replied, 'You should take the precepts as your teacher.' That means everyone should follow the precepts."

The Venerable Master selflessly offered up his entire life. Now his disciples are left with grief, remembrance, gratitude, and a perfect model of deportment and cultivation.

The Venerable Master came from empty space and returned to empty space. Therefore, I know that now the Venerable Master is truly everywhere.

偈成
A Casually Composed Verse

今年花似去年好　今年人比去年老　誰知人老不如花　可惜花落君莫掃

This year's flowers are as pretty as last year's,
But this year I am older than last year.
Do you know that when people get old, they are not as good as flowers?
Have pity on the petals that fall to the ground; please don't sweep them away.

宣公上人作於一九七〇年一月一日
Composed by the Venerable Master Hua on January 1, 1970

他助不如自助

BEING HELPED BY OTHERS IS NOT AS GOOD AS HELPING ONESELF

釋恆友　Shi Hengyo

終於能來到美國，這完全是師父上人慈悲的鼓勵與教化所致。

記得在一九九一年時就連續簽了四次的簽證，但都沒有理由地被拒絕了。接著九二年再次請求（每天在上人法相前跪求）。來美國之前，有一天夢到上人請一位正在被羯磨中的比丘來告訴我：「師父上人很不高興，叫你不要一直打電話給他。」醒來一看，時間是清晨三點多。這個夢非常地清楚並且讓我思索了好幾天。心想為何請一個正在羯磨中的比丘來告訴我呢？啊！終於想通了，原來是自己平常不持戒，也不守規矩。雖然當時未出家，但已入佛學院（正法佛學院）讀書了，應該要持戒、更要懂規矩。而夢中所說的打電話並不是真的打電話，而是打電波。由此可知上人是無所不知，無所不曉的，也時時刻刻都在默默地隨機教化眾生的。

去年有同學想來美國參加上人的華誕，一位師兄又幫我向上人請示是否可來美？上人答「可以！」當時我聽到此話後很高興地想，這次一定可以來美國了。因為每當有師兄弟要到美國前，只要是上人准了，都能得到簽證。所以內心也就沒打失敗的念頭。一心地去簽證。然而非常意外的是－－又被拒絕了。此時我的內心開始對上人的話有了懷疑！我不懂為何他老人家說可以，但我卻是頭一個失敗者？令我無法接受與面對這個事實。當下不知如何面對未來的前途，感到非常迷惘。心想，若這生中無法到美國受戒，那跟上人出家有何意義呢？於是悲從心起，就生起病來。後來向常住請了長假到外面去調養身心。這段時間也沒給常住去電話，但內心卻開始有點不安了，因為色身好調好養，但法身則須以法水來長養。

My coming to America is completely due to the Venerable Master's kind encouragement and teaching.

I tried four times to get a visa in 1991, but each time I was turned down for no apparent reason. In 1992, I continued to seek (I knelt before the Venerable Master's photograph and prayed every day). Before coming to America, one day I suddenly dreamed that the Venerable Master sent a Bhikshu who was undergoing a formal repentance ceremony to tell me, "The Master is very upset. He says you shouldn't keep making phone calls to him." When I woke up, I saw that it was three o'clock in the morning. The dream had been extremely clear and I pondered over it for several days. I wondered why a Bhikshu who was in repentance had been sent to tell me. Aha! It finally dawned on me that it was because I usually didn't hold the precepts or follow the rules. Even though I hadn't left home yet, I'd already entered the Buddhist Academy, so I should hold the precepts and be very orderly. The "phone calls" in a dream didn't really mean phone calls, but "telegrams" sent by the mind. From this, we can know that the Venerable Master is aware of everything and is at all times teaching living beings according to their potentials.

Last year some of my classmates were thinking of coming to the United States to attend the Venerable Master's birthday celebration. My Dharma-brother asked the Venerable Master whether I could come as well, and the Master replied, "Yes!" I was extremely happy, thinking that I would certainly be able to come to America this time. Whenever our Dharma-brothers wanted to come to America, as long as they received the Venerable Master's permission, they would be able to get a visa. Therefore, I didn't even consider the possibility of failure as I single-mindedly went to apply for a visa. Very unexpectedly, I was turned down again. I began to doubt the Venerable Master's words then. I didn't understand why I was the first one to fail after the Venerable Master had said, "Okay." Faced with that kind of test, I couldn't face the situation. I didn't know how to deal with the future. I felt lost and confused. If I couldn't come to America to take the precepts, what point was there in leaving home with the Venerable Master? Thinking like this, I became very sad and fell sick again. I requested a leave of absence from the temple in order to nurse my health. Although I didn't call the temple during that time, I started feeling a bit uneasy, because while it was easy to take care of my physical body, my Dharma body needed the water of Dharma in order to grow.

Finally, I couldn't wait any longer and so I called the temple. The person there just happened to say, "When the Master heard that you were turned down for a visa, he himself said over the phone, 'She shouldn't be like that, giving up on herself so easily! All she needs to

終於忍不住，打了電話給常住，很意外得到一句話：「師父上人聽到妳簽證沒過的消息了，他老人家親自在電話中說：不要這樣子嘛！自暴自棄，多念觀音聖號就可以了。」就是這些話，讓我鼓起勇氣，再次去簽證。而今年剛好有位師兄從美國回臺，她熱心地幫助我們準備了許多資料，讓我們能順利取得簽證。給了我很大的支持與協助，非常的感謝她，也感謝在臺的師兄們幾次有形與無形的幫助。

回到話題，我想說的是，師父上人確實是無時無刻地運用善巧方便，幫助我們成長道業。例如他老人家看我這位愚癡的眾生，只好藉此事來教化我。我為簽證之事而忽略了一點，即「他助不如自助」。我總想要別人來幫助我取得簽證，沒想到自己幫助自己才是最穩當的。這件事後讓我體會到，我們常希望別人協助念佛往生西方，而忽略了應自己念佛生西。

打從小至今，就一直有依賴的心態。小時候靠母親持佛庇佑……，現在長大了還想靠師父慈悲加持，一點也不對自己負起責任。因此師父才觀機教化，讓我終於明白凡事要靠自己，唯有自己努力才有希望。因為這次再去簽證時，就非常的專心持念觀音聖號，不再東看西看心不在焉了，所以能順利過關取得簽證。經歷此事後自己才懂得如何長大、獨立。

後又遇到此次上人圓寂之事，也就比較能夠坦然面對了。我想師父在與不在是我們凡夫的肉眼生分別，最重要的是師父的精神是不息的，分分秒秒都在救度眾生，他老人家並沒有捨棄我們。從〈宇宙白〉的字義上可看出，上人是真的流血汗，不休息。

do is recite Guanyin's holy name more!'" Hearing that, I plucked up courage and went to apply for a visa yet again. This year, one of our Dharma-brothers who returned to Taiwan from America helped us prepare a great deal of material, so we were all able to get visas without any problem. I'm very grateful for her support and help, and also for the help of my Dharma-brothers in Taiwan.

At all times, the Venerable Master uses skill-in-means to help us grow in our cultivation of the Way. For example, seeing such a stupid living being as myself, he used this matter to teach me a lesson. In trying to get a visa, I overlooked one point— "being helped by others is not as good as helping oneself." I always depended on others to help me get my visa. It never occurred to me that it would be more reliable to depend on myself. This incident also made me see that we always hope others will recite the Buddha's name to help us be reborn in the West, instead of reciting the Buddha's name ourselves to obtain rebirth in the West.

From my childhood all the way till now, I have always been dependent on others. When I was little, I relied on my mother's recitation of the Buddha's name to bring us protection... Now that I've grown up, I rely on the Venerable Master's compassionate aid. I haven't taken responsibility for myself at all. Thus, the Master perceived my disposition and taught me to understand that I should always rely on myself. There is hope only if I make an effort myself. This time when I went to apply for a visa, I recited Guanyin Bodhisattva's name with great concentration instead of looking here and there and being distracted, and so I passed the test and got my visa. From this experience, I have learned to grow up and be independent.

Later, when the Venerable Master completed the stillness, I was able to face it more calmly. In my opinion, it is ordinary people with their ordinary flesh eyes who discriminate whether the Venerable Master is present or absent. The important thing is that the Venerable Master's spirit is saving living beings in every minute and second, without ever resting. He has not renounced us. As it says in "White Universe," the Venerable Master truly "spares no blood or sweat and never pauses to rest."

萬物因道生　　得者自通靈　　悟徹個中理　　菩提不減增

宣公上人作

All the myriad things are born from the Tao;
One who attains this naturally penetrates the universe
Once the principles within this are understood,
One realizes that Bodhi neither decreases nor increases

by the Venerable Master Hua

飛來天鵝綻蓮華

「從前我曾經見過你，在那地球的光中，在那人類的慈愛裡。」

How the Swan Came and the Lotuses Bloomed

"I've seen you before, in the light of earth, in the love of man."

張文毅寫於一九九五年七月二十八日

Wen-I Chang　　July 28, 1995

大約十年前的一天，一位朋友建議我，和一位高僧結緣，時間定在下一個星期天。不知是我思想之「能波」走在 Minkowski 的三世（過去、現在、未來）同存的「光錐」（Light cone）平面？還是我乘著超光速的「迅子」（Tachyon）回到未來？當晚即清晰地夢見一位連照片都沒見過的高僧，表情嚴肅的在坐禪，如如不動。剃光的頭上有三座像是「〰」（山的象形文字）的金屬物，以等距插在頭上。到真正見面的那一天，眼前的這位高僧，果然就是夢中的那位。他們對我說：「他就是宣化上人。」他慈祥的笑著問道：「聽說你看見我頭上有「〰」的東西？」「是的，那是什麼？」「那就是佛眼，佛已經事先看見你了！」佛？哪尊佛？在哪裡？……！？莫非是……咫尺天涯的闌珊燈火？

這段奇緣，使我能在日後，常以超時空的角度去觀看、研究這位「佛哲」。

語絲軼事

現在讓我舉一些日常小事，及一些親近上人的人對他的認識，加上讀者的想像力與判斷力，來認識這位，既讓人敬畏又讓人敢於去親近的正知覺者及這位覺者的智慧：

（一）易象乾博士（曾任法界佛教大學校長），是最早追隨上人的眾多白人弟子之一。在上人身邊數月後，有一驚奇的發現：「他（上人）根本沒有他自己這個人。」

（二）有一次，上人坐在我車子的後座上，從後視鏡中可以看到上人閉著眼睛。當車子正要超越前面一輛靈柩車時，上人口中念念有詞，以一連串的手

One day about ten years ago, a friend suggested that I meet with an eminent monk the following Sunday. I don't know if my thought waves were traveling on Minkowski's light-cone surface, which contains the past, present, and future, or if I was going back to the future by riding on a tachyon, which travels faster than the speed of light. That night I had a dream in which I clearly saw a great monk sitting perfectly still in meditation with a stern expression on his face. Resting on his shaved head was a metallic object resembling a pictograph of the Chinese character "mountain" (three mountain peaks). On the day of the meeting, the eminent monk I saw was indeed the one in my dream. They said, "This is the Venerable Master Hsuan Hua." He smiled kindly and said, "They say you saw a mountain-like object on my head." "Yes, what was it?" "That's the Buddha-eye. The Buddha has already seen you!" The Buddha? Which Buddha? Where? ...!?...!? Could it be that the person I've been searching for all along is right here, amidst the glittering lights?

This rare experience allowed me to observe and study this Buddhist philosopher from a time-and-space-transcending perspective.

Random Conversations and Incidents

Let me bring up some ordinary incidents and things that others have said, so that the reader may, with his own imagination and judgement, come to recognize the wisdom of this enlightened one whom people hold in awe and yet wish to draw near.

1. Dr. Ron Epstein, one of the Chancellors of Dharma Realm Buddhist University, was the earliest of the many Caucasian disciples who followed the Venerable Master. After being around the Master for several months, he came to realize with amazement, "He (the Venerable Master) simply doesn't have any sense of self."

2. Once, the Venerable Master was riding in the backseat of my car, and from the rearview mirror I could see that the Master's eyes were closed. Just as I was driving past a hearse, the Master recited something and made a series of hand gestures to liberate

勢對著靈柩車揮著，超度車裡面的亡魂。他對眾生慈悲的定義，包括了中陰身階段的亡魂，「同舟必有前世因，擦身而過也是緣。」

（三）另一次也是在我的車上。當車行駛在曲折而風景優美的山路上時，上人忽然問我：「你對克林頓和范士丹意見如何？」一向直言直語的我，立即回答上人：想當三軍統帥的克林頓，年輕的時候曾逃過兵役，現在克林頓支持墮胎合法化，是傷國本。克林頓以其「只吸不吞」（Never inhale）的吸大麻哲學，被人貽為笑柄。關於范士丹的問題，我是這樣回答師父的：她為爭選票，支持同性戀者，而間接滋生愛死病患者，為道德喪淪。上人聽完後，加了兩句：「他做什麼事，都會反反覆覆。」「你該是歸隊的時候了！」

（四）上人曾就上述兩個政見，和許多人討論過。這些人包括市眾參議員、教授、學者等。在此論點上有異議者，上人會立即毫不猶豫、毫不保留地反駁，一點面子都不給：「請問市長先生，兩個太陽或是兩個月亮在一起，還能滋生萬物嗎？」上人單刀直入的獅子吼，並不是嫉惡如仇，而是來自他的大慈大悲，為那些被墮掉的胎兒及愛死病患者吶喊求救。

（五）美國作家 Rick Field，在其書中提到上人的一位（白人）弟子。有一次偷藏了一塊「派」（餡餅）。晚課完後，偷偷地從防火梯溜到屋頂，正要吃時，上人亦爬上屋頂，該弟子裝著雙手合十，慢走默誦佛經，上人則作相反方向繞行。到第三圈繞完時，上人大笑，問了四個字：「感覺如何？」(How do you feel?)數年後，這位弟子完成了一項祈求世界和平，三步一拜的壯舉。最後到達目的地時，上人手上拿了一塊「派」，又大笑著，對在場所有人士說：「這位僧侶叩頭了千里，就是為了吃這一塊『派』！」這就是上人的幽默。

（六）開放的胸襟：上人常聽弟子們，以音樂來表達佛偈之美；上人的弟子，小沙彌們也以小歌劇的方式，讓眾人了解行者（孫悟空）隨唐三藏取經的歷程。在國際譯經學院與萬佛聖城，也常有科學家們集聚一堂，討論科學與佛法的涇渭難

the soul of the deceased in the hearse. His compassion towards living beings extends even to the souls of those who have left their physical body. "Those in the same boat must have affinities from past lives. Even a brush of the shoulders in passing is a condition."

3. Another time when the Master was in my car and I was driving along the winding and scenic mountain road, the Master suddenly asked me, "What do you think of Clinton and Feinstein?" Being a very forthright person, I immediately replied, "Clinton wants to be the Chief Commander of the Armed Forces (President), but he dodged the military draft in his youth. He supports the legalization of abortion, but this is harmful to the country. He's become a laughingstock with his argument that he "never inhaled" when he smoked marijuana. Regarding Feinstein, I said, "In order to get more votes, she is supporting homosexuality and thus indirectly causing the spread of the AIDS virus and the decline of morality." The Venerable Master added, "He always goes back and forth and cannot make up his mind." "It's about time you returned to the fold!"

4. The Venerable Master discussed these two candidates with many people, including city council members, assembly members, senators, professors, and scholars. When he disagreed with them, he would not hesitate to criticize them and overthrow their views, not giving them any face: "Mr. Mayor, if there are two suns or two moons in the sky, how can the myriad things of creation survive?" The Venerable Master's 'lion's roar,' which cuts straight to the heart of the matter, is not motivated by self-righteousness. Rather, it comes from his great kindness and compassion—he is crying for help on behalf of aborted babies and AIDS victims.

5. In his book, the American author Rick Fields tells the story of a Caucasian disciple. One day he secretly stored away a piece of pie, and after evening lecture, he stealthily climbed the fire escape ladder and snuck onto the roof of the building. Just as he was about to bite into the pie, the Master climbed onto the roof, too. His disciple joined his palms and pretended to be reciting as he walked slowly. The Master did likewise but walked in the opposite direction. After the third round, the Master gave a laugh and asked his disciple, "How do you feel?" Several years later, this disciple completed a pilgrimage in which he bowed once every three steps to pray for world peace. When he reached his destination, the Master, holding a piece of pie in his hand, laughed again and said to the assembly, "This monk has bowed a thousand miles for the sake of this piece of pie!" That was the Master's humor.

6. His open-mindedness: The Venerable Master often listened to his disciples express the beauty of Buddhist poetry through music. The Master's young novice disciples have performed plays about Monkey's journey to obtain Sutras. At the International Translation Institute and at the Sagely City of Ten Thousand Buddhas, he often met with scientists to discuss the points where science and the Buddhadharma are indistinguishable. Whenever there was an important decision to be made, the Master would use democratic

分之處。每當有重大決定時，上人亦以民主方式，以「腦力激盪」來集思廣益。最後，則以最常用的一句話：「用你們的智慧去辦！」來考驗及培養弟子們的能力。

（七）布希總統一九九二年競選的第二次辯論會，曾提到「我再度當選總統後，我要領先將我的年薪立刻減百分之二十」。這即是回應上人的「總統不受薪」的建議。上人曾經希望布希成為「無薪」總統，以為國人、世人之表率。

（八）一九九四年十二月五日時，在身體極度虛弱的情況下，上人仍然捨己為人：「我現在就好像兩個人，一個人現在仍然到處救眾生，我這一個人，我是不會管他的，我是不會幫助自己的！」

蓮花初開

在兩千五百年前，釋迦牟尼佛曾說：「在我滅度後的兩千五百年，至高的教義（佛教）將在一個住有紅臉人的國度發展開來。」這個紅臉人的國度，就是住著印第安人的美國。

美國作家 Mr. Rick Fields 在其著作《天鵝投湖心》(How the Swans Came to the Lake) 一書，推薦宣公上人為第一個來美傳揚佛法的中國和尚。書裡提到宣公上人曾在一九六八年於舊金山預言：「今年美國將有五朵蓮花綻開！」就在一九六九年，有五位白人徒弟到臺灣基隆海會寺受具足戒，開美國白人受佛教具足戒的先河。這件事情的歷史意義重大，因為只有當地的人傳法給當地的人，佛教才能算是在該地紮下根來。

佛教就在這第一隻「天鵝」的飛投湖心後，一步一步地發展開來，隨著別的中國僧侶（尤其最近）相繼地來到美國傳授教理、弘揚佛法，一片興旺景象。套一句優美的西洋詩句：「黃鶯初啼響徹雲霄，而十姐妹（鳥）的吱叫，也增加了樹林的熱鬧氣氛。」

惠能大師的出現

當年這位為母守孝的白孝子，有一天參禪靜坐時，見到六祖來到他的面前說：「你會把五宗變成十

methods and have a brainstorming session to gather everyone's ideas. Finally, he would use his most common phrase, "Use your own wisdom to decide!" to test and to nurture his disciples' capabilities.

7. During President Bush's re-election campaign in 1992, he mentioned in the second debate, "After I am re-elected as President, I will take a twenty-percent cut in my salary." This was in response to the Venerable Master's suggestion that the President not take a salary. The Master had hoped President Bush would become an unsalaried President, a model for the people of the nation and the world.

8. On December 5, 1994, when the Venerable Master's condition was already extremely weak, he still wanted to renounce himself to help others: "I am like two people right now. One person is still going around saving living beings. As for this person who is me, I don't care about him. I will not help myself!"

The Lotuses Begin to Bloom

About 2500 years ago, Shakyamuni Buddha said, "2500 years after my Nirvana, the highest doctrine (Buddhism) will develop and expand in a country where red-faced people live." The country of red-faced people refers to America, the home of red-skinned American Indians.

American author Rick Fields, in his book *How the Swans Came to the Lake*, named the Venerable Master Hsuan Hua as the first Chinese monk to come to America and transmit the Buddhadharma to Westerners. The book mentions the prophecy that the Venerable Master made in 1968 in San Francisco: "This year, five lotuses will bloom in America." In 1969, five Caucasian disciples travelled to Haihui Monastery in Keelung, Taiwan to receive the complete precepts, thus becoming the first fully ordained Caucasian Buddhist monks and nuns in America. This event is of great historical importance, for it is only when the Dharma is transmitted by local people to local people that Buddhism will be considered to have sent its roots down.

After this first swan flew over and landed in the lake, Buddhism has been developing step by step, and other Chinese Sangha members have begun (especially recently) to follow it to America to transmit the teachings and propagate the Buddhadharma. The scene is one of prosperity. There's a beautiful saying: "The voice of the nightingale sings through the sky. The calling of the sparrow adds to the joyfulness of the forest."

Great Master Huineng Appears

When Filial Son Bai (the Venerable Master) was living by his mother's grave, one day while meditating he saw the Sixth Patriarch come before him and say, "You will turn the five schools

宗……，你的弟子將數如恆河沙。你將到西方弘揚佛法，是佛法在西方真正的開始。」等他送走了六祖時，他才頓然想起六祖已圓寂久遠（在西元七三一年）。

世界公民及人道主義者史懷哲，被稱為是自耶穌以後的，最能實踐基督真理的一位偉大信徒。

在《觀世音菩薩普門品》裡，有這麼一首優美的偈頌：

瓶中甘露常遍灑，手內楊柳不計秋；
千處祈求千處應，苦海常作渡人舟。

「渡人舟」與「度輪」都是佛菩薩實踐大悲願力的工具。度輪即宣化上人之法名，以此推敲，宣化上人——這位昔日長白山的乞士，為母守墓的白孝子，把自己身體當做可以讓人踐踏走過的「螞蟻」，不就是釋迦牟尼佛以來，最能實踐其悲憫、慈愛、清淨、莊嚴的無我覺者麼？

大道日逝

今年（一九九五）三月二十二日，我在日記中寫道：「昨日夢見師父圓寂，（我雖沒皈依，但是都以師父稱呼他），我手推車上山（車，其實是一圓桶），師父往雲端走，我對師父說，我還想寫信給他……；前兩星期亦夢見師父穿著白色的衣服，躺在一張檯上（大家去看他時），有點不好意思地對大家笑著……。」做了這個夢後不久，有一天（約四月初），我帶一位沈姓友人到萬佛聖城去，回來後，聽到電話留言有兩個師父的弟子的留言，師父要我立刻回電，師父只有短短的三句話：

「我快回去了，你要珍重，你還有事做！」

沒想到，這是竟我和宣公的最後一次對話。難道師父曉得他在這地球上的旅程表？或是旅程自定？

臨終遺言

一九四八年，宣化上人跋涉三千多公里來到

into ten... Your disciples will be as numerous as the sands of the Ganges. You will go to the West to propagate the Buddhadharma, and that will be the genuine beginning of Buddhism in the West." Only after he had escorted the Sixth Patriarch out of his hut did he remember that the Patriarch had entered Nirvana long ago (in A.D. 713).

The "world citizen" and humanist Schweitzer was praised as a great disciple who was most able to practice the teachings of Jesus.

In the "Universal Door Chapter of Guanshiyin Bodhisattva," there is a lovely Buddhist verse:

Sweet dew sprinkles constantly from her vase.
In her hand she holds the willow branch for countless autumns.
Prayers come from a thousand places, and in a thousand places
*   she manifests.*
In the sea of suffering, she is a ship that crosses people over.

A "ship that crosses people over" and a "saving ferry" are all tools by which the Buddhas and Bodhisattvas carry out their vows of great compassion. "Saving ferry" (To Lun) is the Venerable Master Hua's Dharma name. If we think about it, isn't the Venerable Master Hua—as the Mendicant from Changbai Mountain, as Filial Son Bai who stayed by his mother's grave, as the "ant" who allowed others to walk over his body—the most compassionate, caring, pure, adorned, and selfless enlightened one since Shakyamuni Buddha?

The Great Way Flows Away

On March 22 of this year (1995), I wrote in my diary, "Yesterday I dreamed that the Master completed the stillness (even though I haven't taken refuge, I call him the Master). I was pushing a car up a hill (actually, it was a barrel). The Master was walking towards the clouds. I told the Master I wanted to write to him... Two weeks ago I also dreamed of the Master dressed all in white and lying on a platform (when everyone went to visit him). He seemed a bit embarrassed as he smiled at everyone..." Not long after this, one day (in early April), I brought a friend by the surname of Shen to the Sagely City of Ten Thousand Buddhas. When I returned from Ukiah, there were messages from two of the Master's disciples on the answering machine. The Master wanted me to call right away. The Master only said three short lines:

I'm about to leave. Take care of yourself. You still have work to do!

I didn't realize that would be my last conversation with the Venerable Master Hua. Did the Master know his itinerary on this planet? Did he plan his own itinerary?

Final Words

In 1948, the Venerable Master Hua travelled over three thousand kilometers to pay respects to the Elder Master Hsu Yun, a greatly virtuous monk of the Chan School, at Nanhua Monastery in Baolin, Guang-

廣東寶林南華寺拜見禪宗大德虛雲老和尚。兩位大德相見如故，虛雲老和尚知宣化上人是載法之器，故於幾年後即以燈傳上人。這件事一時在佛教界為人津津樂道，傳為美談。因為當時宣公上人只是三十多歲的年輕和尚。

時光仍然荏苒，四十多年過去了，當師父化緣將盡，病臥在床時，曾鄭重的提名恆律法師做為法界佛教總會的主席。師父以英文president（總統）解釋了他的意願，「你們都要好好支持他」，聲音稍弱，但言詞懇切，字字鏗鏘，猶迴繞不絕於耳。 New star（新星）；New president（新方丈）。尤其最後這句話，師父的聲音似乎提高了一點。我們以虔敬之心，期望萬佛聖城的每一份子，都能以師父的意願為意願，好好護持這位年輕的方丈。

這件事意味著一段時期的結束，就是另一段時期的開始，事情就是這樣繼續下去。誠如科學家所言：「一切有為法都只是事項與流程。」

乘願再來

「我從虛空來，回到虛空去」，這是何等即色即空、解脫自在的圓融大美，可是我總遐想老子的「大曰逝，逝曰遠，遠曰返」，這九個字是宇宙曠古以來最美的道悟：道之美在於它的流逝無常，流逝到極遠之處，又要回返本原。

我很執著！師父的十八大願尚未全了，在逝、遠、返的道上，他一定會再乘願而來，這是可以兌現的預言。讓我以一首泰戈爾獨有的美麗的詩句，來表達我期待在一個未知的時空連續區（time-space continuum），恭敬重逢宣化上人的法喜情境：

總有一天，在另外一個世界的旭光裡，我將為你唱頌一首歌：「從前我曾經見過你，在那地球的光中，在那人類的慈愛裡。」

---

dong Province. When the two worthies met, they were like old friends. The Elder Master Hsu Yun knew that the Master was a vessel of Dharma, and several years later, transmitted the Dharma to him. This event was widely talked about by everyone in Buddhism, for at that time the Master was only a young monk in his thirties.

More than forty years have passed. When the Venerable Master's affinities for teaching were about to come to an end and he was lying sick in bed, he solemnly named Dharma Master Heng Lyu as the Chairman of the Dharma Realm Buddhist Association. The Master used the term "president" in stating his intent, saying, "All of you must support him well." Although his voice was weak, his words were in earnest—every word resonated endlessly in my ear: "new star, new president [new abbot]." In particular, the Master's voice seemed to rise in pitch when he said the last phrase. We sincerely hope that every member of the Sagely City of Ten Thousand Buddhas will take the Master's wish as his or her wish, and support this young Abbot.

This indicates that the end of an era is the beginning of another era. Things continue to move ahead; as modern scientists say, "All things and beings are nothing but events and processes."

Coming Back on His Vows

"I came from empty space, and I will return to empty space." This is the great and perfect beauty of liberation and self-mastery, in which form is just emptiness, but it always makes me think of Laozi's line: "Being great, it flows. Flowing, it goes afar. Going afar, it returns." These words are the most beautiful expression of awakening to the Tao that the universe has ever seen from ancient times until now. The beauty of the Tao lies in its flowing and impermanence. When it flows to the farthest point, it will return to its original source.

I'm very attached! The Master has not fulfilled his eighteen great vows yet. On the path of flowing, going afar, and returning, he is certain to come back riding on his vows. This is a prophecy that is sure to come true. Let me use a beautiful verse by Tagore to express the Dharma-bliss I will feel if I, as I hope, reverently meet with the Venerable Master Hua again in an unknown time-space continuum.

Someday, I shall sing to you in the sunrise of some other world: "I have seen you before, in the light of earth, in the love of man."

師父沒有離開我們

THE VENERABLE MASTER HAS NOT LEFT US

許麗玲　Xu Lilin

我自己認為，我的身體還算是健康的，可是年初幾次念佛聖號時，突然覺得心臟有一種抽痛感。當時懷疑心臟是不是有問題，害怕會不會因心絞痛而死。直到七月初，在師父的法體旁，在大眾念佛聲中，由於悲痛，我淚流滿面，那種心痛的感覺又出現了。我才知道，那是在警告我，我將失去一位無上導師，我將無所依怙。面對巨大的悲哀，我完全不能控制自己的淚水！害怕自己會像小孩似的號啕大哭，我趕緊退出靈堂。自此，我不敢再去無言堂看師父。

我很聽師父的話，乖乖地在大殿誦《華嚴經》。我學佛的時間很短，曾誦過《華嚴經》的一小部份。雖家裡有整部《華嚴經》，可是由於福智淺薄，從沒想到要去讀完這部經。這次對我可是千載難逢的機會。我把誦經當成是在上課，可是比一般死板的上課有趣。誦經，有唱有誦有拜，有靜的一面，也有動的一面。尤其對唱「華嚴四十二字母」，我深有感觸。開始時，我不懂頌偈中說，唱四十二字母可利人天。而且唱得時候，音拖的很長，摸不著順序，發音也不確定。經過幾次揣摩後，我唱得好高興。竟然不知道我原來也有這麼美好的嗓子，真是充滿法喜。對於維那師們連日來的辛苦引導，以及同修們的指點、鼓勵，內心更是充滿溫暖感激之情。

從去年幾次打七的經驗中，曾獲極大啟示。從此，對人生的看法有了很大的轉變。知道了一個生命的結束，只是另一個生命的開始。所謂「萬般帶不去，唯有業隨身」的因果關係，是絲毫不爽。拜佛的確不是迷信。更體悟出，以自己拙劣的根性，應該好好地待在大殿內，安分的隨眾作息。

所以，在這次法會中，依自己體能許可，我儘量睡得少、吃得少、說得少、盡力去洗碗、

I consider myself to be in pretty good health. However, at the beginning of the year, sometimes when I recited the Buddha's holy name, I would suddenly feel a wrenching pain in my heart. At the time I suspected that something was the matter with my heart, and I worried that I might die of a heart spasm. In early July, when the assembly was reciting the Buddha's name next to the Venerable Master's body, tears of grief covered my face, and I experienced that same kind of heart pain. Only then did I realize that it was warning me that I was about to lose an unsurpassed guide and teacher and be left without a refuge. Facing that overwhelming sorrow, I couldn't control my tears. I was afraid I would burst out sobbing like a child, so I quickly left the hall. From then on I didn't dare to go to No Words Hall to behold the Venerable Master.

I obeyed the Venerable Master's instructions and recited the *Flower Adornment Sutra* in the main Buddhahall. At that time I had studied Buddhism for only a short time and had only recited a small portion of the *Flower Adornment Sutra* before. Although I had a complete set of the *Flower Adornment Sutra* at home, due to my scant blessings and wisdom, I had never thought to try to read the entire Sutra. This time I had an opportunity that would be hard to encounter in a thousand years. I treated the Sutra recitation as a class, but it was more interesting than ordinary, unimaginative classes. The recitation of Sutras includes singing, reciting, and bowing. There is both a still aspect and a moving aspect. I was especially impressed by the singing of the forty-two syllables of the Flower Adornment Syllabary. At the start, I didn't understand why the verse said that singing the forty-two syllables could benefit humans and gods. And when it was sung, the sounds were dragged out, and I couldn't figure out the order. I wasn't sure of the pronunciation either. After practicing several times, I was singing very joyfully. I never knew I had such a fine voice. I was truly filled with the joy of Dharma. My heart is also filled with gratitude for the painstaking guidance of the cantor and the tips and encouragement from my fellow cultivators over successive days.

From my experience in several retreats last year, I gained a great insight. My perspective on life underwent a major change. I realized that the end of one life is merely the beginning of another life. As the saying goes, "Everything must be left behind. Only your karma will follow you." The relationship between cause and effect is not off by a hair. Bowing to the Buddhas is definitely not superstition. Another thing I realized was that given my dull and inferior disposition, I should stay in the Buddhahall and follow the assembly in cultivation.

During the Dharma session this time, as far as my strength would allow, I tried to sleep less, eat less, and talk less; I did my best to wash dishes, pull weeds, tidy up the Buddhahall, and wash the toilets in order to eradicate my karmic obstacles. At first, I kept wanting to rest.

去拔草、去整理大殿、去洗廁所，以消除業障。剛開始時，只想找時間休息，到了後來，反而精神愈來愈好。尤其，洗廁所後，自己像是脫了層皮，好像把自己的身上的污垢都給沖刷走了。我感覺到師父對我說：「馬桶是我的臉！」那麼，洗馬桶，就等於是在幫他老人家擦臉一樣，我何其有幸。而師父所用的字句，更是讓我多麼慚愧、惶恐。骯髒的、愚癡的，應該是我！

在「讚頌紀念法會」中，高僧大德們的珍貴教誨，字字打動我的心，這輩子從沒有聽受過這麼好的開示。尤其對法師帶引大眾唱校歌時的印象，極為深刻。為什麼昨天覺得難聽的歌，今天聽起來卻很動人，於是趕緊拿一本課誦本跟著唱。無知的我，淚水又灑了一地，真是一切唯心造呀！

我明明知道，焚化爐中荼毘的，只是師父的肉身。而仍然認為，兔子進入大殿聽我們念經，以及孔雀凝視著幻燈片，是種種的瑞相。我提醒自己，這只是自己的幻想罷了。直到謁見了上人最後一面，我非常肯定的是：師父在這裡！因為當我觀想時，我總看到一個空殼頭，而在謁見的那一剎那，有很強的感應，我所觀想到的就是師父呀！我們所誦的《華嚴經》，師父聽到了；所唱的「華嚴字母」，師父也聽到了；甚至在烈日下掃地，師父也看到了。這個傻子不悲哀了！也不孤獨了！可是，當靈柩經過我面前時，當荼毘的火要點燃時，當骨灰要灑盡時，我怎麼也抑制不住那股悲痛！我流著淚，虔誠地叩著頭。

當師父的骨灰隨著熱氣球上升到空中時，聽到師父對我說：「上面很好玩！」這時，我看到在熱氣球的下面，棋盤式的分佈著藏在發亮泡泡中的諸佛菩薩，天上有座大轎，出現巨大的龍、鳳、仙鶴來迎接師父。我問師父：「師父，您要乘什麼回去？」師父說：「啊！飛機也可以！」於是，我又像是看到一架飛機的雙翼，朝西南而去。師父像是個快樂的小孩，出外遠足似的。

儀式結束後，我心裡很平靜。一抬頭，看到一位善知識在向一位義工人員致謝，是呀！能參與這次盛大法會的大眾，不就都是活菩薩嗎？除了讚美感激這些發心工作的活菩薩外，我更應「見賢思齊」。於是當場我向兩位義工人員表達了我的感謝、佩服。可是，念頭一動，是在攀緣嗎？這時，我感到師父說：「要控制心！」

In the end, I became more and more energetic. After washing the toilets, I felt like I had shed a layer of skin. It was as if I had rinsed the filth off my body. I felt the Venerable Master was saying, "The toilet is my face!" Thus, washing the toilet is equivalent to helping the Master wipe his face. How could I be that fortunate! The Venerable Master's choice of words made me feel so ashamed and afraid. The filthy one and stupid one ought to be me!

During the Ceremony in Praise and Recognition, every word of the cherished instructions of the lofty monks and virtuous laypeople stirred my heart. I had never in my life heard such fine instructions. I was especially impressed when a Dharma Master led the assembly in singing the school song. Why is it that the song which had sounded bad to me before was suddenly so moving? I quickly picked up a Recitation Handbook and began to sing along. Ignorant me, my tears again sprinkled the ground. Truly, everything is made from the mind!

I clearly knew that it was only the Venerable Master's flesh body burning in the crematory. I kept thinking that the rabbit which came into the Buddhahall to hear us reciting the Sutra and the peacock that was captivated by the slide show were auspicious omens. Then I reminded myself that it was probably just my fantasy. When I beheld the Venerable Master's visage, however, I was positive about one thing: The Venerable Master is here! During my contemplations, I had always seen an empty shell of a figure. The instant I saw the Venerable Master, I had a very strong feeling--what I had seen in my contemplation was the Master! When we recited the *Flower Adornment Sutra*, the Venerable Master heard it. When we sang the Flower Adornment Syllabary, the Master also heard it. Even when we were sweeping the grounds under the blazing sun, the Master saw it. This simpleton was no longer sad or lonely! Yet when the casket passed before me, when the fire was about to be lit in the crematory, and when they were about to finish scattering the ashes, I couldn't repress an overwhelming sense of grief! With tears flowing, I prostrated myself sincerely.

When the Master's ashes were being carried up into the air by the hot air balloon, I heard the Master say to me, "It's fun up here!" At that time, I saw Buddhas and Bodhisattvas hidden in shining bubbles arranged in chessboard formation below the hot air balloon. In the sky there was a large sedan-chair. Giant dragons, phoenixes, and Manchurian cranes appeared to welcome the Venerable Master. "Master, what are you going to ride in to go back?" I asked. The Master said, "Ah! A plane would do!" Then I seemed to see the two wings of a plane which was heading southwest. The Master was like a happy child going on a trip.

After the ceremony was over, I felt very peaceful. I looked up and saw a good knowing advisor saying thanks to a volunteer worker. Indeed, aren't the people who were able to participate in this great Dharma session all living Bodhisattvas? In addition to praising and thanking these living Bodhisattvas who had volunteered to work, I ought to try to emulate them. I immediately expressed my gratitude and admiration to two volunteer workers. But then I thought, was this exploiting conditions? I felt the Master was saying, "You've got to control your mind!"

The Venerable Master hasn't left us at all! He is everywhere! He

師父根本沒有離開我們！他無處不在！他老人家仍時時督導著我和所有大眾。在這崎嶇不平的學佛路上，師父不時地把我們從偏離的方向，引回正道。而眼前又有這麼多的高僧、大法師、大護法護持這個道場。我深深感覺，這道場將會愈來愈好。由於師父的強大的凝聚力量，定會有人以信心、毅力來實踐師父的遺志，秉承如來家業！

南無阿彌陀佛

五戒弟子叩泣合十

is guiding me and the assembly at all times. As we tread the crooked and uneven paths in studying Buddhism, the Master is constantly leading us back onto the proper path when we go astray. There are so many lofty monks, great Dharma Masters, and great Dharma protectors supporting and protecting this Way-place. I am firmly convinced that this Way-place will become better and better. Given the Venerable Master's great power to gather in and unify people, I am sure there will be faithful and resolute people to carry out the Venerable Master's vows and carry on the Thus Come One's mission!

Namo Amitabha Buddha

Five-precepts disciple bows tearfully and joins her palms

師恩宣公上人圓寂
恭獻輓詩　七律

On the completion of stillness of my kind teacher the Venerable Master Hua,
I respectfully offer this elegy:

一代聖僧歸極樂，環球震起大鏞聲。

無私無我離塵俗，忍渴忍瘁扶眾生。

萬佛城中宣妙法，大千世界履雲程。

荼毗舍利數千顆，德水慈光共月明。

A sagely monk returns to ultimate bliss;
The tolling of the great bell shook up the world.
Without selfishness or ego, he transcended the mundane world.
He bore hunger and toil in order to aid living beings.
At the City of Ten Thousand Buddhas, he proclaimed the wonderful Dharma.
In the great thousand worlds, he journeyed through the clouds.
His cremation yielded thousands of sharira.
His water of virtue and light of compassion are as bright as the moon.

三寶弟子　妙果居士應國鈞頂禮
一九九五年十月七日

Disciple of the Triple Jewel, Upasaka Miao Guo (Ying Guojun) bows in respect
October 7, 1995

忘己濟群生

FORGETTING HIMSELF TO SAVE THE MULTITUDES

林果明　Lin Guoming

一九九四年夏天，上人不顧自己的健康，強忍病痛，為弘揚大法，至溫哥華，接著又到西雅圖。沒想到，這竟是最後一次與此地的弟子們會面。師父當時的開示記憶猶新，他老人家語重心長的說：末法時代的眾生，還是以念佛法門最易得度，而對沒有時間的人，則以十念法門（以十息為準，每息不斷念佛至十息為止）最方便。感恩師父臨走之前給我們這個法寶。

金峰聖寺舊址是一棟年久失修的老舊旅館，市政府於年前指令，必須在指定的時間內換除可能致癌的天花板，耗資頗巨，因而勢必搬遷，在短時間內要找到合適的道場，確實不易。法師與居士們努力不懈，看了一百多個地方，仍找不到合適的。上人殷切關懷，由加州不斷地叮囑尋寺事宜，又因體恤弟子，不讓弟子擔心諸事，視弘法為己任。上人無言的身教，在尋找道場過程中，讓弟子們深深的感動與敬佩。家父本不諳佛法，有緣與上人見了一面而感於師父的德行，次日即皈依上人時，年已七十歲了。皈依的當天，有幸陪著上人到處看樓房找寺地。從早上到天黑一直陪在身邊。家父說上人雖然身上衣服陳舊，卻不時的發出一股自然的清香，這是他一生與人交往未曾有過的經驗，而且從早到晚忙了一天，上人沒到過廁所，這對一位年近八十歲的長者而言，是不太可能的。

西雅圖的道場終於有了著落，在居士們發心出錢出力整修道場的同時，師父因操心寺院改修經費及臨時用款，拿出五千元對我說：「這是裝修新寺的臨時用款，你先收下，日後錢不夠時再通知我。」當時看到上人虛弱的示疾之身，肩負著近三十所寺廟的大小寺務，時時不忘引導眾生走向正道，發願代

In the summer of 1994, the Venerable Master came to Vancouver and then to Seattle to propagate the great Dharma, neglecting his own health and holding up under sickness. I didn't realize that it would be the last time he came to see his disciples here. I remember the Venerable Master's instructional talk as if I had just heard it. He very solemnly said, "In the Dharma-ending Age, the Dharma door of reciting the Buddha's name is the easiest way for living beings to attain liberation. For people without much time, the Dharma door of ten recitations (recite the Buddha's name nonstop in each breath, for a total of ten breaths) is most convenient." I thank the Master for giving us these Dharma treasures before he left.

The old Gold Summit Monastery was an old hotel that had fallen into disrepair over the years. One year ago the city government ruled that the ceiling, which contained a cancer-causing substance, had to be replaced within a certain time period. Due to the huge cost of such a project, the Monastery was forced to move. However, it was not easy to to find a suitable Way-place in such a short time. The Dharma Masters and laypeople worked very hard, looking at over one hundred sites, but still didn't find a suitable one. The Venerable Master was very concerned and called repeatedly from California to bid them to continue searching. During the time they were searching for a Way-place, the Venerable Master sympathized with his disciples and didn't want them to worry about too many things. He considered propagating the Dharma to be his own responsibility, and he taught by example. Thus, his disciples were deeply moved and filled with respect. My seventy-year-old father, who didn't know anything about the Buddhadharma, was influenced by the Venerable Master's virtue at their first meeting and took refuge with him the next day. That day, he had the fortune of accompanying the Venerable Master to look at various buildings and properties. He stayed by the Master's side from morning till night that day. My father noted that although the Master's clothes were old and worn, his body constantly emitted a natural and pure fragrance. Of all the people he'd known in his life, he had never seen anything like this. What was more, during the entire busy day, the Venerable Master didn't use the restroom once. This is quite incredible for an elder nearly eighty years of age.

A place was finally found for Gold Summit Monastery in Seattle. When the laypeople volunteered to contribute both money and manpower to renovate the Way-place, the Master was still worried about the funds and handed me five thousand dollars, saying, "Here is some cash for renovating the monastery. Take this first, and when it runs out, let me know." When I saw the Venerable Master weakened by sickness, bearing responsibility for nearly thirty temples, never forgetting to guide living beings onto the proper path, vowing to take the sufferings and sicknesses of all living beings upon himself without the slightest regard for his own health, showing concern even for the details of renovating our new Way-

受一切眾生的苦難與病痛，卻一點也不顧自己的身體，連改修新寺之事也無微不至，內心甚感難過。於是我跪下來堅持把錢交還上人，心想這事可由護法團分擔。能有機會讓居士們護法修寺，機緣難逢，弟子們感恩都來不及，怎忍心讓上人操勞！於是各方善士積極參與改修事宜，不分老幼，日以繼夜，有些人還受傷流血，卻沒有一句怨言，法喜充滿。很快的，新寺整修完成，上人卻離開了我們，未能來寺開示，留給我們無限的懷恩！

上人，弟子此生萬幸，得以皈依您的座下，今您雖示圓寂，想著您慈悲眾生的願力，弟子堅信您很快又會乘願再來。我們將本著您的六大宗旨：不爭、不貪、不求、不自私、不自利、不打妄語，互相警惕，精進修持，在往後修行的路上向前邁進！

place, I felt very bad. I knelt down and insisted on returning the money to the Venerable Master, thinking that the Dharma-protectors could take care of it. The laypeople are only too thankful for this rare opportunity to protect the Dharma and renovate the temple; how could we bear to see the Venerable Master worry about it? Therefore the laypeople, both old and young, actively worked on the renovation both day and night. Some people were even injured, but not a single complaint was heard. Everyone was filled with the joy of the Dharma. The new monastery's renovation was soon completed. And yet the Venerable Master has left us and cannot come to give a lecture at the monastery. We are filled with endless memories of his kindness.

Venerable Master, your disciple is so fortunate to have taken refuge with you. Although you have completed the stillness, when I think of your vows of compassion for living beings, I believe that you will come back on your vows very soon. We shall follow your six great principles—no fighting, no greed, no seeking, no selfishness, no pursuit of personal advantage, and no lying—as we encourage each other, practice vigorously, and advance on the path of cultivation!

行道修身莫外尋　自性般若深密因
白浪沖霄黑波止　涅槃彼岸任運登
時分時分勿錯過　慎之慎之取天真
杳杳冥冥通消息　恍恍忽忽見本尊

宣公上人《般若波羅密多心經非台頌解》

In practicing the Way and cultivating yourself, do not search outside.
The Prajna of your own nature is the deep and secret cause.
White billows soar to the heavens; the black waves cease.
Nirvana, the other shore, effortlessly is climbed.
Time, O precious time! Don't let it pass in vain!
With great caution and care, approach the divine truth.
Silently, the news arrives from afar;
Now it's there, now it's not—what is originally esteemed is revealed.

From the Venerable Master Hua's Verses without a Stand for the *Heart of Prajna Paramita Sutra*

跟著上人走

FOLLOWING THE VENERABLE MASTER

果秋　Guo Qiu

自己是一個既懶惰又愚昧的佛弟子，但有幸獲得宣化上人的開示，至今尚懂得一點禮佛、念經、拜懺。為了報答上人在世時，對佛教付出的偉大貢獻，我這個文學膚淺的愚人，也只好硬著頭皮，寫出對上人禮敬的心聲。

六年前，有緣至西雅圖金峰聖寺與大眾共修，因此隨著大家參加萬佛聖城的浴佛盛典。當時見上人坐在佛堂中央，很多信眾跪在地上頂禮上人，上人逐一在每位弟子頭上拍了一下，以示加持。我站在遠處看著，直至所有人都離去了，上人仍端坐在那兒，我才上前跪下頂禮，他微笑的望著我，也在我頭上拍了一下，旁邊有位弟子跪下來問上人：「為什麼拍他那一下比較重？」上人微笑著又在他頭上重重的拍了一下，我想上人對待每位弟子都是平等心，只是自己的貪心作祟，上人又很慈悲，看透了我，於是重重的拍了一下。那時我手上有照相機，大家叫我給上人拍照，我便傻傻的走到上人的前面拍了一照，鎂光燈一閃，上人看著我說偷拍我的照，臉上卻流露出慈祥的微笑，我當時嚇得趕緊跪下來頂禮上人，怪自己實在太失禮儀。

第二次見到上人是在幾年前，金峰聖寺剛拜完〈梁皇寶懺〉，下午上人便從加州到西雅圖來看我們，那天有很多人皈依和受五戒，我也受了五戒。上人在我心中是一位持戒德行高深的聖僧，能拜這樣的高僧實在是我的非常榮幸。希望自己好好的守戒，從他那兒學習，增長智慧，做一個守戒的佛教徒。

第三次拜見上人，是在去年（一九九四年）的法界聖城祝壽會，雖然我只見過上人三次，但是從上人的一生事蹟和他開示錄中，上人在我心目中留下了極深的印象，上人是一位慈悲為懷，持戒森嚴，捨己為眾生的一位大德，一生宣揚佛法，教導眾生無數，更使佛教在美國有了穩固的地位，令下一代的青年認識了佛法

I am a lazy and dull-witted disciple of the Buddha. Fortunately, I came upon the Venerable Master's instructional talks and thus understand a bit about worshipping the Buddhas, reciting Sutras, and bowing in repentance. In order to repay the Venerable Master for the great contributions that he made to Buddhism, I am writing about my feelings regarding making obeisance to the Venerable Master, despite my poor literary skills.

Six years ago, I had an opportunity to cultivate with the assembly at Gold Summit Monastery in Seattle. I also joined them to attend the Bathing the Buddha Festival (Buddha's Birthday) at the Sagely City of Ten Thousand Buddhas. I saw the Venerable Master sitting in the center of the Buddhahall and many people kneeling and bowing to him. The Master struck each person on the head with his hand as a gesture of bestowing aid. I stood and watched from a distance. When the people had all gone, the Venerable Master was still sitting there, and so I walked up, knelt in front of him, and bowed. The Master smiled at me and struck my head as well. A disciple beside me knelt down and asked the Master, "Why did you hit him harder?" The Master smiled and struck him hard on the head. I reflected, "The Master treats all his disciples equally, yet when our greed takes over, he is still very compassionate and understands us. That's why he struck him hard." Since I was carrying a camera, everyone told me to take a picture of the Venerable Master. I foolishly walked up in front of the Venerable Master and took his picture. When the flash went off, the Venerable Master looked at me and said I was taking his picture on the sly. He was smiling benevolently. I was so scared that I quickly knelt down and bowed to the Master, reproaching myself for being so discourteous.

The second time I saw the Venerable Master was a few years ago. Gold Summit Monastery had just completed the Jewelled Repentance of the Emperor of Liang, and the Venerable Master had travelled from California to Seattle to see us in the afternoon. Many people took refuge and received the five precepts that day. I also received the five precepts. I regard the Venerable Master as a holy monk who upheld the precepts and had exalted virtue. I am truly honored to have this eminent monk as my teacher. I hope that I will uphold the precepts well, learn from him, and increase my wisdom, so that I will be a Buddhist who observes the precepts.

The third time I saw the Venerable Master was during the Birthday Celebration at the Sagely City of the Dharma Realm last year (1994). Although I have only seen the Venerable Master three times, the Master's biography and instructional talks have impressed me deeply. The Venerable Master was a greatly virtuous one who based himself on compassion, upheld the precepts rigorously, and gave himself up for others. Throughout his life, he propagated the Buddhadharma, taught countless living beings, and established a solid foundation for Bud-

和中國傳統的倫理道德。在此世風日下的社會，適時的注入一股清流；如今上人圓寂，是我們佛教徒的損失，可是我們不應該傷心，應該化悲憤為力量，應該更團結，跟著上人的教導去做，上人的六大宗旨：不爭、不貪、不求、不自私、不自利、不打妄語，說著容易，要真能受用才不辜負上人的一番苦心。

上人的假體已逝，然而他的法身長存。他仍看著我們所做的一切，我們要更加精進，讓未認識佛法的人，也因上人對佛法的獻身，而皈依三寶，擁護正法。讓佛法的種子在西方生生不息，發揚光大，我願以微薄的力量跟大家共同勉勵！

dhism in America. He introduced the Buddhadharma and traditional Chinese ethics to the next generation of young people. A clear stream now infuses this progressively decadent society. While the Venerable Master's completion of stillness is a great loss to Buddhist disciples, we should not feel sad. Rather, we should transform our sorrow into strength. We should be even more united and follow the Master's teachings. It's easy to talk about the Master's Six Great Principles—no fighting, no greed, no seeking, no selfishness, no pursuit of personal advantage, and no lying—but only if we can truly benefit from them will we not disappoint the Venerable Master's great pains.

The Venerable Master's false body is gone, but his Dharma body is eternal. He is watching everything we do. We must be even more vigorous in bringing the Buddhadharma to those who don't know it, causing them to be inspired by the Venerable Master's self-sacrifice for the Buddhadharma, take refuge with the Triple Jewel, and support the Proper Dharma, so that the seeds of the Buddhadharma will thrive and prosper in the West. I wish to use my feeble strength to encourage everyone!

妙智方可達彼岸　　真心自能契覺源
法喻立名超對待　　空諸法相體絕言
宗趣原來無所得　　力用驅除三障蠲
熟酥判作斯教義　　摩訶逆轉般若船

宣公上人《般若波羅密多心經非台頌解》

Only with wonderful wisdom can one reach the other shore;
With a true mind, one naturally can merge with enlightenment's source.
Dharma and analogy comprise the title of this Sutra,
　　which transcends the relative.
Empty of the characteristics of all dharmas
　　is this substance beyond words.
Non-attainment is its purpose and intent;
Its function is to eradicate the three obstacles.
The "butter division" is determined to be
　　the meaning of this teaching,
A Maha turning around: this is the Prajna boat.

From the Venerable Master Hua's Verses without a Stand for the *Heart of Prajna Paramita Sutra*

盡你最大的努力！

TRY YOUR BEST!

王果宿　Wang Guosu

那天早上在金峰聖寺拜完〈大悲懺〉後，一位師兄對我說師父圓寂了，心中一陣震驚！強自鎮靜，忍住悲痛，因為我知道高僧圓寂了是不可悲傷的。但是這個消息卻一直在我腦子裡打轉，想到才皈依七個月的我，竟然無緣見師父一面，真是既傷感又沮喪。

去年到長堤聖寺參加壽誕時，已知師父病重，就想到如何為師父分擔一點。學佛以來，自己每天在家裡早晚念佛拜佛，於是就在拜佛時祈求觀音菩薩保佑師父法體健康，長久住世。這樣做了一個多月。就在獲知師父圓寂的前幾天，自己突然覺得師父不需要我這樣做而停止了祈求，原來師父要走了！故感應到自己不必為此禱告了。後來看到師父的遺言中說，他不會為了救自己的身體，而動一根手指頭！師父為眾生承擔苦業，我這愚痴的弟子，竟傻傻的去求菩薩替師父分憂解勞，不過，無論如何我是做了，像師父常說的一句英文：「Try your best!」（盡你最大的努力！）

自己活了六十幾歲，對佛法，佛經一無所知，印象中只有觀世音菩薩，阿彌陀佛。去年退休後，聽好友談起，在萬佛聖城可學習打坐，才開始結了佛緣。於是到聖城參訪，那兒正好舉辦三天的坐禪法會，大概是機緣吧！初次參禪，真是苦不堪言，如坐針氈，鬼混了二、三枝香便敗下陣來。第二天法師教授了一些些輔助打坐的體操運動，再坐時方勉強忍痛，用雙盤坐完一個小時。回西雅圖後，抱著忍痛贖罪的心情，天天和兩條腿掙扎苦鬥。有一天在金峰寺打坐，法師見我雙盤是左腳在上，於是對我說，師父是右腳在上，於是我又從頭練習，經數週的苦鬥，終於可坐一個小時。

在上人的開示錄中學習到，能恆常保有持戒、布施、忍辱、精進之心以及時常觀照自心，逐漸息滅貪、瞋、癡等惡習，打坐時的痛楚自

What a great shock it was that morning when I had finished bowing the Great Compassion Mantra at Gold Summit Monastery and a Dharma brother told me the Venerable Master had completed the stillness. I forced myself to remain calm and held back the feelings of grief, because I knew that when a lofty monk completes the stillness, one cannot be sad. Yet this news kept spinning around in my head. When I thought of how I had taken refuge with the Master only seven months before and didn't have the affinity to see the Master even once, I was extremely bereaved and depressed.

I already knew the Venerable Master was gravely ill when I attended the Venerable Master's Birthday Celebration at Long Beach Sagely Monastery last year. I wondered how I could share the Master's burden. Ever since I began studying Buddhism, I have bowed to the Buddha and recited the Buddha's name every morning and evening at home. So when I bowed to the Buddha, I prayed to Guanshiyin Bodhisattva to keep the Master in good health so that he could dwell long in the world. I did that for over a month. A few days before I found out about the Master's completion of stillness, I suddenly felt that the Master didn't need me to pray anymore, so I stopped. As it turned out, the Master was about to leave! That's why I felt there was no need to pray anymore. The Master was bearing suffering for living beings, and I, his stupid disciple, was foolish enough to beg the Bodhisattva to lighten his burden. Well, no matter what, I did it. As the Master often says in English, "Try your best!"

I lived for sixty-some years without understanding anything about the Buddhadharma or Sutras. I knew only about Guanshiyin Bodhisattva and Amitabha Buddha. It was only when my good friend mentioned that one could learn meditation at the Sagely City of Ten Thousand Buddhas last year, after my retirement, that I created affinities with Buddhism. When I went to visit the Sagely City, there happened to be a Three-day Chan Meditation Session going on. The conditions were probably ripe! My first experience with meditation was unspeakably painful. It was like sitting on a pincushion. I struggled for two or three sitting periods before admitting defeat. The second day, a Dharma Master taught us some warm-up exercises. Again, I endured the pain and managed to sit in full lotus for one hour. When I returned to Seattle, I battled with my legs every day, determined to bear the pain and pay for my offenses. One day when I was meditating at Gold Summit Sagely Monastery, a Dharma Master noticed that my left leg was on top when I sat in full lotus, and he told me that the Master sat with his right leg on top. I started over, and after several weeks of bitter struggle, I could finally sit for one hour.

From the Venerable Master's instructional talks, I learned that if one can constantly maintain the resolve to uphold the precepts, practice giving, be patient under insult, and be vigorous, and if one can

然會減低很多；又說眾生，凡夫都執著自己的身體，師父用房子來比喻身體，「我」住在房子裡，不能說那座房子就是「我」吧！明白照覺自性才是真的，破了這個我相，色蘊也就空了。因而師父雖然圓寂了，他留給我們的法卻是永恆的！上人的法語將永留弟子們的心中，師父的話更是一盞明燈，照亮弟子們修行的路！感恩追思永永遠遠……。

constantly contemplate one's own mind, then one will gradually extinguish such bad habits as greed, anger, and stupidity. Moreover, there will be a lot less pain when one meditates. The Master also said that ordinary living beings are attached to their bodies, and he used the analogy of a house: 'I' live in the house, but the house cannot be said to be 'me'! The understanding, enlightened self-nature is what is real. Once we destroy the mark of self, the form skandha will be empty. Hence, even though the Master has completed the stillness, the Dharma he has given us is eternal! The Venerable Master's Dharma will remain forever in our minds. The Master's words are a bright lamp lighting up the path of cultivation for his disciples. We will remember and be grateful forever and ever...

色不異空有若無　　空不異色體用殊
色即是空眞源徹　　空即是色妄流枯
山河大地唯識現　　夢幻泡影如是乎
愼勿外求持中道　　放下染緣即來如

宣公上人《般若波羅蜜多心經非台頌解》

"Form does not differ from emptiness": "is" is like "is not."
"Emptiness does not differ from form":
　　the distinction is of substance and function.
"Form itself is emptiness": its true source is fathomed.
"Emptiness itself is form": the false flow has dried up.
Mountains, rivers, and the great earth are only
　　manifestations of consciousness.
"Dream, illusion, bubble, shadow"—so it is!
Be careful not to seek outside; maintain the Middle way.
To cast down stained threads of cause is to come toward the Thus.

From the Venerable Master Hua's Verses without a Stand for the *Heart of Prajna Paramita Sutra*

哀痛與思念

IN GRIEF AND REMEMBRANCE

西雅圖佛友

A Buddhist from Seattle

由世界各國，各個分支道場來參加師父上人的追思大會暨荼毗大典的人數不斷增加，使得萬佛聖城原來的萬佛寶殿不敷使用。於是在萬佛寶殿外面廣場上，用帳蓬搭蓋一座大佛堂，以便容納二，三千人。整個會場佈置得秩序井然，莊嚴肅穆。法會期間一些拜墊，座椅不夠使用，而且會場上的土地凹凸不平，再加上加州天氣特別炎熱，氣溫高達九十到一百度。每個人在帳棚下雖然熱得汗流浹背，但是這些都阻止不了大家對師父上人的思念與哀痛。

每天上午的禮拜〈華嚴懺〉，由不同的法師帶領，而唱誦的調子不一樣，各有千秋。很遺憾沒有帶錄音機，否則就可以將它錄下。「人身難得，佛法難聞。」我何其有幸，人身難得今已得，佛法難聞今已聞，禮拜各種不同的經懺，誦經，懺悔以祈消除業障。

中午的傳供，對大多數人來說，不曾見過，如今有機會參與傳供各式各樣的供品，由每個人手中一一傳到佛前，真的很殊勝。

放大蒙山，在晚間七點舉行，眾多的僧眾聚集一堂。而另一旁則聚集多種供品，法會由明暘法師主持，會場莊嚴，秩序井然，大眾虔誠的念咒，藉著僧眾念咒的力量，施食與六道群生，願他們得食後，能早日脫離苦海，發菩提心，早成佛道。

涅槃堂內，日夜念佛，二十四小時佛號不斷，法師們輪班念佛，四眾弟子有空都到涅槃堂內先瞻仰師父上人遺容，然後加入念佛行列。當我看到一百零七歲的高僧達摩瓦拉，來瞻仰師父遺容時，我的淚水直流，心中想著，一百零七歲的老法師尚健在，而我們的師父卻入涅槃了，今後再也聽不到師父的法音及教誨了。唉！真地是人生無常，相信老法師有同樣感嘆，在他來說，他失去一位道友，在我們來說卻痛失大慈悲父。

As more and more people from around the world and from various branch Way-places came to attend the Memorial and Cremation Ceremonies for the Venerable Master, the Hall of Ten Thousand Buddhas at the Sagely City of Ten Thousand Buddhas could not accommodate everyone. Then a large tent-cover was set up over the plaza outside the Hall of Ten Thousand Buddhas, making a spacious makeshift Buddhahall that could hold two to three thousand people. The entire area was arranged in a very orderly and adorned way. During the Dharma session, there were not enough bowing cushions and chairs, the ground was pitted and uneven, and the California weather was especially hot, with temperatures from 90 to 100 degrees. Even though everyone was sweating profusely under the tent-cover, it did not stop their remembrances of and grief for the Venerable Master.

Every morning the assembly bowed the Flower Adornment Repentance, which was led by various Dharma Masters. Each had his or her own tune and style. I regretted that I didn't bring a tape recorder, for I would have liked to record it. "It is difficult to obtain a human body. It is difficult to get to hear the Buddhadharma." How fortunate I am! I have obtained a human body, heard the Buddhadharma, bowed in various repentance ceremonies, recited Sutras, and repented in the hope of dispelling karmic hindrances.

The offering ceremony before the noon meal was a new experience for the vast majority of the assembly. It was truly rare to have the opportunity to participate in the ceremony, in which assorted offerings were passed from person to person, all the way up to the front, before the Buddhas.

During the Great Meng Mountain Ceremony, which began at 7:00 p.m., a multitude of Sangha members was assembled, and a great variety of offerings were arranged at the other end of the Buddhahall. The ceremony was hosted by Dharma Master Mingyang. The scene was adorned and orderly, as the assembly sincerely recited mantras. Aided by the power of the mantras being recited by the Sangha, food was offered to beings in the six paths, in the hope that after they obtained the food, they would soon leave the sea of suffering, bring forth the Bodhi resolve, and attain the Buddha Way.

In the Nirvana Hall, recitation of the Buddha's name continued day and night, twenty-four hours without break. The Dharma Masters recited in shifts, and the fourfold assembly of disciples went to the Nirvana Hall when they had time to behold the Venerable Master's visage and join in the recitation. When I saw the 107-year-old Venerable Bhante Dharmawara come in to behold the Venerable Master's visage, tears rolled down my cheeks. I thought that while the 107-year-old Venerable Bhante was still healthy, our Master had already entered Nirvana, and we would never be able to hear his Dharma or his teach-

茶毗大典，當儀隊將師父的棺木移到茶毗場，緩緩將棺木移火爐內，明晹法師一聲令下「燒」。我的心都碎了，師父的法體，從此將化為灰燼，這時的我，才真正的相信師父是入涅槃了。炎熱的太陽，吐著高溫，可是四眾弟子們的哀痛非筆墨可形容，汗水淚水早已分不清了，引領唱誦的維那也泣不成聲。唉！我要我們的師父啊！

撒骨灰前，大眾在法師們的帶領下念著〈大悲咒〉從佛堂移步到大齋堂。在大齋堂前面的廣場上，一位法師手捧師父上人的骨灰，隨著其他五位法師進入熱氣球下面繫著的籃子內，大氣球緩緩升空，法師們把師父的骨灰撒到遍虛空界，讓我感到師父上人在虛空裡，無處不與我們同在。此次撒骨灰儀式，雖不敢說是絕後，但可謂空前未曾有。

從萬佛聖城回到西雅圖，在星期日下午，送一位法師到達摩中心，抬頭一看天空一片淡藍色，風和日麗的好天氣。在達摩中心正上空看到一片白色雲形成一隻鳳的樣子，另一邊又看到有兩隻角，天龍的雲彩，只可惜當時身邊沒有照相機無法拍下。可是當時所看見的龍鳳，卻一直留在我腦海中，其中一位法師說今天真是吉祥日，我回答說：「或許師父上人知道我們回到西雅圖，所以有天龍、天鳳示現。」

ings again. Ah! Life is impermanent! I think the Venerable Bhante must feel the same way. While he has lost a friend in the Way, we have bitterly lost our greatly compassionate father.

During the Cremation Ceremony, the Venerable Master's casket was slowly carried to the cremation site and slowly placed into the crematory. When Dharma Master Mingyang gave the order: "Light the fire!" my heart was shattered: The Master's body would be burned to ashes. Then I really believed the Master had entered Nirvana. The hot sun was blazing, but the fourfold assembly's grief cannot be described in words: their sweat and tears were indistinguishable. Even the cantor himself burst into tears. Ah! I yearn for my Master!

Before the scattering of ashes, the assembly moved from the Buddha-hall to the main dining hall, reciting the Great Compassion Mantra under the leadership of the Dharma Masters. In the meadow in front of the dining hall, a Dharma Master who respectfully carried the Venerable Master's ashes, and five other Dharma Masters climbed into the basket of the hot-air balloon. As the balloon gradually rose up into the sky, the Dharma Masters scattered the Venerable Master's ashes into the air, giving us the feeling that the Venerable Master is always with us, pervading all of empty space. The ritual of scattering the ashes was the first of its kind, although it may not be the last.

On a Sunday afternoon, I drove from the Sagely City of Ten Thousand Buddhas back to Seattle, and then sent a Dharma Master to the Bodhidharma Center. Looking up, I saw the clear blue skies. It was a perfect day, sunny and breezy. In the air directly above the Bodhidharma Center, I saw a white cloud shaped like a phoenix, and another cloud shaped like a heavenly dragon with two horns. Too bad I didn't have my camera, but the dragon and phoenix will remain in my memory. One of the Dharma Masters commented, "Today is a very auspicious day." I said, "Maybe the Venerable Master knows we've returned to Seattle, and so this dragon and phoenix have appeared in the sky."

度過苦海出輪迴　雨霽天晴月正輝　乾元道體人中聖　不壞金軀世上稀
脫生何須千年藥　證滅豈待萬劫期　二死永亡五住盡　逍遙法界任東西

宣公上人《般若波羅密多心經非台頌解》

Across the sea of suffering, one leaves the revolving wheel,
The rains disperse, the heavens clear; just then the moon is fully bright.
The Chien source is the Way-substance, among people the sage.
His undecaying golden body is rare in the world.
Cast off birth; what need of thousand-year elixirs?
Attain extinction; why wait ten thousand kalpas?
Five dwellings ended, the two deaths disappear forever.
Roam at will from East to West, throughout the Dharma Realm.

From the Venerable Master Hua's Verses without a Stand for the *Heart of Prajna Paramita Sutra*

宣公上人救了我！

THE VENERABLE MASTER SAVED MY LIFE!

陳果璞採訪

Interviewed by Chen Guopu

一九八八年，宣公上人在臺灣桃園妙法寺傳授三皈依，那是恆泉師第一次有機緣拜見上人。當時恆泉師正值重病服藥期間，上人一見她，就勸道：「不要吃藥了，吃藥只是拖時間。」

第二天，恆泉師再去拜見上人。上人問她：「妳要死還是要活？」恆泉師說：「死，活都可以。」當時恆泉師在臺灣東勢圓通精舍辦培生幼稚園，深受東勢地方民眾的歡迎。上人對她開示說：「出家人要幫國家，社會做事，最好的方式就是辦教育。不管是多是少，盡心就好。」

接著上人以柺杖打恆泉師的頭，她的頭上立刻起了一個疙瘩。回到東勢後，恆泉師發現肩膀上原先長瘤的地方，竟出現一顆類似青春痘的膿包。有一天午睡中，這顆「青春痘」破了，膿水源源流出，恆泉師趕緊以衛生紙不斷擦拭，用髒了的衛生紙很快堆滿了整個垃圾桶。恆泉師剎時感到胸口血液通暢無阻，身心無比清涼自在。治療了許久都不見起色的痼疾，就這樣好了。

恆泉師回憶道：「師父打了我的頭之後，回去我就沒再吃藥。這是師父第一次救我的命。」

一九九三年農曆春節期間，恆泉師因為嚴重的肺病，只得入院接受治療。有一天，吃了醫生開的藥之後，感覺全身發熱，極不舒服。於是，恆泉師便觀想自己去游泳，全身泡在清涼的水中，精神便好一些了。這天晚上八點十分左右，恆泉師看見上人手持籐製搖籃，搖籃內是個男孩。上人對恆泉師說：

這個男孩就是妳。妳的壽命到今晚為止，等一下妳就要去那裡。這個男孩命很好，生活會很幸福。

恆泉師一聽，忙說：「那很好啊！」
上人：「好是好，還在六道裡。」
恆泉師：「我不要在六道，我要去極樂世界。」

Bhikshuni Heng Quan first met the Venerable Master in 1988, when he was transmitting the Three Refuges at Wonderful Dharma Monastery in Taoyuan, Taiwan. At that time, Bhikshuni Heng Quan was seriously ill and taking medication. Upon seeing her, the Venerable Master urged her,

Don't take medicine. Taking medicine only makes it last longer.

The following day, Bhikshuni Heng Quan went to see the Venerable Master again. The Master asked her, "Do you want to die or live?" She said, "Either one is okay." Bhikshuni Heng Quan was then heading the Peisheng (Nurturing Life) Kindergarten at the Yuantong (Perfect Penetration) Hermitage in Dongshi, and the local people there deeply appreciated her. The Master instructed her,

Left-home people should help the nation and work for society, and the best way to do that is to organize and administer schools. It doesn't matter how much you do, as long as you do your best.

Then the Master hit Bhikshuni Heng Quan's head with his cane, and a lump immediately swelled up there. Returning to Dongshi, she discovered that a small pimple-like blister had formed on the tumor on her shoulder. One afternoon, the pimple burst while she was taking a nap, and a great deal of pus flowed from it. She tried to wipe up the pus with tissues, and soon the used tissues filled the wastebasket. In that instant, She felt the blood circulation in her chest cavity become very free and unhindered, and she experienced an incomparable coolness and comfort both physically and mentally. Thus, that was how she recovered from the chronic disease that had long been treated without any sign of improvement.

Bhikshuni Heng Quan recalls, "After the Venerable Master struck me on the head, I went back and took no more medicine. That was the first time the Master saved my life."

During the Chinese New Year Festival of 1993, Bhikshuni Heng Quan suffered a severe case of lung disease and had to be taken to the hospital for treatment. One day after she had taken the medicine prescribed by the doctor, she felt her whole body become hot. It was extremely uncomfortable. She imagined that she was swimming and her body was soaked in cool water, and she felt better. That evening around ten minutes past eight o'clock, she saw the Venerable Master holding a cradle in his hands. In the cradle was a boy. The Master said to her,

This boy is you. Your life will end tonight, and in a moment you will go there. This boy has a very good life, full of blessings.

宣化老和尚追思紀念專集

這時觀世音菩薩現身，站在上人身側。恆泉師一轉念，想到許多俗務未了，連忙討價還價說：「我不要現在就去極樂世界，我還有很重要的事要做。」上人聽了，帶著為難的神色，轉身走了。走時，恆泉師注意到上人手中拿著兩張紙。

兩個小時後，恆泉師因為身體極度難過，從假寐中清醒過來，睜眼一看，上人又在前面。這次，上人手中已不拿紙，只是吩咐道：「藥不能吃，那個藥就是要妳的命，現在趕快叫五兄弟來分擔。」

說也奇怪，恆泉師一聽就明白五兄弟是指五臟。因此便請照顧她的恆星師倒水給她喝，她將全部的水都喝了。當晚恆星師照顧她到夜裡兩點，正準備睡時，上人對恆泉師說：叫她不要睡，今晚不能睡，趕快念「觀世音菩薩」！這時，上人和觀世音菩薩都出現在恆泉師的病房。恆泉師感覺病房中有許多陰界眾生，可是，上人和觀世音菩薩對待這些陰界眾生，和對待恆泉師的態度是一樣平等的，並不偏向恆泉師。

天亮後，恆泉師和主治醫生商量：「我在醫院睡不著，想回去。」醫生答應了。出院回去後，恆泉師為那些陰界眾生念誦《阿彌陀經》迴向，但病情似未好轉，咳得連想停五分鐘都辦不到。

恆泉師便求佛菩薩加持。當天中午睡午覺時，夢中見上人帶著一大群比丘，比丘尼，圍繞著恆泉師念誦：「喃，室喇多，室喇多，軍刹利，娑婆訶。」醒來時，誦咒聲猶在耳際，但上人及那群比丘，比丘尼的形相已消失。不久，一位比丘尼師兄來看她，發現她的身體已奇蹟般地痊癒了。

Upon hearing that, Bhikshuni Heng Quan quickly said, "That's good!"

Venerable Master: "Sure, it's good, but it's still in the six paths."

Bhikshuni Heng Quan: "I don't want to stay in the six paths. I want to go to the Land of Ultimate Bliss."

At that moment Guanshiyin Bodhisattva appeared and stood beside the Venerable Master. Suddenly Bhikshuni Heng Quan remembered that she still had many worldly affairs to take care of, so she hurriedly tried to bargain, "I don't want to go to the Land of Ultimate Bliss just yet. I still have many important things to do." Hearing her, the Venerable Master turned and walked away, looking disappointed. As he walked away, she noticed that he was carrying two slips of paper in his hand.

Two hours later, Bhikshuni Heng Quan was awakened from a fitful sleep by the extreme physical discomfort. When she opened her eyes, she again saw the Venerable Master before her. The Master was no longer carrying the slips of paper and simply said to her,

"That medicine cannot be taken, for it will take your life. I will quickly call upon the five brothers to share the burden."

Strange to say, but she immediately understood that the "five brothers" meant the five organs. She then asked Shramanerika Heng Xin, who was taking care of her, to give her some water to drink. She drank all the water. That night, Shramanerika Heng Xin took care of her until two o'clock in the morning and was preparing to go to sleep. Just then, the Venerable Master said to Bhikshuni Heng Quan:

Tell her not to sleep! She cannot sleep tonight. Recite "Guanshiyin Bodhisattva," quickly!

At that time, the Venerable Master and Guanshiyin Bodhisattva were both in Bhikshuni Heng Quan's room. She sensed that there were many beings of the underworld in the room as well, yet she felt that the Venerable Master and Guanshiyin Bodhisattva treated the underworld beings and herself equally, without showing her any favoritism.

When day broke, Bhikshuni Heng Quan negotiated with the chief doctor, saying, "I have trouble falling asleep at the hospital, so I'd like to leave." The doctor agreed to discharge her. After she returned to the temple, she recited the *Amitabha Sutra* and transferred the merit to those underworld beings. Nevertheless, she showed no signs of recovery, and five minutes didn't go by without her coughing.

She prayed for aid from the Buddhas and Bodhisattvas. That day, during her afternoon nap, she dreamed of the Venerable Master bringing a large group of Bhikshus and Bhikshunis to gather around her and recite: "Nan, shi li duo, shi li duo, jun zha li, suo po he." When she woke up, the sound of the mantra being recited was still in her ears, but the vision of the Venerable Master and the Bhikshus and Bhikshunis was gone. Not long after, a fellow Bhikshuni came to see her and discovered that she had miraculously recovered.

HE WAS TRUE IN EVERY WAY
一眞一切眞

Sarah Babcock
貝慧學

What I really want to say about the Venerable Master Hsuan Hua, is impossible to say in words. We all know in our hearts what a rare being he was. I did not even know him well, and still, just by reading his books, listening to his tapes, and looking at photographs of him, I know that he was true in every way.

I have only been a disciple for a year and a half, but both my parents have been disciples for many years. I do not know what stopped me from becoming his disciple earlier. I guess I had to learn more about the religion my parents were promoting before I officially became a Buddhist. But actually I always knew it was the truth.

I had two dreams about Shih Fu. Other than that I haven't had many experiences with him personally, but I consider these dreams as very important.

The first dream I had was after I had recited the Great Compassion Mantra very sincerely before I went to sleep. The dream was very clear; not like any other kind of dream I'd had before. I was in the Buddha Hall at the City of Ten Thousand Buddhas. Shih Fu walked by on my right and I faced him. He did not say anything, but I knew he wanted me to show him my breathing. So I carefully inhaled and then exhaled. When I inhaled my breath was strong. When I exhaled it was very shaky and unsteady. Shih Fu was showing me that I needed to practice my breathing. There was a second part to the dream. Shih Fu stood before me and I opened my mouth. He placed his pointer finger on my two bottom front teeth and pressed down. I remember very clearly the feeling of my teeth being pressed on my jaw. He then took his finger out and said, "Ahh, you're going to get sick." I was not frightened or even surprised, just aware.

I was very grateful for this dream, but didn't really understand the teeth pressing. Anyhow, I knew I should practice my breathing. I kept reminding myself that I had better practice, but never really did. I wouldn't humble myself to practice something so basic. So I felt guilty. About a month later, I had another dream.

In this second dream I was also in the Buddha Hall at the City of Ten Thousand Buddhas. Shih Fu was in the middle. A few other people and I were standing at the bowing cushions. Shih Fu stood next to us. We turned to face him. As he looked at me, I felt incredible shame; it was as if every part of me was covered in shame. The corners of my mouth slowly turned down and my head very slowly lowered. I felt nothing but shame. That was the entire dream. After I woke up I felt very fortunate that I was able to repent to Shih Fu.

I learned many things from these two dreams. (1) Practice breathing. (2) Be more aware of the mouth: eating and talking. (3)

對於宣公上人，我真正想說的是無法用語言來表達的。在心裡我們都知道上人是多麼地不尋常。雖然我對上人的了解不深，可是看他的書、聽他的錄音帶，以及看他的相片。我知道他在各方面都是真的。

我成為師父的弟子只有一年半的時間，可是我父母是上人多年的老弟子。我不知道為什麼我沒有早點皈依上人。我想大概是在正式成為佛教徒之前，我想對父母所推崇的宗教有多一點的瞭解。而實際上，我早已知道佛教是真的。

我夢到過師父兩次，除此之外，我沒有什麼其他的個人經驗。可是我認為這兩個夢是很重要的。

第一個是我在睡前很虔誠地念〈大悲咒〉之後做的。這個夢跟我其他的夢不同，它很清楚：我在萬佛城的大殿，師父從我的右邊走過，我轉身面對他。他沒有說話可是我知道他要我做給他看我是怎麼呼吸的。所以我很小心的吸氣、吐氣。我吸的時候很有力，可是吐氣的時候不太穩定。師父是在告訴我，要多練習呼吸。這個夢的第二部份是師父站在我前面，我的嘴巴是張開的。他把食指放在我的兩顆下門牙上往下壓。我記得很清楚牙齒被壓的感覺。然後他把手指拿出來，說：「啊！妳要生病了。」我不覺得害怕，也不覺得驚訝。只是知道這麼回事而已。

我很感激這個夢，雖然我不明白按牙齒的意思，但是我知道我應該練習呼吸。我一直提醒自己要練習呼吸，可是從來沒有真正做到。我是不會讓自己謙下到去花時間在那麼簡單的事情上的，因此我覺得很內咎。一個月後我作了另一個夢。

在這第二個夢裡，我還是在萬佛城的佛殿裡，師父站在殿中央，在我和另外幾個人的旁邊，我們站在拜墊前。我們轉身向著師父。在他看著我的時候，我感到非常地慚愧好像全身都被那種羞恥的感覺包圍住了。我的嘴角慢慢地垂下來，頭也慢慢地低

Don't take what Shih Fu says lightly. These dreams made me more aware that I should not only try to understand what Shih Fu says, but also put it into practice.

Because of Shih Fu and my parents, I have become very interested in the Buddha Dharma. I feel very fortunate to have a good path to follow. Now the only thing left is to follow it!

了下來。除了羞愧，我沒有其他的感覺。整個夢就是如此。醒來後自覺能向師父懺悔是很幸運的。

從這兩個夢裡我學到了要，一、練習呼吸，二、注意嘴巴的吃和說。三、不要不把師父的話當回事。這兩個夢讓我更警覺我不但要了解師父所說的，同時應實際去作。

因為師父及我父母，使我對佛法非常感興趣。我很幸運能找到一條正道，現在要做的就是去行了！

REMEMBRANCE AND GRATITUDE
思念與感恩

Ocean Epstein (Guo Han)　易果涵

I came to San Francisco in the middle of August 1968. It was close to the end of the first Shurangama Summer Session. That was when I first met Shifu.

In January 1969 on Amitabha Buddha's birthday, Shifu presided over the wedding ceremony for me and my husband. Ever since then he took care of, guided, and helped me and my family in an infinity of ways. There are so many stories I could recount, but I will only mention a couple of them: one about Shifu healing my mother and one about my own illness.

In 1982 during my annual physical exam, the doctor found a small cyst in my abdomen. The doctor suggested doing an exploratory operation to see what the cyst consisted of. I went to see Shifu to ask his opinion. He said, "No, you don't need an operation. Everything will be okay. You should recite Gwan Shr Yin Bodhisattva's Universal Door Chapter of the *Lotus Sutra* often." I followed his instructions and did not seek any more medical advice. In the meantime, however, the cyst grew and the entire left half of my abdomen became hard, but it didn't hurt. I felt fine. At that time, I became pregnant with my second child and I was worried, but I had faith in what Shifu had told me.

The pregnancy went along fine until about eleven weeks before the baby was due. At that time I started going into premature labor and was hospitalized. Over the years, we always let Shifu know about our problems no matter how big or small they were. Of course we told Shifu about this serious situation. There is no question in my mind that Shifu was aiding me through this difficult time. One day Shifu told my husband that our baby could be born at that time without problems. My son was born soon after, and all went well. He was healthy and there were no complications. After my son was born, the cyst also disappeared.

During 1985–1986, my mother became seriously ill. First she went to see a Western physician who was 99% sure that she had liver cancer. The doctor advised against a biopsy both because he was sure of the diagnosis and because he did not want to cause her unnecessary pain. He said she would live six months at most. My mother has been a devout Buddhist and vegetarian for a long time. She often recites the name of Guan Yin Bodhisattva, and during this period she would often go to the Sagely City of Ten Thousand Buddhas to bow the Great Compassion Repentance. At that time, one of my parents' friends introduced them to a Chinese medicine cancer specialist. My mother started seeing the specialist twice a week and taking Chinese medicine. The Chinese doctor also thought it was liver cancer. After a few

我於一九六八年八月中旬來到舊金山時，正是第一次夏季「楞嚴講習班」快要結束的時候，也是我第一次晉謁師父上人。

一九六九年正月彌陀誕日，師父為外子和我舉行婚禮。從此以後，師父在各方面不斷地照顧、指導，和幫助我們。我可以述說許許多多所發生過的故事，但是現在只簡述其中兩件：一是師父治癒家母之病，一是有關我自己的病症。

一九八二年在每年例行身體檢查時，醫生在我腹部中發現一個小小的瘤，他建議開刀檢查。於是我去請教師父的意見，師父上人說：「不要動手術，不會有什麼問題，應該多念念《觀世音菩薩普門品》……。」我當然遵從師父的指示，就沒有再去看醫生。之後，瘤卻逐漸長大，直至整個左腹部都變成硬塊。但是並不痛，我的身體和精神都很好。在此期間，我身懷次子，我有些擔心，但對師父所說的話深具信心。

懷孕期間情況非常順利，直到最後的十一個星期左右，因有早產現象而住進醫院。多年以來，如果我們有問題，不論問題大小，都一一請教於師父。當然外子將此嚴重情形稟告上人，在我心裡是毫無疑問地相信師父在幫助我度過這段困難的時期。一天，上人告訴外子：「孩子可以出生了，現在不會有問題了。」不久次子出生，健康無恙，同時腫瘤也消失了。

在一九八五、八六年間，家母病重。她先去看西醫。醫生百分之九十九確定是肝癌，並說最多能活六個月。當時，醫生覺得穿刺檢查都不需要，一者因為他很有把握他的診斷是正確的，再者不願意增加母親的痛苦。家母是虔誠的佛教徒，茹素多年，經常念觀音菩薩的名號，生病期間常到萬佛聖城拜〈大悲懺〉。那時，父母經朋友介紹認識一位在舊金山的中醫，她是醫癌症專家，因此家母開始前往治病。每週兩次，並服中藥，這位中醫也確定母親得了肝癌。經過一段時期的治療，醫生對家父說，

weeks of treatment, the doctor informed my father that my mother's situation was very critical; she also told my husband that in such cases there was not much hope. Of course my father was very agitated. At that time my husband and I went to see Shifu and told him about my mother's situation. The first thing he said was, "Did you come of your own volition or did your parents ask you to come?" I replied that I had decided to come on my own. Then Shifu very compassionately said, "Don't worry, it will be okay. It's not necessarily cancer." After that my mother slowly recovered. She is still alive and healthy today.

Shifu had such a great heart; his compassion and patience were inexhaustible. I will be eternally grateful for all Shifu did for me and my family. I have seen Shifu teach, transform, and help many, many other people as well. Never even once did I see him do anything to benefit himself.

家母情況危急，並對外子說母親的希望渺茫。家父震驚不已，不知所措。此時，外子和我去見師父，稟告家母情況後，上人首先問的是：「是你自己來的，還是你的父母要你來的。」我回答：「是我自己決定來的」。然後師父很慈悲地說：「不要擔心，不會有問題的，不一定就是癌症」。

從那之後，家母慢慢復原，直至今日仍然健在。師父上人胸襟廣大，他用無窮盡的慈悲和耐心來教化和幫助許許多多的人，但從不為自己著想。我將永遠感激不忘師父對我及家人的恩惠。

三光普照透三才　　一歸合處復一來
見色即空受納是　　妄想遷流行業排
識乃了別五陰具　　鏡花水月絕塵埃
空而不空明大用　　見猶未見樂快哉

宣公上人《般若波羅密多心經非台頌解》

The three lights shine everywhere, permeating the three forces.
The one returns to the place of union, yet the one comes forth again.
See that form is emptiness and that feeling is the same way;
False thoughts and shifting currents: cognition and formation are arranged together;
With consciousness, which understands differences, the five skandhas are completed.
Like flowers in the mirror or the moon in water, they are basically beyond defiling dust:
Empty and yet not empty the great function is understood;
Seeing as if not seeing happiness indeed!

From the Venerable Master Hua's Verses without a Stand for the *Heart of Prajna Paramita Sutra*

感念吾師教誨恩

IN GRATITUDE AND REMINISCENCE OF MY MASTER

孔果成　Kong Guocheng

自從上人圓寂之後，我每天都在長堤聖寺念佛，有時至夜裡兩三點才回家。

我既非人才，又無錢財，更無口才，上人願收我為弟子，心中非常感恩。我一向身體不好，不能坐車、搭飛機或乘船，不得已坐了之後，必得在床上躺兩天，所以不願意出遠門。即使女兒們說破了嘴，也不動心。六月十六日傍晚，眾弟子們護送上人的法體回萬佛聖城，我心裡告訴上人：「我這次很想跟您去萬佛城，希望去後不要讓我躺兩天。」當我將這決定告訴女兒時，她們都很驚訝。

一路上，我沒吃藥，心中默默地告訴上人。五、六個小時過去了。中途停車休息時，我從迷糊中醒來，也沒覺得暈車。次日清晨六時許抵達萬佛聖城，我到大殿禮佛。一連在萬佛城住了四十多天，一直沒有不舒服。平日按照萬佛聖城的作息時間，早晚必定到無言堂，有時夜裡一點多也還在那兒繞佛念佛。

當時我住在菩提精舍，人不太多，樓下住了三、四位老太太，其中一位越南太太，不會中文，廣東話也難懂，我又不會越南話，平日溝通時只好比手劃腳。她的法名叫果潔，已七十多歲，由法國來，有風濕病。我告訴她，我的法名叫果成，可是她始終不記得，便說：「我就叫你『朋友』吧！」

一天晚齋之後，回到精舍，果潔指著一個花圃說：「這是我一九九一年種的。」又接著說：「師父救了我的命，我那時住在加拿大，患子宮癌，醫生告訴我用止痛藥，但至多可活六個月。於是我每天拿著師父的照片，對著師父說：「師父我不想死！」我打電話到加拿大金佛寺，告訴法師我得了子宮癌，快死了，心裡很難過。後來法師將此事當面告訴師父，師父馬上吩咐法師在加拿大的金佛寺，連續念兩個月《華嚴經》，並回向給我。但我當時在醫院

After Shr Fu entered stillness, I went to Long Beach Sagely Monastery every day. Sometimes I would stay till two or three o'clock in the morning reciting the Buddha's name before going home. I am not a talented person. I am neither affluent nor eloquent in speech. I am just an ordinary layperson. I feel grateful enough that Shr Fu took me as his disciple. For years, my body has not been in good health. I cannot travel long distance either by land, by water, or by air. When I have no choice but to make those trips, I always end up two days in bed. For this reason, I dislike long-distance travel. No matter how my daughters try to persuade me, I never give in. Around dusk on July 16, the multitude of disciples escorted Shr Fu's Dharma body back to the Sagely City of Ten Thousand Buddhas. At that time, I conveyed this message to Shr Fu: "I really want to escort you back to the Sagely City of Ten Thousand Buddhas. Please don't let me stay sick in bed for two days afterwards." When I told my daughters this decision, they were very surprised.

During the trip, I did not take any medication. I just kept Shr Fu in my thoughts constantly. When the bus stopped at a rest area after five or six hours, I half woke up from sleep and did not feel nauseated. We arrived at the Sagely City at 6:00 a.m. the following morning; I went to the Buddha Hall to bow to the Buddhas and to express my gratitude. I stayed at the Sagely City for more than forty days, never getting sick. I followed the routine schedule of the Sagely City. Every morning and every evening I went to No Words Hall. Sometimes I stayed there reciting the Buddha's name till one o'clock in the morning.

During that time, I stayed at the Bodhi House. There were not many people living there, just three or four elderly women. One of them was an old Vietnamese lady. She did not understand Mandarin or Cantonese, and I did not understand Vietnamese, so we communicated through sign language. Her Dharma name is Guo Jie. She is over seventy years old. She came from France, and she has rheumatism. I told her my Dharma name is Guo Cheng. But she had a hard time remembering, so she said that she would just call me "friend."

One day after coming back from dinner, she pointed to a garden lot and said, "I planted this in 1991." She continued, "Shr Fu saved my life. At that time I was staying in Canada. I was diagnosed with ovarian cancer. The doctor told me to take pain suppressant medication and said that I had only six months to live. During those times, I held onto Shr Fu's photograph every day, crying, 'Shr Fu! I do not want to die!' Later on, I called Canada's Gold Buddha Monastery and told the Dharma Master that I had ovarian cancer and would soon die. I was very down-hearted. The Dharma Master informed Shr Fu of my condition. Immediately, Shr Fu instructed the Dharma Master to recite the *Avatamsaka Sutra* at Gold Buddha Monastery consecutively for two months and transfer the merit and virtue to me. I was not even

，並不知道這件事，住院一個月左右，醫生叫我出院，並說：「我檢查過了，你現在什麼都沒有了。」我聽了十分著急說：「完了，完了！醫生叫我回家去等死啊！」但醫生卻說：「我沒什麼藥給你，因為都好了。」後來我到金佛寺，法師見到我很驚訝地說：「為什麼你來了？」我答：「是醫生叫我出院的。」法師說：「師父要我們連續念兩個月的《華嚴經》。您怎麼一個月就出院了？我當時聽了，對師父感激不已，那是一九八八年的事。」聽完這位越南老太太的敘述，內心十分感動。

望著前方一個荒蕪的花圃，心中想著，師父荼毗大典那幾天，會有很多人從世界各地來參加。人們平時都會經過這裡。若能將那個花圃也整理好，該有多好。我將這想法比手劃腳一番告訴果潔，她似乎聽懂了。第二天便見到她找來剷子、耙子等工具。

那個荒蕪的花圃約二十呎長，十二至十四呎寬，其中長滿了爛草。並有成堆的石頭，我們二人發心翻土、撿石，第一天的天氣熱得不得了。上午做到十點上供前，下午忙到七、八點，但是還有許多乾土未翻，果潔告訴我：「你相不相信，明天一定很涼快！」我心想，會有什麼好天氣，但沒說出來，各人還是做各人的。

第二天早上起來，天空陰陰的，做完早課，用早齋後，又去草地上繼續翻土挑石。直到七、八點，心裡想：「太陽還沒起來呀？」果潔說：「今天一定是好天氣！」我本是容易流汗的人，但那天微風一陣陣吹來，十分清爽。我說：「師父保佑呀！」我們二人很高興地工作到十點，再去上供。下午又繼續再做，天氣仍然是陰涼的。到了晚上，果潔說：「你信不信，明天還是這樣的好天氣！」

果然，第三天仍然是好天氣。我們倆很高興，因為眼看著工作就快做完了，最後我們必須將石頭及雜草用獨輪車運到指定的地方。

第四天上午，天氣仍是涼涼的。心想：「這種天氣應是春天才有的，怎麼在此炎夏有這樣的天氣？」果潔後來告訴我：「我那天跟你講會有好天氣，你不相信，對不對？每天夜裡我回到宿舍，都去求師父，說：『師父我們一個六十多歲，一個七十多歲，想要整理花圃，好讓佛友們來萬佛城時賞欣悅目，師父您一定要幫助我們呀！』所以我有這個自信！」我們二人說著十分高興。

我們第四天一直忙到約十一點才完工，之後還到

aware of this happening because I was in the hospital at that time. After approximately one month, the doctor released me from the hospital saying, 'I examined you, and you're all well.' Hearing this, I got very nervous. I thought, 'That's it! That's it! The doctor is sending me home to wait for my death.' But then, the doctor said, 'I'm not giving you any medication because you are completely well now.' After that, I went to Gold Buddha Monastery. The Dharma Master was startled to see me, "Shr Fu instructed us to recite the *Avatamsaka Sutra* continuously for two months. How come you are already out after one month?" When I heard that, I felt an infinite sense of gratitude towards Shr Fu. This incident took place in 1988." Listening to this elderly Vietnamese lady's narration with sign language, I was deeply moved.

One day, looking at a barren garden lot, I thought, "During Shr Fu's Cremation Ceremony, lots of people will come from all over the world to attend. They will be passing by this corner. Wouldn't it be nice if we could tend this garden lot?" I passed this idea to Guo Jie. The next day, she came bringing shovels and rakes.

The lot is about twenty feet long, and twelve to fourteen feet wide. It was full of dried-up grasses and piles of stones. The two of us resolved to clean it. On the first day, the weather was extremely hot. In the morning, we worked until the Meal Offering, and continued after lunch until seven or eight o'clock in the evening. We still had a long ways to go. Guo Jie told me, "Believe it or not, the weather will be nice and cool tomorrow." I thought to myself, "What good weather will there be?!" I kept the thought to myself, and the two of us were preoccupied with our own chores.

When I woke up the next day, the sky was cloudy. After Morning Recitation and breakfast, we continued toiling on the lot. Around seven or eight o'clock, I commented, "The sun is not up yet!" Guo Jie replied, "I am sure the weather will be nice today!" I am one who sweats easily. But on that day there was a gentle breeze that kept us comfortable. I said, "This is Shr Fu's blessing." The two of us worked happily till ten o'clock, and then attended the Meal Offering. We continued in the afternoon. The weather stayed cool. That night, Guo Jie said, "Believe it or not, the weather will remain nice and cool tomorrow."

True indeed! The weather remained nice on the third day. We were both elated, seeing that our work would soon be completed. Finally, we needed to move all the stones and weeds to the designated spot.

On the morning of the fourth day, the weather was still cool. I thought, "This is spring weather. How can we have this weather in the summertime?" It was later on that Guo Jie told me, "You did not believe me when I said the weather would be nice, did you? Every night when I retire to my room. I always begged Shr Fu, saying, 'Shr Fu! The two of us would like to fix the lot to let our Dharma friends enjoy the scenery when they come to the City of Ten Thousand Buddhas. One of us is over sixty years of age and the other is over seventy. Please help us out!' That's why I had such confidence." The two of us kept

師父面前道歉並告訴師父：「真感謝您啊！」午齋後，約十二時四十五分左右，天氣便熱得不得了，一時四十五分，大眾一齊誦念《華嚴經》，約兩點左右有二人熱得昏倒了。那天下午，人人都連連擠去喝水。

果潔說：「上人就是如此慈悲，恩待我們，讓我們完工，我的師父就是你的師父，我們都應該感謝。」她接著說：「師父雖然色身走了，還是能聽到我們說的話。」

真是不可思議，一連兩天半，天氣如初春一般，一點汗都沒有，花圃的地整好了，並種上很多花，為此我作了短短一偈，以表達感恩的心

聲聲阿彌陀
剷剷懺悔心
雜草亂石一併除
不負吾師教誨恩

在萬佛城住了四、五十天，身體沒什麼不舒服，來回路上也不暈車，這是我沒有想到的。人與人之間不要分別語言的不同，每個人所發的心，真心都是一樣的。我們二人萍水相逢於萬佛城，由於都是懷著感恩心而來，所以任何問題也都因此化解了。

talking, and we were very happy.

On the fourth day, we toiled till 11:30 a.m. and completed our work. Then we went to bow to Shr Fu, to apologize and to thank him. After lunch, around 12:45 p.m., the weather turned incredibly hot. During the afternoon session of the *Avatamsaka Sutra* Recitation, two people passed out. There was a high demand for water.

Guo Jie said, "Shr Fu was so very kind and compassionate to us. He helped us finish our job. He is my Shr Fu and he is your Shr Fu. We should be thankful to him. Even though his flesh body has departed, still he can hear us."

It is really inconceivable! For two and a half days, the weather was like that of springtime. Without even a drop of sweat, the gardening job was accomplished. Many flowers were planted. For this, I came up with a short verse to express my deep-felt gratitude.

With Amitabha Buddha in every sound,
With a mind of repentance in every act of digging,
The weeds and scattered stones are all cast aside.
Let us repay our Master's kindness;
*   let not his teaching be in vain.*

I stayed in the Sagely City for forty to fifty days, but not even once did I feel any discomfort. The journey back and forth was peaceful as well. I did not experience nausea, which was something unthought of before. When interacting with people, we should not discriminate because of language, for the resolves brought forth from true minds do not differ. By chance, the two of us met at the Sagely City. We both shared the same sense of gratitude toward our Master; therefore all our differences could be resolved.

是故空中無色相　受想行識亦亡蠲　六根六塵並六識　三心三止透三關
白牛大車磷磷轉　黃臉小兒跳跳鑽　若問個中何旨趣　前三三接後三三

宣公上人《般若波羅密多心經非台頌解》

Therefore in emptiness there are no characteristics of form.
Feeling, cognition, formation, and consciousness disappear also,
As well as the six faculties and six objects, together with six consciousnesses.
With three minds in three ceasings, three closures are passed through.
The great cart of the white ox turns with the sound lin-lin.
A little yellow-faced child jumps and thumps in agitation.
What instructive meaning is there in this?
The front double-three and the back double-three meet.

From the Venerable Master Hua's Verses without a Stand for the *Heart of Prajna Paramita Sutra*

THE MASTER—A PERSONAL FRIEND
我的朋友 —— 師父

Dolores Krieger, Ph.D., R.N., Professor Emerita of Nursing, New York University
紐約大學護理系名譽教授　多羅瑞絲.柯瑞格　博士

On June 26, 1977, I took refuge with Shr Fu at the Gold Mountain Monastery in San Francisco. It was a formal act of acceptance of a life way I had found to be a closest agreement with my own yearnings after many years of deep study of Mahayana Buddhism. Shortly after that ceremony, I had a personal interview with Shr Fu and took the Five Precepts. For several years I was given the privilege of frequently joining with the Sangha at the City of Ten Thousand Buddhas when I was in the Bay Area, including several months while I was on sabbatical leave from New York University.

During the years of my studies of Buddhism, my interest had focused on Kuan Yin Bodhisattva, and the research, teaching, and practice of a method of healing I developed—Therapeutic Touch—became and continues to be, my major postdoctoral focus. In discussion with Shr Fu and a Bhikhshuni, it was decided that I study the Forty-two Hands and Eyes as the theme of my sabbatical work. Shr Fu gave me permission to view and contemplate the remarkable paintings that he had done, and the Bhikshuni tutored me in the mantras and the mudras and explained the analogies.

During this time I was privileged to join in the daily activities of the Sangha, and it was then that I began to appreciate the depth of Shr Fu's teachings, the profound compassion of his guidance, and the delightful humor that he liberally interspersed throughout his lectures. These amusing comments were frequently followed by his assurance, "Everything's okay!" as he joined in the laughter too. However, we knew even as we laughed, that the point he had made was not trivial and that we would be well advised to remember it, meditate on it, and make it our own.

Indeed, as I look back upon those years, I realize that the most valuable gift that Shr Fu gave me was the opportunity to make that time of deep learning my own. It was Shr Fu's great compassion that taught me compassion, his insight and wisdom that helped me to recognize my dharma, and his beguiling sense of humor that helped me to declare my humility. I am very grateful for the refuge I found under his tutelage. I know I shall remember his counsel "...to cultivate as if Kuan Yin were a personal friend," for he was a model of this "personal friend."

一九七七年六月二十六日，我在舊金山的金山寺皈依了師父上人。這是一種以正式的儀式，來深切表達我個人多年來深究大乘佛學後，對人生追求的渴望。皈依儀式後不久，我和師父面談了一次，並受了五戒。接下來的幾年中，我曾有幸在紐約大學休假的幾個月中，來到灣區，與萬佛城的僧眾生活在一起。

在我學佛的這些年裡，我的興趣集中在研究觀音法門，和專注於研究、教學，和實驗我自己研究出來的「觸摸療法」。這些也一直是我博士後的研究重心。在我和師父及一位尼師商討後，上人決定讓我修習觀音菩薩四十二手眼法門，做為我在大學休假期間的課題，師父允許我觀摩他自己繪的四十二手眼的圖，並且由這位尼師教導我咒語，並解釋其中的異同。

在這段期間，我很榮幸參與了僧眾的日常作息活動。也就是在那段時間，我開始領會到師父深邃的智慧，和他說法時那種隨機應變的風趣。這些有趣的註腳往往跟隨在他和大家一塊兒開懷大笑，並肯定地說「一切都沒問題」之後。然而我們都知道儘管我們笑了，但師父希望我們了解的課題並非如此簡單，他是希望我們好好牢記它，領悟它，把它轉化成我們自己的智慧。

確實當我回顧過去的歲月，我了解到師父給我最珍貴的禮物，就是讓我去深刻地認識我自己。師父的大慈悲教導，慈悲為懷，他的大智慧幫助我找到適合我的法。他循循善誘的幽默指引我了解到我的卑微。我非常慶幸能皈依在師父的護座下，我將永遠記得他的教導……。「修行時要把觀音當做是一個朋友，因為上人就是這樣的一個朋友。」

一切是考驗

EVERYTHING IS A TEST

釋恆堅　Shi Heng Jian

一九八七年，我到萬佛聖城參加觀音七法會。我到總辦公室時，剛好見到師父在給弟子們上課。我就把簽證不順的事，告訴了師父。師父說：「這是你的業障！」我說：「師父，我很怕落因果。」師父說：「**OK**！我把你的業障消掉，你去教化眾生。」隨後師父為我加持了有半個鐘頭之久。我只是一個世俗凡夫之人，也不懂得如何去教化眾生。

有一天，早課後，我回宿舍休息。這個時候，有位法師來叫我，說：「我們去聽師父開示！」我當時睡眼惺忪，也不知道那位法師去哪裡了。我趕到萬佛殿一看，全部的門都已上鎖。當時我想：「師父一定不要我了！是在考驗我了！」

> 一切是考驗，看爾怎麼辦？
> 覿面若不識，須再重頭煉。
> —— 宣公上人

當時心裡就想，自己怎麼這麼愚鈍，於是就用頭去撞門。甚至想，乾脆就死在聖城。我的眼淚不停地流著，只管打門。這時，正好有位居士從廚房工作回來，說：「師父就在妙語堂講經！」我才趕緊到妙語堂。剛要進門，師父已在門口等著。我進去找椅子坐下。師父拿著手杖在我前一排的一位小男孩頭上比一下，又在我頭上加持很久。當時我的感覺是：「師父已使我重新復活了！」師父上台開示完後，我就回佛殿上供、工作、做晚課，跟平常一樣，好像根本不覺得發生過什麼事情。

> 大放光明轉法輪，師子吼聲萬世尊；
> 六道眾生齊聞得，成就無上解脫門。
> —— 宣公上人

打完觀音七，從萬佛聖城回臺灣之後，由於家務和事業的繁瑣，加上「法界佛教印經會」法務

In 1987, I came to the Sagely City of Ten Thousand Buddhas to attend a Guanyin Recitation Session. When I went to the Administrative Office, I happened to see the Venerable Master teaching a class to his disciples. I told the Master about my difficulty in getting a visa. The Master said, "That's your karmic obstacles!" I said, "Master, I'm scared of being caught in cause and effect." The Master said, "Okay! I'll eradicate your karmic obstacles. Go on and teach living beings." Afterwards, the Venerable Master bestowed aid on me for as long as half an hour. I'm only a common, worldly person who doesn't know how to teach living beings.

One day after morning recitation, I went back to the dorm to rest. A Dharma Master came to call me, saying, "We're going to hear the Venerable Master give a talk!" I was still blurry-eyed and half-asleep, and I had no idea where the Dharma Master had gone. When I got to the Hall of Ten Thousand Buddhas, all the doors were locked. I thought, "The Venerable Master must not want me! He must be testing me!"

Everything is a test to see what you will do.
If you don't recognize what's before you,
*   you'll have to start anew.*

—Venerable Master Hua

At the time I asked myself how I could be so stupid, and I hit my head against the door. I even thought: I might as well die in the Sagely City. My tears kept flowing, and I kept knocking on the door. A layperson who happened to be coming back from the kitchen said, "The Master is lecturing in Wonderful Words Hall!" I rushed to Wonderful Words Hall. When I got to the door, the Venerable Master was already waiting at the door. I went in and found a seat. The Master used his cane to tap the head of a little boy sitting one row in front of me, and then bestowed aid on my head for a long time. I felt, "The Venerable Master has already brought me back to life!" After the Venerable Master gave his lecture, I returned to the Buddhahall to do the meal offering, chores, and evening ceremony. Everything was the same as usual, as if nothing at all had happened.

Emitting great light, he turns the Dharma wheel.
The lion's roar is honored throughout the ages.
Living beings in the six paths all hear the sound
And attain the door of supreme liberation.

—Venerable Master Hua

After the Guanyin Recitation Session, I returned to Taiwan. With the myriad household and business affairs and the hectic work at

忙碌，實在感覺很累，也就起了煩惱心。一向沉默的我，回到家中，跪在師父法相前，眼淚直流，不斷地喃喃念著師父名號，這時突然想起師父的偈頌：

> 真認自己錯，莫論他人非；
> 他非即我非，同體名大悲。

就在這一剎那，天空烏雲密佈，一時雷雨交加，一道光明出現在客廳的佛像前，就在這耀眼的光中，看見了宣公上人舉手來教化我，又出現文字「對師信心九十分」。我眨眨眼，想再看清楚，那文字並沒有消失，接著又出現了《金剛經》的偈頌：

> 若以色見我，以音聲求我；
> 是人行邪道，不能見如來。

師父的影像一直停留在空中，當這些文字出現時，天空放晴了，當時是下午二點鐘，我感覺是那麼地輕安舒暢。第二天，身心的一切病痛完全消失，心情非常地愉快。

Dharma Realm Buddhist Text Distribution Association, I felt very tired and afflicted. Being quiet by nature, I returned home and knelt in front of the Venerable Master's image. With tears rolling down my cheeks, I kept murmuring the Venerable Master's name. I suddenly thought of the Venerable Master's verse:

> *Truly recognize your own faults;*
> *Don't discuss the faults of others.*
> *Others' faults are just my own.*
> *To be one with all is called great compassion.*

At that moment, the sky filled with dark clouds. In the midst of the thunder and rain, a ray of light shone in front of the Buddha image in the living room. In this dazzling ray of light, I saw the Venerable Master raising a hand to teach me, and the words "You have ninety percent faith in the Master" appeared. I blinked my eyes, hoping to see more clearly. The words didn't disappear, and a verse from the *Vajra Sutra* also appeared:

> *Those who see me in form or seek me in sound*
> *Practice a deviant way and cannot see the Thus Come One.*

The Venerable Master's image remained in the air, and when the words appeared, the sky had cleared up. It was two o'clock in the afternoon. I felt extremely comfortable. The following day, all the pains and illnesses of my body and mind disappeared, and I felt very happy.

> 舍利子是堅固徵　　譯作鶖鷺母儀型
> 戒定圓明珠光現　　行解相應體玲瓏
> 大智之何因愚表　　善辯已在娘腹生
> 人皆具此真實慧　　取諸曹溪寶林峰
>
> 宣公上人《般若波羅密多心經非台頌解》

Shariputra is the solid and durable proof;
The name means pelican the demeanor of his mother.
With precepts and samadhi complete and bright, the pearl-light appears;
Practice and understanding interact, and his body is transparent.
How does there come to be great wisdom? Because the stupid make their mark.
Already in his mother's womb a fine eloquence had been born;
This real wisdom is complete within all people;
Grasp it at Jewelled Wood Peak at Tsao Creek.

From the Venerable Master Hua's Verses without a Stand for the *Heart of Prajna Paramita Sutra*

MY CLOSE ENCOUNTER WITH A BENEVOLENT SAGE
我與慈悲聖者的巧遇

Sy Piac Hua　施碧華（譯音）

With thoughts of constant faith and joy in the Buddha
and a mind that never retreats,
One draws near to all Thus Come Ones;
This is the karma that should be done.

　　—Chapter Nine, Light Enlightenment, *Flower Adornment Sutra*

We were interviewed and approved by the U.S. Consulate to emigrate to America on Guanyin Bodhisattva's birthday. A month later, upon our arrival in the United States, my husband received his job on Shakyamuni Buddha's birthday. With my strong faith and constant recitation of Buddha's name, our goals in life are arranged accordingly. Whenever problems arrive, solutions unexpectedly follow.

　　After finishing my assigned paper during the early spring of 1991, I visited the fifth floor of the Central Public Library in downtown Los Angeles, where I came across Venerable Master Hsuan Hua's name while browsing through some Buddhist books on the shelves. A book entitled *The Ten Dharma Realm Are Not Beyond a Single Thought* caught my attention. I took it out and enthusiastically read the entire book.

One contemplates the three periods of time, which are boundless,
And studies those Buddhas' merit and virtue
With a mind that is never weary:
This is the karma that should be done.

On that same day, I found three additional books: the *Shurangama Sutra*, the *Dharma Flower Sutra*, and *Records of the Life* of the Master. I yearned to deepen my understanding of the Buddha's teaching, which I had never studied before. So, I checked out eight books and kept renewing them. I was enchanted by the Master's explanation of every Sutra; the language is very easy to understand.

A true and actual Good Knowing Advisor
Is one whom the Thus Come Ones praise,
For it is because of his awesome spirit
That one gets to hear all Buddhadharmas.

　　—Chapter Twenty-four, Praises in the Tushita Heaven Palace,
　　Flower Adornment Sutra

One day, I decided to write a letter to Shr Fu. Although I waited in anticipation, I did not receive his response; I believe my conditions had not yet ripened. As my concentration in studying Buddhism deep-

意常信樂佛。其心不退轉。
親近諸如來。如是業應作。
　　　　《華嚴經》〈光明覺品第九〉

　　我們在觀音誕的那一天，去美國領事館面談，被核准移民美國。一個月後，當我們到達美國後，我先生在釋迦牟尼佛誕的那一天找到一份工作。我因為信願深切又常持佛名，所以我們生活中的希望，總是有好的結果，問題一發生，解答總不期而至。

　　一九九一年初春，我完成論文後，到洛杉磯城中心中央圖書館五樓參觀，在瀏覽架上的佛書時，看到宣公上人的名字，我抽出一本吸引我注意力的書，書名是《十法界不離一念心》，我興奮地讀完了全書。

觀無邊三世。學彼佛功德。
常無厭倦心。如是業應作。

　　在同一天，我興趣盎然地又找到了三本書，《楞嚴經》、《華嚴經》和上人《事蹟》，我對佛法求知若渴，也讓我更渴望去深入瞭解聞所未聞的佛陀教化，我一共借了八本書，不斷續借，我沉浸於上人對每本經書淺顯的開示。

真實善知識。如來所稱讚。
以彼威神故。得聞諸佛法。
　　　《華嚴經》〈兜率宮中偈讚品第二十四〉

　　有一天，我決定寫一封信給上人，但卻未得到我所祈盼的回音，我以為是因果未熟。當我學佛日深，我強烈希望見到上人。很意外地，一天晚上做了一個奇異的夢，夢中父親和我見

ened, I grew eager to see him personally. Surprisingly, a strange dream came one night. My father and I saw a tall monk in a yellow robe approaching and greeting us from a pavilion in an oriental setting. I introduced my father to Shr Fu, and we paid courteous respect to him. The response I'd hoped for came not by mail, but through a dream.

In March 1992, my parents came to visit us in America. We went to see Shr Fu at Long Beach Sagely Monastery, which was still under renovation, but we didn't get a chance to see Shr Fu because he was occupied with his work. The sad look on my father's face did not affect me, for my faith with the Buddha became stronger and I kept on reciting Buddha's name endlessly.

The Good Knowing Advisor is difficult to see
and difficult to encounter

I was informed unexpectedly one day that Shr Fu would be giving a Dharma talk at Long Beach Sagely Monastery, and so I happily called my friend to give us a ride. The day before Shr Fu's Dharma talk, I saw Earth Store Bodhisattva approaching me in my dream. When I woke up that morning, I became speechless and yet continued doing my regular morning recitation. The following day, my parents and I saw Shr Fu for the first time in our life.

On the night of January 16, 1994, at 9:32 p.m., a Dharma Master called and asked if I could go to Long Beach Sagely Monastery the next day because Shr Fu would be holding a Triple Jewel Refuge ceremony. I happily said "yes" without considering whom I could get a ride with. Since my husband had to work and would not be able to take me to Long Beach, I called my colleague and inquired if he could give me a ride, explaining to him about the special occasion. He was very happy to comply and anticipated participating in the ceremony with me.

Unfortunately, in the early morning of January 17 at 4:20 am., a strong earthquake struck Los Angeles, the Northridge quake. I thought I had missed my opportunity to take refuge. Suddenly, I was overcome with chills and numbness. I maintained calm and quietly called Shr Fu to help me. My strength came back. I called my colleague and cancelled the ride, saying I couldn't attend due to the power outage in the apartment.

Everything's a test to see what you will do;
If you don't recognize what's before your face,
You'll have to start anew.

I will never forget my colleague's response over the phone, which was similar to the above quotation. I had never heard him speak like that, for he is a very quiet gentleman. He asserted sternly that he would attend the ceremony with or without me, regardless of the outcome of the quake, because such a special event does not happen all the time. His solemn words led me to reconsider. January 17, 1994 was a day to be remembered for Californians. It was a phenomenal day for me, for I took the Triple Jewel Refuge under the great sage of the West, Venerable Dharma Master Hsuan Hua.

I have the utmost admiration not only for the Master's wonderful,

到一個身材高高、著黃僧袍的出家人從圍帳中出來歡迎我們，四周的背景是東方宮殿式的，我向上人介紹了我父親，我們禮拜上人。我期望上人的回音，卻由夢境中而不是經由郵件而成真實。

一九九二年三月，我父親來美探親，我們去長堤聖寺晉見師父，那兒正在翻修，上人正忙著，所以沒有機會見著上人，父親失望的臉孔並不影響我，因為我對佛信願更深，我不斷的誦持佛名。

善知識難見難遇

有一天，得知上人要去長堤聖寺開示，我很高興地請朋友載我一起去。在前一天晚上夢裡我夢見地藏菩薩，早上醒來，我講不出話來，但是我還是開始做早課，第二天早晨，我和父母生平第一次見到了上人。

一九九四年一月十六日晚上九點三十二分，一位法師打電話來問我能不能去長堤聖寺，因為第二天上人要主持三皈依。我高興地答應了，卻忘了考慮誰能開車帶我去，我的先生早上要上班不可能帶我去長堤，我打電話給同事告訴他這殊勝的儀式，問他能不能開車帶我去，他高興地答應了並且要和我一起皈依上人。

很不幸地，一月十七早清晨四點二十分，強烈的地震襲擊了洛杉磯，我以為會錯失皈依了。忽然間，全身冰冷麻木，肌肉僵硬，我強自鎮定，默求師父救我，我的知覺漸漸恢復。同時我打電話給寺裡和那位要送我的同事說明，因為公寓停電，所以不能參加皈依。

一切是考驗，看爾怎麼辦？
覿面若不識，須再從頭煉。

電話裡，同事的反應就如同上面的引用文，讓我永難忘懷，我從來沒有聽過他那樣說話，我一直以為他是一個很沉默的人，他很嚴峻地說不管我去不去，也不管地震的後果，他一定會去參加皈依，因為這三皈依並不常舉行。他的深沉之語，讓我重新考慮了這趟短行。一九九四年一月十七日是值得南加州的人記憶的一天，對我而言，皈依在西方聖人宣化上人的門下，這卻是珍貴的一天。

spiritual response, but for his superb explanations of the Buddhadharma, which enable me to distinguish between proper and improper knowledge. For example, if you recite the Buddha's name often, in times of sickness you will naturally meet a good doctor. When the doctor is inspired, he will naturally give you the right medicine. So when a doctor cures an illness, that is also the Buddhadharma. This is very true; I have had such an experience.

Four years ago, when I was throwing out the trash, I was bitten by a poisonous insect which caused my physiological condition to change dramatically. A red spot immediately emerged on my right arm, where I had been bitten. Due to my ignorance, I paid no attention even though the pain from the bite was persistent. Within minutes, the red spot began to swell up. I silently called Guanyin Bodhisattva for help and recited the Great Compassion Mantra to relieve my fear. I knelt before Guanyin Bodhisattva and told him everything was in his hands.

I found an outdated newspaper lying on the floor, turned the page, and saw a list of medical help. I randomly chose a doctor, without considering whether or not he would help me. To my surprise, he answered the phone personally when I called. I gave him my name and described the situation briefly. He did not ask many questions, but said that he would prescribe a medicine and asked me to obtain it at the drugstore immediately; otherwise, my chance of survival was uncertain. I told the doctor that I didn't have medical insurance, and he did not even charge me.

That evening, I went to get the medicine with my husband. I fell asleep after taking the medicine. The following morning, I woke up at four as usual and did my morning recitation. The red spot had disappeared. Later, my husband and I went to see the doctor and thanked him for everything he had done.

In thought after thought, we have no doubt,
Guan Shr Yin is pure and sagely,
In times of suffering, agony, danger, and death,
He is our refuge and protector.

—The Universal Door of Guanshiyin Bodhisattva
(The Bodhisattva Who Contemplates the Sounds of the World.)

我對上人最深的仰慕，不止於精神的感應，更在於他的開示，使我對正見邪見具有分辨能力。譬如，如果一個人常持佛名，生病時自然能遇到良醫，而醫生也常會心領神會的對症下藥。所以所謂醫術高明，有時也是佛法的示現，這的確是千真萬確的，因為我自己曾經病過，有過這樣的經歷。

四年前，當我倒垃圾時發生了意外，我被不知名的毒蟲叮咬，全身情況急遽地轉變，右手臂馬上出現紅點，幾分鐘之內，開始持續疼痛，最初由於我的忽略，情況開始變得嚴重，紅點開始腫脹，心跳加速，體溫升高。我默默地向觀世音菩薩求救，同時誦〈大悲咒〉以驅憂。我跪在觀世音菩薩前告訴他，一切由他處理。

我從地上找到了一份舊報紙，翻到了醫藥欄，隨便找了一位醫生，也沒有想到他是不是能幫我，讓我吃驚的是，我打電話去時，他親自接聽，我報上姓名，又大略解釋了蟲咬的情形，他沒有多問問題，只告訴我他開個藥方要我馬上去買藥，不然生死未卜。我告訴醫生說我沒有醫藥保險，他甚至不收費。當天晚上，我和先生一起去買藥，吃了藥後，我就睡了。第二天早上，我跟平常的時間一樣醒過來，做早課，手臂上的紅點消失了。後來我和先生一起去向醫生當面道謝。

念念勿生疑。觀世音淨聖。
於苦惱死厄。能為作依怙。

——《法華經》〈觀世音菩薩普門品〉

念念真誠念念通　默默感應默默中
直至山窮水盡處　逍遙法界任西東
宣公上人作

When every thought is sincere, every thought penetrates;
In silence, responses are quietly received.
When you reach the end of the mountains and rivers,
You are free to roam throughout the Dharma Realm.

by Venerable Master Hua

菩薩清涼月，常遊畢竟空

THE BODHISATTVA IS A CLEAR AND COOL MOON
CONSTANTLY TRAVELLING IN ULTIMATE SPACE

釋恆茂　Shi Heng Mao

「師父，他真的走了嗎？」

「師父，您走了，我們怎麼辦？」

「師父在為我們演說微妙甚深大法，就看我們認識不認識？！」

　　師父上人圓寂的消息，很快地傳遍世界各地，此起彼落的弟子心聲，訴說不完對上人的追思和感恩。有人哀慟，頓失帶領我們走出三界的大導師；有人懷疑，師父在對我們開玩笑；有人認為，這是師父在給我們考試；也有人覺得師父的境界是華嚴境界，盡虛空遍法界，無在無不在，只要我們和往常一樣發心用功，不論他老人家是在美國亦是在常寂光淨土都是一樣的，佛光常普照。有謂「眾裡尋他千百劫，對面不識耐思量」，你是否參得透這件事？你過關了沒？

　　上人這一病就是六年，在這六年中他仍然不停止休息到處在弘法利生，「我現在就好像兩個人，一個人現在仍然到處救度眾生，我在床上這一個人我是不會管他的，我不會幫助自己的。」

　　這種大公無私的精神就是戒律的精神。為什麼會犯戒破齋造業受輪迴呢？就是因為有自私自利的心。有自私自利才會想去貪、去爭、去求、去打妄語，去做出種種顛倒、令自己後悔的事。戒律就是智慧、就是光明，如果不自私不自利，自自然然就持戒清淨如滿月。佛陀臨涅槃時教示「以戒為師」，上人是戒而不戒，所以才會感化這麼多人前去美國依止上人修行。以了生脫死、離苦得樂，就算上人的色身不在世上，只要把師父這種無私精神學起來，你就是上人千百億化身之一。

　　「不要老是想求佛菩薩加被，老是求師父加被，要自己加被自己，再去加被別人」這

"Did the Master really leave?"

"Master, what are we going to do now that you've gone?"

"The Master is expounding the subtle, wondrous, and profound great Dharma to see if we recognize it or not!"

　　The news of the Venerable Master's completion of stillness rapidly spread around the world. His disciples are talking nonstop, expressing their endless remembrance and gratitude towards the Venerable Master. Some people are grieved at the sudden loss of the great teacher who was leading us out of the Triple Realm. Some people are suspicious, wondering if the Venerable Master is playing a joke on us. Others think the Venerable Master is giving us a test. Some think the Venerable Master's state is the Flower Adornment State—exhausting empty space and pervading the Dharma Realm, that he is nowhere and yet everywhere, and that as long as we continue to apply effort, it's the same whether he is in America or in the Pure Land of Eternal Stillness and Light, because the Buddha's light constantly shines everywhere. It has been said "We searched for him among the multitudes for thousands of eons. Yet facing him we fail to recognize him—shouldn't we reflect on this?" Have you been able to fathom this matter? Have you passed the test?

　　The Venerable Master's illness lasted for six years, yet during these six years he continued to travel around propagating the Dharma for the benefit of living beings, never stopping to take a rest. "Right now I'm like two people. One person is still going everywhere and rescuing living beings. As for this person who is lying in bed, I don't care about him. I won't help myself out."

　　This public-spirited and unselfish attitude is the spirit of precepts. Why do people transgress the precepts, break the rules of pure eating, create karma, and undergo birth and death? Because of selfishness and the desire for personal benefit. That's why they will be greedy, fight, seek, lie, and do all sorts of confused things that they later regret. The precepts are wisdom and light. If one is unselfish and doesn't seek personal benefit, one will naturally uphold the precepts as purely as the full moon. Before the Buddha entered Nirvana, he instructed his disciples to take the precepts as their teacher. The Venerable Master followed the precepts and yet was free of precepts, and thus he influenced many people to go to America and cultivate under his guidance in order to end birth and death, leave suffering, and attain bliss. Even if the Venerable Master is not physically in the world, as long as you can learn the Venerable Master's unselfish spirit, you will be one of the Venerable Master's hundreds of millons of transformation bodies.

　　"Don't always seek for aid from the Buddhas and Bodhisattvas. Don't always pray for your teacher's aid. You should aid yourself and then go out and aid others." This was the medicine prescribed by the Venerable

是弟子五年前第一次拜見上人時，上人所開的藥方，直至最近，弟子才明瞭大醫王的苦心。我們不能老是依賴善知識，尤其在善知識捨壽入滅後，更是要學著站起來，等自己站穩後再去幫助他人也站起來。自己如何站起來呢？就是隨時隨地，一舉一動都要迴光返照。檢點自己有無令他人起煩惱？障礙他人修行？如果有，趕緊認錯，改過自新。遇順境莫生歡喜，遇逆境要認帳，隨緣消舊業，要和眾生廣結善緣，不要再造惡緣。「善知識教如芳池日，能開一切善心蓮華」上人教法，不高談闊論，都是做人基本道理，做弟子要把它放在日常生活中躬行實踐，把自己的本分做好才是。

慈悲普度信者得救成正覺
過化存神禮之獲福悟無生

要皈依上人必須要禮一萬拜，才算是他的弟子，殊不知道這正是他老人家度化眾生善巧方便法門之一，禮佛可以培養謙沖之志，消滅我慢習，更可消除業障，改往修來，自然罪消福生、獲得身心莊嚴。

「你們要先成佛，我才成佛；不要混吃等死熬歲月、要勇猛精進，不要連累師父晚成佛。」這更是上人悲智雙運的大流露－－總是用深入淺出的話，來激勵弟子改過自新、返迷歸覺。

「你們大家都有脾氣，我就有病，但是我更見不得別人發脾氣，若大家都沒有脾氣，我的病就會好。要改正自己的思想行為，大家要從最基本做起。」師父如是教，弟子當依教奉行，方不愧為拜在當代明眼善知識的教下，方不負師恩、不負己靈。」

華嚴法會楞嚴壇場四十二手眼安天立地
妙覺世尊等覺菩薩千百億化身變海爲山

這是萬佛聖城山門的對聯，為上人所作，道盡上人一生的行誼。上人的弘願生生世

Master five years ago when I first met him. Only recently have I understood the pains taken by the Great King of Physicians. We cannot rely on our Wise Advisor forever. After our Wise Advisor has entered Quiescence, it's even more important for us to stand up on our own feet. Once we have a steady footing, we can help others stand up as well. How should we stand up? By constantly reflecting on ourselves in every move we make wherever we are. Ask ourselves if we have afflicted others. Have we hindered their cultivation? If so, we should quickly acknowledge our mistakes and reform and renew ourselves. We shouldn't be delighted by favorable conditions. We should acknowledge our debts when we run into adverse states. According with conditions, we should get rid of old karma. And we should extensively create wholesome conditions. "The teaching of a Wise Advisor is like the sun shining on a pond of flowers. It can cause all the lotuses of wholesome mind to bloom." When the Venerable Master taught the Dharma, he talked not about abstract theories, but about basic human principles that disciples should put into practice in their daily lives in order to fulfill their roles and duties.

His kindness and compassion cross over all;
Believers are liberated and perfect the Right Enlightenment.
Transforming beings wherever he goes, his spirit remains intact,
Those who venerate him obtain blessings and
awaken to the Unproduced.

Those who wished to take refuge with the Venerable Master had to make ten thousand bows to the Buddhas before they would be considered his disciples. Little did they know that this was one of the Master's skillful expedients for teaching and rescuing living beings. The act of bowing to the Buddhas can help us to nurture a humble mind, get rid of self-conceit, eradicate karmic hindrances, and correct past mistakes and cause us not to repeat them in the future. Naturally, our offenses will disappear and blessings will arise, and we will obtain adornments of body and mind.

"All of you must become Buddhas first, and then I will become a Buddha. Don't just eat your fill and wait to die, passing the time in vain. You should advance vigorously. Don't delay your teacher from becoming a Buddha." This is an manifestation of the Venerable Master's simultaneous application of compassion and wisdom. He always used simple words of profound meaning to exhort his disciples to reform and renew themselves, to turn from confusion and go towards enlightenment.

"All of you have bad tempers. If everyone can be without a temper, I will get well. You must reform your own thinking and behavior. Everyone must start with the basics." This is what the Venerable Master taught, and we should follow it. Then we will not feel remorse for being disciples of this Bright-eyed Wise Advisor of our time. Then we will not have been ungrateful to the Master for his kindness, and we will not let down our own spiritual nature.

The Flower Adornment Dharma Assembly, the Shurangama Platform,
and the Forty-two Hands and Eyes establish the
Heavens and the Earth.
The World Honored Ones of Wonderful Enlightenment and the
Bodhisattvas of Equal Enlightenment, with a billion transformation
bodies, can turn oceans into mountains.

This is the couplet engraved on the mountain gate of the Sagely City of Ten Thousand Buddhas. It was composed by the Venerable Master and completely describes the Master's life and deeds. The Venerable Master's vast vow is to

世弘揚楞嚴大法，宣講楞嚴大義，因為《楞嚴經》、〈楞嚴咒〉是正法住世的代表；臺灣分支道場自去年十二月，也有自今年師父誕辰起持誦〈楞嚴咒〉不斷，以此迴向祈請上人住世，正法住世。遵照上人遺囑，舉行「華嚴法會」將圓滿四十九日念誦《華嚴經》三大部，這是上人臨走前，送給弟子們累劫享用不盡的無上法寶，讓弟子們種下成佛妙因，只要依照《華嚴經》的義理去修行，一定成佛；否則，經是經，你是你，一點都沒有得到大饒益。所謂「師父引進門，修行在自己」。

以從如來功德生，
令其見者樂佛智；
不離一剎詣眾土，
如月普現照世間。

何其幸運，我們竟能在這個黑暗的時代遇到大善知識，當依教奉行 ── 說真話、做真事、行真理，一切要真到極點，才能脫胎換骨了生死、出三界，現在就要勤修善根，來世才有大因緣，再跟著上人修行，祈請上人乘願再來廣度眾生。

propagate the Great Shurangama Dharma and proclaim the Great Shurangama Meaning in life after life, because the *Shurangama Sutra* and the Shurangama Mantra are symbols of the proper Dharma's perpetuation in the world. The branch monasteries in Taiwan began nonstop recitation of the Shurangama Mantra, some in December of last year and some on the Venerable Master's birthday this year, dedicating the merit to the Venerable Master and praying for him to stay in the world and for the proper Dharma to remain in the world. Following the Venerable Master's last instructions, a Flower Adornment Assembly of forty-nine days is being held during which the *Flower Adornment Sutra* will be recited three times. Before he left, the Venerable Master gave his disciples this supreme Dharma treasure which they can use for countless eons, allowing them to plant the wonderful cause for Buddhahood. As long as we cultivate in accordance with the principles of the *Flower Adornment Sutra*, we will surely become Buddhas. If you do not, you and the Sutra will remain two separate things, and you won't be able to gain great benefit. As the saying goes, "The Master leads you in the door, but you yourself must cultivate."

Born from the merit and virtue of the Thus Come One,
He causes those who see him to delight in the Buddha's wisdom.
Without leaving one kshetra, he goes to the myriad lands,
Just like the moon appearing everywhere and shining on all the world.

How fortunate we are to have met such a great and wise advisor in this dark age. We should follow his teachings—speak true words, do true deeds, practice true principle. We must be true to the utmost in all we do, for only then can we be liberated from birth and death and escape the Triple Realm. We must diligently cultivate good roots now so that in our next life we will have the great affinity to follow the Venerable Master in cultivation and request the Venerable Master to come back riding on his vows to widely save living beings.

無底坑

貪心猶如無底坑　填之難滿瞋恨生
五欲紛陳顛倒想　癡然不覺法器崩

宣公上人作

Bottomless Pit

A greedy mind is like a bottomless pit.
Because it is hard to fill, anger arises.
A profusion of the five desires leads to upside-down thinking.
Without our realizing it, the Dharma vessel disintegrates.

by Venerable Master Hua

悲心切切望回心

COMPASSIONATELY HOPING FOR A TURNAROUND OF THE MIND

陳玉滿寫於一九九五年七月十四日萬佛聖城

Written by Chen Yuman on July 14, 1995 at the Sagely City of Ten Thousand Buddhas

本人是在一九八九年十月份，上人回臺時，在花蓮皈依上人的。一晃數年過去了，至今仍然愚癡顛倒、懈怠無知，仍在不停地造孽，讓上人為弟子擔待無數的重罪。雖然自己也知道，上人的千百億化身永遠住世常在，但是弟子寧願用自己罪孽深重的，凡夫之體去換回慈父般的上人。

I took refuge with the Venerable Master in Hualian, Taiwan, in October of 1989 when the Master returned to Taiwan. In the twinkling of an eye, several years have passed, and yet I am still stupid and confused, lazy and ignorant. I am still ceasefully committing evil, burdening the Venerable Master with my countless heavy offenses. Even though I know that the Venerable Master's hundreds of thousands of millions of transformation bodies are ever present in the world, I wish I could trade my own offense-laden, ordinary person's body for the Venerable Master who was like a kindly father.

* * *

記得上人一九八九年回臺弘法時，第一天的開示，是在花蓮的體育館。待法會結束時，有好多人列隊到上人跟前頂禮。當時我並沒有準備好供養上人，也就不敢去頂禮，就走到體育館後面的出口，等著恭送上人及法師們。上人和法師們經過時，我就地頂禮，當我抬頭要起身時，發現：哇！上人的雙腳怎麼那麼大？大概有兩，三尺或更大，從沒見過。再抬起頭來看上人，哇！只覺得非常非常高，大約有一丈多或兩丈這麼高，從沒有見過這麼巍巍莊嚴的高僧。到現在仍然非常清楚地在腦海裡。

還有一件不可思議的事：有一天，雨下得很大，下了班，穿上雨衣，急著騎機車去聽上人講法，卻覺得忘了帶錄音機，左看右看，機車箱子沒有，就趕緊返回去拿，可是翻遍了家裡也沒有找到。心裡很著急，而且時間已過了七點，心想：「不管了！不找了！」於是又匆匆忙忙騎著機車往外跑。到了寺院，下了車，脫下雨衣，打開機車箱子，咦！錄音機、錄音帶竟然在裡面。心裡很放心，我便匆匆地走到大殿左邊的門邊上，還沒坐好，就聽到上人說：「做事情不要慌慌張張的，要不急不緩。」啊！這不正是在說我嗎？心裡好感激！

無論心裡有多少疑惑，都會在上人開示中，一一得到明確的回應。還有一次，當上人為眾

When the Venerable Master returned to Taiwan in 1989, he lectured at the Hualian Stadium the first day. After the Dharma lecture, many people lined up to bow to the Venerable Master. Since I had not prepared an offering for the Venerable Master, I didn't dare go and bow. Instead, I walked to the exit in the back of the stadium and waited to send off the Venerable Master and other Dharma Masters. When the Venerable Master and other Dharma Masters walked past, I bowed my head to the ground. When I raised my head, I discovered that the Venerable Master's feet were two to three feet long. I'd never seen such large feet and wondered, "Oh! How can the Venerable Master's feet be so huge?" When I looked up at the Venerable Master, he seemed to be extremely tall, probably ten or twenty feet tall. I'd never seen such an awesome high monk. This sight is still very clear in my mind.

There's another inconceivable thing: One day it was pouring rain. After work, I put on my raincoat and was in a hurry to ride my motorcycle to hear the Venerable Master's lecture. I seemed to have forgotten my tape recorder in my rush. I looked around and couldn't find it in the motorcycle's storage compartment, so I rushed back home to get it. I looked all over the house and couldn't find it. I was very anxious, and it was already past seven o'clock, so I thought, "Forget it! I won't look anymore!" I hurriedly left on the motorcycle. When I got there, I got off the bike, took off my raincoat, opened up the motorcycle's storage compartment, and the tape recorder and tapes were all there. I was greatly relieved, and quickly walked to the door on the left side of the Buddhahall. Even before I could seat myself properly, I heard the Venerable Master say, "Don't do things in a rushed or nervous way. You should be neither too fast nor too slow." Ah! He must have been talking to me! I was filled with gratitude!

No matter how many doubts I had, I would always find a clear response in the Venerable Master's lecture. One time, after the Venerable Master had given a talk, many people surrounded the Master and were asking questions. I was next to the altar bowing to the Buddhas,

生做完開示後，好多人圍著上人請教，我當時在供桌旁拜佛，心裡想：「我就在這頂禮師父吧！」叩了一個頭起來時，發現上人慈祥和藹地微笑著，已站在大殿外廊上，剛巧就在我的正前方。

上人律儀嚴謹、德行高超，能皈依上人，實在是我的幸運。想當初，在佛學中我還是童蒙初學，蒙朋友送我一套《修行者的消息》。從書中我才知道，世界上有這麼一位很好很好的師父。

一九九〇年五月八日，因為在花蓮農會服務滿了十年，得到一次出國旅遊的機會。剛巧這次旅遊是到美西十二天。一看旅程表上有舊金山，即和臺北法界佛教印經會連絡，看是否有東西可以順道帶到聖城。我一心想，假如十二天都到聖城該多好，無奈罪障深重，無法如願，只能到聖城一天而已。

我於五月八日順利成行，第一天到夏威夷是早上七點半左右，剛被大雨沖洗過的夏威夷，空氣清新涼快。預計在夏威夷停留三天，導遊介紹這裡有三好：「空氣好，氣候好，水質好。」當時我心裡想：「這麼好的地方，沒有上人的法，太可惜了！就缺師父的法。」

十日傍晚到達舊金山，停留時間是一天兩夜。第二天，因為想去聖城，我離開了旅行團，首先要去的是金山聖寺（事先已和金山聖寺的法師連絡好）。雖然語言不通，可是一路上都會遇到非常熱心的人，所以非常順利地到了中國城。一位先生幫我把東西提下來，付了車資，也不知要付小費就走了。一轉身「金山禪寺」四個大字正好在頭上，原來就在金山聖寺門口。那種喜悅真無法形容！

提著東西，走上樓梯，有種回家的感覺。到櫃台登記後，把要給聖城的東西交給法師，然後去禮佛，隨著法師的指點，轉彎往前一看，上人就坐在正前方。我心中的那份歡喜，就像是看見自己久已未見的慈父，真說不出是什麼感受，頓時淚水如泉水般的湧出，雙膝一跪，頂禮在上人面前。

上人很慈祥地說：「好了！起來吧！你哭什麼？」弟子：「不知道。」我連頭都不敢抬起來見上人。上人：「我明天早上八點，坐飛機到檀香山（夏威夷）。」太妙了。上人問：「妳叫什麼名字？做什麼工作？……」我一一回答。上人告訴我有關一九九〇年十月份回臺弘法的大致的行

and I thought to myself, "I'll bow to the Venerable Master from here!" When I bowed and rose, I discovered the Venerable Master smiling kindly, standing right in front of me in the hallway outside the Buddhahall.

The Venerable Master strictly observed the precepts and possessed exalted virtue. I am truly fortunate to have taken refuge with the Venerable Master. When I was still a beginning student of Buddhism, a friend gave me a set of the books *News from True Cultivators*. It was through these books that I discovered there was such a wonderful teacher in the world.

As a reward for ten years of service at the Hualian Farmers' Association, I was given a chance to travel abroad on May 8, 1990. By coincidence, the trip was to be twelve days in the United States. When I saw San Francisco on the itinerary, I contacted the Dharma Realm Buddhist Books Distribution Society in Taipei to ask if there was anything they needed me to bring to the Sagely City. I thought of how fine it would be if I could stay in the Sagely City for a full twelve days. However, due to my heavy karmic hindrances, my wish could not be realized and I went to the Sagely City for only one day.

On May 8, 1990, the trip began smoothly, and we stopped in Hawaii at around 7:30 a.m. on the first day. After a recent great rain, Hawaii's air was clear and refreshing. We stayed there for three days. The tour guide explained that there were three good things there—good air, good climate, and good water. I thought, "It's a pity such a fine place lacks the Venerable Master's Dharma. The Master's Dharma is the only thing that's missing."

On the evening of the tenth, we arrived in San Francisco for a stay of two nights. I left the tour group because I wanted to go to the Sagely City on the second day. I first went to Gold Mountain Sagely Monastery (I'd already contacted the Dharma Masters there). Even though I didn't know the language, I met very helpful and friendly people on the way and so I was able to reach Chinatown easily. A gentleman helped to carry my luggage off the bus. I paid the fare and left, not knowing if I was supposed to pay a tip. When I turned around, I saw a sign with the words "Gold Mountain Dhyana Monastery" right above me. I was already at the door of monastery. I was overjoyed!

Carrying my things and walking up the stairs, I felt as if I were returning home. After signing in at the front desk, I turned over the things for the Sagely City to the Dharma Master and went to bow to the Buddhas. Following the Dharma Master's directions, I went around the corner and there was the Venerable Master sitting in front of me. I felt as delighted as if I were seeing my father again after a long time. There's no way to describe my feeling. My tears welled up, and I knelt on both knees and bowed to the Venerable Master.

The Venerable Master kindly said, "Okay! Please get up! What are you crying for?" Disciple: "I don't know." I didn't even dare to lift my head to look at the Venerable Master. Venerable Master: "Tomorrow at eight o'clock in the morning, I'll be taking a plane to Hawaii." What a coincidence. Venerable Master: "What's your name? What kind of work do you do?..." I answered the questions one by one. The Venerable Master told me the general schedule of the October 1990 Dharma Propagation Tour in Taiwan, and introduced the Dharma Masters from Baojie Monastery of Wugu,

程，並向我介紹了在場的臺北五股寶擷寺的法師等等。上人：「想不想到萬佛城？」弟子：「想！」上人：「想不想在那兒住？」弟子：「想！」上人：「就在那兒住吧！」於是馬上派法師聯絡人，開車送我進萬佛城。上人：「吃完午飯再去聖城。」臨走前，上人說：「祝妳一路順風！」

到了聖城，巍峨的山門，清幽的環境，簡樸的建築，一片恬淡、寧靜、祥和的氣息。莊嚴、簡樸的大雄寶殿裡，牆上塑滿一尊尊莊嚴的佛像，共有一萬尊。

聖城的法師們說話總是那麼親切，儀表威嚴、一絲不苟。我發現這裡的人，珍惜節儉每一張小紙片、每一小截繩子。功課、工作的時間緊湊而井然有序，毫不浪費時間。萬佛聖城的四眾弟子，為我樹立了學習的典範。

做完晚課，考慮到事先沒有去登記住宿，當晚上就離開了萬佛聖城。臨離開聖城時，發願一定要再來聖城。

一九九〇年，上人返臺主持護國息災大法會時，我參加義工的行列。原本我是被安排到機場迎接上人和法師們，等上人及弘法團們上車後，直接到臺中清涼寺做準備工作。待上人及法師們乘車先行，我們義工分配到事先安排好的車輛。奇怪的是，當時有一位義工拉著我說：「就上這輛。」我問：「是要直接到清涼寺的嗎？」她說：「沒關係！你就上這部車。」等我下車時才知道是到了臺北五股寶擷寺。上人竟然也在這兒。就這樣一路跟著上人的弘法團到了大興善寺、清涼寺，再到高雄。上人風塵僕僕，為法忘軀，馬不停蹄地為教化眾生，利益群倫。眾生的福報實在是太好了！太大了！看見上人疲倦、瘦弱的身體，心中一陣痛楚。

*

一九九五年七月七、八日左右，二姊打電話來，談到一件不可思議的感應：在一個星期以前，二姊因為身體不適，看醫生、吃藥都未見效。當時她就坐在椅子上想：「這樣也不好，那樣也不好，不知道阿滿她師父有沒有辦法？」當她正這麼想的時候（當時是下午），在她院子的半空中出現了一尊佛，告訴二姐說：「妳不要吃肉，妳

Taipei, who were present. Venerable Master: "Do you want to go to the City of Ten Thousand Buddhas?" Disciple: "Yes!" Venerable Master: "Do you want to stay there?" Disciple: "Yes!" Venerable Master: "Then you can stay there!" He immediately asked the Dharma Master to arrange for someone to drive me to the City of Ten Thousand Buddhas. Venerable Master: "You'll be going to the Sagely City after lunch." Before I left, the Venerable Master said, "Hope you have a good trip!"

When we reached the Sagely City, I saw the majestic front gate, the secluded environment, the simple buildings, and the peaceful and serene atmosphere. Inside the dignifed yet simple main Buddhahall, ten thousand adorned Buddha images lined the walls.

The Dharma Masters at the Sagely City spoke in such a gentle, friendly manner. They behaved with dignified decorum and were not casual in the least. I found them to be very thrifty, saving every small piece of paper and string. The schedule of ceremonies and work was tight, yet orderly, and no time was wasted. The fourfold assembly of disciples at the Sagely City of Ten Thousand Buddhas set a good example for me to follow.

I had not signed up for lodging, because I was leaving the Sagely City after the evening ceremony. Right before leaving, I vowed that I would definitely come back.

In 1990, when the Venerable Master hosted the Dharma Session for Protecting the Nation and Quelling Disasters, I joined the group of volunteer workers. I had originally been assigned to welcome the Venerable Master and other Dharma Masters at the airport and see them into their cars, and then go directly to Qingliang Monastery in Taichung to make preparations. After the Venerable Master and other Dharma Masters had already been driven off, the volunteer workers went to their assigned cars. At that time, one of the volunteers said to me, "Just get in this car." "Is it going straight to Qingliang Monastery?" I asked. She said, "Don't worry! Just get in." When I got out of the car, we were at Baojie Monastery in Wugu, Taipei. The Venerable Master was also there. Thus I was able to follow the Venerable Master's delegation to Daxingshan Monastery, Qingliang Monastery, and Kaohsiung. The Venerable Master travelled from place to place, forgetting himself for the Dharma, teaching living beings and benefitting the multitudes without rest. The blessings of living beings are truly fine! Truly great! My heart was pained to see the Venerable Master's fatigued and haggard body.

*　　　*　　　*

Around July 7 or 8 of 1995, my sister called and told me an inconceivable response she'd had: About a week before, she had not felt well, but seeing the doctor and taking medicine had no effect. She had sat and thought, "Nothing seems to work. I wonder if my sister's Master can help." As she was thinking this (in the afternoon), the vision of a Buddha appeared in mid-air in her backyard and told her, "Don't eat meat, and you'll get well." My sister had already planned to stop eating meat, but she hadn't been able to put it down. This time, she really stopped eating meat and then got well.

的病就會好！」二姐原本打算不吃肉了，但一直放不下，這回也就真的不吃了，接著病也好了。

還有很多很多不可思議感應和教化……

一九九五年農曆大年初六，張惠玲居士由聖城回來，告訴我：「金山聖寺法師提到妳：當年上人是特地在金山聖寺等妳的。上人要妳在聖城住下，妳沒有。」（只在聖城呆了一天）聽完張居士的話，我頓時感傷不已，我有何福何德承蒙上人如此抬舉、厚待？如今上人已離我們而去，又深覺自己罪孽深重，不配出家。為報答上人，唯願盡未來際，生生世世追隨上人，童真入道，深入經藏，護持正法。（本人現已有家庭）

上人圓寂以後，奉行師父的遺訓，聖城的四眾弟子，連續持誦了四十九天的《華嚴經》。整部《華嚴經》，就是對上人的行儀風範的寫照：

> 於法於義悉善知。為利群生轉勤習。
> 菩薩所修眾善行。無量無數種種別。
> 於此一切分別知。為利群生故迴向。
> 以妙智慧恆觀察。究竟廣大真實理。
> 哀愍一切諸眾生。令於實法正思惟。

上人為法捐軀的精神，在當今的佛教界獨樹風範：剛毅、堅忍、勤儉、樸實。上人所制定的三大宗旨、六大條款、教育宗旨，是我畢生應遵循的；宣揚正法，讓上人的法豎窮三際，量周沙界，橫遍十方，遍滿盡虛空一切處，應是我終生為之奮鬥的目標。

There have been many, many other inconceivable responses and teachings...

On the sixth day of the lunar new year in 1995, Laywoman Zhang returned from the Sagely City and told me, "The Dharma Master at Gold Mountain Sagely Monastery spoke of you: That year, the Venerable Master had been waiting especially for you at Gold Mountain Monastery. The Venerable Master wanted you to stay at the Sagely City, but you didn't." (I stayed only for one day.) I was deeply affected by Laywoman Zhang's words. What blessings and virtue did I have to deserve such concern from the Venerable Master? Now that the Venerable Master has left us, I deeply feel how heavy my offenses are, making me unfit to leave the home-life. In order to repay the Venerable Master, I vow that in life after life to the end of time, I will follow the Venerable Master, enter the path of cultivation as a pure youth, deeply enter the Sutra Treasury, and protect the Proper Dharma. (I already have my own family.)

After the Venerable Master's completion of stillness, the fourfold assembly of disciples honored the Master's final instructions and recited the *Flower Adornment Sutra* for forty-nine days. The entire *Flower Adornment Sutra* is a portrayal of the Venerable Master's life and conduct:

> *He completely knows all dharmas and meanings.*
> *In order to benefit sentient beings, he diligently cultivates.*
> *The myriad wholesome conducts cultivated by a Bodhisattva*
> *Are immeasurable, uncountable, and of all different kinds.*
> *He distinguishes and knows all of these,*
> *And dedicates the merit to benefit beings.*
> *With wonderful wisdom he constantly contemplates*
> *The ultimate, vast, true and actual principle.*
> *Pitying all living beings,*
> *He brings them to reflect properly upon the actual Dharma.*

With his spirit of sacrificing himself for the sake of the Dharma, the Venerable Master was a singular example of resoluteness, endurance, diligent frugality, and honest sincerity in the contemporary Buddhist world. Throughout my life, I shall honor the Three Principles, Six Guidelines, and the principles of education that the Venerable Master established. All my life, I shall work energetically to propagate the proper Dharma and cause the Venerable Master's Dharma to pervade worlds as many as grains of sand in the ten directions throughout the past, present, and future.

天地之母曰道生　　日月並明而運行
萬物本體亦如是　　生生化化妙無窮
宣公上人作

The mother of heaven and earth is called the originator of the Way of Nature.
The sun and moon are both bright and move in orbit.
The basic substance of the myriad things is also like this.
Its creations and transformations are infinitely wondrous.
by the Venerable Master Hua

寫在上人圓寂之後

WRITTEN AFTER THE VENERABLE MASTER COMPLETED THE STILLNESS

李果鴻　Li Guohong

六月七日的下午，驟聞上人圓寂的消息，一下子有點不能接受，但這畢竟是事實，或許是上人住院的事早已時有所聞，所以悲傷的心情也就很快地平復下來。

回想上人這一輩子，他把他所有的一切都給了眾生，從來沒為自己打算過，也因為這樣，才使得無數的中外人士紛紛皈依其門下，而接受佛法的薰陶。

我景仰上人的是，上人總是不計個人利益，而為大我著想，以及他的「嚴以律己，寬以待人」的胸襟。例如他老人家也知道西方人難度難調服，然而為使正法久住世間，他毅然隻身飄洋過海，扛下使佛法紮根於美國的荷負。以後陸續創辦了國際譯經學院、育良小學、培德中學、法界佛教大學，為這個教育已開始走下坡的國家（美國）點燃一絲復興的希望。

另外一件讓我感動的事，是為使世界宗教能和平共處，為人類作最大的貢獻，上人邀請了天主教的神父在萬佛殿內作天主教的彌撒儀式，這樣的胸襟實是當今這種功利社會少有的。

上人對自己的要求非常嚴格，打從出家一開始便立下日中一食，夜不倒單的誓願，打下這樣的基礎，為的是將來能利益更多的眾生。因為上人曾說過：「願將自己應享受的一切福樂，普施一切眾生；願一切眾生的苦難，悉由自己一人代受。」所以沒有高尚無我的精神怎能做到？相信很多人對上人的能力一直很欽羨。其實上人早開示過，人人能在六大宗旨──「不爭、不貪、不求、不自私、不自利、不打妄語」上下功夫，日子一久，大家成佛做祖師有餘。

在上人示疾住院當中，曾對我們做這樣的開示：「只要你們大家不發脾氣，我的病自然就會好了！」我常在想上人辛辛苦苦地創建萬佛

In the afternoon of June 7, 1995, when I heard the news that the Venerable Master had completed the stillness, I found it a bit difficult to accept. However, it was a fact, and perhaps because I had long known that the Venerable Master was in the hospital, I was soon able to calm down my feelings of grief.

Throughout his life, the Venerable Master gave everything he had to living beings. He never thought on his own behalf. For this reason, countless Chinese people and people of other nationalities came to take refuge under him and receive the influence of the Buddhadharma.

What I admire about the Venerable Master is that he always considered the benefit of everyone and never thought of personal gain. He was strict with himself, but lenient with others. For example, although he knew that Westerners were hard to teach, he wished to perpetuate the Proper Dharma in the world, so he resolutely crossed the ocean alone and took on the responsibility of planting the roots of Buddhism in American soil. Later on he successively founded the International Institute for the Translation of Buddhist Texts, Instilling Goodness Elementary School, Developing Virtue Secondary School, and the Dharma Realm Buddhist University, giving a tiny hope of renewal to a country whose educational system was on the decline (the United States).

Another thing that moved me was that the Venerable Master, hoping that the religions of the world will dwell in harmony and make great contributions to humankind, invited a Catholic priest to perform Catholic Mass in the Hall of Ten Thousand Buddhas. This kind of spirit is very rare in today's utilitarian society.

The Venerable Master made extremely exacting demands on himself. From the time he left the home-life, he vowed to take one meal a day at noon and not to lie down at night. He set down that kind of foundation, hoping he would be able to benefit more living beings in the future. As the Venerable Master has said, "I vow to bestow upon all living beings of the Dharma Realm all of the blessings and happiness I am destined to receive. I vow to take upon myself the miseries of all living beings of the Dharma Realm, that I alone may endure them on their behalf." How could someone without a lofty and selfless spirit be able to do this? I'm sure many people admire the Venerable Master's powers. Yet the Venerable Master said long ago that as long as a person applies effort in practicing the Six Principles—no fighting, no greed, no seeking, no selfishness, no pursuit of personal advantage, and no lying—he or she will eventually be more than qualified to become a Buddha or a Patriarch.

When the Venerable Master was manifesting illness and staying in the hospital, he once instructed us, "As long as none of you lose your temper, I will recover!" I often reflect on how the Venerable Master

城，為的是要成就我們的道業，然而做弟子的我們何曾體會、懂得過上人的一片苦心。仍終日紛紛擾擾，分別你我，或許也就因為這樣，上人才現了個死相，希望我們因此而更精進，因為成就道業全靠自己。

arduously established the City of Ten Thousand Buddhas in order to help us achieve our work in the Way. Yet, as disciples, have we ever realized or understood the pains taken by the Master? We continue to be confused and afflicted, discriminating between self and others all day long. Perhaps that is why the Venerable Master manifested death, in the hope that we will be more vigorous, for it is up to us alone to succeed in our cultivation.

WHY DO YOU WANT TO GO TO HEAVEN?
妳爲什麼要上天堂？

Young Shramanerika Shi Guohe
小沙彌尼　釋果荷

It was at the age of nine that I came to know the City of Ten Thousand Buddhas. People were taking the ten precepts. The Venerable Master called my sister and me first. I remember he asked us, "Why do you want to live in the City?" My sister was too shy, so I answered. I said, "Because I want to cultivate and go to heaven." The Venerable Master laughed and said, "Why do you want to go to heaven? There's a lot of trash there. Do you want to clean it?" I was speechless. Then I moved to the City.

When I was ten, I had a dream. I went to a very weird temple, where a lot of people sat eating. It was sort of like a party. So I sat down and ate some cake. Then I saw the Venerable Master with two disciples. There was something that looked like a big cushion, and it opened when Shr Fu came. Inside was a small Buddhahall. Then he walked very fast and the door closed behind him. I should have bowed to him, but I ran away instead because I was afraid Shr Fu would scold me for eating cake. When I left home, Shr Fu shaved the little part of hair on my head. It isn't easy to leave home under a high Sanghan.

I feel lucky to have such a good knowing advisor to teach me, and although he entered Nirvana so quickly—only one year after I left home—at least I am a disciple of the Venerable Master Hua.

我九歲的時候，開始知道萬佛聖城。大眾在受十戒，上人叫姊姊和我。我記得上人問我們：「為什麼你們要住在聖城？」當時我姊姊很害羞，所以我就回答：「因為我要修行，而且上天。」上人笑了，而且說：「為什麼妳要上天堂，那裡堆滿了垃圾，妳要去清理嗎？」我頓時啞口無言。後來我們搬進了聖城。

當我十歲時，我作了一個夢，我夢見自己到了一個很奇怪的廟，很多人坐著吃東西，就好像在開宴會，所以我也坐下來吃蛋糕。然後我看見上人和他的兩個弟子。當他們進來時，兩個看起來好像很大很大的拜墊之類的東西打開了，裡面是個小佛堂。然後上人走了進去，門馬上關起來。其實我應該向他頂禮，但是我很怕上人會罵我吃蛋糕，所以我跑走了。我出家時，上人幫我圓頂，要在一位高僧座下出家是很不容易的一件事。

雖然我才出家一年後，師父很快就入涅槃了，但是我很幸運能有這麼一位善知識來教我。因為畢竟我還是上宣下化老和尚的弟子。

不留痕跡萬世宗

HE LEFT NO TRACES, BUT A TEACHING THAT WILL LAST FOR TEN THOUSAND GENERATIONS

林漢堂　Lin Hantang

師父圓寂，我心哀傷。曾有過妄想：「希望有一天也能跟上人出家。」記得上人在《開示錄》中曾說：「若我活到百歲，願焚身供佛。」我盤算過，等我的孩子長大以後，上人尚且住世，應該還有機會吧！一九九三年初，聖城弘法團在臺北縣板橋體育館做法會期間，一天晚上有位居士請求上人最起碼活到一百二十歲，但上人答以：「我絕對不願意活到一百二十歲，這是很抱歉的，不能遵命。」那時候我有點懊喪。不禁想起一九九一年七月，有一次師父在萬佛殿的開示：「人家都已經來到這裡精進多時了，你還在後頭趕不上人家！」

仔細追思師父的恩德，實在很深。只可惜自己讀書不多，不擅寫作，無法把自己的經歷生動地描述出來，但又不忍眾生不能分享上人的感人的事蹟，故不揣淺陋，作此紀念文。

自一九八八年皈依師父上人後，就開始恭敬閱讀上人的《開示錄》。每一篇開示都極為珍貴，淺顯易懂。不但容易理解，而且很快地就能在日常生活中運用，並有了自己思想、行為上依循的標準。當看到師父的書中：「任何人想修道就一定要受戒，守護清淨的戒體，就好像守護摩尼寶珠一樣。」心裡就希望早點受五戒，於是把有關五戒的戒律學看了一遍。碰巧又在一位蔡居士的鼓勵下，於一九九〇年九月，終於受了五戒。

師父的法語，是永遠活在眾生心裡的。

今年七月一日，臺北法界佛教印經會的一位林居士問我：「師父圓寂了，但我並不感覺他走了，你覺得怎樣？」上人的慈悲是遍一切處的，老人家曾有偈言：

> 隨類現身示普門，
> 對面不識法王親；

My heart is saddened by the Venerable Master's completion of stillness. I once had the idle thought, "I hope one day I can leave the home-life under the Venerable Master." I remember a line in the Venerable Master's *Instructional Talks*: "If I live to be a hundred, I will burn my entire body as an offering to the Buddhas." I calculated that by the time my children grew up, the Venerable Master would still be alive, so I should still have a chance! When the Dharma-propagation delegation from the Sagely City of Ten Thousand Buddhas was holding a Dharma session at the Banqiao gymnasium in Taipei county in early 1993, one night a layman requested the Venerable Master to live to be at least 120. The Venerable Master had replied, "I certainly won't live to be 120. I'm very sorry, but I can't follow your order." I felt a bit depressed by that. I couldn't help thinking of what the Venerable Master said in July of 1991 in the Hall of Ten Thousand Buddhas: "Other people have already been here cultivating vigorously for a long time. You are still behind, unable to catch up!"

When I reflect carefully, I realize how truly profound the Venerable Master's kindness is. I regret that I didn't receive much education and am a poor writer. I cannot describe my experiences very vividly. However, I must share with living beings the moving deeds of the Master, and so I have written this memorial essay despite my inadequacies.

After taking refuge with the Venerable Master in 1988, I began respectfully reading the Venerable Master's *Instructional Talks*. Every single talk was extremely precious and very easy to understand. They were also immediately applicable in my daily life, serving as standards for my thinking and conduct. When I read in the Venerable Master's book, "Anyone who wants to cultivate the Way must definitely take the five precepts and guard the pure precept substance as if guarding a precious mani pearl," I wished to quickly take the five precepts. I read some books talking about the five precepts, and at the encouragement of Layperson Chai, I received the five precepts in September 1990.

The Venerable Master's Dharma-words will live forever in the hearts of living beings.

On July 1 of this year, a layperson named Lin from the Dharma Realm Buddhist Books Distribution Association in Taipei said to me, "The Venerable Master has completed the stillness, yet I don't feel that he's gone. What do you feel?" The Venerable Master's compassion pervades all places. He has a verse:

> He manifests in accordance in kind among living beings, revealing
> the universal door.
> Meeting face to face, we fail to recognize the Dharma King
> as our relative.

有緣無緣皆救度，
悲心切切望回心。

Saving both those with and without affinities,
He compassionately lingers on, hoping they will turn their minds
around.

像我這般愚癡的人，也能依上人受三皈五戒，實在是幸運啊！我只能說，這是上人度生心量廣大所使然。

回想當年收到皈依三寶證明書時的感受，至今還是法喜充滿的。證書裡面記載了師父上人的十八大願，剛看完第一條：「願盡虛空，遍法界，十方三世一切菩薩等，若有一未成佛時，我誓不取正覺。」時，我就呆住了！該是多麼偉大的賢德，才能發出這種慈悲的大願啊！非佛菩薩倒駕慈航，其誰也！

師父的第十四條大願是：「願一切眾生，見我面，乃至聞我名，悉發菩提心，速得成佛道。」記得當時閱讀《開示錄》，讀到上人開示我們應該受菩薩戒，便生出想求受菩薩戒的心。現在我終於明白這是上人願力的成就。唉！師父的德行，是如此感召修行人在菩提道上精進不息。

皈依的那一天，是在臺中中興堂。師父當時教導我們，先要不發脾氣，再就是不要玩「大家樂」、不炒股票。所謂：「爭是勝負心，與道相違背；便生四相心，由何得三昧。」師父又開示說：「我們皈依三寶，不但要皈依佛、皈依法、皈依僧，也要皈依戒。」師父的話使人天生信服，好像一種電波感應似的，令人有一種自我覺察的力量。記得我十多歲的時候，常愛發脾氣。稍大一點，居然養成生悶氣、好挑剔別人的習氣。修行，就是把這些習氣毛病去掉。幸好遇到明眼善知識，從師父的書中，漸漸我體會到：「真認自己過，莫論他人非；他非即我非，同體名大悲。」「若是盡看他人的不對，就是自己的苦根未盡！」的道理。

上人的言行，是弟子們修行的典範。師父自己也說：「正因為如此，所以我夠得上做你們的師父。」上人依教奉行，身體力行，正如《開示錄》中所說：「若是只能說而不能做，那簡直就是在佛教裡頭胡鬧。」這是真實語！

師父的方便、化導眾生，是超越時空的。記得萬佛聖城弘法團將要到臺灣來弘法，就

Such a stupid person as myself is truly fortunate to have taken the three refuges and received the five precepts from the Venerable Master. This was possible only because of the Venerable Master's vast capacity for saving living beings.

I remember my feelings when I received the certificate of Taking Refuge with the Triple Jewel; even now, I am still filled with the joy of Dharma. The certificate includes the Venerable Master's Eighteen Great Vows. When I finished reading the first vow, which says, "I vow that as long as there is a single Bodhisattva in the three periods of time throughout the ten directions of the Dharma Realm, to the very end of empty space, who has not accomplished Buddhahood, I too will not attain Right Enlightenment," I was dumbstruck. How great must be the virtuous worthy one who made such a greatly compassionate vow! How could this be anyone but a Buddha or Bodhisattva coming back riding on the boat of compassion!

The Venerable Master's fourteenth great vow says, "I vow that living beings who see my face or even hear my name will bring forth the Bodhi mind and quickly realize the Buddha Way." I remember when I read to the part in the *Instructional Talks* where the Venerable Master advises us to receive the Bodhisattva precepts, I conceived the wish to take the Bodhisattva precepts. Now, I finally understand that this was the realization of the Venerable Master's vow. Ah! This is how the Venerable Master's virtue influences cultivators to vigorously advance on the Bodhi Way without rest.

I took refuge at Zhongxing Hall in Taichung (Taiwan). At that time the Venerable Master instructed us not to lose our tempers, not to play the lottery, and not to play the stock market. As the saying goes, "Fighting involves the thought of victory and defeat; / Thus it goes against the Way. / One produces the thought of the four marks: / How then can one attain samadhi?" The Venerable Master also said, "When we take refuge with the Triple Jewel, we take refuge not only with the Buddha, the Dharma, and the Sangha, but also with the precepts." The Venerable Master's words are trustingly accepted by humans and gods. They are like a small electric shock, causing people to have self-awareness. I remember when I was an adolescent, I often lost my temper. When I grew older, I held my anger inside and liked to pick on others' faults. Cultivation consists of changing these bad habits and faults. Fortunately, I met a Bright-eyed Good Knowing Advisor. From the Venerable Master's books, I have gradually come to understand these principles: "Truly recognize your own faults. Don't discuss the faults of others. Others' faults are just my own. To be of the same substance with all is called great compassion." "If you're always looking at other people's wrongs, you haven't ended your own suffering yet!"

The Venerable Master's words and conduct are a model of cultivation for his disciples. The Master himself said, "It is because of this that I am qualified to be your teacher." The Venerable Master truly practices his teachings. As he said in the *Instructional Talks*, "One who only talks without practicing is simply up to no good in Buddhism." These are true words!

The Master's expedients in teaching living beings transcend the limits of time and space. A week or so before the delegation from the Sagely

在法會前一個禮拜左右，夜裡夢見上人：他老人家一下車就開始頂禮。從夢中醒來，我就想：「連上人都這樣頂禮，我也應該頂禮。否則，我執、我慢等壞習氣，如何能除去？的確應該常頂禮。」又有一天夜裡，睡夢中，看到師父慈祥地坐在椅子上，我於是請教師父：「弟子資質不好，這麼多經典，我該從哪一部經下手？」師父微笑著說：「《金剛經》、《法華經》嘛！」臺灣和美國時差約十二個小時左右，臺灣的晚上，正好是美國的白天。師父人在美國，卻還撥空入我夢中指點，雖然為時短暫，但卻讓人深切地感受到師父救度眾生，是不知疲倦，不分晝夜的。

師父為使眾生了生脫死、離苦得樂，不厭其煩，告訴我們要革除物欲，降伏淫欲心，把內心骯髒的東西都掃光。要努力實踐不爭、不貪、不求、不自私、不自利、不打妄語六大條款。我誠心祈求十方諸佛菩薩，於默默中加持於我，奉行師父的六大宗旨。

師父您走了，弟子我真地很悲傷：

師父！師父！您從虛空來，又回虛空去，就像不來亦不去。真實語言、當頭棒喝，只為化眾生。長我善根，降伏魔軍，濟渡同倫登法船，真個無緣大慈，同體大悲。望穿虛空不見空，覽觀法海歸無言，宣無宣，化無化，不留痕跡萬世宗。

City of Ten Thousand Buddhas came to Taiwan to propagate the Dharma, I dreamed of the Venerable Master. As soon as the Master got out of the car, he started to bow. When I awoke, I thought, "Even the Venerable Master is bowing. I should bow, too. Otherwise, how will I ever be able to get rid my bad habits of self-attachment and pride? I should really bow more often." On another night, I saw the Venerable Master in my dream, sitting in a chair with a kind expression. I asked the Master, "I am not well-educated. There are so many Sutras; which Sutra should I start with?" The Master smiled and said, "Why, the *Vajra Sutra* and the *Dharma Flower Sutra!*" There is a twelve-hour time difference between Taiwan and the United States. When it is nighttime in Taiwan, it is daytime in America. The Venerable Master, who was physically in America, allocated time to instruct me in my dream. Even though it was very brief, I am very deeply moved to see how the Master teaches and saves living beings without fatigue and without differentiating between day and night.

In order to enable living beings to end birth and death, leave suffering, and attain bliss, the Venerable Master patiently taught us that we must get rid of desires, subdue thoughts of lust, and sweep the filth out of our minds. We must diligently practice the Six Guidelines of not fighting, not being greedy, not seeking, not being selfish, not pursuing personal advantage, and not lying. I silently pray to the Buddhas and Bodhisattvas to aid me in practicing the Venerable Master's Six Guidelines.

Venerable Master, I am truly grieved by your leaving:

Master, Master, you came from empty space and returned to empty space, as if you neither came nor went. With honest words and direct "blows on the head," you lived only to teach and transform living beings. You nurtured our good roots and subdued the armies of demons, rescuing beings onto the Dharma ship. This is truly great kindness for those without affinities and great compassion of being the same substance with all. You looked through space without seeing the emptiness. Gazing upon the sea of Dharma, one becomes wordless. You proclaimed without proclaiming and transformed without transforming, leaving no traces, but a teaching for ten thousand generations.

迴光返照觀自在　　覺諸有情即薩埵　　如如不動心君泰　　了了常明主人公
六種神通渾閒事　　八方風雨更無驚　　卷之則退藏於密　　放之則彌六甲中

宣公上人《般若波羅密多心經非台頌解》

Directing the light to shine within, Avalokiteshvara
Enlightens all the sentient beings; thus he is a Bodhisattva.
Thus, thus, unmoving; the superior one's mind is at peace;
With total understanding of the ever-shining, he is host and master.
Six types of psychic power are an ordinary matter,
And even less can the winds and rains of the eight directions cause alarm.
Roll it up, and it secretly hides it away;
Let it go, and it fills the entire universe.

From the Venerable Master Hua's Verses without a Stand for the *Heart of Prajna Paramita Sutra*

BRINGING FORTH THE BODHI RESOLVE
初發菩提心

Mee Win Chang

張美雲

If anybody had said to me eleven years ago that I would be called away to a city some 1000 miles away, I would not have believed it. Being away from the nest of my family, let alone living on my own, was not even in my imagination at that time.

That time was 1984. I was just another ignorant person occupied with studying at a college in Pomona, California, to get ready to earn money. That was the normal path that everybody around me seemed to be striving for, I guess.

Being an introvert, I was inept at making friends in college, and had just enough ability to keep up and complete the engineering studies. The final hurdle was to "pass" the job interviews. So it was a complete surprise for me and for my family members when a job offer, the one and only one, came from a company in Seattle. After letting the happy news sit for a while, my father felt comfortable to let me go, with an understanding that I would come back with a couple of years of experience. My mother was to go with me and help me settle in a foreign city. (In the back of my mind, I had a suspicion that there must be another purpose in my going to Seattle, since it was unusual for a person like me to leave my family.)

About two years passed, and I started to look for a job back in Los Angeles where my family lived, but without success. Almost three years later, in 1987, a religious proselytizer came knocking at my apartment door. After he left, I started to wonder about myself: I considered myself a Buddhist, and yet I did not know about Buddhism. With that thought I started to investigate the depths of Buddhism.

I was born in Burma (Myanmar), a country rich in Buddhist faith, as seen in many stupas and pagodas. I remember going to pagodas and paying respect to the Buddha; I remember offering food to the monks when they solemnly came up in front of my family residence. So ignorant was I that I had never had enough curiosity to look into the deep meaning of the root of suffering and the working of Cause and Effect.

My Bodhi seed aroused (fourteen years after I left Myanmar), I made a wish to look for a Buddhist temple that I could attend. One Saturday I saw a religious note in a newspaper. There was in small print an announcement for the Ten Thousand Buddhas Repentance ceremony at Gold Summit Monastery. The next day I went and visited the place.

I found books and Sutras in English at the monastery. When I started reading *Three Steps, One Bow*, I found myself constantly thinking about it, even when walking from my car to my office and from morning to night. That account of true practice caused me to

假如有人在十一年以前,對我說我會讓人叫到一個一千哩以外的城市,我絕對不會相信。那時候從不敢想像自己會離開自己的窩巢,至於自己單獨生活,那更是不用提了。

那時是一九八四年,我不過是眾多無知的人之一,正在加州波摩那市一間大學念書,準備以後能掙錢。我猜這是我身邊人人都想走的一條正常的路。

我是很內向的,在校時不善交友,勉勉強強讀完工程系課程,就等著通過求職的最後一關——面談。所以當我接到這份唯一的工作通知,卻是來自西雅圖時,我家人和我自己都很吃驚。我父親答應讓我外出去工作幾年,積些經驗再回來。因為要到外地,所以我母親就陪我一起去幫忙安頓住處。(在我心深處有一種感覺,覺得像我這樣的人要離家遠走,是很不平常的事,所以這裡面一定有什麼作用。)

兩年之後,我開始在洛杉磯我家附近找工作,但也沒找著。幾乎三年以後,一九八七年有一個曾改變過宗教信仰的人來找我。他走了之後,我開始反省自己,我雖然說自己是佛教徒,但我對佛教卻一點都不明白,因此我就開始深入研究佛教。

我出生在緬甸,在那兒住了十三年,緬甸這個國家是信佛的,那兒有許多佛塔。我記得有時我去佛塔拜佛,有時有僧人威儀肅穆地來到我們家門口,我就拿食物供養。我是這麼愚癡,直到在西雅圖住了幾乎三年,我才生起好奇心想要深究苦的因和因果循環的道理。

在我離開緬甸十三年之後,我的菩提心才發芽,我決心要找一間寺廟。有一個星期六我在報紙上看到一個小啟,字體很小,上頭說金峰聖寺在拜萬佛懺。第二天我就上那廟上去了。

那廟上有英文版的佛書和經典,我開始看三步

see through the clouds of delusion and inspired me to study further. I am grateful that I had a chance to listen to the taped lectures of the Venerable Master on the *Sixth Patriarch Sutra* and the *Shurangama Sutra*. It is said "It is difficult to encounter the Buddhist Sutras."

In the English class at Gold Summit Monastery, *Three Steps, One Bow* and later *Herein Lies the Treasure-Trove*, a collection of Venerable Master Hsuan Hua's instructional talks, were used as reading textbooks. Each person would take turn reading a paragraph; the contents were then discussed in terms of English usage as well as Buddhist context. There was always something in the passages that kept the class alive and charged. To me it was like an introduction to Buddhism.

The more I studied and contemplated on the principles in the Sutras, the more I became aware of the law of Cause and Effect. I became a vegetarian and took refuge with the Triple Jewel in October 1988. Three of my sisters and my mother also became vegetarians, and we all became Master's disciples.

Along with fellow Dharma friends from the monastery, we would take trips to Vancouver, Canada, to listen to Venerable Master's lectures. The Venerable Master's kindness and compassion extends even to the smallest matter. I remember one time I took a friend to go to a lecture at the University of British Columbia. I went along with her to see her friend. After a long visit and finding our way on unfamiliar streets, we arrived late at the lecture hall. We took our seats. Determined to capture the words of Dharma, I hurried to record the lecture. As I fumbled to insert a tape in my cassette tape recorder, suddenly as if on cue, the lecture stopped. The speaker, a Dharma Master sitting next to Venerable Master, stopped abruptly. In those several seconds that I was awkwardly setting up the recorder, everything was quiet and no one spoke, except my friend next to me, who said, "They're waiting for you." After I inserted the tape and was ready to record, the speaker resumed talking as if on cue. Thus was Venerable Master's wordless teaching of the paramita of Kindness.

Venerable Master's lectures were always vigorous. He spoke with full concentration and energy, and one could not fail to pay attention. During one of my visits to my family, one of my younger sisters played a video tape of Venerable Master in Malaysia lecturing on the Great Compassion Mantra. She decided to light incense at the altar next to the television. As the incense burned, from the beginning of the lecture, the ash from the incense stayed unbroken, bending toward the video being played. We watched as it slowly came down; the unbroken incense ash continued bending until, at the end of the lecture and at the bottom end of the incense, it kept its straight-line formation, making a 90-degree angle from the leg of the incense. That lasted for about thirty minutes. It was like a confirmation of the Master's unbroken, constant concentration and single-minded effort in his speaking of Dharma.

The Master has taught, "If you concentrate, it is efficacious. If you get scattered, the effort is lost." "Everything is made from the mind." In *Herein Lies the Treasure Trove,* the Master said about a 'single thought': "Good and evil are each contained in a single thought. I often say people's minds are like motes of dust, knocked

一拜的書，看了之後，我腦海裡日夜不停的，不斷縈迴著這椿事，甚至於當我下車走進辦公室的這段路，我都在想這件真實修行的事。這使我看清了幻覺的雲翳，也因而使我想更深入地去研究。我感到很幸運，也很感激能有機會聽到上人講解的《六祖壇經》和《楞嚴經》，佛經實在是「難遭難遇」。

金峰聖寺的英文課，採用三步一拜的書及上人開示錄來做教材，每一個人輪流念一段，然後討論其內容及其英文結構。每次書中的材料都很生動活潑，使上課的人都很有精神，對我來說，這門課可以說是一門佛教概論的課。

我越深入思考佛經中的道理，我越瞭解因果定律，我終於開始吃素，皈依三寶。在一九八八年十月，我的母親和三個姐妹也開始吃素，我們都成為上人的弟子了。

廟裡的法友們，也常集體到加拿大溫哥華聽上人講法。上人的慈悲是普及眾生無微不至的。我記得有一回，我帶了一位朋友去溫哥華卑詩大學聽講演，我先跟她去看她的一位朋友，因為在那兒待了很久，又加上對路不熟，等我們到講堂時，已經晚了。我們坐下後，我拿出錄音機來決心要把每一句法語都錄下來。我正在忙亂地將一片錄音帶放入錄音機裡去時，忽然好像有默契似的，講法停了，當時說法的人是坐在上人身邊的一位法師，他忽然就不講了。所以在我忙亂地準備錄音那幾秒鐘的時間，他什麼話都沒有講，靜悄悄的。我的朋友小聲地在我旁邊說著：「他們在等妳。」當我把錄音帶放進去，可以開始錄音時，那位說法的人才又開始講法，好像他知道似的，又好像有人給他打了訊號似的，這豈不是上人慈悲的無言之教嗎？

上人講法一向都是很精進的，他說法的時候，總是專心致志很有力的，讓人不能不注意。有一次回家時，我妹妹放了一片錄音帶，是上人在馬來西亞講解的〈大悲咒〉，她點了一支香插在電視機旁邊的佛桌上。當播放錄影帶時，從一開始那支香的香灰就沒有斷落過，並且朝向播放中的錄影帶方向彎下去，我們看著香灰漸漸彎下去，一直到最後錄影帶播完了，香灰也彎成九十度角，持續了三十分鐘才斷落。這好似象徵著上人說法時心不旁鶩，專心致志的精神集中力。

around in space. Suddenly you're in the heavens, then suddenly among the animals, hungry ghosts, or in the hells. There's no end to the bitter sea of suffering, so hurry up and come back to the other shore. There's nothing esoteric about it. It's simply a matter of getting rid of your bad habits and faults."

How straightforward is this advice and yet how difficult to practice under innumerable circumstances! However, I will do my best in this aspect and be mindful of my three karmic actions of body, mouth, and mind to bring harmony and benefit to others. May all beings joyously receive the Dharma. Sadhu, Sadhu, Sadhu!

上人曾說：「專一則靈，分馳則弊。」又說：「一切唯心造。」在《開示錄》中，上人說及「一念」，「善惡都在一念之間，我常說人心就像空中的浮塵一樣，忽爾在天，忽爾在地獄、餓鬼、畜生道裡。苦海無邊，回頭是岸，這沒有什麼稀奇的，只要除去壞習氣毛病就行了。」

上人講得多麼直率，可是在不同的環境之下，行起來又是多麼不容易。但是我仍願盡我最大的努力，謹守身口意三業清淨，為人謀福利，願一切眾生歡喜受持法寶。善哉！善哉！善哉！

幸運的選擇

A FORTUNATE CHOICE

Young Shramanera Shi Guorong

小沙彌　釋果榮

記得第一次在臺北法界佛教印經會見到了師父，當時我很想距離師父更近一點，好跟師父說說話，可是當我和師父第一次說話時，我卻緊張得說不出話來。

出家之後，跟著上人一段時間，我發覺師父好像一個慈祥的父親，令我有一種安穩的感覺。

師父常勉勵我「轉陰成陽」；因為每當我閉上眼睛時，所見到的是一片黑漆漆的。師父說：「應該讓自己就算閉上眼睛，都能看到是一片白色，或者還能看到彩色的光，或是蓮花，甚至一尊佛。」我相信那是很奇妙的。換句話說，如果能到這種境界，那就是我身心更健康的時候了。

我覺得我這一生能跟著上人出家，是很難得的。我應該好好珍惜這個機會努力用功，不要把光陰空過了才對。

I still remember the first time I visited Dharma Realm Buddhist Books Distribution Association in Taipei. I was not familiar with the place, but after some time I started liking it. That was where I met the Venerable Master. I wanted to draw closer to the Master so that I could talk with him, but the first time I had a chance to speak to the Master, I was so excited that I became tongue-tied.

Later, after I had left the home-life with the Venerable Master for some time, I realized that the Master is like a kind and compassionate father who makes me feel peaceful and secure.

The Master often urges me to "turn the darkness (yin) into brightness (yang)" because whenever I close my eyes, I see a pitch-black expanse. The Master said, "Even when your eyes are closed, you should be able to see a white expanse, colorful light, lotus flowers, or even a Buddha." I believe it must be very rare and wonderful. In other words, if I can reach this kind of state, then my body and mind will be even more healthy.

I realize that in this life, I have had a very rare opportunity to leave the home-life with the Venerable Master. I should treasure this opportunity and work diligently. I should not just allow the time to pass in vain.

往菩提大道邁進

ADVANCING TOWARDS THE GREAT BODHI WAY

蕭果盛　Su Guosheng

我於一九八八年，在臺灣桃園皈依了宣公上人。未接觸佛法以前，不知道什麼是真理，直到皈依佛門，學習經典以後才知道：佛陀之所以來到人間，是要教導眾生，覺悟宇宙永恆的真理。

皈依前的我，相當的主觀，常常輕視別人，造了很多的身、口、意惡業。當上人率領的弘法團在桃園體育場說法時，沒有一位講演者的發言讓我滿意。輪到上宣下化法師講法時，我也抱著同樣的輕視心態。

我的視力一向正常，從不使用眼藥之類的。這個時候彷彿有了翳病似的，看到老和尚眼睛奇大，臉面兇巴巴的。我用手揉揉眼睛，再看看老和尚，很正常並沒有變。停了一下，同樣的情形發生了 —— 老和尚的眼睛大大的，臉面兇巴巴的。當時的我，並不知道師父是在示現金剛怒目相給我看。演講完畢，大眾要皈依時，上人講：「如果皈依我的弟子。有一位尚未成佛，我要等他成佛，我才要成佛。」多麼大的願力！當天法會結束，回家的路上，我決定在星期日的法會皈依宣化上人。

星期日的早晨，我騎機車到皈依地點。本以為到得相當早，結果大眾早已在念〈大悲咒〉了，大家比我到得更早。在懺悔、禮拜、皈依、開示後，師父慇勤地囑咐每位皈依弟子要好好做人。最後說：「你們今天皈依師父，以前所作的罪業，師父替你們承當。」

師父！你為了承當皈依弟子們的罪業，所以你病了。弟子我，不努力懺悔業障，精進修行，所以你示現病相並過早地離開了我們，為了是讓弟子當下警覺起來！

大慈大悲的師父！你訶護著弟子及每位皈依你的眾生，往菩提大道邁進！

In 1988, I took refuge with the Venerable Master Hua in Taoyuan, Taiwan. Before I came into contact with the Buddhadharma, I didn't know what the truth was. It was only after taking refuge in Buddhism and studying the Sutras that I realized the Buddha had come to the world to teach living beings to awaken to the eternal truth of the universe.

Before I took refuge, I had been quite opinionated and tended to look down on others. I had created a lot of bad karma with my body, mouth, and mind. When the members of the delegation led by the Venerable Master spoke the Dharma at the Taoyuan Gymnasium, none of their speeches satisfied me. When it was the Venerable Master's turn to speak, I harbored the same attitude of contempt.

My eyesight has always been normal, and I've never had to use eyedrops or anything. But at that time, it was as if I had a cataract, for I saw that the Venerable Master's eyes were very large and his face was very mean-looking. I rubbed my eyes with my hand and took another look at the Venerable Master: This time he appeared normal. But after a while, it happened again—the Venerable Master's eyes were huge and his expression was very fierce. At that time, I didn't realize the Master was manifesting the angry appearance of a Vajra spirit for me to see. After the lecture was over and everyone was preparing to take refuge, the Venerable Master said, "If even one disciple who has taken refuge with me has not become a Buddha, I will wait for him to become a Buddha before I become a Buddha." What a magnificent vow! On my way home after the Dharma session that day, I decided to go take refuge with the Venerable Master Hua on Sunday.

I rode my motorcycle to take refuge on Sunday morning. I had thought I was early, but everyone else had arrived even earlier and was already reciting the Great Compassion Mantra. After the repentance, bowing, refuge-taking, and lecture, the Venerable Master earnestly reminded every disciple to be a good person. At the end he said, "Today you've taken refuge with me, and I will take upon myself all the offense karma you created in the past."

Venerable Master! You took on the offense karma of your refuge disciples, and so you became ill. Because your disciple has not worked hard to repent of his karmic hindrances and to vigorously cultivate, you have manifested illness and left us early, in order to allow us to wake up right away!

Greatly kind and compassionate Master! Out of concern, you admonished me and every living being who has taken refuge with you to make us advance towards the Great Bodhi Way!

THE MASTER'S GIFT TO US
上人的禮物

Frederick Klarer (Kuo Hu) 果護

Three incidents of my years with the Abbot stand out in my mind and have served as a basis for my practice. Because they may be of interest to others, I relate them below. The first was in the fall/winter of 1970–71.

Following the summer session of 1970, there were perhaps as many as fifteen men living and practicing at the Buddhist Lecture Hall on Waverly Place in San Francisco's Chinatown. A similar number of women lived in a private home not too far away and spent their days at the Buddhist Lecture Hall. At any given moment there could be twenty or more people crowded into that one room. To escape the crowding, several of the men had moved up onto the roof, where we built sleeping boxes out of wooden packing crates and slept sitting up. This was the beginning period of cultivation for all of us, a first attempt, and tensions ordinarily ran high, as we each struggled with our private demons and projected them out on each other. As the cold of winter closed in, the tension became unbearable. We each began to fantasize of a wonderful, quiet, spacious forest monastery, where we could do nothing but cultivate day and night and would be free of the supposed obstacles of the Buddhist Lecture Hall. That fantasy quickly blossomed into an obsession for some of us.

Then, one evening, after the formal sutra lecture, the Abbot announced that he had a special present for us. He laughed in his inimitable way, his eyes twinkled, and we all slavered in anticipation. He told us that we would have to wait, that it would be a Christmas present, but that it would be something beyond price—the best present that we would ever receive.

During this period we had been looking at real estate all over California, and beyond. Some of us clever ones quickly put the disparate facts together and decided that the Abbot was going to give us a wonderful mountain monastery for Christmas. Once we had figured that out, anticipation grew daily. As we looked at various country properties we delighted in the anticipation. Life would be wonderful. We would have the perfect circumstances to cultivate. All the obstacles facing us would disappear with a move to a perfect environment and all would be well.

As Christmas approached the Abbot would remind us of the gift that we could expect and we all became happier and happier, expecting our new toys for Christmas. At last the Abbot announced that, on a certain day, he would give us our present. The night of that lecture the Buddhist Lecture Hall was packed. Everyone was there, each anticipating the inevitable announcement that we were all moving to the country for the perfect contemplative life. The Abbot delivered the evening

在我跟隨上人的這些年中，有三件事給我的印象特別深刻，奠定了我修行的基礎。我想或者也有人有興趣知道，所以我寫出來。其中第一件事發生在一九七〇年及一九七一年秋冬之際。

一九七〇年暑假班結束時，在三藩市中國城天后廟街的佛教講堂，大約有十五位男眾住在那兒修行；又有大約同樣多的女眾住在附近另一幢房子，白天到佛教講堂共修。佛教講堂只有那一間房，所以經常都有二十多個人擠在一起。為了怕擠，有些人就搬到屋頂去住，用運貨的木箱子改裝一下，晚間就坐單睡在裡面，這就是我們剛開始修行時的情況。

那時氣氛比較緊張一點，每一個人都跟自己的魔交戰，並將自己的魔互相在別人身上投射出來。寒冬來了，形勢更是緊張得令人不能忍受。大家都夢想著能在森林中有一座廟，在那裡，寬敞、安靜，什麼也不用幹，大家整天就專心修行，沒有佛教講堂那些修行上的障礙。不久，有的人成天就心心念念做著這樣的夢想。

然後有一晚，上人講完經之後，就宣佈他有一件特別的禮物要送給我們。上人以他那種別人學不來的笑容說著，眼裡閃著光，我們都嚥著口水，焦急地等待著。上人又說，我們得耐心等，這是我們的耶誕禮物，是一份無價的禮物，是我們從未收過的最好禮物。

在這一段時間，我們不只在加州，也在別的地方到處看房地產。有些聰明一點的人，將各方面的情形湊合起來，就猜想上人一定會給我們一座在山上的寺廟做為耶誕禮物。一旦我們有了這念頭之後，我們的焦慮一天比一天增長。以後我們會有一個完美的地方修行，日子會過得多愜意！一切一切的障礙都會沒有了。只要我們搬到一個完美的環境去，什麼問題都會消失了。

耶誕日漸漸接近了，上人也提醒大家我們所期待的禮物，我們一天比一天快活，想著我們耶誕時就要有新玩具了。有一天，終於上人宣佈說他在某一天就會把禮物給我們。到了給禮物的那一晚，佛教講堂裡擠

lecture, as usual. The translators finished translating. The Abbot lectured again and, once again, the translators finished translating. Still no mention of our country monastery. We were all beginning to worry a bit. The Venerable Shih Fu put his hands together to recite the transference of merit—then stopped. "Oh." he said. He had forgotten. Today was the day he would give us our present. We all sighed a great sigh of relief. The end to our problems was at hand.

The Venerable Shih Fu then said, "Today I am giving each of you two beautiful, hand-written scrolls. They are a precious gift that you must never put down." This wasn't a monastery, but it was a good start. At least something special and valuable. He continued, "On the first scroll is written "Birth." On the second scroll is written "Death." You are to hang those scrolls, one behind each eyelid, so that you see them at every moment. If you are able to see those scrolls at every moment, you will certainly attain enlightenment in this very life."

We were all taken aback. That was all well and good, but was this a joke? Surely there was more. Then Shih Fu laughed, and looked out over the assembly, and then made as if to speak again. Clearly, that was not the main event. The big present was yet to come. He continued, "But if you are going to meditate night and day you will need a place to do it. You will need a Ch'an Hall." Ah, we each thought, now comes the real present—what we have all been waiting for all these months—the country awaits. "To meditate you will need a Ch'an Hall, so I am giving you a Ch'an Hall," At last, this is it we all thought. He continued, "For the pillars of your Ch'an Hall, I give you the four directions; for its roof, the sky. For your sitting mat I give you the broad earth." He beamed at us, as if he had just opened a box of the most luscious chocolates and offered each of us the best one in the box. He then continued. "You have your topic, you have your place. Now—WORK!!" He then laughed his inimitable laugh, put his palms together, and began to recite the transference of merit. We were all in a state of shock—stunned. Ch'an humor was one thing—but this was serious. The evening's lecture ended and we were each left with our private thoughts. Some thought the whole event a big Ch'an joke—designed to shake us out of attachments. Others were simply disappointed. Each one of us dealt with our disappointment, our shock, in a different way, and the event passed into the past. A few months later we purchased the property at 1731 Fifteenth Street and began to build a new place for cultivation in earnest. Gold Mountain Monastery came into being.

I have thought over that story many, many times, and slowly understood the precious gift that Shih Fu offered each of us that day. It has taken me more than twenty years to begin to make use of that gift, but it still is as fresh as one of those imagined chocolates when the box was first opened. Every moment, every place, every event, is nothing but opportunity to cultivate, if we have the heart and resolve to experience life that way. Entrance into the Dharma-realm is available at every moment; we need simply to recognize our constant opportunities. I have related this story because a gift takes its real meaning when it is passed on to another. For those who were absent that day, I pass on Shih Fu's gift, and hope that you will make better use of it than I have.

滿了人，每一個人都到齊了，期待著上人宣佈我們可以搬到鄉下，一處十全十美適合過冥想生活的地方。那晚上人照常講經，英文翻譯完畢之後，上人又講了一些，接著又是英文翻譯，上人還是不提鄉下寺廟的事。大家都有點著急，上人合掌開始念迴向功德偈，忽然停下來說：「哦……。」原來上人忘了今天是該給我們禮物的日子，我們鬆了一口氣，我們的苦惱終於要結束了。

上人接著說：「今天我要給你們每一個人兩個漂亮的手書卷軸。這份珍貴的禮物，你們永遠不可以放棄。」上人說的不是廟，但也還不錯，至少也是一份別緻而又有價值的東西。上人又接著說：「第一個卷軸上寫『生』字，第二個卷軸上寫著『死』字，你們把這兩個字掛在眉樹上，一邊一個字，所以時時刻刻你們都可以看到這兩幅卷軸，你們在今生就一定能證悟。」

我們都很驚訝。當然這都不錯，但是上人是不是和我們開玩笑，上人一定還有東西要給我們。上人笑了，看著大眾好像又要講話的樣子。很明顯地剛才給的不是主要的禮物，大的禮物還在後頭。上人接著說：「假如你們要日夜坐單，那一定得有個地方才行，得有個禪堂。」對了，我們都心想：現在真正的禮物要來了！我們等了幾個月，終於等到了一個鄉下地方。「要坐禪，你們一定得有個禪堂，所以我給你們一個禪堂。」對了，一定是了！我們都這樣忖量著。

上人又說了：「這四方，我給你們做禪堂的支柱，天空就是屋頂，大地就是你們的坐墊。」上人笑著說，好像打開了一盒最美味的巧克力糖，給我們每一個人盒裡最好的一顆。上人又說：「你們有了話頭，也有了坐禪的地方，現在用功去罷！」上人又閃著那令人沒法模仿的笑容，雙手合十，開始唱迴向功德偈；我們都還在震驚狀態中尚未甦醒。禪幽默是一回事，但這椿事不是開玩笑的。

晚間講經完畢，各人想著心事，有的人覺得這椿事是個禪玩笑，目的在解除我們的執著；有的人則很失望。每個人對這樣的震驚和失望，都有自己的應對之道，這椿事也就過去了。幾個月之後，我們添置了座落在第十五街一七三一號的地方，改建成一處修行的地方，成立了金山寺。

這椿事我後來想了很多次，也漸漸地瞭解到那天上人所給我們的那份珍貴禮物。我花了二十多年時

The second incident that I constantly recall was a trip that Heng Ch'ien, Heng Shou, and I took to look at property in Northern California, Oregon, and Idaho. We were traveling in a Volkswagen bus, sleeping in the bus or camping, looking at various possible sites for a country monastery. Finally, after we had located a few sites that Shih Fu, with whom Heng Ch'ien had communicated by telephone, thought sounded promising, he came up to meet us and spent a couple of days with us driving around. One morning we had stopped by a beautiful stream in northern Idaho to make our one meal of the day. Shih Fu, as was his practice when traveling, ate virtually nothing—a banana and perhaps another piece of fruit. I was, at the time, practicing eating at a single sitting, and made sure that I ate enough to last the better part of the kalpa before I had to get up or the clock hit noon. Heng Ch'ien and Heng Shou, neither of whom had any great interest in food, wandered away from where we had stopped and set up our meal, over to the side of the stream, and were idly skipping rocks over the surface of the water, taking a well deserved rest from hours of driving. Shih Fu and I sat together on a log, he eating his banana and I eating everything that I could get my hands on. Shih Fu was watching Heng Ch'ien and Heng Shou skip rocks, and asked me what it was that they were doing. I explained how and why one went about skipping rocks on water. He asked if they were any good at it and I gave my evaluation. He then said to me, "Why don't you go play with your friends?" sounding like a solicitous parent, concerned that I had been left out. I replied that, when it was time to eat, I ate; that "I knew what was important." He turned his head to me with a delighted twinkle in his eye, "Oh, you know what is important. Kuo Hu knows what is important. Kuo Hu knows what is important." He repeated this phrase over and over again, chuckling. He then finished his banana and went over to Heng Ch'ien and Heng Shou, announcing to them as he came, "I have something important to tell you. This is very important. Kuo Hu knows what is important. Kuo Hu knows what is important." I sat and ate, very pleased with myself for knowing what was important, eating when it was time to eat rather than wasting my time at play. While I ate Shih Fu stood to one side of Heng Ch'ien and Heng Shou, watching them continue to skip rocks. After watching a few throws Shih Fu stepped a couple of feet away, examined the ground carefully, and picked up a large, irregularly shaped stone weighing at least several pounds. He then walked up to the stream's edge and heaved the stone in. It sank without a trace. He then looked directly at Heng Ch'ien and Heng Shou, who were watching the ripples spread. Heng Ch'ien and Heng Shou then looked up from the stream to Shih Fu. The three of them stood there for a moment, looking at each other, then all laughed at the same time. The three of them then ambled back to where I was still eating, Shih Fu telling them both very earnestly how I knew what was important. Heng Ch'ien and Heng Shou then had their lunch as well. I finished eating, then went over to the stream's edge and skipped several stones with great skill, demonstrating, once I had finished the important matter, my prowess with secondary matters as well.

間才開始懂得那份禮物的意思。可是那意義還是像當初打開那盒想像中的巧克力糖那麼新鮮。如果我們立志以身修行的話，那時時刻刻、處處事事，都是修行的機會。如果我們能認得出的話，其實任何時間都是入法界的機會。

因為一件禮物能與人分享則更有意義，所以我將這件事講出來。那些當時不在場的人，我現在將上人的禮物轉給你們，希望你們會比我明白得更多。

第二樁事，我常記得的是我和恆謙、恆授去北加州、奧立岡州，及愛達荷州看房地產的時候。我們開的是一輛旅行車，沿途有時露營，有時就睡在車裡，到處看地，想找一處鄉下地方蓋廟。最後我們終於找到一處地方，恆謙電話告知上人，上人也覺得蠻理想。於是上人就來和我們過幾天，一塊兒到處看看。

一天早上，我們在愛達荷州北邊停下準備用齋。上人就和往常出門的慣例一樣，幾乎什麼都不吃，除了吃根香蕉或一樣別的什麼水果。我那時學習一坐食，在時針指向十二點以前不站起來，所以我一坐下來吃，就一定要吃個夠。恆謙和恆授二個人對吃東西沒有什麼大興趣，就離開我們吃飯的地方，走到一處溪邊打水漂，也好在長途開車之後休息休息。

我和上人坐在一塊木頭上，他吃著香蕉，我則什麼都吃。上人看著恆謙和恆授在用石子打水漂玩，就問我他們在幹什麼？我講給上人聽了，並且解釋怎麼玩法。上人又問我，他們倆玩得好不好，我也告訴上人。然後上人說：「你為什麼不過去和你的朋友一塊兒呢？」上人聽起來好像一個父親，恐怕他的孩子被排擠在外。我回說該吃飯的時候，我就吃飯；我說：「我知道哪個重要。」上人轉過頭來，眼裡閃著愉悅的光采說：「哦，你知道哪個重要，果護知道什麼事重要。」上人笑著不斷重複這句話，上人把香蕉吃完，走到恆謙及恆授那兒宣佈說：「我有件很重要的事要告訴你們，很重要的。果護知道什麼事是要緊的，果護知道什麼事是要緊的。」

我坐在那兒吃著中飯，對自己很滿意，因為我知道哪樁事是要緊的。吃飯的時候就該吃飯，我不會浪費時間去玩。我吃的時候，上人站在恆謙和恆授旁邊，看著他們打水漂玩。上人看了一會兒，就走到旁邊幾尺遠的地方，仔細地查看地面，然後撿起一塊不規則形狀的石頭，至少幾磅重，走到溪邊拋入溪水中。石塊沉入水，再也不見蹤影。恆謙、恆守望著水中的漣漪散開，上人則直視著他們，他們也轉視上人。三個

From then on, at each property we examined, Shih Fu would very seriously turn to me and ask my opinion of the property, announcing, "Kuo Hu knows what is important." When we all eventually returned to Gold Mountain Shih Fu announced on several occasions when we were discussing some problem, that everyone should ask me, since "Kuo Hu knows what is important." Eventually that particular teaching died down and life went on.

But I have considered that incident many, many times. Shih Fu's real teaching there was a demonstration of sympathy with living beings. He recognized what was important to each of us, whether it was self-importance and eating, or relaxing from hard work by skipping rocks across a stream, and responded to each with as much teaching as was possible. What was really important was not, as I felt at the time, my self-discipline, but rather to recognize that Shih Fu taught each of us individually, and that what was most important was to recognize what teaching was for me and what was for someone else—to not confuse the two, to not expect someone else to live up to what he had taught me to strive for, and to not seek to strive for someone else's goals. That teaching was a deep and vivid expression of compassion and *bodhicitta* (Bodhi mind), and one that, as I have slowly come to understand, that I seek to emulate in every moment.

The third incident that has stuck with me all these years occurred while we were building Gold Mountain, at Fifteenth Street. The building was an old mattress factory, full of years of dirt and dust. We were able to clean it up to a great extent, but a problem that seemed insurmountable was that of the brick walls themselves. The building had been cheaply built, and the bricks were a bit crumbly. Much worse, the mortar was crumbling. The building wasn't about to fall down, but every brush against the walls brought bits of mortar and sand. There was no way to keep the interior clean if we could not solve this problem. Heng Ch'ien brought the problem to Shih Fu's attention, and he instantly had a solution. He ordered a bucket brought, some pure cement, water, and an old broom. He had us mix a very thin solution of cement in water. He then took the broom, dipped it into the bucket, and then slammed the soaked broom agianst the brick wall. A few experiments with more or less cement, different stroke techniques, and a couple of old brooms, and he pronounced the process a success. He carefully instructed us to mix the cement with the water in precisely the proportions he had established, use an old broom as he had selected, and to hit the mixture-soaked broom against the walls as he had demonstrated. We then split up into several work groups and proceeded with the task. However, it quickly became apparent that the solution was so thin that most of it dripped down and off the walls. It looked as if it would take forever to cover all the walls. So one of us got the bright idea to thicken the mixture a bit so that it would hold better. Sure enough, the thickened mixture went on much more easily and covered much more quickly. The process would not take nearly as long as we had feared. We also discovered that a new broom, which would hold a greater load of mixture, sped up

人就那麼站著互相看，然後一起笑起來，漫步回到我還在吃飯的地方。上人起勁地告訴他們倆，我怎麼樣地知道什麼事是重要的。恆謙和恆授也吃了午齋，我吃完了，也走到溪邊打水漂玩，漂得很漂亮。一旦我把要緊的事做完了，次要的事我也能做得很漂亮。

從那以後，每次我們看地的時候，上人會很認真地問我對那片地的意見，並說：「果護知道什麼是要緊的。」後來我們去金山寺的時候，有好幾次，當我們討論問題時，上人總會對大家宣佈，有事應該來問我，因為「果護知道什麼是要緊的」。經過一陣子，最後這個教誡才中止，生活才恢復正常。

我為這樁事想了許多次，在上人的教誨中，顯出了對眾生的慈悲。他知道我們每個人都有自認為最要緊的事，不論是自我重視，或是吃東西，或是打水漂玩，以便從辛勤的工作中鬆弛一下。上人總是應量施教。當時我認為真正重要的事，不是我的自制力，而是認知到上人對我們行的是個別教導。最要緊的是能認識什麼教導是針對我個人的，什麼是針對其他人的，不能搞混了。也不要把上人針對我們的教導拿去要求別人；更不要把上人給別人的教誨，拿來做自己努力的目標。上人這樣的教誨，也是有生動深遠的慈悲及菩提心；我逐漸體會到，這也是我們時刻想效法的。

常在我腦海中縈迴多年的第三樁事，是在我們改造第十五街那座金山寺時。這幢建築物原是一家陳舊的床墊工廠，積著多年的塵垢，我們徹底清掃了一番。但是有一個問題始終不能解決，就是那些磚牆；因為這幢建築物蓋得便宜，磚頭也鬆，尤其是磚塊間的水泥也剝落了。雖然這幢建築物還不會倒塌，但是每往牆上刷一下，都會剝落許多磚縫中的水泥。這個問題若不解決，那根本就沒辦法保持室內乾淨。

恆謙告訴了上人，上人馬上就有解決之道。上人要了一個桶子、一些水泥、一些水，和一把舊掃帚。上人教我們調了一些很稀的水泥，然後他拿起舊掃帚，浸入稀水泥中，然後再抹在磚牆上。上人又試了幾次，有時用多點水泥，有時用不同的技巧，又換了幾支不同的舊掃帚，最後上人宣佈試驗成功。上人小心地教我們根據他定的水泥和水的比例混合稀水泥，用他選定的舊掃帚，然後照他示範的方法塗到牆上去。

我們大家分組工作，不一會兒，因為水泥太稀，就沿牆流了下來，這樣子下去，看樣子一輩子也塗不完牆。所以有人就想出一個好方法，就是將水泥調厚一點，就不會流下來。的確水泥厚一點，不但容易塗上

the process even more. Once again, modern American ingenuity and know-how would save the day.

Some time later Shih Fu came by to see how we were doing. One look and he exploded, "Stupid, really stupid," he exclaimed. "That's not how to do it." We objected, explaining all the advantages of our improvements. He just repeated, "Stupid, really stupid." Sure enough, as the mixture dried on the walls, where we had used the thin mixture and the old broom the pure cement dried into a hard, very thin coating that subsequently lasted for years. Where we had used the thicker mixture and the new broom the coating dried as thick flakes that could be easily picked or peeled off. Eventually we had to remove all of those sections and do them over. Our attempt at efficiency caused nothing but more work and a waste of resources.

What was so important about that teaching was not Shih Fu's knowledge of wall coating techniques—I am not sure whether he had ever used that technique before or not. What was important was the clarity—the concentration and insight—that he applied to the task. He perceived directly what the problem was, exactly how much was enough to solve that problem, and applied just the right amount to solve it. He pointed out to us exactly how to apply the techniques of cultivation. It is that ability to perceive a situation as it truly is, not otherwise, that directs one's cultivation to be most effective. Recognizing precisely what needs to be done, the appropriate tools for the task, and the proper application lies at the heart of what Shih Fu taught. Again, it has taken me most of my life simply to recognize this lesson and to begin to apply it in my own work.

I have sought to cultivate according to those simple lessons that Shih Fu taught. To understand that there is only one issue—that of birth and death—and that every moment of every day in every place is the right time and the right place to resolve that issue, that doing one's own work, and not someone else's, is the job at hand, and one cannot understand the mind or actions of a sage with respect to others if one does not even understand them with respect to oneself, and finally, that the tools of cultivation are useful only when one understands the problem to be solved, selects the appropriate tools, and applies them properly, and that concentration and insight are the means to that realization.

With these words I am simply passing along three of my experiences with Shih Fu, hoping that the record of those experiences will benefit others, as they have been of such benefit to me. If there were others present at those occurrences who remember them differently, I can only apologize for my partial perception and experience and trust that they will correct my report. I have repeated those experiences as faithfully as I remember them.

去，而且也塗得比較快。進度比我們所擔心的要快，我們又發現新的掃帚一次可以載多點水泥，使工作進度更快，美國的萬能術又解了我們的難。

過了一會兒，上人來察看我們做得怎樣了，他看了一眼就炸開了，他說：「真笨，笨得可以，不是這樣的。」我們爭辯地說著我們改良後的方法怎麼樣地好，可是上人一再重複地說：「真笨！真笨！」果不其然，我們用稀水泥、舊掃帚塗的地方，乾了之後，成為薄薄的一層外殼，經過好幾年都不落。用厚水泥、新掃帚塗的地方，乾了之後，成為厚厚的碎片，很容易剝落。最後我們還得將這些厚水泥片全剝落下來，重新再塗一層。真是欲速則不達，結果一無所獲，浪費了更多的人力、物力。

上人對塗牆的技巧不是要點所在，我也不敢確定上人以前是不是用過這個技巧。要點在於上人對這件工作的明確認識，上人看清楚問題的癥結，確實知道得用多少材料才能解決問題，然後不多不少就用恰當的份量把問題給解決了。上人指明了得用什麼修行技巧。這種能看清真實情況，然後教人用最有效的方法修行的這種能力；能認知到底該怎麼做，該用什麼適當的器具，上人教導的核心就是在怎樣運用這些。我用了大半生的時間，學這門課，然後運用到我的工作上。

我用上人教的這些簡單的課來修行，認識到只有一樁大事－－生死。又任何時刻，任何地方都是解決生死大事的時刻及地方。自己用自己的功，不在他人用功處用功，這才是我們該做的。凡夫不能瞭解聖人對自己的心行，更不會瞭解聖人對他人的心行。最後一點，是修行的各種工具，只有在人認清各人自己問題的所在時，才能選擇恰當的工具發揮其作用。心志的集中及覺知，才是證得了生死的方法。

上面敘述的是我與上人間的三個經歷，希望能對他人有益，因我由這三次經驗蒙益甚多。如果當時有其他人在場而對當時的情形記得比我清楚，那我要為自己的一知半解向大家道歉，並請糾正。我已盡我所記得的真實地敘述出來了。

THE VENERABLE MASTER'S MAGNIFICENT TRANSMISSION OF A CURE

妙手回春憶上人

Sy Piac Hua

施碧華

I always share the words of wisdom from Venerable Master Hua's instructional talks with Rhosita.

Early last year, she was diagnosed with a tiny cyst in her body. Mortified and depressed, she called me from overseas; I told her to keep reciting the Buddha's name, calm down, and not panic.

The following day, on my way home from work, fear began to reign within me, but I kept reciting Buddha's name until I reached home. I put down my personal belongings, washed my hands, and bowed before the Buddha. Later, I called Long Beach Sagely Monastery to speak to a Dharma Master. I told her the reason why I needed to talk to her; suddenly, on the another phone line, I heard a voice that I knew was the Master's. Overwhelmed, I broke into tears and knelt down before the Buddha's altar.

I said in tears, "Master, please help us...we have kept this situation from our parents for we do not want them worry about us. Please help us, Master...."

The Master's compassionate response was indescribably potent as he transferred aid through me for Rhosita's ailment. Before he hung up, he asked the Dharma Master if I was still crying. I was relieved and overjoyed. Never in my life had I ever encountered anyone as humble and benevolent as the Venerable Master. My conversation with the Master was a miracle and an unforgettable experience. In fact, I didn't know that the Master was in Long Beach Sagely Monastery on that day.

The following morning, Rhosita called me and I told her to follow the Master's instructions by reciting Guanyin's name a full ten thousand times. When she had her final physical exam, the doctors found that the cyst has disappeared. The situation puzzled the doctors. They set another date to verify their test conclusively, and the result showed no sign of the presence of the cyst.

On January 17, 1994, at Long Beach Sagely Monastery, Rhosita took refuge with the Triple Jewel and received the Dharma name Kuo Mong, "Dreamer." Since she was residing in Switzerland at the time, my daughter, Hazel, took refuge on her behalf through the Master's generous and compassionate consent.

我經常與蘿茜達分享《宣化上人開示錄》裡的智慧之語。

去年年初經過檢驗，醫生診斷蘿茜達的體內有一個腫瘤。沮喪之餘，她打越洋電話給我，我要她念佛，靜下來，不要慌。

第二天下班回家的路上，我開始害怕了，可是我不斷的念佛直到回到家裡。放下東西，洗了手，我開始拜佛。稍後我打電話到長堤聖寺找一位法師，我告訴她我打電話的原因。在我們談話時，另一條線上我突然聽到一個確定是師父的聲音，我忍不住哭了，在佛前跪了下來。

我哭著說：「師父，請幫幫我們……。我們瞞著父母，因為怕他們為我們擔心。請救救我們，師父……。」

師父慈悲的答覆是，是由我將師父的加持力傳給蘿茜達，那種力量是無法形容的。在上人掛電話之前，他問法師我是不是還在哭，我感到無比的喜悅。我一生中從未遇到比上人更謙虛、更和藹的法師。我與師父的談話是一個奇蹟，也是難以忘懷的經驗。事實上，那天我根本不知道師父在長堤。

第二天蘿茜達打電話給我，我要她依師父的指示念一萬聲觀音菩薩的聖號。蘿茜達複檢的日子到了，醫生發覺腫瘤不見了，困惑之餘，他們安排了另一次檢查以便下結論。這次檢查也沒有找到腫瘤的蹤跡。

一九九四年一月十七日，蘿茜達與我一同皈依了三寶，法名果夢。雖然她住在瑞士，但經師父慈允後，我女兒榛代她皈依了。

永恆的感恩

日記數則

ETERNAL GRATITUDE

Several Pages from a Diary

羅果旋　Luo Guoxuan

一九九四年七月

去洛杉磯探望師父，那時師父剛動完手術，身體十分虛弱。令我驚訝的是，上人雖然因病臥床，但仍然時時為身旁的弟子們轉法輪。一天，醫院為師父送來簡單的食物：一盤水果，一杯果汁，幾片麵包。師父笑著說：「大概只有在醫院裡，才吃得較好。」

一九九四年八月九日

今天早上，師父的精神很好，一見面，師父就說：「Good morning！」（早安！）雖然身體不適，但師父仍然很關心地問：「今天風雨這麼大，你們來幹什麼？最近聖荷西佛學班如何？某某人生病，有沒有去看醫生？⋯⋯」聽到師父的這些話，心中非常難過。師父從不為自己著想，卻時時想著佛教的事、道場的事、眾生的事。

跪在師父床前，望著師父瘦弱的身體，不禁令我想起一件事。一次，馬來西亞來了一批人，到萬佛城求見上人。這些人多數有病，臉色黯淡無光。上人一見，便知道問題所在。這些人經上人加持後，有的人臉色立即好轉，甚至有一位坐輪椅的人，也可以站起來慢慢走。但他們可曾知道，師父當時整個身體顛抖，臉色鐵青地回寮房去了。看到這種情形，我悲淚盈眶，師父忽然回頭對我說：「要好好研究佛法，少哭一點。你可知道，有多少人能真正明白萬佛城山門的那兩句話。」又說：「你不要難過，自己生死自己了。真正要難過的，是那些不知好好用功辦道的人。」對我而言，又是一記當頭棒喝。

July 1994

I went to Los Angeles to visit the Venerable Master. The Master had just had an operation and was very weak. What surprised me was that even though the Master was lying sick in bed, he was still continuously turning the Dharma wheel for the disciples at his side. One day, the hospital sent the Master a simple meal: a plate of fruit, a glass of juice, and a few slices of bread. The Master said with a smile, "Probably it's only in the hospital that I can eat a little better."

August 9, 1994

The Master was in good spirits this morning. As soon as he saw us, he said, "Good morning!" Even though the Master wasn't feeling well, he still asked us with concern, "The weather is so stormy today. What did you come for? How has the San Jose Buddhist Study Group been? Did so-and-so see the doctor when he was sick? ..." When I heard the Master's words, I felt very bad. The Master never thought of himself. He was always thinking of the affairs of Buddhism, the affairs of Way-places, and the affairs of living beings.

Kneeling by the Master's bed and looking at the Master's thin and feeble body, I couldn't help thinking of a certain incident. One time, a group of people from Malaysia came to the City of Ten Thousand Buddhas and asked to meet with the Venerable Master. Most of them were sick and had a pallor to their faces. When the Master saw them, he knew immediately what they had come for. After receiving aid from the Venerable Master, some of them regained the color in their faces right away. There was one person in a wheelchair who was even able to stand up and walk slowly. What they didn't know was that the Master's body was trembling and his face was green as he returned to his room. I wept to see his state. The Master abruptly turned his head and said to me, "Study the Buddhadharma well and cry a little less. You should know how few people truly understand the two sentences on the main gate of the City of Ten Thousand Buddhas." He also said, "Don't be sad. Each person must end his own birth and death. Those who will truly be in trouble are those who don't know how to apply effort and cultivate." I had just been dealt another blow to the head.

Every instruction from the Venerable Master affords endless benefit for all my life.

上人的每一句法語，都令弟子終生受用無窮。

《華嚴經》〈十迴向品〉中說：

> 菩薩一切皆周給，內外所有悉能捨，必使其心永清淨，不應暫爾生狹劣。或施於頭，或施眼，或施於手，或施足，皮肉骨髓及餘物，一切皆捨心無吝。

師父以他崇高的德行和慈悲的願力，擔負起眾生的業。將自己的身體化成無量的國土，讓各類難調難伏的眾生，依此國土而住。上人捨棄了自身的健康，換來眾生身心得到安穩。

《華嚴經》〈阿僧祇品〉：

> 於一微塵毛端處，有不可說諸普賢，一切毛端悉亦爾，如是乃至遍法界。彼毛端處諸國土，無量種類差別住。有不可說異類剎，有不可說同類剎……於彼一一諸法中，調伏眾生不可說。或復於一毛端處，不可說劫常安住……菩薩如是大慈悲，利益一切諸世間。

《華嚴經》〈普賢行願品〉更提到：

> 若此惡業有體相者，盡虛空界不能容受。

由此可知，師父為眾生所承擔的，是多麼大的業啊！

愚癡的自己，常常為沒有機會親聞師父講經而悔恨。直到目睹師父躺在病床上，才突然醒悟：其實，無論在健康或病重時，師父的行住坐臥，時時刻刻都在為眾生演說無字真經，轉華嚴大法，真是「有眼不識觀世音，有耳不聞圓頓教。」雖悔之，已晚矣！

一九九五年六月九日

南下洛杉磯，瞻仰上人的法相，心情非常沉重。見上人躺在殯儀館冷冰冰的鐵板上，難道這就是〈宇宙白〉所言：「冰天雪地……大慈悲普度，流血汗，不休息。」的境界

The "Ten Transferences Chapter" in the *Flower Adornment Sutra* says,

> The Bodhisattva is able to give away everything. He can give away all that he has both internally and externally. He must cause his mind to be forever pure, and never for an instant give rise to petty or lowly thoughts. He may give away his head, eyes, hands, or feet. Whether it be his skin, flesh, bones, marrow, or other things, he can give them all away without stinginess.

With his exalted virtue and compassionate vows, the Venerable Master has taken upon himself the karma of living beings. He would transform his body into limitless lands so that all kinds of living beings who are difficult to teach and subdue could dwell in them. The Venerable Master sacrificed his own health in order to give living beings peace in body and mind.

The "Asamkhyeya Chapter" of the *Flower Adornment Sutra* says,

> On the tip of one fine hair in one mote of dust, there are ineffable numbers of Universal Worthys. This is true of every hairtip throughout the Dharma Realm. In the countries on the tip of one hair, limitless beings of different species dwell. There are ineffably many kshetras where those of different species dwell, and there are ineffably many kshetras where those of the same species dwell...Within each dharma, they teach and subdue ineffably many beings. Or on the tip of one hair, they may constantly dwell for ineffable kalpas. ... With such great compassion, Bodhisattvas benefit all those in the world.

The "Chapter on the Conduct and Vows of Universal Worthy" in the *Flower Adornment Sutra* says,

> If this evil karma had substance and form, all of empty space could not contain it.

From this, we can know how great must be the karma that the Venerable Master is shouldering for living beings!

Foolish me, I have often regretted the fact that I haven't had the opportunity to hear the Master lecture on the Sutras. Only after seeing the Venerable Master lying sick in bed did I suddenly wake up! I realize now that, whether the Master is healthy or sick, in his every gesture and move, he constantly speaks the true, wordless Sutra and expounds the great Flower Adornment Dharma for living beings. I was truly one who "had eyes but didn't recognize Guanshiyin Bodhisattva, who had ears but didn't hear the Sudden Perfect Teaching." Although I regret it, it's too late!

June 9, 1995

Going south to Los Angeles to behold the Venerable Master, I felt very depressed. I saw the Venerable Master lying on a cold metal table in the mortuary. Was this the state mentioned in White Universe: "Ice in the sky, snow on the ground...With great compassion rescue everyone, sparing neither blood nor sweat, and never pausing to rest"? Why is it that

嗎？為什麼師父能救眾生的法身慧命，眾生卻不能「請佛住世」？一定是眾生的業力太重，一定是我們沒有真正的「懺悔業障」，沒有福報請上人長久住世。

一九九五年八月

清晨，陽光灑遍了萬佛聖城，和煦的晨光中，似乎又見到上人慈悲的面容。四眾弟子們，又開始了忙碌的一天。師父留下的正法及六大宗旨，將由這些四眾弟子發揚光大。

太陽，只是暫時隱沒，當陽光再次衝破黑暗的時候，將把光和熱灑遍三千大千世界。

但願師父的每一位弟子，將師父所傳的法寶，時時持之於心，身體力行。將來也都能夠成為另一個太陽，照破無明黑暗，帶給眾生無限的光明。

the Master can rescue the Dharma body and wisdom life of living beings, yet living beings cannot request the Buddhas to remain in the world? It must be that living beings' karma is too heavy. It must be that we haven't truly repented of our karmic hindrances and don't have the blessings to request the Venerable Master to remain in the world.

August 1995

At dawn, the rays of sun shined over the Sagely City of Ten Thousand Buddhas. In the gentle morning light, I seemed to see the Venerable Master's kind face again. The fourfold assembly of disciples began another busy day. These disciples will cause the proper Dharma and the Six Principles left by the Venerable Master to spread and flourish.

The sun was temporarily obscured. When the rays of sunlight shined through the darkness again, they spread warmth and light throughout the three thousand great thousand worlds.

I hope that every disciple of the Venerable Master will constantly cherish in his heart the Dharma jewels transmitted by the Master and will truly practice them. That way, each one can eventually become another sun that can shine through the darkness of ignorance and bring boundless light to living beings.

藏教菩薩事六度　　圓修妙覺理頓明
無智破執空諸相　　不得非證了法融
於一毫端現寶剎　　坐微塵裡轉法輪
此語說出鮮誠信　　未悉知音有幾人

宣公上人《般若波羅密多心經非台頌解》

The Storehouse-Teaching Bodhisattvas cultivate the Six Paramitas
at the level of phenomena,
While the Perfect-Teaching Bodhisattvas of wonderful enlightenment
cultivate with an understanding of the noumena.
With attachment to Prajna destroyed, all characteristics are emptied.
Without any attainment or verification, he comprehends the fusion of dharmas.
He makes a jeweled realm appear on the tip of a single hair.
And he turns the Dharma-wheel while sitting on a speck of dust.
These words are spoken, yet few believe them;
I do not know how many really understand.

From the Venerable Master Hua's Verses without a Stand for the *Heart of Prajna Paramita Sutra*

恩師宣化上人涅槃感言

ON THE NIRVANA OF OUR KIND TEACHER, THE VENERABLE MASTER HUA

張果梅　Zhang Guomei

自從得知恩師宣公上人圓寂的訊息，我們馬來西亞森美蘭州芙蓉市，一群「果」字輩皈依宣公上人座下的三寶弟子，以及一般信眾，震撼之餘，也很感慨！一代高僧乘願來此娑婆世界，數十年期間，為弘大法，不辭勞苦，聖跡處處，創設道場寺院，廣收僧徒，而於美國萬佛聖城興辦大學、中學、小學各級教育；招賢納德，設立譯經院，續佛慧命，弘法利生。恩師宣公上人與此娑婆緣盡，捨世而歸佛國。

記得恩師宣公上人，前後曾四次蒞臨馬來西亞弘法，那個時候，正法開示，禪風吹拂，萬眾景仰。上人恩澤的感召，大家無不至心歸命信受，奉持佛法。上人加被眾生甘露法雨，振奮社會人心，一時雲集上人座下信佛、念佛者，何止千萬計。聞風所至，使人心向善。

大悲、大智、大雄力，為佛陀的三大宏力。回想恩師宣公上人，倒駕慈航，普度眾生，恢弘佛教正法於東西方各土，法界聞名，這就是在實踐三大宏力。我等信徒，望風瞻仰，恭敬禮拜，以至誠的心意，護持三寶，依教奉行，以期離苦得樂。

閱讀恩師的《開示錄》，我獲得寶貴的人生價值觀，瞭解佛道的無量。感謝佛恩，也感謝恩師宣公上人留給我的「忍、佛、法」三字教誨，能隨時讓無知、無明的我，得到啟發。

一九九五年九月八日

Ever since we received news of the Venerable Master Hua's completion of stillness, those of us in Seremban, Negeri Sembilan, Malaysia who had taken refuge with the Venerable Master and have Dharma names beginning with "Guo," as well as other followers, were shocked and saddened. An eminent monk of this age came to the Saha World and spared no effort to propagate the great Dharma during the several decades that he was here. Wherever he went, he set up Way-places and temples and accepted left-home disciples on a vast scale. At the Sagely City of Ten Thousand Buddhas in America, he established a university, secondary schools, and elementary schools. Attracting worthy and virtuous people, he set up the Institute for the Translation of Buddhist Texts and propagated the Dharma to benefit beings and perpetuate the Buddhas' wisdom. And when his conditions with this Saha world came to an end, he left the world and returned to the Buddhaland.

The Venerable Master came to Malaysia a total of four times to propagate the Dharma. He lectured on the Proper Dharma, stirred up interest in meditation, and won the admiration of the multitudes. Under the influence of the Venerable Master's kindness and virtue, everyone wholeheartedly took refuge in, believed, accepted, and upheld the Buddhadharma. Bestowing the sweet dew and Dharma rain upon living beings, he roused the minds of people throughout the society. The Buddhists who gathered to hear him numbered in the tens of thousands. Attracted by what they heard, people were inspired to become good.

Great compassion, great wisdom, and great courage—these are the three great powers of the Buddha. The Venerable Master Hua compassionately turned the boat around and came to universally save living beings. He propagated the proper Dharma to the people in the East and West, and his renown spread throughout the Dharma Realm. That was the three great powers in action. I and all followers look up to the Master, respectfully make obeisance, and with utmost sincerity protect the Triple Jewel and practice according to the teachings, in the hope of leaving suffering and attaining bliss.

From reading our kind Teacher's instructional talks, I have realized the values of human life and come to understand the boundlessness of the Buddha Way. I am grateful to the Buddha's kindness, and I thank the Venerable Master for the teaching of three words that he left me—patience, the Buddha, and the Dharma—which constantly inspires me in my ignorance.

September 8, 1995

*　　　　*　　　　*

聞知恩師宣公上人於一九九五年六月七日圓寂之後，馬來西亞森美蘭州芙蓉市，一群「果」字輩皈依宣公上人座下的三寶弟子，即時召集會議，發起設立恭奉宣公上人蓮位。訂於七月二日、農曆六月初五上午九時，在森美蘭州佛教支會會所，恭請馬來西亞佛教總會主席兼森美蘭州佛教支會主席上寂下晃長老，暨開基法師、悟輝法師、洞安法師、照圓法師、開信法師和開音法師等領導下，居士信徒們二百餘人，一心禮誦《佛說阿彌陀經》。下午一時則由開基法師率領眾等禮拜《金剛寶懺》，回向恩師宣化上人。當日道場肅穆莊嚴，氣氛殊勝感人，下午四時法會圓滿結束。惟祈望恩師宣公上人乘願再來，化度眾生。

設立恭奉宣公上人蓮位誦經禮懺法會，籌備工委會發起人：李果萍、張果梅。

After hearing of the Venerable Master Hua's completion of stillness on June 7, 1995, a group of disciples in Seremban, Negeri Sembilan, Malaysia, who had taken refuge with the Master and had Dharma names beginning with "Guo," immediately called a meeting and began to make arrangements to set up an altar to the Venerable Master. On July 2 at 9:00 a.m., at the Buddhist Association of Negeri Sembilan, under the leadership of the Elder Master Venerable Ji Noble Huang, Chairman of the Malaysian Buddhist Association and Buddhist Association of Negeri Sembilan, as well as Dharma Masters Kaiji, Wuhui, Dongan, Zhaoyuan, Kaixin, and Kaiyin, the assembly of over two hundred lay followers single-mindedly recited the *Buddha Speaks of Amitabha Sutra*. At 1:00 p.m., Dharma Master Kaiji led the assembly in bowing the Vajra Jewelled Repentance and dedicated the merit to the Venerable Master. The Way-place on that day was solemn and adorned, and there was a sublime feeling that was very touching. The Dharma session ended at 4:00 p.m. We only pray the Venerable Master Hua will come back on his vows to teach and save living beings.

A committee for setting up the altar for worshipping the Venerable Master Hua and organizing the Dharma session for reciting Sutras and bowing in repentance was initiated by Li Guoping and Zhang Guomei.

咒乃密分匪思量　如王詔旨僉同遵

亦似軍中祕密令　問答不符便執行

大乘妙理離分別　凡夫知見妄緣真

因指望月指非月　藉咒明心咒即心

宣公上人《般若波羅密多心經非台頌解》

As part of the esoteric, the mantra is beyond thought;
It is followed by everyone together, like the edict of a monarch
And like a secret password among the troops.
If one's reply to the question is not fitting,
*　　one is quickly put in line.*
The wonderful truth of the Great Vehicle is apart from distinctions,
Yet ordinary people take the false as the true.
Follow the finger's pointing to see the moon; don't take the finger as the moon.
When one understands the mind by means of the mantra, the mantra is just the mind.

From the Venerable Master Hua's Verses without a Stand for the *Heart of Prajna Paramita Sutra*

THE BODHISATTVA'S COMPASSION
菩薩的悲憫

Shi Heng Shou　釋恆授

In the early spring of 1974 I was living in Hong Kong at the Buddhist Lecture Hall when the Master returned after many years in America.

Shortly after the Master returned to Hong Kong, his disciples requested that he perform a Liberating Life Ceremony at Western Bliss Gardens, one of the temples he had founded years ago. Along with two other monks, I assisted with the chanting and playing of the Dharma instruments as the Master led the ceremony in the midst of a large crowd of lay disciples. The beings released that day were a kind of small bird whose flesh was used in Chinese cooking. A little way into the ceremony, on turning my head to pick up any ceremonial cues, I observed the Master standing next to the cages of birds. To my great surprise I noticed that he was weeping. There was no apparent expression of anguish. In fact his countenance was almost placidly and blissfully neutral. But still, there was no mistake about the fact that he really was weeping. Naturally, I was somewhat bewildered.

Since I had met the Master in the early summer of 1968, I had witnessed him displaying nearly every emotion in the course of his work as a Bodhisattva and spiritual instructor. I had seen him speaking very softly and gently to very timid disciples, at which times his voice would sound as comforting as the quiet purr of a kitten. I had seen him speak very harshly and powerfully to very arrogant disciples. At those times his voice could sound as terrifying as the roar of a lion. Sometimes he would tell jokes to lighten a disciple's overly leaden mood. Sometimes he would be very stern in discouraging frivolousness where there was inattention to important details. Sometimes his presence was so beatific that everyone in his presence enjoyed a state of nearly intoxicating blissfulness even without him speaking a word. Sometimes his demeanor was so grave that anyone present spontaneously experienced a sort of glacial solemnity.

So, anyway, I had seen all of these "emotions" in the Master and in many different permutations. But I had never seen the Master weeping. I felt rather disturbed by what I had seen, but of course forged on with the rest of the ceremony, chanting and beating the wooden fish. When the ceremony came to an end, I turned and looked again at the Master who was now smiling radiantly through the traces of his recent tears. I had not been the only one who had noticed the Master weeping. In fact, I think nearly everyone was a bit confused. Then the Master offered a brief explanation (which I paraphrase here), saying, "Some of you probably noticed that I was crying as we were performing the Liberating Life Ceremony and you may have wondered why. Well, I'll tell you. The reason I wept was that I realized that one of these birds had been a monastic disciple of mine in a previous life. But this monastic strayed from the path, and eventually strayed so far that now he has taken rebirth as a bird. It was because of this that I couldn't help but weep out pity."

一九七四年早春，我住在香港佛教講堂。那時，在美國多年的上人，剛剛返回香港。

不久，上人應眾弟子的邀請，在西樂園寺舉行放生法會。西樂園寺是上人多年前建立的道場。法會中，我與另外兩位師兄弟，負責領唱及打法器。那次放生的是一種鳥，中國人用這種鳥的肉做菜。法會剛進行不久，我轉過頭來，去看敲擊法器的適當時間，卻看到上人站在鳥籠邊，流著眼淚。我大吃一驚！事實上，當時上人的表情看起來十分平靜祥和，但是上人的確哭了，這是不會錯的。我有點迷惑了？！

從一九六八年初夏認識上人以來，這位菩薩兼心靈導師所示現的種種「情感」，我均見過。我見過他柔聲細語地對膽小的弟子開示，聲音溫和得像打咕嚕的小貓；也見過他聲色俱厲對貢高我慢的弟子吆喝，就如獅子吼般地令人怖畏；有時，他講講笑話，舒減弟子們過於沉悶的心情；有時，他嚴厲地指責輕率的弟子，疏於留意重要的細節；有時，他的情緒裡，洋溢著某種喜氣，即使未發一言，也令周遭的人感受到那份欣悅；有時，他又神情肅穆，令人畏然起敬。

上人這些「情感」的流露，我均見過，但我從未見上人哭過，所以心神十分不寧。法會繼續進行，我也隨著唱誦及打木魚。當法會快要結束時，我轉過頭再看上人，此時他已破涕為笑，但淚痕猶在。事實上，不只我一個人看見上人哭了，我想幾乎每個人都有點困惑。上人於是稍做解釋：「法會時，也許有的人看見我哭，就想，師父為什麼哭呢？我告訴你們，放生的小鳥裡，有一隻是我前世的出家弟子。他誤入歧途，以致今生做鳥。今日與他在此種場合見面，不禁悲憫落淚。」

That ceremony at Western Bliss Gardens was an unforgettable experience for me. That he would be brought to tears over the karmic fate of one of his disciples shows the depth and genuineness of his concern for them. That he was weeping for a little bird shows me that the Master's compassion is so far-reaching that it really does extend to all living beings.

西樂園寺的放生法會，是我終生難忘的一次經歷。上人對業力所縛的弟子那種關愛，是如此地強烈而深切。不僅僅是為一隻小鳥，上人的慈悲是遠達一切眾生的！

THE SIX GUIDING PRINCIPLES:
EASY TO KNOW BUT DIFFICULT TO PRACTICE
易知難行的六大宗旨

Peter Schmitz 史彼得

Shr Fu taught simple basic principles that were easy to understand but difficult to practice. To be a good person according to the principles Shr Fu taught was a completely new style of living and thinking and reacting to the surroundings. The meaning and depth of purpose contained in the five precepts were taught in a way that was always fresh and useful as a way to gain self control. Shr Fu taught a whole new life awareness, an appreciation of the methods of cultivation. Shr Fu was the example of the truth he taught and the result of pure practice. Understanding causes and conditions, the purpose of meditation, ceremonies, reciting mantras and sutras, all these practical methods Shr Fu taught over and over so even the most stubborn could come to understand at least a little. The very bad qualities that ruin our lives, Shr Fu taught us, are the material that is transformed into wholesome goodness and better understanding and are cause for us to see how to improve. Shr Fu taught ordinary simple rules that had range and depth.

Shr Fu said "everything is okay," although anyone who heard knew that within "everything is okay," we have to improve. Shr Fu wanted disciples to work hard, but always taught that we should make our own decisions. Shr Fu not only wanted His disciples to be able to make choices on their own but always to try to be in accord with the precepts and principles of Buddhism. Shr Fu gave comfort and safety and peace. But it was also clear that you had to work to improve, to become a better person according to how much you understood the teaching. Shr Fu introduced the practice and meaning of the five precepts and the purpose for trying to change our bad habits and learn how to be more pure. It was easier for young Americans new to the study of Buddhism to listen and gradually accept what Shr Fu taught because he was the example of purity. Shr Fu radiated virtue so it was easier to believe that what he said was true.

師父常常教導一些簡單、易懂，而難行的道理。如何去奉行實踐這些教理，做一個好人，是全然一新的生活、思想、及應對環境的方式。師父以一種新的、容易啟發自律的方法，來教導弟子們五戒的深廣義理。師父也使弟子們重新估評修行的方法，去體會生命的意義。師父修清淨行，躬行實踐真理。師父一再重覆地教導弟子們實際修行的方法：要深信因果、參禪打坐、各種法事的儀軌、持咒誦經等，以便即使是最剛強的弟子也能多少明白一些道理。師父說，那些使生命頹喪荒廢的壞習氣：能轉化為善根、也能使我們更明理，及令我們改進。事實上，這些平平無奇、簡單的原則，包含了極深廣的義理。

師父常說「一切都好」。雖然「一切都好」，我們還必須勇猛地改過自新。師父不但要弟子們精進、獨立自主，同時也要遵守戒律，依教奉行。師父給予弟子們：鼓勵、安全感與和平。大家要盡其所能，依照自己所能理解的道理去改進，做一個更好的人。師父解釋了遵守五戒的意義；改變習氣毛病的目的，及如何去淨化身心。師父清淨的行持，使剛剛學習佛法的美國年輕人，聽從和接受了師父的教導。師父的德行，足以令人相信師父所說的每一句話都是真實的。

鍥而不捨地追求

NEVER GIVE UP

李克勤　Christine Lee

在沒認識佛法以前，我生長在一個天主教家庭裡，小時候身體很不好，去的醫院也是天主教的醫院，給我看病的大夫都是修女，所以我跟天主教的因緣是很深的。

我所做的工作，是經常要代表公司到國外去做業務考察，常常要出遠門。這在十多年前，對一個東方女子來講，是一份很不容易、很艱辛的工作。我最遠到過南葉門，那是一個非常落後的國家；我也去過黎巴嫩，那是一個為了宗教一直都在打仗的國家。

有一天，我問自己：「我每日這樣奔波，這樣忙碌，究竟為了什麼？」

我看過戰爭，也看過戰爭後的滿目瘡痍；還有共產國家，還有一些非常有福報的歐洲國家，美國也是很有福報；可是還有很多地區是很落後的。我就問我自己：「我這一生當中，到底在追求什麼？到底在找什麼東西？」我不知道自己到底得到了些什麼？我覺得好像來來去去都是一場空，覺得這個娑婆世界非常非常苦，於是乎我覺得天主教的教義，已經不能滿足我的疑問。

我就由民間的信仰開始，一直尋找我所追求的理念。有一天，在我同學家裡，我第一次知道有關佛教的事。她的先生是學佛的，她家的頂樓有一個佛堂，她介紹給我看，我就請教她怎麼供佛等等。然後我問她：「那妳的師父是誰啊？」她指著師父的照片說：「我的師父就是這位。」我說：「啊！這位就是妳師父啊？」當時覺得好奇，而且很新鮮。我對那張照片的印象非常地深刻，為什麼呢？因為師父手上拿著一把拂塵，我小時候很喜歡扮成七仙女，所以對那把拂塵很有興趣，我說：「我沒有看過和尚手上拿拂塵的哪？」我對這個拂塵就特別有好感。她就告訴我她的一些感應，她說：「我師父要回臺灣的時候，我都會夢到他。」我說：「真的啊？」覺得很有興趣，我又說：「那妳能不能介紹，有沒有妳師父的書，或者生平事蹟，我可以對這個出家人有所瞭解啊？」她說：「有。」就是她唯一的兩本佛書，其中一本是師父上人的《開示錄》第一冊。

當天晚上，我住在她們家，閱讀了兩頁以後，我的淚水就沒有止住過，一個晚上就已經看了三分之二了。我

Before I learned about the Buddhadharma, I grew up in a Catholic family. As a child I often got sick. I went to a Catholic-run hospital and my doctor was a nun, so my conditions with Catholicism ran very deep.

In my work, I regularly represented my company on trips abroad to perform business inspections. For an Asian woman, this was a very difficult job to do over ten years ago. The farthest I travelled was to South Yemen, an extremely underdeveloped country. I've also been to Lebanon, a nation beset by unending religious wars.

One day I asked myself, "What am I so busily running around and working for? Ultimately, what's the point?"

I've seen wars, and I've seen the ravages left by war. I've also seen Communist countries, some European countries where people are very well off, and the United States, which is also very prosperous. There are also many very poor and underdeveloped areas. So I asked myself, "What do I want in this life? What am I seeking for?" I didn't know what I had gained. I felt that despite all the coming and going, everything was empty. I felt that the Saha World was extremely miserable. And I also felt the doctrines of Catholicism could not resolve my doubts satisfactorily.

I began with popular belief and kept searching until I found my ideal. One day, I came across a Buddhist book for the first time at my classmate's house. Her husband was a Buddhist, and they had a shrine on the top floor. She showed it to me and I asked her about how to make offerings to the Buddha and so on. Then I asked her, "Who is your teacher?" She pointed to the Master's photo and said, "This is my teacher." I was very curious. The photo made a deep impression on me, because the Master was holding a whisk. When I was little I liked to dress up and pretend I was one of the seven fairies, so I was very interested in the whisk. I said, "I've never seen a monk holding a whisk." I took a liking to that whisk. She told me about some of the responses she'd had. She said, "When the Master came to Taiwan, I dreamed about him." "Really?" Quite interested, I asked, "Do you have some books by your Master, or his biography, that I can read to find out more about him?" She said, "Yes." She gave me one of her only two Buddhist books—the first volume of the Master's *Instructional Talks*.

That evening, I stayed at their home. After reading two pages, my tears came without stop. In one night, I read

所要問的問題，我所苦苦尋求的答案，全部都在那本書裡。那時候我就告訴自己：「這就是我的師父！可是要去哪裡找這位師父呢？」書上面的地址又不是很清楚，因為那本書已經非常破舊了，可是她還保存得很好，當寶貝一樣。我說：「你師父在美國，我怎麼去美國呢？」這一段時間，對我來講，是人生的一個重大的轉變。但短期內，我根本不可能去美國。於是我就對自己說：「不管怎樣困難，哪怕歷盡千辛萬苦，我也一定要到美國去找我的師父。」當時我對師父並不是非常瞭解，我只覺得他講的每一句話、每一個字、每一件事都這麼平實，全部解答了我一生所要尋找的問題。他所講的話，真地是直指人心。

我那個時候非常慚愧，心想：「喔！原來人生就是這麼一回事，到頭來什麼都是空的，什麼都不屬於自己！」當時我想見師父，是很單純的一個念頭，我見師父不是為了什麼，只是想看看他老人家一眼，「哦！這就是我的師父。」我當時甚至不明白什麼叫皈依。可是我就在這兩年當中，照著師父的方法去做。他要求他的弟子這麼嚴厲，我說：「喔，一天只要吃一餐，還要吃齋，還要背經、背咒，還要打坐參禪呀……。那他的弟子們一定很辛苦啊，一天到底睡幾個鐘頭的覺？」我那時候有很多的疑問：還要是大學畢業的，還有很多其他的要求，我不知道有沒有要求身高啊，因為我個子很矮。

我就這樣，在兩年時間裡，改我的習氣毛病，修正自己。改正自己為的就是要見師父一面。我沒有經過任何人的介紹，很誠心的，就這樣來到了萬佛聖城。那是一九九二年的十月，在舊金山金山寺時，我就是一路哭進來的。當我到萬佛城的時候，我覺得簡直太熟悉這個地方了，我好像曾經來過，簡直是熟悉得不能再熟悉了，那種感覺，就像是一隻迷途的羔羊，找到牠自己的家一樣，那就是我當時的感覺。

在金山寺的時候，我對一位法師說：「我希望求見師父。」她說：「那看你的誠心囉！」我聽了以後，心裡涼了一半，心想：「我還不夠誠心嗎？準備了兩年，千里迢迢地從臺灣來到美國，我難道還不夠誠心嗎？好吧，如果見到師父，就是我的福報；見不到師父，那麼也只好作罷！」當時，我就是這樣想的。於是我就在佛殿拜佛，接著就來到萬佛城住了兩天，然後就到柏林根國際譯經學院去拜見師父。說也奇怪，師父看到我，好像知道我的事情，但是我那時不瞭解師父，他們所謂的高僧，到底高到什麼程度，真地不

two-thirds of the book. All the questions I wanted to ask, all the answers I'd been searching for so diligently, were in this book. At that time I told myself, "This is my teacher! But where could I go to find him?" The address on the books wasn't very clear because the book was very old, although she took good care of it and treated it as a treasure. I said, "Your teacher is in America. How can I go to America?" That was a major turning point in my life. However, there was no way I could go to America in the short term. So I said to myself, "No matter how difficult it is, no matter how much hardship it involves, I must go to America to find my teacher." At that point I didn't really understand who the Master was. I just knew that every sentence and every word he said, and every thing he did, was so ordinary and honest, yet he had given me all the answers I had been searching for in my life. The words that he said truly pointed straight at the mind.

At that time I felt very remorseful as I thought, "Oh! So this is what life's all about. When the time comes, everything is empty. Nothing belongs to us!" My wish to see the Master was a very innocent thought. I didn't want to see the Master for any particular reason, but just to see him and think, "Ah! This is my teacher!" I didn't even know what it meant to take refuge. But during the next two years, I did things according to the Master's method. He was so strict with his disciples. I thought, "They eat only one meal a day, and a vegetarian meal at that, and they also memorize Sutras and mantras, and sit in meditation...His disciples must work very hard; just how many hours of sleep do they get each day?" I had a lot of doubts. There were a lot of other requirements, such as having a college degree. I didn't know if being tall was also a requirement, because I am very short.

In this way, during those two years, I corrected my faults and bad habits and reformed myself. I did this all for the sake of seeing the Master. Without anyone introducing me, I very sincerely came to the Sagely City of Ten Thousand Buddhas. That was in October of 1992. I cried all the way from Gold Mountain Monastery in San Francisco to the Sagely City. When I arrived at the Sagely City, it seemed entirely familiar, as if I had been here before. I couldn't have been more familiar with it. I felt like a lost lamb who had found its way back home.

When I was at Gold Mountain Monastery, I said to a Dharma Master, "I hope to see the Master." She said, "Well, it all depends on your sincerity!" I felt I had been doused with cold water. I thought, "Am I still not sincere enough? I prepared for two years and came all the way from Taiwan to America. Do you mean to say I'm not sincere enough? Fine. If I get to see the Master, then it's my blessings. If I don't get to see the Master, then so be it!" That's what I thought. Then I bowed in the Buddhahall. Afterwards I came to the City of Ten Thousand Buddhas for two days, and then went to the International Translation Institute in Burlingame to see the Master. Strangely enough, the Master seemed to know all

知道，那個時候真地是很愚癡的。

師父見到我，第一句就說：「妳來啦！」我說：「是啊！我來啦！」就好像家裡的人在講話。「妳幾號來的？到了萬佛城？」我說：「是啊！」

第二句話，師父又說：「喔！妳找師父找到美國來囉！妳花很多錢哦。」我說：「是啊，我花很多錢。我準備了兩年來見師父呢！」「嗯，妳找師父找到美國來了，師父也要找弟子啊！」我想師父的意思就是說，你這麼會挑師父，師父也要挑他的弟子的，你合不合格做他的弟子啊。

第三句話，師父跟我講：「妳要出家。」我說：「哦？」我不知道該怎麼回答，因為當時的念頭只是要來見見師父，我說：「師父您說我要出家，那我什麼時候出家？」「看妳囉！妳什麼時候，我怎麼能替妳決定呢？」我沒有說話。

後來師父還跟我講了一些事情，這些事情我記在本子裡面，到目前為止，我還沒有參透到底是什麼意思？指的什麼？將來會怎麼樣子？師父用幾句話，把我這一生的事情都勾畫出來了。我接著就告訴師父說：「我要皈依師父。」師父說：「好啊，不過今天很忙啊，今天有記者招待會。」

後來，師父說他要去洛杉磯，我也跟著去了。但是因為金輪寺當時沒有皈依儀式，我就跪在師父法座旁邊，師父對我說：「我不能為你一個人打皈依。」那時候我心想：「我就回臺灣皈依。」我仍跪在那邊，看師父是不是有什麼話要跟我說，師父只跟我講了幾個字，我到現在都記得很清楚，雖是幾個字，但是對我來講，可以說是終身受用的幾句很平實的話：「見賢思齊，見不賢內自省。」

回到臺灣以後，於一九九三年一月在板橋體育館皈依了師父。自從皈依師父以後，我想要做的事情，沒有一件事情不是遂了我的願。那個時候我想去念佛學院，可是她們說我年齡已超過，沒有辦法。我自己就生了驕傲心，心想：「你們既然不要我的話，那也就罷了，我就不去念了。」於是我就一心一意想瞭解佛教，想瞭解為什麼跟這個宗教有這麼深的因緣？為什麼看到師父的書，就覺得那麼地熟悉？而且從內心裡發出來的那種震撼，是那樣地不可言喻。

我在謄寫《法華經》的這一年當中，感觸相當地深，就像法師剛才說的：「師父，他是很有學問的人。」我可以舉一個很簡單的例子，就知道師父的學問好到什麼程度。各位知道「圓圈」的「圈」，

about me when he saw me. I, however, didn't understand the Master. I didn't understand how lofty a monk he was. I really didn't know. I was really stupid then.

When the Master saw me, the first thing he said was, "You've come!" I said, "Yes, I've come!" It was like talking with my family. "What day did you arrive? Have you been to the City of Ten Thousand Buddhas?" "Yes!" I replied.

The second thing the Master said was, "Ah! So your search for your teacher has brought you to America! It's cost you a lot of money!" I said, "Yes, I've spent a lot of money. I spent two years getting ready to see the Master!" "You've come to America to find your teacher. The teacher also has to search for his disciple, you know?" I think what the Master meant was, "You're very selective about your teacher. Well, your teacher is also very selective about disciples. Are you qualified to be my disciple?"

The Master's third statement was, "You have to leave the home-life." "Huh?" I didn't know what to reply, because my only thought had been to see the Master. I said, "Master, you say I have to leave home. When should I leave home then?" "It's up to you! How can I decide for you?" I said nothing.

Later the Master said some things to me, which I wrote down in a notebook. Even now I haven't been able to completely understand exactly what they mean. What was he referring to? What would happen in the future? In a few words, the Master had delineated my whole life's affairs. Then I said, "I wish to take refuge with the Master." The Master said, "Okay, but I'm very busy today. There's a press conference."

Later the Master said he was going to Los Angeles, and I went along. However, because there was no refuge ceremony at Gold Wheel Monastery, I knelt beside the Master's Dharma seat. The Master said, "I can't hold the refuge ceremony for you alone." I thought to myself, "Then I'll go back to Taiwan and take refuge." I continued kneeling there, waiting to see if the Master had anything to say to me. The Master only said a few words, but I remember them very clearly to this day. Even though they are just a few words, I can benefit from them all my life: "When you see those who are worthy, strive to emulate them. When you see those who are not worthy, reflect upon yourself."

I returned to Taiwan, and in January of 1993, I took refuge with the Master at the Banqiao Stadium. Ever since I took refuge with the Master, everything I wanted to do went according to my wishes. I wanted to study at a Buddhist Academy, but they said I was too old and they couldn't accept me. I felt very arrogant, thinking, "Well, if you don't want me, then forget it. I won't study either." I single-mindedly sought to understand the Buddhadharma and to discover why I had such deep affinity with this religion. Why did I feel the Master's books were so familiar? And why did they stir me up in such an ineffable way?

I have a deep impression of the one year that I spent transcribing the Master's commentary on the *Dharma Flower Sutra*. As the Dharma Master mentioned earlier, the Master is a very learned person. I can give a very simple example to illustrate

名詞是讀ㄑㄩㄢ，師父在講《法華經》的時候，他講「圈（ㄐㄩㄢ）起來」，我為了這個字，在筆記上空了很久，怎麼想都想不出來這到底是哪個ㄐㄩㄢ，我知道不是那個「堅固」的「堅」，我怎麼想都想不出來是什麼字。直到有一天，我翻字典試看看這個「圈」字，才發現原來這個字用在動詞是念ㄐㄩㄢ，「把他圈（ㄐㄩㄢ）起來」，就是坐牢的意思。

從這個很微細的地方，可以知道師父不但上知天文，下知地理，譯經就更不用講了。他老人家的學問，真地是非常非常地淵博。如果各位有人在做經典的謄稿和校對工作，請你們很用心、很專注地去做。這樣你的收穫，包括你自己的修行，都會有無上的進步。同時，你自己也可以從這一面鏡子，非常非常清楚地，照到你自己在修行當中所要改的習氣毛病。

how erudite the Master is. You all know that the Chinese character 圈 "circle" is pronounced *quan*. When the Master was explaining the *Dharma Flower Sutra*, he pronounced it *juan*. I had to leave a blank in my transcription for a long time because I couldn't figure out what the word was. I knew it wasn't the word *jian* "firm," but I couldn't think of any other word. One day, when I looked up the word 圈 "circle" in the dictionary, I discovered that it was pronounced *juan* when used as a verb, meaning "to imprison."

From this small incident, we can see that not only does the Master know the lore of the heavens and earth, explaining the Sutras is no problem at all for him. His learning is extremely profound and vast. If any of you are transcribing or proofreading commentaries on the Sutras, I hope you will be very careful and concentrated. What you gain out of this will enable you to advance greatly in your cultivation. At the same time, you will be able to see very, very clearly, as if in a mirror, the faults and bad habits that you need to get rid of in your cultivation.

*　　　　*　　　　*

接下來我要提到我的一個上司，他的脾氣非常暴躁。在《金剛菩提海》雜誌裡，師父講一句話，他說：「為什麼你愚癡？因為你有脾氣！（Why are you stupid? Because you have temper.）」我就把它影印放大給公司的同事看。上司看了以後，就告訴我說：「我不要愚癡！」我說：「你不要愚癡的話，就要改你的脾氣。」

我提到這件事，是因為我們現在出版的中英對照佛書和《金剛菩提海》雜誌，對於一些不懂佛法的人和一些外國人來講，是很好的讀物，這些都是很淺顯、很平易的。我這位上司被師父這句話影響到什麼程度呢？到目前為止，只要一發脾氣，他就會一直雙手握緊拳頭說：「我不可以發脾氣，我絕對不可以發脾氣，因為這個有智慧的人說，絕對不可以發脾氣，一發脾氣就會做錯很多的決策。」一直到一年多以後，他還常問我說：「我有沒有進步，我的脾氣有沒有好一點。」

從這件事可以看出，翻譯師父的經典解釋，或開示法語，或《金剛菩提海》雜誌，其影響是多麼地深遠！這只是我日常生活中小小的片段，但從此就可以看出翻譯工作的重要性。

還有我們的《永嘉大師證道歌》，外國人看了就說：「我從來不曉得，佛法原來是這麼單純，我們都把它想得非常複雜。」阿彌陀佛！

Now I'd like to tell about one of my supervisors, who has a very bad temper. In the monthly journal *Vajra Bodhi Sea*, I read something the Master said, "Why are you stupid? Because you have a temper!" I made an enlarged photocopy of it and showed it to my colleagues. When my supervisor saw it, he said, "I don't want to be stupid!" I said, "If you don't want to be stupid, then you've got to change your temper."

I brought this up because I want to point out that the Buddhist books and the monthly journal *Vajra Bodhi Sea* that we publish in bilingual (Chinese and English) format are very good reading material for Westerners. They are very simple and easy to understand. To what degree was my supervisor influenced by the Master's statement? As soon as he's about to lose his temper, he balls his fists up and says, "I can't lose my temper. I must not get angry, because this wise person said we can't lose our temper. As soon as we get mad, we will make a lot of wrong decisions." Even more than a year afterwards, he still asked me often, "Have I made any progress? Is my temper getting better?"

From this, we can see what a far-reaching influence the translations of the Master's explanations of Sutras, his Dharma talks, and *Vajra Bodhi Sea*, can have! This is just a small episode from my daily life which illustrates how important the work of translation is.

After reading our publication of the *Song of Enlightenment by Great Master Yongjia*, some Westerners said, "We never knew the Buddhadharma was this simple! We always thought it was very complicated." Amitabha Buddha!

憶念恩師

IN REMEMBRANCE OF OUR KIND MASTER

釋恆尚　Shi Hengxiao

一九九三年十二月一日，在三藩市萬佛君康素菜館，有義工果德居士提議，同修的居士大家來學持咒。我隨喜了三星期後，某日早晨在佛殿內正持〈六字大明咒〉時，突然悲從中來，淚水泉湧，我走到師父法相前，求助於師父。突然眼前一亮，看見遠處師父上人手持錫杖，非常莊嚴，帶領著無數的人。這些人中，有的是在萬佛聖城認識的法師、居士，更多的是不認識的，我亦在其中。上人口中持咒，我們一群人隨著上人之後，經過一片森林，這片森林就如同《阿彌陀經》所描述的西方極樂世界七重行樹一樣。最後我們來到大海邊，咒聲仍然持續……。這時我身感輕安愉悅，惟覺空明無煩惱。經過這樣的感應之後，我持咒信心大增。所以每當煩惱一來，就持咒，瞬間煩惱煙消雲散，心無罣礙。

師父上人圓寂之後，法體從長堤聖寺被接回萬佛聖城的第二天：我推著放有飯菜的推車，從大齋堂回老人院，我和往常一樣念著佛號。剎那間，師父出現在我的眼前，他很自在地漫步於「精進路」與「悲路」（萬佛聖城裡的路名）之間。我下意識地要向師父頂禮，可是師父面帶微笑，稍微向上提起手中的柺杖，所以我就沒有頂禮。雖然我沒有頂禮師父，而他老人家還是一樣慈祥地看著我。

師父的法體停放在無言堂，每當去看師父時，我內心如果有困難，我會向師父請求，希望能得到師父的開示和指點。

未來的歲月，我將會依照師父的六大宗旨去修行。

On February 1, 1993, at the Ten Thousand Buddhas Chun Kang Vegetarian Restaurant, Laywoman Guode, a volunteer worker, suggested that her fellow lay cultivators learn to recite mantras. After three weeks of practicing with them, one morning when I was reciting the Great Bright Six-syllable Mantra in the Buddhahall, I was suddenly overcome with sadness and started crying. I walked over to the Venerable Master's image and sought aid from the Master. All of a sudden it became very bright, and I saw the Venerable Master at a distance. He was very adorned, holding a tin staff and leading countless people. Among them were Dharma Masters and laypeople I knew from the Sagely City of Ten Thousand Buddhas, but there were many more that I didn't recognize. I was also among them. The Venerable Master was reciting a mantra. Following behind him, we passed through a grove resembling the seven rows of trees in the Land of Ultimate Bliss as described in the *Amitabha Sutra*. Finally, as the sound of the mantra continued, we reached the shore of an ocean. I felt very light and happy. My mind was clear and bright, without afflictions. After experiencing this response, my faith in reciting mantras increased. Whenever afflictions come, I recite a mantra, and the afflictions vanish like smoke or clouds being dispersed, leaving my mind free of impediments.

The day after the Venerable Master's body was moved from Long Beach Sagely Monastery to the Sagely City of Ten Thousand Buddhas, I was pushing a cart of food from the main dining hall to the seniors' home. I was reciting the Buddha's name, as I usually do. All of a sudden, the Venerable Master appeared in front of me. He was walking in a slow and leisurely way between Vigor Way and Compassion Way (names of streets in the Sagely City). I instinctively wanted to bow to the Master, but the Master smiled and slightly lifted the staff he was holding in his hand, so I didn't bow. Even though I didn't bow, he continued to look at me in a very kindly way.

The Venerable Master's body was temporarily placed in No Words Hall. When I went to behold the Master, if I had any difficulties on my mind, I would ask for advice, hoping the Master would instruct me.

In the days to come, I shall cultivate according to the Venerable Master's Six Great Principles.

宣化老和尚追思紀念專集

COMMEMORATIVE ESSAY
追 思 短 文

Martin Verhoeven (Kuo Ting) 馬丁（果廷）

Like the China of Great Master Hsuan-tsang's time, America in the late 20th century is awash with a staggering variety of Buddhisms. Just as wave after wave of divergent Indian Buddhist schools and sects inundated China from the end of the Han up through the Tang, so have we witnessed in the West an equally rich and perplexing infusion of schools and teachings—all purporting to be genuine, orthodox, the "real teaching." Great Master Hsuan-tsang (c. 586-664) sought to resolve the confusion of so many conflicting opinions by pilgrimaging to India to seek out the genuine Dharma for himself at its source, and to bring back the sacred scriptures to his homeland.

A great scholar and translator and one of the few Chinese to have mastered Sanskrit, Great Master Hsuan-tsang's stupendous journey marked a high point in the transmission of Buddhism from one culture to another. Americans now, like the Chinese of the Sui and Tang, long for the same clarity and voice of authority. Ironically, the venerable Hsuan-tsang may have had an easier time in his quest than contemporary seekers.

For even when the texts became readily available to Americans (available in a quantity and quality perhaps unequaled in history), the "reading" of those texts proved far more difficult and daunting than we imagined. As the Great Master Hsuan-tsang discovered, and as we Americans are belatedly discovering, Buddhism—the real and vital Buddhism—is penetrated not simply through reading texts (however carefully) and learned exegeses, but through a far more subtle and interior process called "self-cultivation." Great Master Hsuan-tsang's insight and understanding of the written discourses derived from two complementary sources: his own virtuous life of spiritual practice, and his intimate contact with genuine "good knowing advisors" (*kalamitryana*) he encountered throughout his incredible journey.

As it is said, "The Way and the response inconceivably intertwine; practice and understanding mutually respond." Reading Great Master Hsuan-tsang's journal, one cannot avoid the impression that "good knowing advisors," true personifications of the Buddha-Way, were more numerous and accessible then than now. Moreover, in perhaps that less materialistic and "primitive" time, love of one's spiritual nature seemed more cherished; self-cultivation more refined. Thus, although our libraries and bookstores abound with Buddhist texts and works on Buddhism, our knowledge of, and more significantly our cultivation of, that sacred teaching does not for all of that seem proportionately advanced. Nor does our desire for the "unsurpassed,

就像玄奘大師時期的中國一樣，二十世紀晚期的美國，也氾濫著不同種類的佛教。中國在漢末及唐朝時，一波又一波不同的佛教教派，由印度傳到中國。現在在西方，我也看到了豐富雜亂的各宗各派的教法，都各自宣稱是道地的真正佛教。玄奘大師（西元五八六至六六四年）為了尋找真正的佛教和起源，並為解決佛教教理眾說紛紜的困擾，到印度去朝聖，同時將神聖的經典帶回祖國。

玄奘大師為大學者、大翻譯家，是少數精通梵文的中國人之一。他偉大的旅程，為佛法由一個文化至另一個文化的傳揚，創下了佛教史上的高峰。現代的美國人正如隋唐時代的中國人一般，渴望著有一位覺明、資歷深的人來匡正視聽。說起來荒謬，但是現代人追求正法的情形，比玄奘大師當時取經的過程，或者還更困難一些。

就算現代的美國人已經可以讀到許多佛書（其數量、質量可說是空前未有的），但是「閱讀」的困難卻是我們想像不到的。像玄奘大師當初所發現的一樣，我們美國人現在也發現了真正活的佛教，不是經由閱讀佛書、學習論典所能貫通的，不論你怎麼樣仔細閱讀也貫通不了。佛教只有經由微細的內心「自修」才能貫通。玄奘大師對經典的洞察力及理解力，得自於兩個相輔相成的來源：（一）他自己的德行及修持。（二）他在那段難以想像的旅程上與多位善知識的接觸。

正如常說的兩句話「感應道交難思議，修行信解相感應。」讀玄奘大師的日記使人感到，「佛道人性化」的善知識，在那個時代比現代要多，而且比較容易碰上。或者在那種物欲不高，比較「原始」的時代，人們比較注重愛護自己的靈性，自身的修持也更嚴謹。所以我們的圖書館和書店雖充滿了佛經及佛書，但是和我們對聖教的智識和修持似乎不成比例。我們對「無上甚深微妙法」的渴求，也比不上幾世紀前的善男信女那麼熱切。

還有一件荒謬的事，是玄奘大師那時得冒生命的

wonderful Dharma" seem as hungry as that of the men and women who lived centuries before ours.

Another irony: Where Great Master Hsuan-tsang had to risk life and limb traversing god-forsaken deserts and freezing mountains to find the teachings of enlightenment and wise mentors, we in America find both teachings and teachers arriving practically on our doorsteps. Since the 1890s and especially since World War II, Buddhism and Buddhist masters have clearly set the Dharma on a new course: from East to West, from Asia to America. This fragile transfer of ancient wisdom to the New World, as with all previous migrations of the Dharma to new lands, however, depends for its success on transplanting not simply the scriptures, but transmitting the "living tradition." Only on the strength and inspiration of living examples of Buddhism does the Dharma take root in fresh soil and grow in new hearts. Such an exemplar was Venerable Master Hsuan Hua. And such was the scope of his vow: to bring the Dharma to America.

*　　　　　*　　　　　*

My first meeting with the Master in 1976 underscored the importance of the direct and personal encounter. (Interestingly, I "met" the Master in a dream months before I actually met him in San Francisco at the Gold Mountain Monastery.) As was customary and proper, nearly everyone present at the monastery that afternoon to hear him lecture, bowed to the Master, showing their respect for the Dharma he inherited and passed along. I chafed at the thought of bowing to another. "How unbecoming and demeaning," I thought as I watched others bow. "That's so self-abasing and superstitious; I would never kowtow like that to a person!" I suppose in the back of my mind stood the Christian admonition of my childhood catechism lessons not to "worship false gods."

Then during the sutra lecture, the Master, as if out of the blue, digressed in his commentary (or so it seemed) to observe that, "Some people come to the temple seeking the Way, but are so full of self and their own self-importance that they cannot receive the Way. Like a tea cup already full to the brim in which the water of Dharma only spills over the side, they only wish to be noticed, to be praised and given a 'high hat' to wear. They are arrogant and proud and so, 'having eyes they cannot see; having ears they cannot hear.'"

These words struck to my heart. I felt they were surgically directed right at me. I didn't enjoy hearing this criticism, yet strangely I didn't really mind either. Somehow hearing such an honest and direct truth about myself made me forget for the moment the sting of their bitterness to my ego.

Good medicine is bitter to the taste;
Honest words grate on the ears.

I had never before thought of myself as arrogant, but I recognized immediately the Master's skillful perception of my state of mind. After the lecture I went up to the Master and bowed. I thought to myself, "Anyone who knows me better than I know my-

危險，橫越荒漠和冰山來尋求聖教的明師，而我們在美國，聖教和明師幾乎可以說是送到我們的門口。從一八九〇年代，特別是在第二次世界大戰時，佛教和法師們明白地為佛法設了一條新路程：就是由東到西，由亞洲到美洲。就像以前法流傳到新的國度時一樣，這脆弱的法傳到新土地上時，其成功與否，不在於是否只將經典傳到而已，而在於能否把那「活的傳統」傳到新土地上。要佛法在新的土地上，在新的人心裡生根，完全得靠佛教中身教的力量和啟發才能成功。宣化上人就是這樣的一個例子，他的願力就是要將佛法帶到美國。

*

我第一次遇見上人是在一九七六年，那次會面預示了與上人直接個別接觸的重要性。（很有趣地，我在舊金山金山寺遇見上人之前，我已在夢中「見到」上人了。）照一般的習慣及規矩，那天每一個在廟裡聽上人說法的人，都向上人頂禮，表示對他所傳承的法的尊敬。我對向上人叩頭頂禮這事很厭惡，「多難看！多卑賤！」我一面看著別人叩頭，一面心裡這麼想，「簡直作賤自己，多迷信，我永遠都不會向人叩頭！」大概在我心靈深處，我還保留了幼時上「基督教義」課中學到的基督教「不崇拜假神」的告誡。

一次，上人在講經時，忽然好像無緣無故離題而講著：「有的人到廟上來求道，但是卻充滿了我相和自大，不能接受道。好像一杯茶已經滿到了茶杯口的邊緣了，注入的法水會流溢到外邊來。他們只求人認識他，讚美他，只想戴高帽子，又貢高又驕慢，所以『有眼不識，有耳不聞』。」

這些話直打入我的心裡，是衝著我來的。我並不喜歡這些批評，但是很奇怪我也不在意。這些對我所作的忠實又直接的真話，使我暫時忘卻了受到傷害的自尊心。

良藥苦口利於病，忠言逆耳利於行。

我以前從不覺得自己驕傲，但是我立刻就感覺到上人一眼就看穿了我的心境。講完經後，我上

self, deserves my respect. Truly I received an invaluable gift today from this curious monk." The Master just smiled.

I continued to come to the Master's lectures and discovered a teaching that surpassed my expectations. For the first time in my life I felt totally intellectually free to inquire and explore—without dogma, without doctrine, without creed or the abandonment of reason. The Master was then explaining the *Avatamsaka Sutra*, and I felt myself inexorably drawn into its "understanding and expanding of the mind and all its states...the unattached, unbound, liberated mind." The Master was my introduction to Buddhism; his profound and expansive teaching my understanding of what Buddhism was. That impression was shattered when I traveled to Asia the following year.

*　　　　*　　　　*

In 1977 I was part of a delegation that accompanied the Master on a lecture tour of Malaysia, Singapore, Hong Kong, Indonesia, and Thailand. I wasn't prepared for the acculturated forms of Buddhism that have come to dominate the Asian Buddhist world. Centuries of accretion, absorption, and cross-fertilization with indigenous customs and beliefs, local cults, and downright superstition has resulted in "Buddhisms" one would never find in any sutra.

In one particular temple the gaudy display and wai-tao (lit. 'outside the Way') hoopla was especially disturbing and out-of-hand. Dead ducks and bottles of wine covered the altars as offerings to the Buddha (whose precepts enjoin against intoxicants and the taking of life), choking clouds of incense smoke filled the air, making it painful to breathe and sooting the gilded images so heavily that they no longer appeared golden radiant but sticky, ocher brown. Messy oil lamps spilled all over the altars and floors as each devotee struggled to empty his or her gallon bottle into the tiny lanterns. In the corners of the temple people huddled, shaking "fortune sticks" out of cups onto the floor to divine their fate and future. Bereaved relatives burned wads of paper money to "buy off" the angry and vengeful ghosts of the underworld who they believed obstructed their departed ones from rebirth in the heavens. Outside, huge papier-mache boats, cars, houses, planes, and palaces were set to torch and "sent" to the dead to appease them and confer on them riches and wealth. The whole temple-scene resembled a circus or carnival atmosphere. There was even a Gwan-yin Bodhisattva pinball machine where for a coin one could mechanically manipulate a plastic goddess along a track to shovel out a toy ball containing a blessing or prediction of blessings and eternal reward. This was the nadir of my disillusionment with "Buddhism."

When the Master addressed the audience, however, his tone resembled the "lion's roar." With humor softening a patriarch's

前向上人頂禮。我對自己說：「如果有人能認識我，比我自己認識我自己還清楚，我應該向這個人頂禮。今天我從這個令人好奇的和尚那兒，的確得到了一件無價的禮物。」上人微笑不語。

以後我就經常到上人這兒來聽經了，並發覺上人的法出乎意料地好。在我的生命中，這是第一次可以完全自由自在地去諮問探討，既不受教條、教義、教理的約束，又不須放棄理性。上人那時正在講解《華嚴經》，我自己覺得逃不了似地投入那「瞭解、擴大心量及其心的境界……，沒有執著、沒有束縛、解脫了的心。」上人將我引入佛門，他廣大、深邃的教誨，使我明白了什麼是佛教。可是次年，我的亞洲之行，完全粉碎了我對佛教的印象。

一九七七年，我隨上人的弘法團赴馬來西亞、新加坡、香港、印尼、泰國等各國。這些國家的佛教，是一種經過幾個世紀與當地習俗、信仰、迷信相結合，混雜了許多附加物的佛教；一種已經完全變質的佛教，不是我們在經典中找得到的那種佛教。對這種盛行在亞洲的佛教，當時我一點心理準備都沒有。

我們曾去一間寺廟參觀，那間廟的俗艷裝飾及那種外道蠱惑人心的宣傳，特別地令人心煩，無法控制。佛桌堆滿了酒肉等供品（佛制戒殺禁酒），大把大把香放出的濃煙，使人窒息，簡直讓人喘不過氣來。濃煙將金色的佛像薰得沒有了昔日的光澤，成為一種赫褐色且又黏黏的。虔誠的信徒們，爭先恐後地將大罐大罐的油，注入小小髒亂的油燈，油燈裡的油，滿溢出來流了一桌。在廟的各各角落，人們圍在一起，搖著「杯筊桶」，在地上擲筊以卜吉凶。哀傷的人們以一綑一綑的紙錢來「賄賂」鬼，恐怕他們生氣報仇，拉住已死的親人不得往生天堂。外面又焚燒著許多紙紮的船、車、房子、飛機、宮殿，焚燒給死去的親人，讓他們在陰間享用。這廟上的情形就像個馬戲團似的，又像玩雜耍的。還有一種機器，投入一枚硬幣就會有一尊塑膠做的女神，沿著一條軌道擲出一個玩具球，球裡裝有預測福報的來臨的訊息，這一切使我對「佛教」徹底地絕望。

在東南亞，上人對聽眾的開示，是以一位祖師的

righteous duty to protect the Proper Dharma, he took issue with nearly everything we were witnessing in the name of Buddhism.

"If you offer a stick of incense," he began "it is symbolic—symbolic of your desire to become pure of mind and body, pure in the precepts, so as to be a worthy vessel of the Buddha-Way. Incense-lighting signifies your sincere wish to cleanse your own mind and thoughts and to evoke thereby a response from the Buddhas and Bodhisattvas. It's symbolic, a gesture. The smoke doesn't by itself 'purify' nor does it please the Buddha in the way that we people are pleased by perfume and fragrant food. To think that is to be totally confused about true principle. That actually slanders the Buddha. Think about it. How could the Buddha be the Buddha if he was still 'flowing in sights and smells,' still turning in the dust of the senses? Even an *arhat* has gone beyond enslavement to the senses! Do you think that if one incense stick smells good and pleases the Buddha, then a hundred will please him even more—like bribing an official with a present or enticing a child with candy? The Buddha isn't greedy for good things the way ordinary people are. To think and act that way really looks down on the Buddha." Some people began to shift nervously in their seats; others, began to sit up and take notice.

The Master continued, "Look at the Buddha statues! They're all black and tarnished from all the incense smoke! They're choking on it. Instead of a Pure Land we are creating a polluted land—all due to greed and ignorance." At this point you could hear a pin drop.

Some people, obviously offended and upset over what they were hearing, actually got up and walked out. Others, however, especially the younger and better-educated in the audience, applauded enthusiastically and beamed.

The Master went on, "Even though I do not like to speak this way, I cannot not say this. I have made a vow that as long as I have breath and can speak, the proper Dharma will not vanish from this world."

The Venerable Master continued, "As for burning paper money for ghosts, ask yourself: Is that reasonable? Does it make sense? Aren't ghosts immaterial? So what use would they have for things material, especially fake money? Even children can't be taken in by phony money; so how would ghosts who have ghostly psychic powers be fooled?! What use have the dead, whose bodies have returned to the elements, for paper houses, cars, boats, and airplanes? This is truly silly and superstitious!"

Then in a calm and compassionate voice the Master closed: "What is Buddhism? It's just the teaching of wisdom. Shakyamuni Buddha said upon his enlightenment, 'All living beings have the Buddha-nature; all can become Buddhas. It's only because of confused thinking and attachments that they don't realize the Tathagata's state.' Buddha just means 'awakened one'; so don't confuse the branches for the root; don't forsake the near-at-hand and seek far and distant. Return the light to illumine within; seek the Buddha of your mind. That's all I wish to say for now."

Next morning as I washed my face at the water sink I met the Master. He smiled and asked me, "Well, what did you think of my talk last night?"

"Well, Shifu," I replied, "it upset a lot of people, but it also

身份作獅子吼，義不容辭地護持正法。上人以幾分幽默的語言來緩和氣氛，並且拿我們所見到的每一件打著佛教招牌的事，做為講演的話題。

上人說：「假如你上炷香，這炷香是一種象徵，象徵你願意身意清淨，戒行清淨，所以可以成為佛法的載法之器。點香的意義，在於表示你的誠心誠意，想清淨你的意念，引起佛菩薩的感應，這是一種象徵、表徵。香的煙本身不會使佛歡喜，佛不像我們歡喜香水，想吃香的東西。如果你這樣想的話，那你就完全誤解了，你根本就是謗佛。你想一想，如果佛還在色塵、香塵裡轉的話，怎麼能成佛？就是阿羅漢都不會被五塵所奴役。如果一炷香的香味，能使佛歡喜，一百炷香就更使佛歡喜了，就好像賂賄作官的，或拿糖來引誘小孩。佛不像凡夫那樣貪好的東西，凡夫的這種想法和做法是藐視佛。」聽到這兒，有的人坐立不安，有的人則坐直了身子專心地聽著。

上人繼續說：「你看那些佛像，都給薰黑了！佛都給煙嗆住了。本來就是淨土，現在都污染成穢土了，都是給貪心和無明給弄的。」四周鴉雀無聲，連針落地的聲音都聽得見。

有的人一定聽得很不愉快，所以站起來走了。剩下來的人，尤其是一些年輕的，受過一些教育的人，帶著笑容熱烈地鼓掌。

上人又說：「至於給鬼燒紙錢，問問你自己這合理不合理？有沒有道理？鬼不是無形的嗎？那它要有形的東西做什麼？要紙錢做什麼？這假錢連小孩都騙不了，又怎麼騙得了有「鬼通」的鬼呢？死人的身體都分散了，還要那些紙房子、紙車、紙船、紙飛機幹什麼？這真是愚癡，真是迷信！」

最後上人用平靜悲愍的口吻說：「佛教是什麼？就是智慧教。釋迦牟尼佛在開悟時說：『一切眾生皆有佛性，皆堪作佛，但以妄想執著，不能證得。』佛就是「覺者」。所以不要捨本逐末，捨近求遠，要迴光返照，向自性中去找佛，今天我就說這麼多。」

第二天早上我在洗臉時，上人笑著問我：「你覺得我昨晚講得怎麼樣？」「師父，有很多人不高興，但是也有很多人很高興。」

上人又說：「我講話的目的不是要人高興，也不是要人不高興。我只講真話，合乎真理的話，我一向就只會這麼做。」

made many people happy."

The Master said, "I don't speak to upset nor to please; I only speak what is true, what accords with true principle. That's all I know how to do; I have always been that way."

I then confessed my disillusionment with the Buddhism I was seeing on the tour in Asia. I told him that I expected to find the pure and lofty teaching here in the East, in the 'holy land,' so to speak, of Buddhism. But instead I encountered many of the same superstitions and strange beliefs I met in other religions. He said softy and very deliberately, "Everything is made from the mind alone. Buddhism is just the teaching of wisdom, the teaching of the mind. Buddhism is meant to liberate the mind, to activate one's inherent wisdom. I want my students to have wisdom, to discover their inner wisdom, not to become superstitious or attached. Don't follow me, don't follow him. Listen to yourself—your True Self, your Buddhanature—learn to follow true principle and to use your own wisdom. If it's the Tao, advance; if it's not the Tao, turn back. Remember what it says in the *Vajra Sutra*: 'Those seeking me in sights or seeking me in sounds, walk a deviant path and will never find the Thus Come One.' Do you understand?" he asked with a gentle smile.

A few weeks later on the same tour I was riding with the Master in a car en route to a lecture in the countryside. The driver, a local devout layman, asked the Master, "Master, the Theravada school says there is only one Buddha, the historical Buddha. The Mahayana school says there are many Buddhas. Which is correct? Is there one Buddha or are there lots of Buddhas?" He was, it seemed, slightly baiting the Master, yet also sincere in his query.

The Master replied, "There are no Buddhas." The layman was stunned; the car jerked.

"Huh!? How can you say there are no Buddhas?!" he asked incredulously.

The Master smiled and said, "'Basically there's not one thing, so where can dust alight?' Originally there is just great wisdom. Whoever has great wisdom, whoever can find and use their innate wisdom is a Buddha. Whoever remains confused is just a living being. Potentially every living being is a Buddha. Whoever remains confused is just a living being. Potentially every living being is a Buddha, so I say there are limitless Buddhas. But Buddha just means 'awakened one.' Awakened to what? Awakened to the truth of no-self. So fundamentally you could say there are no Buddhas; all Buddhas are not." The Master paused to see if the layman understood. Then he continued, "You eat to satisfy your own hunger; you wear clothes to keep yourself warm, and you cultivate to save yourself. So whether there is one Buddha or a thousand, unless you cultivate there are still Buddhas and you are still a living being—the two are unrelated and the question of one or many is irrelevant. What do you think of my answer?"

The layman thought quietly for a long time, and then shaking his head said, "Hmm. That's really good; really good." I to myself said the same.

*　　　　　*　　　　　*

我告訴上人，在亞洲旅途上所看到的「佛教」使我的希望幻滅。我又說，我原以為在東方，在這個所謂聖地，會看到清淨高尚的佛教，可是我看到的，卻是在其他宗教裡同樣存在的一些迷信奇怪的信仰。

上人從容地說：「一切唯心造，佛教就是智慧教、心教。佛教就是心的解脫，將潛在的智慧發掘出來。我要我的弟子們有智慧，去發掘他們本有的智慧，不要弄得那麼迷信，那麼執著。你們不要跟我，也不要跟他，你們要聽自己的真我，自己的佛性。你們要學習真理，運用自己的智慧，是道則進，非道則退。要記得《金剛經》上說的：『若以色見我，以音聲求我，是人行邪道，不能見如來。』你懂了嗎？」上人微笑著問我。

數星期後，我和上人坐車到鄉下去說法。司機是當地一位虔誠的佛教徒，他問上人：「師父，南傳（小乘）佛教說只有一尊佛，就是歷史上的那尊佛，北傳（大乘）佛教說有許多佛，到底哪一個對？究竟是只有一尊佛？還是有多尊佛？」看起來司機好像有一點要為難上人似的。

上人說：「根本沒有佛！」聽了上人的回答，那位司機呆了，車子也頓了一下。

「什麼？！你怎麼可以說沒有佛？！」司機懷疑地說。

上人笑著說：「『本來無一物，何處惹塵埃』？本來就只有大智慧。誰有大智慧，誰能運用他本有的大智慧，誰就是佛，迷者為眾生，每一個人都有成佛的可能，所以我說佛有無量無邊那麼多。佛的意思就是「覺者」，覺什麼？覺知「無我」的真理。所以基本上你可以說根本就沒有佛，所有的佛都是不存在的。」上人頓了一下，看看這位司機懂了沒有？接著又說：「自己吃飯自己飽，自己穿衣自己暖，自己修行自己了。不管是一尊佛，或是一千尊佛，除非你修行，不然佛還是佛，你還是凡夫，佛和你不相關。到底是一尊或多尊，這個問題根本就不是問題，你覺得我的回答怎麼樣？」

司機想了許久，然後點點頭說：「嗯，真好，真好！」我心裡也這麼說著。

Finally, I remember observing the Master sitting in at a conference on children and education. Upon hearing the statistics and reports on the deteriorating condition of children throughout the world—children suffering from hunger, poverty, abuse, parental neglect, exposed to increasing levels of violence and depravity—the Master quietly bowed his head and began to softly weep. As the tears came streaming down his face, I was reminded of that other aspect of Buddhism the Master so often taught and embodied: great compassion. His deep sense of "being one with everyone" led me to imagine that his tears were no doubt for the children, and for those who hurt them, and for the children of those children yet to come. But he cried (incredibly) out of shame for his own "lack of virtue," as he would say, for not having done a good enough job in his own cultivation or by the example and output of his own life, to have prevented such a tragedy.

It was this living example of a great soul "manifesting a body to speak the Dharma," that made Buddhism come alive for me and I am sure for many others who met the Master. And it is in those meetings, those person-to-person encounters, that the Master's spirit continues to live. What he instilled by his example and tireless giving to each individual he met, insures in some ineffable way that the Dharma will continue to live—to live not just in translations, but in the boundless living beings who had the privilege and opportunity to be kindled and transformed by his light.

最後，記得有一次在討論「兒童及教育」的座談會上，當上人聽到世界各地兒童悲慘的情況及統計數字：捱餓、受窮、被虐待、被父母棄而不顧……，生活在暴力及邪行的環境中，我注意到上人低下了頭輕聲飲泣。當上人的眼淚流下來時，讓我看到了佛陀的大慈悲，這就是上人所具有的廣闊胸襟，這就是上人常常教導我們的：慈悲。上人「同體大悲」的精神，使我相信他的眼淚不僅是為這些兒童而流，也為那些傷害他們的人們而流，也為這些兒童將來所生的兒童而流。但是上人居然責怪自己沒有德行而哭泣，上人常常說因為自己修行沒修好，不能發揮以身作則的能力，來防止這一類的悲劇發生。上人的現身說法和活生生的榜樣，使我覺得佛教是活的；我相信許多其他遇見上人的人，也覺得佛教是活的，就在與上人接觸時，我們可以感覺到上人的精神永存。

慈恩唐三藏玄奘法師偈頌
Verse in Praise of Tripitaka Master Hsuan-tsang
of Ci En Monastery of the Tang Dynasty

古今中外無二人　　爲法忘軀涉險辛　　精誠感動諸天護　　佳願堪回大地春
百折不撓金剛志　　萬魔難退菩提心　　六度桃開徵祥瑞　　仰望慈恩再來臨

There's no other person like him throughout the history of the world.
Forgetting himself, he underwent a myriad hardships for the sake of the Dharma.
His utmost sincerity moved all the gods to protect him.
His vows were so vast that they brought spring back to the great earth.
With a will like Vajra, he was not deterred by a hundred setbacks.
Even ten thousand demons could not make him retreat from his resolve for Bodhi.
The peach trees blossomed six times an auspicious sign.
We gaze up at the Kind One and hope he will come back again.

宣公上人作於一九七二年九月二十三日
Composed by the Venerable Master Hua on September 23, 1972

I WILL REMEMBER YOU SMILING
我將記住您的微笑

Brian Conroy (Guo Kang)
果康

I will remember you smiling,
Broad grin about to burst
Into full unrestrained laughter;
A jolly, happy man
With soft round features;
A modern day Ho Tai,
Showering the sweetness of Dharma
*   on all your childen.*

Once, in Santa Clara,
We assembled in a round pavilion out of doors;
Early in the day I watched your kind eyes
Following the path of a soccer ball
Kicked playfully by a tiny energetic child.
And all the while you smiled,
*   beaming at the child's sport,*
Composing a silent thesis on the benefit of play;
I half expected that at any moment you might run out
Onto the grass and show us all
*   how the game was played.*

You taught me then and ever after:
One who brings forth the Bodhi mind
Must have the heart of a child.

Disciple Brian Conroy (Guo Kang) respectfully bows
in mourning and gratitude for the teachings of
the Venerable Master Hsuan Hua.

我將記住您的微笑
開朗綻放
完全無拘無束微笑的人
高興快樂的一個人
有著圓潤柔和的面容
一個現代的聖誕老人
遍撒甘露法雨給您的孩子們

曾經在聖塔克拉拉
我們聚集在門外的圓形敞棚下
一早我看到您慈祥的眼神
看著路上一個活潑的小孩子
踢著足球玩耍
您一直笑
愉快地看著孩子的運動
組合了一個無言的主題
關於遊戲的利益
我半期望著隨時您會跑出
到草地上來告訴我們如何玩遊戲

從那時起您教了我
一個發菩提心的人
必須要有一顆孩子的心

弟子果康哀傷稽首感激宣公上人的教誨
一九九五年九月三日

THE VENERABLE MASTER
HEARS AND RESPONDS
聞聲救苦的上人

Wang Guo Aun 王鴻安（果安）

I believe that the Venerable Master has spiritual penetrations and that he shows kindness and compassion in every matter provided we are sincere in our thoughts and actions. He helps everyone without us knowing it. Here are some events which occurred and although they may appear trivial, they do show the ways in which the Venerable Master is kind and compassionate so long as we are sincere.

Event 1: My wife and I were discussing certain matters pertaining to Dharma work in our house in Kuala Lumpur. We could not decide on the next course of action and it was pertinent then to have a reply from the Venerable Master. However we decided not to telephone the Master right then, as it was about midnight in San Francisco. To our surprise, the Venerable Master asked his attendant to telephone us from San Francisco about four hours later to give us the necessary guidance!

Event 2: Tze Yun Tung temple was a vacant temple that needed renovation and cleaning up before the official opening ceremony could be conducted. The temple was infested with white ants and these ants had been eating into several places including the altar. We used all means to coax the white ants to move out of the premises without having to exterminate them, which is against our principle of compassion. We were not successful and there was the fear that the ants would take a liking to the Dharma books. When my wife was in CTTB, she remembered to report to the Venerable Master about Tze Yun Tung being infested by white ants that were attacking the timber structure with voracious appetite.

At that time the Venerable Master just brushed this request aside, appearing not to want to be concerned about white ants. But by the time she came back to Malaysia, there was not a single white ant in Tze Yun Tung. The ants had just shifted out for no apparent reason.

Event 3: My mother went to CTTB. She bowed 30,000 times to Guan Yin Bodhisattva in three weeks. One day she had the thought of wondering if Guan Yin Bodhisattva could hear what she said. That very night, the Venerable Master asked a disciple to convey to my mother that Guan Yin Bodhisattva can hear everything anywhere, even just a whisper. My mother also had worried whether her prayers would be answered. The Venerable Master again asked a disciple to convey a message that her prayers had been answered.

Amitabha!

我相信上人有神通，只要我們誠心誠意的話，在每一件事上，都會感受到上人的慈悲。上人默默地幫助每一個眾生，我們甚至都不知道。下面幾則事實，可能是微不足道的，但也足以表達上人對我們的慈悲心。

第一則：我和內人打算在家裡（吉隆坡）作佛事，但卻不知道該怎麼做。於是想請教上人，得到上人的指點。當時，由於時差的關係，美國舊金山已是午夜時分了，所以不便打電話。四小時以後，上人主動叫他的弟子，從舊金山打電話給我們，告訴我們應當怎樣做，那正是我們所期待的，真是不可思議！

第二則：紫雲洞以前是一座空廟，後被改做佛教道場，開幕之前，必須進行改建、整理、清掃。可是廟裡滿是白蟻，好多地方甚至佛桌，都被蛀蝕了。因為殺生是很不慈悲的行為，所以我們想盡方法，誘使這些白蟻遷離他處，但沒有成功。我們擔心經書也會被那些白蟻蛀蝕，所以當我的內人去萬佛城時，她向上人報告說，紫雲洞的木料結構已經被白蟻破壞得很嚴重了。上人對這件事輕輕避過，顯得莫不關心的樣子。但是等內人返回馬來西亞後，紫雲洞裡邊連一隻白蟻也沒有了，不知為什麼都搬走了。

第三則：家母曾去萬佛聖城，在三個星期內，禮觀世音菩薩三萬拜。有一天，她動了一個念頭：觀世音菩薩真地能聽見我說什麼嗎？當天晚上，上人讓徒弟傳話給家母說，無論在什麼地方，觀世音菩薩什麼都能聽見，哪怕是輕聲的耳語。家母又擔心她的祈求得不到感應，上人又讓徒弟傳話給家母說，她的祈求已經有了感應了。

阿彌陀佛

宣公上人二三事

A FEW RECOLLECTIONS OF
THE VENERABLE MASTER HUA

魏果時　Wei Guoshi

六月七日下午驚聞上人圓寂，心裡一直想著：不可能呀！上人怎麼這麼快就捨我們而去？接著就是大家一陣的忙碌。上人的法體在殯儀館裡停放了一個星期，洛城信眾有幸得以瞻禮上人，六月十六日移靈回萬佛聖城，七月二十八日舉行荼毗大典，二十九日上午遵照上人遺囑，把骨灰撒向天空。看著上人的骨灰，從熱氣球上飄下來，在天空中飛揚，然後便不知所蹤，心中的感慨真是好深好深！一代高僧就如此離我們而去……。

上人修為的高深，非我等所能揣測，但能肯定的一件事，就是他早已生死自在。沒想到他為了度我們，卻選擇最艱難的方式－－示現病態而走。以前的馬祖道一禪師也是如此，座下出了八十四位善知識，他棒打威喝，踏殺天下，神通廣大，度人無數，可是他自己卻常年生病，想來真令人心酸。

往昔與上人的接觸對話，一幕幕在腦海裡浮現出來。記得一九八六年初，海燈法師來美國，上人在聖城說：「我和他有很深的因緣！」於是特地南下，來探望他的老友，約四、五人忙著打理金輪聖寺的會客室。當時我正搬著一張小圓桌，由牆角移到中央，上人看了，馬上過來幫我搬，我急忙跟上人說：「師父！沒有關係！這不重，我一個人就可以了。」上人答道：「一樣的，人多好做事！」就這樣我們便一起搬，把小圓桌從這兒搬到那兒。上人那種事事身體力行，毫無一點架子的風範，給那些不做事，只是一味使喚別人的人，留下一個很好的榜樣。

海燈法師來了以後，上人與他聊起當年一起在南華寺虛老座下時的情形，我們在旁聽得津津有味。上人提起南華寺以前有一個小

I was shocked to hear the news of the Venerable Master's completion of stillness on June 7. I kept thinking: "It can't be! How could he leave us so soon?" Then there was a hectic period. The Master's body was kept in the mortuary for a week and Los Angeles disciples had the opportunity to gaze upon it. Then on June 16, the Master's body was moved back to the Sagely City of Ten Thousand Buddhas. The cremation ceremony was held on July 28, and the ashes were scattered in the skies, following the Master's instructions, on the morning of the twenty-ninth. Watching the Venerable Master's ashes scattered from the hot-air balloon and drifting in the air, I was even more at a loss. What deep melancholy! A great monk of this age has left us all.

The depth of the Venerable Master's cultivation is not something that we can fathom. However, we can be sure of one thing: The Master had control over his own birth and death. I never expected that he would choose the most painful and difficult way of leaving—manifesting illness—in order to teach us. In the past, Chan Master Mazu Daoyi did the same. Under his teaching, eighty-four Good Knowing Advisors were produced. He was known for beating and shouting, and for scaring everyone away. His spiritual penetrations were extensive, and he taught countless people. Despite all of this, he was constantly suffering from illness. Thinking of this makes me sick at heart.

My interactions and conversations with the Venerable Master appear in my mind, scene after scene. In early 1986, when Dharma Master Haideng came to America, I remember the Venerable Master saying at the City of Ten Thousand Buddhas, "I have deep affinities with him!" The Master then made a trip south to visit his old friend. Four or five of us were hurriedly cleaned up the reception room at Gold Wheel Monastery. As I was in the process of moving a small round table from the corner to the middle of the room, the Venerable Master noticed and came over to help me. I hastily said, "Master, it's okay! It's not heavy. I can do it myself." The Master said, "It's no matter! It's easier to do things when there are more people!" And so we moved the table together. The Venerable Master's willingness to do everything himself set a very good example for those who only ordered other people around but never did anything themselves.

When Dharma Master Haideng arrived, he and the Master chatted about the days when they were together at Nanhua Monastery studying under the Elder Master Hsu Yun. Those of us who were present listened with great interest. The Venerable Master told of a child at Nanhua Monastery who took twenty-one days to memorize the *Shurangama Sutra* and another twenty-one days to memorize the *Dharma Flower Sutra*. (The Master called him a child, but how old was he? It's not known.)

孩子（被上人稱為小孩子的，到底有多大年紀，則不得而知），花二十一天的功夫，把整部《楞嚴經》背起來，又花二十一天把《法華經》全背起來，想來真是不可思議，不知這位神童現在何處？當年天臺智者大師十八歲出家，他師父給他三部經典——《法華經》、《無量義經》及《普賢觀經》，他只二十天便全都背得滾瓜爛熟，他師父都不知如何教他是好？

上人與海燈法師又提到，有一次元宵節下午，一位老婆婆顯得愁苦無比，帶了一大臉盆的湯圓來供養。虛老請在座的出家眾們吃，可是人人過午不食，眾僧沒有表情，不食不動，只是靜靜地坐著。虛老一看，便自己拿起湯匙，一口一口地把整臉盆的湯圓全吃完。虛老九十五歲進駐南華寺，試想一個近百歲的高齡老人，為了滿某人的願，那種難消化的湯圓，吃一碗都很為難了，更何況一大臉盆，而他又是過午不食，想想真是難為他了！

海燈法師自幼習武，練就了一身硬功夫，據說學過一指禪神功及草上飛（輕功）的功夫。他以一指可穿破沙袋，以食指、中指頂地而倒立，凡見過他的人都要請他表演一下。海公慈悲，經常令人滿願，卻苦了自己。一次，有位同參要遠遊海外，不知何時才能回來，只可惜從未聽過《法華經》。海公一生最愛《法華經》，聽說如此，便邀他到山洞裡，為他講解《法華經》，兩人對坐講了三天三夜，一個高興講，一個高興聽。山洞潮濕，海公出來後，右手有發抖現象，從此無法練倒立功夫。上人一聽，即刻抓著他的右手，加持了好久，然後說道：「你再到萬佛聖城住一段時間，很快就會好了！」上人那種對同參道友的關懷，很令人感動！

海公一直讚歎上人講《華嚴經》講了九年，真是不可思議，又讚歎上人將來一定是全身舍利，上人則回答了一句頗耐人尋味的話：「將來我的舍利會像土一樣地多！」上人當時的語氣、手勢，還依舊在腦海裡，清清楚楚。

海公提起虛老雖上百歲，依然事事親自而為，不假他人手，天一亮便到田裡工作，天黑才收工回寮房。從田裡到寺裡，其間必經一橋，此橋簡陋，只用一根長竹，兩頭擱在兩岸邊。海公說他自己雖有草上飛的功夫，天一黑還是

This is truly inconceivable. Who knows where this child prodigy is now? When Great Master Zhizhe left the home-life at eighteen, his teacher gave him three Sutras—the *Dharma Flower Sutra*, the *Sutra of Limitless Meanings*, and the *Sutra of the Contemplation of Universal Worthy*. In a mere twenty days, he had them thoroughly committed to memory. His teacher didn't know quite how to teach him.

The Venerable Master and Dharma Master Haideng also recounted that once, in the afternoon of the fifteenth day of the first lunar month [a holiday on which Chinese people eat small round dumplings of rice flour], an old woman who seemed to be in great suffering and distress brought a large basin of dumplings and offered them to the Sangha. The Elder Master Hsu invited his left-home disciples to eat. But everyone there maintained the practice of not eating after noon. Showing no expression on their faces, the monks just sat quietly without making any move to eat. Seeing this, the Elder Hsu himself picked up a spoon and proceeded to eat the entire basinful of dumplings. The Elder Hsu had gone to Nanhua Monastery to live when he was ninety-five. For someone nearly a hundred years old, even one bowl of dumplings would have been difficult to eat, for they are not easy to digest, how much the more an entire basin of them! He also maintained the practice of not eating after noon, yet he ate them for the sake of fulfilling one person's wish. Truly a difficult deed!

Dharma Master Haideng had practiced martial arts since early childhood, and his skill was very great. It is said that he had mastered the skill of standing on his finger and of running swiftly without touching the ground. He could pass his finger through a sandbag, and do a handstand supported only by his index and middle fingers. People who met him always asked him to perform, and the compassionate Master Haideng always granted their request, despite the suffering it caused him. Once, a fellow cultivator was about to travel abroad for an indefinite time and lamented only that he had never heard the *Dharma Flower Sutra* explained. The *Dharma Flower Sutra* was Master Haideng's favorite, and when he heard this, he invited that person to his cave in the mountains and explained the Sutra to him. The two of them sat for three days and nights without getting up. One happily explained the Sutra and the other happily listened. Due to the dampness of the cave, Master Haideng's right hand began trembling when he came out of the cave, and for that reason he could not practice handstands anymore. When the Venerable Master heard this, he grasped Master Haideng's right hand and aided it for a long time. Then he said, "Stay at the City of Ten Thousand Buddhas for a period, and your hand will soon get well!" We were truly moved by the Venerable Master's concern for his fellow cultivator.

Master Haideng kept praising the Venerable Master, saying it was truly inconceivable that the Master had lectured on the *Avatamsaka Sutra* for nine years. He also said the Venerable Master's entire body would turn into sharira (relics after cremation). The Venerable Master's reply inspired reflection: "My sharira will be as numerous as particles of dirt." The Master's tone of voice and the way he moved his hands when he said that are still very clearly imprinted in my memory.

Master Haideng commented that despite being over a hundred years old, the Elder Master Hsu continued to do everything himself without relying on others. As soon as it was light outside, he would go work in the fields; and only when it was dark would he stop working and retire

不敢過此橋，可是只見虛老挑著扁擔，在一片漆黑，伸手不見五指的情況下，一搖一幌地走過獨木橋，自在得很，一點恐懼也沒有，看見此景，他才相信學了一身功夫，不如好好地去修行。

當晚海公開示《法華經》裡的〈妙莊嚴王本事品〉，講完下座時，上人帶領大眾向他頂禮致謝。

去年（一九九四年），有人從大陸來美拜見上人，談到海燈法師遭人種種的誤會，最後還因醫生誤醫而死。他童貞出家，自幼練功，丹田地方鼓起一大塊圓圓的硬肉，醫生卻說是瘤，硬是開刀，以致血流不止而亡；但他由始至終，卻沒發出半句怨言。上人聽後，說道：「我和他同時都是虛老的接法人，他真是毀譽不動心，順逆皆精進。」這十個字也可說是道盡海公一生的為人。

以上是記載當年上人與海燈法師的一段因緣，相信由此可看得出，高僧大德們的言行風範，他們的一言一行，在在處處，都足以為我們後人的楷模。

to his room. There was a certain bridge that he had to cross regularly. The bridge was very scantily made with bamboo sticks. Master Haideng said that even though he had the skill of "flying over the grass" (walking without touching the ground), he didn't dare to walk on that bridge after dark. However, he had seen Elder Master Hsu, with his bag slung over his shoulder, ambling in a carefree and without a trace of fear over the precarious bridge in pitch-dark, when one couldn't even see the fingers of one's own extended hand. This sight convinced him that mastering all those martial arts was not as good as concentrating on cultivation.

That evening, Master Haideng lectured on the Chapter of the Past Life of Wonderful Adornment King in the *Dharma Flower Sutra*. When he finished the lecture and left the Dharma-seat, the Venerable Master led the assembly to bow to him in gratitude.

Last year (1994), someone from mainland China paid a visit to the Venerable Master and mentioned that Dharma Master Haideng had been misunderstood in various ways and in the end had died from medical mistreatment. He had left the home-life as a pure youth and had practiced martial arts since childhood. When a hard lump of flesh had swelled up on his *dantian* (lower abdomen), the doctor said it was a tumor and insisted on performing surgery. During the operation, he bled uncontrollably and died. Yet he never uttered a single complaint. Hearing this account, the Venerable Master said, "He and I both received the Dharma from the Elder Master Hsu. He truly was one who was unmoved by slander and praise, and who was vigorous in favorable as well as adverse states." This statement could also describe Master Haideng's whole life.

The above has been an account of the Venerable Master's relationship with Dharma Master Haideng. I believe that from this, we can see the exemplary words and conduct of lofty and greatly virtuous Sanghans. Their every word and deed is a worthy example for future generations to follow.

尸棄佛傳法偈
The Dharma Transmission Verse of Shikhin Buddha

起諸善法本是幻　造諸惡業亦是幻　身如聚沫心如風　幻化無根無實性

The wholesome dharmas we create are basically illusory.
The evil deeds we commit are also illusory.
The body is like a clump of foam, the mind like the wind.
They are illusory transformations, with no root and no reality.

毘舍浮佛傳法偈
The Dharma Transmission Verse of Vipashyin Buddha

假借四大以為身　心本無生因境有　前境若無心亦無　罪福如幻起亦滅

We take the four elements as our body.
The mind basically is unreal; it exists only due to states.
If the states before us do not exist, the mind does not exist either.
Offenses and blessings are like illusions which arise and perish.

千百億化生

A HUNDRED MILLION TRANSFORMATION BODIES

詹果花　Zhan Guohua

師父上人上宣下化老和尚涅槃的消息，來的那麼突然，那麼令人震驚，那麼令人心痛，但事實畢竟是事實。回想起師父的慈悲，師父的恩惠，我哭了！

幾年前，看到一般的素食餐館做菜時都使用蛋類，為了方便他人能吃到清淨的素食，自己就於去年開了一家正宗的素食餐館。因為毫無這方面的經驗，加上操勞過度，於是就病倒了，到醫院檢查才發現卵巢生了腫瘤。因失血過多，醫生所給的藥已經沒有功效。後來遇到一位法師教我誦持〈大悲咒〉一百零八遍，然後服用咒力加持過的大悲水。我花了一天的時間來持誦〈大悲咒〉一百零八遍，以大悲水當藥水服下去。第二天，我已經停止流血。一個星期後，我的血紅蛋白由八點升到十二點（普通人是十四點）。

經由佛友介紹，今年三月七日，我進了一間很有名的私家醫院，三月八日很順利地動了手術。手術後第三天，負責照顧我的一位護士（基督徒），問我是否請了一位和尚來為我念經，因為她看到一位和尚坐在我的床邊為我念經。一個星期後，回到家裡，連續三個晚上都夢到師父上人來馬來西亞。而事實上是：當時，美國洛杉磯的長堤聖寺正在舉行〈梁皇寶懺〉大法會，但因師父上人病重，不能親自在法會上開示。但是師父仍然抱著大慈、大悲、大喜、大捨的精神，千百億化生普度有難的眾生。無明的眾生，顛顛倒倒，難調難伏，但師父無私地奉獻一生，使四眾弟子普被無限的恩澤。

師父上人臨走時，囑四眾弟子恭誦《華嚴經》。當我隨大眾拜《華嚴懺》時，懺文中的每一句每一字，都彷彿是針對我的無明，我的愚癡。當時我全身冒冷汗，手發抖，我真地不能控制我的眼淚，我又哭了。師父您太慈悲了！

一九九五年九月十八日

The news of the Venerable Master Hua's Nirvana came so suddenly, so shockingly, and so painfully. Yet facts are facts. When I thought of the Venerable Master's compassion and grace, I cried!

A few years ago, I observed that most vegetarian restaurants use egg products in their dishes. In order to make it easy for people to eat pure vegetarian food, I opened an orthodox vegetarian restaurant last year. Due to lack of experience and overexhaustion, I collapsed from illness. A hospital checkup showed that I had an ovarian tumor. Because I had lost an excessive amount of blood, the medicine prescribed by the doctor was ineffective. Later I met a Dharma Master who told me to recite the Great Compassion Mantra 108 times and then drink water that had been aided by the power of the mantra. I spent one day's time reciting the Great Compassion Mantra 108 times and then drank the Great Compassion Water as medicine. By the next day, I had stopped bleeding. After a week, my red blood protein count rose from eight points to twelve points (healthy people have fourteen points).

Through the introduction of a Buddhist friend, I entered a well-known private hospital on March 7 of this year. The operation that was performed on me on March 8 went well. Three days after the operation, the nurse (a Christian) who was taking care of me asked me if I had asked a monk to come and recite Sutras for me, because she'd seen a monk sitting at my bedside reciting for me. One week later, I went home and dreamed for three nights in a row that the Venerable Master had come to Malaysia. In reality, the Jewelled Repentance Ceremony of the Emperor of Liang was being held at Long Beach Sagely Monastery in America at the time, but the Venerable Master was seriously ill and could not personally be present at the Dharma assembly to give a talk. Nevertheless, the Venerable Master still had the spirit of great kindness, great compassion, great joy, and great giving, and his hundred million transformation bodies saved living beings who were in difficulty. Ignorant living beings are confused and difficult to teach and subdue, yet the Master unselfishly committed his whole life to aiding the fourfold assembly of disciples with boundless grace.

Before the Venerable Master left, he instructed us to recite the *Flower Adornment Sutra*. When I was bowing the Flower Adornment Repentance with the assembly, it seemed that every sentence and word was directed at my ignorance and stupidity. My body broke out in a cold sweat, my hands were trembling, and I couldn't control myself from crying again. Venerable Master, you're too compassionate!

September 18, 1995

依稀夢中情

SCENES FROM DREAMS

蕭優香　Xiao Youxiang

一九八○年喪夫之後，獨自撫養三個小孩，倍感艱辛。一九八二年恭逢上人正法，覺得心中有了依靠與寄託。

最初親近上人的法，是由一位師姐拿一本上人的事蹟給我看，那時心中有一種欣悅之情。之後，每有空閒時間就拜讀上人的書，並將上人法相供於佛堂頂禮膜拜。心中很想見到上人，但因為家事和孩子的牽絆，去美國萬佛城幾乎是不可能的事。於是便每天期待上人再回臺灣弘法，到時一定去皈依他……。

今年四月，大眾為病中的上人誦持〈大悲咒〉，請上人住世之後，心裡覺得很難過，再一次覺得要見到上人是不可能的了。

不久，上人圓寂的消息傳來。沒有能親覲上人，成了我終生的憾事！值得慶幸的是，我曾數次在夢中拜見上人，並蒙教誨。開始總以為是自己平時太渴望見到上人，以至於有這些夢境，所謂「日有所思，夜有所夢。」但自從我來到聖城以後，一切不可思議的事都似乎是上人早已安排好的。

上人涅槃之後，每次一想到上人的離去，就會淚流滿面，自嘆福薄，今生與上人無緣。上人真是不可思議，甚至對一位從未見面的人，他亦讓她在夢境中感受到菩薩的慈悲喜捨。

一直嚮往萬佛城，但又考慮到三個孩子無人照顧，故始終未能成行。一次在圓通精舍遇見一位師姐，她鼓勵我去萬佛城，辦理好一切手續後，終於順利地來到聖城。

來到聖城，如同到了另一個世界。這裡林木青幽，清明恬靜，有一種回到家裡的感覺。從住在萬佛城的第一天開始，我在臺灣時所祈盼的事情，皆一一實現了。受了三皈五戒，正式成為上人的弟子，心中的那份喜悅

After my husband passed away in 1980, I raised our three children by myself. It was very difficult for me. In 1982 I encountered the Venerable Master's Proper Dharma and felt I had gained a place of refuge.

The first time I was introduced to the Venerable Master's Dharma was when a fellow cultivator gave me a copy of the Venerable Master's biography. When I read it, my heart was filled with delight. Whenever I had spare time I would read the Venerable Master's books. I also placed the Venerable Master's image on the Buddha altar and bowed in homage to it. I really wanted to meet the Venerable Master, but my obligations to the home and children made it virtually impossible. So I wished every day that the Venerable Master would return to Taiwan to propagate the Dharma. I would certainly take refuge with him then...

In April of this year, the assembly recited the Great Compassion Mantra for the Venerable Master during his illness, requesting the Master to stay in the world. I felt very sad. I again thought I probably wouldn't get to meet the Venerable Master.

A little later, the news of the Venerable Master's completion of stillness came. My greatest regret in this life is that I didn't get to see the Venerable Master in person. However, I am fortunate because I did see the Venerable Master and receive teachings from him several times in my dreams. At first I thought these dreams were a result of my constant and strong yearning to see the Venerable Master. As it is said, "What one dreams about at night is determined by what one thinks about during the day." However, ever since I came to the Sagely City of Ten Thousand Buddhas, it has seemed to me that all the inconceivable things that have happened were arranged long ago by the Venerable Master.

Ever since the Venerable Master's Nirvana, every time I think of his leaving, tears roll down my cheeks, and I sigh that my blessings are so scarce and that I have no affinity with the Venerable Master in this life. The Venerable Master is truly inconceivable. He can cause someone who has never even met him to realize in dreams the kindness, compassion, joy, and giving of a Bodhisattva.

I had always wished to come to the City of Ten Thousand Buddhas, but was never able to do so, because I worried that my three children would have no one to care for them. Once I went to the Yuantong Hermitage and saw a Dharma sister who encouraged me to go to the City of Ten Thousand Buddhas. After all the arrangements were made, I finally made it to the Sagely City without any problem.

Coming to the Sagely City is like entering another world. The woods here are secluded, pure, and tranquil. I feel as if I've returned home. Starting on the first day of my stay at the City of Ten Thousand Buddhas, all the things I'd wished for in Taiwan began coming true one by one. I received the Three Refuges and Five Precepts and formally became the Venerable Master's disciple. My feeling of joy is truly indescribable. All of this happened after the Venerable Master had com-

，真是筆墨難以形容……。所有這一切雖然都發生在上人圓寂之後，但彷彿都是事先安排好了的。

第三日，到無言堂瞻仰上人的法體，見到上人安詳的遺容，心裡的那份自責、那份悔恨……！來得太遲了，未能一睹上人昔日的風采！

只有親身來到聖城，才能切實深深地感覺到上人的魄力與偉大，只有菩薩轉世才可能有如此作為。

二十八日請靈，大眾沿途夾道跪拜，想到自己福薄，未能親奉善知識，於是嘶聲痛哭。下午茶毗大典中天氣非常炎熱，熱心的居士們用濕紙巾給大家擦拭，並沿途供水，讓人感到這道場與眾不同。當大眾胡跪，上人靈柩移送到茶毗場時，飄來一陣陣的香味，心想哪裡來的香味？事後問一位師姐有否聞到，才知是一種異香。

當時大家都猜想，上人的骨灰中是否有舍利子。因為師父上人曾說：「在世上我不要留什麼痕跡！我從虛空而來，回到虛空去。」哪知二十九晚，拜願後，法師向大眾公佈上人留有舍利的事，大家真是欣喜萬分……。

法會功德圓滿。其間雖然忙碌，但精力充沛，法喜充滿，反而不覺得勞累。這次聖城之行，收穫是太多太多，發生的每一件事，都好像師父上人的無言開示……。

三十一日就要離開聖城，真捨不得走呢！

pleted the stillness, but it seems as if it had all been arranged beforehand.

On the third day I went to No Words Hall to behold the Venerable Master. When I saw the Venerable Master's peaceful countenance, what self-reproach and regret I felt! I've come too late to see the Venerable Master's exemplary deportment!

Only by coming to the Sagely City in person can one truly and deeply sense the Venerable Master's courage and greatness. Only a Bodhisattva could do what he has done.

On the twenty-eighth, when the casket was being carried, the assembly knelt and bowed on both sides of the path. I thought of what few blessings I had for not being able to personally serve a Good Knowing Advisor, and then I cried bitterly. The cremation ceremony was held in the afternoon, and the weather was extremely hot. Sincere laypeople went about offering wet towels and water to the assembly, making people feel that this Way-place is truly different from the others. As everyone knelt and the Venerable Master's body was being carried to the cremation site, there was wave after wave of fragrance. I wondered where the fragrance could be coming from. Afterwards I asked a fellow cultivator if she had smelled it, and she told me it was a rare fragrance (not the usual kind found in the world).

Everyone was wondering if the Venerable Master's ashes contained sharira. The Master had said, "I don't want to leave any traces in the world! I came from empty space, and I will return to empty space." Who would have expected that after the bowing in the evening on the twenty-ninth, a Dharma Master would announce that the Venerable Master had sharira?! Everyone was ecstatic.

The Dharma session has concluded. Even though it was very hectic, I felt energetic and filled with the joy of the Dharma. I didn't feel tired at all. I have gained tremendous benefit from this trip to the Sagely City. Each thing that happened seemed like a wordless teaching from the Venerable Master...

I have to leave the Sagely City on the thirty-first. I can hardly bear to go.

九九惑盡歇心狂　　靜慮思惟是誰忙
八萬四千由他去　　自在無往覺性王
〈客塵頌〉宣公上人作

Nine times nine delusions stop, and the mad mind is put to rest.
When anxieties are quieted down, consider who was busy.
Now let go of the 84,000 afflictions.
The King of the Enlightened Nature will be at ease, unmoving.

The Guest-dust Verse by Venerable Master Hsuan Hua

萬法唯心

THE MYRIAD DHARMAS ARE MADE FROM THE MIND ALONE

徐淑清　Xu Shuqing

讀了上人的遺言後，掩卷沉思：人，來到這世界上，什麼都沒帶來；走的時候，有形的東西也什麼都沒有帶走！但上人從來到這個世界，到他離開這個世界，他實踐了中國人所說的「立功、立德、立言」三種不朽的德性。也許上人生前沒有刻意這樣做，但他真地給我這份感受。

同樣的一份遺言，每個人的感受不同：

有人說，他很欣賞、很喜歡上人，認為上人好瀟灑。

有人說，上人來去自如，他走後，會有更多靈驗感應的事發生。

有人說，他不希望上人的舍利，成為弟子們爭先供請的對象。

突然覺得同樣的幾句遺言，每個人讀後的心得不同，所以很多事情沒有絕對的答案。也許每個人的出生、成長環境不同，對同樣的話語，反應就不一樣了。我不知道其他人的心得如何？

上人家父雙辭世，滿腹疑團遺心中，一心祈願生時會，無奈事與心願違。
菩薩未憐孩兒心，生時未能盡孝道，未能折壽求父壽，徒留懊悔在心頭。

徐淑清寫於父親往生三七前夜
七月二十九日

After reading the Venerable Master's last instructions, I sank into deep reflection: When a person comes to this world, he doesn't bring anything with him. When he leaves, he cannot take anything tangible with him, either! Yet from the time the Venerable Master came to this world until he left it, he achieved the three imperishable features praised by the Chinese: "establishing merit, establishing virtue, and establishing teachings." Perhaps the Venerable Master didn't intentionally think of doing this in his life, yet this is what I really feel he did.

The same last instructions elicit different reactions from different people:

Some people admire the Venerable Master. Others like the Venerable Master. Others feel the Venerable Master was casually elegant.

Some people think that after the Venerable Master's leaving, there will be even more efficacious responses, for the Venerable Master is free to come and go as he wishes.

Some people hope the Master's disciples will not struggle among themselves to be the first to make offerings to the Master's sharira.

The few sentences of these last instructions have provoked such different feelings from the people who read them. In many cases, there is no definite answer. Perhaps people have different reactions because they were born in different places, have different backgrounds, and speak different languages. I don't know what others think of this.

Now that the Venerable Master and my father have both left the world,
My heart is filled with doubts.
I had sincerely wished that I would meet him when he was alive.
What can I do if the reality is not as I wished?
The Bodhisattvas take no pity on my childish heart;
They only allow living beings to be disappointed.
I failed to fulfill my filial duty when they were alive.
My remembrance and regret are boundless and without end.

Written by Xu Shuqing on July 29 (Three weeks after my father's passing)

I Am Only Able to Help
Those People in Real Need
我只能幫助眞正需要的人

Jerri-Jo Idarius   June 9, 1995
艾潔莉   一九九五年六月九日

Although I was not a disciple of Shr Fu, I was privileged to have the benefit of his friendship and assistance during a time of need. I began working for CTTB in the fall of 1979 as a teacher of calligraphy. Later I was allowed to set up a graphics art studio with Linda Pecaites in the building adjoining the ceramics studio. I believe it is now called Wonderful Words Hall. There I taught classes and worked on publication projects for *Vajra Bodhi Sea*, the *Lotus Sutra* and other books. The time between the fall of 1979 and the summer of 1981 was difficult for me personally. I was leaving a ten-year marriage and transitioning into single motherhood. My son Bodhi was three to five years old during this period and was also going through a difficult time of adjustment.

Although I have hints of the history of my relationship with Shr Fu from past lives, I have to rely on the dream he sent me shortly after beginning to teach calligraphy to the nuns. In this dream he said, "Please come here and bring your friends. You bring a nice family feeling to this place." This resulted in the formation of a pre-school taught by two nuns, which Bodhi and his Ukiah friends attended. I also brought many friends to the Master's lectures through the next several years. I always felt welcome and unencumbered by rules, as long as I showed appropriate respect for others.

In the winter of 1980 my best friend from childhood, Barbara Mayginnes, had a second child. She had moved to Ukiah from Portland, Oregon, in the 1970's, had married a friend in my spiritual group, and had become a disciple of the same spiritual Master. In January 1975 she had a son named Shamaz. My son was born exactly one and a half years later. Our boys spent two years in Instilling Virtue School during the time I worked at CTTB. Barbara's second child was born caesarean. After the birth she was weak and was not recovering in a normal fashion. She soon found out that the doctor had cut a ureter (the tube that transfers urine from the kidney to the bladder) during the operation. Therefore a second operation had to be performed. During the recovery period in the hospital, complications set in. Barbara's body began producing blood clots, and the doctors decided to put her on the blood thinning drug, heparin. This in turn caused internal hemorrhaging in the abdominal cavity. Again she was in a life threatening situation. During this critical

雖然我不是上人的弟子，但是在我困難的時候，我很幸運地受到了他的恩惠及幫助。一九七九年秋天，我開始在萬佛聖城教書法。後來我和琳達在城內一間陶藝工作室旁，設立一間藝術工作室，現在叫做妙語堂。我在那裡教課，並參與《金剛菩提海》、《妙法蓮華經》及其他書籍的出版工作。在一九七九年到一九八一年間，是我生命中一段艱苦的時期。因為那時我結束了十年的婚姻，轉入單身母親的行列。而我的兒子菩提那時正是三歲到五歲之間，適應上也有一些困難。

雖然我覺得自己和師父在前世有一些關係，但我還是仰賴師父在夢中給我的示現。在我開始教尼眾書法後不久，有一天在夢裡上人說：「到這裡來，也帶你的朋友一塊兒來，你給這個地方帶些家庭的氣氛來。」因為這樣，所以就成立了幼稚園，我的兒子菩提，和他在瑜伽市的小朋友們就來這裡上學，當時由兩位尼師任教。接著幾年我也帶了很多朋友來聽上人說法。只要我對人尊重，人家也對我很友善，我也不覺得城裡的規矩有什麼不方便。

一九八〇年冬天，童年好友芭芭拉產下第二胎，她在一九七〇年由奧立岡州的波特蘭搬到瑜伽市。她嫁給我的一位道友，也成為我師父的弟子。一九七五年一月，她生了一個兒子，名叫山姆士；我的兒子則晚他一年半出世。我在萬佛聖城工作的時期，我們兩家的孩子都在育良小學讀了兩年。芭芭拉的第二個小孩是剖腹生產的，產後她很虛弱，並且沒有正常地復原。不久她發現手術時，醫生切除了輸尿管（將尿液由腎臟排到膀胱的管子），所以要動第二次手術。不料手術後，在醫院復原時，芭芭拉身上產生了血凝塊。醫生決定給她服食清血制凝素，此舉轉而引起腹腔出血，她再次有生命危險。

period, the doctors were undecided as to what to do, and time was running out. We were losing Barbara.

On the morning of February 14, 1980, I phoned a nun at the City of Ten Thousand Buddhas and told her about Barbara's condition. She, in turn, notified Shr Fu, who was in San Francisco that day. Later the same day, I called Gold Mountain and asked a monk to relay more details to Shr Fu. I was told that this was not customary and that he probably would not respond. However, I was insistent. A call was returned by the same monk within ten minutes, telling me that Shr Fu said I should recite the name of Kuan Yin Bodhisattva. I did so.

The doctors had decided that the only possibility of saving Barbara was to perform a third surgery, this time clamping the vena cava to protect her heart from a large blood clot. I recall a visible cloud of darkness in the hospital and the feeling of being surrounded by death. I had the sudden realization that I might never see my friend again. I recalled many scenes from our childhood and our lives together and became very sad at the thought of losing her. This was a stark possibility. My emotional reaction was very strong, and I almost panicked.

During the third operation, I received a page to pick up a telephone in a waiting room. It was Shr Fu himself. I always recognized his phone calls by the vastness of the silence before he spoke. It was like picking up the phone and listening to empty space. He told me to recite for Barbara with sincere single-mindedness—"Namo Kuan Shih Yin Pu Sa"—no other thought. He then told me not to worry but to see Kuan Yin coming to help my friend. Three other close friends and I recited, and immediately the energy changed. The darkness left as powerful waves of light and healing began to flood the hospital. Again, this was both visible and palpable to me. We knew that the critical period was over. The operation was successful. Barbara came out from the operating room slightly conscious and was able to give us the "hi" sign.

Shr Fu called the next day to find out how she was. He then recommended that she also recite to regain her strength and for the optimum benefit. She did this. Later on Shr Fu told me that it is the trueness of heart that is most important in reciting. If one is sincere and selfless, help will always come. A mantra without proper attitude and state of mind is empty.

As Barbara recovered, she was in pain but she emanated a special radiance and peace that I have seen around certain people who have suffered greatly or come close to death. I was struck by her compassion and concern for the well-being of others. At one point, she said, "I've been knocked around and it's a blessing. I never thought I'd say that. The past is all gone. The past doesn't exist anymore. It has been wiped out completely."

Shr Fu kept tabs on Barbara for several months without her knowing, asking me about her state of health each time he called. He intimated that I could tell him about people who needed help and that if he could, he would help them secretly. He said that he was only able to help those people in real need. Barbara was such a person. Therefore he had responded and called me to advise me about her after I had requested his help.

醫師不能決定怎麼應急，此刻時間急迫，眼看我們就要失去她了。

一九八〇年二月十四日早晨，我打電話給萬佛聖城的一位尼師，告訴她芭芭拉的情況，她轉告在三藩市的師父。稍晚，我又打電話到金山寺，請一位比丘向師父補充詳細情況。他告訴我沒有這種慣例，可能師父不會回應，不過我堅持要他報告。十分鐘後，這位比丘回電話來說，師父要我誦觀世音菩薩聖號，我照做了。

醫師已決定唯一可能救芭芭拉的辦法是動第三次手術，這次是夾住胸腔靜脈，以保護她的心臟，以免產生大血塊。我想起在醫院裡看見一片烏黑，又有被死亡包圍的感覺，忽然我領悟到：我可能再也見不到我的朋友了。我回想起很多我們兒時的情景，和一塊生活的情形，一想到很可能要失去她，我非常憂傷；我的情緒反應很激烈，驚慌不已。

第三次手術時，我在等候室聽到廣播去接電話，是師父打來的。因為師父在電話中未開口說話以前，總是沈默一陣子，所以我知道是他打來的電話。那感覺就好像是拿起電話來傾聽虛空。上人告訴我要一心真誠地為芭芭拉誦「南無觀世音菩薩」——一心無旁鶩。然後又告訴我不要擔心，只要觀想觀音菩薩來到，幫助我的朋友就可以了。當時有其他三位好友就和我一起誦持，立刻氣氛就轉變了，強大的醫治光波充遍醫院，黑暗就離去了。這是我看得見，又感覺得到的。我們知道危險期過去了，手術成功了。芭芭拉由手術室推出時，神識已經有點清醒，還能跟我們打招呼。

師父隔天又打電話來問她情況如何。他也要她誦持觀音菩薩名號，以恢復體力，也是為她好；她也照做了。後來師父告訴我，念誦最重要是真心，要是一個人真誠無私，總會得助；態度不正或沒有誠心，念咒是不靈的。

當芭芭拉復原時，雖然在痛苦中，她仍然散發著一種光輝和寧靜，那種樣子我在一些受大痛苦或臨終者身上也曾見過。她對旁人福祉的慈悲與關心使我深受感動。有次，她說：「我時常遭受打擊，其實那是一種福氣。我沒有想到自己會這麼說，過去的就過去了，已經完全磨滅了。」

以後幾個月，師父沒讓她知道，總是打電話問我她的健康狀況。上人親切地說如果有人需要幫助，可以告訴他，只要能力所及，他會默默幫助。他說他只能幫助那些有真正需要的人，芭芭拉就是其一

The last time I met with Shr Fu privately was after he had been very sick with a kidney condition in 1992. At that time, he asked me to write down an account of this story. It is only now, just after his passing, that I am coming to understand why. Kuan Yin helps all people who are sincere and in need. This is not obvious to the outer eye. Many people look like they need help, but are not ready to receive it. Others suffer quietly and do not outwardly show their receptivity, yet from within, they are ready. Shr Fu was able to look within the hearts and minds of others and was compassionate. He took time out for many more people than was obvious, even to those very close to him. His compassion reached well beyond the limits of the "Buddhist" community.

I had the privilege of a special view of his work as an outsider and insider. He helped me, my son, and my friends. He worked with me in dreams, gave me forewarnings of things to come, and showed me a large picture of his working. He was not concerned with reputation, nor with being understood by our small minds, yet his method of teaching was simple from the vantage of higher truth. He knew when to be fierce and strict and when to be soft and forgiving. The Masters use expedient means that are not understood by the measure or standards of the world. If we do not listen with the inner ear, we miss the greatness of their teachings. This means remembrance, faith and surrender when we are most attached and blind.

I hope that everyone at the City of Ten Thousand Buddhas will keep alive the spirit of openness and friendship that Shr Fu demonstrated in his dealings with people from all spiritual paths. Times of transition offer an opportunity for jumping to levels of understanding and functioning that were heretofore undreamed of. The challenge before us all is to be true to our commitments and ideals while honoring every soul we contact on the journey. Taking this principle a step further, the synergy created by joining forces across imaginary barriers of mental constructs has the power to transform our communities and the world. This is the power of the future I see.

I am so grateful to have known Shr Fu again and to have received his love and graciousness. My Master, Kirpal Singh, left the body in 1975. Knowing what I went through at that time, I have sympathy for those who are suffering this loss of their venerable Master and teacher. I can think of no greater pain in a lifetime. My love to all of you.

。所以每次我為芭芭拉的事求助於上人時，他都會有所回應。

我最後一次單獨見到上人，是在一九九二年師父腎臟病重時。那時他要我寫下這個故事，直到現在上人圓寂了，我才明白為什麼。觀世音菩薩幫助所有真心求助的有難者，這不是凡夫肉眼所能見的。很多求助的人看來需要幫助，但其實心裡還沒有真正準備好；有些人默默地受苦，外表上看不出來，但他們的內在已經能接受幫助了。師父既能透視人的心底，又慈悲。他花很多時間在無數人身上，即使在他身邊的人也不得而知，他對眾生的慈悲遠遠超過「佛教徒」的範圍。

身為一個當事人及非當事人，我有幸能看到上人工作不尋常的一面。他曾幫助我、我兒和我的友人。他在夢中，向我預先警示未來之事，也讓我看到他工作的大範圍。他不在乎名譽，也不在乎我們的小心量是否能了解他。而他的教導簡單明白，源於高明的真理。他知道何時該兇厲、嚴格，何時該柔和、寬恕。大師們所用的權巧方便法，不是世俗的尺度或標準所能理解的。我們若不用心來聽，就會錯失他們偉大的教化。也就是當我們最執著盲目時，我們應該憶念、信從與接受他們的教誨。

上人對各種不同宗教信仰的人，所表現的開放與友善精神，我希望每位在萬佛城的人，都能持續下去。時勢變遷時，反而有機會增加我們之間相互的瞭解，發揮更大的功用，這是以前所意想不到的。在我們人生旅程上遇到的每一個人，我們要尊重他們，但同時也不能放棄自己的誓願與理想，要同時兼顧這兩者，是我們面臨的最大難題。更進一步，如果我們能克服人我分別的妄見，將我們的力量凝聚起來，就可以改變這個社會與世界。這種凝聚的力量，我相信在將來一定會有的。

我心中充滿感激，今生能再次認識師父，並蒙受上人的愛護和恩惠。我以前的師父於一九七五年離世，我深深了解失去師父的痛苦，所以我對失去上人的朋友深表同情。我想這是人生中最悲痛的事。祝福大家。

THE VENERABLE MASTER'S FOURTEENTH VOW

宣公上人的第十四大願

Rosaline Kang
黃果玲

My life took a significant turn when I was fortunate enough to meet the Venerable Master. It has been the Master's fourteenth vow that has influenced me and changed my life the most. That vow says, "I vow that all living beings who see my face or even hear my voice will fix their thoughts on Bodhi and quickly accomplish the Buddha Way."

I remember that the first time I met the Master was in 1978, on his first visit to Malaysia. At that time I was emotionally upset because I had discovered that my husband was not true to his marriage vows. My marriage and relationship with my husband deteriorated day by day until it reached an unbearable stage which sent me to the verge of insanity. Destiny and past conditions brought me to meet the All-Knowing Advisor—our Venerable Master. The Master advised me to chant Guanshiyin Bodhisattva's name and walk upon the Buddhist path. In following the Master's advice, I worked earnestly each day at chanting Guanshiyin Bodhisattva's name and turned my focus towards the higher values of life. To my surprise I was able to control my anger, and I developed great tolerance and patience to the extent that harmony in the family was restored. I was able to cope with my husband's ways until he passed away in 1984.

In 1986, I met the Master again in the City of Ten Thousand Buddhas (CTTB) for the celebration of CTTB's tenth anniversary. I asked the Master, "Do you remember me?" The Master, without any hesitation, told me what I had confided in him eight years ago. I was struck with awe as I realized the meaning of spiritual penetrations.

Prior to my encounters with the Master, I had sought enjoyment associating with high society and leading a superficial lifestyle. After these years of following Master's teaching and practices, I have discovered a transcendental peace through bowing daily to the Buddhas, reciting the Sutras, and going on a full vegetarian diet. These have brought about a joy and happiness which I've never experienced before.

The best thing that has happened in my life is my taking refuge with the Master. The strength and determination of his great vows have been instrumental in setting me on the path of Buddhist cultivation and in teaching me to lead a happy and meaningful life. I am very grateful to the Venerable Master and will always be indebted to him.

當我很幸運地遇到上人時，我的命運有了重大的轉變。上人的第十四大願，對我最有影響力，改變了我的一生，這個願是：「願一切眾生，見我面、乃至聞我名，悉發菩提心，速得成佛道。」

第一次遇見上人是在一九七八年，他初次訪問馬來西亞時。那時正值我情緒惡劣，因為我發現丈夫不信守婚約，我們的婚姻關係日趨惡化，已經到了忍無可忍的地步，使我精神瀕臨崩潰錯亂。但我命中的因緣，使我遇到了上人，並能親聞這位無所不知的善知識說法。上人要我念觀世音菩薩的聖號，又要我行菩薩道。所以我就依教奉行，每日虔誦觀音菩薩名號，也開始注意到人生有更高的價值。令我驚異的是，我不但能控制自己的怒氣，並且也有了更大的忍耐力，因此我的家庭又重新恢復和諧，在一九八四年我先生去世之前，我和他一直都能和平相處。

一九八六年，萬佛聖城十週年慶時，我再次見到上人。我請問上人：「您還記得我嗎？」上人毫不猶豫地說出我在八年前告訴他的祕密。他的神通使我敬畏不已。

在未遇上人之前，我追求著上流社會的享受，過著膚淺的生活。這些年來，我奉行上人的教導與修行，每天拜佛、誦經、素食，使我經歷到一種超脫世俗的平靜感，和前所未有的欣悅。

在我這一生中，最有價值的一件事就是皈依上人。他的大願力，幫助我安住於道，過著快樂、有意義的人生。我非常感激上人，並永遠感念他的恩澤。

震撼我心的師父上人

THE VENERABLE MASTER HUA, WHO STIRRED MY HEART

游國楨　You Guozhen

下面介紹我學佛的因緣：是受了我太太的影響開始學佛的，我太太看了師父的《開示錄》，生出歡喜心，就如法地依照萬佛聖城的作息做早晚課。初期我是不懂佛法的，但是我會讚歎我太太那種禮佛。她一到寺廟禮佛，大家似乎都注意她，就好像偈頌裡頭的「能禮所禮性空寂」，我雖不懂佛法，但我看了都會讚歎。這樣我也慢慢地去了解佛法。

師父還沒有到臺灣弘法以前，我太太就依照上人的修持的方法來修持佛法。一九八八年上人到臺灣弘法。在臺中舉辦法會時，我太太跟臺中的一些信眾一起去護持。那時，我雖也沒有參與，但是因為我太太的關係，我也皈依了師父上人。皈依的時候，師父規定說每一皈依他的弟子都要拜一萬拜。我就有的時候，一天十拜，或二十拜，或五十拜，時間拖得很長的。就這樣慢慢地走進師父的微妙法裡。

有一次我跟內人到圓山開會。會議結束後，內人跟我就跪在師父的跟前，那時的本意是想得到師父的加持。師父是明眼善知識，他知道眾生的根器，末學跪在師父的跟前，師父好像視若無睹，我跪在前面他連看都不看我。我就生出一種煩惱，因為那時候也不懂什麼叫佛法。但是我太太經常把佛經裡面的偈頌講解給我聽，然後她寫下來。最初，我也沒在意。當我的心比較平靜時，我就慢慢地看她寫下來的偈頌。看了以後，就生出一種歡喜的心，而發出內心的稱讚如來。我跪在師父跟前，覺得跪了很長的時間。後來，我太太就問師父說：「我先生修什麼法門好？」師父就講：「念阿彌陀佛。」後來又重複地講了一次，我跟內人就頂禮師父，接受師父的加持。剛才我還起煩惱，但在師父加持的一剎那，我就生起一種不求的心。

後來，我看到師父的《開示錄》說：「人到無求品自高，到無求處便無憂。」當下我就發了願：「我以後絕不再接受師父的加持。」這是我初期學佛時對我影響很大的一件事情。後來也有因緣接受師

I'd like to talk about how I came to study Buddhism. It was due to my wife's influence. My wife was very happy when she read the Venerable Master's *Instructional Talks*, and she began to do morning and evening ceremonies following the practice of the Sagely City of Ten Thousand Buddhas. In the beginning I didn't know anything about the Buddhadharma, but my wife's worship of the Buddhas won my praise. Whenever she went to the temple to bow to the Buddhas, everyone seemed to take notice of her. It was as the verse says, "The one bowing and the one bowed to are both empty and still in nature." Even though I didn't understand the Dharma, I praised her bowing. Gradually, I also began to understand the Buddhadharma.

Even before the Master came to Taiwan to propagate the Dharma, my wife was already following the Master's teaching to cultivate the Buddhadharma. When the Master came to Taiwan in 1988, my wife and some other devotees in Taichung went to support his Dharma session in Taichung. Though I didn't take part, because of my wife's involvement I also took refuge with the Master. During the taking refuge ceremony, the Master stated that every disciple of his had to bow 10,000 times. Some days I would bow ten bows, or twenty bows, or fifty days, so it took a long time. In this way, I slowly entered the Master's wonderful Dharma.

Once my wife and I went to attend a meeting at Yuanshan. After the meeting, my wife and I knelt in front of the Master, hoping the Master would give us his blessing. The Master, a Bright-eyed Wise Advisor who knew living beings' dispositions, acted as if he didn't even see me kneeling there. He didn't even look at me. I became rather vexed, because I didn't really understand the Buddhadharma then. My wife would often explain verses from the Buddhist scriptures to me and write them out. At first I wouldn't pay attention to them, but when my mind was calm, I would look at the verses she'd written out and be filled with delight. I would praise the Thus Come Ones in my heart. I knelt before the Master for what seemed like a very long time. Finally my wife asked the Master, "What Dharma-door should my husband practice?" The Master said, "Recite Amitabha Buddha's name." He repeated this, and then my wife and I bowed and accepted the Master's blessing. I had been vexed a moment before, but when the Master blessed us, I instantly attained a state of nonseeking.

Later I read in the Master's *Instructional Talks*: "When people reach the place of no seeking, they will naturally be noble in character. At the place of no seeking, there are no worries." I immediately vowed, "I will never again accept the Master's

父的加持，但是跪在師父跟前向師父頂禮的時候，我默默地告訴自己，不要接受師父的加持。但是師父還是很慈悲地給我加持了三次。

記得第一次接受師父加持時，產生了很大的震憾。當時師父為臺灣的眾生祈福絕食，他老人家已經很久沒有吃飯，手有一點抖動。師父加持我的時候，只是輕輕地打，結果我感覺到「轟……」的那種震動。因為那時候是在臺北，回來的一路上，差不多有一天的時間，頭一直感到「轟…轟轟…轟」的。這是我第一次受到師父的震憾。

有一天，我太太就告訴我說：「法會結束以後，我們跟師父上人的緣可能就盡了。」但是很微妙的，就是王金平的家族把臺灣高雄六龜鄉的別墅奉獻給上人。師父就派兩位法師去六龜的道場，就這樣，我跟內人有機會在師父的法蔭下，接受正法的薰陶，差不多有三個月之久。

在那三個月當中，我跟內人和另一位居士，每個星期日都到六龜的道場去護法。我們是去誦經的。但因為房子有很多地方需要整修，如地上的磚塊，因長時間沒有使用，已經脫落了；鐵門，也生鏽了。當地的護法卻非常發心來整理別墅的周圍。當時，蛇非常多，令人有點恐怖，如果沒有相當的定力，這房子是沒有辦法住的。在這三個月當中，經常聽經，很幸運學到了很多以前未學到的東西，所學到的法，每一次都用一種喜悅的心來深入經藏，所以使末學對佛法有了更多的瞭解。

後來兩位法師被調回美國，當時我們覺得跟師父的緣可能又斷了。可是女眾的佛學院又遷入六龜的道場。我太太又跟那兒的女眾法師結下了善緣，一直到今天。因為這個緣，臺中才有每月最後一個禮拜的水懺法會。

最後，我要感謝師父。去年法界聖城成立的時候，末學也有參與此會，法會結束以後，末學到譯經院跟師父上人辭行。師父上人很慈悲就告訴末學說：「多待幾天。」接著說：「不要忘了修行！」最後這句話，今天末學又回想起來，好像是末學再不可能見到師父了。今天的感覺是如此地沉重，那師父上人前一句所講的「多待幾天」，當時我只想著機票都已經訂了，不可能不回去的。事實上，師父的妙法深深地震撼我的心，師父的「多待幾天」，意味深長。如果我能夠把身心放下來，聽師父的話

blessing." This matter made a great impression on me during my initial study of Buddhism. Later I had another chance to receive the Master's blessing, but when I knelt in front of the Master to bow, I told myself silently that I wouldn't accept the blessing. Yet the Master was still very compassionate and blessed me three times.

The first time I received the Master's blessing, I was deeply moved. At the time, the Master was fasting on behalf of the living beings of Taiwan. He had not eaten anything for a long time, and his hands were trembling slightly. When the Master blessed me, he hit me very lightly, but I felt a rumbling "Hong..." within me. We were in Taipei, and on the way home and for the duration of the following day, there was a roaring sound in my head—"Hong, hong, hong..." That was the first time I was stirred by the Master.

One day my wife said to me, "When the Dharma session ends, our conditions with the Master will probably be over." Yet, very wonderfully, Wang Jinping's family donated their villa in Liugui to the Master. The Master asked two Dharma Masters to stay at that Way-place. Thus my wife and I had a chance to immerse ourselves in the Proper Dharma under the Master's Dharma-protection for about three months.

During those three months, my wife and I and Upasika Hong Ziyin would go to the Way-place in Liugui every Sunday to support the Dharma there. We would recite Sutras. The house was in great need of repairs. The floor tiles had become dislodged, and the iron door was rusty. The local laypeople were very eager to help with the repairs. There were a lot of snakes in the area, which was a bit nerve-wracking. People without samadhi power could not have lived in that house. We often recited Sutras in those three months and were fortunate to learn many new things. With great delight, we studied the Sutra Treasury and gained a better understanding of the Buddhadharma.

The two Dharma Masters were later recalled to America, and we thought our conditions with the Master were over. But then the women's Buddhist Academy moved to the Way-place in Liugui. My wife developed good relations with the nuns, which have continued to the present. Due to those circumstances, a Water Repentance Ceremony came to be held in the last week of every month.

Finally, I would like to thank the Master. Last year, after the Sagely City of the Dharma Realm was established, I went to attend the Dharma session. After it was over, I went to the International Translation Institute to say goodbye to the Master. The Master very kindly said, "Stay a few more days." Then he said, "Don't forget to cultivate!" When I think of this last sentence, it seemed to imply that I would never see the Master again. I'm so sad today, for the Master had said, "Stay a few more days," but I had only thought that my ticket was set and I couldn't not go back. In fact, the Master's wonderful Dharma has deeply stirred my heart. The Master's words, "Stay a few more days" carries deep and lasting meaning. If I can let go of

，我就能夠更上一層樓。

　　願大眾能把師父叮嚀我的話，做為叮嚀各位的一樣，「不要忘了修行！」阿彌陀佛！

body and mind and listen to the Master, then I will be able to advance a level higher.

I hope everyone will take the Master's admonishment to me as your own admonishment: "Don't forget to cultivate!" Amitabha Buddha!

眞實的故事

A TRUE STORY

湯雅齡
Una Irons

　　我始終沒有機會與緣份真正見到宣化上人本人，但是有關他的書倒是看了一些。由於因緣促使，我認識了上人的一位出家弟子，我們全家經常到國際譯經院聽法師講經。就在五月的某個星期天，法師要大家講一些曾經被菩薩幫助過的親身經歷及故事，有些同修就陸續地敘述了受宣化上人救助的故事。這使我猛然想起在維吉尼亞州時得癌症病重的朋友，事後我向法師請了一些宣化上人的照片，連同一卷阿彌陀佛聖號的錄音帶，用快遞方式寄給我的朋友。同時在電話中告訴我的朋友說，你不認識他不要緊，求他幫助你。

　　就在一天午後奇蹟出現了，正當她小睡之時，冥冥中她感到有個人走進她的房間，拿了一個用樹葉卷成的東西塞進她的嘴裡，依稀她還可以嘗到奶油的香甜，醒來後她馬上衝到廁所小瀉，（那時她已經是癌症末期，身體內嚴重積水，苦不堪言）之後，她感到從未有過的舒適。毫無信仰的她，事後發電告我此事，充滿了驚訝及感激！不久之後，她雖仍然去逝了，但容顏卻十分安詳、平靜。

　　我相信受過宣化上人幫助的人不在少數，上人一生，致力於講經說法，教化及幫助我們，對社會大眾的貢獻不是我這支拙筆可以形容的。在我心目中他是一位活菩薩，他從未生也從未死。他的教化將是我一生中行為舉止的標準及警惕。

I never had the opportunity or affinity to meet the Venerable Master Hua in person, but I did read some books about him. Certain conditions led me to meet a certain left-home disciple of the Venerable Master. Later our family went regularly to hear the Dharma Masters lecture on Sutras at the International Translation Institute. One Sunday in May, the Dharma Master wanted everyone to tell about their personal experiences of being helped by Bodhisattvas. Some fellow cultivators gave accounts of how they'd been rescued and helped by the Venerable Master Hua. This made me suddenly think of a friend I had in Virginia who had cancer. Afterwards I asked the Dharma Master for some photographs of the Venerable Master Hua and a tape of the recitation of Amitabha Buddha's name, which I sent by express mail to my friend. I also called my friend and said, "It doesn't matter if you don't know him. Just pray to him to help you."

The miracle happened one day after noon. As she was taking a nap, she had a vision of someone walking into her room. He took something wrapped in leaves and stuffed it in her mouth. She seemed to taste a slight butter flavor. When she awakened, she ran to the bathroom with a case of diarrhea (at that point she was already in the final stages of the cancer and her body was seriously bloated with water, a condition which entailed unspeakable suffering). Afterwards, she felt more comfortable than she had ever felt before. She had no religious faith, but when she called to tell me what had happened, she was amazed and grateful. Although she still passed away not long afterwards, her face was very peaceful.

I believe that the people who have been helped by the Venerable Master are not a few. He devoted his life to lecturing on the Sutras and speaking the Dharma, to teaching and helping us, and his contributions to the society are not something that my clumsy pen could describe. In my mind, he is a living Bodhisattva. He was never born and never died. His teachings are the standard and reminder for my conduct throughout my life.

BRINGING FORTH THE RESOLVE FOR THE UNSURPASSED WAY
發 無 上 道 心

Shi Heng Cheng   釋恆正

I met the Venerable Master in October 1976 at Gold Mountain Monastery in San Francisco when I was attending college. I had been involved with psychology and philosophy on the campus I was attending, and one day my philosophy instructor gave me a list of spiritual centers in San Francisco. The second place I went to was Gold Mountain.

At the time I went, the Master was lecturing on *The Flower Adornment Sutra.* I did not understand anything that was going on. However, I knew at that time that the Master was my teacher. The second or third time that I went to Gold Mountain Monastery, I saw the Venerable Master sitting on the Dharma Seat as a five-year-old child.

I was invited to go with the Bhikshunis to take a look at the new Way-place in Talmage, California. There was a group of Korean students who came to visit Gold Mountain Monastery, and so the Venerable Master took them to the City of Ten Thousand Buddhas. I liked the place immediately, and the Master also knew this. It was very cold that day, and I took my heavy coat with me, but I didn't need it. Everyone was hovering around the heater in one of the rooms up at Dragon Tree House, but I was very warm without the heater. Later, I was to return to San Francisco in the same car with the Master, but I stood outside waiting to find out in what car I was supposed to return. The Master was already in the car, and asked, "Kuo K'ai, are you going to stay here?"

During the Winter Semester Break, I attended my first Buddha Recitation Session at Gold Mountain. As I remember, this was my second personal encounter with the Venerable Master. I took refuge with the Triple Jewel during this time, and within two or three days I wanted to leave the home-life. I spoke with one of the nuns at that time, and I was granted an audience with the Master. A Bhikshuni acted as the translator for me. One of the first things the Venerable Master asked me was, "Do you have a boyfriend?" I expressed my wish to leave the home-life, and the Master replied that he wanted me to finish school, and that he wanted to watch me for a while.

I had only six months left of school, and was planning to continue my studies in psychology by transferring to a major university. After that Buddha Recitation Session, and upon returning to my apartment, I began to mentally and physically make arrangements to leave home after I graduated in June.

Early in the spring of 1977 there was a Dharma gathering at San Francisco's Golden Gate Park to pray for the ending of a serious drought in California. At the end of the day, some of us returned to Gold Mountain Monastery. I came face to face with the Master, and he directly said, "You came back."

On June 25, 1977, I went to the women's Way-place with my belongings, and a week later moved to the City of Ten Thousand Buddhas to help start the first summer school at the City. It was during this summer—one and a half months later—that I left the home-life. I took a bus back to San Francisco, and the event took place at Gold Mountain

第一次遇見上人是一九七六年在三藩市的金山寺，那時我還在上大學，在學校裡，我選修了心理學和哲學。一位教哲學的老師給了我們一張三藩市的宗教中心名單，金山寺是我第二個去參訪的地方。

那時上人正在講解《華嚴經》，我雖然一點都聽不懂，但我直覺地就知道上人是我的師父。以後，我再去金山寺的時候，我看見上人坐在座位上，好像五歲的童子。

有人邀我和比丘尼們一起去看位於加州瑜伽鎮的新道場。當時恰好有一群韓國學生在金山寺，所以上人也帶他們一起去萬佛聖城。我一見聖城，就很喜歡，上人也知道。那天很冷，我帶了厚大衣，但卻用不上。在龍樹精舍，大家都圍著暖器取暖，我卻沒去取暖，仍覺得很暖和。離開萬佛城上車時，上人已先坐在車裡，他看見我時，便說：「果楷，你想留下嗎？」

放寒假時，我在金山寺參加了生平第一次的佛七，這是我第二次見到上人，就皈依了師父。過了兩三天，興起出家的念頭，於是我去見上人，通過翻譯，上人問我：「你有男朋友嗎？」我說我想出家，上人說我應該先完成學業，他還要再觀察我一段時期。

再有六個月，我就可以從大學預科畢業，本打算轉到大學去修心理學。但打完佛七，回到住處後，在心理上和身體上，開始做出家的準備。

加州那時鬧旱災，所以於一九七七年初春，上人在三藩市的金門公園舉行祈雨法會。法會結束後，回到金山寺，上人對我說：「妳回來吧！」

一九七七年六月二十五日，我從女眾道場遷居萬佛城，去幫助在聖城舉辦的第一次暑期佛學班。一個半月之後，那年夏天，我在金山寺出家了，有人跟我說我那天看起來像

Monastery on the anniversary of Gwan Shr Yin Bodhisattva's Enlightenment. Someone told me that I looked like a soldier during that day. After the ceremony, the Venerable Master told me that I couldn't get angry any more. Two days later, I returned to the City, and the person I was working with asked me, "Well, how does it feel to leave home?" I immediately replied, "You know, I don't feel that I have done anything different." The next time that the Master came to the City, she told him what I said, and he laughed and said that I had been a cultivator in the past.

Between the winter of 1979 on through to the end of June 1990, I was in a situation which forced me to take a good look at myself, and to learn what I was really supposed to be doing as a left-home person. What was really memorable for me during this time was that I was able to observe the Venerable Master's all-encompassing virtuous conduct. As I now try to write this, I must admit that there is no real way to express what has happened to me because of such a teacher.

I have been memorizing *The Wonderful Dharma Lotus Flower Sutra* now for many years, and have observed the Venerable One's adornments through my memorization. Not only have I been able to "taste" the wonderful flavor of this Sutra, but my reverence and respect for the Venerable Master has greatly transformed me.

I also learned how important it is to attend the Dharma activities that the Venerable Master has established in the Hall of Ten Thousand Buddhas. I have mentioned to others that, "In times of difficulty, the safest place to be is in the Buddha Hall." Often times, I try to repay the Venerable Master's great kindness and compassion by transferring the merit from work that was difficult for me to do, to the Master. The last time that I did this in the presence of the Master was during the Jeweled Repentance before the Ten Thousand Buddhas in 1990. The Master had come into the Buddha Hall at the end of a day's session. He stood about four rows of bowing cushions in front of me and looked directly at me with a smile on his face. After the above session took place, I experienced something of such awesome magnitude with regard to the Venerable Master's great spiritual powers that I cannot present it here. However, during these past eleven and a half years, my faith, reverence, and respect for the Triple Jewel have increased to such a degree that I don't want anything to prevent me from going forward in my cultivation for the Unsurpassed Way of all Buddhas.

There are verses at the end of Chapter Four of *The Wonderful Dharma Lotus Flower Sutra* in which the Venerable Mahakashyapa talks about the difficulty in repaying the Buddha's kindness. I believe that this is also true with a Good Knowing Advisor. Just in these past almost eighteen years, I ask myself how am I going to repay my teacher's kindness and patience with me for so many years? The debt of kindness only increases day by day.

It is easy to say, "If I had known then, what I know now..." I remember that when the Master first started teaching Americans, someone told him that this is an impossible task. However, I am an American, born and raised in the San Francisco Bay Area. Although I have made many serious and not so serious mistakes in the past, and will make many more in the future, I can firmly and confidently say that the Venerable Master has taught and transformed me in many ways. He has been my teacher in the past, in the present, and will be my teacher throughout all of future time until I myself embody *The Wonderful Dharma Lotus Flower Sutra* and the power of Gwan Shr Yin Bodhisattva. Only then will I truly be able to help him in his work.

個士兵。剃度時，上人告誡我不可以再發脾氣了。我回聖城之後，有人問我：「出家的滋味如何？」我立刻回答：「我一點也不覺得有什麼不同的感覺！」上人知道後，笑著說我以前是修行人。

從一九七九年冬天，到一九九〇年之間，周遭發生的一些事情，逼使我好好檢討自己，思考今後該如何做一個名符其實的出家人。那段時期，最值得紀念的是我能夠親眼見到上人的無微不至的德行。上人對我的影響，實非筆墨所可形容。

過去幾年，我一直都在背誦《妙法蓮華經》，而體會到上人的萬德莊嚴。我不但領略到了這部經的微妙法味。我對上人的恭敬，也深深地改變了我。

上人經常強調上佛殿早晚功課的重要性，我對此深有體會。我曾對人講：「在有困難時佛殿是最安全的地方。」我常常在做了有意義的事情之後，將功德迴向給上人以報答上人的慈悲。一九九〇年，我將拜萬佛寶懺的功德迴向給上人。有一天功課完後，我正迴向功德給上人時，上人駕臨佛殿，當他的視線轉到我身上時，我看見他在微笑。在拜完懺之後，我感覺到上人的大神通力，但不便在這兒講述。在過去十一年中，我對三寶的恭敬、信心日增，我將永遠沿菩提道修淨梵行。

在《妙法蓮華經》第四品中，大目犍連尊者講述佛恩難報，我認為善知識的恩也難報。過去這十八年我常問自己應如何回報上人多年的恩德及耐心。對師父上人，我實在虧欠得太多了。

常聽人說：「如果我那時知道的話……」，我記得上人剛開始教化美國人時，有人告訴上人，美國人難調難伏。我是土生土長在舊金山灣區的美國人，過去雖然我犯了很多錯誤，將來也許還會再犯，但是我堅信上人在許多方面已教化、改變了我。上人是我過去生的師父，現在生中的師父，在無窮盡的將來，直到我能證到《妙法蓮華經》裡的諸佛境界，及具足觀世音菩薩的大威神力，只有到那時，我才真正能輔佐上人的事業。

參禪見佛

INVESTIGATING CHAN AND SEEING THE BUDDHA

孫東柏　Sun Dongbo

十七年前，西曆一九七八年，是我來美遊學的年底。

十二月二十二日，我到了金山寺。當時，還在十五街，比起臺灣的廟，金山寺顯得非常簡陋。

找不到進去寺內的大門，站在似門又似窗的寺前，我猶疑不前。突然，一陣陣的暖流，注入前胸，透散全身，頓時，精神奕奕，神清氣爽。有人從裡面向我招手，踏入右側小門，一個白人和尚，跟我說了一些簡單的中國話，說他是老和尚的美國弟子。我表明要參加萬佛聖城為期三週的冬季禪七。法師微笑著帶我進去，見幾個中國人，及一個剛從倫敦來打七的年輕英國人。連我五個人，我們就搭便車前往萬佛城。一路上，他們就說：「萬佛城打七，從未有在家人能呆過二、三天的。」

念了十五年的佛，就是沒參加過禪七，一時，心頭忐忑不安，到底什麼是禪七呢？他們到底在暗示什麼呢？

冬天，天黑得很早。傍晚時分，在車上聞到又沉又濃的檀香味，久久不散。車子又走了約三十分鐘，才到了目的地。

當時的萬佛城，是很簡陋的。

禪七期間，每個晚上，老和尚都會講一小段《華嚴經》及開示。在第二個禮拜天晚上，老和尚說，明天他必須往洛杉磯一趟。就在那個晚上，他特別說了四句偈：

一九七八打禪七，不緊不慢不焦急；
綿綿密密勤精進，不久當至諸佛地。

並特別開示：參禪不要害怕，不可懶惰，你們之間一定有人，會得二十五圓通的法門。

就在開示後，禮佛時，我見到了五尊大佛，於老和尚等肩高處，懸空而坐，紫金身光，襯托著老和尚的大紅祖衣，互相輝映。

Seventeen years ago (1978), my year of study in America ended.

On December 22, I went to Gold Mountain Monastery, which was still on Fifteenth Street then. Compared to temples in Taiwan, Gold Mountain Monastery appeared very poor and humble.

I couldn't find the front door of the monastery. Standing in front of what looked like both a door and a window, I couldn't decide what to do. Suddenly, waves of warm energy passed through my chest and spread through my body. All of a sudden, I became very alert and clear-minded. Someone inside waved to me and stepped out through a small door on the right side. A Caucasian monk spoke a few simple sentences in Chinese to me, telling me he was an American disciple of the Venerable Master. I indicated that I wished to attend the three-week Winter Chan Session at the Sagely City of Ten Thousand Buddhas. The Dharma Master led me inside with a smile. I saw a few Chinese people and a young Englishman who had just arrived from London for the Chan Session. The five people, including me, got a ride to the City of Ten Thousand Buddhas. On the way there they said, "In the Chan Sessions at the City of Ten Thousand Buddhas, laypeople have never managed to stay for more than two or three days."

I had recited the Buddha's name for fifteen years, but I had never participated in a Chan Session before. All of a sudden, I felt very uneasy. Just what was a Chan Session all about? What were they hinting at?

In the winter, it became dark quite early. At dusk, in the car I smelled a very heavy and strong scent of sandalwood, which didn't disperse for a long time. We drove for another half an hour before reaching our destination.

The City of Ten Thousand Buddhas was very poor and humble then.

During the Chan Session, every night the Venerable Master would lecture on a short passage from the *Flower Adornment Sutra* and give an instructional talk. In the evening of the second Sunday, the Venerable Master said he needed to make a trip to Los Angeles the next day. That night, he especially spoke a four-line verse:

In 1978, we hold a Chan Session.
Be neither fast nor slow, and don't get nervous.
Continuously and without a break, be diligent and vigorous.
Soon you will reach the Buddhas' ground.

He also instructed us: "In investigating Chan, one should not be afraid and one should not be lax. Among you, someone will definitely realize one of the Dharma-doors of the Twenty-five Kinds of Perfect Penetrations.

When I was bowing to the Buddhas after the lecture, I saw five large Buddhas sitting in the air at the level of the Venerable Master's shoulders. A purple-golden aura brought his red sash into relief as the colors inter-reflected.

禮佛畢。老和尚故意問道：「你們有誰看到或有什麼感應的嗎？講出來讓大家知道。」當時，覺得老和尚這個問題有點古怪。並約略記得老和尚說：「修持有感應時，不要說出去，除非師父同意或鼓勵同參，方可點到為止。」云云。

老和尚似乎知道，我在疑惑中，又連問了二次。我還是猶豫不定。最後，他說：「說出來，給大家聽聽，參禪功德絕不唐捐。」我終於說出。

禮佛時，抬頭一看，在老和尚坐的講台上方，於老和尚兩肩高處，水平線上，約有一丈高的圓錐形五尊紫金身佛，懸空跏趺而坐。當時，我離講台約有百呎處。

老實說，那兩個禮拜的禪七，我對老和尚的印象並不深刻。直到見佛後，才恍然警覺，這麼簡陋的道場，老和尚憑什麼道行得五佛護持？

After bowing to the Buddhas, the Venerable Master asked, "Did any of you see any responses? Speak up and tell everyone about it." I felt the Master's question was rather peculiar. I also vaguely remember the Master saying, "If you have any responses in cultivation, don't speak about them, unless your Master agrees or encourages fellow cultivators to do so, but even then, you should just touch upon them," and so forth.

The Venerable Master seemed to know that I was confused. He asked two more times. I still vacillated. Finally, he said, "Speak up and let everyone know that the merit and virtue of Chan meditation is absolutely not in vain." I finally spoke.

When I was bowing to the Buddhas, I looked up. Above the stage where the Venerable Master was sitting, at the height of the Master's shoulders, there were five cylindrically shaped Buddhas with purple-golden bodies about ten feet tall, sitting in full lotus in mid-air. At the time, I was about a hundred feet from the stage.

To tell the truth, the Venerable Master did not make a deep impression on me during those two weeks of Chan. It was only when I saw the Buddhas that I suddenly woke up: In such a humble Way-place, what kind of virtue did the Venerable Master have to receive the protection of five Buddhas?

*　　　　*　　　　*

老和尚，您忽然間走了，聖城信徒頓失依怙，人人哀傷慌亂。在這末法時期，邪師充斥，邪說滔滔，惡法流毒，怵目驚心，混淆惑亂佛子，障礙菩提道心，貽誤學人甚鉅。

老和尚，只有您知道，我一直遲疑不決，不想寫說。一九八四年，您鼓勵我翻譯經典，並說，書一印出來後，頒發榮譽學位來獎勵我。可是英譯二十頁《六祖法寶壇經》後，一九八六年，冥冥中蒙六祖惠能祖師告誡我：「勿諍訟，自平和。」所以九年來，我一直採取明哲保身，自立利己，韜光養晦的原則－－不說不寫。

可這次，不用您老要求，該是義不容辭報答佛祖及老和尚的時刻了。這篇「參禪見佛」將刊入《我所認識的度輪宣化老和尚 —— 感應與事蹟》及《禪為唯一真》（一九八三年，達摩祖師教誡我）二本書中。

老和尚，我會將一切學佛經驗與修持心得發表給大眾。一來報答佛恩及感念您：在這麼惡劣的環境中，以身作則，堅苦卓絕奮鬥不懈，為法忘軀，建立法城，維護正法。您的一言一

Venerable Master, you have suddenly gone. The disciples at the Sagely City have suddenly lost the one they relied on. Everyone is distressed and flustered. In this Dharma-ending Age, deviant teachers and deviant theories are everywhere. The spreading of evil dharmas is frightening to see, deluding disciples of the Buddha, hindering them from bringing forth the resolve for Bodhi, and seriously harming students of Buddhism.

Venerable Master, you alone know that I kept hesitating and didn't want to write or speak about my experience. In 1984, you encouraged me to translate Sutras and said that after a book was printed, you would reward me with an honorary degree. But after I translated twenty pages of the *Sixth Patriarch's Dharma Jewel Platform Sutra*, in 1986 I had a vision in which the Sixth Patriarch Hui Neng warned me, "Don't contend, and you will naturally find peace." Therefore for nine years, I have followed the principle of taking care of myself and hiding my light—I neither spoke nor wrote.

But this time, I didn't need you to ask me. This ought to be the time when I cannot refuse to repay the kindness of the Buddhas and the Venerable Master. This article "Investigating Chan and Seeing the Buddha" will be published in the two books *The Venerable Master Hsuan Hua To Lun—Responses and Deeds* and *Chan Is the Only Truth* (in 1983, Patriarch Bodhidharma instructed me to do this).

Venerable Master, I will tell the public about my experiences in studying Buddhism and what I have gained from cultivation. The first reason is to repay the Buddhas' kindness and to thank you for setting a good example, battling resolutely in the face of hardship, sacrificing yourself for the Dharma, establishing a City of Dharma, and protect-

行，精神與榜樣，都是我們後學的楷模。二來，激勵人心：萬佛城微妙殊勝，佛子們在萬佛城參禪、修道，恆得諸佛威神加被護念，實乃人間稀有難得的正法道場，是值得真佛子肝腦塗地，擁護的法城。三來，鼓舞聖城弟子，人事變遷，毫不動心，依和尚言教，克盡職守，身體力行，守護法城，於法自在。

老和尚，您雖不是我的依止師父，我也不贊同您的一些言教，更少親近於您（您的弟子中沒有人認識我的）。您高風亮節，錚錚鐵骨，為弟子讚歎，欽佩不已。從老和尚您那裡，什麼佛法也沒有學到，就只學到您的硬骨頭精神，骨頭不硬，佛道難成。就是把老和尚殺了，剁了來吃，老和尚您一定會說：「我沒死！」聖城弟子們，老和尚圓寂後，他老人家還是和往常一樣，在我最需要的時刻來啟發、教誨我，真是慈悲的菩薩！

老和尚，您哪裡有死呢！

希望這懷思小文，能帶給大眾一些啟示與感念。

最後，敬祝聖城四眾弟子，法喜無量！

南無阿彌陀佛！

佛弟子
禪學針灸研究院院長
孫東柏敬拜
美國加州沙加緬度
一九九五年九月二十一日

ing the Proper Dharma in this evil environment. Your every word and deed, your spirit and example, serve as a standard for those of future generations to follow. Secondly, I wish to encourage people by telling them how wonderful and sublime the City of Ten Thousand Buddhas is. Buddhists who investigate Chan and cultivate at the City of Ten Thousand Buddhas constantly receive the great spiritual aid and mindful protection of all Buddhas. It is truly a Way-place of the Proper Dharma which is rarely found in the world. Genuine Buddhists ought to sacrifice themselves to protect this City of Dharma. Thirdly, I wish to encourage the disciples at the Sagely City not to be moved by changes in people and affairs, to rely on the Venerable Master's teachings, fulfill their responsibilities, honestly practice, guard and protect the City of Dharma, and be at ease within the Dharma.

Venerable Master, although you are not the Master I study under (I disagree with some of your teachings, and I hardly ever drew near to you; none of your disciples know me), your lofty integrity and your stubborn determination win my praise and endless admiration. I didn't learn any Buddhadharma from you, Venerable Master. All I learned was your "hard bones" spirit. If one's bones are not hard, it's difficult to attain the Buddha Way. Even if someone were to kill you, slice you up and eat you, Venerable Master, you'd probably say, "I'm not dead!" Disciples at the Sagely City, after the Venerable Master's completion of stillness, he is still the same as he has always been. At a time when I needed it most, he inspired and taught me. He's truly a compassionate Bodhisattva!

Venerable Master, how could death touch you?

I hope this brief article will give some revelations and thoughts to the assembly.

Finally, I wish the fourfold assembly at the Sagely City boundless Dharma joy!

Namo Amitabha Buddha!

Bowing in respect,
Sun Dongbo, disciple of the Buddha
Director of the Ch'an Buddhism and Acupuncture Research Center
Sacramento, California, U.S.A.
October 21, 1995

錢
Money

二戈爭金殺氣高　人人因它犯嘮叨　能會用者超三界　不會用者孽難逃

Two spears contending over gold, the killing energy is high.
For its sake, everyone chatters too much.
Those who know how to use it can transcend the Triple Realm.
Those who don't will have difficulty escaping their evil retributions.

無盡的哀思

MY BOUNDLESS SORROW

劉能建　Liu Nengjian

美國加州萬佛聖城開山祖師宣化上人，於一九七四年二月首次來臺，弘揚佛法，聽眾踴躍，盛況非常。我夫婦因次女瑤仙之推介，得睹慈顏，並蒙上人光臨寒舍，使蓬蓽生輝。且收我夫婦為弟子賜名果莊、果嚴。從此皈依三寶，禮佛參禪。曾敬填「瀟湘夜雨」詞一闋呈閱，以紀其盛；上人命我當場向法會聽眾朗誦，詞曰：

> 人欲橫流，漫天浩劫，眾生孽海沉浮。欲登彼岸乏輕舟，欣際遇，雲開天際，沾雨露，法駕東遊。兼旬夜，宏揚佛法，功德長留。天涯寄跡，夢回午夜，顧影堪憂！自皈依三寶，滋慰心頭。談學養，從頭起步，培智慧，全力潛修。從今後，師恩浩蕩，佛澤被同儔。

自一九七九年，我全家移民來美後，曾居住加州瑜伽鎮達七年之久。上人創辦的萬佛聖城及法界佛教大學等即位於此鎮。余夫婦參禪禮佛，受上人之感化殊深；尤以次女瑤仙與女婿易象乾博士，全家食素，虔誠禮佛，信仰堅定。

上人自一九六二年蒞美弘揚佛法已三十餘年，澤被眾生，廣施教化。在美國、加拿大、臺灣、香港及馬來西亞等地，設立道場二十七處之多。中文之佛教經典經被翻譯成各國文字，廣為流通，對宣揚佛法厥功至偉。上人的弟子，來自世界各國，堪稱有教無類。上人的弟子多次赴中國大陸寺廟訪問，而大陸的僧眾也曾來萬佛聖城共同主持法會，相互交流。上人甚至捐資山東濟寧大學與寶相寺。

The Venerable Master Hua, founder of the Sagely City of Ten Thousand Buddhas in California, U.S.A., came to Taiwan for the first time in February of 1974 to propagate the Buddhadharma, bringing delight to living beings. It was an extremely successful occasion. Through the introduction of Yaoxian, our second daughter, my wife and I were honored to meet the Master and have him visit our humble home. He accepted us as disciples and gave us the names Guozhuang and Guoyan. We took refuge with the Triple Jewel and began worshipping the Buddhas and sitting in meditation. I composed a verse based on the pattern of "Night Rain at the Junction of the Xiao and Xiang Rivers" in memory of the occasion. The Master asked me to read it aloud to the assembly during the Dharma session. The verse goes,

> *Human desires run rampant; calamities fill the skies.*
> *Living beings bob up and down in the sea of iniquity.*
> *I wish to ascend to the other shore, but I lack a boat.*
> *Fortunately, there has been an opening in the clouds.*
> *Moistened by the mist, the Dharma ship travels eastwards.*
> *Propagating the Buddhadharma by day and by night, his merit is eternal.*
> *Dwelling in a remote corner of the world, I would wake up at midnight and worry about my plight!*
> *Yet now, having taken refuge with the Triple Jewel, my heart is comforted.*
> *As for learning, I will begin again from the very first step.*
> *To foster wisdom, I will devote myself to cultivation.*
> *From now onwards, may the Master's vast kindness*
> *And the Buddha's grace aid those of the same mind.*

My whole family immigrated to America in 1979, and we lived in Ukiah, the city near which the Master founded the Sagely City of Ten Thousand Buddhas and Dharma Realm Buddhist University, for seven years. My wife and I meditated and worshipped the Buddhas at the Sagely City, and were deeply influenced by the Master. This was especially because my second daughter and her husband, Dr. Epstein, have raised their family as vegetarians and are sincere and devout Buddhists.

It has been over thirty years since the Master came to America to propagate the Buddhadharma. Living beings have benefited by his kindness as he extensively taught and transformed them. He founded as many as twenty-seven Way-places in such countries as the United States, Canada, Taiwan, Hong Kong, and Malaysia. He directed the translation of the Chinese Buddhist Canon into various languages and then saw to its extensive circulation. This is a monumental contribution to the propagation of the Buddhadharma. The Master's disciples come from all over the world; he taught all without discrimination. The Master's disciples have made many trips to visit the monasteries of mainland China, and Sangha members from mainland China have also come to the Sagely City of Ten Thousand Buddhas to co-host Dharma sessions in exchange. The Master even donated funds to Jining College and Baoxiang Monastery in Shandong Province, China.

上人精通國學，尤善詩詞，他不但是宗教家，且是教育家、文學家，一生豐功偉蹟，值得敬仰與效法。如能再多延歲月，則對人類與世界之貢獻愈大！今聞上人於六月七日下午三時許在洛杉磯圓寂，哀慟之餘，遂將本人所知有關上人事蹟略陳於上，以表無盡的哀思。

The Master had a thorough understanding of Chinese culture, history, and literature. Not only was he a religious leader, he was also an educator and a literati worthy of our respect and emulation. If he could have lived a few more years, his contributions to mankind and the world would be even greater! When I heard the Master had completed the stillness at three o'clock on June 7 in Los Angeles, I was deeply grieved. I have briefly written down what I know of the Master to express my endless grief.

MY COMPASSIONATE TEACHER, THE VENERABLE MASTER

上人——我慈悲的導師

Leong Soo Hoong 梁素芬

After leaving high school, I developed an inclination towards philosophical and spiritual ideals. I read many books written by a world renowned English philosopher, mathematician and author. His clarity of thought, impressive eloquence, oratorical prowess, sensitivity, sincerity and courage inspired me greatly. But, I was also aware of the limitations of our thinking processes and science. Upon reading that philosopher's autobiography, I was profoundly disappointed. Despite his high caliber and rare intellectual skills, he was still a victim of love, emotions, and desire. Like most ordinary men, he too gave in completely to his rash impulses and passion.

In my lifelong search for the ultimate truth and perfection, I have always valued purity above everything else. Thus, when I first read the Venerable Master's biography, I knew that I had found my Teacher! Why? Because I have finally encountered One Pure Heart who will always uphold all his vows and precepts even in this Dharma Ending Age. Through him, my faith in the Buddhadharma has deepened; for the strict exemplary life which he leads constantly brings to life all the most wonderful principles that are found in the Buddhist Sutras in such a moving and powerful manner.

Just as in the *Avatamsaka Sutra*, the long and moving section in Chapter Thirty-nine that explains what a Good and Wise Advisor is like, the Venerable Master is also that way:

> The Good and Wise Advisor is like a kind mother, in that he gives rise to the Buddha's seed. He is like a kind father, in that he vastly benefits... He is like a valiant general, in that he banishes all terror... The Good and Wise Advisor illumines the Dharma Realm... A Good and Wise Advisor nourishes the Bodhisattva's body, just as parents nourish their child.

My mother was the kindest and most understanding lady I ever knew. Her sudden death in 1990 left me with a lingering, intense kind of dull and numb pain inside, and I thought then that I could never feel happiness again. But, during that time, I joined a delegation from Malaysia to the City of Ten Thousand Buddhas. Shr Fu was in the administration office when we arrived, and I was surprised that my heart was filled with joy when I saw the Venerable Master. His presence alone was so comforting and soothing. I remember that when I first saw the Venera-

高中畢業後，我開始對哲學、精神理想感到興趣。我讀了一位著名的英國哲學家、數學家兼作家很多的著作。他清晰的思想，動人的流暢，雄辯的本領，他的敏銳、誠摯，及勇氣對我有很大的啟發作用。可是同時我也明白了科學及一般人思維過程的限制，在讀了這位哲學家的自傳後，我大感失望。雖然他有一般的才華及罕有的智力，他仍不免是愛欲的犧牲者。如普通人一般，他也被率性的衝動、熱情所主宰。

在我一生對無上真理的追求中，總是將「真純」列於一切事物之上。因此在第一次讀到上人的傳記時，我就知道終於找到了我的導師！為什麼呢？因為我遇到了一位真心的人，即使在這末法時代，還是願意持戒，實行他的願力。透過上人，我對佛法的信心加深了，上人以堪為典範的嚴謹生活，將佛經裡奧妙的理論，以有力而生動的方式示範於生活中。

一如長而動人的《華嚴經》第三十九品中，所描述的善知識，上人就是這樣的一位善知識：

> 善知識者。如慈母，出生佛種故。如慈父，廣大利益故。……如勇將，殄除一切怖畏故。……善知識者，照明法界。……善知識者，長菩薩身。譬如父母，養育兒子。

一九九〇年，母親的突然死亡，在我心中留下一種徘徊不去的遲鈍、麻木的痛苦，我以為我永遠快樂不起來了。但是就在那時，我加入了馬來西亞去萬佛城的訪問團。當我們到達時，師父正好在辦公室。我很驚訝地發覺，當我看到師父時，我的心裡充滿了快樂，光是見到師父就能使人感到安慰、舒適。我想起在一九八八年十一月，第一次在馬來西

462

ble Master in November 1988 at the airport in Malaysia, I was overwhelmed with great joy too!

In Chapter One of the *Avatamsaka Sutra*, the text reads,

In the past, the Buddha cultivated an ocean of joy,
Vast, boundless, beyond all measure;
Thus those who see are all delighted.

I will never forget the great compassion and gentleness which the Venerable Master showed to me during my first trip to this Sagely City. My heart and spirit was grieving, bleeding and weeping most badly then, and Shr Fu employed the most powerful and effective means to alleviate my pain and mental anguish, which is: "Gentle-compassion." Shr Fu responded to my suffering like a most perfect, kind and gentle parent. During my first appointment with the Venerable Master at this Sagely City, he said to me, "Being filial to me is the same as being filial to your father."

I used to contemplate frequently on the profound meaning behind the Venerable Master's compassionate words. In Chapter Three of *The Wonderful Dharma Lotus Flower Sutra*, the Buddha said,

The Thus Come One has already left
The Three Realms' burning house behind.
Quietly I dwell at ease,
In forest and field at peace.
And now it is, that the Three Realms,
Entirely belong to me,
And in them all the living beings
Are children of mind.

In his commentary to the above text of the Sutra, the Venerable Master explains: "The Buddha is your transcendental father, a pure, greatly compassionate father. He is pure and undefiled. If you can recognize your father, then in the future you too, can obtain purity and non-defilement, and get rid of all filth. So don't run outside and fail to recognize your own father.."

In the past , I looked at my photograph of Shr Fu and beseeched him to help me be more brave before I went upstairs to sleep alone at night in a house which was filled with strange and vengeful ghosts. That night I dreamt of Shr Fu coming to bless me. Later, when I came to the City of Ten Thousand Buddhas, the Master blessed me again in the same manner in his office...only then did I realize that my earlier dream of the Venerable Master was real. After I returned home from that trip, I continued to sleep upstairs in that old haunted house not because I was brave but, because I could somehow feel Shr Fu's protection.

I am very grateful that the Venerable Master's most precious lectures are recorded and preserved on tapes and printed in books. I deeply treasure the chance I have now of listening to the Venerable Master's taped lectures because he is my most Compassionate, Wise and Selfless Teacher; and I have experienced on so many, many occasions and instances where while the Venerable Master's taped lectures were played during mealtimes or in the evenings,

亞的機場見到師父時，我也是同樣地充滿了快樂。

如《華嚴經》第一品中所說：

佛昔修治歡喜海
廣大無邊不可測
是故見者咸欣樂

我永遠不會忘記，在聖城時，師父對我的大悲大仁。當時我心靈的憂苦、哀傷到了極點，而師父以最有力且有效的方法減去了我的痛苦，那就是「溫柔的慈悲」。對我的傷痛，師父如一位最完美、仁慈、和善的父親。第一次在聖城見師父時，他說：「孝順我，就跟孝順妳父親一樣的。」

我經常思考上人慈語中所含的深意，《妙法蓮華經》（第三品）中佛說：

如來已離，三界火宅
寂然閑居，安處林野
今此三界，皆是我有
其中眾生，悉是吾子

在解釋上述經文時，上人說：「佛，就是我們出世之父，具大慈悲之父。他是清淨無染的，若你能認得自己的父親，那麼你也可以清淨無染，去除一切穢垢。因此不要往外跑，而認不出自己的父親。」

過去，我獨自住在一棟滿是奇怪的、復仇心重的鬼房子裡，晚上在上樓睡覺之前，有一次我看著師父的相片，祈求他的加被，讓我更勇敢。當晚我夢到師父來加持我，稍後當我在萬佛城時，師父在他的辦公室以同樣的方式加持我。只有在那時，我才領悟到，早先師父在夢裡給我的加持是真實的。自萬佛城返家後，我仍然在老鬼屋的樓上獨眠，我不是變得比較勇敢，我只是能感覺到師父在保護著我。

我非常感激師父最寶貴的講經說法，被錄製、保存了下來，並印成書出版。我深深珍惜現在我仍有機會聽到上人說法的錄音。因為他是我最慈悲、最具智慧，且最無我的導師。同時，也因為我有很多很多次的經驗：當上人的錄音帶在午齋

Shr Fu spoke and penetrated right through the heart and root of the problems and tests which I was facing at that time. Whether the Venerable Master is speaking to us live or through his tapes or books, I find that he always dispenses the right medicine at the right time. And so, I find listening to his taped lectures and reading his printed commentaries to be most ALIVE, essential and illuminating.

I believe that like the Buddhas and Great Bodhisattvas, the Venerable Master too has already transcended the limitations of time. Thus, when he speaks, he is also constantly able to move the past to the present and move the future to the present, thereby displaying the miraculous interpenetration of the past, present and future. This is probably why I often find that the Sutra I am reviewing or the Venerable Master's commentary I am reading or listening to on tape fits so remarkably well the situation and circumstances of that period of time. In Chapter Twenty-four of the *Avatamsaka Sutra*, Jeweled Banner Bodhisattva says:

The Thus Come One is apart from discriminations;
He is not of this world and transcends all calculations;
All guiding masters of the three periods of time appear in this way.

In Chapter Twenty-seven on "The Ten Samadhis," the Sutra reads:

How do Bodhisattvas Mahasattvas enter into and emerge from this samadhi? Disciple of the Buddha, Bodhisattvas Mahasattvas enter this samadhi...in an instant, and emerge in different times...Entering in the past, they emerge in the future...Entering in a moment, they emerge in the past, present, and future; entering in True Suchness, they emerge in verbalization.

These two excerpts from the Sutra explains the inconceivable, auspicious, transforming, and miraculous effect which occurs each time the Venerable Master speaks and whenever his taped lectures are played.

In the past, I used to regard all animals as being no different from people. In fact, I often viewed many species of animals as being better, kinder, more honest, and more sincere than most *homo sapiens*. I failed to see the unwholesome subtle effects and gross danger behind my stubborn concepts about animals. By being so fond of animals and by being overly sympathetic towards their plight, I ran the risk of ending up in their realm in some future existence.

During my first trip to this Sagely City, the Venerable Master said one sentence to me which broke my unusually strong attachment to animals. He told me, "Do you have to be so close to them in order to help them?"
I realized then that I had always been excessively moved by the beings of the animal kingdom. Although I am now still concerned about animals, I am no longer extremely attached to them as I was before.

On August 2, 1993, I dreamed that Shr Fu was teaching us. In

或在晚上聽經播放時，師父說的話直接穿透我的心，以及當時我所面臨的問題的根源。不論是上人親自說法，或聽錄音帶，或者看書，我發覺上人總是適時予藥。因此，我覺得聽上人的錄音帶，或是看他開示的書，是最活生生的，也是最實在、最發人深省的。

我相信，同佛菩薩一樣，上人也超越了時間的限制。因此，在他開示時，他能不斷地將過去移到現在，也將未來搬到現在，因而能對過去、現在、未來做一種神奇的詮釋。也許這就是為什麼，我經常發覺在聽師父講經的錄音帶，或看師父講解的經書時，師父所說的總是不可思議地契合當時的情況。《華嚴經》（第二十四品）中，寶幢菩薩說：

如來離分別，非世超諸數，
三世諸導師，出現皆如是。

《華嚴經》（十定品第二十七）中說：

菩薩摩訶薩於此三昧。云何入。云何起。佛子。菩薩摩訶薩於此三昧。……同念入。別時起。……前際入。後際起。……剎那入。三世起。真如入。言說起。

這一段經文解釋了每次上人開示，或放錄音帶時，所發生的不可思議、吉祥而神奇的效果。

過去，我視動物與人無有不同。事實上，我常認為很多種類的動物，比大多數的人類來得友好、善良、誠實，也較有誠意。我沒有看到，在我那固執己見的背後，那種細微的不良影響以及重大的危險性。像我那麼喜歡動物，而且對他們的境遇那麼過份同情，使我未來有投生在畜生道的危險。

在我首次的萬佛城之行中，上人對我說的一句話，打破了我對動物不尋常的強烈執著。上人問我：「妳一定要跟牠們那麼接近，才能幫助牠們嗎？」我當下明白了，我一直被畜生界的眾生所轉。現在，雖然我還是很關懷動物，我已不再像以前那樣地執著。

一九九三年八月二日，我夢到師父在給我們上課。夢裡上人問弟子一些問題，然後他要我用「靜止、平靜、油」等字，來解釋或作文。我想了

464

宣化老和尚追思紀念專集

that dream, the Venerable Master asked his disciples some questions. Then, he called me and asked me to explain or compose something using the words "still, peace and oil." I thought for a while and said to the Venerable Master,

The water is still
And the mind is at peace,
But the oil intrudes.

When I woke up I did not know what the dream meant, but during that time I was reviewing the *Amitabha Sutra* again. That morning I reached the part where Shr Fu talked about Maitreya Bodhisattva. When I read that Maitreya Bodhisattva "eats his food plain, without soy sauce, hot sauce, or sesame oil. It doesn't taste like much, but it fills his stomach," I suddenly realized the meaning of my dream. After I had lived in the Sagely City for a while, I developed a greed for butter, and very often, half of my meal consisted of many slices of bread spread with a rich layer of butter. So, one can imagine how much "fat" I was ingesting every day. I knew that butter is virtually all fat and that my high consumption of it was detrimental to my health, yet I could not give it up. The Venerable Master knew in advance the verse I would compose, and he also knew in advance that the meaning of the dream would become evident to me when I continued to read his commentary to the *Amitabha Sutra* that morning. The Venerable Master's incredible power filled me with astonishing delight, gratitude, shame, and deep reverence. Hence, from then on, I never ate bread with butter again. After I altered my diet, I felt a kind of inner calm and peace. "The water is still." Our basic nature is still and unmoving. "And the mind is at peace." When there are no ripples or waves, our mind will naturally be at peace. "But the oil intrudes." But my greed for butter or oily food can cause the water to swell or surge up. When the sea becomes stormy, I can even get drowned in its tidal wave.

The Venerable Master has made a vow that wherever he goes, he will establish the Proper Dharma Age and not allow there to be a Dharma Ending Age. I believe this is one of the reasons the first of the Venerable Master's Six Great Guiding Principles is "No Fighting!" It is said that during the Dharma Ending Age, people will be strong in fighting. We are living in the age of ethical infants and nuclear giants. Thus, if we wish to transform the Dharma Ending Age into the Orthodox Dharma Age, we have to constantly make a stringent and courageous effort to always be tolerant, kind, gentle, patient and forgiving towards all living beings. We cannot harbor hatred, anger or jealousy towards anyone. Otherwise, how could we ever repay even a minute fraction of our Compassionate Teacher's Great Kindness? Chapter Twenty-five of the *Avatamsaka Sutra* describes aptly the Venerable Master's far reaching, vast vows and selfless spirit. Part of the text reads:

I should accept all sufferings for the sake of all living beings, and enable them to escape from the abyss of immeasurable woes of birth and death. I should accept all sufferings for the sake of living beings in all worlds, in all states of misery, till the end of time, and still always cultivate foundations of goodness for the sake of all beings. Why? I would rather take all

一想，就對上人說：「水是靜止的，心是平靜的，而油在搗蛋。」

醒來後，我不明白夢的意思。可是當時我正在研讀《佛說阿彌陀經淺釋》。那天早上當我讀到上人談到彌勒菩薩：「⋯⋯吃沒有油鹽的淡飯，不加香油、醬油、糖、醋等調味料，淡而無味的食物，只要能把肚子填飽⋯⋯」時，我突然明白了我的夢境。我住進萬佛城後，養成了對奶油的貪執，經常我一餐裡，有一半以上是很多片塗了厚厚一層奶油的土司麵包，因此你可以想像我每天吃進多少「油脂」。我知道奶油幾乎全是油脂，而且大量地進食有害於健康，可是我就是放不下。上人事先知道我能作那首偈頌，也知道我那天早上，在看他講解的《阿彌陀經》時明白了夢的意義。上人不可思議的能力，讓我充滿了驚奇的喜悅，羞愧的感激，和深深的敬仰。從那時起，我就不吃塗奶油的麵包了。改變飲食後，我感覺到一種內在的平靜。「水是靜止的」，我們的本性是寂然不動的。「心是平靜的」，我們的心在沒有波浪時，自然是平靜的。「而油在搗蛋」，可是我對奶油，或油質食物的貪著，使水翻騰。在起「暴風雨」的海裡，我可能會淹死在它的浪潮裡。

上人發過一個願，就是不論他到哪兒，都要有正法，他不允許末法存在。我相信這就是為什麼六大宗旨裡，第一個就是「不爭」的原因之一。據說在末法時期是「鬥爭堅固」，我們是活在「核子巨人」、「道德嬰兒」的時代。因此，如果我們想將末法轉變成正法，我們一定要勇猛精進地去寬容、諒解一切眾生，對一切眾生都要溫和、有慈心、耐心，我們不能對任何人起瞋心或嫉妒心。不然我們如何能報答我們導師的大慈悲於萬一。《華嚴經》（第二十五品）適當地描述了上人偉大的弘願和他無我的精神：

⋯⋯我當普為一切眾生備受眾苦，令其得出無量生死大壑。我當普為一切眾生，於一切世界，一切惡趣中，盡未來劫受一切苦，然常為眾生勤修善根。何以故？我寧獨受如是眾生苦，不令眾生墮於地獄。當於彼地獄、畜生、閻羅王等險難之處，以身為質，救贖一切惡道眾生，令得解脫⋯⋯。

this suffering upon myself than to allow living beings to fall into the hells. I should be a hostage in those perilous places: hells, animal realms, the places of King Yama, and so on; as a ransom to rescue all living beings in states of woe and enable them to gain liberation.

Even now, the Venerable Master is still turning the Dharma Wheel. In Chapter Twelve of the *Avatamsaka Sutra* the text reads:

> *In the cases of those with greed, hatred, and stupidity,*
> *The raging fires of these afflictions always blazing,*
> *The Bodhisattvas manifest aging, sickness, and death for them,*
> *To cause those living beings to all be tamed.*

The Venerable Master has manifested passing away in this manner because:

a. He wishes to teach and remind us about impermanence and about the extreme urgency in cultivating hard to end birth and death. A verse of exhortation by the Venerable Master says,

> *In every thought do not forget the pain of birth and death.*
> *With all your heart seek to escape the rim*
>   *of the turning wheel.*
> *Smash to pieces empty space; comprehend the Buddha nature.*
> *Understand, and then the cloud of delusion will fall away;*
> *You'll see the basic nature.*

b. He wants us to cultivate ultimate independence.
c. He wants us to break off our attachment to our false body and self and to beautiful forms, for if we can break through all marks of form, we can arrive at the level of liberation.
d. He wants us to cultivate humility, compassion and patience vigorously.

All the living beings in the nine realms, all the Bodhisattvas, Those Enlightened to Conditions, Sound-Hearers, Gods, Asuras, people, animals, hungry ghosts and beings in the hells are included in the Venerable Master's most compassionate vows. In his commentary to Chapter Fifteen of the *Avatamsaka Sutra*, the Venerable Master says:

> I have said to you all, every one of you: If you see my face, or hear my name, or take refuge with me, and if you have faith, I have vowed that you will all become Buddhas before I do. As long as one of you has not become a Buddha, I will wait for you...

The Venerable Master remains in this Saha world, waiting for all his disciples and living beings to return home to the Land of Limitless Light and Ultimate Bliss.

July 3, 1995

即使現在，上人還是在轉法輪，《華嚴經》（第十二品）中說：

> 或有貪欲瞋恚癡
> 煩惱猛火常熾然
> 菩薩爲觀老病死
> 令彼眾生悉調伏

上人以這種方式示現入滅是因為：
（一）要向我們顯示人生的無常，及了脫生死的緊迫性。上人在一首勸導的偈頌中說：

> 念念莫忘生死苦
> 心心想脫輪迴圈
> 虛空粉碎明佛性
> 通體脫落見本源

（二）要我們修行至究竟的獨立。
（三）要破我們對假身、自我及色相的執著。因為如果我們能破除一切色相，就能得到解脫。
（四）要弟子們謙遜、慈悲、忍耐。

所有九法界的眾生：菩薩、聲聞、緣覺、天、人、阿修羅、畜生、餓鬼及地獄的眾生，都包括在上人的悲願裡。上人在《華嚴經》（第十五品）的解釋中說：

> 我對你們每一個人說，若見我面、若聞我名、若皈依我者，如果你有信心，我願你們都成佛後我才成佛，只要你們有一人未成佛也會等你的……。

上人留在這娑婆世界等著所有他的弟子，及一切眾生返回到究竟快樂的無量光淨土。

一九九五年七月三日

觀世音菩薩讓我重獲光明

GUANSHIYIN BODHISATTVA HELPED ME TO SEE THE LIGHT AGAIN

黃傳濟　一九九五年三月十九日
Huang Chuanji　March 19, 1995

一九九三年四月中旬，我的左眼突然發紅、怕光且隱隱作痛，起初認為是結膜炎，而不以為然。一星期以後，仍不見好轉，開始緊張起來了。自己翻翻醫書，加上以前有發作性的鵝口瘡（口腔黏膜潰瘍）及外陰部潰瘍、自發性毛囊炎等病史，就自我診斷為貝西氏病（見註一）。五月中旬，經省立台北醫院眼科主任診斷，也認為符合貝西氏病的症狀。

類固醇眼藥水是治療此病的首選藥，但這類藥的副作用會引起眼壓增高，進而引起青光眼。到了七月中旬，眼睛和頭痛得更加厲害，不點眼藥不行。眼藥的劑量也愈來愈大。真是痛不欲生，根本無法正常工作。七月底，經親戚介紹，到臺灣中壢找一位陳大師，他家裡供奉著觀世音菩薩、關聖帝君，能替人治病。他也認為此病預後不好，終究會失明。原本他想給我，由觀世音菩薩傳給他家的秘方，但一時就是找不到，於是開了一些符咒叫我化水洗眼睛。並囑每天吃用黑豆、紅豆、綠豆、黃豆、薏仁及糙米混合煮成的飯，早晚喝綠豆沖泡的水。

回到家裡，我想，沒有觀世音菩薩的處方，大約沒希望了。於是就跪在地上誠懇祈求觀世音菩薩能救救我的眼睛，一直念著南無觀世音菩薩的聖號。第二天，陳大師打電話來說，觀世音菩薩托夢給他開了處方：莫簹（見註二）、豆腐、黑糖加水煮，連續服用五天。就這樣，眼睛的腫脹漸漸消退，也不疼痛了。一直持續念聖號一個月，及吃豆米混合的飲食，眼壓也慢慢降下來，我的眼病終於痊癒了。

一次，當我很專心念觀世音菩薩的聖號時，突然耳朵裡也出現觀世音菩薩聖號，真是不可思議。感謝觀世音菩薩及陳大師的大慈大悲，讓我重獲光明。

在臺灣法界佛教印經會，看到師父上人講解

In mid-April of 1993, my left eye became reddened, was afraid of the light, and occasionally hurt. At first I thought it was conjunctivitis and didn't take it seriously. When it still hadn't gotten better after a week, I began to feel worried. I looked through the medical books, and with my past case history of thrush's mouth sore (ulcer of the mouth), ulcers of the male organ, and folliculitis, I diagnosed myself as having Bahcet's disease [see Note 1]. In the middle of May, the director of the opthamology department at the Taipei County Hospital examined me and agreed with my diagnosis.

Corticosteroid eyedrops are the best medicine for this disease, but they have a side effect of increased eye pressure and then glaucoma. In mid-July, my eye and head were hurting even more, and I couldn't survive without the eyedrops. The dosage I needed kept increasing. I was under unbearable pain and had no way to work normally. At the end of July, a relative introduced me to a Master Chen in Zhongli, Taiwan. In his house, he had an altar for Guanshiyin Bodhisattva and Lord Guan, and he could heal people. He agreed that the prognosis was not good in my case, and that I would eventually lose my sight. At first he wanted to give me a secret formula that Guanshiyin Bodhisattva had given his family, but he couldn't find it, so he gave me a charm and told me to burn it, sprinkle the ashes in water, and use the water to wash my eye. He also instructed me to eat a meal of black beans, red beans, green beans, soybeans, seeds of Job's tears, and brown rice mixed and cooked together, and to drink water in which green beans have been boiled every morning and evening.

When I returned home, I thought: If I don't have Guanshiyin Bodhisattva's prescription, I probably don't have any hope. Then I knelt and prayed sincerely for Guanshiyin Bodhisattva to heal my eye. I kept reciting "Namo Guanshiyin Bodhisattva." The next day, Master Chen called and said Guanshiyin Bodhisattva had appeared in his dream and given a prescription: boil *modang* [see Note 2], tofu, and brown sugar in water, and administer for five days. When I did this, the swelling and pain of my eye gradually subsided. I continued reciting the Bodhisattva's name and eating the bean-and-rice formula for another month. The pressure in my eye gradually decreased and my eye healed completely.

One time when I was reciting Guanshiyin Bodhisattva's name with great concentration, I suddenly heard the sound of the name in my ear. It was inconceivable. I thank Guanshiyin Bodhisattva and Master Chen for their great compassion in allowing me to recover my sight.

When I read the Venerable Master's explanations of the Sutras and instructional talks from the Dharma Realm Buddhist Books Distribution Association in Taiwan, I came to realize how frightening karmic obstacles and retribution can be and how important it is to cultivate.

的經書及開示錄，使我了解到業障果報的可怕及修行的重要性。

病中那種可怕的折磨，讓我刻骨銘心。一場大病下來，從此不敢沾酒肉，所有的壞習氣毛病都除掉了。診治病人時，也更能體會病人的痛苦，將心比心地幫助別人。遇到一些業障比較重的病人，我就鼓勵他們學習佛法，告訴他們多禮佛、拜懺，才能消除業障；不要吃肉，多放生，病才會很快好起來。

在觀世音菩薩誕辰之日，寫下我的眼疾治療經過，讓眼科醫師們知道這個事實。如是因，如是果，希望和我患同樣眼疾的人，看了這篇文章以後，趕快效法，稱誦觀世音菩薩的聖號。

當我讀誦《普門品》時，誦到：

眾生被困厄，無量苦逼身，
觀音妙智力，能救世間苦。
具足神通力，廣修智方便，
十方諸國土，無剎不現身。
種種諸惡趣，地獄鬼畜生，
生老病死苦，以漸悉令滅。
真觀清靜觀，廣大智慧觀，
悲觀及慈觀，常願常瞻仰。
無垢清淨光，慧日破諸暗，
能伏災風火，普明照世間。

時，不禁潸然淚下。感謝師父開我智慧，我願追隨師父上人，努力修行，盡形壽護持三寶，未來生生世世護持佛法。

唵，嘛尼唄彌吽

註一：急性色素層膜炎（貝西氏病）：一種發病原因不明的，以反覆性發炎為特徵的，慢性的全身系統性疾病。發病者多為年青男性。

公元二○○年左右，在中國古代醫書中，就已經記載了此病——狐惑「症」（白塞氏綜合症）。公元一九○八年，由土耳其皮膚科醫生 Bahcet 首次報導這種疾病，因而命

The fearful ordeal of being sick will forever be impressed in my mind. After that serious illness, I never touched alcohol or meat again and also got rid of all bad habits. When I treat patients, I am better able to understand their suffering and to put myself in their shoes when I help them. When I encounter people with particularly severe karmic obstacles, I encourage them to study the Buddhadharma, worship the Buddhas and bow in repentance more often to eradicate their karmic obstacles. I tell them that in order to recover rapidly, they should liberate life more and not eat meat.

On Guanshiyin Bodhisattva's birthday, I have written down this account of how I was cured of my eye ailment so that more scientists can know about it. As is the cause, so will be the effect. I hope that when people who have the same disease as I did see this article, they will follow my example and recite the holy name of Guanshiyin Bodhisattva.

When I was reciting the Universal Door Chapter, I burst into tears when I recited to the part:

Living beings are best with hardships
And oppressed by limitless sufferings.
The power of Guanyin's wondrous wisdom
Can rescue the world from suffering.

Complete with the power of spiritual penetrations,
Vastly cultivating wisdom and expedient means,
Going throughout countries in the ten directions,
He manifests everywhere in all places.

The various evil destinies,
Those of the hells, ghosts, and animals,
And the pain of birth, old age, sickness, and death
Are all gradually wiped away.

True Contemplator, Pure Contemplator,
Contemplator with Vast, Great Wisdom,
Compassionate Contemplator, Kind Contemplator,
Constant are your vows, constant is our respect!

Undefiled pure light,
The sun of wisdom that breaks through the darkness
Is able to quell calamities of wind and fire
As it shines on all worlds.

I thank the Venerable Master for opening my wisdom, and I vow to follow the Venerable Master in diligent cultivation, support the Triple Jewel to the end of my life, and support the Buddhadharma in all my future lives.

Om. Mani Padme Hum.

Note 1: Acute Uveitis (Bahcet's Disease or Compatible with Bahcet's Disease): This disease is of unclear origin and is characterized by recurrent infections that slowly spread throughout the entire body. Most people with this disease are young males.

Records of this disease can be found in Chinese medical texts as early as A.D. 200, under the name of "fox delusion sickness." The Turkish doctor Bahcet reported this disease for the first time in 1908, and so it was named after him. The disease attacks the iris. A series of recurrent infections leads to retinodialysis and atrophy of the eyeball.

名。其病變部位在虹膜睫狀體。經反覆發炎後，導致網膜剝離及眼球的嚴重萎縮。

註二：莫簹，因原稿潦草無法辨認，姑且使用此二字。

（編按：作者係小兒科醫生。）

Note 2: Because the original manuscript was written in cursive, the editors could not decipher these two characters and temporarily used the characters *modang* to represent them.

[Editor's Note: The author is a pediatrician.]

恩師是照耀我的明燈

OUR BENEVOLENT TEACHER
IS THE BRIGHT LAMP THAT SHINES ON ME

釋恆年
Shi Hengnian

日子過得真快，匆匆地就過去了，恩師上人圓寂已一個月了。在這期間，每每思念恩師的恩德和教誨，及冥冥之中的指示，想到從此失去依靠，內心就感到徬徨。在我人生最後一站裡，恩師的指示和恩師的六大宗旨，是照耀我的明燈，改變了我的人生觀。修持一切善業，往菩提路上走，才能成就，我要永記心頭。

嘆！人生苦短，何其匆匆！聖人已故。恩師所留下來最珍貴的是，恩師的精神及捨己為人的種種德行。上人領導一大群佛弟子們，盡心綿力，用盡心血，開示教導，期望各弟子能有所成就，紹隆佛種，宣揚佛法，教導一切眾生，離苦得樂。這是恩師的願望，不為自求，而為九法界所有眾生擔當一切的苦難。

恩師的豐功偉績無可限量，恩師的志願是願一切大眾成佛，然後才成佛。

Time passes quickly; it rushes by. It's already been a month since our benevolent teacher, the Venerable Master, entered Nirvana. Every time I think about our benevolent teacher's kindness, virtue, and teachings—his invisible instructions, I find that my place of reliance is gone, and my heart feels at a loss. In the final stage of my life, our benevolent teacher's instructions and his Six Guiding Principles have been a bright light for me: they have changed my view on human life. I will always remember that the way to reach perfection is to cultivate good karma of all kinds and to walk the path to Bodhi.

Ah! Human life is painfully brief. How fast it passes! The Sage is already gone. The most precious things that our benevolent teacher left behind were his spirit and his virtue in renouncing himself for the sake of others. He led a group of Buddhist disciples, exerting his mental and physical strength, using all his heart and soul to instruct and guide them, hoping that each and every disciple would become accomplished; perpetuate the lineage of the Buddhas; propagate the Buddhas' Dharma; and teach and transform all living beings so that they will leave suffering and attain bliss. This is the wish of our benevolent teacher, who never sought for himself, but bore sufferings and difficulties on behalf of all living beings in the nine Dharma realms.

Our benevolent teacher's magnificent accomplishments are limitless, and his vow is that he will not become a Buddha until all living beings have become Buddhas.

LIKE A THUNDERSTORM, A MOUNTAIN, OR AN OCEAN

如電，如山，如海

Elizabeth Babcock (Guo Zai)　果在

Now that we no longer have the physical presence of the Master to lean on, it may become clear what it means to have had such a teacher. Rare as it is to encounter the Dharma in this world, it is rarer still to encounter a great teacher like him.

After I heard the news of his passing, I thought of the gatha spoken by Shakyamuni Buddha:

Those who by my form did see me,
　and those who followed me by voice,
Wrong the efforts they engaged in,
　me those people will not see.
By the Dharma should one see
　the Buddha...

Although the Master advised his disciples on their problems and intervened in their disagreements, this was mere expediency. His great sacrifices were made in order to awaken beings to their danger in the Saha world, just as did the kind father in the *Lotus Sutra* who used playthings to tempt his children to leave the burning house.

His immense labor throughout his life on behalf of the Dharma is awesome to contemplate. In fact, if I had to describe the Master in one word, "awesome" would be that word. Meeting him seems the only important event in my life.

At fourteen or so I bought a copy of *The Teachings of the Compassionate Buddha*. After reading these excerpts from the Sutras, I decided I would go to Asia someday and devote my life to the study of these teachings, which were the first explanations of existence that made sense to me. Later I met a student of Chinese literature, the future Guo Jan, who was studying Buddhism at the University of Washington with Edward Conze, the distinguished Prajnaparamita scholar. When I went there, I attended his lectures and began to acquire an intellectual grasp of Buddhist doctrine, but was unable even to stop eating meat, still less consider giving up other bad habits.

In the summer of 1969, I heard about the *Shurangama Sutra* session. A friend got a postcard which described the Master playfully chasing the tiny daughter of a student around the

現在我們不再有上人的色身可以依靠了。這樣的話，或許對有這樣的一位老師所代表的意義，理解得更深刻。在這世上能遇到佛法，是稀有難得的；能遇到像他這樣的一位老師，更是稀有難得。在聽到他圓寂的消息後，我想到釋迦牟尼佛所說的偈頌：

若以色見我，以音聲求我，
是人行邪道，不能見如來。
若見諸相非相，即見如來。

雖然，上人在弟子有問題時給與忠告，在弟子不和時給予調停，這也只是權宜方便。他所做的最大犧牲，是為了要使眾生在娑婆世界的危險中覺醒。就像《法華經》中的慈父，用玩具將孩子們引誘出火宅。

為了佛法，他窮盡一生所做的巨大付出，既令人敬畏，又使人沉思。假如要我以幾個字來形容上人的話，那就是「凜然敬畏」。能遇見他，可說是我生命中最重要的事。

在十四歲左右，我買了一本書叫《慈悲佛陀的教導》。在讀完這些來自經中的擷語之後，這是第一個講「存在」，而讓我覺得有道理的。我就決定將來有一天要去亞洲，並且我將奉獻一生去研究這些教導。之後，我遇到一個學中國文學的學生，也就是後來的果彰，他在華盛頓大學跟一位傑出的智慧學者Edward Conze學佛學。我去那兒聽他演講，並且開始理解到佛學理論上中知性。但我仍然還是吃肉，也不太願意改掉其他的一些壞毛病。

在一九六九年夏天，我聽說有「楞嚴經研習會」，一個朋友收到一張明信片，上面描寫上人和一位學生的小女兒，繞著寺追著玩。那年秋天，我親自去看了一看，我根本不知道我能否接受這種嚴肅的坐禪、唱誦、說法的生活、及遵守佛教的戒律。

temple. In the fall I went to see for myself, far from sure I was ready to face the heavy regime of sitting meditation, recitation, and lectures.

The Master was not remotely like anyone I had encountered previously. He seemed less like a human being than a thunderstorm, a mountain, or an ocean, but an ocean which talked to you as a kindly uncle might talk to a small child.

Before lecture each evening, the Master would write out on newsprint twenty-four characters of the *Shurangama Sutra* and explain them as a Chinese lesson. Afterwards, some students would copy them with brush and ink. Occasionally the Master would look at our work and mark a few characters which were better than the rest. My copies were very weak, but I was fascinated by the beautiful black strokes on the creamy paper. Probably the Master encouraged my attempts to copy his calligraphy because it helped improve my concentration, which was deplorable.

One day, his writing seemed not especially good and I found my mind wandering as he wrote. Noticing this, I recalled my attention to the paper. It seemed as though the brush began to form characters of exceptional power and grace.

Sometimes greeting me he would teasingly ask, "Ni zai bu zai?" (Are you there or not?), making a pun on my Dharma name, which referred to my absent-mindedness. It was somewhat like the playfulness of a huge tiger, a tiger which has dedicated its teeth and claws to the destruction of ignorance and evil, instead of the devouring of tender prey.

Sometimes the Master made me think of a deep mirror, not like the ordinary kind which only shows the surface of things, but one which reflects inner reality. The presence of the Master was intensely disturbing to my self-esteem. I looked into that reflecting pool and saw pettiness, confusion, and weakness. I saw no purpose, nothing solid, nothing to be proud of. But to sit cross-legged listening to his voice roll out like thunder across the lecture hall was truly blissful.

Like so many of my generation, I have sought freedom above all. Like most, I mistakenly thought freedom meant doing whatever I wanted, and not being ordered around. Yet what enslaves us more than our own desires? No one ignores the commands of birth and death. The suffering in the world is difficult to contemplate, so infinite, so appalling.

The question remains: *Who* is suffering? Ask yourself, "*Who* is not free?"

上人一點都不像我以前所遇到的人，跟其他人比起來，他似乎更像暴風，一座高山，一個大海；一個會跟你說話的大海，就像一個叔叔對孩子說話一樣。

在每天下午開示之前，上人會在報紙上寫出，並解釋《楞嚴經》中的二十四個字作為中文課。然後，一些學生會用毛筆臨摹。偶爾，上人會看我們的作品，並將寫的比較好的字做上記號。我寫的很差，但那乳白色紙上美麗的黑色筆畫，總是深深吸引著我。上人鼓勵我臨摹他的書法，可能是因為它能幫助我、改進我那糟糕的注意力。

一天，上人並沒有寫得特別好，當他寫時，我發現我也心不在焉的。一注意到這點，我就將注意力收回到紙上。那毛筆寫出來的字好像也特別有力和優雅。

有時和我打招呼，上人會開玩笑的說：「你在不在啊？」一語雙關的提及我的法名，指我的心不在焉。

有時，上人令我想到一面鏡子，不是照出表面事物的那種一般的鏡子。而是可以反照內在實體的一種鏡子。上人的出現，會使我的自大心理減少到最小。看入那反照的池中，我見到渺小、迷惑、和懦弱。我沒有目標，沒有一樣是堅固的，沒有值得驕傲的。但是在講堂中盤腿而坐，聽著上人如雷灌耳的聲音，著實是很幸福的一件事。

像我們這一代的許多人一樣，我也極力追尋過自由。並錯誤地認為：自由，就是不必守規矩地做我想要做的事。然而，奴役著我們的，不外乎是我們自身的欲望，不是嗎？沒有人能擺脫生死的控制，這世界的痛苦是如此的不可想像，如此的令人不寒而慄。

問題仍在於，受苦的是誰？問問你自己：不自由的是誰？

GRATEFUL FOR THE MASTER'S GUIDANCE IN MY DREAM

夢中示教感慈恩

Chia Mai Choo   October 4, 1995
謝美珠（譯音）一九九五年十月四日

I first heard about the remarkable Venerable Master Hua through a friend who introduced me the *Wonderful Lotus Sutra*. I was thoroughly overjoyed and fascinated with Buddhism after I completed the first volume. Since then, reading the sutras has become a daily routine.

Over the years, I have always venerated the Venerable Master for his bitter cultivation, vast compassion, and strict teachings. His Eighteen Great Vows convinced me that he truly had the heart of a Bodhisattva. Always forgetting himself (even in poor health), he tirelessly propagated the Buddhadharma, performed boundless and magnanimous Bodhisattva conducts to save all living beings. His sudden Completion of Stillness was a shock and grief to me.

The Venerable Master is my Greatest Wise Knowing Adviser. His compassionate words and guidance in my dream when I was deeply troubled led me to admire and respect him even more; hence my strong faith in Buddhism. My greatest regret is that I have not been able to set foot in the City of Ten Thousand Buddhas to pay homage to the Venerable Master, as that has always been my long-held wish. I must therefore strive to diligently cultivate according to Master's teachings and vow to achieve rebirth in Buddha's Pure Land of Ultimate Bliss to repay his kindness.

I always remind myself of what the Master has continually taught: Filiality is the foremost of the ten thousand virtues and the foundation of all cultivation; the six principles of the City of Ten Thousand Buddhas—not contending, not being greedy, not seeking, not being selfish, not asking for personal benefits, and not lying.

I earnestly hope that the publication *In Memory of the Venerable Master Hsuan Hua* will be a success and, together with all the records of his unceasing compassionate conducts and series of Dharma talks, will eventually be able to reach people all over the world, enabling all living beings to bring forth their Bodhi mind and thus contributing to world peace.

Finally, most importantly, I would also like to express my heartfelt appreciation to all members of the Editorial Board of the Buddhist Text Translation Society for the meritorious task of translating the Venerable Master's Dharma teachings into the world's languages and thus bringing inconceivable benefits to all living beings.

由一位朋友那兒，我第一次聽聞到上人的盛名，這位朋友也介紹我《妙法蓮華經》。看完那部經的第一冊時，我真是大喜過望。從那以後，看經成為我每天必做之事。

多年來我非常欽佩上人所行之苦行，和他的大悲心與嚴格教導。上人的十八大願，讓我深深相信上人真正是有菩薩心腸。即使在健康不良的情況下，上人仍是不顧自身孜孜不倦地弘揚佛法，廣行菩薩道，救度眾生。上人突然地離去，我很震驚，也深感悲痛。

上人是我最大的善知識。在我最困難時，上人在夢中安慰我，給我指引，更加深了我對上人的仰慕與對佛教的信心。我最感遺憾的是未能親自到萬佛聖城，向上人頂禮，這一直是我長久以來的心願。我現在只有依上人的教誨精進修行，發願往生西方淨土，來報答上人的恩惠。

上人經常教導我們「百善孝為先」，還有萬佛城的六大宗旨：不爭，不貪，不求，不自私，不自利及不打妄語，是一切修行的基礎，這是我應該永遠銘記於心的。

我由衷地希望「上人追思紀念專集」能夠順利出版。也願上人無盡的慈悲行跡，與上人開示都能陸續出版，傳送給世界各地的人，使所有眾生都發菩提心，並增進世界之和平。

最後很重要的一點，佛經翻譯委員會將上人的教化開示，翻譯成世界各國語言，帶給所有眾生想像不到的利益，實在是功德無量。我願意在這裡向該委員會的編輯委員們，表示我由衷的感謝。

我不做生意！

I Don't Do Business!

釋恆雲　Shi Hengyun

「這種講條件的，我不要！」越洋電話傳來師父上人斬釘截鐵的聲音。「我不做生意，我給人治病，病好是他自己的事，與我無關！！」數年前有位居士，因見上人在西方弘法，困苦艱難，故要我轉達上人：臺灣有位富比王永慶的大企業家，他的太太患眼疾，醫藥無策。若上人能醫好她的眼疾，那麼這位居士，可鼓舞此企業家護持上人。而上人的回答，只是讓作弟子的更肯定，也更慶幸，能常隨這麼一位清淨無染的善知識修行。

上人一生以入世的精神，行無為之事，所行所作都是無相無罣礙的。老人家做什麼都是沒有目的的，不講條件，不做生意，給末法的佛教，帶來一股清流。以上人的能力，若真要作生意，可以成為企業之王，也可以富可敵國，而他不這麼做。上人身貧道不貧，世間上的財物，對上人來說，如浮雲一樣。

他要給眾生的是無盡功德法財。上人講真話，不怕得罪人，不怕斷了財源，不怕沒有供養，為什麼？老人家說：「我們應該把正確的道理帶給人。」身為一名出家人，這是一個重要的理念，秉持這種正確的知見，才不會以盲引盲，貽誤眾生。在上人無量無邊的悲心中，一切都是「但願眾生得離苦，不為自己求安樂。」

上人的心中，沒有名聞利養，沒有自己，堅持真理，但有利於眾生，無不行之。上人說：「若我有一絲頭髮那麼細的自私心，寧可下地獄。」眾生有難、有病，上人捨命都要救度他們，代眾生受苦，自己有病，卻置之不顧：「我不會幫助自己的。」

今年（一九九五年）二月八日，有幸見到恩師。其時老人家的身體非常地瘦弱，臉上

"I don't want anything that's got conditions tied to it!" The Venerable Master's firm voice came over the long distance wire. "I don't do business. When I cure someone's illness, if they get well, that's their business. It has nothing to do with me!" A few years ago, a layperson, upon observing how difficult it was for the Master to propagate the Dharma in the West, wanted me to tell the Master that the wife of a businessman named Wong Yongqing had an incurable eye illness and that if the Master would cure the wife's illness, that the layperson would encourage the businessman to support the Master. However, the Venerable Master's answer reassured this disciple and made her feel even more fortunate to be able to always follow such a pure and undefiled Good and Wise Advisor to cultivate.

His entire life, the Venerable Master used effort in the mundane world to do things in an unconditioned way. Everything he did was without appearances and without hindrance. The Elder Master never had a motive in what he did. He didn't make deals and he didn't do business. He brought a cool breeze into the Dharma-ending Age. Based on the Venerable Master's ability, if he did business he could be a magnate and amass more than the national wealth, but he didn't want to. Although he was materially poor, spiritually he was not. As far as the Venerable Master was concerned, worldly wealth was like a floating cloud. He preferred to give all living beings the infinite merit and virtue of Dharma wealth. The Venerable Master spoke the truth, was not afraid of offending people, did not fear cutting off financial resources, and was not afraid of there being no offerings. Why? The Elder Master said: "We should give people proper principles." As left-home people, this is a very important principle and so we should hold to proper knowledge and views. In that way we won't be like the blind leading the blind, misleading living beings. In the Venerable Master's limitless, boundless compassionate mind, everything is done "only with the hope that all living beings will leave suffering." He never sought peace and happiness for himself.

In the Venerable Master's mind, there's no thought of fame, profit or offerings. He has no self. Holding to true principle, there's nothing he won't do to benefit living beings. The Venerable Master said, "If I were to have even a hair's worth of selfishness, I would willingly fall into the hells." When beings have difficulties or illnesses, the Venerable Master will give up his life to save them; he will suffer on behalf of living beings, but will never take care of himself when he is sick. "I won't help myself."

On February 8 of this year I had the good fortune of being able to see our kind teacher. At that time one of the Master's hands and one of his feet were small and thin. But his face was full of kindness; his eyes were bright; his energy was stable and his spirit steady. His wisdom was astute and his intelligence keen—just as usual. It's hard to imagine how a person's physical and mental condition could be so different. During the Venerable Master's patient instructions on that day, he said: "You don't know that during the war between Iran and Iraq, although I was sick, I

卻慈光靄靄，兩眼炯炯有神，氣定神閒，聰明睿智，一如平常。你很難想像一個病人怎麼會身首差異這麼大？那一天，上人諄諄教誡時提到：「你們都不知道，兩伊戰爭時，我雖然有病，也在那戰爭中救人。」「是上人精神去？」「是真打戰仗啊！在那軍隊中間，到處救人哪！那時某某跟在我後面，我叫她不要跟，她還哭哭啼啼地跟，她不夠功力，會犧牲的。」

數年來，弟子所見的大都是一位現病相的上人，有時候也難免嘀咕著，親自聆聽上人教誨的機會越來越少了。哪知道上人正代眾生受苦呢？上人圓寂消息一傳來，一位居士即泣不成聲的說，她夢到一位和上人是同參道友的菩薩說：「妳的師父扛眾生業太重了，他要走了。」

凡夫的眼光有限，我們見不到超越時空的事。但一生弘揚楞嚴大法的上人，在解釋〈楞嚴咒〉時，清清楚楚的告訴我們，每一種病後面都有一個鬼。十年前，家父恆維師患有脊髓骨癌，上人告訴弟子說：「叫他到萬佛聖城來，慢慢他就會好了。」後來果真好了，又多活了十年，臨終現瑞相生西。以前不明白為什麼恆維師到上人身邊後會好，現在恍然大悟，原來上人把他身上的病鬼帶走了。同樣的，或是疾病，或是災難，背後都有一種陰的力量。我們常常要上人加持，消業障，那知道上人要代我們受多少苦啊！

上人在默默中所幫助的眾生，更不知道有多少。有一個家庭，年年都要發生凶事，直到上人回臺弘法，母女倆去參加法會，因參加法會的人太多，連到上人面前頂禮的機會都沒有，但回來後家庭就平安無事了，他們對上人的感恩真是無以復加。諸如此類，大至平息國家民族的災劫戰爭，小至去除家庭個人的危難疾病，上人所行所做，真不知道有多少？從不居功，也很少讓人知道。

如今上人走了，我們每一個人是不是都應該反觀自省，到底我們給上人添了多少麻煩？在我們不勤修戒定慧，息滅貪瞋癡，放逸任性時，又讓上人扛多少業呢？

was there at the battle helping people."

"Did the Venerable Master's spirit go there?"

"It was a real war! In the midst of the troops, I went about saving people. At that time so-and-so was following me. I told her not to follow. She was crying and didn't have enough skill. She would have been killed."

For the past several years, what this disciple saw was a Venerable Master who was manifesting illness. Sometimes it's been hard to avoid muttering to myself. The chances of personally getting to hear the Venerable Master's instructions grew fewer and fewer. How would I know that the Master is actually taking on living beings' sufferings? When the news of the Venerable Master's Nirvana came, immediately one layperson sobbed and said that she had dreamed of a Bodhisattva who is one of the Master's fellow cultivators telling her, "Your teacher is carrying too heavy a burden of living beings' karma and so he is leaving."

The eyes of ordinary people are limited, and we cannot see the things that transcend time and space. But the Venerable Master, who spent his entire life propagating the great Dharma of the Shurangama, when explaining the Shurangama Mantra, told us very clearly that behind every sickness is a ghost. Ten years ago, my father, Heng Wei Shi, developed cancer of the spine. The Venerable Master told this disciple, "Tell him to come to the City of Ten Thousand Buddhas, and he will gradually get better." Eventually he did get better and lived for ten more years. At the end of his life there was an auspicious sign, and he was born in the Western Pure Land. Before, I didn't understand why Heng Wei Shi got better when he came to be near the Master. Now I suddenly understand. Basically the Master took away his sickness ghost. In the same way, whether an illness or a disaster, there will be a negative energy behind it. We are always wanting the Master to aid us and to eradicate our karmic obstacles. How can we know how much suffering the Master is undergoing on our behalf!

Even less can we know how many beings the Master is imperceptibly helping. One family was plagued with disasters every year until the Master went to Taiwan to propagate the Dharma. The mother and daughter came to join the Dharma assembly, but never had a chance even to bow before the Master. Yet when they returned, the household was peaceful thereafter. There's absolutely no way to repay the Master's kindness. Other things like this, such as, on a large scale, to quell the natural disasters, man-made calamities, and wars of a country and its citizens; on a small scale, to dispel dangers, difficulties, and illnesses of families and individuals. No one can really know how much the Master has done. Nor did he claim credit, and he rarely let anyone know.

Now that the Master has gone, shouldn't each of us reflect and consider ultimately how much trouble we brought to the Venerable Master? As long as we are not cultivating precepts, samadhi, and wisdom; do not put to rest greed, hatred, and stupidity; are lax and indulgent, how much karma are we letting the Master take on?

人與路

PEOPLE AND ROADS

莊果香 Zhuang Guoxiang

人有千萬萬種人
路有千萬萬條路
路有走不完的人
人有走得完的路

There are thousands of millions of kinds of people
And thousands of millions of roads.
While each road is taken by an unlimited number of people,
There is an end to each person's journey.

我常想也常說，人生中有三件事，是不能由別人代替的：健康、學問、吃飯或服藥。最使人難受的事，莫過於生離死別了。一九九五年六月初，我正在生病，全身從頭部至皮膚、肌肉都痛，尤其八日、九日兩天，連門都不能出，也無法去看醫生。突然接到一通電話，方知師父宣公上人在美國圓寂了……。

我邊哭邊責怪臺灣的媒體不恭不敬不孝。我給臺北法界去電話，法師勸我不要難過，要好好弘揚上人的法，師父的法將會永遠長住在人間的，做弟子的應該化悲痛為行動，身體力行師父之法。國史館胡先生透過大乘精舍樂祕書長（中華佛教居士會）與我聯絡。國史館需要大師的有關資料，撰寫近代高僧傳。我就到位於忠孝東路的法界佛教印經會，得到全套上人之法本及錄音資料，心裡充滿了感恩、感謝之情。法師們為我錄了音，雖是記憶中的點點滴滴，但那是真情流露，接著法師要我將回憶寫下來。說句真話，我的文筆不佳，但仁慈的法師卻一直鼓勵我！

「勤修戒定慧，息滅貪瞋癡。」是師父對弟子們的開示，至今仍不絕於耳。筆者和一

I have often thought and said that there are three aspects of life which no one else can do for one, namely staying healthy, studying, and eating food or taking medicine. The hardest thing to bear is to be separated in life or parted at death. In early June 1995, I became sick and my whole body ached from the head to the skin and muscles. On the eighth and ninth, I could not even get up to go out, nor could I go and see a doctor. All of a sudden, I got a phone call informing me that the Venerable Master had entered into stillness in America.

I wept and blamed the mass media in Taiwan for their lack of respect and filiality. When I called the Dharma Realm Buddhist Books Distribution Association (DRBBDA) in Taipei, the Dharma Master there told me not to feel sorry. She said we should work hard to propagate the Venerable Master's Dharma so that it will abide in the world forever. As his disciples, we should convert our grief into action and practice the Master's Dharma well. Mr. Hu of the National Museum contacted me through Mr. Le, Chief Secretary of Mahayana Hermitage (the Buddhist Lay Association of the Republic of China). The National Museum requested information on the Venerable Master for their biography of renowned contemporary monks. I went to the DRBBDA on Chung-hsiao East Road and obtained a full set of the Venerable Master's books and cassette tapes, for which I was very grateful. The Dharma Masters tape-recorded my conversation. Although these are just some small remembrances, they flow from my heart. The Dharma Masters wanted me to record these incidents. Although I do not write well, those compassionate Dharma Masters kept encouraging me to do so.

The Venerable Master instructed his disciples to "diligently cultivate precepts, concentration and wisdom and put to rest greed, hatred and stupidity." These words continue to echo in my ears. Like many of the others who emigrated from Mainland China to Taiwan in the early days, I grew up in a family of mixed Buddhist and Taoist faith. Since my grandmother's time, my family has cultivated the Dharma-door of the

般居住於臺灣的民眾一樣，早期從大陸遷移來臺的人，家中信仰大多數是佛、道同堂共修的。筆者家裡從祖母起，就專修觀音法門，父母亦然，並樂善好施，尤以施藥最廣；但家裡沒有一人皈依為三寶弟子。直到一九八八年，我邀請姊姊來臺北，參加了在桃園舉辦的皈依後，方開始認識佛法，並持〈大悲咒〉。

一九八二年師父曾來過臺北，直到一九八八年秋季，師父才又來臺，以觀音法門舉辦護國息災大法會。接著我代表財團法人中國文化博物館，隨著楊英風教授、陸劍剛教授等，籌辦了那次在桃園的法會及皈依，得法名果香。當時臺灣正警報有三個颱風將同時登陸，師父告訴隨他弘法的眾出家弟子說：你們可以不吃不喝不睡，不可不誦〈大悲咒〉祈禱上蒼。若我到中正機場時，颱風登陸了，你等當受重罰。果然一個颱風都未登陸，而轉向菲律賓去了。

更殊勝的是在桃園舉行大法會時，天氣晴朗，數千名信眾繞佛、唱誦〈大悲咒〉，然後舉行皈依儀式。儀式中突然刮起好幾陣大風，我看見站在我身前的婦女抱著小孩的裹巾好幾次不停地掀起，口中喃喃自語。事後據云：原來南京大屠殺中被害的卅萬亡魂來皈依。（書上記錄被殺害人數為十萬，頗有出入，少報了約二十萬。）

當天下午在雙方都聯繫不上的情況下，幾經周折，我們陪同監察院長余俊賢見到師父。兩人相見甚歡，敘說家常。接著多位長者、同事（尤其包括多位基督徒、天主教徒）在見了師父後，開始對佛教有所認識，更有因而皈依師父，從此專修觀音法門的。

有二次我們清晨五點就出發去看地，因為師父非常慈悲，計劃在臺灣建立道場，師父也隨時以方便法門替弟子們消災解厄。

師父在中山堂開示時，人山人海（好多人都進不去）。會後，請人書寫師父的即興之作。我建議由以前曾任國父秘書的林先生的兒子代筆揮毫，他寫了一手好毛筆字，我請示師父，師父很肯定地說：「先別正式下筆，寫好的初稿拿過來我看看，會有幾個錯別字，等我修改後，方可正式下筆，我再落款。」

果然錯了三個字：「弦」寫成「閒」、「宦」寫成「患」，「溯」寫成「塑」。師父落款

Bodhisattva Who Regards the Sounds of the World. My parents also do charitable works, especially the giving of medicine. However, no one in the family had taken refuge with the Triple Jewel. In 1988, I invited my sister to Taipei, and we took refuge at Taoyuan. That was when I began to learn more about Buddhism and started to recite the Great Compassion Mantra.

The Master came to Taipei in 1982. He came again in the fall of 1988 and presided over the Dharma Session for Protecting the Nation and Quelling Disasters, based on the Guanyin Dharma-door. I, as a representative of the Chinese Cultural Museum Corporation, and Professors Yang Yingfeng and Lu Jiangang and others organized the Dharma Session and Refuge Ceremony at Taoyuan. I was given the Dharma name Guoxiang. At that time, it was reported that three hurricanes were going to reach Taiwan simultaneously. The Master told his left-home disciples: "All of you may go without food, drink, and sleep, but you may not stop reciting the Great Compassion Mantra and praying to the heavens above. If a hurricane hits Taiwan when I reach the Zhongzheng Airport, you will all be punished severely." Sure enough, none of the hurricanes hit Taiwan; they all changed course and headed towards the Phillipines.

Something remarkable happened during the Great Dharma Session held at Taoyuan. On that day, the weather was fine. Several thousand devotees circumambulated the Buddha while reciting the Great Compassion Mantra. Afterwards there was a refuge-taking ceremony. During the ceremony, several strong gusts of wind flapped the bib of the child in the arms of a woman standing in front of me, who kept mumbling to herself. Afterwards, it was said that about three hundred thousand souls of people killed during the Nanjing massacre had come to take refuge. (The books record the incorrect figure of one hundred thousand, which is two hundred thousand less than the actual number.)

That afternoon, we tried to contact the Master but failed, so finally we accompanied the Director of the Judicial Assembly, Mr. Yu Junxian, to meet the Master. They were glad to see each other and began to discuss ordinary matters. After that, many of my elders and colleagues (including many Christians and Catholics) came to see Master. Through meeting the Master, they began to understand more about Buddhism, and some of them even took refuge with Master and began to cultivate the Dharma-door of the Bodhisattva Who Regards the Sound of the World.

One day, we set out at five o'clock in the morning to look at some land, because the Master had kindly planned to establish a Way-place in Taiwan. The Master used expedient dharmas to resolve the troubles of his disciples whenever he saw a chance.

The Chungcheng Memorial Hall was packed for the Master's lecture. Many people couldn't even get in. Later, they wanted to find someone to write some verses composed by the Master. I suggested the son of Mr. Lin, the secretary of the Founding Father, because his calligraphy is very good. When I asked the Master's opinion, he said, "Don't write it formally yet. First have him write a draft and show it to me. There will be some wrong characters. After I correct them, he can write it formally and then I'll sign."

Sure enough, there were three wrong characters. They were the characters for "lute-string," "politicians," and "trace." After they were

中華混亂數十年，傷時感事淚成泉，

此身愧具回天手，往昔難彈落日弦。

世途崎嶇人鬼詐，官海浮沉彼此煎，

出家未忘忠貞志，不改國籍溯本源。

China has been in turmoil for several decades.
Anguished by the affairs of the times, my tears flow like a river.
I regret that in this life, I haven't been able to turn the tide of events.
In the past, I failed to play the lute of the setting sun.
The roads of the world twist and turn, as people and ghosts deceive each other.
The sea of politicians surges and rolls, as they fight each other.
Though I've left the home-life, I haven't forgotten my heart's allegiance.
Not changing my nationality, I trace my roots back to their source.

後，又加蓋印章。據師父表示，那顆玉印是他離開北京前刻的，一直隨身帶著，未曾落過任何款。寫好的字幅共五份：蔣家一份、余院長一份、臺北市長吳伯雄一份、中國文化博物館一份，和我果香一份，共五份，一併交由師父落款。

師父最愛國，更關心全世界人類安危。美國有三位總統見過師父，並向師父請教，也多次表示請師父加入美國籍。可是師父卻在六龜妙通寺住持廣欽國寶法師圓寂後，馬上申請拿到中華民國之護照。

中東連年戰爭，聯合國決定參與調停之際，我請示師父可否由師父轉達布希總統，請美國不要派軍去中東參戰。師父來長途電話說：非打不可，因中東造了太多共業。但只要全人類，尤其是佛教徒不殺生、做早晚課、多生歡喜心、不生氣、多說好話……，那麼戰爭的傷害會降至最低、最輕。（後來我得知師父親自到中東去救人）。

中正紀念堂法會時，我在場親眼目睹，傍晚時分會場天空出現光彩絢麗的霞光。又有一位失明的婦女在師父開導下，大懺悔後，雙目就復明了。

大法會中大眾齊聲誦持〈大悲咒〉，感應天空祥雲呈龍，清清楚楚的，有人證、物證（照片）為憑。

一九九三年元月師父來臺灣弘法，回美國萬佛城後，突然又來電話，當時我不在。事

corrected, the Master signed and added his chop. According to the Master, he had that jade chop carved before he left Beijing. He had always carried it with him, but never used it to sign anything. He signed five copies, one for the Chiang family, one for Director Yu, one for Wu Boxiong (the mayor of Taipei), one for the Chinese Cultural Museum, and one for myself. All of them have the Master's signature and chop.

The Master was the most patriotic person, and he was even more concerned about the safety of the entire human race. Three U.S. Presidents met the Master and asked for his advice. Several times, they asked the Master to become naturalized as an American citizen. However, the Master applied for and got his Chinese passport right after the "National Treasure" Elder Dharma Master Guangqin, the Abbot of Miaotong Monastery in Liugui, completed the stillness.

During the recent war in the Middle East, the United Nations decided to serve as a mediator. I asked the Master if he could ask President Bush not to send troops to the Middle East. The Master called long-distance and said, "There's no way to stop the war, because too much collective karma has accrued in the Middle East. However, if the entire human race, especially the Buddhists, would stop killing, do morning and evening recitation, maintain a happy spirit and not get angry, and speak more kind words, then the harm caused by the war will be reduced to a minimum." (Later I learned that the Master went to the Middle East personally to rescue people.)

During the Dharma Assembly held in the Chungcheng Memorial Hall, I witnessed an extremely spectacular and colorful light in the evening sky. I also witnessed a blind woman repent under the Master's guidance and regain her sight. During the assembly, everyone recited the Great Compassion Mantra together. As a response, a very vivid image of a dragon appeared in the sky. People witnessed this with their own eyes, and photographs were also taken.

In January 1993, the Master came to Taiwan to propagate the Dharma. After he had returned to the United States, he suddenly called me from the City of Ten Thousand Buddhas (CTTB), but I wasn't there to answer the phone. Later I called the Master back and told him that in Taiwan there were reports in the media misinterpreting the Master's intent and compassion. The Master was not angry. He merely said, "Is it

後我回電話去美國，告訴師父說臺灣這兒有媒體報導，曲解了師父的原意和慈悲。師父沒有生氣，只在電話那頭說：可能嗎？有人能利用我嗎？我可能被利用嗎？誰又利用得了我？……。

我的女兒於一九八八年拜見過師父，一九九〇年留學舊金山音樂學院時，師父對她說可常來聖城。她與幾名臺灣留學生，慕名前往後，她們都得到了獎學金。另一件事是：余院長告訴師父他身體不太好時，師父告訴他：你年紀比我大，你來住萬佛城，我會將你當做長輩，因我從小無父；並且你身體會好起來，不必開刀。結果前年余院長往生前，他的秘書告訴我說余院長總共開了三次刀。（他一直未去萬佛城）。

回憶上人曾經給我機會面對面聊天，曾提到：萬佛城到某一城市之間，有一座橋是這麼規定的：一部車二人以下多一毛，三人以上少收一毛。上人知道了，每次為了節省一毛錢的過橋費，親自湊合三個人才去買菜；到那一年為止，已省下好幾千元美金了。尤其該特別一提的是，萬佛城是不買青菜葉的，而是上人帶弟子到菜市場，去撿菜販剝剩的菜葉，回去後再仔細清理、加工料理。

另一件事是上人出家之前，每日清晨在院子裡叩頭：上報四重恩，下濟三途苦。十九歲出家後，立志發大願，其中有兩件不是一般修行者能徹底做到的。一是從此只穿三層衣服：冬天時東北是冰天雪地。一是日中一食：年輕時上人每餐可吃五碗飯，發願日中一食後，飯量不超過三碗。因為當時日本人佔領中國部份國土，欺壓中國人民，所以上人發此大願，祈願中國同胞豐衣足食，寧可自己挨餓受凍，不願中國人挨餓受凍。還有上人出家後，夜不倒單，這也是大家都知道的。

師父經常為了消除臺灣的共業和吵鬧的社會風氣，隨時準備來臺弘揚佛法，護國息災。然而大部份的弟子都知道，上人來一趟是何等不易，何等辛苦，並且曾受過臺灣佛教界的誤解及不公平的待遇。但佛、菩薩有知，師父的法將會永留人間的。

人生原來只是夢　來去去來兩手空
任你方寸不停跳　跳進跳出還是空

possible? Who could have used me? Could I be used?"

My daughter went to visit the Master in 1988. In 1990, when she was studying at a music academy in San Francisco, the Master told her to visit the CTTB often. Out of admiration for the Master, she and several students from Taiwan went to visit the Master. They all got scholarships later on. Another time Director Yu told the Master his health was not good. The Master told him, "You are older than I am. Come to live at CTTB, and I'll treat you as my elder, because I lost my father when I was young. Then your health will improve, and you won't need an operation."

The year before last, before Director Yu passed away, his secretary told me that he underwent three operations (Director Yu didn't go to CTTB).

When I think back to the opportunities the Master gave me to talk with him face to face, the Master mentioned, "Between CTTB and a city [San Francisco], there is a bridge with this rule: If there are two people or less in the car, they collect one dime more. If there are three people or more, they collect one dime less. Once the Master learned about this, he would get three people together to do grocery shopping in order to save on the toll. Over the years, he saved several thousand U.S. dollars this way. It is worth mentioning that the CTTB did not buy its vegetables. Rather, the Master would let his disciples go to the market to pick up discarded vegetables, take them back, and then clean and process them.

Before the Master left the home-life, every morning he would kowtow in the yard. He bowed to repay the four kinds of kindness above and to aid those suffering in the three paths below. When he left home at nineteen years of age, he made great vows. Two of the vows are not something that ordinary cultivators could practice thoroughly. One was that from then on, he would only wear three layers of clothing. The Manchurian winters were icy cold and snow would cover the ground. The other was that he would only take one meal a day in the middle of the day. During his youth, the Master could eat five bowls of food at one meal. After he resolved to take one meal a day, he didn't eat more than three bowls. The Master had made this great vow because the Japanese were occupying part of China and bullying the Chinese people at that time. He hoped his fellow countrymen would have enough food and clothing. He would rather endure hunger and cold himself than see his fellow countrymen do so. It is also common knowledge that after the Master left the home-life, he did not lie down at night.

In order to eradicate the collective karma and social disorder in Taiwan, the Master was ready to come to Taiwan to propagate the Buddhadharma at any time to protect the nation and dispel disasters. Most of his disciples know how difficult and exhausting it was for the Master to come to Taiwan. They know that he was misunderstood and treated unjustly by the Buddhists of Taiwan. But the Buddhas and Bodhisattvas know that the Master's Dharma will remain in this world forever.

Life is basically nothing but a dream.
You come and you go, always with your two hands empty.
Although your heart beats without cease,
It can beat and beat, and still it's all empty.

跳到天上空一切　　　It can beat its way to the heaven: Everything is empty.
跳落地下一場空　　　It can beat its way into the ground: Emptiness is all there is.
空無妙有真如境　　　Emptiness and wonderful existence are the state of True Suchness.
應知諸法皆相空　　　One should know that all dharmas are devoid of characteristics.

人生百年間　生死兩相連　　　A hundred years of human life
顯達方富貴　平凡即自然　　　Birth is always followed by death.
得意又失意　榮如地循環　　　When you're prosperous, you enjoy wealth and position.
功名如糞土　聲名似雲煙　　　When you're just ordinary, you return to nature.
際遇皆幻夢　何須苦戀求　　　Sometimes you're in a favorable state; sometimes you meet adversity.
朝夕參禪佛　傳道福延綿　　　Glory is like the earth's rotation

High position is like manure and dirt.
Name and fame are like clouds and smoke.
All your life is like a dream.
What need is there to linger on?
Meditate, bow to the Buddhas in the morning and evening,
And transmit the Way, and your blessings will be perpetuated.

萬事隨緣觀自在　一心正念證菩提

If you let everything take its course, then you can contemplate at ease.
With single-mindedness and proper thought, you certify to Bodhi.

世事滄桑皆歷盡　心中妄識盡放下
人間表態如塵沙　法風掃盡心自在

The rise and fall of everything in the world—I have experienced it all.
The illusory knowledge in my mind—I shall put it all down.
The phenomena in this world are as numerous as dust and sand.
Once they are swept away by the Dharma wind, my mind will be at ease.

上聯：白水泉中一大天（師父）
下聯：黑土墨地二山出（果香）

In the white water spring, one big sky appears. [The Master's line]
In the dark black soil, two mountains protrude. [Guoxiang's line]

四海忙奔飛　犬馬累盡驅
法緣昌盛益　行跡遇修羅
一劫身心疲
豬年年中驪聲起　菩薩心憂淚灑地
此年天際殞一星　一代金剛到西天

Hastily running throughout the four seas,
Like the dogs and horses being driven to exhaustion.
The conditions of Dharma are more and more prosperous.
Running into asuras wherever he went,
Throughout his life, he exhausted his body and mind.
The sound of farewell is heard in the year of the pig.
We worry the Bodhisattva so much that his tears fall on the ground.
This year, a shooting star fell to the ground.
The Vajra king of this time ascended to the Western heaven.

白皓山川柳成蔭　靈鷲依畔水映天
刻骨銘心隨願造　翌日青山識經心
山川依舊佈新氣　綠水常流貯淨心
心氣合一山水映　法性東起西來意
氣度增廣水長流　肚量放寬任鳥飛
真心懺下世間怨　包容諸相證涅槃
一代高僧不識相　一代大德不知趣
不為瘴氣為法脈　何不抬頭應朝陽
群山本有主峰頭　頭視寰宇涵蒼松
香氣繚繞五峰山　山中惠存共鳴音
音律滋潤花蕊心　凡心早已入雲宵
正知確立迷中定　正見崢立鬧中靜

Below the white, snowcapped mountain,
The willow trees line the river, forming a shady canopy.
Next to the Vulture Peak, the waters reflect the sky.
My vows are engraved in my bones and my mind:
The next day, by the green mountains, I will recognize my heart's wish.
The mountains and rivers assume a new energy.
Constantly flowing green waters purifty my mind.
My mind and energy unite, just like the mountains reflected in water.
The Dharma that arose in the East has come to the West.
Our minds have expanded; the water flows freely.
Our capacities have broadened; birds can soar at ease.
Truly repent of the animosities in the world.
Encompassing all phenomena, one attains Nirvana.
An eminent Sanghan of this age—no one recognized him.
A greatly virtuous one of this time—no one knew his intent.
He perpetuated the Dharma lineage, despite the hostile energies.
Why not raise your head and greet the rising sun?

定靜廣涵天地人　一切自在無言中

仰天俯地　心地法門
心地一體　擎天一柱
天地共鳴　再創佛音
一舉譽世　心懷娑婆
領導眾生　除舊佈新
宗教革新　政治中興
中國互融
邁向世紀連線的曙光
一併而躍娑婆
中國睏虎覺醒
非宣化帶動莫屬

覺

修持在生活
點滴在心頭
涅槃在懺悔
行深在般若

悟

六根在一心
六道在一念
眞如在見性
成佛在明心

無礙

妄念不空　何期見性
妄念不止　何期明心
覺悟之道　絕無二法
涅槃之境　絕無二心

On the main peak of the mountain range,
Through the black pines, there's a panoramic view of the universe.
A fragrance encircles the Five-Peaked Mountain;
An echo resounds in the mountain.
The melody nourishes the flower pistils;
The ordinary mind ascends above the clouds.
With proper knowledge, one has samadhi in the midst of confusion;
With proper views, everything is still in the hubbub.
In the stillness of samadhi, heaven, earth, and people come forth.
Without a word, everything exists.

In the sky above and on the earth below,
There's the Dharma-door of the mind only.
With the mind and earth united in one substance,
The sky is supported.
With heaven and earth in resonance,
The Buddha's sound is heard once more.
His fame prevailed throughout the world.
Yet his heart was with the Saha world.
He led living beings to renew themselves.
He worked to reform religion and restore statesmanship.
Uniting China, marching toward the dawn of the new century,
Leaping out of the Saha world,
And waking up the sleeping tiger of China—
Who else but the Venerable Master Hua could do this?

On Enlightenment

Cultivation is done in daily life;
Every minute detail is in the mind.
Nirvana lies in repentance;
Deep practice is in Prajna.

On Awakening

The six faculties are all created from the mind;
The six paths are not beyond one thought.
True Suchness lies in seeing the nature;
Understanding the mind, one becomes a Buddha.

On Non-obstruction

With random thoughts not empty,
When can you see your nature?
With random thoughts not stopped,
When can you understand your mind?
On the path to enlightenment, there is no duality of dharmas.
In the state of Nirvana, there is no duality of mind.

THE GIFT OF DHARMA IS THE HIGHEST OF ALL

諸布施中，法布施最

Ng Soh Joo   October 4, 1995
黃素珠（譯音）   一九九五年十月四日

I am truly grateful to the Venerable Master, whose Bodhisattva conduct and vows and boundless kindness awakened my faith in Buddhism. The Master's goal of translating the entire Buddhist canon into English has indeed enabled me to obtain the greatest of all gifts—the gift of Dharma.

It started in early 1992 when I attended (at the encouragement of my colleague, to whom I am especially thankful) the final session of a four-day talk by the Venerable Master's disciples, who were in Singapore on a Dharma Propagation Tour. I was overjoyed at hearing the wonderful sound of proper Dharma for the first time. After reading *Records of the Life of the Venerable Master Hsuan Hua* and the *Buddha Root Farm* which were available for free distribution at that time, I was immediately inspired to cultivate the Buddhadharma in accordance with the Master's compassionate teaching.

The Master's dedication of merits and blessings to world peace through his tough ascetic lifestyle profoundly touched and planted the seeds of Bodhi in the hearts of countless living beings. Forgetting about himself for the sake of propagating the orthodox Buddhadharma to all living beings, he was the most remarkable and vigorous cultivator of this era.

I earnestly wish that the Master's transmission of the orthodox Dharma to the West will dwell eternally in the world to liberate all beings from sufferings, and that they cultivate pure practices, so that all can be reborn in the Ultimate Land of Bliss.

Last, but not least, may the Sagely City of Ten Thousand Buddhas always remain as the international spiritual community to unite all religious people as a single family. It was with this purpose of promoting vast affinities and harmony among mankind that the Venerable Master established the monasteries and educational institutions in the City.

我真誠地感激上人，他的菩薩行願和無量慈悲，使我對佛教生起了信心。上人要將三藏十二部經翻譯成英文，給了我最大的禮物——法布施最。

一九九二年初上人的弟子前來亞洲弘法時，有四天在新加坡，我在一位同事鼓勵之下，去聽了最後一場講法，我真是很感謝他。那是我第一次聽聞正法，心裡充滿了法喜。當時有免費贈閱的書，我請了《上人事蹟》及《佛根地》兩本書，看完之後，我就立刻發心依照上人的慈悲教導來修行佛法。

上人以自己的苦行功德迴向世界和平，深深感動了無量眾生，也在他們心田播下了菩提種子。為了將佛教正法帶給眾生，他忘了自己的存在，上人可以說是本世紀最精進、最非凡的修行人。

我衷心希望上人帶給西方的正法能長久住世，解救眾生於苦難之中，令他們修行清淨行，往生極樂世界。

最後希望萬佛聖城能夠始終做一個國際性的宗教中心，聯合各宗教人士為一家人。上人在萬佛城建立道場，設立學校，其目的也正是為了與人類廣結善緣，增進和諧。

忍耐　忍耐　多多忍耐　娑婆訶
——宣公上人作

Patience, patience, gotta have patience, suo po he!
Venerable Master Hua

流血汗，不休息

NOT SPARING BLOOD OR SWEAT AND NEVER PAUSING TO REST

陳果安　Chen Guo An

在追求真理的過程中，經歷了許多曲折。雖有一些收穫，總覺得不全面、不究竟。後來有幸接觸佛法，才終止了摸索。皈依宣公上人後，才開始潛心向佛。

由同事的介紹，認識了宣化上人。當時並沒有急著到金山寺去親近上人。直到一九八九年春天的一個早上，從睡夢中忽然覺得被人推動，催促我快去金山寺。大驚而醒，方知是夢。匆匆趕到金山寺，見到上人時，突覺心頭一亮，意識到這位法師就是我尋找多年的老師。當時即蒙上人殷殷垂詢近況，慈悲的指出我走錯的路。剎那間，一股浪子返家的情懷，如洪水決堤，洶湧而出，不能自己。事後回想，也許是感傷自己愚癡庸碌，無所長進，而愧對故人吧！

此後又有幾次親近上人的機會，受益良多。上人也常常一針見血的指出我犯的錯誤，使我深自警惕。不僅單獨請益上人時，會得到寶貴的指示，神奇的是，即便上人對大眾開示時，我也彷彿覺得是針對我的情況而說法，其他同修也常有這種經驗。

一次，向上人請教後，從金山寺出來，看到工人將一整隻豬推到一家烤豬店的地下室。突然之間，我看到的彷彿不是豬，而是一位中年男子。當下大懼，也更明瞭上人苦口婆心勸人吃素的緣由。

前幾年臺灣政爭，大有一觸即發之勢，上人趕赴臺灣，絕食一個多月。這種悲天憫人，為眾生捐軀的壯舉，令人由衷景仰。

上人風塵僕僕奔赴世界各地，為人類和平做了許多貢獻，卻鮮為人知。譬如，為祈求世界和平，上人在印度建造了許多舍利塔。更是沒日沒夜的為眾生超度、消業、治病、祈福。

將佛法傳到西方世界，是上人最大的心願

In my search for the truth, I encountered numerous complications. Although I did obtain something, I always felt it wasn't complete and ultimate. Fortunately, I later encountered Buddhism and was finally able to end my search. After taking refuge with the Venerable Master Hua, I began to inquire deeply into Buddhism.

Through a friend, I came to know of the Venerable Master Hua. However, at that time I wasn't in any rush to go to Gold Mountain Monastery to meet the Venerable Master. It was not until one morning in the spring of 1989, that I dreamed someone was urging me to quickly go to Gold Mountain Monastery. I woke up in a fright, only to realize that it was a dream. I rushed to Gold Mountain Monastery. When I saw the Venerable Master, my heart lit up and I knew this Dharma Master was the teacher I had been searching for all these years. The Venerable Master concernedly asked about my recent situation and kindly pointed out where I had gone astray. I was suddenly overwhelmed with the feeling that I was a prodigal son returning home. This feeling welled up in my heart, beyond my control. This was probably because I lamented the fact that I was such a dull person unable to improve myself and a disgrace to my elders!

I had several other opportunities to draw near the Venerable Master after that, and I benefited greatly each time. The Venerable Master often pointed out with great precision the errors I had made, startling me greatly. Not only would I obtain treasured advice when I personally sought instruction from the Venerable Master, but the remarkable thing was that, even when the Venerable Master was lecturing to the assembly, I felt as if his words of Dharma were specifically aimed at my own situation! My fellow cultivators have often had the same experience.

Once when I walked out of Gold Mountain Monastery after seeking counsel from the Venerable Master, I saw a worker pushing a pig into the basement of a shop that sold roast pig. Suddenly, I seemed to see not a pig, but a middle-aged man. It gave me a big fright, and I understood why the Venerable Master so earnestly urged people to be vegetarian.

During the political fighting in Taiwan a few years ago, the slightest thing could have triggered an explosive crisis. The Venerable Master rushed to Taiwan and fasted for over a month. Such compassionate concern for people, such great self-sacrifice for the sake of living beings, is truly admirable.

The Venerable Master travelled throughout the world, making many contributions to the peace and harmony of mankind without letting people know. For instance, the Venerable Master commissioned the building of numerous stupas (pagodas) for housing sharira (relics) in India for the sake of world peace. Day and night without stop, he saved living beings, eradicated their karma, healed them of illness, and prayed for blessings on their behalf.

The Venerable Master's greatest vow was to bring the Buddhadharma

。幾十年來，上人為培養佛教人才、翻譯經典、創辦教育、廣設道場，「流血汗，不休息」，奠定了佛教在美國得以弘揚的千秋之業。上人魄力之大，眼光之遠，令弟子無比敬佩。能成為上人的弟子，我感到無上榮光。

上人對佛教經典的闡揚，也是深入淺出、旁徵博引、乾淨俐落，一改世人認為佛經艱深晦澀的觀點，倡導了一種新的傳播佛法的方法。

上人的慈悲大願力，非筆墨能形容：「……曾經皈依我者，若有一未成佛時，我誓不取正覺。」（第十大願）所有皈依他的弟子成佛後，他才成佛。

上人常為眾生指點迷津，解除疑難。眾生中有善根深厚者，對上人之教誨，聞即信受，切實奉行，事情自然會出現轉機。難調難伏剛強之徒，則徒事強辯，本末倒置，最後只是自食惡果。

上人以他的智慧，不僅為平民百姓排憂解難，也經常為前來向他請教的達官顯貴提供治國良方及施政方針。有時，因上人的開示寓意深妙，頗讓人難以明白、接受，但事後，事物發展結果卻正如上人所預料。

上人曾做過多項預言，無不應驗。如預言如共產主義陣營的瓦解，愛滋病在全世界的漫延，乃至各種天災人禍等等。近年來上人又預言，比愛滋病厲害百倍的疫病即將流行，並嚴肅地指出其病源是同性戀。而世人愚癡，仍沉迷不醒。

上人一生嚴持戒律，勤修苦行，上求下化，拔濟苦難。對弟子個人而言，得上人庇護，愚癡稍減，心神日安。對國家而言，上人匡正人心，移風易俗，力挽狂瀾，安定社稷。凡追隨上人者，當以上人言教，身教為宗，為佛教事業盡一己之力，庶幾報上人宏恩於萬一。

to the Western world. For several decades, the Venerable Master toiled tirelessly, training people in Buddhism, translating the Buddhist canon, founding schools and promoting education, and establishing Way-places in order to lay a foundation for the propagation of Buddhism in America a thousand years into the future. I have the highest admiration for the Venerable Master's great courage and far-reaching vision. I feel supremely honored to be the Venerable Master's disciple.

The Venerable Master's explanations of the Buddhist scriptures are very easy to understand. He uses all kinds of examples, and yet his words are concise and to the point. He has changed the notion that worldly people have of the scriptures as being difficult to understand and has promoted an innovative method of propagating the Buddhadharma.

The Venerable Master's greatly compassionate vows cannot be described in words: "I vow that I will not attain the Right Enlightenment if there is even one being who has taken refuge with me and has not yet become a Buddha." (the eighteenth great vow) He will only become a Buddha after all his refuge disciples have done so.

The Venerable Master often helped living beings to clear up their confusion and resolve their doubts. When those with abundant good roots hear the Venerable Master's teaching, they immediately accept it with faith and earnestly practice it, and as a result things take a turn for the better. When headstrong disciples argue back and confuse the head and tail of things, they end up suffering the unpleasant consequences themselves.

The Venerable Master not only used his wisdom to dispel the worries and difficulties of ordinary people, he also offered wise advice on government to political leaders and high officials who came to seek his counsel. Sometimes the implications of the Venerable Master's talks were too mysterious and deep for people to understand and accept, yet things would always turn out just as the Master had predicted.

The Venerable Master made many prophecies, and all of them came true. For example, he predicted the disintegration of the Communist bloc, the spread of AIDS throughout the world, and all sorts of natural and manmade disasters. In recent years the Venerable Master also predicted the outbreak of an epidemic a hundred times worse than AIDS, pointing out sternly that homosexuality would be the cause of this disease. Yet worldly people remain sunk in confusion and fail to awaken.

The Venerable Master upheld the precepts strictly throughout his life, diligently cultivated asceticism, sought the Buddhadharma above and taught living beings below, saving them from suffering and hardship. In my personal case, under the Venerable Master's protective aid, my stupidity has decreased slightly and my peace of mind grows daily. In terms of the country, the Venerable Master has rectified people's minds, reformed the trends, averted chaos and confusion, and brought peace and security to society. Those who have followed the Venerable Master should faithfully uphold the Master's teachings, whether he gave them verbally or by example, and do their best for Buddhism in the hopes of repaying a small fraction of the Venerable Master's great kindness.

感恩與願望

MY GRATITUDE AND WISHES

余果昌　Yu Guochang

感謝上人，在弟子學佛的菩提大道上，各種有形無形的教誨。未皈依前，就曾接觸上人弘法的書籍與錄音帶，感動佩服「直指人心」及「對症下藥」的正法傳授，所以在一九九〇年，上人來臺度眾且舉行皈依儀式時，見機緣不可失，雖知上人表示過「不收已皈依三寶的弟子」，但仍貪求師父的大願及瞭解「人身難得，中土難生，佛法難聞，明師難遇」，所以虔誠地在五股一間寺廟，皈依上人。

還記得，上人在八德路中央日報大樓的一場開示，曾提及「電視對我們危害甚大」。那時心頭一震，不是很了解，但先把疑問放著。直到最近自己坐在電視機前，原先想做的事都沒做時，才恍然大悟。想起法會當時有一聽眾請教：「想好好的學佛，又想把事業做好，該如何才能同時做到？」上人答了一句：「魚與熊掌不可兼得」，這句話，我獲益匪淺。

在一九九一年，曾讀了不少手邊的一些佛書，因為筆者深感若不能解行並重的話，看更多的書，即使是簡易的佛理，也只是增加心頭的負擔，所以決定換工作。從單純的研究發展部門，調到複雜的業務銷售部門，去體會何謂眾生？何謂萬法？何謂貪瞋癡？何謂戒定慧？

如此過了兩年，在一九九三年底，忽然覺得自己該開始閱讀僧寶銓釋的大乘經典，那時法喜充滿地看完南亭法師的《佛說阿彌陀經講話》，及道源法師的《佛說觀無量壽佛經講話》後，碰到一個難題。市面上的許多經典，大都是以文言文詮釋文言文，總讓我這個文學底子甚差的人，望之卻步，不知大乘經典能看多久？後來走了一趟未曾去過的「法界佛教印經會」，這一趟使我的問題迎

I am grateful to the Venerable Master for the various teachings, both visible and invisible, that he has given me in my study of Buddhism on the great path of Bodhi. Even before I took refuge, I had read books and heard tapes of the Venerable Master's Dharma talks, and I admired the Master for his style of "directly pointing at the mind" and "prescribing medicine according to the illness" in propagating the Proper Dharma. When the Venerable Master held a Taking Refuge ceremony in Taiwan in 1990, I didn't miss the opportunity. Though the Master had said he would not accept people who had already taken refuge with the Triple Jewel, I was greedy to benefit from the Master's great vows and was aware of how difficult it is to gain a human body, to be born in a central country, to hear the Buddhadharma, and to encounter a wise teacher. I sincerely took refuge with the Venerable Master at a temple in Wugu.

I still remember that during a lecture given at the headquarters of the *Chinese Daily*, the Venerable Master said, "Television is very harmful to us." This statement startled me, and I didn't quite understand it, but I had set my doubt aside then. Recently I sat in front of the television and didn't get done any of the things I wanted to do. I suddenly understood the Master's meaning then. I also remember someone asking the Master during that lecture, "If I want to study Buddhism and also do well in my business, how can I do both?" The Master had said, "You cannot have both fish and bear's paw. [You cannot have your cake and eat it too.]" I have gained great benefit from this answer.

In 1991, after avidly reading some Buddhist books, I felt that if I didn't emphasize practice as well as understanding, the more books I read—even if they were simple Buddhist principles—the greater my mental burden would be. Thus I decided to change my line of work. I transferred from the "simple research and development department" to the "complex business and sales department." I wanted to understand: What are living beings? What are the myriad dharmas? What are greed, anger, and delusion? What are precepts, samadhi, and wisdom?

Two years passed, and at the end of 1993, I suddenly felt I should start reading the Mahayana (Great Vehicle) Sutras as explained by members of the Sangha. After reading *The Buddha Speaks of Amitabha Sutra* explained by Dharma Master Nanting and *The Buddha Speaks of Contemplating the Buddha of Limitless Life Sutra* explained by Dharma Master Daoyuan, and being filled with the joy of Dharma, I ran into a problem. Most of the Sutra commentaries available on the market used classical Chinese to explain the original classical Chinese Sutra text. Since my literary background is not that good, I didn't know how long I could keep on reading the Mahayana Sutras. Later I happened to go to the Dharma Realm Buddhist Books Distribution Association, which I had never visited before, and my problem was solved. At the Association, there was a whole wall of bookshelves filled with the Venerable Master's Dharma talks and commentaries on Sutras such as the *Vajra Sutra*, the *Shu-*

刃而解，印經會有一整面牆壁的書櫃裡，都是上人的法語，曩括《金剛經》、《楞嚴經》、《法華經》、《華嚴經》……等許多大乘經典，真是一個大寶藏，皆是上人用淺顯易懂的白話、道理來精闢講解原先不易看懂的經文，於是心想這下可法喜充滿好幾年了。感謝上人及法界教印經會的常住法師及師兄師姊的發心。

*　　　　*　　　　*

今年四月，曾出差至美，返國途中，利用休假在萬佛聖城住了三天。在這裡，第一次感受到四眾至誠持誦〈楞嚴咒〉是那麼莊嚴。回臺後不久，就在早課中加念〈楞嚴咒〉，至今短短幾個月，深感其殊勝處。在聖城中，也第一次打了有將近十幾分鐘之久的雙盤，竟然全程感覺舒適，不痛不痠不麻，所以現在在惟覺老和尚的精舍打坐，就一直用雙盤姿勢。在此感恩萬佛聖城的殊勝與法師義工的開導照顧。

聽到上人圓寂的消息，想到廣欽老和尚膾炙人口的名言：「沒來也沒去，沒代誌（閩南話：沒事！」在此，秉受著普賢菩薩十大行願中的「七者，請佛住世」，懇請上人乘願再來，回到娑婆世界，開導愚迷的我們，使我們能福慧雙修、增長而最終福慧圓滿。弟子深受上人的法語，及所屬道場的法師們的教誨而稍有長進，惟妄想執著實是太多，真是慚愧萬分。上人將長存我心。筆者願生生世世受持《楞嚴經》，也更懇請大眾讀誦受持《楞嚴經》或咒中之王〈楞嚴咒〉，反聞聞自性。再者一心念佛，一心憶佛，一心認定阿彌陀佛的西方極樂淨土是我們的唯一歸宿，相信定可加速摧毀無明妄想，早登無上西方極樂淨土。

阿彌陀佛。

rangama Sutra, the *Dharma Flower Sutra*, the *Flower Adornment Sutra*, and many other Mahayana Sutras. It was truly a great treasure trove. The Venerable Master used very simple, easy-to-understand language and principles to explain the essentials of the original text of the Sutras, which was difficult to understand. I reckoned that these would probably keep me "filled with the joy of Dharma" for several years. I am grateful for the efforts of the Venerable Master and the Dharma Masters and volunteers at the Dharma Realm Buddhist Books Distribution Association.

In April of this year, I went to the United States on business. On my way home, I spent three days of my vacation at the Sagely City of Ten Thousand Buddhas. This was the first time I noticed the adorned atmosphere when the fourfold assembly sincerely recited the Shurangama Mantra. After returning to Taiwan, I soon added the Shurangama Mantra to my morning ceremony. In these few months, I have deeply perceived its sublimity. At the Sagely City, I also sat in full lotus for almost twenty minutes for the first time, and it felt very comfortable, with no pain, no soreness, and no numbness. So now when I meditate at the hermitage of Venerable Weijue, I always sit in full lotus. I would like to express my appreciation for the sublime conditions at the Sagely City and for the guidance and care of the Dharma Masters and volunteers there.

When I received news of the Venerable Master's completion of stillness, I thought of the well-known quote from the Elder Master Guangqin: "No coming, no going, nothing happening at all." Based on the seventh of the ten great vows of Universal Worthy Bodhisattva, to request that the Buddhas dwell in the world, I sincerely request the Venerable Master to ride upon his vows and return to the Saha world to teach us, these deluded ones, to cultivate and ultimately perfect our blessings and wisdom. I have deeply accepted the Venerable Master's words of Dharma and the instructions of the Dharma Masters at his Way-places, and I have made a bit of progress. However, my false thoughts and attachments are truly too numerous, and I am greatly ashamed. The Venerable Master will forever be in my heart. I vow to receive and uphold the *Shurangama Sutra* in life after life, and I earnestly request the great assembly to read, recite, receive, and uphold the *Shurangama Sutra* or the Shurangama Mantra (the king of mantras), and direct the hearing inwards to hear the inherent nature. In addition, if we single-mindedly recite the name of the Buddha, single-mindedly recollect the Buddha, and single-mindedly acknowledge Amitabha Buddha's Western Pure Land of Ultimate Bliss as our one and only refuge, we will surely be able to quickly destroy our ignorance and false thoughts and soon ascend to the supreme Western Pure Land of Ultimate Bliss.

Amitabha!

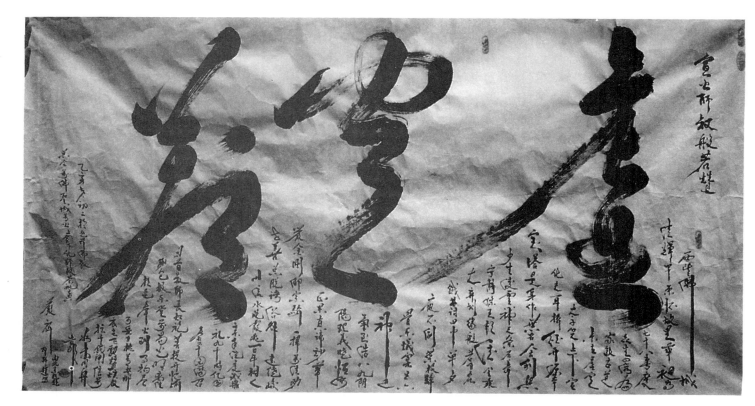

虛空萬有

EMPTINESS AND EXISTENCE

宣公師叔般若贊

In Praise of the Prajna of the Venerable Master, my Teacher-Uncle

嚴新　by Yan Xin

西望佛城清輝早，東懷故里華昶高；七十八春度眾生，四海爲家效古道。
來去虛空太子笑，上下宣化夫耳橋；經開源本寶塔是，身座無名舍利照。
少生凌雲補天條，後養寧靜滌王朝；德全乘大棄划緣，般若自在餓弗討。
日中單餐夜不倒，菜根罈骨樂蟻窯；五六神通氣至浩，八九陰陽理義曉。
恆河正果眞諦妙，華嚴金剛仰宗驕；一掃萬法勸世善，總脫諸俗解迷繞。
峻山流水晚霞兆，百年樹人親手澆；虔誠鼎禮九千時，億國泰平圓滿召。
回首叔師長虹袍，菩提開懷瑜珈包；極樂堂前易光明，離住相見奉公到。
事物盡可岳自挑，尊者腳底塵飛飄；贊頌啓拉千鈞開，信步如來同舟靠。

乙亥七月初二於世界佛教總會
萬佛聖城尊公上宣下化師叔茶毗大典
嚴新　由北京趕赴即拜題寫

Looking to the West, I saw the Buddhas' City in the clear moonlight.
Thinking of the East, I longed for my home village under the bright noon sun.

For seventy-eight springs, he saved living beings.
Taking the four seas as his home, he followed the path of the ancients.

Coming and going in empty space, he was greeted by the smile of the prince.
Proclaiming and transforming, he served as a bridge.

Through the Sutras, he traced back to the source where the jewelled pagoda was.
Although he was without fame, his sharira shine.

Even as a youth, he made a heroic resolve as high as the clouds to make up
*   for the deficiencies of the universe.*
Calm and serene, he penetrated afar and worked to cleanse the world's affairs.

His virtue replete and his Vehicle Great, he never solicited from others.
With Prajna, he was at ease; he never begged even in hunger.

He took one meal at midday and didn't lie down to sleep.
Although he himself would eat only the vegetable roots,
He wanted to have his bones taken out of the urn to delight the ants.

With the Five Eyes and Six Spiritual Penetrations, his energy was vast.
He understood the eight trigrams and the nine chambers, and penetrated yin and yang.

He attained the fruition of the Ganges River—the wonder of the truth.
He attained the Avatamsaka Vajra body and was the pride of the Weiyang Sect.

He swept away the myriad dharmas and exhorted people to do good.
He liberated the mundane and dissolved their confusion.

[His virtue and kindness are like] high mountains and flowing waters reflecting the rosy sunset.
Dedicated to education, he personally nurtured the people.

[His disciples] completed a journey of nine thousand hours
Of sincere bowing to pray for peace among all nations.

I look back at my Teacher-Uncle's long red sash;
Hidden in Ukiah is the blossoming Bodhi.

In front of the Hall of Ultimate Bliss, there's a new light.
Neither apart from nor dwelling in marks, he arrived.

When he investigated all things to the utmost, the mountains moved by themselves.
Under the Venerable One's feet, the dust flew up.

Through our praise, we can pull up the heavy floodgates;
Strolling with the Thus Come One, we arrive at the shore in the same boat.

Written respectfully by Yan Xin
Upon arriving at the World Buddhist Association from Beijing on July 28, 1995
For the Cremation Ceremony of the Venerable Hsuan Noble Hua, my Teacher-Uncle

師父上人的
創校與教學之法

HOW THE VENERABLE MASTER ESTABLISHED SCHOOLS
AND THE WAY HE TAUGHT STUDENTS

易瑞華　一九九五年七月二十七日講於萬佛聖城宣公上人讚頌報恩法會
A talk given by Shari Epstein in the Ceremony in Praise and Recognition of the Venerable Master's Kindness
at the Sagely City of Ten Thousand Buddhas on July 27, 1995

我今天只要談一下師父創立學校與教導學生的方法，因為我每次看師父的遺言，看到最後幾句，就會覺得非常感動，他說：「你們大家要組織起來，把小學辦好，把中學辦好，大學更要辦好！」為什麼我會覺得非常感動呢？這是因為我很幸運有機會在師父身邊長大，也有機會在育良小學與培德中學受教育。

我六歲的時候，就是一九七六年，育良小學設立那一年，我從那一年到十八歲高中畢業，都是在這裡上課，有機會觀察這兩個學校的演變，更幸運的是：有機會親自體驗師父教導學生的方法。大概在座的人，都曾經聽過許多師父的開示，師父有許多關於教育的開示，因為我們都知道他常常強調教育的重要性，常常鼓勵人做義務老師。可是近幾年來，人所可能不知道的是，師父談教育的時候，不是只空談理論而已，他自己年輕的時候，十八歲，在東北，也當過義務老師，有三十幾個學生，完全由他自己來教。

育良小學、培德中學設立以後，不管多忙，師父也幾乎每個禮拜，都從舊金山來到萬佛城，給我們學生上課，這是我不能夠忘記的。

師父上課的方法，是非常活潑有趣的！你都不知道那天他會做什麼新的事情，一點都不無聊。我記得有一陣子，師父告訴我們學生說：「你們不管多小，都要練習，要學習怎麼演講。」所以有幾個月，每個禮拜五，男校、女校都要選一個代表，到大殿坐在師父旁邊，不管懂不懂雙語，都得用中、英語在台上演講。對八歲、九歲、十歲、十一歲的小

Today I just want to say a few words about how Shr Fu (the Venerable Master) established schools and the way he taught students. Every time I see his final instructions, I feel really moved when I get to the very last part, in which he says, "You must organize yourselves. You must manage and administer the schools well, both the elementary and the secondary schools and even more so the university." Why? Because I was very fortunate to have the opportunity to grow up near Shr Fu and to be educated in Instilling Goodness Elementary and Developing Virtue Secondary Schools.

From the time I was six years old, in 1976, the year Instilling Goodness Elementary School was established, until I graduated from high school at eighteen, I attended these two schools. So I had the opportunity to watch the evolution of the schools. I was even more fortunate to personally experience the methods that Shr Fu used to teach us. Probably many of the people who are present have heard Shr Fu's instructional talks. There are many instructional talks on education, because, as we all know, he emphasized the importance of education and encouraged people to be volunteer teachers. I think some of the people who have come in recent years might not know that when Shr Fu talked about education, he wasn't just talking about empty theories. When he was eighteen in Manchuria, he also taught as a volunteer teacher. He had over thirty students, and he taught them all himself.

And then, after Instilling Goodness and Developing Virtue Schools were established, no matter how busy he was, he came up to the City of Ten Thousand Buddhas from San Francisco almost every week and taught us. This is something I can never forget.

His classes were always extremely lively, very creative, and very interesting. You never knew what new things he would do. It wasn't the least bit boring. In particular I remember once there was a period of a few months during which he told us, "No matter how little you are, you should all practice giving speeches." So for several months, every Friday we'd pick a representative from the girls' school and from the boys' school. You had to go

孩來講，這是非常難得的機會與經驗。

我也記得有一陣子，師父給我們上「論語課」，他用什麼方法呢？平常我們上課，坐的方法，是法師坐在前面，然後坐著穿海青的居士、不穿海青的居士，學生可能在最後面。可是那個時候呢，他說：「這堂課是特別為學生開的，學生坐在前面。」那時我們以為坐在在家居士的前面，可是事實不是！師父要我們坐在最前面！喔！那個時候很小，覺得好光榮，可以有機會坐在最前面。我長大以後才想到，由一個老師的角度來看，這是多麼好的方法。因為平時我們坐在最後面嬉戲、講話、遞字條，現在我們不單比較靠近師父，所以他可以看著我們；也有那麼多法師、居士，與家長坐在我們後面，沒有一個學生敢搗蛋，我們又覺得是非常光榮。

師父上課的時候，總是有很多變化。不單只是專門為學生上課的時候，他會跟學生講話，他總讓學生覺得自己很有價值，平時給大眾上課的時候，他也鼓勵學生參加「對聯課」。這是每個禮拜上一兩次的課，每次師父都鼓勵學生對對聯，如果我們不上去對，他都會特別提出我們的名字：「安安、果陀，你們有沒有對對聯？」或者有的小孩不夠高，不能夠在黑板上寫他們的對聯，他會說：「你不要怕你太矮，我把一張椅子搬上來，你站在椅子上對。」上人就真地搬一張椅子上來，讓四歲的小孩站在椅子上，在黑板上寫對聯。他對小孩對的對聯和大人對的對聯一視同仁，平等看待。

這不過是個例子，表示上人如何用出人意外的方法和智慧來教導小孩。

還有一次，我記得有一陣子師父鼓勵大家背經，特別是《楞嚴經》，那個時候他也鼓勵我們背《地藏經》，還有其他的經典，大家都很用功背經。為了鼓勵大家，晚上在大殿，他會讓人上臺背經給大眾聽，用這樣子的方法鼓勵人，所以每隔一兩天，每個人就一個一個地上臺背經。可是過了幾天，他就改變方法了，他說：「好！現在我們要用新的方法，今天是三、四個人一起上去背。」可是他們所背的不是一樣的經，一個人背《地藏經》，一個人背《楞嚴經》，一個人背〈楞嚴咒〉，我們都覺得很驚訝！如果有那麼多人念那麼多不一樣的東西，怎麼行呢？他就解釋給我們聽，他說：「一個人上來背，很容易。如果

up onto the stage and sit next to Shr Fu and give a speech in Chinese and English, whether you knew both languages or not! And when you're a little kid of eight, nine, ten, or eleven years old, it's a very rare opportunity and a very special experience.

Afterwards, I also remember there was a period when he had a class on the *Analects*. What method did he use? Ordinarily in a class, the Dharma Masters sit in the front, then the laypeople with black robes, the laypeople without robes, and then the students at the very back. He told the whole assembly (it took the assembly several times to realize he was really serious), "This class is for the children, and so the children are going to sit in front." We thought, "Well, this must mean in front of the laypeople. We couldn't *possibly* sit in front of the Bhikshus and Bhikshunis." But no, he wanted us right up in front! Oh, we were really little then, and we felt *so* special to be right up in front. As I got older, I thought about it from a teacher's perspective: what better method than to have the children sit in front! Usually we sit in the back of everyone and play and write notes and talk. But here he had us right up close to him, and he had all the Dharma Masters and all the parents in back of us, so nobody dared to goof off. It was a really, really good thing to do with us at that point. At the same time we didn't even realize that we were being watched. We were really happy!

It wasn't just in these classes that he had especially for students that he paid attention to children. He *always* treated the children like we were really worthwhile, and even when he gave classes for the adults, he encouraged the children to attend. For example, in the matched couplets class that was held once or twice a week, he always encouraged us to write couplets. If we didn't write couplets, he would notice. We thought we'd get away with it, but he'd call people by name, "An An, Guo Tuo, did you write couplets?" Sometimes there were children who were too short to reach the board, so he would say, "Don't worry if you're too short. I'll put a chair up by the blackboard for you," and he would—he'd bring up a chair and you'd have four-year-olds standing up there matching couplets! He paid just as much attention to the little kids' couplets as to the adults'.

These are just a few examples, but they give you a taste of the amazing wisdom and creativity and enthusiasm that he brought to teaching children.

I also remember there was a time when Shr Fu encouraged us to memorize Sutras, especially the *Shurangama Sutra*. He also encouraged us to memorize the *Earth Store Sutra* and other Sutras. We all worked really hard at memorizing Sutras. In order to exhort us, in the evenings in the Buddhahall he would ask people to go up to the stage and recite Sutras from memory for the assembly. Every one or two days, one by one people would go up to the stage to recite Sutras from memory. But after a few days he changed his method. He said, "Okay, now we're going to use a new method. Today three or four people are going to come up and recite Sutras from memory." However, they would all be reciting different things. One might be reciting the *Earth Store Sutra*, one would be reciting the *Shurangama Sutra*, and another would be reciting the Shurangama Mantra. We were all very surprised! How could so many people recite different Sutras at the same time? He then ex-

你真地背得很熟，即使有人坐在你旁邊背別的經典，你一定還是能夠背得出來，我要考你們！」這個時候他也讓小孩上去背。這是很好玩的！

當然，師父他是因人施教，看當時情況，他教人的方法就是完全適合那個時候的那個人。有的時候，他可能會很嚴肅，我記得我小時候，大概兩三歲，那個時候還沒有萬佛城，每天師父講完經，我爸爸媽媽都載師父回他住的地方。我那麼小也不懂事，可能有一天在吵，說：「嗯！我要先回家！為什麼我們要等那麼久？」我記得那時候師父很嚴厲很嚴厲地罵了我一頓：「你這樣不行，你要懂禮貌！」當時我覺得非常慚愧，我永遠不會忘記！

可是多半的時候，他是苦口婆心，很慈悲的。等我大一點，我記得有一天當我演講完之後，他叫我到他身邊，他就說：「你要記得！隨時你有什麼事情要告訴我，你都可以來跟我講。」他是非常慈悲，像祖父一樣。

所以我們可以看得出，他花了很多心血教化人，他不要人被動的學習，不管是美國人、中國人，小孩五歲的、兩歲的、三歲的、七十五歲的，他都給所有的人機會發揮他們的潛能。

師父已經盡心竭力教導我們，所以現在我們需要負起責任來，繼承他所開始的工作，「組織起來，把小學辦好，把中學辦好，大學更要辦好！

plained, "For one person to come up and recite is very easy. If you have truly committed the Sutra to memory, then even if someone is beside you reciting another Sutra, if you are very concentrated and have memorized it well, you will still be able to recite it from memory. I'm testing you!" During that time he let children go up to recite, too. It was a lot of fun.

Of course, Shr Fu taught according to people's potentials and the situation. He based his teaching entirely on the person and the time. Sometimes he would be very stern. I remember when I was about two or three years old, which was before we had the City of Ten Thousand Buddhas, after Shr Fu finished lecturing on the Sutras every day, my parents would drive him back to where he lived. I was very little and didn't know anything. One day I was making a fuss and complaining, "I want to go home first. Why should we wait so long?" At that time I remember he scolded me very, very sternly, "You can't act this way. You have to know your manners." I felt very ashamed, and I'll never forget it.

But most of the time he was very kind and very compassionate. When I got older, I remember that one day after I gave a speech, he called me to his side and said, "Remember, anytime you have something you want to tell me, you can come and talk to me." He was very compassionate, just like a grandfather.

So we can see, he spent so much effort in teaching people. He didn't want people to learn passively. Whether it was Americans; Chinese; a child of two, three, or five years old; or a seventy-five year-old, he gave everyone a chance to realize his or her potential.

Shr Fu exhausted all his strength to teach us. Now we should take responsibility for continuing the work he started. We must, "organize ourselves, and manage and administer the schools well, both the elementary and the secondary schools, and even more so the university."

I LIKE MY TEACHER

吾愛吾師

Young Shramanerika Shi Guorou   aged 7
小沙彌尼　釋果柔　七歲

When I met Shr Fu I liked him. He likes kids. I don't know why, but I wish he will be a Buddha next life.
The first day I met Shr Fu, he put me on his lap and I was so shy, but I liked him.
Now Shr Fu has died, but I don't think he really died—maybe because he always laughed and yet didn't laugh...
He is the best Shr Fu I ever saw.

我遇到師父，我喜歡他。他喜歡小孩子。我不知道為什麼，但是我希望來世他就是佛。
我第一次看到師父時，他把我抱到他的腿上，我非常害羞，但是我喜歡他。
現在師父走了，但是我不覺得他真地走了。可能因為他常常笑，但也不是真的笑，他是我所見過最好的師父。

一切是考驗 看爾怎麼辦

EVERYTHING IS A TEST TO SEE WHAT YOU WILL DO

謝果福　Xie Guofu

一切是考驗　看爾怎麼辦
覿面若不是　須再從頭煉

這是上人作的一首偈誦，他老人家常以這首偈誦來開示教化四眾弟子，面對任何境界都是一種考驗，如果沒有定力，馬上就被境界所轉，如果沒有智慧，就會茫然不知所措，當面錯過，就會失之交臂，前功盡棄。

現在上人圓寂了，他老人家給所有弟子出了一道大題目：「我走了，看看你們怎麼辦？」就像上人在聖城的妙語堂，氣定神閒的在黑板上寫好上聯，等著所有弟子上台交卷，他好整以暇的來驗收成果。那麼現在上人的上聯已經完成了，所有四眾弟子該如何來對這下聯呢？

上人在最近幾年，一再示疾，有意無意地提示我們，世緣將盡，要弟子們有個心理準備。上人很多在家皈依弟子，一提起師父，都覺得師父非常了不起，是一個大修行者，神通廣大，無所不能。一逢病痛或稍不如意，就想倚賴師父加持、開示，或是打妄想，認為如果自己墮落不成佛，還有個師父來救度他，殊不知「師父引進門，修行在個人。」《楞嚴經》上阿難尊者也是犯了這個毛病，所以說：「自我從佛，發心出家，恃佛威神，常自思惟，無勞我修，將謂如來，惠我三昧，不知身心，本不相代。」

諸佛菩薩、祖師大德，應化度世，示生示滅，種種遊戲神通三昧，無非是要眾生生稀有心，難遭想。做為上人的弟子，何其殊勝，是大因緣，是大福報。因為「人身難得今已得，佛法難聞今已聞，善知識難遇今已遇，清淨道場難求今不求自得」，這都是上人願力所成就的，也是上人德

Everything is a test to see what you will do.
If you don't recognize what's before you, you'll have to start anew.

This verse was composed by the Venerable Master. He often used this verse to instruct and teach the fourfold assembly of disciples. No matter what state we encounter, it is a test. If we lack samadhi power, we will immediately be turned by the state. If we lack wisdom, we will be at a loss for what to do. We will miss opportunities that come right before us, and we will waste the efforts we have applied.

With his completion of stillness, the Venerable Master is giving all of his disciples a big test problem: "Now that I've gone, let's see what all of you will do." It's just like when the Venerable Master was at Wonderful Words Hall in the Sagely City. He would write the first line of a couplet on the blackboard in a calm and leisurely manner and then wait for his disciples to come up and write their matching lines, which he would examine with unruffled composure. Now the Venerable Master has written the first line. What kind of matching line will his disciples come up with?

In the past few years the Venerable Master manifested illness many times, intentionally or unintentionally reminding us that his affinities with the world were nearly over and that we should be psychologically prepared. The Venerable Master has many lay disciples who feel that the Master is a very extraordinary person, a great cultivator with extensive spiritual powers who is all-capable. Whenever they get sick or run into a small problem, they rely on the Venerable Master's aid or instruction. Some of them may even think that if they fall and do not become Buddhas, they still have a Master who will save them. What they don't know is that "the teacher leads you in the door, but you yourself have to cultivate." In the *Shurangama Sutra*, the Venerable Ananda made the same mistake and said, "Since I followed the Buddha and left home, what I have done is to rely on the Buddha's awesome spirit. I have often thought, 'There is no reason for me to toil at cultivation' expecting that the Tathagata would bestow samadhi upon me. I never realized that he could not stand in for me in body and mind."

The Buddhas, Bodhisattvas, Patriarchs, and Greatly Virtuous Ones manifest transformations in order to save the world. They manifest birth and death, various spiritual powers, and roaming in samadhi in order to cause living beings to appreciate the rarity of their teaching. How fortunate we are to be disciples of the Venerable Master! These are great affinities and great blessings. "It is difficult to obtain a human body, but I have obtained one. It is difficult to get to hear the Buddhadharma, but I have heard it. It is difficult to meet a Wise Advisor, but I have met one. It is difficult to find a pure Way-place, but I have found one without even searching." This is all brought about by the power of the Venerable Master's vows and his virtue.

The Venerable Master often spoke of the City of Ten Thousand Buddhas as a site for selecting Buddhas. It is where we pan for gold in the sand. It is a Way-place of the Proper Dharma where living Patriarchs, living Arhats,

行所感被。

上人常說萬佛城是選佛場，是在沙裡澄金，是造就活祖師、活阿羅漢、活菩薩、活佛的正法道場。可是如果我們要成就道業，不是說皈依了上人或去了萬佛城就夠了，還要遵照六大宗旨「不爭、不貪、不求、不自私、不自利、不打妄語」這十六字真言切實修行，才能成就這些聖果，上人雖然不住世了，我們更要精進修行，依法不依人，才不辜負上人一片苦心。

上人一生都是實實在在的修行，不在口頭上用功夫，一步一腳印，絕不驚世駭俗，嘩眾取寵，教化弟子亦復如是，所以這樣的大修行人，大善知識，完全是以德服人，來攝受眾生，與他老人家有緣的眾生，都會被他的德行所感召，所調伏，我自己未學佛前，毛病習氣很多，皈依上人後，就知錯則改，有一天我姊姊對我母親說：「你撿到了一個兒子。」

上個月重新拜讀了上人的事蹟，對上人一生中難行能行、難忍能忍、難捨能捨的苦行，更加景仰，內心深覺慚愧。忝為上人弟子，不是躲懶偷安，就是盡打妄想。於是下定決心，每天禮《法華經》千拜，來懺悔自己的業障，而上人卻於此時捨壽人滅。上人的一言一行，常能感化眾生於無形，師恩浩蕩，窮劫難報，弟子發心，願禮《法華經》一部，祈請上人於常寂光淨土，早日乘願重返娑婆世界，繼續度化有情眾生。

綜觀上人一生，可以「大忠、大孝、大慈、大悲、大智、大仁、大勇、大願」來概括。上人對國家忠心耿耿，旅居美國三十餘年，始終不忘自己是中國人。他關懷這個多難而分崩離析的國家，所以至死不改中華民國國籍，以明其志，這是大忠。

從十二歲起，每天早晚給父母叩頭頂禮，悔過認錯，報答父母養育劬勞之恩，十九歲母逝後，於墓旁披緇結廬守孝三年，人稱「白孝子」，遠近慕名求皈依者，絡繹不絕，這是大孝。

上人發願要把他應享的福樂，迴向給所有法界眾生。並以善巧方便法門，廣度眾生，使趨向菩提，證涅槃樂，畢竟成佛，這是大

living Bodhisattvas, and living Buddhas will be created. However, if we wish to accomplish our work in the Way, it is not enough merely to take refuge with the Venerable Master or go to the City of Ten Thousand Buddhas. We must also follow the Six Guiding Principles, the true words: "no fighting, no greed, no seeking, no selfishness, no pursuit of personal advantage, and no lying" to cultivate honestly, before we can achieve such sagely fruitions. Although the Venerable Master is no longer in the world, we should be even more vigorous in cultivation, relying on the Dharma and not on people. Then we will not disappoint the Venerable Master for all the pains he took.

The Venerable Master led a life of honest cultivation. He wasn't one to pay mere lipservice to matters. In every step he took, he was careful never to frighten or alarm people. He didn't try to impress people or to gain favors. He also taught his disciples this way. A great cultivator and great wise teacher such as this gathers people in and wins their respect entirely by means of virtue. Living beings who have affinities with the Venerable Master will be influenced and subdued by his virtue. Before I myself studied Buddhism, I had many faults and bad habits. After taking refuge with the Master, I recognized my wrongs and corrected them. One day my sister said to my mother, "You've gained a son."

Last month I read the Venerable Master's biography again and admired even more than before the Venerable Master's ascetic practice of doing what is difficult to do, enduring what is difficult to endure, and giving away what is difficult to give away. I felt ashamed and remorseful. As the Venerable Master's disciple, I was either being lazy or indulging in fanciful thinking all the time. Hence I resolved to bow a thousand times to the *Dharma Flower Sutra* every day to repent of my karmic hindrances. And yet, right at that time, the Venerable Master entered quiescence. The Venerable Master's every word and deed could invisibly influence living beings. The Master's kindness is vast indeed, and it would be difficult to repay even in endless eons. I vow to bow the entire *Dharma Flower Sutra*, and I pray that the Venerable Master in the Pure Land of Eternal Stillness and Light will soon return to the Saha World to continue teaching and rescuing sentient beings.

The Venerable Master's life can be summed up in the words "great loyalty, great filiality, great kindness, great compassion, great wisdom, great humaneness, great courage, and great vows." The Venerable Master was ardently patriotic to his country. Although he lived in America for over thirty years, he never forgot that he was a Chinese. He was extremely concerned about this tumultous country, which has gone through so many ordeals and crises. Hence, to his death he kept his citizenship in the Republic of China in order to express his resolve. This is great loyalty.

Starting from the age of twelve, he would bow every morning and evening to his parents in order to repent of his faults and repay his parents' kindness for raising him. After his mother died when he was nineteen, he built a simple hut by his mother's grave and lived there for three years in observance of filial piety. People called him Filial Son Bai. As his renown spread, an unending succession of people came from far and near seeking to take refuge with him. This is great filiality.

The Venerable Master vowed to dedicate the blessings and happiness he was due to receive to all the living beings of the Dharma Realm. With skillful expedient means, he rescued living beings on a vast scale, causing them to head towards Bodhi and ultimately attain the bliss of Nirvana

慈。

也發願要代眾生受一切的苦，使他們離苦得樂。更以清淨法音開示教化頑冥眾生，出離生死險道，脫離輪迴之苦，這是大悲。

上人觀機逗教，應病予藥，使眾生皈依三寶，返迷歸覺。早期蟄居美國六年，自稱墓中僧，待因緣成熟，開講楞嚴大法，度化五位美國弟子出家修道，這是大智。

上人提倡敬老懷少，使老有所終，幼有所長。上人要所有弟子有悲天憫人的胸懷，人人都能做到「老吾老以及人之老，幼吾幼以及人之幼」，這是大仁。

上人言人所不敢言，並對近代許多知名學者妄言《楞嚴經》是偽經，口誅筆伐，痛下針砭，以免無智者受其蠱惑，斷佛種性，這是大勇。

上人發十八大願，從菩薩、緣覺、聲聞、天、人、阿修羅、惡鬼、畜生、地獄等九法界，若有一未成佛，則不取正覺，乃至聞名見面，悉發菩提心，速得成佛道，這是大願。

上人一生行誼，可謂「道貫古今，德配天地。」弟子不敏，試作一偈，贊曰：

and Buddhahood. This is great kindness.

He also vowed to take upon himself all the sufferings of living beings so that they could leave suffering and attain bliss. He used the pure sound of Dharma to instruct dull and stubborn living beings to leave the dangerous path of birth and death and to escape the suffering of transmigration. This is great compassion.

The Venerable Master bestowed teachings according to the individual and prescribed medicine that was appropriate for each illness, causing living beings to take refuge with the Triple Jewel and turn from confusion to enlightenment. During the first six years of his stay in America, he called himself "A Monk in the Grave." When the conditions ripened, he expounded the Great Shurangama Dharma and inspired five Americans to leave the home-life and cultivate the Way. This is great wisdom.

The Venerable Master advocated that we respect the elderly and cherish the young. That way, the elderly will have a refuge and the young will be nurtured. The Venerable Master wanted all of his disciples to have compassion and pity for the people of the world. He wished everyone could "be filial to others' parents the way they are filial to their own parents; care for others' children the way they care for their own children." This is great humaneness.

The Venerable Master said what other people didn't dare to say. He orally rebuked and criticized in writing the famous contemporary scholars who claim that the *Shurangama Sutra* is an inauthentic Sutra, for he didn't want them to delude ignorant people into cutting off their Buddha-nature. This is great courage.

The Venerable Master made eighteen great vows, vowing that if any Bodhisattva, Pratyekabuddha, Hearer, god, human, asura, hungry ghost, animal, or hell-being—any being in the nine Dharma Realms—has not become a Buddha, he will not attain the Right Enlightenment. He also vowed that any living being who merely heard his name or saw his face would bring forth the Bodhi mind and quickly attain the Buddha Way. These are great vows.

It could be said of the Venerable Master's lifelong conduct: "His Way extends from the past to the present. His virtue matches that of Heaven and Earth." This is my clumsy attempt to write a verse in praise:

大忠我師志氣昂　生逢亂世愍國殤　飄洋過海三十載　不拿綠卡為哪樁
大孝宣公好榜樣　童齡朝暮禮高堂　母逝心中無罣礙　結廬守墓成道場
大慈上人度冥盲　三根普被法中王　誓予眾生涅槃樂　本有家鄉見風光
大悲菩薩懷柔腸　教化群迷遍十方　為拔六道輪迴苦　法音宣流四海揚
大智我師通三藏　觀機逗教作津梁　蟄居墓中待時節　楞嚴大法化彼邦
大仁宣公性慈祥　敬老懷少澤鄰坊　鰥寡孤獨皆蒙恩　人間淨土成仙鄉
大勇上人毅力強　頭陀苦行如家常　一夫當關師子吼　誰叫群魔把經謗
大願菩薩萬德相　般若船上導迷航　聞名見面悉成佛　九品蓮花綻清香

Our greatly loyal teacher had a lofty resolve.
Born in an age of turmoil, he pitied his dying country.
Although he crossed the ocean thirty years ago,
Why did he refuse to apply for permanent residence?

The greatly filial Master Hua was a good model;
As a child he bowed to his parents at dawn and at dusk.
When his mother passed away, his mind was free of worries.
He built a hut and stayed by her grave, making it a place of the Way.

In Memory of Venerable Master Hua

The greatly kind Venerable One saved the dull and blind.
Aiding the three kinds of faculties, he was the King of Dharma.
He vowed to bestow the joy of Nirvana upon living beings,
So that they could see the scenery of their inherent hometown.

The greatly compassionate Bodhisattva was gentle and tender at heart
As he taught the confused masses throughout the ten directions.
Pulling beings out of the suffering of the six paths of rebirth,
The sound of Dharma circulates throughout the four seas.

Our greatly wise teacher mastered the Tripitaka.
Contemplating potentials and bestowing teachings, he served as a bridge and pillar
Hibernating in a grave, he waited for the right time
To transform this country with the great Shurangama Dharma.

The greatly humane Master Hua had a kind and merciful nature.
Revering the elderly and cherishing the young, he enriched the neighborhood.
Widowers, widows, orphans, and the solitary all received his kindness.
The world became a pure land and a village of immortals.

The greatly courageous Venerable Master was firm and resolute.
Dhuta or ascetic practices were his ordinary style.
One man shouldering the job, he gave the Lion's Roar.
Who told the hordes of demons to slander the Sutras?

A Bodhisattva of great vows with ten thousand virtues,
He guides the lost boats from the Prajna ship.
Those who have heard his name or seen his face will all become Buddhas.
Nine grades of lotuses bloom with a subtle fragrance.

夢中示教

A TEACHING IN A DREAM

釋恆尚　　Shi Hengshang

我只懂閩南語，師父通常說的話我並不懂，都是由別人翻譯給我聽的。
但是一天晚上，睡夢中，卻聽到師父用閩南語對我說：「四十二手眼，你要好好修！」
我依教奉行。

I only understand Taiwanese. I don't understand what the Venerable Master usually says. Someone else always   translates for me.

One night, in a dream, I heard the Master say to me in Taiwanese, "You should do a good job of cultivating the Forty-two Hands and Eyes!" I will follow his instruction.

煩勞迷者度慈航

THOSE WHO ARE AFFLICTED, WEARIED, AND CONFUSED RIDE HIS SHIP OF KINDNESS

李果昌一九九五年八月記於 Temple City
Li Guochang August 1995 Temple City

親睹上人的法體被送進荼毗窰，數小時後，換得從熱氣球上遍撒虛空的骨灰，及五彩繽紛的舍利，令人不得不接受上人已圓寂的殘酷事實。當初還抱著一絲希望，希望上人只是入定，畢竟上人的世壽不過七十又八！娑婆世界還有太多的事須上人操心，還有太多的眾生等著上人度化……。

常慶幸自己有大福報，從小到大，曾受教於多位好老師，對我的一生有巨大的影響。然而這些傳授世間法的好老師，和六年前始得親近的上人，畢竟無法相提並論！

上人說過，他要在美國造活佛、活菩薩及活祖師。是故上人法之高、藥之猛，往往非一般凡夫所能立即接受。以萬佛城的方丈一職為例，自六年前末學首次參訪以來，不知已換過多少位，幾乎每一年半載就換個新方丈！甚至老遠從臺灣、大陸請來不搭衣、不上堂的法師來立新規矩，事後眾弟子始恍然大悟，原來又是一場考驗！方丈一職尚且如此，更遑論請氣功師及其他外道來說法了！

三年前無遮懺悔大法會中，上人的嚴酷無情，不知嚇走多少圈外人。慶幸的是，二位知過改悔的比丘，通過了這難值難遇的嚴峻考驗。上人病重的時候，曾召喚其中一位至跟前問道：「戲演得怎樣了？」言畢，師徒倆相擁而泣。上人的苦心，豈是一般凡夫俗子所能體悟的！

上人悲心切切，不捨每一位和他有緣的眾生。因上人聲名遠播，往往不免有趨炎附勢者，藉著親近上人，以提高自己的地位。常有弟子因受不了此等人的氣而生怨言，甚至生退道之心。然而上人是何等的明眼善知識，豈有不明白的道理！上人卻以其大悲心，

After personally seeing the Venerable Master's body being placed in the crematory, and several hours later, seeing his ashes being scattered from a hot air balloon, and seeing his five-colored shining sharira, one has no choice but to accept the cruel fact that the Venerable Master has already completed the stillness. At first, I held to the thread of hope that the Venerable Master was only in samadhi, for after all, he was no more than seventy-eight years old! The Saha world still has so many things for the Venerable Master to worry about, so many living beings waiting for the Master to teach and rescue them...

I often congratulate myself for being very blessed: When I was growing up, I had many good teachers who taught me and influenced my life in a very great way. Nevertheless, these good teachers of worldly subjects cannot compare to the Venerable Master, whom I met six years ago.

The Venerable Master said he wanted to create living Buddhas, living Bodhisattvas, and living Patriarchs in America. For that reason, the loftiness of his Dharma and the strength of his medicine were not something that most people could immediately accept. Consider, for example, the abbotship of the City of Ten Thousand Buddhas. Since I first visited the City six years ago, it's not known how many abbots have come and gone. There is a new abbot just about every year or half year. Dharma Masters who didn't wear their sashes or eat in the formal way were invited from Taiwan and mainland China to come and set up new rules at the City, and only afterwards did everyone wake up and realize that it was another test! If even the abbot's position is this way, need we mention the qigong masters and other externalist teachers who are invited to come and give lectures?

During the Unrestrained Repentance Ceremony three years ago, the Venerable Master's severe and merciless manner scared away many who didn't know the situation. Fortunately, two Bhikshus who recognized their faults and corrected them passed this rigorous test. During the period when the Venerable Master was gravely ill, he summoned one of them to him and asked, "How has the play-acting been going?" After he said that, the Master and disciple embraced each other and wept. How could ordinary people understand the pains taken by the Venerable Master?

The Venerable Master's earnest compassion was such that he would not forsake any living being who had affinities with him. Because the Venerable Master's fame was so widespread, there were those who tried to use his influence, who drew near him in order to raise their own status. Such people would often cause his disciples to get mad and complain, and even to retreat from the Way. Yet, consider what kind of Bright-eyed Good Knowing Advisor the Venerable Master is. How could he not un-

耐心地教化此輩眾生，絕不輕言放棄。一方面，上人欲慈悲攝受有過錯的弟子，給他們改過遷善的機會；另一方面，又要藉此考驗眾弟子。上人說過：「若師兄弟的氣尚且不能忍，又怎能成就道業呢？」由此可見上人為度眾生用心之良苦！

上人示現病相期間，熱心的弟子或毛遂自薦，或請來中西名醫，欲為上人診療。上人本是倒駕慈航的大醫王，為隨機度化眾生，卻還是慈悲地滿弟子們的願，接受這些無謂的治療。究竟誰醫誰的病，由觀音菩薩的偈頌應可窺出端倪：

老僧閒來無甚事，
捉個迷藏臥病床；
胸裡常懷虛空志，
眉頭緊鎖聚靈光。
一俯一仰痛難當，
利物度生終不忘；
眾裡尋他百千劫，
對面不識耐思量。
見有觀空空不空，
診病問源源非源；
隨緣應對無起落，
煩勞迷者度慈航。

上人所講經典的內容，包括經律論，極為廣博。上人說法，深入淺出，生動活潑，舉世無匹，無論初學或老參，均可從中同霑法益。值得慶幸的是，上人講經的錄音帶，保存得極為完整。聆聽上人講演的錄音，彷彿親蒙上人教誨，我們應將這些法寶廣為流傳。

上人更慈悲地留下數千的舍利，不但可供千秋萬世後人瞻仰，更為弟子們留下取之不盡、用之不竭的寶藏，吾等怎能不感激涕零呢？

derstand? The Venerable Master, with his heart of great compassion, patiently taught these disciples and never gave up on them lightly. On the one hand, the Venerable Master wished to compassionately draw in the disciples who were at fault and give them a chance to reform. On the other hand, he wanted to use this to test his disciples. The Master said, "If one cannot endure even the temper of one's Dharma-brothers, how can one accomplish one's work in the Way?" From this, we can see the great pains taken by the Venerable Master to teach and save living beings!

During the time when the Venerable Master was manifesting illness, many devoted disciples either tried to treat the Master themselves or invited well-known Chinese and Western doctors to treat the Master. The Venerable Master is actually a great king of doctors who compassionately turned the ship around. Yet in order to teach and transform living beings according to their potentials, he kindly did as his disciples wished and accepted the unnecessary treatments. Ultimately, who was treating whom? Perhaps Guanyin Bodhisattva's verse will give us a hint:

The old monk has come in leisure, with nothing much to do.
He plays hide-and-seek and lies on the sickbed.
In his heart, he constantly cherishes a resolve
*   as vast as empty space.*
On his creased forehead, a spiritual light gathers.
Tossing and turning, he can barely endure the pain.
Yet he never forgets to benefit and rescue living beings.
For hundreds of thousands of eons, we have sought him
*   in the multitudes.*
Coming face to face we fail to recognize him:
*   This is worth reflecting on.*
Look at existence and contemplate emptiness:
*   the emptiness isn't empty.*
They treat the illness and seek the cause,
*   but the cause is not the cause.*
According with conditions and responding to matters,
*   there is neither rising nor falling.*
Those who are afflicted, wearied, and confused
*   ride his ship of kindness.*

The Venerable Master has lectured on an extensive range of scriptures, which includes Sutras, the Vinaya, and Shastras. When the Master speaks the Dharma, he expresses profound principles in a simple and lively way which no one else in the world can match. Beginners as well as old pros alike can benefit from his Dharma. Fortunately, most of the Venerable Master's lectures on the Sutras have been well preserved on tape. Listening to the Venerable Master's lectures on tape is almost like listening to the Master in person. We should circulate these treasures of Dharma on a wide scale.

The Venerable Master has kindly left behind several thousand sharira for people in thousands of future generations to behold. They are also an inexhaustible treasury the Venerable Master left for his disciples. How can we not be moved to tears by this?

法雨拾零

DROPS OF DHARMA RAIN

釋化來　　Shi Hualai

總綱

「從虛空來，還歸虛空去。」意思是說的自性，也就是本心。如虛空，空無一物；而能千變萬化，妙用無窮；雖有無窮的變化，終歸是空無所有。所謂：「無不從此法界流，無不還歸此法界。」如果說師父的生，是從虛空來，圓寂是歸虛空去，未免欠妥。人，本來就是幻化不實的，如鏡中影像，並非真實，並無來去，有時非有，無時非無，鏡體是常住不動的。以鏡像為真，便失了鏡體。希望大家以此體會師父的生死的幻化，真認本源自性。會此，師父並未離開我們，這是諸佛出世本懷，也是師父說法的本意。故曰總綱。

綱目

（一）一次，我在大悲道掃樹葉，師父駕了高爾夫車，停在我旁，下車即問曰：「做什麼？」我說：「掃葉子。」師父說：「還可以。」這事，我一直在默思著，最近才有所明白。只答對一半。為什麼？因為我當時用了直心，而未用心去想，衝口而出。以當時情況來說，師父停車時，我已擁帚而待，並未掃葉。師父問的是當時，而我答的是過去。不過，以當時情況來講，若在旁人，恐開口不得，我能開口，所以師父說還可以。這是我初攀玉階，而未入門。

（二）又一次，午供時，我剛走過五觀堂。師父駕了車子，停在我旁，下車後，手裡拿了一只瓜果，問曰：「是什麼？」我說：「不識。」這次，我是通過觀看後而答的，但只看到外面，沒有看裡面，以外面來講，是

General Outline:

"Coming from empty space, and returning to empty space." This means that the self-nature—the original mind, is like empty space, which has nothing in it but is capable of a myriad transformations and infinite wonderful functions. Although it undergoes a myriad transformations, in the end it returns to emptiness. As it is said, "There is nothing that does not flow forth from the Dharma Realm, and nothing that does not return to the Dharma Realm." If one were to say that the Venerable Master's birth was a coming from empty space, and that his completion of stillness was a return to empty space, that wouldn't be appropriate. People are fundamentally illusory and unreal, like images in a mirror. They have no actuality and do not come or go. When they exist, they do not really exist, and when they cease to exist, they are not really nonexistent. The substance of the mirror is eternal and unmoving. If the images in the mirror are taken to be real, the substance of the mirror is lost. I hope everyone will understand from this that the Master's birth and death are illusory and will truly recognize their original self-nature. If we understand this, then the Master has not left us. This is the original intention of all Buddhas in coming into the world, and it is also the Venerable Master's purpose in speaking the Dharma. Thus, this is called the "General Outline."

Contents:

1. Once when I was sweeping leaves in the Great Compassion Courtyard, the Venerable Master drove his golf cart up and stopped beside me. He got out and asked, "What are you doing?" I said, "Sweeping the leaves." The Master said, "Not bad." I've been musing over this, and recently I've come to some understanding of it. My answer was only half correct. Why? Because although I used a straight mind, I blurted out the answer without thinking. When the Master had stopped the golf cart, I was holding the broom and waiting, not sweeping leaves. The Master had asked about the present, while I had replied about the past. However, if it had been someone else in that situation, perhaps he wouldn't have dared to say anything at all. At least I was able to say something, so the Master said, "Not bad." That time, I had gone up the steps, but I didn't get in the door.

2. Another time, when it was time for the Noon Meal Offering, I had just walked by the Five Contemplations Dining Hall when the Master drove up, stopped beside me, and got out of the cart. Holding a melon up, he asked, "What's this?" I said, "I don't recognize it." This time, I reflected on my answer before giving it, but I only saw the outside, not the inside. Externally speaking my answer was correct, but internally it wasn't. My own intrinsic mind is constantly before me; how can I not recognize it?

對了，內裡即不是。自己的本心，無時無刻不在眼前，那能不識呢？然而，欲說是什麼？這就很難形容的。如古德靈嶽禪師，被六祖一問，將什麼物來？尚目瞪口呆，回答不出。八年後才回答：「說是一物即不准。」這次我入門，而未升堂入室。

當時，師父將瓜果遞給我，我去接，但不知何用？問曰：「供佛嗎？」師父未說話，我轉身送往廚房。這是師父暗示我普利有情。

（三）法會期間，我從大帳棚回到萬佛殿，有女子，要我和她合照，我連說：「不行！不行！」這是我不能善巧方便，滿眾生願。是不是不知道善巧方便的做法呢？不是的。不過總免不了做作，與師父無做作、無安排，還有些差距。這是我升堂而未入室。

（四）法會期間有人要我寫四句偈頌送他，以為勉勵。我即寫道：「開示悟證，行解相應，行住坐臥，念茲在茲。」這是內外四法為初基。

（五）如師父說：「我從虛空來，回到虛空去。」作麼生道，偈曰：

宣有宣無空泯跡，
化去化來別有天，
奉下兩點不是秦，
心月孤圓照漢天。

又偈曰：

掃葉初攀踏，觀是始入門。
方便常善巧，內外依無依。
有無泯跡後，來去皆妙明，
休為兩點疑，孤月照空城。

總之，做什麼，是什麼，即是從虛空來，還歸虛空去的寫照，會此，通達一切法。

And yet, it would be difficult to describe in words. When the Sixth Patriarch asked the ancient worthy, Chan Master Linyou, what he came from, he was struck dumb and couldn't reply. Eight years later, he answered that even a single thing was impermissible. This time, I got in the door, but didn't ascend the hall or enter the inner rooms yet.

At the time, the Master gave the melon to me and I took it, but I didn't know what it was for. "Is this to be offered to the Buddhas?" I asked. The Master said nothing, so I turned around and took it to the kitchen. This was a hint from the Master that I should benefit all sentient beings.

3. During a Dharma session, as I was walking from the large tent to the Buddhahall, a girl asked to have her picture taken with me. I said, "I can't do that!" That's a case in which I cannot be expedient in order to fulfill living beings' wishes. Is it because I don't know how to use expedient skill-in-means? No. However, I cannot avoid some deliberation on this; I'm still a ways off from the Master's lack of premeditation and arrangement. That time, I ascended the hall but had yet to enter the inner rooms.

4. During the Dharma session, someone wanted me to write a four-line gatha for him as an exhortation, so I wrote, "Opening, demonstrating, awakening, and certifying: practice and understanding mutually correspond. Walking, standing, sitting, and reclining: be mindful in thought after thought." These are the four internal and external dharmas, which serve as an initial foundation.

5. As the Master said, "I came from empty space, and I will return to empty space." I have written a verse,

Proclaiming existence and nonexistence, all traces of emptiness
*   are obliterated.*
Transforming back and forth, another world is reached.
Two dots under the word feng 奉 *is not qing* 秦.
The moon of the mind, lonely and round, shines in the skies of Han.

Another verse says,

Sweeping leaves was the initial ascending of the steps.
Reflection was the entering of the door.
With constantly skillful expedients,
*   there is reliance and yet no reliance inside and out.*
After the traces of existence and nonexistence are destroyed,
*   there is wonderful brightness everywhere one goes.*
When the two points of doubt are put to rest,
*   the lonely moon shines on the city of emptiness.*

In brief, whatever we do, we should do just that. That's a description of coming from empty space and returning to empty space. One who understands this will completely fathom all dharmas.

「斷欲」

"CUT OFF DESIRE!"

釋恆有　Shi Hengyou

今天我有一點高興，又有一點悲傷。高興的是能與諸位大善知識在一起；悲傷的是因為以前我也來萬佛城與金山寺，常常被叫上來講講我所瞭解的佛法。那時下面總是坐著一個人，有時他一句話也不講，只耐心地聽我講；也有時他改正我，有時他也替我補充一些。今天我坐在這裡，可是那個人不在了，他永遠不會再來那樣改正我、教導我了！在人的一生中，能找到一位可以改正你錯誤的人，機會是非常難得的。今天我失去的正是這麼一個人，那人就是我的師父，也是各位的師父。

我不像各位住在萬佛城、金山寺的人那麼幸運，常常在師父身邊，能夠常聽師父的教誨。因為我業障很深，還必須在社會上為生活掙扎，不能來萬佛城親近師父。也正因為這原因，所以師父所告訴我的幾句話，我把它看做是寶貝一樣。因為太少了、太稀有了，所以我就盡力把這很少的幾句話，看看如何能運用在生活上。因為師父給我的話很少，所以我非常珍惜。

一九七七年四月，我去加拿大開會，並發表一篇力學的文章。會期一週，文章報告完畢，我就去金山寺見師父。一見之下，我就感覺非常親切，當時金山寺在十五街，隱隱約約覺得這個地方自己來過。在那之前，我從來沒有見過和尚，也從來沒有進過佛教寺廟，所以那次是我第一次接觸佛教，第一次見到和尚－－就是上人。我十二歲離家，為生活奔波，非常艱苦。十二歲起就沒有再向誰叩頭，連想也沒有想過要給人叩頭。我和上人一見面，就有說不出的親切與自在，好像回到家一樣。各位或許都有溫暖的家庭，無法體會，只有我自己才知道那感受，於是我立刻給他叩頭了。師父一邊笑，一邊說：「教授向我叩頭！」

叩下去站起來，我覺得自己好像變了一個人似的。因為我是一個非常剛強、不容易屈服的人。我就想我怎麼給這個和尚叩頭呢？那個感覺說不出，就覺得自己好像變了，一個突變。我很開心，就皈依他。當天晚上，做完晚課後，十點多鐘大家都睡覺了，我坐在佛堂凳子上，腦子沒有想什麼，覺得空空的，說不出任何感覺，那種發呆的樣子。坐在那裡，師父就來了

Today, I feel kind of happy, and I also feel kind of sad. I'm happy to be together with all of you great, wise teachers. But on the other hand, I feel kind of sad. In the past, when I came to the City of Ten Thousand Buddhas and Gold Mountain Monastery, I was often asked to come up and speak about my understanding of Buddhism. During those times, a certain person always sat there. Sometimes he would just listen to me quietly without saying anything. At other times, he would correct me or make some comments. Today, I'm sitting here, but that person is no longer here. He will never again correct me or teach me. It's really rare to find someone who can correct your mistakes for you. Now I've lost that person, who was my teacher and also your teacher.

I am not as fortunate as those of you who live at the City of Ten Thousand Buddhas and Gold Mountain Monastery, who were often with the Master and heard his teachings. Because of my heavy karmic obstacles, I had to struggle to make a living out in the world. I couldn't come to the City of Ten Thousand Buddhas to be near the Master. Because of that, I really treasured the few sentences that the Master did speak to me. Because they were so rare, I tried my best to apply them in my life. Because the Master's words to me were so few, they were extremely precious to me.

In April 1977, I went to Canada to present a paper on Mechanics at a seven-day conference. Afterwards, I went to Gold Mountain Monastery to see the Master. As soon as I saw him, I felt a great sense of familiarity. Gold Mountain Monastery was on Fifteenth Street then, and somehow I felt that I'd been there before. I had never seen a monk or entered a Buddhist temple before. That was the first time I came into contact with Buddhism and met a monk—the Venerable Master. I had to go out to make a living when I was only twelve years old. It was extremely tough. From the time I was twelve, I never bowed to anyone or even had the thought of bowing to anyone. But as soon as I saw the Master, I had an indescribable feeling of ease and familiarity, as if I'd returned home. Probably you all have caring families, so you cannot imagine how I felt. No one can know that feeling but myself. I immediately bowed to the Master. The Master laughed and said, "Look, here's a professor bowing to me!"

After bowing down and getting up, I felt like a different person. I used to be a very stubborn and unsubmissive person. How could I have bowed to a monk? I can't describe my feeling. A sudden change had occurred in me. I was very happy, and I took the refuge with the Master that same day. At about

，我也沒有跟他講話，他也沒有跟我講話，就坐在我的身邊。我們並坐了十幾分鐘沒有說話，然後他突然大聲說：「斷欲！」當時我沒有害怕，也沒有動一下，但是斷欲的印象，就像獅子吼在我心裡非常深刻，不會忘記！因為我認識佛教是從《六祖壇經》，經中並沒有提到斷欲啊？它說：「淫心本是淨心因。」那次，「斷欲」在我腦海裡非常深刻。

「欲」確實是我的大病，可是我並不覺得，從那天開始我知道自己有一個病。我回去就開始實行，這麼多年了，但是我時時在努力，非常艱苦，它影響到我和我的家庭。後來才知道斷欲是經典中佛陀最基本的教誨，這是師父第一次的教化。

次年，一九七八年，我隨師父到南洋去，共有六個禮拜。這是我接近師父最長久、聽他教化最多的一段時間。在這裡只舉一件事，我們到一間南傳廟，住持是一位在馬來西亞政府很有影響力的Dhammananda法師（達摩難陀）。到他的廟上，師父和這位法師坐在中央，我們九個人就圍著師父坐，我和師父座下兩位法師閉著眼睛在打坐。這位Dhammananda法師的一位在家徒弟，他的大護法，是一位教授，他就起來質問師父：為什麼大乘法師不禮拜小乘法師，不尊重他們？他還說了很多，我不記得了。師父沒有回答他，他還繼續說著。我正在打坐，沒有聽他講話，不知道他講什麼，也不知道為什麼，就站起來了，在他面前給他叩頭。然後我問他：「請問你，我在叩頭前是大乘，還是小乘？我在叩頭後是小乘，還是大乘？」他有點呆了，不能回答我。於是乎他的問題就解決了，他不再問了。同時在旁邊有一位黃姓居士，他是師父到南洋的請法者。黃居士對他說：「他也是一位教授。」從那時開始，他就對我非常好，也不再問師父問題了。

那次旅程中，每天早上我們都會開個小小的會議，師父高坐，我們坐在地板上，檢討一下前一天的工作。那天師父坐好了，就從椅子上挪下來，坐在地板上我身邊，他說：「昨天你做得真是太好了！」我說：「師父您不要誇獎我，好不好？誰誇獎我，我都不怕，因為我不執著，我不需要。不過您誇獎我，我有點受不了，我會執著，因為我太高興了！」師父說：「哎！我不是誇獎你，我是說真話啊！」這比誇獎還厲害！

ten-o'clock that night, after everyone had gone to sleep, I sat on the bench in the Buddhahall. My mind was blank. I was in a daze—I can't describe my feeling. Then the Master walked over and sat down beside me. I didn't say a word, nor did he. We sat there for about ten minutes, and all of a sudden he shouted, "Cut off desire!" I was not scared, and I didn't move, but his hollering of "cut off desire" was like a lion's roar. It made a deep impression on me. I will never forget it! I learned Buddhism from the *Sixth Patriarch Platform Sutra,* which doesn't mention desire directly, but says, "The mind of lust is basically the cause for the mind of purity." That time, the idea of "cutting off desire" really impressed me. Desire was truly my great illness, but I didn't realize it before. From that day on, I recognized this illness. I worked on that teaching for many years. I applied effort constantly, and it was very difficult. It affected not only me, but my whole family. Later on, I realized that the cutting off of desire is the Buddha's basic teaching in all the Sutras. That was the first teaching the Master gave me.

The following year, 1978, I joined the Master's delegation on a six-week visit to Southeast Asia. That was the longest time I was near the Master and also the time when I received the most teachings. Here, I'll just mention one thing that happened. We went to a Theravadan temple whose abbot, the Venerable Sri Dhammananda, was quite influential in the Malaysian government. In the temple, the Master and the Venerable Sri Dhammananda sat in the center. The nine of us sat around the Master. Two left-home disciples of the Master and I were sitting in meditation with our eyes closed. A layman, who was a professor and a great Dharma protector of the temple, asked the Master, "Why don't the Dharma Masters of Mahayana Buddhism respect and bow to Theravadan Dharma Masters?" He said a lot more that I don't remember. The Master didn't reply, and the layman kept asking. I had been meditating and not paying attention to the conversation, but for some unknown reason, I stood up and bowed to the person. I asked him, "Please tell me, before I bowed, was I a Mahayana or a Theravadan Buddhist? After my bowing, am I a Theravadan or a Mahayana Buddhist?" He couldn't answer me. A Mr. Wong, who had made the request for the Master's trip to Malaysia, told him, "He is also a professor." From then on, that layman was very kind to me and didn't ask any more questions.

On that trip, every morning we would hold a small meeting to discuss what we had done the day before. The Master would sit on a high chair and we would sit on the floor. The next morning, the Master got off his chair and sat down on the floor beside me. He said, "What you did yesterday was really good!" I said, "Master, please don't praise me. I'm not afraid of anyone else's praise, because I have no attachments and I don't care. But, Master, I can't take it when you praise me. I'll be attached, because I'll be too happy." He said, " I'm not praising you. I am telling the truth." That's even worse than praising!

THE GOOD AND WISE ADVISOR'S TEACHINGS FOR ME

善知識對我的教誨

Shi Heng Sure 釋恆實

Many disciples experienced the Venerable Abbot's teachings in person and know the dynamic experience of drawing near a Good and Wise Advisor; many others did not, but knew the Master through his books or by reputation only. Scolding is perhaps the most misunderstood aspect of his teachings when viewed by those who did not understand its use among the many skillful expedient means of a true Wise Teacher.

At that time the Youth Good Wealth bowed at his feet, stood, put his palms together, and said, "Sagely One, I have already brought forth the resolve for Anuttara-samyak-sambodhi, but I still do not know how a Bodhisattva studies the Bodhisattva Conduct and how he cultivates the Bodhisattva path. I heard that the Sagely One is skilled at guiding and teaching. I wish you would explain this for me."

The Brahman said, "Good Man, if you can now go up this mountain of knives and throw yourself into the mass of fire, then all your Bodhisattva conduct will be purified."

Chapter on Entering the Dharma Realm,
The *Flower Adornment Sutra*

Shr Fu taught in many skillful ways; one of the more dramatic was his "scoldings." I am one of several disciples who frequently got the benefit of Shr Fu's focused energy via the expedient of scoldings.

In the world, scolding is something universally feared; for that reason a tongue-lashing is effective as a means of discipline and behavior modification. It only works, however, if the one doing the scolding has personal virtue. If there is real anger behind the words, then scolding will produce hatred and anger in return.

We disciples knew that the thundering storm of anger was a technique, because the Abbot could be blasting away to correct a mistake by one disciple, and then in a twinkling turn his head to gently encourage another disciple in the crowd. In another eyeblink, he would return to the fault of the miscreant and send more lightning shafts towards him. These two modes of teaching—(1) subduing and humbling the arrogant and hard; and (2) enticing and embracing the timid and cautious—appear in Sutra descriptions of the Buddha's own two methods of teaching: hard and soft, turned on and off at will. Those who watched closely would see the compassionate, impassive, kindly teacher behind the heat.

很多的弟子曾親自受到上人的教誨，有活生生親近善知識的經驗；也有很多弟子沒這個機會，但他們卻從上人的書中得到受益；有的只是聽過上人的名字罷了；訶責是上人教法中，最容易讓人產生誤解的部分，而這些誤解的人，卻不明白這是大智者善巧法門的運用。

爾時善財童子頂禮其足，合掌而立。自言聖者，我已先發阿耨多羅三藐三菩提心。而未知菩薩。云何學菩薩行。云何修菩薩道。我聞聖者善能誘誨。願唯我說。婆羅門言。汝今若能上此刀山投身火聚。諸菩薩行悉得清淨。

——《華嚴經》〈入法界品〉

上人用各種不同方式教化弟子，其中最戲劇性的，就是上人的「訶責」。眾弟子中，我是常從師父的「訶責」中得到受益的一個。

在世間法上，「訶責」為眾生所懼怕。然而，口頭上的鞭策確實是一種很有效的訓練方式和改變行為的方法。不過，只有具有德行的人才可以用這個方法。假使在「訶責」弟子的時候，帶有真脾氣，「訶責」就會引起仇恨與氣憤。

上人的弟子，都瞭解上人雷雨般的脾氣，只是一種善巧方便。上人往往在嚴厲地批評某個弟子後，回過頭來給另一個弟子很溫和的鼓勵，突然上人轉而又指出另一個弟子的錯誤。佛陀使用這兩種教法：降伏、折服貢高頑固的人，包容、教誨害羞謹慎的人。弟子們常能見到發脾氣後的上人，又顯得慈悲而平靜。

實際上，最親近師父的弟子，通常都受到最

In fact only the closest disciples got scolded harshly at all; and among them, it seemed that scolding came in a sense as a reward for hard work. We "earned" our scoldings. But this did not make them any easier to take.

I recall being scolded once on live television (Channel 5), at the San Francisco airport, and several times while translating on a lecture stage before thousands of people. In my memory, the worst scoldings came overseas: in Hong Kong, in Taiwan, in Calgary. No time was ever too public, too embarrassing to prevent a chance to teach a student who was ripe for a scolding. Sometimes those well-timed tongue-lashings marked an unexpected turning point in a disciple's life.

Once at Gold Mountain an error I made brought on a public reprimand that kept the entire assembly standing at their bowing benches for ninety minutes. The volume and the impact of the rebuke created distaste in some of the onlookers and listeners, but not in the recipient. Strangely enough, its effects, besides producing shame and a wish to change, were clear seeing, lightness, and calm, like the state at the eye of the tornado. Of course it helped to know about the proverbial Chinese father who "*pan zi cheng long*" "reprimands his children to turn them into dragons." That is, scolding strengthens one's bones. Most often the scolding produced a memorable opportunity to get priceless instructions.

For example, once I sent away an important guest by mistake, and got scolded so hard I thought I should run away, or perhaps die. I didn't die, and the next morning the Abbot frowned and asked me how I felt.

"I felt like I ought to die. I felt inadequate, useless, and forlorn. Maybe I *would* rather die," I said.

"You won't die. That would just be cheating. Dying would be easier than changing your bad habits. Where is your copy of the *Ultimate End of the Dharma Sutra*? Get it and read to me." I ran to my desk and found the requested text. I knelt in the Buddhahall in front of the Master. I read the story of the future day when Buddhism will completely disappear from the planet.

The Abbot sat with a distant gaze, keeping a half dozen disciples waiting, each of whom had urgent business—real estate, banking, international phone calls, and offerings—to settle, while he listened to my recitation of the text in clumsy Chinese.

As I read, I felt sweat break out on my face and body. My temperature rose and I felt faint, as if something were being purged and carried out of me. I kept reading and the sensation passed, leaving me lighter, cooler, and calmer. All traces of my earlier mood of self-pity were gone.

The Master exhorted in a stern voice, "You have left home to follow me, and now you are not like you were before; now you have to cultivate the Way; You are a disciple of the Buddha, you belong to the Buddha's family. Do you see how important your words and actions are? In this country you represent the Buddha, the Dharma, and the Sangha. Do you understand? You're not living just for yourself any longer. How can you be heedless and selfish? Don't you see the road you are on?" Great Master Yung Chia saw it,

大的訶叱。這似乎成了一種努力工作後的回報。看起來上人的責罵是我們以努力工作「換取」得來的，雖然這麼說，但捱罵還是常常令人很不好受的。

我還記得，在電視節目（第五頻道）中、在舊金山機場、在上千人的法筵上被上人罵。記憶中最嚴厲的責備都是在海外：香港、臺灣、卡加利。上人不會因為弟子做的事太醜陋，而不予以公開訶叱，這是上人教育學生的特別機會。很多時候，因為罵得正是時候，反而成為弟子生命中，預想不到的轉捩點。

有一次在金山寺，因為我的過失，整整九十分鐘，大眾陪我站著，接受上人的訓叱。如此嚴厲的訓叱，引起旁觀者和聽眾們的反感。奇怪的是，我心中除了慚愧與懺悔之外，同時產生一種輕安和明瞭的見地，有如在龍捲風的風眼裡。當然，這幫助我懂得中國諺語「望子成龍」的意思，父親罵孩子是希望他們成材。不過被罵之後，都會在記憶中印上無價的教誨。

一次，我誤把一位重要客人趕走，我被罵得幾乎想捲鋪蓋走路，要不就乾脆死了算了。可惜我並沒有死，第二天早上，上人皺著眉頭問我覺得怎麼樣？

「我覺得我該死，我做得很不恰當、很沒用、很可憐，我想我應該死了算了。」我說。

上人說：「你不會死的，不要自己欺騙自己。想去死，那太便宜你了，你應該改你的壞習氣。你那本《法滅盡經》在哪裡？拿來讀給我聽！」我拿著那部經，在佛殿裡，跪在上人面前，念了一段有關：佛法如何在地球上消失無遺的經文。上人坐著，凝視著遠方，讓半打的弟子等在佛殿外面。每個人都有要緊的事情要呈報：房地產、銀行、國際電話、供養等，但上人卻在聆聽我笨拙的中文念誦。

我一邊念，一邊感到汗水從臉上、身上流下來，我的體溫上升，我覺得快要暈倒了，體內的什麼東西像是被滌除掉了。我繼續念下去，這種感受就消失了，留下的是輕安、清涼、平靜，先前的自憐已經不存在了。

上人用很堅定的語氣說：「你已經跟我出家了，不可以跟以前一樣。你現在必須修道，你是佛的弟子，屬於佛的家族。難道你沒意識到你的一言一行有多重要嗎？在這個國家，你代表著佛、法、僧，你懂嗎？你已經不是為你自己而活了，你怎麼可以這麼大意，這麼自私？難道你看不到你所走的這條

Once I saw the road to Tsao Creek, I recognized the phenomenon of birth and death and had nothing further to do with them.

The Venerable Abbot continued: "You've got to try harder. A casual effort like before won't get you over the Dragon Gate. I've got high expectations for you. How can you just muddle through, like somebody who is simply eating his fill and waiting for death to catch up to him? Living like somebody born drunk and dying in a dream is good enough for others, but disciples of the Buddha have to be models for both humans and gods. You have to surpass the ordinary and excel the standards. You have to endure what others can't endure, eat food that others can't eat, take on suffering that others can't take on, and practice what others can't practice. You have to be patient where others cannot be patient. Only then will you pass the tests ahead. Take propagating the Dharma as your personal responsibility. Otherwise, Buddhism won't take root in this country."

Good Wealth said, "Strange indeed, Sagely One. When my body came into contact with this mountain of knives and great mass of fire, I felt peaceful, serene, and joyous.

Chapter on Entering the Dharma Realm,
The *Flower Adornment Sutra*

The scolding may have been the catalyst that jolted the memory of my past vows into awareness, because several days later I had the vision that led to my making the resolve to begin the "Three Steps, One Bow" pilgrimage for world peace. The Venerable Abbot observed that night after the Sutra lecture,

All of you in the past have been together with Vairochana Buddha. We have been together investigating the Buddhadharma. And way back then I said we should all go to America and do it. Some of you made the vows of monks and some the vows of nuns. Some made the vows of Dharma-protectors. Others made the vows to be translators. Some of you made vows to build Way-places; and others to teach school.

Now we are all here to fulfill our vows. From limitless kalpas past our causes and conditions with one another have been deep. They create a strength of togetherness that endures... And in the Hall of Ten Thousand Buddhas you can make vows, so in the future we can all become Ten Thousand Buddhas. Three-Steps-One-Bow are seeking Ten Thousand Buddhas to protect ten thousand peoples. In the midst of a dream, we are all here doing the Buddhas' work...

This phrase rings loudest in my mind recently among all the many instructions I've received from the Venerable Abbot in the last twenty years:

Here we are, in the midst of a dream doing the work of the Buddhas.

路？」永嘉大師說：

自從認得曹溪路。了知生死不相關。

上人又接著說：「你應該更努力，偶而的努力不會使你越過龍門的，我對你有更高的期望，你怎麼可以像那些混吃等死的人一樣。對他們來說，醉生夢死已經夠了。可是身為佛子，要做人天師表，要出類拔萃。你必須擔人所不能擔、吃人所不能吃、受人所不能受、行人所不能行、忍人所不能忍，唯有這樣，才能通過考驗。要以弘法為己任，不然佛法是不會在這個國家紮根的。

善財白言：甚奇！聖者，如是刀山及大火聚。我深觸時安穩快樂。
——《華嚴經》〈入法界品〉

責備或許是一種催化劑，喚起我對過去所發誓願的覺知。因為，幾天以後，我觀到一種境界，引發了我為祈求世界和平而行「三步一拜」的決心。那天晚上聽經以後，上人說：

你們以前都跟隨過毗盧遮那佛，我們曾在一起研究佛法。那時候，我說我們應該去美國弘法。當時，有人發願做比丘，有人發願做比丘尼，有人發願做護法，有人發願作翻譯，有人發願建立道場，有人發願教書……。

所以，現在我們都在這裡還願。從無量劫以來，我們彼此都有很深的因緣，這種因緣強而有力，持續地維繫著我們之間的關係……。你可以在萬佛殿發一個願，將來我們都能成為萬佛之一。三步一拜為的是祈求萬佛來護持萬人，我們都在這裡大作夢中佛事。

這幾段話，是上人二十多年來給我的教誨中，我印象最深刻的。幾天來，這幾句話一直在我的腦海裡迴蕩著。

我們在這裡，大作夢中佛事。

*　　　*　　　*

I recall kneeling in the aisle of a bus on a sweltering sunny afternoon in Taoyuan, Taiwan, outside the gate of a monastery. The delegation from Dharma Realm Buddhist University was caught in a titanic traffic jam, caused by our visit to the Republic of China. The cars were coming to listen to the Venerable Abbot speak Dharma and transmit the precepts. People had gotten out of their cars to scratch their heads and to discuss the scene. I was kneeling in the aisle because the Venerable Abbot, to pass the time constructively, had asked the members of the delegation to stand up and give Dharma-talks. "Anywhere and anytime is a good place to cultivate the Way" was one of the Master's favorite travel maxims.

I had been receiving mighty scoldings since before we got on the plane in San Francisco, and I had been apprehensive day and night, fearing to do anything else wrong and anxious to escape the withering glare and lion's roar of the Good and Wise Advisor. The Master had called me out first and ordered me to speak Dharma. I felt exhausted and overwhelmed. The heat, the diarrhea, the pressure of my faults grinding against my teacher's will that I change for the Dharma, for the better, all put my head in a spin, and I couldn't utter a sound. I could only kneel there mute and limp.

"Kuo Chen!" said the Abbot, and suddenly I entered another zone, and as if transported in time I recalled a moment in Malibu on my bowing pilgrimage alongside the highway when the California Highway Patrol pulled up to tell us to be careful of the road ahead because it was narrow and fast. The officer was a slow-speaking, sun-browned cowboy with a twinkle in his eye. "You fellers had better stay way over on the shoulder, and tell that Chinese gentleman behind you to do the same. His red robe helps make him a bit more visible, but this is a fast road, and I don't want any accidents on my shift. Our CHP attorney called on his way to work, said he had spotted you and wanted us to make sure you get safely through Malibu. My wife saw you, too, and told me to remind the three of you to be careful. Take care, fellas."

We thanked him, and, after he left, sheepishly looked behind us for the third member of our team, the "Chinese gentleman." We couldn't see anyone, let alone somebody in a red robe.

"Three monks, he said?"

"Strange. I wonder who they saw."

Only months later in San Francisco did a laywoman tell us the other side of the story. During that time of the pilgrimage, frequently in the mornings or afternoons the Venerable Abbot would be speaking with them and would suddenly stand up and walk into his room and shut the door. They would never know what he did inside, but usually after an hour or so, he would emerge and say, "They're all right now, *mei you shi qing,* it's okay." The CHP officers' request suggested that the Venerable Abbot's vows were helping him supervise the pilgrimage of two young monks from six hundred miles away. The Abbot's seventeenth vow says, "I vow in this life to attain the Five Eyes and Six Penetrations, and the ability to fly freely."

The image brought me back to the stifling bus in Taoyuan, and I believe the Venerable Abbot was observing my insight, because now he was smiling and his tone was gentle, instead of severe. "Kuo Chen here speaks from experience. You should listen to what he has to say, because he knows that without a Good and Wise Advisor he would

我記得是一個酷熱的下午，在臺灣桃園一座寺廟門外，來自美國法界佛教大學的弘法團的車隊，引起了交通阻塞，我們的巴士被夾在車隊中間。車裡的人，都是來聽上人說法或準備受戒的。當時，我在一輛巴士裡面跪在走道上。因為上人善加利用時間，要弘法團在車上隨機說法，任何時候、任何地方都是可以修道的，這是上人旅行時的原則。

在舊金山上機之前，我就已經結結實實地捱了幾頓罵。所以，我日夜都在擔心，怕做錯事，怕善知識的怒目相向和大獅子吼。這一次，上人最先點到我，要我為大眾說法。由於天氣很熱，又瀉肚子，我覺得很累；我的過失，以及上人要求我改過所帶來的壓力，這一切，使我的頭都大了。我一句話也講不出來，只是軟弱無力地跪在那兒，像啞羊似的。

「果真」，上人叫我的名字。忽然，我好像進入了另一個時空。記得在加州，一天，沿一條公路三步一拜到馬力布時，一位公路警察停在我們身邊，告訴我們要小心，因為前面的路很窄，車速又快。這位路警講話慢條斯理，眼睛閃著光。他說：「你們最好沿路邊走，叫那位跟在你們後面的中國先生，也沿路邊走。他身上穿的紅色衣服，雖然使他比較醒目，但這是一條快車道，我希望我值班的這段時間不要有車禍。我們路警的律師，今天早上打電話來說，在路上看到你們，要我確保你們安全的通過馬力布地區。我太太也看到你們了，她告訴我，要提醒你們三個人小心點，所以你們多保重了。」

我們向他道了謝，他便離開了。我們怯生生地往後看，想看看那第三個人——那位「中國先生」是誰？但我們什麼都沒有看到，更別說穿紅袍的人。

「他說三個人？」

「奇怪，他看到的到底是誰？」

幾個月以後在舊金山，一位女居士告訴我們這故事的另外一面。就在三步一拜朝聖的那段時間裡，常常出現這樣的情形：上人正在和人們交談時，往往會突然站起來，走進他自己的房間，把門關上。沒有人知道上人進去做什麼？通常在一小時以後，上人出來說：「好了，他們沒事了！」加州那位路警的話，證實了上

probably be foundering in the Saha world's sea of suffering by now. Isn't that right, Kuo Chen? You were already full of bad habits when you came through the door of Gold Mountain Monastery, don't you remember? You might have sunk beneath the current of birth and death if it weren't for your affinities with a Good Advisor, right? Why don't you tell these people about it?"

I nodded in agreement and looked at my teacher. That week in Taiwan he was not eating any solid food because he was fasting and dedicating the merit to Taiwan and her people, hoping to delay the disaster that pundits were predicting. He was sick as well, which only the monks who attended him were aware of. Once the bus arrived, he would be surrounded by clouds of disciples and seekers, each of whom brought his special request for healing, for a blessing, for help, seeking the Master's powers and abilities.

Often in Taiwan he wouldn't sleep for days, choosing instead to stay up and talk with the line of seekers outside his door, which did not diminish day and night. They came hoping for a chance to draw near and make their request, and to be touched by his compassion.

None of us disciples could stand in for him or pick up even a finger's worth of his burden. Yet he feared no toil or pain. He existed only to dispense the teachings of sweet dew. The teaching of the Great Good and Wise Advisor relieves the suffering of living beings. I opened my mouth and spoke the following lines from the *Avatamsaka Sutra* that I had memorized long ago on a hot Sunday afternoon on a highway outside San Luis Obispo:

The Youth Good Wealth contemplated and reflected upon the instructions of his Good and Wise Advisor: He was like the great sea, which receives the rains from the great clouds without satiation. He had the following thought:

The Good and Wise Advisor's teaching is like a spring sun in that it produces and makes grow the roots and sprouts of all good Dharmas;

The Good and Wise Advisor's teaching is like a full moon, in that it refreshes and cools everything it shines on;

The Good and Wise Advisor's teaching is like a snow mountain in summer, in that it can dispel the heat and thirst of all beasts;

The Good and Wise Advisor's teaching is like the sun on a fragrant pool, in that it can open the lotus flower of the mind of all goodness;

The Good and Wise Advisor's teaching is like a great jeweled continent, in that the various Dharma jewels fill his heart;

The Good and Wise Advisor's teaching is like the Jambu tree, in that it amasses the flowers and fruits of all blessings and wisdom;

The Good and Wise advisor's teaching is like a great dragon king, in that he playfully roams with ease and comfort in empty space;

The Good and Wise Advisor's teaching is like Mt. Sumeru, in that limitless wholesome dharmas of the Heaven of the Thirty-three are situated in its midst;

The Good and Wise Advisor's teaching is like Lord

人在六百哩以外，護持著他的兩位年輕弟子。上人的第十七大願：「願此生即得五眼六通，飛行自在。」

我從回憶中回到現實，仍然跪在沉悶的巴士裡。此時上人面帶微笑，非常溫和，不再那麼嚴厲了。我相信上人已經洞察到我在想什麼，上人說：「這是果真的經驗之談，你們應該聽他講，因為他知道，如果沒有一位善知識，他可能已經沉淪到娑婆世界的苦海中了，對不對？果真，當你走進金山寺的時候，帶著一身壞習氣，記不記得？要不是你和善知識的這種緣份，你早就沉沒在生死流中了，你覺得怎麼樣？為什麼不跟大家講一講？」我點點頭，看了我的善知識一眼。

上人在臺灣的那一個星期，沒有吃固體的食物，上人絕食，將功德迴向給臺灣的眾生，希望能延遲臺灣將面臨的災難。上人身體有病，但只有隨侍身邊的出家人才知道。弘法團的巴士每到一處，上人都被大群的人包圍著。這些人當中，有上人的弟子，有來求治病的、求福的、求幫助的……。

在臺灣，上人常常連續幾天徹夜不眠，和有求於他的人們通宵長談。要求幫助的人越來越多，他們希望親近上人、求助於上人，或被上人的慈悲所感動……。

上人的弟子中，沒有一個人能替代上人，甚至不能分擔上人所負荷的，那怕是一個小指頭那樣少的負擔。上人不畏艱辛、不畏勞苦，上人活著就是為了灑甘露水，大善知識的教化能解救眾生的痛苦。我隨口背出了很久以前，一個炎熱的星期日下午，在聖路易匹茲堡附近的公路上，所記誦的《華嚴經》經文：

爾時善財童子，觀察思惟善知識教，
猶如巨海，受大雲雨，無有厭足，作是念言：
善知識教，猶如春日，生長一切，善法根苗。
善知識教，猶如滿月，凡所照及，皆使清涼。
善知識教，如夏雪山，能除一切諸歡熱渴。
善知識教，如芳池日，能開一切善心蓮華。
善知識教，如大寶洲，種種法寶充滿其心。
善知識教，如閻浮樹，積集一切福智華果。
善知識教，如須彌山，無量善法，三十三天於中止住。

Shakra, who is circumambulated by his multitudes and assemblies, in that none can overshadow him, and who can subdue bizarre cults and hosts of Asura armies. In this way he reflected.

I brought the verses out from my memory effortlessly, I was too tired to think up any doubts or my usual discursive thoughts. The Venerable Abbot seemed very happy, as with a broad grin he said, "See? Everything I teach you has its function and its purpose. Now do you understand?"

As the bus started to roll on up the hill, he said, "Who else wants to speak the Dharma? Don't be lazy. These people have spared no expense to bring you all the way here from America. Can you just eat your fill and wait to die? You owe them some teachings to repay their kindness. Who will be the next Wise Advisor? Don't wait for me to spoon-feed you all your life. All right, who will it be? Step up here. Next!"

善知識教，猶如帝釋，眾會圍繞，無能映蔽，能伏異道修羅軍眾，如是思惟，漸次遊行。

我輕易地背出這一段經文。此時，我累得再也不能胡思亂想了。看起來上人似乎很滿意，笑著說：「你知道了吧！我教你的那些事，都有它的作用和目的的，你現在明白了吧？」弘法團的巴士開始爬坡，上人又說：「還有誰要講法？不要偷懶。這些人費了這麼大的功夫，把你們從美國請到這兒來，你們怎麼能坐吃等死？你們要教他們，來回報他們。誰是下一個善知識？別指望依賴我一輩子。好了，下一個是誰？快上來！」………。

普賢菩薩
Verse on Universal Worthy Bodhisattva

眾生界盡願無窮	煩惱斷時行更深
禮敬諸佛誠懇切	稱讚如來誓大伸
廣修供養培福德	懺悔業障除罪根
普賢菩薩歎難盡	倒駕慈航轉法輪

The realm of living beings may be exhausted, but his vows have no end.
When afflictions are severed, his practice only goes deeper.
He bows to all Buddhas in sincere reverence.
In praising the Tathagata, he greatly extends his vow.
Vastly cultivating the giving of offerings, he develops his blessings.
He repents of karmic hindrances, eradicating his offenses.
It is difficult to finish praising Universal Worthy Bodhisattva.
He compassionately reverses his ship and comes back to turn the Dharma wheel.

宣公上人作
by the Venerable Master Hua

宣化老和尚追思紀念專集 第二冊

西曆1995年11月11日・中英文版
佛曆3022年 9月19日・觀音菩薩出家日・初版

發行人	法界佛教總會
出　版	法界佛教總會/佛經翻譯委員會/法界佛教大學
地　址	1777 Murchison Drive
	Burlingame, CA 94010-4504 U.S.A.
電　話	(415) 692-5912

倡　印	萬佛聖城
地　址	2001 Talmage Road
	Talmage, CA 95481-0217 U.S.A.
電　話	(707) 462-0939